FIFTH EDITION

Advanced Accounting

JOE B. HOYLE

CSX Professor of Management and Accounting
Robins School of Business
University of Richmond

THOMAS F. SCHAEFER

Deloitte & Touche Professor of Accounting
College of Business
Florida State University

TIMOTHY S. DOUPNIK

Professor of Accounting
College of Business Administration
University of South Carolina

Irwin
McGraw-Hill

Boston   Burr Ridge, IL   Dubuque, IA   Madison, WI   New York   San Francisco   St. Louis
Bangkok   Bogotá   Caracas   Lisbon   London   Madrid
Mexico City   Milan   New Delhi   Seoul   Singapore   Sydney   Taipei   Toronto

Irwin/McGraw-Hill

A Division of The **McGraw·Hill** *Companies*

ADVANCED ACCOUNTING

Material from the Uniform CPA Examination, Questions and Unofficial Answers, copyright © 1990, 1991, 1992, and 1993 by American Institute of Certified Public Accountants, Inc., is reprinted (or adapted) with permission.

This book is printed on acid-free paper.

2 3 4 5 6 7 8 9 0 VNH/VNH 9 0 9 8

ISBN 0-256-18150-0

Vice president and Editorial director: *Michael W. Junior*
Publisher: *Jeffrey J. Shelstad*
Sponsoring editor: *George Werthman*
Editorial assistant: *Irene Baki*
Marketing manager: *Rhonda Seelinger*
Senior project manager: *Jean Lou Hess*
Production supervisor: *Michael R. McCormick*
Designer: *Michael Warrell*
Compositor: *GAC/Shepard Poorman*
Typeface: *10/12 Times Roman*
Printer: *Von Hoffmann Press, Inc.*

Library of Congress Cataloging-in-Publication Data

Hoyle, Joe Ben.
    Advanced accounting / Joe B. Hoyle, Thomas F. Schaefer. Timothy S.
Doupnik. — 5th ed.
      p.   cm.
    Includes bibliographical references and index.
    ISBN 0-256-18150-0
    1. Accounting.   I. Schaefer, Thomas F. II. Doupnik, Timothy S.
III. Title.
HF5635.H863   1998
   657′.046—dc21   97-32416

http://www.mhhe.com

To our  *families*

The real purpose
of books is to trap
the mind into
doing its own
thinking.

Christopher Morley

Joe B. Hoyle is the CSX Professor of Management & Accounting at the University of Richmond where he has taught a variety of accounting courses including Advanced Accounting since 1979. Prior to that, Joe was a professor at the College of William and Mary. In addition to authoring *Advanced Accounting,* Joe writes and maintains a very successful CPA review course which he teaches each semester.

Thomas F. Schaefer is the Deloitte & Touche Professor of Accounting at Florida State University. Professor Schaefer has a Ph.D. in accounting from the University of Illinois and a CPA certificate. He has written a number of articles in scholarly journals such as *The Accounting Review, Journal of Accounting Research, Journal of Accounting & Economics, Accounting Horizons,* and others. His primary teaching and research interests are in financial accounting and reporting. Beginning in 1997 he serves on the executive committee of the Financial Accounting and Reporting Section of the American Accounting Association.

Timothy S. Doupnik is Professor of Accounting at the University of South Carolina where he oversees the International Master of Business Administration Program. Tim's primary teaching and research interest is in international accounting. He has published extensively in this area in journals such as *Advances in International Accounting,* the *International Journal of Accounting,* and the *Journal of International Business Studies.* He also has written two research monographs on foreign currency translation published by the FASB. Tim is active in the American Accounting Association and has held a variety of positions in the International Accounting Section.

In this fast-paced information age, how do you entice, engage, and challenge students without sacrificing quality and sophistication? This was our challenge when we wrote the Fifth Edition of *Advanced Accounting.* The Fifth Edition features many changes and advancements in authorship, content, and design. Despite these changes, now more than ever the book fulfills Joe's vow of 1980 to create an accounting text that stimulates, challenges, and excites.

To help meet the challenge to engage and inform, this edition inaugurates a new co-authorship. Tom Schaefer of Florida State University and Tim Doupnik of the University of South Carolina, both recognized accounting researchers and educators, lend their research expertise, teaching experience, and pedagogical ingenuity to this text. In addition to new co-authorship, we have created and implemented a new design that will appeal to students while underscoring important concepts. We believe, and hope you agree, that our new layout and two-color design makes the text more accessible for students. The contemporary look, feel, and content of the Fifth Edition are sure to keep active minds engaged.

This edition incorporates many accounting standards that resulted from many FASB and GASB pronouncements. Fluid writing style, real-world examples, introduction to controversial topics, thorough discussion questions and techniques that were successfully developed in prior editions remain in tact. Innovation is important, but in our innovation we have not sacrificed the elements that made *Advanced Accounting* the authority in its field.

UPDATING THIS EDITION

In general, we continue to provide relevant observations from business periodicals and numerous updated annual report examples to reflect current trends in financial reporting. We have incorporated all recent FASB and GASB Exposure Drafts and Standards. Listed below are specific changes that appear in the text:

Chapter 1 has been updated to incorporate relevant provisions of SFAS No. 115, *Accounting for Certain Investments in Debt and Equity Securities.*

In **Chapter 2,** a new section presents and discusses underlying motivations for business combinations. The recent combinations of IBM and Lotus, Disney and Capital Cities/ABC, and Chase Manhattan and Chemical Bank provide examples demonstrating business characteristics that often lead firms to combine.

In addition, **Chapter 2** contains a presentation and discussion of the definition of control of an entity according to *FASB Exposure Draft, Consolidated Financial Statements: Policy and Procedures* (and subsequent amendments).

In **Chapter 3,** coverage of SFAS No. 121, *Accounting for the Impairment of Long-Lived Assets and for Long-Lived Assets to be Disposed Of* has been added. Issues relating to the impairment of goodwill are discussed in particular with an example of an annual report disclosure by American Greetings Corporation.

Chapter 3 concludes with a new computer project relating alternative consolidation procedures to the parent's investment accounting method choice.

Chapter 4 expands coverage of the economic unit concept recommended in the 1995 FASB Exposure Draft, *Consolidated Financial Statements: Policy and Procedures.* An appendix to the chapter details a chronology of the FASB's efforts to change the way consolidated entities present their financial reports. The appendix also discusses the definition of control, assessing the existence of control, consolidated valuation of subsidiary assets and liabilities, the valuation and presentation of noncontrolling interests, and accounting for changes in a parent's ownership in a subsidiary.

Chapter 4 concludes with a new computer project that compares financial reporting between the parent company concept and the economic unit concept.

Chapters 5, 6, and 7 all contain references to the FASB Exposure Draft, *Consolidated Financial Statements: Policy and Procedures* where applicable.

Chapter 6 has been updated to include SFAS No. 128, *Earnings per Share*.

Chapter 7 has been updated for changes in U.S. tax laws.

Chapter 9 from the previous edition: "Foreign Currency Translation and Remeasurement" has been split into two new chapters. Chapter 9 in the Fifth Edition covers "Foreign Currency Transactions and Hedging Foreign Exchange Risk" and Chapter 10 in the Fifth Edition covers "Translation of Foreign Currency Financial Statements."

The new **Chapter 9** expands the discussion of foreign exchange markets. There is an emphasis on reading and understanding foreign exchange quotes in the newspaper. Also included is a discussion on the use of forward contracts and options to hedge against foreign exchange risk, and a brief discussion of the valuation of foreign currency options.

Chapter 9 then moves into the accounting for foreign currency transactions emphasizing the concept of exposure to foreign exchange risk. There is a more conceptual presentation of the accounting for foreign currency transactions that focuses on the one-transaction and two-transaction perspectives. There is also a more conceptual presentation of the accounting for hedging activities.

Amerco is an example of an export sale denominated in foreign currency and is used throughout the chapter to demonstrate the accounting for foreign currency transactions and hedging.

The discussion of foreign currency transactions and forward contract hedges focuses on the procedures required by FASB Statement 52. The discussion related to the accounting for option hedges is based on the FASB Exposure Draft, *Accounting for Derivatives and Similar Financial Instruments and for Hedging Activities* issued in June of 1996. The concept of hedge accounting as well as the concept of a hedge of a forecasted transaction both of which are introduced in the exposure draft are also described and explained. Amendments to FASB 52 proposed in the Exposure Draft are also described.

The discussion related to hedging concludes with two sections which demonstrate the Use of Hedging Instruments in actual practice and the Off Balance Sheet Nature of Forward Contracts.

The new **Chapter 10** begins by discussing the issue of translating foreign currency financial statements from a conceptual perspective. The focus is on the two issues of determining which translation method to use and deciding where to report translation adjustments in consolidated financial statements.

Emphasis is placed on explaining and showing how the use of the current exchange rate in translation creates a balance sheet exposure to foreign exchange risk and how this exposure causes translation adjustments to arise.

There is an expanded, more conceptual discussion of the various translation methods and the nature of the balance sheet exposure associated with each of them.

A new section called Complicating Aspects of the Temporal Method shows that the temporal method is mechanically more cumbersome than the current rate method. The discussion of SFAS 8 is more systematic and there is an expanded discussion of SFAS 52's highly inflationary economy rule with an example illustrating why this rule is necessary.

The translation process is illustrated by first translating a hypothetical foreign entity's financial statements using the current rate method. New to this edition, the illustration includes translation of the statement of cash flows in addition to the balance sheet and income statement. The same entity's financial statements are then remeasured using the temporal method. The results from applying these two methods are then compared to demonstrate their conceptual differences.

The discussion of hedging balance sheet exposure has been expanded and the paradox associated with that type of hedge is explained.

A new section summarizing disclosures related to financial statement translation has been added.

The chapter concludes with a new section in which the procedures used to consolidate the financial statements of a foreign subsidiary with those of its parent are demonstrated. This integrates the issues covered in Chapter 10 with the principles and procedures learned in Chapters 2 and 3.

Chapter 11 is organized into two parts. The first part discusses worldwide accounting diversity (without focusing on individual countries) and the development of international standards. This part has been completely reorganized, expanded, and updated presenting topics as follows: Problems created by accounting diversity, Evidence of accounting diversity, Reasons for accounting diversity, Accounting clusters, International harmonization of financial reporting, European Union, and IASC.

Also included in the first part of **Chapter 11** is a discussion of the major problems caused by accounting diversity and a systematic discussion of the arguments for and against harmonization.

As in previous editions, the second part of the chapter begins with a description of the accounting profession and financial reporting practices in three important countries: U.K., Germany, and Japan. The discussion of German accounting practice has been expanded to explain the type-of-cost format income statement used by German companies and to provide specific examples of how German companies create hidden reserves to smooth income. The section on Japan now includes a discussion of the problems associated with interpreting financial ratios calculated from Japanese financial statements.

Chapter 12 has been rewritten and updated to conform to the new segment reporting rules introduced by the FASB in SFAS 131 in June of 1997.

As in previous editions, this chapter begins with a historical background on segment reporting. The section entitled "Usefulness of Disaggregated Financial Information" has been updated to describe the concerns and recommendation made by AIMR and the AICPA Special Committee on Financial Reporting regarding segmental reporting which led to the FASB to reconsider this issue.

SFAS 131's management approach is thoroughly described, concentrating on the definition of "operating segment" and the tests designed to determine which operating segments are separately reportable. The expanded disclosures related to operating segments are outlined.

The substantial changes related to geographic segment reporting are also described.

Chapter 13 has been rewritten and updated to include the Bankruptcy Reform Act of 1994.

Chapter 16 has been updated to include a discussion of GASB Statement 22: "Accounting for Taxpayer-Assessed Tax Revenues in Governmental Funds" and GASB Statement 24: "Accounting and Financial Reporting for Certain Grants and Other Financial Assistance."

Chapter 17 has been updated to include a discussion of the 1997 GASB Exposure Draft: "Basic Financial Statements and Management's Discussion and Analysis for State and Local Governments." The chapter includes examples of entitywide perspective financial statements and reconciliations between fund perspective and entitywide perspective financial statements.

Chapter 18 has been redesigned, focusing on the unique accounting and reporting characteristics of public colleges and universities. It includes a discussion of GASB Statement 15: "Governmental College and University Accounting and Financial Reporting Models" and is updated to reflect standards prescribed by the AICPA audit guide: "Audits of Colleges and Universities."

Chapter 18 also includes a discussion of the 1997 GASB Exposure Draft: "Basic Financial Statements and Management's Discussion and Analysis for Public Colleges and Universities."

Chapter 19 has been redesigned, focusing on the unique accounting and reporting characteristics of not-for-profit organizations. It includes a detailed discussion of the accounting and reporting requirements of the three FASB Statements specifically issued for not-for-profit organizations; 116, 117, and 124.

The chapter stresses the accounting and reporting requirements that are common across different types of private not-for-profit organizations. The emphasis is on the financial statements required by GASB Statement 117: "Financial Statements of Not-for-Profit Organizations." Additionally, there is significant discussion and illustrations of accounting for contributions. Financial statements issued by well-known not-for-profit organizations are incorporated into the chapter.

A section of the chapter describes the unique reporting characteristics of health care organizations including a discussion of the differences between not-for-profit, public, and investor-owned health care organizations.

The chapter is updated for the 1996 AICPA Accounting and Audit Guides: "Not-for-Profit Organizations" and "Health Care Organizations."

EDUCATIONAL APPROACH

Many of the pedagogical elements of the four previous editions of *Advanced Accounting* have been retained, expanded, and refined. Each of these features is intended to get students involved in their own education; to encourage them to ask why a particular approach to reporting is considered appropriate rather than just how the numbers are calculated.

Introduction of Controversies   At many points throughout the book, the controversial side of accounting is introduced. The development of financial reporting is shown as a result of a history of considered debate that continues today and into the future. Dissents to official pronouncements are described as are comment letters to the FASB. Published articles are discussed, many of which criticize GAAP.

Writing Style   The writing style of the four previous editions was highly praised. We have made every effort to ensure that the writing style remains engaging, lively, and consistent.

Real-World Examples   As in earlier editions, we have incorporated information from actual situations so students better relate what they learn to what they will be encountering in the business world. Quotations and articles from *Forbes, The Wall Street Journal, Time,* and *Business Week* are incorporated throughout the text. Data has been pulled from business and government financial statements as well as official pronouncements.

Discussion Questions   Students and professors alike have praised the inclusion of discussion questions found in each chapter. Similar to mini-cases, these questions help explain the issues at hand in practical terms. Many times these cases are designed to demonstrate to students why a problem is a problem and worth considering. Often accounting rules are relatively easy to read and learn mechanically but are extremely difficult to apply in the business world. The Discussion Question feature facilitates student understanding of the underlying accounting principles at work in particular business events.

Library Assignments   Student research assignments and related suggested readings are listed at the end of each chapter. These assignments encourage students to take a proactive role in their education.

End-of-Chapter Materials   As in previous editions, the homework material remains a strength of the text. Most of the material has been class tested by us in our own classes. Many of the questions from the fourth edition have been revised, rewritten, and updated to offer greater variety.

INSTRUCTOR SUPPLEMENTS

Instructor's Resource Manual (ISBN: 0072901969): Includes the solutions to all discussion questions, end-of-chapter questions, and problems. In addition, chapter outlines are provided to assist instructors in preparing for class.

Solutions Transparencies (ISBN: 0-256-218002-1): To help clarify and reinforce the processes involved in solving the more complex problems in the text, the answers to selected problems are replicated on acetates that can be used in classroom presentations.

Test Bank (ISBN: 0-256-21803-X): The test bank contains a variety of questions ranging from multiple-choice questions to short answer questions to detailed problems.

Computerized Testing Software (0-256-21802-1): This is a computerized version of the printed test bank for more efficient use, available in a Windows version.

Check Figures: A list of Check figures gives key amounts for the problems to assist students in working through homework problems. Check figures are available in bulk, free to adopters.

FOR THE STUDENT

Study Guide/Working Papers (ISBN: 0-256-26667-0): This combination study guide and working papers reinforces the key concepts of the book by providing students with chapter outlines, multiple-choice questions, and problems for each chapter in the text. In addition, this paperback contains all the forms necessary for completing the end-of-chapter material.

Spreadsheet Application Template Software (SPATS) (ISBN: 0-256-14583-0): This software package, developed by Doris deLespinasse of Adrian College, is available in 3.5″ disk. The software includes an Excel tutorial and innovatively designed templates that may be used with Excel 5.0 to solve many complicated problems found in the book. These problems are identified by a logo in the margin such as the one shown here. Upon adoption, master disks of this package are available to instructors for classroom or laboratory use.

Web Site: http://www.mhhe.com/business/accounting/hoyle

ACKNOWLEDGEMENTS

We could not produce a textbook of the quality and scope of *Advanced Accounting* without the help of a great number of people. We extend a special thank you to Paul Copley of the University of Georgia for his assistance on the Governmental and Not-for-Profit chapters in this edition. We also want to thank the many people who participated in phone surveys, completed questionnaires, and reviewed the manuscript. Our sincerest thanks to them all:

Leonard Bacon
California State University—
Bakersfield

Gus Bahramis
DeVry Institute of Technology

Betty Smith Banks
Aquinas College

Patrick B. Bauer
DeVry, Kansas City

Susan Budak
Formerly, Project Manager
Financial Accounting Foundation

Lynn H. Clements
Florida Southern University

Paul Copley
University of Georgia

David G. Coy
Adrian College

Wagih G. Dafashy
College of William & Mary

John Dawson
Christopher Newport University

Doris deLespinasse
Adrian College

Jim Emig
Villanova University

Lou Fowler
Missouri Western State College

Sally W. Gilfillan
Longwood College

Bonnie L. Givens
Avila College

William A. Grubbs
Guilford College

Donna J. Guydan
Valparaiso University

David O. Jenkins
California State University—Stanislaus

Greg Lowry
Troy State University

Richard Rand
Tennessee Tech.

Raymond Slager
Calvin College

Judson Stryker
Stetson University

Martin Stub
DeVry Institute of Technology

Margaret Tanner
University of Northern Iowa

Roger A. Woods
Northwest Missouri State University

We also pass along a word of thanks to all the people at Irwin/McGraw-Hill who participated in the creation of this edition. In particular, Irene Baki, Editorial Assistant; Jean Lou Hess, Senior Project Manager; Michael McCormick, Production Supervisor; Rhonda Seelinger, Marketing Manager; Jeff Shelstad, Publisher; Michael Warrell, Designer; and George Werthman, Sponsoring Editor, all contributed significantly to the project and we appreciate their efforts.

BRIEF CONTENTS

CONTENTS

Consolidated Financial Statements—Intercompany Asset Transactions, 209

Intercompany Debt and Other Consolidation Issues, 253

Ownership Patterns and Income Taxes, 303

Branch and Consignment Accounting, 355

Foreign Currency Transactions and Hedging Foreign Exchange Risk, 395

CHAPTER

11

Partnerships: Formation and Operation, 613

Partnerships: Termination and Liquidation, 651

Accounting for State and Local Governments (Part One), 687

Accounting for State and Local Governments (Part Two), 733

Accounting for Government-Owned Colleges and Universities, 779

Accounting and Reporting for Private Not-for-Profit Organizations, 817

Accounting for Estates and Trusts, 853

Financial Reporting and the Securities and Exchange Commission, 885

The Equity Method of Accounting for Investments

The first eight chapters of this text present the accounting and reporting for investment activities of businesses. The focus is on investments where one firm possesses either significant influence or control over another through ownership of voting shares. When one firm owns enough voting shares to be able to affect the decisions of another, accounting for the investment becomes challenging and often complex. The source of such complexities typically stems from the fact that transactions among the firms affiliated through ownership cannot be considered independent, arm's-length transactions. As in all matters relating to financial reporting, we look to transactions with *outside parties* to provide a basis for accounting valuation. When firms are affiliated through a common set of owners, objectivity in accounting calls for measurements that recognize the relationships among the firms.

REPORTING INVESTMENTS IN CORPORATE EQUITY SECURITIES

A footnote to recent financial statements of Anheuser-Busch Companies, Inc., informed readers of "the purchase of a 25 percent equity investment and distribution alliance with the Redhook Ale Brewery, Inc., of Seattle, Washington, for $17.9 million. Under the agreement, Redhook products will be distributed exclusively through Anheuser-Busch wholesalers in all new U.S. markets entered by Redhook. The company is accounting for its investment under the equity method."

Such information is hardly unusual in the business world; corporate as well as individual investors frequently acquire ownership shares of both domestic and foreign businesses. These investments can range from the purchase of a few shares to the acquisition of 100 percent control. Although purchases of corporate equity securities (such as the one made by Anheuser-Busch) are not uncommon, they pose a considerable number of problems for the accountant because a close relationship has been established without the investor gaining actual control. These issues are currently addressed by the **equity method.** This chapter deals with the procedures utilized in accounting for stock investments that fall under the application of this method.

At present, accounting standards recognize three different approaches to the financial reporting of investments in corporate equity securities:

The fair-value method.
The equity method.
The consolidation of financial statements.[1]

These three are not interchangeable; a specific method is required by any given situation. The reporting of a particular investment depends on the degree of influence that the investor (stockholder) has over the investee, a factor best indicated by the relative size of ownership.

Fair-Value Method   In many instances, an investor possesses only a small percentage of an investee company's outstanding stock, perhaps only a few shares. Because of the limited level of ownership, the investor cannot expect to have a significant impact on the investee's operations or decision making. These shares are bought in anticipation of cash dividends or in appreciation of stock market values. Such investments are recorded at cost and periodically adjusted to fair value according to the Financial Accounting Standards Board (FASB) in its *Statement of Financial Accounting Standards No. 115* (*SFAS 115*), "Accounting for Certain Investments in Debt and Equity Securities," May 1993.

Since a full coverage of *SFAS 115* is presented in intermediate accounting textbooks, only the following basic principles are noted here.

- Initial investments in equity securities are recorded at cost and subsequently adjusted to fair value if fair value is readily determinable, otherwise the investment remains at cost.
- Equity securities held for the purpose of selling them in the short term are classified as *trading securities* and reported at fair value, with unrealized gains and losses included in earnings.
- Equity securities not classified as trading securities are classified as *available-for-sale securities* and reported at fair value, with unrealized gains and losses excluded from earnings and reported in a separate component of shareholders' equity.
- Dividends received are recognized as income for both trading and available-for-sale securities.

These procedures are required for equity security investments when neither significant influence nor control is present. The recognition of unrealized gains and losses for *SFAS 115* investments represents a departure from past procedures that prevented the anticipation of income. As will be shown, the procedures for significant influence investments in equity securities, while somewhat complex, adhere more closely to traditional accrual accounting.

---

[1]More than three methods of accounting for stock investments are found in actual practice. Consolidations, for example, are reported by either the purchase or the pooling of interests method, depending on specific criteria. In addition, under certain circumstances stock investments may be reported at cost or some other specialized process. Thus, the three methods shown here represent only the broad categories generally encountered.

Consolidation of Financial Statements Although many investments involve only a small percentage of stock, an investor can acquire enough shares to gain actual control over an investee's operation. In financial accounting, such control is recognized whenever a stockholder accumulates more than 50 percent of an organization's outstanding voting stock. At that point, rather than simply influencing the decisions of the investee, the investor clearly can direct the entire decision-making process. A review of the financial statements of America's largest organizations indicates that legal control of one or more subsidiary companies is an almost universal practice. PepsiCo, Inc., as just one example, holds a majority interest in the voting stock of literally hundreds of corporations.

A level of ownership large enough to enable an investor to control an investee presents an economic situation not adequately addressed by *SFAS 115*. Normally, when a majority of voting stock is held, the investor-investee relationship has become so closely connected that the two corporations are viewed as a single entity for reporting purposes. Hence, an entirely different set of accounting procedures is applicable. According to *Accounting Research Bulletin No. 51 (ARB No. 51)*, "Consolidated Financial Statements," August 1959, control generally requires the consolidation of the accounting information produced by the individual companies. Thus, a single set of financial statements is created for external reporting purposes with all assets, liabilities, revenues, and expenses being brought together.[2] The various procedures applied within this consolidation process are examined in subsequent chapters of the textbook.

Equity Method Finally, another investment relationship is appropriately accounted for using the equity method. Anheuser-Busch's ownership of 25 percent of the voting stock of Redhook is less than enough to control the voting stock. Anheuser-Busch is not even close to the level that indicates the need for consolidation. Yet, despite the lack of voting control, Anheuser-Busch maintains a large interest in this investee company. Through its ownership, Anheuser-Busch can undoubtedly have an impact on the decisions and operations of Redhook.

Especially important is the investor's ability to influence the timing of dividend distributions. Because of this influence, the receipt of a dividend from an investee may not qualify as an objective basis for recording income to the investor firm. Because managerial compensation contracts often are based on net income, incentives exist for managers to use whatever discretion they have available in reporting net income. *Thus, to provide an objective basis for reporting investment income, the equity method requires that income be recognized by the investor as it is earned by the investee, not when dividends are received.*

In today's business world, many corporations such as Anheuser-Busch hold significant ownership interests in other companies without having actual control. Just a few examples include Bell South's holding of 43.8 percent of Houston Cellular Telephone Company and Ameritech's ownership of 25 percent of New Zealand Telecom. Sears, Roebuck & Company alone holds between 20 and 50 percent ownership in dozens of separate corporations. Many other large investments are created through joint ventures whereby two or more companies form a new enterprise to carry out a specified operating purpose. For example, in January 1995, Rubbermaid, Inc., formed a joint venture with Royal Plastics Group Limited of Canada to manufacture and market modular plastic components and kits. Each partner owns 50 percent of the joint venture.

---

[2] As is discussed in the next chapter, owning a majority of the voting shares of an investee does not always lead to consolidated financial statements. The FASB is also considering whether control can be established without majority ownership.

For each of these investments, the investors do not possess absolute control because they hold less than a majority of the voting stock. Thus, the preparation of consolidated financial statements is inappropriate. However, the large percentage of ownership indicates that each investor possesses some ability to affect the decision-making process of the investee. To reflect this relationship, such investments are accounted for by the equity method as officially established by *Opinion 18,* "The Equity Method of Accounting for Investments in Common Stock," issued by the Accounting Principles Board (APB) in March of 1971.

APPLYING THE EQUITY METHOD

An understanding of the equity method is best gained by initially examining the APB's treatment of two questions:

1. What parameters identify the area of ownership where the equity method is applicable?
2. How should the investor report this investment and the income generated by it to reflect the relationship between the two companies?

Criteria for Utilizing the Equity Method

In sanctioning application of the equity method, the APB reasoned that an investor begins to gain the ability to influence the decision-making process of an investee as the level of ownership rises. According to *APB Opinion 18* (par. 17), achieving this "ability to exercise significant influence over operating and financial policies of an investee even though the investor holds 50 percent or less of the voting stock" is the sole criterion for requiring application of the equity method.

Clearly a term such as *the ability to exercise significant influence* is nebulous and subject to a variety of judgments and interpretations in practice. At what point does the acquisition of one additional share of stock give an owner the ability to exercise significant influence? This decision becomes even more difficult in that only the *ability* to exercise significant influence need be present: The pronouncement does not specify that any actual influence must have ever been applied.

APB Opinion 18 provides guidance to the accountant by listing several conditions that indicate the presence of this degree of influence:

- Investor representation on the board of directors of the investee.
- Investor participation in the policy-making process of the investee.
- Material intercompany transactions.
- Interchange of managerial personnel.
- Technological dependency.
- Extent of ownership by the investor in relation to the size and concentration of other ownership interests in the investee.

No single one of these guides should be used exclusively in assessing the applicability of the equity method. Instead, all are evaluated together to determine the presence or absence of the sole criterion: the ability to exercise significant influence over the investee.

These guidelines alone do not eliminate the leeway available to each investor when deciding whether use of the equity method is appropriate. To provide a degree of consistency in applying this standard, the APB established a general ownership test. *If an investor holds between 20 and 50 percent of the voting stock of the investee, significant influence is normally assumed and the equity method applied.*

The Board recognizes that determining the ability of an investor to exercise such influence is not always clear and applying judgment is necessary to assess the status of each investment. In order to achieve a reasonable degree of uniformity in application, the Board concludes that an investment (direct or indirect) of 20 percent or more of the voting stock of an investee should lead to a presumption that in the absence of evidence to the contrary an investor has the ability to exercise significant influence over an investee. Conversely, an investment of less than 20 percent of the voting stock of an investee should lead to a presumption that an investor does not have the ability to exercise significant influence unless such ability can be demonstrated.[3]

At first, the 20 percent rule may appear to be an arbitrarily chosen boundary established merely to provide accountants with a consistent method of reporting all investments. However, the essential criterion is still the ability to significantly influence the investee, rather than 20 percent ownership.[4] If the absence of this ability is proven, the equity method should not be applied regardless of the percentage of shares held. Conversely, whenever this ability can be demonstrated, the equity method is appropriate without concern for the degree of ownership.

As an example, in 1996 the Hallwood Company accounted for its investment in ShowBiz using the equity method despite holding only a 13 percent interest. In its annual report, Hallwood explained it utilizes the equity method of accounting for its investment in ShowBiz "because the Company maintains significant influence by virtue of having five company directors sitting on the nine-member board of ShowBiz."

Further guidance on the precise applicability of the equity method was provided in May 1981 when the FASB issued its *Interpretation 35,* "Criteria for Applying the Equity Method of Accounting for Investments in Common Stock." This pronouncement dealt specifically with using the equity method for investments in which the owner holds more than 20 percent of the outstanding shares. It is important because companies had tended to apply the equity method to all investments in the 20 to 50 percent range with little regard for the degree of influence actually present.

According to *Interpretation 35* (par. 3), above the 20 percent level of ownership, "the presumption that the investor has the ability to exercise significant influence over the investee's operating and financial policies stands until overcome by predominant evidence to the contrary." However, the pronouncement then went on to offer clarification by listing examples of occurrences that would provide evidence to nullify this presumption. *Interpretation 35* specifically states that the equity method is not appropriate for investments that demonstrate any of the following characteristics regardless of the investor's degree of ownership:

- An agreement exists between investor and investee whereby the investor surrenders significant rights as a shareholder.
- A concentration of ownership operates the investee without regard for the views of the investor.
- The investor attempts but fails to obtain representation on the investee's board of directors.

To summarize, the following table indicates the method of accounting that is applicable to various stock investments:

---

[3]*APB Opinion 18,* par. 17.

[4]Not everyone agrees with the wisdom of this rule. Two members of the APB, George R. Catlett and Charles T. Horngren, voted for *Opinion 18* but argued in an attached statement that "they do not agree with the arbitrary criterion of 20 percent combined with a variable test of 'significant influence' in paragraph 17, because such an approach is not convincing in concept and will be very difficult to apply in practice."

Criterion	Normal Ownership Level	Applicable Accounting Method
Lack of ability to significantly influence	Less than 20%	Fair-value (*FASB SFAS 115*)
Presence of ability to significantly influence	20%—50%	Equity method (*APB Opinion 18*)
Control	Over 50%	Consolidated financial statements* (*ARB No. 51* and *APB Opinion 16*)

*As discussed in subsequent chapters, voting control over another company does not always lead to the consolidation of financial statements, for example, when such control may be only temporary.

Accounting for an Investment—the Equity Method

Now that the criteria leading to the application of the equity method have been identified, a review of its reporting procedures is appropriate. Knowledge of this accounting process is especially important to users of the investor's financial statements because the equity method affects both the timing of income recognition as well as the carrying value of the investment account.

In applying the equity method, the accounting objective is to report the investor's investment and investment income reflecting the close relationship between the companies. After recording the cost of the acquisition, two equity method entries periodically record the investment's impact:

■ The investor's investment account is *increased as the investee earns and reports income*. Also, investment income is recognized by the investor using the accrual method—that is, in the same time period as it is *earned* by the investee. If an investee reports income of $100,000 in 1998, a 30 percent owner should immediately increase its own income by $30,000. This earnings accrual reflects the essence of the equity method by emphasizing the connection between the two companies; as the owners' equity of the investee increases through the earnings process, so the investment account also increases. Although the acquisition is initially recorded by the investor at cost, upward adjustments in the asset balance are recorded as soon as the investee makes a profit. A reduction is necessary if a loss is reported.

■ The investor's investment account is *decreased whenever a dividend is collected*. Since distribution of cash dividends reduces the book value of the investee company, the investor mirrors this change by recording the receipt as a decrease in the carrying value of the investment rather than as revenue. Once again, a parallel is established between the investment account and the underlying activities of the investee: the reduction in owners' equity of the investee creates a decrease in the investment. Furthermore, since income is recognized immediately by the investor when it is earned by the investee, double counting would occur if subsequent dividend collections also were recorded by the investor as revenue. Importantly, because of the investor's significant influence over the investee, the collection of a cash dividend is not an appropriate point for income recognition. Because the investor can influence the timing of investee dividend distributions, the receipt of a dividend is not an objective measure of the income generated from the investment.

Application of Equity Method

Investee Event	Investor Accounting
Income is earned.	Proportionate share of income is recognized.
Dividends are distributed.	Dividends received are recorded as a reduction in investment.

Exhibit 1-1 Comparison of Equity Method and Fair-Value Method

Year	Income of Little Company	Dividends Paid by Little Company	Accounting by Big Company When Influence Is Not Significant (available-for-sale security)			Accounting by Big Company When Influence Is Significant (equity method)	
			Dividend Income	Carrying Value of Investment	Fair-Value Adjustment to Stockholders' Equity	Equity in Investee Income	Carrying Value of Investment
1998	$200,000	$ 50,000	$10,000	$235,000	$ 35,000	$ 40,000*	$230,000†
1999	300,000	100,000	20,000	255,000	55,000	60,000*	270,000†
2000	400,000	200,000	40,000	320,000	120,000	80,000*	310,000†
Total income recognized			$70,000			$180,000	

*Equity in investee income is 20 percent of the current year income reported by Little Company.

†The carrying value of an investment under the equity method is the original cost plus income recognized less dividends received. For 1998, as an example, the $230,000 reported balance is the $200,000 cost plus $40,000 equity income less $10,000 in dividends received.

Application of the equity method causes the investment account on the investor's balance sheet to fluctuate in direct relation to changes occurring in the equity of the investee company. As an illustration, assume that an investor acquires a 40 percent interest in a business enterprise. If the investor has the ability to significantly influence the investee, the equity method must be utilized. If the investee subsequently reports net income of $50,000, the investor increases the investment account (and its own net income) by $20,000 in recognition of a 40 percent share of these earnings. Conversely, a $20,000 dividend collected from the investee necessitates a reduction of $8,000 in this same asset account (40 percent of the total payout).

In contrast, the fair-value method reports investments at market value if readily determinable. Also, income is only recognized on receipt of dividends. Consequently, financial reports can vary depending on whether the equity method or fair-value method is appropriate for reporting purposes.

To illustrate, assume that Big Company owns a 20 percent interest in Little Company purchased on January 1, 1998, for $200,000. Little then reports net income of $200,000, $300,000, and $400,000 in the next three years while paying dividends of $50,000, $100,000, and $200,000. The fair values of Little, as determined by market prices, were $235,000, $255,000, and $320,000 at the end of 1998, 1999, and 2000, respectively.

Exhibit 1-1 compares the accounting for Big's investment in Little across the two methods. The fair-value method carries the investment at its market values, presumed to be readily available in this example. Because the investment is classified as *an available-for-sale security*, the excess of market value over cost is reported as a separate component of stockholders' equity.[5] Income is recognized as dividends are received.

In contrast, under the equity method, Big recognizes income as it is earned by Little. As shown in Exhibit 1-1, Big recognizes $180,000 in income over the three years and the carrying value of the investment is adjusted upward to $310,000. Dividends received are not considered an appropriate measure of income because of the assumed significant influence when the equity method is applied. Big's ability to influence the decisions of Little applies to the timing of dividend distributions. Therefore, dividends received do not represent an objective measure of Big's income

---

[5] Fluctuations in the market values of *trading securities* are recognized in income in the period in which they occur.

DISCUSSION QUESTION

Does the Equity Method Really Apply Here?

Abraham, Inc., a New Jersey corporation, operates 57 bakeries throughout the northeastern section of the United States. In the past, the company's outstanding common stock has been owned entirely by its founder, James Abraham. However, during the early part of 1997, the corporation suffered a severe cash flow problem brought on by rapid expansion. To avoid bankruptcy, Abraham sought additional investment capital from a friend, Dennis Bostitch, who owned Highland Laboratories. Subsequently, Highland paid $700,000 cash to Abraham, Inc., to acquire enough newly issued shares of common stock for a one-third ownership interest.

At the end of 1997, the accountants for Highland Laboratories are discussing the proper method of reporting this investment. One argues for maintaining the asset at its original cost: "This purchase is no more than a loan to bail out the bakeries. Mr. Abraham will continue to run the organization with little or no attention paid to us. After all, what does anyone in our company know about baking bread? I would not be surprised if these shares are not reacquired by Abraham as soon as the bakery business is profitable again."

One of the other accountants disagrees, stating that the equity method is appropriate. "I realize that our company is not capable of running a bakery. However, the official rules state that we must have only the *ability* to exert significant influence. With one-third of the common stock in our possession, we certainly have that ability. Whether we use it or not, this ability means that we are required to apply the equity method."

How should Highland Laboratories account for its investment in Abraham, Inc.?

from its investment in Little. However, as Little earns income, under the equity method Big recognizes its share (20%) of the income and increases the investment account. The equity method reflects the accrual model: income is recognized as it is earned, not when cash (dividend) is received.

During the three years in Exhibit 1–1, the investor is recognizing $110,000 in income that has not been received yet as dividends ($180,000 reported by the equity method less $70,000 dividends collected). In reality, since most companies routinely retain some amount of earnings for permanent growth purposes, the chances are highly unlikely that all of the $110,000 will ever reach Big as cash dividends. Despite the uncertain nature of this income, the APB believed that the equity method provides the most consistent application of accrual accounting when the ability to exert significant influence over an investee is present.

Not surprisingly, the recognition of income under the equity method is a controversial subject in accounting. Although neither cash nor other assets need be received, income is immediately reported by the investor. In most cases, as in Exhibit 1–1, accrued income is greater than the dividends received. Since this "extra" income ($110,000 in the previous example) is not available to the investor for growth purposes or for payment of its own dividends, the question can be raised as to whether a legitimate basis for recognition actually exists. One discussant of the equity method concludes: "There's nothing equitable about equity accounting. It is grossly misleading."[6]

The primary objective of this textbook is to assist each reader in achieving a basic understanding of financial accounting. However, to appreciate fully the complex nature of the subject, students need to be aware that many accounting principles are still the focus of controversy or, at least, discussion. The wisdom of official accounting pronouncements is debated often in the world of business. Although the APB chose to sanction the equity method for the reporting of investments, arguments are rekindled frequently both for and against its use in practice.

A return to Exhibit 1–1 shows that the carrying value of the investment fluctuates each year under the equity method. This recording parallels the changes occurring in

---

[6]Richard Greene, "Equity Accounting Isn't Equitable," *Forbes*, March 31, 1980, p. 104.

the net asset figures reported by the investee. If the owner's equity of the investee rises through income, an increase is made in the investment account; decreases such as losses and dividends cause reductions to be recorded. Thus, the equity method conveys information that describes the relationship created by the investor's ability to significantly influence the investee.

ACCOUNTING PROCEDURES USED IN APPLYING THE EQUITY METHOD

Once guidelines for the application of the equity method have been established, the mechanical process necessary for recording basic transactions is quite straightforward. The investor accrues its percentage of the earnings reported by the investee each period. Dividend declarations reduce the investment balance to reflect the decrease in the investee's book value.

Referring again to the information presented in Exhibit 1–1, Little Company reported a net income of $200,000 during 1998 and paid cash dividends of $50,000. These figures indicate that Little's net assets have increased by $150,000 during the year. Therefore, in the financial records of Big Company, the following journal entries are made in applying the equity method:

Investment in Little Company	40,000	
Equity in Investee Income		40,000
To accrue earnings of a 20 percent owned investee ($200,000 × 20%).		
Cash	10,000	
Investment in Little Company		10,000
To record receipt of cash dividend from Little Company ($50,000 × 20%).		

In the first entry, Big accrues income based on the reported earnings of the investee even though this amount greatly exceeds the cash dividend. The second entry reflects the actual receipt of the dividend and the related reduction in Little's net assets. The $30,000 net increment recorded here in Big's investment account ($40,000 − $10,000) represents 20 percent of the $150,000 increase in Little's book value that occurred during the year.

Although these two entries illustrate the basic reporting process used in applying the equity method, several other issues must be explored for a full understanding of this approach. More specifically, special procedures are required in accounting for each of the following:

1. Reporting a change to the equity method.
2. Reporting investee income from sources other than continuing operations.
3. Reporting investee losses.
4. Reporting the sale of an equity investment.

Reporting a Change to the Equity Method

In many instances, an investor's ability to significantly influence an investee will not be gained through a single stock acquisition. The investor may possess only a minor ownership for some years before purchasing enough additional shares to require conversion to the equity method. Before the investor achieves significant influence, any investment should be reported by the fair-value method. After the investment reaches the point at which the equity method becomes applicable, a technical question arises about the appropriate means of changing from one method to the other.[7]

---

[7] A switch to the equity method also may be required if the investee purchases a portion of its own shares as treasury stock. This transaction can increase the investor's percentage of outstanding stock.

APB Opinion 18 (par. 19) answers this concern by stating that "the investment, results of operations (current and prior periods presented), and retained earnings of the investor should be adjusted retroactively." *Thus, all accounts are restated so that the investor's financial statements appear as if the equity method had been applied from the date of the first acquisition.* By mandating retroactive treatment, the APB is attempting to ensure comparability from year to year in the financial reporting of the investor company.[8]

To illustrate this restatement procedure, assume that Giant Company acquires a 10 percent ownership in Small Company on January 1, 1998. Officials of Giant do not believe that their company has gained the ability to exert significant influence over Small. The investment is properly recorded through the use of the fair-value method as an available-for-sale security. Subsequently, on January 1, 2000, Giant purchases an additional 30 percent of the outstanding voting stock of Small, thereby achieving the ability to significantly influence the investee's decision making. From 1998 through 2000, Small reports net income, pays cash dividends, and has fair values at January 1 of each year as follows:

Year	Net Income	Cash Dividends	Fair Value at January 1
1998	$ 70,000	$20,000	$800,000
1999	110,000	40,000	840,000
2000	130,000	50,000	930,000

In Giant's 1998 and 1999 financial statements, as originally reported, dividend revenue of $2,000 and $4,000, respectively, would be recognized based on receiving 10 percent of these distributions. The investment account is maintained at fair value since it is readily determinable. Also, the change in the fair value of the investment results in a credit to an unrealized cumulative holding gain of $4,000 in 1998 and $13,000 in 1999 reported in Giant's stockholders' equity section. However, after changing to the equity method on January 1, 2000, Giant must restate these prior years to present the investment *as if the equity method had always been applied.* Subsequently, in comparative statements showing columns for previous periods, the 1998 statements should indicate equity income of $7,000 with $11,000 being disclosed for 1999 based on a 10 percent accrual of Small's income for each of these years.

The income restatement for these earlier years can be computed as follows:

Year	Equity in Investee Income (10%)	Income Reported from Dividends	Retroactive Adjustment
1998	$ 7,000	$2,000	$ 5,000
1999	11,000	4,000	7,000
Total adjustment to Retained Earnings			$12,000

Giant's reported earnings for 1998 will be increased by $5,000 with a $7,000 increment needed for 1999. To bring about this retroactive change to the equity method, Giant prepares the following journal entry on January 1, 2000:

Investment in Small Company	12,000	
Retained Earnings—Prior Period Adjustment—Equity in		
Investee Income		12,000

To adjust 1998 and 1999 records so that investment is accounted
for using the equity method in a consistent manner.

---

[8]One member of the APB voted against issuance of *Opinion 18* based in part on this retroactive approach. In his dissent, Newman T. Halvorson contended that "at the time an investment qualifies for use of the equity method, a new reporting entity is created, and the accounts of the investor for periods prior to that time should not be adjusted retroactively to reflect an entity that did not exist."

Unrealized Holding Gain-Shareholders' Equity 13,000
    Fair Value Adjustment (Available-for-Sale)..............   13,000
    To remove the investor's percentage of the increase in fair value
    (10% × $130,000) from stockholders' equity and the available-
    for-sale portfolio valuation account.

The $13,000 adjustment removes the accounts required by *SFAS No. 115* that pertain to the investment prior to the obtaining of significant influence. Because the investment is no longer part of the available-for-sale portfolio, it is carried under the equity method rather than at fair value. Accordingly, the fair value adjustment accounts are reduced as part of the reclassification.

Continuing with this example, Giant will make two other journal entries at the end of 2000, but they relate solely to the operations and distributions of that period.

Investment in Small Company 52,000
    Equity in Investee Income   52,000
    To accrue 40 percent of the year 2000 income reported by the
    Small Company ($130,000 × 40%).

Cash 20,000
    Investment in Small Company   20,000
    To record receipt of year 2000 cash dividend from Small
    Company ($50,000 × 40%).

Reporting Investee Income from Sources Other than Continuing Operations

Traditionally, certain elements of income are presented separately within a set of financial statements. Examples include extraordinary items (see *APB Opinion 30,* "Reporting the Results of Operations," June 1973) and prior period adjustments (see FASB *SFAS 16,* "Prior Period Adjustments," June 1977). A concern that arises in applying the equity method is whether items appearing separately in the investee's income statement require similar treatment by the investor.

To examine this issue, assume that Large Company owns 40 percent of the voting stock of Tiny Company and accounts for this investment by means of the equity method. In 1998, Tiny reports net income of $200,000, a figure composed of $250,000 in income from continuing operations and a $50,000 extraordinary loss. Large Company accrues earnings of $80,000 based on 40 percent of the $200,000 net figure. However, for proper disclosure, the extraordinary loss incurred by the investee must also be reported separately on the financial statements of the investor. This handling is intended, once again, to mirror the close relationship between the two companies.

Based on the level of ownership, Large recognizes $100,000 as a component of operating income (40 percent of Tiny Company's $250,000 income from continuing operations) along with a $20,000 extraordinary loss (40 percent of $50,000). The overall effect is still an $80,000 net increment in Large's earnings, but this amount has been appropriately allocated between income from continuing operations and extraordinary items.

The journal entry to record Large's equity interest in the income of Tiny would be as follows:

Investment in Tiny Company 80,000
Extraordinary Loss of Investee 20,000
    Equity in Investee Income   100,000
    To accrue operating income and extraordinary loss from equity
    investment.

One additional aspect of this accounting should be noted. Even though this loss has already been judged as extraordinary by the investee, Large does not report its $20,000 share as a separate item unless that figure is considered to be material with respect to the investor's own operations.

Reporting Investee Losses

Although most of the previous illustrations have been based on the recording of profits, accounting for losses incurred by the investee is handled by a similar manner. The appropriate percentage of each loss is recognized immediately by the investor with the carrying value of the investment account also being reduced. Even though these procedures are consistent with the concept of the equity method, they fail to take into account all possible loss situations.

Permanent Losses in Value   *APB Opinion 18* recognizes that investments may suffer permanent losses in market value that are not properly reflected through the equity method. Such declines can be caused by the loss of major customers, changes in economic conditions, loss of a significant patent or other legal right, damage to the company's reputation, and the like. Permanent reductions in market value resulting from such adverse events might not be reported immediately by the investor through the normal equity entries discussed previously. Thus, *APB Opinion 18* (par. 19) established the following guideline:

> A loss in value of an investment which is other than a temporary decline should be recognized the same as a loss in value of other long-term assets. Evidence of a loss in value might include, but would not necessarily be limited to, absence of an ability to recover the carrying amount of the investment or inability of the investee to sustain an earnings capacity which would justify the carrying amount of the investment.

Thus, when a permanent decline in an equity method investment's value occurs, the investor must reduce the asset to fair market value. However, *APB Opinion 18* stresses that this loss must be permanent before such recognition becomes necessary. Under the equity method, a temporary drop in the market value of an investment is simply ignored.

Investment Reduced to Zero   Through the recognition of reported losses as well as any permanent drops in market value, the investment account may eventually be reduced to a zero balance. This condition is most likely to occur if extreme losses have been suffered by the investee or if the original purchase was made at a low, bargain price. Regardless of the reason, the carrying value of the investment account could conceivably be eliminated in total.

At the point at which an investment account is reduced to zero, the investor should discontinue using the equity method, rather than establish a negative balance. The investment retains a zero balance until subsequent investee profits eliminate all unrealized losses. Once the original cost of the investment has been eliminated, no additional losses can accrue to the investor (since the entire cost has been written off) *unless* some further commitment has been made on behalf of the investee.

Noise Cancellation Technologies, Inc., for example, in its 1996 financial statements explains the discontinued use of the equity method when the investment account has been reduced to zero:

> When the Company's share of cumulative losses equals its investment and the Company has no obligation or intention to fund such additional losses, the Company suspends applying the equity method. . . . The Company will not be able to record any equity in income with respect to an entity until its share of future profits is sufficient to recover any cumulative losses that have not previously been recorded.

Reporting the Sale of an Equity Investment

At any time, the investor may choose to sell part or all of its holdings in the investee company. If a sale occurs, the equity method continues to be applied until the transaction date, thus establishing an appropriate carrying value for the investment. The investor then reduces this balance by the percentage of shares being sold.

As an example, assume that Top Company owns 40 percent of the 100,000 outstanding shares of Bottom Company, an investment accounted for by the equity method. Although these 40,000 shares were acquired some years ago for $200,000, application of the equity method has increased the asset balance to $320,000 as of January 1, 1998. On July 1, 1998, Top elects to sell 10,000 of these shares (one fourth of its investment) for $110,000 in cash, thereby reducing ownership in Bottom from 40 percent to 30 percent. Bottom Company reports income of $70,000 during the first six months of 1998 and distributes cash dividends of $30,000.

Top, as the investor, initially makes the following journal entries on July 1, 1998, to accrue the proper income and establish the correct investment balance:

Investment in Bottom Company	28,000	
Equity in Investee Income		28,000
To accrue equity income for first six months of 1998 ($70,000 × 40%).		
Cash	12,000	
Investment in Bottom Company		12,000
To record receipt of cash dividends from January through June 1998 ($30,000 × 40%).		

These two entries increase the carrying value of Top's investment by $16,000, creating a balance of $336,000 as of July 1, 1998. The sale of one-fourth of these shares can then be recorded as follows:

Cash	110,000	
Investment in Bottom Company		84,000
Gain on Sale of Investment		26,000
To record sale of one-fourth of investment in Bottom Company (¼ × $336,000 = $84,000).		

After the sale has been consummated, Top continues to apply the equity method to this investment based on 30 percent ownership rather than 40 percent. However, if the sale had been of sufficient magnitude to cause Top to lose its ability to exercise significant influence over Bottom, the equity method ceases to be applicable. For example, if Top Company's holdings were reduced from 40 percent to 15 percent, the equity method might no longer be appropriate after the sale. The shares still being held are reported according to the fair-value method with the remaining book value becoming the new *cost* figure for the investment rather than the amount originally paid.

If an investor is required to change from the equity method to the fair-value method, no retroactive adjustment is made. Although, as previously demonstrated, a change to the equity method mandates a restatement of prior periods, the treatment is not the same when the investor's change is to the fair-value method.

EXCESS OF INVESTMENT COST OVER BOOK VALUE ACQUIRED

After the basic concepts and procedures of the equity method are mastered, more complex accounting issues can be introduced. Surely one of the most common problems encountered in applying the equity method concerns investment costs that exceed the proportionate book value of the investee company.[9]

---

[9] Although encountered less frequently, investments can be purchased at a cost that is less than the underlying book value of the investee. Accounting for this possibility is explored in later chapters.

Unless the investor acquires its ownership at the time of the investee's conception, paying an amount equal to book value is rare. Dell Computer Corporation, as just one example, reported a book value of approximately $16 per share on January 29, 1995, but near that date, the company's common stock was routinely selling for over $40 per share on the New York Stock Exchange. To obtain Dell Computer shares as well as the stock of many other businesses, payment of a significant premium is required. In this particular example, market value was approximately two and one-half times that of book value.

A number of possible reasons exist for such a marked difference in the book value of a company and the price of its stock. A company's value at any time is based on a multitude of factors such as company profitability, the introduction of a new product, expected dividend payments, projected operating results, and general economic conditions. Furthermore, stock prices are based, at least partially, on the perceived worth of a company's net assets, amounts that often vary dramatically from underlying book values. Asset and liability accounts shown on a balance sheet tend to measure historical costs rather than current value. In addition, these reported figures are affected by the specific accounting methods adopted by a company. Inventory costing methods such as LIFO and FIFO, for example, obviously lead to different book values as do each of the acceptable depreciation methods.

If an investment is acquired at a price in excess of book value, logical reasons should explain the additional cost incurred by the investor. The source of the excess of cost over book value is important. Income recognition requires matching the income generated from the investment with its cost. Excess costs allocated to fixed assets will likely be expensed over longer periods than costs allocated to inventory. In applying the equity method, the cause of such an excess payment can be divided into two general categories:

1. Specific investee assets and liabilities may have market values that differ from their present book values. The excess payment can be identified directly with individual accounts such as inventory, equipment, or franchise rights.

2. The investor could be willing to pay an extra amount because future benefits are expected to accrue from the investment. Such benefits might be anticipated as the result of factors such as the estimated profitability of the investee or the relationship being established between the two companies. In this case, the additional payment is attributed to an intangible future value generally referred to as *goodwill* rather than to any specific investee asset or liability. For example, on its December 31, 1996, financial statements, Ameritech Corporation disclosed that its long-term investment in New Zealand Telecom, accounted for under the equity method, includes goodwill of approximately $290 million.

As an illustration, assume that Big Company is negotiating the acquisition of 30 percent of the outstanding shares of Little Company. Little's balance sheet reports assets of $500,000 and liabilities of $300,000 for a net book value of $200,000. After investigation, Big determines that Little's equipment is undervalued in the company's financial records by $60,000. One of its patents is also undervalued, but only by $40,000. By adding these valuation adjustments to Little's book value, Big arrives at an estimated worth for the company's net assets of $300,000. Based on this computation, Big offers $90,000 for a 30 percent share of the investee's outstanding stock.

Book value of Little Company (assets minus liabilities [or stockholders' equity])	$200,000
Undervaluation of equipment	60,000
Undervaluation of patent	40,000
Value of net assets	$300,000
Portion being acquired	30%
Acquisition price	$ 90,000

Although Big's purchase price is in excess of the proportionate share of Little's book value, this additional amount can be attributed to two specific accounts: Equipment and Patents. No part of the extra payment is traceable to any other projected future benefit. Thus, the cost of Big's investment is allocated as follows:

Payment by investor		$90,000
Percentage of book value acquired ($200,000 × 30%)		60,000
Payment in excess of book value		30,000
Excess payment identified with specific assets:		
Equipment ($60,000 undervaluation × 30%)	$18,000	
Patent ($40,000 undervaluation × 30%)	12,000	30,000
Excess payment not identified with specific assets—goodwill		–0–

Of the $30,000 excess payment made by the investor, $18,000 is assigned to the equipment whereas $12,000 is traced to a patent and its undervaluation. No amount of the purchase price is allocated to goodwill.

To take this example one step further, assume that the owners of Little reject the $90,000 price proposed by Big. They believe that the value of the company as a going concern is greater than the market value of its net assets. Since the management of Big believes that an especially profitable business relationship can be created through this purchase, the bid price is raised to $125,000 and accepted. This new acquisition price is allocated as follows:

Payment by investor		$125,000
Percentage of book value acquired ($200,000 × 30%)		60,000
Payment in excess of book value		65,000
Excess payment identified with specific assets:		
Equipment ($60,000 undervaluation × 30%)	18,000	
Patent ($40,000 undervaluation × 30%)	12,000	30,000
Excess payment not identified with specific assets—goodwill		$ 35,000

As can be seen from this example, *any extra payment that cannot be attributed to a specific asset or liability is assigned to the intangible asset goodwill.* Although the actual purchase price can be computed by a number of different techniques or simply result from negotiations, goodwill is always the excess amount not allocated to identifiable asset or liability accounts.

Under the equity method, the investor enters total cost in a single investment account, regardless of the allocation of any excess purchase price. If Big's bid of $125,000 is accepted by all parties, the acquisition is initially recorded at that amount despite the internal assignments made to equipment, patents, and goodwill. The entire $125,000 was paid to acquire this investment, and it is recorded as such.

The Amortization Process

The preceding extra payments were made in connection with assets (equipment, patents, and goodwill) having limited useful lives. Even though the actual dollar amounts are recorded within the Investment account, a definite historical cost can be attributed to these assets. With a cost to the investor as well as a specified life, the payment relating to each asset should be amortized over an appropriate time period.

Assume, for illustration purposes, that the equipment has a 10-year remaining life, the patent a 5-year life, and the goodwill an estimated 40-year life.[10] If the straight-

---

[10]According to *APB Opinion 17,* "Intangible Assets," August 1970, intangible assets must be amortized over a period not to exceed 40 years.

line method is used with no salvage value, *the investor's cost* should be amortized initially as follows:[11]

Account	Cost Assigned	Useful Life	Annual Amortization
Equipment	$18,000	10 years	$1,800
Patent	12,000	5 years	2,400
Goodwill	35,000	40 years	875
Annual expense (for five years until patent cost is completely amortized)			$5,075

In recording this annual expense, Big is reducing a portion of the investment balance in the same way it would amortize the cost of any other asset that had a limited life. Therefore, at the end of the first year, the investor records the following journal entry under the equity method:

Equity in Investee Income	5,075	
Investment in Little Company		5,075
To record amortization of excess payment allocated to equipment, a patent, and goodwill.		

Because this amortization relates to assets held by the investee, the investor does not establish a specific expense account. Instead, as shown in the previous entry, the expense is recognized through a decrease in the equity income accruing from the investee company.

To illustrate this entire process, assume that Tall Company purchases 20 percent of Short Company for $200,000. Tall can exercise significant influence over the investee, thus, the equity method is appropriately applied. The acquisition is made on January 1, 1998, when Short holds net assets with a book value of $700,000. Tall believes that the investee's building (10-year life) is undervalued within the financial records by $80,000 and equipment with a 5-year life is undervalued by $120,000. Any goodwill established by this purchase would be amortized over the maximum allowable time period. During 1998, Short reports a net income of $150,000 and pays a cash dividend at year's end of $60,000.

Tall's three basic journal entries for 1998 pose little problem:

January 1, 1998

Investment in Short Company	200,000	
Cash		200,000
To record acquisition of 20 percent of the outstanding shares of Short Company.		

December 31, 1998

Investment in Short Company	30,000	
Equity in Investee Income		30,000
To accrue 20 percent of the 1998 reported earnings of investee ($150,000 × 20%).		
Cash	12,000	
Investment in Short Company		12,000
To record receipt of 1998 cash dividend ($60,000 × 20%).		

An allocation must be made of Tall's $200,000 purchase price to determine if an additional adjusting entry is necessary to recognize annual amortization associated with the extra payment:

---

[11] Unless otherwise stated, all amortization computations are based on the straight-line method with no salvage value.

Payment by investor		$200,000
Percentage of 1/1/98 book value ($700,000 × 20%)		140,000
Payment in excess of book value		60,000
Excess payment identified with specific assets:		
Building ($80,000 × 20%)	$16,000	
Equipment ($120,000 × 20%)	24,000	40,000
Excess payment not identified with specific assets—goodwill		$ 20,000

As can be seen, $16,000 of the purchase price is assigned to a building, $24,000 to equipment, with the remaining $20,000 attributed to goodwill. Each of these assets has a limited useful life; therefore, periodic amortization is required.

Asset	Attributed Cost	Useful Life	Annual Amortization
Building	$16,000	10 years	$1,600
Equipment	24,000	5 years	4,800
Goodwill	20,000	40 years	500
Total for 1998			$6,900

At the end of 1998, Tall must also record the following adjustment in connection with these cost allocations:

Equity in Investee Income	6,900	
Investment in Short Company		6,900
To record 1998 amortization of extra cost of building ($1,600),		
equipment ($4,800), and goodwill ($500).		

Although these entries are shown separately here for better explanation, Tall would probably net the income accrual for the year ($30,000) and the amortization ($6,900) to create a single entry increasing the investment and recognizing equity income of $23,100.

ELIMINATION OF UNREALIZED GAINS IN INVENTORY[12]

Many large stock acquisitions are made for one primary purpose: to establish ties between companies to facilitate the direct purchase and sale of inventory items. Such intercompany transactions may occur either on a regular basis or only sporadically. For example, the Coca-Cola Company disclosed that syrup and concentrate sales of $1.6 billion were made in 1996 to its 45 percent-owned investee Coca-Cola Enterprises Inc.

Regardless of their frequency, inventory sales between investor and investee necessitate the use of special accounting procedures to ensure proper timing of revenue recognition. An underlying principle of accounting is that "revenues are not recognized until earned . . . and revenues are considered to have been earned when the entity has substantially accomplished what it must do to be entitled to the benefits represented by the revenues."[13] In the sale of inventory to an unrelated party, recognition of revenue is normally not in question; substantial accomplishment is achieved when the exchange takes place unless special terms are included in the contract.

Unfortunately, the earning process is not so clearly delineated in sales made between related parties. *Because of the relationship between investor and investee, the seller of the goods is said to retain a partial stake in the inventory for as long as it is*

---

[12]Unrealized gains may involve the sale of items other than inventory. The intercompany transfer of depreciable fixed assets and land are discussed in a later chapter.

[13]FASB, *Statement of Financial Accounting Concepts No. 6,* "Recognition and Measurement in Financial Statements of Business Enterprises" (Stamford, Conn.: December 1984), par. 83.

Exhibit 1–2

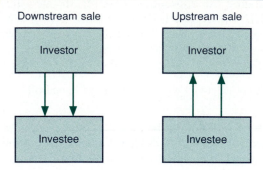

held by the buyer. Thus, the earning process is not considered complete at the time of the original sale. For proper accounting, revenue recognition must be deferred until substantial accomplishment is proven. Consequently, when the investor applies the equity method, reporting of the related profit on intercompany transfers is delayed until the ultimate disposition of the goods by the buyer. When the inventory is eventually consumed within operations or resold to an unrelated party, the original sale is culminated and the gross profit is fully recognized.

In accounting, transactions between related companies are identified as either *downstream* or *upstream*. Downstream transfers refer to the sale of an item by the investor to the investee. Conversely, an upstream sale describes one made to the investor by the investee (see Exhibit 1–2). *Although this distinction is not significant for carrying out the procedures of the equity method, it has definite consequences in the consolidation of financial statements, as discussed in Chapter 5.* Therefore, these two types of intercompany sales are examined separately even at this introductory stage.

Downstream Sales of Inventory

Assume that Big Company owns a 40 percent share of Little Company and accounts for this investment through the equity method. In 1998, Big sells inventory to Little at a price of $50,000. This figure includes a markup of 30 percent, or $15,000. By the end of 1998, Little has sold $40,000 of these goods to outside parties while retaining $10,000 in inventory for sale during the subsequent year.

Downstream sales have been made by the investor to the investee. In applying the equity method, recognition of the related profit must be delayed until these goods are disposed of by the buyer. Although total intercompany transfers amounted to $50,000 in 1998, $40,000 of this merchandise has already been resold to outsiders, thereby justifying the normal reporting of profits. For the $10,000 still in the investee's inventory, the earning process is not finished. In computing equity income, this portion of the intercompany gain must be deferred until the goods are disposed of by Little.

The markup on the original sale was 30 percent of the transfer price; therefore, Big's profit associated with these remaining items is $3,000 ($10,000 × 30%). *However, because only 40 percent of the investee's stock is being held, just $1,200 ($3,000 × 40%) of this gain is unearned.* Big's ownership percentage reflects the intercompany portion of the gain. The total $3,000 gross profit within the ending inventory balance is not the amount deferred. Rather, 40 percent of that gain is viewed as the currently unrealized figure.

Remaining Ending Inventory	Gross Profit Percentage	Gain in Ending Inventory	Investor Ownership Percentage	Unrealized Intercompany Gain
$10,000	30%	$3,000	40%	$1,200

After calculating the appropriate deferral, the investor decreases current equity income by $1,200 to reflect the unearned portion of the intercompany gain. This procedure temporarily removes this portion of the profit from the books of the investor in 1998 until the inventory is disposed of by the investee in 1999. Big accomplishes the actual deferral through the following year-end journal entry:

Deferral of Unrealized Gain

Equity in Investee Income	1,200	
Investment in Little Company		1,200
To defer unrealized gain on sale of inventory to Little Company.		

In the subsequent year, when this inventory is eventually consumed by Little or sold to unrelated parties, the deferral is no longer needed. The earning process is complete and the $1,200 should be recognized by Big. By merely reversing the preceding deferral entry, the accountant succeeds in moving the investor's profit in the appropriate time period. Recognition is shifted from the year of transfer to the year in which the earning process is substantially accomplished.

Subsequent Realization of Intercompany Gain

Investment in Little Company	1,200	
Equity in Investee Income		1,200
To recognize income on intercompany sale that has now been earned through sales to outsiders.		

Upstream Sales of Inventory

Unlike consolidated financial statements (see Chapter 5), the equity method reports upstream sales of inventory in the same manner as downstream sales. Hence, unrealized gains remaining in ending inventory are deferred until the items are used or sold to unrelated parties. To illustrate, assume that Big Company once again owns 40 percent of Little Company. During the current year, Little sells merchandise costing $40,000 to Big for $60,000. At the end of the fiscal period, Big still retains $15,000 of these goods. Little reports net income of $120,000 for the year.

To reflect the basic accrual of the investee's earnings, Big records the following journal entry at the end of this year:

Income Accrual

Investment in Little Company	48,000	
Equity in Investee Income		48,000
To accrue income from 40 percent owned investee ($120,000 × 40%).		

The amount of the gain remaining unrealized at year-end is computed using the markup of $33\frac{1}{3}$ percent of the sales price ($20,000/$60,000):

Remaining Ending Inventory	Gross Profit Percentage	Gain in Ending Inventory	Investor Ownership Percentage	Unrealized Intercompany Gain
$15,000	$33\frac{1}{3}$%	$5,000	40%	$2,000

Based on this calculation, a second entry is required of the investor at year-end. Once again, a deferral of the unrealized gain created by the intercompany transfer is necessary for proper timing of income recognition. *Under the equity method, the direction of the sale has no influence on either the amount or the method of reporting.*

The Coca-Cola Company accounts for its ownership of Coca-Cola Enterprises (CCE) by use of the equity method as described here in Chapter 1. As of December 31, 1996, Coca-Cola held approximately 45 percent of the outstanding stock of CCE. According to the financial statements of CCE, "The products of The Coca-Cola Company account for approximately 91% of our total revenues. Our fourteen-member Board of Directors includes four current or former executives of The Coca-Cola Company, one of whom serves as our chairman. All directors serving on our Board are accomplished individuals and are elected by our share owners."

If Coca-Cola acquires approximately five percent more of CCE, a majority of the stock will be held so that consolidation becomes a requirement. However, given the size of the present ownership and the dependence that CCE has on Coca-Cola for products and marketing, does Coca-Cola truly have no more than "the ability to exercise significant influence over the operating and financial policies" of CCE? Does the equity method fairly represent the relationship that exists? Or, does Coca-Cola actually control CCE despite the level of ownership, and should consolidation be required? Currently, the FASB is reexamining the boundary between the application of the equity method and consolidation. Should the rules be rewritten so that Coca-Cola must consolidate CCE rather than use the equity method? If so, at what level of ownership would the equity method no longer be appropriate?

Deferral of Unrealized Gain

Equity in Investee Income	2,000	
Investment in Little Company		2,000

    To defer recognition of intercompany unrealized gain
    until inventory is used or sold to unrelated parties.

After the adjustment, Big, the investor, reports earnings from this equity investment of $46,000 ($48,000 − $2,000). The income accrual is reduced because a portion of the intercompany gross profit is considered unrealized. When the $15,000 in merchandise is eventually consumed or sold by the investor, the preceding journal entry is reversed. In this way, the effects of the gain are reported in the proper accounting period when the gain is earned by sales to an outside party.

In an upstream sale, the investor's own Inventory account contains the unrealized gain. The previous entry, though, defers recognition of this profit by decreasing Big's investment account rather than the inventory balance. APB *Accounting Interpretation No. 1 of APB Opinion 18,* "Intercompany Profit Eliminations under Equity Method," November 1971, permits the direct reduction of the investor's inventory balance as a means of accounting for this gain. Although this alternative is acceptable, decreasing the investment remains the traditional approach for deferring unrealized gains, even for upstream sales.

As a final note, whether upstream or downstream, the investor's sales and purchases are still reported as if the transactions were carried out with outside parties. Only the unrealized gain is deferred and that amount is adjusted solely through the equity income account. Furthermore, since the companies are not consolidated, the investee's reported balances are not altered at all to reflect the nature of these sales/purchases. Obviously, readers of the financial statements need to be made aware of the inclusion of these amounts in the income statement. Thus, the FASB issued *Statement No. 57,* "Related Party Disclosures," in March 1982; it required reporting companies to disclose certain information about related party transactions. These disclosures include the nature of the relationship, a description of the transactions, the dollar amounts of the transactions, and amounts due to or from any related parties at year-end.

DEFERRED INCOME TAXES[14]

The final issue explored in this chapter concerns the deferral of income taxes. Although the equity method is appropriate for external reporting purposes, the Internal Revenue Code only taxes cash dividends actually collected. The dividend income reported to the tax authorities by the investor normally differs from the investment earnings recognized under the equity method.

To illustrate, assume that Giant owns 30 percent of Small and utilizes the equity method. If this investee reports a $100,000 profit for the current period, Giant immediately recognizes an income accrual of $30,000. However, if Small distributes a total dividend of $20,000 during the same year, Giant reports just the 30 percent received ($6,000) on its tax return.

Because these two methods vary, an important theoretical accounting question arises: Must Giant (the investor) report a liability for future taxes on the remainder of the income being recognized? Or, stated differently, should Giant's tax liability as reported in its financial statements be based on the $30,000 equity income accrual or the $6,000 that is currently taxable?

Most companies routinely retain some portion of their earnings as a permanent basis for future growth. Therefore, an argument can be made that part of the $24,000 difference between the equity income being recognized by Giant ($30,000) and the current cash dividends ($6,000) collected from Small will never be distributed by the investee to the investor. If this portion of equity income is not conveyed, no tax effect will be created in the future. Thus, the assertion has been made that at least some portion of this difference produces no true liability for the investor.

This logic was rejected initially by the APB in *Opinion 24,* "Accounting for Income Taxes—Equity Method Investments," April 1972. A deferred income tax liability was required of the investor to reflect the *entire* amount of potential taxes incurred because of the current recognition of equity earnings. This conservative approach was said to best represent the matching principle: The tax expense is recognized in the same period as the related revenues. In addition, the argument that equity income in excess of current dividends ($24,000 in this example) would never become taxable was virtually impossible to prove. Either through future dividends or the ultimate sale of the investment, an eventual increase in the investor's taxable income seems inevitable.

The FASB reaffirmed this conclusion in *Statement of Financial Accounting Standards No. 109,* "Accounting for Income Taxes," which became effective December 15, 1992. This pronouncement again directs the investor to accrue a liability for future taxes on the excess $24,000 even though the amount is not subject to current taxation. This amount is identified by *Statement 109* (in its glossary) as a *taxable temporary difference,* "differences that result in taxable amounts in future years when the related asset or liability is recovered or settled, respectively."

Thus, utilization of the equity method normally creates a temporary taxable difference between the dividend income reported for tax purposes and the amount accrued by the investor for financial reporting. *Statement 109* requires immediate recognition of a deferred tax effect. Because the income will be taxed in a subsequent period either through a dividend distribution or sale of the stock, the immediate recording of a debt on the $24,000 temporary difference is required. Or, from a different perspective, because an increase in the investment account of $24,000 is reported, it must be

---

[14]The computation and reporting of deferred income taxes is an extremely complex topic that is normally examined in intermediate accounting textbooks. Coverage here is limited to a specific aspect of this issue relevant to the application of the equity method. Consequently, no other differences between taxable income and reported earnings are included in any of the illustrations.

recognized that all of the increase may not be forthcoming to the owners; the tax liability relating to the asset must also be recorded.[15]

Under the present Internal Revenue Code of the United States, a corporation is allowed a reduction of 80 percent for any dividends collected from another domestic corporation if 20 percent or more of the outstanding stock is held.[16] The purpose of this dividends received deduction is to mitigate the effects of taxing two entities for the same income. Assuming a tax rate of 30 percent, the income tax to be paid by the investor (Giant) on the $6,000 received during the year from Small is only $360, computed as follows:

Taxes Currently Payable on $6,000 Dividend

Cash Dividends	80 Percent Deduction	Taxable Income	Tax Rate	Taxes Currently Payable
$6,000	$4,800	$1,200	30%	$360

Although only $360 in income taxes must be paid currently by the owner, *FASB Statement 109* dictates that an additional liability is created by the $24,000 temporary difference. However, computing the amount of this obligation can vary significantly, depending on a single assumption. If the stock is to be held by Giant for an indefinite period so that the investor anticipates the eventual receipt of these earnings as dividends, the 80 percent deduction is applicable to the current tax calculation. Conversely, if the investment is to be sold before these dividends are paid, the $24,000 is expected to be realized by the investor through a higher negotiated price. Thus, the dividend deduction is not relevant in determining the deferred liability.

Deferred Liability—Undistributed $24,000

Investor Anticipates Receiving Future Dividends				
Undistributed Income within Investment	80 Percent Deduction	Income to Be Taxed	Tax Rate	Deferred Tax Liability
$24,000	$19,200	$4,800	30%	$1,440

Investor Anticipates Future Sale of Investment		
Undistributed Income within Investment	Tax Rate	Deferred Tax Liability
$24,000	30%	$7,200

In the first case, the investor's total liability is $1,800 ($360 current and $1,440 future) because the income is to be realized as dividends. For the second possibility, a liability of $7,560 is required ($360 payable now with $7,200 assumed to be payable later when the stock is sold). Using either assumption, the investor's year-end adjusting entry includes a deferred income tax liability resulting from the undistributed earnings of the equity investee within the Investment in Small account.

Dividends to Be Received

Income Tax Expense—Current	360	
Income Tax Expense—Deferred	1,440	
Income Taxes Payable—Current		360
Deferred Income Taxes Payable		1,440
To record taxes on income accruing from equity investment.		

---

[15]*SFAS 109* provides an exception: No deferred tax liability is required for a foreign corporate joint venture accounted for by means of the equity method if the difference is considered to be permanent in duration. As mentioned again in Chapter 7, the same rule applies to foreign subsidiaries.

[16]The corporate dividend received deduction is 70 percent if less than 20 percent of the investee's stock is owned. If 80 percent or more of the stock is held, intercompany dividends are not taxed.

Investment to Be Sold

Income Tax Expense—Current	360	
Income Tax Expense—Deferred	7,200	
Income Taxes Payable—Current		360
Deferred Income Taxes Payable		7,200

    To record taxes on income accruing from equity investment.

SUMMARY

1. The equity method of accounting for an investment reflects the close relationship that may exist between an investor and an investee. More specifically, this approach is applied whenever the owner achieves the ability to apply significant influence to the investee's operating and financial decisions. Significant influence is presumed to exist at the 20 to 50 percent ownership level. However, the accountant must evaluate each situation, regardless of the percentage of ownership, to determine whether this ability is actually present.

2. To mirror the relationship between the companies, the equity method requires the investor to accrue income when earned by the investee. In recording this profit or loss, the investor separately reports items such as extraordinary gains and losses as well as prior period adjustments to highlight their nonrecurring nature. Dividend payments decrease the owners' equity of the investee company; therefore, the investor reduces the investment account when collected.

3. When acquiring capital stock, an investor often pays an amount that exceeds the underlying book value of the investee company. For accounting purposes, such excess payments must be identified with either specific assets and liabilities (such as land or buildings) or allocated to an intangible asset referred to as goodwill. Each assigned cost (except for any amount attributed to land) is then amortized by the investor over the expected useful lives of the assets and liabilities. This amortization reduces the amount of equity income being reported.

4. If the entire investment or any portion is sold, the equity method is applied consistently until the date of disposal. A gain or loss is computed based on the adjusted book value at that time. Remaining shares are accounted for by means of either the equity method or the fair-value method, depending on the investor's subsequent ability to significantly influence the investee.

5. Inventory (or other assets) may be transferred between investor and investee. Because of the relationship between the two companies, the equity income accrual should be reduced to defer the intercompany portion of any markup included on these transfers until the items are either sold to outsiders or consumed. Thus, the amount of intercompany gain in ending inventory decreases the amount of equity income being recognized in the current period although this effect is subsequently reversed.

6. Income taxes are paid by the investor on the amount of dividends received from an investee (less a dividend deduction allowed by law). However, if the equity method is applied, the investor recognizes income for financial reporting purposes at the time it is earned by the investee. Because of this income accrual, the investment account determined for external reporting usually exceeds the asset's cost, the balance appropriate for tax purposes. This excess is viewed as a taxable temporary difference and a deferred tax liability must be recognized by the investor.

COMPREHENSIVE ILLUSTRATION

Problem

(Estimated Time: 30 to 50 Minutes) Every chapter in this textbook concludes with an illustration designed to assist students in tying together the essential elements of the material presented. After a careful reading of each chapter, attempt to work through the comprehensive problem. Then review the solution that follows the problem, noting the handling of each significant accounting issue.

Part A

On January 1, 1998, Big Company pays $70,000 for a 10 percent interest in Little Company. On that date, Little has a book value of $600,000, although equipment, which has a five-year life, is undervalued by $100,000 on its books. Little Company's stock is closely held by a few investors and is traded only infrequently. Because fair values are not readily available on a continuing basis, the investment account is appropriately maintained at cost.

On January 1, 1999, Big acquires an additional 30 percent of Little Company for $264,000. This second purchase provides Big with the ability to exert significant influence over Little. At the time of this transaction, Little's equipment with a four-year life was undervalued by only $80,000.

During these two years, Little reported the following operational results:

Year	Net Income	Cash Dividends Paid
1998	$210,000	$110,000
1999	250,000	$100,000

Additional Information:

- The tax rate is 30 percent.
- Cash dividends are always paid on July 1 of each year.
- Any goodwill will be amortized over a 15-year period.
- Big plans to hold the investment indefinitely.

Required:

a. What income did Big originally report for 1998 in connection with this investment?
b. On comparative financial statements for 1998 and 1999, what figures should Big report in connection with this investment?

Part B (This problem is a continuation of Part A)

In 2000, Little Company reports $400,000 in income from continuing operations plus a $60,000 extraordinary gain. The company pays a $120,000 cash dividend. During this fiscal year, Big sells inventory costing $80,000 to Little for $100,000. Little continues to hold 30 percent of this merchandise at the end of 2000. Big maintains 40 percent ownership of Little throughout the period.

Required:

Ignoring income taxes, prepare all necessary journal entries for Big for the year of 2000.

Solution

Part A

a. Big Company accounts for its investment in Little Company at cost during 1998. Since only 10 percent of the outstanding shares were held, significant influence was apparently not present. Because the stock is not actively traded, fair values are not available and the investment remains at cost. Therefore, only the $11,000 ($110,000 × 10%) received as dividends is recorded by the investor as income in the original financial reporting for that year.

b. To make comparative reports consistent, a change to the equity method is recorded retroactively. Therefore, when the ability to exert significant influence over the operations of Little is established on January 1, 1999, both Big's 1998 and 1999 financial statements must reflect the equity method.

Big first evaluates the initial purchase of Little's stock to determine if either goodwill or incremental asset values need be reflected within the equity method procedures.

Purchase of 10 Percent of Voting Stock on January 1, 1998

Payment by investor	$70,000
Percentage of book value acquired ($600,000 × 10%)	60,000
Payment in excess of book value	10,000
Excess payment identified with specific assets:	
Equipment ($100,000 × 10%)	10,000
Excess payment identified with specific assets—goodwill	–0–

As shown here, the $10,000 excess payment was made in recognition of the undervaluation of Little's equipment. This asset had a useful life at that time of five years; thus, the investor records amortization expense of $2,000 each year.

A similar calculation must be carried out for Big's second stock purchase:

Purchase of 30 Percent of Voting Stock on January 1, 1999

Payment by investor	$264,000
Percentage of book value* acquired ($700,000 × 30%).....................	210,000
Payment in excess of book value	54,000
Excess payment identified with specific assets:	
Equipment ($80,000 × 30%)	24,000
Excess payment not identified with specific assets—goodwill	$ 30,000

*Little's book value on January 1, 1999, is computed by adding the 1998 net income of $210,000 less dividends paid of $110,000 to the previous book value of $600,000.

In this second acquisition, $24,000 of the payment is attributable to the undervalued equipment with $30,000 assigned to goodwill. Since the equipment now has only a four-year remaining life, annual amortization of $6,000 is appropriate ($24,000/4). The goodwill, which has an assumed life of 15 years, will be expensed at the rate of $2,000 per year ($30,000/15). Thus total amortization on this second purchase is initially $8,000 per year.

After the additional shares are acquired on January 1, 1999, Big's financial records for 1998 must be retroactively restated as if the equity method had been applied from the date of the initial investment.

Financial Reporting—1998

Equity in Investee Income (Income Statement)	
Income reported by Little	$210,000
Big's ownership..	10%
Accrual for 1998	$ 21,000
Less: equipment amortization (first purchase)	(2,000)
Equity in investee income—1998	$ 19,000
Investment in Little (Balance Sheet)	
Cost of first acquisition	$ 70,000
1998 Equity in investee income (above)...........................	19,000
Less: Dividends received ($110,000 × 10%)........................	(11,000)
Investment in Little—12/31/98	$ 78,000

The tax effects for 1998 should also be reconsidered. Big collected $11,000 in dividends from Little; thus, the investor's taxable income increased by $2,200 after subtracting the 80 percent deduction. Based on the 30 percent tax rate, Big paid $660 ($2,200 × 30%) in 1998 income taxes relating to this investment. However, *FASB Statement 109* also requires the recording of a liability on the taxable temporary difference that now exists because the equity accrual in the Investment in Little account exceeds the dividend distributed.

As shown, Big is accruing earnings of $19,000, rather than the $11,000 dividend received. Because the investment increases by a net $8,000, recognition of a deferred tax liability on that amount is necessary. After subtracting the 80 percent dividend deduction (applicable because the stock will be held indefinitely), future taxable income is anticipated to increase by $1,600 rather than the entire $8,000. Thus, Big must also retroactively report deferred income taxes of $480 (30%) for 1998 to reflect the change being made to the equity method.

Financial Reporting—1999

Equity in Investee Income (Income Statement)
Income reported by Little $250,000
Big's ownership 40%

    Big's share of Little's reported income $100,000
Less amortization expense:
  Equipment (first purchase) . . . .   (2,000)
  Equipment (second purchase) . . . .   (6,000)
  Goodwill (second purchase) . . . .   (2,000)

    Equity in investee income—1999 . . . . $ 90,000

Investment in Little (Balance Sheet)
Book value—12/31/98 (above) . . . . $ 78,000
Cost of 1999 acquisition   264,000
Equity in investee income (above)   90,000
Less: Dividends received ($100,000 × 40%) . . . .   (40,000)

    Investment in Little—12/31/99 . . . . $392,000

For current taxation purposes, Big reports $8,000 ($40,000 dividends collected less the 80 percent dividend exclusion). The 30 percent tax rate necessitates recognition of $2,400 as the current portion of Big's income tax liability for 1999. However, the reporting of a deferred tax liability also is required. Big's equity income accrual for this same period is $90,000. The $50,000 rise in the investment account ($90,000 income less $40,000 in dividends) is another taxable temporary difference. According to *Statement 109,* this creates an increase in the deferred tax liability related to the investment. Of this $50,000 difference, taxes would be assessed on only $10,000 after subtracting the 80 percent dividend reduction. At a 30 percent tax rate, Big records an additional $3,000 as deferred income tax for 1999.

The total deferred tax liability is thus $3,480 ($480 from 1998 and $3,000 from 1999). From another perspective, the total temporary difference related to the investment is $58,000 ($392,000 carrying value less $334,000 cost). The total deferred tax liability on the temporary difference is $58,000 × (1 − 80%) × 30% = $3,480.

Part B

On July 1, 2000, Big receives a $48,000 cash dividend from Little (40% × $120,000). According to the equity method, receipt of this dividend reduces the carrying value of the investment account:

Cash   48,000
    Investment in Little Company   48,000
  To record receipt of 2000 dividend from investee.

Big records no other journal entries in connection with this investment until the end of 2000. At that time, the annual accrual of income is made as well as the adjustment to record amortization (see Part A for computation of expense). The investee's continuing income is reported separately from the extraordinary item.

Investment in Little Company   184,000
    Equity in Investee Income   160,000
    Extraordinary Gain of Investee   24,000
  To recognize reported income of investee based on a
  40 percent ownership level of $400,000 operating income
  and $60,000 extraordinary gain.

Equity in Investee Income   10,000
    Investment in Little Company   10,000
  To record annual amortization on excess payment made in
  relation to equipment ($2,000 from first purchase and $6,000
  from second) and goodwill ($2,000).

Big only needs to make one other equity entry during 2000. Intercompany sales have occurred and a portion of the inventory continues to be held by Little. Therefore, an unrealized gain exists that must be deferred. The markup on the sales price was 20 percent ($20,000/$100,000). Since $30,000 of this merchandise is still in the possession of the investee, the related gain is $6,000 ($30,000 × 20%). However, Big owns only 40 percent of the outstanding stock of Little; thus, the unrealized intercompany gain at year's end is $2,400 ($6,000 × 40%). That amount must be deferred until the inventory is consumed by Little or sold to unrelated parties in subsequent years.

Equity in Investee Company	2,400	
Investment in Little Company		2,400
To defer unrealized gain on intercompany sale.		

QUESTIONS

1. A company acquires a rather large investment in another corporation. What criteria determine whether the equity method of accounting should be applied by the investor to this investment?

2. What indicates an investor's ability to significantly influence the decision-making process of an investee?

3. Why does the equity method record dividends received from an investee as a reduction in the investment account and not as dividend income?

4. The Jones Company possesses a 25 percent interest in the outstanding voting shares of the Sandridge Company. Under what circumstances might Jones decide that the equity method would not be appropriate to account for this investment?

5. Smith, Inc., has maintained an ownership interest in Watts Corporation for a number of years. This investment has been accounted for by means of the equity method. What transactions or events create changes in the Investment in Watts Corporation account being recorded by Smith?

6. Although the equity method is a generally accepted accounting principle (GAAP), recognition of equity income has been criticized. What theoretical problems can be brought up by opponents of the equity method?

7. Because of the acquisition of additional investee shares, an investor may be forced to change from the fair-value method to the equity method. Which procedures are applied to effect this accounting change?

8. Riggins Company accounts for its investment in Bostic Company by means of the equity method. During the past fiscal year, Bostic reported an extraordinary gain on its income statement. How would this extraordinary item affect the financial records of the investor?

9. During the current year, the common stock of the Davis Company suffers a permanent drop in market value. In the past, Davis has made a significant portion of its sales to one customer. This buyer recently announced its decision to make no further purchases from the Davis Company, an action that led to the loss of market value. Hawkins, Inc., owns 35 percent of the outstanding shares of Davis, an investment that is recorded according to the equity method. How would the loss in value affect the financial reporting of this investor?

10. Wilson Company acquired 40 percent of Andrews Company at a bargain price because of losses expected to result from Andrews's failure in marketing several new products. The price paid by Wilson was only $100,000, although Andrews's corresponding book value was much higher. In the first year after acquisition, Andrews lost $300,000. In applying the equity method, how should Wilson account for this loss?

11. In a stock acquisition accounted for by the equity method, a portion of the purchase price often is attributed to goodwill or to specific assets or liabilities. How are these amounts determined at the time of acquisition? How are these amounts accounted for in subsequent periods?

12. Princeton Company holds a 40 percent interest in the outstanding voting stock of Yale Company. On June 19 of the current year, Princeton sells part of this investment. What accounting should Princeton make on June 19? What accounting will Princeton make for the remainder of the current year?

13. What is the difference between downstream and upstream sales? How does this difference impact application of the equity method?

14. How is the unrealized gain on intercompany sales calculated? What effect does an unrealized gain have on the recording of an investment if the equity method is applied?

15. How are intercompany transfers reported in the separate financial statements of an investee if the investor is using the equity method?

16. How is an investor taxed on the income that accrues from an equity investee?

17. How are deferred income taxes computed in connection with equity income?

LIBRARY ASSIGNMENTS

1. Read "Accounting for Non-Majority-Owned Intercorporate Investments: A Cash Flow Assessment of Alternative Methods," by Sharon McKinnon and Katherine Taylor Halvorsen in *Journal of Business Finance and Accounting*, January 1993. The article compares three methods of accounting for investments and examines their accuracy in predicting future cash flows. Discuss its findings and whether or not this accuracy in prediction should be a primary determinant of the worth of investment accounting methods.

2. Read the following articles and any others available in the library on the equity method:

   "Equity Earnings," *Forbes*, March 31, 1980.
   "Equity Accounting Isn't Equitable," *Forbes*, March 31, 1980.

   Also read *APB Opinion No. 18*, "The Equity Method of Accounting for Investments in Common Stock" (including the dissent and qualifications that follow the pronouncement). Prepare a report to either justify the continued use of the equity method as a generally accepted accounting principle or suggest revisions or abolishment of this approach.

3. Obtain the latest financial statements of The Dow Chemical Company, American Cyanamid Company, or any other corporation holding stock investments reported by the equity method. For these investments, indicate the placement and amount of both the balance sheet and the income statement figures. What percentage of total assets do these investments constitute? Describe the information that is conveyed about these investments in the reporting company's notes to the financial statements.

4. Read "The Influence of Accounting Principles on Management Investment Decisions: An Illustration" in the June 1988 issue of *Accounting Horizons*. The authors state that "The results of this survey indicate that the equity-accounting standard does impact investment decisions by influencing the size of the investment position taken." Should accounting principles affect a company's operating and financing decisions? How can accounting principles be written that would report only a company's activities and have no impact on operating and financing decisions?

PROBLEMS

1. When an investor uses the equity method to account for investments in common stock, cash dividends received by the investor from the investee should be recorded as:
   a. A deduction from the investor's share of the investee's profits.
   b. Dividend income.
   c. A deduction from the stockholders' equity account, dividends to stockholders.
   d. A deduction from the investment account.

   (AICPA adapted)

2. Which of the following is not an indication that an investor company has the ability to significantly influence an investee?
   a. Material intercompany transactions.
   b. The company owns 30 percent of the company but another owner holds the remaining 70 percent.
   c. Interchange of personnel.
   d. Technological dependency.

3. Sisk Company has owned 10 percent of Maust, Inc., for the past several years. This ownership did not allow Sisk to have significant influence over Maust. Recently, Sisk acquires an additional 30 percent of Maust and now does have this ability. How will this change be reported by the investor?

    a. A cumulative effect of an accounting change is shown in the current income statement.

    b. No change is recorded; the equity method is used from the date of the new acquisition.

    c. A retroactive adjustment is made to restate all prior years to the equity method.

    d. Sisk has the option of choosing the method to be used to show this change.

4. On January 1, 1998, Puckett Company paid $1.6 million for 50,000 shares of Harrison's voting common stock which represents a 40 percent investment. No allocation to goodwill or other specific account was made. Significant influence over Harrison is achieved by this acquisition. Harrison distributed a dividend of $2 per share during 1998 and reported net income of $560,000. What is the balance in the Investment in Harrison account found in the financial records of Puckett as of December 31, 1998?

    a. $1,724,000.

    b. $1,784,000.

    c. $1,844,000.

    d. $1,884,000.

5. In January 1998, Wilkinson Corporation acquired 20 percent of the outstanding common stock of Bremm, Inc., for $700,000. This investment gave Wilkinson the ability to exercise significant influence over Bremm. Bremm's assets on that date were recorded at $3,900,000 with liabilities of $900,000. Any excess of cost over book value of Wilkinson's investment was attributed to goodwill having a remaining useful life of 10 years.

    In 1998, Bremm reported net income of $170,000. In 1999, Bremm reported net income of $210,000. Dividends of $70,000 were paid in each of these two years. What is the reported balance of Wilkinson's Investment in Bremm at December 31, 1999?

    a. $728,000.

    b. $748,000.

    c. $756,000.

    d. $776,000.

6. Ace purchases 40 percent of Baskett Company on January 1, 1998, for $500,000. Although not used, this acquisition did give Ace the ability to apply significant influence to the operating and financing policies of Baskett. Baskett reports assets on that date of $1,400,000 with liabilities of $500,000. One building with a seven-year life is undervalued on Baskett's books by $140,000. Any goodwill is to be amortized over 10 years. During 1998, Baskett reports net income of $90,000 while paying dividends of $30,000. What is the Investment in Baskett balance in Ace's financial records as of December 31, 1998?

    a. $504,000.

    b. $507,600.

    c. $513,900.

    d. $516,000.

7. Goldman Company reports net income of $140,000 each year and pays an annual cash dividend of $50,000. The company holds net assets of $1,200,000 on January 1, 1998. On that date, Wallace purchases 10 percent of the outstanding stock for $150,000. On January 1, 2000, the fair value of the 10 percent stock investment is $160,000. Also on January 1, 2000, Wallace buys an additional 20 percent of Goldman's stock for $300,000. This second purchase gives Wallace the ability to significantly influence Goldman. Goodwill is to be amortized over its maximum life. On December 31, 2000, what is the Investment in Goldman balance in Wallace's financial records?

    a. $477,200.

    b. $484,550.

    c. $487,900.

    d. $492,150.

8. Perez, Inc., owns 25 percent of Senior, Inc. During 1998, Perez sold goods with a 40 percent gross profit to Senior. Senior sold all of these goods in 1998. How should Perez report the effect of the intercompany sale on its 1998 income statement?
   a. Sales and cost of goods sold should be reduced by the intercompany sales.
   b. Sales and cost of goods sold should be reduced by 25 percent of the intercompany sales.
   c. Investment income should be reduced by 25 percent of the gross profit on intercompany sales.
   d. No adjustment is necessary.

9. Panner, Inc., owns 30 percent of Watkins and applies the equity method. During the current year, Panner buys inventory costing $54,000 and then sells it to Watkins for $90,000. At the end of the year, only $20,000 merchandise is still being held by Watkins. What amount of unrealized gain must be deferred by Panner in reporting this investment on the equity method?
   a. $2,400.
   b. $4,800.
   c. $8,000.
   d. $10,800.

10. Camato, Inc., buys 40 percent of Swisher Company on January 1, 1998, for $530,000. The equity method of accounting is to be used. The net assets of Swisher on that date were $1.2 million. Any goodwill is to be written off over the maximum possible life. Swisher immediately begins supplying inventory to Camato as follows:

Year	Cost to Swisher	Transfer Price	Amount Held by Camato at Year-End (at Transfer Price)
1998	$70,000	$100,000	$25,000
1999	96,000	150,000	45,000

Inventory held at the end of one year by Camato is sold at the beginning of the next.
   Swisher reports net income of $80,000 in 1998 and $110,000 in 1999 while paying $30,000 in dividends each year. What is the equity income in Swisher to be reported by Camato in 1999?
   a. $34,050.
   b. $39,270.
   c. $46,230.
   d. $51,450.

11. Eastwood, Inc., purchased 35 percent of Tanner Company on July 1, 1998, for $180,000. This purchase was for 60,000 shares of stock and gave Eastwood significant influence over Tanner. This investment is to be held indefinitely. Tanner earned income evenly throughout the year of $250,000. On November 10, 1998, Tanner declared and paid a $.40 per share dividend. Assuming Eastwood has a 40 percent tax rate, what is that company's current tax liability and deferred tax liability?
   a. $1,440 current and $16,060 deferred.
   b. $9,600 current and $7,900 deferred.
   c. $1,920 current and $1,580 deferred.
   d. $1,920 current and $3,950 deferred.

12. On January 3, 1998, Haskins Corporation acquired 40 percent of the outstanding common stock of Clem Company for $990,000. This acquisition gave Haskins the ability to exercise significant influence over the investee. The book value of the acquired shares was $790,000. Any excess cost over the underlying book value was assigned to a patent that was undervalued on Clem's balance sheet. This patent has a remaining useful life of 10 years. For the year ended December 31, 1998, Clem reported net income of $260,000 and paid cash dividends of $80,000. At December 31, 1998, what should Haskins report as its Investment in Clem?

13. On January 1, 1998, Alison, Inc., paid $60,000 for a 40 percent interest in Holister Corporation. This investee had assets with a book value of $200,000 and liabilities of $75,000. A patent held by Holister having a $5,000 book value was actually worth $20,000. This patent had a six-year remaining life. Any goodwill associated with this

acquisition will be amortized over 20 years. During 1998, Holister earned income of $30,000 and paid dividends of $10,000 while in 1999, income was $50,000 and dividends $15,000.

Assuming that Alison has the ability to significantly influence the operations of Holister, what balance should appear in the Investment in Holister account as of December 31, 1999?

14. On January 1, 1998, Ruark Corporation acquired a 40 percent interest in Batson, Inc., for $210,000. On that date, Batson's balance sheet disclosed net assets of $360,000. During 1998, Batson reported net income of $80,000 and paid cash dividends of $25,000. Goodwill is to be amortized over its maximum life. Ruark sold inventory costing $30,000 to Batson during 1998 for $40,000. Batson used all of this merchandise in its operations during 1998. Make all of Ruark's journal entries for 1998 to apply the equity method to this investment.

15. Waters, Inc., acquires 10 percent of Denton Corporation on January 1, 1998, for $210,000 although the book value of Denton on that date was $1,700,000. Denton held land that was undervalued on its accounting records by $100,000. During 1998, Denton earned a net income of $240,000 while paying cash dividends of $90,000. On January 1, 1999, Waters purchased an additional 30 percent of Denton for $600,000. Denton's land is still undervalued on that date but now by $120,000. The investment had been maintained at cost because fair values were not readily available. The equity method will now be applied. Any goodwill is to be amortized by Waters over a 20-year period. During 1999, Denton reported income of $300,000 and distributed dividends of $110,000. Prepare all of the 1999 journal entries for Waters.

16. McKeon Inc. sold $150,000 in inventory to Schilling Company during 1998 for $225,000. Schilling resold $105,000 of this merchandise in 1998 with the remainder to be disposed of during 1999. Assuming McKeon owns 25 percent of Schilling and applies the equity method, what journal entry is recorded at the end of 1999 to defer the unrealized gain?

17. Hager holds 30 percent of the outstanding shares of Jenkins and appropriately applies the equity method of accounting. Goodwill amortization associated with this investment amounts to $9,000 per year. For 1998, Jenkins reports earnings of $80,000 and pays cash dividends of $30,000. During that year, Jenkins acquired inventory for $50,000, which was then sold to Hager for $80,000. At the end of 1998, Hager continues to hold merchandise with a transfer price of $40,000.
  a. What Equity in Investee Income should Hager report for 1998?
  b. How will the intercompany transfer affect Hager's reporting in 1999?
  c. If the inventory had been sold by Hager to Jenkins, how would the above answers have changed?

18. On January 1, 1998, Monroe, Inc., purchased 10,000 shares of Brown Company for $250,000, giving Monroe 10 percent ownership of Brown. On January 1, 1999, Monroe purchased an additional 20,000 shares (20 percent) for $590,000. This latest purchase gave Monroe the ability to apply significant influence over Brown. Assume that no goodwill is involved in either acquisition and the original 10 percent investment was categorized as an available-for-sale security.

Brown reports net income and dividends as follows. These amounts are assumed to have occurred evenly throughout these years.

	Net Income	Cash Dividends
1998	$350,000	$100,000
1999	480,000	110,000
2000	500,000	120,000

On July 1, 2000, Monroe sells 2,000 shares of this investment for $46 per share, thus, reducing its interest from 30 to 28 percent. However, the company retains the ability to significantly influence Brown. What amounts appear in Monroe's 2000 income statement?

19. On January 1, 1998, Wilder, Inc., purchased 100,000 shares of Marple Company for $320,000, giving Wilder 30 percent ownership and the ability to apply significant influence to the operating and financing decisions of Marple. Wilder anticipates holding

this investment for an indefinite time. In making this acquisition, Wilder paid an amount equal to the book value for these shares. The fair market value of each asset and liability was the same as its book value. Dividends and income for Marple for 1998 were as follows:

Dividends	$.35 per share
Income	$330,000

Assuming a 40 percent tax rate, prepare all journal entries for Wilder for 1998.

20. Slice, Inc., owns 40 percent of the outstanding shares of Wilson, an investment accounted for by the equity method. During 1998, Slice earns an operating income (not including any income accrued from its investment in Wilson) of $310,000. For this same period, Wilson reported earnings of $130,000 and paid cash dividends of $50,000. Slice has an effective tax rate of 35 percent and anticipates holding its investment in Wilson for an indefinite period.

What income tax expense journal entry would Slice, Inc., record at the end of 1998?

If Slice expects to sell its interest in Wilson in the near future, how does that decision change the 1998 income tax expense journal entry?

21. Collins, Inc., purchases 10 percent of Merton Corporation on January 1, 1998, for $345,000. Collins acquires an additional 15 percent of Merton on January 1, 1999, for $580,000. The equity method of accounting has now become appropriate for this investment. No intercompany sales have occurred.

a. How does Collins initially determine the income to be reported in 1998 in connection with its ownership of Merton?

b. What factors should have influenced Collins in its decision to apply the equity method in 1999?

c. What factors might have prevented Collins from adopting the equity method after this second purchase?

d. What is the objective of the equity method of accounting?

e. What criticisms have been leveled at the equity method?

f. In comparative statements for 1998 and 1999, how would Collins determine the income to be reported in 1998 in connection with its ownership of Merton? Why is this accounting appropriate?

g. How is the allocation of Collins's payments made?

h. If Merton pays a cash dividend, what impact does it have on the financial records of Collins? Why is this accounting appropriate?

i. On financial statements for 1999, what amounts are included in Collins's Investment in Merton account? What amounts are included in Collins's Equity in Income of Merton account?

22. Parrot Corporation holds a 42 percent ownership of Sunrise, Inc. The equity method is being applied. No goodwill or other allocation occurred in the purchase of this investment. During 1998, intercompany inventory transfers were made between the two companies. A portion of this merchandise was not resold until 1999. During 1999, additional transfers were made.

a. What is the difference in upstream transfers and downstream transfers?

b. How does the direction of an intercompany transfer (upstream versus downstream) affect the application of the equity method?

c. How is the intercompany unrealized gain computed in applying the equity method?

d. How should Parrot compute the amount of equity income to be recognized in 1998? What entry is made to record this income?

e. How should Parrot compute the amount of equity income to be recognized in 1999?

f. If none of the transferred inventory had remained at the end of 1998, how would application of the equity method have been affected by these transfers?

g. How do these intercompany transfers affect the financial reporting of Sunrise?

23. Several years ago, Einstein, Inc., bought 40 percent of the outstanding voting stock of the Brooks Company. The equity method is appropriately applied. On August 1 of the current year, Einstein sold a portion of these shares.

a. How does Einstein compute the book value of this investment on August 1 to determine its gain or loss on the sale.

b. How should Einstein account for this investment after August 1?

    c. If Einstein retains only a 2 percent interest in Brooks so that virtually no influence is held, what figures appear in the investor's income statement for the current year?

    d. If Einstein retains only a 2 percent interest in Brooks so that virtually no influence is held, does the investor have to retroactively adjust any previously reported figures?

24. Palmer Corporation holds a 30 percent interest in Lynn, Inc. The equity method is being applied. No goodwill or other allocations were created by the original purchase.

    During 1998, Lynn reported a net income of $120,000 and paid a cash dividend of $50,000.

    a. Why do these events create a deferred income tax liability for Palmer?

    b. Will this tax ever be paid by Palmer?

    c. In what two ways can the amount of this liability be computed?

    d. If Palmer's tax rate is 28 percent and the company expects to hold this investment indefinitely, what is the year-end income tax entry?

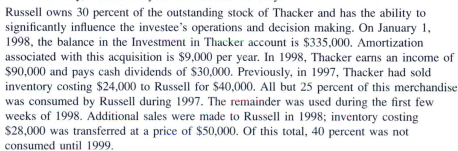

25. Russell owns 30 percent of the outstanding stock of Thacker and has the ability to significantly influence the investee's operations and decision making. On January 1, 1998, the balance in the Investment in Thacker account is $335,000. Amortization associated with this acquisition is $9,000 per year. In 1998, Thacker earns an income of $90,000 and pays cash dividends of $30,000. Previously, in 1997, Thacker had sold inventory costing $24,000 to Russell for $40,000. All but 25 percent of this merchandise was consumed by Russell during 1997. The remainder was used during the first few weeks of 1998. Additional sales were made to Russell in 1998; inventory costing $28,000 was transferred at a price of $50,000. Of this total, 40 percent was not consumed until 1999.

Required:

    a. What amount of income would Russell recognize in 1998 from its ownership interest in Thacker?

    b. What is the balance in the Investment in Thacker account at the end of 1998?

26. Cates owns 40 percent of Zagner, an investment that is being accounted for by the equity method. Zagner follows a policy of paying dividends equal to 30 percent of its income each year. During the current year, Zagner reported earning $180,000 in net income. Cates has an effective tax rate of 38 percent.

    What journal entry would the company record at the end of the current year for income taxes relating to the investment in Zagner? Assume the investment is to be held for an indefinite time.

27. On January 1, 1998, Ace acquires 15 percent of Zip's outstanding common stock for $52,000 and categorizes the investment as an available-for-sale security. Zip earns a net income of $80,000 in 1998 and pays dividends totaling $30,000. On January 1, 1999, Ace buys an additional 10 percent of Zip for $45,000. This second purchase gives Ace the ability to significantly influence the decision making of Zip. During 1999, Zip earns $100,000 and pays $40,000 in dividends. Goodwill is to be amortized over a 10-year life. As of December 31, 1999, Zip reports a net book value of $390,000.

    a. On Ace's December 31, 1999, balance sheet, what balance is reported for the Investment in Zip account?

    b. What amount of equity income should Ace report for 1999?

28. Anderson acquires 10 percent of the outstanding voting shares of Barringer on January 1, 1998, for $92,000 and categorizes the investment as an available-for-sale security. An additional 20 percent of the stock is purchased on January 1, 1999, for $210,000, which gives Anderson the ability to significantly influence Barringer. Barringer has a book value of $800,000 at January 1, 1998, and records net income of $180,000 for the following year. Dividends of $80,000 were paid by Barringer during 1998. The book values of all Barringer's asset and liability accounts are considered as equal to fair market values. Any goodwill is to be amortized to maximize the reported profits each year.

    Barringer reports $210,000 in net income during 1999 and $230,000 in 2000. Dividends of $100,000 are paid in each of these years.

    a. On comparative income statements issued in 2000 by Anderson for 1998 and 1999, what amounts of income would be reported in connection with the company's investment in Barringer?

b. If Anderson sells its entire investment in Barringer on January 1, 2001, for $400,000 cash, what is the impact on Anderson's income?

c. Assume that Anderson sells inventory to Barringer during 1999 and 2000 as follows:

Year	Cost to Anderson	Price to Barringer	Year-End Balance (at Transfer Price)
1999	$35,000	$50,000	$20,000 (sold in following year)
2000	33,000	60,000	40,000 (sold in following year)

What amount of equity income should be recognized by Anderson for the year of 2000?

29. Smith purchases 5 percent of Barker's outstanding stock on October 1, 1998, for $7,475. An additional 10 percent of Barker is acquired for $14,900 on July 1, 1999. Both of these purchases were accounted for as available-for-sale investments. A final 20 percent is purchased on December 31, 2000, for $34,200. With this final acquisition, Smith achieves the ability to significantly influence the decision-making process of Barker.

Barker has a book value of $100,000 as of January 1, 1998. Information follows concerning the operations of this company for the 1998–99 period. Assume all income and dividends occurred evenly throughout the years.

Year	Reported Income	Dividends
1998	$20,000	$ 8,000
1999	30,000	16,000
2000	24,000	9,000

On Barker's financial records, the book values of all assets and liabilities are the same as their fair market values. Any goodwill is to be amortized over a 15-year period. Amortization for a portion of a year should be based on months.

Required:

a. On comparative income statements issued in 2001 for the years of 1998, 1999, and 2000, what would Smith report as its income derived from this investment in Barker?

b. On a balance sheet as of December 31, 2000, what should Smith report as its Investment in Barker?

c. What is the amount of goodwill remaining in the Investment in Barker account as of December 31, 2000?

d. Assume in 2001 Smith records $14,000 of equity income and receives a $3,500 dividend from its share of Barker. If the corporate tax rate is 30 percent, what deferred tax liability should Smith recognize for 2001? Assume that Smith intends to hold its investment in Barker for an indefinite period.

30. Hobson acquires 40 percent of the outstanding voting stock of the Stokes Company on January 1, 1998, for $210,000 in cash. The book value of Stokes's net assets on that date was $400,000, although one of the company's buildings, with a $60,000 carrying value, was actually worth $100,000. This building had a 10-year remaining life. Any goodwill is to be amortized by Hobson over a 20-year life.

Stokes sells inventory to Hobson during 1998 with an original cost of $60,000. This merchandise was sold to Hobson at a price of $90,000. Hobson still holds $15,000 (transfer price) of this amount in inventory as of December 31, 1998. These goods are to be sold to outside parties during 1999.

Stokes reports a loss of $60,000 for 1998, $40,000 from continuing operations and $20,000 from an extraordinary loss. The company still manages to pay a $10,000 cash dividend during the year.

During 1999, Stokes reports a $40,000 net income and distributes a cash dividend of $12,000. Additional inventory sales of $80,000 are made to Hobson during the period. The original cost of the merchandise was $50,000. All but 30 percent of this inventory has been resold to outside parties by the end of the 1999 fiscal year.

Prepare all journal entries for Hobson for 1998 and 1999 in connection with this investment. Assume that the equity method is applied. Ignore income tax effects.

31. Penston Company owns 40 percent (40,000 shares) of Scranton, Inc., which was purchased several years ago for $182,000. Since the date of acquisition, the equity

method has been properly applied and the book value of the investment account as of January 1, 1998, is $248,000. Goodwill amortization of $12,000 is still being recognized each year. During 1998, Scranton reports net income of $200,000, $320,000 in operating income earned evenly throughout the year, and a $120,000 extraordinary loss incurred on October 1. No dividends were paid during the year. Penston sells 8,000 shares of Scranton on August 1, 1998, for $94,000 in cash. However, Penston does retain the ability to significantly influence the investee.

During the last quarter of 1997, Penston sold $50,000 in inventory (which had originally cost Penston only $30,000) to Scranton. At the end of that fiscal year, Scranton's inventory retained $9,000 (at sales price) of this merchandise, which was subsequently sold in the first quarter of 1998.

On Penston's financial statements for the year ended December 31, 1998, what income effects would be reported from its ownership in Scranton? Ignore income taxes.

32. On July 1, 1998, the Abernethy Company acquires 65,000 of the outstanding shares of the Chapman Company for $13 per share. This acquisition gave Abernethy a 25 percent ownership of Chapman and allowed Abernethy to significantly influence the decisions of the investee.

As of July 1, 1998, the investee had assets with a book value of $2 million and liabilities of $400,000. At the time, Chapman held equipment appraised at $120,000 above book value. Company land was valued at $160,000 above book value. The equipment was considered to have an eight-year life with no salvage value. Goodwill is being amortized over 15 years. Depreciation and amortization are computed using the straight-line method.

Chapman follows a policy of paying 50 cents per share as a cash dividend every April 1 and October 1. Chapman's income, earned evenly throughout each year, was 1998—$280,000; 1999—$360,000; and 2000—$380,000.

In addition, Abernethy sold inventory costing $90,000 to Chapman for $150,000 during 1999. Chapman resold $90,000 of this inventory during 1999 and the remaining $60,000 during 2000.

Required:

a. Prepare a schedule computing the equity income to be recognized by Abernethy during each of these years.

b. Compute Abernethy's investment balance as of December 31, 2000.

c. Assume that Abernethy has an effective tax rate of 32 percent and the investment would be held indefinitely. Prepare Abernethy's income tax journal entry for 1998.

33. On January 1, 1998, Plano Company acquired 8 percent (16,000 shares) of the outstanding voting shares of the Sumter Company for $192,000, an amount equal to the underlying book value of Sumter. Sumter pays a cash dividend to its stockholders each year of $100,000 on September 15. Sumter reports net income of $300,000 in 1998, $360,000 in 1999, $400,000 in 2000, and $380,000 in 2001. Each income figure can be assumed to have been earned evenly throughout its respective year. In addition, the market value of these 16,000 shares was indeterminate and therefore the investment account remained at cost.

On January 1, 2000, Plano purchased an additional 32 percent (64,000 shares) of Sumter for $965,750 in cash. This price represented a $50,550 payment in excess of the book value of Sumter's underlying net assets. Plano was willing to make this extra payment to establish better ties with Sumter. All assets were considered appropriately valued on Sumter's books. Any goodwill established by this acquisition is amortized over 15 years.

On July 1, 2001, Plano sold 10 percent (20,000 shares) of the outstanding shares of Sumter for $425,000 in cash. Although this interest was sold, Plano maintained the ability to significantly influence the decision-making process of Sumter. Assume that a weighted average costing system is used by Plano.

Required:

a. Prepare the journal entries for Plano for the years of 1998 through 2001. Ignore income taxes.

b. Assuming an effective tax rate of 35 percent, compute the balance in the deferred income taxes payable account as of December 31, 2000.

34. On January 1, 1998, Lake Company acquired 40 percent of the outstanding voting shares of Slide Company for $600,000. On that date, Slide reports assets and liabilities with book values of $1.8 million and $600,000, respectively. A building owned by Slide had an appraised value of $250,000, although it had a book value of only $100,000. This building had a 12-year remaining life and no salvage value. It was being depreciated on the straight-line method. Any goodwill established by the acquisition of Slide is considered to have a 20-year life.

Slide generated net income of $250,000 in 1998 and a loss of $100,000 in 1999. In each of these two years, Slide paid a cash dividend of $60,000 to its stockholders.

During 1998, Slide sold inventory to Lake that had an original cost of $50,000. The merchandise was sold to Lake for $80,000. Of this balance, $60,000 was resold to outsiders during 1998 and the remainder was sold during 1999. In 1999, Slide sold inventory to Lake for $150,000. This inventory had cost only $90,000. Lake resold $100,000 of the inventory during 1999 and the rest during 2000.

Required:

For 1998 and then for 1999, compute the equity income to be reported by Lake for external reporting purposes.

C H A P T E R

2

Consolidation of Financial Information

QUESTIONS TO CONSIDER

- Why do firms engage in business combinations?

- When one company gains control over another company, how should the relationship between the two parties be presented for external reporting purposes?

- When the relationship between two companies is being assessed, how should control be determined?

- The assets and liabilities of some subsidiary organizations are added directly to the records of the parent company. In other cases, the parent chooses to let the new subsidiary remain in operation as a separate legal entity. How is the accounting process affected by this decision?

- A business combination can be accounted for as either a purchase or a pooling of interests. Why are two methods available? When should each be used? How do they differ? What balances are reported at the date of acquisition for each method? What arguments are made against the pooling of interests method?

- Investment bankers and other financial advisors are paid millions of dollars for assisting one company in acquiring another. What accounting is made of these costs?

- Prior to 1987, many companies chose not to consolidate their finance subsidiaries. Why were these operations omitted from the consolidation process? Why has this practice been changed?

Financial statements, published and distributed to owners, creditors, and other interested parties, appear to report the operations and financial position of a single company. In reality, these statements frequently represent a number of separate organizations tied together through common control (a *business combination*). An example is Time Warner's ownership structure shown here. Time Warner's balance sheet, statement of earnings, and statement of cash flows report financial information gathered from this multitude of companies as if only a single enterprise existed. Whenever financial statements represent more than one corporation, they are said to be *consolidated*.

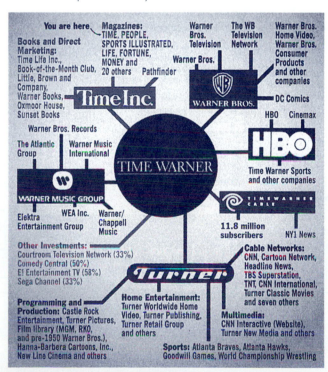

Source: *Time*, October 21, 1996, p. 20. Copyright 1996 Time Inc. Reprinted by permission.

Consolidated financial statements are hardly unusual in today's business world. Most major organizations, and many smaller ones, hold control over an array of organizations. PepsiCo, Inc., as another example, annually consolidates data from more than 100 companies into a single set of financial statements. By gaining control over these companies (often known as *subsidiaries*), which include Pizza Hut, Kentucky Fried Chicken, Taco Bell, and Frito-Lay, a single business combination has been formed by PepsiCo (the *parent*) that should be viewed as a single reporting entity.

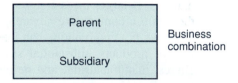

The consolidation of financial information as exemplified by Time Warner and PepsiCo is one of the most complex procedures in all of accounting. To comprehend this process completely, the theoretical logic that underlies the creation of a business combination must be understood. Furthermore, a variety of mechanical steps have to be mastered to ensure that proper accounting is achieved for this single reporting entity. The following coverage introduces both of these aspects of the consolidation process.

EXPANSION THROUGH CORPORATE TAKEOVERS

Why Do Firms Combine?

A common economic phenomenon is the combining of two or more businesses into a single entity under common management and owner control. During recent decades, the United States and the rest of the world have seen an enormous number of corporate mergers and takeovers, transactions in which one company gains control over another. As indicated by Exhibit 2–1, the magnitude of recent combinations continues to be large.

Exhibit 2–1
Recent Notable Business Combinations

Acquirer	Target	Cost (in billions)
Walt Disney Co.	Capital Cities/ABC Inc.	$18.9
AirTouch Communications	US West Inc.	13.5
Bell Atlantic Corp.	NYNEX Corp.	13.0
Wells Fargo & Co.	First Interstate Bancorp.	10.9
Martin Marietta Corp.	Lockheed Martin Corp.	10.0
Chemical Banking Corp.*	Chase Manhattan Corp.	9.9
Time Warner	Turner Broadcasting	7.6
IBM	Lotus Development	3.5
*Merger accounted for as pooling of interests, firms are neither acquirers nor targets.		

As with any other economic activity, business combinations can be part of an overall managerial strategy to maximize shareholder value. Shareholders—the owners of the firm—hire managers to direct resources so that the value of the firm grows over time. In this way, owners receive a return on their investment. Successful firms receive substantial benefits through enhanced share value. Importantly, the managers of successful firms also receive substantial benefits in salaries, especially if their compensation contracts are partly based on stock market performance of the firm's shares.

If the goal of business activity is to maximize the value of the firm, in what ways do business combinations help achieve that goal? Clearly the business community is moving rapidly toward business combinations as a strategy for growth and competitiveness. Size and scale are obviously becoming critical as firms compete in today's markets. If larger firms can be more efficient in delivering goods and services, then they gain a competitive advantage and become more profitable for the owners. For example, if a combination can integrate successive stages of production and distribution of products, substantial savings can result in coordinating raw material purchases, manufacturing, and delivery. For example, when Ford Motor Co. acquired Hertz Rental (one of its largest customers), it not only enabled them to ensure demand for their cars, but also allowed them to closely coordinate production with the need for new rental cars. Other cost savings resulting from elimination of duplicate efforts, such as data processing and marketing, can make a single entity more profitable than the separate parent and subsidiary had been in the past.

Although no two business combinations are exactly alike, many share one or more of the following characteristics that potentially enhance profitability:

- Vertical integration of one firm's output and another firm's distribution or further processing.
- Cost savings through elimination of duplicate facilities and staff.
- Quick entry for new and existing products into domestic and foreign markets.
- Economies of scale allowing greater efficiency and negotiating power.
- The ability to access financing at more attractive rates. As firms grow in size, negotiating power with financial institutions can grow also.
- Diversification of business risk.

Business combinations also result because many firms seek the continuous expansion of their organizations, especially into diversified areas. Acquiring control over a vast network of different businesses has been a strategy utilized by a number of companies (sometimes known as conglomerates) for decades. Entry into new industries is immediately available to the parent without having to construct facilities, develop products, train management, or create market recognition. Many corporations have successfully utilized this strategy to produce huge, highly profitable organizations. Unfortunately, others have discovered that the task of managing a widely diverse group of businesses can prove to be a costly learning experience. Even combinations that purportedly take advantage of operating synergies and cost savings often fail if the integration is not managed carefully.[1]

Overall, the primary motivations for many business combinations can be traced to an increasingly competitive environment. Three recent examples of large business combinations provide interesing examples of some distinct motivations to combine: IBM's acquisition of Lotus Development Corporation, Disney's acquisition of Capital Cities/ABC, and Chemical Bank's merger with Chase Manhattan. Each is discussed briefly in turn.

---

[1]For examples, see "The Case against Mergers," *Business Week,* October 30, 1995.

IBM and Lotus Development Corporation

On June 11, 1996, IBM announced that it had acquired Lotus Development for $3.5 billion. The price paid per share was $64 compared to the price of $31.50 Lotus traded at just 30 days before the acquisition. Clearly some powerful incentives induced IBM to pay such a large purchase premium for Lotus.

First, the acquisition allows IBM quick entry into the client/server software market through the Lotus Notes product line. This software already has dedicated corporate clients in General Motors, Price Waterhouse, and the Central Intelligence Agency. Competition with Microsoft was leaving IBM with rapidly declining software market share and IBM may have viewed the acquisition of Lotus Notes as much more attractive than spending years (and hundreds of millions of dollars) internally developing competing products. As reported in *The New York Times,* "IBM desperately needs to get growth from the software business and that's what the Lotus acquisition was about."[2]

Second, synergistic elements may have helped to motivate the deal. Lotus Notes has the potential to become the basis for IBM's personal computer and network applications. The fact that Lotus Notes complements the IBM PC hardware provides an additional motivation to combine that allows for increased potential for competition with Microsoft. Moreover, IBM has an extensive distribution network with product sales worldwide that may enable it to market the Lotus software more effectively.

Disney and Capital Cities/ABC

Walt Disney Company's acquisition of Capital Cities/ABC Inc. took place late in 1995. The $19 billion takeover vastly overshadows other large media-related acquisitions such as Time Warner's acquisition of Turner for $7.6 billion. However, both combinations reflect the rapid consolidation of the entertainment and information delivery industries. Both firms face difficult challenges from cable and satellite delivery firms in competing for advertising revenues as well as direct consumer revenues. The mergers thus represent the strategy undertaken by media firms for future competitiveness and growth.

Disney's ownership of content and Capital Cities/ABC's ability to distribute the content represents the strategy of vertical integration. As a result of the acquisition, Disney can now make movies, and other entertainment with its own series of network and television stations for distribution purposes. At the date of acquisition, the resulting company included ownership of 11 television stations, a network of 228 affiliates, and 21 radio stations, as well as cable channels ESPN, Lifetime, A&E, and the Disney Channel. Importantly, Capital Cities/ABC is an industry leader in international distribution; this provides an additional vehicle for growth of the new combined entity.

Chase Manhattan and Chemical Bank

In 1995 Chemical Bank announced its agreement with Chase Manhattan for a $10 billion merger pact that created the largest bank in the United States, with almost $300 billion in assets and $20 billion in equity. As with most mergers, the ability of a larger firm to better compete and more quickly grow ranks high among the reasons cited for the combination. Foreign lenders, particularly Japanese and European, have grown to enormous size and offer many of the same services as Chase. The interna-

---

[2]"Manzi's Departure Unlikely to Derail I.B.M.'s Plans" by Steve Lohr, *The New York Times,* October 12, 1995, p. 10.

tional dimension of banking competition cannot be overestimated. Even though the new Chase Manhattan Corporation is the largest U.S. bank, it ranks only 19th worldwide.

Chase Chairman Walter Shipley announced that the merger "will significantly enhance our financial capability and capacity . . . so that we can compete effectively in the increasingly challenging financial services area."[3] The new Chase also takes advantage of synergies in global lending and trading. However, a primary motivation that distinguishes this and other banking mergers is the emphasis on cost cutting through the elimination of duplicate services. Since Chase and Chemical competed in many of the same markets in the northeast, the potential exists for a significant reduction of service activities. Through an aggressive downsizing program, the firms combined operations and thus reduced costs previously incurred in similiar operations.

THE CONSOLIDATION PROCESS

The consolidation of financial information into a single set of statements becomes necessary whenever a single economic entity is created by the business combination of two or more companies. As stated in *Accounting Research Bulletin No. 51* (abbreviated *ARB 51*), "Consolidated Financial Statements," August 1959 (par. 2): "There is a presumption that consolidated statements are more meaningful than separate statements and that they are usually necessary for a fair presentation when one of the companies in the group directly or indirectly has a controlling financial interest in the other companies."

This sentiment was reiterated nearly 30 years later in *Financial Accounting Standards Board Statement No. 94,* "Consolidation of All Majority-Owned Subsidiaries," October 1987 (par. 30): "Consolidated financial statements became common once it was recognized that boundaries between separate corporate entities must be ignored to report the business carried on by a group of affiliated corporations as the economic and financial whole that it actually is."

Thus, in producing financial statements for external distribution, the reporting entity transcends the boundaries of incorporation to encompass all companies where control is present. Even though the various companies may retain their legal identities as separate corporations, the resulting information is more meaningful to outside parties when consolidated into a single set of financial statements.

To explain the process of preparing consolidated financial statements for a business combination, we address three questions:

- How is a business combination formed?
- What constitutes a controlling financial interest?
- How is the consolidation process carried out?

Business Combinations—Creating a Single Economic Entity

A business combination refers to any set of conditions in which two or more organizations are joined together through common control. *APB Statement 4* (chap. 5, par. 3) describes the entity that results from a business combination:

> Accounting information pertains to entities, which are circumscribed areas of interest. In financial accounting the entity is the specific business enterprise. The enterprise is identified in its financial statements. . . . The boundaries of the accounting entity may not be the same

---

[3]"Politicians, Activists Rip New York Megamerger" by Jaret Seiberg, *American Banker,* November 17, 1995, p. 1.

as those of the legal entity, for example, a parent corporation and its subsidiaries treated as a single business enterprise.

Business combinations are formed by a wide variety of transactions with various formats. For example, each of the following is identified as a business combination although differing widely in legal form. In every case, two or more enterprises are being united into a single economic entity so that consolidated financial statements are required.

1. One company obtains the assets, and possibly liabilities, of another company in exchange for cash, other assets, liabilities, stock, or a combination of these. The second organization normally dissolves itself as a legal corporation. Thus, only the acquiring company remains in existence, having absorbed the acquired net assets directly into its own operations. Any business combination in which only one of the original companies continues to exist is referred to in legal terms as a *statutory merger*. A + B = A

2. One company obtains the capital stock of another in exchange for cash, other assets, liabilities, stock, or a combination of these. After gaining control, the acquiring company may decide to transfer all assets and liabilities to its own financial records with the second company being dissolved as a separate corporation.[4] The business combination is, once again, a statutory merger because only one of the companies maintains legal existence. This statutory merger, however, is achieved by obtaining equity securities rather than by buying the target company's assets. Because stock is purchased, the acquiring company must gain 100 percent control of all shares before legally dissolving the subsidiary.

3. Two or more companies transfer either their assets or their capital stock to a newly formed corporation. The original companies both are dissolved, leaving only the new organization remaining in existence. A business combination effected in this manner is a *statutory consolidation.* The use here of the term *consolidation* should not be confused with the accounting meaning of that same word. In accounting, consolidation refers to the mechanical process of bringing together the financial records of two or more organizations to form a single set of statements. A statutory consolidation denotes a specific type of business combination in which two or more existing companies are united under the ownership of a newly created company.

   The business combination of NCNB Corporation and C&S/Sovran Corporation illustrates the formation of a statutory consolidation. The stockholders of these two organizations created a single entity by transferring their ownership interests to a newly established corporation known as NationsBank Corporation. Because only this new company remained in existence as a legal entity, the business combination is a statutory consolidation. A + B = C

4. One company achieves legal control over another by the acquisition of a majority of voting stock. *Although control is present, no dissolution takes place; each company remains in existence as an incorporated operation.* The National Broadcasting Company, as an example, continued to retain its legal status as a corporation after being acquired by General Electric Company. Separate incorporation is frequently preferred to take full advantage of any intangible benefits accruing to the acquired company as a going concern. Better utilization of such factors as trade names, employee loyalty, and the company's reputation may be possible where the subsidiary maintains its own legal identity.

One important aspect of this final type of business combination should be noted. Because the asset and liability account balances are not physically combined as in

---

[4]Although the acquired company has been legally dissolved, it frequently continues to operate as a separate division within the surviving company's organization.

Exhibit 2–2
Business Combinations

Type of Combination	Action of Acquiring Company	Action of Acquired Company
Statutory merger through asset acquisition	Acquires assets and often liabilities	Dissolves and goes out of business
Statutory merger through capital stock acquisition	Acquires all stock and then transfers assets and liabilities to its own books	Dissolves as a separate corporation, often remaining as a division of the acquiring company
Statutory consolidation through capital stock or asset acquisition	Newly created to receive assets or capital stock of original companies	Original companies may dissolve while remaining as separate divisions of newly created company
Acquisition of more than 50 percent of the voting stock	Acquires stock that is recorded as an investment; controls decision making of acquired company	Remains in existence as legal corporation, although now a subsidiary of the acquiring company

statutory mergers and consolidations, each company continues to maintain an independent accounting system. To reflect the creation of the combination, the acquiring company enters the financial impact of the takeover transaction into its own records by establishing a single investment asset account. However, the newly acquired subsidiary omits any recording of this event; the stock being obtained by the parent comes from the subsidiary's shareholders. Thus, the financial records of the subsidiary are not directly affected by a takeover.

As can be seen, business combinations are created in many distinct forms. Since the specific format is a critical factor in the subsequent consolidation of financial information, Exhibit 2–2 provides an overview of the various combinations.

Control—An Elusive Quality

ARB 51, as quoted previously, states that consolidated financial statements are usually necessary when one company has a controlling financial interest over another. However, nowhere in the official accounting pronouncements is a "controlling financial interest" actually defined. Traditionally, in the United States, control is considered to exist if one company holds more than 50 percent of another company's voting stock. Thus, control has been tied directly to ownership. However, in the decades since *ARB 51* was issued, the complexity of business combinations has grown significantly so that control is not always that easy to define.

The FASB has a comprehensive study underway of consolidation issues including the question of control. Chances seem likely that consolidation will eventually be required for less-than-majority-owned subsidiaries if the parent has rights, risks, and benefits equivalent to those that result from majority ownership.

The types of situations that led the FASB to study the issue of control include the following cases. In none of these instances is a majority of the voting stock held. Thus, historically in the United States, consolidation would probably not occur.[5] However, one company certainly does have the potential to exercise a degree of authority over the other. In looking at such cases, two interrelated questions must be

---

[5]In contrast, Australia, Canada, New Zealand, the United Kingdom, and the European Community all have standards specifying control rather than ownership as the basis for consolidation. Japan's Ministry of Finance is to introduce a new accounting standard by 1999, where the basis for determining whether an affiliated firm is a subsidiary will be one of control rather than ownership, and will cover the right to appoint and remove directors. "Consolidated Financial Statements," compiled by Coopers & Lybrand, Tokyo, *Accountancy,* September 1996, p. 86.

addressed: Does one company actually have a controlling financial interest over the other? Has a business combination been created that necessitates the production of consolidated financial statements?

- Company A owns 48 percent of Company B. At the stockholders' meeting each year, only about 90 percent of the outstanding shares are voted so that Company A always casts a majority of the shares on every ballot.
- Company C owns 40 percent of Company D. Ms. Z is president of Company D and owns 11 percent of its stock. Ms. Z is a former vice president and friend of Company C and has always voted her shares in the same manner as Company C.
- Company E owns none of Company F. However, Company E holds convertible bonds issued by Company F. Company E has the option at any time to convert these bonds into 51 percent of the outstanding voting shares of Company F.
- As described in Chapter 1, The Coca-Cola Company holds 44 percent of Coca-Cola Enterprises. Furthermore, the investee is heavily dependent on the investor for products and marketing.

In studying these issues, the Board has described what is meant by control:

Control of an Entity: the possession, direct or indirect, of an exclusive power to direct or cause the direction of the management and policies of another entity through ownership of voting securities or other means.[6]

In studying these issues, the Board describes several elements of control:

- Control of an entity is control over its assets—power to use or direct the use of the individual assets of another entity in essentially the same ways as the controlling entity can use its own assets.
- Control of an entity is an exclusionary power—if A controls B, no other entity can control B. A controlling entity may delegate its control to a manager or another entity, or it may elect not to exercise its control. Neither decision reduces its status as a controlling entity.
- A controlling entity can use or direct the use of the individual assets of its subsidiary in ways that enable it to obtain the service potential or future economic benefit inherent in those assets.
- The powers of a controlling entity need not be unrestricted. Control rarely, if ever, exists without restrictions and even control of a wholly owned subsidiary with no debt may be restricted by laws and regulations and by the nature of the subsidiary's assets.[7]

Consolidation of Financial Information

Whenever one company gains control over another, a business combination is established. Financial data gathered from the individual companies must then be brought together to form a single set of consolidated statements. Although the steps in this process can be numerous, the objectives of a consolidation are rather limited. The asset, liability, equity, revenue, and expense accounts of the companies simply are combined. As a part of this process, reciprocal accounts and intercompany transac-

[6]"Consolidations and Related Matters," FASB Discussion of Board Agenda Projects as of October 1, 1996.

[7]Financial Accounting Standards Board Exposure Draft "Consolidated Financial Statements: Policy and Procedures," October 1995.

tions must be adjusted or eliminated to ensure that all reported balances truly represent the single entity.

Applicable consolidation procedures vary significantly depending on the legal format employed in creating a business combination. *For a statutory merger or a statutory consolidation, where the acquired company (or companies) is legally dissolved, only one accounting consolidation ever occurs.* On the date of the combination, the surviving company simply records the various account balances from each of the dissolving companies. Because all accounts are permanently brought together in this manner, no further consolidation procedures are required. After all of the balances have been transferred to the survivor, the financial records of the acquired companies are closed out as part of the dissolution.

Conversely, in a combination where all companies retain incorporation, a different set of consolidation procedures is appropriate. Because the companies preserve their legal identities, each continues to maintain its own independent accounting records. *Thus, no permanent consolidation of the account balances is ever made. Rather, the consolidation process must be carried out anew each time that the reporting entity prepares financial statements for external reporting purposes.*

Where separate record-keeping is maintained, the accountant faces a unique problem: The financial information must be brought together periodically without disturbing the accounting systems of the individual companies. Since these consolidations are not produced within the financial records, worksheets have traditionally been used to expedite the process. Worksheets are not part of either companies' accounting records or of the resulting financial statements. Instead, they are an efficient structure for organizing and adjusting the information used in the preparation of consolidated statements.

Consequently, the legal characteristics of a business combination have a significant impact on the approach taken to the consolidation process:

What is to be consolidated?

- If dissolution takes place, all account balances are physically consolidated in the financial records of the surviving company.
- If separate incorporation is maintained, only the financial statement information is consolidated and not the actual records.

When does the consolidation take place?

- If dissolution takes place, a permanent consolidation occurs at the date of the combination.
- If separate incorporation is maintained, the consolidation process is carried out at regular intervals whenever financial statements are to be prepared.

How are the accounting records affected?

- If dissolution takes place, the surviving company's accounts are adjusted to include all balances of the dissolved company. The dissolved company's records are closed out.
- If separate incorporation is maintained, each company continues to retain its own records. Using worksheets facilitates the periodic consolidation process without disturbing the individual accounting systems.

PURCHASE VERSUS POOLING OF INTERESTS

Regardless of whether an acquired firm is dissolved or maintains separate incorporation, an additional distinction must be made for accounting purposes. According to *Opinion 16,* "Business Combinations" (par. 42), the APB concluded that "some business combinations should be accounted for by the purchase method and other combinations should be accounted for by the pooling of interests method." The APB's decision to permit both methods is important since widely differing reported balances result.

Not surprisingly, an understanding of both the purchase method and the pooling of interests method is essential in achieving a basic knowledge of the consolidation process. Several aspects of their application must be understood at the beginning of this discussion.

First, purchases and poolings of interests involve contrasting perspectives of the very nature of a business combination.

Second, differences are created in every area of the resulting consolidated financial statements (assets, liabilities, revenues, expenses, and equities), depending on the method in use.

Third, purchases and poolings of interests are not alternatives; each is applied to a specific type of business combination.

The Need for Two Different Consolidation Methods

The term *business combination* encompasses an extremely wide range of transactions. In *Opinion 16,* the APB reasoned that one consolidation method alone could not properly account for all possible combinations. Thus, both the purchase method and the pooling of interests method were designated as appropriate means of reporting business combinations.

In drawing a distinction between these two approaches, paragraph 11 of *Opinion 16* states that "the purchase method accounts for a business combination as *the acquisition of one company by another,*" (emphasis added) whereas paragraph 12 asserts that "the pooling of interests method accounts for a business combination as *the uniting of the ownership interests of two or more companies* by exchange of equity securities. No acquisition is recognized because the combination is accomplished without disbursing resources of the constituents" (emphasis added).

Because purchases and poolings of interests are designed to account for theoretically different types of combinations, the Board went on to specify that "the two methods are not alternatives in accounting for the same business combination" (par. 43). In effect, this pronouncement has divided all business combinations into two distinct classifications. Specific consolidation procedures can then be applied to reflect more closely the essence of a particular combination. Consequently, knowledge of both methods should be based on an understanding of the nature of the business combination that each describes. After the identifying characteristics of these two approaches have been delineated, the mechanical procedures used to carry out a particular consolidation should be easier to comprehend.

The Purchase Method: *Change in Ownership*   The fundamental characteristic of any purchase, whether a single asset or a multibillion dollar corporation, is a change in ownership. In any exchange transaction, a basic accounting principle is the recording of the cost to the new owners. Thus, in a business combination accounted for as a purchase, the acquisition cost to the new owners provides the valuation basis for the net assets acquired. For example, as shown in Exhibit 2–3 Textron Paid $605 million for Cessna Aircraft. This purchase price then served as the basis for valuing Cessna's assets and liabilities in the preparation of consolidated statements.

When a single asset is purchased, application of the cost principle is straightforward. In a business combination, however, the application of the cost principle is complicated because of the literally hundreds of assets and liabilities that often are acquired. *As a result, the purchase method not only establishes cost as the appropriate valuation basis for these items but also must allocate the total acquisition cost among the various assets and liabilities received in the bargained exchange.* The cost allocation procedure employed by the purchase method is based on the fair market

Exhibit 2–3
Business Combination—
Purchase

values of the acquired assets and liabilities at the date of acquisition. Moreover, because income can only accrue to owners after the purchase of an asset (or an entire company), only revenues and expenses generated by these assets and liabilities after the acquisition date are attributed to the business combination.

The Pooling of Interests Method: *Continuity of Ownership*   As business combinations became more common, many transactions did not involve a clean break in ownership. Often former owners of separate firms would agree to combine for their mutual benefit and continue as owners of a combined firm. In such cases, the distinction between acquiring company and acquired company was not always clear. The assets and liabilities of the former firms were never really bought or sold—former owners merely exchanged ownership shares to become joint owners of the combined firm.

The assertion also was made that no bargained transaction actually transpired between the companies when securities alone were exchanged. According to *Opinion 16* (par. 16), "an exchange of stock to effect a business combination is in substance a transaction between the combining stockholder groups and does not involve the corporate entities."

Combinations characterized by exchange of voting shares and continuation of previous ownership became known as pooling of interests. Rather than a purchase and sale transaction where one ownership group replaces another, a pooling of interests is characterized by a continuity of ownership interests before and after the business combination.

Since the basic characteristics of a purchase consolidation did not always appear in every business combination, the idea soon spread that two distinct types of combinations existed. Gradually, alternative consolidation procedures began to emerge based on pooling of interests concepts. Over the decades, this method has been applied to a significant number of business combinations.

For example, the Goodyear Tire & Rubber Company exchanged nearly 25 million shares of its common stock for all of the outstanding common stock of Celeron Corporation to create a combination accounted for as a pooling of interests. As noted in Exhibit 2–4, Goodyear actually issued its stock in exchange for the shares held by the owners of Celeron. Consequently, the combined assets of these two companies were controlled by both the Goodyear shareholders and the previous Celeron owners (who now held Goodyear stock). Regardless of the number of shares exchanged, this same joint control is always found in a pooling of interests.

Exhibit 2–4
Business Combination—
Pooling of Interests*

*This diagram is intended merely to represent the relationship created by a pooling of interests. The shares delivered by Celeron actually came from its owners who in turn received the 24.7 million shares of Goodyear Tire & Rubber directly from the company.

DISCUSSION QUESTION:

Are Purchases and Poolings of Interests Truly Different?

James Atkinson is the sole owner of Acme Taxicab Company, a small organization with 15 vehicles. He wants to expand his operation and approaches Roy Wilbury, owner of Wilbury's Cabs. Wilbury's company operates eight taxicabs in the same city as Acme Taxicab Company.

Scenario One. Atkinson suggests to Wilbury that the two companies join together for their mutual benefit. "We can save money on advertisement, maintenance, and other overhead costs. Instead of two small companies, we will be co-owners of a larger organization operating 23 taxicabs throughout the city. The resulting enterprise will simply be more profitable. I currently own all 1,000 shares of my company's common stock. I will issue another 600 shares to you in exchange for all of the outstanding shares of Wilbury's Cabs."

Scenario Two. Atkinson offers to buy Wilbury's Cabs to expand the Acme Taxicab Company. "I will pay you a fair value in cash for your entire company. I'll buy your assets or buy your stock. You could retire or you can even work for me but I want to have 23 taxicabs operating throughout the city."

What characteristics of a pooling of interests are seen in the first scenario? What characteristics of a purchase are found in the second? In both cases, the two companies would ultimately form a single economic entity with 23 vehicles. Are these transactions sufficiently different to warrant the application of two distinct accounting methods producing widely varying financial results?

Thus, a pooling of interests is characterized as a continuation of ownership where neither a parent nor subsidiary can be easily identified. The combination is created by an exchange of voting stock that is not viewed as a bargained transaction with a precise acquisition price. To reflect these qualities, two important steps are taken in accounting for a combination created as a pooling of interests:

1. The book values of the assets and liabilities of both companies become the book values reported by the comined entity. Because of the continuity of ownership, no new basis of accountability arises.
2. The revenue and expense accounts are combined retroactively as well as prospectively. Again, continuity of ownership allows for the recognition of income accruing to the owners both before and after the combination.

Therefore, in a pooling, reported income is typically higher than under purchase accounting. Under pooling, not only do the firms retroactively combine incomes but the smaller asset bases also result in smaller depreciation and amortization expenses. Because net income reported in financial statements often is used in a variety of contracts, including managerial compensation, the pooling method has been considered an attractive alternative to purchase accounting.

The APB decided in *Opinion 16* that both the purchase and pooling of interest methods are acceptable procedures to account for business combinations. However, the Board placed tight restrictions on the pooling method to prevent managers from engaging in purchase transactions and reporting them as poolings of interest. *Opinion 16* established 12 criteria that must be present in a business combination to justify adoption of the pooling method. By setting strict guidelines, the Board hoped to ensure that only combinations clearly outside the essence of a purchase would fall under the pooling of interests classification. *Business combinations that fail to meet even 1 of these 12 criteria must be accounted for by the purchase method.*

p. 76

These criteria, which are presented in the appendix at the end of this chapter, have two overriding objectives: First, they define a pooling of interests as a single transaction (or series of transactions occurring over a limited time) in which two independent companies are united solely through the exchange of voting common stock. To ensure the complete fusion of the two organizations, one company has to obtain substantially all (90 percent or more) of the voting stock of the other.

The second general objective of these criteria is to prevent purchase combinations from being disguised as poolings. Past experience had shown the APB that combination transactions were frequently manipulated so that they would qualify for pooling of interests treatment (usually to increase reported earnings). However, subsequent events, often involving cash being paid or received by the parties, revealed the true nature of the combination: one company was purchasing the other in a bargained exchange. The APB designed a number of the 12 criteria to stop the possibility of this practice.

For example, to be considered a pooling of interests, no agreement can exist to reacquire any of the shares issued in creating the combination. This rule prevents the parties from eventually receiving cash or other assets as part of the transaction. For the same reason, significant assets of the combined companies cannot be sold for two years unless duplication exists. These restrictions help to ensure that only combinations meeting the essence of a pooling are given that treatment: a continuation of the companies and a continuation of the ownership.

PROCEDURES FOR CONSOLIDATING FINANCIAL INFORMATION

Legal as well as accounting distinctions divide business combinations into at least four separate categories. To facilitate the introduction of consolidation accounting, we present the various procedures utilized in this process according to the following sequence:

1. Purchase method where dissolution takes place.
2. Purchase method where separate incorporation is maintained.
3. Pooling of interests method where dissolution takes place.
4. Pooling of interests method where separate incorporation is maintained.

As a basis for this coverage, assume that Small Company owns one hotel and the land surrounding it. Although the hotel and its furniture have a book value of $400,000, they are worth $600,000. The land is on Small's books at its original cost of $300,000 although currently valued at $400,000. Small also has a mortgage note payable of $200,000 on this property. Because interest rates are currently low, this liability (incurred at a higher rate of interest) has a present value of $250,000.

Giant Company owns two hotels in the same geographic region as Small Company. Giant wants to expand its operations and hopes to acquire Small Company on December 31, 1998. The accounts reported by both Giant and Small on that date are listed in Exhibit 2–5. In addition, the estimated fair market value of Small's assets and liabilities is included.

Small's net assets have a book value of $800,000 but a fair market value of $1,050,000. Only the assets and liabilities have been appraised here; the capital stock, retained earnings, dividend, revenue, and expense accounts represent historical measurements rather than any type of future values. Although these equity and income accounts may give some indication of the overall worth of the organization, none of these figures represents an amount that is actually transferrable by the company.

Purchase Method Where Dissolution Takes Place

The purchase method employs the cost principle in recording a business combination—the total value assigned to the net assets received equals the total cost of the acquisition. The major accounting challenge, however, is the allocation of that cost

Exhibit 2–5
Basic Consolidation
Information

	Giant Company	Small Company	
	Book Value 12/31/98	Book Value 12/31/98	Fair Market Value 12/31/98
Current Assets	$ 400,000	$ 300,000	$ 300,000
Land	500,000	300,000	400,000
Buildings and furniture (net)	1,000,000	400,000	600,000
Mortgage note payable	(300,000)	(200,000)	(250,000)
Net assets......................	$1,600,000	$ 800,000	$1,050,000
Common stock—$10 par value	$ 600,000		
Common stock—$5 par value		$ 200,000	
Additional paid-in capital............	40,000	20,000	
Retained earnings, 1/1/98...........	870,000	470,000	
Dividends paid	110,000	10,000	
Revenues	1,000,000	500,000	
Expenses	800,000	380,000	
Retained earnings, 12/31/98	960,000*	580,000*	

*Retained earnings balance after closing out revenues, expenses, and dividends paid.

among the various assets and liabilities obtained in the acquisition. These allocations depend on the relation between total cost and the fair market values of the acquired firm's assets and liabilities. Therefore, we demonstrate the consolidation procedures in this inital section using four examples, each with a different price relative to fair market value.

a.   **Purchase Price Equals Fair Market Value**   Assume that, after negotiations with the owners of Small, Giant agrees to pay them $1,050,000 for all of Small's assets and liabilities: cash of $250,000 and 20,000 unissued shares of its $10 par value common stock that is currently selling for $40 per share. Small will then dissolve itself as a legal entity.

As with any acquisition, the price established here is based on the value of the consideration paid.

Cash	$ 250,000
Common stock issued (20,000 shares at a $40 per share fair market value)	800,000
Purchase price	$1,050,000

Therefore, Giant's cost is exactly equal to the $1,050,000 fair market value of the individual assets and liabilities being procured.

The purchase method is appropriate for consolidating the financial information of these two companies since all of the essential characteristics are present. A bargained exchange occurred between Giant, the acquiring company, and the owners of Small. This transaction indicates a $1,050,000 purchase price will be the basis used in arriving at consolidated figures for the financial statements of the resulting single economic entity. In addition, since some cash was paid rather than having a pure exchange of voting securities, at least 1 of the 12 criteria for a pooling of interests has not been met.

At the date of acquisition, the purchase method consolidates all subsidiary asset and liability accounts based on their fair market values. The acquired assets and liabilities are recorded as if the parent had simply obtained them by paying market value. Because the negotiated price here equals this total value, the parent records each of these accounts as though purchased individually. As is subsequently demonstrated, variations from this rule do exist if less than market value is paid by the parent.

Because Small Company is to be dissolved, a consolidation entry is made directly onto the financial records of Giant (the surviving company). As a purchase, Small's assets and liabilities are consolidated at market value; original book values are ignored. Revenue, expense, dividend, and equity accounts cannot be transferred to a parent and are omitted in recording the creation of this business combination as a purchase.

Purchase Method—Parent Pays Market Value—Subsidiary Dissolved

Giant Company's Financial Records—December 31, 1998

Current Assets	300,000	
Land	400,000	
Buildings and Furniture	600,000	
Mortgage Note Payable		250,000
Cash (paid by Giant)		250,000
Common Stock (20,000 shares issued by Giant at $10 par value)		200,000
Additional Paid-In Capital (value of shares issued by Giant in excess of par value)		600,000

To record purchase of net assets of Small Company for $1,050,000. Subsidiary accounts are recorded at market value which total to the same $1,050,000. (Dashed line separates the accounts acquired from Small and the consideration paid by Giant. Included for clarification purposes only.)

Giant's financial records now show $900,000 in the Land account ($500,000 former balance + $400,000 acquired), $1,600,000 in Buildings and Furniture ($1,000,000 + $600,000), and so forth. These items have been added into Giant's balances (see Exhibit 2–5) at their fair market values. Conversely, Giant's revenue balance continues to report the company's own $1,000,000 with expenses remaining at $800,000 and dividends of $110,000. *In a purchase, only the subsidiary's revenues, expenses, dividends, and equity transactions that occur subsequent to the takeover affect the business combination.*[8]

Purchase Price Exceeds Fair Market Value   The bargained price in this second illustration is assumed to be $1,140,000 in exchange for all of Small's assets and liabilities. The mode of payment by Giant will be $340,000 in cash plus 20,000 shares of common stock with a market value of $40 per share (or $800,000 in total). The resulting purchase price is $90,000 more than the $1,050,000 fair market value of Small's net assets. In purchase combinations, such excess payments are not unusual. As an example, when Textron acquired Cessna Aircraft, the purchase price of $605 million was $406 million in excess of the fair market value of this subsidiary's net assets.

The $1,050,000 market value of Small's net assets certainly has an influence on the size of any takeover offer. However, Giant's $1,140,000 acquisition price could

---

[8]Chapter 4 describes an alternative method of reporting a purchase that occurs within the current year. All of the subsidiary's revenues and expenses for the entire year are included in the consolidated totals with the income earned prior to the purchase then being subtracted on the income statement as a single Preacquisition Income figure. Thus, consolidated net income is not affected by subsidiary operations occurring before the purchase but the reported revenue and expense balances are more comparable with future periods.

have been affected by any number of other factors such as Small's history of profitability, the company's reputation, the quality of its personnel, or the economic condition of the industry in which it operates. If Small, for example, has demonstrated the ability to generate especially high profits, Giant would probably be willing to pay an extra amount for this company. One additional factor frequently has an impact on an acquisition price: the presence of competitive buyers. If Giant is forced to outbid other companies to acquire Small, the purchase price may be no more than a representation of this bidding war.

Whenever the price paid in a purchase exceeds total fair market value, all of the subsidiary's assets and liabilities are consolidated at fair market value with the additional payment allocated to the intangible asset goodwill. This excess amount may actually reflect the profitability often inherent in a going concern, the creative ability of a research group, market conditions that surrounded the acquisition, or myriad other possible factors. Because the conditions that can influence a purchase price are virtually unlimited, any amount paid in excess of fair market value is simply assigned arbitrarily to goodwill.

Alternative account titles such as Unamortized Cost in Excess of Market Value or some variation have also been widely used in recent years to identify this general allocation of any excess purchase price. Unisys, for example, reported a $1.0 billion asset as a "cost in excess of net assets acquired" on its December 31, 1995, balance sheet. Traditionally, the term *goodwill* has referred to a computationally derived excess payment based on the estimated future profits of a going concern. Since the extra amount paid in the purchase of another company may actually be a function of many other factors, a more descriptive label such as the one reported by Unisys might be preferable. However, goodwill is specifically used in *APB Opinion 16* and is, therefore, incorporated throughout this textbook.

Returning to Giant's $1,140,000 purchase, $90,000 of this price was in excess of the fair market value of Small's net assets. Thus, goodwill of that amount is entered into Giant's accounting system along with the fair market value of each individual account. The actual journal entry made by Giant at the date of acquisition would be:

Purchase Method—Parent Pays More Than Market Value—Subsidiary Dissolved

Giant Company's Financial Records—December 31, 1998

Current Assets	300,000	
Land	400,000	
Buildings and Furniture	600,000	
Goodwill	90,000	
Mortgage Note Payable		250,000
Cash (paid by Giant)		340,000
Common Stock (20,000 shares issued by Giant at $10 par value)		200,000
Additional Paid-In Capital (value of shares issued by Giant in excess of par value)		600,000

To record purchase of net assets of Small Company for $1,140,000. Subsidiary accounts are recorded at market value with $90,000 excess payment attributed to goodwill.

Once again, Giant's financial records show $900,000 in its Land account ($500,000 former balance + $400,000 acquired), $1,600,000 in Buildings and Furniture ($1,000,000 + $600,000), and so forth. As the only change, a Goodwill balance of $90,000 has been established to account for the excess purchase price paid by Giant.

C. **Purchase Price Less Than Fair Market Value**   For this third example, the price paid to the owners of Small is assumed to be $900,000. Giant conveys $100,000 of this amount in cash and issues 20,000 shares of common stock having a $40 per share (or $800,000 total) fair market value. To add a new element to this illustration, Giant is forced to pay $30,000 in accountants' and lawyers' fees directly associated with the combination as well as $10,000 for registering and issuing the shares of common stock.

In this combination, the parent's cost comprises more than one component. According to *APB Opinion 16,* any direct costs of establishing a purchase combination should be included as part of the total acquisition price. Expenditures such as payments to lawyers and accountants as well as finders' fees are necessary to carry out a purchase and are thus capitalized. Such combination costs can be quite significant. In describing the takeover battle for RJR Nabisco, *Time* magazine estimated that the "hundreds of lawyers and investment bankers involved in the bidding stand to earn a total of as much as $1 billion for their expertise."

Based on *APB 16,* the accountants' and lawyers' fees of $30,000 are included by Giant in computing a purchase price of $930,000, the total cost of acquiring Small's assets and liabilities ($900,000 to the owners of Small and $30,000 for these direct costs). However, the remaining $10,000 was paid to register and issue the common stock. This amount is considered a cost associated with these securities rather than a cost of the purchase. As such, the $10,000 is assumed to be a reduction in the paid-in capital recorded for the newly issued shares.

Giant's total purchase price of $930,000 is $120,000 less than the fair market value of Small's net assets. Allocation of full market values to each asset and liability is simply not possible; some reduction must be made. A cost of $930,000 cannot be assigned to accounts having a fair market value of $1,050,000 without an adjustment. Addressing this problem, *APB Opinion 16* (par. 87) states that "the values otherwise assignable to noncurrent assets acquired (except long-term investments in marketable securities) should be reduced by a proportionate part of the excess to determine the assigned values." *Therefore, when a purchase price is less than total fair market value of the net assets, noncurrent accounts, such as land, buildings, and equipment, are consolidated at reduced balances. All remaining assets and liabilities continue to be recorded at their fair market values.*

Since Giant paid $120,000 less than fair market value ($1,050,000 − $930,000), the balances of any noncurrent assets being acquired (other than long-term investments in marketable securities) must be decreased by that amount. As indicated in Exhibit 2–5, the two applicable accounts in this example have a total fair market value of $1,000,000:

Noncurrent Asset Accounts	Fair Market Values	
Land	$400,000	40%
Buildings and Furniture	600,000	60%
Totals	$1,000,000	100%

Because of Giant's payment, these two accounts must be reduced in consolidation by a total of $120,000 (from $1 million to $880,000). The balance reported for land is lowered by $48,000 ($120,000 × 40%). The remaining $72,000 ($120,000 × 60%) is assigned as a decrease to the Buildings and Furniture account. Therefore, for consolidation purposes, Small's land is recorded by Giant at $352,000 ($48,000 less than its $400,000 fair market value). The Buildings and Furniture account is entered as $528,000 ($600,000 − $72,000). All other assets and liabilities are consolidated at their fair market values.

Purchase Method—Parent Pays Less Than Market Value—Subsidiary Dissolved

Giant Company's Financial Records—December 31, 1998

Current Assets	300,000	
Land	352,000	
Buildings and Furniture	528,000	
Mortgage Note Payable		250,000
Cash (paid by Giant to Small's owners)		100,000
Common Stock (20,000 shares issued by Giant at $10 par value)		200,000
Additional Paid-In Capital (value of shares issued by Giant in excess of par value)		600,000
Cash (consolidation costs)		30,000
Additional Paid-In Capital (stock costs)	10,000	
Cash		10,000

To record purchase of net assets of Small Company. Payment includes $30,000 direct combination costs and the $10,000 cost of registering and issuing common stock. Total purchase price of $930,000 is $120,000 less than market value of the net assets, an amount assigned to noncurrent assets (other than long-term investments in marketable securities).

d. **Purchase Price Less Than Fair Market Value—Deferred Credit** In this final illustration, the exchange price for Small's net assets is assumed to be $40,000 with payment made entirely in cash. Obviously, expending this amount for net assets valued at $1,050,000 is an extreme case that indicates an unusual circumstance such as imminent bankruptcy, large contingent liabilities, or an urgent need by the present owners for immediate liquidation. A company, for example, that has its entire business centered on marketing one patent might see the price of its stock drop to nearly zero if the legality of that patent were seriously threatened.

With a purchase price of only $40,000, Small's assets and liabilities must be consolidated at balances $1,010,000 less than their total fair market value of $1,050,000. As was indicated in the previous example, this decrease is initially made in the recording of noncurrent assets. However, these two assets (land and buildings and furniture) have a total worth of only $1,000,000. Even decreasing their balances to zero will not fully account for the $1,010,000 difference between the purchase price and total fair market value. A further reduction of $10,000 has to be assigned within the consolidation process.

Whenever a purchase price is less than fair market value so that the acquired noncurrent asset balances are eliminated entirely, any additional reduction is recorded as a deferred credit. All other assets and liabilities are still brought into the combination at fair market value. This Deferred Credit account results from a bargain purchase, but only comes into existence after the applicable noncurrent assets are first decreased to zero. Thus, before recognition of a credit is necessary, either the price has to be extremely low or the acquired noncurrent assets must be of a relatively small value.

A deferred credit also can be thought of as a credit to income that is being deferred. Given the bargain purchase, it appears that the acquiring firm has made a profit on the acquisition. However, accounting conventions typically require a sale, not a purchase as a prerequisite to income recognition. Therefore, the credit to income is deferred until the underlying assets purchased in the acquisition have been sold to justify the recognition of the deferred credit.

For reporting purposes, the deferred credit is frequently labeled as an "excess of market value over cost of acquisition." The balance is presented within the liability section of the consolidated balance sheet and is often amortized over an arbitrary period of up to 40 years.

Because the $40,000 price in this illustration is $1,010,000 less than fair market value, Giant's journal entry to record its purchase of Small's assets and liabilities would:

1. Recognize no balances for the two noncurrent asset accounts.
2. Allocate the remaining $10,000 reduction to a Deferred Credit account.
3. Report all remaining asset and liability accounts at fair market value.

Purchase Method—Parent Pays Less Than Market Value and Deferred Credit Is Recognized—Subsidiary Dissolved

Giant Company's Financial Records—December 31, 1998

Current Assets	300,000	
Land	-0-	
Buildings and Furniture	-0-	
Mortgage Note Payable		250,000
Deferred Credit—Excess of Market Value over Cost of Acquisition		10,000
Cash (paid by Giant)		40,000

To record acquisition of Small's net assets for $40,000, an amount $1,010,000 below market value.

Summary of the Purchase Method   In a purchase, acquired assets and liabilities are normally consolidated at their fair market values. However, the relationship between purchase price and total market value can necessitate some alterations to this rule. An excess payment, for example, leads to the creation of a Goodwill account. A low purchase price forces a reduction in the recorded balance of noncurrent assets and possibly the recognition of a deferred credit. Exhibit 2–6 summarizes the possible allocation scenarios.

Purchase Method Where Separate Incorporation Is Maintained

When separate incorporation is retained by each company in a purchase combination, many aspects of the consolidation process are identical to those demonstrated in the previous section. Fair market value, as an example, still serves as the basis for initially consolidating the subsidiary's asset and liability accounts. Recognition of goodwill or a deferred credit may again be necessary, depending on the size of the purchase price.

E x h i b i t   2 – 6
Consolidation Values—The Purchase Method

Purchase price equals the fair market value of net assets.	Acquired assets and liabilities are assigned their fair market values.
Purchase price is greater than the fair market value of the net assets.	Acquired assets and liabilities are assigned their fair market values. The excess payment is attributed to goodwill.
Purchase price is less than the fair market value of the net assets.	Current assets, liabilities, and long-term investments in marketable securities are assigned their fair market values. The values of other noncurrent assets are reduced proportionally. If necessary, a deferred credit is recognized.

Despite such similarities, several significant differences do exist in a purchase consolidation in which each company remains a legally incorporated entity. Most noticeably, the consolidation of the financial information is only simulated rather than having the acquiring company physically record the acquired assets and liabilities. Since dissolution does not occur, independent record-keeping continues to be maintained by each company. To facilitate the preparation of consolidated financial statements, a worksheet and consolidation entries are employed using the data gathered from these separate companies.

A worksheet provides the structure for generating information to be reported by the single economic entity. An integral part of this process is the inclusion of consolidation worksheet entries. *These adjustments and eliminations are entered on the worksheet and represent alterations that would be required if the financial records were to be physically united.* Since no actual union occurs, consolidation entries are never formally recorded in the journals of either company. Instead, they are produced solely for use on the worksheet to assist in deriving consolidated account balances of the two separate companies.

To illustrate using the previous information, assume that Giant acquires Small Company on December 31, 1998, by issuing 26,000 shares of $10 par value common stock valued at $40 per share (or $1,040,000 in total). Direct combination costs of $50,000 also are paid by Giant. Hence, the purchase price totals $1,090,000 ($1,040,000 + $50,000). Although only voting stock is being issued to the owners of Small, the assumption is made that at least 1 of the other 12 criteria for a pooling of interests has not been met. Perhaps, Small was a subsidiary of another company and, thus, not autonomous. Or, some agreement might have been made to reacquire the shares issued in this transaction. Consequently, the purchase method is appropriate.

For business reasons, Giant decides to allow Small to continue as a separate corporation. Therefore, whenever financial statements for this combination are to be prepared, a worksheet is utilized in simulating the consolidation of these two companies.

Although the assets and liabilities are not being transferred, Giant must still record the payment made to Small's owners. When the subsidiary remains separate, the parent establishes an Investment account that initially reflects the purchase price.

a. Purchase Method—Subsidiary Is Not Dissolved

Giant Company's Financial Records—December 31, 1998

Investment in Small Company (purchase price)	1,090,000	
Cash (paid for direct combination costs)		50,000
Common Stock (26,000 shares issued by Giant at $10 par value)		260,000
Additional Paid-In Capital (value of shares issued by Giant in excess of par value)		780,000
To record purchase of Small Company, which will maintain its separate legal identity.		

As demonstrated in Exhibit 2–7, a worksheet can be prepared on the date of acquisition to arrive at consolidated totals for this combination. The entire process consists of seven steps:

Step 1 Whenever a worksheet is being constructed, a formal allocation of the purchase price should be made as was done for the equity method in Chapter 1.[9] Thus, the following schedule is appropriate for Giant's purchase of Small:

---

[9] This allocation procedure is helpful but not critical if dissolution occurs. Unless the purchase price is less than total market value, the asset and liability accounts are simply added directly into the parent's books at their assessed worth with any excess assigned to goodwill.

Exhibit 2–7   Purchase Method—Date of Acquisition

GIANT COMPANY AND SMALL COMPANY
Consolidation Worksheet
For Period Ending December 31, 1998

Accounts	Giant Company	Small Company	Consolidation Entries Debits	Consolidation Entries Credits	Consolidated Totals
Income Statement					
Revenues	(1,000,000)				(1,000,000)
Expenses	800,000				800,000
Net income	(200,000)				(200,000)
Statement of Retained Earnings					
Retained earnings, 1/1/98	(870,000)				(870,000)
Net income (above)	(200,000)				(200,000)
Dividends paid	110,000				110,000
Retained earnings, 12/31/98	(960,000)				(960,000)
Balance Sheet					
Current Assets	350,000 *	300,000			650,000
Investment in Small Company	1,090,000 *	–0–		(S) 800,000	–0–
				(A) 290,000	
Land	500,000	300,000	(A) 100,000		900,000
Buildings and furniture	1,000,000	400,000	(A) 200,000		1,600,000
Goodwill	–0–	–0–	(A) 40,000		40,000
Total assets	2,940,000	1,000,000			3,190,000
Mortgage note payable	(300,000)	(200,000)		(A) 50,000	(550,000)
Common stock	(860,000)*	(200,000)	(S) 200,000		(860,000)
Additional paid-in capital	(820,000)*	(20,000)	(S) 20,000		(820,000)
Retained earnings, 12/31/98 (above)	(960,000)	(580,000)	(S) 580,000		(960,000)
Total liabilities and equities	(2,940,000)	(1,000,000)			(3,190,000)

(handwritten annotations: "Allocations" pointing to Debits column; "Stockholders Equity" pointing to (S) entries)

Note: Parentheses indicate a credit balance.

*Balances have been adjusted for issuance of stock and payment of consolidation costs.

Purchase price paid by Giant		$1,090,000
Book value of Small (see Exhibit 2–5)		800,000
Excess of cost over book value		$ 290,000
Allocations made to specific accounts based on difference in fair market values and book values:		
Land ($400,000 − $300,000)	$100,000	
Buildings and furniture ($600,000 − $400,000)	200,000	
Mortgage note payable ($250,000 − $200,000)	(50,000)	250,000
Excess cost not identified with specific accounts—goodwill		$ 40,000

No part of the $290,000 excess payment is attributed to the current assets because the book value and market value are identical. The mortgage note payable shows a negative allocation: since this debt's present value is more than book value, the company's net assets are actually worth *less*.

Step 2   The financial figures from the separate companies as of the date of acquisition (see Exhibit 2–5) are recorded in the first two columns of the worksheet (see Exhibit 2–7). Giant's accounts have been adjusted for the investment entry recorded earlier. As another preliminary step, Small's revenue, expense, and dividend accounts have been closed into retained earnings. In a purchase, the operations of the subsidiary prior to the December 31, 1998, takeover have no direct bearing on the business combination. These activities occurred before Small was obtained; thus, the resulting data should not be reflected as income earned by the new owners in the consolidated statements.

Step 3   Small's stockholders' equity accounts are eliminated through consolidation entry S (S is a reference to beginning subsidiary **S**tockholders' equity). These balances (Common Stock, Additional Paid-In Capital, and Retained Earnings) are historical measurements of subsidiary transactions that occurred prior to the combination. By removing these accounts, only Small's assets and liabilities remain to be combined with the parent company figures.

Step 4   Also in worksheet Entry S, the $800,000 component of the Investment in Small Company account that equates to the book value of the subsidiary's net assets is removed. For external reporting purposes, the combination should report each individual account rather than a single investment balance. In effect, this portion of the Investment in Small Company account is deleted so that it can be replaced by the specific assets and liabilities that it represents.

Step 5   In Entry A, the $290,000 excess payment in the Investment in Small Company is removed and assigned to the specific accounts indicated by the purchase price allocation. Consequently, land is increased by $100,000 to agree with Small's market value; $200,000 is attributed to the buildings and furniture and $50,000 to the mortgage note payable. The unexplained excess of $40,000 is recorded as goodwill. This entry is labeled entry A to indicate that it represents the **A**llocations made in connection with the parent's purchase price. It also completes the elimination of the entire Investment in Small account.

Step 6   All accounts are extended into the "Consolidated Totals" column. For accounts such as Current Assets, this process is no more than the addition of Small's book value to that of Giant. However, where applicable, this extension also includes any allocations to establish the fair market value of Small's asset and liability accounts. Land, as an example, is being increased by $100,000. By raising the subsidiary's book value to market value, the reported balances are the same as in the previous examples where dissolution occurred. The use of a worksheet does not alter the consolidated figures, only the method of deriving those numbers.

Step 7   Consolidated expenses are subtracted from revenues to arrive at a net income of $200,000. Note that because this is a date of acquisition worksheet, no amounts for Small's revenues and expenses are included in the Small Company column. Giant has just purchased Small and therefore Small has not yet earned any income for the owners of Giant. Consolidated revenues, expenses, and net income are identical to Giant's balances. In years subsequent to acquisition, of course, Small's income accounts will be consolidated with Giant's.

In general, totals (such as net income and ending retained earnings) are not directly consolidated on the worksheet. Rather, the components (such as revenues and expenses) are extended across and then combined to derive the appropriate figure. Net income is then carried down on the worksheet to the Statement of Retained Earnings and used (along with beginning retained earnings and dividends paid) to compute this December 31, 1998, equity balance. In the same manner, ending retained earnings of $960,000 is entered into the balance sheet to arrive at total liabilities and equities of $3,190,000, a number which reconciles with the total of consolidated assets.

The balances in the final column of Exhibit 2–7 are used to prepare consolidated financial statements for the business combination of Giant Company and Small Company. The worksheet entries have served as a catalyst for bringing together the two independent sets of financial information. Thus, the actual accounting records of both Giant and Small remain unaltered by this consolidation process.

A Pooling of Interests—Rationale for Different Accounting

As stated previously, the pooling of interests method has evolved over the years as an alternative for reporting business combinations that demonstrate specific characteristics. In theory, a pooling involves the union of two companies so that a continuity of ownership is maintained. The underlying concept is that nothing has been changed by the combination except the composition of the reporting entity. *Thus, the book values of the two companies are simply brought together to form consolidated financial statements.* This approach is in diametric contrast to a purchase where one company clearly acquires another and then utilizes the purchase price as a basis for valuing the subsidiary's assets and liabilities.

ARS 5 (p. 15) explains that

> The "pooling-of-interests accounting" treatment is generally supported by reasoning that no new basis of accountability is required since the two (or more) companies are continuing operations as one company in a manner similar to that which existed in the past. The presumption is that in effect there has been no purchase or sale of assets, but merely a fusion, merging, or pooling of two formerly separate economic entities into one new economic entity.

Since a fusion of the companies rather than a takeover occurs, no purchase price is computed in a pooling of interests. Without a cost figure, no basis exists for either revaluing acquired asset and liability accounts to fair market value or recognizing goodwill. Book values are simply retained. This absence of a purchase price creates many of the significant reporting differences between the pooling of interests method and the purchase method.

The approach to consolidating revenues and expenses also is altered in a pooling of interests. Because a union is occurring, the operations of each company are said to continue in a manner unaffected by the combination. In theory, nothing has changed for either company except the composition of the reporting entity. Since the two companies have merged into one, the financial results of all past operations continue to be relevant information. *Consequently, in a pooling of interests, revenues and expenses are combined on a retroactive basis.* This treatment differs markedly from a purchase where only the operations of the subsidiary after the date of acquisition are attributed to the consolidated entity.

The business combination of AT&T and McCaw Cellular Communications serves as an illustration of this retroactive treatment. Although this pooling of interests did not occur until September 19, 1994, the consolidated income statement for 1994 included all revenues and expenses for both companies for the entire year. In this manner, the operations of the two companies were being reported as one entity. Furthermore, the same restatement procedure was applied to all prior years. In 1993, for example, AT&T disclosed separate revenues of $67.2 billion. When the two companies were subsequently joined, the newly created company (AT&T and Subsidiaries) reported that total 1993 revenues had been $69.3 billion.

In contrast, if AT&T had acquired McCaw Cellular in 1994 through a purchase, the operations of the subsidiary prior to September 19 would have had no effect on the business combination. The revenues reported by AT&T for 1993 would remain at $67.2 billion. However, because the combination was a pooling, the past operating figures for the two companies were brought together. Although the companies were separate entities in 1993, the subsequently consolidated statements do purport to show the financial results of the business combination for that year. By restating the prior years, the operations of the component companies (AT&T and McCaw) are being reported even though their combination had not yet been formed at that particular time.

Pooling of Interests Where Dissolution Takes Place

To demonstrate the formation of a pooling of interests, assume that Giant Company and Small Company decide to join operations on December 31, 1998 (see Exhibit 2–5). This combination is created when Giant issues 19,000 new shares of its common stock, with a $10 par value and a $40 market value per share, to the owners of Small in exchange for all of the company's outstanding common shares. Small transfers its assets and liabilities to Giant and dissolves itself as a separate corporation. Stock registration fees of $5,000 are paid by Giant as well as $3,000 in other costs directly associated with the combination. In creating this business combination, the companies followed all 12 criteria established by *APB Opinion 16* for a pooling of interests (see the appendix at the end of the chapter).

As stated earlier, a pooling of interests consolidates all accounts at their historical book values. Therefore, the reported value of each of Small's accounts (assets, liabilities, revenues, expenses, and dividends paid) simply can be transferred into Giant's financial records through a journal entry. To ensure that adequate disclosure is provided, *APB Opinion 16* does require that the details of the separate operations be presented in a note to the consolidated statements.

In contrast to the purchase method, no part of the $8,000 in consolidation costs is capitalized; the entire amount is recorded here as an expense. According to *APB Opinion 16* (par. 58), "The pooling of interests method records neither the acquiring of assets nor the obtaining of capital. Therefore, costs incurred to effect a combination accounted for by that method and to integrate the continuing operations are expenses of the combined corporation rather than additions to assets or direct reductions of stockholders' equity." To maintain book value, the cost of uniting the organizations is not viewed as a change in either asset or contributed capital accounts; thus, an expense is recorded by the combined entity.

Entering the book values of Small's assets, liabilities, revenues, expenses, and dividends into the records of Giant poses little trouble.[10] Likewise, the $8,000 in direct consolidation costs is simply assigned directly to expense. However, the recording of the 19,000 shares of stock being issued by Giant should be noted. According to Exhibit 2–5, Small is reporting contributed capital (the Common Stock and Additional Paid-In Capital accounts) of $220,000 and retained earnings of $470,000.[11] Because poolings retain book value, Giant uses these same figures in recording the issuance of its own stock. In that way, Small's equity balances are included within the consolidated totals.

Regardless of the amounts reported by Small, Giant's Common Stock account must be increased by $190,000 to reflect the $10 par value of these 19,000 shares. To arrive at the $220,000 figure that corresponds with Small's total contributed capital, Giant also records $30,000 as additional paid-in capital. The entry is then completed with a $470,000 credit to retained earnings. Small's contributed capital

---

[10]As is discussed in Chapter 3, dividends paid between the related companies after a combination is created are intercompany transfers that have to be eliminated. In a pooling of interests, though, any amounts distributed to previous owners before the combination was created continue to be reported as Dividends Paid.

[11]Although the date of the pooling was December 31, Small's Retained Earnings balance as of the first day of the year is recorded by the combination with the company's current revenues, expenses, and dividends being reported separately.

total and retained earnings both have been added into the business combination at book value.

a. Pooling of Interests Method—Subsidiary Dissolved

Giant Company's Financial Records—December 31, 1998

Current Assets	300,000	
Land	300,000	
Buildings and Furniture	400,000	
Dividends Paid	10,000	
Expenses	380,000	
Mortgage Note Payable		200,000
Revenues		500,000
Common Stock (19,000 shares issued by Giant at $10		
par value)		190,000
Additional Paid-In Capital (to equate contributed capital		
with $220,000 amount reported by Small)		30,000
Retained Earnings, 1/1/98 (to record amount equal to		
book value of Small)		470,000
Expenses (consolidation costs)	8,000	
Cash		8,000

To record book value of Small's account obtained through a pooling of interests. Direct consolidation costs are expensed.

After recording these accounts, Giant's financial records show $800,000 in land ($500,000 + $300,000), $1,400,000 in buildings and furniture ($1,000,000 + $400,000), and so on. The Revenues account now holds $1,500,000 ($1,000,000 + $500,000) while expenses are recorded at $1,188,000 ($800,000 + $380,000 + $8,000 in consolidation costs). *Since book values are retained, the various asset, liability, revenue, expense, and dividend balances are not affected by the number of shares issued by Giant.* If 1,900 shares or 190,000 shares had been exchanged rather than 19,000, the same consolidated figures would have still been appropriate for these accounts.

By comparing this consolidation to previous illustrations, several areas of distinct contrast can be seen between the purchase method and the pooling of interests method:

	Consolidation—Purchase Method	Consolidation—Pooling of Interests Method
Assets and liabilities of subsidiary	Recorded at fair value*	Recorded at book value
Goodwill	Excess of purchase price over fair value of subsidiary net assets	Not recognized
Revenues and expenses of subsidiary	Accrued only after date of acquisition	Recognized retroactively
Shares issued to create business combination	Recorded at fair value if any shares are issued	Based on book value of subsidiary's contributed capital and retained earnings at beginning of year
Consolidation costs	Included as part of purchase price unless incurred in connection with issuance of stock, a cost which reduces paid-in capital	Expensed immediately

*If purchase price is less than fair market value, noncurrent assets (except for any long-term investments in marketable securities) are recorded at reduced amounts. A deferred credit also may be required.

DISCUSSION QUESTION:

How Does a Purchase Differ from a Pooling of Interests?

On December 31, 1998, Acme Taxicab Company agrees to form a business combination with Wilbury's Cabs. Acme will exchange 600 shares of its previously unissued, $20 par value stock with Roy Wilbury for all of the outstanding shares of Wilbury's Cabs. Acme's common stock has a fair market value on that date of $100 per share.

The only assets owned by Wilbury's Cabs are eight used taxicabs having a fair market value of $5,000 each. Because of accelerated depreciation, the average book value of these assets is $2,000. Acme has 15 automobiles of its own with a total book value of $60,000 but a fair market value of $74,000.

During 1998, the two companies separately reported the following revenues and expenses:

	Acme	Wilbury
Revenues	$220,000	$95,000
Expenses	150,000	60,000

Based on the information presented here, no determination is possible as to whether a pooling of interests or a purchase has been created.

- On a consolidated balance sheet as of December 31, 1998, how will the reported asset balances differ, depending on the type of method that is appropriate?

- If a business combination is created as a purchase, one set of assets and liabilities is adjusted to fair market value whereas the other is left at book value. Why are both sets of assets and liabilities not revalued?

- On a consolidated income statement for 1998, how will the balances differ, depending on the method considered appropriate?

- Are external decision makers properly served by allowing such widely varying numbers to be reported depending on whether a purchase or a pooling of interests has taken place?

- Based on the facts presented in the case, which set of financial statements best mirrors the economic reality of the business combination that has occurred?

When recording a pooling of interests, one potential variation to the previous entry may be encountered. Although poolings are based on retaining book values, the recording of contributed capital can cause a problem. Because issued shares are always credited for par value, Giant's common stock had to be recorded as $190,000 although Small's balance for this same account was $200,000. As indicated, Giant increased its additional paid-in capital by $30,000 so that total contributed capital equaled Small's $220,000 balance (see Exhibit 2–8).

If Giant had originally issued only 18,000 shares, its Common Stock account would be credited for $180,000 with an accompanying $40,000 added to additional paid-in capital. Once again, the $220,000 total book value of Small's contributed capital is replicated by the entry. Conversely, as shown in Exhibit 2–8, if 23,000 shares with a par value of $230,000 were exchanged by Giant to create this pooling, a $10,000 *reduction* to additional paid-in capital is necessary to arrive at the appropriate $220,000 total. In each case, the book value of Small's total contributed capital is retained by the combination.

A slightly different problem arises in recording total contributed capital for a pooling when the number of issued shares is relatively large. Assume, as an example, that 29,000 shares of common stock are exchanged by Giant to establish this pooling of interests with Small. The $290,000 par value of the stock necessitates a $70,000 reduction in Giant's additional paid-in capital to equal the $220,000 contributed capital reported by Small.

However, Exhibit 2–5 indicates that Giant's Additional Paid-In Capital account only holds a $40,000 balance. Because a negative contributed capital balance is not possible, Giant's additional paid-in capital is first dropped to zero with the remaining $30,000 decrease being made in retained earnings. Exhibit 2–8 shows that only $440,000 in retained earnings (rather than Small's $470,000 balance) is recorded by

Exhibit 2-8
Recording of Shares Issued in a Pooling of Interests

	Small's Book Values (Exhibit 2–5)	Giant Company Issues			
		19,000 Shares	18,000 Shares	23,000 Shares	29,000 Shares
Common stock	$200,000	$190,000	$180,000	$230,000	$290,000
Additional paid-in capital	20,000	30,000	40,000	(10,000)	(40,000)*
Total contributed capital	220,000	220,000	220,000	220,000	250,000
Retained earnings, 1/1/98	470,000	470,000	470,000	470,000	440,000 †

*Giant's Additional Paid-In Capital account is reduced from $40,000 to zero.

†Since the contributed capital of issued shares is $30,000 greater than that reported by Small, retained earnings must be $30,000 lower.

the business combination when 29,000 shares are issued. *Thus, if Giant's issued shares have a total par value greater than Small's total contributed capital, a reduction must be made. Giant initially decreases its own Additional Paid-In Capital account. However, if that amount proves to be insufficient, the Retained Earnings balance must also be reduced.*

④ ### Pooling of Interests Where Separate Incorporation Is Maintained

The combination of Giant Company and Small Company is presented again to demonstrate a pooling of interests, one in which both companies retain their separate legal identities. For this illustration, the same exchange is used as in the purchase consolidation shown in Exhibit 2–7. Thus, Giant issues 26,000 shares of common stock on December 31, 1998, for all of Small's outstanding shares. In addition, direct consolidation costs of $50,000 are incurred. Small's accounts are not transferred to Giant's financial records; both companies continue as separate corporations and maintain independent accounting systems. However, the assumption is made here that the combination meets all 12 requirements for a pooling of interests.

Giant must first record the issuance of 26,000 shares of common stock to create this business combination. Because Small is not being dissolved, Giant establishes an investment balance rather than recording Small's individual accounts. Because the combination is a pooling, this figure is based on Small's $690,000 book value as of the beginning of the year. Using the January 1 total allows the current revenues, expenses, and dividends to be included as separate items in recording the business combination.

The issued shares are recorded by Giant at their par value of $260,000. The Additional Paid-in Capital account is reduced by $40,000 to arrive at total contributed capital of $220,000, the same book value as Small's contributed capital. Retained earnings at January 1, 1998, also are included in this entry since operating activities are retroactively consolidated in a pooling of interests. The direct combination costs are expensed immediately.

a. ### Pooling of Interests Method—Subsidiary Not Dissolved

Giant's Financial Records—December 31, 1998

Investment in Small Company (1/1/98 book value)	690,000	
Additional Paid-In Capital (to align contributed capital with that of Small)	40,000	
Common Stock (26,000 shares at $10 par value)		260,000
Retained Earnings, 1/1/98 (to record balance equal to book value of Small)		470,000
Expenses (direct combination costs)	50,000	
Cash		50,000

To record issuance of 26,000 shares of stock in exchange for all of the outstanding shares of Small in a combination accounted for as a pooling of interests. Direct combination costs are properly expensed.

Exhibit 2 – 9   Pooling of Interests—Date of Acquisition

GIANT COMPANY AND SMALL COMPANY
Consolidation Worksheet
For Period Ending December 31, 1998

Accounts	Giant Company	Small Company	Consolidation Entries		Consolidated Totals
			Debits	Credits	
Income Statement					
Revenues	(1,000,000)	(500,000)			(1,500,000)
Expenses	850,000	380,000			(1,230,000)
Net income	(150,000)	(120,000)			(270,000)
Statement of Retained Earnings					
Retained earnings, 1/1/98	(1,340,000)*	(470,000)	(S) 470,000		(1,340,000)
Net income (above)	(150,000)	(120,000)			(270,000)
Dividends paid	110,000	10,000			120,000
Retained earnings, 12/31/98	(1,380,000)	(580,000)			(1,490,000)
Balance Sheet					
Current Assets	350,000 *	300,000			650,000
Investment in Small Company	690,000 *	–0–		(S) 690,000	–0–
Land	500,000	300,000			800,000
Buildings and furniture (net)	1,000,000	400,000			1,400,000
Total assets	2,540,000	1,000,000			2,850,000
Mortgage note payable	(300,000)	(200,000)			(500,000)
Common stock	(860,000)*	(200,000)	(S) 200,000		(860,000)
Additional paid-in capital	–0– *	(20,000)	(S) 20,000		–0–
Retained earnings, 12/31/98 (above)	(1,380,000)	(580,000)			(1,490,000)
Total liabilities and equities	(2,540,000)	(1,000,000)			(2,850,000)

Note: Parentheses indicate a credit balance.

*Balances have been adjusted for issuance of stock and payment of consolidation costs.

When the common stock shares are exchanged, the combination is formed, and consolidated financial statements can be prepared using the worksheet produced in Exhibit 2–9. This pooling of interests is carried out through the following series of steps:

Step 1   Prior to creating this worksheet, Giant's balances are adjusted to show (1) the effect of its issuance of stock and (2) the direct combination costs. The updated accounts are then entered into the appropriate columns on the worksheet (see Exhibit 2–5 for original book values).

Step 2   The Investment in Small Company account is eliminated as part of the basic consolidation entry(s). In the same manner as the purchase method, the Investment account is not consolidated; rather, the specific accounts that it represents should be reported by the business combination. Therefore, the $690,000 investment is removed on the worksheet so that it can be replaced by the individual balances of Small Company.

Step 3   Small's stockholders' equity balances also are eliminated by this same entry(s). In a purchase, these figures are removed because only assets and liabilities can actually be transferred to the parent. Conversely, for a pooling where a fusion of ownership interests is said to occur, the equity figures for both companies must be included. However, Small's equity accounts have already been brought into the consolidated totals through the recording of Giant's 26,000 shares of issued stock.

The initial investment entry has already added these equity balances to Giant's records prior to consolidating the financial statements. Thus, Small's common stock, additional paid-in capital, and retained earnings must be eliminated on the worksheet to prevent their inclusion in the final figures a second time. The beginning-of-year balance for Small's retained earnings is being removed to allow the 1998 revenues, expenses, and dividends to be reported by the business combination.

Step 4   For a pooling of interests, the consolidation process is carried out by adding together the book values of each account. For example, Giant's revenue of $1,000,000 and Small's revenue of $500,000 are extended for a consolidated total of $1,500,000. Where a consolidation entry affects an account (such as the elimination of Small's equity accounts), the impact of that adjustment also must be reflected in this extension process. However, since a purchase price is not determined in a pooling, no goodwill is recognized and no valuation adjustments are made to any asset or liability.

Step 5   For each of the financial statements on the worksheet, a total is calculated. The income statement ends with a net income balance, the statement of retained earnings computes ending retained earnings, and the balance sheet arrives at total assets as well as total liabilities and equities. As discussed previously, these final figures are not derived by consolidating the respective balances of the separate companies. Instead, the components in each statement are extended and then used to compute the ending balance.

On the income statement demonstrated here, revenues and expenses are added to produce totals of $1,500,000 and $1,230,000, respectively, indicating consolidated net income of $270,000. This figure is moved to the corresponding line within the statement of retained earnings. Each of the other elements constituting this second statement are extended to produce ending retained earnings of $1,490,000. This total is then included within the stockholders' equity section of the consolidated balance sheet enabling it to properly balance.

Step 6   After all accounts have been consolidated, the final balances on the worksheet are used to prepare financial statements for the business combination of Giant Company and Small Company. Exhibit 2–10 provides a comparison of the figures developed for the purchase consolidation shown previously in Exhibit 2–7 and the pooling of interests in Exhibit 2–9.

POOLING OF INTERESTS—THE CONTROVERSY

Now that the basic characteristics of a pooling of interests have been presented, the long history of controversy that has surrounded this method can be better understood. Over the years, the legitimacy of the pooling of interests method has frequently been questioned. One major theoretical problem associated with the pooling method is that it ignores cost figures indicated by the transaction that created the combination. The number of shares exchanged has no impact on consolidated asset and liability balances. What is normally a significant event for both companies is simply omitted from any accounting consideration. *All book values are retained as if nothing has happened. APB Opinion 16* (par. 39) itself admits

The most serious defect attributed to pooling of interests accounting by those who oppose it is that it does not accurately reflect the economic substance of the business combination

E x h i b i t   2 – 1 0
Comparison of Purchase
Method and Pooling of
Interests Method

General Information: 26,000 shares of Giant Company (par value of $10 per share but a market value of $40 per share) issued for all oustanding shares of Small Company on December 31, 1998. Cash of $50,000 paid for direct consolidation costs.

	Purchase Method (Exhibit 2–7)	Pooling of Interests Method (Exhibit 2–9)
Revenues	$1,000,000	$1,500,000
Expenses	(800,000)	(1,230,000)
Net income	$ 200,000	$ 270,000
Retained earnings, 1/1/98	$ 870,000	$1,340,000
Net income (above)	200,000	270,000
Dividends paid	(110,000)	(120,000)
Retained earnings, 12/31/98	$ 960,000	$1,490,000
Current assets	$ 650,000	$ 650,000
Land	900,000	800,000
Buildings and furniture (net)	1,600,000	1,400,000
Goodwill	40,000	–0–
Total assets	$3,190,000	$2,850,000
Mortgage note payable	$ 550,000	$ 500,000
Common stock	860,000	860,000
Additional paid-in capital	820,000	–0–
Retained earnings, 12/31/98 (above)	960,000	1,490,000
Total liabilities and equities	$3,190,000	$2,850,000

transaction. They believe that the method ignores the bargaining which results in the combination by accounting only for the amounts previously shown in accounts of the combining companies.

As a further argument against pooling of interests, many accountants believe that only one accounting approach should be applicable for all business combinations. They hold that all combinations are essentially the same. Even though a variety of formats do exist, critics contend that a parent and an acquisition price can be determined in virtually every case. In addition, conveying freely traded stock is held to be the same as conveying cash. According to this argument, the availability of two radically different accounting methods is simply not warranted. Interestingly, the pooling of interests method is primarily found in the United States. "Of all the major industrialized countries, only Great Britain allows anything resembling pooling, and its rule makers are modifying the rules to prevent most poolings."[12]

The depth of controversy sparked by the pooling of interests method is clearly demonstrated in *Accounting Research Study No. 5 (ARS 5)* where Arthur Wyatt stated that "no basis exists in principle for a continuation of what is presently known as 'pooling-of-interests' accounting *if* the business combination involves an exchange of assets and/or equities between independent parties."[13]

Additionally, in a dissent to *APB Opinion 16,* Sidney Davidson, Charles Horngren, and J. S. Seidman asserted that

The real abuse is pooling itself. On that, the only answer is to eliminate pooling. . . . Elimination of pooling will remove the confusion that comes from the coexistence of pooling and purchase accounting. Above all, the elimination of pooling would remove an

---

[12] Michael Davis, "APB 16: Time to Reconsider," *Journal of Accountancy,* October 1991, p. 99.

[13] Arthur Wyatt, "A Critical Study of Accounting for Business Combinations," *Accounting Research Study No. 5* (New York: AICPA, 1963), p. 105.

aberration in historical cost accounting that permits an acquisition to be accounted for on the basis of the seller's cost rather than the buyer's cost of the assets obtained in a bargained exchange.

As another concern, objective criteria for differentiating between a purchase and a pooling have always been difficult to identify. Despite the vast accounting differences between the two methods, establishing clear-cut boundaries to separate a pooling of interests from a purchase is not really possible. The conditions indicating a pooling lie in very subjective areas such as the intention of the owners and the relationship of the companies. These distinctions are so nebulous that even subtle differences can be crucial in ascertaining whether a true pooling of interests has occurred.[14]

The acceptability of the pooling of interests method might, indeed, have been eliminated years ago except for its popularity in the business world. Preference for the pooling method is based largely on the desirable impact that it usually produces on reported net income. The most obvious effect is the inclusion of the subsidiary's net income as if that company had always been part of the consolidated entity. This retroactive treatment can lead to immediate improvement in the profitability picture being reported. To the extent that managerial compensation contracts are based on accounting measures of profitability, a further motivation to employ the pooling of interests method to accounting for a business combination is provided.

As an illustration, assume that near the end of 1998, the management of Ace Company realizes that net income for that year will amount to only $400,000 compared to $500,000 for 1997. If 100,000 shares of Ace's common stock are outstanding, these income figures represent earnings per share of $4 for 1998, down from $5 in 1997. Assume further that just prior to the end of 1998, Ace issues 40,000 shares of its own common stock in exchange for all of the outstanding common stock of Short Company in a combination meeting all 12 criteria for a pooling of interests. Short had generated a net income of $300,000 for 1998 after suffering a loss of $80,000 in 1997.

To account for this pooling of interests, Ace must retroactively combine the income figures of both companies, thus reporting $700,000 ($400,000 + $300,000) in earnings for 1998 against only $420,000 ($500,000 − $80,000) for 1997. The corresponding earnings per share figures are now $5 for 1998 ($700,000/140,000 shares) versus $3 for 1997 ($420,000/140,000 shares).

Without a single change in operations, Ace has turned a declining profit year into one that appears to indicate a dramatic increase in earnings.[15] Disclosure requirements do dictate that the notes to the consolidated financial statements clearly outline the effect of Short's operations on reported income figures. Many critics, however, feel that such notes are overshadowed by the figures presented on the face of the statements.

Another income effect helps to further account for the popularity enjoyed by the pooling of interests method. In a purchase combination, the subsidiary's assets and liabilities are adjusted to fair market value with goodwill often recognized. Such allocations are viewed as cost figures of the business combination, costs that have only limited useful lives (except when relating to land). Thus, these amounts (which can be extremely large) must be amortized over future accounting periods. The resulting expense, encountered only in the purchase method, serves to reduce consolidated net income year after year.

---

[14]For example, see "Is Now the Time to Revisit Accounting for Business Combinations?" by Richard Dieter in the July 1989 issue of *CPA Journal* beginning on page 44.

[15]A real-life illustration of using poolings of interests to improve reported earnings can be found in "Muddying the Waters" by Abraham J. Briloff in the October 8, 1990, edition of *Barron's* beginning on page 14.

Conversely, a pooling of interests consolidates all accounts at their book values so that no additional amortization expense is ever recognized. Therefore, in most business combinations, the income reported for each succeeding year is higher using the pooling method than would have been the case if consolidated by the purchase method.[16]

Given these reporting advantages, the desire by businesses to create combinations that qualify as poolings is not surprising. Historically, the accounting profession has attempted to define the characteristics of a pooling of interests in such a way as to restrict its use to combinations that were clearly fusions of two independent companies. Over the years, however, the identification of attributes considered to be essential to a pooling of interests has proven to be a difficult task.

Guidance was provided in this area in 1950 when the Committee on Accounting Procedure of the AICPA issued *ARB 40*. This pronouncement suggested that accountants review several factors in judging whether a particular business combination qualified as a true pooling of interests. These factors were (1) continuity of ownership, (2) relative size of the companies, (3) continuity of management, and (4) activities of a similar or complementary nature. *ARB 40* failed, however, to specify the relative importance of each of these four or the means of ascertaining their existence in a particular combination.

With this latitude available, many companies attempted to stretch the pooling criteria to include a wide variety of business combinations. Subsequently, the accounting profession tried to clarify the definition of a pooling in *ARB 48*,"Business Combinations," January 1957 (par. 6), by stating "where one of the constituent corporations is clearly dominant (for example, where the stockholders of one of the constituent corporations obtain 90 percent or 95 percent or more of the voting interest in the combined enterprise), there is a presumption that the transaction is a purchase rather than a pooling of interests."

Despite the efforts to give structure to consolidation accounting, these official pronouncements failed to delineate clearly the boundary separating a purchase from a pooling combination. Thus, during the 1950s and 1960s, many combinations were accounted for as poolings of interests despite having only the barest semblance to the pooling concept. Finally, in 1970 after pressure was applied by the SEC, the Accounting Principles Board issued *Opinion 16* to provide restrictive guidelines for establishing a pooling of interests.

As indicated previously, the APB stated that if any 1 of 12 specified criteria was absent in a combination, the purchase method had to be applied (see appendix at the end of the chapter). Today, this pronouncement continues to limit the pooling approach to combinations that are the complete fusion of two independent companies formed through the exchange of voting common stock. No alteration of assets or liabilities can result (except for consolidation costs) and the owners of the two companies must be the owners of the combined organization.

If *Opinion 16* was designed to limit the use of the pooling of interests method, it was, at least initially successful. *Accounting Trends & Techniques,* in an annual survey of 600 companies, found 144 poolings of interests in 1967 and 184 in 1968. After *APB Opinion 16,* that number had fallen to 31 in 1975 and 43 in 1976. Poolings, however, are experiencing a recent resurgence in popularity, especially among the larger combinations. As reported in *The Wall Street Journal,* since 1992 there have been 357 poolings vs. 36 purchase acquisitions in deals valued at over $100 million. This increase in pooling of interests accounting once again has led the FASB and SEC to consider further restricting its use.[17]

---

[16]For example, see "Anatomy of a Pooling: The AT&T/NCR Merger," by Andrew Fioriti and Thomas Brady, *Ohio CPA Journal,* October 1994, p. 20

[17]*The Wall Street Journal,* "Merger-Accounting Method Under Fire," by Elizabeth McDonald, April 15, 1997, Section A, p. 2. See also *The Wall Street Journal,* "A Modest Proposal to Stop 'Pooling'," by Roger Lowenstein, May 9, 1996, Section C, p. 1.

UNCONSOLIDATED SUBSIDIARIES

Over the years, accountants have attempted to identify situations in which consolidation of financial information might not be appropriate for every subsidiary. The FASB addressed this issue in 1987 when it released *Statement No. 94*. This pronouncement required that all companies more than 50 percent owned must be consolidated with the exception of two cases:

1. An investment where control is only temporary. If the parent company anticipates surrendering control over a subsidiary in the near future through disposition of part or all of its ownership, consolidation would no longer be considered appropriate. As an illustration, a footnote to an annual report of Fuqua Industries, Inc. informed readers that a wholly owned subsidiary, Georgia Federal Bank, was omitted from consolidation because a contract had been signed to sell the operation. The temporary nature of the relationship nullifies any potential informational benefit derived from presenting consolidated financial statements.

2. An investment where control does not actually rest with the majority owners. Without control, the concept of a single economic entity is not applicable. In legal reorganizations and bankruptcies, for example, operational authority over the subsidiary is held by parties other than the parent company. Severe restrictions imposed by foreign governments also limit or remove the power held by the owners. For example, the 1990 financial statements of Unocal Corporation state "the consolidated financial statements of the company include the accounts of subsidiaries more than 50 percent owned, except for certain Brazilian subsidiaries which are accounted for by the cost method due to currency restrictions imposed by the Brazilian government."

Both of these exceptions to the consolidation principle are predicated on the tentative quality of the control held by the parent. The relationship does not indicate the existence of a single economic entity.

Prior to the issuance of *Statement 94,* another important exception to consolidation was allowed. At that time, business combinations were permitted to omit subsidiaries from consolidation because of nonhomogeneity. *ARB 51* had suggested that a subsidiary should remain unconsolidated if the nature of its operations differed so significantly from that of the parent that the combined companies could not be viewed as a single entity. Despite ownership of a majority of voting stock, these companies had to be reported by use of the equity method so that only an investment asset and an equity income balance appeared in the consolidated statements.

Because of the complex nature of the activities in most modern businesses, application of the nonhomogeneity rule was subject to individual judgment. Traditionally, companies gave a broad interpretation to the concept of a single economic entity, so that virtually all subsidiaries were consolidated despite apparent differences in the nature of their operations. However, one important exception to this general rule did exist. *ARB 51* stated, as an example, that "separate statements . . . may be preferable for a finance company where the parent and the other subsidiaries are engaged in manufacturing operations." Following the Board's suggestion, many business combinations segregated finance subsidiaries from their consolidated statements, reporting them on the equity basis. Thus, in 1987, for example, General Motors did not consolidate its finance subsidiary, General Motors Acceptance Corporation (GMAC).

The practice of omitting such subsidiaries from consolidation was criticized vigorously over the years as an excuse for removing large amounts of debt from the entity's balance sheet. Since the individual accounts of an unconsolidated subsidiary are not included in consolidated statements, finance operations could incur significant obligations that would not appear as liabilities of the business combination. One study found, for example, that the debt-to-equity ratio of Borg-Warner in 1985 was .70 without consolidation of a finance subsidiary but 3.06 with it included.[18]

---

[18]Joseph C. Rue and David E. Tosh, "Should We Consolidate Finance Subsidiaries?" *Management Accounting*, April 1987, p. 46.

Consequently, the FASB voted to eliminate this practice. *Statement 94* removed nonhomogeneity as a justification for omitting a subsidiary from consolidation. Thus, finance subsidiaries must now be included in consolidated statements. The topic, though, continues to be debated not only in the United States but also throughout the world. A recent study "reports that financial subsidiaries generally are not consolidated with nonfinancial companies other than in the United States. However, in just the seven months since that survey took place a number of countries, including Canada, New Zealand, and the United Kingdom, have revised their standards to eliminate or minimize diversity of operations as justification for nonconsolidation."[19]

Not surprisingly, *SFAS 94* has not been completely popular with the management of the companies affected.[20] These officials did not relish placing such heavy debt onto their balance sheet. Speaking for the typical corporate accountant, an article by John S. McClenahen, "FASB Faulted," (*Industry Week,* November 7, 1988, p. 17) argued

> *FASB Statement 94,* as the standard is formally known, will make such a mess of balance sheets as to render them "meaningless" complains the corporate CFO. Companies with substantial finance subsidiaries—including General Motors, General Electric, and Westinghouse—will be forced to throw a layer of short-time liability "snow" over the performance of their basic "operating" business he contends . . . "Why anybody would think it's better disclosure to cover up all the really important elements of how they are running their operating business . . . absolutely baffles my mind," he states.[21]

Obviously, when setting standards for financial reporting, the FASB is rarely able to please all of the people.

SUMMARY

1. Consolidation of financial information is required for external reporting purposes whenever one organization gains control of another, thus forming a single economic entity. In many combinations, all but one of the companies is dissolved as a separate legal corporation. Therefore, the consolidation process is carried out only at the date of acquisition to bring together all accounts into a single set of financial records. In other combinations, the companies retain their identities as separate enterprises and continue to maintain their own individual accounting systems. For these cases, consolidation is a periodic process necessary whenever financial statements are to be produced. This periodic procedure is frequently accomplished through the use of a worksheet and consolidation entries.

2. Every business combination must be accounted for as either a purchase or a pooling of interests. To differentiate the applicable use of these methods, 12 criteria were established by the APB. If all 12 are satisfied, the combination must be viewed as a pooling of interests. Otherwise, the purchase method is appropriate. The two methods are not interchangeable; a specific approach is required based on these criteria.

---

[19]FASB, "Consolidation Policy and Procedures," paragraph 38.

[20]Accounting principles can sometimes have a considerable impact on the operations of an entity. As an example, one report found that 30 of 157 surveyed companies chose to sell an unconsolidated subsidiary or drop their ownership level below 50 percent at approximately the time that *SFAS 94* took effect. This report suggested that many of these companies had decided to dispose of some or all of their interest rather than consolidate the extra debt. See "SFAS 94: Did It Produce Its Intended Effect?" *CPA Journal,* April 1992, p. 56.

[21]As is discussed in a subsequent chapter, segment disclosure alleviates some of the possible problems of consolidation by providing financial information about the various components of a business. Chrysler Corporation has addressed this same issue in a different manner by publishing two sets of financial statements side by side. One set properly includes Chrysler Financial Services and the company's car rental operation in the consolidated figures. The other supplemental statements have reported these operations using the equity method.

3. A purchase is said to have been created when one entity acquires control over another. An acquisition price is determined based on the exchange transaction and includes all direct consolidation costs unless expended in the issuance of stock. The assets and liabilities of the acquired company are consolidated based on their fair market values at the date of purchase. If the price paid exceeds the total fair market value of the net assets, the residual amount is recorded in the consolidated financial statements as goodwill, an intangible asset.

4. For a purchase, if the acquisition price is less than total fair market value, a reduction in the consolidated balances is necessary. The acquired company's assets and liabilities are recorded at fair market value, except for noncurrent assets (other than long-term investments in marketable securities). Because of the bargain purchase, these noncurrent assets are consolidated at amounts less than their fair values. The reduction is the difference between the parent's purchase price and the total fair market value of the subsidiary's assets and liabilities. This figure is prorated based on the fair market values of the various noncurrent assets. A deferred credit account is also created if the reduction exceeds the total value of the applicable noncurrent assets.

5. A pooling of interests is formed by uniting the ownership of two companies through the exchange of securities. This method accounts for the new combination by consolidating all accounts at book value. Neither goodwill nor any other account valuation adjustment is recognized because no acquisition price is established. Without a purchase price, direct consolidation costs cannot be capitalized; they must be expensed immediately. For a pooling of interests, all revenues, expenses, and other operational accounts are consolidated on a retroactive basis.

6. The pooling of interests method has been criticized often because it relies on book values only and, therefore, ignores the exchange transaction that formed the economic entity. Poolings also have been questioned because of the retroactive treatment of operating results. Consequently, a company can increase reported earnings by pooling with another company rather than by improving operating efficiency.

7. Subsidiaries can be left unconsolidated if control is only temporary or if it is not actually held by the majority owners. However, nonhomogeneity can no longer be used as a reason for omitting finance subsidiaries from consolidation.

COMPREHENSIVE ILLUSTRATION

Problem

(Estimated Time: 45 to 65 Minutes) Following are the account balances of the Marston Company and the Richmond Company as of December 31, 1998. The appraised values of the Richmond Company assets and liabilities have also been included.

	Marston Company Book Value 12/31/98	Richmond Company Book Value 12/31/98	Richmond Company Appraised Value 12/31/98
Cash	$ 600,000	$ 200,000	$ 200,000
Receivables	900,000	300,000	290,000
Inventory	1,100,000	600,000	720,000
Buildings (net)	3,000,000	800,000	1,000,000
Equipment (net)	6,000,000	500,000	600,000
Accounts payable	(400,000)	(200,000)	(200,000)
Notes payable	(3,400,000)	(1,100,000)	(1,100,000)
Totals	$ 7,800,000	$ 1,100,000	$ 1,510,000
Common stock—$20 par value	$(2,000,000)		
Common stock—$5 par value		$ (720,000)	
Additional paid-in capital	(900,000)	(100,000)	
Retained earnings, 1/1/98	(2,300,000)	(130,000)	
Revenues	(6,000,000)	(900,000)	
Expenses	3,400,000	750,000	

Note: Parentheses indicate a credit balance.

Additional Information (not recorded in the preceding figures):

■ On December 31, 1998, Marston issues 50,000 shares of its $20 par value common stock for all of the outstanding shares of Richmond Company.

■ In creating this combination, Marston pays $10,000 in stock issuance costs and $20,000 in other direct combination costs.

Required:

a. Assume that Marston's stock has a fair market value of $32.00 per share and that this combination does not meet all 12 criteria for a pooling of interests. Prepare the necessary journal entries if Richmond is to dissolve itself as a separate legal entity.

b. Repeat requirement *a.* but with the assumption that this transaction meets all 12 criteria for a pooling of interests.

c. Assume that Marston's stock has a fair market value of $28.52 per share and that this combination does not meet all 12 criteria for a pooling of interests. Richmond will retain separate legal incorporation and maintain its own accounting systems. Prepare a worksheet to consolidate the accounts of the two companies.

d. Repeat requirement *c.* but assume that this transaction meets all 12 criteria for a pooling of interests.

Solution

a. For a purchase, the accountant should first determine the parent company's acquisition price. Since Marston's stock is valued at $32.00 per share, the 50,000 issued shares are worth $1,600,000 in total. The $10,000 stock issuance cost is reported as a reduction to additional paid-in capital. The other $20,000 direct combination costs must be added to the value of the issued shares to arrive at a purchase price of $1,620,000. This total is compared to the $1,510,000 market value of Richmond's assets and liabilities. Since Marston has paid $110,000 over fair market value ($1,620,000 − $1,510,000), that figure would be recognized as goodwill.

    Because dissolution is to occur, Richmond's asset and liability accounts are transferred to Marston and entered at fair market value with the excess recorded as goodwill. The payment of the stock issuance costs is journalized separately to avoid confusion.

Marston Company's Financial Records—December 31, 1998

Cash	200,000	
Receivables	290,000	
Inventory	720,000	
Buildings	1,000,000	
Equipment	600,000	
Goodwill	110,000	
Accounts Payable		200,000
Notes Payable		1,100,000
Common Stock (Marston) (par value)		1,000,000
Additional Paid-In Capital (market value in excess		
of par value)		600,000
Cash (paid for consolidation costs)		20,000
To record purchase of Richmond Company.		
Additional Paid-In Capital	10,000	
Cash (stock issuance costs)		10,000
To record payment of stock issuance costs.		

b. As a pooling of interests, Richmond's account balances (including revenues and expenses) are transferred at their book values. The biggest concern in this process is the recording of contributed capital. Richmond's accounts indicate total contributed capital of $820,000: common stock of $720,000 and additional paid-in capital of $100,000. However, the par value of the 50,000 shares issued by Marston is $1,000,000 (at $20 per share). To arrive at the same $820,000 figure reported by Richmond, Marston's Additional Paid-In Capital account must be reduced by $180,000 in recording these new shares.

    Marston's recording of this combination follows. As this combination is a pooling of interests, all $30,000 of the consolidation costs are recorded as expenses.

Marston Company's Financial Records—December 31, 1998

Cash	200,000	
Receivables	300,000	
Inventory	600,000	
Buildings (net)	800,000	
Equipment (net)	500,000	
Expenses	750,000	
Additional Paid-In Capital (Marston) (to align contributed		
capital totals)	180,000	
Accounts Payable		200,000
Notes Payable		1,100,000
Common Stock (Marston) (par value)		1,000,000
Retained Earnings, 1/1/98		130,000
Revenues		900,000

To establish a pooling of interests with Richmond
Company.

Expenses	30,000	
Cash		30,000

To record payment of combination costs.

c. In this third illustration, a purchase combination is once again created. Since a different value is attributed to the issued shares, a new purchase price must be calculated:

50,000 shares of stock at $28.52 each	$1,426,000
Other direct combination costs	20,000
Purchase price	$1,446,000

As the subsidiary is maintaining separate incorporation, Marston has to establish an investment account to reflect the $1,446,000 purchase price:

Marston's Financial Records—December 31, 1998

Investment in Richmond Company	1,446,000	
Common Stock (Marston) (par value)		1,000,000
Additional Paid-In Capital (market value in excess		
of par value)		426,000
Cash (paid for combination costs)		20,000

To record purchase of Richmond Company.

Additional Paid-In Capital	10,000	
Cash (paid for stock issuance costs)		10,000

To record payment of stock issuance costs.

Separate incorporation is being maintained; thus, a worksheet must be developed for consolidation purposes. The parent needs to analyze the purchase price to determine the allocations required to the individual accounts:

Purchase price paid by Marston		$1,446,000
Book value of Richmond		1,100,000
Excess of cost over book value		$ 346,000
Allocations made to specific accounts based on difference in fair		
market values and book values:		
Receivables ($290,000 − $300,000)	$(10,000)	
Inventory ($720,000 − $600,000)	120,000	
Buildings ($1,000,000 − $800,000)	200,000	
Equipment ($600,000 − $500,000)	100,000	410,000
Bargain purchase		$ (64,000)

Marston's $1,446,000 purchase price is $64,000 less than the $1,510,000 fair market value of Richmond's individual accounts. This reduction must be assigned to the subsidiary's noncurrent assets (other than long-term investments in marketable securities) based on their fair market values:

	Fair Market Value	Percentage of Fair Market Value	Reduction	Percentage of Reduction
Buildings	$1,000,000	62.5%	$64,000	$40,000
Equipment	600,000	37.5	64,000	24,000
Totals	$1,600,000	100.0%		$64,000

Thus, within the consolidation worksheet, the subsidiary's buildings are assigned a reduced value of $960,000 ($1,000,000 − $40,000). The Equipment account is adjusted to $576,000 ($600,000 − $24,000).

Exhibit 2–11 can now be developed using the following steps to arrive at totals for the consolidated financial statements:

Exhibit 2–11   Comprehensive Illustration—Solution—Purchase Method

MARSTON COMPANY AND RICHMOND COMPANY
Consolidation Worksheet
For Period Ending December 31, 1998

Accounts	Marston Company	Richmond Company	Consolidation Entries Debit	Consolidation Entries Credit	Consolidated Totals
Income Statement					
Revenues	(6,000,000)				(6,000,000)
Expenses	3,400,000				3,400,000
Net income	(2,600,000)				(2,600,000)
Statement of Retained Earnings					
Retained earnings, 1/1/98	(2,300,000)				(2,300,000)
Net income (above)	(2,600,000)				(2,600,000)
Retained earnings, 12/31/98	(4,900,000)				(4,900,000)
Balance Sheet					
Cash	570,000 *	200,000			770,000
Receivables	900,000	300,000		(A) 10,000	1,190,000
Inventory	1,100,000	600,000	(A) 120,000		1,820,000
Investment in Richmond Company	1,446,000 *	–0–		(S) 1,100,000 (A) 346,000	–0–
Buildings (net)	3,000,000	800,000	(A) 160,000		3,960,000
Equipment (net)	6,000,000	500,000	(A) 76,000		6,576,000
Total assets	13,016,000	2,400,000			14,316,000
Accounts payable	(400,000)	(200,000)			(600,000)
Notes payable	(3,400,000)	(1,100,000)			(4,500,000)
Common stock	(3,000,000)*	(720,000)	(S) 720,000		(3,000,000)
Additional paid-in capital	(1,316,000)*	(100,000)	(S) 100,000		(1,316,000)
Retained earnings, 12/31/98 (above)	(4,900,000)	(280,000)†	(S) 280,000		(4,900,000)
Total liabilities and equities	(13,016,000)	(2,400,000)			(14,316,000)

Note: Parentheses indicate a credit balance.

*Balances have been adjusted for issuance of stock and payment of consolidation costs.

†Beginning retained earnings plus revenues minus expenses.

- Marston's balances have been updated on this worksheet to include the effect of both the newly issued shares of stock and the combination costs.

- Richmond's revenue and expense accounts have been closed out to retained earnings since this combination is a purchase.

- Entry S on the worksheet eliminates the $1,100,000 book value component of the Investment in Richmond Company account along with the subsidiary's stockholders' equity accounts.

- Entry A adjusts all of Richmond's assets and liabilities to fair market value based on the allocations determined earlier. However, the values attributed to the Buildings account and the Equipment account have been reduced by a total of $64,000 to reflect the bargain purchase made.

d. This final example returns to the pooling of interests concept. As such, the change in value of Marston's common stock (to $28.52 per share) has no impact on consolidated totals; poolings are always based on book values.

   Since separate accounting systems are maintained, Marston records the issuance of its 50,000 shares as an investment. As a pooling, the total is set equal to Richmond's $950,000 book value at January 1, 1998, a figure derived from the company's three stockholders' equity accounts. As in part b., Marston must reduce its own additional paid-in capital so that total contributed capital of $820,000 is recorded, the same figure reported by the subsidiary. The par value of the shares issued by Giant ($1 million) less a reduction here of $180,000 gives this identical balance. Retained earnings as of January 1 of $130,000 also is recorded since poolings are reported on a retroactive basis.

Marston's Financial Records—December 31, 1998

Investment in Richmond Company	950,000	
Additional Paid-In Capital (to align contributed capital totals)	180,000	
Common Stock (Marston) (par value)		1,000,000
Retained Earnings, 1/1/98		130,000
To record the issuance of 50,000 shares to create a pooling of interests with Richmond Company.		
Expenses	30,000	
Cash		30,000
To record payment of combination costs, which are viewed as expenses in a pooling of interests.		

After Marston's entries have been recorded, the consolidation worksheet found in Exhibit 2–12 can be produced. The investment account is eliminated on this worksheet so that the book value of Richmond's individual accounts can be consolidated (assets, liabilities, revenues, and expenses). Richmond's stockholders' equity accounts also are removed on this worksheet since they have already been added to Marston's records through the first journal entry.

Exhibit 2–12   Comprehensive Illustration—Solution—Pooling of Interests Method

MARSTON COMPANY AND RICHMOND COMPANY
Consolidation Worksheet
For Period Ending December 31, 1998

Accounts	Marston Company	Richmond Company	Consolidation Entries		Consolidated Totals
			Debit	Credit	
Income Statement					
Revenues	(6,000,000)	(900,000)			(6,900,000)
Expenses	3,430,000 *	750,000			4,180,000
Net income	(2,570,000)	(150,000)			(2,720,000)
Statement of Retained Earnings					
Retained earnings, 1/1/98	(2,430,000)*	(130,000)	(S) 130,000		(2,430,000)
Net income (above)	(2,570,000)	(150,000)			(2,720,000)
Retained earnings, 12/31/98	(5,000,000)	(280,000)			(5,150,000)
Balance Sheet					
Cash	570,000 *	200,000			770,000
Receivables	900,000	300,000			1,200,000
Inventory	1,100,000	600,000			1,700,000
Investment in Richmond Company	950,000 *	–0–		(S) 950,000	–0–
Buildings (net)	3,000,000	800,000			3,800,000
Equipment (net)	6,000,000	500,000			6,500,000
Total assets	12,520,000	2,400,000			13,970,000
Accounts payable	(400,000)	(200,000)			(600,000)
Notes payable	(3,400,000)	(1,100,000)			(4,500,000)
Common stock	(3,000,000)*	(720,000)	(S) 720,000		(3,000,000)
Additional paid-in capital	(720,000)*	(100,000)	(S) 100,000		(720,000)
Retained earnings, 12/31/98 (above)	(5,000,000)	(280,000)			(5,150,000)
Total liabilities and equities	(12,520,000)	(2,400,000)			(13,970,000)

Note: Parentheses indicate a credit balance.

*Balances have been adjusted for combination transactions and payment of consolidation costs.

APPENDIX

Twelve Criteria for a Pooling of Interests[22]

1. Attributes of combining companies.
   a. Each of the combining companies is autonomous and has not been a subsidiary or division of another corporation within two years before the plan of combination is initiated.
   b. Each of the combining companies is independent of the other combining companies.
2. Characteristics of the combination.
   a. The combination is effected in a single transaction or is completed in accordance with a specific plan within one year after the plan is initiated.
   b. A corporation offers and issues only common stock with rights identical to those of the majority of its outstanding voting common stock in exchange for substantially all of the voting common stock interest of another company at the date the plan of combination is consummated. Substantially all of the voting common stock means 90 percent or more for this condition.

---

[22]Established by *APB Opinion 16*.

c. None of the combining companies changes the equity interest of the voting common stock in contemplation of effecting the combination either within two years before the plan of combination is initiated or between the dates the combination is initiated and consummated; changes in contemplation of effecting the combination may include distributions to stockholders and additional issuances, exchanges, and retirements of securities.

d. Each of the combining companies reacquires shares of voting common stock only for purposes other than business combinations, and no company reacquires more than a normal number of shares between the dates the plan of combination is initiated and consummated.

e. The ratio of the interest of an individual common stockholder to those of other common stockholders in a combining company remains the same as a result of the exchange of stock to effect the combination.

f. The voting rights to which the common stock ownership interests in the resulting combined corporation are entitled are exercisable by the stockholders; the stockholders are neither deprived of nor restricted in exercising those rights for a period.

g. The combination is resolved at the date the plan is consummated and no provisions of the plan relating to the issue of securities or other consideration are pending.

3. Absence of planned transaction.

a. The combined corporation does not agree directly or indirectly to retire or reacquire all or part of the common stock issued to effect the combination.

b. The combined corporation does not enter into other financial arrangements for the benefit of the former stockholders of a combining company, such as a guaranty of loans secured by stock issued in the combination, which in effect negates the exchange of equity securities.

c. The combined corporation does not intend or plan to dispose of a significant part of the assets of the combining companies within two years after the combination other than disposals in the ordinary course of business of the formerly separate companies and to eliminate duplicate facilities or excess capacity.

QUESTIONS

1. What is a business combination?

2. Describe the different types of legal arrangements that can take place to create a business combination.

3. What is meant by consolidated financial statements?

4. Within the consolidation process, what is the purpose of a worksheet?

5. What characteristics are associated with a business combination accounted for as a purchase? What characteristics are associated with a business combination accounted for as a pooling of interests?

6. Jones Company obtains all of the common stock of Hudson, Inc., by issuing 50,000 shares of its own stock. Under these circumstances, why might the determination of an acquisition price be difficult?

7. What is the accounting basis for consolidating assets and liabilities in a business combination recorded as a purchase? What is the accounting basis for consolidating assets and liabilities in a business combination recorded as a pooling of interests?

8. How are a subsidiary's revenues and expenses consolidated in a purchase? How are a subsidiary's revenues and expenses consolidated in a pooling of interests?

9. Richmond Company acquires control over Schmidt Company. How will the determination be made as to whether this combination is to be accounted for as a purchase or as a pooling of interests?

10. Morgan Company purchases all of the outstanding shares of Jennings, Inc. for cash. Morgan pays more than the fair market value of the company's net assets. How should the payment in excess of fair market value be accounted for in the consolidation process?

11. Catron Corporation is having liquidity problems, and as a result, all of its outstanding shares are sold to Lambert, Inc., for cash. Because of Catron's problems, Lambert is able to acquire this stock at less than the fair market value of the company's net assets. How is this reduction in price accounted for within the consolidation process?

12. How is a deferred credit created in a consolidation?

13. Sloane, Inc., issues 25,000 shares of its own common stock in exchange for all of the outstanding shares of Benjamin Company. Benjamin will remain a separately incorporated operation. How does Sloane record the issuance of these shares if this combination is a purchase? How does Sloane record the issuance of these shares if this combination is a pooling of interests?

14. To obtain all of the stock of Molly, Inc., Harrison Corporation issued its own common stock. Harrison had to pay $98,000 to lawyers, accountants, and a stock brokerage firm in connection with services rendered during the creation of this business combination. In addition, Harrison paid $56,000 in costs associated with the stock issuance. If this combination is to be accounted for as a purchase, how will these two costs be recorded? If this combination is to be accounted for as a pooling of interests, how will these two costs be recorded?

15. Two companies that have been in business for a number of years join together to create a new business combination. If this arrangement is appropriately recorded as a pooling of interests, how will the prior operations of the two companies be reported? If this arrangement is appropriately recorded as a purchase, how will the prior operations of the two companies be reported?

16. Under what conditions will a parent company omit a subsidiary from consolidation despite owning over 50 percent of the outstanding voting stock?

LIBRARY ASSIGNMENTS

1. Read "Anatomy of a Pooling: AT&T and NCR Merger," *Ohio CPA Journal,* October 1994. Write a report discussing the ways in which AT&T structured the merger to meet the 12 requirements for a pooling of interests. Include in your report a discussion of whether you believe the accounting for the AT&T and NCR merger reflected form over substance.

2. Read the June 1994 "AICPA Special Committee on Financial Reporting Supplement to the *Journal of Accountancy*: Improving Business Reporting—A Customer Focus. Meeting the Information Needs of Investors and Creditors." Write a brief report on how consolidated financial statements contribute to the needs of investors and creditors. What are the implications of this report for the purchase versus pooling of interests controversy?

3. The June 3, 1996, issue of *The Nation* presents a series of articles concerning the effects of merger and acquisition activities on the media and entertainment industry. Discuss some of the political issues faced as a result of concentration in the media and entertainment industry.

4. Read "What's off, What's on?" in the February 20, 1989, issue of *Forbes* as well as "Consolidations: An Overview of the FASB DM," in the April 1992 issue of the *Journal of Accountancy* and "The Debate Over Consolidating Statements," in the March–April 1992 issue of *Financial Executive*. As indicated, Masco Corporation does not consolidate Masco Industries because less than 50 percent of the voting stock is held. Write a short report discussing whether the FASB should set criteria for control (and consolidation) other than majority ownership.

5. Read the following as well as any other published information on the consolidation of finance subsidiaries:

    "Should We Consolidate Finance Subsidiaries?" *Management Accounting,* April 1987.
    "Unconsolidated Finance Subsidiaries: Characteristics and Debt/Equity Effects," *Accounting Horizons,* March 1988.
    "Mishmash Accounting," *Forbes,* November 27, 1989.
    "FASB Faulted," *Industry Week,* November 7, 1988.

"SFAS 94: The Prodigal Son Becomes Part of the Family Picture," *CPA Journal,*
  February 1989.
"Consolidation of All Majority-Owned Subsidiaries," *FASB Statement No. 94*
  (including the dissent at the end of the pronouncement and both appendices).

Write a report to either justify the FASB's decision to consolidate finance subsidiaries or
offer a preferred alternative.

6. Locate *The Wall Street Journal General Index* for the most recent year. Under the
    heading "Mergers and Acquisitions," find one or more articles describing a recent
    corporate takeover. After reading these stories, answer the following questions:
    - Was the acquisition a purchase or a pooling of interests?
    - What was exchanged to create the combination?
    - Was the takeover hostile or negotiated?
    - If hostile, did the company being acquired take any actions in hopes of preventing
      the takeover?
    - If this transaction was a purchase, does the article specify the amount, if any, of
      goodwill to be recognized?
    - Does the article speculate as to the impact of the acquisition on the acquiring
      company's future profits?
    - What other information is provided?

7. Read the following as well as any other published information concerning the pooling of
    interests method:
    "U.S. Bancorp Switching from Pooling on Takeover,"*American Banker,* May 13, 1996.
    "Equity Issue Helped Sway First Interstate,"*American Banker,* February 27, 1996.
    "APB 16: Time to Reconsider," *Journal of Accountancy,* October 1991.
    "Merger Mania—Should Pooling Be Abolished?" *National Public Accountant,* June
      1990.
    "A History of Pooling of Interests Accounting for Business Combinations in the
      United States," *Accounting Historians Journal,* December 1991.
    "Does Pooling Present Fairly?" *CPA Journal,* December 1974.
    "Is Now the Time to Revisit Accounting for Business Combinations?" *CPA Journal,*
      July 1989.
    "Muddying the Waters," *Barron's,* October 8, 1990.
    "Pooling versus Purchase and Goodwill: A Long-standing Controversy Abates,"
      Mergers & Acquisitions, Fall 1980.

Write a report discussing whether the pooling of interests method should be abolished as
a generally accepted accounting principle.

PROBLEMS

1. Which of the following is the best theoretical justification for consolidated financial
    statements?
    a. In form the companies are one entity; in substance they are separate.
    b. In form the companies are separate; in substance they are one entity.
    c. In form and substance the companies are one entity.
    d. In form and substance the companies are separate.

    (AICPA)

2. What is a statutory merger?
    a. A merger approved by the Securities and Exchange Commission.
    b. An acquisition involving both the purchase of stock and assets.
    c. A takeover completed within one year of the initial tender offer.
    d. A business combination in which only one company continues to exist as a legal
        entity.

3. Which of the following characteristics is not associated with a purchase?
    a. One company acquires either the stock or assets of another company.
    b. A clearly identified cost figure is evident for the transaction.
    c. The distinction as to which organization is the acquiring company and which is the
        acquired is not always clear.
    d. Cash or debt or stocks can be used as payment for the acquired company.

4. Williams Company obtains all of the outstanding stock of Jaminson, Inc., in a purchase transaction. In a consolidation prepared immediately after the takeover, at what value will the inventory owned by Jaminson be consolidated?
   a. Jaminson's historical cost.
   b. A percentage of the acquisition cost paid by Williams.
   c. The inventory will be omitted in the consolidation.
   d. At the fair market value on the date of the purchase.

5. When is the recognition of a deferred credit required in consolidating financial information?
   a. When any bargain purchase is created.
   b. In a pooling of interests that is created in the middle of a fiscal year.
   c. In a purchase, when the value of all assets and liabilities cannot be determined.
   d. When the amount of a bargain purchase is greater than the value of the noncurrent assets (other than marketable securities) held by the acquired company.

6. Haynes, Inc., obtains all of the outstanding common stock of Tallent Company on October 1, 1998. Tallent earns net income of $10,000 per month. A consolidated income statement is to be prepared for the year ended December 31, 1998. What is the impact on net income of including Tallent in the consolidated statements?
   a. Increased by $120,000 in a purchase; increased by $120,000 in a pooling of interests.
   b. Increased by $120,000 in a purchase; increased by $30,000 in a pooling of interests.
   c. Increased by $30,000 in a purchase; increased by $120,000 in a pooling of interests.
   d. Increased by $30,000 in a purchase; increased by $30,000 in a pooling of interests.

7. A business combination is accounted for properly as a pooling of interests. Which of the following costs related to effecting the business combination should enter into the determination of the net income of a combined corporation for the period in which the expenses are incurred?

	Fees of Finders and Consultants	Registration Fees
a.	No	Yes
b.	No	No
c.	Yes	No
d.	Yes	Yes

(AICPA adapted)

8. Which of the following transactions related to a business combination would require that the combination be accounted for as a purchase?
   a. The combination is to be completed within 12 months from the date the plan was initiated.
   b. Ninety-two percent of one company's common stock is exchanged for only common stock in the other company.
   c. The combined company is to retire a portion of the common stock exchanged to effect the combination within 12 months of the combination.
   d. The combined company will dispose of numerous fixed assets representing duplicate facilities subsequent to the combination.

(AICPA)

9. How should equipment obtained in a business combination be shown under each of the following methods?

	Pooling of Interests	Purchase
a.	Recorded value	Recorded value
b.	Recorded value	Fair value
c.	Fair value	Fair value
d.	Fair value	Recorded value

(AICPA adapted)

10. Starten Company has common stock of $300,000 and retained earnings of $400,000. Premtick, Inc., has common stock of $600,000 and retained earnings of $800,000. On January 1, 1998, Premtick issues 31,000 shares of common stock with a $10 par value and a $30 fair market value for all of Starten's outstanding common stock. A pooling of interests has been created. Immediately after the combination is created, what is the balance in consolidated retained earnings? *(no APIC)*
    a. $800,000.
    b. $1,200,000.
    c. $1,190,000.
    d. $1,420,000.

11. Which of the following is not an appropriate reason for leaving a subsidiary unconsolidated?
    a. The subsidiary is in bankruptcy.
    b. The subsidiary is to be sold in the near future.
    c. A foreign government threatens to take over the assets of the subsidiary.
    d. The subsidiary is in an industry that is significantly different than that of the parent.

Problems 12 and 13 are based on the following information: Prior to being united in a business combination, Atkins, Inc., and Waterson Corporation had the following stockholders' equity figures:

	Atkins	**Waterson**
Common stock ($1 par value)	$180,000	$ 45,000
Additional paid-in capital	90,000	20,000
Retained earnings	300,000	110,000

Atkins issues 51,000 new shares of its common stock valued at $3 per share for all of the outstanding stock of Waterson.

12. Assume that Atkins is acquiring Waterson through a purchase. Immediately afterwards, what are consolidated additional paid-in capital and retained earnings, respectively?
    a. $104,000 and $300,000.
    b. $110,000 and $410,000.
    c. $192,000 and $300,000.
    d. $212,000 and $410,000.

13. Assume that Atkins and Waterson are being joined in a pooling of interests. Immediately afterwards, what are consolidated additional paid-in capital and retained earnings, respectively?
    a. $104,000 and $300,000.
    b. $104,000 and $410,000.
    c. $110,000 and $300,000.
    d. $110,000 and $410,000.

Problems 14 and 15 are based on the following information: Hampstead, Inc., has only three assets:

	Book Value	**Fair Market Value**
Inventory	$110,000	$150,000
Land	700,000	600,000
Buildings	700,000	900,000

Miller Corporation purchases Hampstead by issuing 100,000 shares of its $10 par value common stock.

14. If Miller's stock is worth $20 per share, at what value will the inventory, land, and buildings be consolidated, respectively?
    a. $110,000, $600,000, $900,000.
    b. $110,000, $700,000, $700,000.
    c. $150,000, $600,000, $900,000.
    d. $150,000, $700,000, $900,000.

15. If Miller's stock is worth $15 per share, at what value will the inventory, land, and buildings be consolidated, respectively?
    a. $110,000, $695,000, $695,000.
    b. $150,000, $525,000, $825,000.
    c. $150,000, $540,000, $810,000.
    d. $136,363, $545,455, $818,182.

Problems 16 through 23 are based on the following information: Allen, Inc., obtains control over Tucker, Inc., on July 1, 1998. The book value and fair market value of Tucker's accounts on that date (prior to creating the combination) follow, along with the book value of Allen's accounts:

	Allen Book Value	Tucker Book Value	Tucker Market Value
Revenues	$250,000	$130,000	
Expenses	170,000	80,000	
Retained earnings, 1/1/98	130,000	150,000	
Cash and receivables	140,000	60,000	$ 60,000
Inventory	190,000	145,000	175,000
Land	230,000	180,000	200,000
Buildings (net)	400,000	200,000	225,000
Equipment (net)	100,000	75,000	75,000
Liabilities	540,000	360,000	350,000
Common stock	300,000	70,000	
Additional paid-in capital	10,000	30,000	

16. Assume that Allen issues 10,000 shares of common stock with a $5 par value and a $40 fair market value to obtain all of Tucker's outstanding stock. If this transaction is a purchase, how much goodwill should be recognized?
    a. –0–.
    b. $15,000.
    c. $35,000.
    d. $100,000.

17. Assume that Allen issues 10,000 shares of common stock with a $5 par value and a $40 fair market value for all of the outstanding stock of Tucker. What is the consolidated land balance if this transaction is a pooling of interests?
    a. $380,000.
    b. $410,000.
    c. $420,000.
    d. $430,000.

18. For the fiscal year ending December 31, 1998, how will consolidated net income of this business combination be determined if Allen acquires all of Tucker's stock in a pooling of interests?
    a. Allen's income for the past year plus Tucker's income for the past six months.
    b. Allen's income for the past year plus Tucker's income for the past year.
    c. Allen's income for the past six months plus Tucker's income for the past six months.
    d. Allen's income for the past six months plus Tucker's income for the past year.

19. For the fiscal year ending December 31, 1998, how will consolidated net income of this business combination be determined if Allen acquires all of Tucker's stock in a purchase?
    a. Allen's income for the past year plus Tucker's income for the past six months.
    b. Allen's income for the past year plus Tucker's income for the past year.
    c. Allen's income for the past six months plus Tucker's income for the past six months.
    d. Allen's income for the past six months plus Tucker's income for the past year.

20. Assume that Allen issues 16,000 shares of common stock with a $5 per share par value and a $40 fair market value in exchange for all of the outstanding shares of Tucker. What will be the consolidated Additional Paid-In Capital and Retained Earnings (January 1, 1998, balance) if this combination is recorded as a pooling of interests?

a. $10,000 and $130,000.
b. $30,000 and $280,000.
c. $30,000 and $130,000.
d. $40,000 and $280,000.

21. Assume that Allen issues 16,000 shares of common stock with a $10 per share par value and a $40 fair market value in exchange for all of the outstanding shares of Tucker. What will be the consolidated Additional Paid-In Capital and Retained Earnings (January 1, 1998, balance) if this combination is recorded as a pooling of interests?
a. $10,000 and $130,000.
b. –0– and $230,000.
c. –0– and $80,000.
d. $40,000 and $280,000.

22. Assume that Allen issues preferred stock with a par value of $200,000 and a fair market value of $335,000 for all shares of Tucker in a combination accounted for as a purchase. What will be the balance in the consolidated Inventory, Land, and beginning Retained Earnings accounts?
a. $365,000, $410,000, and $130,000.
b. $365,000, $430,000, and $130,000.
c. $352,500, $417,500, and $280,000.
d. $335,000, $430,000, and $280,000.

23. Assume that Allen pays a total of $370,000 in cash for all of the shares of Tucker. In addition, Allen pays $30,000 to a group of attorneys for their work in arranging the acquisition. What will be the balance in consolidated goodwill and retained earnings?
a. –0– and $90,000.
b. –0– and $280,000.
c. $15,000 and $280,000.
d. $15,000 and $130,000.

24. Two methods are used to account for business combinations: purchase and pooling of interests.

Required:

a. A business combination is being accounted for as a purchase.
    (1) What is the theoretical rationale behind this method?
    (2) How should the amount of goodwill be determined at the date of acquisition?
b. A business combination is being accounted for as a pooling of interests.
    (1) What is the theoretical rationale behind this method?
    (2) How should the various stockholders' equity accounts be reported?

(AICPA adapted)

25. Spellman Company will soon acquire Moore, Inc. Spellman will issue shares of its stock for all of the outstanding stock of Moore. Therefore, this combination might be accounted for as either a purchase or a pooling of interests. The fair market value of the shares being issued will exceed the value of Moore's net assets.

Required:

a. How does the method of accounting for a business combination affect the recognition of goodwill?
b. If goodwill is to be reported by this business combination, how is the amount determined?
c. Why should consolidated financial statements be prepared?
d. What condition must first exist before the consolidation of financial statements is necessary?
e. Does the method of accounting for a business combination affect the decision to prepare consolidated financial statements?

(AICPA adapted)

26. Flaherty Company entered into a business combination with Steeley Company during 1998. The combination was accounted for as a pooling of interests.

Flaherty Company also acquired all of the voting common stock of Rubin Company during 1998. This combination was accounted for as a purchase and resulted in goodwill.

Registration fees were incurred in issuing common stock in both of these combinations. Other costs, such as legal and accounting fees, were also paid.

Required:

a. In the business combination accounted for as a pooling of interests, how should the assets and liabilities of the two companies be included within consolidated statements? What is the rationale for accounting for a business combination as a pooling of interests?

b. In the business combination accounted for as a pooling of interests, how should the registration fees and the other direct costs be recorded?

c. In the business combination accounted for as a pooling of interests, how should the results of the operations for 1998 be reported?

d. In the business combination accounted for as a purchase, how should the assets and liabilities of the two companies be included within consolidated statements? What is the rationale for accounting for a business combination as a purchase?

e. In the business combination accounted for as purchase, how should the registration fees and the other direct costs be recorded?

f. In the business combination accounted for as a purchase, how should the results of the operations for 1998 be reported?

(AICPA adapted)

27. Bakel Corporation has the following account balances:

Receivables	$ 80,000
Inventory	200,000
Land	600,000
Building	500,000
Liabilities	400,000
Common stock	100,000
Additional paid-in capital	100,000
Retained earnings, 1/1/98	700,000
Revenues	300,000
Expenses	220,000

Several of Bakel's accounts have market values that differ from book value: land—$400,000; building—$600,000; inventory—$280,000; and liabilities—$330,000. Homewood, Inc., obtains all of the outstanding shares of Bakel by issuing 20,000 shares of common stock having a $5 par value but a $55 fair market value. Stock issuance costs amount to $10,000. The transaction is to be accounted for as a purchase.

a. What is the purchase price in this combination?

b. What is the book value of Bakel's net assets on the date of the takeover?

c. How are the stock issuance costs handled?

d. How does the issuance of these shares affect the stockholders' equity accounts of Homewood, the parent?

e. What allocations are made of Homewood's purchase price to specific accounts and to goodwill?

f. How do Bakel's revenues and expenses affect consolidated totals? Why?

g. How do Bakel's common stock and additional paid-in capital balances affect consolidated totals?

h. In financial statements prepared immediately following the takeover, what impact will this acquisition have on the various consolidated totals?

i. If Homewood's stock had been worth only $40 per share rather than $55, how would the consolidation of Bakel's assets and liabilities have been affected?

28. Harcourt Company has the following account balances:

Receivables	$90,000
Inventory	500,000
Land	700,000
Buildings	200,000
Liabilities	800,000
Common stock	100,000
Additional paid-in capital	90,000
Retained earnings, 1/1/98	440,000
Revenues	400,000
Expenses	340,000

Several of Harcourt's accounts have market values that differ from book value: land—$900,000; building—$400,000; inventory—$470,000; and liabilities—$840,000. Lee Corporation obtains all of the outstanding shares of Harcourt by issuing 20,000 shares of common stock having a $10 par value but a $62 fair market value. Stock issuance costs amount to $10,000. The transaction is to be accounted for as a pooling of interests. Before recording the issuance of these new shares, Lee has a Common Stock account of $2 million and Additional Paid-In Capital of $1.3 million.

   a. What is the book value of Harcourt's net assets on the date of the takeover?
   b. How are the stock issuance costs handled?
   c. Assume that both companies will retain their identities as separate corporations. What journal entry would Lee record for the issuance of its stock?
   d. How would the answer to part c. have changed if Lee's stock had a $1 per share par value rather than $10 per share?
   e. How would the answer to part c. have changed if Lee's stock had a $10 per share par value but Lee issued 30,000 shares rather than 20,000?
   f. How do Harcourt's revenues and expenses affect consolidated totals? Why?
   g. In financial statements prepared immediately following the takeover, what impact would Harcourt's accounts have on the various consolidated totals?
   h. Give 3 of the 12 requirements that must be met for a combination to be accounted for as a pooling of interests.

29. Winston has the following account balances as of February 1, 1998:

Inventory	$600,000
Land	500,000
Buildings (net) (valued at $1,000,000)	900,000
Common stock ($10 par value)	800,000
Retained earnings (January 1, 1998)	1,100,000
Revenues	600,000
Expenses	500,000

Arlington pays $1.4 million cash and issues 10,000 shares of its $30 par value common stock (valued at $80 per share) for all of Winston's outstanding stock. Stock issuance costs amount to $30,000. Prior to recording these newly issued shares, Arlington reports a Common Stock account of $900,000 and Additional Paid-In Capital of $500,000.

Required:

For each of the following accounts, determine what balance would be included in a February 1, 1998, consolidation.
   a. Goodwill.
   b. Expenses.
   c. Retained Earnings, 1/1/98.
   d. Buildings.

30. Use the same information as presented in problem 29 but assume that Arlington pays cash of $2.3 million. No stock is issued. An additional $40,000 is paid in direct combination costs.

Required:

For each of the following accounts, determine what balance would be included in a February 1, 1998, consolidation.

    a. Goodwill.
    b. Expenses.
    c. Retained Earnings, 1/1/98.
    d. Buildings.

31. Use the same information as presented in problem 29 but assume that Arlington pays $2,020,000 in cash. An additional $20,000 is paid in direct combination costs.

Required:

For each of the following accounts, determine what balance will be included in a February 1, 1998, consolidation.

    a. Inventory.
    b. Goodwill.
    c. Expenses.
    d. Buildings.
    e. Land.

32. Use the same information as presented in problem 29 but assume that Arlington issues 30,000 shares of common stock ($30 par value but a fair market value of $80 per share) for all of Winston's outstanding stock in a transaction that qualifies as a pooling of interests. Stock issuance costs of $35,000 are paid along with $24,000 of other direct combination costs. (assume Arlington has no APIC)

Required:

For each of the following accounts, determine what balance will be included in a February 1, 1998, consolidation.

    a. Buildings.
    b. Goodwill.
    c. Expenses.
    d. Retained Earnings, 1/1/98.

33. On December 31, 1998, Bingham Company and Laredo Company have the following account balances:

	Bingham	Laredo
Revenues	$100,000	$ 80,000
Expenses	60,000	50,000
Net income	40,000	30,000
Retained earnings, 1/1/98	$210,000	$ 70,000
Net income	40,000	30,000
Dividends	30,000	–0–
Retained earnings, 12/31/98	220,000	100,000
Cash	$ 80,000	$ 20,000
Receivables	60,000	60,000
Inventory	100,000	70,000
Buildings and equipment (net)	200,000	100,000
Total assets	440,000	250,000
Current liabilities	$ 20,000	$ 10,000
Long-term liabilities	70,000	50,000
Common stock	110,000	90,000
Additional paid-in capital	20,000	–0–
Retained earnings, 12/31/98	220,000	100,000
Total liabilities and equities	440,000	250,000

After these figures were prepared, Bingham issued 10,000 shares of its $10 par value stock for all of the outstanding shares of Laredo. Bingham's stock had a $25 per share fair market value. Bingham also paid $10,000 in direct combination costs and $20,000 in stock issuance costs. Laredo holds a building that is worth $40,000 more than its current book value. *sub*

Required:

a. Assume that this combination is a pooling of interests. Determine consolidated balances for this combination as of December 31, 1998.

b. Assume that this combination is a purchase. Determine consolidated balances for this combination as of December 31, 1998.

34. Following are the financial balances for the Parrot Company and the Sun Company as of December 31, 1998. Also included are fair market values for the Sun Company accounts.

	Parrot Company Book Value 12/31/98	Sun Company Book Value 12/31/98	Sun Company Market Value 12/31/98
Cash	$ 290,000	$ 120,000	$ 120,000
Receivables	220,000	300,000	300,000
Inventory	410,000	210,000	260,000
Land	600,000	130,000	110,000
Buildings (net)	600,000	270,000	330,000
Equipment (net)	220,000	190,000	220,000
Accounts payable	(190,000)	(120,000)	(120,000)
Accrued expenses	(90,000)	(30,000)	(30,000)
Long-term liabilities	(900,000)	(510,000)	(510,000)
Common stock—$20 par value	(660,000)		
Common stock—$5 par value		(210,000)	
Additional paid-in capital	(70,000)	(90,000)	
Retained earnings, 1/1/98	(390,000)	(240,000)	
Revenues	(960,000)	(330,000)	
Expenses	920,000	310,000	

Note: Parentheses indicate a credit balance.

Required:

In the following situations, determine the value that would be shown in consolidated financial statements for each of the accounts listed below. Each problem should be viewed as an independent occurrence. These transactions all take place on December 31, 1998.

Accounts	
Inventory	Revenues
Land	Additional Paid-In Capital
Buildings	Expenses
Goodwill	Retained Earnings, 1/1/98

a. Parrot acquires the outstanding stock of Sun by issuing $760,000 in long-term liabilities.

b. Parrot acquires the outstanding stock of Sun by paying $160,000 in cash and issuing 10,000 shares of its own common stock with a value of $40 per share. Direct combination costs of $20,000 are paid by Parrot as well as $5,000 in stock issuance costs.

c. Parrot obtains the outstanding stock of Sun by issuing 12,000 shares of common stock with a value of $40 per share. This transaction meets all 12 requirements for a pooling of interests.

d. Parrot obtains the outstanding stock of Sun by issuing 16,000 shares of common stock with a value of $40 per share. This transaction meets all 12 requirements for a pooling of interests. Stock issuance costs of $8,000 are paid.

e. Parrot obtains the outstanding stock of Sun by issuing 19,000 shares of its common stock with a value of $40 per share. This transaction meets all 12 requirements for a pooling of interests. Direct combination costs of $9,000 are paid by Parrot.

35. The financial statements for Hope, Inc., and Kaisley Corporation for the year ending December 31, 1998, follow. Kaisley's buildings are undervalued on its financial records by $50,000.

	Hope	Kaisley
Revenues	$ 400,000	$ 400,000
Expenses	240,000	240,000
Net income	$ 160,000	$ 160,000
Retained earnings, 1/1/98	$ 600,000	$ 400,000
Net income	160,000	160,000
Dividends paid	90,000	90,000
Retained earnings, 12/31/98	$ 670,000	$ 470,000
Cash	$ 130,000	$ 100,000
Receivables and inventory	200,000	200,000
Buildings (net)	600,000	300,000
Equipment (net)	600,000	500,000
Total assets	$1,530,000	$1,100,000
Liabilities	$ 200,000	$ 200,000
Common stock	630,000	360,000
Additional paid-in capital	30,000	70,000
Retained earnings	670,000	470,000
Total liabilities and equities	$1,530,000	$1,100,000

On December 31, 1998, Hope issues 45,000 new shares of its $10 par value stock to the owners of Kaisley in exchange for all of the outstanding shares of that company. Hope's shares had a fair market value on that date of $30 per share. Hope paid $30,000 to a bank for assisting in the arrangements. Hope also paid $20,000 in stock issuance costs. This combination meets all 12 requirements of a pooling of interests. What are the appropriate consolidated balances?

36. The financial statements for Willeslye, Inc., and Barrett Company for the year ending December 31, 1998, follow:

	Willeslye	Barrett
Revenues	$ 900,000	$ 300,000
Expenses	660,000	200,000
Net income	$ 240,000	$ 100,000
Retained earnings, 1/1/98	$ 800,000	$ 200,000
Net income	240,000	100,000
Dividends paid	90,000	–0–
Retained earnings, 12/31/98	$ 950,000	$ 300,000
Cash	$ 80,000	$ 110,000
Receivables and inventory	400,000	170,000
Buildings (net)	900,000	300,000
Equipment (net)	700,000	600,000
Total assets	$2,080,000	$1,180,000
Liabilities	$ 500,000	$ 410,000
Common stock	360,000	200,000
Additional paid-in capital	270,000	270,000
Retained earnings	950,000	300,000
Total liabilities and equities	$2,080,000	$1,180,000

On December 31, 1998, Willeslye issues $300,000 in debt and 15,000 new shares of its $10 par value stock to the owners of Barrett to purchase all of the outstanding shares of that company. Willeslye shares had a fair market value of $40 per share.

Willeslye also paid $30,000 to a broker for arranging the transaction. In addition, Willeslye paid $40,000 in stock issuance costs. Barrett's equipment was actually worth $700,000 but its buildings were only valued at $280,000.

What are the consolidated balances for the following accounts?

- Net Income
- Retained Earnings, 1/1/98
- Equipment
- Goodwill
- Liabilities
- Common Stock
- Additional Paid-In Capital

37. Merrill acquires 100 percent of the outstanding voting shares of Harriss Company on January 1, 1998. To obtain these shares, Merrill pays $200,000 in cash and issues 10,000 shares of its own $10 par value common stock. On this date, Merrill's stock has a fair market value of $18 per share. Merrill also pays $10,000 to a local investment company for arranging the acquisition. An additional $6,000 was paid by Merrill in stock issuance costs.

The book values for both Merrill and Harriss as of December 31, 1998, follow. The fair market value of each of Harriss's accounts is also included. In addition, Harriss holds a fully amortized patent that still retains a $30,000 value.

| | Merrill, Inc. Book Value | Harriss Company | |
		Book Value	Fair Market Value
Cash.	$300,000	$ 40,000	$ 40,000
Receivables.	160,000	90,000	80,000
Inventory	220,000	130,000	130,000
Land	100,000	60,000	60,000
Buildings (net)	400,000	110,000	140,000
Equipment (net)	120,000	50,000	50,000
Accounts Payable	160,000	30,000	30,000
Long-Term Liabilities	380,000	170,000	150,000
Common Stock	400,000	40,000	
Retained Earnings	360,000	240,000	

Required:

a. Assume that this combination is a statutory merger so that Harriss's accounts are to be transferred to the records of Merrill with Harriss subsequently being dissolved as a legal corporation. Prepare the journal entries for Merrill that are required to record this merger.

b. Assume that no dissolution is to take place in connection with this combination. Rather, both companies retain their separate legal identities. Prepare a worksheet to consolidate the two companies as of January 1, 1998.

38. The following are preliminary financial statements for Green Company and Gold Company for the year ending December 31, 1998.

	Green Company	Gold Company
Sales	$300,000	$190,000
Expenses	(200,000)	(110,000)
Net income	$100,000	$ 80,000
Retained earnings, 1/1/98	$400,000	$210,000
Net income—above	100,000	80,000
Dividends paid	(30,000)	–0–
Retained earnings, 12/31/98	$470,000	$290,000
Current assets	$300,000	$100,000
Land	100,000	90,000
Buildings (net)	400,000	280,000
Total assets	$800,000	$470,000
Liabilities	$ 90,000	$110,000
Common stock	160,000	60,000
Additional paid-in capital	80,000	10,000
Retained earnings, 12/31/98	470,000	290,000
Total liabilities and equities	$800,000	$470,000

On December 31, 1998 (subsequent to the preceding statements), Green exchanges 8,000 shares of its $10 par value common stock for all of the outstanding shares of Gold. This transaction meets all 12 criteria for a pooling of interests. Green's stock on that date has a fair market value of $55 per share. Green was willing to issue 8,000 shares of stock because Gold's land was appraised at $170,000. Green also paid $12,000 to several attorneys and accountants who assisted in creating this combination.

Required:

a. Assuming that these two companies retain their separate legal identities, prepare a consolidation worksheet as of December 31, 1998.

b. Assuming that Gold's accounts are transferred to the records of Green, prepare the necessary journal entries within Green's accounting system as of December 31, 1998.

39. On January 1, 1998, the Lee Company purchased 100 percent of the outstanding common stock of Grant Company. To acquire these shares, Lee issued $200,000 in long-term liabilities and 20,000 shares of common stock having a par value of $1 per share but a fair market value of $10 per share. Lee paid $30,000 to accountants, lawyers, and brokers for assistance in bringing about this purchase. Another $12,000 was paid in connection with stock issuance costs.

Prior to these transactions, the balance sheets for the two companies were as follows:

	Lee Company Book Value	Grant Company Book Value
Cash..................................	$ 60,000	$ 20,000
Receivables..........................	270,000	90,000
Inventory	360,000	140,000
Land	200,000	180,000
Buildings (net)	420,000	220,000
Equipment (net)	160,000	50,000
Accounts payable	(150,000)	(40,000)
Long-term liabilities	(430,000)	(200,000)
Common stock—$1 par value..........	(110,000)	
Common stock—$20 par value........		(120,000)
Additional paid-in capital	(360,000)	–0–
Retained earnings, 1/1/98	(420,000)	(340,000)

Note: Parentheses indicate a credit balance.

In Lee's appraisal of Grant, three accounts were deemed to be undervalued on the subsidiary's books: inventory by $5,000, land by $20,000, and buildings by $30,000.

Required:

a. Determine the consolidated balance for each of these accounts.

b. To verify the answers found in part a., prepare a worksheet to consolidate the balance sheets of these two companies as of January 1, 1998.

40. The Landover Corporation purchased all of the outstanding shares of Smithers, Inc., on January 1, 1998, for $295,000 cash. Several of Smithers's accounts have market values that differ from their book values on this date:

	Book Value	Fair Market Value
Land	$20,000	$70,000
Buildings	60,000	80,000
Equipment	40,000	30,000
Notes Payable	50,000	55,000

Prepare a consolidation worksheet at the date of acquisition based on the following information:

	Landover	Smithers
Cash	$ 36,000	$ 16,000
Receivables	116,000	52,000
Inventory	144,000	90,000
Investment in Smithers	295,000	–0–
Land	210,000	20,000
Buildings (net)	640,000	60,000
Equipment (net)	308,000	40,000
Total assets	$1,749,000	$278,000
Accounts payable	$ 88,000	$ 8,000
Notes payable	510,000	50,000
Common stock	380,000	80,000
Retained earnings	771,000	140,000
Total liabilities and equities	$1,749,000	$278,000

41. The Lincoln Company obtains all of the outstanding shares of Swathmore, Inc., on December 31, 1998, in exchange for 7,000 shares of common stock. All 12 criteria of a pooling of interests have been met in this combination. Each of Lincoln's shares has a $10 par value and a $40 fair market value. Several of Swathmore's accounts have market values that differ from their book values on this date:

	Book Value	Fair Market Value
Inventory	$70,000	$100,000
Land	30,000	30,000
Equipment	50,000	60,000
Notes payable	50,000	45,000

Financial statements for 1998 for the two companies are as follows:

	Lincoln	Swathmore
Revenues	$ 990,000	$540,000
Expenses	(640,000)	(330,000)
Net income	$ 350,000	$210,000
Retained earnings, 1/1/98	$ 830,000	$110,000
Net income	350,000	210,000
Dividends paid	(220,000)	(130,000)
Retained earnings, 12/31/98	$ 960,000	$190,000
Cash	$ 60,000	$ 29,000
Receivables	150,000	65,000
Inventory	190,000	120,000
Land	310,000	30,000
Buildings (net)	840,000	60,000
Equipment (net)	320,000	50,000
Totals	$1,870,000	$354,000
Accounts payable	$ 110,000	$ 34,000
Notes payable	370,000	50,000
Common stock	400,000	50,000
Additional paid-in capital	30,000	30,000
Retained earnings	960,000	190,000
Totals	$1,870,000	$354,000

Required:

a. Determine the consolidated balance for each of these accounts.

b. To verify the answers found in part *a.*, prepare a worksheet to consolidate the financial statements of these two companies.

42. On December 31, 1998, the Sherman Company exchanges 17,000 shares of its common stock with a market value of $57 per share for 100 percent of the outstanding shares of the Atlanta Company. This transaction meets all 12 of the criteria for a pooling of interest. Prior to the exchange, the trial balances of both companies for the year of 1998 are as follows:

	Sherman Company Book Value	Atlanta Company Book Value
Debits		
Cash	$110,000	$ 20,000
Receivables (net)	300,000	290,000
Inventory	440,000	260,000
Land	280,000	80,000
Buildings (net)	270,000	290,000
Equipment (net)	810,000	320,000
Expenses	540,000	210,000
Dividends	30,000	–0–
Credits		
Accounts payable	120,000	60,000
Long-term liabilities	960,000	330,000
Common stock—$20 par value	520,000	
Common stock—$25 par value		300,000
Additional paid-in capital	110,000	100,000
Retained earnings, 1/1/98	470,000	200,000
Revenues	600,000	480,000

Additional Information:

- After the preparation of these trial balances, Sherman pays $20,000 in cash for costs incurred relating to this exchange. These expenditures covered the fees charged by lawyers and accountants involved with creating the business combination.
- Atlanta possesses land that has greatly appreciated in value since it was acquired. The book value of this land is estimated to be $60,000 less than fair market value.

Required:

a. Prepare a worksheet to consolidate the financial information of these two companies for the year ending December 31, 1998. *do like #33 on wksht*

b. Prepare a worksheet to consolidate the financial information of these two companies for the year ending December 31, 1998, assuming that this combination was actually a purchase.

Consolidations— Subsequent to the Date of Acquisition

n April of 1963, the H. J. Heinz Company acquired Star-Kist Foods, Inc., by exchanging .27 shares of convertible preferred stock for each share of Star-Kist common stock. Although this transaction involved two well-known companies, it was not unique; mergers and acquisitions have long been common in the business world. 2,574 mergers and acquisitions involved U.S. companies in 1992, a number that rose dramatically to 5,859 transactions in 1996 (with a monetary value of $493 billion).[1]

The current financial statements of the H. J. Heinz Company indicate that Star-Kist is still a component of this economic entity. However, Star-Kist continues to be a separately incorporated concern three decades after its purchase. As discussed in Chapter 2, a parent often chooses to let a subsidiary retain its identity as a legal corporation to better utilize the value inherent in a going concern.

For external reporting purposes, maintenance of incorporation creates an ongoing challenge for the accountant. In each subsequent period, consolidation must be simulated anew through the use of a worksheet and consolidation entries. Thus, for more than 35 years, the financial data for Heinz and Star-Kist have been brought together periodically to provide figures for the financial statements that represent this business combination.

---

[1] "Mergers Blast into New Orbit; Rich Stocks, Low Rates Lift Market," by John Schmeltzer, *Chicago Tribune*, January 1, 1997, Business Section page 1.

CONSOLIDATION—THE EFFECTS CREATED BY THE PASSAGE OF TIME

In the previous chapter, consolidation accounting was analyzed but only at the date that a combination was created. The present chapter carries this process one step further by examining the consolidation procedures that must be followed in subsequent periods whenever separate incorporation of the subsidiary is maintained.

Despite complexities created by the passage of time, the basic objective of all consolidations remains the same: to combine asset, liability, revenue, expense, and equity accounts based on the concepts of either the purchase method or the pooling of interests method. From a mechanical perspective, a worksheet and consolidation entries continue to provide structure for the production of a single set of financial statements for the combined business entity.

When a time factor is introduced into the consolidation process, additional complications are encountered. For internal record-keeping purposes, the parent must select and apply an accounting method to monitor the relationship between the two companies. The investment balance recorded by the parent varies over time as a result of the method chosen as does the income subsequently recognized. These differences affect the periodic consolidation process but not the figures to be reported by the combined entity. Regardless of the amount, the parent's Investment account is eliminated on the worksheet so that the subsidiary's actual assets and liabilities can be consolidated. Likewise, the income figure accrued by the parent is removed each period so that the subsidiary's revenues and expenses can be included when creating an income statement for the combined business entity.

INVESTMENT ACCOUNTING BY THE ACQUIRING COMPANY

For external reporting, consolidation of a subsidiary becomes necessary whenever control exists. For internal record-keeping, though, the parent has the choice of three alternatives for monitoring the activities of its subsidiaries: the cost method, the equity method, or the partial equity method. *Since both the resulting investment balance as well as the related income is eliminated as part of every recurring consolidation, the selection of a particular method does not affect the totals ultimately reported for the combined companies.* Rather, this decision dictates the specific procedures subsequently utilized in consolidating the financial information of the separate organizations.

The actual choice of a method is often based on the internal reporting philosophy of the acquiring company. The *cost method* might be selected because it is easy to apply. The investment balance remains permanently on the parent's balance sheet at original cost. The cost method uses the cash basis for income recognition. Therefore only the dividends subsequently received from the subsidiary are recognized as income. No other adjustments are recorded. Thus, this method requires little effort while providing an accurate measure of the cash flows between the two companies.

In contrast, under *the equity method* the acquiring company accrues income when earned by the subsidiary. To match acquisition costs against income, amortization expense stemming from the original acquisition is recognized through periodic adjusting entries. Unrealized gains on intercompany transactions are deferred; dividends paid by the subsidiary serve to reduce the investment balance. As discussed in Chapter 1, the equity method is designed to create a parallel between the parent's investment accounts and the underlying operations of the acquired company.[2]

---

[2] In Chapter 1, the equity method was introduced in connection with the external reporting of investments in which the owner held the ability to apply significant influence over the investee (usually by possessing 20 to 50 percent of the company's voting stock). Here, the equity method is utilized for the *internal* reporting of the parent for investments in which control is maintained. Although the accounting procedures are identical, the reason for using the equity method is different.

By utilizing this approach, the parent's accounts will reflect the income of the entire combined business entity. Consequently, the equity method often is referred to in accounting as a single-line consolidation. The equity method is especially popular in companies where management wants to get a picture of overall profitability by looking at the periodic (such as monthly) figures developed by the parent.

A third method available to the acquiring company is *a partial application of the equity method*. Under this approach, income accruing from the subsidiary is recognized immediately by the parent. Dividends that are collected reduce the investment balance. However, no other equity adjustments (amortization or deferral of unrealized gains) are recorded. Thus, in many cases, earnings figures on the parent's books approximate consolidated totals but without the effort associated with a full application of the equity method.

Each acquiring company must decide for itself the appropriate approach to utilize in recording the operations of its subsidiaries. For example, Alliant Food Service, Inc. applies the equity method. According to Joe Tomczak, vice president and controller of Alliant Food Service, Inc., "we maintain the parent holding company books on an equity basis. This approach provides the best method of providing information for our operational decisions."[3]

In contrast, Reynolds Metals Corporation has chosen to utilize the partial equity method approach. Allen Earehart, director of corporate accounting for Reynolds, states "we do adjust the carrying value of our investments annually to reflect the earnings of each subsidiary. We want to be able to evaluate the parent company on a stand-alone basis and a regular equity accrual is, therefore, necessary. However, we do separate certain adjustments such as the elimination of intercompany gains and losses and record them solely within the development of consolidated financial statements."[4]

Exhibit 3–1 provides a summary of these three reporting techniques. The method adopted only affects the acquiring company's separate financial records. No changes are created in either the subsidiary's accounts or the consolidated totals.

Since specific worksheet procedures differ based on the investment method being utilized by the parent, the consolidation process subsequent to the date of combination will be introduced twice. Initially, consolidations in which the acquiring company uses the equity method are reviewed. All procedures are then redeveloped where the investment is recorded by one of the alternative methods.

Exhibit 3–1 Internal Reporting of Investment Accounts by Acquiring Company

Method	Investment Account	Income Account	Advantages
Equity	Continually adjusted to reflect ownership of acquired company	Income is accrued as earned; amortization and other adjustments are recognized	Acquiring company totals give a true representation of consolidation figures
Cost	Remains at initially recorded cost	Cash received is recorded as Dividend Income	Easy to apply; measures cash flows
Partial equity	Adjusted only for accrued income and dividends received from acquired company	Income is accrued as earned; no other adjustments are recognized	Usually gives balances approximating consolidation figures, but is easier to apply than equity method

[3]Telephone conversation with Joe Tomczak.
[4]Telephone conversation with Allen Earehart.

I. **SUBSEQUENT CONSOLIDATION—INVESTMENT RECORDED BY THE EQUITY METHOD**

a. *Acquisition Made during the Current Year*

As a basis for this illustration, assume that Parrot Company obtains all of the outstanding common stock of Sun Company on January 1, 1998. Parrot acquires this stock for $760,000 in cash but pays an additional $40,000 in direct combination costs. Because cash is paid, the purchase method is applicable; a pooling of interests requires that the business combination be created only through the exchange of voting common stock.

The book values as well as the appraised values of Sun's accounts are as follows:

	Book Value 1/1/98	Fair Market Value 1/1/98	Difference
Current assets	$ 320,000	$ 320,000	–0–
Land	200,000	250,000	+ 50,000
Buildings (10-year life)	320,000	400,000	+ 80,000
Equipment (5-year life)	180,000	150,000	(30,000)
Liabilities	(420,000)	(420,000)	–0–
Net book value	$ 600,000	$ 700,000	$100,000
Common stock—$40 par value	$(200,000)		
Additional paid-in capital	(20,000)		
Retained earnings, 1/1/98	(380,000)		

For this combination, the assumption is being made that any amortization relating to purchase price allocations is calculated using the straight-line method with no estimated salvage value.[5] Goodwill is to be amortized over a 20-year period.

With the inclusion of the $40,000 direct consolidation costs, a total of $800,000 has been paid by Parrot in this purchase of Sun Company. As shown in Exhibit 3–2, individual allocations are used to adjust Sun's accounts from their book values on January 1, 1998, to fair market values. Since the total value of these assets and liabilities was only $700,000, goodwill of $100,000 must be recognized for consolidation purposes.

Each of these allocated amounts (other than the $50,000 attributed to land) represents a cost incurred by Parrot that is associated with an account having a limited useful life. As discussed in Chapter 1, Parrot must amortize each of these cost figures over their expected lives. The expense recognition necessitated by this purchase price allocation is calculated in Exhibit 3–3.

Exhibit 3–2

PARROT COMPANY
Allocation of Purchase Price
January 1, 1998

Purchase price by Parrot Company		$ 800,000
Book value of Sun Company		(600,000)
Excess of cost over book value		200,000
Allocation to specific accounts based on fair market values:		
Land	$ 50,000	
Buildings	80,000	
Equipment (overvalued)	(30,000)	100,000
Excess cost not identified with specific accounts—goodwill		$ 100,000

[5]Unless otherwise stated, all amortization expense computations in this textbook are based on the straight-line method with no salvage value.

DISCUSSION QUESTION

Is the Amortization of Goodwill Bad for the Country?

Curiously, many argue that recognition of amortization expense in connection with goodwill has a significant impact on global economics. In some countries, amortization of goodwill is not required to be recognized as a reduction in net income. Thus, purchase takeovers appear to be more profitable subsequent to the acquisition. Some suggest that foreign investors, therefore, have an apparent advantage over U.S. companies.

For example, Steve Wells et al. ("Accounting Differences: U.S. Enterprises and International Competition for Capital," *Accounting Horizons*, June 1995, pp. 25–39) discuss the acquisition of Chesebrough-Pond by Unilever, a company owned by both Dutch and British citizens. The total purchase price of $3.1 billion included $2.4 billion for goodwill. U.S. accounting would require an annual $60 million charge to earnings. There was speculation that U.S. enterprises could not successfully compete in the acquisition because the future goodwill amortizations would negatively affect profits—and therefore cast a negative evaluation due to the acquisition.

Others indicate that goodwill amortization involves no cash outflow and since the value of a company ultimately is solely dependent on its cash flows, such amortizations can have only limited impacts. The important event is the purchase of goodwill, not whether it is amortized. As indicated in the *Banking Policy Report* (November 18, 1996), "While the amortization of goodwill in a purchase transaction will result in lower reported net income, amortization is not a cash expense and the 'true' earnings power of the company . . . is not affected by goodwill amortization." Seha Tinic ("A Perspective on the Stock Market's Fixation on Accounting Numbers," *The Accounting Review*, October 1990, pp. 781–796) further discusses the view that the market is efficient with respect to accounting information and only reacts when cash flows are affected.

Discuss whether the U.S. requirement of goodwill amortization is a disadvantage in global market competition or simply a matter of form over substance.

One aspect of this amortization schedule warrants explanation. The fair market value of Sun's Equipment account was $30,000 *less* than book value. Therefore, instead of attributing an additional cost to this asset, the $30,000 allocation actually reflects a cost reduction. As such, the amortization shown in Exhibit 3–3 relating to Equipment is not an additional expense but rather an expense reduction.

Having determined the allocation of the purchase price in the previous example as well as the associated amortization, the parent's separate record-keeping for 1998 can be constructed as shown on next page. Assume that Sun earns income of $100,000 during the year and pays a $40,000 cash dividend on August 1, 1998.

In this initial illustration, Parrot has adopted the equity method. Apparently, this company believes that the information derived from using the equity method is useful in their evaluation of Sun.

Exhibit 3–3
Annual Amortization

PARROT COMPANY
Amortization Schedule—Allocation of Purchase Price

Account	Allocation	Useful Life	Annual Amortization
Land	$ 50,000	Permanent	–0–
Buildings	80,000	10 years	$ 8,000
Equipment	(30,000)	5 years	(6,000)
Goodwill	100,000	20 years	5,000
1995 amortization			$ 7,000*

*Amortization will be $7,000 annually for five years until the equipment allocation is fully removed. At the end of each asset's life, future amortization will change.

Application of the Equity Method

Parrot's Financial Records

1/1/98	Investment in Sun Company	800,000	
	Cash		800,000

To record purchase of Sun Company including direct consolidation costs.

8/1/98	Cash	40,000	
	Investment in Sun Company		40,000

To record receipt of cash dividend from subsidiary, an investment that is being accounted for by means of the equity method.

12/31/98	Investment in Sun Company	100,000	
	Equity in subsidiary earnings		100,000

To accrue income earned by 100 percent owned subsidiary.

12/31/98	Equity in subsidiary earnings	7,000	
	Investment in Sun Company		7,000

To recognize amortization on allocations made in purchase of subsidiary (see Exhibit 3–3).

Parrot's application of the equity method, as shown in this series of entries, causes the Investment in Sun Company account balance to rise from $800,000 to $853,000 ($800,000 − $40,000 + $100,000 − $7,000). During the same period, a $93,000 equity income figure (the $100,000 earnings accrual less the $7,000 amortization expense) is recognized by the parent.

The consolidation procedures for Parrot and Sun one year after the date of acquisition are illustrated next. For this purpose, Exhibit 3–4 presents the separate 1998 financial statements for these two companies. Both investment accounts (the $853,000 asset balance and the $93,000 income accrual) have been recorded by Parrot based on applying the equity method.

Determining Consolidated Totals

Before becoming immersed in the mechanical aspects of a consolidation, the objective of this process should be understood. As indicated in Chapter 2, the revenue, expense, asset, and liability accounts of the subsidiary are to be added to the parent company balances. Within this procedure, several important guidelines must be followed:

- Sun's assets and liabilities are adjusted to reflect any allocations originating from the purchase price.
- Because of the passage of time, amortization of these allocations must also be recorded within the consolidation process.
- Any reciprocal or intercompany accounts have to be offset. If, for example, one of the companies owes money to the other, the receivable and the payable balances have no connection with an outside party. Both should be eliminated for external reporting purposes. When the companies are viewed as a single entity, the receivable and the payable are intercompany balances to be removed.

A consolidation of the two sets of financial information in Exhibit 3–4 is a relatively uncomplicated task and can even be carried out without the use of a worksheet. Understanding the origin of each reported figure is the first step in gaining a knowledge of this process.

- *Revenues* = $1,900,000. The revenues of the parent and the subsidiary are added together.

Exhibit 3–4
Separate Records—Equity
Method Applied

PARROT COMPANY AND SUN COMPANY
Financial Statements
For Year Ending December 31, 1998

	Parrot Company	Sun Company
Income Statement		
Revenues	$(1,500,000)	$ (400,000)
Expenses	900,000	300,000
Equity in subsidiary earnings	(93,000)	–0–
Net income	$ (693,000)	$ (100,000)
Statement of Retained Earnings		
Retained earnings, 1/1/98	$ (840,000)	$ (380,000)
Net income (above)	(693,000)	(100,000)
Dividends paid	120,000	40,000
Retained earnings, 12/31/98	$(1,413,000)	$ (440,000)
Balance Sheet		
Current assets	$ 1,040,000	$ 400,000
Investment in Sun Company (at equity)	853,000	–0–
Land	600,000	200,000
Buildings (net)	370,000	288,000
Equipment (net)	250,000	220,000
Total assets	$ 3,113,000	$ 1,108,000
Liabilities	$ (980,000)	$ (448,000)
Common stock	(600,000)	(200,000)
Additional paid-in capital	(120,000)	(20,000)
Retained earnings, 12/31/98 (above)	(1,413,000)	(440,000)
Total liabilities and equities	$(3,113,000)	$(1,108,000)

Note: Parentheses indicate a credit balance.

- *Expenses* = $1,207,000. The expenses of the parent and the subsidiary are added together along with the $7,000 amortization expense for the year indicated in Exhibit 3–3.
- *Equity in subsidiary earnings* = –0–. The investment income recorded by the parent is eliminated so that the subsidiary's revenues and expenses can be included in the consolidated totals.
- *Net income* = $693,000. Consolidated revenues less consolidated expenses.
- *Retained earnings, 1/1/98* = $840,000. The parent figure only because the subsidiary was not owned prior to that date.
- *Dividends paid* = $120,000. The parent company balance only because the subsidiary's dividends were paid intercompany to the parent and not to an outside party.
- *Retained earnings, 12/31/98* = $1,413,000. Consolidated retained earnings as of the beginning of the year plus consolidated net income less consolidated dividends paid.
- *Current assets* = $1,440,000. The parent's book value plus the subsidiary's book value.
- *Investment in Sun Company* = –0–. The asset recorded by the parent is eliminated so that the subsidiary's assets and liabilities can be included in the consolidated totals.
- *Land* = $850,000. The parent's book value plus the subsidiary's book value plus the $50,000 allocation within the purchase price.

- *Buildings* = $730,000. The parent's book value plus the subsidiary's book value plus the $80,000 allocation within the purchase price less 1998 amortization of $8,000.
- *Equipment* = $446,000. The parent's book value plus the subsidiary's book value *less* the $30,000 cost reduction allocation plus the 1998 expense reduction of $6,000.
- *Goodwill* = $95,000. The residual allocation shown in Exhibit 3–2 less $5,000 amortization expense for 1998.
- *Total assets* = $3,561,000. Summation of consolidated assets.
- *Liabilities* = $1,428,000. The parent's book value plus the subsidiary's book value.
- *Common stock* = $600,000. The parent's book value since this combination was a purchase.
- *Additional paid-in capital* = $120,000. The parent's book value since this combination was a purchase.
- *Retained earnings, 12/31/98* = $1,413,000. Computed above.
- *Total Liabilities and Equities* = $3,561,000. Summation of consolidated liabilities and equities.

 ## Consolidation Worksheet

Although the consolidated figures to be reported can be computed as just shown, accountants normally prefer to use a worksheet. A worksheet provides an organized structure for this process, a benefit that becomes especially important in consolidating complex combinations.

For Parrot and Sun, only five consolidation entries are needed to arrive at the same figures previously derived for this business combination. As discussed in Chapter 2, *worksheet entries are the catalyst for developing totals to be reported by the entity but are not physically recorded in the individual account balances of either company.*

Consolidation Entry S

Common Stock (Sun Company)	200,000	
Additional Paid-In Capital (Sun Company)	20,000	
Retained Earnings, 1/1/98 (Sun Company)	380,000	
Investment in Sun Company..................		600,000

As shown in Exhibit 3–2, Parrot's $800,000 purchase price reflects two components: (1) a $600,000 amount equal to Sun's book value and (2) a $200,000 figure attributed to the difference, at January 1, 1998, between the book value and market value of Sun's assets and liabilities (with a residual allocation made to goodwill). Entry S removes the $600,000 component of the Investment in Sun Company account so that the *book value* of each subsidiary asset and liability can be included in the consolidated figures. A second worksheet entry (Entry A) eliminates the remaining $200,000 portion of the purchase price, allowing the specific allocations to be recorded along with any goodwill.

Entry S also removes Sun's stockholders' equity accounts as of the beginning of the year. As a purchase, subsidiary equity balances generated prior to the acquisition are not relevant to the business combination and should be deleted. The elimination is made through this entry because the equity accounts and the $600,000 component of the Investment account represent reciprocal balances: both provide a measure of Sun's book value as of January 1, 1998.

Before moving to the next consolidation entry, a clarification point should be made. In actual practice, worksheet entries are usually identified numerically. However as in the previous chapter, the label "Entry S" used in this example refers to the elimination of Sun's beginning Stockholders' equity. As a reminder of the purpose being served, all worksheet entries are identified in a similar fashion. Thus, throughout this textbook, "Entry S" always refers to the removal of the subsidiary's beginning stockholders' equity balances for the year against the book value portion of the Investment account.

Consolidation Entry A

Land	50,000	
Buildings	80,000	
Goodwill	100,000	
Equipment		30,000
Investment in Sun Company		200,000

As indicated previously, the second worksheet entry removes the $200,000 component of the purchase price, replacing it with the specific allocations from the original purchase price (see Exhibit 3–2). In this manner, the individual assets and liabilities of the consolidated entity now reflect the cost incurred by Parrot in making this purchase. Sun's accounts are adjusted based on the $200,000 paid at the time of acquisition that was in excess of Sun's book value. No basis exists for continually revaluing the accounts to newly determined market values at the date of each subsequent consolidation.

This entry is labeled "Entry A" to indicate that it represents the Allocations made in connection with the parent's purchase price.

Consolidation Entry I

Equity in subsidiary earnings	93,000	
Investment in Sun Company		93,000

"Entry I" (for Income) removes the subsidiary income recognized by Parrot during the year so that the underlying revenue and expense accounts of Sun (and the current amortization expense) can be brought into the consolidated totals. The $93,000 figure eliminated here represents the $100,000 income accrual recognized by Parrot, reduced by the $7,000 in amortization. For consolidation purposes, the one-line amount appearing in the parent's records is not appropriate and is removed so that the individual balances can be included. The entry originally recorded by the parent is simply reversed on the worksheet to remove its impact.

Consolidation Entry D

Investment in Sun Company	40,000	
Dividends Paid		40,000

The dividends distributed by the subsidiary during 1998 also must be eliminated from the consolidated totals. The entire $40,000 payment was made to the parent so that, from the viewpoint of the consolidated entity, it is simply an intercompany transfer of cash. The distribution did not affect any outside party. Therefore, "Entry D" (for Dividends) is designed to offset the impact of this transaction by removing the subsidiary's Dividends Paid account. Because the equity method has been applied, receipt of this money by Parrot was recorded originally as a decrease in the Investment in Sun Company account. To eliminate the impact of this reduction, the Investment account is increased here.

Consolidation Entry E

Expenses	7,000	
Equipment	6,000	
Buildings		8,000
Goodwill		5,000

This final worksheet entry records the current year amortization expense relating to Parrot's purchase price. Since the equity method amortization was eliminated within Entry I, "Entry E" (for **E**xpense) now records the 1998 expense attributed to each of the specific account allocations (see Exhibit 3–3).

Thus, the worksheet entries necessary for consolidation when the parent has applied the equity method are as follows:

Entry S—Eliminates the subsidiary's stockholders' equity accounts as of the beginning of the current year along with the equivalent book value component within the parent's purchase price in the Investment account.

Entry A—Recognizes the unamortized allocations as of the beginning of the current year, costs that were associated with the original purchase price.

Entry I—Eliminates the impact of intercompany income accrued by parent.

Entry D—Eliminates the impact of intercompany dividend payments made by the subsidiary.

Entry E—Recognizes amortization expense for the current period on the allocations within the original purchase price.

Exhibit 3–5 provides a complete presentation of the December 31, 1998, consolidation worksheet developed for Parrot Company and Sun Company. The series of entries just described successfully brings together the separate financial statements of these two organizations. Note that the consolidated totals are the same as those computed previously for this combination.

One aspect of this worksheet should be explained. Parrot is separately reporting net income of $693,000 as well as ending retained earnings of $1,413,000, figures that are identical to the totals generated for the consolidated entity. However, in a purchase combination, subsidiary income earned after the date of acquisition is to be *added* to that of the parent. Thus, a question arises in this example as to why the parent company figures alone equal the consolidated balances of both operations.

In reality, Sun's income for this period is contained in both Parrot's reported balances as well as in the consolidated totals. Through the application of the equity method, the 1998 earnings of the subsidiary have already been accrued by Parrot along with the appropriate amortization expense. *The parent's Equity in Subsidiary Earnings account is, therefore, an accurate representation of Sun's effect on consolidated net income.* If the equity method is employed properly, the worksheet process simply replaces this single $93,000 balance with the specific revenue and expense accounts that it represents. Consequently, *the parent's net income and retained earnings mirror consolidated totals.*

Consolidation Subsequent to Year of Acquisition—Equity Method

In many ways, every consolidation of Parrot and Sun prepared after the date of acquisition incorporates the same basic procedures outlined in the previous section. Unfortunately, the continual financial evolution undergone by the companies prohibits an exact repetition of the consolidation entries demonstrated in Exhibit 3–5.

As a basis for analyzing the procedural changes necessitated by the passage of time, assume that Parrot Company continues to hold its ownership of Sun Company as of December 31, 2001. This date was selected at random; any date subsequent to 1998 would serve equally well to illustrate this process. As an additional factor, assume that Sun now has a $40,000 liability that is payable to Parrot.

For this consolidation, assume that the January 1, 2001, retained earnings balance of Sun Company has risen to $600,000. Since that account had a reported total of only $380,000 on January 1, 1998, Sun's book value apparently has increased by $220,000 during the 1998–2000 period. Although knowledge of individual operating

Exhibit 3-5

PARROT COMPANY AND SUN COMPANY
Consolidation Worksheet
For Year Ending December 31, 1998

Consolidation: Purchase Method
Investment: Equity Method

Accounts	Parrot Company	Sun Company	Consolidation Entries Debit	Consolidation Entries Credit	Consolidated Totals
Income Statement					
Revenues	(1,500,000)	(400,000)			(1,900,000)
Expenses	900,000	300,000	(E) 7,000		1,207,000
Equity in subsidiary earnings	(93,000)	–0–	(I) 93,000		–0–
Net income	(693,000)	(100,000)			(693,000)
Statement of Retained Earnings					
Retained earnings, 1/1/98	(840,000)	(380,000)	(S) 380,000		(840,000)
Net income (above)	(693,000)	(100,000)			(693,000)
Dividends paid	120,000	40,000		(D) 40,000	120,000
Retained earnings, 12/31/98	(1,413,000)	(440,000)			(1,413,000)
Balance Sheet					
Current assets	1,040,000	400,000			1,440,000
Investment in Sun Company	853,000	–0–	(D) 40,000	(S) 600,000 (A) 200,000 (I) 93,000	–0–
Land	600,000	200,000	(A) 50,000		850,000
Buildings (net)	370,000	288,000	(A) 80,000	(E) 8,000	730,000
Equipment (net)	250,000	220,000	(E) 6,000	(A) 30,000	446,000
Goodwill	–0–	–0–	(A) 100,000	(E) 5,000	95,000
Total assets	3,113,000	1,108,000			3,561,000
Liabilities	(980,000)	(448,000)			(1,428,000)
Common stock	(600,000)	(200,000)	(S) 200,000		(600,000)
Additional paid-in capital	(120,000)	(20,000)	(S) 20,000		(120,000)
Retained earnings, 12/31/98 (above)	(1,413,000)	(440,000)			(1,413,000)
Total liabilities and equities	(3,113,000)	(1,108,000)			(3,561,000)

Note: Parentheses indicate a credit balance.

Consolidation entries:
(S) Elimination of Sun's stockholders' equity accounts as of January 1, 1998, and book value portion of purchase price.
(A) Allocation of Parrot's cost in excess of Sun's book value.
(I) Elimination of intercompany equity income.
(D) Elimination of intercompany dividends.
(E) Recognition of amortization expense on purchase price allocations.

figures in the past is not required, Sun's reported totals help to clarify the consolidation procedures.

Year	Sun Company Net Income	Dividends Paid	Increase in Book Value	Ending Retained Earnings
1998	$100,000	$ 40,000	$ 60,000	$440,000
1999	140,000	50,000	90,000	530,000
2000	90,000	20,000	70,000	600,000
	$330,000	$110,000	$220,000	

For 2001, the current year, the assumption will be made that Sun reports net income of $160,000 and pays cash dividends of $70,000. Because it applies the equity method, earnings of $160,000 are recognized by Parrot. Furthermore, as shown in Exhibit 3–3, amortization expense of $7,000 is applicable to 2001 and must

Exhibit 3–6

PARROT COMPANY Investment in Sun Company Account As of December 31, 2001 *Equity Method Applied*		
Purchase price		$ 800,000
Entries recorded in prior years:		
Accrual of Sun Company's income		
1998	$100,000	
1999	140,000	
2000	90,000	330,000
Sun Company—Dividends paid		
1998	$ 40,000	
1999	50,000	
2000	20,000	(110,000)
Amortization expense		
1998	$ 7,000	
1999	7,000	
2000	7,000	(21,000)
Entries recorded in current year—2001:		
Accrual of Sun Company's income	$160,000	
Sun Company—Dividends paid	(70,000)	
Amortization expense	(7,000)	83,000
Investment in Sun Company, 12/31/01		$1,082,000

also be recorded by the parent. Consequently, Parrot reports an Equity in Subsidiary Earnings balance for the year of $153,000 ($160,000 − $7,000).

Although this income figure can be reconstructed with little difficulty, the current balance in the Investment in Sun Company account is more complicated. Over the years, the initial $800,000 purchase price has been subjected to adjustments for:

1. The annual accrual of Sun's income.
2. The receipt of dividends from Sun.
3. The recognition of annual amortization expense.

However, by analyzing these changes, Exhibit 3–6 can be developed to show the components of the balance in the Investment in Sun Company account as of December 31, 2001.

Following the construction of the Investment in Sun Company account, the consolidation worksheet developed in Exhibit 3–7 should be easier to understand. Current figures for both companies are presented in the first two columns. The parent's investment balance and equity income accrual as well as Sun's income and stockholders' equity accounts correspond to the information given previously. Worksheet entries (lettered to agree with the previous illustration) are then utilized to consolidate all balances.

Several steps are necessary to arrive at these reported totals. The subsidiary's assets, liabilities, revenues, and expenses are added to those same accounts of the parent. The unamortized portion of the original purchase price allocations are included along with current amortization expense. The investment and equity income balances are both eliminated as is the subsidiary's stockholders' equity accounts. Intercompany dividends are removed with the same treatment required for the debt existing between the two companies.

Consolidation Entry S   Once again, this first consolidation entry offsets reciprocal amounts representing the subsidiary's book value as of the beginning of the current year. Sun's January 1, 2001, stockholders' equity accounts are eliminated against the

Exhibit 3–7

Consolidation: Purchase Method
Investment: Equity Method

PARROT COMPANY AND SUN COMPANY
Consolidation Worksheet
For Year Ending December 31, 2001

Accounts	Parrot Company	Sun Company	Consolidation Entries Debit	Consolidation Entries Credit	Consolidated Totals
Income Statement					
Revenues	(2,100,000)	(600,000)			(2,700,000)
Expenses	1,300,000	440,000	(E) 7,000		1,747,000
Equity in subsidiary earnings	(153,000)	–0–	(I) 153,000		–0–
Net income	(953,000)	(160,000)			(953,000)
Statement of Retained Earnings					
Retained earnings, 1/1/01	(2,044,000)	(600,000)	(S) 600,000		(2,044,000)
Net income (above)	(953,000)	(160,000)			(953,000)
Dividends paid	420,000	70,000		(D) 70,000	420,000
Retained earnings, 12/31/01	(2,577,000)	(690,000)			(2,577,000)
Balance Sheet					
Current assets	1,705,000	500,000		(P) 40,000	2,165,000
Investment in Sun Company	1,082,000	–0–	(D) 70,000	(S) 820,000	–0–
				(A) 179,000	
				(I) 153,000	
Land	600,000	240,000	(A) 50,000		890,000
Buildings (net)	540,000	420,000	(A) 56,000	(E) 8,000	1,008,000
Equipment (net)	420,000	210,000	(E) 6,000	(A) 12,000	624,000
Goodwill	–0–	–0–	(A) 85,000	(E) 5,000	80,000
Total assets	4,347,000	1,370,000			4,767,000
Liabilities	(1,050,000)	(460,000)	(P) 40,000		(1,470,000)
Common stock	(600,000)	(200,000)	(S) 200,000		(600,000)
Additional paid-in capital	(120,000)	(20,000)	(S) 20,000		(120,000)
Retained earnings, 12/31/01 (above)	(2,577,000)	(690,000)			(2,577,000)
Total liabilities and equities	(4,347,000)	(1,370,000)			(4,767,000)

Note: Parentheses indicate a credit balance.

Consolidation entries:
  (S) Elimination of Sun's stockholders' equity accounts as of January 1, 2001, and book value portion of Investment account.
  (A) Allocation of Parrot's cost in excess of Sun's book value, unamortized values as of January 1, 2001.
  (I) Elimination of intercompany income.
  (D) Elimination of intercompany dividends.
  (E) Recognition of amortization expense on purchase price allocations.
  (P) Elimination of intercompany receivable/payable balances.

book value portion of the parent's Investment account. Here, though, the amount eliminated is $820,000 rather than the $600,000 shown in Exhibit 3–5 for 1998. Both balances have changed during the 1998–2000 period. Sun's operations caused a $220,000 increase in retained earnings. Parrot's application of the equity method created a parallel effect on its Investment in Sun Company account (the income accrual of $330,000 less dividends collected of $110,000).

Although Sun's retained earnings balance is removed in this entry, the income earned by this company since the date of purchase is still included in the consolidated figures. Parrot accrues these profits annually through application of the equity method. Thus, elimination of the subsidiary's entire retained earnings is necessary; a portion was earned prior to the purchase and the remainder has already been recorded by the parent.

Entry S removes these balances as of the first day of 2001 rather than at the end of the year. The consolidation process is made a bit simpler by segregating the effect of

E x h i b i t   3 – 8
Amortization Relating to
Individual Accounts as of
January 1, 2001

| Accounts | Original Allocation | Annual Amortization | | | Balance 1/1/01 |
		1998	1999	2000	
Land	$ 50,000	–0–	–0–	–0–	$ 50,000
Buildings	80,000	$ 8,000	$ 8,000	$8,000	56,000
Equipment	(30,000)	(6,000)	(6,000)	(6,000)	(12,000)
Goodwill	100,000	5,000	5,000	5,000	85,000
	$200,000	$ 7,000	$ 7,000	$7,000	$179,000
			$21,000		

preceding operations from the transactions of the current year. *Thus, all worksheet entries relate specifically to either the previous years (S and A) or the current period (I, D, E, and P).*

Consolidation Entry A   In the initial consolidation (1998), cost allocations amounting to $200,000 were recorded but these balances have now undergone three years of amortization. As computed in Exhibit 3–8, expenses for these prior years totaled $21,000, leaving a balance of $179,000. Allocation of this amount to the individual accounts is also determined in Exhibit 3–8 and reflected in worksheet Entry A. As with Entry S, these balances are calculated as of January 1, 2001, so that the current year expenses may be recorded separately (in Entry E).

Consolidation Entry I   As before, this entry eliminates the equity income recorded currently by Parrot ($153,000) in connection with its ownership of Sun. The subsidiary's revenue and expense accounts are left intact so they can be included in the consolidated figures.

Consolidation Entry D   This worksheet entry offsets the $70,000 intercompany dividend payment made by Sun to Parrot during the current period.

Consolidation Entry E   Amortization expense figures relating to Parrot's purchase price are individually recorded for 2001.
   Before progressing to the final worksheet entry, note the close similarity of these entries with the five incorporated in the 1998 consolidation (Exhibit 3–5). Except for the numerical changes created by the passage of time, the entries are identical.

Consolidation Entry P   This last entry (labeled "Entry P" because it eliminates an intercompany **P**ayable) introduces a new element to the consolidation process. As noted earlier, intercompany debt transactions do not relate to outside parties. Therefore, Sun's $40,000 payable and Parrot's $40,000 receivable are reciprocals that must be removed on the worksheet because the companies are being reported as a single entity.
   In reviewing Exhibit 3–7, note several aspects of the consolidation process:

■ The stockholders' equity accounts of the subsidiary are removed.
■ The Investment in Sun Company and the Equity in Subsidiary Earnings are both removed.
■ The parent's retained earnings balance is not adjusted. Since the equity method has been applied, this account should be correct.
■ The original allocations created by the purchase price are recognized but only after adjustment for annual amortization.
■ Intercompany transactions such as dividend payments and the receivable/payable are offset.

SUBSEQUENT CONSOLIDATIONS—INVESTMENT RECORDED ON OTHER THAN THE EQUITY METHOD

Acquisition Made during the Current Year

As discussed at the beginning of this chapter, the parent company may opt to use the cost method or the partial equity method for internal record-keeping rather than the equity method. Application of either alternative changes the balances recorded by the parent over time and, thus, the procedures followed in creating consolidations. However, *choosing one of these other approaches does not affect any of the final consolidated figures to be reported.*

Where the equity method is utilized, all reciprocal accounts are eliminated, unamortized cost allocations are assigned to specific accounts, and amortization expense is recorded for the current year. Application of either the cost method or the partial equity method has no effect on this basic process. For this reason, a number of the consolidation entries remain the same regardless of the accounting method being applied by the parent.

In reality, just three of the parent's accounts actually vary because of the method applied:

- The investment account.
- The income recognized from the subsidiary.
- The parent's retained earnings (in periods after the initial year of the combination).

Only the differences found in these balances affect the consolidation process when another method is applied. Thus, any time after the date of purchase, accounting for these three accounts is of special importance.

To illustrate the modifications required by the adoption of an alternative accounting method, the consolidation of Parrot and Sun as of December 31, 1998, is reconstructed. Only one differing factor is introduced: the method by which Parrot accounts for its investment. Exhibit 3–9 presents the 1998 consolidation based on Parrot's use of the cost method. Exhibit 3–10 demonstrates this same process assuming that the partial equity method was applied by the parent. Each entry on these worksheets is labeled to correspond with the 1998 consolidation in which the parent used the equity method (Exhibit 3–5). Furthermore, differences with the equity method (both on the parent company records and with the consolidation entries) are highlighted on each of the worksheets.

Cost Method Applied—1998 Consolidation   Although the cost method theoretically stands in marked contrast to the equity method, just a narrow range of reporting differences actually result. In the year of acquisition, Parrot's income and investment accounts relating to the subsidiary are the only accounts altered.

Under the cost method, income recognition in 1998 is limited to the $40,000 dividend received by the parent; no equity income accrual is made. At the same time, the Investment account retains its $800,000 cost. Unlike the equity method, no adjustments are recorded within this asset in connection with the current year operations, the dividends paid by the subsidiary, or amortization of any purchase price allocations.

After the composition of these two accounts has been established, worksheet entries can be used to produce the consolidated figures found in Exhibit 3–9 as of December 31, 1998.

Consolidation Entry S   As with the previous Entry S in Exhibit 3–5, the $600,000 component of the Investment account is eliminated against the beginning stockholders' equity of the subsidiary. Both are equivalent to Sun's net assets at January 1,

Exhibit 3–9

			Consolidation: Purchase Method Investment: Cost Method	

PARROT COMPANY AND SUN COMPANY
Consolidation Worksheet
For Year Ending December 31, 1998

Accounts	Parrot Company	Sun Company	Consolidation Entries		Consolidated Totals
			Debit	Credit	
Income Statement					
Revenues	(1,500,000)	(400,000)			(1,900,000)
Expenses	900,000	300,000	(E) 7,000		1,207,000
Dividend income	(40,000)*	–0–	(I) 40,000*		–0–
Net income	(640,000)	(100,000)			(693,000)
Statement of Retained Earnings					
Retained earnings, 1/1/98	(840,000)	(380,000)	(S) 380,000		(840,000)
Net income (above)	(640,000)	(100,000)			(693,000)
Dividends paid	120,000	40,000		(I) 40,000*	120,000
Retained earnings, 12/31/98	(1,360,000)	(440,000)			(1,413,000)
Balance Sheet					
Current assets	1,040,000	400,000			1,440,000
Investment in Sun Company	800,000*	–0–		(S) 600,000 (A) 200,000	–0–
Land	600,000	200,000	(A) 50,000		850,000
Buildings (net)	370,000	288,000	(A) 80,000	(E) 8,000	730,000
Equipment (net)	250,000	220,000	(E) 6,000	(A) 30,000	446,000
Goodwill	–0–	–0–	(A) 100,000	(E) 5,000	95,000
Total assets	3,060,000	1,108,000			3,561,000
Liabilities	(980,000)	(448,000)			(1,428,000)
Common stock	(600,000)	(200,000)	(S) 200,000		(600,000)
Additional paid-in capital	(120,000)	(20,000)	(S) 20,000		(120,000)
Retained earnings, 12/31/98 (above)	(1,360,000)	(440,000)			(1,413,000)
Total liabilities and equities	(3,060,000)	(1,108,000)			(3,561,000)

Note: Parentheses indicate a credit balance.
*Boxed items highlight differences with consolidation in Exhibit 3–5.
Consolidation entries:
(S) Elimination of Sun's Stockholders' Equity Accounts as of January 1, 1998, and book value portion of purchase price.
(A) Allocation of Parrot's cost in excess of Sun's book value.
(I) Elimination of intercompany dividends recognized by parent as income.
(D) Entry is not needed when cost method is applied because Entry I eliminates intercompany dividends.
(E) Recognition of amortization expense on purchase price allocations.

1998, and are, therefore, reciprocal balances that must be offset. This entry is not affected by the accounting method in use.

Consolidation Entry A Parrot's $200,000 excess payment is allocated to Sun's assets and liabilities based on the fair market values at the date of acquisition. The $100,000 residual is attributed to goodwill. This procedure is also identical to the corresponding entry in Exhibit 2–5 where the equity method was applied.

Consolidation Entry I Under the cost method, the parent records dividend collections as income. Entry I removes this Dividend Income account along with Sun's Dividends Paid. From a consolidated perspective, these two $40,000 balances represent an intercompany transfer of cash that had no financial impact outside of the entity. In contrast to the equity method, subsidiary income has not been accrued by

Parrot nor has amortization been recorded; thus, no further income elimination is needed.

Dividend Income	40,000	
Dividend Paid		40,000
To eliminate intercompany income.		

Consolidation Entry D   When the cost method is applied, intercompany dividends are recorded by the parent as income. Since these distributions were already removed from the consolidated totals by Entry I, no separate Entry D is required.

Consolidation Entry E   Regardless of the parent's method of accounting, the reporting entity must recognize amortization for the current year in connection with the original purchase price allocations. Thus, Entry E serves to bring the 1998 expense into the consolidated financial statements.

Consequently, using the cost method rather than the equity method changes only Entries I and D in the year of acquisition. Despite the change in methods, reported figures are still derived by (1) eliminating all reciprocals, (2) allocating the excess portion of the purchase price, and (3) recording amortization on these allocations. As indicated previously, the consolidated totals appearing in Exhibit 3–9 are identical to the figures produced previously in Exhibit 3–5. Although the income and the investment accounts on the parent company's separate statements vary, the consolidated balances are not affected.

One significant difference between the cost method and equity method does exist: the parent's separate statements do not reflect consolidated income totals when the cost method is used. Since equity adjustments (such as amortization) are ignored, neither Parrot's reported net income of $640,000 nor its retained earnings of $1,360,000 provides an accurate portrayal of consolidated figures.

2. Partial Equity Method Applied—1998 Consolidation   Exhibit 3–10 presents a worksheet to consolidate these two companies for 1998 (the year of acquisition) based on the assumption that Parrot applied the partial equity method. Again, the only changes from previous examples are found in (1) the parent's separate records for this investment and its related income and (2) worksheet Entries I and D.

As discussed earlier, under the partial equity approach the parent's record-keeping is limited to two periodic journal entries: the annual accrual of subsidiary income and the receipt of dividends. Hence, within the parent's records, only a few differences exist when the partial equity method is applied rather than the cost method. The entries recorded by Parrot in connection with Sun's 1998 operations illustrate both of these approaches.

<table>
<tr><td colspan="3">Parrot Company
Cost Method
1998</td><td colspan="3">Parrot Company
Partial Equity Method
1998</td></tr>
<tr><td>Cash . . . .</td><td>40,000</td><td></td><td>Cash . . . .</td><td>40,000</td><td></td></tr>
<tr><td>Dividend Income . .</td><td></td><td>40,000</td><td>Investment in Sun</td><td></td><td></td></tr>
<tr><td>Dividends collected</td><td></td><td></td><td>Company . . . . . .</td><td></td><td>40,000</td></tr>
<tr><td>from subsidiary.</td><td></td><td></td><td>Dividends collected</td><td></td><td></td></tr>
<tr><td></td><td></td><td></td><td>from subsidiary.</td><td></td><td></td></tr>
<tr><td></td><td></td><td></td><td></td><td></td><td></td></tr>
<tr><td></td><td></td><td></td><td>Investment in Sun</td><td></td><td></td></tr>
<tr><td></td><td></td><td></td><td>Company . . . .</td><td>100,000</td><td></td></tr>
<tr><td></td><td></td><td></td><td>Equity in Subsidiary</td><td></td><td></td></tr>
<tr><td></td><td></td><td></td><td>Earnings . . . .</td><td></td><td>100,000</td></tr>
<tr><td></td><td></td><td></td><td>Accrual of subsidiary</td><td></td><td></td></tr>
<tr><td></td><td></td><td></td><td>income.</td><td></td><td></td></tr>
</table>

Exhibit 3–10

	PARROT COMPANY AND SUN COMPANY				
Consolidation: Purchase Method	Consolidation Worksheet				
Investment: Partial Equity Method	For Year Ending December 31, 1998				

			Consolidation Entries		
Accounts	**Parrot Company**	**Sun Company**	**Debit**	**Credit**	**Consolidated Totals**
Income Statement					
Revenues	(1,500,000)	(400,000)			(1,900,000)
Expenses	900,000	300,000	(E) 7,000		1,207,000
Equity in subsidiary earnings	(100,000)*	–0–	(I) 100,000*		–0–
Net income	(700,000)	(100,000)			(693,000)
Statement of Retained Earnings					
Retained earnings, 1/1/98	(840,000)	(380,000)	(S) 380,000		(840,000)
Net income (above)	(700,000)	(100,000)			(693,000)
Dividends paid	120,000	40,000		(D) 40,000	120,000
Retained earnings, 12/31/98	(1,420,000)	(440,000)			(1,413,000)
Balance Sheet					
Current assets	1,040,000	400,000			1,440,000
Investment in Sun Company	860,000*	–0–	(D) 40,000	(S) 600,000	–0–
				(A) 200,000	
				(I) 100,000*	
Land	600,000	200,000	(A) 50,000		850,000
Buildings (net)	370,000	288,000	(A) 80,000	(E) 8,000	730,000
Equipment (net)	250,000	220,000	(E) 6,000	(A) 30,000	446,000
Goodwill	–0–	–0–	(A) 100,000	(E) 5,000	95,000
Total assets	3,120,000	1,108,000			3,561,000
Liabilities	(980,000)	(448,000)			(1,428,000)
Common stock	(600,000)	(200,000)	(S) 200,000		(600,000)
Additional paid-in capital	(120,000)	(20,000)	(S) 20,000		(120,000)
Retained earnings, 12/31/98 (above)	(1,420,000)	(440,000)			(1,413,000)
Total liabilities and equities	(3,120,000)	(1,108,000)			(3,561,000)

Note: Parentheses indicate a credit balance.

*Boxed items highlight differences with consolidation in Exhibit 3–5.

Consolidation entries:
   (S) Elimination of Sun's Stockholders' Equity Accounts as of January 1, 1998, and book value portion of purchase price.
   (A) Allocation of Parrot's cost in excess of Sun's book value.
   (I) Elimination of parent's equity income accrual.
   (D) Elimination of intercompany dividend payment.
   (E) Recognition of amortization expense on purchase price allocations.

Therefore, by applying the partial equity method, the Investment account on the parent's balance sheet rises to $860,000 by the end of 1998. This total is comprised of the original $800,000 purchase price adjusted for the $100,000 income recognition and the $40,000 cash dividend payment. The same $100,000 equity income figure appears within the parent's income statement. These two balances are appropriately found in Parrot's records in Exhibit 3–10.

Because of the handling of income recognition and dividend payments, Entries I and D again differ on the worksheet. For the partial equity method, the $100,000 equity income is eliminated (Entry I) by reversing the parent's entry. Removing this accrual allows the individual revenue and expense accounts of the subsidiary to be reported without double-counting. The $40,000 intercompany dividend payment must also be removed (Entry D). The Dividend Paid account is simply deleted. However, elimination of the dividend from the Investment in Sun Company actually causes an increase because receipt was recorded by Parrot as a reduction in that account. All other consolidation entries (Entries S, A, and E) are the same for all three methods.

b. Consolidation Subsequent to Year of Acquisition—Other than the Equity Method

By again incorporating the December 31, 2001, financial data for Parrot and Sun (presented in Exhibit 3–7), consolidation procedures for the cost method and the partial equity method can be examined for years subsequent to the date of acquisition. *In both cases, establishment of an appropriate beginning retained earnings figure becomes a significant goal of the consolidation.*

This concern was not faced previously when the equity method was adopted. Under that approach, the parent's retained earnings balance mirrors the consolidated total so that no adjustment is necessary. In the earlier illustration, the $330,000 income accrual for the 1998–2000 period as well as the $21,000 amortization expense were recognized by the parent based on employment of the equity method (see Exhibit 3–6). Having been recorded in this manner, these two balances form a permanent part of Parrot's retained earnings and are included automatically in the consolidated total. Consequently, if the equity method is applied, the process is simplified; no worksheet entries are needed to adjust the parent's retained earnings to record subsidiary operations or amortization for past years.

Conversely, if a method other than the equity method is used, a worksheet change must be made to the parent's beginning retained earnings (in every subsequent year) to equate this balance with the consolidated total. To quantify this adjustment, the parent's recognized income for these past three years under each method is first determined (Exhibit 3–11). For consolidation purposes, beginning retained earnings must then be increased or decreased to create the same effect as the equity method.

1. Cost Method Applied—Subsequent Consolidation   As shown in Exhibit 3–11, if the cost method is applied by Parrot during the 1998–2000 period, $199,000 less income is recognized than under the equity method ($309,000 − $110,000). This difference has two causes. First, the $220,000 increase in the subsidiary's book value in the period prior to the current year has not been accrued by Parrot. Although the $110,000 in dividends were recorded as income, the remainder of the $330,000 earned by the subsidiary was never recognized by the parent.[6] Second, no accounting

---

Exhibit 3–11

PARROT'S INCOME RECOGNITION Previous Years—1998–2000			
	Equity Method	**Cost Method**	**Partial Equity Method**
Equity accrual	$330,000	–0–	$330,000
Dividend income	–0–	$110,000	–0–
Amortization expense	(21,000)	–0–	–0–
Increase in parent's retained earnings	$309,000	$110,000	$330,000

---

[6]Two different methods are indicated here for determining the $220,000 in nonrecorded income for prior years: (1) subsidiary income less dividends paid and (2) the change in the subsidiary's book value as of the first day of the current year. The second method only works if the subsidiary has had no other equity transactions such as the issuance of new stock or the purchase of treasury shares. Unless otherwise stated, the assumption is made that no such transactions have occurred.

has been made of the $21,000 amortization expense. Thus, the parent's beginning retained earnings are $199,000 ($220,000 − $21,000) below the appropriate consolidated total and must be adjusted.[7]

To simulate the equity method so that the parent's beginning retained earnings agree with that of the combination, this $199,000 increase is recorded through a worksheet entry. The cost method figures reported by the parent are effectively being converted into equity method balances.

Consolidation Entry *C

Investment in Sun Company	199,000	
Retained Earnings, 1/1/01 (Parrot Company)		199,000
To convert parent's beginning retained earnings from cost method to equity method.		

This adjustment has been labeled Entry *C. The C refers to the conversion being made to equity method totals. The asterisk indicates that this equity simulation relates solely to transactions of prior periods. Thus, *Entry *C should be recorded before the other worksheet entries to align the beginning balances for the year.*

Exhibit 3–12 provides a complete presentation of the consolidation of Parrot and Sun as of December 31, 2001, based on the parent's application of the cost method. After Entry *C has been recorded on the worksheet, the remainder of this consolidation follows the same pattern as previous examples. Sun's stockholders' equity accounts are eliminated (Entry S) while the allocations stemming from the $800,000 purchase price are recorded (Entry A) at their unamortized balances as of January 1, 2001 (see Exhibit 3–8). Intercompany dividend income is removed (Entry I) and current year amortization expense is recognized (Entry E). To complete this process, the intercompany debt of $40,000 is offset (Entry P).

In retrospect, the only new element introduced here is the adjustment of the parent's beginning retained earnings. For a consolidation produced after the initial year of acquisition, an Entry *C is required if the equity method has not been applied by the parent.

Partial Equity Method Applied—Subsequent Consolidation   Exhibit 3–13 demonstrates the worksheet consolidation of Parrot and Sun as of December 31, 2001, where the investment accounts have been recorded by the parent using the partial equity method. This approach accrues subsidiary income each year but records no other equity adjustments. Therefore, as of December 31, 2001, Parrot's Investment in Sun Company account has a balance of $1,110,000:

Purchase price.		$ 800,000
Sun Company's 1998–2000 increase in book value:		
Accrual of Sun Company's Income	$330,000	
Collection of Sun Company's Dividends	(110,000)	220,000
Sun Company's 2001 operations:		
Accrual of Sun Company's income	$160,000	
Collection of Sun Company's dividends.	(70,000)	90,000
Investment in Sun Company, 12/31/01 (Partial equity method)		$1,110,000

As indicated here and in Exhibit 3–11, the yearly equity income accrual has been properly recognized by Parrot but amortization has not. Consequently, if the partial

---

[7]Since neither the income in excess of dividends nor amortization is recorded by the parent under the cost method, its beginning retained earnings are $199,000 less than the $2,044,000 reported under the equity method (Exhibit 3–7). Thus, a $1,845,000 balance is shown in Exhibit 3–12 ($2,044,000 − this $199,000). Conversely if the partial equity method had been applied, Parrot's failure to record amortization would cause retained earnings to be $21,000 higher than the figure derived by the equity method. For this reason, Exhibit 3–13 shows the parent with beginning retained earnings of $2,065,000 rather than $2,044,000.

E x h i b i t   3 – 1 2

Consolidation: Purchase Method *Investment: Cost Method*	**PARROT COMPANY AND SUN COMPANY** **Consolidation Worksheet** **For Year Ending December 31, 2001**				

Accounts	Parrot Company	Sun Company	Consolidation Entries Debit	Consolidation Entries Credit	Consolidated Totals
Income Statement					
Revenues	(2,100,000)	(600,000)			(2,700,000)
Expenses	1,300,000	440,000	(E) 7,000		1,747,000
Dividend income	(70,000)*	–0–	(I) 70,000*		–0–
Net income	(870,000)	(160,000)			(953,000)
Statement of Retained Earnings					
Retained earnings, 1/1/01:					
Parrot Company	(1,845,000)†*			(*C) 199,000*	(2,044,000)
Sun Company		(600,000)	(S) 600,000		–0–
Net income (above)	(870,000)	(160,000)			(953,000)
Dividends paid	420,000	70,000		(I) 70,000*	420,000
Retained earnings, 12/31/01	(2,295,000)	(690,000)			(2,577,000)
Balance Sheet					
Current assets	1,705,000	500,000		(P) 40,000	2,165,000
Investment in Sun Company	800,000*	–0–	(*C) 199,000*	(S) 820,000	–0–
				(A) 179,000	
Land	600,000	240,000	(A) 50,000		890,000
Buildings (net)	540,000	420,000	(A) 56,000	(E) 8,000	1,008,000
Equipment (net)	420,000	210,000	(E) 6,000	(A) 12,000	624,000
Goodwill	–0–	–0–	(A) 85,000	(E) 5,000	80,000
Total assets	4,065,000	1,370,000			4,767,000
Liabilities	(1,050,000)	(460,000)	(P) 40,000		(1,470,000)
Common stock	(600,000)	(200,000)	(S) 200,000		(600,000)
Additional paid-in capital	(120,000)	(20,000)	(S) 20,000		(120,000)
Retained earnings, 12/31/01 (above)	(2,295,000)	(690,000)			(2,577,000)
Total liabilities and equities	(4,065,000)	(1,370,000)			(4,767,000)

Note: Parentheses indicate a credit balance.

*Boxed items highlight differences with consolidation in Exhibit 3–7.

†See footnote 7.

Consolidation entries:

(*C) To recognize additional earnings and amortization relating to ownership of subsidiary for years prior to 2001.

(S) Elimination of Sun's Stockholders' Equity accounts as of January 1, 2001, and book value portion of Investment account.

(A) Allocation of Parrot's cost in excess of Sun's book value, unamortized values as of January 1, 2001.

(I) Elimination of intercompany dividends recognized by parent as income.

(D) Entry is not needed when cost method is applied because Entry I eliminates intercompany dividend income.

(E) Recognition of amortization expense on purchase price allocations.

(P) Elimination of intercompany receivable/payable balances.

equity method is in use, the parent's beginning retained earnings must be adjusted to include this expense. The $21,000 amortization is recorded through Entry *C to simulate the equity method and, hence, consolidated totals.

Consolidation Entry *C

Retained Earnings, 1/1/01 (Parrot Company).............	21,000	
Investment in Sun Company......................		21,000

To convert parent's beginning retained earnings from partial equity method to equity method by including amortization.

PARROT COMPANY AND SUN COMPANY

Consolidation: Purchase Method   **Consolidation Worksheet**
Investment: Partial Equity Method   **For Year Ending December 31, 2001**

Accounts	Parrot Company	Sun Company	Consolidation Entries Debit	Consolidation Entries Credit	Consolidated Totals
Income Statement					
Revenues	(2,100,000)	(600,000)			(2,700,000)
Expenses	1,300,000	440,000	(E) 7,000		1,747,000
Equity in subsidiary earnings	(160,000)*	–0–	(I) 160,000 *		–0–
Net income	(960,000)	(160,000)			(953,000)
Statement of Retained Earnings					
Retained earnings, 1/1/01:					
Parrot Company	(2,065,000)† *		(*C) 21,000 *		(2,044,000)
Sun Company		(600,000)	(S) 600,000		–0–
Net income (above)	(960,000)	(160,000)			(953,000)
Dividends paid	420,000	70,000		(D) 70,000	420,000
Retained earnings, 12/31/01	(2,605,000)	(690,000)			(2,577,000)
Balance Sheet					
Current assets	1,705,000	500,000		(P) 40,000	2,165,000
Investment in Sun Company	1,110,000 *	–0–	(D) 70,000	(*C) 21,000 *	–0–
				(S) 820,000	
				(A) 179,000	
				(I) 160,000 *	
Land	600,000	240,000	(A) 50,000		890,000
Buildings (net)	540,000	420,000	(A) 56,000	(E) 8,000	1,008,000
Equipment (net)	420,000	210,000	(E) 6,000	(A) 12,000	624,000
Goodwill	–0–	–0–	(A) 85,000	(E) 5,000	80,000
Total assets	4,375,000	1,370,000			4,767,000
Liabilities	(1,050,000)	(460,000)	(P) 40,000		(1,470,000)
Common stock	(600,000)	(200,000)	(S) 200,000		(600,000)
Additional paid-in capital	(120,000)	(20,000)	(S) 20,000		(120,000)
Retained earnings, 12/31/01 (above)	(2,605,000)	(690,000)			(2,577,000)
Total liabilities and equities	(4,375,000)	(1,370,000)			(4,767,000)

Note: Parentheses indicate a credit balance.

*Boxed items highlight differences with consolidation in Exhibit 3–7.

†See footnote 7.

Consolidation entries:

(*C) To record amortization of acquisition price allocations for years prior to 2001.

(S) Elimination of Sun's Stockholders' Equity accounts as of January 1, 2001, and book value portion of Investment account.
(A) Allocation of Parrot's cost in excess of Sun's book value, unamortized values as of January 1, 2001.
(I) Elimination of parent's equity income accrual.
(D) Elimination of intercompany dividend payment.
(E) Recognition of amortization expense on purchase price allocations.
(P) Elimination of intercompany receivable/payable balances.

By recording Entry *C on the worksheet, all of the subsidiary's operational results for the 1998–2000 period are included in the consolidation. As shown in Exhibit 3–13, the remainder of the worksheet entries follow the same basic pattern as that illustrated previously for the year of acquisition (Exhibit 3–10).

Summary of Investment Methods   Having three investment methods available to the parent means that three sets of entries must be understood to arrive at reported figures appropriate for a business combination. The process may initially seem like a confusing overlap of procedures. However, at this point in the coverage, only three

DISCUSSION QUESTION:

How Does a Company Really Decide Which Investment Method to Apply?

During the early stages of 1998, Pilgrim Products, Inc., buys a controlling interest in the common stock of Crestwood Corporation. This transaction fails to meet all of the 12 criteria of a pooling of interests and will, therefore, be recorded as a purchase. Shortly after the acquisition, a meeting of Pilgrim's accounting department is convened to discuss the internal reporting procedures required by the ownership of this subsidiary. Each member of the staff has a definite opinion as to whether the equity method, cost method, or partial equity method should be adopted. To resolve this issue, Pilgrim's chief financial officer outlines several of her concerns about the decision.

"I already understand how each methods works. I know the general advantages and disadvantages of all three. I realize, for example, that the equity method provides more detailed information whereas the cost method is much easier to apply. What I need to know are the factors specific to our situation that should be considered in deciding which method to adopt. I must make a recommendation to the president on this matter, and he will want firm reasons for my favoring a particular approach. I don't want us to select a method and then find out in six months that the information is not adequate for our needs or that the cost of adapting our system to monitor Crestwood outweighs the benefits derived from the data."

What are the factors that Pilgrim's officials should evaluate when making this decision?

worksheet entries actually are affected by the choice of either the equity method, partial equity method, or cost method: Entries *C, I, and D. Furthermore, accountants should never get so involved with a worksheet and its entries that they lose sight of the balances that this process is designed to calculate. These figures are never impacted by the parent's choice of an accounting method.

Consolidated Totals Subsequent to Acquisition—Purchase Method*

Current revenues	Parent revenues are included. Subsidiary revenues are included but only for the period since the acquisition.
Current expenses	Parent expenses are included. Subsidiary expenses are included but only for the period since the acquisition. Amortization expense on the purchase price allocations is included by recognition on the worksheet.
Investment (or dividend) income	Income recognized by parent is eliminated on the worksheet so that the balance is not included in consolidated figures.
Retained earnings, beginning balance	Parent balance is included. Subsidiary balance since the acquisition is included either as a regular accrual by the parent or through a worksheet entry to increase parent balance. Past amortization expense on the purchase price allocations is included either as a part of parent balance or through a worksheet entry.
Assets and liabilities	Parent balances are included. Subsidiary balances are included. Remaining unamortized purchase price allocations are included. Intercompany receivable/payable balances are eliminated.
Goodwill	Remaining unamortized purchase price allocation is included.
Investment in subsidiary	Asset account recorded by parent is eliminated on the worksheet so that the balance is not included in consolidated figures.
Capital stock and additional paid-in capital	Parent balances only are included although they will have been adjusted at date of purchase if stock was issued.

*The next few chapters discuss the necessity of altering some of these balances for consolidation purposes. Thus, this table is not definitive but only included to provide a basic overview of the consolidation process as it has been described to this point.

Exhibit 3-14   Consolidation Worksheet Entries—Purchase Method

	Equity Method Applied	Cost Method Applied	Partial Equity Method Applied
Any time during year of acquisition:			
Entry S	Beginning stockholders' equity of subsidiary is eliminated against book value portion of investment account	Same as equity method	Same as equity method
Entry A	Excess purchase price is allocated to assets and liabilities based on difference in book values and fair market values; residual is assigned to goodwill	Same as equity method	Same as equity method
Entry I	Equity income accrual (including amortization expense) is eliminated	Dividend income is eliminated	Equity income accrual is eliminated
Entry D	Intercompany dividends paid by subsidiary are eliminated	No entry—intercompany dividends are eliminated in Entry I	Same as equity method
Entry E	Current year amortization expense of cost allocations is recorded	Same as equity method	Same as equity method
Entry P	Intercompany payable/receivable balances are offset	Same as equity method	Same as equity method
Any time following year of acquisition:			
Entry *C	No entry—equity income for prior years has already been recognized along with amortization expense	Increase in subsidiary's book value during prior years as well as amortization expense are recognized (conversion is made to equity method)	Amortization expense for prior years is recognized (conversion is made to equity method)
Entry S	Same as initial year	Same as initial year	Same as initial year
Entry A	Unamortized cost at beginning of year is allocated to specific accounts and to goodwill	Same as equity method	Same as equity method
Entry I	Same as initial year	Same as initial year	Same as initial year
Entry D	Same as initial year	Same as initial year	Same as initial year
Entry E	Same as initial year	Same as initial year	Same as initial year
Entry P	Same as initial year	Same as initial year	Same as initial year

Once the appropriate balance for each account is understood, worksheet entries assist the accountant in deriving these figures. To help clarify the consolidation process required under each of the three accounting methods, Exhibit 3–14 describes the purpose of each worksheet entry: first during the year of acquisition and second for any period following the year of acquisition.

PURCHASE PRICE—CONTINGENT CONSIDERATION

A footnote to the 1995 financial statements of SPS Technologies discloses the following contingency:

On August 16, 1995, the Company acquired approximately 48 percent of the outstanding stock of Metalac S.A. located in Sao Paulo, Brazil. With this acquisition, the Company increased its ownership to approximately 95 percent. The Company paid $4,000,000 in cash and issued 141,666 shares of the Company's common stock (approximate market value on August 16, 1995, of $5,667,000). The Stock Purchase Agreement also contains additional payments contingent on the future earnings performance of Metalac. Any additional payments made, when the contingency is resolved, will be accounted for as additional costs of the acquired assets and amortized over the remaining life of the assets.

DISCUSSION QUESTION:

Is This Income?

Artilio Corporation pays $1 million for all of the outstanding stock of Zepthan, Inc. Because of an urgent need for cash, the owners of Zepthan are forced to accept this price although the company's net assets have a value of $1.6 million.

Based on the guidelines for a bargain purchase previously demonstrated in Chapter 2, the $600,000 reduction is assigned to the subsidiary's noncurrent assets (other than long-term investments in marketable securities). Consequently, assume that the consolidated value of Zepthan's land is reduced by $50,000 with its buildings and equipment decreased by a total of $550,000. If the buildings and equipment have a life of 10 years, these negative allocations reduce amortization expense by $55,000 per year and, hence, increase income by that amount. Consolidated net income for the combination is projected to be approximately $250,000 per year for the foreseeable future. Thus, 22 percent is attributable to the bargain purchase ($55,000/$250,000). Despite the positive impact on income, amortization of bargain purchase figures is required.

Because of the annual decrease from amortization, a bargain purchase creates a consolidated entity that reports more income than the sum of the two component companies. As in the case of Artilio and Zepthan, the amount can be very significant.

Should a business combination be allowed to increase reported earnings based on paying a bargain price to acquire a new subsidiary? Does this practice distort earnings? Does a reasonable alternative exist?

A business combination has been formed here but, as this footnote describes, a portion of the purchase price being paid by the parent will not be finalized until several years after the date of acquisition.

Where a subsequent payment, such as that described by SPS Technologies' statements, is based solely on future earnings, the contingency has no initial impact on the purchase price or the consolidated figures. The potential disbursement should be disclosed only in a note to the financial statements similar to the one just presented. When the contingency is ultimately resolved, any further payment made by the parent is simply added to the purchase price.

Thus, if goodwill was recognized at the date of acquisition, any later disbursement is assigned to this same intangible asset. Should another $100,000 be paid, for example, reported goodwill is increased by this amount. Conversely, if the original price was below fair market value so that the balances assigned to noncurrent assets were reduced (and possibly a deferred credit established), a subsequent payment serves to decrease the amount of these reductions. In either case, an increase in the initial purchase price resulting from a contingency of this type is not accounted for in a retroactive manner. Any resulting amortization expense is only recorded over the *remaining* life of the appropriate account.

A contingency can also result from the acquisition of a subsidiary if the price is based on the future value of the stock issued. Such arrangements are designed to ensure that the previous owners receive compensation that retains a minimum value for a specified period. For example, in discussing an earlier acquisition, financial statements of Munsingwear, Inc., once stated that "the Company is obligated to issue additional shares of common stock . . . in the event of a decline in the market value of the common stock." From an accounting perspective, this second type of extra payment is not viewed as an increase in the parent's purchase price. Rather, the possible distribution is a guarantee of the value of the consideration conveyed in the original transaction. Thus, no change is made in goodwill or any other allocations.

If additional shares of the parent's stock must be issued because of a subsequent drop in price, the parent records the new shares at fair market value. At the same time, the total attributed to the shares originally issued at the date of purchase is reduced by a corresponding amount to reflect the decrease in value. The net effect is that the parent's stock account is increased by the par value of the new shares issued with additional paid-in capital reduced by the same amount. The purchase price does not change.

To illustrate, assume that Large issues 10,000 shares of its $10 par value stock to acquire Small. This stock had a value on that date of $25 per share ($250,000 in total). In recording this transaction, Large increases:

■ Its Common Stock account by the $100,000 par value of these shares.
■ Additional Paid-In Capital by $150,000 to reflect the value in excess of par ($25 − $10).

Subsequently, the market value of this stock drops to $20 per share. Assume that the purchase agreement specified that the market value of the shares issued could not be reduced for a given period. To maintain the total value at $250,000, 2,500 more shares are issued to Small's previous owners. At $20 per share, the new total of 12,500 shares has the appropriate value of $250,000. The new shares are recorded at par value ($25,000 or 2,500 shares at $10 per share) with an accompanying reduction in additional paid-in capital. Therefore, total contributed capital from this purchase remains at $250,000.

Large's Financial Records—Subsequent Issuance of Shares

Additional Paid-In Capital	25,000	
Common Stock (par value)		25,000

To record issuance of 2,500 new shares of stock in connection with previous acquisition of Small. Additional shares were required because of drop in market value of shares originally issued.

SUBSEQUENT CONSOLIDATIONS—POOLING OF INTERESTS

For consolidations prepared after the date of combination, a pooling of interests requires a slightly less complex set of procedures than does the purchase method. By reflecting on the fundamental concepts of a pooling, the essential differences between the subsequent consolidation entries employed by these two methods can be understood.

In Chapter 2 the purchase method is identified as applicable to combinations involving a takeover with the pooling of interests method appropriate when the combination is formed by a union of companies. Since a takeover does not occur, no acquisition price is ever calculated for a pooling. All assets and liabilities are simply consolidated at their book values. No allocations based on fair market value are computed nor is any goodwill recognized. Hence, amortization that would be associated with such cost factors is not encountered in a pooling of interests.

In mechanical terms, the absence of a purchase price means that worksheet entries relating to cost allocations (Entry A) and subsequent amortization expense (Entry E) are never found in a pooling. Obviously, as with push-down accounting, alleviating the necessity of working with these entries simplifies the entire consolidation process.

The company that issues its stock to consummate a pooling of interests must record these shares along with the resulting investment. This company must then adopt a method to account for this investment. One possibility is to apply the equity method to accrue income as it is earned by the other company and to adjust for intercompany transactions (as discussed in Chapter 5). The partial equity method also might be selected so that recording is limited to the periodic accrual of income.

However, any reference to a cost method would be a misnomer since, in a pooling of interests, no acquisition cost is ever established. Thus, for internal reporting purposes, the cost method is replaced by a *book value method* that has the same essential

Exhibit 3–15

| Consolidation: Pooling of Interests Method Investment: Book Value Method | BROTHER COMPANY AND SISTER COMPANY Consolidation Worksheet For Year Ending December 31, 2001 |

Accounts	Brother Company	Sister Company	Consolidation Entries		Consolidated Totals
			Debit	**Credit**	
Income Statement					
Revenues	(1,600,000)	(550,000)			(2,150,000)
Expenses	1,220,000	440,000			1,660,000
Dividend income	(40,000)	–0–	(I) 40,000		–0–
Net income	(420,000)	(110,000)			(490,000)
Statement of Retained Earnings					
Retained earnings, 1/1/01	(2,260,000)	(910,000)	(S) 910,000	(*C) 610,000	(2,870,000)
Net income (above)	(420,000)	(110,000)			(490,000)
Dividends paid	60,000	40,000		(I) 40,000	60,000
Retained earnings, 12/31/01	(2,620,000)	(980,000)			(3,300,000)
Balance Sheet					
Cash and receivables	590,000	140,000		(P) 90,000	640,000
Inventory	940,000	480,000			1,420,000
Investment in Sister Company	700,000	–0–	(*C) 610,000	(S) 1,310,000	–0–
Land	600,000	340,000			940,000
Buildings (net)	970,000	270,000			1,240,000
Equipment (net)	730,000	520,000			1,250,000
Total assets	4,530,000	1,750,000			5,490,000
Liabilities	(810,000)	(370,000)	(P) 90,000		(1,090,000)
Common stock	(800,000)	(300,000)	(S) 300,000		(800,000)
Additional paid-in capital	(300,000)	(100,000)	(S) 100,000		(300,000)
Retained earnings, 12/31/01 (above)	(2,620,000)	(980,000)			(3,300,000)
Total liabilities and equities	(4,530,000)	(1,750,000)			(5,490,000)

Note: Parentheses indicate a credit balance.

Consolidation entries:
  (*C) To recognize increase in book value of affiliate company during years prior to 2001.
  (S) Elimination of Sister's Stockholders' Equity accounts as of January 1, 2001, and book value portion of Investment account.
  (I) Elimination of intercompany dividends recognized by Brother as income.
  (P) Elimination of intercompany receivable/payable balances.

characteristics: the investment account permanently retains its initial balance (the book value of the other company) with any dividends received being recognized as income.

To illustrate the consolidation techniques employed in a pooling of interests, assume that Brother Company obtains 100 percent of the outstanding voting shares of Sister Company on January 1, 1998. To create this combination, Brother issues 10,000 shares of its own common stock in an exchange that meets all 12 requirements for a pooling of interests. On that date, Sister reports a total book value of $700,000 although market value is $950,000. For reporting purposes, the additional $250,000 is unimportant; only book value is relevant in accounting for a pooling of interests. Consequently, $700,000 is recorded by Brother as an investment. The book value method is applied by Brother; thus, this balance remains unchanged over the years.

For this example, consolidated financial statements are prepared as of December 31, 2001. Sister's book value has risen by $610,000 to $1,310,000 as of the first day of 2001. Assume also that Sister owes $90,000 to Brother at the end of this year. Exhibit 3–15 presents the worksheet for the 2001 consolidation of these two companies under the pooling of interests concept. Once again, the entries have been labeled to parallel the earlier consolidation examples, although neither Entry A nor Entry E is applicable to a pooling.

Because Brother applies the book value method, no recognition has been made of the increase in Sister's book value since the date of combination. Consequently, Brother's retained earnings at January 1, 2001, do not reflect a consolidated total; the $610,000 increment is not included. An Entry *C must be recorded on the worksheet to accrue this income that has been earned by Sister in excess of dividends distributed (the increase in net book value). After Brother's beginning retained earnings have been properly adjusted in this manner, the remaining consolidation entries eliminate Sister's stockholders' equity (Entry S), the intercompany dividend income (Entry I), and the intercompany debt (Entry P).

IMPAIRMENT OF LONG-LIVED ASSETS INCLUDING GOODWILL

Subsequent to a business combination, it is possible that the fair value of the acquired entity falls below its carrying value (acquisition cost less excess amortization). Such a loss in market value to the owners of the firm is referred to as an impairment and may result from declines in the fair values of specific subsidiary assets or a decline in the fair value of the subsidiary as a whole. In either case, SFAS No. 121, "Accounting for the Impairment of Long-Lived Assets and for Long-Lived Assets to Be Disposed Of," describes the applicable methods of determining when an impairment occurs, and the accounting treatment for recognizing the loss in the combined entity's financial statements.[8]

According to *SFAS No. 121*, several factors may indicate that an asset impairment has occurred. For example, a significant change in the business climate or legal factors could affect the value of an asset. A current period operating or cash flow loss combined with a history of operating or cash flow losses may point to further losses in the future that were not expected when the asset was purchased.

SFAS No. 121 describes a two-step process for determining whether an impairment loss should be recognized. First, if circumstances in the business suggest that the carrying amount of an entity may not be recoverable, a cash flow test is performed. If the sum of the expected *net* future cash flows (undiscounted and without interest charges) is less than the carrying amount of the asset, the entity is required to recognize an impairment loss. Second, an impairment loss is measured as the amount by which the carrying amount of the asset exceeds the fair value of the asset.

In applying the cash flow test for recoverability, assets must be assigned to groups to provide a reasonable basis for isolating independent cash flows to the firm from identifiable activities. In some circumstances, the test is applicable at only the entity level because the asset being tested for recoverability does not have identifiable cash flows that are largely independent of other asset groupings. In this case, *SFAS No. 121* states:

> If an asset being tested for recoverability was acquired in a business combination accounted for using the purchase method, the goodwill that arose in that transaction shall be included as part of the asset grouping in determining recoverability. . . . In instances where goodwill is identified with assets that are subject to an impairment loss, the carrying amount of the identified goodwill shall be eliminated before making any reduction of the carrying amounts of impaired long-lived assets and identifiable intangibles.

Therefore, if goodwill is part of an asset grouping that has suffered an impairment, the goodwill is written off first in recognizing the impairment loss. Only after the associated goodwill is eliminated may other assets be written down.

---

[8]For further discussion and examples see "Asset Impairment and SFAS 121" by Barbara Scofield in the December 1995 *Ohio CPA Journal* and "Auditing Considerations of FASB 121" by Hugo Nurnberg and Nelson Dittmar in the July 1996 *Journal of Accountancy*.

For example, American Greeting Corporation's 1996 annual report had the following disclosure:

> In accordance with Statement of Financial Accounting Standards No. 121, "Accounting for the Impairment of Long-Lived Assets and for Long-Lived Assets to Be Disposed Of," the Corporation recorded an impairment loss on the long-lived assets of its CreataCard business. The trends in the CreataCard business indicated that the undiscounted future cash flows from this business would be less than the carrying value of the long-lived assets related to that business. Accordingly, on November 1, 1995, the Corporation recognized an asset impairment loss of $52,061,000 ($35,094,000 net of tax, and $.47 per share). This loss is the difference between the carrying value of the CreataCard machines and related goodwill and other intangibles, and the fair value of these assets based on discounted estimated future cash flows.

In considering the appropriate income statement treatment for impairment losses, the FASB decided to require loss recognition as part of income from continuing operations.

PUSH-DOWN ACCOUNTING

External Reporting

In the analysis of business combinations to this point, discussion has focused on (1) the recording by the parent company and (2) required consolidation procedures. Unfortunately, official accounting pronouncements give virtually no guidance as to the impact of a purchase on the separate financial statements of the subsidiary.

This issue has become especially significant in recent years because of a rash of management led buy-outs as well as corporate reorganizations. An organization, for example, might acquire a company and subsequently offer the shares back to the public in hopes of making a large profit. What should be reported in the subsidiary's financial statements being distributed with this offering? Such deals have reheated a long-standing debate over the merits of *push-down accounting*, the direct recording by a subsidiary of purchase price allocations and subsequent amortization.

For this reason, the FASB has been exploring the various possible methods of reporting by a company that has been acquired or reorganized. To illustrate, assume that Yarrow Company owns one asset: a building with a book value of $200,000 but a fair market value of $900,000. Mannen Corporation pays exactly $900,000 in cash to acquire Yarrow. Consolidation offers no real problem here: the building will be reported by the business combination at $900,000.

However, if Yarrow continues to issue separate financial statements (for example, to its creditors or potential stockholders), should the building be reported at $200,000 or $900,000? If adjusted, should the $700,000 increase be reported as a gain by the subsidiary or as an addition to contributed capital? Should depreciation be based on $200,000 or $900,000? If the subsidiary is to be viewed as a new entity with a new basis for its assets and liabilities, should retained earnings be returned to zero? If the parent acquires only 51 percent of Yarrow, does that change the answers to the previous questions? These questions represent just a few of the difficult issues currently being explored.

Proponents of push-down accounting provide justification founded on the contention that a change in ownership creates a new basis for subsidiary assets and liabilities. An unadjusted balance ($200,000 in the preceding illustration) is a cost figure applicable to previous stockholders. That total is no longer relevant information. Rather, according to this argument, it is the historical cost *paid by the current owner* that is important, a figure that is best reflected by the expenditure made in acquiring the subsidiary. Balance sheet accounts should be reported at the cost incurred by the present stockholders ($900,000 in the illustration) rather than the cost incurred by the company.

Currently, primary guidance concerning push-down accounting for external reporting purposes is provided by the Securities and Exchange Commission (SEC). Through Staff Accounting Bulletin No. 54 (*Application of "Push Down" Basis of Accounting in Financial Statements of Subsidiaries Acquired by Purchase*) and Staff Accounting Bulletin No. 73 (*"Push Down" Basis of Accounting for Parent Company Debt Related to Subsidiary Acquisitions*), the SEC has indicated that

> push down accounting should be used in the separate financial statements of a "substantially wholly owned" subsidiary. . . . That view is based on the notion that when the form of ownership is within the control of the parent company, the accounting basis should be the same whether the entity continues to exist or is merged into the parent's operations. If a purchase of a "substantially wholly owned" subsidiary is financed by debt of the parent, that debt generally must be pushed down to the subsidiary. . . . As a general rule, the SEC requires push down accounting when the ownership change is greater than 95 percent and objects to push down accounting when the ownership change is less than 80 percent. However, if the acquired subsidiary has outstanding public debt or preferred stock, push down accounting is encouraged by the SEC but not required.[9]

Thus, the SEC requires the use of push-down accounting for the separate financial statements of any subsidiary where no substantial outside ownership exists of the company's common stock, preferred stock, and publicly held debt. Apparently, the SEC believes that a change in ownership of that degree justifies a new basis of reporting for the subsidiary's assets and liabilities. Until the FASB takes action, though, application is only required when the subsidiary desires to issue securities (stock or debt) to the public as regulated by the SEC.

Push-Down Accounting—Internal Reporting

Although the use of push-down accounting for external reporting is limited, this approach has gained significant popularity in recent years for internal reporting purposes.

> Subsidiaries owned by the Chesapeake Corporation are recorded using push-down accounting. Under this theory, the subsidiary adjusts its assets and liabilities to current value at the time of the acquisition while also recording the necessary goodwill. The subsidiary's net assets, as adjusted, would equal the amount recorded by the parent as the investment in subsidiary.[10]
>
> At the time of acquisition of each subsidiary, purchase method accounting is applied by James River Corporation on a push-down basis. The parent's investment equals the net book value of the subsidiary through an allocation of the purchase price to the net assets of the subsidiary on a fair market value basis.[11]

Push-down accounting has several advantages for internal reporting. For example, it simplifies the consolidation process. Because the allocations and amortization are already entered into the records of the subsidiary, worksheet Entries A (to recognize the allocations originating from the purchase price) and E (amortization expense) are not needed. Therefore, except for eliminating the effects of intercompany transactions, the assets, liabilities, revenues, and expenses of the subsidiary can be added directly to those of the parent to derive consolidated totals.

More importantly, push-down accounting provides better information for internal evaluation. Since the subsidiary's separate figures include amortization expense, the net income reported by the company is a good representation of the impact that the

---

[9]FASB Discussion Memorandum, *An Analysis of Issues Related to New Basis Accounting,* December 18, 1991, p. 54.

[10]Letter from Timothy M. Harhan, senior corporate accountant with Chesapeake Corporation.

[11]Letter from Catherine M. Freeman, manager—financial projects with James River Corporation.

acquisition has on the earnings of the business combination. As an example, assume that Ace Corporation owns 100 percent of Waxworth, Inc. Waxworth uses push-down accounting and reports net income of $500,000: $600,000 from operations less $100,000 in amortization expense resulting from purchase price allocations. Thus, officials of Ace Corporation know that this acquisition has added $500,000 to the consolidated net income of the business combination. They can then evaluate whether these earnings provide a sufficient return for the parent's investment.

However, the recording of amortization expense by the subsidiary can lead to dissension. Members of the subsidiary's management may argue that they are being forced to record a large expense over which they have no control or responsibility. This amortization comes directly from the purchase price paid by the parent and is not a result of any action taken by the subsidiary. Chesapeake Corporation has considered this problem and resolved it in the following manner: "For internal reporting of income statement activity, earnings from operations are identified separately from amortization. This allows management to analyze the subsidiary's results without the effect of amortization."[12]

SUMMARY

1. The procedures used to consolidate financial information generated by the separate companies in a business combination are affected by both the passage of time and the method applied by the parent in accounting for the subsidiary. Thus, no single consolidation process can be described that is applicable to all business combinations.

2. The parent might elect to utilize the equity method to account for a subsidiary. As discussed in Chapter 1, income is accrued by the parent when earned by the subsidiary and dividend receipts are recorded as reductions in the Investment account. The effects of amortization or any intercompany transactions also are reflected within the parent's financial records. The equity method provides the parent with accurate information concerning the subsidiary's impact on consolidated totals; however, it is usually somewhat complicated to apply.

3. The cost method and the partial equity method are two alternatives to the equity method. The cost method recognizes only the subsidiary's dividends as income while the asset balance remains at cost. This approach is simple and provides a measure of cash flows between the two companies. Under the partial equity method, the parent accrues the subsidiary's income as earned but does not record adjustments that might be required by amortization or intercompany transfers. The partial equity method is easier to apply than the equity method but, in many cases, the parent's income is a reasonable approximation of the consolidated total.

4. For a consolidation in any subsequent period, all reciprocal balances have to be eliminated. Thus, the subsidiary's equity accounts, the parent's investment balance, and intercompany income, dividends, and liabilities are removed. In addition, the remaining unamortized portions of the purchase price allocations are recognized along with amortization expense for the period. If the equity method has not been applied, the beginning retained earnings of the parent also must be adjusted for any previous income or amortization that has not yet been recorded.

5. The purchase price of a subsidiary can be based, at least in part, on future income levels or stock prices. If a subsequent payment is made because a specified amount of income is earned, consolidated goodwill is increased. However, if additional shares are issued because of a drop in the price of the parent's stock, the Common Stock and Additional Paid-In Capital accounts are realigned to agree with the new price.

6. Push-down accounting is the adjustment of the subsidiary's account balances to recognize allocations and goodwill stemming from the parent's purchase price. Subsequent amortization of these cost figures also is recorded by the subsidiary as an expense. At this

---

[12]Letter from Timothy H. Harhan.

time, push-down accounting is required by the SEC for the separate statements of the subsidiary only when no substantial outside ownership exists. The FASB is currently studying push-down accounting and may issue more specific rules on its application. However, for internal reporting purposes, push-down accounting is gaining popularity because it aids company officials in evaluating the impact that the subsidiary has on the business combination.

7. Subsequent to the purchase of a subsidiary, the parent must make periodic reviews of asset recoverability to determine when a possible impairment must be recognized as a loss. *SFAS No. 121* establishes accounting standards for the impairment of long-lived assets, certain identifiable intangibles, and goodwill related to those assets to be held and used and for long-lived assets and certain identifiable intangibles to be disposed of. If acquired goodwill is part of a group of assets that has suffered an impairment, the goodwill is written off before any of the other long-lived assets and identifiable intangibles in the group.

COMPREHENSIVE ILLUSTRATION

Problem

(Estimated Time: 40 to 65 Minutes) On January 1, 1998, Top Company acquired all of the outstanding common stock of Bottom Company for $800,000 in cash. As of that date, one of Bottom's buildings with a five-year remaining life was undervalued on its financial records by $30,000. Equipment with a 10-year life was undervalued but only by $10,000. The book values of all of Bottom's other assets and liabilities were equal to their fair market values at that time. Any goodwill indicated by this purchase is assumed to have the maximum life allowed for amortization purposes.

During 1998, Bottom reported net income of $100,000 and paid $30,000 in dividends. Earnings were $120,000 in 1999 with $20,000 in dividends distributed by the subsidiary. As of December 31, 2000, the companies reported the following selected balances:

	Top Company December 31, 2000		Bottom Company December 31, 2000	
	Debit	Credit	Debit	Credit
Buildings	$1,540,000		$460,000	
Cash and receivables	50,000		90,000	
Common stock		$ 900,000		$400,000
Dividends paid	70,000		10,000	
Equipment	280,000		200,000	
Expenses	600,000		180,000	
Inventory	280,000		260,000	
Land	330,000		250,000	
Liabilities		480,000		260,000
Retained earnings, 1/1/00		1,360,000		490,000
Revenues		900,000		300,000

Required:

a. If the equity method is applied by Top, what are its investment account balances as of December 31, 2000?

b. If the cost method is applied by Top, what are its investment account balances as of December 31, 2000?

c. Regardless of the accounting method in use by Top, what are the consolidated totals as of December 31, 2000, for each of the following accounts:

Buildings	Revenues
Equipment	Net Income
Land	Investment in Bottom
Expenses	Dividends Paid

d. If this combination had met the 12 criteria for a pooling of interests, what would be the consolidated totals as of December 31, 2000, for the accounts listed in requirement *c*?

e. Prepare the worksheet entries required on December 31, 2000, to consolidate the financial records of these two companies. Assume that Top applied the equity method to its investment accounts and that the combination is a purchase.

f. How would the worksheet entries in requirement *e.* be altered if Top has used the cost method?

Solution

a. To determine the investment balances under the equity method, four items must be known: the original cost, the income accrual, dividend payments, and amortization expense. Although the first three are indicated in the problem, amortization must be calculated separately. However, the book value of Bottom Company as of the date of acquisition is not given, and that figure is needed to determine the presence of goodwill.

Bottom's book value at January 1, 2000, totaled $890,000 (common stock of $400,000 plus retained earnings of $490,000). During the 1998–99 period, the subsidiary earned income of $220,000 ($100,000 in 1998 and $120,000 in 1999) while paying $50,000 in dividends ($30,000 in 1998 and $20,000 in 1999). These figures indicate a $170,000 net increase; thus, Bottom had a book value of $720,000 when acquired on January 1, 1998 ($890,000 − $170,000).

Following this computation, an allocation of Top's purchase price can be determined as well as the related amortization expense.

		Life (years)	Annual Amortization
Purchase price paid by Top Company	$ 800,000		
Book value of Sun Company, 1/1/98	(720,000)		
Excess cost over book value	80,000		
Excess cost allocated to specific accounts based on fair market values:			
Buildings	30,000	5	$6,000
Equipment	10,000	10	$1,000
Excess cost not identified with specific accounts—goodwill	$ 40,000	40	$1,000
Total annual expense			$8,000

Thus, if Top adopts the equity method to account for this subsidiary, the Investment in Bottom account holds a December 31, 2000, balance of $1,056,000, computed as follows:

Purchase price		$ 800,000
Bottom Company's 1998–99 increase in book value (income less dividends)		170,000
Amortization for 1998–99 ($8,000 per year for two years)		(16,000)
Current year recognition (2000):		
Equity income accrual (Bottom's revenues less its expenses)	$120,000	
Amortization expense	(8,000)	
Dividend from Bottom	(10,000)	102,000
Investment in Bottom Company, 12/31/00		$1,056,000

The $120,000 income accrual for 2000 and the $8,000 amortization expense indicate that an Equity in Subsidiary Earnings balance of $112,000 appears in Top's income statement for the current period.

b. If Top Company applies the cost method, the Investment in Bottom Company account permanently retains its original $800,000 balance and only the intercompany dividend of $10,000 is recognized by the parent as income in 2000.

c. ■ The consolidated Buildings account as of December 31, 2000, holds a balance of $2,012,000. Although the two book value figures total to only $2 million, a $30,000 purchase price allocation was made to this account based on fair market value at date of acquisition. Since this amount is being amortized at the rate of $6,000 per year, the original allocation will have been reduced by $18,000 by the end of 2000, leaving only a $12,000 increase.

■ On December 31, 2000, the consolidated Equipment account amounts to $487,000. The book values found in the financial records of Top and Bottom provide a total of

$480,000. Once again, the allocation ($10,000) established by the purchase price must be included in the consolidated balance after being adjusted for three years of amortization ($1,000 × 3 years or $3,000).

- Land has a consolidated total of $580,000. Since the book value and fair market value of Bottom's land were in agreement at the date of acquisition, no allocation of the purchase price was made to this account. Thus, the book values are simply added together to derive a consolidated figure.
- Consolidated expenses of $788,000 are recognized for 2000. The figures reported by the two companies are added and then increased by $8,000 in amortization expense for the year, a balance that results from the purchase price allocations.
- The Revenues account appears as $1.2 million in the consolidated income statement. None of the worksheet entries in this example affects the individual balances of either company. Consolidation results merely from the addition of the two book values.
- Net income for this business combination is $412,000: consolidated expenses of $788,000 subtracted from revenues of $1.2 million.
- The parent's Investment in Bottom account is removed entirely on the worksheet so that no balance is reported. For consolidation purposes, this account is always eliminated so that the individual assets and liabilities of the subsidiary can be included.
- Dividends paid by the combination should be reported as $70,000, the amount distributed by Top. Because Bottom's dividend payments are entirely intercompany, they are deleted in arriving at consolidated figures.

d. The consolidation of companies under the pooling of interests method is based primarily on the addition of book values. Therefore, consolidated totals for the first five accounts in this question can be determined merely by summing the separate balances:

- Buildings = $2,000,000 ($1,540,000 + $460,000)
- Equipment = $480,000 ($280,000 + $200,000)
- Land = $580,000 ($330,000 + $250,000)
- Expenses = $780,000 ($600,000 + $180,000)
- Revenues = $1,200,000 ($900,000 + $300,000)

- Consolidated net income is calculated by subtracting the $780,000 in expenses (just computed) from revenues of $1.2 million for a reported total of $420,000.
- As in a purchase, the Investment in Bottom account is eliminated so that the subsidiary's individual balances can be included.
- Only the parent's dividend ($70,000) is reported in the consolidated statements since Bottom's payment is an intercompany cash transfer.

e. Consolidation Entries Assuming Equity Method Used by Parent

Entry S

Common Stock (Bottom Company)	400,000	
Retained Earnings, 1/1/00		
(Bottom Company)	490,000	
Investment in Bottom Company		890,000
Elimination of subsidiary's beginning stockholders' equity accounts against book value portion of investment account.		

Entry A

Buildings.	18,000	
Equipment	8,000	
Goodwill	38,000	
Investment in Bottom Company		64,000
To recognize allocation of parent's unamortized cost in excess of subsidiary's book value. Balances represent original allocations less two years of amortization for the 1998–99 period.		

Entry I

Equity in Subsidiary Earnings	112,000	
Investment in Bottom Company		112,000

To eliminate parent's equity income accrual, balance is computed in requirement *a*.

Entry D

Investment in Bottom	10,000	
Dividends Paid		10,000

To eliminate intercompany dividend payment made by subsidiary to the parent (and recorded as a reduction in the investment account since the equity method is in use).

Entry E

Expenses	8,000	
Buildings		6,000
Equipment		1,000
Goodwill		1,000

To recognize amortization expense for 2000.

f. If the cost method rather than the equity method is utilized by Top, three changes are required in the development of consolidation entries:

(1) An Entry *C is required to update the beginning retained earnings of the parent as if the equity method had been applied. Both an income accrual as well as amortization for the prior two years must be recognized since these balances were not recorded by the parent.

Entry *C

Investment in Bottom Company	154,000	
Retained Earnings, 1/1/00 (Top Company)		154,000

To convert cost figures to the equity method by accruing the net effect of the subsidiary's operations (income less dividends) for the prior two years ($170,000) along with amortization expense ($16,000) for this same period.

(2) An alteration is needed in Entry I since, under the cost method, only dividend payments are recorded by the parent as income.

Entry I

Dividend Income	10,000	
Dividends Paid		10,000

To eliminate intercompany dividend payments recorded by parent as income.

(3) Finally, because the intercompany dividends have been eliminated in Entry I, no separate Entry D is needed.

QUESTIONS

1. Bell Corporation acquires a controlling interest in Dawkins, Inc., in a purchase transaction. Bell may utilize any one of three methods to account for this investment. Describe each of these methods, indicating their advantages and disadvantages.

2. Simpson Company obtains 100 percent control over Williams Company. Several years after the takeover, consolidated financial statements are being produced. For each of the following accounts, indicate the values that should be included in consolidated totals. Assume that Simpson acquired Williams in a transaction that must be viewed as a purchase.

   a. Equipment.
   b. Investment in Williams Company.
   c. Dividends paid.
   d. Goodwill.
   e. Revenues.
   f. Expenses.
   g. Common stock.
   h. Net income.

3. Using the information presented in question 2, determine each of the consolidated totals if the combination is to be accounted for as a pooling of interests.

4. When a parent company uses the equity method to account for an investment in a subsidiary, why do both the parent's net income and retained earnings balances agree with the consolidated totals?

5. When a parent company uses the equity method to account for a purchased investment, the amortization expense entry recorded during the year is eliminated on a consolidation worksheet as a component of Entry I. What is the necessity of removing this amortization?

6. When a parent company is applying the cost method or the partial equity method to an investment, an adjustment must be made to the parent's beginning retained earnings (Entry *C) in every period after the year of acquisition. What is the necessity for this entry? Why is no similar entry found when the equity method is utilized by the parent?

7. Several years ago, Jenkins Company acquired a controlling interest in Lambert Company. Lambert recently borrowed $100,000 from Jenkins. In consolidating the financial records of these two companies, how will this debt be handled?

8. Benns Company acquires Waters Company in a combination accounted for as a purchase. Benns adopts the equity method. At the end of six years, Benns reports an investment in Waters of $920,000. What figures constitute this balance?

9. One company is acquired by another in a purchase transaction in which $100,000 of the acquisition price is assigned to goodwill. Several years later a worksheet is being produced to consolidate these two companies. How is the reported value of the goodwill determined at this date?

10. Remo Company purchases Albane Corporation on January 1, 1998. As part of the purchase agreement, the parent states that an additional $100,000 payment to the former owners of Albane may be required in 2001 depending on the outcome of specified conditions. If this payment is subsequently made, how will Remo account for the extra cost?

11. When is the use of push-down accounting required and what is the rationale for its application?

12. How are the individual financial records of both the parent and the subsidiary affected in cases where push-down accounting is being applied?

13. Why has push-down accounting gained popularity for internal reporting purposes?

14. The consolidation process applicable to a pooling of interests often is viewed as easier than that used for a purchase. What creates this perception?

15. When should a parent consider recognizing an impairment loss for goodwill associated with a purchased subsidiary? How should the loss be reported in the financial statements?

LIBRARY ASSIGNMENTS

1. Read the following as well as any other published information concerning goodwill:
   "The Goodwill Game," *Chartered Accountants Magazine*, March 1995.
   "Goodwill Accounting: Time for an Overhaul," *Journal of Accountancy*, June 1992.
   "Goodwill—An Eternal Controversy," *CPA Journal*, April 1993.
   "The Evolution of APB Opinion No. 17, 'Accounting for Intangible Assets': A Study of the U.S. Position on Accounting for Goodwill," *Accounting Historians Journal*, Spring 1981.
   "Accounting for Goodwill," *Accounting Horizons*, March 1988.

Write a report to either justify the current treatment required for the recognition and amortization of goodwill or recommend an alternative method of accounting.

2. Read the following as well as any other published information concerning push-down accounting:

"Push-Down Accounting: FAS 200?" *Management Accounting,* November 1988.

"Business Combinations: Goodwill and Push-Down Accounting," *CPA Journal,* August 1988.

"The Push-Down Accounting Controversy," *Management Accounting,* January 1987.

"Push Down Accounting: A Descriptive Assessment," *Accounting Horizons,* September 1988.

"Push-Down Accounting: Pros and Cons," *Journal of Accountancy,* June 1984.

Write a report suggesting actions that the FASB should take in connection with the future application of push-down accounting.

PROBLEMS

1. A company acquires a subsidiary on January 1, 1998, and will prepare consolidated financial statements for the year ending December 31, 1998. For internal reporting purposes, the company has decided to apply the cost method. Why might the company have made this decision?
   a. It is a relatively easy method to apply.
   b. Operating results appearing on the parent's financial records reflect consolidated totals.
   c. The FASB now requires the use of this particular method for internal reporting purposes.
   d. Consolidation is not required when the cost method is used by the parent.

2. A company acquires a subsidiary on January 1, 1998, and will prepare consolidated financial statements for the year ending December 31, 1998. For internal reporting purposes, the company has decided to apply the equity method during 1998. Why might the company have made this decision?
   a. It is a relatively easy method to apply.
   b. Operating results appearing on the parent's financial records reflect consolidated totals.
   c. The FASB now requires the use of this particular method for internal reporting purposes.
   d. Consolidation is not required when the equity method is used by the parent.

3. Hansen, Inc., buys all of the outstanding stock of Shawnee Company on January 1, 1998, for $214,000. Annual amortization of $16,000 results from this purchase. Hansen reported net income of $60,000 in 1998 and $40,000 in 1999 and paid $18,000 in dividends each year. Shawnee reported net income of $33,000 in 1998 and $39,000 in 1999 and paid $8,000 in dividends each year. What is the Investment in Shawnee balance on Hansen's books as of December 31, 1999, if the equity method has been applied?
   a. $238,000.
   b. $246,000.
   c. $278,000.
   d. $286,000.

4. Barrett Corporation buys 100 percent of Smith, Inc., on January 1, 1998, at a price in excess of the subsidiary's fair market value. On that date, Barrett's equipment (10-year life) has a book value of $300,000 but a fair market value of $400,000. Smith has equipment (10-year life) with a book value of $200,000 but a fair market value of $300,000. Barrett uses the partial equity method to record its investment in Smith. On December 31, 2000, Barrett has equipment with a book value of $210,000 but a fair market value of $330,000. Smith has equipment with a book value of $140,000 but a fair market value of $270,000. What is the consolidated balance for the Equipment account as of December 31, 2000?
   a. $600,000.
   b. $490,000.
   c. $480,000.
   d. $420,000.

5. How would the answer to question 4 have been affected if the parent had applied the cost method rather than the partial equity method?
   a. No effect: the method used by the parent is for internal reporting purposes only and has no impact on consolidated totals.
   b. The consolidated Equipment account would have a higher reported balance.
   c. The consolidated Equipment account would have a lower reported balance.
   d. The balance in the consolidated Equipment account cannot be determined for the cost method using the information given.

6. Brocklin, Incorporated buys all of the outstanding shares of New England Corporation on January 1, 1998, for $700,000 in cash. This price resulted in a $35,000 allocation to equipment and goodwill of $88,000. Because the subsidiary subsequently earned especially high profits, Brocklin was required to pay the previous owners of New England an additional $110,000 on January 1, 2000. How should this extra amount be reported?
   a. The additional $110,000 payment is a reduction in consolidated retained earnings.
   b. A retroactive adjustment is made to record the $110,000 as an additional expense for the year ending December 31, 1998.
   c. Consolidated goodwill as of January 1, 2000, is increased by $110,000.
   d. The $110,000 is recorded as an expense in 2000.

7. Cantalupe Corporation purchases Simon, Inc., on January 1, 1998, by issuing 13,000 shares of common stock with a $10 per share par value and a $23 fair market value. This transaction results in the recording of $62,000 of goodwill. Subsequently, on January 1, 2000, Cantalupe is required to issue an additional 3,000 shares of stock to Simon's previous owners because of a drop in the market value of the initial 13,000 shares. How is this additional issuance of stock recorded?
   a. The fair market value of the newly issued shares increases the Goodwill account balance.
   b. The Investment balance is not affected but the parent's Additional Paid-In Capital is reduced by the par value of the newly issued shares.
   c. All of the subsidiary's asset and liability accounts must be revalued for consolidation purposes based on their fair market values as of January 1, 2000.
   d. The additional shares are assumed to have been issued on January 1, 1998, so that a retroactive adjustment is required.

8. What is push-down accounting?
   a. A requirement that a subsidiary must use the same accounting principles as a parent company.
   b. Inventory transfers made from a parent company to a subsidiary.
   c. Recording by a subsidiary of the market value allocations found within the purchase price paid by a parent as well as subsequent amortization.
   d. The adjustments required for consolidation when a parent has applied the cost method of accounting for internal reporting purposes.

9. Treadway Corporation purchases Hooker, Inc., on January 1, 1998. The parent pays more than the fair market value of the subsidiary's net assets. On that date, Treadway has equipment with a book value of $420,000 and a fair market value of $530,000. Hooker has equipment with a book value of $330,000 and a fair market value of $390,000. Hooker is going to use push-down accounting. Immediately after the acquisition, what Equipment account appears on Hooker's separate balance sheet and on the consolidated balance sheet?
   a. $330,000 and $750,000.
   b. $330,000 and $860,000.
   c. $390,000 and $810,000.
   d. $390,000 and $920,000.

Problems 10 through 12 are based on the following information:

Hans, Inc., purchases all of the oustanding stock of Sysk Corporation, on January 1, 1998, for $310,000. Equipment with a 10-year life was undervalued on Sysk's financial records by $38,000. Goodwill resulting from this combination is $56,000 and will be amortized over its maximum life.

Sysk earned a reported net income of $150,000 in 1998 and $180,000 in 1999. Dividends of $60,000 were paid in each of these two years.

Selected account balances as of December 31, 2000, for the two companies follow.

	Hans	**Sysk**
Revenues	$900,000	$700,000
Expenses	400,000	500,000
Investment Income	not given	—
Retained Earnings, 1/1/00	700,000	500,000
Dividends Paid	110,000	60,000

10. If the partial equity method has been applied, what is the consolidated net income?
   a. $700,000.
   b. $694,800.
   c. $690,600.
   d. $687,400.

11. If the equity method has been applied, what is the Investment in Sysk account balance within the records of Hans at the end of 2000?
   a. $644,400.
   b. $509,600.
   c. $520,000.
   d. $660,000.

12. If the cost method has been applied, what is the consolidated retained earnings balance as of January 1, 2000?
   a. $700,000.
   b. $910,000.
   c. $899,600.
   d. $1,019,600.

13. Herbert, Inc., buys all of the outstanding stock of Rambis Company on January 1, 1998. Annual amortization of $12,000 results from this purchase transaction. On the date of the takeover, Herbert reported retained earnings of $400,000 while Rambis reported a $200,000 balance. Herbert reported income of $40,000 in 1998 and $50,000 in 1999 and paid $10,000 in dividends each year. Rambis reported net income of $20,000 in 1998 and $30,000 in 1999 and paid $5,000 in dividends each year.

Required:
   a. Assume that Herbert's reported income does not include any income derived from the subsidiary.
      - If the parent uses the equity method, what are the consolidated retained earnings on December 31, 1999?
      - If the parent uses the partial equity method, what are the consolidated retained earnings on December 31, 1999?
      - If the parent uses the cost method, what are the consolidated retained earnings on December 31, 1999?
   b. Assume that Herbert's reported income does include income derived from the subsidiary.
      - If the parent uses the equity method, what are the consolidated retained earnings on December 31, 1999?
      - If the parent uses the partial equity method, what are the consolidated retained earnings on December 31, 1999?
      - If the parent uses the cost method, what are the consolidated retained earnings on December 31, 1999?
   c. Under each of the following situations, what is Entry *C on a 1999 consolidation worksheet?
      - The parent uses the equity method.
      - The parent uses the partial equity method.
      - The parent uses the cost method.

14. Haynes, Inc., obtains 100 percent of Turner Company's common stock on January 1, 1998, by issuing 9,000 shares of $10 par value common stock. Haynes's shares had a $15 per share fair market value. On that date, Turner reported a net book value of $100,000. However, its equipment (with a five-year remaining life) was undervalued by

$5,000 in the company's accounting records. Any goodwill would be amortized over 10 years.

The following figures come from the individual accounting records of these two companies as of December 31, 1998:

	Haynes	Turner
Revenues	$600,000	$230,000
Expenses	440,000	120,000
Investment Income	not given	—
Dividends Paid	80,000	50,000

The following figures come from the individual accounting records of these two companies as of December 31, 1999:

	Haynes	Turner
Revenues	$700,000	$280,000
Expenses	460,000	150,000
Investment Income	not given	—
Dividends Paid	90,000	40,000
Equipment	500,000	300,000
Retained Earnings, 12/31/99 Balance	800,000	180,000

Required:

  a. If this combination is viewed as a purchase, what balance does Haynes's Investment in Turner account show on December 31, 1999, when the equity method is applied?
  b. If this combination is viewed as a purchase, what is the consolidated net income for the year ending December 31, 1999?
  c. If this combination is viewed as a purchase, what are the consolidated equipment and consolidated goodwill as of December 31, 1999? How would this answer be affected by the investment method applied by the parent?
  d. If this combination is viewed as a purchase and Haynes has applied the equity method to account for its investment, what are consolidated retained earnings as of December 31, 1999? How would this answer be changed if Haynes had used the partial equity approach?
  e. If this combination is viewed as a pooling of interests, what is the consolidated net income for the year ending December 31, 1999?
  f. If this combination is viewed as a pooling of interests, what are the consolidated equipment and consolidated goodwill as of December 31, 1999?
  g. If this combination is viewed as a purchase and Haynes has applied the cost method to account for its investment, what adjustment is needed to beginning retained earnings on a December 31, 1999, consolidation worksheet? How would this answer change if the partial equity method had been in use? How would this answer change if the equity method had been in use?

15. On January 1, 1998, Pure, Inc., issues 58 shares of previously unissued common stock for all of the outstanding shares of Simple Company. Pure's stock has a par value of $1 per share but a fair market value of $10 per share.

Just prior to the creation of this combination, the following information is known about these two companies:

	Pure, Inc. Book Value	Simple Company Book Value	Simple Company Fair Market Value
Current assets	$150	$ 60	$ 60
Equipment (10-year life)	600	200	260
Buildings (20-year life)	900	300	340
Liabilities	450	160	160
Common stock	500	100	
Additional paid-in capital	100	50	
Retained earnings	600	250	

Any goodwill is to be amortized over a 40-year period.

During 1998, Pure reported $100 in net income (excluding any investment or dividend income) and distributed $30 in dividends; Simple had $80 in net income and $20 in dividends. At the end of 1999, the following figures were reported by the two separate companies. Once again, Pure's figures do not include any investment or dividend income.

	Pure, Inc.	Simple Company
Revenues	$400	$250
Expenses	280	160
Dividends paid	40	30
Equipment	700	220
Buildings	800	280

Required:

a. If this business combination is accounted for as a purchase, what would be the consolidated revenues, expenses, and net income for the year ending December 31, 1999?

b. If this business combination is accounted for as a pooling of interests, what would be the consolidated revenues, expenses, and net income for the year ending December 31, 1999?

c. If this business combination is accounted for as a purchase, what would be the consolidated balance of the Investment in Simple Company account and the Investment Income account as of December 31, 1999?

d. If this business combination is accounted for as a purchase, what would be the consolidated balance of the Buildings account on December 31, 1999?

e. If this business combination is accounted for as a pooling of interests, what would be the consolidated balance of the Buildings account on December 31, 1999?

f. If this business combination is accounted for as a purchase, what would be the consolidated balance of retained earnings at December 31, 1999? What are the consolidated retained earnings if this combination meets all of the criteria for a pooling of interests?

16. Texas, Inc., obtains all of the outstanding stock of Chainsaw Corporation on January 1, 1998. At that date, Chainsaw owned only three assets and had no liabilities:

	Book Value	Fair Market Value
Inventory	$ 30,000	$ 40,000
Equipment (5-year life)	70,000	50,000
Building (10-year life)	100,000	150,000

Required:

a. If Texas pays $250,000 in cash for Chainsaw, what allocation should be assigned to the subsidiary's Building account and its Equipment account in a December 31, 2000, consolidation?

b. If Texas pays $220,000 in cash for Chainsaw, what allocation should be assigned to the subsidiary's Building account and its Equipment account in a December 31, 2000, consolidation?

c. If Texas pays $180,000 in cash for Chainsaw, what allocation should be assigned to the subsidiary's Building account and its Equipment account in a December 31, 2000, consolidation?

d. If Texas issues common stock valued at $180,000 (rather than paying cash) for Chainsaw in a pooling of interests, what allocation should be assigned to the subsidiary's Building account and its Equipment account in a December 31, 2000, consolidation?

Problems 17 through 21 are based on the following data:

Chapman Company obtains 100 percent of the stock of Abernethy Company on January 1, 1998. As of that date, Abernethy has the following trial balance:

	Debit	Credit
Accounts Payable		$ 50,000
Accounts Receivable	$ 40,000	
Additional Paid-In Capital		50,000
Buildings (net) (20-year life)	120,000	
Cash and Short-Term Investments	60,000	
Common Stock		250,000
Equipment (net) (5-year life)	200,000	
Inventory	90,000	
Land.	80,000	
Long-Term Liabilities (mature 12/31/01)		150,000
Retained Earnings, 1/1/98		100,000
Supplies	10,000	
Totals	$600,000	$600,000

Any goodwill will be considered to have a 10-year life.

During 1998, Abernethy reported income of $80,000 while paying dividends of $10,000. During 1999, Abernethy reported income of $110,000 while paying dividends of $30,000.

The following five problems should be viewed as independent situations.

17. Assume that Chapman Company acquired the common stock of Abernethy for $490,000 in cash. As of January 1, 1998, Abernethy's land had a fair market value of $90,000, its buildings were valued at $160,000, and its equipment was appraised at $180,000. Chapman uses the equity method for this investment. Prepare consolidation worksheet entries for December 31, 1998, and December 31, 1999.

18. Assume that Chapman Company acquired the common stock of Abernethy for $500,000 in cash. Assume that the equipment and long-term liabilities had fair market values of $220,000 and $120,000, respectively, on that date. Chapman uses the cost method to account for its investment. Prepare consolidation worksheet entries for December 31, 1998, and December 31, 1999.

19. Assume that Chapman Company acquired the common stock of Abernethy by issuing 10,000 shares of its $30 par value common stock. The stock had a fair market value of $42 per share on January 1, 1998. This transaction meets all 12 requirements for a pooling of interests. Assume that Abernethy's land on that date had a fair market value of $110,000, while the inventory was valued at $120,000. Chapman uses the book value method to account for this investment. Prepare consolidation worksheet entries for December 31, 1998, and December 31, 1999.

20. Assume that Chapman Company acquires the common stock of Abernethy by issuing 10,000 shares of its $30 par value common stock. The stock has a $42 per share fair market value on January 1, 1998. This transaction does not meet all 12 criteria for a pooling of interests. On January 1, 1998, Abernethy's inventory had a fair market value of $150,000. All of this inventory is assumed to have been sold during 1998. Chapman applies the equity method to account for this investment. Prepare the consolidation worksheet entries for December 31, 1998, and December 31, 1999.

21. Assume that Chapman Company acquired the common stock of Abernethy by paying $520,000 in cash. All accounts of Abernethy are estimated to have a value approximately equal to present book values. Chapman uses the partial equity method to account for its investment. Prepare the consolidation worksheet entries for December 31, 1998, and December 31, 1999.

22. Jefferson, Inc., purchases Hamilton Corporation on January 1, 1998. Immediately after the acquisition, the two companies have the following account balances. Hamilton's equipment (with a five-year life) is actually worth $450,000. Any goodwill will be amortized over the maximum allowable time period.

	Jefferson	Hamilton
Current Assets.	$300,000	$210,000
Investment in Hamilton	510,000	
Equipment	600,000	400,000
Liabilities	200,000	160,000
Common Stock	350,000	150,000
Retained Earnings	860,000	300,000

In 1998, Hamilton earns a net income of $55,000 and pays a $5,000 cash dividend. At the end of 1999, selected account balances for the two companies are as follows:

	Jefferson	Hamilton
Revenues	$400,000	$240,000
Expenses	290,000	180,000
Investment Income	not given	
Retained Earnings, 1/1/99	990,000	350,000
Current Assets	360,000	140,000
Investment in Hamilton	not given	
Equipment	520,000	420,000
Liabilities	170,000	190,000

Required:

a. What will be the December 31, 1999, balance in the Investment Income account and the Investment in Hamilton account under each of the three methods described in this chapter?

b. How is the consolidated Expense account affected by the accounting method used by the parent to record ownership of this subsidiary?

c. How is the consolidated Equipment account affected by the accounting method used by the parent to record ownership of this subsidiary?

d. What is the consolidated Retained Earnings balance as of January 1, 1999, under each of the three methods described in this chapter?

e. What is Entry *C on a consolidation worksheet for 1999 under each of the three methods described in this chapter?

f. What is Entry S on a consolidation worksheet for 1999 under each of the three methods described in this chapter?

g. What is consolidated net income for 1999?

23. Following are selected account balances from the Profitt Company and Simon Corporation as of December 31, 1998:

	Profitt	Simon
Revenues	$700,000	$ 400,000
Expenses	400,000	300,000
Investment Income	not given	
Dividends Paid	80,000	60,000
Retained Earnings, 1/1/98	600,000	200,000
Current Assets	400,000	500,000
Buildings (net)	900,000	400,000
Equipment (net)	600,000	1,000,000
Investment in Simon	not given	
Liabilities	500,000	1,380,000
Common Stock	600,000 ($20 par)	200,000 ($10 par)
Additional Paid-In Capital	150,000	80,000

On January 1, 1998, Profitt purchased all of the outstanding stock of Simon for $660,000 in cash and common stock. Profitt also pays $20,000 in lawyers' fees and other combination costs as well as $10,000 in stock issuance costs. At the date of acquisition, Simon's buildings (with a six-year remaining life) have a $440,000 book value but a fair market value of $560,000. Goodwill is assumed to have a 40-year life.

Required:

a. As of December 31, 1998, what is the consolidated Buildings balance?

b. As of December 31, 1998, what is the consolidated Retained Earnings balance?

c. For the year ending December 31, 1998, what is consolidated net income?

d. As of December 31, 1998, what is the consolidated balance to be reported for goodwill?

24. Foxx Corporation purchases all of the outstanding stock of Greenburg Company on January 1, 1998, for $600,000. Greenburg had net assets on that date of $470,000 although equipment with a 10-year life was undervalued on the records by $90,000. Any recognized goodwill will be amortized over its maximum possible life.

Greenburg reports net income in 1998 of $90,000 and $100,000 in 1999. Dividends of $20,000 are paid by the subsidiary in each of these two years.

Financial figures for the year ending December 31, 2000, follow:

	Foxx	Greenburg
Revenues	$ 800,000	$ 600,000
Expenses	(400,000)	(500,000)
Investment income	20,000	
Net Income	$ 420,000	$ 100,000
Retained earnings, 1/1/00	$1,100,000	$ 320,000
Net income	420,000	100,000
Dividends paid	(120,000)	(20,000)
Retained earnings, 12/31/00	$1,400,000	$ 400,000
Current assets	$ 300,000	$ 100,000
Investment in subsidiary	600,000	–0–
Equipment (net)	900,000	600,000
Buildings (net)	800,000	400,000
Land	600,000	100,000
Total assets	$3,200,000	$1,200,000
Liabilities	$ 900,000	$ 500,000
Common stock	900,000	300,000
Retained earnings	1,400,000	400,000
Total liabilities and equities	$3,200,000	$1,200,000

Required:

a. Determine the consolidated balance for each of the following accounts:

Expenses	Buildings
Dividends Paid	Goodwill
Revenues	Common Stock
Equipment	

b. How does the parent's choice of an accounting method for its investment affect the balances computed in requirement *a*?

c. Which method of accounting for this subsidiary is the parent actually using for internal reporting purposes?

d. If a different method of accounting for this investment had been used by the parent company, how could that method have been identified?

e. What would be the consolidated balance for retained earnings as of January 1, 2000, if each of the following methods had been in use?

Cost Method
Partial Equity Method
Equity Method

 25. Big Corporation purchased Little Company on January 1, 1998, for $400,000 in cash. Little reported net assets at that time of $320,000. However, several of Little's accounts had fair market values that differed from book values:

	Book Value	Fair Market Value
Land	$ 60,000	$ 50,000
Buildings (10-year life)	100,000	120,000
Equipment (6-year life)	60,000	90,000

Goodwill is amortized over a 40-year period.

Following are financial statements for these two companies for the year ending December 31, 1998. Credit balances are indicated by parentheses.

	Big	Little
Revenues	$ (600,000)	$(300,000)
Expenses	400,000	180,000
Income of Little	(112,000)	–0–
Net income	$ (312,000)	$(120,000)
Retained earnings, 1/1/98	$ (700,000)	$(220,000)
Net income (above)	(312,000)	(120,000)
Dividends paid	142,000	80,000
Retained earnings, 12/31/98	$ (870,000)	$(260,000)
Cash	$ 176,000	$ 80,000
Receivables	210,000	90,000
Inventory	190,000	130,000
Investment in Little	432,000	–0–
Land	350,000	60,000
Buildings (net)	343,000	90,000
Equipment (net)	190,000	50,000
Goodwill	–0–	–0–
Total assets	$ 1,891,000	$ 500,000
Liabilities	$ (621,000)	$(140,000)
Common stock	(400,000)	(100,000)
Retained earnings (above)	(870,000)	(260,000)
Total liabilities and equity	$(1,891,000)	$(500,000)

a. How was the $112,000 "Income of Little" balance computed?

b. Without preparing a worksheet or consolidation entries, determine the totals to be reported for this business combination for the year ending December 31, 1998.

c. Verify the totals determined in part *b.* by producing a consolidation worksheet for Big and Little for the year ending December 31, 1998.

26. Following are separate financial statements for Mitchell Company and Andrews Company as of December 31, 1998. Mitchell acquired all of the outstanding stock of Andrews on January 1, 1994, by issuing 9,000 shares of its own common stock. This stock was valued at $50 per share while having a par value of $30 per share. In addition, Mitchell paid $20,000 to lawyers, accountants, and other parties for costs incurred in creating the combination. Although the transaction was carried out by the exchange of common stock, it did not meet all 12 criteria for a pooling of interests.

	Mitchell Company 12/31/98	Andrews Company 12/31/98
Revenues	$ 610,000	$ 370,000
Expenses	380,000	220,000
Net income	$ 230,000	$ 150,000
Retained earnings, 1/1/98	$ 880,000	$ 490,000
Net income (above)	230,000	150,000
Dividends paid	90,000	–0–
Retained earnings, 12/31/98	$1,020,000	$ 640,000
Cash	$ 110,000	$ 20,000
Receivables	380,000	220,000
Inventory	560,000	280,000
Investment in Andrews Company	470,000	–0–
Land	460,000	340,000
Buildings and equipment (net)	920,000	380,000
Total assets	$2,900,000	$1,240,000
Liabilities	$ 780,000	$ 470,000
Preferred stock	300,000	–0–
Common stock	500,000	100,000
Additional paid-in capital	300,000	30,000
Retained earnings, 12/31/98	1,020,000	640,000
Total liabilities and equities	$2,900,000	$1,240,000

On the date of purchase, Andrews reported a book value of $360,000, although its buildings and equipment were undervalued by $60,000. This property was assumed to have a six-year life with no salvage value. Additionally, any goodwill recognized in this consolidation was viewed as having a 10-year life.

a. Using the preceding information, prepare a consolidation worksheet for these two companies as of December 31, 1998.

b. Assuming that Mitchell applied the equity method to this investment, what account balances would be altered on the parent's individual financial statements?

c. Assuming that Mitchell applied the equity method to this investment, what changes would be necessary in the consolidation entries found on a December 31, 1998, worksheet?

d. Assuming that Mitchell applied the equity method to this investment, what changes would be created in the consolidated figures to be reported by this combination?

27. Tucson Company has reported the following income and dividend figures during the past few years:

	Net Income	Dividends Paid
1997	$80,000	$30,000
1996	70,000	30,000
1995	40,000	20,000
1994	50,000	20,000

Account balances for Arizona, Inc., and Tucson Company as of December 31, 1998, follow. Some of Arizona's accounts have been omitted from this list.

	Arizona	Tucson
Revenues	$600,000	$400,000
Expenses	400,000	250,000
Investment Income	not given	
Retained Earnings, 1/1/98	900,000	800,000
Dividends Paid	130,000	40,000
Current Assets	200,000	690,000
Land	300,000	290,000
Buildings (net)	500,000	230,000
Equipment (net)	200,000	250,000
Liabilities	400,000	350,000
Common Stock	300,000	40,000
Additional Paid-In Capital	50,000	160,000

On January 1, 1994, Arizona acquired all of Tucson's stock by paying $1 million cash. Tucson's equipment (10-year life) was overvalued at that time by $30,000 but its buildings were undervalued by $50,000. These buildings had a five-year life; goodwill was to be amortized over 20 years.

Required:

a. Assuming that Arizona has applied the cost method, prepare consolidation entries as of December 31, 1998. What is the purpose of Entry *C?

b. Determine the consolidated totals for the following accounts; assume that the parent applies the partial equity method:

   Net Income
   Equipment (net)
   Buildings (net)
   Retained Earnings, 1/1/98

c. Determine the consolidated totals for the following accounts; assume that the parent applies the equity method:

   Net Income
   Equipment (net)
   Buildings (net)
   Retained Earnings, 1/1/98

28. Following are the trial balances for the High Company and the Low Company as of December 31, 1998:

	High Company Trial Balance 12/31/98		Low Company Trial Balance 12/31/98	
	Debit	Credit	Debit	Credit
Accounts Payable		$ 170,000		$ 200,000
Accounts Receivable	$ 440,000		$ 80,000	
Buildings (net)	1,510,000		660,000	
Cash....................	60,000		10,000	
Common Stock		700,000		400,000
Dividends Paid	100,000		20,000	
Expenses.................	440,000		195,000	
Inventory	640,000		610,000	
Investment in Low Company ..	1,260,000		–0–	
Investment Income.........		50,000		–0–
Long-Term Liabilities........		690,000		500,000
Machinery (net)...........	660,000		460,000	
Retained Earnings, 1/1/98.....		2,630,000		690,000
Revenues		870,000		245,000
Totals	$5,110,000	$5,110,000	$2,035,000	$2,035,000

High Company acquired all of the outstanding common stock of Low Company on January 1, 1995, for $940,000 in cash. On that date, Low's buildings (20-year life) were undervalued in the company's records by $100,000 while its machinery (10-year life) was overvalued by $20,000. Low's book value on the date of acquisition was $800,000. Any goodwill recognized in the consolidation is amortized over a 20-year life. High uses the partial equity method to account for this investment.

As of December 31, 1998, Low owes $20,000 to High.

Required:

Determine the consolidated figures that will be reported by the business combination of High Company and Low Company as of December 31, 1998.

29. Giant purchased all of the common stock of Small on January 1, 1998. Over the next few years, Giant applied the equity method to the recording of this investment. At the date of the original purchase, $90,000 of the price was attributed to undervalued land, while $50,000 was assigned to equipment having a 10-year life. The remaining $60,000 unallocated portion of the purchase price ($60,000) was viewed as goodwill to be amortized over a 30-year period.

Following are individual financial statements for the year ending December 31, 2002. On that date, Small owes Giant $10,000. Credits are indicated by parentheses.

	Giant	Small
Revenues	$(1,175,000)	$ (360,000)
Expenses......................................	722,000	220,000
Equity in income of Small	(133,000)	–0–
Net income	$ (586,000)	$ (140,000)
Retained earnings, 1/1/02	$(1,409,000)	$ (620,000)
Net income (above)	(586,000)	(140,000)
Dividends paid	310,000	110,000
Retained earnings, 12/31/02	$(1,685,000)	$ (650,000)
Current assets	$ 398,000	$ 318,000
Investment in Small...........................	985,000	–0–
Land...	440,000	165,000
Buildings (net)	304,000	419,000
Equipment (net)...............................	648,000	286,000
Goodwill.....................................	–0–	–0–
Total assets	$ 2,775,000	$ 1,188,000
Liabilities	$ (840,000)	$ (368,000)
Common stock	(250,000)	(170,000)
Retained earnings (above)......................	(1,685,000)	(650,000)
Total liabilities and equity	$(2,775,000)	$(1,188,000)

a. How was the $133,000 "Equity in Income of Small" balance computed?

b. Without preparing a worksheet or consolidation entries, determine the totals to be reported by this business combination for the year ending December 31, 2002.

c. Verify the figures determined in part *b.* by producing a consolidation worksheet for Giant and Small for the year ending December 31, 2002.

d. If Small had adopted the push-down method of accounting, how would the preceding accounts of the subsidiary have been affected? How would the worksheet process be changed? What impact does the application of push-down accounting have on consolidated financial statements?

30. Following are selected accounts for Mergaronite Company and Hill, Inc., as of December 31, 1998. Several of Mergaronite's accounts have been omitted.

	Mergaronite	**Hill**
Revenues	$600,000	$250,000
Expenses	400,000	150,000
Investment Income	not given	
Retained Earnings, 1/1/98	900,000	600,000
Dividends Paid	130,000	40,000
Current Assets	200,000	690,000
Land	300,000	90,000
Buildings (net)	500,000	140,000
Equipment (net)	200,000	250,000
Liabilities	400,000	310,000
Common Stock	300,000	40,000
Additional Paid in Capital	50,000	160,000

Assume that Mergaronite took over Hill on January 1, 1994, in a purchase by issuing 7,000 shares of common stock having a par value of $10 per share but a fair market value of $100 each. On January 1, 1994, Hill's land was undervalued by $20,000, its buildings were overvalued by $30,000, and equipment was undervalued by $60,000. The buildings had a 10-year life; the equipment had a 5-year life. Goodwill of $100,000 resulted from this purchase and was to be written off over a 20-year period.

Required:

a. What are the December 31, 1998, consolidated totals for the following accounts:

    Revenue
    Expenses
    Buildings
    Equipment
    Goodwill
    Common Stock
    Additional Paid in Capital

b. In requirement *a.,* why can the consolidated totals be determined without knowing which method the parent has used to account for the subsidiary?

c. If the equity method is used by the parent, what consolidation entries would be used on a 1998 worksheet?

31. Alton Company acquired Zeidner, Inc., on January 1, 1994, in a business combination properly accounted for as a purchase. On that date, Zeidner held assets and liabilities with book values of $700,000 and $200,000, respectively. Alton paid a total of $670,000 to acquire all of the outstanding stock of Zeidner. At the date of this purchase, Zeidner possessed equipment (with a five-year life) that had a value $50,000 in excess of its book value. In addition, Zeidner had buildings worth $80,000 more than their book value. These buildings had a remaining life expectancy of 20 years. Any goodwill that results from the acquisition will be amortized over the maximum 40-year period.

Following are the individual financial statements for these two companies for the year ending December 31, 2003. Alton owes Zeidner $30,000 at this point in time. Without preparing consolidation entries or setting up a worksheet, determine the consolidated totals for Alton Company and Zeidner, Inc.

	Alton Company	Zeidner, Inc.
Income Statement		
Revenues	$ 600,000	$ 500,000
Expenses	(300,000)	(300,000)
Investment income from Zeidner Company	200,000	–0–
Net income	$ 500,000	$ 200,000
Statement of Retained Earnings		
Retained earnings, 1/1/03	$1,500,000	$ 650,000
Net income (above)	500,000	200,000
Dividends paid	(200,000)	(50,000)
Retained earnings, 12/31/03	$1,800,000	$ 800,000
Balance Sheet		
Current assets	$ 230,000	$ 300,000
Investment in Zeidner Company	1,270,000	–0–
Land	100,000	200,000
Buildings	300,000	400,000
Equipment	600,000	300,000
Goodwill	–0–	–0–
Total assets	$2,500,000	$1,200,000
Liabilities	$ 300,000	$ 100,000
Common stock	400,000	300,000
Retained earnings, 12/31/03	1,800,000	800,000
Total liabilities and equities	$2,500,000	$1,200,000

32. On January 1, 1998, Romeo, Incorporated, exchanged 10,000 shares of previously unissued common stock for all of the outstanding shares of Juliet Company. This combination met all 12 criteria for a pooling of interests. Romeo's common stock had a $20 par value but a fair market value of $48 per share. On the date of the exchange, Juliet reported $370,000 in stockholders' equity:

Common Stock	$200,000
Additional Paid-In Capital	50,000
Retained Earnings	120,000

Romeo originally offered only 8,000 shares for Juliet's stock but raised that bid based on favorable earnings projections. In addition, equipment held by the subsidiary (with a 10-year remaining life) was estimated to be undervalued on the accounting records by $70,000. Goodwill is always amortized by these companies over a 20-year period.

During 1998, Juliet reported net income of $80,000 and paid cash dividends of $60,000. In accounting for this investment, Romeo utilized the equity method.

Following are the December 31, 1999, trial balances for these two companies. Determine the consolidated balances that would be reported by this combination.

	Romeo Incorporated	Juliet Company
Debits		
Accounts Receivable	$ 140,000	$ 40,000
Buildings	620,000	260,000
Cash	60,000	10,000
Dividends Paid	130,000	60,000
Equipment	490,000	330,000
Expenses	390,000	110,000
Inventory	190,000	110,000
Investment in Juliet Company	420,000	–0–
Land	300,000	200,000
Total Debits	$2,740,000	$1,120,000

(continued)

	Romeo Incorporated	Juliet Company
Credits		
Additional Paid-In Capital	$ 190,000	$ 50,000
Common Stock	600,000	200,000
Investment Income from Juliet Company	90,000	–0–
Liabilities	580,000	530,000
Retained Earnings, 1/1/99	680,000	140,000
Revenues	600,000	200,000
Total Credits	$2,740,000	$1,120,000

33. Broome paid $430,000 cash for all of the outstanding common stock of Charlotte, Inc., on January 1, 1998. The subsidiary had a book value of $340,000 on that date (common stock of $200,000 and retained earnings of $140,000), although equipment recorded at $40,000 (with a five-year remaining life) was assessed as having an actual worth of $70,000. Any goodwill is to be amortized over 20 years.

During the subsequent three years, Charlotte reported the following balances:

	Net Income	Dividends Paid
1998	$65,000	$25,000
1999	75,000	35,000
2000	80,000	40,000

On January 1, 2000, Broome paid an additional $20,000 to the previous owners of Charlotte, an amount that was due because the subsidiary's earnings for the first two years had exceeded $120,000.

a. Prepare consolidation worksheet entries as of December 31, 2000, assuming that Broome has applied the cost method.

b. Prepare consolidation worksheet entries as of December 31, 2000, assuming that Broome has applied the partial equity method.

34. Palm Company acquired 100 percent of the voting stock of Storm Company on January 1, 1994, by issuing 10,000 shares of its $10 par value common stock (having a fair market value of $13 per share). Palm also paid $10,000 in consolidation costs to lawyers and investment analysts. As of that date, Storm had stockholders' equity totaling $105,000. Land shown on Storm's accounting records was undervalued by $10,000. Equipment (with a five-year life) was undervalued by $5,000. Goodwill amortization was to be over a 40-year period.

Following are the separate financial statements for the two companies for the year ending December 31, 1998. Assume that the 12 criteria for a pooling of interests have not been met.

	Palm Company	Storm Company
Revenues	$ 485,000	$190,000
Expenses	(290,000)	(122,000)
Equity in subsidiary earnings *matches equity method* . . .	66,500	–0–
Net income	$ 261,500	$ 68,000
Retained earnings, 1/1/98	$ 661,000	$ 98,000
Net income (above)	261,500	68,000
Dividends paid	(175,500)	(40,000)
Retained earnings, 12/31/98	$ 747,000	$126,000
Current assets	$ 268,000	$ 75,000
Investment in Storm Company	218,500	–0–
Land	427,500	58,000
Buildings and equipment (net)	713,000	161,000
Total assets	$1,627,000	$294,000
Current liabilities	$ 110,000	$ 19,000
Long-term liabilities	80,000	84,000
Common stock	600,000	60,000
Additional paid-in capital	90,000	5,000
Retained earnings, 12/31/98	747,000	126,000
Total liabilities and equities	$1,627,000	$294,000

a. How was the $66,500 balance in the Equity in Subsidiary Earnings account derived?

b. Prepare a worksheet to consolidate the financial information for these two companies. *Consol. entries 3 worksheet*

c. How would Storm's individual financial records differ if the push-down method of accounting had been applied?

35. The Tyler Company acquired all of the outstanding stock of Jasmine Company on January 1, 1998, for $206,000 in cash. Jasmine had a book value of only $140,000 on that date. However, equipment (having an eight-year life) was undervalued by $40,000 on Jasmine's financial records. A building with a 20-year life was overvalued by $10,000. Tyler amortizes all goodwill over the maximum allowable life. Subsequent to the acquisition, Jasmine reported the following:

	Net Income	Dividends Paid
1998	$50,000	$10,000
1999	60,000	40,000
2000	30,000	20,000

In accounting for this investment, Tyler has used the equity method. Selected accounts taken from the financial records of these two companies as of December 31, 2000, are as follows:

	Tyler Company	Jasmine Company
Revenues—Operating	$310,000	$104,000
Expenses	198,000	74,000
Equipment (net)	320,000	50,000
Buildings (net)	220,000	68,000
Common Stock	290,000	50,000
Retained Earnings, 12/31/00 Balance	410,000	160,000

Required:

Determine the following account balances as of December 31, 2000:

a. Investment in Jasmine Company (on Tyler's individual financial records).

b. Equity in subsidiary earnings (on Tyler's individual financial records).

c. Consolidated net income.

d. Consolidated equipment (net).

e. Consolidated buildings (net).

f. Consolidated goodwill (net).

g. Consolidated common stock.

h. Consolidated retained earnings, 12/31/00.

36. During 1998, Abbott Corporation issued shares of its common stock for all of the outstanding stock of Drexel, Inc., in a transaction meeting all of the qualifications for a pooling of interests. Drexel's book value was only $120,000 at the time, but Abbott issued 10,000 shares valued at $18 per share. Abbott was willing to convey these shares because it felt that buildings (10-year life) were undervalued on Drexel's records by $40,000 while equipment (5-year life) was undervalued by $20,000. Goodwill is amortized by this business combination over a 30-year period.

Following are the individual financial records for these two companies for the year ending December 31, 2001.

	Abbott	Drexel
Revenues	$ 310,000	$ 90,000
Expenses................................	(220,000)	(60,000)
Equity in subsidiary earnings	30,000	–0–
Net income	$ 120,000	$ 30,000
Retained earnings, 1/1/01	$ 640,000	$ 85,000
Net income	120,000	30,000
Less: Dividends paid	(70,000)	(20,000)
Retained earnings, 12/31/01	$ 690,000	$ 95,000
Current assets	$ 159,000	$ 57,000
Investment in Drexel	155,000	–0–
Buildings (net)	472,000	71,000
Equipment (net)..........................	404,000	107,000
Total assets	$1,190,000	$235,000
Liabilities	$ 160,000	$ 80,000
Common stock	300,000	60,000
Additional paid-in capital	40,000	–0–
Retained earnings, 12/31/01 (above)	690,000	95,000
Total liabilities and equities	$1,190,000	$235,000

a. Without making consolidation entries or setting up a worksheet, determine the consolidated totals for this business combination.

b. Verify the balances determined in part a. by preparing a worksheet as of December 31, 2001.

COMPUTER PROJECT

Alternative Investment Methods and Consolidated Financial Statements

In this project you are to provide an analysis of alternative accounting methods for controlling interest investments and subsequent effects on consolidated reporting. The project requires the use of a computer and a spreadsheet software package (Microsoft Excel, Lotus 123, etc.). The use of these tools allows assessment of the sensitivity of alternative accounting methods on consolidated financial reporting without the necessity of preparing several similar worksheets by hand. Also by modeling a worksheet process, a better understanding of accounting for combined reporting entities may result.

Consolidated Worksheet Preparation   You will be creating and entering formulas to complete four worksheets. The first objective is to demonstrate the effect of different methods of accounting for the investments (equity, cost, and partial equity) on the parent company's trial balance and on the consolidated worksheet subsequent to acquisition. The second objective is to show the effect on consolidated balances of altering the amortization periods for goodwill and other cost allocations.

The project requires preparation of the following four separate worksheets:

1. Consolidated Information Worksheet (provided below)
2. Equity Method Consolidation Worksheet
3. Cost Method Consolidation Worksheet
4. Partial Equity Method Consolidation Worksheet

If your spreadsheet package has multiple worksheet capabilities (e.g., Excel) separate worksheets can be used; otherwise, each of the four worksheets can reside in a separate area of a single spreadsheet.

In formulating your solution, each worksheet should link directly to the first worksheet. Make sure the cost allocations and amortizations on the first worksheet are linked directly to each of the three consolidating worksheets. Also, feel free to create supplemental schedules to enhance the capabilities of your worksheet.

Project Scenario Palm Company purchased 100 percent of the outstanding stock of Sand for $255,000 cash on January 1, 1997, when Sand Company had the following balance sheet:

Assets		Liabilities and Equity	
Cash	$ 25,000	Liabilities	$260,000
Accounts Receivable	85,000		
Inventory	140,000		
Land	60,000	Common stock	100,000
Buildings (net)	100,000	Retained earnings	110,000
Equipment (net)	60,000		
	$470,000		$470,000

At the purchase date, the fair market values of each identifiable asset and liability that differed from book value were as follows:

Land	$ 50,000	
Building	125,000	(10-year remaining life)
Equipment (net)	75,000	(3-year remaining life)

The following additional information is available:

- It is Palm Company's policy to amortize any goodwill over five years. But management is interested in the effect of alternative amortization periods for goodwill and other cost allocations.

- During 1997, Sand earns $70,000 and pays no dividends.

- Both Palm's and Sand's trial balances at December 31, 1998, are presented in the Consolidated Information Worksheet. All consolidated worksheets are to be prepared as of December 31, 1998, two years subsequent to acquisition.

- Palm's initial trial balance presented on the Consolidated Information Worksheet reflects the use of the cost method. You are to provide alternative trial balances reflecting the use of the equity and partial equity methods. You are also to provide the necessary adjustments and eliminations for each separate method of investment accounting.

Following are the Consolidated Information Worksheet and a template for each of the three subsequent worksheets.

Consolidated Information Worksheet

	A	B	C	D
1	**December 31, 1998, trial balances: Palm uses Cost Method**			
2				
3		**Palm**	**Sand**	
4	Revenues	($ 600,000)	($260,000)	
5	Expenses	$ 400,000	$180,000	
6	Income of Sand	($ 20,000)		
7	Net Income	($ 220,000)	($ 80,000)	
8				
9	Retained earnings—Palm 1/1/98	($ 700,000)		
10	Retained earnings—Sand 1/1/98		($180,000)	
11	Net income (above)	($ 220,000)	($ 80,000)	
12	Dividends paid	$ 142,000	$ 20,000	
13	Retained earnings 12/31/98	($ 778,000)	($240,000)	
14				
15	Cash	$ 116,000	$ 80,000	
16	Receivables	$ 210,000	$ 90,000	
17	Inventory	$ 190,000	$210,000	
18	Investment in Sand	$ 255,000		
19				
20				
21				
22	Land	$ 495,000	$ 60,000	
23	Buildings (net)	$ 343,000	$ 80,000	
24	Equipment (net)	$ 190,000	$ 40,000	
25	Goodwill	$ 0	$ 0	
26	Total assets	$1,799,000	$560,000	
27				
28	Liabilities	($ 621,000)	($220,000)	
29	Common stock	($ 400,000)	($100,000)	
30	Retained earnings (above)	($ 778,000)	($240,000)	
31	Total liabilities and equity	($1,799,000)	($560,000)	
32				
33	**Cost Allocation Schedule**			
34	Price Paid	$ 255,000		
35	Book Value	($ 210,000)		
36	Excess Cost	$ 45,000		
37	to Land	($ 10,000)		**Amortizations**
38	to Building	$ 25,000	10	$ 2,500
39	to Equipment	$ 15,000	3	$ 5,000
40	to Goodwill	$ 15,000	5	$ 3,000
41				$10,500
42				
43	**Sand's RE Changes**	**Income**	**Dividends**	
44	1997	$ 70,000	$ 0	
45	1998	$ 80,000	$ 20,000	

Consolidated Worksheet Template

	A	B	C	D	E	F
				Consolidation Entries		Consolidated
1	**December 31, 1998**					
2				Consolidation Entries		Consolidated
3		**Palm**	**Sand**	**Debit**	**Credit**	**Totals**
4	Revenues					
5	Expenses					
6	Income of Sand					
7	Net Income					
8						
9	Retained earnings 1/1/98 Palm					
10	Retained earnings 1/1/98 Sand					
11	Net income (above)					
12	Dividends paid					
13	Retained earnings 12/31/98					
14						
15	Cash					
16	Receivables					
17	Inventory					
18	Investment in Sand					
19						
20						
21						
22	Land					
23	Buildings (net)					
24	Equipment (net)					
25	Goodwill					
26	Total assets					
27						
28	Liabilities					
29	Common stock					
30	Retained earnings (above)					
31	Total liabilities and equity					

Project Requirements

1. Complete the four worksheets as follows:
   a. Input the **Consolidated Information Worksheet** provided. In preparing the **cost allocation schedule** for Palm's investment in Sand, make sure you state the amortization periods in separate cells so these can be easily changed. Also make sure to use formulas (not just typing in the numbers) for the resulting amortizations. For example, in Excel, cell D40 can be formulated as =B40/C40 so that D40 will change automatically whenever C40 is changed.
   b. Using separate worksheets prepare Palm's December 31, 1998, trial balances for each of the indicated accounting methods (equity, cost, and partial equity). **Use formulas for the Investment in Sand account, the Income of Sand account, and beginning and ending Retained Earnings accounts.**
   c. **Using references to other cells only (either from the Consolidated Information Worksheet or from the separate method worksheets),** prepare for each of the three consolidating worksheets,

- Worksheet adjustments and eliminations.
- Consolidated balances.

    d. Your worksheets should have the capability to adjust immediately for changes in the amortization periods of Goodwill and the other cost allocations as indicated in your cost allocation schedule.

2. Prepare a written report to accompany your worksheets addressing the following:

    a. What are the effects of alternative investment accounting methods on the parent's trial balances and the final consolidated figures?

    b. What is the relation between consolidated retained earnings and the parent's retained earnings under each of the three (equity, cost, partial equity) investment accounting methods?

    c. What is the effect on consolidated income of alternative goodwill amortization periods? What factors should enter into the decision regarding the length of the amortization period?

4

Consolidated Financial Statements and Outside Ownership

QUESTIONS TO CONSIDER

■ Total ownership is not an absolute requirement for consolidation; a parent need only gain control of another company to create a business combination. If less than 100 percent of a subsidiary's voting stock is obtained, how is the presence of the other owners reflected in consolidated financial statements? What accounting is appropriate for this noncontrolling interest? How are these figures computed and where are they reported on the consolidated statements?

■ If a parent holds less than complete ownership, are the subsidiary's assets and liabilities consolidated at 100 percent of their fair market values or should the reported figures be affected by the degree of the parent's ownership?

■ If a parent acquires several blocks of a subsidiary's stock over a period of time prior to gaining control, how are the various purchases consolidated?

■ How are a subsidiary's revenues and expenses reported on a consolidated income statement when the parent gains control within the current year?

■ When a portion, or all, of a subsidiary's stock is sold, how is the resulting gain or loss calculated? By what accounting method are any shares that remain reported?

A note to the 1996 financial statements of 360° Communications Inc. contains the following information:

> The accompanying consolidated financial statements include the accounts of the Company and its wholly owned and majority-owned subsidiaries. The assets, liabilities and results of operations of entities (both corporations and partnerships) in which the Company has a controlling interest have been consolidated. The ownership interests of noncontrolling owners in such entities are reflected as minority interests.

360° Communications includes *all of the financial figures* generated by both its wholly and majority-owned subsidiaries within consolidated financial statements. How does 360° Communications account for the partial ownership interest of the noncontrolling owners of its subsidiaries?

A number of reasons exist for one company to hold less than 100 percent ownership of a subsidiary. The parent may not have had sufficient resources available to obtain all of the outstanding stock. As a second possibility, a few stockholders of the subsidiary could have elected to retain their ownership, perhaps in hopes of getting a better price at a later date.

Lack of total ownership is frequently encountered with foreign subsidiaries. The laws of some countries prohibit outsiders from maintaining complete control of domestic business enterprises. In other areas of the world, a parent may seek to establish better relations with a subsidiary's employees, customers, and local government by maintaining some percentage of native ownership.

Regardless of the reason for owning less than 100 percent, the parent consolidates the financial data of every subsidiary where control is present. As discussed in Chapter 2, *complete ownership is not a prerequisite for consolidation.* A single economic entity is formed whenever one company is able to control the decision-making process of another.

Although most parent companies do possess 100 percent ownership of their subsidiaries, a significant number, such as 360° Communications, establish control with a lesser amount of stock. The remaining outside owners are collectively referred to as a *noncontrolling interest* or by the more traditional term *minority interest.* The presence of these other stockholders poses a number of reporting questions for the accountant. Whenever less than 100 percent of a subsidiary's voting stock is held, how should the subsidiary's accounts be valued within consolidated financial statements? How should the presence of these additional owners be acknowledged?

CONSOLIDATIONS INVOLVING A NONCONTROLLING INTEREST[1]

In any combination in which a noncontrolling interest remains, an intriguing theoretical controversy is created as to (1) the appropriate consolidation values that should be assigned to the subsidiary's accounts and (2) the method of disclosing the presence of the other owners. This debate involves more than a reporting problem; it ultimately concerns the fundamental objectives of consolidated financial statements.

When total ownership exists, the subsidiary's assets and liabilities are always consolidated based on their fair market values at the date of acquisition with any excess cost assigned to goodwill.[2] Since no other owners would exist, disclosure of a noncontrolling interest is not relevant. In contrast, whenever less than 100 percent of a subsidiary is acquired, several different theoretical methods exist to calculate the consolidated values of the acquired accounts. Each of these approaches uses a different technique for reporting the presence of the noncontrolling interest.

As a basis for examining these alternative valuation theories, assume that Small Company possesses net assets as follows:

Book value of net assets $110,000
Fair market value of identifiable net assets   130,000

In the current year, Big Company purchases 70 percent of the outstanding voting stock of Small for $140,000. Big's willingness to pay this price can be viewed as an indication that Small, taken as a whole, has an implied value of $200,000 ($140,000/ 70 percent). *The accounting controversy centers on whether the parent's $140,000 cost or the $200,000 implied value of the subsidiary should serve as the valuation basis for subsequently consolidated figures.*[3]

---

[1]The term *minority interest* has been used almost universally over the decades to identify the presence of other outside owners. However, in the FASB's October 16, 1995, Exposure Draft, *Consolidated Financial Statements: Policy and Procedures*, the term *noncontrolling interest* was applied. Since this newer term is more descriptive, it is used throughout this textbook.

[2]To avoid unnecessary complexities in analyzing this issue, bargain purchases are not illustrated. In addition, this controversy does not relate to a pooling of interests where accounts are always consolidated at their book values.

[3]In a 100 percent purchase, the implied value of the subsidiary is the parent's purchase price. Thus, only one valuation basis is present and, at least from a mechanical perspective, no problem exists.

DISCUSSION QUESTION

How Do We Report This Other Owner?

The Hartstone Company was created 15 years ago and presently owns several large retail clothing stores in and around Lakeland, Minnesota. Hartstone's capital stock is held equally by its four founders: Scott Arnold, Janine Bostio, Garrison Cantleberry, and Ingrid Jorgesson.

Until recently, Thomas Warwick was the sole owner of a competing business in the nearby city of Kalshburg. Because Warwick was nearing retirement age, he opted to sell 90 percent of his company (which encompassed only one store) to Hartstone. Because the business had been in Warwick's family for several generations, he wanted to retain 10 percent ownership. Hartstone paid cash for this acquisition. Based on past profitability, the negotiated price for the shares was set to indicate a total value of $2 million, although the current book value of the store was only $1.4 million.

At the end of the current year, the owners of Hartstone must produce consolidated financial statements for the first time. Consequently, they are having a discussion with their accountant concerning the appropriate method of reporting Thomas Warwick's 10 percent interest in the Kalshburg store.

Scott Arnold: These statements are designed to represent the Hartstone Company and our assets, liabilities, revenues, and expenses. Warwick owns none of our stock. I see no reason to include any figure at all for him. Readers would naturally assume that he controls a portion of Hartstone; we would be misleading them. He has nothing to do with our company.

Janine Bostio: I think you are wrong. Warwick owns 10 percent of one of our stores. He is a partial owner of this asset, and since we are consolidating the entire Kalshburg store, we have to recognize that he has an equity interest. The price indicates a $2,000,000 value; so his ownership should be recognized at $200,000.

Garrison Cantleberry: I agree with Scott; the statements are designed to represent Hartstone Company, and Warwick is certainly not a stockholder of Hartstone. However, we do have a legal obligation to him. If we ever liquidate the Kalshburg store, he would be entitled to a portion of the residual. Even now, when the store pays a dividend, he must be paid 10 percent of each distribution. We have an obligation to him that can only be properly disclosed as a liability.

Ingrid Jorgesson: I have trouble with recording a liability. I understand that we eventually might have a debt to Warwick, but at this point in time we are under no obligation to him. To me, a possible future claim should not be recorded as an actual liability. However, Warwick has retained a $140,000 investment in one of our assets. That is his cost. Since this amount doesn't seem to be either debt or equity, why don't we record it separately between our liabilities and the stockholders' equity? Anyone reading the statements can add this figure to either balance if desired or simply ignore it entirely.

As the accountant, what recommendation would you make to your clients and why? Should Warwick's interest be recognized? If so, where should the figure be reported and what amount should be disclosed?

Incorporating the cost figure suggests that consolidated statements are primarily intended as a report of the parent company and the results of its $140,000 investment. Conversely, by utilizing the $200,000 implied value, the emphasis is focused on accounting for Big and Small as two individual components forming a single economic entity.

Unfortunately, virtually nothing in official accounting pronouncements has ever addressed the issue of valuation theory in combinations involving less than 100 percent ownership. Thus, the positions adopted at present are based on traditional approaches that have evolved over the years. However, this issue was recently opened up for examination by the FASB.[4] This examination might possibly lead to the issuance of an official standard that requires one theory to be used. However, until that time, companies are free to apply any one of several approaches in reporting the accounts of a subsidiary. The following section presents three of the theories outlined by the FASB.[5]

---

[4]See FASB Exposure Draft *Consolidated Financial Statements: Policy and Procedures.*

[5]Variations do exist of each approach presented here. To avoid unnecessary complication, only three of the basic theories are described.

The Economic Unit Concept[6]

If the accounting emphasis in preparing consolidated statements is placed on the business combination being formed (rather than on the parent's investment), an approach referred to as the *economic unit concept* (also known as the *entity theory*) is generally endorsed. This concept is founded on the proposition that the subsidiary and especially the subsidiary's individual accounts cannot be divided along ownership lines. A controlled company must always be consolidated as a whole regardless of the parent's level of ownership.

Proponents argue that this concept provides the most consistent perspective of the consolidation process. It also gives the best view of the assets and liabilities that have come under the control of the parent company. If, in the previous illustration, Small owns land with a book value of $8,000 but a fair market value of $10,000, the economic unit concept requires the $10,000 figure to be reported within consolidated statements whether the parent acquires 70 percent, 100 percent, or any other level of control. The owners of Big control all of the resources of both Big and Small despite holding only 70 percent of the subsidiary's voting stock.

Therefore, in accounting for Big's acquisition of Small, the economic unit concept bases consolidated totals on the $200,000 implied value of the subsidiary taken as a whole. All of the subsidiary's assets and liabilities are included at their fair market values with any excess assigned to goodwill. Because the individual market values total only $130,000 but the implied value of the company as a whole equals $200,000, the excess $70,000 is assigned to goodwill.

Since the total value of every asset and liability is attributed to the consolidated entity, the partial ownership held by outside parties must also be acknowledged. *Including 100 percent of the value of a subsidiary's accounts when only 70 percent of the stock is owned creates an imbalance that requires the recognition of a 30 percent noncontrolling interest.* Hence, $60,000 (30 percent of the total implied value being included in the consolidation) is attributed to the other owners of Small.

Economic Unit Concept

Implied value of Small ($140,000/70%)	$200,000
Fair market value assigned to Small's accounts	130,000
Fair market value not assigned to identifiable accounts—goodwill	$ 70,000
Noncontrolling interest (30% of the $200,000 implied value included in consolidated totals)	$ 60,000

Although Small's outside owners do not possess an equity interest in the parent company, the $60,000 balance is presented within the consolidated stockholders' equity section when the economic unit concept is in use. This placement is based on the assertion that the two companies should be viewed together as a single entity. The outside parties own a component part of the resulting business combination; thus, their interest is viewed as an equity (or ownership) balance to be reported within the consolidated balance sheet.

After the balance sheet valuations are established for the economic unit concept, a logical extension can be made to the construction of a consolidated income statement. Once again this approach recognizes 100 percent of the subsidiary's balances. Its entire income is included. By consolidating every account in total, the fundamental objective of reporting the subsidiary as an indivisible unit within the consolidated

---

[6]In their June 1996 Working Draft revision of the *Consolidated Financial Statements: Policy and Procedures* Exposure Draft, the FASB recommends the adoption of the economic unit concept as discussed in this section. See the appendix to this chapter for further discussion of this issue.

entity is being fulfilled. Furthermore, this approach effectively reports the income that is generated by the net assets under the control of the parent company.

Consequently, for Big's acquisition of Small, 100 percent of the subsidiary's revenues and expenses should be included in the consolidated figures. Because only 70 percent of Small is owned by the parent, a 30 percent claim to the subsidiary's earnings must be deducted separately in recognition of the noncontrolling interest. This portion of consolidated net income is viewed as an allocation to these other owners.

In computing the part of consolidated income to be assigned to the noncontrolling interest, a theoretical question arises concerning the impact of any amortization incurred in connection with the price paid by the parent. As shown in Chapter 3, recognition of an expense is necessitated by the allocations made to specific accounts as well as to goodwill. Within the business combination, is this expense attributed to the parent or to the subsidiary?

A logical extension of the economic unit concept is that each purchase price allocation is perceived as a revaluation of a subsidiary asset or liability to fair market value. Subsequent amortization of these costs, therefore, relate to the subsidiary rather than the parent. Because the expense is viewed as an adjustment to the subsidiary's net income, it affects the computation of the noncontrolling interest's share of these earnings.

For example, what is the noncontrolling interest in the subsidiary's income in the following situation?

Portion of subsidiary owned by parent . . . .   90 percent
Subsidiary's reported net income $300,000
Amortization expense on purchase price allocations $40,000

The economic unit concept presumes that the amortizations relate to the subsidiary's assets. Thus, the allocation of consolidated income made to the noncontrolling interest is $26,000 (or 10 percent of earnings less amortization expense).

Under the economic unit theory, all consolidated totals (except for noncontrolling interest figures) are identical regardless of the degree of parent ownership. The parent controls the entire decision-making process of the subsidiary whenever control exists. Therefore, the economic unit concept views the subsidiary as an indivisible unit within the business combination. As such, fair market value serves as the basis for consolidating each asset and liability, even though the parent's interest may be significantly below 100 percent control. Any contrived division of the subsidiary accounts is, thus, avoided.

The Proportionate Consolidation Concept

The *proportionate consolidation concept* presumes that the ultimate objective of consolidated financial statements is to serve as a report to the stockholders of the parent company. These owners are perceived as being primarily interested in an accounting of parent company resources. Returning to the previous illustration, the accounting emphasis is placed on Big's $140,000 investment to acquire a 70 percent interest in Small.

Under proportionate consolidation, the values utilized for consolidation reflect the parent's payment attributed to each asset and liability. Big is paying for these assets and not for the company. Because 70 percent ownership has been acquired, that percentage of every account's fair market value at the date of purchase forms the basis for consolidated figures. If, for example, Small owns land with a book value of $8,000 but a fair market value of $10,000, a $7,000 component of the price (70 percent of fair market value) is said to have been Big's cost incurred in connection with this asset.

Under proportionate consolidation, goodwill of $49,000 is recognized: the amount of the purchase price in excess of the appropriate portion of the net assets' fair market value.

Proportionate Consolidation Concept

Purchase price	$140,000
Fair market value assigned to Small's accounts ($130,000 × 70%)	91,000
Cost in excess of fair market value—goodwill	$ 49,000
Noncontrolling interest	–0–

Although goodwill is computed here as a residual cost element, a more consistent view of proportionate consolidation is that this figure represents 70 percent of the subsidiary's total goodwill. As shown in the previous section, a goodwill figure of $70,000 is appropriate for the subsidiary as a whole (the $200,000 implied value of the company less the $130,000 market value of its net assets). Thus, the portion of this goodwill that is applicable to Big's investment is $49,000 ($70,000 × 70%).

A unique feature of proportionate consolidation is the reporting of the noncontrolling interest; these outside owners are totally ignored in consolidated statements. Proponents of this theory hold that the presence of a noncontrolling interest is irrelevant to the stockholders of the parent company. An outside owner of a subsidiary has no capital invested in the parent company; furthermore, the parent has no legal obligation to this group. Thus, including any type of balance within consolidated financial statements to reflect a noncontrolling interest is viewed as serving no purpose.

Before leaving this discussion of proportionate consolidation, a quick extension of this concept can be made to income statement reporting. Not surprisingly, Big Company includes 70 percent of each of the subsidiary's revenue and expense accounts in the consolidated balances while showing no amount of the income total as associated with the noncontrolling interest. Within the framework of proportionate consolidation, this presentation is consistent. The parent's ownership entitles it to accrue only 70 percent of the subsidiary's income; the remaining 30 percent is applicable to outside owners. Any recording of this 30 percent share of Small's net income has no apparent relevance to the owners of Big Company.

In actual practice, little evidence exists to indicate significant usage of proportionate consolidation. Although omitting any mention of outside stockholders may be appealing, the division of each subsidiary account based on the ownership percentage is hard to justify. The parent has achieved control over all assets and liabilities, not just a 70 percent interest of each. However, this concept has recently gained some support for use in cases where control is present without majority ownership. As discussed in Chapter 2, a parent may effectively control a subsidiary although holding only 50 percent or even less of the outstanding voting stock. Proponents argue that proportionate consolidation would be a better reflection of the relationship between the two companies than the equity method that is currently required.

The Parent Company Concept

The *parent company concept* is sometimes viewed as a hybrid method because it incorporates a mixture of the assumptions found in the economic unit concept and proportionate consolidation. Two fundamental assertions underlie this approach to consolidation valuation:

1. Holding control of a subsidiary provides the parent with an indivisible interest in that company. This statement is clearly derived from the economic unit concept.

2. Consolidated financial statements are produced primarily for the benefit of parent company stockholders. This idea is, of course, the basic argument used to substantiate proportionate consolidation.

Both of the assertions attributed to the parent company concept appear to have merit. However, as shown in the previous sections, they lead to radically differing sets of consolidated financial statements: one based on the implied value of the entire subsidiary and the other on the cost incurred in a partial acquisition. The parent company approach combines both of these ideas in valuing the consolidated enterprise. The subsidiary's book value and the purchase price paid by the parent are viewed as separate elements that can be accounted for individually within the consolidation process.

The book value of each subsidiary asset and liability is presumed to be indivisible and, therefore, not subject to an artificial allocation because of the specific level of ownership. Conversely, differences between the market value and underlying book value of these same accounts are only recognized because of the purchase price paid by the parent. Thus, if the parent acquires less than 100 percent of the subsidiary's voting stock, allocations attributed to individual accounts at the date of purchase should be based on the resulting ownership percentage. *The subsidiary's book value is consolidated in total along the lines of the economic unit concept whereas any cost in excess of book value is assumed to be a parent company expenditure appropriately allocated as indicated by the proportionate consolidation.*

Returning to Big's acquisition of Small, the appropriate consolidation values to be assigned under the parent company concept are computed as follows:

Parent Company Concept

Purchase price		$140,000
Book value of Small (100%)	$110,000	
Less: Recognition of noncontrolling interest (30%)	(33,000)	(77,000)
Cost in excess of underlying book value		63,000
Allocation based on fair market value in excess of book value ($130,000 − $110,000) × 70%		(14,000)
Goodwill		$ 49,000

The parent company concept includes the entire book value of each of Small's accounts within the consolidated statements but only 70 percent of the difference between fair market value and book value. Proponents justify this approach by pointing out that the subsidiary's cost figures are not affected by the parent's purchase and, therefore, should be consolidated in total. In contrast, the various allocations result solely from the price paid by the parent in a transaction negotiated to acquire 70 percent ownership. Thus, the investment is assumed to reflect only 70 percent of the change in the value of individual accounts.

As a practical example, Small's land, with an $8,000 cost but a fair market value of $10,000, is consolidated at a $9,400 balance: the entire $8,000 book value plus 70 percent of the $2,000 increase in its worth ($10,000 − $8,000). The subsidiary originally expended $8,000 for this land and the parent has now paid an additional $1,400 within the purchase price as a reflection of this change in value. Thus, to the business combination, the land's cost totals $9,400.

In the valuation schedule presented earlier, a noncontrolling interest of $33,000 is computed on the basis of Small's $110,000 book value rather than on either the fair market value of the net assets or the implied worth of the company taken as a whole. Under the parent company concept, only the book value of the subsidiary's accounts is consolidated in total. Although Big holds just 70 percent ownership, 100 percent of each book value is brought into the consolidation. Consequently, the presence of a noncontrolling interest equivalent to 30 percent of that particular total must also be recognized. The payment made by Big in excess of book value, however, has no impact on the remaining outside owners and is not included in this calculation.

Some amount of disagreement exists among the users of the parent company concept as to the appropriate placement of the noncontrolling interest figure within the consolidated balance sheet. Arguments can be made for showing the balance as either a liability or an equity. However, proponents of this theory are most likely to isolate the noncontrolling interest between liabilities and stockholders' equity.

> The parent company concept views the consolidated financial statements as those of the parent—with the assets, liabilities, revenues, and expenses of the subsidiary merely substituting for the parent's investment on the balance sheet. . . . From that perspective, the noncontrolling (minority) interest is not a liability because the parent does not have a present obligation to pay cash or other assets. Nor does it appear to be owners' equity from a parent company perspective because the noncontrolling investors in a subsidiary do not have an ownership interest in the subsidiary's parent. . . . Thus, the parent company concept generally reports noncontrolling interest below liabilities but above stockholders' equity in consolidated statements.[7]

Currently, in practice, the appropriate placement of a noncontrolling interest balance remains an unresolved question. *Statement of Financial Accounting Concepts No. 6 (SFAC 6)*, "Elements of Financial Statements," issued in December of 1985 by the FASB recommends inclusion within equity (par. 254):

> Minority interests in net assets of consolidated subsidiaries do not represent present obligations of the enterprise to pay cash or distribute other assets to minority stockholders. *Rather, those stockholders have ownership or residual interests in components of a consolidated enterprise.* The definitions in this Statement do not, of course, preclude showing minority interests separately from majority interests or preclude emphasizing the interests of majority stockholders for whom consolidated statements are primarily provided. Stock purchase warrants are also sometimes called liabilities but entirely lack the characteristics of liabilities. They also are part of equity. (emphasis added)

Consistent with the *SFAC 6* reasoning, in their 1995 Exposure Draft *Consolidated Financial Statements: Policy and Procedures*, the FASB recommends the following (paragraph 22):

> The aggregate amount of the noncontrolling interest in subsidiaries that are not wholly owned by the parent shall be reported in consolidated financial statements as a separate component of equity. That amount shall be appropriately labeled, for example, as *noncontrolling interest in subsidiaries,* to distinguish it from the components of equity attributable to the controlling interest.

Interestingly, *International Accounting Standard No. 27*, "Consolidated Financial Statements and Accounting for Investments in Subsidiaries," 1989 (par. 33), addresses this same issue as follows: "Minority interests should be presented in the consolidated balance sheet separately from liabilities and parent shareholders' equity." In contrast to *SFAC 6*, this statement rejects the classification of a noncontrolling interest as an equity figure. Placement between the liability and equity sections is recommended in the same manner as used by the parent company concept.

Obviously, disagreement continues to exist as to the appropriate location of this balance sheet item. Today, the placement of a noncontrolling interest continues to vary with the reporting entity. Many companies disclose this figure as a single balance appearing directly after noncurrent liabilities. No accumulated total is provided for liabilities or equities, so that the reader is forced to decide whether the noncon-

---

[7]FASB Discussion Memorandum, *An Analysis of Issues Related to Consolidation Policy and Procedures*, September 10, 1991, paragraphs 69 and 70.

What Decision Should the FASB Make?

Whenever the FASB is studying an accounting issue, the board always seems to get plenty of advice. In response to its discussion memorandum, "An Analysis of Issues Related to Consolidation Policy and Procedures," the FASB received more than 70 letters. A sampling of these letters includes the following recommendations:

M. R. Schools, Jr., Virginia Power: Virginia Power believes that accounting information prepared under the proportionate consolidation approach provides the most relevant accounting information because it includes the interests of only the parent company shareholders.

David K. Owens, Edison Electric Institute: We generally support the "Parent Company Concept" because it emphasizes the interests of the parent shareholders and is most consistent with current practice.

Richard G. Rademacher, Sara Lee Corporation: By purchasing a controlling interest in an entity, management obtains the control of 100 percent of all assets and liabilities. It does not control only a proportionate share of each asset (i. e., 70% of a building) and the value of an asset recorded in consolidation does not vary dependent upon the percentage of ownership obtained. Therefore, we strongly oppose the parent company and proportionate share concepts of consolidation.

J. Michael Kelly, GTE Corporation: GTE has consistently responded in support of the parent company concept. The thrust of our support stems from this concept's emphasis on the interests of the parent's shareholders.

P. J. Lynch, Texaco Inc.: It is Texaco's view that neither the economic unit nor the parent company concept can be applied exclusively to all the issues raised in the DM. Accordingly, any future promulgation concerning consolidation policy should be a hybrid of the two concepts.

Joseph J. Martin, IBM: While we take a parent's view of deciding when to consolidate, we generally favor an economic unit theory approach on the mechanics of consolidation and financial statement presentation.

John J. Mesloh, Pfizer Inc.: You may note that we favor the Parent Company view (which is consistent with our view of current written GAAP) of consolidation, as identified by the FASB. In short, we do not have too many issues with the current state of consolidation accounting.

What should the FASB decide to do?

trolling interest should be included in either classification or viewed as an item separate from both. Although this placement is often encountered in practice, no consensus currently exists as to the appropriate classification of this balance. However, if the FASB eventually takes action on consolidation policies and procedures, a specific location for the noncontrolling interest may well be required in the future.

In constructing a consolidated income statement, the parent company theory again demonstrates characteristics applicable to both the economic unit concept and proportionate consolidation. As with the economic unit concept, the book values of the various subsidiary accounts are included in total. Since these revenues and expenses are consolidated at 100 percent of their recorded balances, a 30 percent share of the subsidiary's net income is identified with the noncontrolling interest.

However, similar to proportionate consolidation, amortization is associated solely with the parent's investment because the allocations that create the expense result from the original payment. Consequently, amortization is not considered to have an impact on the calculation of noncontrolling interest. The additional cost is presumed to be that of the parent company and, thus, the expense is not directly related to the subsidiary's operations. For reporting purposes, the subsidiary's income is simply multiplied times the outside ownership percentage.

Under the parent company concept, the resulting noncontrolling interest figure has traditionally appeared as a reduction in arriving at consolidated net income. For example, following is the bottom portion of a typical income statement as reported by United Technologies:

UNITED TECHNOLOGIES CORPORATION
Year Ended December 31, 1996
(in millions)

Income before income taxes and minority interests	$1,560
Income taxes	523
Minority interests in subsidiaries' earnings	131
Net income	$ 906

As mentioned earlier, the FASB is currently studying valuation theories with the possibility that one concept may be mandated. Until that time, companies are free to select any approach and are not even required to disclose their choice. Although evidence is not readily available, the parent company concept is generally considered to be most commonly used in current practice. Therefore, except where noted, that concept is used throughout the remainder of this textbook. Knowledge of the alternatives is important, though; companies do apply these other approaches and their use may be promoted or required by the FASB in the future (see the appendix to this chapter).

Valuation Theories—Overview

To provide a complete illustration of these three concepts, assume that Anderson Company acquires 60 percent of the voting stock of Zebulon Company on January 1, 1998. Anderson purchases this interest for $360,000 in cash at a time when Zebulon's assets and liabilities have the following values:

	Book Value 1/1/98	Fair Market Value 1/1/98
Current assets less liabilities	$160,000	$160,000
Buildings and equipment (10-year life)	240,000	360,000
	$400,000	$520,000

Since Anderson's $360,000 payment was made to acquire 60 percent interest, Zebulon is apparently worth $600,000 when taken as a whole ($360,000/60 percent). In comparison to the $520,000 appraised value of the net assets, this implied value signifies *total* goodwill associated with Zebulon of $80,000. Any goodwill recognized by this business combination is assumed to be amortized over a life of 20 years.

Exhibit 4–1 presents alternative values that can be attributed to Zebulon's accounts on consolidated statements produced as of the date of acquisition. Quite obviously, differing figures are derived from each of the three valuation theories. The economic unit concept makes no division of any balance, whereas proportionate consolidation includes only 60 percent of subsidiary accounts because that portion represents the parent's ownership. The parent company concept adopts a compromise position: the book values of the subsidiary's assets and liabilities remain intact while all cost allocations (based on the difference in book values and fair market values) are computed using the parent's ownership percentage.

To carry this illustration to a natural conclusion, assume that Zebulon reports the following condensed income statement for the year of 1998:

Revenues	$400,000
Expenses	300,000
Net income	$100,000

These balances permit an examination of the totals to be included in the 1998 consolidated income statement. Exhibit 4–2 presents these figures, once again computed under each of the three theories described in this chapter. The economic unit concept consolidates all accounts and assumes that amortization expense relates to

E x h i b i t   4 – I   Valuation Theories in Practice—Balance Sheet

ANDERSON COMPANY AND ZEBULON COMPANY
Subsidiary Consolidation Figures
Balance Sheet
January 1, 1998

	Economic Unit Concept	Proportionate Consolidation Concept	Parent Company Concept
Current assets and liabilities:			
Book value	$160,000 (100%)	$ 96,000 (60%)	$160,000 (100%)
Allocation based on fair market value	–0–	–0–	–0–
Consolidated value	$160,000	$ 96,000	$160,000
Buildings and equipment:			
Book value	$240,000 (100%)	$144,000 (60%)	$240,000 (100%)
Allocation based on fair market value	120,000 (100%)	72,000 (60%)	72,000 (60%)
Consolidated value	$360,000	$216,000	$312,000
Goodwill*	$ 80,000 (100%)	$ 48,000 (60%)	$ 48,000 (60%)
Noncontrolling interest, 1/1/98	$240,000 (40% of implied value)*	–0–	$160,000 (40% of book value)
Annual amortization of allocations:			
Buildings and equipment (10-year life)	$ 12,000	$ 7,200	$ 7,200
Goodwill (20-year life)	4,000	2,400	2,400
Annual expense	$ 16,000	$ 9,600	$ 9,600

*Implied value of company is $600,000 ($360,000/60%) with the value of net assets only $520,000. Total goodwill is $80,000 ($600,000 – $520,000).

E x h i b i t   4 – 2   Valuation Theory in Practice—Income Statement

ANDERSON COMPANY AND ZEBULON COMPANY
Subsidiary Consolidation Figures
Income Statement
For Year Ending December 31, 1998

	Economic Unit Concept	Proportionate Consolidation Concept	Parent Company Concept
Revenues	$400,000 (100%)	$240,000 (60%)	$400,000 (100%)
Expenses	300,000 (100%)	180,000 (60%)	300,000 (100%)
Amortization expense (see Exhibit 4–1)	16,000	9,600	9,600
Noncontrolling interest in subsidiary's net income			40,000 (40% of subsidiary income, amortization not included)
Net effect on consolidated income	$ 84,000	$ 50,400	$ 50,400
Allocation of income:			
To controlling interest (60%)	$ 50,400		
To noncontrolling interest (40%)	$ 33,600		

the subsidiary. Proportionate consolidation includes only 60 percent of each revenue and expense and discloses no balance for the noncontrolling interest. The parent company concept recognizes all of the subsidiary's income statement accounts but attributes amortization to the parent so that the noncontrolling interest is not affected.

CONSOLIDATIONS INVOLVING A NONCONTROLLING INTEREST—SUBSEQUENT TO ACQUISITION

Having reviewed the basic philosophies of each of these three theories, this textbook now concentrates on the mechanical aspects of the consolidation process when an outside ownership is present. More specifically, consolidations for time periods subsequent to the date of acquisition are examined to analyze the full range of accounting complexities created by a noncontrolling interest. As indicated previously, this discussion centers on the parent company concept because it appears to be the most prevalent method in practice.

Computation of Noncontrolling Interest Balances

The presence of a noncontrolling interest does not dramatically alter the consolidation procedures demonstrated in Chapter 3. The unamortized balance of each purchase price allocation (as well as any goodwill or deferred credit) must still be computed and included within the consolidated totals. Amortization is recognized each year on these allocations. Reciprocal balances are eliminated.

Beyond these basic steps, the valuation and recognition of four noncontrolling interest balances add a new dimension to the process of consolidating financial information. The accountant must determine and then enter each of these figures when constructing a worksheet:

■ (1) Noncontrolling interest in the subsidiary as of the beginning of the current year.
■ (2) Noncontrolling interest in the subsidiary's current year income.
■ (3) Noncontrolling interest in the subsidiary's dividend payments.
■ (4) Noncontrolling interest as of the end of the year (found by combining the three balances above).

To illustrate, assume that King Company acquires 80 percent of the outstanding stock of Pawn Company on January 1, 1998, for $960,000 in cash. The combination is to be accounted for as a purchase. King makes an additional $20,000 payment to lawyers, accountants, and appraisers to cover the direct costs associated with this acquisition. Exhibit 4–3 presents the book value of Pawn's accounts as well as the fair market value of each asset and liability on the date of purchase.

Exhibit 4–3
Subsidiary Accounts—Date of Acquisition

PAWN COMPANY
Account Balances
January 1, 1998

	Book Value	Fair Market Value	Differences
Current Assets	$ 440,000	$ 440,000	–0–
Land	260,000	320,000	+$ 60,000
Buildings (20-year life)	480,000	600,000	+ 120,000
Equipment (10-year life)	110,000	100,000	(10,000)
Long-Term Liabilities (8-year maturity)	(550,000)	(510,000)	+ 40,000
Net Assets	$ 740,000	$ 950,000	+$210,000
Common Stock	$(230,000)		
Retained Earnings, 1/1/98	(510,000)		

Note: Parentheses indicate a credit balance.

Exhibit 4 – 4

KING COMPANY AND PAWN COMPANY			
Purchase Price Allocation and Amortization			
January 1, 1998			
	Allocation	**Estimated Life (years)**	**Annual Amortization**
Purchase price paid by King Company	$ 980,000		
80% of subsidiary book value ($740,000)			
(King Company's ownership)*	592,000		
Cost in excess of book value	388,000		
Allocation to specific accounts based on difference between fair market value and book value:			
Land ($60,000 × 80%)	48,000		
Buildings ($120,000 × 80%)	96,000	20	4,800
Equipment ($10,000 × 80%)	(8,000)	10	(800)
Long-term liabilities ($40,000 × 80%)	32,000	8	4,000
Goodwill	$ 220,000	40	5,500
Annual amortization (initial years)			$13,500

*The parent company concept consolidates 100 percent of all asset and liability book values but also records an offsetting noncontrolling interest of 20 percent. The net effect is equal to 80 percent of the subsidiary's book value.

Including direct consolidation costs, King's payment totals $980,000. This purchase price is attributed to Pawn's accounts as shown in Exhibit 4–4. Annual amortization relating to these allocations also is included in this schedule. Although expense figures are computed for only the initial years, some amount of amortization is recognized in each of the 40 years following the acquisition (since that life is assumed for the goodwill).

Assume that consolidated financial statements are to be produced for the year ending December 31, 1999. This date was chosen arbitrarily. Any time period subsequent to 1998 could have served to demonstrate the applicable consolidation procedures. Having already calculated the purchase price allocations and related amortization, the consolidation of these two companies can be constructed along the lines demonstrated in Chapter 3. Only the presence of the 20 percent noncontrolling interest alters the previously explained process.

To complete the information needed for this combination, assume that Pawn Company reports the following changes in book value since King's acquisition:

Current year (1999)	
Net income	$ 90,000
Less: Dividends paid	(50,000)
Increase in book value	$ 40,000
Prior years (only 1998 in this illustration):	
Increase in book value	$ 70,000

Assuming that King Company has applied the equity method, the Investment in Pawn Company account as of December 31, 1999, can be constructed as shown in Exhibit 4–5.

Exhibit 4–6 presents the separate financial statements for these two companies as of December 31, 1999, and the year then ended based on the information provided.

Consolidated Totals   Although the inclusion of a 20 percent outside ownership complicates the consolidation process, the 1999 totals to be reported by this business combination can still be determined without the use of a worksheet:

Exhibit 4-5

KING COMPANY
Investment in Pawn Company
Equity Method
December 31, 1999

Purchase price		$ 980,000
Prior year (1998):		
Increase in book value (80% × $70,000)	$ 56,000	
Amortization expense (Exhibit 4–4)	(13,500)	42,500
Current year (1999):		
Income accrual (80% × $90,000)	72,000	
Amortization expense (Exhibit 4–4)	(13,500)	
Equity in subsidiary earnings	58,500*	
Dividends received (80% × $50,000)	(40,000)	18,500
Balance, 12/31/99		$1,041,000

*This figure appears in King's 1999 income statement.

Exhibit 4-6

KING COMPANY AND PAWN COMPANY
Separate Financial Statements
For December 31, 1999 and the Year Then Ended

	King	Pawn
Revenues	$ 910,000	$ 430,000
Expenses	(580,000)	(340,000)
Equity in subsidiary earnings (see Exhibit 4–5)	58,500	–0–
Net income	$ 388,500	$ 90,000
Retained earnings, 1/1/99	$ 876,100	$ 580,000
Net income (above)	388,500	90,000
Dividends paid	(60,000)	(50,000)
Retained earnings, 12/31/99	$1,204,600	$ 620,000
Current assets	$ 626,000	$ 445,000
Land	298,000	295,000
Buildings (net)	880,000	540,000
Equipment (net)	290,000	160,000
Investment in Pawn Company (see Exhibit 4–5)	1,041,000	–0–
Total assets	$3,135,000	$1,440,000
Long-term liabilities	$1,080,400	$ 590,000
Common stock	850,000	230,000
Retained earnings, 12/31/99	1,204,600	620,000
Total liabilities and equities	$3,135,000	$1,440,000

- *Revenues* = $1,340,000. The revenues of the parent and the subsidiary are added together. Under the parent company concept, the subsidiary's book value is included in total although only 80 percent of the stock is owned by King.

- *Expenses* = $933,500. The expenses of the parent and the subsidiary are added together along with the $13,500 amortization expense for the year indicated in Exhibit 4–4.

- *Equity in subsidiary earnings* = –0–. The investment income recorded by the parent is eliminated so that the subsidiary's revenues and expenses can be included in the consolidated totals.

- *Noncontrolling interest in subsidiary's income* = $18,000. The outside owners are assigned 20 percent of Pawn's reported income of $90,000. According to the parent company concept, that amount is shown as a reduction within the consolidated income statement.

- *Net income* = $388,500. Both consolidated expenses and the amount allocated to the noncontrolling interest are subtracted from consolidated revenues.

- *Retained earnings, 1/1/99* = $876,100. The parent company figure equals the consolidated total since the equity method was applied. If the cost method or the partial equity method had been used, the parent's balance would require adjustment to include any omitted figures.

- *Dividends paid* = $60,000. Only the parent company balance is reported. Part of the subsidiary's payments (80 percent) were intercompany to the parent and are eliminated. The remaining distribution was made to the outside owners and serves to reduce the balance attributed to them.

- *Retained earnings, 12/31/99* = $1,204,600. Balance is found by adding consolidated net income to the beginning retained earnings balance and then subtracting the consolidated dividends paid. Since the equity method was utilized, the parent company figure reflects the total for the business combination.

- *Current assets* = $1,071,000. The parent's book value is added to the subsidiary's book value.

- *Land* = $641,000. The parent's book value is added to the subsidiary's book value plus the $48,000 allocation within the purchase price (see Exhibit 4–4).

- *Buildings* = $1,506,400. The parent's book value is added to the subsidiary's book value plus the $96,000 allocation within the purchase price less 1998 and 1999 amortization of $4,800 per year (see Exhibit 4–4).

- *Equipment* = $443,600. The parent's book value is added to the subsidiary's book value less the $8,000 cost reduction allocation plus the 1998 and 1999 expense reduction of $800 per year (see Exhibit 4–4).

- *Investment in Pawn Company* = –0–. The balance reported by the parent is eliminated so that the subsidiary's assets and liabilities can be included in the consolidated totals.

- *Goodwill* = $209,000. The residual allocation shown in Exhibit 4–4 is reported after subtracting 1998 and 1999 amortization of $5,500 per year.

- *Total assets* = $3,871,000. This balance is a summation of the consolidated assets.

- *Long-term liabilities* = $1,646,400. The parent's book value is added to the subsidiary's book value less the $32,000 allocation within the purchase price plus 1998 and 1999 amortization of $4,000 per year (see Exhibit 4–4).

- *Noncontrolling interest in subsidiary* = $170,000. The outside ownership is 20 percent of the subsidiary's year-end book value (common stock plus ending retained earnings) of $850,000. This $170,000 total can also be calculated as follows:

Noncontrolling interest at 1/1/99 (20 percent of $810,000 beginning book value—common stock plus 1/1/99 retained earnings)	$162,000
Noncontrolling interest in subsidiary's income (computed above)	18,000
Dividends paid to noncontrolling interest (20 percent of $50,000 total)	(10,000)
Noncontrolling interest at 12/31/99	$170,000

- *Common stock* = $850,000. Only the parent's book value is reported since this combination is a purchase.

- *Retained earnings, 12/31/99* = $1,204,600. Computed above.

- *Total liabilities and equities* = $3,871,000. This total is a summation of consolidated liabilities, noncontrolling interest, and equities.

Worksheet Process   The consolidated totals for King and Pawn also can be determined by means of a worksheet as shown in Exhibit 4–7. A comparison of the

Exhibit 4–7 Noncontrolling Interest Illustrated

Consolidation: Purchase Method
Investment: Equity Method

Ownership: 80%

KING COMPANY AND PAWN COMPANY
Consolidation Worksheet
For Year Ending December 31, 1999

Accounts	King* Company	Pawn* Company	Consolidation Entries Debit	Consolidation Entries Credit	Noncontrolling Interest	Consolidated Totals
Income Statement						
Revenues	(910,000)	(430,000)				(1,340,000)
Expenses	580,000	340,000	(E) 13,500			933,500
Equity in subsidiary earnings	(58,500)	-0-	(I) 58,500			-0-
Noncontrolling interest in Pawn					(18,000)	18,000
Company's income						
Net income	(388,500)	(90,000)				(388,500)
Statement of Retained Earnings						
Retained earnings, 1/1/99:						
King Company	(876,100)					(876,100)
Pawn Company		(580,000)	(S) 580,000			-0-
Net income (above)	(388,500)	(90,000)				(388,500)
Dividends paid	60,000	50,000		(D) 40,000	10,000	60,000
Retained earnings, 12/31/99	(1,204,600)	(620,000)				(1,204,600)

(Handwritten annotations in margin near Noncontrolling Interest and Credit columns: "400,000", "2000 by Pawn Co", "400 x 20% total Pawn paid 400 x 20%")

Balance Sheet

			Debits	Credits	Noncontrolling Interest	Consolidated
Current assets	626,000	445,000				1,071,000
Land	298,000	295,000	(A) 48,000			641,000
Buildings (net)	880,000	540,000	(A) 91,200			1,506,400
Equipment (net)	290,000	160,000	(E) 800 (D) 40,000			443,600
Investment in Pawn Company	1,041,000	-0-		(E) 4,800 (A) 7,200 (S) 648,000 (A) 374,500 (I) 58,500		-0-
Goodwill	-0-	-0-	(A) 214,500	(E) 5,500		209,000
Total assets	3,135,000	1,440,000				3,871,000
Long-term liabilities	(1,080,400)	(590,000)	(A) 28,000			(1,646,400)
Noncontrolling interest in Pawn Company, 1/1/99	-0-	-0-		(E) 4,000 (S) 162,000	(162,000)	
Noncontrolling interest in Pawn Company, 12/31/99	-0-	-0-			(170,000)	(170,000)
Common stock	(850,000)	(230,000)	(S) 230,000			(850,000)
Retained earnings, 12/31/99 (above)	(1,204,600)	(620,000)				(1,204,600)
Total liabilities and equities	(3,135,000)	(1,440,000)				(3,871,000)

*See Exhibit 4–6.

Note: Parentheses indicate a credit balance.

Consolidation entries:
(S) Elimination of subsidiary's stockholders' equity accounts along with recognition of January 1, 1999, noncontrolling interest.
(A) Allocation of parent's cost in excess of subsidiary's book value, unamortized balances as of January 1, 1999.
(I) Elimination of intercompany income (equity accrual less amortization expense).
(D) Elimination of intercompany dividend payments.
(E) Recognition of amortization expense on purchase price allocations.

[handwritten notes in margin: "parent owned"; "90000 × 80% − 1500"; "102000 / 71,000 / 70000 = 170,000"; "credit invest in sub f/v 90 owned"; "subs NI × % owned"]

worksheet entries made in this example with the entries incorporated in Chapter 3 (Exhibit 3–7) indicates that the presence of a noncontrolling interest does not create a significant number of changes in the consolidation procedures.

The worksheet still includes elimination of the subsidiary's stockholders' equity accounts (Entry S) although, as explained next, this entry is expanded to record the beginning noncontrolling interest for the year. The second worksheet entry recognizes the purchase price allocations at January 1 after one year of amortization (Entry A). Intercompany income as well as dividend payments are removed also (Entries I and D), while current year amortization expense is recorded (Entry E). The differences that can be cited with illustrations in the previous chapter relate exclusively to the recognition of four noncontrolling interest balances. In addition, *a separate Noncontrolling Interest column is added to the worksheet to accumulate the components that form the year-end figure to be reported on the consolidated balance sheet.*

Noncontrolling Interest—Beginning of Year   As discussed previously, Pawn's stockholders' equity accounts (common stock and beginning retained earnings) indicate a January 1, 1999, book value of $810,000. Thus, the 20 percent outside ownership is valued at $162,000 ($810,000 × 20 percent) as of the first day of the current year. This balance is recorded on the worksheet by means of Entry S:

Consolidation Entry S

Common Stock (Pawn)	230,000	
Retained Earnings, 1/1/99 (Pawn)	580,000	
Investment in Pawn Company (80%)		648,000
Noncontrolling Interest in Subsidiary, 1/1/99 (20%)		162,000
To eliminate beginning stockholders' equity accounts of		
subsidiary along with book value portion of investment (equal		
to 80 percent ownership). Noncontrolling interest of 20 percent		
is also recognized.		

The $162,000 balance assigned here to the outside owners at the beginning of the year is extended on the worksheet into the Noncontrolling Interest column (see Exhibit 4–7).

Noncontrolling Interest—Current Year Income   Exhibit 4–2 indicates that the parent company concept calculates the noncontrolling interest's share of current year earnings based on the subsidiary's income without regard for amortization. Thus, Pawn's 1999 earnings of $90,000 necessitate an assignment of $18,000 (20 percent) to the outside owners. This figure is shown as a reduction in arriving at consolidated net income. In effect, 100 percent of each subsidiary revenue and expense account is consolidated with an accompanying 20 percent decrease to reflect the presence of the noncontrolling interest. The 80 percent net effect corresponds to King's ownership.

Because this $18,000 portion of consolidated income is viewed as accruing to the noncontrolling interest, an increase is necessary in the $162,000 beginning balance assigned (in Entry S) to these outside owners. The amount attributed to the noncontrolling interest is raised because the subsidiary generated a profit during the period.

Although this allocation could be recorded on the worksheet through an additional entry, the $18,000 is usually shown, as in Exhibit 4–7, by means of a columnar adjustment. The current year accrual is simultaneously entered in the consolidated Income Statement column as a *reduction* and in the Noncontrolling Interest column as an *increase*. This procedure indicates that a portion of the earnings included in the consolidated figures must be assigned to the outside owners rather than to the business combination.

Noncontrolling Interest—Dividend Payments   The $40,000 dividend that went to the parent company is eliminated routinely through Entry D, but the remainder of Pawn's dividend was paid to noncontrolling interest. The impact of the dividend (20 percent of the subsidiary's total payment) distributed to the other owners must be acknowledged. As shown in Exhibit 4–7, this remaining $10,000 is extended directly into the Noncontrolling Interest column on the worksheet as a reduction. It represents the drop in the underlying book value of the outside ownership that resulted from the subsidiary's asset distribution.

Noncontrolling Interest—End of Year The ending assignment for these other owners is calculated by a summation of

1. The beginning balance for the year ($162,000).
2. Plus the appropriate share of the subsidiary's current income ($18,000).
3. Less the dividends paid to the outside owners ($10,000).

The Noncontrolling Interest column on the worksheet in Exhibit 4–7 accumulates these figures. The $170,000 total is then transferred to the balance sheet where it appears in the consolidated statements.

Consolidated Financial Statements Having successfully consolidated the information for King and Pawn, the resulting financial statements for these two companies is produced in Exhibit 4–8. These figures can be computed directly or can be taken from the consolidation worksheet.

Exhibit 4–8
Consolidated Statements with Noncontrolling Interest

KING COMPANY AND CONSOLIDATED SUBSIDIARY
Income Statement
For Year Ending December 31, 1999

Revenues	$1,340,000
Expenses	(933,500)
Noncontrolling interest in subsidiary's income	(18,000)
Consolidated net income	$ 388,500

KING COMPANY AND CONSOLIDATED SUBSIDIARY
Statement of Retained Earnings
For Year Ending December 31, 1999

Retained earnings, January 1, 1999	$ 876,100
Consolidated net income	388,500
Less: Dividends paid	(60,000)
Retained earnings, December 31, 1999	$1,204,600

KING COMPANY AND CONSOLIDATED SUBSIDIARY
Balance Sheet
December 31, 1999

Assets

Current assets	$1,071,000
Land	641,000
Buildings (net)	1,506,400
Equipment (net)	443,600
Goodwill	209,000
Total assets	$3,871,000

Liabilities and Equities

Long-term liabilities	$1,646,400
Noncontrolling interest in subsidiary	170,000
Common stock—King Company	850,000
Retained earnings (above)	1,204,600
Total liabilities and equities	$3,871,000

Effects Created by Alternative Investment Methods

One final aspect of the accounting for a noncontrolling interest needs to be explored. In the King and Pawn illustration, the equity method was utilized by the parent, with all worksheet entries based on that approach. As discussed in Chapter 3, had King incorporated either the cost method or the partial equity method, a few specific changes in the consolidation process would be required although the reported figures are not affected.

Cost Method   As in Chapter 3, two balances are omitted by the parent if the cost method is applied. First, dividend income is recognized rather than an equity income accrual. Thus, the parent fails to accrue the percentage of the subsidiary's income earned in past years in excess of dividends (the increase in book value). Second, amortization expense is not recorded under the cost method and must also be included in the consolidation process if proper totals are to be achieved. Because neither of these figures is recognized in applying the cost method, an Entry *C is added to the worksheet to convert the previously recorded balances to the equity method. The parent's beginning retained earnings is affected by this adjustment as well as the Investment in Subsidiary account. The exact amount is computed as follows.

Conversion to Equity Method from Cost Method (Entry *C)   Combine:

1. The increase during past years since acquisition in the subsidiary's book value (income less dividends) times the parent's ownership percentage.
2. Total amortization expense for these same past years.

One other procedural change is required when the cost method is in use. Since no equity income accrual is recognized, only dividends received from the subsidiary are recorded by the parent as income. Entry I is used on the worksheet to remove this intercompany income. Because the dividends are eliminated in this manner, no Entry D is required.

Partial Equity Method   Again, an Entry *C is needed to convert the parent's retained earnings as of January 1, 1999, to the equity method. In this case, however, only the amortization expense for the prior years must be included. Under the partial equity method, the income accrual is appropriately recognized each period by the parent company so that no further adjustment is necessary.

STEP ACQUISITIONS

The 1996 annual report of Edison Mission Energy describes the creation of a business combination through a series of separate purchases:

> In January, we increased our ownership of Iberian Hy-Power Amsterdam B.V. from 34 percent to 100 percent. Iberian Hy-Power owns 18 run-of-the-river hydroelectric plants that have provided clean, efficient power to the people of Spain for many years.

In all previous consolidation illustrations, control over a subsidiary was assumed to have been achieved through a single transaction. Obviously, Edison Mission's takeover of Iberian Hy-Power shows that a combination also may be the result of a series of stock purchases. These step acquisitions further complicate the consolidation process. The financial information of the separate companies must still be brought together, but no single purchase price exists. How do the initial acquisitions affect this process?

> If a parent-subsidiary relationship is established in a step acquisition, a problem arises that does not exist if the parent-subsidiary relationship is established in a single transaction. *That*

problem is how to include in consolidated financial statements the portion of the parent's interest in the subsidiary that was purchased prior to the date the parent-subsidiary relationship is established. (emphasis added)[8]

For example, in consolidating the accounts of Iberian Hy-Power, the values to be reported could vary significantly depending on Edison Mission's handling of the 34 percent ownership that it held prior to gaining control.

Step Acquisitions—Parent Company Concept

Under the parent company concept, each investment is viewed as an individual purchase (sometimes referred to as a *layer*) with its own cost allocations and related amortization. To illustrate, assume that Art Company purchases 30 percent of Zip Company on January 1, 1998, for $164,000 in cash. As of the date of this acquisition, Zip is reporting a net book value of $400,000.

Assuming that Art has gained the ability to significantly influence the decision-making process of Zip, this investment, for external reporting purposes, is accounted for by means of the equity method as discussed in Chapter 1. Thus, Art must determine any allocations and amortization associated with its purchase price (see Exhibit 4–9). Goodwill is assumed here to represent all excess payments and to have the maximum possible life.

As discussed previously, application of the equity method requires the immediate accrual of investee income by the parent while any dividends received are recorded as a decrease in the Investment account. Art must also reduce both the income and asset balances in recognition of the annual $1,100 amortization indicated in Exhibit 4–9. If, over the next two years, Zip reports a total of $140,000 in net income and pays dividends of $40,000, the subsidiary's book value rises from $400,000 to $500,000. At the same time, the parent's investment account grows to $191,800:

Purchase Price—1/1/98	$164,000
Accrual of 1998–99 Equity Income ($140,000 × 30 percent)	42,000
Dividends Received 1998–99 ($40,000 × 30%)	(12,000)
Amortization ($1,100 per year for 2 years)	(2,200)
Investment in Zip, 12/31/99	$191,800

On January 1, 2000, Art's ownership is raised to 80 percent by the purchase of another 50 percent of the outstanding common stock of Zip Company for $350,000. Although the equity method can still be utilized for internal reporting, this second purchase necessitates the preparation of consolidated financial statements beginning in 2000. Art now controls Zip; the two companies should be viewed as a single economic entity for external reporting purposes.

Exhibit 4–9
Allocation of First Purchase

ART COMPANY AND ZIP COMPANY
Purchase Price Allocation and Amortization
January 1, 1998

Purchase price	$ 164,000
Book value equivalent of Art's ownership ($400,000 × 30%)	(120,000)
Goodwill	$ 44,000
Maximum life	40 years
Annual amortization expense	$ 1,100

---

[8]FASB, *An Analysis of Issues Related to Consolidation Policy and Procedures*, paragraph 289.

Exhibit 4–10
Allocation of Second
Purchase

ART COMPANY AND ZIP COMPANY	
Purchase Price Allocation and Amortization	
January 1, 2000	
Purchase price	$ 350,000
Book value equivalent of Art's ownership ($500,000 × 50%)	(250,000)
Goodwill	$ 100,000
Maximum life	40 years
Annual amortization expense	$ 2,500

Before computing any consolidated balances, Art must make a separate cost allocation for this second purchase (Exhibit 4–10). This schedule does not supersede the allocation made in Exhibit 4–9 but merely supplements it for the price paid in acquiring the 50 percent block of Zip's stock.

Worksheet Consolidation for a Step Acquisition

To complete this example, assume that the subsidiary earns $100,000 in net income during 2000 and distributes $20,000 as a cash dividend. If the parent company continues applying the equity method to this investment, Art reports an Equity in Subsidiary Earnings balance of $76,400 for 2000 and an Investment in Zip Company of $602,200:

Investment in Zip, 12/31/99 (computed above)		$191,800
January 1, 2000—Second Acquisition		350,000
Dividends Received—2000 ($20,000 × 80%)		(16,000)
Equity Income Accrual—2000 ($100,000 × 80%)	$80,000	
2000 Amortization: First Purchase (Exhibit 4–9)	(1,100)	
Second Purchase (Exhibit 4–10)	(2,500)	76,400
Investment in Zip, 12/31/00		$602,200

Once both investment balances have been determined, the worksheet shown in Exhibit 4–11 can be developed. Although this step acquisition might appear to be more complex than a single purchase, the actual consolidation process is the same as in previous examples.

■ No conversion to the equity method (Entry *C) is required since that method has been applied by the parent. If a different approach were used, amortization expense for prior years would have to be recognized along with, possibly, the proportionate increase in the subsidiary's book value for this same period.

■ The stockholders' equity accounts of Zip are removed through Entry S. This worksheet entry also establishes the $100,000 beginning balance for the 20 percent noncontrolling interest that still remains (20 percent multiplied by the $500,000 stockholders' equity as of January 1, 2000).

■ The unamortized purchase price allocations are brought into the consolidation through Entry A. To avoid confusion, two figures are entered on the worksheet for goodwill. The $44,000 balance resulting from the first transaction has already undergone two years of amortization. Thus, only a cost of $41,800 remains at the beginning of the current period. Since the second allocation ($100,000) was made on January 1 of the current year, no expense has been recorded in prior years.

■ Entry I on the worksheet eliminates the $76,400 equity income accrual calculated above.

■ Entry D removes the $16,000 intercompany dividend paid to the parent in 2000. The remaining 20 percent ($4,000) was paid to the outside owners.

Thus, that amount is extended to the Noncontrolling Interest column on the worksheet as a reduction.

■ The final consolidation entry (Entry E) recognizes amortization for the current period. Again, two amounts are shown here for clarification because two separate purchases were made.

■ The noncontrolling interest balances to be reported on the income statement and balance sheet must be computed before the worksheet can be completed. Since Art now holds 80 percent of Zip, the outside owner's share of the subsidiary's income is 20 percent of the $100,000 reported earnings (or $20,000). Once again, this assignment is recorded on the worksheet through a columnar entry: the Noncontrolling Interest column is increased by that amount with a parallel decrease to consolidated net income.

For the balance sheet, the ending amount applicable to these outside owners is determined within the Noncontrolling Interest column: assigned income of $20,000 is added to the $100,000 beginning balance with dividends of $4,000 being subtracted. The $116,000 total then is reported on the balance sheet between the liabilities and stockholders' equity.

Retroactive Treatment Created by Step Acquisition

Because the initial 30 percent acquisition gave Art the ability to maintain significant influence over Zip, the investment balances in 1998 and 1999 were recorded using the equity method. For external reporting, the subsidiary's operations as well as related amortization were accounted for in those years in a manner that parallels the consolidation process. Thus, financial statements prepared and distributed by Art in 1998 and 1999 are considered comparable with the consolidated statements produced for 2000. Consequently, no retroactive adjustment of the earlier figures is required by Art's change in the method of reporting its investment in Zip.

Conversely, if Art had originally secured only a small percentage of Zip's shares (achieving less than significant influence), the market-value method would have been applied during 1998 and 1999. Under this approach, except for amounts received in the form of dividends, subsidiary income is ignored by the owner as is the recording of any amortization. However, gaining control of Zip in 2000 necessitates a transformation to consolidated statements, a change that strains the comparability of the results reported in the earlier years. Thus, to establish a proper degree of consistency, both the investment and income accounts are restated by the parent as if the equity method had been utilized from the date of the first acquisition.

ARB 51 (par. 9) does allow one exception to this restatement policy by indicating that "if small purchases are made over a period of time and then a purchase is made which results in control, the date of the latest purchase, as a matter of convenience, may be considered as the date of acquisition." Therefore, retroactive adjustment is not required when initial acquisition levels are relatively small. The ARB apparently felt that the difficulties encountered in restating such minor amounts outweighed the benefits derived from establishing comparability.

Step Acquisitions—Economic Unit Concept

Although this textbook primarily uses the parent company concept for illustration purposes, comparison with the economic unit concept demonstrates significant differences. Because the FASB is studying the issue of consolidation policies, one method or the other might eventually be mandated or an entirely new approach could be required. The economic unit concept, in particular, has received much attention (see the appendix to this chapter).

Exhibit 4-11   Step Acquisition Illustrated

Consolidation: Purchase Method
Investment: Equity Method

ART COMPANY AND ZIP COMPANY
Consolidation Worksheet
For Year Ending December 31, 2000

Accounts	Art Company	Zip Company	Consolidation Entries Debit	Consolidation Entries Credit	Noncontrolling Interest	Consolidated Totals
Income Statement						
Revenues	(600,000)	(260,000)				(860,000)
Expenses	425,000	160,000	(E) 3,600			588,600
Equity in subsidiary earnings	(76,400)	–0–	(I) 76,400			–0–
Noncontrolling interest in Zip						
Company's income	–0–	–0–			(20,000)	20,000
Net income	(251,400)	(100,000)				(251,400)
Statement of Retained Earnings						
Retained earnings, 1/1/00:						
Art Company	(760,000)					(760,000)
Zip Company		(230,000)	(S) 230,000			
Net income (above)	(251,400)	(100,000)				(251,400)
Dividends paid	126,400	20,000		(D) 16,000	4,000	126,400
Retained earnings, 12/31/00	(885,000)	(310,000)				(885,000)

Balance Sheet

Current assets	505,800	280,000				785,800
Land	205,000	90,000				295,000
Buildings (net)	646,000	310,000	(D) 16,000			956,000
Investment in Zip Company	602,200	–0–		(A) 141,800 (S) 400,000 (I) 76,400 (E) 1,100 (E) 2,500		–0–
Goodwill	–0–	–0–	(A) 41,800 (A) 100,000			138,200
Total assets	1,959,000	680,000				2,175,000
Liabilities	(459,000)	(100,000)				(559,000)
Noncontrolling interest in Zip Company, 1/1/00	–0–	–0–		(S) 100,000	(100,000)	
Noncontrolling interest in Zip Company, 12/31/00					(116,000)	(116,000)
Common stock	(355,000)	(200,000)	(S) 200,000			(355,000)
Additional paid-in capital	(260,000)	(70,000)	(S) 70,000			(260,000)
Retained earnings, 12/31/00 (above)	(885,000)	(310,000)				(885,000)
Total liabilities and equities	(1,959,000)	(680,000)				(2,175,000)

Note: Parentheses indicate a credit balance.

Consolidation entries:

(S) Elimination of subsidiary's stockholders' equity accounts along with recognition of January 1, 2000, noncontrolling interest.

(A) Allocation of parent's cost in excess of subsidiary's book value, unamortized balances as of January 1, 2000, two separate allocations are shown because two purchases were made.

(I) Elimination of intercompany income (equity accrual less amortization expense).

(D) Elimination of intercompany dividend payments.

(E) Recognition of amortization expense on goodwill resulting from purchase price.

To illustrate a step acquisition using the economic unit concept, assume that on January 1, 1998, Amanda Co. purchases 70 percent of Zoe, Inc., for $350,000. Because Zoe's net assets have book values equal to their fair market values of $400,000, under the economic unit concept, goodwill of $100,000 (10-year life) is recognized as the difference between the implied value of $500,000 ($350,000 ÷ 70%) and net asset market value of $400,000. On January 1, 1999, when Zoe's book value has grown to $420,000, Amanda buys another 20 percent of Zoe for $95,000, bringing its total ownership up to 90 percent.

Under the economic unit concept, the valuation basis for Zoe's net assets was established on January 1, 1998, the date Amanda obtained control. Subsequent transactions in the subsidiary's stock (purchases or sales) are now viewed as transactions in the economic unit's own stock. Therefore, no gains or losses are recognized and differences between transaction prices and the underlying subsidiary book value are simply treated as adjustments to additional paid-in capital. The difference between the $95,000 price and the underlying consolidated book value is computed as follows:

1/1/99 Purchase price for 20 percent interest		$ 95,000
Noncontrolling interest acquired:		
Book value (20%) 1/1/99	$84,000	
Unamortized goodwill (20%)	18,000	
Noncontrolling interest book value 1/1/99		102,000
Additional paid-in capital from 20 percent NCI acquisition		$ 7,000

By purchasing 20 percent of Zoe for $95,000 the consolidated entity's owners have acquired a portion of their own firm at a price $7,000 less than consolidated book value (which includes the unamortized excess). From a worksheet perspective, the recognition of the additional $102,000 in consolidated net assets from the 20 percent purchase is offset by the $95,000 purchase price and a $7,000 credit to additional paid-in capital. Importantly, the $95,000 purchase price for the 20 percent interest in Zoe's net assets does *not* affect consolidated asset valuation. From the economic unit perspective, the basis for the reported values in the consolidated financial statements was established on the date control was obtained.

PREACQUISITION INCOME

In virtually all of the previous examples in this textbook, the parent has gained control of the subsidiary on the first day of the fiscal year. How is the consolidation process affected if a purchase is made on April 1 or August 19 or some other day within the year?[9]

If control is gained at a different time, a few obvious changes occur. The subsidiary's book value as of that date has to be computed so that an appropriate comparison with the purchase price can be made to determine allocations and goodwill. Amortization expense as well as any equity accrual and dividend collections are recognized for a period shorter than a year. The real issue to be resolved, though, is in consolidating the subsidiary's revenues and expenses. Obviously, these balances can be included just for the months after the takeover. However, this approach gives totals that may not be comparable to the figures reported in the future when ownership is for a full year.

Paragraph 10 of *ARB 51* addresses this issue by stating

> When a subsidiary is purchased during the year, there are alternative ways of dealing with the results of its operations in the consolidated income statement. One method, which usually is

---

[9] In a pooling of interests, operating results are consolidated retroactively as if the companies had always been together. Therefore, the specific date on which a pooling is formed has no impact on the resulting income statement.

preferable, especially where there are several dates of acquisition of blocks of shares, is to include the subsidiary in the consolidation as though it had been acquired at the beginning of the year, and to deduct at the bottom of the consolidated income statement the preacquisition earnings applicable to each block of stock. This method presents results which are more indicative of the current status of the group, and facilitates future comparison with subsequent years.

Thus, when a purchase combination is created during the current year, this pronouncement recommends that the reporting emphasis be placed on promoting the statement user's ability to compare current and future periods. *To achieve this objective, the income statement accounts should be consolidated as if the parent had possessed its interest for the entire year.* Consequently, revenues and expenses are included in total within the consolidated figures. However, a single-line reduction (often referred to as *preacquisition income*) appears at the bottom of the income statement to remove the portion of these earnings that apply to the previous owners.

For example, Mednet MPC Corporation disclosed in its 1995 financial statements that:

> On September 15, 1995, the Company acquired substantially all of the assets of Home Pharmacy. . . . The Company has consolidated operations of Home Pharmacy retroactively to January 1, 1995; therefore, the preacquisition income of Home Pharmacy of $982,000 has been deducted from the consolidated statement of operations for the year ended December 31, 1995. The effect of this consolidation of operations prior to acquisition was to increase net sales by approximately $30,629,000.

Inclusion of this balance is a means of accounting for the prior group of stockholders in a manner similar to that accorded to any noncontrolling interest that remains. The only difference is that these previous owners ceased during the current year to be associated with the subsidiary. Thus, although an income allocation is reported for the period of their ownership, no end-of-year balance is recognized. Any dividends paid to the previous owners are likewise omitted from consolidation consideration.

To illustrate, assume that Berkeley Company purchases 90 percent of Waltins Company on October 1, 1998. The 1998 operations of this new subsidiary would impact the consolidated income statement as follows:

Impact on Consolidated Income Statement—1998
Berkeley owns 90 percent of Waltins for last three months

Revenues	100% of subsidiary's revenues are included
Expenses	100% of subsidiary's expenses are included plus amortization expense for three months
Noncontrolling interest	Reduction is 10% of subsidiary's income for the entire year
Preacquisition income	Reduction is 90% of subsidiary's income for the first nine months of the year
Net impact on consolidated net income	Increased by 90% of subsidiary's income for the last three months of the year reduced by any amortization expense for this same period

The establishment of a Preacquisition Income account permits comparability between the figures reported for current and future years. The reader of the financial statements is able to measure the full impact of creating this combination through the inclusion of 100 percent of each subsidiary revenue and expense account. By reporting reductions for the noncontrolling interest (10 percent) and the previous owners (90 percent for nine months), consolidated net income successfully mirrors the parent's 90 percent ownership for the last three months of the year. Thus, the *ARB's* suggested handling of this matter has no effect on the amount of consolidated net income. Rather, the pronouncement simply constructs the income statement in a manner that provides comparability with future periods.

Before leaving this illustration, one further comment should be made. The term *preacquisition income* has been incorporated here since it appears to be most prevalent in practice. As can be observed in much of accounting, financial statement terminology is not always particularly descriptive. This allocation could also be reported as: *current year income accruing to previous owners prior to the date subsidiary was acquired*. This title is significantly more wordy but less subject to misinterpretation by the users of the financial data. Most companies, however, elect to stay with traditional terms such as *preacquisition income* when preparing statements for external reporting purposes.

SALES OF SUBSIDIARY STOCK

Although this textbook has concentrated on the acquisition and ownership of large blocks of corporate securities, the eventual sale of these stocks is also encountered in the business world. For example, a note to the 1996 financial statements of Enron Corporation states:

> In December 1995, Enron sold 31 million outstanding shares of its EOG common stock, reducing its ownership interest from 80 percent to 61 percent. . . . During 1996, Enron sold approximately 12 million shares of EOG common stock. Enron's ownership interest in EOG at December 31, 1996 was 53 percent.

Under the parent company concept, accounting for the disposition of such shares parallels the sale of any corporate asset: the investment is adjusted to the appropriate book value as of the date of sale and then removed from the records of the parent company.[10] Any difference in the recorded balance and the consideration being received is recognized as a gain or loss.

Establishment of Investment Book Value

Any needed adjustment to the investment account depends on the accounting method used by the parent for internal reporting purposes. If the equity method has been applied, little problem should exist in recording the transaction. The investment is correctly reported by the parent as of the beginning of the year so that only the normal equity method adjustments are needed to reflect operations and amortization for the current period.

However, if either the cost or the partial equity method has been utilized, the adjustment process is more complicated. As indicated previously, both of these alternatives offer a convenient means to monitor a subsidiary. Unfortunately, neither produces the accurate book value necessary for recording a sales transaction. Therefore, when either of these other methods has been applied, the parent's Investment in Subsidiary account must be updated as if the equity method had been applied since the date of acquisition.

To illustrate, assume that Giant Company owns 80 percent of Tiny Company. Initially, a 50 percent interest was acquired in 1990 for $600,000 with the additional 30 percent being purchased in 1993 for $440,000. If Giant elects to account for this subsidiary using the equity method, the Investment in Tiny account contains a $1,245,000 balance as of January 1, 1998, based on the following assumed figures:

	Cost	Income Accrual Since Acquisition	Dividends	Amortization	Investment Balance 1/1/98
1990 purchase . . .	$ 600,000	$200,000	$ (15,000)	$(40,000)	$ 745,000
1993 purchase . . .	440,000	100,000	(6,000)	(34,000)	500,000
Totals	$1,040,000	$300,000	$ (21,000)	$(74,000)	$1,245,000

---

[10]Unless control is surrendered, the economic unit concept views the sale of a subsidiary's stock as a treasury stock transaction so that no gain or loss is recognized.

Sale Made at Beginning of Year Appropriate application of the equity method signifies that the $1,245,000 is a correctly recorded balance. Assuming that Giant sells this entire interest on January 1, 1998, for $1,400,000, the transaction is recorded as follows:[11]

Giant's Financial Records—January 1, 1998

Cash (or other assets)	1,400,000	
Investment in Tiny Company		1,245,000
Gain on Sale of Investment		155,000
To record January 1, 1998, sale of subsidiary.		

Because the sale is made on the first day of the year, no adjustment is required to recognize the 1998 operations of the subsidiary.

In contrast, if one of the alternative methods has been utilized by Giant, a preliminary entry is needed to establish the appropriate $1,245,000 balance.

Application of the cost method. The $1,040,000 total of the two original payments continues to be reported by the parent for this investment so that a $205,000 increase is necessary (income in excess of dividends and amortization).

Application of the partial equity method. A book value of $1,319,000 (income and dividends are recognized by the parent but not the $74,000 amortization) is found. An adjustment must be made to record the amortization.

Hence, depending on the method in use, one of the following entries is required of the parent prior to recording the sales transaction:

Giant's Financial Records—January 1, 1998
Cost Method Has Been Applied

Investment in Tiny Company	205,000	
Retained Earnings, 1/1/98 (Giant)		205,000
To establish correct equity balance by recognizing income accrual (in excess of dividends) for previous years as well as amortization.		

Partial Equity Method Has Been Applied

Retained Earnings, 1/1/98 (Giant)	74,000	
Investment in Tiny Company		74,000
To establish correct equity balance by recognizing amortization relating to previous years.		

These adjustments are equivalent to the Entry *C used in past consolidations to update the investment account when either the cost or partial equity methods has been applied. However, for a sale, this entry must be recorded directly into the parent's books rather than as a part of the worksheet process. Following the adjustment to $1,245,000, the parent records the sales transaction using the same journal entry presented in connection with the equity method.

Sale Made during the Year If this sale had transpired *within* the fiscal year, Giant still adjusts the investment to $1,245,000 (if necessary) but then extends application of the equity method over the period that the stock is held during 1998. The resulting book value must be correct as of the date of sale. The income accruing to Giant during this portion of the year is reported as a single-line item in the 1998 income statement. In this manner, subsidiary earnings continue to be recognized throughout the period of ownership even though consolidation is no longer applicable.

---

[11]Under the guidelines of *APB Opinion 30*, Giant may have to report this sale as the disposal of a segment. Because this issue is covered in most intermediate accounting textbooks, it is not explored here.

Cost-Flow Assumptions

If less than an entire investment is sold, the parent must select an appropriate cost-flow assumption whenever more than one purchase has been made. In the sale of securities, the use of specific identification based on serial numbers is acceptable, although averaging or FIFO assumptions often are applied. Use of the averaging method is especially appealing in that all shares are truly identical, creating little justification for identifying different cost figures with individual shares.

Returning to Giant's ownership of Tiny Company, assume that the parent sold only a 20 percent portion of the subsidiary on January 1, 1998 (thereby reducing its holdings from 80 to 60 percent). Averaging dictates the removal of $311,250 (20 percent/80 percent × $1,245,000) from the investment account. Conversely, adoption of FIFO requires that $298,000 be written off based on the currently reported value of the initial 1990 acquisition (20 percent/50 percent × $745,000).

Accounting for Shares that Remain

If only a portion of Giant's investment is sold, a determination also must be made as to the proper method of accounting for the shares that remain. Three possible scenarios can be envisioned:

1. Giant's interest may have been so drastically reduced that the parent no longer controls the subsidiary or even has the ability to significantly influence its decision making. For example, assume that Giant's ownership drops from 80 to 5 percent. In the current period prior to the sale, the 80 percent investment is reported by means of the equity method with the market-value method used for the 5 percent that remains thereafter. Consolidated financial statements are no longer applicable.

2. Giant may still be able to apply significant influence over the operations of Tiny, although control is no longer maintained. A drop in the level of ownership from 80 to 30 percent would normally meet this condition. In this case, the equity method is utilized by the parent for the entire year. Application is based on 80 percent until the time of sale and then on 30 percent for the remainder of the year. Again, consolidated statements cease to be appropriate because control has been lost.

3. The decrease in ownership may be relatively small so that the parent continues to maintain control over the subsidiary even after the sale. Giant's reduction of its ownership in Tiny from 80 to 60 percent is an example of this situation. After the disposal, consolidated financial statements are still required but the process is based on the *end-of-year ownership percentage*. As with step acquisitions, the accounting emphasis is placed here on maintaining comparability with future years. However, since only the retained shares (60 percent in this case) are consolidated, separate recognition must be made of any current year income accruing to the parent from its terminated interest. Thus, earnings on this portion of the investment (a 20 percent interest in Tiny for the time during the year that it is held) are shown in the consolidated income statement as a single-line item computed by means of the equity method.

SUMMARY

1. A parent company need not acquire 100 percent of a subsidiary's stock to form a business combination. Only control over the decision-making process is necessary, a level that has historically been achieved by obtaining a majority of the voting shares. Ownership of any subsidiary stock that is retained by outside, unrelated parties is collectively referred to as a noncontrolling interest.

2. A purchase consolidation takes on an added degree of complexity when a noncontrolling interest is present. A decision must be made as to the theoretical approach by which

subsidiary assets and liabilities are to be valued within the financial statements of the business combination. One alternative, the economic unit concept, presumes that the combination is composed of two identifiable companies and should be accounted for as such. Allocations associated with the subsidiary's assets and liabilities are determined using their total fair market value regardless of the degree of parent ownership. The calculation of any noncontrolling interest is based on this total and reported by the business combination as a component of stockholders' equity.

3. The proportionate consolidation concept focuses on the parent company by stressing the cost of buying a portion of the subsidiary. Under this approach, allocations are computed using the ownership percentage of each account's fair market value. No recognition of noncontrolling interest is reported in either the consolidated balance sheet or income statement.

4. In practice, the parent company concept appears to be most popular. According to this method, the book value of each subsidiary asset and liability is included in the total whereas the difference between fair market value and book value is consolidated based on the parent's ownership percentage. Any noncontrolling interest is measured using only the subsidiary's book value and reported between the liabilities and stockholders' equity.

5. Four noncontrolling interest figures actually appear in the annual consolidation process. Calculation of each is derived by multiplying the percentage of outside ownership by the subsidiary's book value. A balance as of the beginning of the year is brought into the worksheet first (through Entry S) followed by the noncontrolling interest's share of the subsidiary's income for the period (recorded by a columnar entry) . A decrease is recognized because of any dividends paid to these unrelated owners (with the amount appearing on the worksheet as the subsidiary's dividends that were not eliminated as intercompany). The final balance for the year is found as a summation of the Noncontrolling Interest column and is presented on the consolidated balance sheet, usually between the Liability and Stockholders' Equity sections. The income figure appears as a reduction within the income statement.

6. A parent may obtain control of a subsidiary by means of several separate purchases occurring over time, a process often referred to as a *step acquisition*. In such cases, each purchase is viewed as an individual investment with separate allocations and amortization.

7. When a purchase is made within a year, operating figures should be reported that are comparable with those of future years. Thus, revenues and expenses can be consolidated as if the acquisition had taken place on the first day of the year. A *preacquisition income* figure is then subtracted within the consolidated income statement to remove the effects of the subsidiary's operations relating to the time prior to the takeover.

8. A parent company also may sell all, or a portion, of a subsidiary. The appropriate book value for the investment must be established within the parent's separate records so that the gain or loss can be computed accurately. If the equity method has not been applied, the parent's investment balance should be restated to recognize any income and amortization previously omitted. The resulting balance is then compared to the amount received for the stock to arrive at the gain or loss. Any shares still being held will subsequently be reported by either consolidation, the equity method, or the market-value method, depending on the influence retained by the parent.

COMPREHENSIVE ILLUSTRATION

Problem

(Estimated Time: 60 to 75 Minutes) On January 1, 1994, Father Company purchased an 80 percent interest in Sun Company for $410,000. As of that date, Sun reported total stockholders' equity of $400,000: $100,000 in common stock and $300,000 in retained earnings. In setting the acquisition price, Father had appraised three accounts as having values different from the balances reported within Sun's financial records.

> Buildings (eight-year life) . . . . Undervalued by $20,000
> Land . . . . Undervalued by $50,000
> Equipment (five-year life) . . . . Undervalued by $12,500

Any goodwill recognized within this combination was to be amortized over a 30-year period.

As of December 31, 1998, the trial balances of these two companies are as follows:

	Father Company	Sun Company
Debits		
Current assets	$ 620,000	$ 280,000
Investment in Sun Company	410,000	–0–
Land	200,000	300,000
Buildings (net)	640,000	290,000
Equipment (net)	380,000	160,000
Expenses	550,000	190,000
Dividends	90,000	20,000
Total debits	$2,890,000	$1,240,000
Credits		
Liabilities	$ 910,000	$ 300,000
Common stock	480,000	100,000
Retained earnings, 1/1/98	704,000	480,000
Revenues	780,000	360,000
Dividend income	16,000	–0–
Total credits	$2,890,000	$1,240,000

Within these figures, Sun has a $20,000 debt to the parent company.

Required

a. Determine consolidated totals for Father Company and Sun Company for the year of 1998. Assume that the parent company concept is to be applied.
b. Prepare worksheet entries to consolidate the trial balances of Father Company and Sun Company for the year of 1998.
c. Assume that Father acquires an additional 5 percent of the outstanding shares of Sun Company on December 31, 1998. Discuss the effects of this transaction on the consolidated figures computed in requirement a.
d. Assume that Father uses the economic unit concept rather than the parent company concept. Discuss the effects of this change on the consolidated figures computed in requirement a.

Solution

a. The consolidation of Father Company and Sun Company should begin with the allocation of the purchase price as shown in Exhibit 4–12. This process is based on the parent company concept and the parent's $410,000 expenditure. Since this consolidation is taking place after several years, the unamortized balances for the various allocations at the start of the current year also should be determined (see Exhibit 4–13).

Next, the parent's method of accounting for its subsidiary should be ascertained. The continuing presence in the investment account of the original $410,000 acquisition price indicates that Father is applying the cost method. This same determination can be made from the Dividend Income account that equals 80 percent of the subsidiary's dividends. Thus, the increase in Sun's book value as well as the amortization expense for the prior periods of ownership have been ignored in Father's accounting records. These amounts have to be added to the parent's January 1, 1998, retained earnings to arrive at a properly consolidated balance.

During the 1994–97 period of ownership, Sun's Retained Earnings account rose by $180,000 ($480,000 − $300,000). Father's 80 percent interest necessitates an accrual of $144,000 ($180,000 × 80 percent) for these years. In addition, the purchase price allocations require the recognition of $19,200 in amortization expense for this same period ($4,800 × 4 years). Thus, a net increase of $124,800 ($144,000 − $19,200) is needed to correct the parent's beginning retained earnings balance for the year.

Once the adjustment from the cost method to the equity method has been determined, the consolidated figures for 1998 can be calculated:

Current assets = $880,000. The parent's book value is added to the subsidiary's book value. The $20,000 intercompany balance is eliminated.

Investment in Sun Company = –0–. The intercompany ownership is eliminated so that the subsidiary's specific assets and liabilities can be consolidated.

Exhibit 4–12

FATHER COMPANY AND SUN COMPANY
Purchase Price Allocation and Amortization
January 1, 1994

	Allocation	Estimated Life (years)	Annual Amortization
Purchase price paid by Father Company	$ 410,000		
80% of subsidiary $400,000 book value (Father Company's ownership)	(320,000)		
Cost in excess of book value	90,000		
Allocation to specific accounts based on fair market value:			
Buildings ($20,000 × 80%)	16,000	8	$ 2,000
Land ($50,000 × 80%)	40,000		
Equipment ($12,500 × 80%)	10,000	5	2,000
Goodwill	$ 24,000	30	800
Annual amortization expense			$ 4,800
1994–97 amortization expense ($4,800 × 4)...			$19,200

Exhibit 4–13

FATHER COMPANY AND SUN COMPANY
Unamortized Cost Allocation
January 1, 1998, Balances

Account	Original Allocation	Amortization 1994–97	Unamortized Balance 1/1/98
Buildings	$16,000	$8,000	$ 8,000
Land	40,000	–0–	40,000
Equipment	10,000	8,000	2,000
Goodwill	24,000	3,200	20,800
Total			$70,800

Land = $540,000. The parent's book value is added to the subsidiary's book value plus the purchase price allocation (see Exhibit 4–12).

Buildings (net) = $936,000. The parent's book value is added to the subsidiary's book value plus the related purchase price allocation (see Exhibit 4–13) after taking into account five years of amortization (1994 through 1998).

Equipment (net) = $540,000. The parent's book value is added to the subsidiary's book value. The purchase price allocation has been completely amortized after five years.

Expenses = $744,800. The parent's book value is added to the subsidiary's book value plus amortization expense on the purchase price allocations for the year (see Exhibit 4–12).

Dividends Paid = $90,000. Only the parent company dividends are consolidated. The subsidiary's dividends that were paid to the parent are eliminated; the remainder serve as a reduction in the Noncontrolling Interest balance.

Goodwill = $20,000. The original residual allocation from the purchase price is recognized after taking into account five years of amortization (see Exhibit 4–13).

Noncontrolling Interest in Subsidiary's Income = $34,000. The outside owners are assigned a 20 percent share of the subsidiary's income (revenues of $360,000 less expenses of $190,000 or $170,000).

Total of Consolidated Debit Balances = $3,784,800. This figure is a summation of the preceding balances.

Liabilities = $1,190,000. The parent's book value is added to the subsidiary's book value. The $20,000 intercompany balance is eliminated.

Common Stock = $480,000. The parent company balance only is reported.

Retained Earnings, 1/1/98 = $828,800. The parent company balance only is reported after a $124,800 increase is made as explained earlier to convert the parent's use of the cost method to the equity method.

Revenues = $1,140,000. The parent's book value is added to the subsidiary's book value.

Dividend Income = –0–. The intercompany dividend receipts are eliminated.

Noncontrolling Interest in Subsidiary, 12/31/98 = $146,000. The beginning balance is $116,000, 20 percent of the subsidiary's 1/1/98 book value ($580,000 as shown by the stockholders' equity accounts). This figure is increased by the noncontrolling interest's share of net income ($34,000 as computed above). The dividends paid to the outside owners (20 percent of $20,000 or $4,000) serve to decrease in the balance. The consolidated total is then derived from these three balances.

Total of Consolidated Credit Balances = $3,784,800. This figure is a summation of the preceding balances.

b. *Six* worksheet entries are necessary to produce a consolidation worksheet for Father Company and Sun Company.

ENTRY *C

Investment in Sun Company	124,800	
Retained Earnings, 1/1/98 (parent)		124,800

As discussed earlier, this increment is required to adjust the parent's retained earnings from the cost method to the equity method. The amount is $144,000 (80 percent of the $180,000 increase in the subsidiary's book value during previous years) less $19,200 in amortization over this same four-year period ($4,800 × 4 years).

ENTRY S

Common Stock (subsidiary)	100,000	
Retained Earnings, 1/1/98 (subsidiary)	480,000	
Investment in Sun Company (80 percent)		464,000
Noncontrolling Interest in Sun Company (20 percent)		116,000

To eliminate beginning stockholders' equity accounts of the subsidiary and recognize the beginning balance attributed to the outside owners (20 percent).

ENTRY A

Buildings	8,000	
Land	40,000	
Equipment	2,000	
Goodwill	20,800	
Investment in Sun Company		70,800

To recognize unamortized purchase price allocations as of the first day of the current year (see Exhibit 4–13).

ENTRY I

Dividend Income	16,000	
Dividends Paid		16,000

To eliminate intercompany dividend payments recorded by parent (using the cost method) as income.

ENTRY E

Amortization Expense	4,800	
Buildings		2,000
Equipment		2,000
Goodwill		800

To record amortization expense for the current year (see Exhibit 4–12).

c. *This* question asks about the impact created by Father's purchase of an additional 5 percent of Sun on December 31, 1998. Three direct effects can be listed:

1. All of the noncontrolling interest balances will be calculated as if only 15 percent of the subsidiary's shares had been held by outside parties during the entire year. This handling allows

for production of financial statements that will be comparable with the results reported in future years.

2. A Preacquisition Income account is established to reflect the portion of Sun's 1998 income (5 percent) accruing to the previous owners. This balance reduces consolidated net income for the current year. In addition, any dividends paid to former stockholders must be eliminated since this group no longer holds an equity interest in Sun.

3. Any cost in excess of book value paid by Father in this latest purchase must be allocated to specific accounts and then recognized within the consolidated balance sheet. Because the acquisition occurs at the end of the fiscal year, no additional amortization expense is necessary for 1998.

d. Recall that under the economic unit concept not only is an implied value for 100 percent of the subsidiary used in allocating market values to subsidiary assets but adjustments also are made for 100 percent of the differences in market and book values. The following cost allocation schedule reflects the economic unit concept for Father's purchase of Sun on January 1, 1994:

	Allocation	Estimated Life (years)	Annual Amortization
Implied value ($410,000 ÷ 80%)	$512,500		
Sun book value (100%)	400,000		
Excess implied value	112,500		
Allocation to specific subsidiary accounts based on fair market value:			
Buildings	$ 20,000	8	$2,500
Land	50,000		
Equipment	12,500	5	2,500
Goodwill	$ 30,000	30	1,000
Annual amortization expense (economic unit concept)			$6,000

Father's consolidated statements would therefore reflect the total market values of the subsidiary at acquisition date less the above amortizations. To offset the increased asset values, a larger noncontrolling interest also is recognized.

The noncontrolling interest would be reported in the December 31, 1998, stockholders' equity section of Father's consolidated balance sheet at $162,500 computed as follows:

NCI in Sun's 1/1/98 book value (20% × $580,000)	$116,000
NCI in unamortized excess allocations (20% × $88,500)	17,700
January 1, 1998, NCI in Sun implied value	$133,700
NCI in Sun's economic unit income 20% × ($360,000 − 196,000)	32,800
NCI dividend share 20% × $20,000	(4,000)
Total noncontrolling interest December 31, 1998	$162,500

Note that the $162,500 noncontrolling interest amount is the same as the $146,000 amount reported in part *a.*, plus 20 percent of the $82,500 unamortized excess allocations at December 31, 1998 ($112,500 − 5 years × $6,000).

The noncontrolling interest's share of the subsidiary's net income is not reported on the consolidated income statement but rather as a separate allocation. This amount is based on the subsidiary's net income after deducting amortization expense which is attributed to the company's asset and liability accounts.

APPENDIX

FASB Proposals to Amend Consolidated Financial Reporting

Throughout the 1990s, the FASB issued several controversial documents in an attempt to standardize financial reporting for consolidated enterprises. Ultimately, the goal was to establish standards determining when entities should be included in consolidated financial statements and how these statements should be prepared. First, in September 1991, a Discussion Memorandum *An Analysis of Issues Related to Consolidation Policy and Procedures* was published. The purpose of the Discussion Memorandum was to present alternative accounting methods to address the many reporting complexities that have arisen since the last comprehensive authoritative pronouncement (*APB Opinion No. 16*) was issued in 1970. Then, in October 1995, an Exposure Draft of a proposed Statement of Financial Accounting Standards entitled *Consolidated Financial Statement: Policy and Procedures*, was issued.

After much controversy regarding several of the Exposure Draft's provisions, in May 1996 a Working Draft of Consolidations Statement was disseminated. The major disagreements revolved around the definition of control, valuation of the noncontrolling interest, and accounting for changes in ownership levels. The Working Draft contained several proposed major modifications of the recommendations in the Exposure Draft. This Working Draft, however, did not result in a timely resolution of the reporting controversies and substantial doubt remains whether its revisions will form the basis for a final pronouncement.

Further FASB discussions have been disseminated through a Discussion of Board Agenda Projects available from the FASB Internet home page (www.fasb.org). Overall, the collective attempts to modify financial reporting for consolidated enterprises relate to the theories and procedures discussed in Chapter 4. Therefore, the recommendations to date, as presented in the Exposure Draft, Working Draft and subsequently, are discussed next.

Definition of Control and Assessing Its Existence

As indicated in both the Exposure Draft and Working Draft, "control of an entity is an exclusionary power over its assets—power to direct the use of the individual assets of another entity in essentially the same ways as the controlling entity can use its own assets." Clearly one entity is presumed to control another entity if it owns, directly or indirectly, a majority voting interest in another entity. In addition, the FASB suggests an expanded set of control situations as follows:

- Ownership of a large minority interest (for example, approximately 40 percent) in another entity, and no other group has a significant voting interest.
- Ownership of securities in the other entity that may be converted into a majority voting interest at the option of the holder.
- An unconditional right to dissolve another entity and assume control of its individual assets.
- A relationship established by the parent with an entity, other than through voting stock, that nonetheless provides substantially all future economic benefits to the parent.
- Ownership of a sole general partnership interest in a limited partnership.

Under this expanded definition of control, many more firms will be required to prepare consolidated financial statements. For example, consolidated reporting may be necessary for a parent and another entity even though the parent owns less than 50 percent of the other entity's voting stock.

On March 19, 1997, the FASB discussed another tentative definition of control as a basis for consolidation—"the power to direct the policies and management that guide the activities of another entity so as to benefit from its activities."[12] Apparently, a fundamental definition of control remains a matter of concern in the FASB deliberations.

Valuation of Subsidiary Assets and Liabilities in Consolidated Reports

As discussed in Chapter 4, firms historically have chosen one of three valuation methods—the economic unit approach, proportionate consolidation, or the parent company approach. In their latest effort, the FASB endorses the economic unit concept for valuing subsidiary assets and liabilities in consolidated financial statements. The most recent proposal is to use the parent's cost as a basis for an implied total subsidiary value. Any excess implied value over book value is then allocated to specific subsidiary assets and liabilities based on their total fair market value.

Application of the economic unit concept under the FASB proposal is the same as presented in Chapter 4 with one additional element—accounting for a control premium. A control premium is an estimable portion of the purchase price paid by the parent representing additional value that

---

[12]FASB, "Discussion of Board Agenda Projects as of April 1, 1997, Consolidations and Related Matters."

derives from obtaining a controlling interest. A parent may be forced to pay an inflated price for the last few shares if it wishes to control another entity. Such control premiums are not to be used in determining the subsidiary's implied value, but are considered additional goodwill to the parent company only.

Valuation and Presentation of Noncontrolling Interests

As presented in Chapter 4, under the economic unit concept, the noncontrolling interest is valued at its proportionate share of the implied value of the subsidiary at the date control by the parent is obtained. Therefore noncontrolling interest valuation is based on the market values of the subsidiary's individual assets and liabilities as well as a proportionate share of goodwill. Importantly, the FASB proposals would require the noncontrolling interest to be presented in the consolidated financial statements as a separate component of owners' equity. Total consolidated net income is allocated to both controlling and noncontrolling interests on the face of the income statement.

The term *noncontrolling interest* replaces the traditional term *minority interest*. In light of the possibility of consolidating entities with less than a 50 percent interest, the new term is more descriptive.

Changes in a Parent's Ownership in a Subsidiary

The latest FASB proposals in accounting for changes in a parent's ownership in a subsidiary also represent a major departure from past procedures. Under the economic unit concept, transactions in the stock of a subsidiary, whether purchases or sales by the parent or issuance of its own stock by the subsidiary, are considered to be transactions in the equity of the consolidated entity. No gains or losses are appropriate under the economic unit concept. As stated in the Working Draft (paragraph 29):

> changes in a parent's proportionate ownership interest in a subsidiary that do not result in a loss of control shall be accounted for as transactions in the equity of the consolidated entity whether they result from subsequent purchases or sales of the subsidiary's stock by the parent or from the acquisition of treasury stock or the issuance of additional shares by the subsidiary.

When shares of a subsidiary held by the parent are sold, with an accompanying loss of control, a gain or loss is recognized. The gain or loss is computed as the difference between the proceeds from the sale and the carrying amount in the consolidated financial statements of the subsidiary's net assets, including unamortized excess allocations. If there had been any adjustments to paid-in capital from previous transactions in a subsidiary's shares, an appropriate amount also is transferred to the gain or loss on the shares sold.

Finally, if a parent acquires a control over a subsidiary in which it already held an investment, the investment account is adjusted to its fair market value on the date control is obtained, and a gain or loss from the adjustment is recognized in earnings. Similarly, if a sale of shares results in relinquishment of control over a subsidiary, the remaining investment should be measured at its fair market value on the date control is given up.

QUESTIONS

1. What is meant by the term *noncontrolling interest*?

2. Atwater Company acquires 80 percent of the outstanding voting stock of Belwood Company. On that date, Belwood possesses a building with a $160,000 book value but a fair market value of $220,000. Assuming that a bargain purchase has not been made, at what value would this building be consolidated under each of the following?
   a. Economic unit concept.
   b. Proportionate consolidation concept.
   c. Parent company concept.

3. Giant Company acquired 70 percent of Small Company at the beginning of 1998. Subsequently, Giant reports net income for 1998 of $60,000 (without regard for the investment in Small). For the same period, this subsidiary reports earnings of $30,000. In acquiring this interest, Giant paid a total of $224,000, although Small's book value

was only $200,000 at the time. A building with a 10-year life was undervalued on Small's accounting records by $10,000. Any other excess amount was attributed to goodwill with a life of 40 years. Under each of the following, what is the consolidated net income for 1998 after reduction is made for the noncontrolling interest's claims?

   a. Economic unit concept.

   b. Proportionate consolidation concept.

   c. Parent company theory.

4. How does the parent company concept merge the ideas put forth under the economic unit concept and proportionate consolidation?

5. Where should the noncontrolling interest's claims be reported in a consolidated set of financial statements.

6. How is the noncontrolling interest in a subsidiary company calculated as of the end of the current year? *Where should it be shown and why*

7. Consolidated financial statements are being prepared by Sandridge Company and its consolidated subsidiary. Preacquisition income of $55,000 is presented within these statements. What does this Preacquisition Income account represent? How was the amount computed?

8. Tree, Inc., has held a 10 percent interest in the stock of Limb Company for several years. Because of the level of ownership, this investment has been accounted for by means of the market value method. At the beginning of the current year, Tree acquires an additional 70 percent interest which provides the company with control over Limb. In preparing consolidated financial statements for this business combination, how is the previous 10 percent ownership interest accounted for by Tree?

9. Duke Corporation owns a 70 percent equity interest in UNCCH, a subsidiary corporation. During the current year, a portion of this stock is sold to an outside party. Before recording this transaction, Duke adjusts the book value of its investment account. What is the purpose of this adjustment?

10. In question 9, how would the parent record the sales transaction?

11. In question 9, how would the parent record the sales transaction if the economic unit concept is being used and control is retained?

12. In question 9, how would Duke account for the remainder of its investment subsequent to the sale of this partial interest?

LIBRARY ASSIGNMENTS

1. Read the following articles and any others that might be available discussing the method of accounting for a noncontrolling interest:

> "Consolidations: An Overview of the FASB DM," *Journal of Accountancy*, April 1992.
>
> "Response to the FASB Exposure Draft: *Proposed Statement of Financial Accounting Standards—Consolidated Financial Statements: Policy and Procedures,*" *Accounting Horizons*, September 1996.
>
> "FASB Presents View on Consolidated Statements," *Journal of Accountancy*, November 1994.
>
> "FASB Proposes Significant Changes in Consolidation Policies and Procedures," *Ohio CPA Journal*, April 1996.
>
> "Consolidated Financial Statements—Understanding Their Theories," *The Woman CPA*, April 1984.
>
> "Proportionate Consolidation and Financial Analysis," *Accounting Horizons*, December 1992.
>
> "Minority Interest: Opposing Views," *Journal of Accountancy*, March 1986.

Prepare a report to justify the selection of one particular concept of consolidated values where a noncontrolling interest is present as well as a preferred placement for the balances reported for the noncontrolling interest.

2. Obtain the latest financial statements for the Atlantic Richfield Corporation, Sara Lee Corporation, or any other company reporting a noncontrolling interest. Indicate the

placement of both the balance sheet and the income statement figures. Describe the information conveyed about the noncontrolling interest within the reporting company's notes to its financial statements.

PROBLEMS

Note: Unless otherwise stated, assume that the parent company concept is being used.

1. Bailey, Inc., buys 60 percent of the outstanding stock of Luebs, Inc., in a purchase that resulted in the recognition of goodwill. Luebs owns a piece of land that cost $200,000 but was worth $500,000 at the date of purchase. For each of the three concepts described in this chapter, what value would be attributed to this land in a consolidated balance sheet at the date of takeover?

	Economic Unit Concept	Proportionate Consolidation	Parent Company Concept
a.	$500,000	$300,000	$500,000
b.	$200,000	$120,000	$500,000
c.	$200,000	$120,000	$380,000
d.	$500,000	$300,000	$380,000

2. Jordan, Inc., holds 75 percent of the outstanding stock of Paxson Corporation. Paxson currently owes Jordan $400,000 for inventory acquired over the past few months. In preparing consolidated financial statements, what amount of this debt should be eliminated?
   a. $0.
   b. $100,000.
   c. $300,000.
   d. $400,000.

3. On January 1, 1998, Brendan, Inc., reports net assets of $760,000 although equipment (with a four-year life) having a book value of $440,000 is worth $500,000. Hope Corporation pays $692,000 on that date for an 80 percent ownership in Brendan. If goodwill is to be written off over a 10-year period, what is the consolidated goodwill balance on December 31, 1999?
   a. $20,800.
   b. $28,800.
   c. $34,200.
   d. $67,200.

4. On January 1, 1998, Turner Inc., reports net assets of $480,000 although a building (with a 10-year life) having a book value of $260,000 is now worth $310,000. Plaster Corporation pays $400,000 on that date for a 70 percent ownership in Turner. On December 31, 2000, Turner reports a Building account of $245,000 while Plaster reports a Building account of $510,000. What is the consolidated balance of the Building account?
   a. $779,500.
   b. $783,500.
   c. $790,000.
   d. $805.000.

5. On January 1, 1998, Hygille, Inc., reports net assets of $880,000 although a building (with a 20-year life) having a book value of $330,000 is now worth $400,000. Nuyt Corporation pays $840,000 on that date for an 80 percent ownership in Hygille. Goodwill is to be written off over its maximum life. On December 31, 2000, Hygille reports total expenses of $621,000 while Nuyt reports expenses of $714,000. What is the consolidated expense balance?
   a. $1,336,000.
   b. $1,338,000.
   c. $1,338,500.
   d. $1,339,800.

6. On January 1, 1998, Neville Inc., reports net assets of $540,000 although equipment (with a five-year life) having a book value of $90,000 is worth $130,000. Chamberlain

Corporation pays $388,000 on that date for a 60 percent ownership in Neville. Goodwill is to be written off over a 10-year period. On December 31, 2000, Neville reports revenues of $400,000 and expenses of $300,000 while Chamberlain reports revenues of $700,000 and expenses of $400,000. The parent figures contain no income from the subsidiary. What is consolidated net income?

   a. $349,600.
   b. $351,200.
   c. $360,000.
   d. $391,200.

7. What is a basic premise of the economic unit concept?

   a. Consolidated financial statements should be primarily for the benefit of the stockholders of the parent company.
   b. Consolidated financial statements should be produced only if both the parent and the subsidiary are in the same basic industry.
   c. A subsidiary is an indivisible part of a business combination and should be included in whole regardless of the degree of ownership.
   d. Consolidated financial statements should not report a noncontrolling interest balance since these outside owners do not hold stock in the parent company.

8. A preacquisition income account.

   a. Is an adjustment to retained earnings when a pooling of interests is created.
   b. Is a reduction in consolidated net income that allows a subsidiary's revenues and expenses to be reported for the entire year even though acquisition took place during the current year.
   c. Is an income figure that requires the parent to pay an additional amount to create a business combination.
   d. Is the balance in a subsidiary's retained earnings account on the date that a business combination is created.

 9. Ames, Inc., has a book value of $400,000 on January 1, 1998, and $550,000 on January 1, 2000. On both dates, the book value of the company's assets and liabilities were the same as fair market value. Hitchcock Corporation acquires 30 percent of Ames on January 1, 1998, for $160,000 in cash. Hitchcock purchases an additional 40 percent of Ames on January 1, 2000, for $240,000. Goodwill is being amortized over its maximum life. On a consolidated balance sheet as of December 31, ~~1998,~~ **2000** what amount of goodwill is reported?

   a. $60,000.
   b. $57,000.
   c. $56,500.
   d. $55,500.

10. A parent buys 32 percent of a subsidiary in 1997 and then buys an additional 40 percent in 1999. In a step acquisition of this type, how does the economic unit concept differ from the parent company concept?

   a. In using the economic unit concept, all subsequent purchases are valued based on the implied value at the time of the first acquisition.
   b. In using the economic unit concept, the two purchases are recorded as separate acquisitions with their own allocations and goodwill.
   c. In using the economic unit concept, the first purchase is adjusted to its implied value based on the acquisition price of the second transaction with a resulting gain or loss being recorded.
   d. The economic unit concept views each company as a whole and, thus, cannot be applied unless 100 percent of the subsidiary's stock is held.

 preacquisition income 11. On April 1, 1998, Guns, Inc., purchases 70 percent of the outstanding stock of Roses Corporation for $430,000. The subsidiary's book value on that date was $500,000. Any resulting goodwill will be amortized over 40 years. During 1998, Roses generates revenues of $600,000 and expenses of $360,000. Both figures occur evenly throughout the year. On a consolidated income statement for the year ending December 31, 1998, what should be reported as the noncontrolling interest in the subsidiary's net income and as preacquisition income?

   a. $72,000 and $42,000.
   b. $70,500 and $60,000.

    c. $70,500 and $40,500.

    d. $72,000 and $41,650.

Use the following information for Problems 12 through 14: David Company acquired 60 percent of Mark Company for $300,000 when Mark's book value was $400,000. On that date, Mark had equipment (with a 10-year life) that was undervalued in the financial records by $60,000. Any goodwill is amortized over 40 years. Two years later, the following figures are reported by these two companies (stockholders' equity accounts have been omitted).

	David Company Book Value	Mark Company Book Value	Mark Company Fair Market Value
Current assets	$ 620,000	$ 300,000	$ 320,000
Equipment	260,000	200,000	280,000
Buildings	410,000	150,000	150,000
Liabilities	(390,000)	(120,000)	(120,000)
Revenues	(900,000)	(400,000)	
Expenses	500,000	300,000	
Investment income	Not Given		

12. What is consolidated net income prior to the reduction for the noncontrolling interest's share of the subsidiary's income?

    a. $455,800.

    b. $460,000.

    c. $494,000.

    d. $495,800.

13. What is the noncontrolling interest's share of the subsidiary's income and what is the ending balance of the noncontrolling interest in the subsidiary?

    a. $42,000 and $196,000.

    b. $40,000 and $212,000.

    c. $38,320 and $217,400.

    d. $37,600 and $224,000.

14. What is the consolidated balance of the Equipment account?

    a. $488,800.

    b. $498,400.

    c. $500,800.

    d. $508,000.

Use the following information for Problems 15 through 19: On January 1, 1998, Polk Corporation and Strass Corporation had condensed balance sheets as follows:

	Polk	Strass
Current assets	$ 70,000	$20,000
Noncurrent assets	90,000	40,000
Total assets	$160,000	$60,000
Current liabilities	$ 30,000	$10,000
Long-term debt	50,000	—
Stockholders' equity	80,000	50,000
Total liabilities and equities	$160,000	$60,000

On January 2, 1998, Polk borrowed $60,000 and used the proceeds to purchase 90 percent of the outstanding common shares of Strass. This debt is payable in 10 equal annual principal payments, plus interest, beginning December 31, 1998. The excess cost of the investment over the underlying book value of the acquired net assets is allocated to inventory (60 percent) and to goodwill (40 percent). On a consolidated balance sheet as of January 2, 1998,

15. Current assets should be:

    a. $99,000.

    b. $96,000.

    c. $90,000.

    d. $79,000.

16. Noncurrent assets should be:
    a. $130,000.
    b. $134,000.
    c. $136,000.
    d. $140,000.

17. Current liabilities should be:
    a. $50,000.
    b. $46,000.
    c. $40,000.
    d. $30,000.

18. Noncurrent liabilities, including noncontrolling interest, should be:
    a. $115,000.
    b. $109,000.
    c. $104,000.
    d. $55,000.

19. Stockholders' equity should be:
    a. $80,000.
    b. $85,000.
    c. $90,000.
    d. $130,000.

    (AICPA adapted)

20. On January 1, 1998, Harrison, Inc., purchased 90 percent of Starr Company. Annual amortization of $8,000 resulted from this transaction. Starr Company reported a Common Stock account of $100,000 and Retained Earnings of $200,000 at that date. The subsidiary earned $70,000 in 1998 and $90,000 in 1999 with dividend payments of $30,000 each year. Without regard for this investment, Harrison had income of $220,000 in 1998 and $260,000 in 1999.
    a. What is consolidated net income in each of these two years?
    b. What is the ending noncontrolling interest balance as of December 31, 1999?

21. Pistol, Inc., purchases 70 percent of Bytvl Company for $400,000. On that date, Bytvl had the following accounts:

	Book Value	Fair Market Value
Current assets	$210,000	$210,000
Land	170,000	180,000
Buildings	300,000	330,000
Liabilities	280,000	280,000

    The buildings have a 10-year life and any resulting goodwill will be amortized over 20 years. In addition, Bytvl holds a patent worth $20,000 that has a five-year life but is not recorded on its financial records.
    a. Assume that the purchase took place on January 1, 1998. At the end of 1998, the two companies report the following balances:

	Pistol	Bytvl
Revenues	$900,000	$600,000
Expenses	600,000	400,000

    What figures would appear in a consolidated income statement for this year?
    b. Assume that the purchase took place on April 1, 1998. At the end of 1998, the two companies report the following balances:

	Pistol	Bytvl
Revenues	$760,000	$590,000
Expenses	540,000	380,000

    What figures would appear in a consolidated income statement for this year?

22. On January 1, 1998, Alva Company has one asset, an invention with a cost of $10,000. The asset has an estimated life of 10 years and a fair market value of $50,000. Menlo, Inc. buys 60 percent of the outstanding stock of Alva on that date for $42,000.

During 1998, Alva generates revenues of $50,000 and expenses of $20,000. Any goodwill is to be amortized over its maximum possible life.

Required

For each of the following, determine the amounts included in the 1998 consolidated financial statements for Alva's revenues, expenses (plus amortization, if applicable), noncontrolling interest in the subsidiary's income, goodwill, and the invention:

    a. Economic unit concept.

    b. Proportionate consolidation.

    c. Parent company concept.

 Mabry, Inc., purchases 60 percent of Thompson Corporation on August 1, 1998, and an additional 30 percent on October 1, 1999. Annual amortization of $6,000 relates to the first acquisition and $10,000 to the second. Thompson reports the following figures for 1999:

Revenues	$600,000
Expenses	420,000
Retained earnings, 1/1/99	540,000
Dividends paid	70,000
Common stock	310,000

Without regard for this investment, Mabry earns $360,000 in net income during 1999.

    a. What is consolidated net income for 1999?

    b. What is the noncontrolling interest as of December 31, 1999?

 Clark Corporation acquired 50 percent of Lamp, Inc. several years ago and an additional 30 percent on April 1 of the current year. Goodwill of $60,000 was computed in connection with the first acquisition, and that amount is being amortized over its maximum life. The following figures are reported by these two companies for the current year. Investment income is not included within the balances for Clark shown here. Income is assumed to have been earned evenly throughout the year, and no dividends were paid.

	Clark Corporation	Lamp Inc.
Revenues	$600,000	$500,000
Expenses	380,000	300,000

    a. What is the noncontrolling interest's share of the subsidiary's net income?

    b. What is the amount of preacquisition income?

    c. What is the consolidated net income for these two companies?

25. Wilson Company acquired 7,000 of the 10,000 outstanding shares of Green Company on January 1, 1994, for $800,000. The subsidiary's book value on that date was $1,000,000. Any cost of this purchase in excess of Green's book value was assigned to goodwill with a 10-year life. On January 1, 1998, Wilson reported a $1,085,000 balance in the Investment in Green Company account based on application of the partial equity method. On October 1, 1998, Wilson sells 1,000 shares of the investment for $191,000. During 1998, Green reported net income of $120,000 and paid dividends of $40,000. These amounts are assumed to have been incurred evenly throughout the year.

    a. How are the 1,000 shares reported for the period from January 1, 1998, until October 1, 1998?

    b. What is the effect on net income of this sale of 1,000 shares?

    c. What accounting is now made of the 6,000 shares that Wilson continues to hold?

26. Robert Palmer and Anita Blackwood are the sole owners of Quinn Corporation. Palmer holds 70 percent of the stock while Blackwood owns the remaining 30 percent. On January 1, 1998, Quinn reports $10,000 in common stock and $90,000 in retained earnings. During each month of 1998, the company earns $15,000 in net income. Dividends of $5,000 are paid every month. At the end of the year, Quinn's net income is $180,000 (revenues of $400,000 less $220,000 in expenses), while $60,000 in dividends have been paid.

The book value of Quinn Corporation on December 1, 1998, is $210,000 ($100,000 beginning balance plus $10,000 growth for 11 months). On that date, Brown, Inc., buys all of Palmer's interest. Blackwood retains her 30 percent share of the company's stock. Brown pays exactly book value for these shares ($147,000 or 70 percent of $210,000). The individual fair market values of Quinn's assets and liabilities are equal to their book values.

Brown, Inc., is currently preparing consolidated financial statements for the year ending December 31, 1998.

a. What amount of Quinn's revenues would be included in the consolidated income statement?

b. What balance should be reported as the noncontrolling interest in Quinn's net income? Who is the noncontrolling interest?

c. For consolidation purposes, what happens to the $3,500 per month in dividends that Palmer received for the first 11 months of the year?

d. What amount of preacquisition income should be reported for consolidation purposes? Where is this figure disclosed? To whom does this income accrue?

27. Narcissus acquired 80 percent of the outstanding stock of Goldmund for $156,000. Just prior to this purchase, the following information is gathered from the two companies:

	Narcissus Book Value	Goldmund Book Value	Goldmund Fair Market Value
Current assets	$500,000	$150,000	$150,000
Land.....................	100,000	30,000	40,000
Buildings and equipment (net)	600,000	160,000	180,000
Liabilities	300,000	200,000	200,000
Common stock	400,000	40,000	
Retained earnings	500,000	100,000	

The buildings and equipment have a 10-year remaining life; any goodwill will be amortized over a 40-year period.

Subsequently, on December 31, 1998, the two companies are reporting the following account balances. Fair market values are presented where applicable.

	Narcissus Book Value	Goldmund Book Value	Goldmund Fair Market Value
Current assets	$300,000	$ 90,000	$ 90,000
Investment in Goldmund	156,000	–0–	–0–
Land.....................	150,000	60,000	74,000
Buildings and equipment (net)	570,000	180,000	216,000
Liabilities	246,000	185,000	185,000
Common stock	400,000	40,000	
Retained earnings, January 1, 1998	470,000	95,000	
Revenues	300,000	100,000	
Expenses..................	200,000	90,000	
Dividends paid	40,000	–0–	

Required:

a. On consolidated financial statements as of the date of acquisition, what balances are reported for the Buildings and Equipment account and the Goodwill account?

b. Assume that the purchase was made on January 1, 1994. What would be the consolidated Buildings and Equipment balance and the consolidated Goodwill balance on December 31, 1998?

c. Assume that the purchase was made during 1997. What is the consolidated net income for 1998 before subtracting the noncontrolling interest's share of the subsidiary's income?

d. Assume that the purchase was made during 1996. What is the noncontrolling interest's share of the subsidiary's income for the year ending December 31, 1998?

e. Assume that the purchase was made on July 1, 1998. Prepare a consolidated income statement for the year ending December 31, 1998.

f. Assume that the purchase was made on January 1, 1997. On October 1, 1998, Narcissus sells one-fourth of these shares for $82,000 in cash. What income effects appear on the consolidated income statement for 1998?

28. On January 1, ~~1997~~ *1996,* Thacker acquires 70 percent of Barker in a purchase transaction. The new subsidiary reported common stock on that date of $300,000 with retained earnings of $180,000. A building was undervalued in the company's financial records by $20,000. This building had a 10-year remaining life. Goodwill of $60,000 is being amortized over its maximum life.

Barker earns income and pays cash dividends as follows:

	Net Income	Dividends Paid	
1996	$ 75,000	$39,000	*30000*
1997	96,000	44,000	*52000*
1998	110,000	60,000	*50000*

On December 31, 1998, Thacker owes $22,000 to Barker. *payable*

a. If the equity method has been applied by Thacker, what are the consolidation entries needed as of December 31, 1998?

b. If the cost method has been applied by Thacker, what Entry *C is needed for a 1998 consolidation?

c. If the partial equity method has been applied by Thacker, what Entry *C is needed for a 1998 consolidation?

d. What noncontrolling interest balances will appear in consolidated financial statements for 1998?

29. The Hearts Company acquired an 80 percent interest in Dylan Company as of January 1, 1997. Hearts paid $620,000 to the owners of Dylan to purchase these shares. In addition, Hearts paid several lawyers and merger analysts $44,000 for assisting in the acquisition.

On January 1, 1997, Dylan reported a book value of $600,000 (common stock— $300,000; additional paid-in capital—$90,000; retained earnings—$210,000). Several of Dylan's buildings were undervalued by a total of $80,000. These buildings had a remaining life of 20 years. Any goodwill resulting from the takeover was assumed to have a 30-year life.

During the 1997–99 time period, Dylan reported the following figures:

Year	Net Income	Dividends Paid
1997	$ 70,000	$10,000
1998	90,000	15,000
1999	100,000	20,000

Required:

Determine the appropriate answers for each of the following questions:

a. What amount of amortization expense would be recognized in the consolidated financial statements for the initial years following this purchase?

b. If a consolidated balance sheet is prepared as of January 1, 1997, what amount of goodwill would be recognized?

c. If a consolidation worksheet is prepared as of January 1, 1997, what Entry S should be included?

d. On the separate financial records of the parent company, what amount of investment income would be reported for 1997 under each of the following accounting methods:
   (1) The equity method.
   (2) The partial equity method.
   (3) The cost method.

e. On the separate financial records of the parent company, what would be the December 31, 1999, balance for the Investment in Dylan Company account under each of the following accounting methods:
   (1) The equity method.
   (2) The partial equity method.
   (3) The cost method.

    f. As of December 31, 1998, Hearts has a Buildings account on its separate records with a balance of $800,000 while Dylan has a similar account with a $300,000 balance. What would be the consolidated balance for the Buildings account? What would be the balance if the economic unit concept is used?

    g. What would be the balance of consolidated goodwill as of December 31, 1999?

    h. Assume that the parent company has been applying the equity method to this investment. On December 31, 1999, the separate financial statements for the two companies present the following information:

	Hearts Company	Dylan Company
Common stock	$500,000	$300,000
Additional paid-in capital	280,000	90,000
Retained earnings, 12/31/99	620,000	425,000

What will be the consolidated balance of each of these accounts?

    i. Answer the same question as in requirement *h.,* but assume that the parent has been applying the partial equity method.

30. Following are several of the account balances taken from the records of Bigston and Lytle as of December 31, 1998. A few asset accounts have been omitted here. All revenues, expenses, and dividends occurred evenly throughout the year. Any goodwill is to be amortized over 30 years.

	Bigston	Lytle
Sales	$ 800,000	$500,000
Cost of goods sold	400,000	280,000
Expenses	200,000	100,000
Investment income	not given	–0–
Retained earnings, 1/1/98	1,400,000	700,000
Dividends	80,000	20,000
Land	600,000	200,000
Buildings (net)	700,000	300,000
Equipment (net)	400,000	400,000
Liabilities	500,000	200,000
Common stock ($10 par value)	400,000	100,000
Additional paid-in capital	500,000	600,000

    On July 1, 1998, Bigston purchased 80 percent of Lytle for $1,300,000 in cash. In addition, Big paid $30,000 in direct consolidation costs. At that time, Lytle's buildings (with a 10-year life) were undervalued on its books by $100,000. On a consolidation prepared at the end of 1998, what balances would be reported for the following:

Preacquisition Income	Net Income
Sales	Retained Earnings, 1/1/98
Expenses	Buildings (Net)
Noncontrolling Interest in	Land
Subsidiary's Net Income	Goodwill

31. Monroe, Inc., acquires 60 percent of Sunrise Corporation for $414,000 cash on January 1, 1998. On that date, Sunrise had the following accounts:

	Book Value	Fair Market Value
Current Assets	$150,000	$150,000
Land	200,000	200,000
Buildings (net) (6-year life)	300,000	360,000
Equipment (net) (4-year life)	300,000	280,000
Liabilities	400,000	400,000

The companies' financial statements for the year ending December 31, 2001, follow. Determine all consolidated balances. Goodwill has a 10-year life.

	Monroe	Sunrise
Revenues	$ 600,000	$ 300,000
Expenses	410,000	210,000
Investment income	42,000	
Net income	$ 232,000	$ 90,000
Retained earnings, 1/1/01	$ 700,000	$ 300,000
Net income	232,000	90,000
Dividends paid	92,000	70,000
Retained earnings, 12/31/01	$ 840,000	$ 320,000
Current assets	$ 330,000	$ 100,000
Land	220,000	200,000
Buildings (net)	700,000	200,000
Equipment (net)	400,000	500,000
Investment in Sunrise	414,000	–0–
Total assets	$2,064,000	$1,000,000
Liabilities	$ 500,000	$ 200,000
Common stock	724,000	480,000
Retained earnings, 12/31/01	840,000	320,000
Total liabilities and equities	$2,064,000	$1,000,000

Answer the following questions:

a. How can the accountant determine that the cost method has been applied by the parent?

b. What is the annual amortization initially recognized in connection with this purchase?

c. If the partial equity method had been applied, what Investment Income would have been recorded by the parent in 2001? What if the equity method had been applied?

d. What is the consolidated balance for retained earnings as of January 1, 2001?

e. What is the noncontrolling interest in the subsidiary's 2001 income?

f. What is consolidated net income for 2001?

g. Within consolidated statements at January 1, 1998, what balance is included for the subsidiary's Buildings account?

h. What is the consolidated Buildings account as of December 31, 2001?

  32. Father, Inc., buys 80 percent of the outstanding common stock of Sam Corporation on January 1, 1998, for $680,000 cash. Total book value of Sam on that date was only $600,000. However, Sam possessed several accounts that had fair market values differing from their book values:

	Book Value	Fair Market Value
Land	$160,000	$225,000
Buildings and equipment (10-year remaining life)	275,000	250,000
Notes payable (due in 8 years)	130,000	120,000

Any goodwill indicated by the purchase price is to be amortized over the maximum possible life. For internal reporting purposes, Father Inc. employs the equity method to account for this investment.

The following account balances are for the year ending December 31, 1998, for both companies. Determine consolidated balances for this business combination (either through individual computations or the use of a worksheet).

	Father	Sam
Revenues	$(1,360,000)	$(540,000)
Expenses	1,004,000	405,000
Equity in income of Sam	(105,000)	–0–
Net income	$ (461,000)	$(135,000)
Retained earnings, 1/1/98	$(1,265,000)	$(440,000)
Net income (above)	(461,000)	(135,000)
Dividends paid	260,000	65,000
Retained earnings, 12/31/98	$(1,466,000)	$(510,000)
Current assets	$ 965,000	$ 528,000
Investment in Sam	733,000	–0–
Land	292,000	160,000
Buildings and equipment (net)	877,000	260,000
Total assets	$ 2,867,000	$ 948,000
Accounts payable	$ (191,000)	$(148,000)
Notes payable	(460,000)	(130,000)
Common stock	(300,000)	(100,000)
Additional paid-in capital	(450,000)	(60,000)
Retained earnings (above)	(1,466,000)	(510,000)
Total liabilities and equities	$(2,867,000)	$(948,000)

Note: Credits are indicated by parentheses.

33. Answer problem 32 again, this time use the economic unit concept.

34. Burke Corporation purchased 90 percent of the outstanding voting shares of Drexel, Inc., on December 31, 1996. Burke paid a total of $602,000 in cash for these shares. As of that date, Drexel had the following account balances:

	Book Value	Fair Market Value
Current assets	$160,000	$160,000
Land	120,000	150,000
Building (10-year life)	220,000	200,000
Equipment (5-year life)	160,000	200,000
Patents (10-year life)	–0–	50,000
Liabilities (5-year life)	200,000	180,000
Common stock	180,000	
Retained earnings, 12/31/96	280,000	

The following adjusted trial balances are for these two companies on December 31, 1998:

	Burke Corporation	Drexel, Inc.
Debits		
Current Assets	$ 611,000	$ 250,000
Land	380,000	150,000
Buildings	490,000	250,000
Equipment	873,000	150,000
Investment in Drexel, Inc.	701,000	–0–
Expenses	620,000	160,000
Dividends Paid	110,000	70,000
Total Debits	$3,785,000	$1,030,000
Credits		
Liabilities	$ 860,000	$ 230,000
Common Stock	510,000	180,000
Retained Earnings, 1/1/98	1,367,000	340,000
Revenues	940,000	280,000
Investment Income	108,000	–0–
Total Credits	$3,785,000	$1,030,000

Required:

    a. Without using a worksheet or consolidation entries, determine the balances to be reported as of December 31, 1998, for this business combination. Any goodwill will be amortized over the maximum possible life.

    b. To verify the figures determined in requirement *a.*, prepare a consolidation worksheet for Burke Corporation and Drexel, Inc., as of December 31, 1998.

35. Using the information presented in problem 34, produce a worksheet to consolidate the financial statements of Burke and Drexel incorporating the economic unit concept rather than the parent company concept.

36. Following are the individual financial statements for Up and Down for the year ending December 31, 1998:

	Up	**Down**
Sales	$ 600,000	$ 300,000
Cost of goods sold	300,000	140,000
Operating expenses	174,000	60,000
Dividend income	24,000	–0–
Net income	$ 150,000	$ 100,000
Retained earnings, 1/1/98	$ 700,000	$ 400,000
Net income	150,000	100,000
Dividends paid	80,000	40,000
Retained earnings, 12/31/98	$ 770,000	$ 460,000
Cash and receivables	$ 250,000	$ 100,000
Inventory	500,000	190,000
Investment in Down	526,000	–0–
Buildings (net)	524,000	600,000
Equipment (net)	400,000	400,000
Total assets	$2,200,000	$1,290,000
Liabilities	800,000	490,000
Common stock	630,000	340,000
Retained earnings, 12/31/98	770,000	460,000
Totals liabilities and stockholders' equity	$2,200,000	$1,290,000

    Up acquired 60 percent of Down on April 1, 1998, for $526,000. On that date, equipment (with a six-year life) was overvalued by $30,000. Goodwill is to be amortized over five years. Income is earned by Down evenly during the year but the dividend was paid entirely on November 1, 1998.

Required:

    a. Prepare a consolidated income statement for the year ending December 31, 1998.

    b. Determine the consolidated balance for each of the following accounts as of December 31, 1998:

        Goodwill   Buildings (net)

        Equipment (net)   Dividends Paid

        Common Stock

37. Bon Air, Inc., acquired 70 percent (2,800 shares) of the outstanding voting stock of Creedmoor Corporation on January 1, 1995, for $250,000 cash. Creedmoor's net assets on that date totaled $230,000, but this balance included three accounts having actual values that differed from their book values:

	Book Value	**Fair Market Value**
Land	$30,000	$40,000
Equipment (20-year life)	50,000	30,000
Liabilities (10-year life)	70,000	50,000

Any goodwill created by this combination will be amortized over a 20-year life.

As of December 31, 1998, the two companies report the following balances:

	Bon Air	Creedmoor
Revenues	$ 694,800	$250,000
Expenses	(630,000)	(180,000)
Investment income	44,200	–0–
Net income	$ 109,000	$ 70,000
Retained earnings, January 1, 1998	$ 760,000	$260,000
Net income	109,000	70,000
Dividends paid	(68,000)	(10,000)
Retained earnings, December 31, 1998	$ 801,000	$320,000
Current assets	$ 72,000	$120,000
Investment in Creedmoor Corp.	321,800	–0–
Land	241,000	50,000
Buildings (net)	289,000	200,000
Equipment (net)	165,200	40,000
Total assets	$1,089,000	$410,000
Liabilities	$ 180,000	$ 50,000
Common stock	50,000	40,000
Additional paid-in capital	58,000	–0–
Retained earnings, December 31, 1998	801,000	320,000
Total liabilities and equities	$1,089,000	$410,000

Required:

(Each of the following are independent questions.)

a. Consolidated financial statements are being prepared on December 31, 1998. What balance should be reported for each of the following figures?

  Expenses
  Noncontrolling interest in Creedmoor's net income
  Revenues
  Retained earnings, January 1, 1998
  Net income
  Dividends paid
  Land
  Equipment
  Liabilities
  Common stock
  Retained earnings, December 31, 1998
  Noncontrolling interest in Creedmoor, December 31, 1998

b. If Bon Air sells 400 shares of this stock on December 31, 1998, for $60,000 cash, what journal entry is recorded?

38. The Seals Corporation purchased 80 percent of the outstanding stock of Croft, Inc., for $384,000. An appraisal of Croft made on that date determined that all book values appropriately reflected the actual worth of the underlying accounts except that a building with a 10-year life was undervalued by $20,000.

Following are the separate financial statements for the year ending December 31, 1998. Croft's income is assumed to have been earned evenly throughout the year. In addition, the subsidiary's dividend payments have been made as four equal quarterly payments. Seals has inappropriately included the receipt of dividends in its Sales account rather than a separate Dividend Income account.

	Seals Corporation	Croft, Inc.
Sales	$ 600,000	$210,000
Cost of goods sold....................	(200,000)	(80,000)
Operating expenses	(246,000)	(70,000)
Dividend income	–0–	–0–
Net income	$ 154,000	$ 60,000
Retained earnings, 1/1/98	$ 700,000	$280,000
Net income (above)	154,000	60,000
Dividends paid	(70,000)	(20,000)
Retained earnings, 12/31/98	$ 784,000	$320,000
Current assets	$ 400,000	$220,000
Investment in Croft, Inc.	384,000	–0–
Buildings (net)	320,000	180,000
Equipment (net).....................	360,000	210,000
Total assets	$ 1,464,000	$610,000
Liabilities	$ 470,000	$190,000
Common stock	210,000	100,000
Retained earnings, 12/31/98 (above) ...	784,000	320,000
Total liabilities and equities	$ 1,464,000	$610,000

Any goodwill indicated by this consolidation will be amortized over the maximum possible life.

Required:

a. *Prepare* a worksheet to consolidate these two companies on the assumption that the purchase was made on January 1, 1998.

b. *Without* using a worksheet determine consolidated totals for these two companies on the assumption that the purchase was made on October 1, 1998.

39. Watson, Inc., acquires 60 percent of Houston, Inc., on January 1, 1995, for $400,000 in cash. On that date, assets and liabilities of the subsidiary had the following values:

	Book Values	Fair Market Values
Current assets	$ 320,000	$320,000
Equipment (net)(10-year life)	410,000	380,000
Buildings (net)(20-year life)	300,000	360,000
Current liabilities....................	190,000	190,000
Bonds payable (due in 10 years)	370,000	350,000

Goodwill will be amortized over a 40-year period.

On December 31, 1998, these two companies report the following figures:

	Watson	Houston
Revenues	$ 640,000	$ 280,000
Expenses.........................	(480,000)	(210,000)
Equity in subsidiary earnings	38,600	–0–
Net income	$ 198,600	$ 70,000
Retained earnings, 1/1/98	$ 690,000	$ 380,000
Net income	198,600	70,000
Dividends paid	(60,200)	(40,000)
Retained earnings, 12/31/98	$ 828,400	$ 410,000
Current assets	$ 215,000	$ 260,000
Investment in Houston	500,400	–0–
Equipment (net)....................	500,000	420,000
Buildings (net)	413,000	520,000
Total assets	$1,628,400	$1,200,000
Current liabilities	$ 390,000	$ 170,000
Bonds payable.....................	100,000	370,000
Common stock	310,000	250,000
Retained earnings, 12/31/98	828,400	410,000
Total liabilities and equities	$1,628,400	$1,200,000

Answer each of the following questions:

a. The parent is recognizing a $38,600 balance as its "equity in subsidiary earnings." How was this balance calculated?

b. Is an adjustment needed to the parent's retained earnings as of January 1, 1998? Why or why not?

c. How much amortization expense should be recognized for consolidation purposes in 1998?

d. What is the noncontrolling interest in the subsidiary's net income?

e. Prepare a consolidated income statement.

f. What allocations were made as a result of the purchase price? What amount of each allocation remains at the end of 1998?

g. What is the December 31, 1998, noncontrolling interest in the subsidiary? What three components make up this total?

h. Prepare a consolidated balance sheet.

40. Good Corporation acquired 80 percent of the outstanding stock of Morning, Inc., on January 1, 1995, for $1,400,000 in cash, debt, and stock. One of Morning's buildings, with a 10-year remaining life, was undervalued on the company's accounting records by $80,000. Any goodwill resulting from this transaction also was to be amortized over a 10-year period.

During subsequent years, Morning reports the following:

	Net Income	Dividends Paid
1995	$180,000	$100,000
1996	200,000	100,000
1997	300,000	100,000
1998	400,000	120,000

The following trial balances are for these two companies as of December 31, 1998. Morning owes Good $100,000 as of this date.

	Good	Morning
Debits		
Cash	$ 300,000	$ 200,000
Receivables	700,000	400,000
Inventory	400,000	500,000
Investment in Morning	1,400,000	–0–
Land	700,000	600,000
Buildings (net)	300,000	700,000
Expenses	400,000	100,000
Dividends paid	380,000	120,000
Total debits	$4,580,000	$2,620,000
Credits		
Liabilities	$ 200,000	$ 620,000
Common stock	1,000,000	460,000
Additional paid-in capital	600,000	40,000
Retained earnings, 1/1/98	1,800,000	1,000,000
Revenues	884,000	500,000
Dividend income	96,000	–0–
Total credits	$4,580,000	$2,620,000

Prepare consolidated financial statements for this business combination.

41. On January 1, 1998, Turner Company bought a 30 percent interest in Atlanta Company. The acquisition price was $257,000 and was negotiated under the assumption that all of Atlanta's accounts were fairly valued within the company's accounting records. During 1998, Atlanta reported net income of $90,000 and paid cash dividends of $60,000. Turner felt that the ability to significantly influence the operations of Atlanta had been achieved and, therefore, accounted for this investment by means of the equity method.

On April 1, 1999, Turner acquired an additional 30 percent interest in Atlanta for $309,000 in cash. As of this date, the parent believed that a patent developed by Atlanta was worth $100,000, even though it was not recorded within the financial records of the subsidiary. This patent is anticipated to have a remaining life of 15 years. Although the financial statements now have to be consolidated, Turner elects to continue applying the equity method to this investment for internal reporting purposes.

The following financial information is for these two companies for 1999. Assume that any goodwill will be amortized over a 10-year life. In addition, all of the subsidiary's operations as well as dividend payments are considered to have occurred evenly throughout the year.

	Turner Company	Atlanta Company
Revenues	$ 660,000	$ 400,000
Expenses	(398,000)	(280,000)
Income of subsidiary	57,250	
Net income	$ 319,250	$ 120,000
Retained earnings, beginning balance	$ 821,000	$ 500,000
Net income (above)	319,250	120,000
Cash dividends paid to stockholders	(148,000)	(80,000)
Retained earnings, ending balance	$ 992,250	$ 540,000
Current assets	$ 481,000	$ 410,000
Investment in subsidiary	588,250	
Land	388,000	200,000
Buildings	700,900	630,000
Total assets	$2,158,150	$1,240,000
Liabilities	$ 660,900	$ 380,000
Common stock	95,000	300,000
Additional paid-in capital	410,000	20,000
Retained earnings, ending balance	992,250	540,000
Total liabilities and equities	$2,158,150	$1,240,000

Answer the following questions:

a. What allocation would Turner have made of the initial $257,000 acquisition price?

b. What is the book value of the Investment in Atlanta account at the end of 1998?

c. What allocation would Turner have made of the second $309,000 acquisition price?

d. On Turner's separate income statement for 1999, the Income of Subsidiary account has a balance of $57,250. How was this amount derived?

e. On Turner's separate balance sheet as of December 31, 1999, the Investment of Subsidiary account reports a balance of $588,250. How was this balance derived?

f. What is the consolidated retained earnings balance as of January 1, 1999? How is this amount determined?

g. Prepare a worksheet to consolidate the financial statements of these two companies as of December 31, 1999.

42. On January 1, 1998, Ace, Incorporated acquired 60 percent of the outstanding shares of Holt Company for $566,000 in cash. At the time of this purchase, Holt held a building (10 year remaining life) that was undervalued in the accounting records by $100,000. During 1998, Holt reported net income of $150,000 and paid cash dividends of $80,000. On May 1, 1999, Ace bought an additional 30 percent interest in Holt for $366,000. Ace reappraised Holt's assets and liabilities on this date and estimated that the company's buildings were currently undervalued by $180,000. At the time of this second purchase, these buildings had a nine-year remaining life. Any goodwill was to be amortized over 40 years.

The following financial information is for these two companies for 1999. Holt issued no additional capital stock during either 1998 or 1999. Income and dividends can be assumed as having been earned and paid evenly throughout each of the years.

	Ace, Incorporated	Holt Company
Revenues	$ 400,000	$ 300,000
Expenses	(200,000)	(120,000)
Investment income (partial equity method)	144,000	
Net income	$ 344,000	$ 180,000
Retained earnings, 1/1/99	$ 800,000	$ 500,000
Net income (above)	344,000	180,000
Dividends paid	(144,000)	(60,000)
Retained earnings, 12/31/99	$1,000,000	$ 620,000
Current assets	$ 200,000	$ 190,000
Investment in Holt Company	1,070,000	
Land	100,000	600,000
Buildings (net)	210,000	300,000
Equipment (net)	380,000	110,000
Total assets	$1,960,000	$1,200,000
Liabilities	$ 500,000	$ 200,000
Common stock	400,000	300,000
Additional paid-in capital	60,000	80,000
Retained earnings, 12/31/99	1,000,000	620,000
Total liabilities and equities	$1,960,000	$1,200,000

Required:

Determine the appropriate balances for consolidated financial statements for Ace, Incorporated, and Holt Company for December 31, 1999, and the year then ended. Show supporting computations in good form.

43. On January 1, 1994, Wilbourne Company acquired 6,000 of the 10,000 outstanding shares of Hampton Corporation. The purchase price included an allocation of $120,000 for goodwill. All of the assets and liabilities of Hampton had fair market values equal to their book values. The goodwill was to be amortized over the maximum life of 40 years.

On January 1, 1997, Wilbourne bought an additional 2,000 shares of Hampton increasing ownership to an 80 percent interest. In making this second acquisition, Wilbourne assigned $40,000 of the purchase price to a patent (life of 10 years) held by Hampton. An additional $40,000 was attributed to goodwill.

In need of raising cash, Wilbourne sold 1,000 shares of its investment in Hampton on April 1, 1998, for $140,000 in cash. A problem arose in connection with the recording of this sale. Wilbourne's accountants could not agree on the appropriate gain or loss to be recognized so they simply debited cash for $140,000 and credited the Investment account for the same amount. Because of the confusion, Wilbourne prepared no other entries for the investment for the year of 1998, although the equity method had been properly applied prior to this time.

The following individual financial records are for these two companies for 1998. Prepare a consolidation worksheet and the resulting financial statements. Assume that an averaging system is used to determine the appropriate book value of the shares that were sold.

	Wilbourne Company	Hampton Corporation
Revenues	$ 920,000	$ 600,000
Expenses.....................................	(650,000)	(440,000)
Equity income of Hampton Corporation.............	–0–	–0–
Net income	$ 270,000	$ 160,000
Retained earnings, 1/1/98	$1,430,000	$ 750,000
Net income (above)	270,000	160,000
Dividends paid	(150,000)	–0–
Retained earnings, 12/31/98	$1,550,000	$ 910,000
Cash...	$ 60,000	$ 98,000
Receivables..................................	430,000	210,000
Inventories	677,000	620,000
Investment in Hampton Corporation	883,000	–0–
Buildings and equipment (net)	620,000	514,000
Patents (net)	40,000	90,000
Total assets	$2,710,000	$1,532,000
Liabilities	$ 690,000	$ 322,000
Common stock	470,000	300,000
Retained earnings, 12/31/98	1,550,000	910,000
Total liabilities and equities	$2,710,000	$1,532,000

COMPUTER PROJECT

A Comparison of Consolidated Financial Statements under the Economic Unit Concept and the Parent Company Concept

The purpose of this project is to assess the sensitivity of alternative concepts of noncontrolling interest valuation on consolidated financial reporting. The project requires the use of a computer and a spreadsheet software package (Microsoft Excel, Lotus 123, etc.). The use of these tools allows assessment of the sensitivity of alternative accounting methods on consolidated financial reporting without the necessity of preparing several similar worksheets by hand. Also by modeling a worksheet process, a better understanding of accounting for combined reporting entities may result.

The project involves preparing two consolidated worksheets for a parent and subsidiary. The first worksheet uses the economic unit concept (as recommended by the FASB exposure draft) for the consolidated entity. The second worksheet uses the parent company concept (most prevalent in current practice). Additional analysis is provided to assess the sensitivity of each approach to changes in the percentage of the subsidiary owned by the noncontrolling interest.

Project Scenario   On January 1, 1998, Pine purchased a controlling interest in Straw, Inc., for $700,000. At that date Straw's book value was $600,000. Straw's assets and liabilities approximated their market values except for the following items:

	Market Value	Book Value
Land	$ 88,000	$100,000
Building (8-year remaining life)	170,000	140,000
Equipment (5-year remaining life).......	370,000	325,000

Pine accounts for its investment in Straw using the equity method and amortizes goodwill over a 10-year period. Straw declared a $25,000 dividend late in 1998. The dividend had not been paid as of December 31, 1998.

Pine and Straw submit trial balances for consolidation as of December 31, 1998, as indicated in the accompanying worksheet template. Note that the trial balance for Pine reflects a 70 percent ownership of Straw. However, to provide insights regarding varying levels of outside ownership, the trial balance must be programmed so that this percentage can vary.

Instructions

1.   Input the information from the **worksheet template** into your spreadsheet as a starting point for two separate consolidation worksheets—one for the economic unit concept and

one for the parent company concept. Use either separate worksheets available in Excel or Lotus, or use distinct areas of a single spreadsheet for each consolidation.

2. Designate a single cell as the percentage of Straw acquired by Pine. Use this cell (e.g., B38 in the worksheet template) as a reference in other cell formulas. **Your worksheets should automatically change when different percentages are entered in this designated cell.**

3. On each worksheet, prepare separate cost allocation schedules using formulas to allow for alternative ownership percentages.

4. To accommodate alternative ownership percentages, the following accounts in Pine's trial balances require formulas: Equity income of Straw, Dividend receivable, Investment in Straw, as well as the carry down figures (income and retained earnings) and the totals. For example, in Excel, cell B17 in Pine's trial balance can be entered as =C12*B38 so that it will change whenever cell B38 changes. No accounts in Straw's trial balances require formulas.

5. Complete the worksheet adjusting and eliminating entries, the noncontrolling interest amounts, and consolidated balances. Be sure to use formulas to enable the worksheets to automatically change when the percentage acquired is changed.

6. Prepare an accompanying written report that compares and explains the differences between the economic unit concept and parent company concept consolidated figures at 70 percent ownership. Describe the effects on the consolidated balances when 100 percent ownership exists. Indicate which concept you believe should be used in financial reporting and why.

Worksheet Template

	A	B	C	D	E	F	G
1	**December 31, 1998**					Noncontrolling	
2		**Pine**	**Straw**	Adjustments & Eliminations		Interest	Consolidated
3	Revenues	($ 700,000)	($490,000)				
4	Expenses	$ 550,000	$290,000				
5	Equity income of Straw	($ 107,485)					
6	Noncontrolling interest in Straw's Income						
7	Net Income	($ 257,485)	($200,000)				
8							
9	Retained earnings—Pine 1/1/98	($ 775,000)					
10	Retained earnings—Straw 1/1/98		($350,000)				
11	Net income (above)	($ 257,485)	($200,000)				
12	Dividends declared	$ 115,000	$ 25,000				
13	Retained earnings 12/31/98	($ 917,485)	($525,000)				
14							
15	Cash	$ 88,000	$ 42,000				
16	Accounts receivable	$ 110,000	$153,000				
17	Dividend receivable	$ 17,500					
18	Inventory	$ 225,000	$195,000				
19	Investment in Straw	$ 789,985					
20							
21							
22							
23	Land	$ 300,000	$100,000				
24	Buildings (net)	$ 650,000	$125,000				
25	Equipment (net)	$ 250,000	$305,000				
26	Goodwill						
27	Total assets	$2,430,485	$920,000				
28							
29	Dividend payable		($ 25,000)				
30	Liabilities	$ 513,000)	($120,000)				
31	Common stock	($1,000,000)	($250,000)				
32	Noncontrolling interest						
33							
34							
35	Retained earnings (above)	($ 917,485)	($525,000)				
36	Total liabilities and equity	($2,430,485)	($920,000)				
37							
38	**Percentage acquired**	**70%**					

C H A P T E R

5

Consolidated Financial Statements— Intercompany Asset Transactions

QUESTIONS TO CONSIDER

■ How does the intercompany transfer of inventory or other assets between parent and subsidiary affect the consolidation process?

■ Gains on intercompany transactions are considered unrealized until the assets are resold to outsiders or consumed. Prior to the realization of these gains, what adjustments are required in producing consolidated financial statements?

■ How does the presence of intercompany transactions affect the balances reported for any noncontrolling interest? What impact does the direction of these transfers (upstream versus downstream) have on the reporting of a noncontrolling interest?

■ The intercompany sale of land and depreciable assets also can occur between the members of a business combination. What impact does the specific type of property being conveyed have on the consolidation process?

■ Why does the transfer of a depreciable asset frequently result in the recording of excess depreciation in subsequent years?

In Chapter 1, the elimination of gains created by inventory transfers between two affiliated companies is analyzed in connection with equity method accounting. The central theme of that discussion is that intercompany profits are not considered to be realized until the earning process is culminated by a sale to an unrelated party. This same accounting logic applies to transactions between companies within a business combination. Because a single economic entity is formed, such sales create neither profits nor losses. In reference to this issue, *ARB 51* (par. 7) states:

> As consolidated statements are based on the assumption that they represent the financial position and operating results of a single business enterprise, such statements should not include gain or loss on transactions among the companies in the group. Accordingly, any intercompany profit or loss on assets remaining within the group should be eliminated; the concept usually applied for this purpose is gross profit or loss.

The elimination of the accounting effects created by intercompany transactions is one of the most significant problems encountered in the consolidation process. The mere volume of transfers within most large enterprises can be staggering. The 1996 annual report for the Ford Motor Company shows the elimination of intersegment sales amounting to over $28 billion!

Such transactions are especially common in companies that have been constructed as a vertically integrated chain of organizations. These entities reduce their costs by developing affiliations where one operation furnishes products to another. As observed by *Mergers and Acquisitions:*

Downstream acquisitions . . . are aimed at securing critical sources of materials and components, streamlining manufacturing and materials planning, gaining economies of scale, entering new markets, and enhancing overall competitiveness. Manufacturers that combine with suppliers are often able to assert total control over such critical areas as product quality and resource planning.[1]

Intercompany asset transactions take several forms. In particular, inventory transfers are especially prevalent. However, the sale of land as well as depreciable assets also can occur between the parties within a combination. This chapter examines the consolidation procedures necessitated by each of these different types of intercompany asset transfers.[2]

INTERCOMPANY INVENTORY TRANSACTIONS

As discussed in previous chapters, companies that make up a business combination frequently retain their legal identities as separate operating centers and maintain their own record-keeping. Thus, any inventory sales between these companies trigger the independent accounting systems of both parties. Revenue is duly recorded by the seller, while the purchase is simultaneously entered into the accounts of the buyer. For internal reporting purposes, recording an inventory transfer as a sale/purchase provides vital data to help measure the operational efficiency of each enterprise.[3]

Despite the informational benefits of accounting for the transaction in this manner, from a consolidated perspective neither a sale nor a purchase has occurred. *An intercompany transfer is merely the internal movement of inventory, an event that creates no net change in the financial position of the business combination taken as a whole.* Thus, in producing consolidated financial statements, the recorded effects of these transfers are eliminated so that consolidated statements reflect only transactions with outside parties. Worksheet entries serve this purpose; they adapt the financial information reported by the separate companies to the perspective of the consolidated enterprise. The entire impact of the intercompany transactions must be identified and then removed. The deleting of the actual transfer is described here first.

The Sales and Purchases Accounts

To account for related companies as a single economic entity, all intercompany sales/purchases accounts are eliminated. For example, if Arlington Company makes an $80,000 inventory sale to Zirkin Company, an affiliated party within a business combination, both parties record the transfer as a normal sale/purchase. The following worksheet entry is then necessary to remove the resulting balances from the consolidated figures. Cost of Goods Sold is reduced here under the assumption that the Purchases account usually is closed out prior to the consolidation process.

---

[1] "Acquiring along the Value Chain," *Mergers & Acquisitions,* June–July 1996, p. 8.

[2] The FASB's 1995 Exposure Draft, *Consolidated Financial Statements: Policy and Procedures,* also addresses intercompany profit issues. However, no major changes in accounting for intercompany profits are recommended in the Exposure Draft. The accounting and reporting procedures in this chapter are consistent with those endorsed in the Exposure Draft.

[3] For all intercompany transactions, the two parties involved view the events from different perspectives. Thus, the transfer is both a sale and a purchase, often creating both a receivable and a payable. To indicate the dual nature of such transactions, these accounts are indicated within this text as sales/purchases, receivables/payables, and so on.

Consolidation Entry TI

Sales	80,000	
Cost of Goods Sold (purchases component)		80,000

To eliminate effects of intercompany transfer of inventory.
(Labeled "TI" in reference to the transferred inventory.)

In the preparation of consolidated financial statements, the preceding elimination must be made for all intercompany inventory transfers. The total recorded (intercompany) sales figure is deleted regardless of whether the transaction was downstream (from parent to subsidiary) or upstream (from subsidiary to parent).[4] Furthermore, the elimination is unaffected by any markup included in the transfer price. Because the entire amount of the transfer was between related parties, the total effect must be removed in preparing the consolidated statements.[5]

Unrealized Gains—Year of Transfer (Year One)

Removal of the sale/purchase is often just the first in a series of consolidation entries necessitated by inventory transfers. Despite the previous elimination, unrealized gains created by such sales may still exist in the accounting records at year's end. These gains initially result when the merchandise is priced at more than historical cost. Actual transfer prices are established in several ways, including the normal sales price of the inventory, sales price less a specified discount, or at a predetermined markup above cost. In a footnote to its 1996 financial statements, Ford Motor Company explains that

> Intercompany sales among geographic areas consist primarily of vehicles, parts, and components manufactured by the company and various subsidiaries and sold to different entities within the consolidated group; transfer prices for these transactions are established by agreement between the affected entities.

Regardless of the method used for this pricing decision, intercompany gains that remain unrealized at year-end must be removed in arriving at consolidated figures.

All Inventory Remains at Year-End   In the preceding illustration, assume that Arlington acquired or produced this inventory at a cost of $50,000 and then sold it to Zirkin, an affiliated party, at the indicated price of $80,000. From a consolidated perspective, the inventory still has a historical cost of only $50,000. However, it is now reported in Zirkin's records as an asset at the $80,000 transfer price. In addition, because of the markup, Arlington has recorded a $30,000 gross profit as a result of this intercompany sale. Because the transaction did not occur with an outside party, recognition of this profit is not appropriate for the combination as a whole.

Thus, although the sale/purchase figures are eliminated by consolidation entry TI shown earlier, the $30,000 inflation created by the transfer price still exists in two areas of the individual statements:

- Ending inventory remains overstated by $30,000.
- Gross profit is artificially overstated by this same amount.

---

[4]Downstream and upstream transactions were introduced in Chapter 1. Although the direction of the transfer did not influence the equity method of accounting (for external reporting), the distinction is significant in the preparation of consolidated statements.

[5]As is shown in the appendix to this chapter, the FASB's discussion memorandum, *An Analysis of Issues Related to Consolidation Policy and Procedures,* does identify alternative theoretical approaches to consolidation that advocate removing only the parent's portion of intercompany sales/purchases when a noncontrolling interest is present. In current practice, elimination of all intercompany sales/purchases (as shown here) appears to predominate and is recommended in the FASB's Exposure Draft, *Consolidated Financial Statements: Policy and Procedures.*

Correction of the ending inventory only requires a reduction in the asset. How-ever, before decreasing gross profit, the accounts affected by the unrealized gain must be identified. The ending inventory total serves as a negative component within the Cost of Goods Sold computation; it represents the portion of acquired inventory that was not sold. Thus, the $30,000 overstatement of the inventory that is still held incorrectly lowers this expense (the inventory that was sold). *Despite Entry TI, the inflated ending inventory figure causes cost of goods sold to be too low and, thus, profits to be too high by $30,000.* For consolidation purposes, the expense must be raised by this amount, through a worksheet adjustment that properly removes the unrealized gain from consolidated net income.

Consequently, if all of the transferred inventory is retained by the business combi-nation at the end of the year, the following worksheet entry also has to be included to eliminate the effects of the gain that remains unrealized within ending inventory.

Consolidation Entry G—Year of Transfer (Year One)
All Inventory Remains

Cost of Goods Sold (ending inventory component)	30,000	
Inventory (balance sheet account)		30,000
To remove unrealized gain created by intercompany sale.		

This entry (labeled G for gain) reduces the consolidated Inventory account to its original $50,000 historical cost. Furthermore, increasing cost of goods sold by $30,000 effectively removes the unrealized gain from gross profit. Thus, both report-ing problems created by the transfer price markup are resolved by this worksheet entry.

Only a Portion of Inventory Remains Obviously, a company does not buy inven-tory to hold it for an indefinite time. The acquired items are used within the com-pany's operations or resold to unrelated, outside parties. Intercompany gains ultimately are realized by the subsequent consumption or reselling of these goods. Therefore, only the transferred inventory still held at year's end continues to be recorded in the separate statements at a value more than the historical cost. For this reason, *the elimination of unrealized gains (Entry G) is not based on total intercom-pany sales but only on the amount of transferred merchandise retained within the business at the end of the year.*

To illustrate, assume that Arlington transferred inventory costing $50,000 to Zirkin, a related company, for $80,000, thus recording a gross profit of $30,000. Assume further that by year's end Zirkin has resold $60,000 of these goods to unrelated parties but retains the other $20,000 (for resale in the following year). From the viewpoint of the consolidated company, the gain on the $60,000 portion of the intercompany sale has now been earned and no adjustment is required for consol-idation purposes.

Conversely, any gain recorded in connection with the $20,000 in merchandise that remains is still a component within Zirkin's Inventory account. Because the markup was 37½ percent ($30,000 gross profit/$80,000 transfer price), this retained inventory is stated at a value $7,500 more than its original cost ($20,000 × 37½%). The required reduction (Entry G) is not the entire $30,000 shown previously but only the $7,500 unrealized gain that remains in ending inventory.

Consolidation Entry G—Year of Transfer (Year One)
40% of Inventory Remains (replaces previous entry)

Cost of Goods Sold (ending inventory component)	7,500	
Inventory		7,500
To remove portion of intercompany gain which is unrealized in year of transfer.		

II.

Unrealized Gains—Year Following Transfer (Year Two)

Whenever an unrealized intercompany gain is present in ending Inventory, one further consolidation entry is eventually required. Although Entry G removes the gain from the *consolidated* inventory balances in the year of transfer, the $7,500 overstatement remains within the separate financial records of the buyer and seller. The effects of this gain are carried into their beginning balances in the subsequent year. Hence, another worksheet elimination is necessary in the period following the transfer. For consolidation purposes, the unrealized portion of the intercompany gain must be adjusted in two successive years (from ending inventory in the year of transfer and from beginning inventory of the next period).

Referring again to Arlington's sale of inventory to Zirkin, the $7,500 unrealized gain is still in Zirkin's Inventory account at the start of the subsequent year. Once again, the overstatement is removed within the consolidation process but this time from the beginning inventory balance (which appears in the financial statements only as a positive component of cost of goods sold). This elimination is termed *Entry *G*. The asterisk indicates that the intercompany gain was created by a transfer made in a previous year.

Consolidation Entry *G—Year Following Transfer (Year Two)

Retained Earnings (beginning balance of seller) 7,500
    Cost of Goods Sold (beginning inventory component)   7,500
        To remove unrealized gain from beginning figures so that it can be recognized currently in the period in which the earning process is completed.

By reducing cost of goods sold (beginning inventory) through this worksheet entry, the gross profit reported for this second year is increased. For consolidation purposes, the gain on the transfer is recognized in the period in which the items are actually sold to outside parties. As shown in the following diagram, Entry G initially deferred the $7,500 gain because this amount was unrealized in the year of transfer. Entry *G now increases consolidated net income (by decreasing cost of goods sold) to reflect the earning process in the current year.

In Entry *G, removal of the $7,500 from beginning inventory (within cost of goods sold) appropriately increases current income and should not pose a significant conceptual problem. However, the rationale for decreasing the seller's beginning retained earnings deserves further explanation. This reduction removes the unrealized gain (recognized by the seller in the year of transfer) so that the profit is reported in the period when it is earned. Despite the consolidation entries in Year One, the $7,500 gain remained on this company's separate books and was closed to retained earnings at the end of the period. Recall that consolidation entries are never posted to the individual affiliate's books. Therefore, from a consolidated view, the buyer's inventory and the seller's retained earnings as of the beginning of Year Two contain the unrealized profit and must both be reduced in Entry *G.

Intercompany Beginning Inventory Gain Adjustment—Downstream Sales When Parent Uses Equity Method

The worksheet elimination of the sales/purchases balances (Entry TI) as well as the entry to remove the unrealized gain from ending inventory in Year One (Entry G) are both standard, regardless of the circumstances of the consolidation. Conversely, in one specific situation, the procedure used to eliminate the intercompany gain from Year Two's beginning accounts differs from the Entry *G just presented. If (1) the original transfer is downstream (made by the parent) and (2) the equity method has been applied for internal accounting purposes, the Investment in Subsidiary account replaces beginning retained earnings in Entry *G.

When using the equity method, the parent maintains appropriate income balances within its own individual financial records. Thus, any unrealized gain is removed by the parent at the end of Year One through an equity method adjustment that also decreases the Investment in Subsidiary account. With the gain eliminated, the retained earnings of the parent/seller at the beginning of the following year is correctly stated.[6] The account does not contain the unrealized gain and needs no adjustment. For consolidation purposes, cost of goods sold is still decreased in Entry *G but the Investment in Subsidiary account is increased (to offset the equity method reduction).

Consolidation Entry *G—Year Following Transfer (Year Two)
(replaces previous Entry *G when transfers have been downstream and the equity method is in use)

Investment in Subsidiary	7,500	
Cost of Goods Sold (beginning inventory component)		7,500

To remove impact of previously deferred unrealized gain to allow for recognition in the current period. The Investment account replaces retained earnings here because the equity method has been applied and the transfers were downstream. The retained earnings of the parent (the seller) have already been corrected by an equity adjustment.

Unrealized Gains—Effect on Noncontrolling Interest Valuation

The effects of intercompany inventory transfers on business combinations are appropriately accounted for by the worksheet entries just described. However, one question remains: What impact do these procedures have on the valuation of a noncontrolling interest? In regard to this issue, paragraph 13 of *ARB 51* states:

> The amount of intercompany profit or loss to be eliminated in accordance with paragraph 7 is not affected by the existence of a minority interest. The complete elimination of the intercompany profit or loss is consistent with the underlying assumption that consolidated statements represent the financial position and operating results of a single business enterprise. The elimination of the intercompany profit or loss *may be allocated proportionately* between the majority and minority interests. (Emphasis added.)

The last sentence indicates that alternative approaches are available in computing the noncontrolling interest's share of a subsidiary's net income. According to this pronouncement, recognition of outside ownership *may or may not be* affected by unrealized gains resulting from intercompany transfers. Because consolidated net income is reduced by the amount attributed to a noncontrolling interest, the handling of this issue can affect the reported profitability of a business combination.

---

[6]If intercompany transfers are upstream, the subsidiary is the seller. Because application of the equity method affects only the records of the parent, the actual unrealized gain is not eliminated and must be removed from the retained earnings of the subsidiary/seller through Entry *G.

To illustrate, assume that Large Company owns 70 percent of the voting stock of Small Company. To avoid extraneous complications assume that no amortization expense resulted from this purchase. Assume further that Large reports current net income (from separate operations) of $500,000, while Small earns $100,000. During the current period, intercompany transfers of $200,000 occur with a total markup of $90,000. At the end of the year, an unrealized intercompany gain of $40,000 remains within the inventory accounts.

Clearly, the consolidated net income prior to the reduction for the 30 percent noncontrolling interest is $560,000, the two income balances less the unrealized gain. The problem facing the accountant is the computation of the noncontrolling interest's share of Small's income. Because of the flexibility allowed by *ARB 51,* this figure may be reported as either $30,000 (30 percent of the $100,000 earnings of the subsidiary) or $18,000 (30 percent of reported income after that figure is reduced by the $40,000 unrealized gain).

To determine an appropriate valuation for this noncontrolling interest allocation, an analysis must be made of the relationship between an intercompany transaction and the outside owners. If a transfer is downstream (the parent sells inventory to the subsidiary), a logical view would seem to be that the unrealized gain is that of the parent company. The parent made the original sale, therefore, the gross profit is included in its financial records. Because the subsidiary's income is unaffected, little justification exists for adjusting the noncontrolling interest to reflect the deferral of the unrealized gain. Consequently, in the example of Large and Small, if the transfers were downstream, the 30 percent noncontrolling interest would be $30,000 based on Small's reported income of $100,000.

In contrast, if inventory is sold by the subsidiary to the parent (an upstream transfer), the gross profit would be recognized in the subsidiary's financial records, even though part of this income remains unrealized from a consolidation perspective. Because the outside owners possess their interest in the subsidiary, a reasonable conclusion would be that valuation of the noncontrolling interest is calculated on the income actually earned by this company. The 1995 FASB Exposure Draft, *Consolidated Financial Statements: Policy and Procedures,* supports allocating a proportionate amount of the intercompany profit adjustments (from upstream sales) to the noncontrolling interest:

> The effects on equity of eliminating intercompany profit and losses on assets that remain within the group shall be allocated between the controlling interest and the noncontrolling interest on the basis of their proportionate interest in the selling affiliate.

Thus, in this textbook, the noncontrolling interest's share of consolidated net income is computed based on *the reported income of the subsidiary after adjustment for any unrealized upstream gains*. Returning to Large Company and Small Company, if the $40,000 unrealized gain was the result of an upstream sale from subsidiary to parent, only $60,000 of Small's $100,000 reported income actually has been earned by the end of the year. The allocation to the noncontrolling interest is, therefore, reported as $18,000, or 30 percent of this realized income figure.

[handwritten annotation: but not for downstream sales]

Alternative Concepts of a Noncontrolling Interest

Although the noncontrolling interest figure is based here on the subsidiary's reported income adjusted for the effects of upstream intercompany transfers, *ARB 51,* as quoted earlier, does not require this treatment. Giving effect to upstream transfers in this calculation but not to downstream transfers is no more than an attempt to select the most logical approach from among acceptable alternatives. Over the years a number of possible methods of consolidating the results of intercompany transfers have been considered. Several of these alternatives are in the appendix at the end of this chapter.

Intercompany Inventory Transfers Summarized

To assist in overcoming the complications created by intercompany transfers, the consolidation process is demonstrated in three different ways:

- Before proceeding to a numerical example, the impact of intercompany transfers on consolidated figures is reviewed. Ultimately, the accountant must understand how the balances to be reported by a business combination are derived when unrealized gains result from either upstream or downstream sales.

- Next, two different consolidation worksheets are produced: one for downstream transfers and the other for upstream. The various consolidation procedures used in these worksheets are explained and analyzed.

- Finally, several of the worksheet entries used in developing a consolidation worksheet are shown side by side so that the differences created by the direction of the transfers can be better understood.

The Development of Consolidated Totals   The following summary discusses only the accounts impacted by intercompany transactions:

A. *Revenues.* The parent's balance is added to the subsidiary's balance but all intercompany transfers are then removed.

B. *Cost of Goods Sold.* This expense is one of the most difficult figures computed within the consolidation process. The parent's balance is added to the subsidiary's balance but all intercompany transfers are removed. The resulting total is decreased by any beginning unrealized gain (thus, raising net income) and increased by any ending unrealized gain (to reduce net income).

C. *Expenses.* The parent's balance is added to the subsidiary's balance plus any amortization expense for the year recognized on the purchase price allocations and goodwill.[7]

D. *Noncontrolling Interest in Subsidiary's Net Income.* The subsidiary's reported net income is adjusted for the effects of unrealized gains on upstream transfers (but not downstream transfers) and then multiplied by the percentage of outside ownership.

E. *Retained Earnings at the Beginning of the Year.* As in previous chapters, if the equity method has been applied, the parent's balance mirrors the consolidated total. When any other method is used, the parent's beginning retained earnings must be converted to the equity method by Entry *C. Accruals for this purpose are based on the income actually earned by the subsidiary in previous years (reported income adjusted for any unrealized upstream gains).

F. *Inventory.* The parent's balance is added to the subsidiary's balance. Any unrealized gain remaining at the end of the current year is removed to lower the reported balance to historical cost.

G. *Land, Buildings, and Equipment.* The parent's balance is added to the subsidiary's balance. This total is adjusted for any purchase price allocations and subsequent amortization.[8]

---

[7]As discussed later in this chapter, consolidated expenses also have to be reduced to remove excess depreciation recognized whenever a depreciable asset is transferred between the companies within a business combination at a price more than the book value.

[8]As discussed later in this chapter, if land, buildings, or equipment have been transferred between parent and subsidiary, the separately reported balances must be returned to historical cost figures in deriving consolidated totals.

H. *Noncontrolling Interest in Subsidiary at End of Year.* The final total begins with the noncontrolling interest at the beginning of the year. This figure is based on the subsidiary's book value on that date after removing any unrealized gains on upstream sales. The beginning balance is updated by adding the portion of the subsidiary's income assigned to these outside owners (computed above) and subtracting the noncontrolling interest's share of the subsidiary's dividend payments.

Intercompany Inventory Transfers Illustrated

To examine the various consolidation procedures relative to intercompany inventory transfers, assume that Top Company purchases 80 percent of the voting stock of Bottom Company on January 1, 1998. The parent pays a total of $400,000, a price that includes all directly related consolidation costs. Goodwill of $40,000 results from this purchase, a figure amortized at the rate of $1,000 per year for 40 years.

The subsidiary reports net income of $30,000 in 1998 and $70,000 in 1999, the current year. Dividend payments are $20,000 in the first year and $50,000 in the second. Top applies the cost method so that dividend income of $16,000 ($20,000 × 80 percent) and $40,000 ($50,000 × 80 percent) is recorded by the parent during these two years. Using the cost method in this initial example avoids the problem of computing the parent's investment account balances. However, this illustration is extended to demonstrate the changes necessary if the parent applies the equity method.

After the takeover, intercompany inventory sales occurred between the two companies as shown in Exhibit 5–1. A $10,000 intercompany debt also exists as of December 31, 1999.

The 1999 consolidation of Top and Bottom is presented twice. First, the transfers are assumed to be downstream from parent to subsidiary. Second, consolidated figures are recomputed with the transfers being viewed as upstream. This distinction is only significant because of a noncontrolling interest.

Downstream Sales In the first example, all inventory transfers are assumed to have been *downstream* from Top to Bottom. Based on that perspective, the worksheet to consolidate these two companies for the year ending December 31, 1999, is in Exhibit 5–2.

Most of the worksheet entries found in Exhibit 5–2 are described and analyzed in previous chapters of this textbook. Thus, only four of these entries are examined in detail along with the computation of the noncontrolling interests in the subsidiary's income.

Entry *G Entry *G removes the unrealized gains carried over from the previous period. As $16,000 in transferred merchandise was retained by Bottom at the first of the current year, any related gain is unearned and must be deferred. The 1998 markup on these items was 25 percent ($20,000 gross profit/$80,000 transfer price) indicating

Exhibit 5–1
Intercompany Transfers

	1998	1999
Transfer prices	$80,000	$100,000
Historical cost	60,000	70,000
Gross profit	$20,000	$ 30,000
Inventory remaining at year's end (at transfer price)	$16,000	$ 20,000

Exhibit 5–2   Downstream Inventory Transfers

Consolidation: Purchase Method
Investment: Cost Method

TOP COMPANY AND BOTTOM COMPANY
Consolidation Worksheet
For Year Ending December 31, 1999

Ownership: 80%

Accounts	Top Company	Bottom Company	Consolidation Entries Debit	Consolidation Entries Credit	Noncontrolling Interest	Consolidated Totals
Income Statement						
Sales	(600,000)	(300,000)	(TI) 100,000			(800,000)
Cost of goods sold	320,000	180,000	(G) 6,000	(*G) 4,000		402,000
				(TI) 100,000		
Expenses	170,000	50,000	(E) 1,000			221,000
Dividend income	(40,000)	–0–	(I) 40,000			–0–
Noncontrolling interest in Bottom Company's income	–0–	–0–			(14,000) ‡	14,000
Net income	(150,000)	(70,000)				(163,000)
Statement of Retained Earnings						
Retained earnings, 1/1/99:						
Top Company	(650,000)		(*G) 4,000	(*C) 7,000		(653,000)
Bottom Company		(310,000)	(S) 310,000 †			–0–
Net income (above)	(150,000)	(70,000)				(163,000)
Dividends paid	70,000	50,000		(I) 40,000	10,000	70,000
Retained earnings, 12/31/99	(730,000)	(330,000)				(746,000)

Balance Sheet

Account	Top Company	Bottom Company	Debit	Credit	Noncontrolling Interest	Consolidated Totals
Cash and receivables	280,000	120,000		(P) 10,000		390,000
Inventory	220,000	160,000		(G) 6,000		374,000
Investment in Bottom Company	400,000	-0-	(*C) 7,000	(S) 368,000 / (A) 39,000		-0-
Land	410,000	200,000				610,000
Plant assets (net)	190,000	170,000				360,000
Goodwill	-0-	-0-	(A) 39,000	(E) 1,000		38,000
Total assets	1,500,000	650,000				1,772,000
Liabilities	(340,000)	(170,000)	(P) 10,000			(500,000)
Noncontrolling interest in Bottom Company, 1/1/99	-0-	-0-		(S) 92,000	(92,000)	
Noncontrolling interest in Bottom Company, 12/31/99					(96,000)	(96,000)
Common stock	(430,000)	(150,000)	(S) 150,000			(430,000)
Retained earnings, 12/31/99 (above)	(730,000)	(330,000)				(746,000)
Total liabilities and equities	(1,500,000)	(650,000)				(1,772,000)

Note: Parentheses indicate a credit balance.

† Boxed items highlight differences with upstream transfers examined in Exhibit 5–3.

‡ Because intercompany sales are made downstream (by the parent), the subsidiary's earned income is the $70,000 reported figure with the 20% noncontrolling interest being allocated ($14,000).

Consolidation entries:

(*G) Removal of unrealized gain from beginning figures so that it can be recognized in current period. Downstream sales attributed to parent.

(*C) Recognition of increase in book value and amortization relating to ownership of subsidiary for year prior to 1999.

(S) Elimination of subsidiary's stockholders' equity accounts along with recognition of January 1, 1999, noncontrolling interest.

(A) Allocation of parent's cost in excess of subsidiary's book value, unamortized balance as of January 1, 1999.

(I) Elimination of intercompany dividends recorded by parent as income.

(E) Recognition of amortization expense for current year on goodwill.

(P) Elimination of intercompany receivable/payable balances.

(TI) Elimination of intercompany sales/purchases balances.

(G) Removal of unrealized gain from ending figures so that it can be recognized in subsequent period.

an unrealized gain of $4,000 (25 percent of the remaining $16,000 in inventory). Thus, Entry *G reduces cost of goods sold (or the beginning inventory component of that expense) by that amount as well as the January 1, 1999, Retained Earnings of Top (the seller of the goods).

Two effects are created by Entry *G: First, last year's profits, as reflected by the seller's beginning retained earnings, are reduced because the $4,000 gain was not earned at that time. Second, through the reduction in cost of goods sold, an increase in current year income is created. From a consolidation perspective, the gain is being correctly recognized in 1999 when the inventory is sold to an outside party.

Entry *C   Entry *C is introduced in Chapter 3 as an initial consolidation adjustment required whenever the equity method is not applied by the parent company. Entry *C converts the parent's beginning retained earnings to a consolidated total. In the current illustration, Top did not accrue its portion of the 1998 increase in Bottom's book value [($30,000 income less $20,000 paid in dividends) × 80% or $8,000] or record the $1,000 amortization expense for this same period. Because neither number has been recognized within the parent's individual records, both must be brought into the consolidation process through a $7,000 adjustment (Entry *C). The intercompany transfers did not affect this entry because they were downstream; the gains had no impact on the income recognized in connection with the subsidiary.

Entry TI   The intercompany sales/purchases for 1999 are eliminated by Entry TI. The entire $100,000 transfer recorded by the two parties during the current period is removed to arrive at consolidated figures for the business combination.

Entry G   Entry G defers the unrealized gain remaining at the end of 1999. The $20,000 in transferred merchandise retained by Bottom has a markup of 30 percent ($30,000 gross profit/$100,000 transfer price); thus, the unrealized gain amounts to $6,000. On the worksheet, Entry G eliminates this overstatement in the Inventory asset balance as well as the ending inventory (negative) component of cost of goods sold. Because the gain remains unrealized, the increase in this expense account has the appropriate effect of lowering consolidated income.

Noncontrolling Interest's Share of the Subsidiary's Income   In this first illustration, the intercompany transfers are downstream. Thus, the unrealized gains are considered to relate solely to the parent company, creating no effect on the subsidiary or the outside ownership. For this reason, the noncontrolling interest's share of consolidated income is recorded as a columnar entry of $14,000, 20 percent of the $70,000 net income reported by Bottom.

By including these entries along with the other routine worksheet eliminations and adjustments, the accounting information generated by Top and Bottom can be brought together into a single set of consolidated financial statements. However, this process does more than simply delete intercompany transactions; reported income is affected. A $4,000 gain is being removed on the worksheet from 1998 figures so that it can be recognized in 1999 (Entry *G). A $6,000 gain is deferred in a similar fashion from 1999 and subsequently recognized in 2000 (Entry G). However, these changes do not affect the noncontrolling interest since the transfers were downstream.

Upstream Sales   A different set of consolidation procedures is necessary if the intercompany transfers are upstream from Bottom to Top. As previously discussed, upstream gains are attributed to the subsidiary rather than to the parent company. Therefore, had these transfers been upstream, the $4,000 gain moved from 1998 into the current year (Entry *G) as well as the $6,000 unrealized gain deferred from 1999 into the future (Entry G) are both considered adjustments to Bottom's reported totals.

Tying upstream gains to Bottom's income may be a logical perspective, but such treatment complicates the consolidation process in several ways:

- Deferring the $4,000 gain from 1998 into 1999 dictates that the beginning retained earnings balance of the subsidiary (as the seller of the goods) should be adjusted to $306,000 rather than $310,000 found in the company's separate records on the worksheet.

- Because $4,000 of the income reported for 1998 was unearned at that time, Bottom's book value did not increase by $10,000 during the previous period (income less dividends as stated in the introduction) but only by an earned amount of $6,000.

- Bottom's earned income for the year of 1999 is $68,000 rather than the $70,000 found within the company's separate financial statements. This $68,000 figure is based on adjusting the timing of the reported income to reflect the deferral and recognition of the intercompany gains.

Earned Income of Subsidiary—Upstream Transfers

Income Reported by Bottom Company, 1999	Add: Gain from Previous Period Realized in 1999	Less: Gain Reported in 1999 to Be Realized in Later Period	1999 Income of Bottom Company from Consolidated Perspective
$70,000	$4,000	$(6,000)	$68,000

Determining Bottom's beginning retained earnings (realized) to be $306,000 and its 1999 income as $68,000 are preliminary calculations made in anticipation of the consolidation process. These newly computed totals are significant because they serve as the basis for several of the worksheet entries. However, the financial records of the subsidiary remain unaffected. In addition, because the cost method has been applied, no change is required in any of the parent's accounts on the worksheet.

To illustrate the effects of upstream inventory transfers, in Exhibit 5–3 we consolidate the financial statements of Top and Bottom once again. *The individual records of the two companies are unchanged from Exhibit 5–2: the only difference in this second worksheet is that the intercompany transfers are assumed to have been made upstream from Bottom to Top.* This single change creates several important differences between Exhibits 5–2 and 5–3:

1. Because the intercompany sales are made upstream, the $4,000 deferral of the beginning unrealized gain (Entry *G) is no longer a reduction in the retained earnings of the parent company. Bottom was the seller of the merchandise; thus, the elimination made in Exhibit 5–3 reduces that company's January 1, 1999, equity balance. Following this entry, Bottom's beginning retained earnings on the worksheet is $306,000 which is, as discussed earlier, the appropriate total from a consolidated perspective.

2. Because $4,000 of Bottom's 1998 income is being deferred into 1999, the increase in the subsidiary's book value in the previous year is only $6,000 rather than $10,000 as reported. Consequently, conversion to the equity method (Entry *C) requires an increase of just $3,800:

> $6,000 earned increase in subsidiary's
> book value during 1998 × 80% $4,800
> 1998 amortization expense . . . .   (1,000)
> Increase in parent's beginning retained
> earnings (Entry *C) $3,800

3. Within Entry S, the valuation of the initial noncontrolling interest as well as the portion of the parent's investment account to be eliminated differ from the previous

Exhibit 5-3   Upstream Inventory Transfers

TOP COMPANY AND BOTTOM COMPANY
Consolidation Worksheet
For Year Ending December 31, 1999

Consolidation: Purchase Method
Investment: Cost Method

Ownership: 80%

Accounts	Top Company	Bottom Company	Consolidation Entries Debit	Consolidation Entries Credit	Noncontrolling Interest	Consolidated Totals
Income Statement						
Sales	(600,000)	(300,000)	(TI) 100,000			(800,000)
Cost of goods sold	320,000	180,000	(G) 6,000	(*G) 4,000 / (TI) 100,000		402,000
Expenses	170,000	50,000	(E) 1,000			221,000
Dividend income	(40,000)	-0-	(I) 40,000			-0-
Noncontrolling interest in Bottom Company's income	-0-	-0-			(13,600) ‡	13,600
Net income	(150,000)	(70,000)				(163,400)
Statement of Retained Earnings						
Retained earnings, 1/1/99:						
Top Company	(650,000)					(653,000)
Bottom Company		(310,000)	(*G) 4,000 / (S) 306,000 †	(*C) 3,800		-0-
Net income (above)	(150,000)	(70,000)				(163,000)
Dividends paid	70,000	50,000		(I) 40,000	10,000	70,000
Retained earnings, 12/31/99	(730,000)	(330,000)				(747,200)

Balance Sheet

			Consolidation Entries (Debit)	Consolidation Entries (Credit)	Noncontrolling Interest	Consolidated Totals
Cash and receivables	280,000	220,000		(P) 10,000		390,000
Inventory	120,000	160,000	(*C) 3,800	(G) 6,000		374,000
Investment in Bottom Company	400,000	-0-		(S) 364,800 (A) 39,000		-0-
Land	410,000	200,000	(A) 39,000			610,000
Plant assets (net)	190,000	170,000				360,000
Goodwill	-0-	-0-	(E) 1,000			38,000
Total assets	1,500,000	650,000				1,772,000
Liabilities	(340,000)	(170,000)	(P) 10,000			(500,000)
Noncontrolling interest in Bottom Company, 1/1/99	-0-	-0-		(S) 91,200	(91,200)	
Noncontrolling interest in Bottom Company, 12/31/99					(94,800)	(94,800)
Common stock	(430,000)	(150,000)	(S) 150,000			(430,000)
Retained earnings, 12/31/99 (above)	(730,000)	(330,000)				(747,200)
Total liabilities and equities	(1,500,000)	(650,000)				(1,772,000)

Note: Parentheses indicate a credit balance.

† Boxed items highlight differences with downstream transfers examined in Exhibit 5-2.

‡ Because intercompany sales are made upstream (by the subsidiary), the subsidiary's realized income is the $68,000 ($70,000 reported balance plus $4,000 gain deferred from previous year less $6,000 deferred into next year) with the 20% noncontrolling interest being allocated $13,600.

Consolidation entries:

(*G) Removal of unrealized gain from beginning figures so that it can be recognized in current period. Upstream sales attributed to subsidiary.

(*C) Recognition of earned increase in book value and amortization relating to ownership of subsidiary for year prior to 1999.

(S) Elimination of adjusted stockholders' equity accounts along with recognition of January 1, 1999, noncontrolling interest.

(A) Allocation of parent's cost in excess of subsidiary's book value, unamortized balance as of January 1, 1999.

(I) Elimination of intercompany dividends recorded by parent as income.

(E) Recognition of amortization expense for current year on goodwill.

(P) Elimination of intercompany receivable/payable balances.

(TI) Elimination of intercompany sales/purchases balances.

(G) Removal of unrealized gain from ending figures so that it can be recognized in subsequent period.

example. This worksheet entry removes the stockholders' equity accounts of the subsidiary as of the beginning of the current year. Thus, the $4,000 reduction made to Bottom's retained earnings to remove the 1998 unrealized gain must be taken into account in developing Entry S. After posting Entry *G, only $456,000 remains as the subsidiary's January 1, 1999, book value (the total of common stock and beginning retained earnings after adjustment for Entry *G). This figure forms the basis for the 20 percent noncontrolling interest ($91,200) and elimination of the 80 percent parent company investment ($364,800).

4. Finally, to complete the consolidation, the noncontrolling interest's share of the subsidiary's net income is recorded on the worksheet as $13,600. This balance represents a 20 percent allocation of the $68,000 earned income figure attributed to Bottom. Upstream transfers affect this computation although the downstream sales in the previous example did not. Thus, the noncontrolling interest balance reported previously in the income statement in Exhibit 5–2 differs from the allocation in Exhibit 5–3.

Consolidations—Downstream versus Upstream Transfers.

To help clarify the effect of downstream and upstream transfers, the worksheet entries that differ can be examined in greater detail.

Downstream Transfers (Exhibit 5–2)	Upstream Transfers (Exhibit 5–3)
Entry *G	**Entry *G**
Retained earnings, 1/1/99—Top 4,000	Retained earnings, 1/1/99—Bottom 4,000
Cost of goods sold 4,000	Cost of goods sold 4,000
To remove 1998 unrealized gain from beginning balances of the seller.	To remove 1998 unrealized gain from beginning balances of the seller.
Entry *C	**Entry *C**
Investment in Bottom . . 7,000	Investment in Bottom . . 3,800
Retained earnings, 1/1/99—Top 7,000	Retained earnings, 1/1/99—Top 3,800
To convert 1/1/99 cost figures to the equity method. Income accrual is 80% of reported income of $10,000 less $1,000 amortization.	To convert 1/1/99 cost figures to the equity method. Income accrual is 80% of earned income of $6,000 (after removal of unrealized gain) less $1,000 amortization.
Entry S	**Entry S**
Common stock—Bottom 150,000	Common stock—Bottom 150,000
Retained earnings, 1/1/99—Bottom . . . 310,000	Retained earnings, 1/1/99—Bottom (as adjusted) 306,000
Investment in Bottom (80%) 368,000	Investment in Bottom (80%) 364,800
Noncontrolling interest—1/1/99 (20%) 92,000	Noncontrolling interest—1/1/99 (20%) 91,200
To remove subsidiary's stockholders' equity accounts and portion of investment balance. Book value at beginning of year is appropriate.	To remove subsidiary's stockholders' equity accounts (as adjusted in Entry *G) and portion of investment balance. Adjusted book value at beginning of year is appropriate.
Noncontrolling Interest in Subsidiary's Income = $14,000. 20 percent of Bottom's reported income.	**Noncontrolling Interest in Subsidiary's Income** = $13,600. 20 percent of Bottom's earned income (reported income after adjustment for unrealized gains).

DISCUSSION QUESTION

What Price Should We Charge Ourselves?

Slagle Corporation is a large manufacturing organization. Over the past several years, Slagle has obtained an important component used in its production process exclusively from Harrison, Inc., a relatively small company in Topeka, Kansas. Harrison charges $90 per unit for this part:

Variable cost per unit	$40.00
Fixed cost assigned per unit	30.00
Markup	20.00
Total price	$90.00

In hopes of reducing manufacturing costs, Slagle purchases all of the outstanding common stock of Harrison. This new subsidiary continues to sell merchandise to a number of outside customers as well as to Slagle. Thus, for internal reporting purposes, Harrison is being viewed as a separate profit center.

A controversy has now arisen among company officials about the amount that Harrison should charge Slagle for each component. The administrator in charge of the subsidiary wants to continue with a price of $90.00 as in the past. He believes this figure best reflects the profitability of the division: "If we are to be judged by our profits, why should we be punished for selling to our own parent company? If that occurs, my figures will look better if I forget Slagle as a customer and try to market my goods solely to outsiders."

In contrast, the vice president in charge of Slagle's production wants the price set at variable cost, total cost, or some derivative of these numbers. "We bought Harrison to bring our costs down. It only makes sense to reduce the transfer price, otherwise the benefits of acquiring this subsidiary are not apparent. I pushed the company to buy Harrison; if our operating results are not improved, I will get the blame."

Will the decision about the transfer price affect consolidated net income?

Which method would be easiest for the company's accountant to administer?

As the company's accountant, what advice would you give to these officials?

Effects on Consolidation of Alternative Investment Methods

In Exhibits 5–2 and 5–3, the cost method was utilized. However, when using either the equity method or the partial equity method, consolidation procedures normally continue to follow the same patterns analyzed in the previous chapters of this textbook. As described earlier, though, a variation in Entry *G is required when the equity method is applied and downstream transfers have occurred. The investment account is increased rather than recording a reduction in the beginning retained earnings of the parent/seller. Otherwise, the specific accounting method in use creates no unique impact on the consolidation process for intercompany transactions.

The major complication when the parent uses the equity method is not always related to a consolidation procedure. Frequently, the composition of the investment balances appearing on the parent's separate financial records proves to be the most complex element of the entire process. Under the equity method, the investment accounts are subjected to (1) income accrual, (2) amortization, (3) dividends, and (4) adjustments required by unrealized intercompany gains. Thus, if Top Company applies the equity method and the transfers are downstream, the Investment in Bottom Company account would grow from $400,000 to $416,000 by the end of 1999. For that year, the Equity Income—Bottom Company account registers a $53,000 balance. Both of these totals result from the accounting shown in Exhibit 5–4.

If transfers are upstream, the individual investment accounts reported by the parent can be determined in the same manner as in Exhibit 5–4. Because of the change in direction, the gains are now attributed to the subsidiary. Thus, both investment accounts hold balances that vary from the totals computed earlier. The Investment in

Investment in Bottom Company, 12/31/99		
Cost.		$400,000
Increase in Bottom Company book value:		
12/31/99 book value	$ 480,000	
1/1/98 book value	(450,000)	
Increase	30,000	
Top Company ownership	80%	24,000
Deferral of Top's 12/31/99 unrealized gain (downstream sale) . . .		(6,000)
Amortization of goodwill, 1998–99		(2,000)
Investment in Bottom Company, 12/31/99		$416,000

Equity in Income of Bottom Company, 1999		
1999—income accrual by Top Company:		
Reported income of Bottom Company	$ 70,000	
Top Company's ownership	80%	$ 56,000
Recognition of gain deferred from 1998 into 1999		4,000
Deferral of Top's 1999 unrealized gain into 2000		(6,000)
Amortization, 1999		(1,000)
Equity in Income of Bottom Company, 1999		$ 53,000

E x h i b i t   5 – 5
Investment Balances—Equity
Method—**upstream sales**

Investment in Bottom Company, 12/31/99		
Cost.		$400,000
Increase in Bottom Company book value:		
12/31/99 book value	$ 480,000	
1/1/98 book value	(450,000)	
Increase	30,000	
Deferral of Bottom's 12/31/99 unrealized gain (upstream sale) . .	(6,000)	
Earned increase	$ 24,000	
Top Company's ownership	80%	19,200
Amortization of goodwill, 1998–99		(2,000)
Investment in Bottom Company, 12/31/99		$417,200

Equity in Income of Bottom Company, 1999		
1999—income accrual by Top Company:		
Reported income of Bottom Company	$ 70,000	
Recognition of Bottom's gain deferred from 1998 into 1999 . .	4,000	
Deferral of Bottom's 1999 unrealized gain into 2000	(6,000)	
Realized income	68,000	
Top Company's ownership	80%	$ 54,400
Amortization, 1999		(1,000)
Equity in Income of Bottom Company, 1999		$ 53,400

Bottom Company balance becomes $417,200, whereas the Equity Income—Bottom Company account for the year is $53,400. The differences are the result of having upstream rather than downstream transactions. The components of these accounts are identified in Exhibit 5–5.

INTERCOMPANY LAND TRANSFERS

Although not as prevalent as inventory transactions, intercompany sales of other assets occur occasionally. The final two sections of this chapter examine the work-sheet procedures necessitated by noninventory transfers. Land transactions are analyzed followed by a discussion of the effects created by the intercompany sale of depreciable assets such as buildings and equipment.

Accounting for Land Transactions — Not on test

The consolidation procedures necessitated by intercompany land transfers partially parallel those for intercompany inventory. As with inventory, the sale of land creates a series of effects on the individual records of the two companies. The worksheet process must then adjust the account balances to present all transactions from the perspective of a single economic entity.

By reviewing the sequence of events occurring in an intercompany land sale, the similarities to inventory transfers can be ascertained as well as the unique features of this transaction.

1. A gain (losses are rare in intercompany asset transfers) is reported by the original seller of the land, even though the transaction occurred between related parties. At the same time, the acquiring company capitalizes the inflated transfer price rather than the land's historical cost to the business combination.

2. The unrealized gain recorded by the seller is closed into retained earnings at the end of the year. From a consolidated perspective, this account has been artificially increased. Thus, both the Land account of the buyer and the Retained Earnings of the seller continue to contain the unrealized profit.

3. Only when the land is subsequently disposed of to an outside party is the gain on the original transfer actually earned. Therefore, appropriate consolidation techniques must be designed to eliminate the intercompany gain each period until the time of resale.

Clearly, two characteristics encountered in inventory transfers also are present in intercompany land transactions: inflated book values and unrealized gains subsequently culminated through sales to outside parties. Despite these similarities, significant differences exist. Because of the nature of the transaction, no sales/purchases balances are recorded by the individual companies when land is transferred. Instead, a separate gain account is established by the seller. Because this gain is unearned, the balance has to be eliminated when preparing consolidated statements.

In addition, the subsequent resale of land to an outside party does not always occur in the year immediately following the transfer. Although inventory is normally disposed of within a relatively short time, land is often held by the buyer for years if not permanently. Thus, the overvalued Land account can remain on the books of the acquiring company indefinitely. As long as the land is retained, elimination of the effects of the unrealized gain (the equivalent of Entry *G in inventory transfers) must be made for each subsequent consolidation. By repeating this worksheet entry every year, both the Land and the Retained Earnings accounts are properly stated in the consolidated financial statements.

Eliminating Unrealized Gains—Land Transfers

To illustrate these worksheet procedures, assume that Hastings Company and Patrick Company are related parties. On July 1, 1998, land that originally cost $60,000 is sold by Hastings to Patrick at a $100,000 transfer price. The seller reports a $40,000 gain; the buyer records the land at the $100,000 acquisition price. At the end of this fiscal period, the intercompany effect of this transaction must be eliminated for consolidation purposes:

Consolidation Entry TL (year of transfer)

Gain on Sale of Land	40,000	
Land		40,000

To eliminate effects of intercompany transfer of land.
(Labeled "TL" in reference to the transferred land.)

This worksheet entry eliminates the unrealized gain from the consolidated statements of 1998. However, as with the transfer of inventory, the effects created by the original transaction remain in the financial records of the individual companies for as long as the property is held. The gain recorded by Hastings carries through to retained earnings while Patrick's Land account retains the inflated transfer price. *Therefore, for every subsequent consolidation until the land is eventually sold, the elimination process must be repeated.* By including the following entry on each subsequent worksheet, the unrealized gain is removed from the asset and from the earnings reported by the combination.

Consolidation Entry *GL (every year following transfer)

Retained Earnings (beginning balance of seller)	40,000	
Land		40,000

    To eliminate effects of intercompany transfer of land made in a
    previous year. (Labeled as "*GL" in reference to the gain on a
    land transfer occurring in a prior year.)

As in the handling of inventory transfers, the reduction in retained earnings is changed to an increase in the Investment account whenever the original sale is downstream and the equity method has been applied by the parent. In that specific situation, equity method adjustments have already corrected the timing of the parent's unrealized gain. Removing the gain has created a reduction in the Investment account that must be eliminated on the worksheet. Conversely, if sales were upstream, the retained earnings of the seller (the subsidiary) continue to be overstated even if the parent applies the equity method.

One final consolidation concern exists in accounting for intercompany transfers of land. If the property is ever sold to an outside party, the company making the sale records a gain or loss based on its recorded book value. However, this cost figure is actually the internal transfer price. The gain or loss being recognized is incorrect for consolidation purposes; it has not been computed by comparison to the land's historical cost. Once again, the separate financial records fail to reflect the transaction from the perspective of the single economic entity.

Therefore, if the land is eventually sold, the gain deferred at the time of the original transfer must be recognized. This profit finally has been earned by the sale of the property to outsiders. On the worksheet, the gain is removed one last time from beginning retained earnings (or the Investment account, if applicable). In this instance, though, the entry is completed by reclassifying the amount as a realized gain. The timing of income recognition has been switched from the year of transfer into the fiscal period in which the land is sold to the unrelated party.

Returning to the previous illustration, land was acquired by Hastings for $60,000 and sold to Patrick, a related party, for $100,000. Consequently, the $40,000 unrealized gain was eliminated on the consolidation worksheet in the year of transfer as well as in each succeeding period. However, if this land is subsequently sold to an outside party for $115,000, Patrick would recognize only a $15,000 gain. From the viewpoint of the business combination, the land (having been bought for $60,000) was actually sold at a $55,000 gain. To correct the reporting, the following consolidation entry must be made in the year that the property is sold to the unrelated party. This adjustment increases the $15,000 gain recorded by Patrick to the consolidated balance of $55,000.

Consolidation Entry *GL (year of sale to outside party)

Retained Earnings (Hastings)	40,000	
Gain on Sale of Land		40,000

    To remove intercompany gain from year of transfer so that total
    profit can be recognized in the current period when land is sold to
    an outside party.

As in the accounting for inventory transfers, the entire consolidation process demonstrated here accomplishes two major objectives:

1. Historical cost is reported for the transferred land for as long as it remains within the business combination.
2. Income recognition is deferred until the land is sold to outside parties.

Effect on Noncontrolling Interest Valuation—Land Transfers

The preceding discussion of intercompany land transfers has ignored the possible presence of a noncontrolling interest. In constructing financial statements for an economic entity that includes outside ownership, the guidelines already established for inventory transfers remain applicable.

If the original sale was a *downstream* transaction, neither the annual deferral nor the eventual recognition of the unrealized gain has any effect on the noncontrolling interest. The rationale for this treatment, as previously indicated, is that profits from downstream transfers relate solely to the parent company.

Conversely, if the transfer is made *upstream,* deferral and recognition of gains are attributed to the subsidiary and, hence, to the valuation of the noncontrolling interest. As with inventory, all noncontrolling interest balances are to be computed on the reported earnings of the subsidiary after adjustment for any upstream transfers.

To reiterate, the accounting consequences stemming from land transfers are:

1. In the year of transfer, any unrealized gain is deferred and the land account is reduced to historical cost. When the gain is created by an upstream sale, the amount also is excluded in calculating the noncontrolling interest's share of the subsidiary's net income for that year.
2. Each year thereafter, the unrealized gain will be removed from the beginning retained earnings of the seller. If the transfer was upstream, eliminating this earlier gain directly affects the balances recorded within both Entry *C (if conversion to the equity method is required) and Entry S. The additional equity accrual (Entry *C, if needed) as well as the elimination of beginning stockholders' equity (Entry S) must be based on the newly adjusted balance in the subsidiary's retained earnings. This deferral process also has an impact on the noncontrolling interest's share of the subsidiary's income but only in the year of transfer and the eventual year of sale.
3. In the event that the land is ever sold to an outside party, the original gain is earned and must be reported by the consolidated entity.

INTERCOMPANY TRANSFER OF DEPRECIABLE ASSETS

Just as land can be transferred between related parties, the intercompany sale of a host of other assets is possible. Equipment, patents, franchises, buildings, as well as other long-lived assets may be involved. Accounting for these transactions resembles that demonstrated for land sales. However, the subsequent calculation of depreciation or amortization provides an added challenge in the development of consolidated statements.[9]

The Deferral of Unrealized Gains

When faced with intercompany sales of depreciable assets, the accountant's basic objective remains unchanged: *the deferral of unrealized gains to establish both historical cost balances and appropriate income recognition within the consolidated statements.* More specifically, gains created by these transfers are deferred until such time as the subsequent use or resale of the asset consummates the original transac-

---

[9]To avoid redundancy within this analysis, all further references are made to depreciation expense alone, although this discussion is equally applicable to the amortization of intangible assets or the depletion of wasting assets.

tion. For inventory sales, the culminating disposal normally occurs currently or in the year following the transfer. In contrast, transferred land is quite often never resold, thus permanently deferring the recognition of the intercompany profit.

For depreciable asset transfers, the ultimate realization of the gain normally occurs in a different manner; the property's use within the buyer's operations is reflected through depreciation. Recognition of this expense reduces the asset's book value every year and, hence, the overvaluation within that balance.

The depreciation systematically eliminates the unrealized gain not only from the asset account but also from retained earnings. For the buyer, excess expense results each year because the computation is based on the inflated transfer cost. This depreciation is then closed annually into retained earnings. *From a consolidated perspective, the extra expense gradually offsets the unrealized gain within this equity account. In fact, over the life of the asset, the depreciation process eliminates all effects of the transfer from both the asset balance as well as the Retained Earnings account.*

Depreciable Asset Transfers Illustrated

To examine the consolidation procedures required by the intercompany transfer of a depreciable asset, assume that Able Company sells equipment to Baker Company, a related party, at the current market value of $90,000. The equipment originally had been acquired by Able for $100,000 several years ago; since that time, $40,000 in accumulated depreciation has been recorded. The transfer is made on January 1, 1998, when the equipment has a 10-year remaining life.

Year of Transfer   The 1998 effects on the separate financial accounts of the two companies can be quickly enumerated:

1. Baker, as the buyer, enters the equipment into its records at the $90,000 transfer price. However, from a consolidated view, the $60,000 book value ($100,000 cost less $40,000 accumulated depreciation) is still appropriate.

2. Able, as the seller, reports a profit of $30,000, although nothing has yet been earned by the combination. This gain is then closed into the company's Retained Earnings account at the end of 1998.

3. Assuming application of the straight-line method of depreciation with no salvage value, Baker records expense of $9,000 at the end of 1998 ($90,000 transfer price/10 years). The buyer recognizes this amount rather than the $6,000 depreciation figure applicable to the consolidated entity ($60,000 book value/10 years).

To report these events as seen by the business combination, both the $30,000 unrealized gain and the $3,000 inflation in depreciation expense must be eliminated on the worksheet. For clarification purposes, two separate consolidation entries are shown here for 1998. However, they can be combined into a single adjustment.

Consolidation Entry TA: (year of transfer)

Gain on Sale of Equipment	30,000	
Equipment	10,000	
Accumulated Depreciation		40,000

To remove unrealized gain and return equipment accounts to balances based on original historical cost. (Labeled "TA" in reference to transferred asset.)

Consolidation Entry ED: (year of transfer)

Accumulated Depreciation	3,000	
Depreciation Expense		3,000

To eliminate overstatement of depreciation expense caused by inflated transfer price. (Labeled "ED" in reference to excess depreciation.)
Entry must be repeated for all 10 years of the equipment's life.

From the viewpoint of a single entity, these entries accomplish several objectives.

- The asset's historical cost of $100,000 is reinstated.
- By recording accumulated depreciation of $40,000, the January 1, 1998, book value is returned to the appropriate $60,000 figure.
- The $30,000 unrealized gain recorded by Able is eliminated so that this intercompany profit does not appear in the consolidated income statement.
- Depreciation for the year is reduced from $9,000 to $6,000, the appropriate expense based on historical cost.

Years Following Transfer   Once again, the preceding worksheet entries do not actually remove the effects of the intercompany transfer from the individual records of these two organizations. Both the unrealized gain and the excess depreciation expense remain on the separate books and are closed into the retained earnings of the respective companies at year's end. Similarly, the Equipment account along with the related accumulated depreciation continue to hold balances based on the transfer price and not historical cost. *Thus, for every subsequent period, the separately reported figures must be adjusted on the worksheet to present the consolidated totals from the perspective of a single entity.*

To derive worksheet entries at any future point, the balances in the accounts of the individual companies must be ascertained and compared to the figures appropriate for the business combination. As an illustration, the separate records of Able and Baker two years after the transfer (December 31, 1999) follow. Consolidated totals are calculated based on the original historical cost of $100,000 and accumulated depreciation of $40,000.

Individual Records, 12/31/99

Equipment—transfer price		$ 90,000
Accumulated depreciation (2 years) . .		$ 18,000
Effect on retained earnings, 1/1/99		
Unrealized gain	$(30,000)	
Depreciation expense (1998)	9,000	$ (21,000)

Consolidated Perspective, 12/31/99

			Difference with Individual Records
Equipment—cost		$100,000	$ 10,000
Accumulated depreciation:			
Originally reported	$(40,000)		
For 1998–99	(12,000)	$ (52,000)	$(34,000)
Effect on retained earnings, 1/1/99			
Depreciation expense (1998)		$ 6,000	$ 27,000

Note: Parentheses indicate a credit.

Because effects of the transfer continue to exist in the separate financial records, the various accounts have to be corrected in each succeeding consolidation. However, the amounts involved must be updated every period because of the continual impact that depreciation has on these balances. As an example, to adjust the individual figures to the consolidated totals derived earlier, the 1999 worksheet must include the following entry. The two entries shown for 1998 are combined in this second illustration.

Consolidation Entry *TA (year following transfer)

Retained Earnings, 1/1/99—Able		
(as original seller of asset) 27,000		
Equipment 10,000		
Depreciation Expense................................		3,000
Accumulated Depreciation		34,000

To eliminate remaining effects of 1998 transfer so that consolidated
accounts are based on the original historical cost figures. See
previous computations.

Although adjustments of the asset and depreciation expense remain constant, the
change in beginning retained earnings and accumulated depreciation vary with each
succeeding consolidation. At December 31, 1998, the individual companies closed
out both the unrealized gain of $30,000 and the initial $3,000 overstatement of
depreciation expense. Therefore, as reflected in Entry *TA, the beginning retained
earnings account for 1999 is overvalued by a net amount of only $27,000 rather than
$30,000. *Over the life of the asset, the unrealized gain in retained earnings will be
systematically reduced to zero as excess depreciation expense ($3,000) is closed out
each year.* Hence, on subsequent consolidation worksheets, the beginning retained
earnings account is decreased by $27,000 in 1999, by $24,000 in 2000, and $21,000
in the following period. This reduction continues until the effect of the unrealized
gain no longer exists at the end of 10 years.

If this equipment is ever resold to an outside party, the remaining portion of the
gain would be consummated. As in the previous discussion of land, the intercompany
profit that exists at that date must be recognized on the consolidated income statement to arrive at the appropriate amount of gain or loss on the sale.

Effect on Noncontrolling Interest Valuation—Depreciable Asset Transfers

Because of the lack of official guidance, no easy answer exists about the assignment
of any income effects created within the consolidation process. Consistent with the
previous sections of this chapter, and with the 1995 FASB Exposure Draft, all
income is assigned here to the original seller. In Entry *TA, for example, the beginning retained earnings account of Able (the seller) is reduced. Both the unrealized
gain on the transfer and the excess depreciation expense subsequently recognized are
assigned to that party.

Thus, once again, downstream sales are assumed to have no effect on any noncontrolling interest values. The parent made the sale rather than the subsidiary. Conversely, the impact on income created by upstream sales must be taken into account
in computing the balances attributed to these outside owners. Currently, this approach is one of many acceptable alternatives. However, in its future deliberations on
consolidation policies and procedures, the FASB may possibly mandate a specific
allocation pattern.

SUMMARY

1. The transfer of assets, especially inventory, between the members of a business
   combination is a common practice. In producing consolidated financial statements, any
   effects on the separate accounting records created by such transfers must be removed
   because the transactions did not occur with an outside, unrelated party.

2. Inventory transfers are the most prevalent form of intercompany asset transaction. Despite
   being only a transfer, one company records a sale while the other reports a purchase.
   These balances are reciprocals that have to be offset on the worksheet in the process of
   producing consolidated figures.

3. Additional accounting problems result if inventory is transferred at a markup. Any portion of the merchandise still held at year-end would be valued at more than historical cost because of the inflation in price. Furthermore, the gross profit reported by the seller on these goods is unrealized from a consolidation perspective. Thus, this gain must be removed from ending inventory, a figure that appears as an asset on the balance sheet and as a negative component within cost of goods sold.

4. Unrealized inventory gains also create a consolidation problem in the year following the transfer. Within the separate accounting systems, the seller closes the gross profit to retained earnings. The buyer's ending inventory becomes the beginning balance (within cost of goods sold) of the next period. Therefore, the inflation must be removed again but this time in the subsequent year. Beginning retained earnings of the seller is decreased to eliminate the unrealized gain while cost of goods sold is reduced to remove the overstatement from the beginning inventory component. Through this process, the intercompany profit is deferred from the year of transfer so that recognition can be made at the point of disposal or consumption.

5. The deferral and subsequent realization of intercompany gains raises a question concerning the valuation of noncontrolling interest balances: Does the change in the period of recognition alter these calculations? Although the issue is being studied by the FASB, no formal answer to this question is yet found in official accounting pronouncements. In this textbook, the deferral of gains from upstream transfers (from subsidiary to parent) is assumed to affect the noncontrolling interest whereas downstream transactions (from parent to subsidiary) do not. When upstream transfers are involved, noncontrolling interest values are based on the earned figures remaining after adjustment for any unrealized gains.

6. Inventory is not the only asset that can be sold between the members of a business combination. For example, transfers of land sometimes occur. Once again, if the price exceeds original cost, the asset is stated on the buyer's records at an inflated value while an unrealized gain is recognized by the seller. As with inventory, the consolidation process must return the asset's recorded balance to cost while deferring the gain. Repetition of this procedure is necessary in every consolidation for as long as the land remains within the business combination.

7. The consolidation process required by the intercompany transfer of depreciable assets differs somewhat from that demonstrated for inventory and land. Unrealized gain created by the transaction must still be eliminated along with the overstatement of the asset. However, because of subsequent depreciation, these adjustments systematically change from period to period. Following the transfer, depreciation is computed by the buyer based on the new inflated transfer price. Thus, expense is recorded that reduces the carrying value of the asset at a rate in excess of appropriate depreciation; the book value moves closer to the historical cost figure each time that depreciation is recorded. Additionally, because the excess depreciation is closed annually to retained earnings, the overstatement of the equity account resulting from the unrealized gain is constantly reduced. To produce consolidated figures at any point in time, the remaining inflation in these figures (as well as in the current depreciation expense) must be determined and removed.

COMPREHENSIVE ILLUSTRATION

Problem

(Estimated Time: 45 to 65 Minutes) On January 1, 1993, Daisy Company purchased 80 percent of Rose Company for $594,000 in cash. The total book value of Rose on that date was $610,000. The newly acquired subsidiary possessed equipment (10-year remaining life) that was undervalued by $75,000 in the company's accounting records and land that was undervalued by $15,000. Any goodwill associated with this purchase will be amortized over 10 years.

   Daisy decided to acquire Rose so that the subsidiary could furnish component parts for the parent's production process. During the ensuing years, Rose sold inventory to Daisy as follows:

Year	Cost to Rose Company	Transfer Price	Markup on Transfer Price	Transferred Inventory Being Held at End of Year (at transfer price)
1993	$ 60,000	$ 90,000	33.3%	$10,000
1994	80,000	100,000	20.0	15,000
1995	90,000	120,000	25.0	10,000
1996	100,000	140,000	28.6	20,000
1997	100,000	150,000	33.3	30,000
1998	96,000	160,000	40.0	40,000

Any transferred merchandise retained by Daisy at the end of a year was always put into production during the following period.

On January 1, 1996, Daisy sold several pieces of equipment to Rose. These assets had a 10-year remaining life and were being depreciated on the straight-line method with no salvage value. This equipment was transferred at an $80,000 price, although it had an original cost to Daisy of $100,000 and a book value at the date of exchange of $44,000.

On January 1, 1998, Daisy sold land to Rose for $60,000, the fair market value at that date. The original cost had been only $40,000. By the end of 1998, no payment had yet been made by Rose.

The following separate financial statements are for Daisy and Rose as of December 31, 1998. Daisy has applied the equity method to account for this investment.

	Daisy Company	Rose Company
Sales	$ 900,000	$ 500,000
Cost of goods sold	(600,000)	(300,000)
Operating expenses	(210,000)	(80,000)
Gain on sale of land	20,000	–0–
Income of Rose Company	65,400	–0–
Net income	$ 175,400	$ 120,000
Retained earnings, 1/1/98	$ 620,000	$ 430,000
Net income	175,400	120,000
Dividends paid	(55,400)	(50,000)
Retained earnings, 12/31/98	$ 740,000	$ 500,000
Cash and accounts receivable	$ 380,000	$ 410,000
Inventory	421,600	190,000
Investment in Rose Company	711,600	–0–
Land	452,800	280,000
Equipment	270,000	190,000
Accumulated depreciation	(180,000)	(50,000)
Total assets	$2,056,000	$1,020,000
Liabilities	716,000	120,000
Common stock	600,000	400,000
Retained earnings, 12/31/98	740,000	500,000
Total liabilities and equities	$2,056,000	$1,020,000

Required:

Answer the following questions:

a. By how much did Rose's book value increase during the period from January 1, 1993, through December 31, 1997?

b. During the initial years after the takeover, what annual amortization expense was recognized in connection with the parent's purchase price?

c. What amount of unrealized gain exists within the parent's inventory figures at the beginning and at the end of 1998?

d. Equipment has been transferred between the companies. What amount of excess depreciation is recognized in 1998 because of this transfer?

e. The parent reports Income of Rose Company for 1998 of $65,400. How was this figure calculated?

f. Without using a worksheet, determine consolidated totals.

g. Prepare the worksheet entries required at December 31, 1998, by the transfer of inventory, land, and equipment.

Solution

a. The subsidiary's book value on the date of purchase was given as $610,000. At the beginning of 1998, the company's common stock and retained earnings total to $830,000 ($400,000 and $430,000, respectively). In the previous years, Rose's book value has apparently grown by $220,000 ($830,000 − $610,000).

b. To determine amortization, an allocation of the purchase price must first be made. The following allocations to equipment ($60,000) and goodwill ($34,000) lead to an annual expense of $9,400 for the initial years of the combination. The $12,000 assigned to land is not subject to amortization.

Cost Allocation and Amortization Schedule

Purchase price . . . . . . $ 594,000
Book value of
  Rose Company
  ($610,000 × 80%)   (488,000)
Excess cost over book
  value   106,000

		Life (years)	Annual Amortization	Amortization 1993–98	Unamortized Value, 12/31/98
Equipment undervaluation ($75,000 × 80%) . .	60,000	10	$6,000	$36,000	$24,000
Land undervaluation ($15,000 × 80%) . .	12,000				
Goodwill	$ 34,000	10	3,400	20,400	13,600
			$9,400		

c. Of the inventory transferred to Daisy during 1997, $30,000 is still held at the beginning of 1998. This merchandise contains an unrealized gain of $10,000 ($30,000 × 33.3% [rounded] markup for that year). At year's end, $16,000 ($40,000 remaining inventory × 40% markup) is viewed as an unrealized gain.

d. Excess depreciation for 1998 is $3,600. Equipment with a book value of $44,000 was transferred at a price of $80,000. The addition of $36,000 to this asset's account balance would be written off over 10 years for an extra $3,600 per year.

e. According to the separate statements given, the subsidiary reports net income of $120,000. However, in determining the income allocation between the parent and the noncontrolling interest, this reported figure must be adjusted for the effects of any *upstream* transfers. Since the inventory was sold upstream from Rose to Daisy, the $10,000 gain deferred in requirement *c.* from 1997 into the current period is attributed to the subsidiary (as the seller). Likewise, the $16,000 unrealized gain at year's end is viewed as a reduction in Rose's income.

All other transfers are downstream and not considered to have an effect on the subsidiary. Therefore, the Income of Rose Company balance can be verified as follows:

Rose Company's reported income—1998	$120,000
Recognition of 1997 unrealized gain	+10,000
Deferral of 1998 unrealized gain	(16,000)
Earned income of subsidiary from consolidated perspective	114,000
Parent's ownership percentage	80%
Equity income accrual	$ 91,200
Adjustments attributed to parent's ownership:	
Amortization expense—1998 (see requirement *b.*)	(9,400)
Deferral of unrealized gain—land	(20,000)
Removal of excess depreciation (see requirement *d.*)	+3,600
Income of Rose Company—1998	$ 65,400

f. Each of the 1998 consolidated totals for this business combination can be determined as follows:

Sales = $1,240,000. The parent's balance is added to the subsidiary's balance less the $160,000 in intercompany transfers for the period.

Cost of Goods Sold = $746,000. The computation begins by adding the parent's balance to the subsidiary's balance less the $160,000 in intercompany transfers for the period. The $10,000 unrealized gain from the previous year is deducted to recognize this income currently. Next, the $16,000 ending unrealized gain is added to cost of goods sold to defer the income until a later year when the goods are sold to an outside party.

Operating Expenses = $295,800. The parent's balance is added to the subsidiary's balance. Annual amortization of $9,400 on the purchase price allocations (see requirement *b.*) must also be included. Excess depreciation of $3,600 resulting from the transfer of equipment (see requirement *e.*) is removed.

Gain on Sale of Land = –0–. This amount is eliminated for consolidation purposes because the transaction was intercompany.

Income of Rose Company = –0–. The equity income figure is removed so that the actual revenues and expenses of the subsidiary can be included in the financial statements without double-counting.

Noncontrolling Interest in Subsidiary's Income = $22,800. In requirement *d.*, the earned income of the subsidiary was computed as $114,000 after adjustments were made for unrealized upstream gains. Because outsiders hold 20 percent of the subsidiary, an allocation of $22,800 ($114,000 × 20%) is necessary.

Net Income = $175,400. This total is derived from the previous consolidated balances. Because the equity method has been applied, consolidated net income is also equal to the balance reported by the parent.

Retained Earnings, 1/1/98 = $620,000. The equity method has been applied; therefore, the parent's balance is equal to the consolidated total.

Dividends Paid = $55,400. Only the amount the parent paid is shown in the consolidated statements. Distributions made by the subsidiary to the parent are eliminated as intercompany transfers. Any payment to the noncontrolling interest reduces in the ending balance attributed to these outside owners.

Cash and Accounts Receivable = $730,000. The two balances are added after removal of the $60,000 intercompany receivable created by the transfer of land.

Inventory = $595,600. The two balances are added after removal of the $16,000 ending unrealized gain (see requirement *c.*).

Investment in Rose Company = –0–. The investment balance is eliminated so that the actual assets and liabilities of the subsidiary can be included.

Land = $724,800. The two balances are added. The $20,000 unrealized gain created by the transfer is removed. The $12,000 allocation from the purchase price is added.

Equipment = $540,000. The two balances are added. Because of the intercompany transfer, $20,000 must also be included to adjust the $80,000 transfer price to the original $100,000 cost of the asset. A $60,000 allocation within the purchase price must also be recognized.

Accumulated Depreciation = $311,200. The balances are added together along with the $36,000 that has been written off in connection with the purchase price allocation to equipment ($6,000 per year for six years). The $56,000 in accumulated depreciation on the equipment (before its transfer) must also be reinstated. A reduction of $10,800 is made to remove the excess depreciation subsequently recorded on this same equipment ($3,600 per year for three years).

Goodwill = $13,600. The $34,000 allocation is recognized less six years of amortization ($20,400 or $3,400 per year for six years).

Total Assets = $2,292,800. This figure is a summation of the preceding consolidated assets.

Liabilities = $776,000. The two balances are added after removal of the $60,000 intercompany payable created by the transfer of land.

Noncontrolling Interest in Subsidiary, 12/31/98 = $176,800. This figure is composed of several different balances:

Book value of subsidiary, 1/1/98 (common stock and beginning retained earnings)	$830,000	
Unrealized gain on upstream transfer as of beginning of year	(10,000)	
Earned book value of subsidiary, 1/1/98	$820,000	
Noncontrolling interest	20%	
Noncontrolling interest, 1/1/98	$164,000	
Noncontrolling interest in subsidiary's income (see above)	22,800	
Less: Dividends paid to noncontrolling interest ($50,000 × 20%)	(10,000)	
Noncontrolling interest, 12/31/98	$176,800	

Common Stock = $600,000. The parent company balance only is reported within the consolidated statements.

Retained Earnings, 12/31/98 = $740,000. Retained earnings are found by adding consolidated net income to the beginning retained earnings balance and then subtracting the dividends paid. All of these figures have been computed previously.

Total Liabilities and Equities = $2,292,800. This figure is the summation of all consolidated liabilities and equities.

g.

CONSOLIDATION WORKSHEET ENTRIES—
INTERCOMPANY TRANSACTIONS
December 31, 1998

Inventory

Entry *G

Retained Earnings, 1/1/98—Subsidiary	10,000	
Cost of Goods Sold		10,000

To remove 1997 unrealized gain from beginning balances of the current year. Because transfers were upstream, retained earnings of the subsidiary (as the original seller) is being reduced. Balance is computed in requirement *c*.

Entry TI

Sales	160,000	
Cost of Goods Sold		160,000

To eliminate current year intercompany transfer of inventory.

Entry G

Cost of Goods Sold	16,000	
Inventory		16,000

To remove 1998 unrealized gain from ending accounts of the current year. Balance is computed in requirement *c*.

Land

Entry TL

Gain on Sale of Land	20,000	
Land		20,000

To eliminate gain created on first day of current year by an intercompany transfer of land.

Equipment

Entry *TA

Equipment	20,000	
Investment in Rose Company	28,800	
Accumulated Depreciation		48,800

To remove unrealized gain (as of January 1, 1998) created by intercompany transfer of equipment and to adjust equipment and accumulated depreciation to historical cost figures.

    Equipment is increased from the $80,000 transfer price to $100,000 cost.

    Accumulated depreciation of $56,000 was eliminated at time of transfer. Excess depreciation of $3,600 per year has been recorded for the two prior years ($7,200); thus, the accumulated depreciation is now only $48,800 less than cost based figure.

    The unrealized gain on the transfer was $36,000 ($80,000 less $44,000). That figure has now been reduced by two years of excess depreciation ($7,200). Because the parent used the equity method and this transfer was downstream, the adjustment here is to the investment account rather than the parent's beginning retained earnings.

Entry ED

Accumulated Depreciation	3,600	
Operating Expenses (depreciation)		3,600

To eliminate the current year overstatement of depreciation created by inflated transfer price.

APPENDIX

Transfers—Alternative Approaches

In this chapter, we use one method in consolidating the effects of intercompany transfers and unrealized gains when a noncontrolling interest is present. This approach was chosen because it is consistent with the guidelines put forth in *ARB 51* and the 1995 Exposure Draft. Over the years, several other possibilities have been devised and considered. The FASB's discussion memorandum, *An Analysis of Issues Related to Consolidation Policy and Procedures,* describes eight methods of consolidating intercompany transactions (three for downstream transfers and five for upstream). The following table indicates the range of potential effects on consolidated totals by demonstrating six of these approaches (two for downstream and four for upstream). All methods except for proportionate consolidation have been included.

The figures used in this illustration are the same as in the Large Company and Small Company example in the first section of this chapter.

- Large owns 70 percent of the outstanding stock of Small.
- Intercompany inventory transfers during the year amount to $200,000.
- The remaining unrealized gain at the end of the year is $40,000.
- Subsidiary reported income is $100,000.

Downstream Transfers (from parent to subsidiary)

	ARB 51* Economic Unit Concept One Variation of Parent Company Concept (method used in this textbook)	Another Variation of Parent Company Concept
Sales	Eliminate all $200,000 transfers	Eliminate $140,000 (70%) of the transfers
Purchases	Eliminate all $200,000 transfers	Eliminate $140,000 (70%) of the transfers
Unrealized gain	Eliminate all $40,000	Eliminate $28,000 (70%)
Income assigned to noncontrolling interests	30% of $100,000 reported income or $30,000	30% of $100,000 reported income or $30,000

Upstream Transfers (from subsidiary to parent)

	ARB 51 Economic Unit Concept (method used in this textbook)	One Variation of Parent Company Concept	Another Approach Based On ARB 51	Another Variation of Parent Company Concept
Sales	Eliminate all $200,000 transfers	Eliminate $140,000 (70%) of the transfers	Eliminate all $200,000 transfers	Eliminate all $200,000 transfers
Purchases	Eliminate all $200,000 transfers	Eliminate $140,000 (70%) of the transfers	Eliminate all $200,000 transfers	Eliminate all $200,000 transfers
Unrealized gain	Eliminate all $40,000	Eliminate $28,000 (70%)	Eliminate all $40,000	Eliminate $28,000 (70%)
Income assigned to noncontrolling interests	30% of $60,000 realized income after removing $40,000 unrealized gain or $18,000	30% of $100,000 reported income or $30,000	30% of $100,000 reported income or $30,000	30% of $100,000 reported income or $30,000

*Titles indicate authority for each approach.

QUESTIONS

1. Intercompany transfers between the component companies of a business combination are quite common. Why do these intercompany transactions occur so frequently?

2. Barker Company owns 80 percent of the outstanding voting stock of Walden Company. During the current year, intercompany sales amount to $100,000. These transactions were made with a markup equal to 40 percent of the transfer price. In consolidating the two companies, what amount of these sales would be eliminated?

3. How are unrealized inventory gains created, and what consolidation entries are necessitated by the presence of these gains?

4. James, Inc. sells inventory to Matthews Company, a related party. The inventory was sold at James's standard markup. At the end of the current fiscal year, some portion of this inventory is still being held by Matthews. If consolidated financial statements are to be prepared, why are worksheet entries required in two different fiscal periods?

5. When intercompany gains are present in any year, how are the noncontrolling interest calculations affected?

6. A worksheet is being developed to consolidate Williams, Incorporated, and Simpson Company. Considerable intercompany transactions have been made between these two organizations. How would the consolidation process be affected if these transfers were downstream? How would the consolidation process be affected if these transfers were upstream?

7. King Company owns a 90 percent interest in the outstanding voting shares of Pawn Company. Pawn reports a net income of $110,000 for the current year. Intercompany sales are made at regular intervals between the two companies. Unrealized gains of $30,000 were present in the beginning inventory balances, whereas $60,000 in similar gains were recorded at the end of the year. What is the noncontrolling interest's share of the subsidiary's net income?

8. When a subsidiary sells inventory to a parent, the intercompany profit is removed from the subsidiary's income and reduces the income allocation to the noncontrolling interest. Is the profit permanently eliminated from the noncontrolling interest or is it merely shifted from one period to the next? Explain.

9. The consolidation process that is applicable when intercompany land transfers have occurred is somewhat different from that used for intercompany inventory sales. What differences should be noted?

10. A subsidiary sells land to the parent company at a significant gain. The parent holds the land for two years and then sells it to an outside party, also for a gain. How are these events accounted for by the business combination?

11. Why does an intercompany sale of a depreciable asset (such as equipment or a building) require subsequent adjustments to depreciation expense within the consolidation process?

12. If an intercompany sale of a depreciable asset has been made at a price above book value, the beginning retained earnings of the seller are reduced when preparing each subsequent consolidation. Why does the amount of the adjustment change from year to year?

LIBRARY ASSIGNMENTS

1. Read Chapter 6, "Intercompany Transactions," of the FASB discussion memorandum *An Analysis of Issues Related to Consolidation Policy and Procedures*. Select an approach that should be used in preparing consolidated financial statements where intercompany transfers occur and then justify its adoption.

2. Read the following as well as any other published materials that might be available concerning transfer pricing:

    "Transfer Pricing by Multinational Marketers: Risky Business," *Business Horizons*, January 1996.

    "Setting the Right Transfer Price," *Management Accounting*, December 1994.

    "Transfer Pricing in the 1990s," *Management Accounting*, February 1992.

    "Transfer Pricing in a Dynamic Market," *Management Accounting*, February 1988.

Write a report outlining several methods of setting transfer prices on intercompany transfers. Select one approach as preferable and justify its application.

PROBLEMS

1. What is the impact on consolidated financial statements of upstream and downstream transfers?
   a. No difference exists in consolidated financial statements between upstream and downstream transfers.
   b. Downstream transfers affect the computation of the noncontrolling interest's share of the subsidiary's income but upstream transfers do not.
   c. Upstream transfers affect the computation of the noncontrolling interest's share of the subsidiary's income but downstream transfers do not.
   d. Downstream transfers may be ignored since they are made by the parent company.

2. King Corporation owns 80 percent of Lee Corporation's common stock. During October 1998, Lee sold merchandise to King for $100,000. At December 31, 1998, 50 percent of this merchandise remains in King's inventory. For 1998, gross profit percentages were 30 percent for King and 40 percent for Lee. The amount of unrealized intercompany profit in ending inventory at December 31, 1998, that should be eliminated in the consolidation process is:
   a. $40,000.
   b. $20,000.
   c. $16,000.
   d. $15,000.

(AICPA adapted)

3. When intercompany transfers occur, how is the noncontrolling interest's share of the subsidiary's income computed?
   a. The subsidiary's reported income is adjusted for the impact of upstream transfers prior to computing the noncontrolling interest's allocation.
   b. The subsidiary's reported income is adjusted for the impact of all transfers prior to computing the noncontrolling interest's allocation.
   c. The subsidiary's reported income is not adjusted for the impact of transfers prior to computing the noncontrolling interest's allocation.
   d. The subsidiary's reported income is adjusted for the impact of downstream transfers prior to computing the noncontrolling interest's allocation.

4. Bellgrade, Inc., acquired a 60 percent interest in the Hansen Company several years ago. During 1997, Hansen sold inventory costing $75,000 to Bellgrade for $100,000. A total of 16 percent of this inventory was not sold to outsiders until 1998. During 1998, Hansen sold inventory costing $96,000 to Bellgrade for $120,000. A total of 35 percent of this inventory was not sold to outsiders until 1999. In 1998, Bellgrade reported cost of goods sold of $380,000 while Hansen reported $210,000. What is consolidated cost of goods sold?
   a. $465,600.
   b. $473,440.
   c. $474,400.
   d. $522,400.

5. Top Company holds 90 percent of the common stock of Bottom Company. In 1998, Top reports sales of $800,000 and cost of goods sold of $600,000. For this same period, Bottom has sales of $300,000 and cost of goods sold of $180,000. During 1998, Top sold merchandise to Bottom for $100,000. The subsidiary still possesses 40 percent of this inventory at the end of 1998. Top had established the transfer price based on its normal markup. What are consolidated sales and cost of goods sold?
   a. $1,000,000 and $690,000.
   b. $1,000,000 and $705,000.
   c. $1,000,000 and $740,000.
   d. $970,000 and $696,000.

6. Use the same information as in problem 5 except assume that the transfers were from Bottom Company to Top Company. What are the consolidated sales and cost of goods sold for 1998?

    a. $1,000,000 and $720,000.
    b. $1,000,000 and $755,000.
    c. $1,000,000 and $696,000.
    d. $970,000 and $712,000.

7. Hardwood Inc., holds a 90 percent interest in Pittstoni Company. During 1997, Pittstoni sold inventory costing $77,000 to Hardwood for $110,000. A total of $40,000 of this inventory was not sold to outsiders until 1998. During 1998, Pittstoni sold inventory costing $72,000 to Hardwood for $120,000. A total of $50,000 of this inventory was not sold to outsiders until 1999. In 1998, Hardwood reported net income of $150,000 while Pittstoni reported $90,000. What is the noncontrolling interest in the income of the subsidiary?

    a. $8,000.
    b. $8,200.
    c. $9,000.
    d. $9,800.

8. Dunn Corporation owns 100 percent of Grey Corporation's common stock. On January 2, 1998, Dunn sold to Grey, for $40,000, machinery with a carrying amount of $30,000. Grey is depreciating the acquired machinery over a five-year life by the straight-line method. The net adjustments to compute 1998 and 1999 consolidated net income would be an increase (decrease) of

	1998	1999
a.	($ 8,000)	$2,000
b.	($ 8,000)	–0–
c.	($10,000)	$2,000
d.	($10,000)	–0–

    (AICPA adapted)

9. Wallton Corporation owns 70 percent of the outstanding stock of Hastings, Incorporated. On January 1, 1996, Wallton acquired a building with a 10-year life for $300,000. No salvage value was anticipated and the building was to be depreciated on the straight-line method. On January 1, 1998, Wallton sold this building to Hastings for $280,000. At that time, the building had a remaining life of eight years but still no expected salvage value. In preparing financial statements for 1998, how does this transfer affect the computation of consolidated net income?

    a. Income must be reduced by $32,000.
    b. Income must be reduced by $35,000.
    c. Income must be reduced by $36,000.
    d. Income must be reduced by $40,000.

Use the following data for questions 10–15:

    On January 1, 1998, Jarel buys 80 percent of the outstanding voting stock of Suarez for $260,000. Of this payment, $20,000 was allocated to equipment (with a five-year life) that had been undervalued on Suarez's books by $25,000. Any goodwill would be amortized over its maximum life.

    As of December 31, 1998, the financial statements appeared as follows:

	Jarel	Suarez
Revenues	$ 300,000	$200,000
Cost of goods sold	140,000	80,000
Expenses	20,000	10,000
Net income	$ 140,000	$110,000
Retained earnings, 1/1/98	$ 300,000	$150,000
Net income	140,000	110,000
Dividends paid	–0–	–0–
Retained earnings, 12/31/98	$ 440,000	$260,000

	Jarel	Suarez
Cash and receivables	$ 210,000	$ 90,000
Inventory	150,000	110,000
Investment in Jarel	260,000	–0–
Equipment (net)	440,000	300,000
Total assets	$1,060,000	$500,000
Liabilities	$ 420,000	$140,000
Common stock	200,000	100,000
Retained earnings, 12/31/98	440,000	260,000
Total liabilities and equities	$1,060,000	$500,000

During 1998, Jarel bought inventory for $80,000 and sold it to Suarez for $100,000. Only half of this purchase has been paid for by Suarez by the end of the year. Sixty percent of these goods are still in the company's possession on December 31.

10. What is the total of consolidated revenues?
  a. $500,000.
  b. $460,000.
  c. $420,000.
  d. $400,000.

11. What is the total of consolidated expenses?
  a. $30,000.
  b. $35,000.
  c. $34,000.
  d. $38,000.

12. What is the total of consolidated cost of goods sold?
  a. $140,000.
  b. $152,000.
  c. $132,000.
  d. $145,000.

13. What is the consolidated total of noncontrolling interest appearing on the balance sheet?
  a. $72,000.
  b. $69,600.
  c. $67,000.
  d. $70,600.

14. What is the consolidated total for equipment (net) at December 31?
  a. $680,000.
  b. $756,000.
  c. $764,000.
  d. $848,000.

15. What is the consolidated total for inventory at December 31?
  a. $240,000.
  b. $248,000.
  c. $250,000.
  d. $260,000.

16. Following are several figures reported for Pop and Sam as of December 31, 1998:

	Pop	Sam
Inventory	$300,000	$100,000
Sales	700,000	500,000
Investment income	not given	
Cost of goods sold	300,000	200,000
Expenses	200,000	200,000

Pop acquired 80 percent of Sam on January 1, 1991. Goodwill of $180,000 resulting from that transaction is being amortized over its maximum life. During 1998, Sam sells inventory costing $100,000 to Pop for $150,000. Of this inventory, 10 percent remains at year's end. On a 1998 consolidation, what totals would be reported for the following accounts:

Inventory.

Sales.

Cost of Goods Sold.

Expenses.

Noncontrolling Interest in the Subsidiary's Net Income.

17. Smith Corporation acquired 80 percent of the outstanding voting stock of Huss, Inc., on January 1, 1991, when Huss had a net book value of $400,000. Goodwill established by this acquisition is being amortized at a rate of $5,000 per year.

Smith reports net income for 1998 of $300,000 while Huss reports $110,000. Smith distributed $100,000 in dividends during this period; Huss paid $40,000. At the end of the year, selected figures from the two companies' balance sheets were as follows:

	Smith Corporation	Huss, Inc.
Inventory	$140,000	$ 90,000
Land	600,000	200,000
Equipment (net)	400,000	300,000
Common stock	400,000	200,000
Retained earnings, 12/31/98	600,000	400,000

During 1997, intercompany sales of $90,000 (original cost of $54,000) were made. Only 20 percent of this inventory was still being held at the end of 1997. In 1998, $120,000 in intercompany sales were made with an original cost of $66,000. Of this merchandise, 30 percent had not been resold to outside parties by the end of the year.

Each of the following questions should be considered as an independent situation.

a. If the intercompany sales were upstream, what would be the noncontrolling interest's share of the subsidiary's 1998 net income?

b. What is the consolidated balance in the ending Inventory account?

c. If the intercompany sales were downstream, what would be the noncontrolling interest's share of the subsidiary's 1998 net income?

d. If the intercompany sales were downstream, what would be the consolidated net income prior to the reduction for the noncontrolling interest's share of the subsidiary's income? Assume that Smith uses the cost method to account for this investment.

e. If the intercompany sales were downstream, what would be the consolidated balance for retained earnings as of the end of 1998? Assume that Smith uses the partial equity method to account for this investment.

f. If the intercompany sales were upstream, what would be the consolidated balance for retained earnings as of the end of 1998? Assume that Smith uses the partial equity method to account for this investment.

g. Assume that no intercompany inventory sales occurred between Smith and Huss. Instead, in 1995, Huss sold land costing $30,000 to Smith for $50,000. On the 1998 consolidated balance sheet, what value should be reported for land?

h. Assume that no intercompany inventory or land sales occurred between Smith and Huss. Instead, on January 1, 1997, Huss sold equipment (that originally cost $100,000 but had a $60,000 book value on that date) to Smith for $80,000. At the time of sale, the equipment had a remaining useful life of five years. What worksheet entries are made for a December 31, 1998, consolidation of these two companies to eliminate the impact of the intercompany transfer? For 1998, what is the noncontrolling interest's share of Huss's net income?

18. Rockney owns 60 percent of the outstanding stock of Dabney. Dabney reports net income for 1998 of $120,000. Since being acquired, the subsidiary has regularly supplied inventory to Rockney at 20 percent more than cost. Sales to Rockney amounted to $252,000 in 1997 and $288,000 in 1998. Approximately one tenth of the inventory purchased during any one year is not used until the following period.

Required:

a. What is the noncontrolling interest's share of the Dabney's income in 1998?

b. Prepare the 1998 and 1999 consolidation entries that would be required by the preceding intercompany inventory transfers.

19. Several years ago Penguin, Inc., purchased an 80 percent interest in Snow Company. The book values of Snow's asset and liability accounts at that time were considered to be equal to their fair market values. Penguin paid an amount corresponding to the underlying book value of Snow so that no allocations or goodwill resulted from the purchase price.

    The following selected account balances are from the individual financial records of these two companies as of December 31, 1998:

	Penguin	Snow
Sales	$640,000	$360,000
Cost of goods sold	290,000	197,000
Operating expenses	150,000	105,000
Retained earnings, 1/1/98	740,000	180,000
Inventory	346,000	110,000
Buildings (net)	358,000	157,000
Investment income	not given	

Each of the following problems is an independent situation.

a. Assume that Penguin sells inventory to Snow at a markup equal to 40 percent of cost. Intercompany transfers were $90,000 in 1997 and $110,000 in 1998. Of this inventory, $28,000 of the 1997 transfers were retained and then sold by Snow in 1998 while $42,000 of the 1998 transfers were held until 1999.

   On consolidated financial statements for 1998, what balances would appear for the following accounts:

   Cost of Goods Sold.

   Inventory.

   Noncontrolling Interest in Subsidiary's Net Income.

b. Assume that Snow sells inventory to Penguin at a markup equal to 40 percent of cost. Intercompany transfers were $50,000 in 1997 and $80,000 in 1998. Of this inventory, $21,000 of the 1997 transfers were retained and then sold by Penguin in 1998, whereas $35,000 of the 1998 transfers were held until 1999.

   On consolidated financial statements for 1998, what balances would appear for the following accounts:

   Cost of Goods Sold.

   Inventory.

   Noncontrolling Interest in Subsidiary's Net Income.

c. Penguin sells a building to Snow on January 1, 1997, for $80,000, although the book value of this asset was only $50,000 on this date. The building had a five-year remaining life and was to be depreciated using the straight-line method with no salvage value.

   On consolidated financial statements for 1998, what balances would appear for the following accounts:

   Buildings (net).

   Expenses.

   Noncontrolling Interest in Subsidiary's Net Income.

20. Allen, Inc. owns all of the outstanding stock of Bowen Corporation. Amortization expense of $9,000 per year resulted from the original purchase. For 1998, the companies had the following account balances:

	Allen	Bowen
Sales	$900,000	$500,000
Cost of goods sold	400,000	300,000
Operating expenses	300,000	120,000
Investment income	not given	–0–
Dividends paid	60,000	40,000

Intercompany sales of $200,000 occurred during 1997 and again in 1998. This merchandise cost $140,000 each year. Of the total transfers, $60,000 was still held on December 31, 1997, with $45,000 unsold on December 31, 1998.

Required:

    a. For consolidation purposes, does the direction of the transfers (upstream or downstream) affect the balances to be reported here?

    b. Prepare a consolidated income statement for the year ending December 31, 1998.

21. Plimpton holds 100 percent of the outstanding shares of Stanger. On January 1, 1996, Plimpton transferred equipment to Stanger for $70,000. The equipment had cost $110,000 originally but had a $40,000 book value and five-year remaining life at the date of transfer. Depreciation expense is computed according to the straight-line method with no salvage value.

    Consolidated financial statements for 1998 currently are being prepared. What worksheet entries are needed in connection with the consolidation of this asset? Assume that the parent applies the partial equity method.

22. On January 1, 1998, Slaughter sold equipment to Bennett (a wholly owned subsidiary) for $120,000 in cash. The equipment had originally cost $100,000 but had a book value of only $70,000 when transferred. On that date, the equipment had a five-year remaining life. Depreciation expense is computed using the straight-line method.

    Slaughter earned $220,000 in net income in 1998 (not including any investment income) while Bennett reported $90,000.

Required:

    a. What is the consolidated net income for 1998?

    b. What is the consolidated net income for 1998 if Slaughter owns only 90 percent of Bennett?

    c. What is the consolidated net income for 1998 if Slaughter owns only 90 percent of Bennett and the equipment transfer had been upstream?

    d. What is the consolidated net income for 1999 if Slaughter reports $240,000 (does not include investment income) and Bennett $100,000 in income? Assume that Bennett is a wholly owned subsidiary and the equipment transfer was downstream. = $350,

23. Anchovy purchased 90 percent of Yelton on January 1, 1996. Of the original price paid by the parent, $60,000 was allocated to undervalued equipment (with a 10-year life) and $80,000 was attributed to goodwill (to be written off over a 20-year period).

    Since the takeover, Yelton has transferred inventory to its parent as follows:

Year	Cost	Transfer Price	Remaining at Year-End
1996	$20,000	$ 50,000	$20,000 (at transfer price)
1997	49,000	70,000	30,000 (at transfer price)
1998	50,000	100,000	40,000 (at transfer price)

    On January 1, 1997, Anchovy sold a building to Yelton for $50,000. The building had originally cost $70,000 but had a book value at the date of transfer of only $30,000. The building is estimated to have a five-year remaining life (straight-line depreciation is used with no salvage value).

    Selected figures from the December 31, 1998, trial balances of these two companies are as follows:

	Anchovy	Yelton
Sales	$600,000	$500,000
Cost of goods sold	400,000	260,000
Operating expenses	120,000	80,000
Investment income	not given	
Inventory	220,000	80,000
Equipment (net)	140,000	110,000
Buildings (net)	350,000	190,000

    Determine consolidated totals for each of these account balances.

24. On January 1, 1998, Sledge has common stock of $120,000 and retained earnings of $260,000. During that year, Sledge reported sales of $130,000, cost of goods sold of $70,000, and operating expenses of $40,000.

    On January 1, 1993, 80 percent of Sledge's outstanding voting stock was acquired by Percy, Inc. At that date, $60,000 of the purchase price was assigned to goodwill (with a 40-year life) and $20,000 to an undervalued building (with a 10-year life).

In 1997, Sledge sold inventory costing $9,000 to Percy for $15,000. Of this merchandise, Percy continued to hold $5,000 at the end of that period. During 1998, inventory costing $11,000 was transferred to Percy for $20,000. Half of these items are still being held at year's end.

On January 1, 1997, Percy sold equipment to Sledge for $12,000. This asset originally cost $16,000 but had a January 1, 1997, book value of $9,000. At the time of transfer, the equipment's remaining life was estimated to be five years.

Percy has properly applied the equity method to the investment in Sledge.

Required:

a. Prepare worksheet entries to consolidate these two companies as of December 31, 1998.

b. Compute the noncontrolling interest in the subsidiary's income for 1998.

25. Big purchased 90 percent of the outstanding shares of Little on January 1, 1996, for $345,000 in cash. The subsidiary's stockholders' equity accounts totaled $330,000 on that day. However, a building held by Little (with a nine-year remaining life) was undervalued in the accounting records by $20,000. Any goodwill resulting from the purchase price is to be amortized over a 10-year period.

Little reported net income of $60,000 in 1996 and $80,000 in 1997. The company followed a policy of paying dividends each year equal to 30 percent of income.

Little sells inventory to Big as follows:

Year	Cost to Little	Transfer Price to Big	Inventory Remaining at Year's End (at transfer price)
1996	$69,000	$115,000	$25,000
1997	81,000	135,000	37,500
1998	92,800	160,000	50,000

At December 31, 1998, Big owes Little $16,000 for inventory acquired during the current period.

The following separate account balances are for these two companies for December 31, 1998, and the year then ended. Credits are indicated by parentheses.

	Big	Little
Sales revenues	$ (862,000)	$(366,000)
Cost of goods sold	515,000	209,000
Expenses	186,600	67,000
Investment income—Little	(70,600)	—
Net income	$ (231,000)	$ (90,000)
Retained earnings, 1/1/98	$ (488,000)	$(278,000)
Net income (above)	(231,000)	(90,000)
Dividends paid	136,000	27,000
Retained earnings, 12/31/98	$ (583,000)	$(341,000)
Cash and receivables	$ 146,000	$ 98,000
Inventory	255,000	136,000
Investment in Little	456,000	—
Land, buildings, and equipment (net)	959,000	328,000
Total assets	$ 1,816,000	$ 562,000
Liabilities	$ (718,000)	$ (71,000)
Common stock	(515,000)	(150,000)
Retained earnings, 12/31/98	(583,000)	(341,000)
Total liabilities and equities	$(1,816,000)	$(562,000)

Answer each of the following questions:

a. How much did the book value of the subsidiary increase during the previous two years of ownership (1996 and 1997)?

b. What was the annual amortization resulting from the purchase price allocations?

c. Were the intercompany transfers upstream or downstream?

d. What unrealized gain existed as of January 1, 1998?

e. What was the subsidiary's realized retained earnings as of January 1, 1998?
f. What unrealized gain existed as of December 31, 1998?
g. What was the subsidiary's realized net income for 1998?
h. What amounts make up the $70,600 Investment Income—Little account balance for 1998?
i. What was the noncontrolling interest's share of the subsidiary's net income for 1998?
j. What amounts make up the $456,000 Investment in Little account balance as of December 31, 1998?
k. What Entry S is required in producing a 1998 consolidation worksheet?
l. Without preparing a worksheet or consolidation entries, determine the consolidation balances for these two companies.

26. Asphalt acquired 70 percent of Broadway on June 11, 1987. Based on the purchase price, goodwill of $300,000 was recognized which is being amortized at the rate of $10,000 per year. The 1998 financial statements are as follows:

	Asphalt	Broadway
Sales	$ 800,000	$ 600,000
Cost of goods sold	(535,000)	(400,000)
Operating expenses	(100,000)	(100,000)
Dividend income	35,000	–0–
Net income	$ 200,000	$ 100,000
Retained earnings, 1/1/98	$1,300,000	$ 850,000
Net income	200,000	100,000
Dividends paid	(100,000)	(50,000)
Retained earnings, 12/31/98	$1,400,000	$ 900,000
Cash and receivables	$ 400,000	$ 300,000
Inventory	298,000	700,000
Investment in Broadway	902,000	–0–
Fixed assets	1,000,000	600,000
Accumulated depreciation	(300,000)	(200,000)
Totals	$2,300,000	$1,400,000
Liabilities	$ 600,000	$ 400,000
Common stock	300,000	100,000
Retained earnings	1,400,000	900,000
Totals	$2,300,000	$1,400,000

Asphalt sells inventory costing $72,000 to Broadway during 1997 for $120,000. At year's end, 30 percent is left. Asphalt sells inventory costing $200,000 to Broadway during 1998 for $250,000. At year's end, 20 percent is left. Under these circumstances, what are the consolidated balances for the following accounts:

    Sales.
    Cost of Goods Sold.
    Operating Expenses.
    Dividend Income.
    Noncontrolling Interest in Consolidated Income.
    Inventory.
    Noncontrolling Interest in Subsidiary, 12/31/98.

27. Compute the balances in problem 26 again assuming that the intercompany transfers were all made from Broadway to Asphalt.

28. Following are financial statements for Topper Company and Kirby Company for 1998:

	Topper	Kirby
Sales and other income	$ 800,000	$ 600,000
Cost of goods sold	500,000	400,000
Operating and interest expense	100,000	160,000
Net income	$ 200,000	$ 40,000

	Topper	Kirby
Retained earnings, 1/1/98	$ 990,000	$ 500,000
Net income	200,000	40,000
Dividends paid	130,000	–0–
Retained earnings, 12/31/98	$1,060,000	$ 540,000
Cash and receivables	$ 220,000	$ 170,000
Inventory	224,000	160,000
Investment in Kirby	654,000	–0–
Equipment (net)....................	600,000	400,000
Buildings	1,000,000	800,000
Accumulated depreciation—buildings ...	(100,000)	(200,000)
Other assets	200,000	100,000
Total assets	$2,798,000	$1,430,000
Liabilities	$1,138,000	$ 590,000
Common stock	600,000	300,000
Retained earnings, 12/31/98	1,060,000	540,000
Total liabilities and equity	$2,798,000	$1,430,000

■ Topper purchased 90 percent of Kirby on January 1, 1987, for $654,000 in cash. On the date of acquisition, Kirby held equipment (5-year life) which was undervalued on the financial records by $50,000 and liabilities (20-year life) that were overvalued $30,000. Any goodwill is being amortized over its maximum life.

■ Between January 1, 1987, and December 31, 1997, Kirby earned a net income of $600,000 and paid dividends of $340,000.

■ Kirby sells inventory each year to Topper with a markup equal to 20 percent of the transfer price. Intercompany sales were $145,000 in 1997 and $160,000 in 1998. On January 1, 1998, 30 percent of the 1997 transfers were still on hand and, on December 31, 1998, 40 percent of the 1998 transfers remained in inventory. Topper still owes $20,000 on the final shipment.

■ Topper sold a building to Kirby on January 1, 1997. It had cost Topper $100,000 but had $90,000 in accumulated depreciation at the time of this transfer. The price was $25,000 in cash. At that time, the building had a five-year remaining life.

Required:

Determine all consolidated balances either computationally or by the use of a worksheet.

29. Atkins, Inc., and Smith, Inc., formed a business combination on January 1, 1992, when Atkins acquired a 60 percent interest in the common stock of Smith for $372,000. The book value of Smith on that day was $350,000. Patents held by the subsidiary (with a 12-year remaining life) were undervalued within the company's accounting records by $120,000. Any goodwill indicated by the acquisition price is to be amortized over 10 years.

Intercompany inventory sales between the two companies have been made as follows:

Year	Cost to Atkins	Transfer Price to Smith	Ending Balance (at transfer price)
1992	$ 60,000	$ 72,000	$15,000
1993	70,000	84,000	25,000
1994	80,000	100,000	20,000
1995	100,000	125,000	40,000
1996	90,000	120,000	30,000
1997	120,000	150,000	50,000
1998	112,000	160,000	40,000

Smith sold a building to Atkins on January 1, 1996, for $80,000. The building had a net book value of $30,000 on that date and a five-year life. No salvage value was expected for this asset which was being depreciated by the straight-line method.

The individual financial statements for these two companies as of December 31, 1998, and the year then ended follow:

	Atkins, Inc.	Smith, Inc.
Sales	$ 700,000	$ 300,000
Cost of goods sold........................	(460,000)	(205,000)
Operating expenses	(170,000)	(70,000)
Income of Smith	15,000	–0–
Net income	$ 85,000	$ 25,000
Retained earnings, January 1, 1998	$ 690,000	$ 400,000
Net income (above)	85,000	25,000
Dividends paid	(45,000)	(5,000)
Retained earnings, December 31, 1998	$ 730,000	$ 420,000
Cash and receivables	$ 185,000	$ 142,000
Inventory	233,000	229,000
Investment in Smith......................	474,000	–0–
Buildings (net)	308,000	202,000
Equipment (net)..........................	220,000	86,000
Patents (net)	–0–	20,000
Total assets	$1,420,000	$ 679,000
Liabilities	$ 390,000	$ 159,000
Common stock	300,000	100,000
Retained earnings, December 31, 1998	730,000	420,000
Total liabilities and equities	$1,420,000	$ 679,000

For each of the following accounts, determine the 1998 consolidated balance:

a. Cost of Goods Sold.
b. Operating Expenses.
c. Net Income.
d. Retained Earnings, January 1, 1998.
e. Inventory.
f. Buildings (net).
g. Patents (net).
h. Common Stock.
i. Noncontrolling Interest in Smith, December 31, 1998.

30. Tall Company purchased 60 percent of the outstanding stock of Short, Inc., on January 1, 1996. A $70,000 portion of the purchase price was allocated to equipment with a 10-year remaining life while $40,000 was attributed to a building having a 20-year life. Goodwill of $60,000 was also recognized and has been amortized over a 30-year period.

Short sells inventory to Tall at a markup equal to 25 percent of the transfer price. Sales have been as follows:

Year	Transfer Price to Tall	Inventory Remaining at Year's End (at transfer price)
1996	$ 90,000	$30,000
1997	120,000	20,000
1998	140,000	40,000

Tall still owes $30,000 to Short for the last inventory shipment.

Following are the account balances at December 31, 1998, for both companies. Credit balances are indicated with parentheses.

	Tall	Short
Revenues	$ (984,000)	$(438,000)
Cost of goods sold........................	551,000	286,000
Operating expenses	198,000	112,000
Equity earnings of Short....................	(10,000)	–0–
Net income	$ (245,000)	$ (40,000)

	Tall	Short
Retained earnings, 1/1/98	$ (871,000)	$(350,000)
Net income (above)	(245,000)	(40,000)
Dividends paid	110,000	25,000
Retained earnings, 12/31/98	$(1,006,000)	$(365,000)
Cash and receivables	$ 239,000	$ 57,000
Inventory	454,000	95,000
Investment in Short	440,000	–0–
Land and buildings (net)	722,000	394,000
Equipment (net).............	328,000	257,000
Total assets	$ 2,183,000	$ 803,000
Liabilities	$ (686,000)	$(288,000)
Common stock	(320,000)	(90,000)
Additional paid-in capital	(171,000)	(60,000)
Retained earnings	(1,006,000)	(365,000)
Total liabilities and stockholders' equity	$(2,183,000)	$(803,000)

Required:

    a. The parent applies the equity method. How was the $10,000 balance in the Equity Earnings of Short account determined?

    b. Construct a worksheet to arrive at consolidated figures to be used for external reporting purposes.

31. On December 31, 1995, the Silvey Company acquired 70 percent of the outstanding common stock of the Young Company for $665,000. The stockholders' equity accounts reported by Young on that date were as follows:

Common stock—$10 par value	$300,000
Additional paid-in capital	90,000
Retained earnings	410,000

In establishing the purchase price, Silvey appraised the assets of Young and ascertained that a building (with a five-year life) was undervalued within the accounting records by $50,000. Any goodwill recognized in this acquisition was to be amortized over 10 years.

    During the subsequent years, Young sold inventory to Silvey at a 30 percent markup on the transfer price. Silvey consistently resold this merchandise in the year of acquisition or in the period immediately following. Transfers for the three years after this business combination was created amounted to:

Year	Transfer Price	Remaining Inventory— Year-End (at transfer price)
1996	$60,000	$10,000
1997	80,000	12,000
1998	90,000	18,000

In addition, Silvey sold several pieces of fully depreciated equipment to Young on January 1, 1997, for $20,000. The equipment had originally cost Silvey $50,000. Young plans to depreciate the cost of these assets over a five-year period.

    In 1998, Young earns a net income of $160,000 while distributing $50,000 in cash dividends. These figures increase the subsidiary's retained earnings to a $740,000 balance at the end of 1998. During this same year, Silvey reported dividend income of $35,000 and an investment account containing the original cost balance of $665,000.

Required:

Prepare the 1998 consolidation worksheet entries for Silvey and Young. In addition, compute the noncontrolling interest's share of the subsidiary's net income for 1998.

32. Assume the same basic information as presented in problem 31 except that Silvey has employed the equity method of accounting. Hence, investment income is being reported for 1998 as $100,740 with an investment account balance of $838,220. Under these circumstances, prepare the worksheet entries required for the consolidation of Silvey Company and Young Company.

33. The individual financial statements for Bumpus Company and Keller Company for the year ending December 31, 1998, follow. Bumpus acquired a 60 percent interest in Keller on January 1, 1993. Goodwill of $100,000 was recognized within the original purchase price. This intangible asset is being amortized over 20 years.

    Bumpus sold land with a book value of $60,000 to Keller on January 1, 1995, for $100,000. Keller still holds this land at the end of the current year.

    Keller annually transfers inventory to Bumpus. In 1997, inventory costing $100,000 was shipped to Bumpus at a price of $150,000. During 1998, intercompany shipments totaled $200,000, although the original cost to Keller was only $140,000. In each of these years, 20 percent of the merchandise was not resold to outside parties until the period following the transfer. Bumpus owes Keller $40,000 at the end of 1998.

	Bumpus Company	Keller Company
Sales	$ 800,000	$ 500,000
Cost of goods sold	(500,000)	(300,000)
Operating expenses	(100,000)	(60,000)
Income of Keller Company	84,000	–0–
Net income	$ 284,000	$ 140,000
Retained earnings, 1/1/98	$1,116,000	$ 620,000
Net income (above)	284,000	140,000
Dividends paid	(115,000)	(60,000)
Retained earnings, 12/31/98	$1,285,000	$ 700,000
Cash	$ 177,000	$ 90,000
Accounts receivable	316,000	410,000
Inventory	440,000	320,000
Investment in Keller Company	766,000	–0–
Land	180,000	390,000
Buildings and equipment (net)	496,000	300,000
Total assets	$2,375,000	$1,510,000
Liabilities	$ 480,000	$ 400,000
Common stock	610,000	320,000
Additional paid-in capital	–0–	90,000
Retained earnings, 12/31/98	1,285,000	700,000
Total liabilities and equities	$2,375,000	$1,510,000

Required:

a. Prepare a worksheet to consolidate the separate 1998 financial statements produced by Bumpus and Keller.

b. How would the consolidation entries in requirement a. have differed if Bumpus had sold a building with a $60,000 book value (cost of $140,000) to Keller for $100,000 instead of land as the problem reports? Assume that the building had a 10-year remaining life at the date of transfer.

34. Greene, Inc., obtained 100 percent of Meadow Corporation on January 1, 1994, in an exchange that did not meet all requirements for a pooling of interests. Meadow reported total stockholders' equity on this date of $300,000 although the stock issued by Greene in the transaction had a $170,000 par value but a fair market value of $450,000. On January 1, 1994, Meadow held land that was undervalued in the company's accounting records by $30,000. Any goodwill indicated by this takeover is to be amortized over the maximum possible life.

    Inventory has been regularly transferred by Meadow to Greene. In 1997, merchandise costing $60,000 was sold to Greene for $100,000. Of this total, 30 percent was not resold to unrelated parties until the following year. In 1998, $75,000 in inventory was shipped to Greene for $150,000 with $20,000 (transfer price) still held at the end of the period.

    On June 19, 1998, Greene sold land costing $12,000 to Meadow for $17,000. This money has not yet been paid.

The following account balances are for both companies as of December 31, 1998, and the year then ended. The parent has used the equity method to record this investment. Produce a worksheet to arrive at consolidated financial statements for this business combination. Credit balances are indicated by parentheses.

	Greene	Meadow
Revenues	$ (477,000)	$(358,000)
Cost of goods sold	289,000	195,000
General and administrative expenses	170,000	75,000
Gain on sale of land	(5,000)	–0–
Investment income	(82,000)	–0–
Net income	$ (105,000)	$ (88,000)
Retained earnings, 1/1/98	$ (365,000)	$(292,000)
Net income	(105,000)	(88,000)
Dividends distributed	70,000	20,000
Retained earnings, 12/31/98	$ (400,000)	$(360,000)
Cash and receivables	$ 169,000	$ 210,000
Inventory	281,000	232,000
Investment in Meadow	630,000	–0–
Land, buildings, and equipment (net)	487,000	284,000
Total assets	$ 1,567,000	$ 726,000
Liabilities	$ (466,000)	$(216,000)
Common stock	(410,000)	(120,000)
Additional paid-in capital	(291,000)	(30,000)
Retained earnings, 12/31/98	(400,000)	(360,000)
Total liabilities and stockholders' equity	$(1,567,000)	$(726,000)

CHAPTER

6

Intercompany Debt and Other Consolidation Issues

QUESTIONS TO CONSIDER

- When an affiliate's debt instrument is bought from an outside party, the reciprocal balances (investment and debt, interest revenue and expense, etc.) usually do not agree. How is the consolidation process carried out in the year of acquisition as well as in each succeeding period?

- Some preferred stocks are viewed as equity interests but others, because of the rights conveyed, are considered to be equivalent to debts. How is this distinction drawn, and what impact does the nature of a subsidiary's preferred stock have on the consolidation process?

- What effect does the inclusion of a subsidiary have on the preparation of a consolidated statement of cash flows?

- If a subsidiary has debt or preferred stock or other items outstanding that can be exchanged for common stock, how are basic and diluted earnings per share computed for the business combination?

- Why would a subsidiary buy or sell more shares of its own stock after coming under the control of a parent company? What effect do such transactions have on consolidated financial statements?

The consolidation of financial information can be a highly complex process often encompassing a number of practical challenges. This chapter examines the procedures required by several additional issues:

- Intercompany debt.

- Subsidiary preferred stock.

- The consolidated statement of cash flows.

- Computation of consolidated earnings per share.

- Subsidiary stock transactions.

Each of these can create potential difficulties for an accountant attempting to produce fairly presented financial statements for a business combination.

INTERCOMPANY DEBT TRANSACTIONS

The previous chapter explored the consolidation procedures required by the intercompany transfer of inventory, land, and depreciable assets. In consolidating these transactions, all resulting gains were deferred until earned through either use of the asset or its resale to outside parties. Deferral was necessary because these gains, although legitimately recognized by the individual companies, were unearned from the perspective of the consolidated entity. The separate financial information of each company was adjusted on the worksheet to be consistent with the view that the related companies actually composed a single economic concern.

This same objective applies in consolidating all intercompany transactions: the financial statements must represent the business combination as one enterprise rather than as a group of independent organizations. Consequently, in designing consolidation procedures for intercompany transactions, the effects recorded by the individual companies first must be isolated. After the impact of each action is analyzed, the

253

worksheet entries necessary to recast these events from the vantage point of the business combination are developed. Although this process involves a number of nuances and complexities, the desire for reporting financial information solely from the perspective of the consolidated entity remains constant.

The intercompany sale of inventory, land, and depreciable assets was introduced together (in Chapter 5) because these transfers result in similar consolidation procedures. In each case, one of the affiliated companies recognizes a gain prior to its actually being earned by the consolidated entity. The worksheet entries required by these transactions simply realign the separate financial information to agree with the viewpoint of the business combination. The gain is removed and the inflated asset value is reduced to historical cost.

The first section of this chapter examines the intercompany acquisition of bonds and notes. Although accounting for the related companies as a single economic entity continues to be the central goal, the consolidation procedures applied to intercompany debt transactions are in diametric contrast to the process utilized in Chapter 5 for asset transfers.

Before delving into this topic, note that *direct* loans used to transfer funds between affiliated companies create no unique consolidation problems. Regardless of whether such amounts are generated by bonds or notes, the resulting receivable/payable balances are necessarily identical. Because no money is owed to or from an outside party, these reciprocal accounts must be eliminated in each subsequent consolidation. A worksheet entry simply offsets the two corresponding balances. Furthermore, the interest revenue/expense accounts associated with direct loans also agree and are removed in the same fashion.

Acquisition of Affiliate's Debt from an Outside Party

The difficulties encountered in consolidating intercompany liabilities relate to a specific type of transaction: the purchase from an outside third party of an affiliate's debt instrument. A parent company, for example, might acquire a bond previously issued by a subsidiary on the open market. Despite the intercompany nature of this transaction, the debt remains an outstanding obligation of the original issuer while simultaneously being recorded as an investment by the acquiring company. Thereafter, even though related parties are involved, interest payments pass periodically between the two organizations.

Although the individual companies continue to report both the debt and the investment, from a consolidation viewpoint this liability is retired as of the date of acquisition. From that time forward, the debt is no longer owed to a party outside of the business combination. Subsequent interest payments are simply intercompany cash transfers. To create consolidated statements, worksheet entries must be developed that adjust the various balances to report the effective retirement of the debt.

Acquiring an affiliate's bond or note from an unrelated party poses no significant consolidation problems if the purchase price equals the corresponding book value of the liability. Reciprocal balances within the individual records would always be identical in value and easily offset in each subsequent consolidation.

Realistically though, such reciprocity is rare when a debt is purchased from a third party. A variety of economic factors typically produces a difference between the price paid for the investment and the carrying amount of the obligation. The debt is originally sold under market conditions at a particular time. Any premium or discount associated with this issuance is then amortized over the life of the bond creating a continuous adjustment to book value. The acquisition of this instrument at a later date is made at a price influenced by current economic conditions, prevailing interest rates, and myriad other financial and market factors.

Therefore, the cost paid to purchase the debt might be either more or less than the book value of the liability currently found within the financial records of the issuing

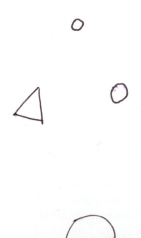

[handwritten: Sub]

company. *To the business combination, this difference is a gain or loss because the acquisition effectively retires the bond; the debt is no longer owed to an outside party.* For external reporting purposes, this gain or loss must be recognized immediately by the consolidated entity as required by *APB Opinion 26*, "Early Extinguishment of Debt," October 1972.

[handwritten: is extraordinary if it is material]

Accounting for Intercompany Debt Transactions—Individual Financial Records

[handwritten: all 4 change each year]

The accounting problems encountered in consolidating intercompany debt transactions are fourfold:

[handwritten: change constant]

[handwritten left margin: rare that sub would buy parent]

1. Both the investment and debt accounts have to be eliminated now and for each future consolidation despite containing differing balances.
2. Subsequent interest revenue/expense (as well as any interest receivable/payable accounts) must be removed although these balances also fail to agree in amount.
3. Changes in all of the preceding accounts occur constantly because of the amortization process.
4. The gain or loss on retirement of the debt must be recognized by the business combination, even though this balance does not appear within the financial records of either company.

To illustrate, assume that Alpha Company possesses an 80 percent interest in the outstanding voting stock of Omega Company. On January 1, 1996, Omega issues $1 million in 10-year term bonds paying cash interest annually of 9 percent. Because of market conditions prevailing on that date, the debt is sold for $938,555 to yield an effective interest rate of 10 percent per year. Shortly thereafter, the prime interest rate begins to fall, and by January 1, 1998, the decision is made to retire this debt prematurely and refinance it at the currently lower rates. To carry out this plan, Alpha purchases all of these bonds in the open market on January 1, 1998, for $1,057,466. This price was based on an effective yield of 8 percent, which is assumed to be in line with the interest rates at the time.

Many reasons could exist for having Alpha, rather than Omega, reacquire this debt. For example, company cash levels at that date might necessitate Alpha's role as the purchasing agent. Also, contractual limitations may prohibit Omega from repurchasing its own bonds.

In accounting for this business combination, an early extinguishment of the debt has occurred. Thus, the difference between the $1,057,466 payment and the January 1, 1998, book value of the liability must be recognized in the consolidated statements as a gain or loss. The exact account balance reported for the debt on that date depends on the amortization process. Although the issue was recorded initially at the $938,555 exchange price, after two years the carrying value has increased to $946,651, calculated as follows:[1]

Bonds Payable—Book Value—January 1, 1998

Year	Book Value	Effective Interest (10 percent rate)	Cash Interest	Amortization	Year-End Book Value
1996	$938,555	$93,855	$90,000	$3,855	$942,410
1997	942,410	94,241	90,000	4,241	946,651
1998	*946,651*	*94,665*	*90,000*	*4,665*	*951,316*

[1]The effective rate method of amortization is demonstrated here because this approach is theoretically preferable. However, the straight-line method can be applied if the resulting balances are not materially different than the figures computed using the effective rate method.

Since Alpha paid $110,815 in excess of the recorded liability ($1,057,466 − $946,651), a loss of this amount must be recognized by the consolidated concern. If material, the $110,815 is highlighted as an extraordinary item. After the loss has been acknowledged, the bond is considered to be retired and no further reporting would be necessary by the *business combination* after January 1, 1998.

Despite the simplicity of this approach, neither company accounts for the event in this manner. Omega retains the $1 million debt balance within its separate financial records while amortizing the remaining discount each year. Annual cash interest payments of $90,000 (9 percent) continue to be made. At the same time, the investment is recorded by Alpha at the historical cost of $1,057,466, an amount that also requires periodic amortization. Furthermore, as the owner of these bonds, Alpha receives the $90,000 interest payments made by Omega.

To organize the accountant's approach to this consolidation, a complete analysis of the subsequent financial recording made by each of these companies should be produced. Only two journal entries would be recorded by Omega during 1998 if the assumption is made that interest is paid each December 31.

Omega Company's Financial Records

12/31/98	Interest Expense	90,000	
	Cash		90,000
	To record payment of annual cash interest on $1 million, 9 percent bonds payable.		
12/31/98	Interest Expense	4,665	
	Bonds Payable (or Discount on Bonds Payable)		4,665
	To adjust interest expense to effective rate based on original yield rate of 10 percent ($946,651 book value for 1998 × 10% = $94,665). Book value increases to $951,316.		

Concurrently, Alpha journalizes entries to record its ownership of this investment:

Alpha Company's Financial Record

1/1/98	Investment in Omega Company Bonds	1,057,466	
	Cash		1,057,466
	To record acquisition of $1,000,000 in Omega Company bonds paying 9 percent cash interest, acquired to yield an effective rate of 8 percent.		
12/31/98	Cash	90,000	
	Interest Income		90,000
	To record receipt of cash interest from Omega Company bonds ($1,000,000 × 9%).		
12/31/98	Interest Income	5,403	
	Investment in Omega Company Bonds		5,403
	To reduce $90,000 interest income to effective rate based on original yield rate of 8 percent ($1,057,466 book value for 1998 × 8% = $84,597). Book value decreases to $1,052,063.		

Even a brief review of these entries indicates that the reciprocal accounts to be eliminated within the consolidation process do not agree in amount. You can see the dollar amounts appearing in each set of financial records in Exhibit 6–1. Despite the presence of these recorded balances, none of the four intercompany accounts (the liability, investment, interest expense, and interest revenue) appear in the consolidated financial statements. *The only figure to be reported by the business combination is the $110,815 loss created by the extinguishment of this debt.*

Exhibit 6–1

<table>
<tr><td colspan="3" align="center">ALPHA COMPANY AND OMEGA COMPANY
Effects of Intercompany Debt Transaction
1998</td></tr>
<tr><td></td><td align="center">Omega Company
Reported Debt</td><td align="center">Alpha
Company
Investment</td></tr>
<tr><td>1998 interest expense* . . . .</td><td align="right">$ 94,665</td><td align="right">$ –0–</td></tr>
<tr><td>1998 interest income† . . . .</td><td align="right">–0–</td><td align="right">84,597</td></tr>
<tr><td>Bonds payable* . . . .</td><td align="right">(951,316)</td><td align="right">–0–</td></tr>
<tr><td>Investment in bonds, 12/31/98† . . . .</td><td align="right">–0–</td><td align="right">1,052,063</td></tr>
<tr><td>Loss on retirement . . . .</td><td align="right">–0–</td><td align="right">–0–</td></tr>
<tr><td colspan="3">Note: Parentheses indicate credit balances.</td></tr>
<tr><td colspan="3">*Company total is adjusted for 1998 amortization of $4,665 (see journal entry).</td></tr>
<tr><td colspan="3">†Adjusted for 1998 amortization of $5,403 (see journal entry).</td></tr>
</table>

Effects on Consolidation Process

As indicated in previous discussions, consolidation procedures serve to convert information generated by the individual accounting systems to the perspective of a single economic entity. A worksheet entry is, therefore, required on December 31, 1998, to eliminate the intercompany balances shown in Exhibit 6–1 and to recognize the loss resulting from the repurchase. Mechanically, the differences in the liability and investment balances as well as the interest expense and interest income accounts stem from the $110,815 deviation between the purchase price of the investment and the book value of the liability. Recognition of this loss, in effect, bridges the gap between the divergent figures.

Consolidation Entry B (December 31, 1998)

Bonds Payable . . . . . . *F.V. – unamort discount*	951,316	
Interest Income . . . . *Cash –*	84,597	
Extraordinary Loss on Retirement of Bond *purchase price – BV*	110,815	
Investment in Omega Company Bonds *CV at end of 1st year*		1,052,063
Interest Expense . . *Payment + amort*		94,665

To remove intercompany bonds and related interest accounts
and record loss on the early extinguishment of this debt.
(Labeled "B" in reference to bonds.)

The preceding entry successfully transforms the separate financial reporting of Alpha and Omega to that appropriate for the business combination. The objective of the consolidation process has been met: the statements present the bonds as having been retired on January 1, 1998. The debt as well as the corresponding investment is eliminated along with both interest accounts. Only the loss now appears on the worksheet to be reported within the consolidated financial statements.

Assignment of Retirement Gain or Loss   *read only ✳*

Perhaps the most intriguing issue to be addressed in accounting for intercompany debt transactions concerns the assignment of any gains and losses created by the retirement. Should the $110,815 loss just reported be attributed to Alpha or to Omega? From a practical perspective, this assignment is only important in the calculation and reporting of noncontrolling interest figures. However, the FASB's Discussion Memorandum, "An Analysis of Issues Related to Consolidation Policy and Procedures," identifies four possible allocations (paragraph 384), each of which demonstrate theoretical merit.

First, a strong argument can be made that the liability being extinguished is that of the issuing company and, thus, any resulting income relates solely to that party. This

DISCUSSION QUESTION

Who Lost This $300,000?

Several years ago, the Penston Company purchased 90 percent of the outstanding shares of Swansan Corporation. The acquisition was made because Swansan produced a vital component used in Penston's manufacturing process. Penston wanted to ensure an adequate supply of this item at a reasonable price. The remaining 10 percent of Swansan's stock was retained by the former owner, James Swansan, who agreed to continue managing this organization. He was given responsibility over the subsidiary's daily manufacturing operations but not any of the financial decisions.

The takeover of Swansan has proven to be a successful undertaking for Penston. The subsidiary has managed to supply all of the parent's inventory needs as well as distribute a variety of items to outside customers.

At a recent meeting, the president of Penston and the company's chief financial officer began discussing Swansan's debt position. The subsidiary had a debt to equity ratio that seemed unreasonably high considering the significant amount of cash flows being generated by both companies. Payment of the interest expense, especially on the subsidiary's outstanding bonds, was a major cost, one that the corporate officials hoped to reduce. However, the bond indenture specified that Swansan could only retire this debt prior to maturity by paying 107 percent of face value.

This premium was considered prohibitive. Thus, to avoid contractual problems, Penston acquired a large portion of Swansan's liability on the open market for 101 percent of face value. Penston's purchase created an effective loss on the debt of $300,000: the excess of the price over the book value of the debt as reported on Swansan's books.

Company accountants currently are computing the noncontrolling interest's share of consolidated net income to be reported for the current year. They are unsure about the impact of this $300,000 loss. The subsidiary's debt was retired but the decision was made by officials of the parent company. Who lost this $300,000?

approach assumes that only the debtor is affected by the retirement of any obligation. Proponents of this position hold that the acquiring company is merely serving as a purchasing agent for the original issuer of the bonds. Accordingly, in the previous illustration, the benefits derived from paying off the liability should accrue to Omega because that company's interest rate has been reduced through refinancing. The loss was incurred solely to obtain these lower rates. Therefore, under this assumption, the entire $110,815 is assigned to Omega, the issuer of the debt. This assignment is usually considered to be consistent with the economic unit concept and was recommended in the 1995 FASB Exposure Draft, "Consolidated Financial Statements: Policy and Procedures."

Second, other accountants argue that the loss should be assigned solely to the investor (Alpha). According to proponents of this approach, the income effect is created by the acquisition of the bonds and the price negotiated by the buyer.

A third hypothesis is that the resulting gain or loss should be split in some manner between the two companies. This approach is consistent with both the parent company concept and proportionate consolidation. Since both parties are involved with the debt, this proposition contends that assigning income to only one company is arbitrary and misleading. Normally, such a division is based on the original face value of the debt. Hence, $57,466 of the loss would be allocated to Alpha with the remaining $53,349 assigned to Omega:

Alpha		Omega	
Purchase price	$1,057,466	Book value	$ 946,651
Face value	1,000,000	Face value	1,000,000
Loss—Alpha	$ 57,466	Loss—Omega	$ 53,349

Allocating the loss in this manner is an enticing solution; the subsequent accounting process creates an identical division within the individual financial records. Be-

Exhibit 6–2

	ALPHA COMPANY AND OMEGA COMPANY Effects of Intercompany Debt Transactions 1999	
	Omega Company Reported Debt	**Alpha Company Investment**
1999 interest expense*	$ 95,132	–0–
1999 interest income†	–0–	$ (84,165)
Bonds payable*	(956,448)	–0–
Investment in bonds, 12/31/99†	–0–	1,046,228
Income effect within retained earnings, 1/1/99‡	94,665	(84,597)

Note: Parentheses indicate credit balance.

*Company total is adjusted for 1999 amortization of $5,132 (see journal entry).

†Adjusted for 1999 amortization of $5,835 (see journal entry).

‡The balance shown for the Retained Earnings accounts of the individual companies represents the 1998 reported interest figures.

cause both Alpha's premium and Omega's discount must be amortized, the loss figures eventually affect the reported earnings of the respective companies. Over the life of the bond, the $57,466 is recorded by Alpha as an interest income reduction while Omega increases its own interest expense by $53,349 because of the amortization of the discount.

 A fourth perspective takes a more practical view of intercompany debt transactions: all repurchases are ultimately orchestrated by the parent company. As the controlling party in a business combination, the ultimate responsibility for retiring any obligation lies with the parent. The gain or loss resulting from the decision should, thus, be assigned solely to the parent regardless of the specific identity of the debt issuer or the acquiring company. In the current example, Alpha maintains control over Omega. Therefore, according to this theory, the financial consequences of reacquiring these bonds rest with Alpha so that the entire $110,815 loss must be attributed to that party.

Each of these arguments does have conceptual merit, and if the FASB eventually sets an official standard, any one approach (or possibly a hybrid) might be required. Unless otherwise stated, however, all income effects in this textbook relating to intercompany debt transactions are assigned solely to the parent company, as discussed in the final approach. Consequently, the results of extinguishing debt always are attributed to the party most likely to have been responsible for the action.

Intercompany Debt Transactions—Subsequent to Year of Acquisition

Even though the preceding Entry B correctly eliminates Omega's bonds in the year of retirement, the debt remains within the financial accounts of both companies until maturity. Therefore, in each succeeding time period, all balances must again be consolidated so that the liability is always reported as having been extinguished on January 1, 1998. Unfortunately, a simple repetition of Entry B is not possible. Developing the appropriate worksheet entry is complicated by the amortization process that produces continual change in the various account balances. Thus, as a preliminary step in each subsequent consolidation, current book values, as reported by the two parties, must be identified.

To illustrate, the 1999 journal entries for Alpha and Omega follow. Exhibit 6–2 shows the resulting account balances as of the end of that year.

Omega Company's Financial Records—December 31, 1999

Interest Expense	90,000	
Cash		90,000

To record payment of annual cash interest on $1 million, 9
percent bonds payable.

Interest Expense	5,132	
Bonds Payable (or Discount on Bonds Payable)		5,132

To adjust interest expense to effective rate based on an original
yield rate of 10 percent ($951,316 book value for 1999 × 10%
= $95,132). Book value increases to $956,448.

Alpha Company's Financial Records—December 31, 1999

Cash	90,000	
Interest Income		90,000

To record receipt of cash interest from Omega Company
bonds.

Interest Income	5,835	
Investment in Omega Company Bonds		5,835

To reduce $90,000 interest income to effective rate based on
an original yield rate of 8 percent ($1,052,063 book value for
1999 × 8% = $84,165). Book value decreases to $1,046,228.

After the information in Exhibit 6–2 has been assembled, the necessary consolidation entry as of December 31, 1999, can be produced. This entry removes the balances reported at that date for the intercompany bonds, along with both of the interest accounts, to reflect the extinguishment of the debt on January 1, 1998. Since retirement took place in a prior period, the adjustment on the worksheet must also create a $110,815 reduction in retained earnings to represent the original loss.

Consolidation Entry *B (December 31, 1999)

Bonds Payable .... [FV - unamort dis.]	956,448	
Interest Income	84,165	
[par] Retained Earnings, 1/1/99 (Alpha)	100,747	
Investment in Omega Company Bonds		1,046,228
Interest Expense		95,132

To eliminate intercompany bond and related interest accounts
and to adjust retained earnings from $10,068 (currently
recorded net balance) to $110,815. (Labeled as "*B" in
reference to prior year bond transaction.)

In analyzing this latest consolidation entry, several important factors should be emphasized:

1. The individual account balances change during the present fiscal period so that the current consolidation entry differs from Entry B. These alterations are a result of the amortization process. To ensure the accuracy of the worksheet entry, the adjusted balances are isolated in Exhibit 6–2.

2. As indicated previously, all income effects arising from intercompany debt transactions are assigned to the parent company. For this reason, the adjustment to beginning retained earnings in Entry *B is attributed to Alpha as is the $10,967 increase in current income ($95,132 interest expense elimination less the $84,165 interest revenue elimination).[2] Consequently, the noncontrolling interest balances are not altered by Entry *B.

---

[2]Had the effects of the retirement been attributed solely to the original issuer of the bonds, the $10,967 reduction in current income would have been assigned to Omega (the subsidiary), thus creating a change in the noncontrolling interest computations.

3. The 1999 reduction to beginning retained earnings in Entry *B ($100,747) does not agree with the original $110,815 retirement loss. A net deficit balance of $10,068 (the amount by which previous interest expense exceeds interest revenue) has already been recorded by the individual companies at the start of 1999. To achieve the proper consolidated total, an adjustment of only $100,747 is required ($110,815 − $10,068).

Retained earnings balance—consolidation perspective		
(loss on retirement of debt)		$110,815
Individual retained earnings balances, 1/1/99:		
Omega Company (interest expense—1998)	$ 94,665	
Alpha Company (interest income—1998)	(84,597)	10,068
Adjustment to consolidated retained earnings, 1/1/99		$100,747

Parentheses indicate a credit balance.

The periodic amortization of both the bond payable discount and the premium on the investment impacts the interest expense and revenue recorded by the two companies. As shown in this schedule, these two interest accounts do not offset exactly; a $10,068 net residual amount remains in retained earnings after the first year. Because this balance continues to grow each year, the subsequent consolidation adjustments to record the loss decrease to $100,747 in 1999 and constantly get smaller thereafter. *Over the life of the bond, the amortization process gradually brings the totals in the individual Retained Earnings accounts into agreement with the consolidated balance.*

4. Entry *B as shown is appropriate for consolidations in which the parent has applied either the cost or the partial equity method. However, a deviation is required if the parent uses the equity method for internal reporting purposes. As discussed in Chapter 5, proper application of the equity method ensures that the parent's income and, hence, its retained earnings are correctly stated prior to consolidation. Alpha would have already recognized the loss in accounting for this investment. Consequently, no adjustment to retained earnings is needed. In this one case, the $100,747 debit in Entry *B is made to the Investment in Omega Company because the loss has become a component of that account.

STOP!

SUBSIDIARY PREFERRED STOCK

When Kohlberg Kravis Roberts & Company purchased the outstanding common stock of Owens-Illinois Inc. for $60.50 per share, they also acquired all of the preferred stock of Owens-Illinois for $363 per share or a total of $25.8 million. Although preferred shares are routinely issued by both small and large corporations, their presence within the equity structure of a subsidiary adds a new dimension to the consolidation process. What accounting should be made of a subsidiary's preferred stock and the parent's payments, such as this $25.8 million, that are made to acquire these shares?

The consolidation measures required to report the preferred stock of a subsidiary depend on the specific nature of the shares. Controversy has long existed as to whether such issues are more akin to equity or debt, a distinction that depends on the specified rights granted to the holders. The characteristics of many preferred shares resemble those attributed to long-term liabilities rather than to equity securities. For example, a stock with a call value and no rights except for a set, cumulative dividend is in substance almost identical to a bond payable. Conversely, preferred shares that offer voting and/or participation rights clearly demonstrate essential characteristics associated with an ownership interest.

However, not all preferred stocks lend themselves to easy classification: the legal rights given to shareholders often vary significantly from issue to issue. For example,

Ford Motor Company in its 1996 annual report shows both Series A and Series B preferred stock outstanding, each with specific rights as to dividends, convertibility to common stock, and redemption prices. Such attributes can make the distinction between debt and equity quite nebulous. Because of this identification problem, the FASB has plans to study the issue within its financial instruments project. However, until a guideline is established, as is utilized in earnings per share computations, determining the true nature of many types of preferred stock still requires considerable individual judgment.

In consolidating subsidiary preferred stock, the accountant must evaluate whether the shares are more similar to debt or to equity. If the stock resembles a debt, any shares acquired by the parent are recorded as if retired. Conversely, if a preferred stock is truly an equity instrument, the combination accounts for the purchased shares in the same manner as common stock: allocations are made to specific assets and liabilities with any residual payment assigned to goodwill.

Preferred Stock Viewed as a Debt Instrument

If a subsidiary's preferred stock has characteristics that primarily resemble a liability, consolidation techniques should parallel the process previously demonstrated for intercompany debt. To illustrate, assume that on January 1, 1998, High Corporation acquires control over Low Company by purchasing 80 percent of its outstanding common stock as well as 60 percent of its nonvoting, cumulative, preferred stock. Low owns land that is undervalued in its records by $100,000.

The purchase price paid by High was $1 million for the common shares and $62,400 for the preferred. On the date of acquisition, Low reported the following stockholders' equity balances. Note that the 1,000 shares of preferred stock outstanding have a $100 par value but can be called (retired) by Low for $110 per share.

Common stock, $20 par value (20,000 shares outstanding)	$ 400,000
Preferred stock, 6% cumulative with a par value of $100 and a $110 call value (1,000 shares outstanding)	100,000
Additional paid-in capital	200,000
Retained earnings	516,400
Total stockholders' equity (book value)	$1,216,400

Low's preferred stock carries no rights other than its cumulative dividend; thus, this issue is considered a debt instrument in nature. The $62,400 price paid by High is handled in a manner consistent with that of an intercompany bond. The payment made for these shares has no influence on the valuation of specific subsidiary accounts (such as the undervalued land) or the recognition of goodwill. Instead, the preferred stock acquired by the parent is eliminated on each subsequent worksheet as if the shares had been retired.

Although this handling parallels that of a long-term liability, one important distinction must be drawn. Preferred stock is legally an equity; thus, its retirement cannot result in the reporting of a gain or loss to the consolidated entity. Instead, the difference between the stock's par value and the acquisition price paid by the parent must be recorded as an adjustment to Additional Paid-In Capital (or to Retained Earnings if a reduction is required and the Additional Paid-In Capital account is not of sufficient size).

The consolidation entry to account for this preferred stock acquisition follows. *Since the stock is viewed as the equivalent of debt, these shares (60 percent of the 1,000 outstanding) are simply eliminated as if retired.*

Preferred Stock (the 60 percent owned by High)	60,000	
Additional Paid-In Capital	2,400	
Investment in Low Company's Preferred Stock		62,400
To eliminate preferred stock of Low Company acquired by the parent company.		

This entry assumes that no part of the cumulative dividend is in arrears at the date of purchase. If a dividend had been owed on the preferred stock, a reduction in the subsidiary's retained earnings equal to that amount would have been included here rather than assigning the entire $2,400 difference to additional paid-in capital. This alteration presumes that a portion of the purchase price is paid to reimburse the former owners for the missed dividends.

Although the preceding worksheet entry removes the effects of High's acquisition, it ignores the residual 40 percent noncontrolling interest in the preferred stock. In recording an allocation to these outside owners, the appropriate amount to be recognized must be determined. When preferred stock is viewed as a debt, the call value (if present) is considered to be more relevant to the consolidated entity than par value. Thus, the outside owners are assigned a balance equal to the call value of the securities (plus any dividends in arrears). In the current illustration, the $110 figure reflects the cost required to retire each of the remaining 400 shares (40% of 1,000). Thus, the worksheet entry to recognize this noncontrolling interest is as follows:

Preferred Stock (40% owned by outsiders)	40,000	
Additional Paid-In Capital	4,000	
Noncontrolling Interest in Low Company (call value)		44,000

To recognize the outside ownership of 40 percent of Low Company's preferred stock.

These entries have been presented separately to clarify the difference in consolidating parent-owned and outside-owned shares. In practice, these figures are combined to eliminate all of the subsidiary's preferred stock. Thus, a single consolidation entry actually should be incorporated in this illustration:

Consolidation Entry PS

Preferred Stock	100,000	
Additional Paid-In Capital	6,400	
Investment in Low Company's Preferred Stock		62,400
Noncontrolling Interest in Low Company		44,000

To eliminate preferred stock of subsidiary (viewed as a debt) and record noncontrolling interest. (Labeled as "PS" in reference to preferred stock.)

Having accounted for Low's preferred stock, now the elimination of the company's remaining stockholders' equity accounts can be made. As with any purchase combination, a preliminary allocation of the purchase price paid for the common stock is essential. Because of the amounts attributed to preferred stock, only $1,110,000 of Low's total book value is assigned to the common stock at the date of acquisition:

Total book value of Low Company, 1/1/98		$1,216,400
Allocated to preferred stock ownership:		
Acquisition price of High Company's interest	$62,400	
Call value of noncontrolling interest	44,000	(106,400)
Book value allocated to common stock		$1,110,000

Based on this book value, the $1 million paid by High for 80 percent of Low's common stock is allocated as shown in Exhibit 6–3. As indicated previously, land owned by Low is assumed here to be undervalued on the subsidiary's records by $100,000.

By utilizing the information from Exhibit 6–3, basic worksheet entries can be constructed as of January 1, 1998 (the date of purchase). After Entry PS removes the preferred shares and recognizes the noncontrolling interest in that stock, the remainder of Low's stockholders' equity accounts are eliminated by Entry S. In addition, a 20 percent noncontrolling interest in Low's common stock is established as $222,000 (20 percent of the $1,110,000 book value). The allocations made to the undervalued

Exhibit 6–3

HIGH COMPANY AND LOW COMPANY
Allocation of Common Stock Purchase Price
January 1, 1998

Purchase price paid for common stock	$1,000,000
Common stock book value equivalent to High's ownership	
($1,110,000 × 80%)	(888,000)
Cost in excess of book value	112,000
Allocation to specific accounts based on fair market value:	
Land ($100,000 × 80%)	80,000
Excess cost not identified with specific accounts—goodwill	$ 32,000

land and to goodwill then are recognized in Entry A. No other consolidation entries are needed as no time has passed since the acquisition took place.

Consolidation Entry S

Common Stock (Low Company)	400,000	
Additional Paid-In Capital (Low Company)	193,600	
Retained Earnings (Low Company)	516,400	
Investment in Low Company's Common Stock (80%)		888,000
Noncontrolling Interest in Low Company (20%)		222,000

To eliminate remaining stockholders' equity accounts after removal of preferred stock and to recognize noncontrolling interest in common stock.

Consolidation Entry A

Land	80,000	
Goodwill	32,000	
Investment in Low Company's Common Stock		112,000

To allocate excess cost paid for Low's common stock to specific account based on fair market value and to goodwill (see Exhibit 6–3).

In working with this illustration, note the structure that is followed in consolidating a subsidiary's preferred stock. First, a determination is made of the nature of the stock. Identifying Low Company's issue as a debt-type instrument significantly influenced the development of the consolidation process. Second, the subsidiary's book value is divided between the preferred and common stock interests. Assigning $106,400 of Low's book value to the preferred stock (the price of the purchased shares plus the call value of remainder) and the residual $1,110,000 to common stock led directly to the valuations and eliminations incorporated in this consolidation. As is subsequently demonstrated, this allocation of book value can vary considerably depending on the specific rights granted to the preferred shareholders.

Allocation of Subsidiary Income   The final factor influencing a consolidation that includes subsidiary preferred shares is the allocation of the company's income between the two types of stock. A division must be made for every period subsequent to the takeover (1) to compute the noncontrolling interest's share and (2) for the parent's own recognition purposes. For a cumulative, nonparticipating preferred stock such as the one presently being examined, only the specified annual dividend is attributed to the preferred stock with all remaining income assigned to common stock. Consequently, if the assumption is made that Low reports earnings of $100,000 in 1998 while paying the annual $6,000 dividend on its preferred stock, income is allocated for consolidation purposes as follows:

	Income
Subsidiary total	$100,000
Preferred stock (6% dividend × $100,000 par value of the stock)	$ 6,000
Common stock (residual amount)	94,000

During 1998, High Company, as the parent, would be entitled to $3,600 in dividends from Low's preferred stock because of its 60 percent ownership. In addition, High holds 80 percent of Low's common stock so that another $75,200 of the income ($94,000 × 80 percent) is attributed to the parent. The noncontrolling interest in the subsidiary's income can be calculated in a similar fashion:

		Percent Outside Ownership	Noncontrolling Interest
Preferred stock dividend	$ 6,000	40%	$ 2,400
Income attributed to common stock	94,000	20	18,800
Noncontrolling interests in subsidiary's income ...			$21,200

Preferred Stock Viewed as an Equity Interest

Having established basic principles for a consolidation that includes subsidiary preferred stock that resembles debt, a second example can be utilized in which the stock is considered an equity. Continuing to employ High's acquisition of Low, assume now that the dividends of the subsidiary's preferred stock are fully participating as well as cumulative. Furthermore, the stock is not callable. Because the preferred shares convey additional rights, the relative values of the two classes of stock differ from that of the previous example. Therefore, High is assumed to have paid only $894,496 for an 80 percent interest in Low's common stock but $149,968 for 60 percent of the preferred.

The ability to participate in the earnings of Low Company provides the preferred shareholders with an ownership interest that is akin to that of common stock. Thus, altering the rights of this issue has changed its essential nature to that of an equity interest rather than a debt. When subsidiary preferred stock is viewed as an equity, the consolidation process differs significantly from that examined in the previous illustration. *The preferred stock is handled in the same manner as common stock: any purchase price in excess of underlying book value is allocated to specific accounts as well as to goodwill. Income is accrued by the owners based on subsidiary earnings rather than on dividends.*

The cumulative participation rights entitle the holders of Low's preferred shares to a portion of the subsidiary's earnings each year. The specific division of income would be stipulated on the preferred stock certificate. That percentage is often based on the ratio of the total par values of the two classes of equity. Thus, 20 percent ($100,000 par value of the preferred stock divided by $500,000 total par value) of Low's annual income is assigned to the preferred shares. Additionally, because of the cumulative right, 20 percent of the subsidiary's retained earnings should also be attributed to the preferred stock (assuming that both classes of stock were originally issued on the same date). With these particular rights in force, allocation of the January 1, 1998, book value of Low Company is as follows:

Total book value of Low Company, 1/1/98		$1,216,400
Allocated to preferred stock ownership:		
Par value of preferred stock (no call value)	$100,000	
20% of total retained earnings ($516,400) based on cumulative, participation rights	103,280	(203,280)
Book value allocated to common stock (residual)		$1,013,120

Once the division of the subsidiary's book value has been established, High must allocate each of the acquisition payments. In this manner, the preferred stock is being accounted for as a true equity interest. Exhibit 6–4 analyzes both purchases: the $149,968 price paid for the preferred stock is shown first followed by the $894,496 amount invested in common stock. To complete this allocation, one theoretical question must be addressed: How is the undervaluation of the subsidiary's land to be

HIGH COMPANY AND LOW COMPANY
Allocation of Preferred and Common Stock Purchase Prices
January 1, 1998

Preferred Stock

Purchase price paid for preferred stock	$ 149,968
Preferred stock book value equivalent to High's ownership	
($203,280 × 60%)	(121,968)
Cost in excess of book value	$ 28,000
Allocation to specific accounts:	
Land ($20,000 × 60%)...................................	12,000
Excess cost not identified with specific accounts—goodwill	$ 16,000

Common Stock

Purchase price paid for common stock	$ 894,496
Common stock book value equivalent to High's ownership	
($1,013,120 × 80%)	(810,496)
Cost in excess of book value	$ 84,000
Allocation to specific accounts:	
Land ($80,000 × 80%)...................................	64,000
Excess cost not identified with specific accounts—goodwill	$ 20,000

treated? Since both stocks are considered equity interests, the $100,000 undervaluation is assumed to be reflected in each purchase price. Because of the participation feature of the preferred shares, the logical approach is to divide this $100,000 unrealized gain between the two stocks according to the par value ratio (20:80) or $20,000 to preferred stock and $80,000 to common.

From the information produced in Exhibit 6–4, the following consolidation entries for January 1, 1998 (the date of purchase) can be developed. Note that Entry A has been split into "A1" and "A2" to identify the allocations resulting from the preferred stock and common stock, respectively. This segregation is made merely to clarify the process; these two worksheet entries could easily be combined.

Consolidation Entry PS

Preferred Stock (Low Company)	100,000	
Retained Earnings (Low Company) (20%)	103,280	
Investment in Low Company Preferred Stock (60% ownership)		121,968
Noncontrolling Interest in Low Company (40%)		81,312

To eliminate subsidiary's preferred stockholders' equity accounts
($203,280) and recognize noncontrolling interest in preferred
stock. Retained earnings is based on par value assignment.

Consolidation Entry S

Common Stock (Low Company)	400,000	
Additional Paid-In Capital (Low Company)................	200,000	
Retained Earnings (Low Company) (80%)	413,120	
Investment in Low Company Common Stock (80% ownership)		810,496
Noncontrolling Interest in Low Company (20%)		202,624

To eliminate subsidiary's remaining stockholders' equity
accounts ($1,013,120) and recognize noncontrolling interest in
common stock. Retained earnings reflects Entry PS.

Consolidation Entry A1

Land	12,000	
Goodwill	16,000	
Investment in Low Company Preferred Stock		28,000

To allocate cost paid for preferred stock in excess of book value.
(See Exhibit 6–4.)

Consolidation Entry A2

Land	64,000	
Goodwill	20,000	
Investment in Low Company Common Stock		84,000

To allocate cost paid for common stock in excess of book value.
(See Exhibit 6–4.)

Allocation of Subsidiary Income   The specific rights granted to the owners of the preferred stock also affect the subsequent allocation of the subsidiary's income each year. If the assumption is again made that Low reports net income for 1998 of $100,000, this amount must be divided between the two ownership interests based on the cumulative, participating rights of the preferred stock. These shares constitute 20 percent of the subsidiary's total par value with the remaining 80 percent coming from the holders of the common stock. Thus, net income is prorated according to this same ratio.

	Income
Subsidiary totals	$100,000
Preferred stock—possesses rights to 20% of total (based on relative par values) ...	$ 20,000
Common stock—residual 80% interest	80,000

Based on this allocation of the subsidiary's income for 1998, the noncontrolling interest's share of consolidated income can be determined:

		Percent Outside Ownership	Noncontrolling Interest
Income attributed to preferred stock	$20,000	40%	$ 8,000
Income attributed to common stock	80,000	20	16,000
Noncontrolling interests in subsidiary's income ...			$24,000

CONSOLIDATED STATEMENT OF CASH FLOWS

In November of 1987, the Financial Accounting Standards Board issued its *Statement No. 95*, "Statement of Cash Flows," mandating that companies include a statement of cash flows within a set of financial statements. Because of this pronouncement, details of an organization's cash flows must be reported for each period in which an income statement is presented.

To this point in the coverage of consolidated financial statements, no mention has been made of cash flows for two reasons:

First, production of the statement of cash flows is a topic covered in detail in intermediate accounting textbooks.

Second, this consolidated statement is not prepared from the individual cash flows of the separate companies. Instead, the income statements and balance sheets are first brought together on the worksheet. The cash flows statement is based then on the resulting consolidated figures. *Thus, this statement is not actually produced by consolidation but rather it is created from numbers generated by that process.*

Although not directly created by the consolidation process, preparing a statement of cash flows for a business combination does introduce several accounting issues. In preparing this statement, noncontrolling interest balances, amortization, and intercompany transactions must all be properly handled.

Noncontrolling Interest   On the consolidated income statement, the outside ownership of a noncontrolling interest is reflected as a decrease in net income. This reduction represents the earnings accrual assigned to these other owners. However, the only cash actually distributed to the noncontrolling interest is the portion of dividends paid to them by the subsidiary. Although the income statement presents the accrual rather than the dividend, the opposite is true of the cash flow statement: only cash transactions are included. *Thus, for this statement, two adjustments are made. First, the noncontrolling interest's share of the subsidiary's net income must be eliminated; second, the dividends paid to the outside owners are included.*

The noncontrolling interest's income accrual can be removed from the statement of cash flows in either of two ways. If the business combination is using the direct approach to disclose cash generated by operations, the specific cash inflows and outflows are identified. For example, the cash collected from customers is disclosed along with the cash paid for inventory and expenses. Because the noncontrolling interest's share of consolidated income is a noncash item, this balance is simply omitted from the statement.

The business combination could also, instead, determine the cash from operations by applying the indirect approach. Under this alternative, noncash as well as non-operational items are removed from net income, which leaves a residual figure representing the increase or decrease in cash resulting from operations. If the indirect approach is used, the noncontrolling interest's share of consolidated income must be eliminated from net income since this reduction in earnings is a noncash account. The noncontrolling interest balance does not represent an actual cash payment or collection. Because the earnings assigned to these outside owners is a decrease (or negative) within consolidated income, the amount is eliminated by adding the number to net income.

Regardless of which approach is used, the noncontrolling interest income accrual is removed in computing the cash derived from operations. However, any dividend paid to the other owners during the period is an actual cash outflow incurred by the combination and must be included on the statement. Since this distribution is made to an owner, the amount is listed separately under the "Cash Flows from Financing Activities" section of the statement of cash flows.

Amortization   The amortization of allocations made to specific accounts as well as to goodwill is recorded in the consolidation process by means of a worksheet adjustment (Entry E). This expense does not appear on either set of individual records but is still included in the income statement of the business combination. As a noncash decrease in income, this expense impacts the statement of cash flows in the same manner as the noncontrolling interest's share of consolidated income. If the direct approach is used by the business combination, the balance is omitted because this expense does not affect the amount of cash. In contrast, if the indirect approach is applied, the amortization expense is removed by adding the balance to net income.

Intercompany Transactions   As discussed previously in this text, a significant volume of transfers often occur between the related companies composing a business combination. The resulting effects of this intercompany activity must be eliminated on the worksheet so that the consolidated income statement and balance sheet reflect only transactions with outside parties. Likewise, the consolidated statement of cash flows should not include the impact of these transfers. Although the cash flows may be large, intercompany sales and purchases do not change the amount of cash being held by the business combination when viewed as a whole.

Because the statement of cash flows is derived from the consolidated balance sheet and income statement, the impact of all transfers has been removed prior to producing this last statement. Therefore, no special adjustments are needed to arrive at a proper presentation of cash flows. The elimination entries made on the worksheet have the added effect of providing correct data for the consolidated statement of cash flows.

Illustration   A complete illustration of the production of a consolidated statement of cash flows is presented in the second comprehensive illustration at the end of the chapter. This example examines the effect on this statement created by the presence of a noncontrolling interest, amortization expense, and intercompany transactions.

CONSOLIDATED EARNINGS PER SHARE

One other intermediate accounting topic, the computation of earnings per share (EPS), is affected by the consolidation process. As required by *Statement of Financial Accounting Standards No. 128* (March 1997), "Earnings Per Share," publicly held companies must disclose EPS each period.

Such figures are calculated through the following steps:

- Basic earnings per share is determined by dividing net income (after reduction for preferred stock dividends) by the weighted average number of common stock shares outstanding for the period. If the reporting entity has no dilutive options, warrants or other convertible items, only basic EPS is presented on the face of the income statement. However, diluted earnings per share also must be presented if any dilutive convertibles are present.

- Diluted earnings per share is computed by combining the effects of *any dilutive securities* with basic earnings per share. Stock options, stock warrants, convertible debt and convertible preferred stock often qualify as dilutive securities.[3]

In most instances, the computation of earnings per share for a business combination follows the same general pattern. Consolidated net income along with the number of outstanding parent shares provides the basis for calculating basic EPS. Any convertibles, warrants, or options for the parent's stock that can possibly dilute the reported figure must be included as described earlier in determining diluted EPS.

However, a problem arises if warrants, options, or convertibles are outstanding that can dilute the subsidiary's earnings. Although the parent company is not directly affected, the potential impact of these items on consolidated net income must be given weight in computing diluted earnings per share for the business combination as a whole. Because of possible conversion, the subsidiary earnings figure included in consolidated net income is not necessarily applicable to the diluted earnings per share computation. *Thus, the accountant must make a separate determination of the amount of subsidiary income that should be used in deriving diluted earnings per share for the business combination.*

Earnings per Share Illustration   Assume that Big Corporation has 100,000 shares of its common stock outstanding during the current year. The company also has issued 20,000 shares of nonvoting preferred stock paying an annual cumulative dividend of $5 per share ($100,000 total). Each of these preferred shares is convertible into two shares of Big's common stock.

Assume further that Big owns 90 percent of Little's common stock and 60 percent of its preferred stock (which pays $12,000 in dividends per year). Annual amortization is $24,000. EPS computations currently are being made for 1998. During the year, Big reported separate income of $600,000 while Little earned $100,000. A

---

[3]Complete coverage of the earnings per share computation can be found in virtually any intermediate accounting textbook. To achieve an adequate understanding of this process, a number of complex procedures must be mastered including:

- Calculation of the weighted average number of common shares outstanding.
- Understanding the method of including stock rights, convertible debt, and convertible preferred stock within the computation diluted earnings per share.
- Determination of whether a convertible is antidilutive.

simplified consolidation of the figures for the year indicates net income for the business combination of $662,400:

Big's separate income for 1998		$600,000
Amortization expense resulting from original purchase price		(24,000)
Little's separate income for 1998	100,000	
Noncontrolling interest in Little—common stock (10% of income after $12,000 in preferred stock dividends)	(8,800)	
Noncontrolling interest in Little—preferred stock (40% of dividends)	(4,800)	86,400
Consolidated net income		$662,400

Little has 20,000 shares of common stock and 4,000 shares of preferred stock outstanding. The preferred shares pay a $3 per year dividend and each can be converted into 2 shares of common stock (or 8,000 shares in total). Since Big owns only 60 percent of Little's preferred stock, a $4,800 dividend is distributed each year to the outside owners (40 percent of $12,000 total payment).

Assume finally that the subsidiary also has $200,000 in convertible bonds outstanding that were originally issued at face value. This debt has a cash and an effective interest rate of 10 percent ($20,000 per year) and can be converted by the owners into 9,000 shares of Little's common stock. None of these bonds are owned by Big. The tax rate applicable to Little is 30 percent.

To better visualize these factors, the convertible items are scheduled as follows:

Company	Item	Interest or Dividend	Conversion	Big Owns
Big	Preferred stock	$100,000/year	40,000 shares	Not applicable
Little	Preferred stock	12,000/year	8,000 shares	60%
Little	Bonds	14,000/year*	9,000 shares	–0–

*Interest on the bonds is shown net of the 30 percent tax effect ($20,000 interest less $6,000 tax savings). No tax is computed for the preferred shares because distributed dividends do not create a tax impact.

Because the subsidiary has convertible items that may affect the company's outstanding shares and net income, Little's diluted earnings per share must be derived *before* consolidated diluted EPS can be determined. As shown in Exhibit 6–5, Little's diluted earnings per share are $3.08. Two aspects of this schedule should be noted:

■ The individual impact of the convertibles ($1.50 for the preferred stock and $1.56 for the bonds) did not raise the earnings per share figures. Thus, neither the preferred stock nor the bonds are antidilutive and both are properly included in these computations.

■ Determining diluted earnings per share of the subsidiary is only necessary because of the possible dilutive impact. Without the subsidiary's convertible bonds and preferred stock, consolidated net income would form the basis for computing EPS for the business combination and only basic EPS would be reported.

According to Exhibit 6–5, Little's income is $114,000 for diluted EPS. The issue for the accountant is how much of this amount should be included in computing consolidated diluted earnings per share. This allocation is based on the percentage of shares controlled by the parent. Note that if the subsidiary preferred stock and bonds are converted into common shares, Big's ownership falls from 90 to 62 percent. For diluted EPS, 37,000 shares are appropriate. Big's 62 percent ownership (22,800/37,000) is the basis for allocating the subsidiary's $114,000 income to the parent.

Exhibit 6–5
Subsidiary's Diluted Earnings
per Share

LITTLE COMPANY Diluted Earnings per Common Share For Year Ending December 31, 1998			
	Earnings	**Shares**	
As reported	$100,000	20,000	
Preferred stock dividends	(12,000)		
Effect of possible preferred stock conversion:			
Dividends saved...........	12,000	New Shares 8,000	$1.50 Impact (12,000/8,000)
Effect of possible bond conversion:			
Interest saved (net of taxes) ..	14,000	9,000	$1.56 Impact (14,000/9,000)
Diluted EPS	$114,000	37,000	$3.08 (rounded)

Supporting Calculations for Diluted Earnings per Share

	Little Company Shares	Big's Percentage	Big's Ownership
Common stock	20,000	90%	18,000
Possible new shares—preferred stock ...	8,000	60	4,800
Possible new shares—bonds	9,000	–0–	–0–
Total	37,000		22,800

Big's ownership (diluted): 22,800/37,000 = 62% (rounded)
Income assigned to Big (diluted earnings per share computation):
   $114,000 × 62% = $70,680

Consolidated earnings per share now can be determined. Only $70,680 of subsidiary income is appropriate for the diluted EPS computation. Since two different income figures are utilized, basic and diluted calculations are made separately as shown in Exhibit 6–6. Consequently, as determined in these schedules, this business combination should report basic earnings per share of $5.62 with diluted earnings per share of $4.62.

SUBSIDIARY STOCK TRANSACTIONS

A footnote to the financial statements of the Gerber Products Company disclosed a transaction carried out by one of the organization's subsidiaries: "The Company's wholly owned Mexican subsidiary sold previously unissued shares of common stock to Grupo Coral, S.A., a Mexican food company, at a price in excess of the shares' net book value." The footnote went on to state that Gerber had increased consolidated additional paid-in capital by $432,000 as a result of this stock sale.

As shown by this illustration, subsidiary stock transactions can alter the level of parent ownership. A subsidiary, for example, may decide to sell previously unissued stock to raise needed capital. Although the parent company may acquire a portion or even all of these new shares, such issues frequently are marketed entirely to outsiders. A subsidiary might also be legally forced to sell additional shares of its stock. As an example, companies holding control over foreign subsidiaries occasionally encounter this problem because of laws found in the individual localities. Issuance of new shares may be mandated if regulations require a certain percentage of local ownership as a prerequisite for operating within a country. Of course, changes in the level of parent ownership do not result solely from stock sales: a subsidiary also can repurchase its own stock. The acquisition, and possible retirement, of such treasury shares serves as a means of reducing the percentage of outside ownership.

Exhibit 6–6

BIG COMPANY AND CONSOLIDATED SUBSIDIARY
Consolidated Basic Earnings per Common Share
For Year Ending December 31, 1998

	Earnings	Shares	
Consolidated net income	$662,400		
Big's shares outstanding		100,000	
Preferred stock			
dividends (Big)	(100,000)		
Basic EPS	$562,400	100,000	$5.62

BIG COMPANY AND CONSOLIDATED SUBSIDIARY
Consolidated Diluted Earnings per Common Share
For Year Ending December 31, 1998

	Earnings	Shares	
Computed below	$646,680*		
Big's shares outstanding		100,000	
Preferred stock			
dividends (Big)	(100,000)		
Effect of possible preferred			
stock (Big) conversion:			
Dividends saved	100,000	New shares 40,000	$2.50 impact
			(100,000/40,000)
Diluted EPS	$646,680	140,000	$4.62 (rounded)
*Net income computation:			
Big's separate income			
for 1998	$600,000		
Amortization expense resulting			
from original purchase price . .	(24,000)		
Portion of Little's income			
assigned to diluted earnings			
per share calculation	70,680	(computed previously)	
Earnings of the business			
combination applicable			
to diluted earnings			
per share	$646,680		

Changes in Subsidiary Book Value—Stock Transactions

When a subsidiary subsequently buys or sells its own stock, a nonoperational increase or decrease occurs in the company's book value. Because the transaction need not involve the parent, the effect of this change is not automatically reflected in the parent's investment account. *Thus, a separate adjustment must be recorded to maintain reciprocity between the subsidiary's stockholders' equity accounts and the parent's investment balance.* The accountant measures the impact that the stock transaction has on the parent to ensure that this effect is appropriately recorded within the consolidation process.

An example demonstrates the mechanics of this issue. Assume that on January 1, 1998, Small Company's book value is $700,000 as follows:

Common stock ($1.00 par value with 70,000 shares issued and outstanding)	$ 70,000
Retained earnings	630,000
Total stockholders' equity	$700,000

Based on the 70,000 outstanding shares, Small's book value at this time is $10 per common share ($700,000/70,000 shares).

On this same date, Giant Company acquired in the open market an 80 percent interest in Small Company (56,000 of the outstanding shares). To avoid unnecessary complications, the price of this stock is assumed to be $560,000, or $10 per share, exactly equivalent to the book value of the purchased shares. The assumption also is made that no goodwill or other revaluations are indicated by this acquisition.

Under these conditions, the consolidation process is uncomplicated. On the purchase date only a single worksheet entry is required. The investment account is eliminated and the 20 percent noncontrolling interest recognized through the following routine entry:

Consolidation Entry S (January 1, 1998)

Common Stock (Small Company)	70,000	
Retained Earnings (Small Company)	630,000	
Investment in Small Company (80%)		560,000
Noncontrolling Interest in Small Company (20%)		140,000

   To eliminate subsidiary's stockholders' equity accounts and record noncontrolling interest balance on this date.

A subsidiary stock transaction is now introduced to demonstrate the effect created on the consolidation process. Assume that on January 2, 1998, Small sells 10,000 previously unissued shares of its common stock to outside parties for $16 per share.[4] Because of this transaction, Giant no longer possesses an 80 percent interest in a subsidiary having a $700,000 net book value. Instead, the parent now holds 70 percent (56,000 shares out of a total of 80,000) of a company with a book value of $860,000 ($700,000 previous book value plus $160,000 capital generated by the sale of additional shares). *Independently of any action by the parent company, the book value equivalency of this investment has risen from $560,000 to $602,000 (70% of $860,000).* This increase has been created by Small's ability to sell shares of stock at $6.00 more than the book value.

Small's new stock issuance has increased the underlying book value component of Giant's investment by $42,000 ($602,000 − $560,000). Thus, even with the rise in outside ownership, the business combination has grown in size by this amount, a change that must be reflected within the consolidated financial figures. As indicated by the Gerber example, this adjustment is frequently recorded to additional paid-in capital. Because the subsidiary's stockholders' equity is eliminated on the worksheet, any equity increase accruing to the business combination must be recognized by the parent. Therefore, the $42,000 increment is entered into Giant's financial records as an adjustment in both the investment account (since the underlying book value of the subsidiary has increased) as well as additional paid-in capital.

Giant Company's Financial Records—January 2, 1998

Investment in Small Company	42,000	
Additional Paid-in Capital (Giant Company)		42,000

   To recognize change in equity of business combination created by issuance of 10,000 additional shares of common stock by Small Company, the subsidiary, at above book value.

Once the change in the parent's records has been made, the consolidation process can be carried out in a normal fashion. If, for example, the financial statements are brought together immediately following the sale of these additional shares, the following worksheet Entry S can be constructed. *Although the investment and subsid-*

---

[4]This example has been created solely for demonstration purposes. Obviously, having the parent acquire stock at book value on one day with an outsider paying $6 per share more than book value on the following day is an unlikely situation. Normally, the prices would be similar or a greater length of time would transpire between the two acquisitions. In either case, the consolidation process is fundamentally unchanged.

iary equity accounts are removed here, the change recorded earlier in Giant's additional paid-in capital remains within the consolidated figures. Thus, the subsidiary's issuance of stock at more than the book value has increased the reported equity of the business combination.

Consolidation Entry S—January 2, 1998—after subsidiary's stock issuance

Common Stock (Small Company)	80,000	
Additional Paid-In Capital (Small Company)	150,000	
Retained Earnings (Small Company)	630,000	
Investment in Small Company (70%)		602,000
Noncontrolling Interest in Small Company (30%)		258,000

To eliminate subsidiary's stockholders' equity accounts and record noncontrolling interest balance on this date. Small's capital accounts have been updated to reflect the issuance of 10,000 shares of $1 par value common stock at $16 per share. The investment balance has also been adjusted for the $42,000 increment recorded earlier by the parent.

In 1983, because of a lack of formal guidance, the staff of the SEC decided that an adjustment necessitated by subsidiary stock transactions could be made to either additional paid-in capital or to a gain or loss account. For example, Atlantic Richfield Company disclosed that a previously wholly owned subsidiary had "completed an initial public offering of 19,550,000 shares of its common stock, thereby decreasing ARCO's percentage ownership to 80.4 percent. The Company recognized an after-tax gain of $185 million from this transaction."

In its October 1995 Exposure Draft, "Consolidated Financial Statements: Policy and Procedures," however, the FASB clearly supported the view that the effects on a parent of a subsidiary's transactions in its own stock should be reported as adjustments to additional paid-in capital, not as gains and losses. As stated in the Exposure Draft:

> Transactions in the stock of a subsidiary by any of the affiliates, whether purchases or sales by the parent or another subsidiary or reacquisitions or issuances of its own stock by the subsidiary, are transactions in the equity of the reporting entity comprising a parent and its subsidiaries. . . . Therefore, no gains or losses should be recognized on those transactions (paragraph 128).

The FASB thus recommended the following for reacquisition or issuance of additional shares by a subsidiary:

> The amount of the change in a parent's proportionate ownership interest in a subsidiary is reported as an increase or decrease in additional paid-in capital and as a corresponding decrease or increase in the noncontrolling interest (paragraph 29).

Consistent with the recommendation in the Exposure Draft, this textbook treats the effects from subsidiary stock transactions on the consolidated entity as adjustments to additional paid-in capital.

Subsidiary Stock Transactions—Illustrated

No single example can demonstrate the many possible variations that could be created by different types of subsidiary stock transactions. To provide a working knowledge of this process, several additional cases are analyzed briefly. The original balances presented for Small (the 80 percent-owned subsidiary) and Giant (the parent) as of January 1, 1998, serve as the basis for these illustrations:

Small Company (subsidiary):	
Shares outstanding.....................	70,000
Book value of company..................	$700,000
Book value per share...................	$10.00
Giant Company (parent):	
Shares owned of Small Company	56,000
Book value of investment	$560,000 (80%)

Each of the following cases should be viewed as an independent situation. In addition, all adjustments are made here to additional paid-in capital although, as discussed, recognition of a gain or loss remains a possible alternative.

Case 1 Assume that Small Company sells 10,000 shares of previously unissued common stock to outside parties for $8 per share.

Small is issuing its stock here at a price below the company's current book value of $10 per share. Selling shares to outsiders at a discount necessitates a drop in the recorded value of consolidated additional paid-in capital. The parent's ownership interest is being diluted, thus creating a decrease in the underlying book value of the parent's investment. This reduction can be measured as follows:

Adjusted book value of subsidiary ($700,000 + $80,000)	$780,000
Current parent ownership (56,000 shares/80,000 shares)	70%
Book value equivalency of ownership	546,000
Current book value of investment account	560,000
Required *reduction*	$ 14,000

In the original illustration, new shares were sold by the subsidiary at $6 more than book value, thus increasing consolidated equity. Here, the opposite transpires; the shares are issued at a price less than book value, creating a decrease.

Giant Company's Financial Records

Additional Paid-In Capital (or Retained Earnings)		
(Giant Company)	14,000	
Investment in Small Company		14,000

To recognize change in equity of business combination created by issuance of 10,000 additional shares of Small's common stock at less than book value.

Case 2 Assume that Small issues 10,000 new shares of common stock for $16 per share. Of this total, Giant acquires 8,000 shares to maintain its 80 percent level of ownership. Giant pays a total of $128,000 (8,000 × $16) for this additional stock. The remaining shares are bought by outside parties.

Under these circumstances, both the parent's investment account and the book value of the subsidiary are altered by the stock transaction. Thus, both figures must be updated prior to determining the necessity of an equity revaluation:

Adjusted book value of subsidiary ($700,000 + $160,000)	$860,000
Current parent ownership (64,000 shares/80,000 shares)	80%
Book value equivalency of ownership	688,000
Current book value of investment (after including additional $128,000 acquisition)	688,000
Required change	$ –0–

No adjustment is required in this case because Giant's underlying interest remains properly aligned with the subsidiary's book value. Any time that new stock is sold to the parent in the same ratio as previous ownership, consolidated additional paid-in capital is unaffected. No proportionate increase or decrease is created by the transaction.

Case 3 Assume that Small issues 10,000 additional shares of common stock solely to Giant for $16 per share.

A different type of situation is faced here. As shown in the following computational schedule, this issuance causes the parent's investment account to again be in excess of the subsidiary's underlying book value (as in Case 1). However, in this latest example, the $10,500 difference is created by a parent company purchase rather than by the subsidiary's sale of common stock to outside parties. Thus, the reporting of this impact has to be altered to reflect Giant's acquisition of these new shares.

Adjusted book value of subsidiary ($700,000 + $160,000)	$860,000
Current parent ownership (66,000 shares/80,000 shares)	82.5%
Book value equivalency of ownership	709,500
Current book value of investment (after including additional $160,000 acquisition).......................................	720,000
Differences in subsidiary book value and investment book value after second purchase	$ 10,500

The $14,000 reduction in Case 1 was caused by the subsidiary's sale of stock to outsiders at a price less than book value, a transaction that mathematically diluted the value of the parent's investment. Because this action realigned the ownership interests to the apparent detriment of the business combination, additional paid-in capital was reduced. This result was achieved for consolidation purposes through a decrease in the parent's equity account as well as in the Investment in Small Company.

Conversely, in Case 3, the $10,500 difference has been created solely by an expenditure made by the parent. Since the price paid was more than the corresponding book value of the subsidiary, the excess is attributed to goodwill (unless the amount can be traced to specific asset or liability accounts). As in any purchase combination, Giant records the entire $160,000 payment as an investment and then utilizes Entry A on the consolidation worksheet to report the allocation. Because the parent made the acquisition, the transaction is handled differently than a subsidiary's sale of stock to outsiders at less than book value.

Case 4 Assume that instead of issuing new stock, Small reacquires 10,000 shares from outside owners. The price paid for this treasury stock is $16 per share.

This illustration is designed to present another type of subsidiary stock transaction: the acquisition of treasury stock. Although the subsidiary's actions have changed, the basic accounting procedures are unaffected.

Adjusted book value of subsidiary ($700,000 − $160,000)	$540,000
Current parent ownership (56,000 shares/60,000 shares)	93⅓%
Book value equivalency of ownership	504,000
Current book value of investment	560,000
Required *reduction*	$ 56,000

The subsidiary paid an amount in excess of the treasury stock's $10 per share book value. Consequently, the parent's interest is once again being diluted. This effect is created by a transaction between the subsidiary and the noncontrolling interest; the reduction is not the result of a purchase made by the parent. As in Case 1, the change must be reported as an adjustment in the parent's additional paid-in capital accompanied by a corresponding decrease in the investment account (to $504,000 in this case). Again, for reporting purposes, this transaction results in lowering consolidated additional paid-in capital.

Giant Company's Financial Records

Additional Paid-In Capital (Giant Company)	56,000	
Investment in Small Company		56,000
To recognize change in equity of business combination created by acquisition of 10,000 treasury shares by Small at above book value.		

This fourth illustration represents a different subsidiary stock transaction, the purchase of treasury stock. Therefore, display of consolidation Entry S should also be presented. This entry demonstrates the worksheet elimination required when the subsidiary holds treasury shares.

Consolidation Entry S

Common Stock (Small Company)	70,000	
Retained Earnings (Small Company)	630,000	
Treasury Stock (Small Company) (at cost)		160,000
Investment in Small Company (93⅓%—subsequent to		
adjustment)		504,000
Noncontrolling Interest (6⅔% of net book value)		36,000

To eliminate equity accounts of Small Company and recognize appropriate noncontrolling interest. Book value of Small is now $540,000.

Case 5   Assume that Small issues a 10 percent stock dividend (7,000 new shares) to its owners at a time when the fair market value of the stock is $16 per share.

This final case illustrates that not all subsidiary stock transactions produce discernible effects on the consolidation process. A stock dividend, whether large or small, serves to capitalize a portion of the issuing company's retained earnings and, thus, does not alter book value. Shareholders recognize the receipt of a stock dividend only as a change in the recorded cost of each share rather than as any type of adjustment in the investment balance. Because no net effect is perceived by either party, the consolidation process proceeds in a routine fashion. Therefore, a subsidiary stock dividend requires no special treatment prior to development of a worksheet.

Book value of subsidiary (no adjustment required)	$700,000
Current parent ownership (adjusted for 10% stock dividend—	
61,600 shares/77,000 shares)	80%
Book value equivalency of ownership	560,000
Current book value of investment	560,000
Adjustment required by stock dividend	$ –0–

The consolidation Entry S that would be made just after the issuance of this stock dividend follows. The $560,000 component of the investment account continues to be offset against the stockholders' equity of the subsidiary. Although the parent's investment was not affected by the dividend, the equity accounts of the subsidiary have been realigned in recognition of the $112,000 stock dividend (7,000 shares of $1 par value stock valued at $16 per share).

Consolidation Entry S

Common Stock (Small Company)	77,000	
Additional Paid-In Capital (Small Company)................	105,000	
Retained Earnings (Small Company)	518,000	
Investment in Small Company (80%)		560,000
Noncontrolling Interest (20%)		140,000

To eliminate stockholders' equity accounts of subsidiary and recognize noncontrolling interest following issuance of stock dividend.

SUMMARY

1. If one member of a business combination acquires an affiliate's debt instrument (a bond or note, for example) from an outside party, the purchase price usually differs from the book value of the liability. Thus, a gain or loss has been incurred from the perspective of the business combination. However, both the debt and investment remain in the individual

financial accounts of the two companies while the gain or loss goes unrecorded. In the consolidation process, all balances must be adjusted to reflect the effective retirement of the debt.

2. Following the acquisition of one company's debt by a related party, interest income and expense are recognized. Because these accounts result from intercompany transactions, they also must be removed in every subsequent consolidation along with the debt and investment figures. Retained earnings also requires adjustment in each year after the purchase to record the impact of the gain or loss.

3. Amortization of intercompany debt/investment balances often is necessary because of discounts and/or premiums. Consequently, the interest income and interest expense figures reported by the two parties will not agree. The closing of these two accounts into retained earnings each year gradually reduces the consolidation adjustment that must be made to this equity account.

4. When acquired, many subsidiaries have preferred stock outstanding as well as common stock. The method of handling any subsidiary preferred shares within the consolidation process is dependent on the nature of the stock. Preferred issues that have a call value, no voting rights, and a set cumulative dividend are not easily distinguished from a debt. Conversely, preferred shares with a voting or participation right are clearly an ownership interest resembling common stock.

5. If a subsidiary's preferred stock is viewed as a debt-type instrument, any shares acquired by the parent are eliminated on the worksheet as if the stock had been retired. Because a gain or loss cannot be recognized in connection with a company's own stock transactions, the difference between par value and the parent's cost is adjusted through additional paid-in capital or retained earnings. Any shares still held by outside parties are reported as a noncontrolling interest, based on the call value of the stock.

6. A subsidiary preferred stock that is perceived as an equity interest is accounted for in the same manner as a common stock purchase. Any excess acquisition price paid for the preferred stock is assigned to specific accounts based on fair market value with any residual reported as goodwill. As a prerequisite to this process, the book value of the subsidiary must be divided between the two equity interests. This calculation is based on the rights specified for the preferred shareholders.

7. A statement of cash flows is required of every business combination. This statement is not created by consolidating the individual cash flows of the separate companies. Instead, both a consolidated income statement and balance sheet are produced and the cash flows statement is developed from these figures. Within this statement, the noncontrolling interest's share of the subsidiary's income is not included because no cash flows result. However, the dividends paid to these outside owners must be listed as a financing activity.

8. For most business combinations, the determination of consolidated earnings per share follows the normal pattern presented in intermediate accounting textbooks. However, if the subsidiary has potentially dilutive items outstanding (stock warrants, convertible preferred stock, convertible bonds, etc.), a different process must be followed. The subsidiary's own diluted earnings per share are computed as a preliminary procedure. The earnings used in each of these calculations are then allocated between the parent and the outside owners based on the ownership levels of the subsidiary's shares and the dilutive items. The portion of income assigned to the parent is included in determining the diluted earnings per share figures to be reported for the business combination.

9. A subsidiary may enter into stock transactions after the combination is created such as the issuance of additional shares or the acquisition of treasury stock. Such actions normally create a proportional increase or decrease in the subsidiary's equity when compared with the parent's investment. The change is measured and then reflected in the consolidated statements through the Additional Paid-In Capital account. Recognition of a gain or loss is also a possibility. To achieve the appropriate accounting, the parent adjusts the Investment in Subsidiary account as well as its own additional paid-in capital. Since this equity balance is not eliminated on the worksheet, the required increase or decrease is created in the consolidated figures.

COMPREHENSIVE ILLUSTRATION

Because several topics have been covered in this chapter, two comprehensive illustrations are presented.

Problem One: Intercompany Bonds, Preferred Stock, and Stock Transactions

(Estimated Time: 50 to 65 Minutes) The individual financial statements for Big Company and Little Corporation for the year ending December 31, 1998, follow:

	Big Company	Little Corporation
Revenues	$ 900,000	$ 389,026
Expenses	(702,000)	(200,000)
Interest income	–0–	10,974
Dividend income—Little Corporation preferred stock	2,400	–0–
Income of subsidiary—Little Corporation common stock	116,400	–0–
Net income	$ 316,800	$ 200,000
Retained earnings, 1/1/98	$1,300,000	$ 700,000
Net income (above)	316,800	200,000
Dividends—preferred stock	–0–	(6,000)
Dividends—common stock	(136,800)	(24,000)
Retained earnings, 12/31/98	$1,480,000	$ 870,000
Current assets	$ 484,525	$ 850,000
Investment in Big Company bonds	–0–	108,711
Investment in Little Corporation preferred stock	26,800	–0–
Investment in Little Corporation common stock	958,000	–0–
Land, buildings, and equipment (net)	600,000	750,000
Total assets	$2,069,325	$1,708,711
Current liabilities	$ 202,000	$ 138,711
Bonds payable ($200,000 face value)	177,325	–0–
Preferred stock—$60 par value; 1,000 shares outstanding	–0–	60,000
Common stock—$4 par value; 50,000 shares outstanding	200,000	
Common stock—$10 par value; 24,000 shares outstanding		240,000
Additional paid-in capital	10,000	400,000
Retained earnings (above)	1,480,000	870,000
Total liabilities and equities	$2,069,325	$1,708,711

Note: Parentheses indicate a reduction.

Additional Information:

On January 1, 1993, Big Company purchased 14,400 shares of Little's common stock (80 percent of the 18,000 shares outstanding at that date). Big also bought 40 percent of the company's outstanding preferred stock (400 shares). A total of $530,800 was paid by Big for these two investments: $504,000 for the common stock and $26,800 for the preferred. At the date of acquisition, Big believed that no significant difference existed between the book value of Little's assets and liabilities and their fair market values. Little Corporation reported the following stockholders' equity accounts on January 1, 1993:

Preferred stock—$60 par value, 10% cumulative dividend, nonparticipating, nonvoting; call value of $72 per share; 1,000 shares outstanding	$ 60,000
Common stock—$10 par value; 18,000 shares outstanding	180,000
Additional paid-in capital	100,000
Retained earnings	260,000
Total stockholders' equity	$600,000

On January 1, 1997, Little acquired on the open market half of the $200,000 outstanding bonds payable of Big Company. The bonds pay 12 percent cash interest each December 31 but were originally issued at a price yielding an effective rate of 15 percent. On the date of Little's purchase, Big was reporting a total book value for this debt of $173,100. Because of a recent decline in the prime interest rate, Little had to pay $110,670 for these bonds. This price was calculated to produce a 10 percent yield. Each company uses the effective interest rate method of amortization.

To raise new capital for expansion, Little Corporation issued an additional 6,000 shares of common stock to outsiders on January 1, 1998. Because of the company's profitability, the stock was sold for $60 per share. Because none of these shares were acquired by Big, the parent did not record the transaction.

Big has applied the partial equity method to the investment in Little's common stock while using the cost method for preferred shares. From 1993 through 1997, Little's retained earnings went up $440,000. Since preferred stock dividends were paid in full each year, the entire increase was directly attributable to the common shares (80 percent owned by Big).

Because of Little's sale of additional shares at the beginning of 1998, Big now holds only 60 percent of the common stock (14,400/24,000). Thus, the parent recognized equity income of $116,400 in 1998 in connection with its ownership of the subsidiary's common stock, 60 percent of the $194,000 income applicable to common stock (the $200,000 reported total less the $6,000 preferred stock dividend). The year-end investment in the common stock balance is made up of the following components:

Purchase price—common stock	$504,000
Increase in book value during prior years ($440,000 × 80%)	352,000
Equity accrual for current year	116,400
Dividends paid on common stock during current year ($24,000 × 60%)	(14,400)
Investment in Little Corporation common stock—12/31/98	$958,000

Any goodwill will be amortized over a 40-year period.

Required:

Prepare consolidated balances for Big and Little for 1998 financial statements.

Solution (One)

Specifying a single definitive approach to consolidating a complex business combination is not realistically possible. Clearly, though, certain aspects of the process should be handled first. Allocation of the purchase price routinely has been an initial step in previous examples. In this illustration, the allocation is complicated by the presence of Little's preferred stock. The nature of these shares must be identified as a prerequisite for the valuation of the common stock acquisition.

As the preferred stock is listed as nonvoting and nonparticipating, it possesses the basic characteristics of a debt issue and is handled in a corresponding manner. Thus, the price paid for the preferred shares does not directly affect the calculation of goodwill. Instead, 40 percent of the subsidiary's preferred stock is viewed as having been retired by Big's acquisition. Under this assumption, $70,000 of the January 1, 1993, book value is allocated to this stock.

Acquisition price paid by Big Company—400 shares of preferred stock (40% ownership)	$26,800
Call value of remaining 600 shares—$72 per share (noncontrolling interest)	43,200
Book value attributable to preferred stock	$70,000

Having allotted $70,000 to the preferred stock interest, the remaining $530,000 of Little's January 1, 1993, book value is applicable to the common shares. Based on this residual value, Exhibit 6–7 can be constructed to allocate the $504,000 purchase price paid by Big to acquire 80 percent ownership in Little's common stock. No similar schedule is necessary for the preferred shares because that stock is viewed, in this case, as a debt-type instrument.

E x h i b i t   6 – 7

BIG COMPANY AND LITTLE CORPORATION
Common Stock Purchase Price Allocation
January 1, 1993

Purchase price of common stock	$ 504,000
Common stock book value equivalent to Big's ownership ($530,000 × 80%)	(424,000)
Cost in excess of book value—all allocated to goodwill	$ 80,000
Assumed life of goodwill	40 years
Annual amortization	$ 2,000

A second concern to be addressed at the start of this consolidation revolves around the subsidiary stock transaction. Since Big (as stated in the problem) made no entry to reflect the change on the business combination, an adjustment must be recorded. Big originally acquired 80 percent of Little's outstanding common stock (14,400 shares out of a total of 18,000). However, the issuance of 6,000 new shares to outsiders reduces the parent's level of ownership to 60 percent (14,400/24,000 shares). Selling this stock for $60 per share also has increased Little's book value by $360,000. The impact of the subsidiary stock transaction can be measured as follows:

Little Corporation's 1/1/98 book value prior to stock sale ($600,000 book value at acquisition plus the $440,000 increment for the 1993–97 period)	$1,040,000
Little Corporation's 1/1/98 book value subsequent to stock issuance ($1,040,000 + $360,000)	$1,400,000
Little Corporation's book value applicable to preferred stock (see above)	(70,000)
Residual book value applicable to common stock	1,330,000
Current ownership by Big	60%
Book value equivalency of Big's common stock ownership	798,000
Unadjusted book value of Big's common stock investment [($1,040,000 previous book value − $70,000) × 80%]	776,000
Required increase in investment account created by subsidiary stock issuance	$ 22,000

The issuance of these new shares has created a $22,000 increase in the underlying equity of Little Corporation that is held by the parent. This transaction creates a change in the additional paid-in capital reported by the business combination. Although the increase could have been recorded by the parent at the time of sale, no entry was made. Consequently, an adjustment of $22,000 must be made to Big's additional paid-in capital.

After accounting for the previous computations, an analysis should be made of the intercompany bond transaction. Little's payment of $110,670 to retire a liability with a book value on Big's records of only $86,550 (half of the $173,100 total) produced an immediate loss of $24,120 on January 1, 1997. However, since the companies are being accounted for as two separate entities, neither the retirement nor the loss were recognized by either party. Both the debtor and creditor continue to account for these bonds as if they were still outstanding. Interest payments are made periodically as required while each company amortizes the difference between the book value of the bonds and their face value.

The bond and interest accounts found in Big's December 31, 1998, accounting records have been calculated in the following schedule. This presentation determines these balances for only one-half of the bonds payable because only that amount currently is held within the business combination.

Big Company's Financial Records—Bonds Payable

Year	Beginning Book Value	Effective Interest (15 percent rate)	Cash Interest (12 percent rate)	Amortization	Year-End Book Value
1997	$86,550	$12,983	$12,000	$ 983	$87,533
1998	87,533	13,130	12,000	1,130	88,663

During this time, Little would have accounted for the investment in these same bonds as follows:

Little Corporation's Financial Records—Investment in Bonds

Year	Beginning Book Value	Effective Interest (10 percent rate)	Cash Interest (12 percent rate)	Amortization	Year-End Book Value
1997	$110,670	$11,067	$12,000	$ 933	$109,737
1998	109,737	10,974	12,000	1,026	108,711

After the financial figures relative to the intercompany bonds have been isolated, an appropriate elimination can be produced. Consolidated balances must report these bonds as having been retired on the date they were acquired by the subsidiary. Thus, the current $88,663 book value of the liability is removed as well as the $108,711 investment balance. At the same time, both the $13,130 interest expense reported by Big for the current period and the $10,974 interest income recognized by Little are eliminated.

To complete the handling of this bond, a $22,204 reduction is made to the parent's beginning retained earnings. Although the loss was actually $24,120, the previous $983 amortization of the bond payable discount in 1997 and the $933 amortization of the investment premium have already reduced the 1998 beginning retained earnings by a total of $1,916. A decrease of only $22,204 is needed to reflect the loss on retirement.

As the final step in establishing appropriate 1998 balances, Big's beginning retained earnings must be restated to be in conformity with application of the equity method for this investment. The $22,204 adjustment necessitated by the bond retirement was just explained. In addition, a $10,000 reduction is needed to recognize $2,000 of goodwill amortization (as computed in Exhibit 6–7) for each of the five years from 1993 through 1997.

Having analyzed this information, consolidated balances for the business combination of Big and Little for December 31, 1998, and the year then ended can be developed:

Revenues = $1,289,026. Since no intercompany inventory transfers took place between Big and Little, the two account balances are simply added together.

Expenses = $890,870. Amortization expense of $2,000 must be added to the book values while $13,130 in interest expense on the intercompany bond is removed.

Interest income = –0–. The amount reported by Little is an intercompany figure produced by the investment in Big's bonds. For consolidation purposes, this figure is removed entirely.

Dividend income—Little preferred stock = –0–. This intercompany cash transfer is eliminated.

Equity income—Little common stock = –0–. The accrual recorded by the parent is eliminated so that the specific revenues and expenses of the subsidiary can be included in the consolidated figures.

Noncontrolling interest in income attributed to Little's preferred stock = $3,600. This figure is 60 percent of the amount of dividends paid since the parent owns only 40 percent.

Noncontrolling interest in income attributed to Little's common stock = $77,600. This figure is 40 percent of the income earned by the subsidiary after payment of the preferred stock dividend ($200,000 − $6,000 or $194,000). Although Big originally purchased 80 percent of Little, the subsequent issuance of additional shares has reduced the parent's ownership to 60 percent.

Net income = $316,956. Consolidated expenses and the amounts attributed to the outside owners are subtracted from consolidated revenues.

Retained earnings, 1/1/98 = $1,267,796. Because the parent is applying the partial equity method, the amortization expense for the five previous years must be recognized ($2,000 for five years or $10,000) as well as the $22,204 reduction in connection with the loss on bond retirement (computation made above).

Dividends paid on preferred stock = –0–. The dividends paid by the subsidiary are eliminated as intercompany (40 percent) or attributed to the noncontrolling interest (60 percent).

Dividends paid on common stock = $136,800. This balance represents the amount distributed by the parent. The subsidiary's dividends are eliminated as intercompany or are attributed to the noncontrolling interest.

Retained earnings, 12/31/98 = $1,447,952. The consolidated beginning retained earnings balance plus net income for the year less the dividends paid.

Current assets = $1,334,525. The book values are added together.

Investment in Big Company bonds = –0–. The balance is eliminated as an intercompany account.

Investment in Little Corporation preferred stock = –0–. The balance is eliminated as an intercompany account.

Investment in Little Corporation common stock = –0–. The balance is eliminated so that the individual assets and liabilities of the subsidiary can be included in the consolidated figures.

Land, buildings, and equipment = $1,350,000. The two book values are added.

Goodwill = $68,000. The original allocation to goodwill was $80,000, an amount which has now been reduced by six years of amortization at $2,000 per year.

Total assets = $2,752,525. This figure is a summation of the consolidated asset balances.

Current liabilities = $340,711. The book values are added.

Bonds payable = $88,662. Half of the reported bonds are eliminated as an intercompany investment.

Noncontrolling interest in Little's preferred stock = $43,200. This figure is the call value of the shares held by outsiders (600 shares at $72 per share).

Noncontrolling interest in Little's common stock = $600,000. This balance is computed as follows:

40% of subsidiary's common stock book value at 1/1/98 ($1,330,000—based on stockholders' equity accounts at beginning of year after subtracting $70,000 applicable to preferred shares)	$532,000
Noncontrolling interest in Little's net income— common stock (computed above)	77,600
Noncontrolling interest in Little's dividends— common stock ($24,000 × 40%)	(9,600)
Year-end balance	$600,000

Preferred stock = –0–. Only parent figure is reported for contributed capital and Big has no preferred stock.

Common stock = $200,000. Parent company balance only is presented.

Additional paid-in capital = $32,000. Parent company balance is reported after the $22,000 adjustment is made because of the subsidiary's sale of additional shares of stock.

Retained earnings, 12/31/98 = $1,447,952. Amount is computed above.

Total liabilities and stockholders' equity = $2,752,525. Summation of the consolidated liabilities and equity accounts.

COMPREHENSIVE ILLUSTRATION

Problem Two: Consolidated Statement of Cash Flows and Earnings per Share

(Estimated Time: 35 to 45 Minutes) Pop, Inc., acquires 90 percent of the 20,000 shares of Son Company's outstanding common stock on December 31, 1997. Of the purchase price, $80,000 was allocated to goodwill, a figure amortized at the rate of $2,000 per year. Immediately following the purchase, a consolidated balance sheet was constructed:

Cash	$ 130,000
Accounts receivable	220,000
Inventory	278,000
Land, buildings, and equipment (net)	1,120,000
Goodwill	80,000
Total assets	$1,828,000
Accounts payable	$ 296,000
Long-term liabilities	550,000
Noncontrolling interest	34,000
Preferred stock (2,000 shares outstanding)	100,000
Common stock (26,000 shares outstanding)	520,000
Retained earnings, 12/31/97	328,000
Total liabilities and stockholders' equity	$1,828,000

During 1998, Pop transferred inventory costing $60,000 to Son for $100,000. By year's end, all but 10 percent of this merchandise had been sold to outside parties.

On January 17, 1998, Pop borrowed $100,000 from a local bank. Several months later, the parent acquired equipment for $60,000 cash. On November 10, 1998, Son sold a building with a $40,000 book value, receiving cash of $50,000. These transactions were all with outside parties.

Pop pays a $10,000 dividend each year to the holders of the company's preferred stock. Each share of this stock can be converted into three shares of common. Son's long-term debt also is convertible. Interest expense in 1998 (net of taxes) was $16,000. The debt can be exchanged for 10,000 shares of the subsidiary's common stock. Pop owns none of this debt.

Presented in Exhibit 6–8 is the 1998 consolidation worksheet for Pop and Son. Pop applies the equity method to account for the investment in Son. The $48,000 equity income figure

Exhibit 6–8

Consolidation: Purchase Method
Investment: Equity Method

POP, INC., AND SON COMPANY
Consolidation Worksheet
Year Ending December 31, 1998

	Pop, Inc.	Son Company	Consolidation Entries Debit	Consolidation Entries Credit	Noncontrolling Interest	Consolidated Totals
Revenues	600,000	300,000	(TI) 100,000	(TI) 100,000		800,000
Cost of goods sold	(400,000)	(180,000)	(G) 4,000			(484,000)
Depreciation and amortization	(20,000)	(30,000)	(E) 2,000			(52,000)
Other expenses	(56,000)	(40,000)				(96,000)
Gain on sale of building	-0-	10,000				10,000
Equity in Son's income	48,000	-0-	(I) 48,000			-0-
Noncontrolling interest in Son's income	-0-	-0-			6,000	(6,000)
Net income	172,000	60,000				172,000
Retained earnings, 1/1/98	328,000	140,000	(S) 140,000			328,000
Net income	172,000	60,000				172,000
Dividends paid	(50,000)	(20,000)		(D) 18,000	(2,000)	(50,000)
Retained earnings, 12/31/98	450,000	180,000				450,000
Cash	180,000	30,000				210,000
Accounts receivable	260,000	90,000				350,000
Inventory	254,000	70,000		(G) 4,000		320,000
Investment in Son	416,000	-0-	(D) 18,000	(S) 306,000		-0-
				(A) 80,000		
				(I) 48,000		

	Parent	Son	Debits	Credits	NCI	Consolidated
Land, buildings, and equipment (net)	640,000	450,000				1,090,000
Goodwill	-0-	-0-	(A) 80,000	(E) 2,000		78,000
Total assets	1,750,000	640,000				2,048,000
Accounts payable	210,000	80,000				290,000
Long-term liabilities	470,000	180,000				650,000
Noncontrolling interest in Son, 1/1/98	-0-	-0-		(S) 34,000	34,000	
Noncontrolling interest in Son, 12/31/98	-0-	-0-			38,000	38,000
Preferred stock	100,000	-0-				100,000
Common stock	520,000	200,000	(S) 200,000			520,000
Retained earnings (above)	450,000	180,000				450,000
Total liabilities and stockholders' equity	1,750,000	640,000				2,048,000

Note: Parentheses indicate a reduction.

Consolidation entries:
(S) Elimination of subsidiary's stockholders' equity accounts along with recognition of January 1, 1998, noncontrolling interest.
(A) Allocation of parent's cost in excess of subsidiary's book value.
(I) Elimination of intercompany income.
(D) Elimination of intercompany dividends.
(E) Recognition of amortization expense for 1998.
(TI) Elimination of intercompany sales/purchases balances.
(G) Deferral of unrealized gain so that it can be recognized in 1999.

reported by the parent is derived from the $54,000 annual accrual (90 percent of the $60,000 reported income of the subsidiary) less the $2,000 amortization and the $4,000 unrealized gain (10 percent of the original intercompany gross profit). The noncontrolling interest in Son's income is 10 percent of the subsidiary's reported income for 1998.

Required:

a. Prepare a consolidated statement of cash flows for Pop, Inc., and Son Company for the year ending December 31, 1998. Use the indirect approach for determining the amount of cash generated by normal operations.[5]

b. Compute basic earnings per share and diluted earnings per share for this business combination.

Solution (Two)

a. *Consolidated Statement of Cash Flows*

The problem specifies that the indirect approach should be used in preparing the consolidated statement of cash flows. Therefore, all items that do not represent cash flows from operations must be removed from the $172,000 consolidated net income. For example, the depreciation and amortization both are eliminated (noncash items) as well as the gain on the sale of the building (a nonoperational item). As discussed in the chapter, the noncontrolling interest's share of Son's net income is another noncash reduction that also is removed. In addition, the changes in consolidated accounts receivable, inventory, and accounts payable each produce a noncash impact on net income. The increase in accounts receivable, for example, indicates that the sales figure for the period was larger than the amount of cash collected so that adjustment is required in producing this statement.

From the information given, only five nonoperational changes in cash can be determined: the bank loan, the acquisition of equipment, the sale of a building, the dividend paid by Son to the minority interest, and the dividend paid by the parent. These transactions are each included in the consolidated statement of cash flows shown in Exhibit 6–9 that explains the $80,000 increase in cash experienced by the entity during 1998.

b. *Consolidated Earnings per Share*

The subsidiary's convertible debt has a potentially dilutive effect on earnings per share. Therefore, diluted EPS cannot be determined for the business combination directly from consolidated net income. First, the diluted EPS figure must be calculated for the subsidiary. This information then is used in the computations made by the consolidated entity.

Diluted earnings per share of $2.53 for the subsidiary is determined as follows:

Son Company—Diluted Earnings per Share

	Earnings		Shares	
As reported.	$60,000		20,000	$3.00
Effect of possible debt conversion:				
Interest saved (net of taxes)	16,000	New shares	10,000	$1.60 impact
				(16,000/10,000)
Diluted EPS	$76,000		30,000	$2.53 (rounded)

The parent owns none of the convertible debt included in computing diluted earnings per share. Pop holds only 18,000 (90 percent of the outstanding common stock) of the 30,000 shares used in this EPS calculation. Consequently, in determining diluted EPS for the entire business combination, just $45,600 of the subsidiary's income is applicable:

$$\$76,000 \times 18,000/30,000 = \$45,600$$

Exhibit 6–10 reveals consolidated basic earnings per share of $6.62 and diluted EPS of $5.11. Because the subsidiary's earnings figure is included separately in the computation of diluted EPS, the individual income of the parent must be identified in the same manner. Thus, the effect of the equity income, intercompany (downstream) transactions, and amortization are taken into account in arriving at the parent's earnings alone.

---

[5]Prior to attempting this problem, a review of an intermediate accounting textbook might be useful to obtain a complete overview of the production of a statement of cash flows.

Exhibit 6–9

POP, INC., AND SON COMPANY
Consolidated Statement of Cash Flows
Year Ending December 31, 1998

Cash flows from operating activities		
Net income		$ 172,000
Adjustments to reconcile net income to net cash provided by operating activities:		
Depreciation and amortization	$ 52,000	
Gain on sale of building	(10,000)	
Noncontrolling interest in Son's income	6,000	
Increase in accounts receivable	(130,000)	
Increase in inventory	(42,000)	
Decrease in accounts payable	(6,000)	(130,000)
Net cash provided by operations		$ 42,000
Cash flows from investing activities		
Purchase of equipment	$ (60,000)	
Sale of building	50,000	
Net cash used in investing activities		(10,000)
Cash flows from financing activities		
Payment of cash dividend—Pop	$ (50,000)	
Payment of cash dividend to noncontrolling owners of Son . .	(2,000)	
Borrowed from bank	100,000	
Net cash provided by financing activities		48,000
Net increase in cash		$ 80,000
Cash, January 1, 1998		130,000
Cash, December 31, 1998		$ 210,000

Exhibit 6–10

POP, INC., AND SON COMPANY
Consolidated Earnings per Share
Year Ending December 31, 1998

	Earnings		Shares	
	Basic Earnings per Share			
Basic EPS	$172,000		26,000	$6.62 (rounded)
	Diluted Earnings per Share			
Pop's reported income	$172,000			
Remove equity income	(48,000)			
Remove unrealized gain	(4,000)			
Recognize amortization expense	(2,000)			
Preferred stock dividend	(10,000)			
Common shares outstanding (Pop, Inc.)				
Common stock income—Pop (for EPS computations)	$108,000		26,000	
Income of Son (above—for diluted EPS)	45,600			
	$153,600		26,000	$5.91 (rounded)
Effect of possible preferred stock conversion:				
Dividends saved	10,000	New shares	6,000	$1.67 impact (10,000/6,000)
Diluted EPS	$163,600		32,000	$5.11

QUESTIONS

1. A parent company acquires from a third party bonds that had been issued originally by one of its subsidiaries. What accounting problems are created by this purchase?

2. In question 1, why is the consolidation process simpler if the bonds had been acquired directly from the subsidiary rather than from a third party?

3. When one company's debt instruments are acquired by an affiliated company from a third party, how is the gain or loss on extinguishment of the debt calculated? When should this balance be recognized?

4. Several years ago, Bennett, Inc., bought a portion of the outstanding bonds of Smith Corporation, a subsidiary organization. The acquisition was made from an outside party. In the current year, how should these intercompany bonds be accounted for within the consolidation process?

5. One company purchases the outstanding debt instruments of an affiliated company on the open market. This transaction creates a gain that is appropriately recognized in the consolidated financial statements of that year. Thereafter, a worksheet adjustment is required to correct the beginning balance of the consolidated retained earnings. Why is the amount of this adjustment reduced from year to year?

6. A parent acquires the outstanding bonds of a subsidiary company directly from an outside third party. For consolidation purposes, this transaction creates a gain of $45,000. Should this gain be allocated to the parent or the subsidiary? Why?

7. Some preferred stocks possess characteristics that resemble an equity or ownership interest. Others, however, demonstrate traits similar to a debt instrument. How is the distinction drawn as to whether the preferred stock is actually an equity or a debt?

8. Perkins Company acquires 90 percent of the outstanding common stock of the Butterfly Corporation as well as 55 percent of its preferred stock. Because of the rights being conveyed, the preferred stock is considered to be a debt-type instrument. How should these preferred shares be accounted for within the consolidation process? How should the book value of Butterfly be allocated between the common and the preferred stock?

9. Assume the same information as in question 8 except that the preferred stock is viewed as an equity interest. How is the preferred stock now accounted for within the consolidation process? How should the book value of Butterfly be allocated between the common and the preferred stock?

10. A consolidated statement of cash flows is not produced using a worksheet as are the income statement and the balance sheet. What process is followed in preparing a consolidated statement of cash flows?

11. How do noncontrolling interest balances affect the consolidated statement of cash flows?

12. In many cases, consolidated earnings per share is computed based on consolidated net income and parent company shares and convertibles. However, a different process must be used for some business combinations. When is this alternative approach required?

13. A subsidiary has (1) a convertible preferred stock and (2) a convertible bond. How are these items factored into the computation of earnings per share for the business combination?

14. Why might a subsidiary decide to issue new shares of common stock to parties outside of the business combination?

15. Washburn Company owns 75 percent of the outstanding common stock of Metcalf Company. During the current year, Metcalf issues additional shares to outside parties at a price more than book value. How does this transaction affect the business combination? How is this impact recorded within the consolidated statements?

16. Assume the same information as in question 15 except that the new shares are issued primarily to Washburn. How does this transaction affect the business combination?

17. Assume the same information as in question 15 except that Metcalf issues a 10 percent stock dividend instead of selling new shares of stock. How does this transaction affect the business combination?

18. If a parent must increase its investment because a subsidiary issues additional shares of stock, in what two ways can the adjustment be recorded?

LIBRARY ASSIGNMENTS

1. Read the following as well as any other published materials that might be available concerning the characteristics of preferred stocks:

    "Innovative Forms of Preferred Stock: Debt or Equity?" *Commercial Lending Review*, Fall 1995.

    "New Instruments Create New Questions in Preferred Stock Investments," *Journal of Taxation Investments*, Autumn 1994.

    "Usefulness of Hybrid Security Classifications: Evidence from Redeemable Preferred Stock," *The Accounting Review*, January 1995.

    "Financial Instruments: A Report on the Liability-Equity Comment Letters and Public Hearings," (Status Report published by FASB), *Financial Accounting Series No. 103*, May 31, 1991.

    Write a report outlining an approach that can be taken to determine whether a preferred stock issue should be considered a debt instrument or an equity interest.

2. Read paragraphs 380–84 of the FASB's discussion memorandum, *An Analysis of Issues Related to Consolidation Policy and Procedures*. Write a short report justifying one method of allocating any gains and losses that result from an intercompany bond transaction.

PROBLEMS

1. A subsidiary has a debt outstanding that was originally issued at a discount. At the beginning of the current year, the debt was acquired at a slight premium from outside parties by the parent company. Which of the following statements are true?
    a. Whether the balances agree or not, both the subsequent interest income and interest expense should be reported in a consolidated income statement.
    b. The interest income and interest expense will agree in amount and should be offset for consolidation purposes.
    c. In computing any noncontrolling interest allocation, the interest income should be included but not the interest expense.
    d. Although subsequent interest income and interest expense will not agree in amount, both balances should be eliminated for consolidation purposes.

2. A subsidiary issues a bond directly to its parent at a discount. Which of the following statements is true?
    a. Elimination is not necessary for consolidation purposes since the bond was acquired directly from the subsidiary.
    b. Because of the discount, the various interest accounts on the two sets of financial records will not agree.
    c. Since the bond was issued by the subsidiary, the amount attributed to a noncontrolling interest is always affected.
    d. All interest balances exactly offset for consolidation purposes.

3. A bond that had been issued by a parent company at a discount was acquired several years ago by its subsidiary from an outside party at a premium. Which of the following statements is true?
    a. The bond has no impact on a current consolidation because the acquisition was made in the past.
    b. The original loss would be reported in the current year's consolidated income statement.
    c. For consolidation purposes, retained earnings must be reduced at the beginning of the current year but by an amount smaller than the original loss.
    d. The various interest balances exactly offset so that no adjustment to retained earnings or to income is necessary.

4. A parent company acquires all of a subsidiary's common stock but only 70 percent of its preferred shares. This preferred stock is callable and pays a 7 percent annual cumulative dividend. No dividends are in arrears at the current time. How is the noncontrolling interest's share of the subsidiary's income computed?

a. As 30 percent of the subsidiary's preferred dividend.
b. No allocation is made since the dividends have been paid.
c. As 30 percent of the subsidiary's income after all dividends have been subtracted.
d. Income is assigned to the preferred stock based on total par value and 30 percent of that amount is allocated to the noncontrolling interest.

5. Aceton Corporation owns 80 percent of the outstanding stock of Voctax, Inc. During the current year, Voctax made $140,000 in sales to Aceton. How does this transfer affect the consolidated statement of cash flows?
a. The transaction should be included if payment has been made.
b. Only 80 percent of the transfers should be included because the sales were made by the subsidiary.
c. Because the transfers were from a subsidiary organization, the cash flows are reported as investing activities.
d. Because of the intercompany nature of the transfers, the amount is not reported in the consolidated cash flow statement.

6. Warrenton, Inc., owns 80 percent of Aminable Corporation. On a consolidated income statement, the Noncontrolling Interest in the Subsidiary's Income is reported as $37,000. Aminable paid a total cash dividend of $100,000 for the year. How is the consolidated statement of cash flows impacted?
a. The dividends paid to the outside owners is reported as a financing activity but the noncontrolling interest figure is not viewed as a cash flow.
b. The noncontrolling interest figure is reported as an investing activity but the dividends paid to the outside owners is omitted entirely.
c. Neither figure is reported on the statement of cash flow.
d. Both dividends paid and the noncontrolling interest are viewed as financing activities.

7. Thuoy Corporation is computing consolidated earnings per share. One of its subsidiaries has stock warrants outstanding. How do these convertible items affect the consolidated earnings per share computation?
a. No effect is created since the stock warrants were for the shares of the subsidiary company.
b. The stock warrants are not included in the computation unless they are antidilutive.
c. The effect of the stock warrants must be computed in deriving the amount of subsidiary income that is to be included in making the consolidated diluted earnings per share calculation.
d. The stock warrants are only included in basic earnings per share but never in diluted earnings per share.

8. A parent company owns a controlling interest in a subsidiary whose stock has a book value of $31 per share. At the end of the current year, the subsidiary issues new shares entirely to outside parties at $45 per share. The parent still holds control over this subsidiary. Which of the following statements is true?
a. Since the shares were all sold to outside parties, the parent's Investment account is not affected.
b. Since the parent now owns a smaller percentage of the subsidiary, the parent's Investment account must be reduced.
c. Since the shares were sold for more than book value, the parent's Investment account must be increased.
d. Since the sale was made at the end of the year, the parent's Investment account is not affected.

9. Rodgers, Inc., owns Ferdinal Corporation. For 1998, Rodgers reports net income (without consideration of its investment in Ferdinal) of $200,000 while the subsidiary reports $80,000. The parent had a bond payable outstanding on January 1, 1998, with a book value of $212,000. The subsidiary acquired the bond on that date for $199,000. During 1998, Rodgers reported interest income of $22,000 while Ferdinal reported interest expense of $21,000. What is consolidated net income?
a. $266,000.
b. $268,000.
c. $292,000.
d. $294,000.

10. Thompkins, Inc., owns Pastimer Company. The subsidiary had a bond payable outstanding on January 1, 1997, with a book value of $189,000. The parent acquired the bond on that date for $206,000. Subsequently, Pastimer reported interest income of $18,000 in 1997 while Thompkins reported interest expense of $21,000. Consolidated financial statements are being prepared for 1998. What adjustment is needed for the retained earnings balance as of January 1, 1998?
   a. Reduction of $20,000.
   b. Reduction of $14,000.
   c. Reduction of $3,000.
   d. Reduction of $22,000.

11. Ace Company reports current earnings of $400,000 while paying $40,000 in cash dividends. Byrd Company earns $100,000 in net income and distributes $10,000 in dividends. Ace has held a 70 percent interest in Byrd for several years, an investment that it originally purchased at a price equal to the book value of the underlying net assets. Ace uses the cost method to account for these shares.

   On January 1, of the current year, Byrd acquired in the open market $50,000 of Ace's 8 percent bonds. The bonds had originally been issued several years ago for 92, reflecting a 10 percent effective interest rate. On the date of purchase, the book value of the bonds payable was $48,300. Byrd paid $46,600 based on a 12 percent effective interest rate over the remaining life of the bonds.

   What is consolidated net income for this year prior to reduction for the noncontrolling interest's share of the subsidiary's net income?
   a. $492,160.
   b. $493,938.
   c. $499,160.
   d. $500,258.

12. Using the same information presented in problem 11, what is the noncontrolling interest's share of the subsidiary's net income?
   a. $27,000.
   b. $28,290.
   c. $28,620.
   d. $30,000.

13. Able Company possesses 80 percent of the outstanding voting stock of Baker Company. Able uses the partial equity method to account for this investment. On January 1, 1995, Able sold 9 percent bonds payable with a $10 million face value (maturing in 20 years) on the open market at a premium of $600,000. On January 1, 1998, Baker acquired 40 percent of these same bonds from an outside party at 96.6 of face value. Both companies use the straight-line method of amortization. For a 1999 consolidation, what adjustment should be made to Able's beginning retained earnings as a result of this bond acquisition?
   a. $320,000 increase.
   b. $326,000 increase.
   c. $331,000 increase.
   d. $340,000 increase.

14. A company has common stock with a total par value of $400,000 and preferred stock with a total par value of $100,000. The book value of the company is $890,000. The preferred stock pays an 8 percent annual dividend whereas the common stock normally distributes a dividend each year that is equal to 10 percent of its par value. If this company is acquired by another, what portion of the book value should be assigned to the preferred stock? The preferred stock is considered an equity. (Round to the nearest dollar.)
   a. $100,000.
   b. $395,555.
   c. $148,333.
   d. $178,000.

15. Top Company spent a total of $4,384,000 to acquire control over Bottom Company. This price was based on paying $424,000 for 20 percent of Bottom's preferred stock and $3,960,000 for 90 percent of its outstanding common stock. As of the date of purchase, Bottom's stockholders' equity accounts were as follows:

Preferred stock—9%, $100 par value, cumulative and participating;
  10,000 shares outstanding $1,000,000
Common stock—$50 par value; 40,000 shares outstanding 2,000,000
Retained earnings 3,000,000
    Total stockholders' equity $6,000,000

The owners of the preferred stock vote on any issues considered by the owners of the common stock.

Top believes that all of Bottom's accounts are correctly valued within the company's financial statements. What amount of consolidated goodwill should be recognized?
a. $300,000.
b. $316,000.
c. $364,000.
d. $384,000.

16. On January 1, 1998, Mitchell Company has a net book value of $1,500,000 as follows:

1,000 shares of preferred stock; par value $100 per share; cumulative,
  nonparticipating, nonvoting; call value $108 per share .... $ 100,000
20,000 shares of common stock; par value $40 per share 800,000
Retained earnings 600,000
    Total $1,500,000

Andrews Company acquires all of the outstanding preferred shares for $106,000 and 60 percent of the common stock for $916,400. Andrews believed that one of Mitchell's buildings, with a 12-year life, was undervalued on the company's financial records by $50,000.

What amount of consolidated goodwill would be recognized from this purchase?
a. $50,000.
b. $51,200.
c. $52,400.
d. $56,000.

17. Aedion Company owns control over Breedlove, Inc. Aedion reports sales of $300,000 during 1998 while Breedlove reports $200,000. Inventory costing $20,000 was transferred from Breedlove to Aedion (upstream) during the year for $40,000. Of this amount, 25 percent is still in ending inventory at year's end. Total receivables on the consolidated balance sheet were $80,000 at the first of the year and $110,000 at year-end. No intercompany debt existed at the beginning or ending of the year. Using the direct approach, what is the consolidated amount of cash collected by the business combination from its customers?
a. $430,000.
b. $460,000.
c. $490,000.
d. $510,000.

18. Ames owns 100 percent of Nestlum, Inc. Although the Investment in Nestlum account has a balance of $596,000, the subsidiary's 12,000 shares have an underlying book value of only $40 per share. On January 1, 1998, Nestlum issues 3,000 new shares to the public for $50 per share. How does this transaction affect the Investment in Nestlum account?
a. It is not affected since the shares were sold to outside parties.
b. It should be increased by $24,000.
c. It should be decreased by $119,200.
d. It should be increased by $30,000.

Problems 19 through 21 are based on the following information:

Chapman Company purchases 80 percent of the common stock of Russell Company on January 1, 1992, when Russell has the following stockholders' equity accounts:

Common stock—40,000 shares outstanding $100,000
Additional paid-in capital 75,000
Retained earnings 340,000
    Total stockholders' equity $515,000

To acquire this interest in Russell, Chapman pays a total of $487,000 with any excess cost being allocated to goodwill.

On January 1, 1998, Russell reports a net book value of $795,000. Chapman has accrued the increase in Russell's book value through application of the equity method.

The following problems should be viewed as independent situations.

19. On January 1, 1998, Russell issues 10,000 additional shares of common stock for $25 per share. Chapman acquires 8,000 of these shares. How will this transaction affect the additional paid-in capital of the parent company?

    a. –0–.
    b. Increase it by $20,500.
    c. Increase it by $36,400.
    d. Increase it by $82,300.

20. On January 1, 1998, Russell issues 10,000 additional shares of common stock for $15 per share. Chapman does not acquire any of this newly issued stock. How would this transaction affect the additional paid-in capital of the parent company?

    a. –0–.
    b. Increase it by $16,600.
    c. Decrease it by $31,200.
    d. Decrease it by $48,750.

21. On January 1, 1994, Russell reacquires 8,000 of the outstanding shares of its own common stock for $24 per share. None of these shares belonged to Chapman. How would this transaction affect the additional paid-in capital of the parent company?

    a. –0–.
    b. Decrease it by $22,000.
    c. Decrease it by $30,500.
    d. Decrease it by $33,000.

22. Darges owns 51 percent of the voting stock of Walrus, Inc. The parent's interest was acquired several years ago on the date that the subsidiary was formed. Consequently, no goodwill or other allocation was recorded in connection with the purchase price.

    On January 1, 1996, Walrus sold $1,000,000 in 10-year bonds to the public for 105. The bonds had a cash interest rate of 9 percent payable every December 31. Darges acquired 40 percent of these bonds on January 1, 1998, for 96 percent of face value. Both companies utilize the straight-line method of amortization.

Required

    a. What consolidation entry would be recorded in connection with these intercompany bonds on December 31, 1998?
    b. What consolidation entry would be recorded in connection with these intercompany bonds on December 31, 1999?
    c. What consolidation entry would be recorded in connection with these intercompany bonds on December 31, 2000?

23. Highlight, Inc., owns all of the outstanding stock of Kiort Corporation. The two companies report the following balances for the year ending December 31, 1998:

	Highlight	Kiort
Revenues and interest income	$670,000	$390,000
Operating and interest expense	(540,000)	(221,000)
Other gains and losses	120,000	32,000
Net income	$250,000	$201,000

On January 1, 1998, Highlight acquired bonds on the open market for $108,000 originally issued by Kiort. This investment had an effective rate of 8 percent. The bonds had a face value of $100,000 and a cash interest rate of 9 percent. At the date of acquisition, these bonds were shown as liabilities by Kiort with a book value of $84,000 (based on an effective rate of 11 percent). Determine the balances that should appear on a consolidated income statement for 1998.

24. Several years ago Absalom, Inc., sold $800,000 in bonds to the public. Annual cash interest of 8 percent ($64,000) was to be paid on this debt. The bonds were issued at a

discount to yield 10 percent. At the beginning of 1998, McDowell Corporation (a wholly owned subsidiary of Absalom) purchased $100,000 of these bonds on the open market for $121,655, a price that was based on an effective interest rate of 6 percent. The bond liability had a book value on that date of $668,778.

Required

a. What consolidation entry would be required for these bonds on December 31, 1998?

b. What consolidation entry would be required for these bonds on December 31, 2000?

 25. Opus, Incorporated, owns 90 percent of Bloom Company. On December 31, 1998, Opus acquires half of Bloom's $500,000 in outstanding bonds. These bonds had been sold on the open market on January 1, 1996, at a 12 percent effective rate. The bonds pay a cash interest rate of 10 percent every December 31 and are scheduled to come due on December 31, 2006. Bloom issued this debt originally for $435,763. Opus paid $283,550 for this investment indicating an 8 percent effective yield.

Required

a. Assuming that both parties use the effective rate method, what gain or loss should be reported on the consolidated income statement for 1998 from the retirement of this debt?

b. Assuming that both parties use the effective rate method, what balances should appear in the Investment in Bloom Bonds account on Opus's records and the Bonds Payable account of Bloom as of December 31, 1999?

c. Assuming that both parties use the straight-line method, what consolidation entry would be required on December 31, 1999, because of these bonds? Assume that the parent is not applying the equity method.

26. Hapinst Corporation has the following stockholders' equity accounts:

Preferred stock (6% cumulative dividend)	$500,000
Common stock	750,000
Additional paid-in capital	300,000
Retained earnings	950,000

The preferred stock is participating and, therefore, is considered an equity instrument. Westyln Corporation buys 90 percent of this common stock for $1,600,000 and 70 percent of the preferred stock for $800,000. All of the subsidiary's assets and liabilities are viewed as having market values equal to their book values. What amount is attributed to goodwill on the date of acquisition?

27. Mace, Inc., acquires 90 percent of the outstanding common stock of Blade Company from the company's president for $2,520,000 and 40 percent of the preferred stock for $250,000. On the date of purchase, Blade had the following stockholders' equity accounts:

Common stock	$ 800,000
Preferred stock	200,000
Retained earnings	2,000,000
Total	$3,000,000

Required

a. Assume that the preferred stock is both cumulative and fully participating and is, therefore, considered an equity interest. What is the total amount of goodwill to be recognized within consolidated financial statements?

b. Assume that the preferred stock is callable at 120 percent of par value and is, therefore, considered a debt instrument. What is the total amount of goodwill to be recognized within consolidated financial statements?

c. Assume that the preferred stock is callable at 120 percent of par value and is, therefore, considered a debt instrument. What is the total value assigned to the noncontrolling interests on the date of acquisition?

28. Smith, Inc., has the following stockholders' equity accounts as of January 1, 1998:

Preferred stock—$100 par, nonvoting and nonparticipating, 8 percent cumulative dividend	$ 2,000,000
Common stock—$20 par value	4,000,000
Retained earnings	10,000,000

Haried Company purchases all of the common stock of Smith on January 1, 1998, for $14,040,000. The preferred stock (which is callable at 108) remains in the hands of outside parties. Any goodwill indicated by this acquisition is to be amortized over the maximum possible period of time.

During 1998, Smith reports earning $450,000 in net income and pays $360,000 in cash dividends. Haried applies the equity method to this investment.

Required

    a. What is the noncontrolling interest's share of consolidated net income for this period?

    b. What is the balance in the Investment in Smith account as of December 31, 1998?

    c. What consolidation entries would be needed for 1998?

29. Through the payment of $10,468,000 in cash, Drexel Company acquires voting control over Young Company. This price was paid for 60 percent of the subsidiary's 100,000 outstanding common shares ($40 par value) as well as all 10,000 shares of 8 percent, cumulative, $100 par value preferred stock. Of the total payment, $3.1 million was attributed to the fully participating and fully voting preferred stock with the remainder paid for the common. This purchase is carried out on January 1, 1998, when Young reports retained earnings of $10 million and a total book value of $15 million. On this same date, a building owned by Young (with a 5-year remaining life) is undervalued in the financial records by $200,000, while equipment with a 10-year life is overvalued by $100,000. Goodwill is assumed to have a 20-year life.

During 1998, Young reports net income of $900,000 while paying $400,000 in cash dividends. Drexel has used the cost method to account for both of these investments.

Required

Prepare consolidation entries that would be appropriate for the year of 1998.

30. The following information has been taken from the consolidation worksheet of Peak and its 90-percent-owned subsidiary, Valley:

- Peak reports a $12,000 gain on the sale of a building. The building had a book value of $32,000 but was sold for $44,000 cash.
- The noncontrolling interest in Valley's Income is reported as $23,000.
- Intercompany inventory transfers of $129,000 occurred during the current period.
- A $30,000 dividend was paid by Valley during the year with $27,000 of this amount going to Peak.
- Amortization of the goodwill created by Peak's purchase was $16,000 for the current period.
- Consolidated accounts payable decreased by $11,000 during the year.

Required

Indicate how each of these events is reflected on a consolidated statement of cash flows.

31. Ames Company and its 80 percent owned subsidiary, Wallace, have the following income statements for 1998:

	Ames	Wallace
Revenues	$ 500,000	$ 230,000
Cost of goods sold	(300,000)	(140,000)
Depreciation and amortization	(40,000)	(10,000)
Other expenses	(20,000)	(20,000)
Gain on sale of equipment	30,000	–0–
Equity in earnings of Wallace	48,000	–0–
Net income	$ 218,000	$ 60,000

Additional Information:

- Intercompany transfers during 1998 amounted to $90,000 and were downstream from Ames to Wallace.
- Unrealized inventory gains at January 1, 1998, were $6,000, but at December 31, 1998, unrealized gains are $9,000.
- Annual amortization expense resulting from the purchase price is $11,000.
- Wallace paid dividends totaling $20,000.

■ The noncontrolling interest's share of the subsidiary's income is $12,000.
■ During 1998, consolidated inventory rose by $11,000 while accounts receivable and accounts payable declined by $8,000 and $6,000, respectively.

Required

Using either the direct or the indirect approach, determine the amount of cash generated from operations during the period by this business combination.

32. Parent Corporation owns all 30,000 shares of the common stock of Subsid, Inc. Parent has 60,000 shares of its own common stock outstanding. In 1998, Parent earns income (without any consideration of its investment in Subsid) of $150,000 while Subsid reports $130,000. Annual amortization of $10,000 is recognized each year on the consolidation worksheet based on allocations within the original purchase price. Both companies have convertible bonds outstanding. During 1998, interest expense (net of taxes) is $32,000 for Parent and $24,000 for Subsid. Parent's bonds can be converted into 10,000 shares of common stock; Subsid's bonds can be converted into 12,000 shares. Parent owns 20 percent of Subsid's bonds. For consolidation purposes, what are basic and diluted earnings per share for this business combination?

33. Primus, Inc., owns all of the outstanding stock of Sonston, Inc. For 1998, Primus reports income (exclusive of any investment income) of $600,000. Primus has 100,000 shares of common stock outstanding. Sonston reports net income of $200,000 for the period with 40,000 shares of common stock outstanding. Sonston also has 10,000 stock warrants outstanding that allow the holder to acquire shares at $10 per share. The value of this stock was $20 per share throughout the year. Primus owns 2,000 of these warrants. What is the consolidated diluted earnings per share?

34. Garfun, Inc., owns all of the stock of Simon, Inc. For 1998, Garfun reports income (exclusive of any investment income) of $480,000. Garfun has 80,000 shares of common stock outstanding. Garfun also has 5,000 shares of preferred stock outstanding that pay a dividend of $15,000 per year. Simon reports net income of $290,000 for the period with 80,000 shares of common stock outstanding. Simon also has a liability for 10,000 $100 bonds that pay annual interest of $8 per bond. Each of these bonds can be converted into three shares of common stock. Garfun owns none of these bonds. Assume a tax rate of 30 percent. What is the consolidated diluted earnings per share?

35. The following separate income statements are for Mason and its 80 percent owned subsidiary, Dixon:

	Mason	Dixon
Revenues	$ 400,000	$ 300,000
Expenses	(290,000)	(225,000)
Gain on sale of equipment	–0–	15,000
Equity earnings of subsidiary	72,000	–0–
Net income	$ 182,000	$ 90,000
Outstanding common shares	50,000	30,000

Additional Information:

■ Amortization expense resulting from the purchase price paid by Mason is $20,000 per year.
■ Mason has convertible preferred stock outstanding. Each of these 5,000 shares is paid a dividend of $4.00 per year. Each share can be converted into four shares of common stock.
■ Stock warrants to buy 10,000 shares of Dixon are also outstanding. For $20, each warrant can be converted into a share of Dixon's common stock. The fair market value of this stock is $25 throughout the year. Mason owns none of these warrants.
■ Dixon has convertible bonds payable that paid interest of $30,000 (after taxes) during the year. These bonds can be exchanged for 20,000 shares of common stock. Mason holds 15 percent of these bonds.

Required

Compute basic and diluted earnings per share for this business combination.

36.   Alice, Inc., owns 100 percent of Rughty, Inc. On Alice's books, the Investment in Rughty account currently is shown as $731,000 although the subsidiary's 40,000 shares have an underlying book value of only $12 per share.

Rughty issues 10,000 new shares to the public for $15.75 per share. How does this transaction affect the Investment in Rughty account that appears on Alice's financial records?

37.   Davis, Incorporated, acquired 16,000 shares of Maxwell Company several years ago. At the present time, Maxwell is reporting $800,000 as total stockholders' equity which is broken down as follows:

Common stock ($10 par value)	$200,000
Additional paid-in capital	230,000
Retained earnings	370,000
Total	$800,000

The following cases should be viewed as independent situations:

a.   Maxwell issues 5,000 shares of previously unissued common stock to the public for $50 per share. None of this stock is purchased by Davis. What journal entry should Davis make to recognize the impact of this stock transaction?

b.   Maxwell issues 4,000 shares of previously unissued common stock to the public for $25 per share. None of this stock is purchased by Davis. What journal entry should Davis make to recognize the impact of this stock transaction?

c.   Maxwell issues 5,000 shares of previously unissued common stock for $42 per share. All of these shares are purchased by Davis. How would this transaction affect a consolidation prepared immediately thereafter?

38.   On January 1, 1996, Abraham Company purchased 90 percent of the outstanding shares of Sparks Company. Sparks had a net book value on that date of $480,000: common stock ($10 par value) of $200,000 and retained earnings of $280,000. Sparks also possessed a tract of land that was undervalued by $80,000 on its financial statements.

Abraham paid $584,000 for this investment. Goodwill created by the acquisition price was to be amortized over a 20-year period. Subsequent to the purchase, Abraham applied the cost method to its investment accounts.

In the 1996–97 period, the subsidiary's book value rose by $100,000. During 1998, Sparks earned income of $80,000 while paying $20,000 in dividends. Also, at the beginning of the year, Sparks issued 4,000 new shares of common stock for $36 per share to finance the expansion of its corporate facilities. None of these additional shares were sold to Abraham and, hence, no entry was recorded by the parent company.

Required

a.   Prepare the consolidation entries that would be appropriate for these two companies for the year of 1998.

b.   Assume that Sparks actually issued 5,000 new shares of stock (rather than 4,000 shares) at the beginning of 1998 for $25 per share. Abraham purchased 4,500 of these shares and recorded the acquisition at cost. Under these altered circumstances, prepare consolidation entries for 1998.

39.   Giant purchases all of the outstanding shares of Little on January 1, 1995, for $460,000 in cash. Of this price, $30,000 was attributed to equipment with a 10-year remaining life. Goodwill of $40,000 has also been identified and will be expensed over a 20-year period. Giant applies the partial equity method so that income is accrued each period based solely on the earnings reported by the subsidiary.

On January 1, 1998, Giant reports $200,000 in bonds outstanding with a book value of $188,000. Little purchases half of these bonds on the open market for $97,000.

During 1998, Giant begins to sell merchandise to Little. During that year, inventory costing $80,000 was transferred at a price of $100,000. All but $10,000 (at sales price) of these goods were resold to outside parties by year's end. Little still owes $36,000 for inventory shipped from Giant during December.

The following financial figures are for the two companies for the year ending December 31, 1998. Prepare a worksheet to produce consolidated balances. (Credits are indicated by parentheses.)

	Giant	Little
Revenues	$ (639,000)	$(466,000)
Cost of goods sold....................	345,000	198,000
Expenses.........................	134,000	161,000
Interest expense—bonds	24,000	–0–
Interest income—bond investment	–0–	(11,000)
Equity in income of Little	(118,000)	–0–
Net income	$ (254,000)	$(118,000)
Retained earnings, 1/1/98	$ (345,000)	
Retained earnings, 1/1/98		$(361,000)
Net income (above)	(254,000)	(118,000)
Dividends paid	155,000	61,000
Retained earnings, 12/31/98	$ (444,000)	$(418,000)
Cash and receivables	$ 133,000	$ 78,000
Inventory	171,000	87,000
Investment in Little	608,000	–0–
Investment in Giant bonds	–0–	98,000
Land, buildings, and equipment (net)........	249,000	541,000
Total assets	$ 1,161,000	$ 804,000
Accounts payable.....................	$ (225,000)	$(166,000)
Bonds payable......................	(200,000)	(100,000)
Discount on bonds	8,000	–0–
Common stock	(300,000)	(120,000)
Retained earnings (above)...............	(444,000)	(418,000)
Total liabilities and stockholders' equity	$(1,161,000)	$(804,000)

40. Fred, Inc., and Bub Corporation formed a business combination on January 1, 1994, when Fred purchased a 60 percent interest in the common stock of Bub for $310,000 in cash. The book value of Bub's assets and liabilities on that day totaled $300,000. Patents being held by Bub (with a 12-year remaining life) were undervalued by $100,000 within the company's financial records. Any goodwill indicated by this acquisition is to be amortized over a 10-year period.

Intercompany inventory transfers have been made between the two companies on a regular basis. Merchandise that is carried over from one year to the next is always sold in the subsequent period.

Year	Original Cost to Bub	Transfer Price to Fred	Ending Balance at Transfer Price
1994	$ 60,000	$ 72,000	$15,000
1995	70,000	84,000	25,000
1996	80,000	100,000	20,000
1997	100,000	125,000	40,000
1998	90,000	120,000	30,000

Half of the 1998 inventory transfers have not been paid for by Fred by the end of the year.

On January 1, 1995, Fred sold $15,000 in land to Bub for $22,000. Bub is still holding this land.

On January 1, 1998, Bub acquired $20,000 (face value) of Fred's bonds on the open market. These bonds had an 8 percent cash interest rate. On the date of repurchase, the liability was shown within Fred's records at $21,386, indicating an effective yield of 6 percent. Bub's acquisition price was $18,732 based on an effective interest rate of 10 percent.

Bub indicated earning a net income of $15,000 within its 1998 financial statements. The subsidiary also reported a beginning retained earnings balance of $300,000, dividends paid of $5,000, and common stock of $100,000. Bub has not issued any additional common stock since its takeover. Parent company has applied the equity method to record its investment in Bub.

Required

a. Prepare consolidation entries for 1998.

b. Calculate the 1998 balance for the noncontrolling interest's share of consolidated net income. In addition, determine the ending 1998 balance for noncontrolling interest in the consolidated balance sheet.

c. Determine the consolidation entry needed in 1999 in connection with the intercompany bonds.

41. On January 1, 1998, Mona, Inc., purchased 80 percent of Lisa Company's common stock as well as 60 percent of its preferred shares. Mona paid $65,000 in cash for the preferred stock which is considered a debt-type instrument (because no voting rights were granted and the stock has a call value of 110 percent of the $50 per share par value). Mona also paid $552,800 for the common stock, a price that indicated goodwill of $40,000. This intangible asset is being amortized over a 40-year period. Lisa pays all preferred stock dividends (a total of $8,000 per year) on an annual basis. During 1998, Lisa's book value increased by $50,000.

On January 2, 1998, Mona acquired one-half of Lisa's outstanding bonds payable to reduce the debt position of the business combination. Lisa's bonds had a face value of $100,000 and paid cash interest of 10 percent per year. These bonds had been issued to the public to yield 14 percent. Interest is paid each December 31. On January 2, 1998, these bonds payable had a total book value of $88,350. Mona paid $53,310, an amount indicating an effective interest rate of 8 percent.

On January 3, 1998, Mona sold fixed assets to Lisa. These assets had originally cost $100,000 but had accumulated depreciation of $60,000 when transferred. The transfer was made at a price of $120,000. These assets were estimated to have a remaining useful life of 10 years.

The individual financial statements for these two companies for the year ending December 31, 1999, are as follows:

	Mona, Inc.	Lisa Company
Sales and other revenues	$ 500,000	$ 200,000
Expenses	(220,000)	(120,000)
Dividend income—Lisa common stock	8,000	–0–
Dividend income—Lisa preferred stock	4,800	–0–
Net income	$ 292,800	$ 80,000
Retained earnings, 1/1/99	$ 700,000	$ 500,000
Net income (above)	292,800	80,000
Dividends paid—common stock	(92,800)	(10,000)
Dividends paid—preferred stock	–0–	(8,000)
Retained earnings, 12/31/99	$ 900,000	$ 562,000
Current assets	$ 130,419	$ 500,000
Investment in Lisa—common stock	552,800	–0–
Investment in Lisa—preferred stock	65,000	–0–
Investment in Lisa—bonds	51,781	–0–
Fixed assets	1,100,000	800,000
Accumulated depreciation	(300,000)	(200,000)
Total assets	$1,600,000	$1,100,000
Accounts payable	$ 400,000	$ 144,580
Bonds payable	–0–	100,000
Discount on bonds payable	–0–	(6,580)
Common stock	300,000	200,000
Preferred stock	–0–	100,000
Retained earnings, 12/31/99	900,000	562,000
Total liabilities and equities	$1,600,000	$1,100,000

Required

a. What consolidation entry (or entries) would have been required as of January 1, 1998, to eliminate the subsidiary's common and preferred stocks?

b. What consolidation entry (or entries) would have been required as of December 31, 1998, to account for Mona's purchase of Lisa's bonds?

c.   What consolidation entry (or entries) would have been required as of December 31, 1998, to account for the intercompany sale of fixed assets?

d.   Assume that consolidated financial statements are being prepared for the year ending December 31, 1999. Calculate the consolidated balance for each of the following accounts:

     Goodwill.
     Fixed Assets.
     Accumulated Depreciation.
     Expenses.
     Noncontrolling Interest in Lisa's Net Income.
     Net Income.

42. Rogers Company holds 80 percent of the common stock of Andrews, Inc., and 40 percent of this subsidiary's convertible bonds. The following consolidated financial statements are for 1998 and 1999:

Rogers Company and Consolidated Subsidiary

	1998	1999
Revenues	$ 760,000	$ 880,000
Cost of goods sold	(510,000)	(540,000)
Depreciation and amortization	(90,000)	(100,000)
Gain on sale of building	–0–	20,000
Interest expense	(30,000)	(30,000)
Noncontrolling interest	(9,000)	(11,000)
Net income	$ 121,000	$ 219,000
Retained earnings, 1/1	300,000	$ 371,000
Net income	121,000	219,000
Dividends paid	(50,000)	(100,000)
Retained earnings, 12/31	$ 371,000	$ 490,000
Cash	$ 80,000	$ 140,000
Accounts receivable	150,000	140,000
Inventory	200,000	340,000
Buildings and equipment (net)	640,000	690,000
Goodwill	150,000	145,000
Total assets	$1,220,000	$1,455,000
Accounts payable	140,000	100,000
Bonds payable	400,000	500,000
Noncontrolling interest in Andrews	32,000	41,000
Common stock	100,000	120,000
Additional paid-in capital	177,000	204,000
Retained earnings	371,000	490,000
Total liabilities and equities	$1,220,000	$1,455,000

Additional Information:

■ Bonds were issued during 1999 by the parent for cash.
■ Amortization of goodwill amounts to $5,000 per year.
■ A building with a cost of $60,000 but a $30,000 book value was sold by the parent for cash on May 11, 1999.
■ Equipment was purchased by the subsidiary on July 23, 1999, using cash.
■ Late in November of 1999, the parent issued stock for cash.
■ During 1999, the subsidiary paid dividends of $10,000.

Required

Prepare a consolidated statement of cash flows for this business combination for the year ending December 31, 1999. Either the direct or the indirect approach may be used.

43. Following are separate income statements for Alexander, Inc., and Raleigh Corporation as well as a consolidated statement for the business combination as a whole.

	Alexander	**Raleigh**	**Consolidated**
Revenues	$700,000	$500,000	$1,000,000
Cost of goods sold	(400,000)	(300,000)	(495,000)
Operating expenses	(100,000)	(70,000)	(190,000)
Equity in earnings of Raleigh	104,000	–0–	–0–
Noncontrolling interest in Raleigh's income	–0–	–0–	(26,000)
Net income	$304,000	$130,000	$ 289,000

Additional Information:

- Intercompany inventory transfers are all downstream.
- The parent applies the partial equity method to this investment.
- Alexander has 50,000 shares of common stock and 10,000 shares of preferred stock outstanding. Owners of the preferred are paid an annual dividend of $40,000, and each share can be exchanged for two shares of common stock.
- Raleigh has 30,000 shares of common stock outstanding. The company also has 5,000 stock warrants outstanding. For $10, each warrant can be converted into a share of Raleigh's common stock. Alexander holds half of these warrants. The price of Raleigh's common stock was $20 per share throughout the year.
- Raleigh also has convertible bonds, none of which is owned by Alexander. During the current year, total interest expense (net of taxes) was $22,000. These bonds can be exchanged for 10,000 shares of the subsidiary's common stock.

Required

Determine basic and diluted earnings per share for this business combination.

44. On January 1, 1998, Paisley, Inc., paid $560,000 for all of the outstanding stock of Skyler Corporation. This cash payment was based on a price of $180 per share for Skyler's $100 par value preferred stock and $38 per share for the company's $20 par value common stock. The preferred shares are voting, cumulative, and fully participating; they have no set call value. At the date of purchase, the book values of Skyler's accounts equaled their market values. Any goodwill will be amortized over a 10-year period.

    During 1998, Skyler sold inventory costing $60,000 to Paisley for $90,000. All but $18,000 (measured at transfer price) of this merchandise has been resold to outsiders by the end of the year. At the end of 1998, Paisley continues to owe Skyler for the last shipment of inventory priced at $28,000.

    Also, on January 2, 1998, Paisley sold equipment to Skyler for $20,000 although it had a book value of only $12,000 (original cost of $30,000). Both companies depreciate such property according to the straight-line method with no salvage value. The remaining life at this date was four years.

    The following financial statements are for each company for the year ending December 31, 1998. Determine consolidated financial totals for this business combination.

	Paisley, Inc.	Skyler Corporation
Sales	$ (800,000)	$(400,000)
Costs of goods sold	528,000	260,000
Expenses.....................................	180,000	130,000
Gain on sale of equipment	(8,000)	–0–
Net income	$ (100,000)	$ (10,000)
Retained earnings, 1/1/98	$ (400,000)	$(150,000)
Net income	(100,000)	(10,000)
Dividends paid	60,000	–0–
Retained earnings, 12/31/98	$ (440,000)	$(160,000)
Cash..	$ 30,000	$ 40,000
Accounts receivable	300,000	100,000
Inventory	260,000	180,000
Investment in Skyler Corporation	560,000	–0–
Land, buildings, and equipment................	680,000	500,000
Accumulated depreciation.....................	(180,000)	(90,000)
Total assets	$ 1,650,000	$ 730,000
Accounts payable.............................	$ (140,000)	$ (90,000)
Long-term liabilities..........................	(240,000)	(180,000)
Preferred stock	–0–	(100,000)
Common stock	(620,000)	(200,000)
Additional paid-in capital	(210,000)	–0–
Retained earnings, 12/31/98	(440,000)	(160,000)
Total equities...............................	$(1,650,000)	$(730,000)

Parentheses indicate a credit balance.

Ownership Patterns and Income Taxes

Consolidated Financial Statements

QUESTIONS TO CONSIDER

- A parent holds control over a subsidiary which, in turn, owns a majority of the voting stock of another company. Hence, the parent indirectly controls both of these subsidiaries. How does this type of ownership pattern affect the consolidation process for a business combination?

- If a subsidiary possesses stock of its parent company, what impact does the mutual ownership have on consolidated financial statements?

- How does a business combination qualify to file a consolidated income tax return? What advantages are gained by filing in this manner?

- Why does the filing of separate tax returns by the members of a business combination frequently create the need to recognize deferred income taxes?

Coverage of the accounting for business combinations is concluded here in Chapter 7 by analyzing two additional aspects of consolidated financial statements. First, the various patterns of ownership that can exist within a combination are presented. Indirect control of a subsidiary, connecting affiliations, and mutual ownership are all examined along with the consolidation procedures applicable to each of these organizational structures. The chapter then presents an overview of the income tax considerations relevant to the members of a business combination. Income tax accounting for both consolidated and separate corporate returns is discussed in light of current laws.

INDIRECT SUBSIDIARY CONTROL

Throughout previous chapters, only one type of relationship has been presented for every business combination. Specifically, a parent has always held a direct financial interest in a single subsidiary. This ownership pattern has been assumed to expedite the explanation of consolidation theories and techniques. In actual practice, though, much more elaborate corporate structures commonly exist. Time Warner, Inc., for example, controls literally scores of subsidiaries. However, Time Warner owns voting stock in a relatively small number of these companies. Control is maintained often through indirect ownership; Time Warner's subsidiaries hold the stock of many of the companies within this business combination. For example, Time Warner, the parent company, owns the voting stock of Turner Broadcasting, Inc., which in turn has total ownership of Castle Rock Entertainment and many other companies (see Chapter 2 for a graphic display). This type of corporate configuration is often referred to as a father-son-grandson relationship (or sometimes as a pyramid) because of the pattern created by the descending tiers.

Forming a business combination as a series of indirect ownerships is not an unusual practice. Many businesses organize their operations in this manner to group individual companies along product lines, geographic districts, or some other logical criteria. The philosophy behind this structuring is that clearer lines of communication and responsibility reporting can be developed by placing direct control in proximity to each subsidiary. However, other indirect ownership patterns are simply the result of years of acquisition and growth. As an example, in purchasing General Foods, Philip Morris Companies, Inc., actually gained control over a number of corporations (including Oscar Mayer Foods Corporation, Maxwell House Coffee Company, and Birds Eye, Inc.). This control was not achieved directly by Philip Morris but rather indirectly through the acquisition of their parent company.

The Consolidation Process When Indirect Control Is Present

Regardless of a company's reason for establishing indirect control over a subsidiary, a new accounting problem is encountered: the financial information generated by several connecting corporations must be consolidated into a single set of financial statements. Fortunately, indirect ownership does not introduce any new conceptual issues but affects only the mechanical elements of this process. For example, a purchase price allocation, as well as an annual amortization expense figure, must be computed and recognized for every investment. In addition, all of the worksheet entries previously demonstrated continue to apply. For business combinations involving indirect control, the entire consolidation process is basically repeated for each separate acquisition.

Calculation of Realized Income Although most consolidation procedures are unchanged by the presence of an indirect ownership, the isolation of each subsidiary's realized income does pose an added degree of difficulty. Appropriate determination of this figure is essential because it serves as the basis for calculating (1) equity income accruals and (2) the noncontrolling interest's share of consolidated income.

In previous chapters, the subsidiary's realized income has been determined by adjusting reported earnings for the effects of any upstream intercompany transfers. *However, where indirect control is involved, at least one company within the business combination (and possibly many) holds both a parent and a subsidiary position.* Any company in that position must first give proper recognition to the equity income accruing from its subsidiaries before computing its own realized income total. This guideline is not a theoretical doctrine but merely a necessary arrangement for calculating income totals in a predetermined order. The process begins with the grandson, then moves to the son, and finishes with the father. Only by following this systematic approach can the correct amount of realized income be determined for each individual company.

Realized Income Computation Illustrated For example, assume that three companies form a business combination: Top Company owns 70 percent of Midway Company which, in turn, possesses 60 percent of Bottom Company. As can be seen from the following display, both subsidiaries are under the control of Top, although the parent's relationship with Bottom is only of an indirect nature.

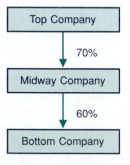

For illustration purposes, assume that the following information has been elicited from the 1998 individual financial records of the three companies making up this combination:

	Top Company	Midway Company	Bottom Company
Operating income	$600,000	$300,000	$100,000
Dividend income from investment in subsidiary (based on cost method)	80,000	50,000	
Reported net income	$680,000	$350,000	$100,000
Additional information:			
Net unrealized intercompany gains within current year income	$110,000	$ 80,000	$ 20,000
Amortization expense relating to purchase price of investment	20,000	15,000	–0–

Beginning, as specified, with the grandson of the organization, a calculation is made of each company's 1998 realized income. For example, from the perspective of the business combination, Bottom's income for the period would be only $80,000 after removing the $20,000 effect of the company's unrealized intercompany gains. Thus, $80,000 is the basis for the equity accrual by its parent as well as any noncontrolling interest recognition.

Once the grandson's income has been derived, this figure then can be used in computing the realized earnings of the son, Midway:

Operating income—Midway Company	$300,000
Equity income accruing from Bottom Company—60% of realized income of $80,000	48,000
Recognition of amortization expense relating to purchase of Bottom Company (above)	(15,000)
Removal of Midway's unrealized intercompany gain (above)	(80,000)
Realized income of Midway Company	$253,000

The $253,000 realized income figure determined for Midway varies significantly from the company's reported profit of $350,000. This difference is not unusual and is merely the result of establishing an appropriate consolidation perspective in viewing both the investment in its subsidiary and the effects of intercompany transfers. The recognition of all transactions is being brought into line with the company's vantage point within this business combination.

Continuing with this systematic calculation of each company's earnings, Top's realized income now can be determined. Only after the appropriate figure is computed for the son can the father's earnings within the business combination be derived.

Operating income—Top Company	$600,000
Equity income accruing from Midway Company—70% of realized income of $253,000	177,100
Recognition of amortization expense relating to purchase of Midway Company (above)	(20,000)
Removal of Top's unrealized intercompany gain (above)...................	(110,000)
Realized income of Top	$647,100

Having established realized income figures for each of these three companies, several aspects of this data should be noted:

1. Within the 1998 income statement reported for Top Company and its consolidated subsidiaries, a $107,900 balance would be disclosed as the "noncontrolling interests' share of subsidiary income." This total is based on the realized income figures of the two subsidiaries and is computed as follows:

	Realized Income	Outside Ownership	Noncontrolling Interests in Income
Bottom Company	$ 80,000	40%	$ 32,000
Midway Company	253,000	30	75,900
Total			$107,900

2. Although the cost method was applied to both of the investments in this illustration, the parents' individual accounting is not a factor in determining realized income totals. The cost figures were omitted and replaced with equity accruals in preparation for consolidation. The selection of a particular method is only relevant for internal reporting purposes; computation of realized earnings, as shown here, is based entirely on the equity income accruing from each subsidiary.

3. As demonstrated previously, if appropriate equity accruals are recognized, the parent's realized income can serve as a "proof figure" for the consolidated total. Parent earnings calculated in this manner equal the net income for the entire business combination. Thus, if the consolidation process is carried out correctly, the earnings to be reported by this entire organization should equal $647,100 as indicated previously for Top.

4. Whenever indirect control is established, a discrepancy exists between the percentage of stock being held and the income contributed to the business combination by a subsidiary. In this illustration, Midway possesses 60 percent of Bottom's voting stock but, mathematically, only 42 percent of Bottom's income is attributed to Top's controlling interest (70 percent direct ownership of Midway × 60 percent indirect ownership of Bottom). The remaining income earned by this subsidiary is assigned to the owners outside of the combination.

The validity of this 42 percent accrual is one aspect of the consolidation that is not readily apparent. Therefore, an elementary example can be constructed to demonstrate the mathematical accuracy of this percentage. Assume that neither Top nor Midway reports any earnings during the year but that Bottom has $100 in realized income. If Bottom declares a $100 cash dividend, $60 goes to Midway with the remaining $40 distributed to Bottom's noncontrolling interest. Assuming then that Midway uses this $60 to pay its own dividend, $42 (70 percent) is transferred to Top with $18 going to the outside owners of Midway.

Thus, 58 percent of Bottom's income should be attributed to parties outside of the business combination. An initial 40 percent belongs to Bottom's own noncontrolling interest while an additional 18 percent is eventually accrued by the other shareholders of Midway. Consequently, only 42 percent of Bottom's original income is considered as having been earned by the combination. Consolidated financial statements reflect this allocation by including 100 percent of the subsidiary's revenues and expenses while simultaneously recognizing a reduction for the 58 percent noncontrolling interests' in the subsidiary's net income.

Consolidation Process—Indirect Control

Having analyzed the calculation of realized income within a father-son-grandson configuration, a full-scale consolidation now can be produced. As is demonstrated, the worksheet process is not significantly altered by this type of ownership pattern. In reality, most worksheet entries are simply made twice; first for the son's investment in the grandson and then for the father's ownership of the son. Although this sudden doubling of entries may initially seem overwhelming, close examination reveals that the individual procedures remain unaffected.

As an illustration, assume that on January 1, 1995, Big purchases 80 percent of the outstanding common stock of Middle for $640,000. On that date, Middle has a book value (total stockholders' equity) of $700,000, which indicates the parent paid $80,000 in excess of the subsidiary's underlying $560,000 book value ($700,000 × 80 percent). This $80,000 is assigned to goodwill and amortized at the rate of $2,000 per year.

Following the acquisition, Middle's book value rises to $1,080,000 by the end of 1998, denoting a $380,000 increment during this three-year period ($1,080,000 − $700,000). Big applies the partial equity method; therefore, a $304,000 ($380,000 × 80%) increase in the investment account (to $944,000) is accrued by the parent over this same time span.

On January 1, 1997, Middle acquires 70 percent of Little for $461,000. Little's stockholders' equity accounts total $630,000, indicating that Middle has paid $20,000 more than the applicable book value of $441,000 ($630,000 × 70%). This entire $20,000 is allocated to goodwill so that, over a 40-year assumed life, amortization expense of $500 is recognized each year by the business combination. During 1997–98, Little's book value increases by $150,000 to a $780,000 total. Because Middle also is applying the partial equity method, $105,000 ($150,000 × 70%) has been added to the investment account to arrive at a $566,000 balance ($461,000 + $105,000).

To complete the introductory information for this illustration, assume that a number of intercompany upstream transfers have occurred over the past two years. The dollar volume of these transactions is chronicled here as well as the unrealized gain in each year's ending inventory.

	Little Company Transfers to Middle Company		Middle Company Transfers to Big Company	
Year	Transfer Price	Year-End Unrealized Gain	Transfer Price	Year-End Unrealized Gain
1997	$ 75,000	$20,000	$200,000	$30,000
1998	120,000	25,000	250,000	40,000

The worksheet to consolidate these three companies for the year ending December 31, 1998, is presented in Exhibit 7–1. The first three columns represent the individual statements for each of the organizations. This information is followed by the entries required to consolidate the various balances. To help identify the separate procedures, entries concerning the relationship between Big (father) and Middle (son) are marked with a "B," whereas an "L" denotes Middle's ownership of Little (grandson). The duplication of entries in this exhibit is done primarily to facilitate a clearer understanding of this consolidation. A number of these dual entries can be combined once a familiarity with the entire process is achieved.

To arrive at consolidated figures, Exhibit 7–1 incorporates the worksheet entries described next. By analyzing each of these adjustments and eliminations, the consolidation procedures necessitated by a father-son-grandson ownership pattern can be identified. Despite the presence of indirect control over Little, financial statements can be created for the business combination as a whole utilizing the process described in previous chapters.

Consolidation Entry *G Entry *G defers the unrealized intercompany gains contained in the beginning financial figures. Within their separate accounting systems, two of the companies prematurely recorded income ($20,000 by Little and $30,000 by Middle) in 1997 at the time of transfer. For consolidation purposes, a worksheet entry must be included in 1998 to eliminate these unrealized gains from both beginning retained earnings as well as cost of goods sold (the present location of the beginning inventory). Consequently, this gross profit is being appropriately recognized on the consolidated income statement of the current period.

Exhibit 7–1

Consolidation: Purchase Method
Investment: Partial Equity Method

BIG COMPANY AND CONSOLIDATED SUBSIDIARIES
Consolidation Worksheet
For Year Ending December 31, 1998

Accounts	Big Company	Middle Company	Little Company	Consolidation Entries Debit	Consolidation Entries Credit	Noncontrolling Interest	Consolidated Totals
Income Statement							
Sales	(800,000)	(500,000)	(300,000)	(LTI) 120,000 (BTI) 250,000 (LG) 25,000			(1,230,000)
Cost of goods sold	300,000	220,000	140,000	(BG) 40,000	(L*G) 20,000 (LTI) 120,000 (B*G) 30,000 (BTI) 250,000		305,000
Expenses	200,000	80,000	60,000	(LE) 500 (BE) 2,000 (LI) 70,000 (BI) 216,000			342,500
Income of Little Company	–0–	(70,000)	–0–				–0–
Income of Middle Company	(216,000)	–0–	–0–				–0–
Noncontrolling interest in Little Company's net income	–0–	–0–	–0–			(28,500)	28,500
Noncontrolling interest in Middle Company's net income	–0–	–0–	–0–			(51,200)	51,200
Net income	(516,000)	(270,000)	(100,000)				(502,800)
Statement of Retained Earnings							
Retained earnings, 1/1/98:							
Big Company	(900,000)	–0–	–0–	(B*C) 39,600 (B*G) 30,000 (L*C) 14,500 (BS) 755,500 (L*G) 20,000 (LS) 580,000			(860,400)
Middle Company	–0–	(800,000)	–0–				–0–
Little Company	–0–	–0–	(600,000)				
Net income (from above)	(516,000)	(270,000)	(100,000)				(502,800)
Dividends paid:							
Big Company	120,000	–0–	–0–				120,000
Middle Company	–0–	90,000	–0–		(BD) 72,000	18,000	–0–
Little Company	–0–	–0–	50,000		(LD) 35,000	15,000	–0–
Retained earnings, 12/31/98	(1,296,000)	(980,000)	(650,000)				(1,243,200)

Balance Sheet

	Big Company	Middle Company	Little Company	Debit Entries	Credit Entries	Noncontrolling Interest	Consolidated
Cash and receivables	600,000	300,000	280,000	(BD) 72,000			1,180,000
Investment in Middle Company	944,000	-0-	-0-		(B*C) 39,600 (BS) 684,400 (BI) 216,000 (BA) 76,000		-0-
Investment in Little Company	-0-	566,000	-0-	(LD) 35,000	(L*C) 14,500 (LS) 497,000 (LI) 70,000 (LA) 19,500 (LG) 25,000 (BG) 40,000		-0-
Inventory	300,000	260,000	290,000	(LA) 19,500			785,000
Land, building, equipment	192,000	154,000	510,000	(BA) 76,000			856,000
Goodwill	-0-	-0-	-0-		(LE) 500 (BE) 2,000		93,000
Total assets	2,036,000	1,280,000	1,080,000				2,914,000
Liabilities	(340,000)	(200,000)	(300,000)				(840,000)
Noncontrolling interest in Little Company, 1/1/98	-0-	-0-	-0-		(LS) 213,000	(213,000)	
Noncontrolling interest in Middle Company, 1/1/98	-0-	-0-	-0-		(BS) 171,100	(171,100)	
Total noncontrolling interest, 12/31/98	-0-	-0-	-0-			(430,800)	(430,800)
Common stock:							
Big Company	(400,000)	-0-	-0-				(400,000)
Middle Company	-0-	(100,000)	-0-	(BS) 100,000			-0-
Little Company	-0-	-0-	(130,000)	(LS) 130,000			-0-
Retained earnings (above)	(1,296,000)	(980,000)	(650,000)				(1,243,200)
Total liabilities and equities	(2,036,000)	(1,280,000)	(1,080,000)				(2,914,000)

Note: Parentheses indicate credit balance.

Consolidation Entries: Entries labeled with a "B" refer to the investment relationship between Big and Middle. Entries with an "L" refer to Middle's ownership of Little.

(*G) Removal of unrealized gain from beginning inventory figures so that it can be recognized in current period.

(*C) Conversion of partial equity method to equity method. Amortization for prior years is recognized along with effects of beginning unrealized upstream gains.

(S) Elimination of subsidiaries' stockholders' equity accounts along with recognition of January 1, 1998, noncontrolling interests.

(A) Allocation to goodwill, unamortized balance being recognized as of January 1, 1998.

(I) Elimination of intercompany income accrued during the period.

(D) Elimination of intercompany dividends.

(E) Recognition of amortization expense for the current period.

(TI) Elimination of intercompany sales/purchases balances created by the transfer of inventory.

(G) Removal of unrealized inventory gain from ending figures so that it can be recognized in subsequent period.

Consolidation Entry *C   Neither Big nor Middle has applied the full equity method to their investments; therefore, the figures recognized during the years prior to the current period (1998) must now be updated on the worksheet. This process begins with the son's ownership of the grandson. Hence, Middle must reduce its 1997 income (now closed into retained earnings) by $500 to reflect the amortization applicable to that year. This expense would not have been recorded by Middle in applying the partial equity method.

In addition, since $20,000 of Little's previously reported earnings have just been deferred (in preceding Entry *G), the effect of this reduction on Middle's ownership must also be recognized. The parent's original equity accrual for 1997 was based on reported rather than realized profit; thus, too much income was recorded. Little's deferral necessitates a parallel $14,000 decrease ($20,000 × 70%) by Middle. Consequently, Middle's retained earnings balance as of January 1, 1998, as well as the Investment in Little account are reduced on the worksheet by a total of $14,500:

Reduction in Middle's Beginning Retained Earnings

1997 amortization expense	$ 500
Income effect created by Little's deferral of 1997 unrealized gain (reduction of previous accrual) ($20,000 × 70%)	14,000
Required reduction to Middle's beginning retained earnings (Entry L*C)	$14,500

A similar equity adjustment also must be made in connection with Big's ownership of Middle. The calculation of the specific amount to be recorded follows the same procedural path identified earlier for Middle's investment in Little. Once again, amortization expense for all prior years (1996 and 1997, in this case) has to be brought into the consolidation as well as the income reduction created by the deferral of Middle's $30,000 unrealized gain (Entry *G). *However, recognition also must be given to the effects associated with the $14,500 decrease in Middle's pre–1998 earnings described in the previous paragraph.* Although only recorded on the worksheet, this adjustment is a change in Middle's originally reported income. To reflect Big's ownership of Middle, the effect of this reduction must be included in arriving at the income balances actually accruing to the parent company. Thus, a decrease of $39,600 is needed in Big's beginning retained earnings to establish the proper accounting for its subsidiaries.

Reduction in Big's Beginning Retained Earnings

Amortization expense relating to acquisition of Middle Company—1996–1997 ($2,000 per year)	$ (4,000)
Income effect created by Middle Company's deferral of unrealized gain ($30,000 × 80%)	(24,000)
Income effect created by Middle Company's adjustment to its prior year's investment income ($14,500 × 80%) (above)	(11,600)
Required reduction to Big's beginning retained earnings (Entry B*C)	$(39,600)

Consolidation Entry S   The beginning stockholders' equity accounts of each subsidiary are eliminated here and noncontrolling interest balances as of the beginning of the year are recognized. As in previous chapters, the amounts involved in this entry have been directly affected by the preliminary adjustments described earlier. Because Entry *G removed a $20,000 beginning unrealized gain, Little's January 1, 1998, book value on the worksheet is $710,000 and not $730,000. This realized total serves as the basis for recording a $213,000 beginning noncontrolling interest (30 percent) as well as the $497,000 elimination (70 percent) from the parent's investment account.

In a similar vein, Middle's book value has already been decreased by $44,500 through Entries *G ($30,000) and *C ($14,500). Thus, the beginning stockholders' equity accounts for this company have now been adjusted to a total of $855,500 ($900,000 − $44,500). This balance leads to a $171,100 initial noncontrolling interest valuation (20 percent) and a $684,400 (80 percent) offset against Big's Investment in Middle account.

Consolidation Entry A   The unamortized goodwill balances remaining as of January 1, 1998, are removed from the two investment accounts so that this intangible asset can be identified separately on the consolidated balance sheet. Because amortization expense for the previous periods has already been recognized in Entry *C, only beginning totals for the year of $19,500 ($20,000 − $500) and $76,000 ($80,000 − $4,000) still remain from the original amounts paid.

Consolidation Entry I   This entry eliminates the current intercompany income figures accrued by each of the parents through their application of the partial equity method.

Consolidation Entry D   Intercompany dividends distributed during the year are removed here from the consolidated financial totals.

Consolidation Entry E   The annual amortization expense relating to each of the goodwill balances is recorded.

Consolidation Entry TI   The intercompany sales/purchases figures created by the transfer of inventory during 1998 are eliminated on the worksheet.

Consolidation Entry G   This final consolidation entry defers the intercompany inventory gains that remain unrealized as of December 31, 1998. The profit on these transfers is removed until the merchandise is subsequently sold to unrelated parties.

Noncontrolling Interests' Share of Consolidated Income   To complete the steps that constitute this consolidation worksheet, recognition must be given to the 1998 income accruing to owners outside of the business combination. This allocation is based on the realized earnings of the two subsidiaries which, as previously discussed, is calculated beginning with the grandson (Little) followed by the son (Middle).

Little Company's Realized Income and Noncontrolling Interest

Reported operating income (from Exhibit 7–1)	$100,000
Realization of gains previously deferred from 1997 (Entry L*G)	20,000
Deferral of gains unrealized as of 12/31/98 (Entry LG)	(25,000)
Little Company's realized income, 1998	95,000
Outside ownership	30%
Noncontrolling interest in Little Company's income	$ 28,500

Middle Company's Realized Income and Noncontrolling Interest

Reported operating income (from Exhibit 7–1 after removing income of Little Company)	$200,000
Amortization expense relating to acquisition of Little Company, current year	(500)
Realization of gains previously deferred from 1997 (Entry B*G)	30,000
Deferral of gains unrealized as of 12/31/98 (Entry BG)	(40,000)
Equity income accruing from Little Company (70% of $95,000 realized income [above])	66,500
Middle Company's realized income, 1998	256,000
Outside ownership	20%
Noncontrolling interest in Middle Company's income	$ 51,200

Although computation of Big's realized earnings is not required here, as previously noted, this figure does provide a means of verifying the accuracy of the income total reported for the consolidated entity.

Big Company's Realized Income

Reported operating income (from Exhibit 7–1 after removing income of Middle Company)	$300,000
Amortization expense relating to acquisition of Middle Company, current year	(2,000)
Equity income accruing from Middle Company (80% of $256,000 realized income [above])	204,800
Big Company's realized income, 1998	$502,800

This $502,800 figure represents the income derived by the parent from its own operations plus the earnings accrued from the company's two subsidiaries (one directly owned and the other indirectly controlled). If calculated correctly, this balance equals the consolidated income of the business combination. As shown in Exhibit 7–1, the income reported by Big Company and consolidated subsidiaries does, indeed, net to this same total: $502,800. Although not completely conclusive, the agreement of these balances serves as strong evidence of the validity of the final figures on the consolidation worksheet.

INDIRECT SUBSIDIARY CONTROL—CONNECTING AFFILIATION

The father-son-grandson organization is hardly the only corporate ownership pattern that can be encountered. The number of possible configurations found in the modern world of business is almost limitless. To assist in illustrating the consolidation procedures necessitated by these alternative patterns, a second basic ownership structure referred to as a *connecting affiliation* is discussed briefly.

A connecting affiliation exists whenever two or more companies within a business combination own an interest in another member of that organization. The simplest form of this configuration is frequently drawn as a triangle:

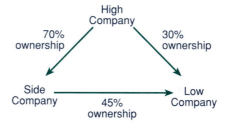

In this example, both High Company and Side Company maintain an ownership interest in Low Company, thus creating a connecting affiliation. Although neither of these individual companies possesses enough voting stock to establish direct control over Low's operations, a total of 75 percent of the outstanding shares is held by members of the combination. Consequently, control lies within the boundaries of the single economic entity, and the inclusion of Low's financial information as a part of consolidated statements is necessary.

Despite the potential for numerous variations in this basic ownership pattern, the process for consolidating a connecting affiliation is essentially unchanged from that demonstrated for a father-son-grandson organization. Perhaps, the most noticeable alteration is that more than two investments are always going to be present. In this triangular business combination, High possesses an ownership interest in both Side and Low while Side also maintains an investment in Low. Thus, unless combined in some manner, three separate sets of consolidation entries would appear on the worksheet. Although the added quantity of entries certainly provides a degree of mechanical complication, the basic concepts involved in the consolidation process remain the same regardless of the number of investments involved.

As with the father-son-grandson structure, one key aspect of the consolidation process warrants additional illustration: the determination of realized income figures for the individual companies. Therefore, assume that High, Side, and Low have separate operating incomes (without inclusion of any earnings from their subsidiaries) of $300,000, $200,000, and $100,000, respectively. Each company also retains a $30,000 net unrealized gain in their current year income figures. Assume further that annual amortization expense of $10,000 has been identified within the purchase price paid for each of the three investments.

In the same manner as a father-son-grandson organization, determination of realized earnings should begin with any companies that are solely in a subsidiary position (Low, in this case). Next, realized income is computed for companies that are both parents as well as subsidiaries (Side). Finally, this same calculation should be made for the one company (High) that has ultimate control over the entire combination. Realized income figures for the three companies in this combination would be derived as follows:

Low Company's Realized Income and Noncontrolling Interest

Reported operating income	$100,000
Deferral of Low Company's net unrealized gain	(30,000)
Low Company's realized income	70,000
Outside ownership	25%
Noncontrolling interest in Low Company's income	$ 17,500

Side Company's Realized Income and Noncontrolling Interest

Reported operating income	$200,000
Deferral of Side Company's net unrealized gain	(30,000)
Equity income accruing from Low Company (45% of $70,000 realized income)	31,500
Amortization expense relating to Side Company's acquisition of Low Company	(10,000)
Side Company's realized income	191,500
Outside ownership	30%
Noncontrolling interest in Side Company's income	$ 57,450

High Company's Realized Income

Reported operating income	$300,000
Deferral of High Company's net unrealized gain	(30,000)
Equity income accruing from Side Company (70% of $191,500 realized income)	134,050
Amortization expense relating to High Company's acquisition of Side Company	(10,000)
Equity income accruing from Low Company—direct ownership (30% of $70,000 realized income)	21,000
Amortization expense relating to High Company's acquisition of Low Company	(10,000)
High Company's realized income (and consolidated net income)	$405,050

Even though a connecting affiliation exists in this illustration, the basic tenets of the consolidation process remain the same:

■ All effects from intercompany transfers are removed.
■ The parents' beginning retained earnings figures are adjusted to recognize the equity income resulting from ownership of the subsidiaries in prior years. The

determination of realized earnings for this period is necessary to properly align the balances with the perspective of a single economic entity.

- The beginning stockholders' equity accounts of each subsidiary are eliminated and the noncontrolling interests' figures as of the first day of the year are recognized.

- All unamortized allocation balances created by the original purchase prices are entered onto the worksheet.

- Amortization expense for the current year is recorded.

- Intercompany income and dividends are removed.

- The noncontrolling interests' share of the subsidiaries' net income is computed (as just shown) and included in the financial statements of the business combination.

MUTUAL OWNERSHIP

One specific corporate structure that does require further analysis is a mutual ownership. This type of configuration exists whenever two companies within a business combination hold an equity interest in each other. This ownership pattern was sometimes created as a result of the financial battles that occurred during many of the takeover attempts prevalent during the 1980s. A defensive strategy (often referred to as the *Pac-Man Defense*) was occasionally adopted whereby the target company would attempt to avoid takeover by reversing roles and acquiring shares of its investor. Consequently the two parties came to hold shares of each other with one usually gaining control.

Two typical mutual ownership patterns follow. In situation A, the parent and the subsidiary possess a percentage of each other's voting shares; whereas in situation B, the mutual ownership exists between two subsidiary companies.

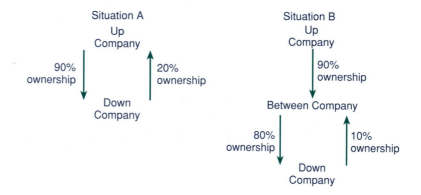

In accounting for a mutual ownership, unique conceptual issues are raised. These concerns center on the handling of any parent company stock owned by a subsidiary. *ARB 51* (par. 12) states that "shares of the parent held by a subsidiary should not be treated as outstanding stock in the consolidated balance sheet." The FASB's Exposure Draft (October 1995) agrees with this approach and recommends that "shares of a parent held by a subsidiary shall not be reported as outstanding stock in consolidated statements." (paragraph 21) This guidance is theoretically appropriate because the shares are not owned by parties outside of the business combination. Unfortunately, the actual reporting of such internally held stock can vary significantly, depending on the perspective taken as to the substance of the subsidiary's purchase. Until formal guidance is provided by standard setters, variations in practice will continue.

Mutual Ownership: What Do Those Shares Represent?

During 1998, Pierpont Corporation began a plan to acquire control over Sandstone, Inc., a competing company of similar size. An offer of $27 per share (to be paid in a combination of cash and stock) was initially made for Sandstone's common stock. In an attempt to maintain its independence, Sandstone began a counterattack by purchasing the outstanding common stock of Pierpont on the open market. Pierpont increased its offer to $31 and, finally, to $38 per share before successfully winning control over Sandstone. Eventually, 80 percent of Sandstone's shares were obtained. However, during the takeover struggle, Sandstone managed to acquire 30 percent of Pierpont's stock (75,000 shares) at a total cost of $8 million.

Following the purchase, Sandstone remained a relatively autonomous organization. The president and administrative officers retained their positions with the company, and Sandstone's principal stockholder before the takeover is now on the board of directors of Pierpont.

Within Sandstone's separate accounting records, the investment in Pierpont's stock is reported using the equity method. Thus, at the end of 1999, the asset's balance has risen to $8.7 million. Accounting officials of Pierpont, who currently are preparing consolidated financial statements, are attempting to determine the proper accounting for these 75,000 shares. According to the controller, "these shares are our own stock and they are being held within the business combination. The acquisition is no more than the intercompany purchase of treasury shares. Reporting should be simple; we show $8 million as the cost of treasury stock and eliminate all other related figures."

The assistant vice president for finance does not agree. "If we just remove all the balances, we will be using an income for Sandstone that has not been correctly calculated. Sandstone owns this investment and it generates a profit; that profit must be assigned to Sandstone in some manner or we are understating the income that this subsidiary's assets are producing."

The controller is not convinced: "Sandstone has no earnings from this investment. The dividends that we pay them are just intercompany cash transfers and they should not even be recognizing equity income accruals. We control them; Sandstone certainly does not have significant influence over us."

In computing the noncontrolling interest in Sandstone's income, how should the ownership of these 75,000 shares affect the determination of the subsidiary's realized income?

Treasury Stock Approach

Interestingly, when parent shares are obtained by a subsidiary, both of the prevalent methods of accounting take the same perspective: financial reporting should not vary based on the specific identity of the purchasing agent. For consolidation purposes, no legitimate accounting distinction can be drawn between an acquisition by the parent and the same transaction if it is made by a subsidiary. However, these two methods disagree as to the underlying nature of a subsidiary's purchase of the parent's stock: should the shares be viewed as treasury stock or as an investment?

The *treasury stock approach* assumes that both parties should account for this transaction as the parent would record a purchase of its own stock. Conversely, according to the *conventional approach,* both the parent and the subsidiary must record all intercompany investments in the same manner. Because the parent recognizes income based on its ownership of the subsidiary, the subsidiary should recognize income from an investment in the parent. Although the distinction between these two approaches may seem subtle, the resulting financial figures can vary appreciably.

The treasury stock approach to mutual ownership focuses on the parent's control over the subsidiary. Even though the companies maintain separate legal incorporation, only a single economic entity actually exists, and it is under the dominance of the parent. Hence, according to proponents, stock or other items can be purchased by either company but all reporting for the business combination has to be from the parent's perspective. Although the subsidiary may serve as the purchasing agent, the acquisition of parent shares is still viewed as treasury stock in the consolidated statements. This perspective is firmly grounded in the parent company concept (discussed in Chapter 4), which accounts for all transactions from the vantage point of the parent's stockholders.

In present accounting practice, the treasury stock approach appears to predominate, although this popularity is undoubtedly based as much on the ease of application as on theoretical merit. *The cost of parent shares held by the subsidiary is merely reclassified on the worksheet into a treasury stock account.* Any dividend payments on this stock are considered intercompany cash transfers that must be eliminated. This reporting technique is simple and the shares are, indeed, no longer accounted for as if they were outstanding.

Conventional Approach

The conventional approach provides a different view of a subsidiary's ownership of parent shares. This alternative theory presumes that the acquisition of parent stock is no more than another equity purchase made in one of the affiliated companies within a business combination. Thus, the consolidation of a mutual ownership should parallel the process that has been demonstrated already for a connecting affiliation: two investments are present rather than one. *In effect, this argument contends that accounting for the parent's investment and a subsidiary's investment by totally different methods is inconsistent.*

Proponents of the conventional approach believe that introducing a unique process, such as the treasury stock approach, simply because of the subsidiary's location within the corporate structure is not justified. To rectify this situation, the internally held shares of the parent company are consolidated in the same manner as an investment in a subsidiary. The conventional approach is aligned with the economic unit concept which contends that each company should be accounted for as an individual component within the business combination.

Probably the most distinctive aspect of the conventional approach is the determination of realized income figures. Because of the mutual ownership, each company occupies both a parent and a subsidiary position within the combination. Immediately, a paradox is created by this relationship. The income of neither company can be computed first; each is partially dependent on the final balance of the other. Unlike the previous indirect ownership examples, no systematic calculation of earnings is possible. Rather, mutual income accruals can be derived only by solving two simultaneous equations.

Clearly, these two approaches represent alternative perceptions of the same event: the subsidiary's purchase of parent stock. However, the underlying question here concerns the theoretical concept that should provide the basis for consolidated statements. What is the purpose of a consolidation and for whom are the financial statements prepared? After these central issues have been resolved, the handling of mutual ownerships (as well as other theoretical concerns) should follow as logical extensions of the selected concept.

Mutual Ownership Illustrated

To illustrate both the treasury stock and the conventional approaches, assume that on January 1, 1998, Sun Company purchases 10 percent of Pop Company. Sun pays $120,000 for these shares, an amount that exactly equals the proportionate book value of Pop. Many possible reasons could exist for this transaction. The acquisition may be simply an investment or possibly an attempt by Sun to forestall a takeover move by Pop. Regardless, Sun subsequently accounts for these shares according to *SFAS 115*. To simplify the illustration, it is assumed that Pop's shares are not traded actively and therefore continuous market values are unavailable.

Under these circumstances, the investment in Pop is carried appropriately on Sun's books at original cost.

On January 1, 1999, Pop manages to gain control over Sun by acquiring a 70 percent ownership interest, thus creating a business combination. Details of Pop's purchase are as follows:

Purchase price of 70% interest, 1/1/99 . . . . $500,000
Sun Company's reported book value, 1/1/99   600,000
Excess cost over book value—assumed to be goodwill . . . . 40-year life
Investment is being accounted for internally by means of the cost method.

During the ensuing years, these two companies report the following balances and transactions:

| | Sun Company | | | Pop Company | | |
| | Reported Operating | Dividend Income (10 percent | Dividends | Reported Operating | Dividend Income (70 percent | Dividends |
Year	Income	ownership)	Paid	Income	ownership)	Paid
1998	$20,000	$3,000	$ 8,000	$ 90,000	–0–	$30,000
1999	30,000	5,000	10,000	130,000	$ 7,000	50,000
2000	40,000	7,000	15,000	160,000	10,500	70,000

Treasury Stock Approach Illustrated   One possible consolidation of Pop and Sun for the year of 2000 is presented in Exhibit 7–2. This worksheet has been developed under the treasury stock approach to mutual ownerships so that Pop's investment in Sun is consolidated along routine lines. This process begins with the determination of goodwill and the computation of annual amortization:

Purchase price . . . . $ 500,000
Proportionate interest in Sun's book value ($600,000 × 70%) . . . . (420,000)
Goodwill, January 1, 1999 . . . . $ 80,000
Annual amortization—40-year life . . . . $ 2,000
Unamortized balance, January 1, 2000 . . . . $ 78,000

Following the calculation of goodwill and amortization, regular worksheet entries can be developed for Pop's investment. Since the cost method has been applied, the $7,000 dividend income recognized in the prior years of ownership (only 1999, in this case) is converted to an equity accrual in Entry *C. The parent should recognize 70 percent of the subsidiary's $35,000 income for 1999, or $24,500.[1] However, inclusion of the $2,000 amortization expense (computed above) dictates that $22,500 is the appropriate equity accrual. Because $7,000 in dividend income has already been recognized by the parent, Entry *C records the necessary increase as $15,500 ($22,500 − $7,000).[2]

---

[1]Although an intercompany transfer, the $5,000 dividend received from Pop is included here in measuring the subsidiary's previous income. Sun's book value was increased by this cash distribution; thus, some accounting must be made within the consolidation process. In addition, at the time of payment, the parent reduced its retained earnings. Hence, the intercompany portion of this dividend has to be reinstated or consolidated retained earnings will be too low.

[2]The necessary adjustment to beginning retained earnings also can be computed as follows:

Income of subsidiary—1999 . . . . $ 35,000
Dividends paid . . . .   (10,000)
Increase in book value . . . . $ 25,000
Ownership percentage 70%
Income accrual . . . . $ 17,500
Amortization—1999 . . . .   (2,000)
Increase in beginning retained earnings . . . . $ 15,500

Exhibit 7–2

Investment: Cost Method
Mutual Ownership: Treasury
* Stock Approach*

POP AND CONSOLIDATED SUBSIDIARY
Consolidation Worksheet
For Year Ending December 31, 2000

Accounts	Pop Company	Sun Company	Consolidation Entries Debit	Consolidation Entries Credit	Noncontrolling Interest	Consolidated Totals
Income Statement						
Revenues	(900,000)	(400,000)				(1,300,000)
Expenses	740,000	360,000	(E) 2,000			1,102,000
Dividend income	(10,500)	(7,000)	(I) 17,500			–0–
Noncontrolling interest in Sun Company's income ($47,000 × 30%)	–0–	–0–			(14,100)	14,100
Net income	(170,500)	(47,000)				(183,900)
Statement of Retained Earnings						
Retained earnings, 1/1/00:						
Pop Company	(747,000)	–0–		(*C) 15,500		(762,500)
Sun Company	–0–	(425,000)	(S) 425,000			–0–
Net income (above)	(170,500)	(47,000)				(183,900)
Dividends paid:						
Pop Company	70,000	–0–		(I) 7,000		63,000
Sun Company	–0–	15,000		(I) 10,500	4,500	–0–
Retained earnings, 12/31/00	(847,500)	(457,000)				(883,400)
Balance Sheet						
Current assets	855,500	331,000				1,186,500
Investment in Sun Company	500,000	–0–	(*C) 15,500	(S) 437,500 (A) 78,000		–0–
Investment in Pop Company	–0–	120,000		(TS) 120,000		–0–
Land, building, equipment (net)	642,000	516,000				1,158,000
Goodwill	–0–	–0–	(A) 78,000	(E) 2,000		76,000
Total assets	1,997,500	967,000				2,420,500
Liabilities	(550,000)	(310,000)				(860,000)
Noncontrolling interest in Sun Company, 1/1/00	–0–	–0–		(S) 187,500	(187,500)	
Noncontrolling interest in Sun Company, 12/31/00	–0–	–0–			(197,100)	(197,100)
Common stock	(600,000)	(200,000)	(S) 200,000			(600,000)
Retained earnings, 12/31/00 (above)	(847,500)	(457,000)				(883,400)
Treasury stock	–0–	–0–	(TS) 120,000			120,000
Total liabilities and equities	(1,997,500)	(967,000)				(2,420,500)

Note: Parentheses indicate a credit balance.

Consolidation entries:

(*C) Conversion of cost method to equity method. This entry recognizes 70 percent of the 1999 increase in Sun Company's book value ($25,000 × 70% = $17,500) less $2,000 amortization expense applicable to that year.

 (S) Elimination of subsidiary's stockholders' equity accounts along with recognition of January 1, 2000, noncontrolling interest.

(TS) Reclassification of Sun Company's ownership in Pop Company into a Treasury Stock account.

 (A) Allocation to goodwill, unamortized balance being recorded as of January 1, 2000.

 (I) Elimination of intercompany dividend income for the period.

 (E) Recognition of amortization expense for the current year.

The remaining entries relating to Pop's investment are standard: the stockholders' equity accounts of the subsidiary are eliminated (Entry S), the goodwill allocation is recognized (Entry A), and so on. Only two facets of Exhibit 7–2 have actually been affected by the existence of the mutual ownership. First, the $120,000 payment made by Sun for the parent's shares is reclassified into a Treasury Stock account (through Entry TS). Second, the $7,000 intercompany dividend flowing from Pop to Sun during the current year of 2000 is eliminated within Entry I (Entry I is used because the collection was recorded as income). The simplicity of applying the treasury stock approach should be apparent from this one example.

Before leaving the treasury stock approach, a final comment needs to be made in connection with the computation of the noncontrolling interest's share of Sun's income. In Exhibit 7–2, this balance is recorded as $14,100, or 30 percent of the subsidiary's $47,000 net income figure. A question can be raised as to the validity of including the $7,000 dividend within this income total since that payment is eliminated within the consolidation.

These dividends, although intercompany in nature, do increase the book value of the subsidiary company (see footnote 1). Therefore, the increment must be reflected in some manner to indicate the change in the amount attributed to the outsider owners. For example, the increase could have been recognized through a direct adjustment of $2,100 (30 percent of $7,000) in the noncontrolling interest balance being reported. More often, as shown here, such cash transfers are considered to be income *when viewed from the perspective of these other unrelated parties.*

Conventional Approach Illustrated   Exhibit 7–3 presents the consolidation of this same business combination based on the conventional method of reporting mutual holdings. Although many aspects of the worksheet also are routine, several entries involve procedures unique to the conventional approach. These distinctive elements concern the investment income accruals recorded for both Pop and Sun. According to the conventional approach, these figures must be calculated by identical methods to avoid any inconsistency.

Because each of the stock purchases is maintained at cost, equity accruals (Entry *C) must be established to correct the recording of all pre-2000 investment earnings. This process should begin with the earliest acquisition: the purchase made by Sun. According to the schedule presented previously, Sun reported $23,000 in total earnings (operating income plus dividends) for 1998. However, based on the data given, Sun's *realized* income for that year was actually $29,000: its own $20,000 operating profit plus an accrual of 10 percent of Pop's earnings ($9,000 or 10 percent of $90,000). To record the appropriate investment income for this initial period, a $6,000 ($29,000 − $23,000) increase in Sun's beginning retained earnings must be included on the worksheet. No special difficulty is encountered in arriving at this first amount since the mutual ownership did not yet exist in 1998.

Before leaving this 1998 adjustment, an explanation is warranted concerning the validity of making an equity income accrual for a time period in which only 10 percent ownership was maintained. The business combination formed by these two companies did not come into existence until Pop's subsequent purchase on January 1, 1999.

Despite the limited level of ownership at the time, a $6,000 equity accrual is still required for 1998 to report the subsequently created combination. As discussed in Chapter 1, retroactive adjustment to the equity method is mandated when such changes occur in the relationship between two companies. Only by applying this approach consistently can comparable financial statements be produced from year to year. Consequently, this $6,000 income accrual is recorded within the 2000 consolidation as an increase in the subsidiary's beginning retained earnings. The amount is included as a component of Entry *C1 found on the worksheet.

Computation of equity income accruals becomes significantly more involved in 1999 upon the creation of the mutual ownership. Since neither company's realized

E x h i b i t   7 – 3

Investment: Cost Method
Mutual Ownership:
Conventional Approach

POP AND CONSOLIDATED SUBSIDIARY
Consolidation Worksheet
For Year Ending December 31, 2000

Accounts	Pop Company	Sun Company	Consolidation Entries Debit	Consolidation Entries Credit	Noncontrolling Interest	Consolidated Totals
Income Statement						
Revenues	(900,000)	(400,000)				(1,300,000)
Expenses	740,000	360,000	(E) 1,895			1,101,895
Dividend income	(10,500)	(7,000)	(I) 17,500			–0–
Noncontrolling interest in Sun						–0–
Company's income	–0–	–0–			18,003	18,003
Net income	(170,500)	(47,000)			(18,003)	(180,102)
Statement of Retained Earnings						
Retained earnings, 1/1/00:						
Pop Company	(747,000)		(SS) 77,033	(*C2) 23,328		(693,295)
Sun Company		(425,000)	(S) 442,033	(*C1) 17,033		–0–
Net income (above)	(170,500)	(47,000)				(180,102)
Dividends paid:						
Pop Company	70,000			(I) 7,000		63,000
Sun Company		15,000		(I) 10,500	4,500	–0–
Retained earnings, 12/31/00	(847,500)	(457,000)				(810,397)

Balance Sheet

	Pop Company	Sun Company	Debit	Credit	Noncontrolling Interest	Consolidated Totals
Current assets	855,500	331,000				1,186,500
Investment in Sun Company	500,000	-0-	(*C2) 23,328	(S) 449,423 (A) 73,905		-0-
Investment in Pop Company	-0-	120,000	(*C1) 17,033	(SS) 137,033		-0-
Land, building, equipment (net)	642,000	516,000				1,158,000
Goodwill	-0-	-0-	(A) 73,905	(E) 1,895		72,010
Total assets	1,997,500	967,000				2,416,510
Liabilities	(550,000)	(310,000)				(860,000)
Noncontrolling interest in Sun Company, 1/1/00	-0-	-0-		(S) 192,610	(192,610)	-0-
Noncontrolling interest in Sun Company, 12/31/00					(206,113)	(206,113)
Common stock: Pop Company	(600,000)		(SS) 60,000			(540,000)
Sun Company		(200,000)	(S) 200,000			-0-
Retained earnings, 12/31/00 (above)	(847,500)	(457,000)				(810,397)
Total liabilities and equities	(1,997,500)	(967,000)				(2,416,510)

Note: Parentheses indicate a credit balance.

Consolidation entries:

(*C1) Conversion of cost method to equity method for Sun's investment in Pop. This accrual for prior years (1998–1999) is computed by solving a set of simultaneous equations.

(*C2) Conversion of cost method to equity method for Pop's investment in Sun. This accrual for the prior year (1999) is computed by solving a set of simultaneous equations.

(S) Elimination of subsidiary's stockholders' equity accounts along with recognition of January 1, 2000, noncontrolling interest.

(SS) Elimination of 10 percent of Pop's stockholders' equity in recognition of intercompany holdings of Sun.

(A) Allocation to goodwill, unamortized balance being recorded as of January 1, 2000.

(I) Elimination of intercompany dividend income for the period.

(E) Recognition of amortization expense for the current year.

earnings can be determined first, they must be solved simultaneously. The following set of equations provides the appropriate realized income figures for each company:

Sun's realized income
= Sun's operating income + 10% of Pop's realized income

and

Pop's realized income
= Pop's operating income + 70% of Sun's realized income

Only two of the balances needed in these equations are available for 1999: Sun's operating income for this year already has been reported as $30,000 while Pop's profits amounted to $128,105. The total for Pop comes from the $130,000 figure indicated previously for 1999 less $1,895 in amortization expense relating to its investment in Sun. This expense differs from the annual $2,000 charge previously derived in producing Exhibit 7–2. The change is necessary because the $6,000 accrual attributed above to Sun for 1998 alters the realized book value of the subsidiary on the date of the parent's purchase to $606,000. This adjustment, based on application of the conventional approach, was not made in the treasury stock approach.

Purchase price—70% of Sun Company		$ 500,000
Proportionate interest in Sun Company's book value:		
Reported book value, 1/1/99	$600,000	
Adjustment to book value—1998 equity income		
accrual relating to investment	6,000	
Adjusted book value, 1/1/999.	606,000	
Ownership interest.	70%	(424,200)
Goodwill		$ 75,800
Annual amortization—40-year life		$ 1,895

By inserting the two operating income figures, the simultaneous equations can be restated as follows. SRI and PRI are used here to indicate Sun's realized income and Pop's realized income, respectively.

SRI = $30,000 + 10% of PRI
and
PRI = $128,105 + 70% of SRI

To arrive at a single equation containing only one unknown, the equivalency of PRI formulated in the second equation can be used as a replacement within the first. In addition, to facilitate making the necessary mathematical computations, all percentages are restated in their decimal equivalents. Through these two alterations, the first equation can be solved to derive Sun's realized income for 1999:

SRI = $30,000 + .10 ($128,105 + .70 SRI)

SRI = $30,000 + $12,810.50 + .07 SRI

.93 SRI = $42,810.50

SRI = $46,033 (rounded)

A quick comparison of Sun's 1999 realized income of $46,033 with the reported earnings of $35,000 (from operations and dividends) indicates a required increase in the subsidiary's retained earnings of $11,033. *This increment properly records the 1999 income of Sun derived from the investment in the parent company.* Thus, to consolidate the pre-2000 earnings of Sun, a total increase of $17,033 is recognized in Entry *C1 as of January 1, 2000, $6,000 in connection with 1998, and $11,033 for 1999.

Accrual of Sun's Equity Income for Years Prior to 2000

Year	Sun's Realized Income	Sun's Reported Income	Accrual
1998	$29,000	$23,000	$ 6,000
1999	46,033	35,000	11,033
Total increase in subsidiary's 2000 beginning retained earnings—Entry *C1			$17,033

A 1999 equity accrual for Pop's income also is required under the conventional approach because of the mutual ownership at that time. This adjustment must be determined in an identical manner. The second simultaneous equation is incorporated for this purpose along with the appropriate replacement from the first:

$$PRI = \$128,105 + .70\ (\$30,000 + .10\ PRI)$$
$$PRI = \$128,105 + \$21,000 + .07\ PRI$$
$$.93\ PRI = \$149,105$$
$$PRI = \$160,328\ \text{(rounded)}$$

Based on this calculated total of $160,328, Pop's originally reported income of $137,000 (operations plus dividends) must be updated on the worksheet by $23,328 (Entry *C2). Through this adjustment, the 1999 income earned from the investment in the subsidiary is correctly included in the consolidated retained earnings.

Having accounted for the pre-2000 operations of this business combination, the remaining consolidation entries utilized in Exhibit 7–3 are mostly routine. However, the elimination of Sun's Investment in Pop (Entry SS) merits further attention. The worksheet shows the parent with beginning stockholders' equity for 2000 of $1,370,328: common stock of $600,000 plus a January 1 retained earnings balance of $770,328 (after increasing the previously recorded income through Entry *C2). Since Sun's original purchase price was equal to Pop's proportionate book value, the newly adjusted investment balance of $137,033 necessarily equates to 10 percent of this same total. The investment was 10 percent of Pop's book value when acquired and Entry *C1 (based on the solution of the simultaneous equations) maintains this agreement.

Consequently, Sun's investment account can be eliminated on the worksheet (Entry SS) by a direct write-off against this portion of Pop's stockholders' equity; 10 percent of the company's common stock and 10 percent of its beginning retained earnings are eliminated. Although this process is more complicated than recording the cost of the intercompany purchase as treasury stock, the same goal is achieved: parent shares held by the subsidiary are not reported as outstanding on the consolidated statements. However, income is assigned to the subsidiary in the same manner that Pop used in recognizing income on its investment.

One final aspect of the consolidation process presented in Exhibit 7–3 should be analyzed: the 2000 computation of the noncontrolling interest in Sun's income (shown on the worksheet as $18,003). As in all previous illustrations, this allocation is based on the realized income of the subsidiary. However, under the conventional approach, the figure must be determined by solving two simultaneous equations. For this computation, Pop's operating income for the period ($160,000) has, once again, been reduced by $1,895 in amortization.

$$SRI = \$40,000 + 10\%\ \text{of PRI}$$
$$\text{and}$$
$$PRI = \$158,105 + 70\%\ \text{of SRI}$$
$$\text{therefore}$$
$$SRI = \$40,000 + .10\ (\$158,105 + .70\ SRI)$$
$$SRI = \$40,000 + \$15,810.50 + .07\ SRI$$
$$.93\ SRI = \$55,810.50$$
$$SRI = \$60,011\ \text{(rounded)}$$

The subsidiary's realized income is $60,011. Since the noncontrolling interest possesses 30 percent of Sun's voting stock, $18,003 ($60,011 × 30%) of the consolidated income is assigned to these outside owners. This balance varies significantly from the $14,100 allocation that was calculated under the treasury stock approach and recognized in Exhibit 7–2. Indeed, several of the consolidated totals (retained earnings, net income, etc.) will differ depending on the method adopted. Under the conventional approach, a portion of the parent's income is being assigned to the subsidiary. Consequently, a higher realized earnings figure is normally calculated for the subsidiary each year, an increase that produces an impact on the consolidated income balances.

Although the discussion here has focused exclusively on mutual ownerships between a parent and a subsidiary, similar relationships can exist between two subsidiaries within a business combination. The consolidation principles that are applicable in this circumstance are not altered substantially. The only major difference created by this configuration is that the treasury stock approach is no longer a viable option because parent shares are not being held. Rather, the conventional approach must be utilized based, once again, on determining realized income figures through the solution of two simultaneous equations.

INCOME TAX ACCOUNTING FOR A BUSINESS COMBINATION

This textbook has not attempted to analyze the income tax implications involved in corporate mergers and acquisitions. Numerous complexities inherent in the tax laws in this area necessitate that only a comprehensive tax course can provide complete coverage. Furthermore, essential accounting issues may become overshadowed by intermingling an explanation of the financial reporting process with an in-depth study of related tax consequences.

Thus, coverage to this point of business combinations and consolidated financial statements has been designed solely to develop a basic understanding of the reporting that is required when one company gains control over another. The effort to isolate the examination of conceptual accounting matters is not intended to minimize the importance of the tax laws as they concern consolidated entities. In reality, one of the motives behind the creation of many business combinations is the reduction of tax liabilities.

Despite the desire to focus attention on basic accounting issues, income taxes can never be ignored. Certain elements of the tax laws have a direct impact on the financial reporting of any business combination. At a minimum, recognition of current income tax expense figures as well as deferred income taxes are required to present fairly the financial statements of the consolidated entity. Therefore, an introduction to the income taxation of a business combination is necessary for a complete understanding of the financial reporting process.

Affiliated Groups

A central issue in accounting for the income taxes of a business combination is the method by which the entity's tax returns are filed. For many combinations, only a single consolidated return is required whereas in other cases separate returns are prepared for some, or even all, of the component corporations. According to current tax laws, a business combination may elect to file a consolidated return encompassing all companies that comprise an *affiliated group* as defined by the Internal Revenue Code. All other corporations are automatically required to submit separate income tax returns. Consequently, a first step in working with the taxation process is the delineation of the boundaries of an affiliated group. Because of specific requirements outlined in the tax laws, this designation does not necessarily cover the same constituents as a business combination.

According to the Internal Revenue Code, the essential criterion for including a subsidiary within an affiliated group is the parent's ownership of at least 80 percent of the voting stock as well as at least 80 percent of each class of nonvoting stock. This ownership may be direct or indirect, although the parent must meet these requirements in connection with at least one directly owned subsidiary. As another condition, each company included in the affiliated group has to be a domestic (rather than a foreign) corporation. A company's options can be described as follows:

- Domestic subsidiary, 80 percent to 100 percent owned: may file as part of consolidated return or may file separately.
- Domestic subsidiary, less than 80 percent owned: must file separately.
- Foreign subsidiary: must file separately.

Clearly, a distinction can be drawn between business combinations (identified for financial reporting) and affiliated groups as defined for tax purposes. In Chapter 2, a business combination was described as containing all subsidiaries controlled by a parent company unless control was only temporary. Control is normally evidenced by the possession (either directly or indirectly) of a mere majority of voting stock. Conversely, the 80 percent rule established by the Internal Revenue Code creates a smaller circle of companies qualifying for inclusion in an affiliated group.

For the companies that compose an affiliated group, the filing of a consolidated tax return provides several distinct benefits:

- Intercompany profits are not taxed until realized, although in a similar manner, intercompany losses (which are rare) are not deducted until finally culminated.
- Intercompany dividends are nontaxable (this exclusion applies to all dividends between members of an affiliated group regardless of whether a consolidated return is filed).
- Losses incurred by one affiliated company can be used to reduce taxable income earned by other members of that group.

Many companies can't resist the lure of consolidated tax returns. When corporate parent companies file such returns, they can offset profits with losses from any members of their affiliated groups.[3]

Deferred Income Taxes

Some of the deviations between generally accepted accounting principles and income tax laws create *temporary differences* whereby (1) a variation exists between an asset or liability's recorded book value and its tax basis and (2) this difference results in taxable or deductible amounts in future years. Whenever a temporary difference is present, the recognition of a deferred tax asset or liability is required for financial reporting purposes. The specific amount of this income tax deferral depends somewhat on whether consolidated or separate returns are being filed. Thus, the tax consequences of several common transactions are analyzed here as a means of demonstrating the recording of income tax expense by a business combination.

Intercompany Dividends   For financial reporting, dividends between the members of a business combination always are eliminated; they represent intercompany transfers of cash. In tax accounting, dividends also are removed from income but only if at least 80 percent of the subsidiary's stock is held. Consequently, with this level of ownership, no difference exists between financial and tax reporting; all intercompany dividends are eliminated in both cases. Income tax expense is not recorded. Deferred tax recognition is also ignored because no temporary difference has been created.

However, if less than 80 percent of subsidiary's stock is held, tax recognition becomes necessary. Any intercompany dividends are taxed partially because, at that

---

[3]*Journal of Accountancy,* Tax Briefs, October 1993.

level of ownership, 20 percent is taxable. The dividend received deduction on the tax return (the nontaxable portion) is only 80 percent.[4] Thus, an income tax liability is immediately created for the recipient. *In addition, deferred income taxes are required for any of the subsidiary's income not paid currently as a dividend.* A temporary difference has been created because tax payments will be necessary in future years when the earnings of this investment eventually are distributed to the parent. Hence, a current tax liability is recorded based on the dividends collected and a deferred tax liability is recorded for the taxable portion of any income not paid to the parent during the year.

Amortization of Goodwill   In a business combination, goodwill is amortized over an expected life of up to 40 years. Historically goodwill has not been deductible for tax purposes; however, the Revenue Reconciliation Act of 1993 now allows the deduction of goodwill and other purchased intangibles over a 15-year period. If the period of deduction for tax and financial reporting purposes is the same, there is no deferred income tax recognition from goodwill amortization.

Unrealized Intercompany Gains   Taxes on the unrealized gains that can result from transfers made between the related companies within a business combination create a special accounting problem. On consolidated financial statements, the impact of all such transactions is deferred. The same handling is true for a consolidated tax return; the gains are removed until realized. No temporary difference is created.

If separate returns are filed, though, tax laws require the profits to be reported in the period of transfer even though unearned by the business combination. Thus, the income is taxed immediately, prior to being earned from a financial reporting perspective. This "prepayment" of the tax creates a deferred income tax asset.[5]

Consolidated Tax Returns—Illustration

As an illustration of the accounting effects created by the filing of a consolidated tax return, assume that Great Company possesses 90 percent of Small Company's voting and nonvoting stocks. Subsequent to the acquisition, the two companies continued normal operations, which included significant intercompany transactions. Each company's operational and dividend incomes for the current time period follow as well as the effects of unrealized gains. No income tax accruals have been recognized within these totals.

	Great Company	Small Company (90% owned)
Operating income (excludes equity or dividend income from subsidiary)	$160,000	$40,000
Net unrealized gains in current year income (included in operating income above)	30,000	8,000
Dividend income (from Small)	9,000	–0–
Dividends paid	20,000	10,000

---

[4]If less than 20 percent of a company's stock is owned, the dividend received deduction is only 70 percent. However, this level of ownership is not applicable to a subsidiary within a business combination.

[5]In *SFAS 109,* the FASB required deferral of the amount of taxes paid on the unrealized gain by the seller. This approach was taken rather than computing the deferral based on the future tax effect caused by the difference between the buyer's book value and tax basis, a procedure consistent with the rest of the pronouncement. According to paragraph 124, this decision was made to help "eliminate the need for complex cross-currency deferred tax computations" when the parties are in separate tax jurisdictions.

From the perspective of the single economic entity, Great's individual income for the period amounts to $130,000, $160,000 in operational earnings less $30,000 in unrealized gains. Using this same approach, Small's income is calculated as $32,000 after removing the effects of the intercompany transfers ($40,000 operating income less $8,000 in unrealized gains). Thus, the income to be reported in consolidated financial statements before the reduction for noncontrolling interest is $162,000 ($130,000 + $32,000). For financial reporting, both intercompany dividends and unrealized gains have been omitted in arriving at this total. Income prior to the noncontrolling interest has been computed here since any allocation to these other owners is not deductible for tax purposes.

Because the parent owns more than 80 percent of Small's stock, the dividends collected from the subsidiary are tax free. Likewise, the intercompany gains are not taxable presently since a consolidated return is being filed. Hence, *financial and tax accounting are the same for both items;* neither of these figures produces a temporary difference so that recognition of a deferred income tax is ignored.

The affiliated group pays taxes on $162,000. Assuming an effective rate of 30 percent, $48,600 ($162,000 × 30%) must be conveyed to the government this year. Because no temporary differences are present, deferred income tax recognition is not applicable. Consequently, $48,600 is the only expense reported in connection with current income. This amount should be recorded as the income tax expense for the consolidated entity by means of a worksheet entry or through an individual accrual recorded by each company.

Assigning Income Tax Expense—Consolidated Return

Whenever a consolidated tax return is filed, an allocation of the total expense between the two parties must be determined. This figure is especially important to the subsidiary if it has to produce separate financial statements for a loan or a future issuance of equity. The subsidiary's expense also is needed as a basis for calculating the noncontrolling interest's share of consolidated income.

Several techniques exist to accomplish this proration. For example, the expense charged to the subsidiary often is based on the percentage of the total taxable income that comes from each company (the percentage allocation method) or on the taxable income figures that would be appropriate if separate returns were filed (the separate return method).[6]

To illustrate, the figures from Great and Small in the previous example are again utilized. Great owned 90 percent of Small's outstanding stock. Based on filing a consolidated return, total income tax expense of $48,600 was recognized. How should this figure be allocated between these two companies?

Percentage Allocation Method   Total taxable income on this consolidated return was $162,000. Of this amount, $130,000 was applicable to the parent (operating income after deferral of unrealized gain) while $32,000 came from the subsidiary (computed in the same manner). Thus, 19.8 percent ($32,000/$162,000, rounded) of total expense should be assigned to the subsidiary, an amount that equals $9,622.80 (19.8 percent of $48,600).

Separate Return Method   On separate returns, intercompany gains are taxable. Therefore, the separate returns of these two companies would appear as follows:

---

[6]For other methods, see "How to Allocate a Consolidated Tax Liability among Members of the Affiliated Group," in the October 1986 issue of *The Practical Accountant;* or "Uncharted Territory: Subsidiary Financial Reporting," in the October 1989 issue of *Journal of Accountancy.*

	Great	Small	Total
Operating income	$160,000	$40,000	
Assumed tax rate	30%	30%	
Income tax expense—separate returns	$ 48,000	$12,000	$60,000

By filing a consolidated return, an expense of only $48,600 is recorded for the business combination. Because 20 percent of taxable income on the separate returns ($12,000/$60,000) came from the subsidiary, $9,720 of the expense ($48,600 × 20%) should be assigned to Small.

Under this second approach, the noncontrolling interest's share of this subsidiary's income is computed as follows:

Small Company—reported income	$40,000
Less: Unrealized intercompany gains..................................	(8,000)
Less: Assigned income tax expense	(9,720)
Small Company—realized income	22,280
Outside ownership..	10%
Noncontrolling interest in Small Company's income	$ 2,228

Filing Separate Tax Returns

Despite the advantages of filing as an affiliated group, a single consolidated return cannot be used always to encompass every member of a business combination. Separate returns are mandatory for foreign subsidiaries as well as for domestic corporations not meeting the 80 percent ownership rule. However, even if the conditions for inclusion within an affiliated group are met, a company may still elect to file separately. If all companies in an affiliated group are profitable and few intercompany transactions occur, separate returns may be preferred. By filing in this manner, the various companies have more flexibility in their choice of accounting methods as well as fiscal tax years.[7] Tax laws, though, do not allow a company to switch back and forth between consolidated and separate returns. Once a company elects to file a consolidated tax return as part of an affiliated group, obtaining permission from the Internal Revenue Service to file separately can be difficult.

The filing of a separate tax return by a member of a business combination often creates temporary differences because of (1) the immediate taxation of unrealized gains (and losses) and (2) the possible future tax effect of any subsidiary income in excess of dividend payments. Since temporary differences can result, recognition of a deferred tax asset or liability may be necessary. For example, as mentioned previously, intercompany gains and losses must be included on a separate return at the time of transfer rather than when the earning process is culminated. These gains and losses appear on both sets of records but, if unrealized at year's end, in different time periods. A temporary difference is produced between the transferred asset's book value and tax basis that affects future tax computations; thus, deferred taxes must be reported.

For dividend payments, deferred taxes are not required if 80 percent or more of the subsidiary's stock is owned. The transfer is nontaxable even on a separate return; no expense recognition is required.

If the amount distributed by a subsidiary that is less than 80 percent owned is equal to current earnings, 20 percent of the collection is taxed immediately but no temporary difference is created because no future tax effect is produced. Hence, again, deferred income tax recognition is not appropriate.

---

[7]At one time, the filing of separate returns was especially popular as a means of taking advantage of reduced tax rates on lower income levels. However, in the early part of the 1970s, Congress eliminated the availability of this tax saving.

Conceptually, though, as discussed in Chapter 1, questions arise about the recognition of deferred taxes when a subsidiary less than 80 percent owned pays fewer dividends than its current income. If a subsidiary earns, for example, $100,000 but pays dividends of only $60,000, will the parent's share of the $40,000 remainder ever become taxable income? Do these undistributed earnings represent temporary differences? If so, immediate recognition of the associated tax effect is required even though payment of this $40,000 may not be anticipated for the foreseeable future.

In response to these concerns, *FASB Statement No. 109*, "Accounting for Income Taxes," February 1992 (par. 32) states that "a deferred tax liability shall be recognized for . . . an excess of the amount for financial reporting over the tax basis of an investment in a domestic subsidiary." Therefore, other than one exception noted later in this chapter, a temporary difference is created by any portion of the subsidiary's income not distributed in the form of dividends. These earnings would not be taxed until a later date; thus, a deferred tax liability is created. Because many companies retain a substantial portion of their income to finance growth, an expense is recognized here that might never be paid.

Deferred Tax on Undistributed Earnings—Illustrated   Accounting for the income tax effect created by undistributed earnings probably is demonstrated best through a practical example. Assume that Parent Company owns 70 percent of Child Company. Because ownership is less than 80 percent, the filing of separate tax returns for the two companies is mandatory. In the current year, Parent's operational earnings (excluding taxes and any income from this investment) amount to $200,000 while Child reports a pretax net income of $100,000. During the period, the subsidiary paid a total of $20,000 in cash dividends, $14,000 (70 percent) to Parent, with the remainder going to the other owners. To avoid complications in this initial example, the assumption is made that no unrealized intercompany gains and losses are present.

The reporting of Child's income taxes does not provide a significant difficulty because no temporary differences are involved. Using an assumed tax rate of 30 percent, the subsidiary accrues income tax expense of $30,000 ($100,000 × 30%), leaving an after-tax profit of $70,000. *Because only $20,000 in dividends were paid, undistributed earnings for the period amount to $50,000.*

For Parent, Child's undistributed earnings represent a temporary tax difference. The following schedules have been developed to calculate Parent's current tax liability and deferred tax liability:

Income Tax Currently Payable—Parent Company

Reported operating income—Parent Company		$200,000
Dividends received	$ 14,000	
Less: Dividend deduction (80%)	(11,200)	2,800
Taxable income—current year		202,800
Tax rate		30%
Income tax payable—current period (Parent)		$ 60,840

Deferred Income Tax Payable—Parent Company

Undistributed earnings of Child Company	$ 50,000
Parent Company's ownership	70%
Undistributed earnings accruing to Parent	35,000
Dividend deduction upon eventual distribution (80%)	(28,000)
Income to be taxed—subsequent dividend payments	7,000
Tax rate	30%
Deferred income tax payable	$ 2,100

These computations indicate a total income tax expense of $62,940: a current liability of $60,840 and a deferred liability of $2,100. The deferred balance results entirely from the undistributed earnings of Child. Although the subsidiary had an after-tax income of $70,000, only $20,000 was distributed in the form of dividends. According to *FASB Statement 109,* just quoted, the $50,000 being retained by Child represents a temporary tax difference to the stockholders. Thus, recognition of the deferred income tax associated with these undistributed earnings is required. The income is earned now; therefore, the liability must be recorded in the current period.

FASB Statement 109 is not completely inflexible on this matter; in connection with a subsidiary's undistributed income, one important exception to the recognition of deferred income taxes is provided. The pronouncement (par. 31) states that a deferred tax liability is not recognized for the excess of the amount for financial reporting over the tax basis of an investment in a *foreign* subsidiary unless the reversal of those temporary differences in the foreseeable future becomes apparent.

Thus, in the previous example, if the subsidiary is foreign and if the retention of these excess earnings seems to be permanent, the $2,100 deferred tax liability is omitted, reducing the total reported expense to $60,840.

Separate Tax Returns Illustrated   The full accounting impact created by the filing of separate tax returns can be demonstrated best by a complete example. As a basis for this illustration, assume that the following data has been reported by Lion Corporation and its 60 percent owned subsidiary, Cub Company (a domestic corporation), for the year of 1998.

	Lion Corporation	Cub Company (60/% owned by Lion)
Operating income	$500,000	$200,000
Unrealized intercompany inventory gains (included in operating income)	40,000	30,000
Dividend income from Cub Company	24,000	not applicable
Dividends paid	not applicable	40,000
Applicable tax rate	30%	30%

Subsidiary's Income Tax Expense   Because separate tax returns must be filed, the unrealized gains are not deferred but left within the operating incomes of both companies. Thus, Cub's taxable income for 1998 is $200,000, an amount that creates a current payable of $60,000 ($200,000 × 30%). The unrealized gain is a temporary difference for financial reporting purposes, creating a deferred income tax asset (payment of the tax comes before the income actually is earned) of $9,000 ($30,000 × 30%). Therefore, the appropriate expense to be recognized by the subsidiary for the period is only $51,000:

Income Tax Expense—Cub

Income currently taxable	$ 200,000	
Tax rate	30%	$ 60,000
Temporary difference (unrealized gain is taxed before being earned)	(30,000)	
Tax rate	30%	(9,000)
Income tax expense—Cub		$ 51,000

Consequently, Cub reports after-tax income of $119,000 ($200,000 operating income less $30,000 unrealized gain less $51,000 in income tax expense). This profit figure serves as the basis for recognizing $47,600 ($119,000 × 40% outside ownership) as the noncontrolling interest's share of consolidated income.

Parent's Income Tax Expense   On Lion's separate return, its own unrealized gains remain within income. The taxable portion of the dividends received from Cub also must be included. Hence, the parent's taxable earnings for 1998 would be $504,800, a balance that creates a $151,440 current tax liability for the company.

Income Tax Currently Payable—Lion

Operating income—Lion Corporation (includes $40,000 unrealized gains)		$ 500,000
Dividends received from Cub Company (60%)	$ 24,000	
Less: 80% dividend deduction	(19,200)	4,800
Taxable income		504,800
Tax rate		30%
Income tax payable—current (Lion)		$ 151,440

Although Lion's tax return information is presented here, the total tax expense to be reported for the period can be determined only by accounting for the impact of the two temporary differences: the parent's $40,000 in unrealized gains and the undistributed earnings of the subsidiary. The undistributed earnings amount to $47,400 computed as follows:

After-tax income of Cub (above)	$ 119,000
Dividends paid	(40,000)
Undistributed earnings	79,000
Lion's ownership	60%
Lion's portion of undistributed earnings	$ 47,400

The deferred income tax effects to be recorded by the parent now can be derived.

Deferred Income Taxes—Lion Company

Unrealized Gains

Amount taxable now prior to being earned	$ 40,000
Tax rate	30%
Deferred income tax asset	$ 12,000

Undistributed Earnings of Subsidiary

Undistributed earnings of Cub—to be taxed later (computed above)	$ 47,400
Dividend received deduction upon distribution (80%)	(37,920)
Income eventually taxable	$ 9,480
Tax rate	30%
Deferred income tax liability	$ 2,844

The two temporary differences exert opposite effects on Lion's reported income taxes. Because separate returns are filed, the unrealized gains are taxable in the current period despite not actually having been earned. From an accounting perspective, paying the tax on these gains now creates a deferred income tax asset of $12,000 ($40,000 × 30%). In contrast, the undistributed earnings are recognized currently by the parent (through consolidation of the investment). However, this portion of the subsidiary's income is not yet taxable to the parent. Because the tax payment is not required until the dividends are received, a deferred income tax liability of $2,844 is necessary ($9,480 × 30%).

The deferred tax asset is reported as a current asset since it relates to inventory whereas the deferred tax liability is long-term because it was created by ownership of the investment. Lion's reported income tax expense results from the creation of these three accounts:

Lion's Financial Records

Deferred Income Tax Asset—Current	12,000	
Income Tax Expense	142,284	
Deferred Income Tax Liability—Long-Term		2,844
Income Tax Currently Payable		151,440

To record current and deferred taxes of parent company.

Temporary Differences Generated by Business Combinations

Based on the nature of the transaction, some purchase combinations are deemed tax free (to the seller) by the tax laws whereas others are taxable. In most tax-free purchases and in a few taxable purchases, the resulting book values of the acquired company's assets and liabilities differ from their tax bases. Such differences result because the subsidiary's cost is retained for tax purposes (in tax-free exchanges) or because the allocations for tax purposes vary from those used for financial reporting (a situation found in some taxable transactions).

Thus, temporary differences may be created at the time that a business combination is formed. Any deferred income tax assets and liabilities previously recorded by the subsidiary are not at issue; these accounts are consolidated in the same manner as other assets and liabilities. The question addressed here concerns differences in book value and tax basis that stem from the takeover.

As an illustration, assume that Son Company owns a single asset, a building. This property has a tax basis of $150,000 (cost less accumulated depreciation) but it presently has a fair market value of $210,000. Pop Corporation conveys a total value of $300,000 to acquire this company. The exchange is structured to be tax free. After this transaction, the building continues to have a tax basis of only $150,000. However, its consolidated book value is $210,000, an amount $60,000 more than the figure applicable for tax purposes. How does this $60,000 difference affect the consolidated statements?

In 1992, the FASB issued *Statement of Financial Accounting Standards No. 109,* "Accounting for Income Taxes," which established guidelines for the reporting of deferred income tax assets and liabilities created in a business combination. According to paragraph 127:

> Values are assigned to identified assets and liabilities when a business combination is accounted for as a purchase. The assigned values frequently will be different from the tax bases of those assets and liabilities. The Board concluded that a liability or asset should be recognized for the deferred tax consequences of differences between the assigned values and the tax bases of the assets and liabilities (other than goodwill and leveraged leases) recognized in a purchase business combination.

Thus, according to this pronouncement, a deferred tax asset or liability is created by any temporary difference such as is found in Pop's purchase of Son. Because the tax basis of the asset is $150,000, but its recorded value within consolidated statements is $210,000, a temporary difference of $60,000 exists. Assuming that a 30 percent tax rate is appropriate, a deferred income tax liability of $18,000 ($60,000 × 30%) must be recognized by the newly formed business combination. Before *Statement 109,* this $18,000 would have been reported as a reduction in the consolidated value of the Buildings account. However, a liability is recorded now to reflect the future effect of recognizing lower depreciation for tax purposes (thus creating higher taxable income and additional payments). The FASB also apparently felt that this placement was more consistent with the asset and liability approach required by *Statement 109.*

Consequently, in a consolidated balance sheet prepared immediately after Pop obtains control over Son, the building would be recorded at fair market value of $210,000. In addition, the new deferred tax liability of $18,000 computed earlier is recognized. Because the net value of these two accounts is $192,000, goodwill of $108,000 also is recorded as the figure remaining from the $300,000 purchase price.

This $18,000 liability systematically declines to zero over the life of the building. Depreciation for tax purposes must be computed on the $150,000 cost figure and would, therefore, be less each year than the expense shown for financial reporting purposes (based on $210,000). With less expense, taxable income would be more than book income for the remaining years of the asset's life. However, according to *Statement 109,* the extra payment that results is not charged to expense. Rather, the deferred tax liability (initially established at the date of purchase) is reduced by the additional amount.

To illustrate, assume that revenues of $40,000 per year are generated from this building. Assume also that it has a life of 10 years and that the straight-line method of depreciation is in use.

	Financial Reporting	Income Tax Reporting
Revenues	$ 40,000	$ 40,000
Depreciation expense:		
10% of $210,000	21,000	
10% of $150,000		$ 15,000
Income	$ 19,000	$ 25,000
Tax rate	30%	30%
Tax effect	$ 5,700	$ 7,500

Although $7,500 must be paid to the government, currently reported income would have caused only $5,700 of that amount. The other $1,800 ($6,000 reversal of temporary difference × 30%) resulted because of the use of the previous basis for tax purposes. Therefore, the following entry is made:

Income Tax Expense	5,700	
Deferred Income Tax Liability (to remove part of balance created at		
date of purchase)	1,800	
Income Tax Currently Payable		7,500

To accrue current income taxes as well as impact of temporary difference in asset of subsidiary.

Business Combinations and Operating Loss Carryforwards

Tax laws in the United States provide a measure of relief for companies incurring net operating losses (NOLs) when filing current tax returns. Such losses may be carried back for three years and applied as a reduction to taxable income figures previously reported. This procedure generates a cash refund of income taxes paid by the company during these earlier periods.

If a loss still exists after the carryback (or if the taxpayer elects not to carry the loss back), a carryforward for the subsequent 15 years also is allowed.[8] Carrying the loss forward reduces subsequent taxable income levels until the NOL is eliminated entirely or the time period expires. *Thus, NOL carryforwards can benefit the company only if taxable income can be generated in the future.* The immediate recognition of NOL carryforwards has always been controversial because it requires the company to anticipate making profits. In 1992, *Statement 109* of the Financial Accounting Standards Board established reporting rules for the appropriate recognition of such carryforwards.

---

[8] If a taxpayer believes that tax rates will be higher in the future, choosing not to carry a loss back in favor of only a carryforward may be financially preferable.

Until recently, some business combinations were created, at least in part, to take advantage of tax carryforwards. If an acquired company had an unused NOL while the parent projected significant profitability, the carryforward was used on a consolidated return to reduce income taxes after the acquisition. However, U.S. laws have now been changed so that virtually all of an NOL carryforward can be used only by the company that reported the loss. Hence, the acquisition of companies with an NOL carryforward has ceased to be a popular business strategy. However, since the practice has not disappeared, reporting rules for a subsidiary's NOL carryforward are still needed.

Statement 109 requires the recording of a deferred income tax asset for any NOL carryforward. In addition, though, a valuation allowance also must be recognized

> if, based on the weight of available evidence, it is *more likely than not* (a likelihood of more than 50 percent) that some portion or all of the deferred tax assets will not be realized. The valuation allowance should be sufficient to reduce the deferred tax asset to the amount that is more likely than not to be realized. (par. 17e)

As an example, assume that a company has one asset (a building) worth $500,000. Because of recent losses, this company has an NOL carryforward of $200,000. The assumed tax rate is 30 percent so that a benefit of $60,000 ($200,000 × 30%) will be derived if future taxable profits are earned.

Assume that this company is purchased for $640,000. In accounting for the acquisition, the parent must anticipate the likelihood that some portion or all of the NOL carryforward will ever be utilized by the new subsidiary. If it is more likely than not that the benefit would be realized, goodwill of $80,000 results:

Purchase price		$640,000
Subsidiary assets:		
Building	$500,000	
Deferred income tax asset	60,000	560,000
Goodwill		$ 80,000

Conversely, if the chances that this subsidiary will use the NOL carryforward are only 50 percent or less, a valuation allowance must be recognized and consolidated goodwill is $140,000:

Purchase price			$640,000
Subsidiary assets:			
Building		$500,000	
Deferred income tax asset	$ 60,000		
Valuation allowance	(60,000)	–0–	500,000
Goodwill			$140,000

In this second case, a question arises if future taxes are successfully reduced by this carryforward: How should the valuation allowance be removed? *Statement 109* requires that these subsequent benefits be recorded as a reduction to goodwill. Only if this asset is decreased to zero should income tax expense be reduced.

SUMMARY

1. For consolidation purposes, a parent need not possess majority ownership of each of the component companies constituting a business combination. Often, control is of an indirect nature; a majority of one subsidiary's shares are held by another subsidiary. Although the parent might own stock in only one of these companies, control has been established over both. Such an arrangement often is referred to as a father-son-grandson or a pyramid configuration.

2. The consolidation of financial information for a father-son-grandson business combination does not differ conceptually from a consolidation involving only direct ownership. All intercompany, reciprocal balances are eliminated. Goodwill, other allocations, and amortization usually must be recognized if a purchase has taken place. Because more than one investment is involved, the quantity of worksheet entries increases, but that is more of a mechanical inconvenience than a conceptual concern.

3. One aspect of a father-son-grandson consolidation that does warrant attention is the determination of realized income figures for each of the subsidiaries. Any company within a business combination that holds both a parent and subsidiary position must determine the income accruing from ownership of its subsidiary before computing its own realized earnings. This procedure is important because realized income is the basis for each parent's equity accruals as well as noncontrolling interest allocations.

4. If a subsidiary possesses shares of its parent, a mutual affiliation exists. Although this investment is intercompany in nature and must be eliminated for consolidation purposes, the amount to be removed and the income allocated to the subsidiary can be computed in two different ways. The treasury stock approach simply reclassifies the cost of these shares as treasury stock with no equity accrual being recorded. In contrast, the conventional approach accounts for the shares as a regular investment in a related party. Under this second method, equity income accruals are attributed to the subsidiary in connection with ownership of the parent. Because the companies are both in parent and subsidiary positions, the amount of realized income cannot be directly derived by either party. These figures can be found only by solving two simultaneous equations.

5. Under present tax laws, a single consolidated income tax return can be filed by an affiliated group. Only domestic corporations are included and 80 percent of the voting stock as well as 80 percent of the nonvoting stock must be controlled (either directly or indirectly) by the parent. A consolidated return allows the companies to defer recognition of intercompany gains until realized. Furthermore, losses incurred by one member of the group reduce taxable income earned by the others. Intercompany dividends are also nontaxable on a consolidated return, although such distributions are never taxable when paid between companies within an affiliated group.

6. For some members of a business combination, separate tax returns are applicable. Foreign corporations, as an example, must report in this manner as well as any company not meeting the 80 percent ownership rule. In addition, a company might simply elect to file in this manner if no advantages are gained from a consolidated return. For financial reporting purposes, a separate return often necessitates recognition of deferred income taxes because temporary differences can result from unrealized transfer gains as well as intercompany dividends (if 80 percent ownership is not held).

7. When a purchase combination is created, the subsidiary's assets and liabilities sometimes have a tax basis that differs from their assigned values. In such cases, a deferred tax asset or liability must be recognized at the time of acquisition to reflect the tax impact of these differences.

COMPREHENSIVE ILLUSTRATION

Problem

(Estimated Time: 60 to 75 Minutes) On January 1, 1998, Gold Company purchased 90 percent of Silver Company for $570,000. This price indicated goodwill of $30,000 based on the subsidiary's total book value of $600,000. The goodwill is expensed over a 15-year period at the rate of $2,000 per year.

Subsequently, on January 1, 1999, Silver acquired 10 percent of Gold for $150,000. This price equaled the appropriately adjusted book value of Gold's underlying net assets. Consequently, no allocation was made to either goodwill or any specific accounts.

On January 1, 2000, Gold and Silver each purchased 30 percent of the outstanding shares of Bronze for $105,000 apiece. Bronze had a book value on that date of $300,000 so the underlying book value of each acquisition was $90,000 ($300,000 × 30%). Hence, goodwill of $15,000 was recognized as a component of each investment. Both goodwill balances are to be amortized over a 15-year period, necessitating an annual expense of $1,000 for Gold and Silver.

After the formation of this business combination, significant intercompany inventory sales were made from Silver to Gold. The volume of these transfers has been as follows:

Year	Transfer Price to Gold Company	Markup on Transfer Price	Inventory Retained at End of Year (at transfer price)
1998	$100,000	30%	$120,000
1999	160,000	25	90,000
2000	200,000	28	120,000

In addition, on July 1, 2000, Gold sold a tract of land to Bronze for $25,000. This property originally had cost $12,000 when acquired by the parent several years ago.

The cost method is used to account for all investments. Income from the investments is recognized by the individual firms when dividends are received. Because consolidated statements are prepared for the business combination, accounting for the investments affects internal reporting only. During 1998 and 1999, Gold and Silver individually reported the following information:

	Gold Company	Silver Company
1998:		
Operational income	$180,000	$120,000
Dividend income—Silver Company (90%)	36,000	–0–
Dividends paid	80,000	40,000
1999:		
Operational income	240,000	150,000
Dividend income—Gold Company (10%)	–0–	9,000
Dividend income—Silver Company (90%)	27,000	–0–
Dividends paid	90,000	30,000

The 2000 financial statements for each of the three companies composing this business combination are presented in Exhibit 7–4. Income tax effects have been ignored in deriving these figures.

Exhibit 7–4
Individual Financial Statements—2000

	Gold Company	Silver Company	Bronze Company
Sales	$ 800,000	$ 600,000	$ 300,000
Cost of goods sold	(380,000)	(300,000)	(120,000)
Operating expenses	(193,000)	(100,000)	(90,000)
Gain on sale of land	13,000	–0–	–0–
Dividend income from Gold Company	–0–	10,000	–0–
Dividend income from Silver Company	36,000	–0–	–0–
Dividend income from Bronze Company	6,000	6,000	–0–
Net income	$ 282,000	$ 216,000	$ 90,000
Retained earnings, 1/1/00	$ 923,200	$ 609,000	$ 200,000
Net income (above)	282,000	216,000	90,000
Dividends paid	(100,000)	(40,000)	(20,000)
Retained earnings, 12/31/00	$1,105,200	$ 785,000	$ 270,000
Cash and receivables	$ 295,000	$ 190,000	$ 130,000
Inventory	459,000	410,000	110,000
Investment in Silver Company	570,000	–0–	–0–
Investment in Gold Company	–0–	150,000	–0–
Investment in Bronze Company	105,000	105,000	–0–
Land, buildings, and equipment (net)	980,000	670,000	380,000
Total assets	$2,409,000	$1,525,000	$ 620,000
Liabilities	$ 603,800	$ 540,000	$ 250,000
Common stock	700,000	200,000	100,000
Retained earnings, 12/31/00	1,105,200	785,000	270,000
Total liabilities and equities	$2,409,000	$1,525,000	$ 620,000

Required

a. Prepare worksheet entries to consolidate the 2000 financial statements for this combination. Assume that the mutual ownership between Gold and Silver is accounted for by means of the conventional approach. Compute the noncontrolling interests in Bronze's income and in Silver's income.

b. Assume that consolidated net income (before deducting any balance for the noncontrolling interests) amounts to $501,900. Assume further that the effective tax rate is 40 percent and that Gold and Silver file a consolidated tax return while Bronze files separately. Calculate the income tax expense to be recognized within the consolidated income statement for 2000.

Solution

a. The 2000 consolidation entries for Gold, Silver, and Bronze follow.

Entry *G The consolidation process begins with Entry *G that recognizes the intercompany gain (on transfers from Silver to Gold) created in the previous period. The unrealized gain within ending inventory is deferred from 1999 into the current period.

*Consolidation Entry *G*

Retained earnings, 1/1/00 (Silver Company) 22,500
    Cost of goods sold 22,500
    To defer unrealized gains on intercompany sales made from Silver
    to Gold during the preceding year (25% markup × $90,000).

Entry *C1 Gold's ownership of Silver has been recorded using the cost method. This worksheet entry converts that number to a balance appropriate for the equity method. According to the information provided, Gold has recognized dividend income on its 90 percent investment in Silver of $36,000 (1998) and $27,000 (1999). However, Silver's total operational income for these prior years, after adjustment for intercompany transfers, amounted to $102,000 and $145,000, respectively:

1998 reported operational income—Silver .... $ 120,000
Less: Unrealized gains (30% markup × $60,000) .... (18,000)
1998 operational income—Silver .... $ 102,000

1999 reported operational income—Silver .... $ 150,000
Add: 1998 gains actually realized in 1999 (from above) 18,000
Less: 1999 unrealized gains (25% markup × $90,000) .... (22,500)
1999 operational income—Silver .... $ 145,500

As the mutual relationship between these two companies did not exist in 1998, the solving of simultaneous equations is not applicable for this initial period. Gold's equity income can be computed directly: 90 percent of Silver's $102,000 in realized earnings ($91,800) less the $2,000 amortization expense associated with this acquisition. The resulting $89,800 balance indicates the need for an additional accrual of $53,800 on the worksheet to correct the $36,000 figure recognized by Gold.

In contrast, Gold's 1999 equity accrual should reflect the mutual relationship that has come into existence. As the conventional approach is to be applied, simultaneous equations will be incorporated. These equations include Silver's 1999 operational income of $145,500 (calculated above) and the $238,000 operational income of Gold (reported earnings for the year less the annual amortization expense).

Gold's 1999 realized income = $238,000 + 90% of Silver's realized income
and
Silver's 1999 realized income = $145,500 + 10% of Gold's realized income
therefore
GRI = $238,000 + .9 ($145,500 + .1 GRI)
GRI = $238,000 + $130,950 + .09 GRI
.91 GRI = $368,950
Gold's realized income = $405,440 (rounded)

Gold recorded income in 1999 of only $267,000 ($240,000 from operations plus $27,000 in dividend income). Its realized income is computed to be $405,440 here; therefore, an additional accrual of $138,440 ($405,440 − $267,000) is required to reflect ownership in Silver during this period. Combined with the $53,800 accrual calculated previously for 1998, a total worksheet adjustment of $192,240 must be made for Gold (Entry *C1) to recognize the appropriate equity income for these two prior years.

Consolidation Entry *C1 (Gold)

Investment in Silver Company	192,240	
Retained Earnings, 1/1/00 (Gold Company)		192,240

To convert Gold's investment income figures for the two preceding years to equity income accruals.

Entry *C2   At the beginning of 1999, Silver obtained a 10 percent interest in Gold, an investment that also has been recorded using the cost method. To apply the conventional approach, Silver must solve the same simultaneous equations as Gold to determine the correct equity accrual. Using these equations, a realized income figure for Silver of $186,044 can be calculated for 1999.

$$SRI = \$145,500 + 10\% \text{ of GRI}$$

and

$$GRI = \$238,000 + 90\% \text{ of SRI}$$

therefore

$$SRI = \$145,500 + .1 \ (\$238,000 + .9 \ SRI)$$
$$SRI = \$145,500 + \$23,800 + .09 \ SRI$$
$$.91 \ SRI = \$169,300$$

Silver's 1999 realized income = $186,044 (rounded)

Consequently, total investment income of $40,544 ($186,044 realized earnings less $145,500 operating income) should be recognized by Silver for 1999. However, only the $9,000 received in the form of dividends actually was recorded during that period. Therefore, Entry *C2 is included on the worksheet to rectify the consolidated figures for this preceding year by recording $31,544 in additional earnings ($40,544 − $9,000).

Consolidation Entry *C2 (Silver)

Investment in Gold Company	31,544	
Retained Earnings, 1/1/00 (Silver Company)		31,544

To convert Silver's investment income figures for the prior year to equity income.

Remaining Consolidation Entries   After the three previous entries have been recorded, the remainder of the worksheet entries to consolidate these companies are relatively uncomplicated.

Consolidation Entry S1

Common Stock (Silver Company)	200,000	
Retained Earnings, 1/1/00 (Silver Company) (as adjusted above)	618,044	
Investment in Silver Company (90%)		736,240
Noncontrolling Interest in Silver Company, 1/1/00 (10%) . .		81,804

To eliminate the beginning stockholders' equity accounts of Silver and to recognize a 10 percent noncontrolling interest in the subsidiary. Retained earnings has been adjusted for Entry *G and Entry *C2.

Consolidation Entry S2

Common Stock (Gold Company) (10%)	70,000	
Retained Earnings (Gold Company) (10% of 1/1/00 balance as		
adjusted above)	111,544	
Investment in Gold Company (as adjusted above)		181,544

To eliminate the January 1, 2000, equity of Gold Company's shares being held by Silver Company. Retained earnings has been adjusted for Entry *C1.

Consolidation Entry S3

Common Stock (Bronze Company)	100,000	
Retained Earnings, 1/1/00 (Bronze Company)	200,000	
Investment in Bronze Company (60%)...............		180,000
Noncontrolling Interest in Bronze Company, 1/1/00 (40%)		120,000

To eliminate beginning stockholders' equity accounts of Bronze and to recognize outside ownership of the company's remaining shares. The investments of both Gold and Silver are being accounted for concurrently through this one entry.

Consolidation Entry A

Goodwill	56,000	
Investment in Silver Company		26,000
Investment in Bronze Company		30,000

To recognize January 1, 2000, goodwill balances. Although $30,000 was originally allocated to goodwill in the purchase of Silver, the recognition of amortization for 1998 and 1999 has reduced that figure by $4,000 ($2,000 per year). Conversely, as of the beginning of 2000, no expense has been recorded yet on the $30,000 in goodwill associated with the acquisitions of Bronze. Thus, a total allocation of $56,000 is appropriate as of January 1, 2000.

Consolidation Entry I

Dividend Income from Gold Company	10,000	
Dividend Income from Silver Company	36,000	
Dividend Income from Bronze Company	12,000	
Dividends Paid (Gold Company)....................		10,000
Dividends Paid (Silver Company)		36,000
Dividends Paid (Bronze Company)		12,000

To eliminate dividend payments made between the companies and recorded as income based on application of the cost method.

Consolidation Entry E

Amortization Expense	4,000	
Goodwill......................................		4,000

To recognize the 2000 amortization expense for the various goodwill balances. Amortization of $2,000 is recognized on the $30,000 allocation made in the acquisition of Silver while an additional $1,000 expense is associated with each of the two investments made in Bronze.

Consolidation Entry TI

Sales	200,000	
Cost of Goods Sold		200,000

To eliminate the intercompany transfer of inventory made in 2000 by Silver.

Consolidation Entry G

Cost of Goods Sold	33,600	
Inventory		33,600

To eliminate intercompany gains remaining in the December 31, 2000, inventory of Gold. The unrealized gain is 28 percent (the markup for 2000) of the $120,000 ending inventory balance held by the parent.

Consolidation Entry GL

Gain on Sale of Land	13,000	
Land..		13,000

To eliminate gain on intercompany transfer of land made from Gold Company to Bronze during the year.

Noncontrolling Interest in Bronze Company's Income   As in all past examples, the noncontrolling interest's claim to a portion of consolidated income must be calculated based on the realized income of the subsidiary. In this illustration, the combination is a father-son-grandson configuration; therefore, computation of income must begin with Bronze. Because this subsidiary has neither unrealized intercompany gains nor amortization expense, the $90,000 income figure reported in Exhibit 7–4 is applicable. Thus, $36,000 ($90,000 × 40%) should be reported as the noncontrolling interest's share of Bronze's 2000 income.

Noncontrolling Interest in Silver Company's Income   Because of the mutual ownership with Gold, Silver's realized income for 2000 can be determined only by solving two simultaneous equations (since the conventional approach is being applied). Operational income figures for both parties are required as a prerequisite for this procedure.

Silver's Operational Income

Sales	$ 600,000
Cost of goods sold	(300,000)
Operating expenses	(100,000)
Amortization expense—purchase of Bronze	(1,000)
Equity in earnings of Bronze (30%)	27,000
1999 intercompany gains currently realized (Entry *G)	22,500
2000 intercompany unrealized gains being deferred (Entry G)	(33,600)
Operational income	$ 214,900

Gold's Operational Income

Sales	$ 800,000
Cost of goods sold	(380,000)
Operating expenses	(193,000)
Amortization expense—purchase of Silver	(2,000)
Amortization expense—purchase of Bronze	(1,000)
Equity in earnings of Bronze (30%)	27,000
Operational income	$ 251,000

Using these two income balances, the simultaneous equations can be constructed to determine Silver's realized income for the current year. This total serves as the basis for making the noncontrolling interest calculation.

$$\text{SRI} = \$214,900 + 10\% \text{ of GRI}$$

and

$$\text{GRI} = \$251,000 + 90\% \text{ of SRI}$$

therefore

$$\text{SRI} = \$214,900 + .1 \ (\$251,000 + .9 \ \text{SRI})$$

$$\text{SRI} = \$214,900 + \$25,100 + .09 \ \text{SRI}$$

$$.91 \ \text{SRI} = \$240,000$$

$$\text{Silver's realized income} = \$263,736$$

$$\text{Noncontrolling interest in Silver's income (10\%)} = \$26,374 \text{ (rounded)}$$

b.   For Bronze, no differences exist between book values and tax basis. No computation of deferred income taxes is required; thus this company's separate tax return is relatively straightforward. The $90,000 income figure being reported creates a current tax liability of $36,000 (based on the 40 percent tax rate).

In contrast, the consolidated tax return filed for Gold and Silver must include the following financial information. Where applicable, figures reported in Exhibit 7–4 have been combined for the two companies.

Tax Return Information—Consolidated Return

Sales	$ 1,400,000	
Less: Intercompany sales (2000)	(200,000)	$1,200,000
Cost of goods sold	680,000	
Less: 2000 intercompany purchases	(200,000)	
Less: 1999 intercompany gains recognized in 2000 ($90,000 \times 25\%$)	(22,500)	
Add: 2000 unrealized intercompany gains ($120,000 \times 28\%$)	33,600	491,100
Gross profit		708,900
Operating expenses (including amortization)		297,000
Operating income		$ 411,900
Other income (since Bronze is not part of affiliated group):		
Gain on sale of land		13,000
Dividend income—Bronze Company	$ 12,000	
Less: 80% deduction	(9,600)	2,400
Taxable income		$ 427,300
Tax rate		40%
Income tax payable by Gold Company and Silver Company for 2000		$ 170,920

A total of $206,920 must be paid to the government in 2000 by the members of this business combination ($36,000 by Bronze and $170,920 in connection with the consolidated return of Gold and Silver). However, according to *FASB Statement 109,* accounting for deferred income tax assets and/or liabilities also is necessitated by any temporary differences that originate or reverse during the year. *In this illustration, only the dividend payments from Bronze and the unrealized gain on the sale of land to Bronze actually create such differences.* Other items encountered do not lead to deferred income taxes:

■ Because a consolidated return is being filed by Gold and Silver, the unrealized inventory gains are deferred for both tax purposes and financial reporting so that no difference is created.

■ The dividends paid from Silver to Gold are not subject to taxation because these distributions were made between members of an affiliated group.

However, recognition of a deferred tax liability is required because Bronze's realized income ($54,000 after income tax expense of $36,000) is greater than its $20,000 dividend distribution. Gold and Silver own 60 percent of this subsidiary indicating that $32,400 ($54,000 \times 60\%$) of its income is included on the consolidated income statement. Because this figure is $20,400 larger than the amount of dividends paid to Gold and Silver ($12,000 or 60% of $20,000), a deferred tax liability is required. The temporary difference is actually $4,080 (20% of $20,400) because of the 80 percent dividend deduction. The future tax effect on this difference is $1,632 based on the 40 percent tax rate being applied.

A deferred tax asset also is needed in connection with the intercompany sale of land from Gold to Bronze. Separate returns are being filed by these companies. Thus, the gain is taxed immediately, although this $13,000 will not be realized for reporting purposes until a future resale occurs. From an accounting perspective, the tax of $5,200 ($13,000 \times 40\%$) is being prepaid in 2000.

Recognition of the current payable as well as the two deferrals leads to an income tax expense of $203,352:

Income Tax Expense	203,352	
Deferred Income Tax—Asset	5,200	
Income Taxes Payable—Current		206,920
Deferred Income Tax—Liability		1,632

QUESTIONS

1. What is meant by a father-son-grandson relationship?

2. When an indirect ownership is present, why is a specific ordering necessary for determining the realized incomes of the component corporations?

3. Able Company owns 70 percent of the outstanding voting stock of Baker Company which, in turn, holds 80 percent of Carter Company. Carter possesses 60 percent of the capital stock of Dexter Company. How much income actually accrues to the consolidated entity from each of these companies after giving consideration to the various noncontrolling interests?

4. How does the presence of an indirect ownership (such as a father-son-grandson relationship) affect the mechanical aspects of the consolidation process?

5. What is the difference between a connecting affiliation and a mutual ownership?

6. When a mutual ownership exists, two different views of this relationship can be adopted. What are these two views and how do they differ?

7. In accounting for mutual ownerships, why is the treasury stock approach more prevalent in practice than the conventional approach?

8. Alexander Company holds 80 percent of the outstanding common stock of Baxter Company. Baxter, in turn, owns 30 percent of the stock of Alexander. How is the realized income of these two companies computed if the conventional approach is being utilized?

9. For income tax purposes, how is an affiliated group defined?

10. What are the advantages to a business combination filing a consolidated tax return? Considering these advantages, why do some members of a business combination file separate tax returns?

11. Why is the allocation of the income tax expense figure between the members of a business combination important? By what methods can this allocation be made?

12. If separate income tax returns are filed by a parent and its subsidiary, why will the parent frequently have to recognize deferred income taxes? Why might the subsidiary have to recognize deferred income taxes?

13. In a recent acquisition, the consolidated value of a subsidiary's assets exceeded the basis appropriate for tax purposes. How does this difference affect the consolidated balance sheet?

14. Jones acquires Wilson, in part, because the new subsidiary has an unused net operating loss carryforward for tax purposes. How does this carryforward affect the consolidated figures at the date of acquisition?

15. A subsidiary is acquired that has a net operating loss carryforward. The related deferred income tax asset is $230,000. Because the parent believes that a portion of this carryforward likely will never be used, a valuation allowance of $150,000 also is recognized. At the end of the first year of ownership, the parent reassesses the situation and determines that the valuation allowance should be reduced to $110,000. What effect does this change have on the reporting of the business combination?

LIBRARY ASSIGNMENTS

1. Locate PepsiCo, Inc., or General Electric Company, in the most recent edition of *Moody's Industrial Manual*. Find at least three examples of father-son-grandson ownership patterns. By reading the history of the company in the manual, determine, if possible, the method by which the parents gained control over the three grandson organizations.

    Locate at least one other company in *Moody's Industrial Manual* with a considerable number of subsidiaries. Are most of these subsidiaries controlled directly by the parent or indirectly?

2. Read "Japan's New Wave of Advantages," in the March 1996 *International Tax Review*. Prepare a report that discusses some of the differences between the Japanese and U.S. tax

treatments for consolidated entities. Do these differences affect the relative competitiveness of U.S. firms in comparison to Japanese firms?

3. Read some of the following articles and prepare a report on the elections (annual and one-time) that must be made by entities that prepare consolidated tax returns.

"New Elections Available in Wake of Final Consolidated Return Regulations," *The Tax Adviser,* June 1996.

"Responding to the New Subsidiary Investment and Earnings and Profits Consolidated Return Regulations," *Tax Executive,* March 1995.

"Consolidated Return Intercompany Transaction Regulations: Clearly Reflecting Income Is Clearly Not Simple," *Tax Executive,* September 1994.

PROBLEMS

1. In a father-son-grandson business combination, which of the following statements is true?
   a. The father company always must have its realized income computed first.
   b. The computation of a company's realized income has no effect on the realized income of other companies within a business combination.
   c. A father-son-grandson configuration does not require consolidation unless one company owns shares in all of the other companies.
   d. All companies that are solely in subsidiary positions must have their realized income computed first within the consolidation process.

2. A subsidiary owns shares of its parent company. Which of the following is true concerning the treasury stock approach?
   a. It is considered to be more difficult to apply than the conventional approach.
   b. The original cost of the subsidiary's investment is a reduction in consolidated stockholders' equity.
   c. The subsidiary accrues income on its investment by using the equity method.
   d. The treasury stock approach eliminates these shares entirely within the consolidation process.

3. On January 1, 1998, a subsidiary buys 10 percent of the outstanding shares of its parent company. Although the total book value and fair market value of the parent's net assets were $4 million, the purchase price for these shares was $420,000. Goodwill is amortized in this business combination over a 40-year period. During 1998, the parent reported operational income (no investment income was included) of $510,000 while paying dividends of $140,000. How are these shares reported at December 31, 1998, if the treasury stock approach is used?
   a. The investment is recorded as $457,000 at the end of 1998 and then eliminated for consolidation purposes.
   b. Consolidated stockholders' equity is reduced by $457,000.
   c. The investment is recorded as $456,500 at the end of 1998 and then eliminated for consolidation purposes.
   d. Consolidated stockholders' equity is reduced by $420,000.

4. Which of the following is correct for two companies that want to file a consolidated tax return as an affiliated group?
   a. One company must hold at least 51 percent of the other company's voting stock.
   b. One company must hold at least 65 percent of the other company's voting stock.
   c. One company must hold at least 80 percent of the other company's voting stock.
   d. A consolidated tax return cannot be filed unless one company owns 100 percent of the voting stock of the other.

5. How does the amortization of goodwill affect the computation of income taxes on a consolidated tax return?
   a. It is a deductible expense but only if the parent owns 80 percent of the voting stock of the subsidiary.
   b. It is a temporary tax difference that creates a tax effect in subsequent years.
   c. It is a deductible item over a 15-year period.
   d. It is deductible for tax purposes but only if a consolidated tax return is being filed.

6. Which of the following is not a reason for two companies to file separate tax returns?
   a. The parent owns 68 percent of the subsidiary.
   b. They have no intercompany transactions.
   c. Intercompany dividends are tax free only on separate returns.
   d. Neither company historically has had an operating tax loss.

7. Bassett Company owns 80 percent of Crimson Corporation. Crimson Corporation owns 90 percent of Damson, Inc. Operational income totals for 1998 follow; these figures contain no investment income. Amortization expense was not required by any of these purchases. Included in Damson's income is a $40,000 unrealized gain on intercompany transfers to Crimson.

	Bassett	Crimson	Damson
Operational income	$300,000	$200,000	$200,000

What is Bassett's realized income for the year?
   a. $575,200.
   b. $588,000.
   c. $596,400.
   d. $604,000.

8. Gardner Corporation holds 80 percent of Healthstone which, in turn, owns 80 percent of Icede. Operational income figures (without investment income) as well as unrealized upstream gains included in the income for the current year follow:

	Gardner	Healthstone	Icede
Operational income	$400,000	$300,000	$220,000
Unrealized gains	50,000	30,000	60,000

On a consolidated income statement for the year, what balance is reported for the noncontrolling interest in the subsidiaries' income?
   a. $86,000.
   b. $100,000.
   c. $111,600.
   d. $120,800.

9. Nesbitt Corporation owns 90 percent of Jones, Inc., while Jones owns 10 percent of the outstanding shares of Nesbitt. No goodwill or any other allocations were recognized in connection with either of these acquisitions. Nesbitt reports operational income of $190,000 for 1998 whereas Jones earned $70,000 during the same period. No investment income is included within either of these income totals. On a consolidated income statement, what is the noncontrolling interest in Jones's income if the conventional approach is being used?
   a. $7,000.
   b. $7,740.
   c. $8,900.
   d. $9,780.

10. Horton, Inc., owns 90 percent of the voting stock of Juvyn Corporation. The purchase price was in excess of book value and fair market value by $80,000. Juvyn holds 20 percent of the voting stock of Horton. That purchase price was in excess of book value and fair market value by $20,000. All goodwill is to be amortized over a 20-year period.
    During the current year, Horton reported operational income of $160,000 and dividend income from Juvyn of $27,000. At the same time, Juvyn reported operational income of $50,000 and dividend income from Horton of $14,000.
    If the treasury stock approach is utilized, what will be reported as the Noncontrolling Interest in Juvyn's Net Income?
   a. $5,000.
   b. $5,400.
   c. $6,300.
   d. $6,400.

11. What would be the answer to problem 10 if the conventional approach were being used?
   a. $9,781.
   b. $9,964.

      c. $10,414.

      d. $11,864.

12. Cremmins, Inc., owns 60 percent of Anderson. During the current year, Anderson reported net income of $200,000 but paid a total cash dividend of only $40,000. What deferred income tax liability must be recognized in the consolidated balance sheet? Assume the tax rate is 30 percent.

      a. $5,760.

      b. $9,600.

      c. $12,840.

      d. $28,800.

13. Prybylos, Inc., owns 90 percent of Station Corporation. Both companies have been profitable for many years. During the current year, the parent sold merchandise costing $70,000 to the subsidiary for $100,000. At the end of the year, 20 percent of this merchandise was still being held. Assume that the tax rate is 25 percent and that separate tax returns are filed. What deferred income tax asset is created?

      a. –0–.

      b. $300.

      c. $1,500.

      d. $7,500.

14. What would be the answer to problem 13 if a consolidated tax return were filed?

      a. –0–.

      b. $300.

      c. $1,500.

      d. $7,500.

15. Hastoon Company purchases all of Zedner Company for $420,000 in cash. On that date, the subsidiary has net assets with a $400,000 fair market value but a $300,000 book value and tax basis. The tax rate is 30 percent. Neither company has reported any deferred income tax assets or liabilities. What amount of goodwill should be recognized on the date of the acquisition?

      a. $20,000.

      b. $36,000.

      c. $50,000.

      d. $120,000.

16. On January 1, 1998, Tree Company purchased 70 percent of Limb Company's outstanding voting stock for $250,000. Limb had a $300,000 reported book value on that date. Subsequently, on January 1, 1999, Limb Company acquired 70 percent of Leaf Company for $90,000 when Leaf had a $100,000 book value. All goodwill is assumed to have a maximum life.

    These companies report the following financial information. Investment income figures are not included.

	1998	1999	2000
Sales:			
Tree Company	$400,000	$500,000	$650,000
Limb Company	200,000	280,000	400,000
Leaf Company	Not available	160,000	210,000
Expenses:			
Tree Company	$310,000	420,000	510,000
Limb Company	160,000	220,000	335,000
Leaf Company	Not available	150,000	180,000
Dividends paid:			
Tree Company	$ 20,000	40,000	50,000
Limb Company	10,000	20,000	20,000
Leaf Company	Not available	2,000	10,000

Assume that the following questions are each independent:

    a. If all companies use the equity method for internal reporting purposes, what is the December 31, 1999, balance in the Tree's Investment in Limb Company account?

b. If all companies use the cost method to account for their investments, what adjustments must Limb and Tree make to their beginning retained earnings balances on the 2000 consolidation worksheet?

c. What is the consolidated net income for this business combination for the year of 2000 prior to any reduction for the noncontrolling interests' share of the subsidiaries' net income?

d. What is the noncontrolling interests' share of the consolidated net income in 2000?

e. Assume that Limb made intercompany inventory transfers to Tree that result in the following unrealized gains at the end of each year:

Date	Amount
12/31/98	$10,000
12/31/99	16,000
12/31/00	25,000

What is the realized income of Limb in 1999 and 2000, respectively?

f. Assuming the same unrealized gains as presented in part e, what worksheet adjustment must be made to the January 1, 2000, Retained Earnings account of Tree if that company has applied the cost method to its investment?

17. On January 1, 1998, Uncle Company purchased 80 percent of Nephew Company's capital stock for $500,000 in cash and other assets. Nephew had a book value of $600,000 on that date. Goodwill allocations are amortized over a 10-year period.

On January 1, 2000, Nephew acquired 30 percent of Uncle for $280,000. Uncle's appropriately adjusted book value as of that date was $900,000.

Operational income figures (includes no investment income) for these two companies follow. In addition, Uncle pays $20,000 in dividends to shareholders each year while Nephew distributes $5,000 annually.

Year	Uncle Company	Nephew Company
1998	$ 90,000	$30,000
1999	120,000	40,000
2000	140,000	50,000

The following questions should be viewed as independent problems:

a. Assume that the treasury stock approach is being utilized and that Uncle applies the equity method to account for this investment in Nephew. What is the Income of the Subsidiary being recognized by Uncle in 2000?

b. If the treasury stock approach is applied, what is the noncontrolling interest's share of the subsidiary's 2000 income?

c. Assume that the conventional approach is utilized and that Uncle applies the equity method to this investment in Nephew. What is the Income of the Subsidiary being recognized by Uncle in 2000?

d. If the conventional approach is being applied, what is the noncontrolling interest's share of the subsidiary's 2000 net income?

18. Gaddy, Inc., obtained 60 percent of Mabry Corporation on January 1, 1998. Annual amortization of $25,000 is to be recorded on the allocations made in connection with this purchase. On January 1, 1999, Mabry acquired 90 percent of Tucson Company's voting stock. Amortization on this second purchase amounted to $2,000 per year.

For the year of 2001, these three companies reported the following information as accumulated by their separate accounting systems. Operating income figures do not include any investment or dividend income.

	Operating Income	Dividends Paid
Gaddy...........	$220,000	$120,000
Mabry...........	160,000	50,000
Tucson	90,000	10,000

Required

    a. On consolidated financial statements for 2001, what is the noncontrolling interests' share of the subsidiaries' income?

    b. What is consolidated net income for 2001?

    c. If Mabry's operating income figures for 2001 include a net unrealized gain of $12,000, what is consolidated net income for that year?

19. Fonseca owns 80 percent of the voting stock of Carson. The purchase price exceeded the underlying book value of Carson's assets and liabilities by $60,000. At the same time, Carson holds a 30 percent interest in the outstanding shares of Fonseca. This stock was bought at a price $10,000 in excess of underlying book value. All goodwill is to be amortized over a useful life of 10 years.

    Both of these companies use the cost method to record their investments for internal reporting purposes. During the current year, the following information was reported:

	Operating Income	Dividend Income	Total Reported Income
Fonseca	$80,000	$16,000 (all from Carson)	$96,000
Carson	30,000	15,000 (all from Fonseca)	45,000

Required

    a. If the conventional approach is to be utilized, what reduction should be recorded in the consolidated income statement as the noncontrolling interest in Carson's net income?

    b. If the treasury stock approach is applied, what reduction should be recorded in the consolidated income statement as the noncontrolling interest in Carson's net income?

20. Baxter, Inc., owns 90 percent of Wisconsin, Inc., and 20 percent of the Cleveland Company. Wisconsin, in turn, holds 60 percent of the outstanding stock of Cleveland. Total annual amortization of $17,000 resulted from the purchases made by Baxter. During the current year, Cleveland sold a variety of inventory items to Wisconsin for $40,000 although the original cost had been $30,000. Of this total, $12,000 in inventory (at transfer price) was still held by Wisconsin at year's end.

    During this same period, Wisconsin sold merchandise to Baxter for $100,000 although the original cost had been only $70,000. At the end of the year, $40,000 of these goods (at the transfer price) were still on hand.

    The cost method is used to record each of these investments. No other investments are held by any of the companies.

    Using the following separate income statements, determine the figures that would appear on a consolidated income statement.

	Baxter	Wisconsin	Cleveland
Sales	$1,000,000	$ 450,000	$ 280,000
Cost of goods sold	(670,000)	(280,000)	(190,000)
Expenses	(110,000)	(60,000)	(30,000)
Dividend income:			
Wisconsin	36,000	–0–	–0–
Cleveland	4,000	12,000	–0–
Net income	$ 260,000	$ 122,000	$ 60,000

21. Alice Corporation bought 90 percent of the outstanding shares of Wonderland, Inc., several years ago for $610,000. Wonderland, in turn, acquired 10 percent of Alice for $111,000. Annual amortization expense of $12,000 resulted from Alice's purchase. The cost method is used to record each of these investments. No other investments are held by either company.

Required

    a. Based on the following separate income statements, produce the figures that would appear on a consolidated income statement. Assume that the treasury approach is being used.

	Alice	Wonderland
Sales	$ 1,300,000	$ 500,000
Cost of goods sold	(750,000)	(270,000)
Expenses	(220,000)	(120,000)
Dividend income	45,000	16,000
Net income	$ 375,000	$ 126,000

b. Assuming that the treasury stock approach is still in use, what are the consolidated totals for the following two accounts?

	Alice	Wonderland
Common stock	$880,000	$350,000
Treasury stock	–0–	–0–

22. The following figures are reported by Up and its 80 percent owned subsidiary (Down) for the year ending December 31, 1998. Down paid dividends of $30,000 during this period.

	Up	Down
Sales	$600,000	$300,000
Cost of goods sold	300,000	140,000
Operating expenses	174,000	60,000
Dividend income	24,000	–0–
Net income	$150,000	$100,000

   In 1997, unrealized gains of $30,000 on upstream transfers of $90,000 were deferred into 1998. In 1998, unrealized gains of $40,000 on upstream transfers of $110,000 were deferred into 1999.
   a. What figures appear in a consolidated income statement?
   b. What income tax expense should be shown in the consolidated income statement if separate returns are filed? Assume that the tax rate is 30 percent.

23. Clarke has a controlling interest in the outstanding stock of Rogers. At the end of the current year, the following information has been accumulated for these two companies:

	Operating Income	Dividends Paid
Clarke	$500,000 (includes a $90,000 net unrealized gain on intercompany inventory transfers)	$90,000
Rogers	$240,000	$80,000

   Clarke uses the cost method to account for the investment in Rogers. Neither dividend nor other investment income is included in the operating income figures just presented. The effective tax rate for both companies is 40 percent.

Required

   a. Assume that Clarke owns 100 percent of the voting stock of Rogers and that a consolidated tax return is being filed. What amount of income taxes would this affiliated group pay in connection with the current period?
   b. Assume that Clarke owns 92 percent of the voting stock of Rogers and that a consolidated tax return is being filed. What amount of income taxes would this affiliated group pay in connection with the current period?
   c. Assume that Clarke owns 80 percent of the voting stock of Rogers but the companies have elected to file separate tax returns. What is the total amount of income taxes that these two companies pay for the current period?
   d. Assume that Clarke owns 70 percent of the voting stock of Rogers so that separate tax returns are required. What is the total amount of income tax expense to be recognized in the consolidated income statement for the current period?
   e. Assume that Clarke owns 70 percent of the voting stock of Rogers so that separate tax returns are required. What amount of income taxes does Clarke have to pay in connection with the current year?

24. On January 1, 1998, Piranto acquires 90 percent of the outstanding shares of Slinton. Financial information for these two companies for the years of 1998 and 1999 are as follows:

	1998	1999
Piranto Company:		
Sales	$600,000	$800,000
Operational expenses	400,000	500,000
Unrealized gains as of end of year (included in above figures)	120,000	150,000
Dividend income—Slinton Company	18,000	36,000
Slinton Company:		
Sales	200,000	250,000
Operational expenses	120,000	150,000
Dividends paid	20,000	40,000

Assume that a tax rate of 40 percent is applicable to both companies.

Required

  a. On consolidated financial statements for 1999, what would be the income tax expense and the income tax currently payable if Piranto and Slinton file a consolidated tax return as an affiliated group?
  b. On consolidated financial statements for 1999, what would be the income tax expense and income tax currently payable for each company if they choose to file separate returns?

25. Lake acquired a controlling interest in Boxwood several years ago. During the current fiscal period, these two companies have individually reported the following income figures (exclusive of any investment income):

Lake	$300,000
Boxwood	100,000

  Lake paid a cash dividend of $90,000 during the current year while Boxwood distributed $10,000.
  Boxwood sells inventory to Lake each period. Unrealized intercompany gains of $18,000 were present in Lake's beginning inventory for the current year while its ending inventory carried $32,000 in unrealized profits.
  The following questions should be viewed as independent situations. The effective tax rate for both companies is 40 percent.

  a. If Lake owns a 60 percent interest in Boxwood, what total income tax expense must be reported on a consolidated income statement for this period?
  b. If Lake owns a 60 percent interest in Boxwood, what total amount of income taxes must be paid by these two companies for the current year?
  c. If Lake owns a 90 percent interest in Boxwood and a consolidated tax return is being filed, what amount of income tax expense would be reported on a consolidated income statement for the year?
  d. Assume that Lake owns a 90 percent interest in Boxwood while Boxwood possesses a 20 percent interest in Lake. Using the conventional approach to mutual ownership, determine the noncontrolling interest in Boxwood's income for the year. Ignore income taxes.

26. Garrison holds a controlling interest in the outstanding stock of Robertson. For the current year, the following information has been gathered about these two companies:

	Garrison	Robertson
Operating income	$300,000 (includes a $50,000 net unrealized gain on an intercompany transfer)	$200,000
Dividends paid	32,000	50,000
Tax rate	40%	40%

Garrison uses the cost method to account for the investment in Robertson. Dividend income for the current year is not included in Garrison's operating income figure.

Required

a. Assume that Garrison owns 80 percent of the voting stock of Robertson. On a consolidated tax return, what amount of income taxes would be paid?
b. Assume that Garrison owns 80 percent of the voting stock of Robertson. On separate tax returns, what is the total amount of income taxes to be paid?
c. Assume that Garrison owns 70 percent of the voting stock of Robertson. What is the total amount of income tax expense to be recognized on a consolidated income statement?
d. Assume that Garrison holds 60 percent of the voting stock of Robertson. On a separate income tax return, what amount of income taxes would Garrison have to pay?

27. Leftwich recently purchased all of the stock of Kew Corporation and is now in the process of consolidating the financial data of this new subsidiary. Leftwich paid a total of $650,000 for the company, which has the following accounts:

	Fair Market Value	Tax Basis
Accounts receivable	$110,000	$110,000
Inventory	130,000	130,000
Land	100,000	100,000
Buildings	180,000	140,000
Equipment	200,000	150,000
Liabilities	220,000	220,000

Assume that the effective tax rate is 30 percent. On a consolidated balance sheet prepared immediately after this takeover, what impact would the acquisition of Kew have on the individual asset and liability accounts reported by the business combination?

28. House Corporation was created in 1950 and has been operating profitably since that time. At the beginning of 1998, House purchased a 70 percent ownership in Room Company. Room's financial accounts as of that date were as follows:

	Book Value	Fair Market Value
Cash and receivables	$300,000	$300,000
Inventory	380,000	380,000
Buildings (20-year life)	200,000	260,000
Equipment (4-year life)	160,000	140,000
Land	260,000	260,000
Liabilities	510,000	510,000

House paid $701,000 in cash for this investment. Goodwill is to be amortized over the maximum allowable life.

During 1998 and 1999, Room earned net income totaling $160,000 while paying cash dividends of $50,000.

House has made regular acquisitions of inventory from Room at a markup of 25 percent more than cost. House's purchases during 1998 and 1999 as well as related ending inventory balances are as follows:

Year	Intercompany Purchases	Retained Intercompany Inventory—End of Year
1998	$120,000	$40,000
1999	150,000	60,000

On January 1, 2000, House and Room acted together as coacquirers of 80 percent of the outstanding common stock of Wall Company. The total price of these shares was $200,000, indicating that no goodwill or other specific valuation allocations were needed. Each company put up-one half of this purchase price.

During 2000, House acquired additional inventory at a price of $200,000 from Room. Of this merchandise, 45 percent is still being held at year's end.

Room loaned Wall $40,000 on a 10 percent note on October 1, 2000. Although interest has been properly recorded, no part of this debt has been repaid as of December 31, 2000.

Wall's preferred stock is owned entirely by outside parties. This stock pays an 8 percent annual cumulative dividend. The stock is neither participating nor voting, although it does have a call value of 106 percent of par value. No dividends are currently in arrears on these shares.

Following are the financial records for these three companies for 2000. Prepare a consolidation worksheet. The partial equity method based on *operational earnings* has been applied to each investment.

	House Corporation	Room Company	Wall Company
Sales and other revenues	$ 900,000	$ 700,000	$ 300,000
Cost of goods sold	(551,120)	(300,000)	(140,000)
Operating expenses	(218,400)	(268,400)	(90,000)
Income of Room Company	92,120	–0–	–0–
Income of Wall Company	26,400	26,400	–0–
Net income	$ 249,000	$ 158,000	$ 70,000
Retained earnings, 1/1/00	$ 820,000	$ 590,000	$ 153,000
Net income (above)	249,000	158,000	70,000
Dividends paid	(100,000)	(96,000)	(50,000)
Retained earnings, 12/31/00	$ 969,000	$ 652,000	$ 173,000
Cash and receivables	$ 244,880	$ 354,000	$ 70,000
Inventory	390,200	320,000	103,000
Investment in Room Company	802,920	–0–	–0–
Investment in Wall Company	108,000	108,000	–0–
Buildings	385,000	320,000	144,000
Equipment	310,000	130,000	88,000
Land	180,000	300,000	16,000
Liabilities	632,000	570,000	98,000
Preferred stock	–0–	–0–	50,000
Common stock	820,000	310,000	100,000
Retained earnings, 12/31/00	969,000	652,000	173,000

29. Mighty Company purchased a 60 percent interest in Lowly Company on January 1, 1995, for $400,000 in cash. Lowly's book value at that date was reported as $500,000. Any goodwill resulting from this transaction was to be amortized over 20 years. Subsequently, on January 1, 1996, Lowly acquired a 20 percent interest in Mighty. The price of $240,000 was equivalent to 20 percent of Mighty's book value.

Neither company has paid dividends since these acquisitions occurred. On January 1, 2001, Lowly's book value was $800,000, a figure which rises to $840,000 (common stock of $300,000 and retained earnings of $540,000) by the end of the year. Mighty's book value was $1.7 million at the beginning of 2001 and $1.8 million (common stock of $1 million and retained earnings of $800,000) at December 31, 2001. No intercompany transactions have occurred and no additional stock has been sold. Each company applies the cost method in accounting for the individual investments.

Required

   a. What worksheet entries are required to consolidate these two companies for 2001? What is the noncontrolling interest in the subsidiary's net income for this year? Assume that the treasury stock approach is utilized.

   b. Answer the same questions as in requirement *a* but assume that the conventional approach is being applied to the mutual ownership.

   c. How do the answers in requirement *b* differ if, on January 1, 1999, Mighty sold equipment (costing $80,000) with a remaining life of 10 years and a $20,000 book value to Lowly for $50,000 in cash?

30. On January 1, 1998, Travers Company purchased 90 percent of the outstanding stock of Yarrow Company. On the same date, Yarrow acquired an 80 percent interest in Stookey Company. Although both of these investments are to be accounted for by applying the cost method, no dividends are distributed by either Yarrow or Stookey during 1998 or 1999. Travers follows a policy of paying out cash dividends each year equal to 40 percent of operational earnings. Reported income totals for 1998 are as follows:

Travers Company	$300,000
Yarrow Company	160,000
Stookey Company	120,000

Goodwill is to be amortized over 15 years.

Following are the 1999 financial statements for these three companies. Stookey has made numerous transfers of inventory to Yarrow since the takeover: $80,000 (1998) and $100,000 (1999). These transactions include the same markup applicable to Stookey's outside sales. In each of these years, Yarrow has carried 20 percent of this inventory into the succeeding year before disposing of it.

An effective tax rate of 45 percent is applicable to all companies.

	Travers Company	Yarrow Company	Stookey Company
Sales	$ 900,000	$ 600,000	$ 500,000
Cost of goods sold	(480,000)	(320,000)	(260,000)
Operating expenses	(100,000)	(80,000)	(140,000)
Net income	$ 320,000	$ 200,000	$ 100,000
Retained earnings, 1/1/99	$ 700,000	$ 600,000	$ 300,000
Net income (above)	320,000	200,000	100,000
Dividends paid	(128,000)	–0–	–0–
Retained earnings, 12/31/99	$ 892,000	$ 800,000	$ 400,000
Current assets	$ 423,000	$ 375,000	$ 280,000
Investment in Yarrow Company	741,000	–0–	–0–
Investment in Stookey Company	–0–	349,000	–0–
Land, buildings, and equipment (net)	949,000	836,000	520,000
Total assets	$ 2,113,000	$ 1,560,000	$ 800,000
Liabilities	$ 721,000	$ 460,000	$ 200,000
Common stock	500,000	300,000	200,000
Retained earnings, 12/31/99	892,000	800,000	400,000
Total liabilities and equities	$ 2,113,000	$ 1,560,000	$ 800,000

Required

a. Prepare the 1999 consolidation worksheet for this business combination. Ignore income tax effects.

b. Determine the amount of income taxes to be paid by Travers and Yarrow on a consolidated tax return for the year of 1999.

c. Determine the amount of income taxes to be paid by Stookey on a separate tax return for the year of 1999.

d. Based on the answers to requirements *b* and *c*, what journal entry would be made by this combination to record 1999 income taxes?

31. Several years ago, Daniel Company purchased 90 percent of the outstanding voting stock of Murphy, Inc. At approximately the same time, Murphy acquired 10 percent of the common stock of Daniel. In both cases, the price paid was equal to the book value and fair market value of the underlying net assets. Therefore, no allocations were made to either goodwill or specific asset or liability accounts.

Prior to the current year, the book value of Daniel has increased by $400,000 since the date of acquisition while Murphy's book value has risen by $150,000.

Both companies use the cost method to account for their investments.

Required

Using the following information for the year of 1998, prepare a consolidation worksheet based on the conventional approach to mutual holdings.

	Daniel	Murphy
Sales	$ 600,000	$ 220,000
Expenses	(400,000)	(126,000)
Dividend income	18,000	9,000
Net income	$ 218,000	$ 103,000
Retained earnings, 1/1/98	$ 850,000	$ 200,000
Net income	218,000	103,000
Dividends paid	(90,000)	(20,000)
Retained earnings, 12/31/98	$ 978,000	$ 283,000
Cash............................	$ 20,000	$ 40,000
Receivables.....................	178,000	96,000
Inventory	125,000	108,000
Investment in Murphy	189,000	–0–
Investment in Daniel	–0–	50,000
Property, plant, and equipment (net) ...	651,000	361,000
Total assets	$ 1,163,000	$ 655,000
Liabilities	$ 135,000	$ 212,000
Common stock	50,000	160,000
Retained earnings, 12/31/98	978,000	283,000
Total liabilities and equities ...	$ 1,163,000	$ 655,000

32. Politan Company acquired an 80 percent interest in Soludan several years ago. Any portion of the purchase price in excess of the corresponding book value of Soludan Company was assigned to goodwill. This intangible asset has subsequently undergone annual amortization based on a 15-year life. In recent years, regular intercompany inventory sales have transpired between the two companies. No payment has yet been made on the latest transfer.

Following are the individual financial statements for the two companies as well as consolidated totals for the current year.

	Politan Company	Soludan Company	Consolidated Totals
Sales	$ 800,000	$ 600,000	$ 1,280,000
Cost of goods sold.............	(500,000)	(400,000)	(784,000)
Operating expenses	(100,000)	(100,000)	(202,000)
Income of Soludan	80,000	–0–	–0–
Noncontrolling interest in Soludan Company's income...............	–0–	–0–	(19,200)
Net income	$ 280,000	$ 100,000	$ 274,800
Retained earnings, 1/1	$ 620,000	$ 290,000	$ 607,600
Net income (above)	280,000	100,000	274,800
Dividends paid	(70,000)	(20,000)	(70,000)
Retained earnings, 12/31	$ 830,000	$ 370,000	$ 812,400
Cash and receivables	$ 290,000	$ 90,000	$ 360,000
Inventory	190,000	160,000	338,000
Investment in Soludan Company	390,000	–0–	–0–
Land, buildings, and equipment	380,000	260,000	640,000
Goodwill	–0–	–0–	22,000
Total assets	$ 1,250,000	$ 510,000	$ 1,360,000
Liabilities	$ 270,000	$ 60,000	$ 310,000
Noncontrolling interest in Soludan Company	–0–	–0–	87,600
Common stock	120,000	80,000	120,000
Additional paid-in capital	30,000	–0–	30,000
Retained earnings (above)	830,000	370,000	812,400
Total liabilities and equities ...	$ 1,250,000	$ 510,000	$ 1,360,000

Required

a. By what method is Politan accounting for its investment in Soludan?
b. What is the balance of the unrealized inventory gain being deferred at the end of the current period?

c. What figure was originally allocated to goodwill?
d. What was the amount of the current year intercompany inventory sales?
e. Were the intercompany inventory sales made upstream or downstream?
f. What was the balance of the intercompany liability at the end of the current year?
g. What unrealized gain was deferred into the current year from the preceding period?
h. The consolidated Retained Earnings account shows a balance of $607,600 rather than the $620,000 reported by the parent. What creates this difference?
i. How was the ending Noncontrolling interest in Soludan Company computed?
j. Assuming a tax rate of 40 percent, what income tax journal entry is recorded if these two companies prepare a consolidated tax return?
k. Assuming a tax rate of 40 percent, what income tax journal entry is recorded if these two companies prepare separate tax returns?

33. On January 1, 1998, Alpha acquired 80 percent of Delta. Of the total purchase price, $100,000 was allocated to goodwill. Subsequently, on January 1, 1999, Delta obtained 70 percent of the outstanding voting shares of Omega. In this second acquisition, $80,000 of the payment was assigned to goodwill. All goodwill balances are being amortized over a 20-year life. Delta had a book value of $490,000 at January 1, 1998, whereas Omega reported a book value of $140,000 on January 1, 1999.

Delta has made numerous inventory transfers to Alpha since the business combination was formed. Unrealized gains of $15,000 were present in Alpha's inventory as of January 1, 2003. During the year, $200,000 in additional intercompany sales were made with $22,000 in gains remaining unrealized at the end of the period.

Both Alpha and Delta have utilized the partial equity method to account for their investment balances.

Required

The following individual financial statements are for these three companies for the year 2003 along with consolidated totals. Develop the worksheet entries necessary to derive these reported balances.

	Alpha Company	Delta Company	Omega Company	Consolidated totals
Sales	$ 900,000	$ 500,000	$ 200,000	$ 1,400,000
Cost of goods sold	(500,000)	(240,000)	(80,000)	(627,000)
Operating expenses	(294,000)	(129,000)	(50,000)	(482,000)
Income of subsidiary	144,000	49,000	–0–	–0–
Noncontrolling interest in income of Delta Company	–0–	–0–	–0–	(33,800)
Noncontrolling interest in income of Omega Company	–0–	–0–	–0–	(21,000)
Net income	$ 250,000	$ 180,000	$ 70,000	$ 236,200
Retained earnings, 1/1/03	$ 600,000	$ 400,000	$ 100,000	$ 550,200
Net income (above)	250,000	180,000	70,000	236,200
Dividends paid	(50,000)	(40,000)	(50,000)	(50,000)
Retained earnings, 12/31/03	$ 800,000	$ 540,000	$ 120,000	$ 736,400
Cash and receivables	$ 262,000	$ 210,000	$ 70,000	$ 522,000
Inventory	290,000	310,000	160,000	738,000
Investment in Delta Company	628,000	–0–	–0–	–0–
Investment in Omega Company	–0–	234,000	–0–	–0–
Property, plant, and equipment	420,000	316,000	270,000	1,006,000
Goodwill	–0–	–0–	–0–	130,000
Total assets	$ 1,600,000	$ 1,070,000	$ 500,000	$ 2,396,000
Liabilities	$ 600,000	$ 410,000	$ 280,000	$ 1,270,000
Common stock	200,000	120,000	100,000	200,000
Retained earnings, 12/31/03	800,000	540,000	120,000	736,400
Noncontrolling interest in Delta Company	–0–	–0–	–0–	123,600
Noncontrolling interest in Omega Company	–0–	–0–	–0–	66,000
Total liabilities and equities	$ 1,600,000	$ 1,070,000	$ 500,000	$ 2,396,000

CHAPTER

8

Branch and Consignment Accounting

QUESTIONS TO CONSIDER

- How does the accounting for branch operations differ from consolidation accounting? What similarities can be found?

- What techniques do companies with numerous branch operations use to monitor the intracompany transfers and allocations that can continually occur?

- Why are intracompany inventory shipments frequently recorded at a transfer price in excess of cost? What impact do unrealized gains resulting from such prices have on the financial reporting of the company as a whole?

- What are the enticements to a company to distribute its inventory through a consignment marketing system?

- In consignment marketing, how does the reporting process of the consignor (the owner) differ from that of the consignee (the seller)?

Accounting for the operations of a business can become complicated whenever geographical separation is encountered between the various facets of the organization. This chapter examines the special procedures necessary to record transactions occurring at significant distances from a central office. Branch accounting is analyzed first. This initial section of the chapter describes reporting systems designed to accumulate the financial data generated by operations in widely dispersed locations.

Following the coverage of branches, accounting for consignment sales is investigated. Companies use this marketing technique to place their inventory in retail outlets owned by other parties, an approach intended to achieve a wider distribution of merchandise than might otherwise be possible. Thus, both branch and consignment accounting systems must be capable of gathering information despite the great distances frequently involved.

BRANCH ACCOUNTING

Opening a branch office can prove challenging, exhilarating, and profitable. But you must approach it with the same caution, care, and commitment you would any other business activity. . . . According to the Census Bureau's most recent figures, the United States counts more than 500,000 branch offices among its 3.8 million businesses.[1]

Few aspects of the phenomenal expansion of American business during this century have been more evident than the development of branch operations. Many of today's largest enterprises achieved their present magnitude primarily by establishing

---

[1]Michael Flynn and Linda Kephart Flynn, "Corporate Report—Branching Out," *Ingrams* 21, no. 8 (August 1995), p. 48.

individual branches throughout the country. As just one example, in 1997, the JCPenney Company, Inc., disclosed that it operated 1,228 retail stores, 2,699 drugstores, four catalog distribution centers, and one store distribution center.

Previous chapters have analyzed the consolidation procedures used to produce financial statements when two or more incorporated enterprises form a business combination. As an extension of this coverage, the first section of Chapter 8 examines the accounting process utilized by companies subdivided into identifiable branch operations. Once again, a single economic entity is made up of a number of individual reporting units. In this case, though, the lines of distinction are internal rather than legal. Although titles such as *divisions, chain stores,* or *profit centers* often are applied to these separate operations, the term *branch* has traditionally been applied by accountants to indicate an unincorporated operation within a company that carries out a specific function.

Proliferation of Branch Operations

The extensive use of branch operations is especially common in modern retailing where companies attempt to attract customers by offering the convenience of numerous outlets. McDonald's Corporation, for example, recently reported more than 18,000 separate operations around the world. At that same time, the retail sales of Safeway Stores, Incorporated, were being made through more than 1,000 supermarkets located in the United States and Canada. Development of branch operations for retailing purposes is not limited, though, to giant organizations such as McDonald's and Safeway. Relatively small companies often attempt to expand their market base by establishing additional outlets in nearby communities. This type of internal division is not even restricted to the retail function. Branch operations are commonly found in banking as well as in manufacturing and other industries.

The Structuring of Branch Organizations

Although organizing and expanding a company through the development of separate units is widespread, no uniform model exists for a branch. The specific activities of a branch depend on its purpose as well as the nature of the company's operations. As an example, some branches merely collect cash and receive sales orders, thus acting primarily as agents for the company's home office. To record such routine functions, the accounting system need consist of little more than a cash receipts listing.

In contrast, many companies establish branches to execute a complete range of business activities, including inventory procurement or production, credit sales, advertising, and so forth. This second type of operation is likely to maintain extensive financial records utilizing all of the journals and ledgers normally found in an incorporated concern. Only the omission of stockholders' equity accounts would distinguish this reporting system from that of a corporation.

The development of branch accounting also is influenced by a company's philosophy toward its own internal structuring. For businesses that operate under a policy of decentralization authority, the creation of numerous, relatively independent branches is emphasized. Proponents of this organizational style assign a significant degree of responsibility to each unit and then monitor these operations accordingly, usually through periodically reported summaries.

Conversely, a corporation that stresses centralized management may still elect to establish a large quantity of branch operations but the primary authority for decision making tends to remain with the officials working in the home office. In such organizations, the company's accounting process should be designed to reflect this approach by making detailed operational data available to appropriate individuals. As always, the accountant must create a system that meets the informational needs of the enterprise.

In considering the procedures that a company should apply in accounting for individual branch operations, the sheer number of potential reporting units may appear to pose an overwhelming problem. Upon closer investigation, though, the accounting difficulties that might be associated with large-scale operations such as JCPenney or Safeway can be seen as primarily mechanical rather than conceptual. With the advent and nearly universal utilization of computer systems, most organizations have the capability of maintaining legitimate accounting control over hundreds, or even thousands, of branches located throughout the world.

Accounting for Intracompany Transactions

Although modern computers enable companies to isolate and record the operations of a multitude of separate branches, significant accounting problems still continue to exist. *Of special concern is the recording of the many interface events that can occur between the branch and the corporate home office.* Procedures must be in place to ensure that all intracompany transactions such as transfers and allocations are recorded in a consistent manner by both parties.

This problem is especially significant because the volume of such transactions can become quite large. Just to begin a branch's operations, cash and other assets are normally transferred from the company's home office. In addition, if the branch maintains a stock of inventory, a portion or even all of this merchandise may have to be shipped directly from a central corporate warehouse. Thereafter, should the branch prove to be profitable, excess cash balances might be transferred back to the home office on a regular, perhaps daily, basis.

Frequently, though, the accounting interaction transpiring between the branch and the home office goes beyond periodic asset transfers. Depending on the internal reporting philosophy of the organization, general expenses incurred by the home office may well be allocated, at least in part, to the separate branches. By assigning costs such as corporate accounting, data processing, and advertising to these units, their individual profitability can be measured more precisely. Thus, accurate comparisons are made available to corporate officials on a branch-by-branch or year-by-year basis.

Because of the volume as well as importance of intracompany transactions, the interface existing between the accounting systems of the home office and each branch operation must be monitored closely. To facilitate this process, all reporting units normally establish an intracompany account within their ledgers. Although these accounts are referred to by a variety of different titles, the terms *branch* and *home office* are common and are used in this textbook.

To be more precise, the financial records of the corporation's home office should include a separate Branch account for each of the individual units. These ledger accounts serve to record all intracompany transfers and allocations from the vantage of the home office. Therefore, the balance in a Branch account signifies the corporation's current equity investment in that particular operation. Simultaneously, a parallel Home Office account is maintained by each branch to record these same interface transactions but from the viewpoint of the branch. Hence, the accumulated total also represents the equity investment attributable to the home office.

Since these two accounts are used to record the same transfers and allocations, the Branch and Home Office balances should be equal and offsetting at all times. From a practical perspective, though, such reciprocity frequently does not exist. In many companies, the volume of intracompany transfers and allocations is significant, thus raising the possibility of human errors occurring within the recording process. Additionally, the physical separation that exists between the home office and the various branches can create timing differences in the entering of many intracompany transactions.

Therefore, periodic reconciliation of the Branch and Home Office accounts is a required procedure in most large organizations. Although this agreement of the

How Do We Account for the Store in Greenville?

In 1990, several local investors opened a retail store in Spartanburg, South Carolina, to market fashionable clothes to both men and women. This operation proved to be quite successful; the break-even point in sales was reached in less than 2½ years. By 1998, the business had become well known throughout the region for both the price of its merchandise and the quality of its service. To capitalize on this reputation, the owners decided to open a second store in Greenville, approximately 25 miles away. Prior to beginning this new undertaking, the accounting department was asked to develop a plan that would extend the company's reporting system to encompass the new store. Two different approaches have been proposed, but the accounting department has not yet settled on a recommendation.

Plan One. One member of the accounting department feels that very little formal record-keeping should be carried out at the new store. "Have the Greenville operation monitor its sales, purchases, and expenses. At the end of each day, they can send us the results by fax machine and we will post all transactions to our ledger accounts here in the home office. We can simply create additional accounts where necessary: 'Sales—Greenville,' 'Inventory—Greenville,' and so on. All the records will be here under our control, and we can produce comparable results by store whenever necessary. A lot of work would be duplicated if the company hires more accountants and sets up a separate system for this new operation."

Plan Two. A second accountant argues that the Greenville branch should have an accounting department of its own. "First, you threaten to overload our system by adding all the transactions from this second store. In addition, keeping the multitude of transactions separated by store may prove to be quite difficult. I believe we should account for the home office here and let the company hire someone in Greenville to record the branch. The individual operations will be better monitored in this way, and we can consolidate the results periodically for external reporting purposes. Accounting is more efficient when carried out at the site of the business."

Both of these systems (as well as many variations) would work. Both are used by many companies. What factors should be weighed in deciding which system to adopt to account for the Greenville branch?

Branch and Home Office accounts is necessary prior to financial reporting, reconciliation usually is carried out more often to facilitate the discovery of errors and other recording problems.

Branch Accounting Illustrated

To demonstrate the accounting procedures applicable to branch operations, assume that the Zimmerman Company opens a new retail outlet in Topeka, Kansas, during the early months of 1998. A small building is acquired by the corporation for $200,000 with an additional $50,000 being paid for equipment. Based on company policy, these fixed assets are to be maintained on the financial records of the home office. A cash balance of $10,000 is transferred to the branch to begin operations as well as $80,000 in inventory from Zimmerman's central warehouse.

The following entries should be recorded within the accounting systems of the two parties to reflect these initial transactions:

Home Office Records			Branch Records		
Building	200,000		No entry because		
Equipment	50,000		of company policy.		
Cash		250,000			
Branch—Topeka	90,000		Cash	10,000	
Shipments to Branch		80,000	Shipments from Warehouse	80,000	
Cash		10,000	Home Office		90,000

As even this brief example shows, the Branch/Home Office accounts connect the two accounting systems. Both balances now indicate that the home office has invested $90,000 in the operations of the branch. Since these figures are in agreement, they are directly offset in the preparation of financial statements for external reporting purposes.

The Shipments to Branch account in the preceding entry is the equivalent of "Intracompany Sales," while Shipments from Warehouse is an "Intracompany Purchases" balance. These $80,000 figures also are reciprocals so that both are eliminated as a preliminary step whenever financial statements are being produced.

To provide a more complete illustration of branch operation accounting, assume that the following events subsequently transpire in 1998 in connection with the Topeka branch of the Zimmerman Company:

a. Cash sales of $75,000 are made.
b. A shipment of inventory is received from the home office with a transfer price of $50,000.
c. Salary expenses of $5,000 are paid.
d. Inventory costing $20,000 is acquired on account from outside vendors.
e. Invoices for utilities such as heat and light totaling $4,000 are paid.
f. Additional cash sales of $25,000 are made.
g. The home office pays $6,000 in property taxes assessed on the fixed assets located in Topeka. This cost is assigned to the branch.
h. Cash of $40,000 is transferred from the branch to home office's bank account.
i. The home office computes $10,000 as annual depreciation on the building and equipment located in Topeka. This expense is charged to the branch.
j. The home office assigns $6,000 of the current cost of a nationwide advertising campaign to its Topeka branch. Although this entry is recorded immediately by the home office, the information is not communicated to the Topeka branch until the first days of 1999.
k. The Topeka branch counts year-end inventory. Goods costing $90,000 are held on that date, indicating the cost of goods sold for the year of $60,000:

Initial shipment from home office	$80,000
Second shipment from home office	50,000
Purchase from outside vendors	20,000
Inventory available for sale	150,000
Ending inventory (per count)	(90,000)
Cost of goods sold	$60,000

l. The reciprocity of the Branch/Home Office intracompany accounts must be established by the company with any needed adjustments recorded.
m. After the reciprocal balances are brought into agreement, separate financial statements for the branch are prepared. These statements provide an indication of the operating success achieved by the branch as well as its current financial position.
n. The accounting information from both the home office and the branch are combined at the end of the period into a single set of financial statements to be distributed for external reporting purposes.
o. At the end of the fiscal year, all revenue and expense accounts of the branch operation are closed out. Because stockholders' equity accounts are not maintained by the branch, the resulting net income figure is closed into the company's Retained Earnings account located within the financial records of the home office.

The following journal entries are recorded by Zimmerman Company's home office and its Topeka branch to account for transactions a through k. Detailed explanations are then provided for the last four events: l through o.

Home Office Records		Branch Records	
Home Office Records		**Branch Records**	
a. No entry.		a. Cash 75,000	
		Sales	75,000
		Current branch sales.	
b. Branch—Topeka 50,000		b. Shipments from	
Shipments to		Warehouse 50,000	
Branch	50,000	Home Office	50,000
Inventory shipped to		Inventory shipments	
Topeka branch.		received from central	
		warehouse.	
c. No entry.		c. Salary Expense 5,000	
		Cash	5,000
		Payment of salary	
		expense.	
d. No entry.		d. Purchases 20,000	
		Accounts Payable	20,000
		Inventory acquired	
		from outside vendors.	
e. No entry.		e. Utility Expense 4,000	
		Cash	4,000
		Payment of utility	
		expenses.	
f. No entry.		f. Cash 25,000	
		Sales	25,000
		Current branch sales.	
g. Branch—Topeka 6,000		g. Property Tax Expense 6,000	
Cash	6,000	Home Office	6,000
Paid property taxes		Property taxes paid	
for branch.		by home office.	
h. Cash 40,000		h. Home Office 40,000	
Branch—Topeka	40,000	Cash	40,000
Received cash		Transferred cash to	
transfer from branch.		home office.	
i. Branch—Topeka 10,000		i. Depreciation	
Accumulated		Expense 10,000	
Depreciation	10,000	Home Office . . .	10,000
Computed		Depreciation	
depreciation and		allocated from home	
assigned balance to		office.	
branch.			
j. Branch—Topeka 6,000		j. Not entered prior to	
Advertising		year-end.	
Expense	6,000		
Portion of national			
advertising allocated			
to branch.			
k. No entry.		k. Inventory (balance	
		sheet) 90,000	
		Inventory (income	
		statement)	90,000
		Recording of year-	
		end inventory	
		balance.	

l. Reconciling Branch and Home Office Accounts   At this point, the reciprocity of the Branch/Home Office accounts is verified prior to preparing financial statements. Because of the potential volume of intracompany transactions that can occur during a period of time, reconciliation frequently becomes a very extensive process. Problems often arise within the accounting systems that necessitate adjustments to establish the equality of these accounts.

Disagreements between the Branch/Home Office balances, for example, are created by timing differences: events recorded on one set of financial records have not, as of yet, been entered into the other. In-transit items such as inventory and cash often fall into this category as would any home office expense allocation that has not been communicated to the branch. The recording of the Advertising Expense in *j* is an example of this specific type of accounting problem.

Timing differences are especially prevalent in companies where the branch maintains a separate accounting system. The physical distance between the two parties frequently prohibits the simultaneous recording of all financial events. Such problems usually can be avoided in fully automated systems that utilize a centralized computer. The computer is simply programmed to reject changes to either the Home Office or the Branch account unless an offsetting entry is simultaneously made to the reciprocal account.

Even in such computerized systems, however, occasional human errors can arise within the recording process. Therefore, most companies review and reconcile the Branch/Home Office accounts on a weekly or monthly basis. To facilitate this procedure, especially in companies maintaining separate accounting systems, the branch operation is normally directed to file a periodic, perhaps daily, listing of all entries to the intracompany account. The accuracy of the balance can then be established by matching this list (on an individual item basis, if necessary) against the reciprocal figures on the home office's records.

Returning to the Zimmerman Company illustration, the two intracompany accounts hold the following balances as of the end of 1998:

	Branch Account (home office's records)	Home Office Account (branch's records)
Initial transfer of cash and inventory	$ 90,000	$ (90,000)
Subsequent inventory transfer	50,000	(50,000)
Property tax allocation	6,000	(6,000)
Cash transferred to home office	(40,000)	40,000
Depreciation expense allocation	10,000	(10,000)
Advertising expense allocation	6,000	–0–
End-of-period totals	$122,000	$(116,000)

Because this illustration has only a few transactions, the $6,000 timing difference created by the advertising expense allocation is immediately evident. In many cases, however, a detailed matching of the entries is necessary to isolate all of the deviations within the ending account balances. After the reconciling items have been ascertained, adjustments can be made directly to the financial records of the specific party. For example, the Topeka branch must record the following entry to correct the timing problem identified in the preceding reconciliation.

Home Office Records	Branch Records

l. No adjustment needed since allocation has already been recorded.	*l.* Advertising Expense ... 6,000
	    Home Office 6,000
	    Advertising allocation from home office.

m. Producing Financial Statements for the Branch   After the reciprocity of the intracompany accounts is established, financial statements for the Topeka branch can be prepared as a basis for internal corporate analysis. These statements displayed in Exhibit 8–1 are based on the ledger balances that result from the previous series of journal entries. Since the $131,000 Home Office figure is the equivalent of an ownership interest, this account replaces the stockholders' equity section on the branch's balance sheet. Consequently, a separate statement disclosing the changes made in the Home Office account during the period is included as a substitute for a statement of retained earnings.

TOPEKA BRANCH OF ZIMMERMAN COMPANY
Financial Statements

Income Statement
Year Ending December 31, 1998

Sales		$100,000
Cost of goods sold:		
Beginning inventory	–0–	
Shipments from warehouse	$130,000	
Purchases	20,000	
Goods available for sale	150,000	
Ending inventory	(90,000)	(60,000)
Gross profit		$ 40,000
Operating expenses:		
Salary expense	5,000	
Depreciation expense	10,000	
Utility expense	4,000	
Advertising expense	6,000	
Property tax expense	6,000	(31,000)
Net income of branch		$ 9,000

Home Office Account
Year Ending December 31, 1998

Account balance, January 1, 1998		–0–
Transfers from home office:		
Cash	$ 10,000	
Inventory	130,000	
Expense allocations:		
Property taxes	6,000	
Depreciation	10,000	
Advertising	6,000	$162,000
Transfers to home office:		
Cash		(40,000)
Net income (above)		9,000
Account balance, December 31, 1998		$131,000

Balance Sheet
December 31, 1998
Assets

Cash	$ 61,000
Inventory	90,000
Total assets	$151,000

Liabilities and Equity

Accounts payable	$ 20,000
Home office (above)	131,000
Total liabilities and equity	$151,000

n. Producing Financial Statements for the Entire Company

Once financial statements for the Topeka branch have been developed, the Zimmerman Company can create a single combined set of statements for its entire organization. To achieve this objective, the simulated union of the accounting records for Zimmerman Company's home office and the Topeka branch is presented in Exhibit 8–2.

On this worksheet, only one branch operation is included to avoid unnecessary mechanical complications. Although companies frequently maintain control over a multitude of branches, the individual combination procedures are merely repeated for each separate unit. Therefore, a better understanding of this process can be gained by focusing attention on a single operation. In this illustration, the data gathered from the Topeka branch provides a complete demonstration of the various procedures necessary for arriving at combined financial statements.

A quick perusal of the combination worksheet presented in Exhibit 8–2 indicates that it is considerably less complex than the consolidation examples previously presented in this text. Here, the entire process is limited to offsetting the intracompany accounts that exist within the individual financial records. In Entry 1, the $130,000 balances recorded by both parties in connection with the inventory shipments are eliminated. When viewed from an external perspective, these transactions have created no changes in the company's overall financial position; they were simply internal asset transfers. Similarly, the $122,000 equity balances found in the Home Office and Branch accounts at the end of the period are removed by Entry 2. As with consolidation, the individual account balances of the branch should be included in the financial statements of the single economic entity rather than the lump sum amount invested by the home office.

Since no other reciprocal balances exist in this particular example, the remaining accounts of both parties are merely extended to arrive at combined totals for the organization. Therefore, the figures found in the final three columns of the worksheet in Exhibit 8–2 represent the operations of Zimmerman Company for 1998 and its financial position at the end of that year. A trial balance worksheet is demonstrated here rather than the financial statement format used in previous chapters. This change is included simply to illustrate that worksheets may take different forms.

Before leaving Exhibit 8–2, one final comment should be made about the utilization of a worksheet in home office/branch combinations. Often, as in the Zimmerman illustration, the figures to be reported can be determined by a few relatively uncomplicated elimination entries. In such cases, the worksheet is frequently unnecessary; the combination process consists of little more than the addition of all nonreciprocal balances. Although a worksheet is presented here, its inclusion is mainly to afford a visual display of the procedures being employed. The use of a worksheet is always an optional technique that can take various forms or even be omitted in practice.

o. Recording Closing Entries for the Branch Operation

The last requirement of the Zimmerman Company illustration can now be completed. The 1998 revenue and expense accounts of the Topeka branch must be closed out in anticipation of beginning a new fiscal year. Final balances are found on the worksheet in Exhibit 8–2. Because no equity accounts exist within the branch's own accounting system, the closing process is constructed to utilize the Retained Earnings account of the home office.[2]

---

[2]The individual revenue and expense accounts of the home office must also be closed out. Therefore, the Shipments to Branch balance also is reduced to zero at the end of this year.

Exhibit 8-2

ZIMMERMAN COMPANY
Worksheet to Combine Home Office and Topeka Branch
Year Ending December 31, 1998

Accounts	Home Office	Topeka Branch	Combination Entries Debit	Combination Entries Credit	Income Statement	Statement of Retained Earnings	Balance Sheet
Debits							
Cash	96,000	61,000					157,000
Accounts receivable	112,000	-0-					112,000
Inventory, 12/31/98	166,000	90,000					256,000
Buildings (net)	620,000	-0-					620,000
Equipment (net)	304,000	-0-					304,000
Branch—Topeka	122,000	-0-		(2) 122,000			
Dividends paid	30,000	-0-				30,000	
Inventory, 1/1/98	108,000	-0-			108,000		
Purchases	414,000	20,000			434,000		
Shipments from warehouse	-0-	130,000		(1) 130,000			
Salary expense	46,000	5,000			51,000		
Depreciation expense	34,000	10,000			44,000		
Utility expense	28,000	4,000			32,000		
Advertising expense	41,000	6,000			47,000		
Property tax expense	29,000	6,000			35,000		
Total debits	2,150,000	332,000					1,449,000
Credits							
Accounts payable	(86,000)	(20,000)					(106,000)
Long-term liabilities	(166,000)	-0-					(166,000)
Common stock	(303,000)	-0-					(303,000)
Additional paid-in capital	(83,000)	-0-					(83,000)
Retained earnings, 1/1/98	(544,000)	-0-				(544,000)	
Home office	-0-	(122,000)	(2) 122,000				
Sales	(672,000)	(100,000)			(772,000)		
Shipments to branch	(130,000)	-0-	(1) 130,000				
Inventory, 12/31/98	(166,000)	(90,000)			(256,000)		
Combined net income					(277,000)	(277,000)	
Combined retained earnings, 12/31/98						(791,000)	(791,000)
Total credits	(2,150,000)	(332,000)					(1,449,000)

Note: Parentheses indicate a credit balance.

Home Office Records			Branch Records		
o. Branch—Topeka	9,000		*o.* Sales	100,000	
Retained Earnings		9,000	Inventory (12/31/98) . .	90,000	
To record 1998			Shipments from		
income of Topeka			Warehouse		130,000
branch.			Purchases		20,000
			Salary Expense . .		5,000
			Depreciation		
			Expense		10,000
			Utility Expense . .		4,000
			Advertising		
			Expense		6,000
			Property Tax		
			Expense		6,000
			Home Office		9,000
			To close out 1998 revenue and expense accounts with net income being recorded on home office books.		

These closing entries achieve two basic objectives: each of the branch's revenue and expense accounts is returned to a zero balance and the net income for the period is added to retained earnings. In a manner similar to that of other interface activities, the Home Office and Branch accounts serve here as the connecting agents between the two accounting systems.

Unrealized Gains Created by Intracompany Transfers

As can be seen from a review of the worksheet in Exhibit 8–2, the procedures used in the combination process run somewhat parallel to that of a consolidation. Fortunately, many of the complex consolidation issues analyzed in previous chapters are not present in branch accounting. For example, no allocation is made of a purchase price. Consequently, no related amortization expense has to be recognized.

As exemplified by Exhibit 8–2, the principal function of the combination process is the direct elimination of all reciprocal balances. *However, at least one major complication does carry over from the consolidation area: year-end inventory balances often contain unrealized gains as a result of intracompany transactions.*

Inventory transfers may be priced (as in the Zimmerman example) at historical cost; however, alternative possibilities do exist. As discussed in Chapter 5, a company can elect to record merchandise shipments at the normal sales price, at its variable cost, at cost plus a predetermined markup, or at some other established value. One survey found 11 different systems in use for setting transfer prices with the market price being the most popular (used by 25.1 percent of the respondents) followed by full production cost plus a markup (16.6 percent) and a negotiated price (16.6 percent).[3]

Although the actual transfer pricing decision should be based on the company's policy regarding internal profitability measurement, problems may be encountered with any specific approach. For example, charging the branch with only the cost of transferred goods leaves the home office reporting an unrealistically low income figure and allows the branch to show significant, perhaps undeserved, profit margins. Conversely, recording transfers at an amount more than cost might force the branch to set prices at artificially high levels to maintain a standard gross profit.

Clearly, the transfer pricing issue is an often discussed philosophical issue somewhat removed from financial accounting. However, the resulting management deci-

---

[3]Roger W. Tang, "Transfer Pricing in the 1990s," *Management Accounting,* February 1992, p. 24.

sion directly affects the subsequent combination process. If a profit markup is included by the home office, any transferred inventory held by the branch at year's end has a book value exceeding historical cost. For external reporting purposes, procedures must be applied within the combination process to eliminate these unrealized gains. Only in this manner can ending inventory be returned to its original cost while the intracompany profit is being deferred until the merchandise is eventually sold to outside parties.

Unrealized Gains Not Separately Recorded   Several procedural techniques exist for dealing with unrealized inventory gains created by intracompany transactions. The exact process to be applied in a particular combination depends on the policy of the home office toward recording the gains at the time of transfer. Often, especially if profit margins are set at a standard percentage or amount, the home office makes no attempt to monitor the unrealized gains. Instead, the overvaluation is ignored until year-end and then eliminated from the inventory accounts based on the established markup. This approach is similar to that demonstrated previously in connection with the consolidation of incorporated subsidiaries.

To serve as an example, assume that inventory costing $200,000 is shipped by the home office to one of its branches. All such transfers are priced for internal reporting purposes based on a standard markup of 20 percent of historical cost but no separate recording is made of the transfer gain ($40,000 or 20 percent of $200,000). Under this policy, both parties simply record the intracompany shipments at $240,000. Subsequently, in producing financial statements at year's end, these two accounts are offset in the same manner as Entry 1 in Exhibit 8–2.

However, this elimination does not completely resolve the accounting problem created by the markup. The book value of any merchandise remaining with the branch is still overstated: the recorded account contains a portion of the unrealized gain. If the branch, for example, sells $180,000 of this transferred inventory (75 percent) but retains $60,000, the original cost of the ending balance would have been only $50,000 ($60,000/120%). For external reporting, the $10,000 inflation must be deferred on the combination worksheet through an additional entry.

Combination Entry (year of transfer)

Inventory (12/31/98) (income statement)
 (or Cost of Goods Sold) 10,000
  Inventory (12/31/98) (balance sheet)   10,000
 To remove unrealized intracompany gain from ending inventory
 balances.

As in previous consolidation examples, this $10,000 unrealized gain reappears in the succeeding fiscal period as an element of the branch's beginning inventory balance. For this reason, the gain must be removed again, but this time in the year following the original transfer. Because of the intervening closing entries, the second elimination of the $10,000 intracompany profit is made as follows:

Combination Entry (year subsequent to transfer)

Retained earnings, 1/1/99 10,000
  Inventory (1/1/99) (income statement)
   (or Cost of Goods Sold)   10,000
 To remove unrealized intracompany gain from beginning-of-year
 balances.

Unrealized Gains Separately Recorded   Although the combination entries demonstrated earlier appropriately account for intracompany gains, this method of deferring unrealized profits is not applicable in all cases. A variation of this process is required if the home office chooses to keep an ongoing record of transfer gains. Separately accounting for markups at the time of shipment provides the company with a means of monitoring inventory balances, which may be especially important if a perpetual system is in use. Therefore, the $240,000 transfer could have been re-corded initially by the two parties through the following journal entries:

Home Office Records			**Branch Records**		
Branch	240,000		Shipments from		
Shipments to			Home Office	240,000	
Branch		200,000	Home office . . .		240,000
Unrealized Gains		40,000	To record shipments		
To record shipments			from home office at		
to branch with gains			a transfer price		
separately			above cost.		
monitored.					

Subsequently, if 75 percent of this inventory is sold to outside parties by the branch, the home office reclassifies the appropriate portion of the gain:

Home Office Records			**Branch Records**
Unrealized Gains			No entry recorded.
(75%)	30,000		
Realized Gains		30,000	
To reclassify			
inventory gains that			
have now been			
earned.			

This approach is adopted by some companies as a means of providing better control over inventory balances. By separating the original $40,000 gain, the home office is able to maintain inventory records at historical cost because the Shipments to Branch figure measures the cost of the transferred goods. However, a discrepancy has been introduced between the two reciprocal shipment accounts: one now reports $200,000 while the other shows $240,000. Consequently, in producing combination entries, the two gain accounts must be taken into consideration to establish agreement. They are both eliminated to remove the impact of the intracompany transaction.

Combination Entry (year of transfer)

Shipments to Branch	200,000	
Unrealized Gains	10,000	
Realized Gains	30,000	
Shipments from Home Office		240,000
To eliminate the effects of intracompany inventory transfers.		

Despite the removal here of both home office gain accounts, the book value of any inventory retained by the branch is still inflated by the remaining portion of the intracompany profit. Thus, the $10,000 inventory reduction entry shown previously (to return the balance to cost) must be repeated. Indeed, this entry is necessary regardless of the method incorporated by the home office to monitor realized and unrealized gains.

Combination Entry (year of transfer)

Inventory (12/31/98) (income statement)		
(or Cost of Goods Sold)	10,000	
Inventory (12/31/98) (balance sheet)		10,000
To remove unrealized intracompany gain from ending inventory		
balances.		

When the practice of separately monitoring intracompany gains is applied by the home office, a slightly more complex accounting situation arises in the year *subsequent* to the transfer. The Unrealized Gain account on the home office records is not closed out at the end of the initial period; thus, the Retained Earnings account is correct rather than being $10,000 overstated (as in the previous illustration). For this reason, a different adjustment must be made to eliminate the intracompany profit from the subsequent figures. Assuming that the home office reclassifies the $10,000 to a Realized Gain account during 1999, this figure must be removed in preparing combined financial statements. The accompanying reduction to beginning inventory (within cost of goods sold) effectively increases gross profit in the period of actual realization.

Combination Entry (year subsequent to transfer)

Realized Gains   10,000
       Inventory (1/1/99) (income statement)
        (or Cost of Goods Sold)   10,000
  To remove previous intracompany gain from individual account
balances.

CONSIGNMENT ACCOUNTING

The establishment of branch operations is not the only technique available to a company attempting to achieve the wide-scale distribution of its product line. One alternative that has the potential for placing inventory items into thousands of outlets is consignment marketing. In its simplest form, a manufacturer or distributor (the *consignor*) gives possession of merchandise to a retailer (the *consignee*) while continuing to retain legal ownership. Although the inventory is then physically held by the consignee, title to the goods remains with the consignor.

The consignee serves in the capacity of a sales agent with ownership of the goods passing directly from the consignor to a third-party purchaser. Once the merchandise is sold, the consignor is entitled to any proceeds remaining from the revenue after the consignee has removed a predetermined sales commission and reimbursement for any specified expenses. Traditionally, the inventory is held by the consignee for a stated time with any unsold items then returned to the consignor.

Hanes Corporation, as one example, has achieved significant success in marketing L'eggs panty hose in this manner. The company "decided to distribute L'eggs on consignment. Hanes would own the display and the inventory. The store would provide only the sales space. Route sales representatives, mostly young women, would drive trucks to the stores, where they could refill empty racks on the spot . . . . It has paid off handsomely. L'eggs has captured over 15 percent of the U.S. hosiery market."[4]

Many of the advantages of consignment retailing are readily apparent from the illustration provided by the Hanes Corporation. A company can offer products at a great number of locations with a minimal cost while retaining control over merchandising and pricing. This strategy is especially appealing as a means of introducing a new product to retailers who might be hesitant about investing in an unproven item. The consignor expands the product's market base while the consignee invests little and runs virtually no risk of incurring large losses if the merchandise fails to sell.

Consignment marketing has become especially prevalent over the years in a number of widely varying industries. Antiques and art works, for example, are often sold in this manner as are plant seeds for home gardening. In a recent trend, a significant portion of medical supplies are placed in hospitals on consignment. This technique minimizes inventory losses as well as the amount of money tied up in supplies and, thus, may help reduce the high cost of health care.

Relationship between the Consignor and the Consignee

Prior to the initial transfer of inventory, the consignor and consignee should agree on a written contract clearly establishing the rights and responsibilities of both parties. Although contractual law is not the primary focus of this textbook, an accountant

---

[4]Carol E. Curtis, "Nothing Beats a Great Pair of L'eggs," *Forbes,* September 29, 1980, p. 73.

must be able to advise clients. Furthermore, a thorough knowledge of the various stipulations found in a consignment contract is needed as a basis for understanding and recording subsequent events.

A consignment agreement usually covers the following:

- The price charged to the consignee or the amount of commission to be paid.
- Responsibilities for expenses such as damaged merchandise, bad debts, and product warranties.
- The consignor's responsibility for reimbursing the consignee for costs such as advertising and delivery.
- The consignee's responsibility to store goods safely.
- Procedure for return of unsold goods.
- Invoicing procedures.
- Consignee's responsibility for periodic reporting to consignor.
- Rights upon termination of relationship.[5]

Consignment marketing provides both parties with rather unique accounting situations. The consignor must continue to report inventory that it no longer possesses while the consignee, despite physically holding the goods, has little or no cost to record. To reflect this arrangement, accounting procedures should be designed so that all inventory costs, especially those of the consignor, are correctly maintained. In addition, both reporting systems must ensure that no revenues are recognized until the point of actual sale.

To meet these objectives, companies have devised a wide variety of bookkeeping techniques to record consignment transactions. This textbook examines the general procedures most commonly encountered in practice. However, as long as all cost and revenue figures are properly stated, a degree of accounting flexibility is available in this area.

Because consignment transactions are viewed from two such differing perspectives, the accounting process employed by the consignor is in distinct contrast to that of the consignee. In the following coverage, the procedures applicable to the consignor are examined first. This analysis is followed by a similar presentation of the recording techniques utilized by the consignee. Structuring the material in this manner avoids the confusion that can result from attempting to review both sides of the same transaction simultaneously.

Consignment Accounting—The Consignor

In organizing the accounting process, the consignor must first establish ledger accounts to monitor the various consignment transactions, especially the cost of its transferred inventory. Either of two approaches can be adopted for this purpose.

In many cases, a single holding account (usually referred to as a *Consignment-Out* account) is set up to record all consignment transactions initially: the original cost of the merchandise, sales revenue, commissions, and so on. *Every transaction is entered directly to this account and then appropriately reclassified for reporting purposes at the end of the fiscal period.* Although this method simplifies the day-to-day accounting process, a detailed analysis of the Consignment-Out balance has to be made on a regular basis. If many transactions have occurred, developing this periodic listing may be quite tedious and time consuming.

An alternative approach is available to the consignor for recording these same transactions. A Consignment Inventory account is established to monitor the mer-

[5]Paul R. Kinny, "How To Protect Consigned Inventory," *Business Credit,* January 1991, p. 25.

chandise costs with all other transactions being reported in a normal fashion. Under this approach, consignment revenues and expenses are recorded by the consignor as revenues and expenses. Thus, no extensive end-of-period analysis is required. However, the company's accounting system must be designed to ensure that all consignment transactions are properly classified within the financial records at the time of the event. Consequently, this method is most frequently used by companies with extensive consignment sales.

When reviewing these two methods of recording consignment transactions, a number of differences are noted. However, regardless of the specific procedures utilized in a company's bookkeeping system, all variations are purely mechanical. The resulting financial information is not dependent on the recording method being employed.

Consignment Accounting—Illustrated from the Consignor's Perspective

As a basis for demonstration, assume that Richmond Corporation enters into a consignment arrangement with Lee Company. At the beginning of each month, Richmond (the consignor) is to provide Lee with a stock of inventory having a cost of $50,000. Richmond is responsible for all transportation costs as well as advertising. The agreement also stipulates that Lee is to receive reimbursement for any expenses incurred in connection with a warranty given to customers specifying that defective merchandise will be fixed without charge.

In return, Lee offers the inventory for sale at a price 50 percent in excess of original cost. The contract further states that any credit sales are the responsibility of the consignee: Lee must, therefore, absorb losses resulting from bad debts. At the end of each month, Lee is to deduct all reimbursable expenses along with a 15 percent commission and forward the remainder of the sales revenue to Richmond.

As indicated earlier, the consignor's journal entries depend on the structure of that company's accounting system. To provide a better comparison of the alternative methods, Richmond's record-keeping is shown here in parallel. Thus, the initial shipment of consignment goods sent to Lee can be recorded by Richmond through either of the following two entries:

Consignor's Records (Consignment-Out account is being used)		Consignor's Records (Consignment Inventory account is being used)	
Consignment-Out	50,000	Consignment Inventory	50,000
Inventory	50,000	Inventory	50,000

The direct reduction to the Inventory account shown here is utilized by companies that maintain perpetual records. If the consignor accounts for inventory through a periodic system, the credit portion of this entry is more likely to be made to an account such as Consignments Shipped.

To continue with this illustration, assume that Richmond pays $900 in transportation costs to ship the inventory delivered to Lee. An additional $1,200 is then spent by the consignor for an advertising campaign to promote these products. Subsequently, at the end of the first month of this arrangement, Richmond receives the following statement from Lee in connection with this consignment merchandise:

Consignee's Report		
Consignment sales		$ 60,000
Less: Commissions (15%)	$9,000	
Repair expenses under warranty	2,000	(11,000)
Check enclosed		$ 49,000

Based on the information accumulated about this series of transactions, Richmond records the following three journal entries. Once again, the use of both Consignment-Out and Consignment Inventory accounts are illustrated here.

Consignor's Records (Consignment-Out account)		
Consignment-Out	900	
Cash		900
To record transportation cost for consignment inventory.		
Consignment-Out	1,200	
Cash		1,200
To record advertising made in connection with consignment inventory.		
Cash	49,000	
Consignment-Out		49,000
To record cash received from consignee.		

Consignor's Records (Consignment Inventory account)		
Consignment Inventory	900	
Cash		900
To record transportation cost for consignment inventory.		
Advertising Expense	1,200	
Cash		1,200
To record advertising made in connection with consignment inventory.		
Cash	49,000	
Commission Expense	9,000	
Warranty Expense	2,000	
Consignment Sales		60,000
To record consignment sales and expenses as well as cash received from consignee.		

Adjustment Process—Consignment-Out Approach   At the close of the month, assume that Richmond elects to review and adjust its consignment records immediately rather than wait until year's end. Periodic reclassification is especially important if numerous transactions are involved or if the consignor is producing interim financial statements.

Under the consignment-out approach, Richmond has a single consignment account with a balance of $3,100 at the end of this first month:

Consignment-Out Account	
Inventory shipped	$ 50,000
Transportation	900
Advertising	1,200
Sales revenue	(60,000)
Commissions	9,000
Warranty repairs	2,000
Ending balance	$ 3,100

To achieve a proper accounting of Richmond's consignment transactions, each of these amounts must be reclassified. As stated, the Consignment-Out account merely holds the various transactions. Before an adjustment can be developed for this purpose, a cost of goods sold figure for the period must be calculated. Based on the standard 50 percent markup, the $60,000 revenue reported by the consignee indicates that the merchandise disposed of by the consignee had a base cost of $40,000 ($60,000/150%). Consequently, 80 percent of the original $50,000 shipment has now been sold ($40,000/$50,000). This percentage enables Richmond to compute its cost of goods sold as $40,720 with an ending inventory balance of $10,180:

Total inventory cost (historical cost plus $900 transportation)	$50,900
Cost of goods sold (80% sold)	$40,720
Ending consignment inventory (20% retained)	$10,180

Obviously, verifying the physical existence of this ending inventory is a control problem when consignment marketing is used. Many consignors have inventory at numerous retail locations. Under such conditions, periodic inspection is not always possible. Thus, the accuracy of the $10,180 figure being reported here may depend entirely on data provided by the consignee. Unfortunately, more than one consignor has learned that consignee record-keeping may not be as timely and correct as would be desired.

Having computed the cost of goods sold for the period, Richmond can produce the following reclassification entry to report its consignment transactions for the period. Although the appropriate $10,180 inventory balance is recorded here as a separate asset, the amount also could be left in the Consignment-Out account.

Consignor's Records
(Consignment-Out Approach)

Consignment Inventory	10,180	
Cost of Goods Sold	40,720	
Advertising Expense	1,200	
Commission Expense	9,000	
Warranty Expense	2,000	
Consignment Sales		60,000
Consignment-Out		3,100

To reclassify consignment transactions occurring during the current month to appropriate accounts.

One aspect of this reclassification should be specifically mentioned. Both the consignment sales figure and the related cost of goods sold are explicitly shown. Several alternatives exist for reporting this particular information. Richmond, for example, could net these two figures and record the resulting $19,280 gross profit as a single income item. This procedure is common in companies where consignment transactions make up only a small portion of total revenues.

As a second possibility, the components of the consignor's cost of goods sold can be presented individually: the beginning and ending inventory balances, shipments, freight, and so on. Although the cost of goods sold total would no longer be directly evident within the accounting records, additional information is made available by inclusion of each of these separate figures.

Adjustment Process—Consignment Inventory Approach   If Richmond had chosen to adopt the alternative method of recording these transactions, the Consignment Inventory account would hold an accumulated balance of $50,900 (cost plus transportation). The inventory costs alone are included in this total. Thus, a much less complicated end-of-period recording process is required. Although cost of goods sold has been omitted, sales and expense figures have already been properly classified during the month. Richmond needs to make only a single adjustment for reporting purposes: reclassification of the $40,720 (as just calculated) from an asset to an expense account.

Consignor's Records
(Consignment Inventory Approach)

Cost of Goods Sold	40,720	
Consignment Inventory		40,720

To record cost of goods that were sold on consignment during the month.

Although the entries vary, the consignment-out and consignment inventory approaches produce identical financial results for the consignor:

Consignment sales			$ 60,000
Cost of goods sold:			
Beginning inventory		–0–	
Transfers	$50,000		
Transportation	900	$ 50,900	
Goods available for sale		50,900	
Ending inventory (20%)		(10,180)	(40,720)
Gross profit			$ 19,280
Less: Advertising and commissions			(10,200)
Warranty expense			(2,000)
Consignment net income			$ 7,080

Since reported financial information is not affected, a consignor may select either of these two methods for recording consignment transactions. The simplicity of the consignment-out approach is immediately appealing because so little attention is required. The holding account serves as a balancing figure for all consignment transactions made during the period. Unfortunately, the periodic reclassification process can be a rather pedestrian task, especially if large volumes of consignment shipments and sales are made on a regular basis.

In contrast, establishing a Consignment Inventory account requires more extensive analysis on a day-to-day basis but does not entail a rigorous review prior to preparing any type of financial report. For this reason, companies that engage in a significant amount of consignment transactions often design their accounting systems along the lines of the consignment inventory approach. Other enterprises that use consignment marketing less frequently are likely to rely on a Consignment-Out account rather than investing resources in the development of more extensive bookkeeping techniques.

Accounting Used by the Consignee

The coverage of consignment accounting switches at this point to the reporting procedures utilized by the consignee. Since this party has possession of the merchandise but not the title, an entirely different perspective of these transactions is assumed. The consignee never owns the inventory; thus, the cost of the asset and any associated obligation are simply ignored. Under normal conditions, the consignee does have to account for four events that occur in connection with consignment goods:

1. Expenditures made for reimbursable expenses.
2. Sales of the consignment merchandise.
3. Commissions earned on consignment sales.
4. Transfer of appropriate cash proceeds to the consignor.

To facilitate the recording process, a Consignment-In account is commonly maintained by the consignee. Because this account contains no inventory costs, only amounts due to and from the consignor are included. Thus, an ending debit balance represents a receivable from the consignor while a credit total indicates a liability.

Using the information in the previous example, Lee, as the consignee, would record four transactions in connection with the consignment inventory.

- Sale of goods for $60,000.
- Payment of $2,000 in reimbursable warranty costs.
- Recognition of 15 percent commission.
- Transfer to consignor of remaining $49,000 in cash: $60,000 revenues less $9,000 in commissions (15%) and warranty costs.

In reviewing the entries that follow, note that Lee makes only a memorandum entry to record the initial receipt of the consignment inventory. Since title to these items has not been conveyed, Lee bears none of the cost of these goods.

Consignee's Records

Memorandum entry: Received $50,000 in consignment inventory
  from Richmond Corporation.

Cash (or Accounts Receivable)	60,000	
Consignment-In		60,000
To record sale of merchandise being held on consignment.		
Consignment-In	2,000	
Cash (or Accounts Payable)		2,000
To record expenditure for reimbursable repairs made in connection		
with product warranty on consigned goods.		

Consignment-In	9,000	
Commissions Earned		9,000
To record 15 percent sales commission on consignment sales for the month.		
Consignment-In	49,000	
Cash		49,000
To close out Consignment-In account by forwarding applicable balance to Richmond Corporation, the consignor.		

SUMMARY

1. Geographic separation places special demands on the gathering and reporting of financial information. In this chapter, accounting systems and procedures are examined that record transactions gathered from many, often distant, locations. The reporting process utilized by organizations that have created branch operations is explored first, followed by a similar coverage of consignment marketing.

2. Companies frequently establish individual operations, referred to as *branches,* throughout the country and even the world. Geographic dispersion is especially prevalent in both retailing and banking, which attempt to attract customers by offering merchandise and service at many convenient locations. The most significant accounting problem created by this type of organization is the recording of intracompany transactions and allocations. Normally, cash and inventory are transferred between the parties and common costs are assigned to the individual units. For accounting purposes, a Branch account is established on the home office's records for every branch. Likewise, a Home Office account is maintained by each individual branch operation to serve as the equivalent of an equity balance. Although these two accounts should be equal and offsetting at all times, periodic reconciliations are required to identify and correct any errors and timing differences.

3. Individual financial statements can be prepared for each branch on a regular basis. For external reporting purposes, though, combined statements encompassing all of the company's operations are necessary. Such statements can be produced through the use of a combination worksheet that utilizes simulated journal entries to eliminate all reciprocal balances. The Branch/Home Office accounts should be offset in this manner along with balances created by inventory transfers and any other intracompany transactions.

4. Intracompany inventory shipments may be made at a transfer price above historical cost. If any portion of this merchandise is not resold or used by the end of the fiscal period, the unrealized gain associated with these goods must be removed from the inventory balances. Both the asset account and the ending inventory figure (within cost of goods sold) are reduced. Some enterprises separately record these unrealized gains at the time of transfer. If this approach is followed, these additional account balances are eliminated within the combination process.

5. Wide-scale distribution of products also can be achieved through consignment marketing. A manufacturer or distributor (a *consignor*) transfers physical possession of merchandise to a retailer (a *consignee*) while continuing to maintain legal title. Since the consignee is not required to purchase the inventory, that party faces little risk of loss. The consignee normally holds the goods until sold and then forwards the receipts (less a commission and any reimbursable costs) to the consignor. If any of the inventory fails to sell, it is normally returned after a specified time.

6. As the owner, the consignor should account for the cost of consigned inventory until the time of sale. In addition, all related expenses as well as the resulting revenues must be properly monitored. Many consignors establish a Consignment-Out account in which all transactions are recorded initially. A detailed analysis is periodically required of the resulting balance so that the various components can be reclassified for reporting purposes. This approach is easy to apply, although accurate interim information is not always readily available.

7. A consignor can adopt an alternative accounting approach by using a Consignment Inventory account. Under this method, each consignment transaction is properly classified at the time of the event: sales are recorded as sales, expenses as expenses, and so on. More effort is required to record this data, but accurate information is constantly

maintained. For reporting purposes, an adjusting entry to record ending inventory and cost of goods sold is still necessary.

8. Proper accounting procedures must also be established by the consignee. Since title to the goods is not being held, the consignee need not record inventory costs. Many companies do, however, set up a Consignment-In account for the recording of all sales, commissions, reimbursable costs, and the like. The components of this balance can then be analyzed and adjusted at any time that a report (or payment) is to be made to the consignor.

COMPREHENSIVE ILLUSTRATION

Problem

(Estimated Time: 35 to 50 Minutes) The Rice Corporation is a distributor of widgets in Pueblo, Colorado. Historically, Rice has sold this product exclusively through a local department store on a consignment basis. In 1998, Rice also began to sell widgets in a branch outlet that the company opened in the nearby town of Chester. The trial balance for the Rice Corporation as of December 31, 1999, follows:

	Debits	Credits
Accounts payable		$ 39,000
Accounts receivable	$ 29,000	
Accumulated depreciation		18,000
Advertising expense	16,000	
Branch—Chester	145,000	
Buildings and equipment	66,000	
Cash	7,000	
Common stock		200,000
Consignment-out	120,000	
Depreciation expense	4,000	
Dividends paid	12,000	
Inventory (income statement)	79,000	67,000
Inventory, 12/31/99	67,000	
Land	21,000	
Purchases	246,000	
Repair expense	13,000	
Retained earnings, 1/1/99		275,000
Salary expense	27,000	
Shipments to branch		88,000
Shipments to consignee		170,000
Utility expense	5,000	
Totals	$857,000	$857,000

For accounting purposes, Rice requires both the branch and the consignment dealer to file periodic operating reports. Following (on the left) are summaries of these transactional memos for the year of 1999 as well as the composition of Rice's own reciprocal accounts (on the right).

CHESTER BRANCH OF RICE CORPORATION Home Office Account 1999		RICE CORPORATION Branch—Chester Account 1999	
Beginning balance	$ (71,000)	Beginning balance	$ 71,000
Cash transfer	28,000	Inventory shipped—cost	36,000
Inventory received	(36,000)	Cash received	(28,000)
Allocation of advertising	(6,000)	Inventory shipped—cost	16,000
Inventory received	(19,000)	Allocation of	
Allocation of salary	(8,000)	advertising expense	6,000
Cash transfer	19,000	Allocation of salaries	8,000
Inventory received	(22,000)	Inventory shipped—cost	22,000
		Inventory shipped—cost	14,000
End-of-year balance	$(115,000)	End-of-year balance	$145,000

DEPARTMENT STORE—CONSIGNEE Consignment Report 1999		RICE CORPORATION Consignment-Out Account 1999	
Beginning balance	–0–	Beginning balance (inventory)	$ 35,000
Reimbursable advertising................	$ 3,000	Inventory shipped	98,000
Consignment sales	(128,000)	Packing of shipment	2,000
Partial consignment payment	94,000	Freight for shipment	4,000
Reimbursable insurance.................	2,000	Payment received	(94,000)
Consignment sales	(162,000)	Inventory shipped	72,000
Consignment sales	(40,000)	Freight for shipment	2,000
Commissions earned (20%)	66,000	Packing of shipment	1,000
End-of-year balance	$(165,000)	End-of-year balance...................	$120,000

Note: One-third of last inventory shipment remains at end of year.

Required

Prepare a worksheet to combine the accounting records of the Rice Corporation and its Chester branch so that financial statements can be produced. In creating this worksheet, assume that all parties are using FIFO inventory costing systems. Also assume that any omissions from the records just presented were caused by timing differences occurring at the end of the fiscal year. *Where unexplained discrepancies exist, assume that the account balances of the Rice Corporation's home office are correct.* Since the actual journals and ledgers are not available, any adjusting entries should be made directly on the worksheet. The final 1999 trial balance for the Chester branch follows:

	Debit	Credit
Accounts payable........................		$ 9,000
Accounts receivable	$ 44,000	
Accumulated depreciation.................		6,000
Advertising expense.....................	6,000	
Buildings and equipment	54,000	
Cash.................................	26,000	
Depreciation expense	4,000	
Home office		115,000
Insurance expense	4,000	
Inventory (income statement)	16,000	24,000
Inventory, 12/31/99	24,000	
Salary expense	17,000	
Sales		121,000
Shipments from home office	77,000	
Utility expense	3,000	
Totals	$275,000	$275,000

Solution

As indicated within this chapter, monitoring the interaction between the various reporting systems is an essential activity of both branch and consignment accounting. Thus, as a preliminary step in preparing financial statements, Rice Corporation should reconcile the Home Office and Branch accounts. The Consignment-Out balance also needs to be brought into agreement with the information provided by the consignee. Once these interface accounts have been properly adjusted, the development of combined financial statements should be a rather uncomplicated process.

Branch Operations   Although a number of different approaches are viable here, an analysis of the Home Office/Branch accounts provides a convenient starting point. As can be seen from the two individual trial balances, the home office is reporting a Branch balance of $145,000 whereas the reciprocal Home Office account (on the branch's books) holds a total of only $115,000. A comparison of the detailed listing of entries presented in the problem indicates that three recording errors have created this $30,000 difference:

- A cash transfer of $19,000 from the branch was not recorded by the home office prior to the end of the year.
- A $14,000 shipment of merchandise from the home office has not yet been acknowledged by the branch.
- An inventory transfer was entered by the branch as $19,000 rather than $16,000.

The first two of these problems are merely timing differences. In each case, one of the accounting systems failed to record information in the appropriate fiscal period. Corrections have been made on the combination worksheet (in Exhibit 8–3) through Entries 1 and 2. Since inventory (Entry 2) was in transit at year-end, an additional assumption is made that this merchandise was not included in the physical count, taken by the branch, an oversight rectified through Entry 3.

The final item is apparently a recording error made by the Chester branch (since the financial records of the home office are assumed to be correct). Thus, the $19,000 that was reported by the branch is reduced (in Entry 4) to the correct $16,000 balance. The combination of the home office and branch then can be consummated by the elimination of all reciprocals. Entry 5 offsets the intracompany inventory shipments, Entry 6 removes the adjusted $126,000 Home Office/Branch accounts.

Consignment Sales   Having now produced the entries necessary for combining the financial data of the home office and the branch, Rice's consignment transactions should be analyzed next. Since a Consignment-Out (or holding) account is utilized, a complete breakdown of its contents is a requisite for reclassifying the various balances.

As a basis for this procedure, the Consignment-Out account is compared with the report filed by the consignee. *However, no agreement is sought between the final balances since these accounts are not actually reciprocals.* Rather, reconciliation helps to identify any transactions that the consignor has not recorded properly. By comparing the details of these two accounts, Rice is able to determine

1. The cost of inventory still being held by the consignee.
2. The cost of consignment goods sold.
3. The revenue and expense figures for the period.
4. Any ending receivable balance due from the consignee.

To arrive at the amounts to be reported by the consignor, the following four schedules can be developed:

Ending consignment inventory:
Total cost of last shipment (including freight and packing)	$ 75,000
Inventory remaining (as reported by consignee)	⅓
Cost of ending consignment inventory	$ 25,000

Cost of consignment goods sold:
Beginning inventory (per ledger account)	$ 35,000
Shipments to consignee	170,000
Packing and freight	9,000
Less: Ending inventory (above)	(25,000)
Cost of consignment goods sold	$ 189,000

Consignment revenue and expense balances:
Consignment sales (from consignee's report)	$ 330,000
Cost of goods sold (above)	(189,000)
Gross profit	141,000
Operating expenses (from consignee's report):	
Commissions	(66,000)
Advertising	(3,000)
Insurance	(2,000)
Consignment income	$ 70,000

Ending consignment receivable balance:
Consignment sales	$ 330,000
Less: Commissions—20%	(66,000)
Less: Reimbursable expenses:	
Advertising	(3,000)
Insurance	(2,000)
Amount due from consignee	259,000
Partial payment received during year	(94,000)
Consignment receivable—end of year	$ 165,000

Exhibit 8–3

RICE CORPORATION
Combination Worksheet
For Year Ending December 31, 1999

Accounts	Home Office Debit	Home Office Credit	Chester Branch Debit	Chester Branch Credit	Combination Entries Debit	Combination Entries Credit	Income Statement	Statement of Retained Earnings	Balance Sheet
Accounts payable		39,000		9,000					(48,000)
Accounts receivable	29,000		44,000						73,000
Accumulated depreciation		18,000		6,000					(24,000)
Advertising expense	16,000		6,000		(7) 3,000		25,000		
Branch—Chester	145,000		-0-			(1) 19,000 (6) 126,000			-0-
Buildings and equipment	66,000		54,000						120,000
Cash	7,000		26,000		(1) 19,000				52,000
Commissions expense	-0-		-0-		(7) 66,000		66,000		
Common stock		200,000							(200,000)
Consignment inventory (balance sheet)	-0-		-0-		(7) 25,000				25,000
Consignment inventory (income statement)	-0-		-0-		(7) 35,000	(7) 25,000	(BI) 35,000 (EI) (25,000)		
Consignment-out	120,000		-0-			(7) 120,000			-0-
Consignment receivable	-0-		-0-		(7) 165,000				165,000
Consignment sales		-0-		-0-		(7) 330,000	(330,000)		
Depreciation expense	4,000		4,000				8,000		
Dividends paid	12,000		-0-					12,000	
Freight and packing	-0-		-0-		(7) 9,000		9,000		
Home office	-0-			115,000	(4) 3,000 (6) 126,000	(2) 14,000			-0-

	Home Office	Branch	Consignee	Eliminations Dr	Eliminations Cr	Combined (Income Statement)	Combined (Balance Sheet)
Insurance expense	-0-	4,000		(7) 2,000		6,000	
Inventory (income statement)	79,000	16,000				(BI) 95,000 / (EI) (105,000)	
Inventory, 12/31/99	67,000	24,000	24,000				105,000
Land	21,000	-0-					21,000
Purchases	246,000	-0-				246,000	
Repair expense	13,000	-0-		(3) 14,000	(3) 14,000	13,000	
Retained earnings, 1/1/99	275,000						(275,000)
Salary expense	27,000	17,000				44,000	
Sales	-0-	77,000	121,000			(121,000)	
Shipments from home office	-0-	-0-	-0-	(2) 14,000	(4) 3,000	-0-	
Shipments on consignment	-0-			(7) 170,000 (5) 88,000	(5) 88,000	170,000	
Shipments to branch	88,000					-0-	
Shipments to consignee	170,000					(170,000)	
Utility expense	5,000	3,000				8,000	
Combined net income						(26,000)	(26,000)
Combined retained earnings						(289,000)	(289,000)
Totals	857,000	275,000	275,000			275,000	-0-

Note: Parentheses indicate a credit balance.

"BI" represents beginning inventory; "EI" is ending inventory.

Worksheet entries are discussed in the text.

Exhibit 8-4   Financial Statements

RICE CORPORATION
Income Statement
for Year Ending December 31, 1999

	Home Office and Branch		Consignments		Totals	
Sales		$121,000		$ 330,000		$ 451,000
Cost of sales:						
Beginning inventory	$ 95,000		$ 35,000		$ 130,000	
Purchases	246,000		–0–		246,000	
Shipments on consignment	(170,000)		170,000		–0–	
Freight and packing	–0–		9,000		9,000	
Goods available	171,000		214,000		385,000	
Ending inventory	(105,000)		(25,000)		(130,000)	
Cost of goods sold		(66,000)		(189,000)		(255,000)
Gross profit		$ 55,000		$ 141,000		$ 196,000
Advertising expense						(25,000)
Commissions expense						(66,000)
Depreciation expense						(8,000)
Insurance expense						(6,000)
Repair expense						(13,000)
Salary expense						(44,000)
Utility expense						(8,000)
Net income						$ 26,000

Statement of Retained Earnings
for Year Ending December 31, 1999

Retained earnings, 1/1/99		$275,000
Net income (above)	$ 26,000	
Less: Dividends paid	(12,000)	14,000
Retained earnings, 12/31/99		$289,000

Balance Sheet
December 31, 1999
Assets

Cash		$ 52,000
Accounts receivable		73,000
Consignment receivable		165,000
Inventory		105,000
Consignment inventory		25,000
Land		21,000
Buildings and equipment	$120,000	
Less: Accumulated depreciation	(24,000)	96,000
Total assets		$537,000

Liabilities and Equities

Accounts payable		$ 48,000
Common stock	$200,000	
Retained earnings (above)	289,000	489,000
Total liabilities and equities		$537,000

Note: Although companies are required to report a statement of cash flows for every fiscal period in which an income statement is prepared, insufficient information is included in this illustration for that purpose. Thus, the statement of cash flows has been omitted.

Based on these computations, an extended worksheet entry can be produced by Rice to reclassify the various consignment figures. This entry recognizes consignment revenue, expense, and asset balances that should be reported by the company for the period.

Worksheet Entry 7

Consignment Receivable	165,000	
Commissions Expense	66,000	
Advertising Expense	3,000	
Insurance Expense	2,000	
Shipments on Consignment	170,000	
Freight and Packing	9,000	
Consignment Inventory, 12/31/99 (balance sheet)	25,000	
Consignment Inventory (income statement)	35,000	25,000
Consignment Sales		330,000
Consignment-Out		120,000

Exhibit 8–3 presents the completed worksheet for Rice Corporation and its various operations. The figures in the last three columns can be utilized to produce financial statements for external reporting purposes. The seven entries just discussed have been used to combine the account balances of the company's home office and the Chester branch as well as report the consignment transactions for 1999.

When a company such as Rice relies on more than one method of distributing its products, a question arises as to the best approach to take for reporting the operational figures. Although no single format is applicable in all cases, one possible income statement is presented in the financial statements in Exhibit 8–4. Revenues, cost of goods sold, and gross profit are all disclosed for both branch and consignment transactions. Because no other allocation information has been given, the operating expenses are presented as common costs. In practice, many of these figures also might be divided between the two distributing functions of this company.

QUESTIONS

1. What is meant by the term *branch?*
2. Why is the development of branch operations so prevalent in retailing and banking?
3. When a corporation makes use of branch operations, accounting problems often arise in connection with intracompany transactions. What intracompany transactions are commonly encountered? What difficulties are presented?
4. In accounting for branch operations, many companies assign a portion of their general corporate expenses to the various branches. What is the rationale for such allocations?
5. Home Office and Branch accounts are found frequently in the accounting systems of companies that maintain branch operations. What is the purpose of these two accounts? Why should reciprocity be maintained between their balances?
6. How do the combination procedures applied in connection with branch operations resemble the consolidation process and in what ways are they different?
7. What is consignment marketing? What are the advantages to a company of selling on consignment?
8. What are the major objectives in accounting for consignment transactions?
9. A consignor can adopt either of two different approaches in the recording of consignments. Describe these approaches and indicate the advantages of each.
10. What is the purpose of a Consignment-In account?

LIBRARY ASSIGNMENT

Read "Integrating the Enterprise—'Beam Out This Shipment, Scotty' " in *Industry Week,* September 18, 1995, by John H. Sheridan with Tim Stevens and John Teresko. Prepare a report on the impact that supplier-retailer interconnected information systems have on the proliferation of consignment sales.

PROBLEMS

1. Hayes, Inc., has a branch operation located in Duluth. On the home office financial records, Hayes reports a Duluth—Branch account with a $78,000 debit balance. At that same time, the branch operation is reporting a Home Office account with an $81,000 credit balance. Which of the following statements is true?
   a. Since two different sets of records are being kept, these two accounts are not designed to agree.
   b. The difference indicates that inventory may be in transit from the home office to the branch.
   c. The difference indicates that cash may be in transit from the branch to the home office.
   d. Cash may have been collected by the home office for the branch but not yet reported to the branch.

2. Lewis, Inc., operates a branch in Toledo, Ohio. On the home office financial records at the end of 1998, Lewis reports a Toledo—Branch account with a $167,000 debit balance. The branch operation is reporting on that same date a Home Office account with a $162,000 credit balance. Which of the following statements is true?
   a. Since two different sets of records are being kept, these two accounts are not designed to agree.
   b. The difference indicates that cash may be in transit from the branch to the home office.
   c. Cash may have been collected by the home office for the branch but not yet reported to the branch.
   d. The difference indicates that the home office might have assigned a $6,000 expense allocation to the branch that was incorrectly recorded by the branch as $11,000.

3. A company sells inventory from its home office and also from a branch operation in a nearby city. At the end of the fiscal year, what happens to the Branch account (on the home office's financial records) and the Home Office account (on the branch's financial records) when financial statements for the company as a whole are being produced?
   a. The Home Office account is eliminated but the Branch account balance is reported as an investment.
   b. The two accounts are reconciled and offset against each other.
   c. The Home Office account is reported as an equity account whereas the Branch account is shown as an investment.
   d. On these financial statements, the manner of reporting these two accounts depends on whether they have debit or credit balances.

4. A company has several branch operations that sell merchandise transferred from the home office. This inventory is transferred at a price 20 percent more than cost. In producing financial statements for the company as a whole, what happens at the end of the year?
   a. The unrealized gain on any remaining inventory is eliminated for financial reporting purposes.
   b. The gain remains as reported since the amount would be immaterial.
   c. Any remaining gain is reported as a contra balance to the Purchases account.
   d. Any remaining gain is reported as a contra balance to the Branch account.

5. Consignment marketing is a popular means by which companies can get wide distribution of their products. Which of the following statements is true?
   a. The consignor has no risks.
   b. The consignor is guaranteed that all goods will be sold.
   c. The consignee might be willing to attempt to sell goods that it would otherwise not carry.
   d. The consignor has no costs to record as a result of this type of marketing.

6. What does the balance in a Consignment-Out account represent?
   a. The amount that a consignee owes to a consignor at any time.
   b. The consignor's cost of all consignment inventory being held by consignees.
   c. The amount of consignment sales made by the consignee during the current period.
   d. The net of all consignment costs incurred by a consignor less all receipts from the consignee.

7. Simpson Corporation starts a branch operation in a nearby town. Merchandise costing $80,000 is shipped to this branch along with equipment costing $50,000. During the initial year, the home office assigns $8,000 in expenses to the branch. The branch sells 70 percent of the inventory that it received for $80,000 and remits $40,000 in cash to the home office. What is the correct Home Office account balance on the records of the branch? Closing entries have not been made.
   a. $98,000.
   b. $104,000.
   c. $122,000.
   d. $178,000.

8. Lancaster, Inc., starts a branch operation to sell more of its merchandise. Inventory costing $60,000 is shipped to this branch at a transfer price of $90,000. During the initial year, the home office pays $17,000 in expenses for the branch. The branch sells 80 percent of the inventory that it received for $110,000 and remits $70,000 in cash to the home office. What is the correct Home Office account balance on the records of the branch? Closing entries have not been made.
   a. $7,000.
   b. $37,000.
   c. $75,000.
   d. $147,000.

9. Splicer starts a branch operation on January 1, 1998. Inventory costing $72,000 is shipped to this branch at a transfer price of $100,000. Freight is an additional $6,000. The branch sells 70 percent of this inventory for $110,000 and remits $70,000 in cash to the home office. On Splicer's financial statements for this period, what is the appropriate Cost of Goods Sold figure?
   a. $50,400.
   b. $54,600.
   c. $70,000.
   d. $74,200.

10. Storey Corporation operates a branch in Dallas, Texas. In October, the home office transferred $34,000 in inventory to this branch. Although the home office made the correct journal entry, the branch credited its Home Office account for $43,000. In November, the branch collected $1,000 on an account receivable for the home office. The home office was properly notified but debited its Branch account for $4,000. At the end of the year, the home office paid and recorded a $6,000 expense for the branch but the branch has not yet made the appropriate entry. Also, at year's end, the branch conveyed $25,000 in cash to the home office but the home office has not yet made the necessary entry. What corrections are needed?
   a. The home office needs to credit its Branch account for $24,000 and the branch needs to debit its Home Office account for $9,000.
   b. The home office needs to credit its Branch account for $30,000 and the branch needs to debit its Home Office account for $3,000.
   c. The home office needs to credit its Branch account for $22,000 and the branch needs to debit its Home Office account for $15,000.
   d. The home office needs to credit its Branch account for $28,000 and the branch needs to debit its Home Office account for $3,000.

11. A branch operation buys most of its inventory from outside parties. However, this year the home office transferred merchandise costing $50,000 to the branch for $80,000. At the end of the year, 20 percent of this merchandise was still held by the branch. Although the inventory was correctly counted and reported, the branch did not tell the home office that this portion of the remaining goods came from transfers. Consequently, the home office assumed that all of the transferred merchandise had been sold to outside parties. What is the resulting impact on the net income reported for the company as a whole?
   a. The net income figure would still be correctly calculated.
   b. The net income figure would be $6,000 overstated.
   c. The net income figure would be $30,000 overstated.
   d. The net income figure would be $30,000 understated.

Problems 12 and 13 are based on the following information:

The Simon Company always ships merchandise to a branch outlet in Chicago at a 30 percent markup above cost. During 1998, this branch received $182,000 in such shipments while also acquiring goods from outside vendors at at cost of $96,000. Half of the branch's December 31, 1998, inventory of $57,200 came from home office acquisitions. At the beginning of 1998, the branch held merchandise with a transfer price of $49,400. All of this inventory had been purchased directly from the home office.

12. At the end of 1998, what is the adjusted balance in Simon's Unrealized Gain account?
    a. $4,250.
    b. $5,340.
    c. $6,000.
    d. $6,600.

13. For external reporting purposes, what cost of goods sold figure should be reported by the branch for this period?
    a. $207,846.
    b. $223,400.
    c. $230,000.
    d. $234,800.

14. Cochran, Incorporated, sends 1,000 units of inventory costing $80 each to a consignor to be sold at $120 per unit. Freight costs paid by Cochran total $2,000. The consignor also pays an additional $1,000 in advertising costs. The consignee sells 60 percent of this merchandise. The consignee is entitled to a commission equal to 10 percent of sales price. The consignee only remits $50,000 at this time. What profit has been earned by the consignor?
    a. $13,800.
    b. $14,000.
    c. $14,600.
    d. $15,000.

15. Crescent Corporation ships 2,000 units of inventory costing $30 each to a consignor to be sold at $70 per unit. Freight costs paid by Cochran amount to $8,000. Another $3,000 is paid by the consignor for advertising costs. During the current period, the consignee sells 70 percent of this merchandise. The consignee is entitled to a commission equal to 20 percent of sales price. The consignee remits $78,400 at this time. What is the unadjusted balance in Crescent's Consignment-Out account?
    a. $7,400 credit.
    b. $22,400 credit.
    c. $16,400 debit.
    d. $31,400 debit.

16. Bears, Inc., owns a branch operation in Chicago. As of the end of the current year, the home office has a Chicago—Branch account with a $77,000 debit balance. At the same time, the branch is reporting a Home Office account with a $61,000 credit balance. An investigation uncovers the following:

    ■ During the year, the home office shipped merchandise costing $16,000 to the branch at a transfer price of $28,000. The branch accidently recorded the shipment as $38,000.
    ■ At year's end, the home office assigned $14,000 in expenses to the branch. The branch recorded this allocation as $19,000.
    ■ Also at year's end, the branch transferred $31,000 in cash to the home office. The home office has not yet recorded this money.

Required

    a. What is the reconciled balance of the Chicago—Branch and Home Office accounts?
    b. What correcting entries are needed?

17. Wilson Company's home office has the following transactions with one of its branch operations located in Phoenix:

    1998
    Jan. 1   The beginning Branch account holds a debit balance of $86,000.
    Jan. 2   The home office receives notice of a $32,000 cash transfer deposited on December 31, 1997, by the Phoenix branch. The home office had made no previous recording.

Jan. 6   The home office ships $30,000 in inventory to this branch at a $34,500 transfer price.

Jan. 10   The home office pays $1,000 monthly rent to the owner of the Phoenix branch's building. This cost is assigned to the operations of the branch (communication is made immediately).

Jan. 12   The home office allocates $3,000 of general corporate expenses to the branch (communication is made immediately).

Jan. 24   The home office ships $40,000 in inventory to the Phoenix branch at a transfer price of $46,000. The branch erroneously records the shipment as $64,000.

Jan. 31   The home office allocates $3,000 in transportation costs (that were incurred during January) to the branch. The assignment is not communicated to the branch until February 2, 1998.

Feb. 1   Notification of a $74,000 cash transfer is received by the home office. The deposit was made in Phoenix on January 31, 1998.

Required

a.   What is the unadjusted balance of the Branch—Phoenix account on the home office's books as of January 31, 1998?

b.   What is the unadjusted balance of the Home Office account on the branch's financial records as of January 31, 1998?

c.   What is the reconciled value for the Home Office/Branch accounts as of January 31, 1998?

d.   Assume that a FIFO costing system is being used and that 25 percent of the final inventory shipment remains unsold at year-end. What is the amount of unrealized gain to be eliminated from the branch's ending inventory?

18.   King Company sells its merchandise on consignment. This year the company began operations with $18,000 (8,000 units) of inventory out on consignment. During the year, inventory costing $66,000 (27,500 units) was shipped to the consignee. The related freight cost was $6,050. At the end of the period, King received the following statement from the consignee.

Sales (24,500 units at $6)	$147,000
Delivery cost of units sold	(4,900)
Advertising	(16,300)
Commissions	(29,400)
Check enclosed	$ 96,400

Required

a.   What is King's cost of goods sold if the company employs a FIFO system?

b.   What is King's cost of goods sold if the company employs a LIFO system?

c.   What is the adjusted book value of the Consignment-Out and Consignment-In accounts at the end of the year if both parties use a FIFO costing system?

19.   The Lewis Corporation has a branch operation in Fairfax, Virginia. Because of the high volume of intracompany transactions, the company has encountered difficulty in reconciling its Home Office/Branch accounts. Following is a listing of the components of the Branch balance (from the home office's ledger) followed with the Home Office account as recorded by the branch.

BRANCH—FAIRFAX
Account Composition (on financial records of home office)

Jan.	1	Beginning balance	$ 62,000
Jan.	2	Cash received	(16,000)
Mar.	2	Inventory transferred	42,000
Apr.	1	Salary allocation	9,200
July	2	Inventory transferred	36,000
Sept.	5	Insurance expense allocation	1,000
Oct.	6	Cash received	(21,000)
Nov.	4	Inventory transferred	28,000
Dec.	31	Depreciation allocation	(3,000)
		End-of-year balance (debit)	$138,200

HOME OFFICE

Account Composition (on financial records of branch)

Jan.	1	Beginning balance	$ (35,000)
Jan.	2	Inventory received	(11,000)
Mar.	5	Inventory received	(42,000)
Apr.	5	Salary allocation	(9,000)
Apr.	8	Cash transferred	45,000
July	6	Inventory received	(48,000)
Sept.	10	Insurance expense allocation	(1,000)
Oct.	4	Cash transferred	21,000
Nov.	8	Inventory received	(28,000)
Dec.	31	Cash transferred	15,000
		End-of-year balance (credit)	$ (93,000)

Additional Information:

- A cash transfer received during the year was credited by the home office to Miscellaneous Income.
- The bookkeeper for the branch incorrectly recorded two amounts: a salary allocation and an inventory shipment.

Required

   a. Determine the correct balance for the Home Office/Branch accounts as of December 31.

   b. Prepare adjusting entries for both parties as of December 31 to properly record these intracompany accounts.

20. The Columbia Company recently made the decision to open a branch of its business in Gaffney. Since that time, the following transactions have occurred in connection with this new operation:

- The home office acquired $18,000 in equipment to be used (and recorded) by the branch.
- The home office paid $3,000 to lease a building for the last six months of this year. This cost was charged to the branch.
- Inventory costing $80,000 was shipped to branch by the home office at a transfer price of $100,000. The home office separately records all of its unrealized gains.
- The branch paid $11,000 for various operating expenses.
- The branch sold 75 percent of the inventory received, collecting $105,000 in cash.
- The branch transferred $60,000 in cash to the home office.

Required

   a. Prepare journal entries for both the home office and the branch to record the previous transactions.

   b. Prepare the worksheet entries that would bring about the combination of the home office and branch at the end of the period.

   c. Produce entries to close out the operations of the branch at the end of the period.

21. During the first part of the current year, Nobula, Inc. begins a branch operation in Cherry Hill, New Jersey. Equipment costing $50,000 is immediately sent to this site. In addition, inventory costing $40,000 is transferred but at a price of $60,000. Cash of $10,000 also is conveyed to the branch.

   The following events occur thereafter:

- The branch buys inventory from an outside party at a cost of $30,000. A periodic inventory system is in use.
- The home office pays $10,000 rent on a building for the next eight months. The branch is notified of this payment.
- Sales of $90,000 are made. Cash of $40,000 is collected immediately. The rest of the sales are made on account.
- The branch pays $8,000 for advertising and another $5,000 for salaries.
- The branch transfers $10,000 in cash to the home office. The money is received and recorded.
- A $3,000 receivable is collected by the home office for the branch. The branch is notified of this collection.
- The building rented by the branch is occupied for four months.

Required

  a. Prepare all necessary journal entries for both the branch and the home office.
  b. Assume that one-third of the transferred merchandise and one-fourth of the inventory bought from outsiders remains at year's end. What is the net income of the branch operation?

22. In hopes of improving corporate profitability, Denmark, Inc., has opened a branch operation in the city of Norge. Merchandise is shipped to this branch at a transfer price 50 percent more than the home office's cost. At the end of 1998, Denmark allocated several expenses to the branch but the branch has not yet been notified about these amounts.

Advertising expense . . . . $11,000 allocated to the Norge branch
Rent expense . . . . 7,000 allocated to the Norge branch
Miscellaneous expenses . . . . 6,000 allocated to the Norge branch

   In addition, one $21,000 shipment of inventory has not yet been received or recorded by the Norge branch. A $9,000 cash transfer from the branch has not yet been received or recorded by the home office.
   Following are the various account balances for the home office and the branch. Determine the total for each account to be presented in a set of financial statements prepared for the company as a whole.

	Home Office	Branch
Debits:		
Cash	$ 16,000	$ 11,000
Accounts receivable	81,000	37,000
Inventory, 12/31/98 (balance sheet)	97,000	60,000
Branch—Norge	177,000	–0–
Land, buildings, and equipment	361,000	99,000
Shipments from home office	–0–	159,000
Purchases	429,000	–0–
Depreciation expense	17,000	11,000
Advertising expense	29,000	18,000
Rent expense	14,000	9,000
Miscellaneous expenses	62,000	32,000
Inventory, 1/1/98	121,000	36,000
Total debits	$1,404,000	$472,000
Credits:		
Accumulated depreciation	$ 90,000	$ 18,000
Accounts payable	48,000	56,000
Notes payable	180,000	–0–
Home office	–0–	123,000
Common stock	60,000	–0–
Retained earnings, 1/1/98	260,000	–0–
Sales	489,000	215,000
Shipments to Norge branch	180,000	–0–
Inventory, 12/31/98 (income statement)	97,000	60,000
Total credits	$1,404,000	$472,000

23. The Jiminie Company began in 1998 to sell merchandise through a consignee. Prepare journal entries for Jiminie for the following transactions assuming that a Consignment-Out account is being used. In addition, prepare the year-end reclassification entry that would be needed.

   ■ 1,500 units of inventory costing $30 apiece are transferred to the consignee.
   ■ Jiminie pays $4,500 in freight costs to have these units delivered to the consignee.
   ■ Jiminie pays $3,000 to have the units insured enroute to the consignee.
   ■ The consignee sells 1,000 units owned by Jiminie for $50 each. Consignee retains $5,000 as a commission and $2,000 to cover the cost of a local advertising campaign. The remaining $43,000 is forwarded to Jiminie.

24. During the current year, the Lang Corporation decided to begin selling its inventory on consignment. Hill, Inc., agrees to serve as a consignee. Hill receives a commission of 20 percent on every sale that is made. Lang transfers inventory to Hill having a cost of $55,000 but a sales value of $80,000. Lang pays an additional $4,000 in delivery costs.

Hill sells 60 percent of this inventory for cash and remits the appropriate amount to Lang.

Required

a. Prepare journal entries for both companies. Assume that Lang uses a Consignment Inventory account.
b. Compute the amount of profit earned by Lang from its consignment sales.
c. Determine the ending balance in the Consignment Inventory account on Lang's balance sheet.

25. Financial statement information follows for the Northern Company and its Millburn branch:

	Northern Company	Millburn Branch
Sales	$(300,000)	$(180,000)
Inventory, 1/1	40,000	10,000
Purchases	160,000	–0–
Intracompany shipments	(90,000)	120,000
Inventory, 12/31	(25,000)	(20,000)
Unrealized gains	(30,000)	–0–
Operating expenses	140,000	28,000
Net income	$(105,000)	$ (42,000)
Retained earnings, home office, 1/1	$(620,000)	$ (90,000)
Net income (above)	(105,000)	(42,000)
Dividends (transfers)	70,000	20,000
Ending balance	$(655,000)	$(112,000)
Current assets	$ 225,000	$ 79,000
Millburn branch	122,000	–0–
Fixed assets (net).........................	586,000	93,000
Total assets	$ 933,000	$ 172,000
Liabilities	$(198,000)	$ (60,000)
Home office (above)	–0–	(112,000)
Common stock	(80,000)	–0–
Retained earnings (above)...................	(655,000)	–0–
Total liabilities and equities	$(933,000)	$(172,000)

At the end of the fiscal year, a $10,000 cash transfer from the branch was in transit.

Required

Prepare a combination worksheet for the Northern Company and this branch operation.

26. Addams ships inventory with a cost of $98,000 to a consignee in hopes of generating additional revenues. Freight and transportation costs amounting to $7,000 were paid by Addams.

The consignee subsequently sells 70 percent of this merchandise for $124,000, remitting $102,000 to Addams after subtracting a $20,000 commission and $2,000 in reimbursable selling costs.

No adjusting or reclassification entries have, as of yet, been recorded by Addams.

Required

a. What amount of net income should Addams recognize in connection with these consignment transactions?
b. If Addams uses a single Consignment-Out account, what is the current balance?
c. Assume that Addams uses a single Consignment-Out account. Prepare journal entries for Addams along with any needed adjusting or reclassification entries.
d. Assume that Addams uses a Consignment Inventory account. Prepare journal entries for Addams along with any needed adjusting or reclassification entries.
e. What is the current balance of the Consignment-In account found within the financial records of the consignee?

27. On January 1, 1998, Landon, Inc., opened a branch operation in the nearby community of Belwood. During the year that followed, the home office incurred the following transactions in connection with this newly formed branch:

1998

Jan. 1   Transferred several items to the Belwood branch:

         Cash—$30,000

         Inventory—$36,000 (cost)

         Equipment—$122,000 (cost)

June 2   Transferred inventory costing $18,000 to branch in Belwood.

July 1   Paid 1998 property taxes of $5,000 assessed on assets held by the Belwood branch.

Sept. 1   Transferred inventory costing $26,000 to the branch in Belwood.

Dec. 31   Allocated a $6,000 portion of general corporate expenses to the Belwood branch.

Dec. 31   Received cash transfer from Belwood branch.

During this same period, the Belwood branch recorded the following events:

1998

Jan. 10   Received initial transfers from home office.

Jan. 20   Paid $4,000 rent expense for the year.

Feb. 1   Sold half of inventory on hand for $27,000 cash.

Apr. 1   Sold remaining inventory for $33,000 cash.

May 1   Paid miscellaneous expenses of $7,000.

June 5   Received shipment of inventory.

July 6   Received communication concerning property tax payment.

Sept. 9   Received shipment of inventory.

Oct. 1   Sold the June 5 inventory for $26,000 in cash (a FIFO costing system is used).

Nov. 1   Paid miscellaneous expenses of $4,000.

Dec. 22   Transferred $63,000 cash to home office.

Dec. 31   Calculated and recorded depreciation expense of $4,000.

Dec. 31   Received communication from home office concerning expense allocation.

Required

a.   What amount of net income has been earned by the Belwood branch?

b.   On December 31, 1998, prior to recording closing entries, what is the appropriate balance in the Home Office/Branch accounts?

c.   Prepare journal entries for this period for the Belwood branch. Closing entries are not required. Assume that a perpetual inventory system is being used.

d.   Prepare a balance sheet for the Belwood branch as of December 31, 1998.

e.   Assume that all entries have been recorded properly by both parties. However, the home office has a policy of transferring inventory shipments at a price 20 percent above cost. What are the balances in the Branch and Home Office accounts on December 31, 1998, after all closing entries?

28.   Hopkins, Inc., sells a number of different items from its headquarters in Denver, Colorado. In recent years, in hopes of increasing sales volume, the company has opened two branches in nearby cities: Wilson and Simmons. Merchandise is shipped to these outlets periodically and recorded at a transfer price that includes a 50 percent markup over cost.

     At the end of 1999, Hopkins assigns the following portions of several corporate expenses to these two branches. Although these allocations were recorded by the company headquarters, the branches did not receive this information prior to the end of the year.

Allocations	Wilson	Simmons
Advertising expense	$4,000	$ 5,000
Rent expense	3,000	4,000
Miscellaneous expenses	5,000	5,000

Required

The following financial records are for the home office and these two branches as of December 31, 1999. Produce a worksheet to combine the accounts of these three operations so that a single set of financial statements can be prepared for Hopkins, Inc. Also prepare closing entries for each of the branches.

	Hopkins	Wilson	Simmons
Debits			
Cash..................................	$ 25,000	$ 10,000	$ 30,000
Accounts receivable	94,000	20,000	38,000
Inventory, 12/31/99 (balance sheet)	214,000	35,000	40,000
Branch—Wilson	176,000	–0–	–0–
Branch—Simmons	232,000	–0–	–0–
Land, buildings, and equipment............	330,000	120,000	90,000
Shipments from home office	–0–	90,000	170,000
Purchases	380,000	–0–	–0–
Depreciation expense	20,000	6,000	9,000
Advertising expense.....................	30,000	10,000	10,000
Rent expense...........................	10,000	5,000	15,000
Miscellaneous expenses	50,000	10,000	8,000
Inventory, 1/1/99	186,000	30,000	60,000
Total debits	$1,747,000	$336,000	$470,000
Credits			
Accumulated depreciation................	$ 60,000	$ 12,000	$ 18,000
Accounts payable.......................	20,000	5,000	24,000
Notes payable	240,000	–0–	10,000
Home office	–0–	164,000	218,000
Common stock	100,000	–0–	–0–
Retained earnings, 1/1/99	413,000	–0–	–0–
Sales	440,000	120,000	160,000
Shipments to branch	260,000	–0–	–0–
Inventory, 12/31/99 (income statement)	214,000	35,000	40,000
Total credits	$1,747,000	$336,000	$470,000

29. The Oregon Company has sold merchandise on consignment for a number of years. At the beginning of 1998, $85,000 of Oregon's consignment inventory is being held by Charlotte, Inc. Currently, Charlotte owes $36,000 to Oregon for consignment sales made during the previous year.

Following are the consignment transactions for Oregon that occurred during the first quarter of the new period:

1998

Jan. 9   Received $36,000 check from Charlotte.
Feb. 2   Received the following statement from Charlotte:

Sales	$110,000
Commissions...................	(27,500)
Advertising	(2,200)
Delivery	(1,600)
Amount due	78,700
Current remittance	(40,000)
Amount still due	$ 38,700

Feb. 20   Paid $1,000 insurance on consignment goods.
Feb. 27   Shipped inventory costing $68,000 to Charlotte.
Mar. 2   Paid $1,100 freight cost on the above shipment.
Mar. 6   Received $38,700 check from Charlotte.
Mar. 20   Received following statement from Charlotte:

Sales	$124,000
Commissions...................	(31,000)
Advertising	(2,500)
Delivery	(2,300)
Amount due.................	88,200
Current remittance	(50,000)
Amount still due...........	$ 38,200

Charlotte's latest statement also indicates that 30 percent of the inventory shipped on February 27 remains unsold. Oregon utilizes a FIFO inventory system.

Required

    a. Assume that Oregon uses a Consignment-Out (or holding) account to record its transactions. Prepare the journal entries for the first three months of 1998, including the reclassification entries needed at the end of the quarter.

    b. Compute the net income derived by Oregon from these consignment transactions.

    c. Assume that Oregon uses a Consignment Inventory account to record consignment transactions as they occur. Prepare the journal entries for the first three months of 1998, including the company's cost of goods sold entry.

    d. Prepare journal entries for Charlotte for the first three months of 1998.

30. In hopes of increasing sales volume, the Heyman Company opened a branch outlet several years ago in the nearby city of Dover. Merchandise is shipped to this store periodically and recorded at a transfer price that includes a 40 percent markup over cost. At the end of 1999, Heyman assigns the following corporate expenses to this branch. Although the main office has properly recorded these allocations, no entry has yet been made by the branch.

Expense	Allocation to Dover
Advertising	$9,000
Rent	6,000
Miscellaneous	2,000

    The following trial balances are for the main office and the Dover branch as of December 31, 1999. One $14,000 inventory shipment has not been received or recorded by Dover.

Required

Prepare a worksheet to combine the records of these two operations so that a single set of financial statements can be prepared for Heyman, Inc.

	Heyman	Dover
Debits		
Cash	$ 25,000	$ 18,000
Accounts receivable	108,000	25,000
Inventory, 12/31/99 (balance sheet)	209,000	42,000
Branch—Dover	207,000	—
Land, buildings, and equipment	340,000	112,000
Shipments from home office	—	96,000
Purchases	348,000	—
Depreciation expense	25,000	8,000
Advertising expense	36,000	15,000
Rent expense	12,000	5,000
Miscellaneous expenses	40,000	20,000
Inventory, 1/1/99	175,000	35,000
Total debits	$1,525,000	$376,000
Credits		
Accumulated depreciation	$ 80,000	$ 16,000
Accounts payable	37,000	15,000
Notes payable	220,000	—
Home office	—	176,000
Common stock	100,000	—
Retained earnings, 1/1/99	240,000	—
Sales	529,000	127,000
Shipments to branch	110,000	—
Inventory, 12/31/99 (income statement)	209,000	42,000
Total credits	$1,525,000	$376,000

31. The Brendan Company has always marketed a large percentage of its goods through a branch operation in the city of Davis, Florida. This year, the company also began to distribute some of its merchandise on consignment through Mark, Inc.

Following are the December 31, 1998, trial balances for Brendan and for the Davis branch. From this information as well as the other data presented, construct a worksheet to combine these operations for external reporting purposes.

	Brendan Company	Davis Branch
Debits		
Cash	$ 6,000	$ 27,000
Receivables	29,000	42,000
Inventory	41,000	46,000
Consignment-out	56,000	–0–
Land	23,000	–0–
Buildings	109,000	–0–
Equipment	43,000	127,000
Branch—Davis	111,000	–0–
Dividends paid	16,000	–0–
Inventory, 1/1/99	26,000	21,000
Purchases	275,000	64,000
Shipments from home office	–0–	153,000
Advertising expense	14,000	17,000
Salary expense	31,000	16,000
Depreciation expense	9,000	12,000
Miscellaneous expense	20,000	4,000
Total debits	$ 809,000	$ 529,000
Credits		
Accumulated depreciation	$ (36,000)	$ (27,000)
Accounts payable	(39,000)	(22,000)
Long-term liabilities	(164,000)	(12,000)
Common stock	(60,000)	–0–
Retained earnings, 1/1/98	(102,000)	–0–
Home office	–0–	(94,000)
Unrealized gains	(11,000)	–0–
Realized transfer gains	(45,000)	–0–
Sales	(115,000)	(328,000)
Shipments to branch	(110,000)	–0–
Shipments to consignee	(86,000)	–0–
Inventory, 12/31/98	(41,000)	(46,000)
Total credits	$(809,000)	$(529,000)

Additional Information:

■ The Consignment-Out account measures inventory shipments made during the year. This balance has been reduced recently by a $30,000 payment received at the end of the year from Mark, Inc., accompanied by the following report:

Sold: 80% of consignment inventory		$125,000
Reductions:		
Commissions	$26,000	
Warranty expense	11,000	
Advertising expense	8,000	(45,000)
Check enclosed		(30,000)
Amount due		$ 50,000

■ The branch's beginning inventory balance for the period contained $6,000 in unrealized intracompany gains whereas ending inventory is stated at an amount $11,000 in excess of cost.

■ One intracompany shipment during the year was recorded incorrectly by the branch. The error amounted to $7,000.

■ A $10,000 cash transfer was not recorded by the home office until the money was received on January 5, 1999.

32. Burt Corporation distributes merchandise through a consignment system. The company uses a standard cost accounting and records all inventory at a cost of $1,000 per unit. Following is the Consignment-Out account that Burt has maintained to record transactions with Hassle, Inc., a major consignee.

Date	Amount	Explanation
1/1	$97,000 debit	Beginning balance—89 units plus transportation cost
3/6	40,000 debit	Cost of inventory shipped to Hassle
3/19	6,000 debit	Freight cost on 3/6 shipment
4/8	9,000 debit	Local advertising incurred in connection with sale at Hassle
5/16	61,000 credit	Cash received from Hassle
6/1	20,000 debit	Loan to Hassle—10% annual interest
7/2	66,000 debit	Cost of inventory shipped to Hassle
7/11	6,500 debit	Freight cost on 7/2 shipment
8/3	1,000 credit	Item from last shipment is returned because of damage—loss is recorded
12/6	94,000 credit	Cash received from Hassle
12/31	$88,500 debit	Ending balance

When submitting cash to Burt during the year, Hassle filed the following two reports:

Date: May 10

Sales (at $2,000 per unit)		$104,000
Less: Commission	$20,000	
Delivery to customers	8,000	
Advertising	15,000	43,000
Amount remitted		$ 61,000

Date: December 1

Sales (at $2,000 per unit)		$164,000
Less: Commission	$40,000	
Delivery to customers	16,000	
Advertising	19,000	75,000
Amount currently due		$ 89,000
Loan repayment		5,000
Amount remitted		$ 94,000

Burt uses a FIFO system in recording inventory costs.

Required

a. What cost of goods sold should be recognized by Burt in connection with the consignment sales made by Hassle?

b. What is the recorded cost of Burt's consignment inventory that is being held by Hassle as of December 31?

c. What income should be recognized by Burt in connection with the consignment sales made by Hassle?

d. What reclassification journal entry should Burt record at year's end?

e. What income would be recognized by Hassle in connection with its sales?

Foreign Currency Transactions and Hedging Foreign Exchange Risk

QUESTIONS TO CONSIDER

- How does a company that has transactions in a foreign currency determine the amounts to be reported in the financial statements?

- Does a change in the value of a foreign currency asset or liability held by a company represent a gain or loss that should be reported in income?

- What is foreign exchange risk? How does a company become exposed to foreign exchange risk?

- What is the basic objective of hedging an exposure to foreign exchange risk?

- What is a hedge of a foreign currency transaction? What is a hedge of a foreign currency commitment? How does the accounting for these two types of hedge differ?

- How are foreign currency options used to hedge foreign exchange risk? How do firms account for foreign currency options?

- What is the proper accounting for a foreign currency forward contract entered into for speculative reasons?

Today, our global economy is a reality. Even small businesses are involved in transactions occurring throughout the world. Merchandise is commonly bought and sold in markets from Chile to Australia and from Egypt to Japan. Large organizations rarely limit themselves to individual foreign transactions. They often choose to establish entire operations in other countries. Therefore, either through the development of export and import markets or the creation of foreign subsidiaries, modern business operations extend beyond national boundaries on an almost routine basis. As a result of their international activities, many companies conduct a portion of their business in other countries and maintain some of their accounting records in foreign currencies.

Issues related to the accounting for foreign currency activities are covered in Chapters 9 and 10. Chapter 9 examines the accounting for foreign currency transactions and hedges of those transactions. These accounting issues are important for any company engaged in importing or exporting activities, regardless of whether it has foreign operations. The translation of foreign currency financial statements prepared by foreign operations for purposes of producing worldwide consolidated statements is the topic of Chapter 10.

GLOBAL ECONOMY

In its 1995 annual report, the General Electric Company reported making export sales from the United States of $9.2 billion during the year. This represented 17 percent of sales made by its U.S. operations. In addition, revenues of $19.4 billion were generated by foreign subsidiaries, comprising 26 percent of the company's worldwide revenues. The Gillette Company's 1995 annual report indicated that the company had subsidiaries in Argentina, Australia, Brazil, Canada, England, France,

Germany, Hong Kong, Italy, Jamaica, Japan, Korea, Russia, Switzerland, and Turkey—and that's just a partial list. Sales in 1995 generated by foreign operations comprised 70 percent of Gillette's consolidated total.

For any U.S. business, a portion of its transactions and accounts may be set (or denominated) in a currency other than the U.S. dollar.

- ■ Collections from export sales or payments for imported raw materials and other purchases may not always be made in U.S. dollars but rather in pesos, pounds, yen, and the like depending on the negotiated terms of the transaction.
- ■ The accounting records of a foreign subsidiary are probably maintained in the local currency of that country. An Italian subsidiary of a U.S. parent company, for example, accounts for its transactions and keeps books in Italian lire.

Many companies deal with a vast array of foreign currencies. However, when they produce consolidated financial statements, they report in only a single currency. Regardless of the currency in which a transaction is denominated or the currency used by a foreign subsidiary for keeping its books, U.S. companies prepare their consolidated financial statements in U.S. dollars. Because of the magnitude of the amounts involved, the accounting process of restating balances denominated in a foreign currency into U.S. dollars has become an especially sensitive concern in recent years.

As background information for this important accounting issue, the next section discusses foreign exchange markets. An understanding of foreign exchange rates and various foreign currency financial instruments is necessary to fully comprehend the accounting issues discussed later.

FOREIGN EXCHANGE MARKETS

Each country uses its own currency as the unit of value for the purchase and sale of goods and services. The currency used in the United States is the U.S. dollar, the currency used in Mexico is the Mexican peso, and so on. If a U.S. citizen travels to Mexico and wishes to purchase local goods, Mexican merchants require payment to be made in Mexican pesos. To make a purchase, a U.S. citizen has to purchase pesos using U.S. dollars. The price at which the foreign currency can be acquired is known as the foreign exchange rate. A variety of factors determine the exchange rate between two currencies; unfortunately for those engaged in international business, the exchange rate can fluctuate over time.

Exchange Rate Mechanisms

Exchange rates have not always fluctuated. During the period 1945–1973, countries fixed the par value of their currency in terms of the U.S. dollar and the value of the U.S. dollar was fixed in terms of gold. Countries agreed to maintain the value of their currency within 1 percent of the par value. If the exchange rate for a particular currency began to move outside of this 1 percent range, the country's central bank was required to intervene by buying or selling its currency in the foreign exchange market. Due to the law of supply and demand, the purchase of currency by a central bank would cause the price of the currency to stop falling and the sale of currency would cause the price to stop rising.

The integrity of the system hinged on the U.S. dollar maintaining its value in gold and the ability of foreign countries to convert their U.S. dollar holdings into gold at the fixed rate of $35 per ounce. As the United States began to incur balance of payment deficits in the 1960s, a glut of U.S. dollars arose worldwide and foreign countries began converting their U.S. dollars into gold. This resulted in a decline in the U.S. government's gold reserve from a high of $24.6 billion in 1949 to a low of $10.2 billion in 1971. In that year, the United States suspended the convertibility of the U.S. dollar into gold signaling the beginning of the end for the fixed exchange rate system. In March 1973, most currencies were allowed to float in value.

Today, several different currency arrangements exist. Some of the more important ones and the countries affected are

1. **Independent float**—the value of the currency is allowed to fluctuate freely according to market forces with little or no intervention from the central bank (Canada, Japan, Sweden, Switzerland, United States).

2. **Pegged to another currency**—the value of the currency is fixed (pegged) in terms of a particular foreign currency and the central bank intervenes as necessary to maintain the fixed value. For example, 25 countries peg their currency to the U.S. dollar (including the Bahamas and Syria); 14 former African colonies peg to the French franc.

3. **European Monetary System (EMS)**—the currencies of most of the members of the European Union float jointly against non-EMS currencies. In other words, the exchange rate between, say, the German mark and French franc remains relatively fixed with the central banks intervening when necessary. Both of these currencies float in tandem against non-EMS currencies such as the U.S. dollar. Under the Maastricht Treaty signed in 1991, the EMS countries have agreed to develop a single currency to be used in all member countries.

Foreign Exchange Rates

Exchange rates between the U.S. dollar and most foreign currencies are published on a daily basis in *The Wall Street Journal* and major U.S. newspapers. To better illustrate exchange rates and the foreign currency market, next we examine the exchange rates published in *The Wall Street Journal* for Monday, February 10, 1997, as shown in Exhibit 9–1.

These exchange rates were quoted in New York at 4:00 P.M. Eastern time. The price for one Austrian schilling on Monday, February 10 at 4:00 P.M. in New York was $.08583. The U.S. dollar price for a schilling at 4:01 P.M. Eastern time in New York was probably something different, as was the U.S. dollar price for a schilling in Vienna at 4:00 P.M. Eastern time. These exchange rates are for trades between banks in amounts of $1 million or more; that is, these are interbank or wholesale prices. Prices charged to retail customers, such as companies engaged in international business, are higher. These are selling rates, the rates at which banks in New York will sell currency to one another. The prices banks are willing to pay to buy foreign currency (buying rates) are somewhat less than the selling rates. The difference between the buying and selling rates is the spread through which the banks earn a profit on foreign exchange trades.

There are two columns of information for each day exchange rates are published. The first column, U.S. $ equiv., indicates the number of U.S. dollars needed to purchase one unit of foreign currency. These are known as direct quotes. The direct quote for the Swedish krona on February 10 was $.1359; in other words, one krona could be purchased with $.1359. The second column, Currency per U.S. $, indicates the number of foreign currency units that could be purchased with one U.S. dollar. These are called indirect quotes. Indirect quotes are simply the inverse of direct quotes. If one krona can be purchased with $.1359, then 7.3575 kroner can be purchased with $1.00. (The arithmetic does not work out perfectly because the direct quotes for the Swedish krona published in *The Wall Street Journal* are carried out to only four decimal points.) To avoid confusion, direct quotes are used exclusively in this chapter.

For each currency, comparative exchange rates for two days are presented. In almost all cases, there has been a change in the exchange rate from Friday, February 7, 1997, to Monday, February 10, 1997. Some currencies, such as the British pound,

Exhibit 9–1
The Wall Street Journal
Foreign Exchange Quotes,
February 10, 1997

CURRENCY TRADING

Monday, February 10, 1997

EXCHANGE RATES

The New York foreign exchange selling rates below apply to trading among banks in amounts of $1 million and more, as quoted at 4 p.m. Eastern time by Dow Jones Telerate Inc. and other sources. Retail transactions provide fewer units of foreign currency per dollar.

(handwritten: this week = Mon; last week = Fri)

Country	U.S. $ equiv. Mon	Fri	Currency per U.S.$ Mon	Fri
Argentina (Peso)	1.0012	1.0012	.9988	.9988
Australia (Dollar)	.7583	.7620	1.3187	1.3123
Austria (Schilling)	.08583	.08561	11.651	11.681
Bahrain (Dinar)	2.6525	2.6525	.3770	.3770
Belgium (Franc)	.02925	.02922	34.185	34.225
Brazil (Real)	.9550	.9550	1.0471	1.0471
Britain (Pound)	1.6412	1.6300	.6093	.6135
30-Day Forward	1.6403	1.6291	.6097	.6138
90-Day Forward	1.6383	1.6270	.6104	.6146
180-Day Forward	1.6353	1.6241	.6115	.6157
Canada (Dollar)	.7382	.7404	1.3547	1.3506
30-Day Forward	.7395	.7417	1.3523	1.3482
90-Day Forward	.7424	.7448	1.3469	1.3427
180-Day Forward	.7466	.7490	1.3394	1.3352
Chile (Peso)	.002393	.002396	417.85	417.35
China (Renminbi)	.1202	.1202	8.3216	8.3216
Colombia (Peso)	.0009377	.0009339	1066.44	1070.80
Czech. Rep. (Koruna)	....			
Commercial rate	.03608	.03591	27.715	27.847
Denmark (Krone)	.1583	.1568	6.3154	6.3778
Ecuador (Sucre)	....			
Floating rate	.0002699	.0002699	3705.00	3705.00
Finland (Markka)	.2039	.2019	4.9050	4.9539
France (Franc)	.1789	.1787	5.5890	5.5975
30-Day Forward	.1792	.1789	5.5800	5.5884
90-Day Forward	.1788	.1796	5.5930	5.5669
180-Day Forward	.1809	.1807	5.5270	5.5348
Germany (Mark)	.6041	.6030	1.6553	1.6583
30-Day Forward	.6051	.6040	1.6525	1.6555
90-Day Forward	.6075	.6065	1.6460	1.6488
180-Day Forward	.6114	.6103	1.6357	1.6385
Greece (Drachma)	.003848	.003842	259.88	260.26
Hong Kong (Dollar)	.1291	.1291	7.7465	7.7470
Hungary (Forint)	.005840	.005824	171.23	171.70
India (Rupee)	.02789	.02788	35.850	35.872
Indonesia (Rupiah)	.0004207	.0004205	2377.25	2377.88
Ireland (Punt)	1.6028	1.5903	.6239	.6288
Israel (Shekel)	.3013	.3007	3.3194	3.3252
Italy (Lira)	.0006144	.0006156	1627.50	1624.50

Country	U.S. $ equiv. Mon	Fri	Currency per U.S.$ Mon	Fri
Japan (Yen)	.008151	.008135	122.68	122.93
30-Day Forward	.008183	.008166	122.21	122.46
90-Day Forward	.008253	.008238	121.17	121.39
180-Day Forward	.008363	.008349	119.58	119.77
Jordan (Dinar)	1.4094	1.4094	.7095	.7095
Kuwait (Dinar)	3.3047	3.3047	.3026	.3026
Lebanon (Pound)	.0006455	.0006455	1549.25	1549.25
Malaysia (Ringgit)	.4021	.4013	2.4870	2.4920
Malta (Lira)	2.6490	2.6490	.3775	.3775
Mexico (Peso)	....			
Floating rate	.1283	.1281	7.7930	7.8050
Netherland (Guilder)	.5379	.5366	1.8592	1.8637
New Zealand (Dollar)	.6846	.6849	1.4607	1.4601
Norway (Krone)	.1527	.1525	6.5477	6.5588
Pakistan (Rupee)	.02520	.02520	39.680	39.680
Peru (new Sol)	.3816	.3811	2.6208	2.6238
Philippines (Peso)	.03795	.03795	26.348	26.348
Poland (Zloty)	.3331	.3317	3.0025	3.0152
Portugal (Escudo)	.006009	.005959	166.41	167.81
Russia (Ruble) (a)	.0001773	.0001774	5639.00	5636.00
Saudi Arabia (Riyal)	.2666	.2666	3.7505	3.7505
Singapore (Dollar)	.7096	.7077	1.4092	1.4130
Slovak Rep. (Koruna)	.03080	.03080	32.473	32.473
South Africa (Rand)	.2269	.2255	4.4075	4.4355
South Korea (Won)	.001151	.001153	868.65	867.40
Spain (Peseta)	.007131	.007083	140.23	141.18
Sweden (Krona)	.1359	.1347	7.3575	7.4239
Switzerland (Franc)	.7013	.7005	1.4260	1.4275
30-Day Forward	.7032	.7025	1.4220	1.4235
90-Day Forward	.7077	.7070	1.4130	1.4145
180-Day Forward	.7146	.7137	1.3993	1.4012
Taiwan (Dollar)	.03635	.03635	27.508	27.508
Thailand (Baht)	.03856	.03849	25.935	25.981
Turkey (Lira)	.00000851	.00000851	117555.00	117555.00
United Arab (Dirham)	.2723	.2723	3.6720	3.6720
Uruguay (New Peso)	....			
Financial	.1129	.1129	8.8600	8.8600
Venezuela (Bolivar)	.002107	.002107	474.50	474.53

Source: *The Wall Street Journal,* February 11, 1997, page C16. Reprinted by permission of *The Wall Street Journal* © 1997 Dow Jones & Company, Inc. All Rights Reserved Worldwide.

increased in value or appreciated against the U.S. dollar (to $1.6412 from $1.6300). Other currencies, such as the Canadian dollar, decreased in value or depreciated against the U.S. dollar (to $.7382 from $.7404).

Spot and Forward Rates

Foreign currency trades can be executed on a spot or forward basis. The *spot rate* is the price at which a foreign currency can be purchased or sold today. In contrast, the *forward rate* is the price today at which foreign currency can be purchased or sold sometime in the future. Because many international business transactions take some time to be completed, a company that can lock in a price today at which foreign currency can be purchased or sold at some future date has definite advantages.

Most of the quotes published in *The Wall Street Journal* are spot rates. In addition, it publishes forward rates quoted by New York banks for the major currencies (British pound, Canadian dollar, French franc, German mark, Japanese yen, and Swiss franc) on a daily basis. This is only a partial listing of possible forward contracts. A firm and its bank can tailor forward contracts in other currencies and for other time periods to meet the needs of the firm.

The forward rate can exceed the spot rate on a given date, in which case the foreign currency is said to be selling at a *premium* in the forward market, or the forward rate can be less than the spot rate, in which case it is selling at a *discount*. Currencies sell at a premium or a discount because of differences in interest rates between two countries. When the interest rate in the foreign country exceeds the interest rate domestically, the foreign currency sells at a discount in the forward market. Conversely, if the foreign interest rate is less than the domestic rate, the foreign currency sells at a premium.[1] Forward rates are said to be unbiased predictors of the future spot rate.

The spot rate for British pounds on February 10, 1997, indicates that one pound could have been purchased on that date for $1.6412. On the same day, the 30-day forward rate was $1.6403. By entering into a forward contract on February 10, it was possible to guarantee that pounds could be purchased on March 11 at a price of $1.6403, regardless of what the spot rate turned out to be on March 11. Entering into the forward contact to purchase pounds would have been beneficial if the spot rate on March 11 were greater than $1.6403. On the other hand, such a forward contract would have been detrimental if the spot rate were less than $1.6403. In either case, the forward contract must be honored and pounds must be purchased on March 11 at $1.6403.

Option Contracts

To provide companies more flexibility than exists with a forward contract, a market for *foreign currency options* has developed. A foreign currency option gives the holder of the option *the right but not the obligation* to trade foreign currency in the future. A *put* option is for the sale of foreign currency by the holder of the option; a *call* is for the purchase of foreign currency by the holder of the option. The *strike price* is the exchange rate at which the option will be executed if the holder of the option decides to exercise the option. The strike price is similar to a forward rate. There are generally several strike prices to choose from at any particular time. Foreign currency options may be purchased either on the Philadelphia Stock Exchange or directly from a bank in the so-called over-the-counter market.

Unlike a forward contract, where banks earn their profit through the spread between buying and selling rates, options must actually be purchased by paying an *option premium*. The option premium is a function of two components: *intrinsic value* and *time value*. The *intrinsic value* of an option is equal to the gain that could be realized by exercising the option immediately. For example, if a spot rate for a foreign currency is $1.00, a *call* option (to purchase foreign currency) with a strike price of $.97 has an intrinsic value of $.03, whereas a *put* option with a strike price of $1.00 or less has an intrinsic value of zero. An option with a positive intrinsic value is said to be "in the money." The *time value* of an option relates to the fact that the spot rate can change over time and cause the option to become in the money. Even though a 90-day call option with a strike price of $1.00 has zero intrinsic value when the spot rate is $1.00, it will still have a positive time value if there is a chance that the spot rate could increase over the next 90 days and bring the option into the money.

Option quotes reported in *The Wall Street Journal* on February 10, 1997, indicated that a call option in German marks with a strike price of $.62 could have been purchased by paying a premium of $.0021 per mark. Thus, the right to purchase 10,000 German marks on March 11, 1997, at a price of $.62 per mark could have been acquired by paying $21 ($.0021 × 10,000 marks). If the spot rate for German marks on March 11 is greater than $.62, the option would have been exercised and marks purchased at the strike price of $.62. If, on the other hand, the March 11 spot rate is less than $.62, the option would not be exercised; instead, marks would be purchased at the lower spot rate. The option contract establishes the maximum

---

[1]This relationship is based on the theory of interest rate parity that indicates the difference in national interest rates should be equal to, but opposite in sign to, the forward rate discount or premium. This topic is covered in detail in international finance textbooks.

amount that would have to be paid for German marks but does not lock in a disad-vantageous price should the spot rate fall below the option strike price.

FOREIGN CURRENCY TRANSACTIONS

Export sales and import purchases are international transactions; they are compo-nents of what is called trade. When two parties from different countries enter into a transaction, they must decide which of the two countries' currencies to use to settle the transaction. For example, if a U.S. computer manufacturer sells to a customer in Japan, the parties must decide whether the transaction will be denominated (payment will be made) in U.S. dollars or Japanese yen.

Assume that a U.S. exporter (Amerco) sells goods to a German importer with payment to be made in German marks (deutschemarks or DM). In this situation, Amerco has entered into a foreign currency transaction. It must restate the German mark amount that actually will be received into U.S. dollars to account for this transaction. This is because Amerco keeps its books and prepares financial state-ments in U.S. dollars. Although the German importer has entered into an interna-tional transaction, it does not have a foreign currency transaction (payment will be made in its currency) and no restatement is necessary.

Assume that, as is customary in its industry, Amerco does not require immediate payment and allows its German customer 30 days to pay for its purchases. By doing this, Amerco runs the risk that the German mark might depreciate against the U.S. dollar between the sale date and the date of payment. Then, fewer U.S. dollars are generated from the sale than if the German mark had not decreased in value and the sale is less profitable because it was made on a credit basis. In this situation Amerco is said to have an *exposure to foreign exchange risk*. Specifically, Amerco has a transaction exposure that can be summarized as follows:

- *Export Sale*—a transaction exposure exists when the exporter allows the buyer to pay in a foreign currency and also allows the buyer to pay sometime after the sale has been made. The exporter is exposed to the risk that the foreign currency might depreciate (decrease in value) between the date of sale and the date of payment, thereby decreasing the U.S. dollars ultimately collected.

- *Import Purchase*—a transaction exposure exists when the importer is required to pay in foreign currency and is allowed to pay sometime after the purchase has been made. The importer is exposed to the risk that the foreign currency might appreciate (increase in price) between the date of purchase and the date of payment, thereby increasing the U.S. dollars that have to be paid for the imported goods.

Accounting Issue

The major issue in accounting for foreign currency transactions is how to deal with the change in U.S. dollar value of the sales revenue and account receivable resulting from the export when the foreign currency changes in value. (The corollary issue is how to deal with the change in the U.S. dollar value of the account payable and goods being acquired in an import purchase.) For example, assume that Amerco, a U.S. company, sells goods to a German customer at a price of 1 million German marks when the spot exchange rate is $.55 per mark. If payment were received at the date of sale, Amerco could have converted 1 million marks into $550,000 and this amount clearly would be the amount at which the sales revenue would be recognized. Instead, Amerco allows the German customer 30 days to pay for its purchase. At the end of 30 days, the German mark has depreciated to $.53 and Amerco is able to convert the 1 million marks received on that date into only $530,000. How should Amerco account for this $20,000 decrease in value?

Accounting Alternatives

Conceptually, the two methods of accounting for changes in the value of a foreign currency transaction are the one-transaction perspective and the two-transaction perspective. The *one-transaction perspective* assumes that an export sale is not complete until the foreign currency receivable has been collected and converted into U.S. dollars. Any change in the U.S. dollar value of the foreign currency is accounted for as an adjustment to Accounts Receivable and to Sales. Under this perspective, Amerco would ultimately report Sales at $530,000 and an increase in the Cash account of the same amount. This approach can be criticized because it hides the fact that the company could have received $550,000 if the German customer had been required to pay at the date of sale. The company incurs a $20,000 loss because of the depreciation in the DM, but that loss is buried in an adjustment to Sales. This approach is not acceptable under U.S. GAAP.

Instead, *FASB Statement No. 52* requires companies to use a *two-transaction perspective* in accounting for foreign currency transactions.[2] This perspective treats the export sale and the subsequent collection of cash as two separate transactions. Because management has made two decisions: (1) to make the export sale, and (2) to extend credit in foreign currency to the customer, the income effect from each of these decisions should be reported separately. The U.S. dollar value of the sale is recorded at the date the sale occurs. At that point the sale has been completed; there are no subsequent adjustments to the Sales account. Any difference between the number of U.S. dollars that could have been received at the date of sale and the number of U.S. dollars actually received at the date of payment due to fluctuations in the exchange rate is a result of the decision to extend foreign currency credit to the customer. This difference is treated as a Foreign Exchange Gain or Loss that is reported separately from Sales in the income statement. Using the two-transaction perspective to account for its export sale to Germany, Amerco would make the following journal entries:

Date of Purchase:	Accounts Receivable (DM)	550,000	
	Sales		550,000
	To record the sale and DM receivable at the spot rate of $.55.		
Date of Payment:	Foreign Exchange Loss	20,000	
	Accounts Receivable (DM)		20,000
	To adjust the value of the DM receivable to the new spot rate of $.53 and record a foreign exchange loss resulting from the depreciation in the DM.		
	Cash	530,000	
	Accounts Receivable (DM)		530,000
	To record the receipt of DM 1 million and conversion at the spot rate of $.53.		

Sales are reported in income at the amount that would have been received if the customer had not been given 30 days to pay the 1 million marks, that is, $550,000. A separate Foreign Exchange Loss of $20,000 is reported in income to indicate that because of the decision to extend foreign currency credit to the German customer and because the DM decreased in value, fewer U.S. dollars are actually received.[3]

---

[2]FASB, *Statement of Financial Accounting Standards No. 52,* "Foreign Currency Translation" (Stamford, CT: FASB, December 1981).

[3]Note that the foreign exchange loss results because the customer is allowed to pay in German marks and is given 30 days to pay. If the transaction were denominated in U.S. dollars, no loss would result. Nor would there be a loss if the German marks had been received at the date the sale was made.

Note that Amerco keeps its Account Receivable (DM) account separate from its U.S. dollar receivables. Companies engaged in international trade need to keep separate payable and receivable accounts in each of the currencies in which they have transactions. Each foreign currency receivable and payable should have a separate account number in the company's chart of accounts.

We can summarize the relationship between fluctuations in exchange rates and foreign exchange gains and losses as follows:

Transaction	Type of Exposure	Foreign Currency (FC)	
		Appreciates	Depreciates
Export sale –income	Asset	Gain	Loss
Import purchase –payable	Liability	Loss	Gain

A foreign currency receivable arising from an export sale creates an *asset exposure* to foreign exchange risk. If the foreign currency appreciates, the foreign currency asset increases in U.S. dollar value and a foreign exchange gain arises; depreciation of the foreign currency causes a foreign exchange loss. A foreign currency payable arising from an import purchase creates a *liability exposure* to foreign exchange risk. If the foreign currency appreciates, the foreign currency liability increases in U.S. dollar value and a foreign exchange loss results; depreciation of the currency results in a foreign exchange gain.

Balance Sheet Date before Date of Payment

The question arises as to what accounting should be done if a balance sheet date falls between the date of sale and the date of payment. For example, assume that Amerco shipped goods to its German customer on December 10, 1997, with payment to be received on January 9, 1998. Assume that at December 10, the spot rate for DM is $.55, but by December 31, the DM has appreciated to $.56. Is any adjustment needed at December 31, 1997, when the books are closed to account for the fact that the foreign currency receivable has changed in U.S. dollar value since December 10?

The general consensus worldwide is that a foreign currency receivable or foreign currency payable should be revalued at the balance sheet date to account for the change in exchange rates. Under the two-transaction perspective, this means that a foreign exchange gain or loss arises at the balance sheet date. The next question then is what should be done with these foreign exchange gains and losses that have not yet been realized in cash. Should they be included in net income?

The two approaches to accounting for unrealized foreign exchange gains and losses are the deferral approach and the accrual approach. Under the *deferral approach,* unrealized foreign exchange gains and losses are deferred on the balance sheet until cash is actually paid or received. When cash is paid or received, a *realized* foreign exchange gain or loss would be included in income. This approach is not acceptable under U.S. GAAP.

SFAS 52 requires U.S. companies to use the *accrual approach* to account for unrealized foreign exchange gains and losses. Under this approach, a firm reports unrealized foreign exchange gains and losses in net income in the period in which the exchange rate changes. The statement says: "This is consistent with accrual accounting; it results in reporting the effect of a rate change that will have cash flow effects when the event causing the effect takes place."[4] Thus, any change in the exchange rate from the date of sale to the balance sheet date would result in a foreign exchange gain or loss to be reported in income in that period. Any change in the exchange rate from the balance sheet date to the date of payment would

---

[4]*SFAS No. 52,* paragraph 124.

result in a second foreign exchange gain or loss that would be reported in the second accounting period. The journal entries Amerco would make under the accrual approach would be:

12/10/97	Accounts Receivable (DM)	550,000	
	Sales		550,000
	To record the sale and DM receivable at the spot rate of $.55.		
12/31/97	Accounts Receivable (DM)	10,000	
	Foreign Exchange Gain		10,000
	To adjust the value of the DM receivable to the new spot rate of $.56 and record a foreign exchange gain resulting from the appreciation in the DM since December 10.		
1/9/98	Foreign Exchange Loss	30,000	
	Accounts Receivable (DM)		30,000
	To adjust the value of the DM receivable to the new spot rate of $.53 and record a foreign exchange loss resulting from the depreciation in the DM since December 31.		
	Cash	530,000	
	Accounts Receivable (DM)		530,000
	To record the receipt of DM 1 million and conversion at the spot rate of $.53.		

The net impact on income in 1997 is Sales of $550,000 and a Foreign Exchange Gain of $10,000; in 1998, a Foreign Exchange Loss of $30,000 is recorded. This results in a net increase in retained earnings of $530,000 that is balanced by an equal increase in Cash.

One criticism of the accrual approach is that it leads to a violation of conservatism when an unrealized foreign exchange gain arises at the balance sheet date. In fact, this is one of only two situations in U.S. GAAP where it is acceptable to recognize an unrealized gain in income. (The other situation relates to trading marketable securities reported at market value.) Germany, Austria, and several other countries more strictly adhere to the concept of conservatism than does the United States. In those countries, if at the balance sheet date the exchange rate has changed so that an unrealized gain arises, the change in exchange rate is ignored and the foreign currency account receivable or payable continues to be carried on the balance sheet at the exchange rate that existed at the date of the transaction. On the other hand, if the exchange rate had changed to cause a foreign exchange loss, the account receivable would be revalued and an unrealized loss would have been recorded and reported in income. This is a classic application of conservatism.

SFAS 52 requires restatement at the balance sheet date of all foreign currency assets and liabilities carried on a company's books. In addition to foreign currency payables and receivables arising from import and export transactions, companies might have dividends receivable from foreign subsidiaries, loans payable to foreign lenders, or lease payments receivable from foreign customers that are denominated in a foreign currency and therefore must be restated at the balance sheet date. Each of these foreign currency denominated assets and liabilities is exposed to foreign exchange risk; therefore, fluctuations in the exchange rate result in foreign exchange gains and losses.

Many U.S. companies report foreign exchange gains and losses on the income statement in a line item often titled "Other Income (Expense)." Other incidental gains and losses such as gains and losses on sales of assets would be included in this line item as well. *SFAS 52* requires companies to disclose the magnitude of foreign exchange gains and losses if material. For example, in the Notes to Financial Statements in its 1995 annual report, Merck indicated that the income statement item Other (Income) Expense, Net included a net exchange (gain) loss of $68.2 million, $26.2 million, and ($7.8) million in 1993, 1994, and 1995, respectively.

HEDGE OF A FOREIGN CURRENCY TRANSACTION

In the preceding example, Amerco has an asset exposure in German marks when it sells goods to the German customer and allows the customer 30 days to pay for its purchase. If the German mark depreciates over the next 30 days, Amerco incurs a foreign exchange loss. For many companies, the uncertainty of not knowing exactly how many U.S. dollars will be earned on this export sale is of great concern. To avoid this uncertainty, as soon as the sale is made, Amerco would like to lock in a price at which it can sell the 1 million marks that it will receive on January 9, 1998. Amerco can do this by entering into a 30-day forward contract to sell marks as soon as the goods are shipped to the German customer. *By entering into the forward contract, Amerco eliminates its exposure to foreign exchange risk; it knows with 100 percent certainty the number of U.S. dollars it will receive in 30 days.* The process of eliminating risk exposure is known as *hedging.*

Assume that on December 10, 1997, the 30-day forward rate for marks is $.535 and Amerco signs a contract with New Manhattan Bank to deliver 1 million marks in 30 days in exchange for $535,000. Given that the spot rate on December 10, 1997, is $.55, the mark is selling at a discount in the 30-day forward market (the forward rate is less than the spot rate). With the 30-day forward contract, Amerco locks in a U.S. dollar value for the 1 million marks that it will receive in 30 days. By entering into the forward contract, Amerco has hedged its German mark asset exposure. Amerco knows with 100 percent certainty the number of U.S. dollars it will receive from this export sale; management can sleep soundly at night without worrying about what is happening to the value of the German mark in the spot market.

Given that the future spot rate turns out to be only $.53, selling the marks at a forward rate of $.535 is obviously better than leaving the German mark receivable unhedged—Amerco will receive a $5,000 greater cash inflow as a result of the hedge. Because the mark is selling at a forward discount of $0.15 per mark, Amerco receives $15,000 less than if the goods had been paid for at the time of delivery ($550,000 − $535,000). This $15,000 reduction in cash inflow is considered to be an expense; it is the cost of extending foreign currency credit to a foreign customer.[5] Conceptually, the *discount expense* is similar to the foreign exchange loss that arises on the export sale. It exists only because the transaction is denominated in foreign currency. The major difference is that Amerco knows the exact amount of the discount expense at the date of sale, whereas, when left unhedged, Amerco does not know the size of the foreign exchange loss until 30 days pass. (Possibly the unhedged receivable could result in a foreign exchange gain rather than a foreign exchange loss.)

Accounting for a Hedge of a Foreign Currency Transaction

One issue in accounting for forward contracts used to hedge foreign exchange risk is the treatment of the discount expense. Under a one-transaction perspective, the discount expense would be a reduction in the amount recognized as Sales revenue. For Amerco, the final result would be a credit to Sales of $535,000 and a debit to Cash of $535,000. Once again, this perspective would hide the fact that Amerco could have received $550,000 from this export sale, but received $15,000 less as a result of selling to the foreign customer on a credit basis and allowing payment in foreign currency.

Under a two-transaction perspective, Amerco records the discount expense as a separate expense, thus showing that the decision to sell on account in a foreign currency cost the company $15,000. The discount expense would be recognized over the life of the forward contract using a straight-line approach. The following journal

---

[5]This should not be confused with the cost associated with normal credit risk; that is, the risk that the customer will not pay for its purchase. That is a separate issue unrelated to the currency in which the transaction is denominated.

Exhibit 9–2
Hedge of a Foreign Currency
Account Receivable with a
Forward Contract

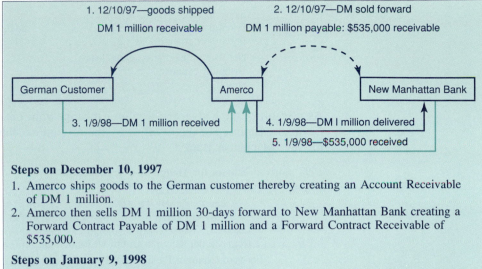

Steps on December 10, 1997

1. Amerco ships goods to the German customer thereby creating an Account Receivable of DM 1 million.
2. Amerco then sells DM 1 million 30-days forward to New Manhattan Bank creating a Forward Contract Payable of DM 1 million and a Forward Contract Receivable of $535,000.

Steps on January 9, 1998

3. The German customer remits DM 1 million to Amerco—the DM Account Receivable has been received and Amerco has DM 1 million reflected in an account Foreign Currency (DM).
4. Amerco delivers DM 1 million to New Manhattan Bank—the Foreign Currency (DM) is used to pay the DM Forward Contract Payable.
5. New Manhattan Bank pays Amerco $535,000—the Forward Contract Receivable ($) has been received.

entries for this approach are required of U.S. companies under *SFAS 52*. The accounting for forward contract hedges is somewhat complicated because the company must account for both the foreign currency transaction and the forward contract used to hedge that transaction. The process can be better understood by referring to the steps involving the three parties—Amerco, the German customer, and New Manhattan Bank—in Exhibit 9–2.

1997 Journal Entries for Hedge of a Transaction

12/10/97	Accounts Receivable (DM)	550,000	
	Sales		550,000
	To record the sale and DM receivable at the spot rate of $.55. (Step 1 in Exhibit 9–2)		
	Forward Contract Receivable ($)	535,000	
	Deferred Discount	15,000	
	Forward Contract Payable (DM)		550,000
	To record the forward contract receivable ($) at the forward rate of $.535, DM payable at the spot rate of $.55, and deferred discount for the difference. (Step 2)		
12/31/97	Accounts Receivable (DM)	10,000	
	Foreign Exchange Gain		10,000
	To adjust the value of the DM receivable to the new spot rate of $.56 and record a foreign exchange gain resulting from the appreciation in the DM since December 10.		
	Foreign Exchange Loss	10,000	
	Forward Contract Payable (DM)		10,000
	To adjust the value of the DM payable to the new spot rate of $.56 and record a foreign exchange loss resulting from the appreciation in the DM since December 10.		
	Discount Expense	10,500	
	Deferred Discount		10,500
	To amortize on a straight-line basis the deferred discount to expense over the life of the forward contract: $15,000 × 21/30 = $10,500.		

The net impact on the income statement for the year 1997 would be as follows:

Sales		$ 550,000
Foreign exchange gain	$10,000	
Foreign exchange loss	(10,000)	
Net foreign exchange gain (loss)		0
Discount expense		(10,500)
Net		$ 539,500

As a result of the hedge, the foreign exchange gain on the DM receivable from the German customer is exactly offset by the foreign exchange loss on the DM payable to New Manhattan Bank.

1998 Journal Entries for Hedge of a Transaction

1/9/98	Foreign Exchange Loss	30,000	
	Accounts Receivable (DM)		30,000
	To adjust the value of the DM receivable to the new spot rate of $.53 and record a foreign exchange loss resulting from the depreciation in the DM since December 31.		
	Forward Contract Payable (DM)	30,000	
	Foreign Exchange Gain		30,000
	To adjust the value of the DM payable to the new spot rate of $.53 and record a foreign exchange gain resulting from the depreciation in the DM since December 31.		
	Discount Expense	4,500	
	Deferred Discount		4,500
	To amortize the remaining deferred discount to expense.		
	Foreign Currency (DM)[6]	530,000	
	Accounts Receivable (DM)		530,000
	To record the receipt of DM 1 million from the German customer as an asset at the spot rate of $.53. (Step 3 in Exhibit 9–2)		
	Forward Contract Payable (DM)	530,000	
	Foreign Currency (DM)		530,000
	To record the remittance of DM 1 million to New Manhattan Bank. (Step 4)		
	Cash	535,000	
	Forward Contract Receivable ($)		535,000
	To record the receipt of $535,000 from New Manhattan Bank. (Step 5)		

The net impact on the income statement in 1998 would be:

Foreign exchange loss	$(30,000)	
Foreign exchange gain	30,000	
Net foreign exchange gain (loss)		0
Discount expense		(4,500)
Net		$(4,500)

Over the two accounting periods, the firm would report Sales at $550,000 and Discount Expense at a total of $15,000. The increase in Retained Earnings of $535,000 is counterbalanced by an equal increase in Cash.

The Essence of Hedging

Note that Amerco has hedged its DM receivable (asset) exposure by selling DM in the forward market. In selling DM forward, Amerco creates a DM payable (liability) exposure. The DM payable offsets (hedges) the DM receivable such that the net

---

[6]The DM 1 million received represents an asset to the company. Amerco could use various account titles to record this asset including Foreign Currency (DM), Investment in DM, and Cash (DM).

The Ahnuld Corporation, a health juice producer, recently has been expanding its sales through exports to foreign markets. Earlier this year, the company negotiated the sale of several thousand cases of turnip juice to a retailer in the country of Tcheckia. The customer is unwilling to assume the risk of having to make payment in U.S. dollars. Desperate to enter the Tcheckian market, the vice president for international sales agrees to denominate the sale in tchecks, the national currency of Tcheckia. The current exchange rate for tchecks is $2.00. In addition, the customer indicates that he cannot make payment until all of the juice has been sold. Payment is scheduled for six months from the date of sale.

Fearful that the tcheck might depreciate in value over the next six months, the head of the risk management department at Ahnuld Corporation enters into a forward contract to sell tchecks in six months at a forward rate of $1.80. Six months later, when payment is received from the Tcheckian customer, the exchange rate for the tcheck is $1.70. The corporate treasurer calls the head of the risk management department into her office.

Treasurer: I see that your decision to hedge our foreign currency position on that sale to Tcheckia was a bad one.

Department Head: What do you mean? We have a gain on that forward contract. We're $10,000 better off from having entered into that hedge.

Treasurer: That's not what the books say. The accountants have recorded a discount expense of $20,000 on that particular deal. I'm afraid I'm not going to be able to pay you a bonus this year. Another bad deal like this one and I'm going to have to demote you back to the interest rate swap department.

Department Head: Those bean counters have messed up again. I told those guys in international sales that selling to customers in Tcheckia was risky, but at least by hedging our exposure, we managed to receive a reasonable amount of cash on that deal. In fact, we ended up with a gain of $10,000 on the hedge. Tell the accountants to check their debits and credits again. I'm sure they just put a debit in the wrong place or some accounting thing like that.

Have the accountants made a mistake? Does the company have an expense, a gain, or both from this forward contract?

exposure to foreign exchange risk is zero. *This is the essence of hedging—reducing exposure by offsetting foreign currency assets with foreign currency liabilities and vice versa.*

To see how a hedge works for an import purchase, assume Amerco also has a French franc (FF) payable from importing goods from a French supplier. Amerco needs to acquire FF to make payment 30 days in the future. The company can lock in a price at which to acquire the FF by buying FF forward. By buying forward, Amerco creates a FF receivable from the foreign currency broker that offsets its FF payable to the French supplier. Gains and losses from the import purchase and forward contract hedge offset one another.

Regarding its export sale to Germany, Amerco has entered into a *perfect hedge* of its DM asset exposure. A perfect hedge exists when the hedging instrument (the forward contract) is of the same size and has the same maturity as the hedged item (the DM receivable). If for some reason Amerco does not sell exactly 1 million marks forward, an imperfect hedge exists and the mismatch gives rise to a net foreign exchange gain or loss reported in net income. For example, if Amerco was able to sell only 800,000 marks forward, the overhang of 200,000 marks will be an unhedged asset exposure. In 1997, when the German mark appreciated $.01, this would have resulted in a net foreign exchange gain of $2,000 being reported in 1997 income.

Discounts and Premiums

In the Amerco example, the German mark is selling at a discount in the 30-day forward market thus yielding a discount expense on the hedge of an export sale transaction. What if the mark were selling instead at a premium? In that event, Amerco could lock into sell its marks 30 days in the future at a higher price than it could obtain at the date of sale. The premium would generate additional revenue for Amerco over and above what was recognized as revenue from the sale. Just as with a discount expense, the premium revenue would be recognized over the life of the forward contract on a straight-line basis.

Hedges of foreign currency payables give rise to discount revenue and premium expense. If the French franc is selling at a forward premium when Amerco enters into a contract to buy francs, then Amerco ends up spending more U.S. dollars than if it had purchased francs at the date the imported goods were received. In this case, the premium results in an expense. If the French franc were selling at a discount, Amerco would spend fewer U.S. dollars than if it purchased francs at the date the goods were received; the discount results in a revenue. The relationship between forward contract discounts/premiums and revenue/expense is as follows:

Nature of Foreign Currency Exposure	Type of Hedge	Forward Rate < Spot Rate Discount	Forward Rate > Spot Rate Premium
Asset	Sell FC forward	Expense	Revenue
Liability	Buy FC forward	Revenue	Expense

FOREIGN CURRENCY OPTION AS HEDGE OF TRANSACTION

As an alternative to a forward contract, Amerco could hedge its exposure to foreign exchange risk arising from the German mark account receivable by purchasing a foreign currency *put* option. A put option would give Amerco the right but not the obligation to sell 1 million marks on January 9, 1998, at a predetermined strike price. Assume that on December 10, 1997, Amerco selects a strike price of $.54 when the spot rate is $.55 and pays a premium of $.009 per mark. Thus, the purchase price for the option is $9,000 [DM 1,000,000 × $.009]. Because the strike price is less than the spot rate, there is no intrinsic value associated with this option. The premium is based solely on time value; that is, it is possible that the DM will depreciate and the spot rate on January 9, 1998, will be less than $.54.

If the spot rate for German marks on January 9, 1998, is less than the strike price of $.54, Amerco will exercise its option and sell its 1 million German marks at the strike price of $.54. If the spot rate for marks in 30 days is greater than the strike price of $.54, Amerco will not exercise its option and sell marks at the higher spot rate. By purchasing the option, Amerco is guaranteed a minimum cash flow of $531,000 [$540,000 from exercising the option less $9,000 to purchase the option]. There is no limit to the maximum number of U.S. dollars that could be received.

Accounting for a Foreign Currency Option Used as a Hedge

SFAS 52 does not cover the accounting for foreign currency options. The FASB did not address this issue until 1996 when it issued an Exposure Draft entitled *Accounting for Derivative and Similar Financial Instruments and for Hedging Activities.* This proposed statement of financial accounting standards covers the accounting for all types of derivative financial instruments including foreign currency options. As this book went to press, the FASB indicated its intention to issue a final statement related to derivatives in late 1997.

The Exposure Draft requires foreign currency options designated as hedges of foreign currency transactions (referred to as a *fair value hedge*) to be recognized as assets. Changes in the value of a foreign currency option must be recognized as gains or losses in net income in the period of change together with an offsetting loss or gain on the asset or liability being hedged. Making sure that the loss or gain on the hedged item (asset or liability) is recognized in the same accounting period as the gain or loss on the hedging instrument (option) is referred to as *hedge accounting*.

The objective of hedge accounting is to have a net gain or loss on the hedging instrument and hedged item equal to zero. To achieve this objective, only the *lesser* of the gain or loss on the hedging instrument or the gain or loss on the hedged item can be recorded in net income in the current period.

The fair value of an option fluctuates over its life as a result of changes in its intrinsic value and time value. For example, as the spot rate for a foreign currency decreases over time, the intrinsic value of a put option in that currency increases. The ability to sell foreign currency at a fixed strike price has more value as the spot rate decreases. On the other hand, as the spot rate increases, the intrinsic value of a put option declines.

Returning to the Amerco illustration, we summarize the changes in value for the DM account receivable and DM put option:

Date	Spot Rate	Accounts Receivable (DM)		Foreign Currency Option	
		U.S. Dollar Value	Change in U.S. Dollar Value	Fair Value	Change in Fair Value
12/10/97	$.55	$ 550,000	—	$ 9,000	—
12/31/97	$.56	$ 560,000	+10,000	$ 5,000	−4,000
1/9/98	$.53	$ 530,000	−30,000	$10,000	+5,000

The fair value of the option at December 10 is the premium paid of $9,000. Appreciation of the DM from December 10 to December 31 causes the fair value of the option contract to fall to $5,000 at December 31, 1997. The subsequent decrease in the DM spot rate from December 31 to January 9, 1998, results in an increase in the value of the foreign currency option. At January 9, 1998, the option's exercise date, the time value of the option is zero. Based on the strike price of $.54 and the spot rate of $.53, the intrinsic value of the option is $10,000 [DM 1 million × ($.54 − $.53)].

At December 31, 1997, the DM receivable has increased in U.S. dollar value by $10,000, but the option has decreased in value by only $4,000. Under hedge accounting, the lower of these two amounts is recognized—a foreign exchange gain on the receivable of only $4,000 is recorded to offset the loss on the foreign currency option. The entries to record these events in 1997 are

1997 Journal Entries—Hedge of Transaction Using Foreign Currency Option

12/10/97	Accounts Receivable (DM)	550,000	
	Sales		550,000
	To record the sale and receivable (DM) at the spot rate of $.55.		
	Foreign Currency Option	9,000	
	Cash		9,000
	To record the purchase of the option contract as an asset.		
12/31/97	Loss on Foreign Currency Options	4,000	
	Foreign Currency Options		4,000
	To adjust the fair value of the foreign currency option from $9,000 to $5,000 and record a loss on foreign currency options.		
	Accounts Receivable (DM)	4,000	
	Foreign Exchange Gain		4,000
	To recognize an offsetting gain on the DM account receivable only to the extent of the option loss.		

As a result of these entries, Accounts Receivable (DM) will be reported as an asset on the balance sheet of $554,000 and Foreign Currency Options would be reported as an asset at $5,000. The net impact on the income statement for the year 1997 is

Sales	$550,000
Foreign exchange gain	4,000
Loss on foreign currency options	(4,000)
Net	$550,000

At January 9, 1998, the option has increased in value by $5,000 and the DM receivable has decreased in value by $30,000. A gain and loss for the lesser of these two amounts will be recognized on that date. The accounting entries made in 1998 are as follows:

1998 Journal Entries—Hedge of Transaction Using Foreign Currency Option

1/9/98:	Foreign Currency Options	5,000	
	Gain on Foreign Currency Options		5,000
	To adjust the fair value of the foreign currency option from $5,000 to $10,000 and record a gain on foreign currency options.		
	Foreign Exchange Loss	5,000	
	Accounts Receivable (DM)		5,000
	To recognize an offsetting loss on the DM account receivable only to the extent of the option gain.		
	Foreign Currency (DM)	530,000	
	Foreign Exchange Loss	19,000	
	Accounts Receivable (DM)		549,000
	To record the receipt of DM 1 million from the German customer as an asset at the spot rate of $.53, close the DM account receivable, and recognize a loss for the difference between the carrying value of the account receivable and the U.S. dollar value of the foreign currency received.		
	Cash	540,000	
	Foreign Currency (DM)		530,000
	Foreign Currency Options		10,000
	To record exercise of the option at the strike price of $.54 and close out the foreign currency options account.		

The option was exercised because the spot rate ($.53) on January 9, 1998, is less than the strike price of $.54. The impact on 1998 net income is

Foreign exchange loss	$(24,000)
Gain on foreign currency options	5,000
Net loss	$(19,000)

Sales of $550,000 are recognized in 1997 and a net loss of $19,000 is recognized in 1998. The net impact on income over the two periods of $531,000 is equal to the net cash inflow arising from the export sale ($540,000 from exercising the option less $9,000 to purchase the option).

Spot Rate Exceeds Strike Price

If the spot rate at January 9, 1998, had been greater than the strike price of $.54, Amerco would allow its option to expire unexercised. Instead it would sell its Foreign Currency (DM) at the spot rate. The fair value of the foreign currency option on January 9, 1998, would be zero. The journal entries for 1997 to reflect this scenario would be the same as above. The option would be reported as an asset on the December 31, 1997, balance sheet at $5,000 and the DM receivable would have a carrying value of $554,000. The entries at January 9, 1998, assuming a spot rate on that date of $.57, would be as follows:

1/9/98	Loss on Foreign Currency Options	5,000	
	Foreign Currency Options		5,000
	To adjust the fair value of the foreign currency option from $5,000 to zero and record a loss on foreign currency options.		
	Accounts Receivable (DM)	5,000	
	Foreign Exchange Gain		5,000
	To recognize an offsetting gain on the DM account receivable only to the extent of the option loss.		

Foreign Currency (DM) 570,000
     Accounts Receivable (DM)   559,000
     Foreign Exchange Gain   11,000
     To record the receipt of DM 1 million from the German
     customer as an asset at the spot rate of $.57, close the DM
     accounts receivable, and recognize a gain for the difference
     in the carrying value of the receivable and the U.S. dollar
     value for the foreign currency received.

Cash 570.000
     Foreign Currency (DM)   570,000
     To record the sale of DM 1 million at the spot rate of $.57.

The net impact on income over the two accounting periods is

$$
\begin{array}{lr}
\text{Sales—1997} & \$550{,}000 \\
\text{Net gain—1998} & \underline{11{,}000} \\
\text{Total} & \underline{\underline{\$561{,}000}} \\
\end{array}
$$

The net amount reflected in income equals the net cash inflow derived from the export sale.

HEDGE OF A FUTURE FOREIGN CURRENCY COMMITMENT

In the examples thus far, Amerco has not entered into a hedge of its export sale until the sale is actually made. Quite often, however, companies engaged in foreign currency transactions enter into hedging arrangements as soon as an order has been accepted. Assume now that Amerco accepts an order in the amount of DM 1 million from the German customer on November 10, 1997, and that it will take Amerco 60 days to fill the order. Assume further that Amerco will ship the goods to the German customer on January 9, 1998, and will receive immediate payment on delivery. In other words, Amerco will not allow the German customer time to pay. Although Amerco will not make the sale until January 9, 1998, it has a German mark *asset exposure* to foreign exchange risk as soon as it accepts the sales order from its German customer on November 10, 1997. On that date, Amerco wants to lock in a price at which it can sell 1 million marks in 60 days. It does this by entering into a 60-day forward contract at the date the goods are ordered.

This scenario differs from the previous hedge of a transaction in that Amerco enters into the forward contract hedge before the transaction actually takes place. This is known as a *hedge of a foreign currency commitment*. The FASB's Exposure Draft amends *SFAS 52* to require the following procedures for forward contract hedges of foreign currency commitments:

- Gains and losses on the forward contract are recognized in income in the period in which the exchange rate changes (similar to hedges of transactions).
- Although there is no transaction to account for, gains and losses on the foreign currency commitment must be recognized and taken to income to offset gains and losses on the forward contract (hedge accounting).

According to *SFAS 52* (par. 21), hedge accounting is allowed only when:

1. The foreign currency commitment is firm.
2. The contract is designated as, and is effective as, a hedge of a foreign currency commitment.

If these two requirements are not met, changes in the fair value of the forward contract are recognized in current income without any recognition of gains and losses on the foreign currency commitment.

The first requirement for a firm foreign currency commitment was established to preclude hedge accounting on hedges of forecasted transactions (expected transactions for which a contractual agreement does not yet exist). Many companies comply with the second requirement by documenting the fact that the forward contract is designed to hedge a specific future foreign currency commitment. Although quite often it is, the forward contract does not have to be in the same currency as the commitment to be effective as a hedge. Currencies that are linked to one another, such as those in the European Monetary System, can serve as effective hedges of one another. For example, Amerco could have hedged its commitment to receive German marks by entering into a forward contract to sell Dutch guilders (or any other currency moving in tandem with the German mark).

In fact, under *SFAS 52*, other types of foreign currency transactions such as foreign currency borrowings could serve as a hedge of a foreign currency commitment, as long as they are designated and effective as such a hedge. For example, Amerco could have hedged its future receipt of German marks (an asset exposure) by taking out a German mark loan (a liability exposure) from a German bank.

Continuing with the Amerco example, assume the following exchange rates at November 10, 1997:

	$ per DM
Spot rate	$.555
60-day forward rate	$.538

With a 60-day forward contract, Amerco locks in a price of $538,000 at which it will sell the 1 million DM when received in 60 days. The exposure to foreign exchange risk has been eliminated. Amerco knows with 100 percent certainty the number of U.S. dollars it will receive from this export sale.

The difference between the spot rate and forward rate at November 10, 1997, gives rise to a discount of $17,000 ($555,000 − $538,000). In a hedge of a foreign currency commitment, *SFAS 52* allows companies two options regarding the treatment of discounts and premiums: (1) amortize to income over the life of the forward contract (two-transaction perspective) or (2) defer until the transaction occurs and then treat as an adjustment to the underlying transaction (one-transaction perspective).

Assuming that Amerco decides to defer the discount until the sale takes place, the journal entries to account for the hedge of a commitment would be as follows:

1997 Journal Entries—Hedge of Foreign Currency Firm Commitment

11/10/97	No entries related to the sales order.		
	Forward Contract Receivable ($)	538,000	
	Deferred Discount	17,000	
	Forward Contract Payable (DM)		555,000
	To record the forward contract: U.S. dollars receivable at the forward rate of $.538, DM payable at the spot rate of $.555, and deferred discount for the difference.		
12/31/97	Foreign Exchange Loss	5,000	
	Forward Contract Payable (DM)		5,000
	To adjust the value of the DM payable to the new spot rate of $.56 and record a foreign exchange loss resulting from the appreciation in the DM since November 10.		
	Firm Commitment (DM)	5,000	
	Foreign Exchange Gain		5,000
	To record a gain on the firm commitment to receive DM 1 million resulting from the appreciation in the DM since November 10.		

Consistent with the objective of hedge accounting, the gain on the firm commitment offsets the loss on the forward contract and the net impact on 1997 income is zero. There is no entry to amortize the deferred discount.

1998 Journal Entries—Hedge of Foreign Currency Commitment

1/9/98	Forward Contract Payable (DM)	30,000	
	Foreign Exchange Gain		30,000

To adjust the value of the DM payable to the new spot rate of $.53 and record a foreign exchange gain resulting from the depreciation in the DM since December 31.

Foreign Exchange Loss	30,000	
Firm Commitment (DM)		30,000

To record a loss on the firm commitment to receive DM 1 million resulting from a depreciation in the DM since December 31.

Foreign Currency (DM)	530,000	
Sales		530,000

To record the sale and receipt of DM 1 million from the German customer at the spot rate of $.53.

Forward Contract Payable (DM)	530,000	
Foreign Currency (DM)		530,000

To record the remittance of DM 1 million to the foreign exchange broker.

Cash	538,000	
Forward Contract Receivable ($)		538,000

To record the receipt of $538,000 from the foreign exchange broker.

Firm Commitment (DM)	25,000	
Deferred Discount		17,000
Sales		8,000

To close the firm commitment (DM) account and deferred discount as adjustments to sales.

Once again, the foreign exchange gain and loss offset. As a result of the last entry, Amerco reports Sales in 1998 net income at $538,000, exactly the number of U.S. dollars received. As noted earlier, this is the objective of a one-transaction perspective to accounting for foreign currency transactions.

If Amerco decided to follow a two-transaction perspective, it would amortize the deferred discount of $17,000 to expense on a straight-line basis: $14,450 in 1997 and $2,550 in 1998. The last journal entry on January 9, 1998, to close the firm commitment account would be:

Firm Commitment (DM)	25,000	
Sales		25,000

This approach would result in Sales being reported on the 1998 income statement at $555,000. This is equivalent to recording the sale at the original spot rate of $.555 when the order was accepted. This amount of U.S. dollars could have been realized from the export sale only if the German customer had paid at the date the order was placed. As this is extremely unlikely, recording sales at the spot rate when the sales order was accepted has little to recommend it. Moreover, recording a separate discount expense as a measure of the cost of extending foreign currency credit to the German customer is conceptually unappealing given that, in this scenario, Amerco does not extend credit to the customer. Consistent with the one-transaction perspective, a majority of U.S. companies choose to defer the discount or premium, treating it as an adjustment to the related transaction.

OPTION USED AS HEDGE OF A COMMITMENT

Now assume that instead of entering into a forward contract to hedge its foreign currency commitment, Amerco purchases a DM 1 million put option on November 10, 1997, that matures on January 9, 1998. The strike price is $.548 and the premium is $.006 per DM. The option, which costs $6,000 [DM 1,000,000 × $.006], gives Amerco the right but not the obligation to sell 1 million marks on January 9, 1998, for $548,000. Amerco is sure to receive a minimum of $542,000 [$548,000 − $6,000] in cash from the sale to be made on January 9.

1977 Journal Entries—Hedge of Commitment Using Foreign Currency Option

11/10/97	No entries related to the sales order.		
	Foreign Currency Options	6,000	
	Cash		6,000
	To record the purchase of the option contract as an asset; the premium is $.006 per DM.		

As of December 31, 1997, as a result of the appreciation of the DM from $.555 to $.56, the value of the foreign currency option decreases to $4,000.

12/31/97	Loss on Foreign Currency Options	2,000	
	Foreign Currency Options		2,000
	To adjust the fair value of the foreign currency option from $6,000 to $4,000 and record a loss on foreign currency options.		
	Firm Commitment (DM)	2,000	
	Foreign Exchange Gain		2,000
	To record an offsetting gain on the firm commitment only to the extent of the option loss.		

From December 31, 1997, to January 9, 1998, the DM depreciates to $.53. The fair value of the foreign currency option at January 9 is its intrinsic value of $18,000 [DM 1 million × ($.548 strike − $.53 spot)]

1998 Journal Entries—Hedge of Commitment Using Foreign Currency Option

1/9/98	Foreign Currency Options	14,000	
	Gain on Foreign Currency Options		14,000
	To adjust the fair value of the foreign currency option from $4,000 to $18,000 and record a gain on foreign currency options.		
	Foreign Exchange Loss	14,000	
	Firm Commitment (DM)		14,000
	To record an offsetting loss on the firm commitment only to the extent of the option gain.		
	Foreign Currency (DM)	530,000	
	Sales		530,000
	To record the sale and receipt of DM 1 million from the German customer at the spot rate of $.53.		
	Cash	548,000	
	Foreign Currency (DM)		530,000
	Foreign Currency Options		18,000
	To record exercise of the foreign currency option at a strike price of $.548 and close out the foreign currency options account.		
	Firm Commitment (DM)	12,000	
	Sales		12,000
	To close the firm commitment account as an adjustment to sales.		

The net impact on the income statement over the two years 1997 and 1998 would be:

Sales	$542,000
Net foreign exchange gain (loss)	(12,000)
Net gain (loss) on foreign currency options	12,000
Net	$542,000

The net cash inflow realized from the export sale is $542,000; $548,000 from exercising the option less $6,000 to purchase the option. Consistent with a one-transaction perspective, Sales is reported at the amount of net cash inflow.

Forecasted Transactions

SFAS 52 does not allow using hedge accounting for forward contracts hedging forecasted transactions that are expected to occur but for which a contractual agreement does not exist. In contrast, provided that certain criteria are met, the FASB's Exposure Draft does allow hedge accounting for a foreign currency option used to hedge a forecasted transaction (referred to as a *cash flow hedge*). For hedge accounting to apply, the forecasted transaction must be probable (likely to occur) and the hedge must be appropriately documented.

To demonstrate the nature of a cash flow hedge, assume that a U.S. company has purchased goods from a foreign supplier for several years. The company anticipates purchases from the foreign supplier in the coming year to be the same as last year. The expected timing and terms of the purchases can be identified, and the purchases are probable. In this case, hedge accounting would be allowed for a foreign currency option used to hedge against adverse fluctuations in the exchange rate.

The accounting for an option hedge of a forecasted transaction (cash flow hedge) differs from the accounting for an option hedge of a foreign currency firm commitment (fair value hedge) in two ways:

- Unlike the accounting for a firm commitment, there is no recognition of gains and losses on a forecasted transaction.
- The foreign currency option is reported at fair value, but because there is no gain or loss on the forecasted transaction to offset against, changes in the fair value of the foreign currency option are not reported as gains or losses in net income. Instead they are reported outside of net income in *comprehensive income*. On the projected date of the forecasted transaction, the cumulative change in fair value is transferred from comprehensive income to net income.

The FASB introduced reporting of comprehensive income in 1997.[7] It defined comprehensive income as all changes in equity from nonowner sources and identified two components: *net income* and *other comprehensive income*. Other comprehensive income consists of income items that under previous FASB statements were required to be deferred in stockholders' equity such as gains and losses on available-for-sale marketable securities. Changes in the fair value of options designated as hedges of forecasted transactions (cash flow hedges) would be reported in other comprehensive income.

USE OF HEDGING INSTRUMENTS

There are probably as many different corporate strategies regarding hedging foreign exchange risk as there are companies exposed to that risk. Some companies simply require hedges of all foreign currency transactions. Others require the use of a forward contract hedge when the forward rate results in a greater cash inflow or smaller cash outflow than with the spot rate. Still other companies have proportional hedging policies that require hedging on some predetermined percentage (e.g., 50, 60, or 70 percent) of transaction exposure.

The notes to financial statements of multinational companies indicate the magnitude of foreign exchange risk and the importance of hedging contracts. The following has been extracted from the Coca-Cola Company's 1995 annual report:

---

[7]FASB Statement No. 130, *Reporting Comprehensive Income,* was issued in June 1997.

Foreign Currency Management (in millions)

Forward contracts	
Assets	$1,927
Liabilities	554
Swap agreements	
Assets	390
Liabilities	1,686
Purchased options	
Assets	1,823
	$6,380

Coca-Cola had $6.38 billion in foreign currency hedging instruments outstanding at December 31, 1995. To better appreciate the significance of this amount, consider that Coca-Cola had total sales of $18 billion and net income of $3 billion in 1995, and that total assets at December 31, 1995, were $15 billion.

Coca-Cola uses a combination of foreign currency forward contracts, swaps, and options in its hedging strategy, and in roughly equal amounts. In its 1995 annual report, Abbott Laboratories reported foreign exchange forward contracts of $7.8 million and options of $10.6 million at December 31, 1995. Colgate-Palmolive Company uses forward contracts only in its management of foreign exchange risk. Its 1995 annual report indicated forward contracts of $972 million outstanding at December 31, 1995.

As can be seen from the Coca-Cola illustration, a third popular means of hedging foreign exchange risk is through a *foreign currency swap*. A currency swap is a mechanism for converting a foreign currency receivable (or payable) into the domestic currency (U.S. dollar) prior to actual settlement. A discussion of the mechanism of foreign currency swaps is beyond the scope of this book. The FASB Exposure Draft requires that swaps be accounted for in a manner similar to foreign currency options.

OFF BALANCE SHEET NATURE OF FORWARD CONTRACTS

In the preceding illustrations of accounting for forward contracts, firms recorded an asset and liability at the date the forward contract was signed with a discount or premium recorded as the difference between the two. In actual practice, because forward contracts are executory contracts, most U.S. companies do not report these assets and liabilities on their balance sheets. A major reason why companies prefer to keep their forward contracts off balance sheet is that it allows them to report a smaller amount of current liabilities thereby improving ratios such as the current ratio and debt-to-equity ratio. Exhibit 9–3 demonstrates the journal entries that would be made if the forward contract used as a hedge of an export sale illustrated earlier in this chapter were kept off balance sheet.

Under the off balance sheet treatment, Amerco does not make an accounting entry when the forward contract is entered into on December 10, 1997. Although the DM forward contract payable has not been recorded, the company must recognize a foreign exchange loss on the unrecorded liability at December 31, 1997. Because the payable has not been recorded, the firm uses a deferred credit (liability) account to offset the foreign exchange loss. It uses the same deferred credit account to offset the discount expense that also must be recognized at year-end.

The forward contract has the same effect on the income statement regardless of whether it is reported on or off balance sheet. By keeping the forward contract off balance sheet, however, the company reports $560,000 less in both current assets and current liabilities at December 31, 1997. As a result, the company has a lower debt-to-equity ratio.

Exhibit 9–3   Illustration of Forward Contract Kept off Balance Sheet

Date	Foreign Currency Transaction	Forward Contract on Balance Sheet	Forward Contract off Balance Sheet

12/10/97	Accounts Receivable (DM) ... 550,000
	  Sales ... 550,000
		Forward Contract Receivable ($) ... 535,000
		Deferred Discount ... 15,000
		  Forward Contract Payable (DM) ... 550,000
			No entry at date of inception.

12/31/97	Accounts Receivable (DM) ... 10,000
	  Foreign Exchange Gain ... 10,000
		Foreign Exchange Loss ... 10,000
		  Forward Contract Payable (DM) ... 10,000
		
		Discount Expense ... 10,000
		  Deferred Discount ... 10,000
			Foreign Exchange Loss ... 10,000
			  Deferred Credit ... 10,000
			
			Discount Expense ... 10,000
			  Deferred Credit ... 10,000

Income Statement 1997

Forward Contract on Balance Sheet		Forward Contract off Balance Sheet	
Sales ...	550,000	Sales ...	550,000
Foreign exchange loss ...	(10,000)	Foreign exchange loss ...	(10,000)
Foreign exchange gain ...	10,000	Foreign exchange gain ...	10,000
Discount expense ...	(10,000)	Discount expense ...	(10,000)
	540,000		540,000

Balance Sheet at 12/31/97

Forward Contract on Balance Sheet

Assets	
Accounts receivable (DM) ...	560,000
Forward contract receivable ($) ...	535,000
Deferred discount ...	5,000
	1,100,000

Liabilities and Equity	
Forward contract payable (DM) ...	560,000
Retained earnings ...	540,000
	1,100,000

Forward Contract off Balance Sheet

Assets	
Accounts receivable (DM) ...	560,000

Liabilities and Equity	
Deferred credit ...	20,000
Retained earnings ...	540,000
	560,000

Date	Forward Contract on Balance Sheet	Forward Contract off Balance Sheet

1/9/98	Foreign Exchange Loss ... 30,000
	  Accounts Receivable (DM) ... 30,000 *(Foreign Currency Transaction)*
	
	Forward Contract Payable (DM) ... 30,000
	  Foreign Exchange Gain ... 30,000
	
	Discount Expense ... 5,000
	  Deferred Discount ... 5,000
	
	Foreign Currency (DM) ... 530,000
	  Accounts Receivable (DM) ... 530,000
	
	Forward Contract Payable (DM) ... 530,000
	  Foreign Currency (DM) ... 530,000
	
	Cash ... 535,000
	  Forward Contract Receivable ($) ... 535,000
		Deferred Credit ... 30,000
		  Foreign Exchange Gain ... 30,000
		
		Discount Expense ... 5,000
		  Deferred Credit ... 5,000
		
		Foreign Currency (DM) ... 530,000
		  Accounts Receivable (DM) ... 530,000
		
		Cash ... 535,000
		Deferred Credit ... 5,000
		  Foreign Currency (DM) ... 530,000

FOREIGN CURRENCY BORROWING

In addition to the receivables and payables that arise from import and export activities, companies often must account for foreign currency borrowings, another type of foreign currency transaction. Companies borrow foreign currency from foreign lenders either to finance foreign operations or perhaps to take advantage of more favorable interest rates. Accounting for a foreign currency borrowing is complicated by the fact that both the principal and interest are denominated in foreign currency and both create an exposure to foreign exchange risk.

To demonstrate the accounting for foreign currency debt, assume that on July 1, 1997, Multicorp International borrowed 1 billion Japanese yen (¥) on a one-year note at a per annum interest rate of 5 percent. Interest is payable and the note comes due on July 1, 1998. The following exchange rates apply:

Date	U.S. Dollars per Japanese Yen Spot Rate
July 1, 1997	$.00921
December 31, 1997	$.00932
July 1, 1998	$.00937

On July 1, 1997 Multicorp borrows 1 billion yen and converts it into $9,210,000 in the spot market. Over the life of the note, Multicorp must record accrued interest expense at year-end and interest payments on the anniversary date of July 1. In addition, the firm must revalue the Japanese yen note payable at year-end, with foreign exchange gains and losses reported in income. These journal entries account for this foreign currency borrowing:

7/1/97	Cash	9,210,000	
	Note Payable (¥)		9,210,000
	To record the ¥ note payable at the spot rate of $.00921 and the conversion of ¥ 1 billion into U.S. dollars.		
12/31/97	Interest Expense	233,000	
	Accrued Interest Payable (¥)		233,000
	To accrue interest for the period July 1–December 31, 1997: ¥ 1 billion × 5% × 1/2 year = ¥ 25 million × $.00932 = $233,000.		
	Foreign Exchange Loss	110,000	
	Note Payable (¥)		110,000
	To revalue the ¥ note payable at the spot rate of $.00932 and record a foreign exchange loss of $110,000 [¥ 1 billion × ($.00932 − $.00921)].		
7/1/98	Interest Expense	234,250	
	Accrued Interest Payable (¥)	233,000	
	Foreign Exchange Loss	1,250	
	Cash		468,500
	To record the interest payment of ¥ 50 million acquired at the spot rate of $.00937 for $468,500; interest expense for the period January 1–July 1, 1998—¥ 25 million × $.00937; and a foreign exchange loss on the ¥ accrued interest payable—¥ 25 million × ($.00937 − $.00932).		
	Foreign Exchange Loss	50,000	
	Note Payable (¥)		50,000
	To revalue the ¥ note payable at the spot rate of $.00937 and record a foreign exchange loss of $50,000 [¥ 1 billion × ($.00937 − $.00932)].		
	Note Payable (¥)	9,370,000	
	Cash		9,370,000
	To record repayment of the ¥ 1 billion note through purchase of ¥ at the spot rate of $.00937.		

Foreign Currency Loan

At times companies might lend foreign currency to related parties, creating the opposite situation as with a foreign currency borrowing. The accounting involves keeping track of a note receivable and interest receivable both of which are denominated in foreign currency. Fluctuations in the U.S. dollar value of the principal and interest generally give rise to foreign exchange gains and losses that would be included in income. Under *SFAS 52,* an exception arises when the foreign currency loan is being made on a long-term basis to a foreign branch, subsidiary, or equity method affiliate. Foreign exchange gains and losses on "intercompany foreign currency transactions that are of a long-term investment nature (that is, settlement is not planned or anticipated in the foreseeable future)" are deferred in the stockholder's equity section of the balance sheet until the loan is repaid.[8] Only the foreign exchange gains and losses related to the interest receivable are recorded currently in net income.

SPECULATIVE FOREIGN CURRENCY FORWARD CONTRACT

A forward exchange contract does not necessarily have to serve as a hedge. Companies also can acquire such contracts as investments for speculative purposes. If a fluctuation is anticipated in the value of a particular currency, a forward exchange contract can be negotiated in hopes of realizing a profit from the expected movement. However, because no hedge has been created, hedge accounting is not appropriate and all subsequent changes in the value of the contract are recognized immediately as foreign exchange gains or losses.

To demonstrate the procedures used in accounting for a forward exchange contract that is acquired as an investment, assume that on December 1, 1997, exchange rates between the Swiss franc (Sfr) and U.S. dollar are as follows:

	Spot	90-Day Forward	60-Day Forward
December 1, 1997	$.80	$.81	$.809

Mega Company believes that the Swiss franc will actually appreciate by more than $.01 against the U.S. dollar over the next 90 days. The company therefore enters into a 90-day forward contract to buy 1 million Swiss francs at $.81 per franc, betting that it will be able to sell the francs at a higher spot rate in 90 days. Mega Company has no business need for the Swiss francs. The company is not importing any goods from Switzerland—this is pure speculation.

In accounting for a speculative forward contract, *SFAS 52* (par. 19) indicates that both the forward contract payable and forward contract receivable shall be recorded at the forward rate. The premium (or discount) is not recorded. The signing of the forward contract is recorded as follows:

12/1/97	Forward Contract Receivable (Sfr)	810,000	
	Forward Contract Payable ($)		810,000
	To record the forward contract to buy Sfr 1 million at a forward rate of $.81.		

In this initial entry, the foreign currency receivable is recorded at the forward exchange rate rather than the December 1, 1997, spot rate that would have been applicable for a hedge. Because of the speculative nature of the purchase, the contract is viewed as an investment rather than a receivable. In many cases, the company does not anticipate holding the contract until maturity. Instead, the company resells the contract when it believes the highest possible price has been reached. Therefore,

[8]*SFAS 52,* par. 20(*b*).

revaluation is based on the market value of the contract (the forward rate) rather than the current value of the francs (the spot rate).

At the end of the fiscal period, December 31, 1997, Mega Company must close its books and record any gain or loss on the Swiss franc forward contract receivable. According to *SFAS 52,* the gain or loss is determined by reference to the value of a forward contract with a life remaining to the maturity date. In this example, at December 31, 1997, the 90-day forward contract has 60 days remaining to maturity. The current value of the forward contract can be determined by reference to the 60-day forward rate on December 31, 1997. Relevant exchange rates are

	Spot	90-Day Forward	60-Day Forward
December 31, 1997	$.805	$.819	$.817

The 1 million Swiss franc receivable has a current value of $817,000 and must be adjusted accordingly. Through the following adjusting entry, the company records the increase in U.S. dollar value of the forward contract as a foreign exchange gain in 1997 income:

12/31/97	Forward Contract Receivable (Sfr)	7,000	
	Speculative Gain		7,000
	To revalue the Sfr receivable at 60-day forward rate of $.817 and record a gain.		

On March 1, 1998, the spot rate is $.82. Mega Company purchases 1 million Swiss francs for $810,000 under the forward contract and then sells them at the spot rate for $820,000. Mega realizes a net gain of $10,000 through speculation; $7,000 was recognized in 1997 and the remaining $3,000 will be recognized in 1998.

3/1/98	Forward Contract Receivable (Sfr)	3,000	
	Speculative Gain		3,000
	To revalue the Sfr receivable at the spot rate of $.82 and record a gain.		
	Investment in Sfr	820,000	
	Forward Contract Receivable (Sfr)		820,000
	To record receipt of the Sfr from the bank.		
	Forward Contract Payable ($)	810,000	
	Cash		810,000
	To record payment of U.S. dollars to the bank.		
	Cash	820,000	
	Investment in Sfr		820,000
	To record sale of the Sfr in the spot market.		

The net impact on the balance sheet is an increase in cash of $10,000, offset by an increase in retained earnings from the $10,000 gain recognized over the two-year period.

SUMMARY

1. There are a variety of exchange rate mechanisms in use around the world. A majority of national currencies are allowed to fluctuate in value against other currencies over time.

2. Exposure to foreign exchange risk exists when a payment to be made or a payment to be received is denominated (stated) in a foreign currency. Appreciation in a foreign currency results in a foreign exchange gain on a foreign currency receivable and a foreign exchange loss on a foreign currency payable. Conversely, a decrease in the value of a foreign currency results in a foreign exchange loss on a foreign currency receivable and a foreign exchange gain on a foreign currency payable.

3. Under *SFAS 52,* foreign exchange gains and losses on foreign currency balances are recorded in income in the period in which an exchange rate change occurs; this is a two-transaction perspective, accrual approach. Foreign currency balances must be revalued to

their current U.S. dollar equivalent using current exchange rates whenever financial statements are prepared. This approach violates the conservatism principle when unrealized foreign exchange gains are recognized as income.

4. Exposure to foreign exchange risk can be eliminated through hedging. A foreign currency asset (receivable) exposure is hedged by creating a foreign currency liability (payable) of similar magnitude and maturity. A foreign currency liability exposure is hedged by creating an offsetting foreign currency asset.

5. One popular means of hedging is the forward exchange contract, an agreement to exchange currencies in the future at a predetermined rate. In a forward exchange contract, either a receivable or payable (depending on the terms of the agreement) is created in a specified foreign currency. The forward contract receivable or payable is revalued periodically based on current exchange rates. The resulting foreign exchange gain or loss on the forward contract serves to offset part (or all) of the foreign exchange loss or gain created by the foreign currency transaction being hedged.

6. If a foreign currency firm commitment (either a purchase or sale) is being hedged, gains and losses on the hedging instrument as well as on the underlying firm commitment should be recognized in net income as exchange rate changes occur. The firm commitment account created to offset the gain or loss on firm commitment is treated as an adjustment to the underlying transaction when it takes place.

7. A forward exchange contract also can be acquired for speculative purposes and not as a hedge. In this situation, gains and losses are recognized immediately. However, revaluation is carried out using the market value of the contract rather than the spot rate for the forward contract receivable or payable.

8. Foreign currency options are another popular tool for hedging foreign exchange risk. The FASB Exposure Draft on derivatives requires foreign currency options to be recorded as an asset when purchased. When a foreign currency transaction or firm commitment is being hedged (fair value hedge), changes in the value of the foreign currency option are recorded as gains or losses in net income. If a forecasted transaction is being hedged (cash flow hedge), changes in the value of the option are reported in other comprehensive income. The cumulative change in fair value reported in other comprehensive income is included in net income in the period in which the forecasted transaction was originally anticipated to take place.

COMPREHENSIVE ILLUSTRATION

Problem

(Estimated Time: 55 to 65 Minutes) The Zelm Company is a U.S. company that primarily imports and exports miscellaneous products. During the first quarter of 1998, the company engaged in the following foreign currency transactions.

Part A

On January 15, Zelm places an order to purchase 10,000 board feet of teakwood at a total price of 2 million baht (BT) from a lumber company in Thailand. Delivery will be made in three months on April 15. The spot rate at the date the order was placed was $.25 per baht. On that date, Zelm signed a 90-day forward contract to buy 2 million baht at a forward rate of $.242 per baht. The spot rate for baht is $.254 on March 31 and $.240 on April 15.

Part B

Zelm imports a truckload of footwear from Mexico on February 15. Payment of 200,000 Mexican pesos (MP) will be made on March 15 after the footwear has been sold in the U.S. market. The spot rate on February 15 is $.13 per peso. Assuming that the peso would not appreciate over the next 30 days, Zelm decided to leave its peso liability exposure unhedged. At March 15, the spot rate is $.118 per peso.

Part C

Zelm sells 10 1969 Ford Mustangs to a Danish automobile dealer on February 1 at a price of 900,000 Danish kroner (DK), with payment to be received on March 1. The spot rate at the date of sale is $.175 per krone. Zelm would like to lock in a price at which it can sell the kroner when received in 30 days but it is unable to find a foreign currency broker willing to buy Danish kroner forward. To hedge its foreign currency asset exposure, Zelm signs a contract to sell 215,000 German marks (DM) 30 days forward. Zelm designates the German mark forward contract as a hedge of its Danish kroner exposure. It is effective as a hedge because both currencies are part of the European Monetary System and tend to fluctuate in tandem. On February 1, the DM spot rate is $.73 and the 30-day forward rate is $.74. On March 1, the DK spot rate is $.179 and the DM spot rate is $.746.

Part D

On March 1, to take advantage of lower interest rates in Switzerland, Zelm negotiates a two-year 100,000 Swiss franc (SFR) loan at 4 percent. Principal and interest are to be paid quarterly, with the first payments on June 1. The spot rate at the date of the loan is $.80 per franc. By March 31, the franc has depreciated to $.78, but recovers somewhat to $.786 by June 1.

Part E

Zelm completes the sale of computer printer ink cartridges to a Canadian computer parts store on March 10. The sales price of 100,000 Canadian dollars (C$) will be received in 30 days. On March 10, when the spot rate for the Canadian dollar is $.73, Zelm purchases a put option on 100,000 Canadian dollars at a strike price of $.73, paying a premium of $.005 per unit. The spot rate is $.727 on March 31 and $.723 on April 9. Due to the depreciation in the Canadian dollar, the foreign currency option had a fair value of $600 on March 31 and $700 on April 9.

Required

Prepare journal entries for each of these foreign currency activities in accordance with *SFAS 52* and the FASB's Exposure Draft on derivatives and determine the amounts to be reported in income for the quarter ending March 31, 1998.

Solution

Part A. Forward Contract Hedge of a Foreign Currency Purchase Commitment

(Zelm elects to treat the discount on the forward contract as an adjustment of the underlying transaction.)

1/15/98:	No journal entries related to the purchase order.			
	Forward Contract Receivable (BT)		500,000	
	Forward Contract Payable ($)			484,000
	Deferred Discount			16,000
	To record the forward contract payable at the forward rate of $.242, BT receivable at the spot rate of $.25, and deferred discount for the difference.			
3/31/98	Forward Contract Receivable (BT)		8,000	
	Foreign Exchange Gain			8,000
	To adjust the value of the BT receivable to the new spot rate of $.254 and record a deferred foreign exchange gain resulting from the appreciation in the BT since January 15.			
	Foreign Exchange Loss		8,000	
	Firm Commitment (BT)			8,000
	To record a loss on the firm commitment to pay BT resulting from the appreciation in the BT since January 15.			
	No entry to amortize the premium.			
4/15/98	Foreign Exchange Loss		28,000	
	Forward Contract Receivable (BT)			28,000
	To adjust the value of the BT receivable to the new spot rate of $.240 and record a deferred foreign exchange loss resulting from the depreciation in the BT since March 31.			
	Firm Commitment (BT)		28,000	
	Foreign Exchange Gain			28,000
	To record a gain on the firm commitment to pay BT resulting from the depreciation in the BT since March 31.			
	Forward Contract Payable ($)		484,000	
	Cash			484,000
	To record the purchase of BT 2 million at the forward rate of $.242 from the foreign currency broker.			

Foreign Currency (BT) 480,000
    Forward Contract Receivable (BT)   480,000
  To record receipt of BT 2 million from the foreign
  currency broker at the spot rate of $.240.

Inventory 484,000
Deferred Discount 16,000
    Foreign Currency (BT).   480,000
    Firm Commitment (BT)   20,000
  To record payment of BT 2 million to the Thai supplier
  and close the deferred discount and firm commitment (BT)
  accounts as adjustments to the cost of the inventory.

Summary—Consistent with the one-transaction perspective, Inventory is carried at a cost of $484,000, the exact amount of cash paid. There is no impact on income.

Part B. Foreign Currency Purchase Transaction

2/15/98   Inventory 26,000
            Accounts Payable (MP)   26,000
         To record the purchase of inventory and MP payable at the
         spot rate of $.13.

3/15/98   Accounts Payable (MP) 26,000
            Cash   23,600
            Foreign Exchange Gain   2,400
         To record the purchase of MP 200,000 at the spot rate of
         $.118, payment to the Mexican supplier, and a foreign
         exchange gain resulting from the depreciation in the MP
         since February 15.

Summary—Inventory is recorded at a cost of $26,000, the amount that would have been paid if the inventory had been paid for when received. The first quarter 1998 income statement will include a foreign exchange gain of $2,400 as a result of this transaction.

Part C. Forward Contract Hedge of a Foreign Currency Sale Transaction

2/1/98   Accounts Receivable (DK) 157,500
            Sales   157,500
         To record the sale and DK receivable at the spot rate
         of $.175.

         Forward Contract Receivable ($) 159,100
            Forward Contract Payable (DM)   156,950
            Deferred Premium   2,150
         To record the DM forward contract receivable at the
         forward rate of $.74, DM payable at the spot rate of $.73,
         and deferred premium for the difference.

3/1/98   Accounts Receivable (DK) 3,600
            Foreign Exchange Gain   3,600
         To adjust the value of the DK receivable to the new spot
         rate of $.179 and record a foreign exchange gain resulting
         from the appreciation in the DK since February 1.

         Foreign Exchange Loss 3,440
            Forward Contract Payable (DM)   3,400
         To adjust the value of the DM payable to the new spot rate
         of $.746 and record a foreign exchange loss resulting from
         the appreciation in the DM since February 1.

         Deferred Premium 2,150
            Premium Revenue   2,150
         To amortize the deferred premium to revenue.

         Cash 161,100
            Account Receivable (DK)   161,100
         To record the receipt and conversion of DK 900,000 at the
         spot rate of $.179.

         Forward Contract Payable (DM) 160,390
            Cash   160,390
         To record the purchase of DM 215,000 at the spot rate of
         $.746 and payment to the foreign currency broker.

```
Cash ................................................ 159,100
     Forward Contract Receivable ($) ..................        159,100
     To record the receipt of $159,100 for the foreign currency
     broker.
```

Summary—the net impact on income in the first quarter 1998 would be:

Sales		$157,500
Foreign exchange gain	$3,600	
Foreign exchange loss	(3,440)	
Net foreign exchange gain (loss)		160
Premium revenue		2,150
Net		$159,810

The net impact on income is equal to the net cash inflow of $159,810 ($161,100 − $160,390 + $159,100).

Part D. Foreign Currency Borrowing

```
3/1/98    Cash ......................................... 80,000
              Notes Payable (SFR) ..........................         80,000
              To record the SFR note payable at the spot rate of $.80 and
              the conversion of SFR 100,000 into U.S. dollars.

3/31/98   Interest Expense .................................   260
              Accrued Interest Payable (SFR) ...................         260
              To accrue interest for the month of March 1998: SFR
              100,000 × 4% × 1/12 year = SFR 333.33 × $.78 = $260.

          Notes Payable (SFR) ............................. 2,000
              Foreign Exchange Gain ........................       2,000
              To revalue the SFR note payable at the spot rate of $.78
              and record a foreign exchange gain of $2,000 [SFR
              100,000 × ($.78 − $.80)]

6/1/98    Notes Payable (SFR) ............................. 9,750
          Foreign Exchange Loss ............................    75
              Cash .......................................       9,825
              To record the first principal payment of SFR 12,500
              acquired at the spot rate of $.786 ($9,825); remove one-
              eighth of the carrying value of the note payable ($9,750)
              from the books; and record a foreign exchange loss
              resulting from an appreciation in the SFR since March
              31—SFR 12,500 × ($.786 − $.78).

          Interest Expense .................................   524
          Accrued Interest Payable (SFR) ....................   260
          Foreign Exchange Loss ............................     2
              Cash .......................................       786
              To record the first interest payment of SFR 1,000 acquired
              at the spot rate of $.786; interest expense for the period
              March 31–June 1: SFR 666.66 × $.786; and a foreign
              exchange loss on the SFR accrued interest payable—SFR
              333.33 × ($.786 − $.78).
```

Summary—the income statement for the quarter ended March 31, 1998, would include interest expense of $260 and a foreign exchange gain of $2,000.

Part E. Foreign Currency Option Hedge of Export Sale Transaction

```
3/10/98   Accounts Receivable (C$) ......................... 73,000
              Sales .......................................        73,000
              To record the sale and C$ receivable at the spot rate
              of $.73.

          Foreign Currency Options .........................   500
              Cash .......................................        500
              To record the purchase of the option contract (C$100,000 ×
              $.005) as an asset.
```

3/31/98	Foreign Currency Options	100	
	Gain on Foreign Currency Options		100
	To adjust the fair value of the foreign currency option from $500 to $600 and record a gain on foreign currency options.		
	Foreign Exchange Loss	100	
	Accounts Receivable (C$)		100
	To recognize an offsetting loss on the C$ payable only to the extent of the option gain.		
4/9/98	Foreign Currency Options	100	
	Gain on Foreign Currency Options		100
	To adjust the fair value of the foreign currency option form $600 to $700 and record a gain on foreign currency options.		
	Foreign Exchange Loss	100	
	Accounts Receivable (C$)		100
	To recognize an offsetting loss on the C$ receivable only to the extent of the option gain.		
	Foreign Currency (C$)	72,300	
	Foreign Exchange Loss	500	
	Accounts Receivable (C$)		72,800
	To record the receipt of C$100,000 from the Canadian customer at the spot rate of $.723, close the C$ account receivable, and recognize a loss for the difference between the carrying value of the account receivable and the U S. dollar value of the foreign currency received.		
	Cash	73,000	
	Foreign Currency (C$)		72,300
	Foreign Currency Options		700
	To record exercise of the option at the strike price of $.73 and close the foreign currency options account.		

(The option was exercised because the spot rate on April 9, 1998, of $.723 is less than the strike price of $.73.)

Summary—the impact on net income for the first quarter 1998 would be:

Sales	$73,000	
Foreign exchange loss	(700)	
Gain on foreign currency options	200	
Net	$72,500	

This net impact on income is equal to the net cash inflow ($73,000 strike price less $500 option premium).

Overall, the first quarter 1998 income statement would include the following:

	B	C	D	E	Total
Sales		$157,500		$73,000	$ 230,500
Interest expense			$ (260)		(260)
Net foreign exchange gain (loss).	$2,400	160	2,000	(700)	3,860
Gain on foreign currency options				200	200
Net premium revenue		2,150			2,150
	$2,400	$159,810	$1,740	$72,500	$ 236,450

QUESTIONS

1. What is the concept underlying the two-transaction perspective to accounting for foreign currency transactions?

2. Brown Company makes export sales denominated in several different foreign currencies. How are fluctuations in exchange rates handled under the two-transaction perspective, accrual approach?

3. What creates a foreign exchange gain and a foreign exchange loss, and where are these figures reported in a set of financial statements?

4. What does the term *hedging* mean, and why do companies elect to follow this strategy?

5. What is a forward exchange contract?

6. Why would a company enter into a forward exchange contract?

7. A forward exchange contract creates both a payable and a receivable. Why is only one of these balances revalued at the balance sheet date?

8. What is the proper accounting treatment for a forward contract discount on a hedge of a foreign currency receivable?

9. How is the economic benefit, that is, increase in cash flow, from the hedge of a foreign currency transaction accounted for?

10. What are the major differences in the accounting treatment of a hedge of a foreign currency transaction and a hedge of a foreign currency commitment?

11. Casper Corporation uses a forward contract to hedge a foreign currency commitment resulting from ordering machinery from a foreign manufacturer. How is the cost of the imported machinery determined?

12. How does the accounting for a forward exchange contract differ if the agreement is acquired for speculation rather than as a hedge?

13. What is a foreign currency put option?

14. How does a foreign currency option differ from a foreign currency forward contract?

15. Why might a company prefer to use an option rather than a forward contract? Why might a company prefer a forward contract over an option?

16. What is the proper accounting treatment for the premium paid for a foreign currency option?

17. What is hedge accounting?

18. How are changes in the fair value of a foreign currency option accounted for in a fair value hedge? In a cash flow hedge?

19. How do most companies present forward contract payables and receivables on the balance sheet?

LIBRARY ASSIGNMENTS

1. As the manager of international sales for Compex Global Corporation, you have made a major sale to a new customer in Great Britain. Payment of 500,000 British pounds will be received in 30 days. You must decide which of the following strategies to use: (*a*) leave the foreign currency exposure unhedged, (*b*) hedge the risk using a forward contract, or (*c*) hedge using a foreign currency option.

    To help make your decision, review current foreign exchange quotes published in *The Wall Street Journal* (or another major newspaper). Select one of the three strategies—*a, b,* or *c.* Prepare journal entries for all three strategies at the date of sale.

    At the end of 30 days, determine the current spot rate for British pounds. Prepare journal entries for all three strategies at the date that payment is received. Which strategy resulted in the greatest amount of cash inflow? Was your strategy the best?

2. Read the following as well as any other published articles on hedging and hedge accounting:

    "Indecent Exposure," *Institutional Investor,* September 1991.
    "Foreign Exchange Exposure Management," *CPA Journal* (Accounting for International Operations section), August 1988.
    "The Challenges of Hedge Accounting," *Journal of Accountancy,* November 1989.
    "(Dangerous) Fun and Games in the Foreign Exchange Market," *Forbes,* August 22, 1988.
    "Foreign Exchange Rate Hedging and *SFAS No. 52*—Relatives or Strangers?" *Accounting Horizons,* December 1988.

    Write a report describing the various reasons for creating hedges and the methods by which hedges can be established.

PROBLEMS

1. Leickner Company ordered parts costing FC100,000 from a foreign supplier on May 12 when the spot rate was $.20 per FC. A one-month forward contract was signed on that date to purchase FC100,000 at a forward rate of $.21. On June 12, when the parts are received, the spot rate is $.23. At what amount should the parts be carried on Leickner's books?
   - a. $20,000.
   - b. $21,000.
   - c. $22,000.
   - d. $23,000.

2. Which of the following combinations correctly describes the relationship between foreign currency transactions, exchange rate changes, and foreign exchange gains and losses?

	Type of Transaction	Foreign Currency	Foreign Exchange Gain or Loss
a.	Export sale	Appreciates	Loss
b.	Import purchase	Appreciates	Gain
c.	Import purchase	Depreciates	Gain
d.	Export sale	Depreciates	Gain

3. A U.S. exporter has a French franc account receivable resulting from an export sale on April 1, 1998, to a French customer. The exporter signed a forward contract on April 1, 1998, to sell French francs. The spot rate was $.22 on that date and the forward rate was $.23. Which of the following would the U.S. exporter have reported in 1998 income?
   - a. Discount revenue.
   - b. Premium expense.
   - c. Discount expense.
   - d. Premium revenue.

4. In accounting for foreign currency transactions, which of the following approaches is used in the United States?
   - a. One-transaction perspective; accrue foreign exchange gains and losses.
   - b. One-transaction perspective; defer foreign exchange gains and losses.
   - c. Two-transaction perspective; defer foreign exchange gains and losses.
   - d. Two-transaction perspective; accrue foreign exchange gains and losses.

Use the following information for problems 5 and 6.

MNC Corp. (a U.S.-based company) sold parts to a Korean customer on December 16, 1998, with payment of 10 million Korean won to be received on January 15, 1999. The following exchange rates apply:

Date	Spot Rate	One-Month Forward Rate
December 16, 1998	$.0035	$.0034
December 31, 1998	.0033	.0037
January 15, 1999	.0038	.0039

5. Assuming no forward contract was entered into, how much foreign exchange gain or loss should MNC report on its 1998 income statement with regard to this transaction?
   - a. $5,000 gain.
   - b. $3,000 gain.
   - c. $2,000 loss.
   - d. $1,000 loss.

6. Assuming a forward contract was entered into to hedge this foreign currency transaction, what would be the net impact on income in 1998?
   - a. No impact on income.
   - b. $500 decrease in income.
   - c. $1,000 decrease in income.
   - d. $5,000 increase in income.

7. On October 1, 1998, Mud Co., a U.S. company, purchased parts from Terra, a Portuguese company, with payment due on December 1, 1998. If Mud's 1998 operating income included no foreign exchange gain or loss, the transaction could have
   a. Resulted in an extraordinary gain.
   b. Been denominated in U.S. dollars.
   c. Caused a foreign exchange gain to be reported as a deferred charge on the balance sheet.
   d. Caused a foreign exchange gain to be reported as a separate component of stockholders' equity.

(AICPA adapted)

Use the following information for problems 8 through 10.

On December 12, 1996, Pumper Co. entered into three forward contracts each to purchase 100,000 cruzodas in 90 days. The relevant exchange rates are as follows:

	Spot Rate	Forward Rate (for 3/12/97)
December 12, 1996	$1.50	$1.08
December 31, 1996	$1.15	$1.11

8. Pumper entered into the first forward contract to hedge a purchase of inventory in November 1996, payable in March 1998. At December 31, 1996, what amount of foreign exchange gain should Pumper include in income from this forward contract?
   a. $0.
   b. $3,000.
   c. $5,000.
   d. $10,000.

9. Pumper entered into the second forward contract to hedge a commitment to purchase equipment being manufactured to Pumper's specifications. At December 31, 1996, what amount of foreign exchange gain should Pumper include in income from this forward contract?
   a. $0.
   b. $3,000.
   c. $5,000.
   d. $10,000.

10. Pumper entered into the third forward contract for speculation. At December 31, 1996, what amount of foreign exchange gain should Pumper include in income from this forward contract?
    a. $0.
    b. $3,000.
    c. $5,000.
    d. $10,000.

(AICPA adapted)

11. Post, Inc., had a receivable from a foreign customer that is payable in the local currency of the customer. On December 31, 1997, this receivable for 200,000 local currency units (LCU) was correctly included in Post's balance sheet at $110,000. When the receivable was collected on February 15, 1998, the U.S. dollar equivalent was $120,000. In Post's 1998 consolidated income statement, how much should be reported as a foreign exchange gain?
    a. $0.
    b. $10,000.
    c. $30,000.
    d. $40,000.

(AICPA adapted)

12. On July 1, 1998, Haywood Company borrowed 1,680,000 lire from a foreign lender, evidenced by an interest-bearing note due on July 1, 1998. The note is denominated in lire. The U.S. dollar equivalent of the note principal is as follows:

Date	Amount
July 1, 1998 (date borrowed)	$210,000
December 31, 1998 (Haywood's year-end)	$240,000
July 1, 1999 (date repaid)	$280,000

In its 1999 income statement, what amount should Haywood include as a foreign exchange gain or loss?

a. $0.
b. $70,000 gain.
c. $70,000 loss.
d. $40,000 gain.
e. $40,000 loss.

(AICPA adapted)

13. Slick Co. had a Japanese yen receivable resulting from exports to Japan and a Belgian franc payable resulting from imports from Belgium. Slick recorded foreign exchange gains related to both its yen receivable and franc payable. Did the foreign currencies increase or decrease in dollar value from the date of the transaction to the settlement date?

	Yen	Franc
a.	Increase	Increase
b.	Decrease	Decrease
c.	Decrease	Increase
d.	Increase	Decrease

(AICPA adapted)

14. Grete Corp. had the following foreign currency transactions during 1998:

■ Merchandise was purchased from a foreign supplier on January 20, 1998, for the U.S. dollar equivalent of $60,000. The invoice was paid on April 20, 1998, at the U.S. dollar equivalent of $68,000.

■ On September 1, 1998, Grete borrowed the U.S. dollar equivalent of $300,000 evidenced by a note that was payable in the lender's local currency on September 1, 1998. On December 31, 1998, the U.S. dollar equivalents of the principal amount and accrued interest were $320,000 and $12,000, respectively. Interest on the note is 10 percent per annum.

In Grete's 1998 income statement, what amount should be included as a foreign exchange loss?

a. $4,000.
b. $20,000.
c. $22,000.
d. $30,000.

15. The Pankow Corporation (a U.S. company) received an order to manufacture a special piece of equipment for a customer in Sweden. The machine is to be delivered in three months with payment of 1 million Swedish kronor on that date. On the date the order is accepted, the spot rate is $.15 per krona, and Pankow acquires a three-month option to sell 1 million Swedish kronor. The option strike price is $.15 and the premium is $.005 per unit. At the end of three months, Pankow delivers the equipment and receives 1 million kronor. The spot rate at that date is $.143 per krona. What is the amount that Pankow would report in income as a result of this transaction?

a. $140,000.
b. $143,000.
c. $145,000.
d. $150,000.

16. The Palmer Corporation operates as a U.S. corporation. Palmer recently acquired a forward exchange contract. The company promised to pay 200,000 ramda in six months in exchange for $31,000. This contract was entered into because the company has a firm commitment to sell merchandise to a customer in six months for 200,000 ramda. At the date of acquiring the forward contract, $.17 = 1 ramda. After two months, $.18 = 1 ramda. How does Palmer reflect the change in the value of the ramda?

a. Recognizes a $2,000 foreign exchange loss.

b. Recognizes a $2,000 foreign exchange gain.

c. Recognizes a $2,000 foreign exchange loss and a $2,000 foreign exchange gain.

d. Recognizes a $2,000 deferred foreign exchange loss.

17. Deveto Corporation acquired merchandise from a foreign supplier on November 12, 1998, for 60,000 LCU (local currency units). The debt was paid on January 19, 1999. The following currency rates are known:

November 12, 1998	$1 = .29 LCU
December 31, 1998	$1 = .33 LCU
January 19, 1999	$1 = .28 LCU

How is the 1998 income statement of Deveto affected by the fluctuations in currency values? How is the 1999 income statement of Deveto affected by the fluctuation in currency values?

18. On December 20, 1997, Butanta Company (a U.S. company headquartered in Miami, Florida) sold parts to a foreign customer at a price of 50,000 ostras. Payment is received on January 10, 1998. Currency exchange rates are as follows:

December 20, 1997	1 ostra = $1.05
December 31, 1997	1 ostra = $1.02
January 10, 1998	1 ostra = $.98

How is the 1997 income statement of Butanta affected by the fluctuations in currency values? How is the 1998 income statement of Butanta affected by the fluctuations in currency values?

19. New Colony Corporation (a U.S. company) made a sale to a foreign customer on September 15, 1998, for 100,000 foreign currency units (FCU). Payment was received on October 15, 1998. The following exchange rates apply:

September 15, 1998	FCU 1 = $.40
September 30, 1998	FCU 1 = $.42
October 15, 1998	FCU 1 = $.37

Required

Prepare all journal entries for New Colony in connection with this sale assuming that the company closes its books on September 30 to prepare interim financial statements.

20. On December 1, 1997, the Dresden Company (an American company in Albany, New York) purchases inventory from a foreign supplier for 60,000 local currency units (LCU). Payment will be made in 90 days after Dresden has sold this merchandise. Sales are made rather quickly and Dresden pays this entire obligation on January 28, 1998. Currency exchange rates are as follows:

December 1, 1997	$.88 = 1 LCU
December 31, 1997	$.82 = 1 LCU
January 28, 1998	$.90 = 1 LCU

Required

Prepare all journal entries for the Dresden Company in connection with the purchase and payment.

21. A U.S. company carries out a set of transactions in a foreign country during 1997. Prepare all journal entries in U.S. dollars along with any December 31, 1997, adjusting entries.

Exchange rates:	
June 1, 1997	$.52 = 1 ertu
August 1, 1997	$.55 = 1 ertu
October 1, 1997	$.60 = 1 ertu
November 1, 1997	$.64 = 1 ertu
December 31, 1997	$.65 = 1 ertu

June 1	Bought inventory of 20,000 ertus on credit.
Aug. 1	Sold all inventory for 30,000 ertus on credit.
Oct. 1	Paid 10,000 ertus on 6/1 purchase.
Nov. 1	Collected 10,000 ertus from 8/1 sale.

22. The Acme Corporation (a United States company in Sarasota, Florida) has the following import/export transactions in 1997:

Mar. 1	Bought inventory costing 50,000 pesos on credit.
May 1	Sold 60 percent of the inventory for 45,000 pesos on credit.
Aug. 1	Collected 40,000 pesos from customers.
Sept. 1	Paid 30,000 pesos to creditors.

Currency exchange rates are as follows:

March 1, 1997.............	$.17 = 1 peso
May 1, 1997	$.18 = 1 peso
August 1, 1997	$.19 = 1 peso
September 1, 1997.........	$.20 = 1 peso
December 31, 1997	$.21 = 1 peso

For each of the following accounts, what will Acme report on its 1997 financial statements?

Inventory	Accounts Receivable
Cost of Goods Sold	Accounts Payable
Sales	Cash

23. The Brandlin Company of Anaheim, California, sells parts to a foreign customer on December 1, 1998, with payment of 20,000 korunas to be received on March 1, 1999. Brandlin enters into a forward contract on December 1, 1998, to sell 20,000 korunas on March 1, 1999. The three-month forward rate on that date was $2.15 per koruna. The spot rates for the koruna (K) on various dates are as follows:

P.405

December 1, 1998	$2.00
December 31, 1998	$2.10
January 15, 1999	$2.20
March 1, 1999.............	$2.25

Required:

Prepare journal entries for these transactions in U.S. dollars assuming that December 31 is Brandlin's year-end. What is the impact on 1998 income? What is the impact on 1999 income?

like
23

xerux

24. On November 10, 1997, the Ace Company sells inventory to a customer in a foreign country. Ace agrees to accept 80,000 matejkas (MJ) in full payment for this inventory. Payment is to be made on February 1, 1998. On December 1, 1997, Ace enters into a forward exchange contract wherein 80,000 matejkas will be delivered to a currency broker in two months. The two-month forward exchange rate on that date was MJ 1 = $0.25. The spot rates on various dates are as follows:

November 10, 1997	MJ 1 = $0.29
December 1, 1997	MJ 1 = $0.27
December 31, 1997	MJ 1 = $0.24
February 1, 1998	MJ 1 = $0.26

Required:

 a. What is the 1997 income effect created by the company's dealings in their foreign currency?
 b. What is the 1998 income effect created by the company's dealings in this foreign currency?
 c. What would be the effect on net income in 1997 if the sale had originally occurred on December 1, 1997, the same date that the forward exchange contract was acquired?
 d. Assume that the customer had made a firm commitment on December 1, 1997, to pay MJ 80,000 for the inventory when delivered on February 1, 1998. The forward exchange contract was acquired on that date to hedge this commitment. What would have been the effect on 1997 net income?

25. The Bartlett Company in Cincinnati, Ohio, has occasional transactions with companies in foreign countries. Prepare journal entries for the following transactions in U.S. dollars. Also prepare any necessary adjusting entries caused by fluctuations in the value of the

foreign currencies. Assume that December 31 is Bartlett's year-end and that the company uses a perpetual inventory system.

1997

Feb. 1	Bought equipment for 40,000 lire on credit.
Apr. 1	Paid for the above equipment.
June 1	Bought inventory for 30,000 lire on credit.
Aug. 1	Sold 70 percent of above inventory for 40,000 lire on credit.
Oct. 1	Collected 30,000 lire from the sales made on August 1, 1995.
Nov. 1	Paid 20,000 lire on the debts incurred on June 1, 1995.

1998

Feb. 1	Collected remaining 10,000 lire from August 1, 1995, sales.
Mar. 1	Paid remaining 10,000 lire on the debts incurred on June 1, 1995.

Currency exchange rates are as follows:

February 1, 1997	$.44 = 1 lira
April 1, 1997	$.45 = 1 lira
June 1, 1997	$.47 = 1 lira
August 1, 1997.	$.48 = 1 lira
October 1, 1997	$.49 = 1 lira
November 1, 1997	$.50 = 1 lira
December 31, 1997.	$.52 = 1 lira
February 1, 1998	$.54 = 1 lira
March 1, 1998	$.55 = 1 lira

26. On June 1, 1997, Alexander Corporation sold goods to a customer in the country of Jungland at a price of 1,000,000 jungs (the local currency of Jungland—abbreviated JG). Payment will be received in three months on September 1, 1997. On June 1, 1997, Alexander enters into a contract to sell JG 1,000,000 in three months at a forward rate of $.049. The company must close its books and prepare its second-quarter financial statements on June 30. Spot exchange rates are as follows:

June 1, 1997.	JG 1 = $.045
June 30, 1997	JG 1 = $.048
September 1, 1997	JG 1 = $.044

Required:

    a. Determine the impact the change in the value of the JG has on Alexander's second-quarter 1997 income.

    b. Determine the impact the change in the value of the JG has on Alexander's third-quarter 1997 income.

    c. What is Alexander's net economic benefit (or loss) from hedging its foreign currency transaction? How is this benefit (or loss) recognized in the accounts?

27. On November 1, 1997, an American company buys inventory from a supplier in the country of Spagnola. The price of this inventory was 10,000 thads (the local currency of Spagnola—abbreviated TD) to be paid in three months on February 1, 1998. Currency values are as follows:

November 1, 1997	TD 1 = $.21
December 1, 1997	TD 1 = $.24
December 31, 1997.	TD 1 = $.28
February 1, 1998	TD 1 = $.25

Required:

    a. How is the American company's net income affected in 1997 by the changes in the relative value of the thad? How is the American company's net income affected in 1998?

    b. Assume that on December 1, 1997, the American company enters into a two-month forward exchange contract whereby 10,000 thads will be received on February 1, 1998, in exchange for $2,600. How is the American company's net income affected in 1997 by the acquisition of the inventory and the forward exchange contract? How is the American company's net income affected in 1998?

28. On October 1, 1996, a forward exchange contract was acquired whereby the Hawkins Company was to pay 100,000 LCU in four months (on February 1, 1997) and receive $65,000 in U.S. dollars. The spot rate for the LCU is as follows:

    > October 1, 1996 . . . . LCU 1 = $.69
    > December 31, 1996 . . . . LCU 1 = $.71
    > February 1, 1997 . . . . LCU 1 = $.72

    a. What journal entries are recorded if the forward exchange contract was entered into to hedge a LCU 100,000 receivable?
    b. What journal entries are recorded if the forward exchange contract was entered into to hedge a commitment related to a LCU 100,000 cash sale that will be made on February 1, 1997? Include entries for both the sale and the forward contract. Assume that Hawkins defers the forward contract premium/discount as an adjustment to the underlying transaction.

29. On November 1, 1997, Tompson (a company with the U.S. dollar as its reporting currency) enters into a four-month forward exchange contract whereby the company will receive 20,000 LCUs (the currency of a foreign country) on March 1, 1998. In exchange, Tompson agrees to pay for these LCUs at the rate of 1 LCU = $.68. The actual spot rate on November 1, 1997, is 1 LCU = $.62 but rises to 1 LCU = $.64 by December 31, 1997, and 1 LCU = $.69 on March 1, 1998. On December 31, 1997, a two-month forward exchange contract has a rate of 1 LCU = $.72.

Required:

    a. Assume that Tompson entered into the four-month forward exchange contract to hedge the effects of a 20,000 LCU liability that was incurred on November 1, 1997, and will be paid on March 1, 1998. What amount of income should Tompson recognize in each of these two years?
    b. Assume that Tompson entered into the four-month forward exchange contract to hedge the effects of a 20,000 LCU commitment that was made on November 1, 1997, to buy inventory on March 1, 1998. What amount of income would Tompson recognize in each of these two years? At what amount will the inventory be recorded on March 1, 1998?
    c. Assume that Tompson entered into the four-month forward exchange contract for investment purposes and that the contract was sold on January 11, 1998, for $610 cash. What amount of income should Tompson recognize in each of these two years?

30. Benjamin, Inc., operates an export/import business. The company, located in Mobile, Alabama, has considerable dealings with companies in the country of Camerrand. All transactions with these companies are denominated in alaries (AL), the currency in use in Camerrand. During 1997, Benjamin acquires 20,000 widgets at a price of 8 alaries per widget with payment to be made when the items are sold. Currency exchange rates are as follows:

    > September 1, 1997 . . . . AL 1 = $.46
    > December 1, 1997 . . . . AL 1 = $.44
    > December 31, 1997 . . . . AL 1 = $.48
    > March 1, 1998 . . . . AL 1 = $.45

Required:

    a. Assume that Benjamin's acquisition took place on December 1, 1997, with payment being made on March 1, 1998. What is the effect of the rate fluctuations on reported income in 1997 and in 1998?
    b. Assume that Benjamin's acquisition took place on September 1, 1997, with payment being made on December 1, 1997. What is the effect of the rate fluctuations on reported income in 1997?
    c. Assume that Benjamin's acquisition took place on September 1, 1997, with payment being made on March 1, 1998. What is the effect of the rate fluctuations on reported income in 1997 and in 1998?
    d. Assume that Benjamin's acquisition took place on December 1, 1997, with payment being made on March 1, 1998. Assume that on December 1, 1997, Benjamin entered

into a three-month forward exchange contract to buy AL 160,000 at an exchange rate of AL 1 = $.47. Considering the acquisition of widgets, payment of the debt, and the forward exchange contract, what is the effect on income in 1997 and in 1998?

31. On November 1, 1997, the Derek Corporation of San Francisco acquires a six-month forward exchange contract. Under the terms of this agreement, Derek agrees to purchase 20,000 milazzos (MZ) at a forward rate of $.42 per MZ. The spot rate on that date is $.48 per MZ. Subsequent exchange rates are as follows:

> December 31, 1997 (spot rate) . . . . $.45 = 1 milazzo
> December 31, 1997 (four-month forward rate) . . . . . . $.40 = 1 milazzo
> May 1, 1998 (spot rate) . . . . $.50 = 1 milazzo

Required:

a. Make all of the journal entries for Derek if the contract was acquired for speculative purposes.

b. Make all of the journal entries for Derek if the company had incurred a commitment on November 1, 1997, to acquire equipment on May 1, 1998, for 20,000 milazzos.

c. Make all of the journal entries for Derek if the company acquired land on November 1, 1997, for 20,000 milazzos with payment to be made on May 1, 1998.

32. Eximco Corporation (based in Champaign, Illinois) has a number of transactions with companies in the country of Mongagua. On November 15, 1997, Eximco sold equipment at a price of 500,000 mongs to a Mongaguan customer with payment to be received on January 15, 1998. In addition, on December 1, 1997, Eximco purchased raw materials from a Mongaguan supplier at a price of 300,000 mongs; payment will be made on February 1, 1998. To hedge its net asset exposure in mongs, Eximco entered into a two-month forward contract on December 1, 1997, wherein Eximco will deliver 200,000 mongs to the foreign currency broker in exchange for $100,000. The following spot rates apply:

> November 15, 1997 . . . .   1 mong = $.53
> December 1, 1997 . . . .   1 mong = $.51
> December 31, 1997 . . . .   1 mong = $.50
> January 15, 1998 . . . .   1 mong = $.49
> February 1, 1998 . . . .   1 mong = $.48

Required:

Prepare all journal entries including December 31 adjusting entries to record these transactions. What is the net impact on net income in 1997? In 1998?

33. On September 30, 1997, the Ericson Company negotiated a two-year, 1,000,000 dudek loan from a foreign bank at an interest rate of 2 percent per annum. Interest payments are made annually on September 30 and the principal will be repaid on September 30, 1999. Ericson prepares U.S. dollar financial statements and has a December 31 year-end. Prepare all journal entries related to this foreign currency borrowing assuming the following exchange rates:

> September 30, 1997 . . . .   1 dudek = $.10
> December 31, 1997 . . . .   1 dudek = $.105
> September 30, 1998 . . . .   1 dudek = $.120
> December 31, 1998 . . . .   1 dudek = $.125
> September 30, 1999 . . . .   1 dudek = $.150

What is the effective cost of borrowing in dollars in each of the years 1997, 1998, and 1999?

34. The Big Arber Company ordered parts from a foreign supplier on May 25, 1998, at a price of 50,000 pijios when the spot rate was $.20 per pijio. Delivery and payment were scheduled for June 25, 1998. On May 25, 1998, Big Arber acquired a call option on 50,000 pijios at a strike price of $.19 and premium of $.008 per unit. The parts are delivered and paid for according to schedule.

a. Assuming a spot rate of $.21 per pijio on June 25, 1998, at what amount will the parts be recorded when received?

    b. Assuming a spot rate of $.18 per pijio on June 25, 1998, at what amount will the parts be recorded when received?

35. On November 15, 1998, Anderson Company sold merchandise to a foreign customer for 100,000 LCU to be received on January 15, 1999. At the date of sale, when the spot rate was $1.10 per LCU, Anderson acquired a put option to sell 100,000 LCU in two months. Given a strike price of $1.12, the premium paid for the option was $.025 per LCU. The following information was gathered:

	Spot Rate	**Fair Value of Option**
December 31, 1998	$1.095	$2,750
January 15, 1999	$1.103	$1,700

Required

    a. Prepare all journal entries for the sale and option hedge assuming December 31 is Anderson's year-end. What is the impact on 1998 income? What is the impact on 1999 income?

    b. Assume the spot rate on January 15, 1999, is $1.123 and the option has a fair value of zero on that date. Prepare all journal entries for the sale and option hedge.

36. Based on past experience, the Leickner Company expects that it will need to purchase component parts from a foreign supplier at a cost of 1,000,000 marks on March 15, 1999. To hedge this forecasted transaction, a three-month call option to purchase 1,000,000 marks is acquired on December 15, 1998. Leickner selects a strike price of $.58 per mark, paying a premium of $.005 per unit, when the spot rate is $.57. The spot rate increases to $.58 at December 31, 1998, causing the fair value of the option to increase to $8,000. By March 15, 1999, when the parts are purchased, the spot rate has climbed to $.59 resulting in a fair value for the option of $10,000.

Required

Prepare all journal entries for the option hedge of a forecasted transaction and for the purchase of component parts assuming that December 31 is Leickner's year-end. What is the impact on 1998 income? What is the impact on 1999 income? What is the carrying value of the component parts inventory? What is the net cash outflow to acquire the component parts?

CHAPTER

10

Translation of Foreign Currency Financial Statements

QUESTIONS TO CONSIDER

■ What is a translation adjustment? How is it computed? Where should it be reported in a set of consolidated financial statements?

■ What is balance sheet exposure and how does it compare with transaction exposure to foreign exchange risk?

■ What are the different concepts underlying the temporal and current rate methods of translation? How does balance sheet exposure differ under these two methods of translation?

■ What is a company's functional currency? How is this functional currency identified?

■ When is remeasurement appropriate rather than translation of foreign currency balances?

■ How does a remeasurement differ from a translation?

■ Why would a company hedge a balance sheet exposure and how is this accounted for?

H.J. Heinz Company added to its roster of international affiliates with the opening of a factory in Russia, and the acquisition of an infant formula and dairy products company in the Czech Republic.[1]

During the year, Gillette augmented its thriving business in India, the world's largest blade market, with the acquisition of Wiltech India, Ltd.[2]

Under an agreement with the Israeli government announced in November, Intel will build a $1.6 billion plant in Kiryat Gat, thirty-five miles outside Jerusalem.[3]

Recent announcements like these have become more the norm than the exception in today's global economy. Companies establish operations in foreign countries for a variety of reasons including the development of new markets for their products, taking advantage of lower production costs, or gaining access to raw materials. Some multinational companies have reached a stage in their development in which domestic operations are no longer considered to be of higher priority than international operations. For example, U.S.-based International Flavors and Fragrances Inc. has operations in 33 countries and has 64 percent of its assets outside of the United States. The Coca-Cola Company generates over 70 percent of its sales and almost 80 percent of its profits from foreign operations.

For the parent company foreign operations create numerous managerial problems that do not exist for domestic operations. Some of these problems arise from cultural differences between the home and foreign countries. Other problems exist because foreign operations generally are required to comply with the laws and regulations of the foreign

---

[1]H.J. Heinz, First Quarter 1996 Report, p. 1.
[2]The Gillette Company, 1995 Annual Report, p. 7.
[3]KPMG Peat Marwick, "Border Crossings," *World Business,* May–June 1996, p. 50.

country. For example, in most countries, companies are required to prepare financial statements in the local currency using local accounting rules.

To prepare worldwide consolidated financial statements, a U.S. parent company must (1) convert the foreign GAAP financial statements of its foreign operations into U.S. GAAP, and (2) translate the financial statements from the foreign currency into U.S. dollars. This conversion and translation process must be carried out regardless of whether the foreign operation is a branch, joint venture, majority owned subsidiary, or affiliate accounted for under the equity method. Differences in GAAP and problems associated with those differences are discussed in the next chapter. This chapter deals with the issue of translating foreign currency financial statements into the parent's reporting currency.

There are two major theoretical issues related to the translation process: (1) which **translation method** should be used and (2) where the resulting **translation adjustment** should be reported in the consolidated financial statements. In this chapter, these two issues are examined first from a conceptual perspective and second by the manner in which these issues have been resolved by the FASB in the United States.

EXCHANGE RATES USED IN TRANSLATION

Two types of exchange rate are used in translating financial statements:

1. **Historical exchange rate**—the exchange rate that exists when a transaction occurs.
2. **Current exchange rate**—the exchange rate that exists at the balance sheet date.

Translation methods differ as to which balance sheet and income statement accounts are translated at historical exchange rates and which are translated at current exchange rates.

Assume that the company described in the discussion question on the next page began operations in Gualos on December 31, 1997, when the exchange rate was $.20 per vilsek. When Southwestern Corporation prepares its consolidated balance sheet at December 31, 1997, it has no choice about the exchange rate it uses to translate the Land into U.S. dollars. Land carried on the foreign subsidiary's books at 150,000 vilseks is translated at an exchange rate of $.20; $.20 is both the *historical* and *current* exchange rate for Land at December 31, 1997.

Consolidated Balance Sheet: 12/31/97
Land (150,000 vilseks × $.20) $30,000

During the first quarter of 1998, the vilsek appreciates relative to the U.S. dollar by 15 percent; the exchange rate at March 31, 1998, is $.23 per vilsek. In preparing its balance sheet at the end of the first quarter of 1998, Southwestern now must decide whether Land carried on the subsidiary's balance sheet at 150,000 vilseks should be translated into dollars using the *historical exchange rate* of $.20 or the *current exchange rate* of $.23.

If the historical exchange rate is used at March 31, 1998, Land continues to be carried on the consolidated balance sheet at $30,000 with no change from December 31, 1997.

DISCUSSION QUESTION

How Do We Report This?

The Southwestern Corporation operates throughout Texas buying and selling widgets. In hopes of expanding into more profitable markets, the company recently decided to open a small subsidiary in the nearby country of Gualos. The currency in Gualos is the vilsek. For some time, the government of that country held the exchange rate constant: 1 vilsek equaled $.20 (or 5 vilseks equal $1.00). Initially, Southwestern invested cash in this new operation; its $90,000 was converted into 450,000 vilseks ($90,000 × 5). One-third of this money (150,000 vilseks or $30,000) was used to purchase land to be held for the possible construction of a plant, one-third was invested in short-term marketable securities, and one-third was spent in acquiring inventory for future resale.

Shortly thereafter, the Gualos government officially revalued the currency so that 1 vilsek was worth $.23. Because of the strength of the local economy, the vilsek gained buying power in relation to the U.S. dollar. Now the vilsek was considered more valuable than in the past. The accountants for Southwestern realized that a change had occurred; each of the assets was now worth more in U.S. dollars than the original $30,000 investment: 150,000 vilseks × $.23 = $34,500. Two of the company's top officers met to determine the appropriate method for reporting this change in currency values.

Controller: Nothing has changed. Our cost is still $30,000 for each item. That's what we spent. Accounting uses historical cost wherever possible. Thus, we should do nothing.

Finance director: Yes, but the old rates are meaningless now. We would be foolish to report figures based on a rate that no longer exists. The cost is still 150,000 vilseks for each item. You are right; the cost has not changed. However, the vilsek is now worth $.23 so our reported value must change.

Controller: The new rate only affects us if we take money out of the country. We don't plan to do that for many years. The rate will probably change 20 more times before we remove money from Gualos. We've got to stick to our $30,000 historical cost. That's our cost and that's good, basic accounting.

Finance director: You mean that for the next 20 years we will be translating balances for external reporting purposes using an exchange rate that has not existed for years? That does not make sense. I have a real problem using an antiquated rate for the investments and inventory. They will be sold for cash when the new rate is in effect. These balances have no remaining relation to the original exchange rate.

Controller: You misunderstand the impact of an exchange rate fluctuation. Within Gualos, no impact occurs. One vilsek is still one vilsek. The effect is only realized when an actual conversion takes place into U.S. dollars at a new rate. At that point, we will properly measure and report the gain or loss. That is when realization takes place. Until then our cost has not changed.

Finance director: I simply see no value at all in producing financial information based entirely on an exchange rate that does not exist. I don't care when realization takes place.

Controller: You've got to stick with historical cost, believe me. The exchange rate today isn't important unless we actually convert vilseks to dollars.

How should Southwestern report each of these three assets on its current balance sheet? Does the company have a gain because the value of the vilsek has increased relative to the U.S. dollar?

Historical Rate—Consolidated Balance Sheet: 3/31/98

Land (150,000 vilseks × $.20) $30,000

If the current exchange rate is used, Land is carried on the consolidated balance sheet at $34,500, an increase of $4,500 from December 31, 1997.

Current Rate—Consolidated Balance Sheet: 3/31/98

Land (150,000 vilseks × $.23) $34,500

Translation Adjustments

To keep the accounting equation (A = L + OE) in balance, the increase of $4,500 on the asset (A) side of the consolidated balance sheet when the current exchange rate is used must be offset by an equal $4,500 *increase* in owners' equity (OE) on the other side of the balance sheet. The increase in owners' equity is called a **positive translation adjustment.** It has a *credit* balance.

The increase in dollar value of the Land due to appreciation of the vilsek creates a positive translation adjustment. This is true for any asset on the Gualos subsidiary's balance sheet that is translated at the *current* exchange rate. *Assets translated at the current exchange rate when the foreign currency has appreciated generate a positive (credit) translation adjustment.*

Liabilities on the Gualos subsidiary's balance sheet that are translated at the current exchange rate also increase in dollar value when the vilsek appreciates. For example, Notes Payable of 10,000 vilseks would be reported at $2,000 on the December 31, 1997, balance sheet and at $2,300 on the March 31, 1998, balance sheet. To keep the accounting equation in balance, the increase in liabilities (L) must be offset by a *decrease* in owners' equity (OE), giving rise to a **negative translation adjustment.** This has a *debit* balance. *Liabilities translated at the current exchange rate when the foreign currency has appreciated generate a negative (debit) translation adjustment.*

Balance Sheet Exposure

Balance sheet items (assets and liabilities) translated at the *current* exchange rate change in dollar value from balance sheet to balance sheet as a result of the change in exchange rate. These items are *exposed* to translation adjustment. Balance sheet items translated at *historical* exchange rates do not change in dollar value from one balance sheet to the next. These items are *not* exposed to translation adjustment. Exposure to translation adjustment is referred to as balance sheet, *translation,* or accounting exposure. **Balance sheet exposure** can be contrasted with the **transaction exposure** discussed in Chapter 9 that arises when a company has foreign currency receivables and payables in the following way: *Transaction exposure gives rise to foreign exchange gains and losses that are ultimately realized in cash; translation adjustments arising from balance sheet exposure do not directly result in cash inflows or outflows.*

Each item translated at the current exchange rate is exposed to translation adjustment. In effect, a separate translation adjustment exists for each of these exposed items. However, positive translation adjustments on assets when the foreign currency appreciates are offset by negative translation adjustments on liabilities. If total exposed assets are equal to total exposed liabilities throughout the year, the translation adjustments (although perhaps significant on an individual basis) net to a zero balance. The *net* translation adjustment needed to keep the consolidated balance sheet in balance is based solely on the *net asset* or *net liability* exposure.

A foreign operation has a **net asset balance sheet exposure** when assets translated at the current exchange rate are greater in amount than liabilities translated at the current exchange rate. A **net liability balance sheet exposure** exists when liabilities translated at the current exchange rate are greater than assets translated at the current exchange rate. The relationship between exchange rate fluctuations, balance sheet exposure, and translation adjustments is summarized as follows:

Balance Sheet Exposure	Foreign Currency (FC)	
	Appreciates	**Depreciates**
Net Asset	Positive Translation Adjustment	Negative Translation Adjustment
Net Liability	Negative Translation Adjustment	Positive Translation Adjustment

Exactly how the translation adjustment should be handled in the consolidated financial statements is a matter of some debate. The major question is whether the translation adjustments should be treated as a *translation gain or loss reported in income* or whether the translation adjustment should be treated as a *direct adjustment to owners' equity without affecting income.* We consider this issue in more detail later after examining methods of translation.

TRANSLATION METHODS

Four major methods of translation have been used worldwide: (1) the current/noncurrent method, (2) the monetary/nonmonetary method, (3) the temporal method, and (4) the current rate (or closing rate) method. We discuss each of these methods from the perspective of a U.S.-based multinational company translating foreign currency financial statements into U.S. dollars.

Current/Noncurrent Method

The rules for the **current/noncurrent method** are as follows: current assets and current liabilities are translated at the current exchange rate; noncurrent assets, noncurrent liabilities, and stockholders' equity accounts are translated at historical exchange rates. There is no theoretical basis underlying this method. Although once the predominant method, the current/noncurrent method has been unacceptable in the United States since 1975 and is seldom used in other countries.

Monetary/Nonmonetary Method

To remedy some of the theoretical flaws in the current/noncurrent method, Samuel Hepworth developed an alternative method of translation in 1956.[4] Under the **monetary/nonmonetary method** of translation, *monetary assets and liabilities* are translated at *current* exchange rates; *nonmonetary assets, nonmonetary liabilities, and stockholders' equity* are translated at *historical* exchange rates. Monetary assets are those assets whose monetary value does not fluctuate over time—primarily cash and receivables. Nonmonetary assets are assets whose monetary value can fluctuate. They consist of marketable securities, inventories, prepaid expenses, investments, fixed assets, and intangible assets; that is, all assets other than cash and receivables. Monetary liabilities are those liabilities whose monetary value cannot fluctuate over time, which is true for most payables.

Under the monetary/nonmonetary method, *cash, receivables, and payables* carried on the foreign operation's balance sheet are *exposed* to translation adjustment. There is a *net asset exposure* when cash plus receivables are greater than payables, and a *net liability exposure* exists when payables are greater than cash plus receivables.

Cash + Receivables > Payables   →   Net Asset Exposure
Cash + Receivables < Payables   →   Net Liability Exposure

One way of understanding the concept of exposure underlying the monetary/nonmonetary method is to pretend that the foreign operation's cash, receivables, and payables are actually carried on the parent's balance sheet. For example, consider the Japanese subsidiary of a U.S. parent company. The Japanese subsidiary's yen receivables that result from sales in Japan may be thought of as Japanese yen receivables of the U.S. parent resulting from export sales to Japan. If the U.S. parent had yen receivables on its balance sheet, a decrease in the value of the yen would result in a *foreign exchange* loss. There also would be a foreign exchange loss on the Japanese yen held in cash by the U.S. parent. These foreign exchange losses would be offset by a foreign exchange gain on the parent's Japanese yen payables resulting from foreign purchases. Whether a net gain or a net loss exists depends on the relative size of yen cash and receivables versus yen payables. Under the monetary/nonmonetary method, the translation adjustment measures the net foreign exchange gain or loss on the foreign operation's cash, receivables, and payables, *as if those items were actually carried on the books of the parent.*

---

[4] Samuel R. Hepworth, *Reporting Foreign Operations* (Ann Arbor: University of Michigan, Bureau of Business Research, 1956).

As mentioned earlier, the major difference between the translation adjustment and a foreign exchange gain or loss is that the translation adjustment is not necessarily realized through inflows or outflows of cash. The U.S. dollar translation adjustment *could be realized* as a gain or loss only if: (1) the parent sends U.S. dollars to the Japanese subsidiary to pay off all its yen liabilities, and (2) the Japanese subsidiary collects all its yen receivables and then sends this amount plus its yen cash to the parent in the United States where the yen are converted into U.S. dollars.

Temporal Method

The basic objective underlying the **temporal method** of translation is to produce a set of U.S. dollar translated financial statements as if the foreign subsidiary had actually used U.S. dollars in conducting its operations. Continuing with the Gualos subsidiary example presented earlier, Land should be reported on the consolidated balance sheet at the amount of U.S. dollars that would have been spent if the U.S. parent had sent dollars to the subsidiary to purchase Land. Because Land had a cost of 150,000 vilseks at a time when one vilsek could be acquired with $.20, the parent would have sent $30,000 to the subsidiary to acquire the land—this is the land's historical cost *in U.S. dollar terms.* Consistent with the temporal method's underlying objective is the following rule:

1. Assets and liabilities on the foreign operation's balance sheet at *historical cost* are translated at *historical* exchange rates to yield an equivalent historical cost in U.S. dollars.
2. Conversely, assets and liabilities carried at a *current or future value* are translated at the *current* exchange rate to yield an equivalent current value in U.S. dollars.

In addition, Owners' Equity accounts are translated at historical exchange rates. Application of this rule maintains the underlying valuation method (current value or historical cost) used by the foreign subsidiary in accounting for its assets and liabilities.

Cash, marketable securities, receivables, and most liabilities are carried at current or future value and translated at the *current* exchange rate under the temporal method.[5] The temporal method generates either a net asset or a net liability balance sheet exposure depending on whether cash plus marketable securities plus receivables are greater than or less than liabilities. Assuming that liabilities (current plus long-term) generally are greater than assets translated at current rates, *a net liability exposure generally exists when the temporal method is used.*

Cash + Marketable Securities + Receivables < Liabilities $\rightarrow$ Net Liability Exposure

By coincidence, the temporal method and the monetary/nonmonetary method result in fairly similar translation rules. The two methods diverge from one another only when nonmonetary assets are carried at current value which is the case with marketable securities and when inventory is written down to market value under the lower-of-cost-or-market rule. The monetary/nonmonetary method translates these items at historical rates, whereas the temporal method translates them at the current rate. Because of the similarity of the two methods, and the fact that the monetary/nonmonetary method has not been used in the United States since 1975, further discussion concentrates on the temporal method.

---

[5]Under *SFAS 105,* all marketable equity securities and marketable debt securities classified as "trading" or "available for sale" are carried at current market value. Marketable debt securities classified as "hold-to-maturity" are carried at cost. Throughout the remainder of this chapter we assume that all marketable securities are reported at current value.

Under the temporal method, income statement items are translated at exchange rates that exist when the revenue is generated or the expense is incurred. For most items, an assumption can be made that the revenue or expense is incurred evenly throughout the accounting period and an average-for-the-period exchange rate can be used for translation. Some expenses, such as cost of goods sold, depreciation of fixed assets, and amortization of intangibles, are related to assets carried at historical cost. Because the related assets are translated at historical exchange rates, these expenses must be translated at historical rates as well.

Current Rate Method

The fourth major method used in translating financial statements is the **current rate method.** The basic assumption underlying the current rate method is that a company's *net investment* in a foreign operation is *exposed* to foreign exchange risk. In other words, a foreign operation represents a foreign currency net asset and if the foreign currency *decreases* in value against the U.S. dollar, then there is a *decrease in the U.S. dollar value of the foreign currency net asset*. This decrease in U.S. dollar value of the net investment is reflected by reporting a *negative* (debit balance) translation adjustment in the consolidated financial statements. If the foreign currency *increases* in value, there is an *increase in the U.S. dollar value of the net asset* that is reflected through a *positive* (credit balance) translation adjustment.

To measure the net investment's exposure to foreign exchange risk, *all assets and all liabilities* of the foreign operation are translated at the *current* exchange rate. As is true for all methods of translation, owners' equity items are translated at historical rates. *The balance sheet exposure under the current rate method is equal to the foreign operation's net asset (total assets minus total liabilities) position.*

Total Assets > Total Liabilities → Net Asset Exposure

The translation adjustment arising when the current rate method is used is also unrealized. It can become a realized gain or loss only if the foreign operation is sold (for its book value) and the foreign currency proceeds from the sale are converted into U.S. dollars.

Under the current rate method, all income statement items are translated at the exchange rate in effect at the date of accounting recognition. In most cases, an assumption can be made that the revenue or expense is incurred evenly throughout the accounting period and a weighted average for the period exchange rate can be used for translation. However, when an income account, such as a gain or loss, occurs at a specific point in time, the exchange rate at that date should be used for translation.[6]

The current rate method and temporal method are currently used in the United States and are the predominant methods used worldwide. A summary of the appropriate exchange rate for selected financial statement items under these two methods is presented in Exhibit 10–1.

Translation of Retained Earnings

Stockholders' equity items are translated at historical exchange rates under both the temporal and current rate methods. This creates somewhat of a problem in translating retained earnings. This figure is actually a composite of many previous transactions: all revenues, expenses, gains, losses, and declared dividends occurring over the life

---

[6]Alternatively, all income statement items may be translated at the current exchange rate. Later we demonstrate that translation at the current rate has a slight advantage over translation at the average-for-the-period rate.

Exhibit 10–1
Exchange Rates for Selected
Financial Statement Items

	Temporal Method Exchange Rate	Current Rate Method Exchange Rate
Balance Sheet		
Assets		
Cash and receivables	Current	Current
Marketable securities	Current*	Current
Inventory at market	Current	Current
Inventory at cost	Historical	Current
Prepaid expenses	Historical	Current
Property, plant, and equipment	Historical	Current
Intangible assets	Historical	Current
Liabilities		
Current liabilities	Current	Current
Deferred income	Historical	Current
Long-term debt	Current	Current
Stockholders' equity		
Capital stock	Historical	Historical
Additional paid-in capital	Historical	Historical
Retained earnings	Composite	Composite
Income Statement		
Revenues	Average	Average
Most expenses	Average	Average
Cost of goods sold	Historical	Average
Depreciation of property, plant, and equipment	Historical	Average
Amortization of intangibles	Historical	Average

*Marketable debt securities classified as hold-to-maturity are carried at cost and translated at the historical exchange rate under the temporal method.

of the company. At the end of the first year of operations, foreign currency (FC) retained earnings is translated as follows:

Net income in FC	[translated per method used to translate income statement items]	= Net income in $
– Dividends in FC	× historical exchange rate when declared	= – Dividends in $
Ending R/E in FC		Ending R/E in $

The ending dollar retained earnings in year one becomes the beginning dollar retained earnings for year two and the translated retained earnings in year two (and subsequent years) is then determined as follows:

Beginning R/E in FC	(from last year's translation)	= Beginning R/E in $
+ Net income in FC	[translated per method used to translate income statement items]	= + Net income in $
– Dividends in FC	× historical exchange rate when declared	= – Dividends in $
Ending R/E in FC		Ending R/E in $

The same approach translates retained earnings under both the current rate and the temporal methods. The only difference is that translation of the current period's net income is done differently under the two methods.

COMPLICATING ASPECTS OF THE TEMPORAL METHOD

Under the temporal method, it is necessary to keep a record of the exchange rates when inventory, prepaid expenses, fixed assets, and intangible assets are acquired because these assets, carried at historical cost, are translated at historical exchange rates. Keeping track of the historical rates for these assets is not necessary under the current rate method. Translating these assets at historical rates makes application of the temporal method more complicated than the current rate method.

Calculation of Cost of Goods Sold (COGS)

Under the *current rate method,* COGS in Foreign Currency (FC) is simply translated using the average-for-the-period exchange rate (ER):

$$\text{COGS in FC} \times \text{Average ER} = \text{COGS in \$}$$

Under the *temporal method,* COGS must be decomposed into beginning inventory, purchases, and ending inventory and each component of COGS must then be translated at its appropriate historical rate. For example, if beginning inventory (FIFO basis) in the year 1997 was acquired evenly throughout the fourth quarter of 1996, then the average exchange rate in the fourth quarter of 1996 is used to translate beginning inventory. Likewise, the fourth quarter (4thQ) 1997 exchange rate is used to translate ending inventory. When purchases can be assumed to have been made evenly throughout 1997, then the average 1997 exchange rate is used to translate purchases:

Beginning inventory in FC	× Historical ER (4thQ 1996)	= Beginning inventory in $
+ Purchases in FC	× Average ER (1997)	= + Purchases in $
− Ending inventory in FC	× Historical ER (4thQ 1997)	= − Ending inventory in $
COGS in FC		COGS in $

No single exchange rate can be used to directly translate COGS in FC into COGS in $.

Application of the Lower-of-Cost-or-Market Rule

Under the *current rate method,* the ending inventory reported on the foreign currency balance sheet is translated at the current exchange rate regardless of whether it is carried at cost or a lower market value. Application of the *temporal method* requires the foreign currency cost and foreign currency market value of the inventory to be translated into U.S. dollars at appropriate exchange rates, and the *lower of the dollar cost and dollar market value* is reported on the consolidated balance sheet. As a result of this procedure, it is possible for inventory to be carried at cost on the foreign currency balance sheet and at market value on the U.S. dollar consolidated balance sheet, and vice versa.

Fixed Assets, Depreciation, Accumulated Depreciation

Under the *temporal method,* fixed assets acquired at different times must be translated at different (historical) exchange rates. The same is true for depreciation of fixed assets and accumulated depreciation related to fixed assets.

For example, assume a company purchases a piece of equipment on January 1, 1997, for FC 1,000 when the exchange rate is $1.00 per FC. Another item of equipment is purchased on January 1, 1998, for FC 5,000 when the exchange rate is $1.20 per FC. Both pieces of equipment have a five-year useful life. Under the temporal method, the amount at which Equipment would be reported on the consolidated balance sheet on December 31, 1999, when the exchange rate is $1.50 per FC, would be:

$$
\begin{aligned}
\text{FC } 1{,}000 \times \$1.00 &= \$1{,}000 \\
\text{FC } 5{,}000 \times \$1.20 &= \$6{,}000 \\
\text{FC } 6{,}000 & \ \ \$7{,}000
\end{aligned}
$$

Depreciation expense for 1999 under the temporal method would be calculated as:

$$
\begin{array}{rl}
\text{FC} \quad 200 \times \$1.00 = & \$ \ \ 200 \\
\text{FC} \ \underline{1,000} \times \$1.20 = & \underline{\$1,200} \\
\text{FC} \ \underline{1,200} & \underline{\$1,400} \\
\end{array}
$$

Accumulated depreciation under the temporal method would be calculated as:

$$
\begin{array}{rl}
\text{FC} \quad 600 \times \$1.00 = & \$ \ \ 600 \\
\text{FC} \ \underline{2,000} \times \$1.20 = & \underline{\$2,400} \\
\text{FC} \ \underline{2,600} & \underline{\$3,000} \\
\end{array}
$$

Similar procedures apply for intangible assets as well.

Under the *current rate method,* Equipment would be reported on the December 31, 1999, balance sheet at: FC 6,000 × $1.50 = $9,000. Depreciation expense would be: FC 1,200 × $1.40 = $1,680, and accumulated depreciation would be: FC 2,600 × $1.50 = $3,900.

In this example, the foreign subsidiary has only two fixed assets requiring translation. For subsidiaries that own hundreds and thousands of fixed assets, the temporal method can require substantial additional work as compared to the current rate method.

Gain or Loss on the Sale of an Asset

Assume that a foreign subsidiary sells land that cost FC 1,000 at a selling price of FC 1,200. A gain on the sale of land of FC 200 is reported in the subsidiary's income statement. The land was acquired when the exchange rate was $1.00 per FC; the sale was made when the exchange rate was $1.20 per FC; and the exchange rate at the balance sheet date is $1.50 per FC.

Under the *currrent rate method,* the gain on sale of land is translated at the exchange rate in effect at the date of sale:

$$
\text{FC } 200 \times \$1.20 = \$240
$$

Under the *temporal method,* the gain on sale of land cannot be translated directly. Instead, the cash received and the cost of the land sold are translated into U.S. dollars separately, with the difference being the U.S. dollar value of the gain. In accordance with the rules of the temporal method, Cash is translated at the current rate and Land is translated at the historical rate:

$$
\begin{array}{lll}
\text{Cash} & \text{FC } 1,200 \times \$1.50 = & \$1,800 \\
\text{Land} & \text{FC } \underline{1,000} \times \$1.00 = & \underline{\$1,000} \\
\text{Gain} & \text{FC } \ \ \underline{200} & \$ \ \ \underline{800} \\
\end{array}
$$

DISPOSITION OF TRANSLATION ADJUSTMENT

The first issue related to the translation of foreign currency financial statements is selecting the appropriate method. The *second issue* in financial statement translation relates to deciding *where the resulting translation adjustment should be reported in the consolidated financial statements.* There are two prevailing schools of thought with regard to this issue:

1. **Translation Gain or Loss**—Under this treatment, the translation adjustment is considered to be a gain or loss analogous to the gains and losses arising from foreign currency transactions and should be reported in income in the period in which the fluctuation in the exchange rate occurs.

The first of two conceptual problems with treating translation adjustments as gains or losses in income is the gain or loss is unrealized; that is, there is no accompanying cash inflow or outflow. The second problem is the gain or loss may not be consistent with economic reality. For example, the depreciation of a foreign currency may have a *positive* impact on the foreign operation's export sales and income, but the particular translation method used gives rise to a translation *loss*.

2. Cumulative Translation Adjustment in Stockholders' Equity—The alternative to reporting the translation adjustment as a gain or loss in income is to take it directly to stockholders' equity. One way of viewing this treatment is that the gain or loss is being deferred in stockholders' equity until realized in some way.

The two major translation methods and the two possible treatments for the translation adjustment give rise to these four possible combinations:

Combination	Translation Method	Treatment of Translation Adjustment
A	Temporal	Gain or loss in income
B	Temporal	Deferred in stockholders' equity
C	Current rate	Gain or loss in income
D	Current rate	Deferred in stockholders' equity

U.S. RULES

Prior to 1975 the United States had no authoritative rules about which translation method to use or where the translation adjustment had to be reported in the consolidated financial statements. Different combinations were used by different companies. As an indication of the importance of this particular accounting issue, the first official pronouncement issued by the newly created FASB in 1973 was *SFAS No. 1,* "Disclosure of Foreign Currency Translation Information." *SFAS 1* did not express a preference for any particular combination, but simply required disclosure of the method used and the treatment of the translation equipment.

SFAS No. 8

The use of different combinations by different companies created a lack of comparability across companies. To eliminate this noncomparability, in 1975 the FASB issued *SFAS No. 8,* "Accounting for the Translation of Foreign Currency Transactions and Foreign Currency Financial Statements." *SFAS 8* mandated use of the *temporal method* with *translation gains or losses* reported in income by all companies for all foreign operations (Combination A).

In developing *SFAS 8,* the FASB determined that the primary objective of the translation process was to generate a set of U.S. dollar financial statements as if the U.S. dollar had actually been used by the foreign subsidiary in its operations—hence, the use of the temporal method. The FASB also believed that the resulting translation adjustment accurately reflected the economic impact of exchange rate changes on the foreign operation's ability to generate future cash flows in U.S. dollars—hence, the gain or loss treatment.

Criticism of *SFAS 8* U.S. multinational companies (MNCs) were strongly opposed to *SFAS 8;* their specific concerns included:

1. Reporting translation gains and losses in income was considered to be inappropriate given that they are unrealized. Moreover, as currency fluctuations often reverse themselves in subsequent quarters, this creates artificial volatility in quarterly earnings. As a case in point, in 1981 ITT

reported the following percentage changes in income from the same quarter of the previous year.[7]

| | Translation Gains or Losses | |
Quarter	Not Included in Income	Included in Income
First	0%	− 45%
Second	−29	+109
Third	+ 2	−119

Whereas ITT's income excluding translation gains and losses would have been the same in the first quarter 1981 as it was in the first quarter 1980 (0 percent change), income as actually reported with translation gains and losses included was 45 percent smaller in the first quarter 1981 than it was in the first quarter 1980. The change in actual reported income from one year to the next was much more volatile as a result of translation gains or losses being included in income.

2. As most foreign operations had a *net liability exposure* under the temporal method, *appreciation* of the foreign currency generated *translation losses*. Yet appreciation of the foreign currency is *likely to generate greater cash flows in U.S. dollars*. This is certainly the case with regard to dividend payments made by the foreign operation to its U.S. parent. The foreign currency dividend increases in U.S. dollar values as the foreign currency appreciates. In this situation, the negative sign of the translation adjustment was considered to be inconsistent with economic reality.

3. The translation of inventory at the historical rate and accounts payable at the current rate was inconsistent given that accounts payable arise from the purchase of inventory. Translation of this asset and liability at different exchange rates resulted in a net exposure to translation adjustment that many argued should not exist.

4. The translation of sales at the average-for-the-current-period rate and cost-of-goods-sold at historical rates was inconsistent and distorted gross profit. This can be seen through the following example:

Sales	FC 100	× 1.20 [Average ER]	=	$120
COGS	FC 80	× 1.00 [Historical ER]	=	$ 80
Gross profit	FC 20 (20%)			$ 40 (33.3%)

Gross profit as a percentage of sales is 20 percent in the foreign currency, but 33.3 percent when translated into U.S. dollars.

A study commissioned by the FASB investigated the impact of *SFAS 8* on U.S. MNCs' behavior.[8] Published in 1978, the study revealed MNCs increased their use of forward contracts to hedge balance sheet exposure and refrained from making foreign direct investments because of the potential for translation losses. *SFAS 8* had an unintended and perhaps dysfunctional effect on multinationals' operating decisions.

In the spring of 1978, the FASB invited companies to provide comments on the first 12 SFASs as part of a postenactment review process. Most of the nearly 200 comments the Board received criticized *SFAS 8*. As a result of this negative reaction, the FASB agreed to reconsider the translation issue. The difficulty in establishing appropriate translation rules was recognized by the FASB:

> For enterprises conducting activities in more than a single currency, the practical necessities of financial reporting in a single currency require that the changing prices between two units

---

[7]Raymond H. Alleman, "Why ITT Likes *FASB 52*," *Management Accounting,* July 1982, pp. 23–29.

[8]Thomas G. Evans; William R. Folks, Jr.; and Michael Jilling, *The Impact of Statement of Financial Accounting Standards No. 8 on the Foreign Exchange Risk Management Practices of American Multinationals: An Economic Impact Study* (Stamford, CT: FASB, 1978).

of currency be accommodated in some fashion. People generally agree on this practical necessity but disagree on concepts and details of implementation. As a result, there is significant disagreement among informed observers regarding the basic nature, information content, and meaning of results produced by various methods of translating amounts from foreign currencies into the reporting currency. Each method has strong proponents and severe critics.[9]

After releasing two exposure drafts proposing new translation rules, the FASB finally issued *SFAS No. 52,* "Foreign Currency Translation," in 1981. This resulted in a complete overhaul of U.S. GAAP with regard to foreign currency translation. *SFAS 52* was approved by a narrow four-to-three vote of the Board indicating how contentious the issue of foreign currency translation has been.

SFAS No. 52

Implicit in the **temporal method** is the assumption that foreign subsidiaries of U.S. MNCs have very close ties to their parent companies and would actually carry out their day-to-day operations and keep their books in the U.S. dollar if they could. To reflect the integrated nature of the foreign subsidiary with its U.S. parent, the translation process should create a set of U.S. dollar translated financial statements as if the dollar had actually been used by the foreign subsidiary. This is the **U.S. dollar perspective** to translation that was adopted in *SFAS 8.*

In *SFAS 52,* the FASB recognized two types of foreign entities. First, some foreign entities are so closely integrated with their parents that they do conduct much of their business in U.S. dollars. *Second, other foreign entities are relatively self-contained and integrated with the local economy; primarily, they use a foreign currency in their daily operations.* For the first type of entity, the FASB determined that the U.S. dollar perspective still applies and, therefore, *SFAS 8* rules are still relevant.

For the second relatively independent type of entity, a **local currency perspective** to translation is applicable. For this type of entity the FASB determined that a different translation methodology, namely the *current rate method,* should be used for translation and that translation adjustments should be reported as a *separate component in stockholders' equity* (Combination D above). In addition, the FASB requires using the *average-for-the-period* exchange rate in translating income when the current rate method is used.

In rationalizing the placement of the translation adjustment in stockholders' equity, *SFAS 52* (pars. 113, 114) offered two contrasting positions on the conceptual nature of the translation adjustment. One view is that the "change in the dollar equivalent of the net investment is an unrealized enhancement or reduction, having no effect on the functional currency net cash flow generated by the foreign entity which may be currently reinvested or distributed to the parent." Philosophically, this position holds that even though gains and losses are created by changes in the exchange rate, they are unrealized in nature and should, therefore, not be included within net income.

The alternative perspective put forth by the FASB "regards the translation adjustment as merely a mechanical by-product of the translation process." This second contention argues that no meaningful effect is created by exchange rate fluctuation; the resulting translation adjustment merely serves to keep the balance sheet in equilibrium.

Interestingly enough, the FASB chose not to express preference for either of these theoretical views. The Board felt no need to offer a hint of guidance as to the essential nature of the translation adjustment because both explanations point to its exclusion from the income statement. Thus, a balance sheet figure that can amount to millions of dollars is basically undefined.[10]

---

[9]*SFAS No. 52,* par. 59.

[10]Beginning in 1998, FASB Statement 130 will require translation adjustments to be reported in "other comprehensive income."

Functional Currency   To determine whether a specific foreign operation is integrated with its parent or self-contained and integrated with the local economy, *SFAS 52* created the concept of the **functional currency.** The functional currency is the primary currency of the foreign entity's operating environment. It can be either the parent's currency (U.S.$) or a foreign currency (generally the local currency). *SFAS 52*'s functional currency orientation results in the following rule:

Functional Currency	Translation Method	Translation Adjustment
U.S. dollar	Temporal method	Gain (loss) in income
Foreign currency	Current rate method	Separate component of stockholders' equity

In addition to introducing the concept of the **functional currency,** *SFAS 52* introduced some new terminology. The **reporting currency** is the currency in which the entity prepares its financial statements. For U.S-based corporations, this is the U.S. dollar. If a foreign operation's functional currency is the U.S. dollar, foreign currency balances must be **remeasured** into U.S. dollars using the temporal method with translation adjustments reported as **remeasurement gains and losses** in income. When a foreign currency is the functional currency, foreign currency balances are **translated** using the current rate method and a **translation adjustment** is reported on the balance sheet.

The functional currency is essentially a matter of fact. However, *SFAS 52* (par. 8) states that for many cases "management's judgment will be required to determine the functional currency in which financial results and relationships are measured with the greatest degree of relevance and reliability." *SFAS 52* provides a list of indicators to guide parent company management in its determination of a foreign entity's functional currency (see Exhibit 10–2). *SFAS 52* provides no guidance as to how these indicators are to be weighted in determining the functional currency. Leaving the decision about identifying the functional currency up to management allows some leeway in this process. Different companies approach this selection in different ways:

> "For us it was intuitively obvious," versus "It was quite a process. We took the six criteria and developed a matrix. We then considered the dollar amount and the related percentages in developing a point scheme. Each of the separate criteria was given equal weight (in the analytical methods applied)."[11]

Research has shown that the weighting schemes used by U.S. multinationals for determining the functional currency might be biased toward selection of the *foreign currency* as the functional currency.[12] This would be rational behavior for multinationals given that, when the foreign currency is the functional currency, the translation adjustment is reported in stockholders' equity and does not affect income.

An alternative to the selection of a single functional currency is allowed by *SFAS 52.* A foreign subsidiary's activities may be reported as if several entities existed, each with its own functional currency. However, this option is only appropriate if each of these operations is "distinct and separable." A European subsidiary, for example, might be divided into a German operation with the deutsche mark as its functional currency and a French operation with the franc as its functional currency. One survey of 179 corporations indicated that 12.3 percent had opted to split at least one foreign subsidiary to report more than one functional currency.[13]

[11]Jerry L. Arnold and William W. Holder, *Impact of Statement 52 on Decisions, Financial Reports and Attitudes* (Morristown, NJ: Financial Executives Research Foundation, 1986), p. 89.

[12]Timothy S. Doupnik and Thomas G. Evans, "Functional Currency as a Strategy to Smooth Income," *Advances in International Accounting,* 1988.

[13]Thomas G. Evans and Timothy S. Doupnik, *Determining the Functional Currency under Statement 52,* (Stamford, CT: FASB, 1986), p. 25.

Exhibit 10-2
SFAS 52 Indicators for Determining the Functional Currency

Indicator	Indication that Functional Currency Is the	
	Foreign Currency	**Parent's Currency**
Cash flow	Primarily in FC and do not affect parent's cash flows	Directly impact parent's cash flows on a current basis
Sales price	Not affected on short-term basis by changes in exchange rate	Affected on short-term basis by changes in exchange rate
Sales market	Active local sales market	Sales market mostly in parent's country or sales denominated in parent's currency
Expenses	Primarily local costs	Primarily costs for components obtained from parent's country
Financing	Primarily denominated in foreign currency and FC cash flows adequate to service obligations	Primarily from parent or denominated in parent currency or FC cash flows not adequate to service obligations
Intercompany transactions	Low volume of intercompany transactions, not extensive interrelationship with parent's operations	High volume of intercompany transactions and extensive interrelationship with parent's operations

Highly Inflationary Economies

For those foreign entities located in a **highly inflationary economy,** it is not necessary to determine the functional currency—*SFAS 52* mandates use of the *temporal method* with *translation gains or losses reported in income.*

A country is defined has having a *highly inflationary economy* when its cumulative three-year inflation exceeds 100 percent. With compounding, this equates to an average of approximately 26 percent per year for three years in a row. Countries that have met this definition at some time since *SFAS 52* was implemented include Argentina, Brazil, Israel, Mexico, and Turkey. In any given year, a country may or may not be classified as highly inflationary depending on its most recent three-year experience with inflation.

One reason for this rule is to avoid a "disappearing plant problem" caused by using the current rate method in a country with high inflation. Remember that under the current rate method, all assets (including fixed assets) are translated at the current exchange rate. To see the problem this creates in a highly inflationary economy, consider the following hypothetical example.

The Brazilian subsidiary of a U.S. parent purchased Land at the end of 1984 for 10,000,000 cruzeiros (Cr$) when the exchange rate was $.001 per Cr$. Under the *current rate method,* the Land would be reported in the parent's Consolidated Balance Sheet at $10,000.

	Historical Cost	Current ER	Consolidated B.S.
1984	Cr$ 10,000,000 ×	$.001 =	$10,000

In 1985, Brazil experienced roughly 200 percent inflation. Accordingly, with the forces of purchasing power parity at work, the cruzeiro plummeted against the U.S. dollar to a value of $.00025 at the end of 1985. Under the current rate method, Land now would be reported in the parent's Consolidated Balance Sheet at $2,500, and a negative translation adjustment of $7,500 would result.

1985	Cr$ 10,000,000 ×	$.00025 =	$2,500

Using the current rate method, Land has lost 75 percent of its U.S. dollar value in one year, and Land is not even a depreciable asset!

High rates of inflation continued in Brazil with the high point of roughly 1,800 percent reached in 1993. As a result of applying the current rate method, the Land originally reported on the 1984 Consolidated Balance Sheet at $10,000 was carried on the 1993 Balance Sheet at less $1.00.

In the exposure draft leading to *SFAS 52,* the FASB proposed requiring companies with operations in highly inflationary countries to first **restate** the historical costs for inflation and then **translate** using the current rate method. For example, with 200 percent inflation in 1985, the Land would have been written up to Cr$ 40,000,000 and then translated at the current exchange rate of $.00025. This would have produced a translated amount of $10,000, the same as in 1984.

Companies objected to making inflation adjustments, however, because of a lack of reliable inflation indices in many countries. The FASB backed off from requiring the **restate/translate** approach; instead *SFAS 52* requires using the temporal method in highly inflationary countries. In the previous example, under the *temporal method,* a firm would use the historical rate of $.001 to translate Land year after year. Land would be carried on the Consolidated Balance Sheet at $10,000 each year, thereby avoiding the disappearing plant problem.

THE PROCESS ILLUSTRATED

To provide a basis for demonstrating the translation and remeasurement procedures prescribed by *SFAS 52,* assume that USCO (a U.S-based company) forms a wholly owned subsidiary in Germany (BERLINCO) on December 31, 1997. On that date, USCO invested $300,000 in exchange for all of the subsidiary's common stock. Given the exchange rate of DM 1 = $.60, the initial capital investment was DM 500,000, of which DM 150,000 was immediately invested in inventory and the remainder held in cash. Thus, BERLINCO begins operations on January 1, 1998, with stockholders' equity (net assets) of DM 500,000 and net monetary assets of DM 350,000.

BERLINCO
Opening Balance Sheet
January 1, 1998

Assets	DM	Liabilities and Equity	DM
Cash	DM 350,000	Common stock	DM 100,000
Inventory	150,000	Additional paid-in capital . .	400,000
	DM 500,000		DM 500,000

During 1998, BERLINCO purchased property and equipment, acquired a patent, and made additional purchases of inventory, primarily on account. A five-year loan was negotiated to help finance the purchase of equipment. Sales were made, primarily on account, and expenses were incurred. Income after taxes of DM 470,000 was generated, with dividends of DM 150,000 declared on October 1, 1998. BERLINCO's financial statements for the year 1998 in German marks appear in Exhibit 10–3.

To properly translate the DM financial statements into U.S. dollars, USCO must gather exchange rates between the DM and U.S. dollar at various points in time. Relevant exchange rates are as follows:

January 1, 1998	$.60
Rate when property and equipment were acquired and long-term debt was incurred, March 15, 1998	$.61
Rate when patent was acquired, April 10, 1998	$.62
Average 1998	$.65
Rate when dividends were declared, October 1, 1998	$.67
Average fourth quarter 1998	$.68
December 31, 1998	$.70

As can be seen, the DM steadily appreciated against the dollar during the year.

Exhibit 10–3
Foreign Currency Financial Statements

BERLINCO
Income Statement
For Year Ending December 31, 1998

	DM
Sales	4,000,000
Cost of goods sold	3,000,000
Gross profit	1,000,000
Depreciation expense	100,000
Amortization expense	10,000
Other expenses	220,000
Income before income taxes	670,000
Income taxes	200,000
Net income	470,000

Statement of Retained Earnings
For Year Ending December 31, 1998

	DM
Retained earnings, 1/1/98	–0–
Net income, 1998	470,000
Less: Dividends, 10/1/98	150,000
Retained earnings, 12/31/98	320,000

Balance Sheet
December 31, 1998

Assets	DM	Liabilities and Equity	DM
Cash	130,000	Accounts payable	600,000
Accounts receivable	200,000	Total current liabilities	600,000
Inventory*	400,000	Long-term debt	250,000
Total current assets	730,000	Total current liabilities	850,000
Property and equipment	1,000,000	Common stock	100,000
Accumulated depreciation	(100,000)	Additional paid-in capital	400,000
Patents, net	40,000	Retained earnings	320,000
Total assets	1,670,000	Total equity	820,000
		Total liabilities and equity	1,670,000

*Inventory is valued at FIFO cost under the lower-of-cost-or-market-value rule; ending inventory was acquired evenly throughout the fourth quarter.

Statement of Cash Flows
For Year Ending December 31, 1998

	DM
Operating activities:	
Net income	470,000
Add: Depreciation expense	100,000
Amortization expense	10,000
Increase in accounts receivable	(200,000)
Increase in inventory	(250,000)
Increase in accounts payable	600,000
Net cash from operations	730,000
Investing activities:	
Purchase of property and equipment	(1,000,000)
Acquisition of patent	(50,000)
Net cash from investing activities	(1,050,000)
Financing activities:	
Proceeds from long-term debt	250,000
Payment of dividends	(150,000)
Net cash from financing activities	100,000
Decrease in cash	(220,000)
Cash at 12/31/97	350,000
Cash at 12/31/98	130,000

Income Statement
For Year Ending December 31, 1998

	DM	Translation Rate*	US$
Sales	DM 4,000,000	0.65 A	$ 2,600,000
Cost of goods sold	(3,000,000)	0.65 A	(1,950,000)
Gross profit	1,000,000		650,000
Depreciation expense	(100,000)	0.65 A	(65,000)
Amortization expense	(10,000)	0.65 A	(6,500)
Other expenses	(220,000)	0.65 A	(143,000)
Income before income taxes	670,000		435,500
Income taxes	(200,000)	0.65 A	(130,000)
Net income	DM 470,000		$ 305,500

*Indicates the exchange rate used and whether the rate is the current (C), average (A), or a historical (H) rate.

Statement of Retained Earnings
For Year Ending December 31, 1998

	DM	Translation Rate	US$
Retained earnings, 1/1/98	DM –0–		$ –0–
Net income, 1998	470,000	above	305,500
Less: Dividends, 10/1/98	(150,000)	0.67 H	(100,500)
Retained earnings, 12/31/98	DM 320,000		$ 205,000

TRANSLATION OF FINANCIAL STATEMENTS—CURRENT RATE METHOD

The first step in translating foreign currency financial statements is determining the functional currency. Assuming that the German mark is the functional currency, the income statement and statement of retained earnings would be translated into U.S. dollars using the current rate method as shown in Exhibit 10–4.

All revenues and expenses are translated at the exchange rate in effect at the date of accounting recognition. The weighted-average exchange rate for 1998 is utilized here because each revenue and expense in this illustration would have been recognized evenly throughout the year. However, when an income account, such as a gain or loss, occurs at a specific point in time, the exchange rate as of that date is applied. Depreciation and amortization expense also are translated at the average rate for the year. These expenses accrue evenly throughout the year even though the journal entry may have been delayed until year-end for convenience.

The translated amount of net income for 1998 is brought down from the income statement into the statement of retained earnings. Dividends are translated at the exchange rate on the date of declaration.

Translation of the Balance Sheet

Looking at BERLINCO's translated balance sheet in Exhibit 10–5, note that all assets and liabilities are translated at the current exchange rate. Common stock and additional paid-in capital are translated at the exchange rate on the day the common stock was originally sold. Retained earnings at December 31, 1998, is brought down from the statement of retained earnings. Application of these procedures results in total assets of $1,169,000, and total liabilities and equities of $1,100,000. The balance sheet is brought back into balance by creating a positive translation adjustment of $69,000 that is treated as an increase in stockholders' equity.

Note that the translation adjustment for 1998 is a *positive* $69,000 (credit balance). The sign of the translation adjustment (positive or negative) is a function of

Exhibit 10–5
Translation of Balance
Sheet—Current Rate Method

Balance Sheet December 31, 1998	DM	Translation Rate	US$
Assets			
Cash	DM 130,000	0.70 C	$ 91,000
Accounts receivable	200,000	0.70 C	140,000
Inventory	400,000	0.70 C	280,000
Total current assets	730,000		511,000
Property and equipment	1,000,000	0.70 C	700,000
Less: Accumulated depreciation	(100,000)	0.70 C	(70,000)
Patents, net	40,000	0.70 C	28,000
Total assets	DM 1,670,000		$1,169,000
Liabilities and Equities			
Accounts payable	DM 600,000	0.70 C	$ 420,000
Total current liabilities	600,000		420,000
Long-term debt	250,000	0.70 C	175,000
Total liabilities	850,000		595,000
Common stock	100,000	0.60 H	60,000
Additional paid-in capital	400,000	0.60 H	240,000
Retained earnings	320,000	above	205,000
Cumulative translation adjustment		plug	69,000
Total equity	820,000		574,000
Total liabilities and equity	DM 1,670,000		$1,169,000

two factors: (1) the nature of the balance sheet exposure (asset or liability) and (2) the change in the exchange rate (appreciation or depreciation). In this illustration, BERLINCO has a *net asset exposure* (total assets translated at the current exchange rate are greater than total liabilities at the current exchange rate), and the DM has *appreciated* creating a *positive translation adjustment.*

The translation adjustment can be derived as a plug figure that brings the balance sheet back into balance. The translation adjustment also can be calculated by considering the impact of exchange rate changes on the beginning balance and subsequent changes in the net asset position:

1. The net asset balance of the subsidiary at the beginning of the year is translated at the exchange rate in effect on that date.

2. Individual increases and decreases in the net asset balance during the year are translated at the rates in effect when those increases and decreases occurred. Only a few events actually change net assets, such as net income, dividends stock issuance, and the acquisition of treasury stock. Transactions such as the acquisition of equipment or the payment of a liability have no effect on total net assets.

3. The translated beginning net asset balance (*a*) and the translated value of the individual changes (*b*) are then combined to arrive at the relative value of the net assets being held prior to the impact of any exchange rate fluctuations.

4. The ending net asset balance is translated then at the current exchange rate to determine the reported value after all exchange rate changes have occurred.

5. The translated value of the net assets prior to any rate changes (*c*) is compared with the ending translated value (*d*). The difference is the result of exchange rate changes during the period. If (*c*) is greater than (*d*), then a negative (debit) translation adjustment arises. If (*d*) is greater than (*c*), a positive (credit) translation adjustment results.

Computation of Translation Adjustment   Based on the process just described, the translation adjustment for BERLINCO in this example is calculated as follows:

Net asset balance, 1/1/98	DM 500,000	× 0.60 =	$ 300,000
Change in net assets:			
Net income, 1998	470,000	× 0.65 =	$ 305,500
Dividends declared, 10/1/98	(150,000)	× 0.67 =	(100,500)
Net asset balance, 12/31/98	DM 820,000		$ 505,000
Net asset balance, 12/31/98 at current			
exchange rate	DM 820,000	× 0.70 =	(574,000)
Translation adjustment, 1998 (positive)			$ (69,000)

Since this subsidiary began operations at the beginning of the current year, the $69,000 translation adjustment is the only amount applicable for reporting purposes. If a balance already had been created by translations in previous years, that beginning balance would have been combined with the $69,000 to arrive at an appropriate year-end total to be presented within stockholders' equity.

The translation adjustment is reported as a separate component of equity only until the foreign operation is sold or liquidated. *SFAS 52* (para. 14) stipulates that, *in the period in which sale or liquidation occurs, the cumulative translation adjustment related to the particular entity must be removed from equity and reported as part of the gain or loss on the sale of the investment.*

Translation of the Statement of Cash Flows

Under the current rate method, all operating items in the statement of cash flows are translated at the average-for-the-period exchange rate (see Exhibit 10–6). This is the same rate used for translating income statement items. Although the ending balance in accounts receivable, inventory, and accounts payable on the balance sheet are

Exhibit 10–6
Translated Statement of Cash Flows—Current Rate Method

Statement of Cash Flows For Year Ending December 31, 1998			
	DM	Translation Rate	US$
Operating activities:			
Net income	DM 470,000	0.65 A	$ 305,500
Add: Depreciation	100,000	0.65 A	$ 65,000
Amortization	10,000	0.65 A	$ 6,500
Increase in accounts receivable	(200,000)	0.65 A	(130,000)
Increase in inventory	(250,000)	0.65 A	(162,500)
Increase in accounts payable	600,000	0.65 A	390,000
Net cash from operations	730,000		474,500
Investing activities:			
Purchase of property and equipment . .	(1,000,000)	0.61 H	(610,000)
Acquisition of patent	(50,000)	0.62 H	(31,000)
Net cash from investing activities . .	(1,050,000)		(641,000)
Financing activities:			
Proceeds from long-term debt	250,000	0.61 H	152,500
Payment of dividends	(150,000)	0.67 H	(100,500)
Net cash from financing activities . .	100,000		52,000
Decrease in cash	(220,000)		(114,500)
Effect of exchange rate change on cash . .		plug	(4,500)
Cash at December 31, 1997	DM 350,000	0.60 C	$ 210,000
Cash at December 31, 1998	DM 130,000	0.70 C	$ 91,000

translated at the current exchange rate, the average rate is used for the *changes* in these accounts because those changes are caused by operating activities (such as sales and purchases) that are translated at the average rate.

Investing and financing activities are translated at the exchange rate on the day the activity took place. Although long-term debt is translated in the balance sheet at the current rate, in the statement of cash flows it is translated at the historical rate when the debt was incurred.

The $(4,500) "effect of exchange rate change on cash" is a part of the overall translation adjustment of $69,000. It represents that part of the translation adjustment attributable to a decrease in cash and is derived as a plug figure.

REMEASUREMENT OF FINANCIAL STATEMENTS—TEMPORAL METHOD

Now assume that a careful examination of the functional currency indicators outlined in *SFAS 52* leads USCO's management to conclude that BERLINCO's functional currency is the U.S. dollar. In that case, the deutsche mark financial statements must be remeasured into U.S. dollars using the temporal method and the remeasurement gain or loss reported in income. To ensure that the remeasurement gain or loss is reported in income, it is easiest to remeasure the balance sheet first (as shown in Exhibit 10–7).

According to the procedures outlined in Exhibit 10–1, under the temporal method, cash, receivables, and liabilities are remeasured into U.S. dollars using the current exchange rate of $.70. Inventory (carried at FIFO cost), property and equipment, patents, and the contributed capital accounts (Common Stock and Additional Paid-In Capital) are remeasured at historical rates. These procedures result in total assets of $1,076,800, and liabilities and contributed capital of $895,000. To balance the balance sheet, retained earnings must be $181,800. The accuracy of this amount is verified later.

Exhibit 10–7

Remeasurement of Balance Sheet—Temporal Method

Balance Sheet December 31, 1998			
	DM	**Remeasurement Rate**	**US$**
Assets			
Cash	DM 130,000	0.70 C	$ 91,000
Accounts receivable	200,000	0.70 C	140,000
Inventory	400,000	0.68 H	272,000
Total current assets	730,000		503,000
Property and equipment	1,000,000	0.61 H	610,000
Less: Accumulated depreciation	(100,000)	0.61 H	(61,000)
Patents	40,000	0.62 H	24,800
Total assets	DM 1,670,000		$1,076,800
Liabilities and Equities			
Accounts payable	DM 600,000	0.70 C	$ 420,000
Total current liabilities	600,000		420,000
Long-term debt	250,000	0.70 C	175,000
Total liabilities	850,000		595,000
Common stock	100,000	0.60 H	60,000
Additional paid-in capital	400,000	0.60 H	240,000
Retained earnings	320,000	plug	181,800
Total equity	820,000		481,000
Total liabilities and equity	DM 1,670,000		$1,076,800

Remeasurement of the Income Statement

The remeasurement of BERLINCO's income statement and statement of retained earnings is demonstrated in Exhibit 10–8. Revenues and expenses incurred evenly throughout the year (sales, other expenses, and income taxes) are remeasured at the average exchange rate. Expenses related to assets remeasured at historical exchange rates (depreciation expense and amortization expense) are themselves remeasured at relevant historical rates.

Cost of goods sold is remeasured at historical exchange rates using the following procedure. Beginning inventory acquired on January 1 is remeasured at the exchange rate from that date ($.60). Purchases made evenly throughout the year are remeasured at the average rate for the year ($.65). Ending inventory (at FIFO cost) purchased evenly throughout the fourth quarter of 1998 and the average exchange rate for the quarter ($.68) are used to remeasure that component of cost of goods sold. These procedures result in cost of goods sold of $1,930,500, calculated as follows:

Beginning inventory, 1/1/98	DM 150,000	× 0.60 =	$ 90,000
Plus: Purchases, 1998	3,250,000	× 0.65 =	2,112,500
Less: Ending inventory, 12/31/98	(400,000)	× 0.68 =	(272,000)
Cost of goods sold, 1998	DM 3,000,000		$1,930,500

The ending balance in retained earnings on the balance sheet and in the statement of retained earnings must reconcile with one another. Given that dividends are remeasured into a U.S. dollar equivalent of $100,500 and the ending balance in retained earnings on the balance sheet is $181,800, net income must be $282,300.

To reconcile the amount of income reported in the statement of retained earnings and in the income statement, a remeasurement loss of $47,000 is required in the calculation of income. Without this remeasurement loss, the income statement, statement of retained earnings, and balance sheet are not consistent with one another.

The remeasurement loss can be calculated by considering the impact of exchange rate changes on the subsidiary's balance sheet exposure. Under the temporal method,

Exhibit 10–8
Remeasurement of Income Statement and Statement of Retained Earnings—Temporal Method

Income Statement
For the Year Ending December 31, 1998

	DM	Remeasurement Rate	US$
Sales	DM 4,000,000	0.65 A	$ 2,600,000
Cost of goods sold	(3,000,000)	above	(1,930,500
Gross profit	1,000,000		669,500
Depreciation expense	(100,000)	0.61 H	(61,000)
Amortization expense	(10,000)	0.62 H	(6,200)
Other expenses	(220,000)	0.65 A	(143,000)
Income before income taxes	670,000		459,300
Income taxes	(200,000	0.65 A	(130,000
Remeasurement Loss		plug	(47,000)
Net income	DM 470,000		$ 282,300

Statement of Retained Earnings
For the Year Ending December 31, 1998

	DM	Remeasurement Rate	US$
Retained earnings, 1/1/98	DM –0–		$ –0–
Net income, 1998	470,000	above	282,300
Dividends	(150,000)	0.67 H	(100,500)
Retained earnings, 12/31/98	DM 320,000		$ 181,800

BERLINCO's balance sheet exposure is defined by its net monetary asset or net monetary liability position. BERLINCO began 1998 with net monetary assets (cash) of DM 350,000. During the year, however, expenditures of cash and the incurrence of liabilities caused monetary liabilities (accounts payable + long-term debt = DM 850,000) to exceed monetary assets (cash + accounts receivable = DM 330,000). A net monetary liability position of DM 520,000 exists at December 31, 1998. The remeasurement loss is computed by translating the beginning net monetary asset position and subsequent changes in monetary items at appropriate exchange rates and then comparing this with the dollar value of net monetary liabilities at year-end based on the current exchange rate.

Computation of Remeasurement Loss

Net monetary assets, 1/1/98	DM	350,000	× 0.60 =	$ 210,000
Increases in monetary items:				
Sales, 1998		4,000,000	× 0.65 =	2,600,000
Decreases in monetary items:				
Purchases, 1998		(3,250,000)	× 0.65 =	(2,112,500)
Other expenses, 1998		(220,000)	× 0.65 =	(143,000)
Income taxes, 1998		(200,000)	× 0.65 =	(130,000)
Purchase of property and equipment, 3/15/98		(1,000,000)	× 0.61 =	(610,000)
Acquisition of patents, 4/10/98		(50,000)	× 0.62 =	(31,000)
Dividends, 10/1/98		(150,000)	× 0.67 =	(100,500)
Net monetary liabilities, 12/31/98	DM	(520,000)		$ (317,000)
Net monetary liabilities, 12/31/98 at the current exchange rate	DM	(520,000)	× .070 =	(364,000)
Remeasurement loss				$ 47,000

If BERLINCO had maintained its net monetary asset position (cash) of DM 350,000 for the entire year, a remeasurement gain of $35,000 would have resulted. The DM held in cash was worth $210,000 (DM 350,000 × $.60) at the beginning of the year and $245,000 (DM 350,000 × $.70) at year-end. However, the net monetary asset position is not maintained. Indeed, a net monetary liability position arises. The *appreciation* of the foreign currency coupled with an increase in *net monetary liabilities* generates a *remeasurement loss* for the year.

Remeasurement of the Statement of Cash Flows

In remeasuring the statement of cash flows (shown in Exhibit 10–9), the U.S. dollar value for net income is taken directly from the remeasured income statement. Depreciation and amortization are remeasured at the rates used in the income statement, and the remeasurement loss is added back to net income because it is a non-cash item. The increases in accounts receivable and accounts payable relate to sales and purchases and are therefore remeasured at the average rate. The U.S. dollar value for the increase in inventory is determined by referring to the remeasurement of cost of goods sold.

The resulting U.S. dollar amount of "net cash from operations" ($474,500) is exactly the same as when the current rate method was used in translation. In addition, the investing and financing activities are translated in the same manner under both methods. This makes sense; the amount of cash inflows and outflows are a matter of fact and are not affected by the particular translation methodology employed.

Non-Local Currency Balances

One additional issue related to the translation of foreign currency financial statements needs to be considered. If any of the accounts of the German subsidiary are denominated in a currency other than the German mark, those balances would first have to

Exhibit 10-9
Remeasurement of Statement
of Cash Flows—Temporal
Method

**Statement of Cash Flows
For the Year Ending December 31, 1998**

	DM	Remeasurement Rate	US$
Operating activities:			
Net income . . . . DM	470,000	from I/S	$ 282,300
Add: Depreciation expense	100,000	0.61 H	61,000
Amortization expense	10,000	0.62 H	6,200
Remeasurement loss		from I/S	47,000
Increase in accounts receivable	(200,000)	0.65 A	(130,000)
Increase in inventory	(250,000)	*	(182,000)
Increase in accounts payable	600,000	0.65 A	390,000
Net cash from operations	730,000		474,500
Investing activities:			
Purchase of property and equipment . .	(1,000,000)	0.61 H	(610,000)
Acquisition of patent	(50,000)	0.62 H	(31,000)
Net cash from investing activities	(1,050,000)		(641,000)
Financing activities:			
Proceeds from long-term debt	250,000	0.61 H	152,500
Payment of dividends	(150,000)	0.67 H	(100,500)
Net cash from financing activities	100,000		52,000
Decrease in cash	(220,000)		(114,500)
Effect of exchange rate changes on cash			(4,500)
Cash at December 31, 1997 . . . . DM	350,000	0.6 C	$ 210,000
Cash at December 31, 1998 . . . . DM	130,000	0.7 C	$ 91,000

*In remeasuring cost of goods sold earlier, beginning inventory was remeasured as $90,000 and ending inventory was remeasured as $272,000; an increase of $182,000.

be restated into marks in accordance with the rules discussed in Chapter 9. Both the foreign currency balance and any related foreign exchange gain or loss would then be translated (or remeasured) into U.S. dollars. For example, a note payable of 10,000 Belgian francs first would be remeasured into German marks before the translation process could commence.

COMPARISON OF THE RESULTS FROM APPLYING THE TWO DIFFERENT METHODS

The determination of the foreign subsidiary's functional currency (and the use of different translation methods) can have a significant impact on consolidated financial statements. The following chart shows differences for BERLINCO in several key items under the two different translation methods:

	Translation Method		
Item	Current Rate	Temporal	Difference
Net income	$ 305,500	$ 282,300	+ 8.2%
Total assets	$1,169,000	$1,076,800	+ 8.6%
Total equity	$ 574,000	$ 481,000	+19.3%
Return on equity	53.2%	58.7%	− 9.4%

In this illustration if the German mark is determined to be BERLINCO's functional currency (and the current rate method is applied), net income reported in the consolidated income statement would be 8.2 percent greater than if the U.S. dollar is the functional currency (and the temporal method is applied). In addition, total assets would be 8.6 percent greater and total equity would be 19.3 percent higher using the current rate method. Because of the larger amount of equity, return on equity using the current rate method is 9.4 percent smaller.

Note that the current rate method does not always result in larger net income and a greater amount of equity than the temporal method. For example, if BERLINCO had maintained its net monetary asset position, a remeasurement gain would have been computed under the temporal method leading to higher income than under the current rate method. Moreover, if the deutsche mark had depreciated during 1998, the temporal method would have resulted in higher net income.

The important point is that the determination of the functional currency and resulting translation method can have a significant impact on the amounts reported by a parent company in its consolidated financial statements. The appropriate determination of the functional currency is an important issue.

> "Within rather broad parameters," says Peat, Marwick, Mitchell partner James Weir, choosing the functional currency is basically a management call. So much so, in fact, that Texaco, Occidental, and Unocal settled on the dollar as the functional currency for most of their foreign operations, whereas competitors Exxon, Mobil, and Amoco chose primarily the local currencies as the functional currencies for their foreign businesses.[14]

Different functional currencies selected by different companies in the same industry could have a significant impact on the comparability of financial statements within that industry. Indeed, one of the concerns raised by those FASB members dissenting on *SFAS 52* was that the functional currency rules might not result in similar accounting for similar situations.

In addition to differences in amounts reported in the consolidated financial statements, the results of the BERLINCO illustration demonstrate several conceptual differences between the two translation methods.

Underlying Valuation Method

Using the temporal method, BERLINCO's property and equipment was remeasured as follows:

$$\text{Property and equipment} \quad DM\ 1,000,000 \times \$0.61\ H = \$610,000$$

By multiplying the historical cost in DM by the historical exchange rate, $610,000 represents the U.S. dollar equivalent historical cost of this asset. It is the amount of U.S. dollars that the parent company would have had to pay to acquire assets having a cost of DM 1,000,000 when the exchange rate was $.61 per DM.

Property and equipment was translated under the current rate method as follows:

$$\text{Property and equipment} \quad DM\ 1,000,000 \times \$0.70\ C = \$700,000$$

The $700,000 amount is not readily interpretable. It does not represent the U.S. dollar equivalent historical cost of the asset; that amount is $610,000. It also does not represent the U.S. dollar equivalent current cost of the asset because DM 1,000,000 is not the current cost of the asset in Germany. The $700,000 amount is simply the product of multiplying two numbers together!

Underlying Relationships

The following table reports the values for selected financial ratios calculated from the original foreign currency financial statements and from the U.S. dollar translated statements using the two different translation methods:

---

[14]John Heins, "Plenty of Opportunity to Fool Around," *Forbes,* June 2, 1986, p. 139.

Ratio	DM	US$ Temporal	US$ Current Rate
Current ratio [current assets/current liabilities]	1.22	1.20	1.22
Debt/equity ratio[total liabilities/total equities]	1.04	1.24	1.04
Gross profit ratio[gross profit/sales]	25%	25.8%	25%
Return on equity[net income/total equity]	57.3%	58.7%	53.2%

The temporal method distorts all of the ratios as measured in the foreign currency. The subsidiary appears to be less liquid, more highly leveraged, and more profitable than it does in DM terms.

The current rate method maintains the first three ratios, but return on equity is distorted. The distortion occurs because income was translated at the average-for-the-period exchange rate whereas total equity was translated at the current exchange rate. In fact, any ratio combining balance sheet and income statement figures, such as turnover ratios, is distorted by the use of the average rate for income and the current rate for assets and liabilities.

Conceptually, when the current rate method is employed, income statement items can be translated at either the average or the current exchange rate. *SFAS 52* requires using the average exchange rate. In this illustration, if revenues and expenses had been translated at the current exchange rate, net income would have been $329,000 (DM 470,000 × $.70), and the return on equity would have been 57.3 percent ($329,000/$574,000), exactly the amount reflected in the DM financial statements. In several countries in which the current rate method is used, companies are allowed to choose between the average exchange rate and the current exchange rate in translating income. This is true, for example, in France and the United Kingdom.

HEDGING BALANCE SHEET EXPOSURE

When the U.S. dollar is the functional currency or when a foreign operation is located in a highly inflationary economy, remeasurement gains and losses are reported in the consolidated income statement. Management of U.S. multinational companies might wish to avoid reporting remeasurement losses in income because of the perceived negative impact this has on the company's stock price. Likewise, when the foreign currency is the functional currency, management might wish to avoid reporting negative translation adjustments in stockholders' equity because of the adverse impact on the debt to equity ratio.

> More and more corporations are hedging their translation exposure—the recorded value of international assets such as plant, equipment and inventory—to prevent gyrations in their quarterly accounts. Though technically only paper gains or losses, translation adjustments can play havoc with balance-sheet ratios and can spook analysts and creditors alike.[15]

Translation adjustments and remeasurement gains or losses are a function of two factors: (1) changes in the exchange rate and (2) balance sheet exposure. Although there is little if anything a company can do to influence exchange rates, parent companies can use several techniques to hedge the balance sheet exposures of their foreign operations. As was true for hedging foreign currency transaction exposure, each of these techniques involves creating an equilibrium between foreign currency asset and liability balances that are translated at current exchange rates.

Forward contracts are a popular means of hedging balance sheet exposure. To illustrate their use, assume that BERLINCO's functional currency is the German mark; this creates a net asset balance sheet exposure. USCO believes that the German

[15]Ida Picker, "Indecent Exposure," *Institutional Investor,* September 1991, p. 82.

mark will depreciate, thereby generating a negative translation adjustment that will be reported in consolidated stockholders' equity.

USCO could hedge this balance sheet exposure by entering into a forward contract with a foreign currency broker to sell German marks, thereby creating a German mark payable to offset the net asset exposure. *SFAS 52* refers to this as a **hedge of a net investment** and stipulates that foreign exchange gains and losses arising from this type of foreign contract are to be treated in the same fashion as the item being hedged. Because the forward contract is designed to hedge a translation adjustment reported in stockholders' equity, any change in the U.S. dollar value of the forward contract resulting from rate fluctuations would be classified as an offsetting translation adjustment rather than as a foreign exchange gain or loss. On the other hand, if a remeasurement-based balance sheet exposure is being hedged, foreign exchange gains and losses on forward contracts used to hedge that exposure are included in income as offsets to the remeasurement gains and losses being hedged.

The paradox of hedging balance sheet exposure is that in the process of avoiding an unrealized negative translation adjustment or remeasurement loss, realized foreign exchange gains and losses result. Returning to USCO and its hedge of a German mark net investment, USCO must deliver German marks to the foreign currency broker when the forward contract matures. Because USCO has no German mark receivable to generate an inflow of marks, it has to purchase marks in the foreign exchange market at the spot rate and then deliver those marks to the foreign currency broker. If the mark depreciates more than was anticipated by the foreign exchange market, USCO can purchase marks at a spot rate lower than the forward rate and realize a gain. This gain offsets the negative translation adjustment created by the depreciation of the mark. If the mark depreciates less than was predicted by the forward rate or even appreciates in value, USCO has to purchase marks at a spot rate exceeding the forward rate and a loss results. This is pure speculation. While this hedge eliminates the possibility of reporting a negative translation adjustment in stockholders' equity, speculative gains and losses realized in cash result.

DISCLOSURES RELATED TO TRANSLATION

SFAS 52 (para. 31) requires firms to present an analysis of the change in the cumulative translation adjustment account in the financial statements or notes thereto. Many companies comply with this requirement by including a translation adjustment column in their Statement of Stockholders' Equity. Other companies provide separate disclosure in the notes; see Exhibit 10–10 for an example of this disclosure for the Gillette Company.

An analysis of Gillette's cumulative translation adjustment account indicates a negative translation adjustment of $154.2 million in 1993, a positive translation adjustment of $43.0 million in 1994, and a negative translation adjustment of $120.4 million in 1995. From the signs of these adjustments one can infer that, in aggregate, the foreign currencies in which Gillette has operations depreciated against the U.S. dollar in 1993 and 1995, and appreciated against the dollar in 1994. On the whole, Gillette's management is probably pleased that the translation adjustment is not reflected in income. Before tax income would have been 9 percent smaller in 1995 and 18 percent smaller in 1993 if translation adjustments had been included in income.

Note that Gillette's cumulative translation adjustment account includes not only "net exchange gains and losses resulting from the translation of assets and liabilities of foreign subsidiaries" but also gains and losses on "intercompany transactions of a long-term investment nature" (as mentioned in Chapter 9) and on "transactions designated as hedges of net foreign investments." Gillette reports its remeasurement gains and losses, which relate primarily to subsidiaries in Brazil, in a line item titled

Exhibit 10–10
The Gillette Company and
Subsidiary Companies 1995
Annual Report

> **Foreign Currency Translation**
>
> Net exchange gains or losses resulting from the translation of assets and liabilities of foreign subsidiaries, except those in highly inflationary economies, are accumulated in a separate section of stockholders' equity titled, "Cumulative foreign currency translation adjustments." Also included are the effects of exchange rate changes on intercompany transactions of a long-term investment nature and transactions designated as hedges of net foreign investments.
>
> An analysis of this account follows:
>
> | (Millions of dollars) | 1995 | 1994 | 1993 |
> |---|---|---|---|
> | Balance at beginning of year .... | $(377.1) | $(415.0) | $(265.2) |
> | Translation adjustments, including the effect of hedging .... | (120.4) | 43.0 | (154.2) |
> | Related income tax effect .... | 20.5 | (5.1) | 4.4 |
> | Balance at end of year..................... | $(477.0) | $(377.1) | $(415.0) |
>
> Included in Other charges are net exchange losses of $17.0 million, $77.4 million, and $105.4 million for 1995, 1994, and 1993, respectively, primarily relating to subsidiaries in highly inflationary countries, principally Brazil.

"Other charges—net" on the income statement. The remeasurement loss of $105.4 million in 1993 was significant, equal to 15 percent of before tax income.

Although there is no specific requirement to do so, many companies include a description of their translation procedures in their "summary of significant accounting policies" in the notes to the financial statements. The following excerpt from Biomet, Inc.'s 1995 annual report illustrates this type of disclosure:

> Translation of Foreign Currency—Assets and liabilities of foreign subsidiaries are translated at rates of exchange in effect at the close of their fiscal year. Revenues and expenses are translated at the weighted-average exchange rates during the year. Translation gains and losses are accumulated as a separate component of shareholders' equity. Foreign currency transaction gains and losses are included in other income, net.

CONSOLIDATION OF A FOREIGN SUBSIDIARY

The final section of this chapter demonstrates the procedures used to consolidate the financial statements of a foreign subsidiary with those of its parent. Special attention should be paid to the treatment of the excess of cost over book value. As an item denominated in foreign currency, translation of the excess gives rise to a translation adjustment recorded on the consolidation worksheet.

On January 1, 1997, Altman Inc., a U.S.-based manufacturing firm, purchased 100 percent of Bradford Ltd. in Great Britain. Altman paid £25,000,000 for its purchase. On January 1, 1997, Bradford had the following balance sheet:

Cash	£ 925,000	Accounts payable	£ 675,000
Accounts receivable.......	1,400,000	Long-term debt	4,000,000
Inventory	6,050,000	Common stock	20,000,000
Plant and equipment (net) ..	19,000,000	Retained earnings	2,700,000
Total	£27,375,000	Total	£27,375,000

The excess of cost over book value of £2,300,000 was due to undervalued land (part of plant and equipment) and therefore is not subject to amortization. Altman uses the equity method to account for its investment in Bradford.

On December 31, 1998, two years after the date of acquisition, Bradford submitted the following trial balance for consolidation (credit balances are in parentheses):

Cash	£	600,000
Accounts receivable		2,700,000
Inventory		9,000,000
Plant and equipment (net)		17,200,000
Accounts payable		(500,000)
Long-term debt		(2,000,000)
Common stock		(20,000,000)
Retained earnings, 1/1/98		(3,800,000)
Sales		(13,900,000)
Cost of goods sold		8,100,000
Depreciation expense		900,000
Other expenses		950,000
Dividends declared, 6/30/98		750,000
	£	–0–

Although Bradford generated net income of £1,100,000 in 1997, no dividends were declared or paid that year. Other than the payment of dividends in 1998, there were no intercompany transactions between the two affiliates. Altman has determined the British pound to be Bradford's functional currency.

Relevant exchange rates for the British pound were as follows:

	January 1	June 30	December 31	Average
1997	$1.51	—	$1.56	$1.54
1998	1.56	$1.58	1.53	1.55

Translation of Foreign Subsidiary Trial Balance

The initial step in consolidating the foreign subsidiary is to translate its trial balance from British pounds into U.S. dollars. Because the British pound has been determined to be the functional currency, this is carried out using the current rate method. The historical exchange rate for translating Bradford's common stock and January 1, 1997, retained earnings is the exchange rate that existed at the date of acquisition—$1.51.

	British Pounds	Rate	U.S. Dollars
Cash	£ 600,000	1.53 C	$ 918,000
Accounts receivable	2,700,000	1.53 C	4,131,000
Inventory	9,000,000	1.53 C	13,770,000
Property and plant (net)	17,200,000	1.53 C	26,316,000
Accounts payable	(500,000)	1.53 C	(765,000)
Long-term debt	(2,000,000)	1.53 C	(3,060,000)
Common stock	(20,000,000)	1.51 H	(3,020,000)
Retained earnings, 1/1/98	(3,800,000)	*	(5,771,000)
Sales	(13,900,000)	1.55 A	(21,545,000)
Cost of goods sold	8,100,000	1.55 A	12,555,000
Depreciation expense	900,000	1.55 A	1,395,000
Other expenses	950,000	1.55 A	1,472,500
Dividends declared, 6/30/98	750,000	1.58 H	1,185,000
Cumulative translation adjustment			(401,500)
	£ –0–		$ –0–
*Retained earnings, 1/1/97	£2,700,000	1.51 H	$4,077,000
Net income, 1997	1,100,000	1.54 A	1,694,000
Retained earnings, 12/31/97	£3,800,000		$5,771,000

A positive (credit balance) cumulative translation adjustment is required to make the trial balance actually balance. The cumulative translation adjustment is calculated as follows:

Net assets, 1/1/97...............	£22,700,000	1.51 H	$ 34,277,000
Change in net assets, 1997:			
Net income, 1997	1,100,000	1.54 A	1,694,000
Net assets, 12/31/97............	£23,800,000		$ 35,971,000
Net assets, 12/31/97 at current exchange rate	£23,800,000	1.56 C	37,128,000

Translation adjustment, 1997 (positive).. $(1,157,000)

Net assets, 1/1/98...............	£23,800,000	1.56 H	$ 37,128,000
Change in net assets, 1998:			
Net income, 1998	3,950,000	1.55 A	6,122,500
Dividends, 6/30/98.............	(750,000)	1.58 H	(1,185,000)
Net assets, 12/31/98............	£27,000,000		$ 42,065,500
Net assets, 12/31/98 at current exchange rate	£27,000,000	1.53 C	41,310,000

Translation adjustment, 1998 (negative) 755,500

Cumulative translation adjustment, 12/31/98 (positive)............... $ (401,500)

The translation adjustment in 1997 is positive because the British pound appreciated that year; the translation adjustment in 1998 is negative because of a depreciation in the British pound.

Determination of Balance in Investment Account—Equity Method

The original cost of the investment in Bradford, the net income earned by Bradford, and the dividends paid by Bradford are all denominated in British pounds. Relevant amounts must be translated from pounds into U.S. dollars so Altman can account for its investment in Bradford under the equity method. In addition, the translation adjustment calculated each year is included in the Investment account to update the foreign currency investment to its U.S. dollar equivalent. The counterpart is recorded as a translation adjustment on Altman's books:

12/31/97	Dr. Investment in Bradford	$1,157,000	
	Cr. Cumulative translation adjustment		$1,157,000
	To record the positive translation adjustment related to the investment in a British subsidiary when the British pound appreciated.		
12/31/98	Dr. Cumulative translation adjustment	$ 755,500	
	Cr. Investment in Bradford.................		$ 755,500
	To record the negative translation adjustment related to the investment in a British subsidiary when the British pound depreciated.		

The carrying value of the investment account in U.S. dollar terms at December 31, 1998, is determined as follows:

Investment in Bradford	British Pounds	Exchange Rate	U.S. Dollars
Original cost...................	£25,000,000	1.51 H	$37,750,000
Bradford net income, 1997.........	1,100,000	1.54 A	1,694,000
Translation adjustment, 1997			1,157,000
Balance, 12/31/97	£26,100,000		$40,601,000
Bradford net income, 1998.........	3,950,000	1.55 A	6,122,500
Bradford dividends, 6/30/98	(750,000)	1.58 H	(1,185,000)
Translation adjustment, 1998			(755,500)
Balance, 12/31/98	£29,300,000		$44,783,000

In addition to the investment in Bradford of $44,783,000, Altman also has equity income on its December 31, 1998, trial balance in the amount of $6,122,500.

Consolidation Worksheet

Once the subsidiary's trial balance has been translated into dollars and the carrying value of the investment is known, the consolidation worksheet at December 31, 1998, can be prepared. As is true in the consolidation of domestic subsidiaries, the investment account, the subsidiary's equity accounts, and the effects of intercompany transactions must be eliminated. The excess of cost over book value at the date of acquisition also must be allocated to the appropriate accounts (in this example, plant and equipment).

Unique to the consolidation of foreign subsidiaries is the fact that the excess of cost over book value, which is denominated in foreign currency, also must be translated into the parent's reporting currency. When the foreign currency is the functional currency, the excess is translated at the current exchange rate with a resulting translation adjustment. The excess is not carried on either the parent or the subsidiary's books but is recorded only in the consolidation worksheet. *The translation adjustment related to the excess has not yet been recognized by either the parent or the subsidiary and must be recorded in the consolidation worksheet.* Exhibit 10–11 presents the consolidation worksheet of Altman and Bradford at December 31, 1998.

Explanation of consolidation entries:

S—Eliminates the subsidiary's stockholders' equity accounts as of the beginning of the current year along with the equivalent book value component within the parent's purchase price in the Investment account.

Exhibit 10–11 Consolidation Worksheet—Parent and Foreign Subsidiary

ALTMAN INC. AND BRADFORD LTD.
Consolidation Worksheet
For Year Ending December 31, 1998

Accounts	Altman	Bradford	Consolidation Entries Debits	Consolidation Entries Credits	Consolidated Totals
Income Statement					
Sales	$ (32,489,000)	$(21,545,000)			$ (54,034,000)
Cost of goods sold	16,000,000	12,555,000			28,555,000
Depreciation expense	9,700,000	1,395,000			11,095,000
Other expenses	2,900,000	1,472,500			4,372,500
Equity income	(6,122,500)		(I) 6,122,500		–0–
Net income	$(10,011,500)	$ (6,122,500)			$(10,011,500)
Statement of Retained Earnings					
Retained earnings, 1/1/98	$ (25,194,000)	$ (5,771,000)	(S) 5,771,000		$ (25,194,000)
Net income (above)	(10,011,500)	(6,122,500)			(10,011,500)
Dividends paid	1,500,000	1,185,000		(D) 1,185,000	1,500,000
Retained earnings, 12/31/98	$ (33,705,500)	$(10,708,500)			$ (33,705,500)
Balance Sheet					
Cash	$ 3,649,800	$ 918,000			$ 4,567,800
Accounts receivable	3,100,000	4,131,000			7,231,000
Inventory	11,410,000	13,770,000			25,180,000
Investment in Bradford	44,783,000			(S) 35,971,500	
				(A) 3,473,500	
			(D) 1,185,000	(I) 6,122,500	
				(T) 401,500	
Plant and equipment (net)	39,500,000	26,316,000	(A) 3,473,000		
			(E) 46,000		69,335,000
Total assets	$102,442,800	$ 45,135,000			$106,313,800
Accounts payable	$ (2,500,000)	$ (765,000)			$ (3,265,000)
Long-term debt	(22,728,800)	(3,060,000)			(25,788,800)
Common stock	(43,107,000)	(30,200,000)	(S) 30,200,000		(43,107,000)
Retained earnings, 12/31/98 (above)	(33,705,500)	(10,708,500)			(33,705,500)
Cumulative translation adjustment	(401,500)	(401,500)	(T) 401,500	(E) 46,000	(447,500)
Total liabilities and equities	$102,422,800	$ 45,135,000	$47,199,000	$47,199,000	$106,313,800

A—Allocates the excess of cost over book value at the date of acquisition to land (plant and equipment) and eliminates that amount within the parent's purchase price from the Investment account.

I—Eliminates the amount of equity income recognized by the parent in the current year and included in the Investment account under the equity method.

D—Eliminates the subsidiary's dividend payment that was a reduction in the Investment account under the equity method.

T—Eliminates the cumulative translation adjustment included in the Investment account under the equity method and eliminates the cumulative translation adjustment carried on the parent's books.

E—Revalues the excess of cost over book value for the change in exchange rate since the date of acquisition with the counterpart recognized as an increase in the consolidated cumulative translation adjustment. The revaluation is calculated as follows:

Excess of Cost over Book Value

U.S. dollar equivalent at 12/31/98	£2,300,000 × $1.53 =	$3,519,000
U.S. dollar equivalent at 1/1/97	£2,300,000 × $1.51 =	3,473,000
Cumulative translation adjustment related to excess, 12/31/98		$ 46,000

SUMMARY

1. Because many companies have significant financial involvement in foreign countries, the process by which foreign currency financial statements are translated into U.S. dollars is of special accounting importance. The two major issues related to the translation process are (1) which method to use, and (2) where the resulting translation adjustment should be reported in the consolidated financial statements.

2. Translation methods differ on the basis of which accounts are translated at the current exchange rate and which are translated at historical rates. Accounts translated at the current exchange rate are exposed to translation adjustment. Different translation methods give rise to different concepts of balance sheet exposure and translation adjustments of differing signs and magnitude.

3. Under the temporal method, assets carried at current value (cash, marketable securities, receivables) and liabilities are translated at the current exchange rate. Assets carried at historical cost and stockholders' equity are translated at historical exchange rates. When liabilities are greater than the sum of cash, marketable securities, and receivables, a net liability balance sheet exposure exists. Appreciation in the foreign currency results in a negative translation adjustment (remeasurement loss). Depreciation in the foreign currency results in a positive translation adjustment (remeasurement gain). By translating assets carried at historical cost at historical exchange rates, the temporal method maintains the underlying valuation method used by the foreign operation, but relationships in the foreign currency financial statements are distorted.

4. Under the current rate method, all assets and liabilities are translated at the current exchange rate giving rise to a net asset balance sheet exposure. Appreciation in the foreign currency results in a positive translation adjustment. Depreciation in the foreign currency results in a negative translation adjustment. By translating assets carried at historical cost at the current exchange rate, the current rate method maintains relationships in the foreign currency financial statements but the underlying valuation method used by the foreign operation is distorted.

5. From 1975 through 1981, the temporal method—as prescribed by *Statement 8* of the Financial Accounting Standards Board—was used to translate the financial statements of foreign operations. Translation adjustments were reported as gains and losses in income. Because this approach came under increasing attack from the business community as well as from many accountants, the FASB eventually replaced it with *Statement 52*.

6. *Statement 52* creates two separate procedures for translating foreign currency financial statements into the parent's reporting currency. *Translation* through use of the current rate

method is appropriate when the foreign operation's functional currency is a foreign currency. In this case, the translation adjustment is reported in a separate component of stockholders' equity. *Remeasurement* through use of the temporal method is appropriate when the operation's functional currency is the U.S. dollar. Remeasurement also is applied when the operation is in a country with a highly inflationary economy. In these situations, the translation adjustment is treated as a remeasurement gain or loss in income.

7. Some companies hedge their balance sheet exposures to avoid reporting remeasurement losses in income and/or negative translation adjustments in stockholders' equity. One popular hedging tool is the forward exchange contract. Foreign exchange gains and losses on forward contracts employed to hedge translation-based exposure are treated as part of the cumulative translation adjustment in stockholders' equity. Foreign exchange gains and losses on forward contracts used to hedge remeasurement-based exposure are offset against remeasurement gains and losses.

COMPREHENSIVE ILLUSTRATION

Problem

(*Estimated Time: 55 to 65 Minutes*) The Arlington Company is an American-based organization with numerous foreign subsidiaries. As a preliminary step in preparing consolidated financial statements for 1997, the financial information from each of these foreign operations must be translated into the parent's reporting currency, the U.S. dollar.

Arlington owns a subsidiary in Sweden that has been in business for several years. On December 31, 1996, this entity's balance sheet was translated from Swedish kronor (SKr) (its functional currency) into U.S. dollars as prescribed by *SFAS 52*. Equity accounts at that date were as follows (all credit balances):

Common stock	SKr 110,000	=	$21,000
Retained earnings	194,800	=	36,100
Cumulative translation adjustment			3,860

At the end of 1997, the Swedish subsidiary produced the trial balance that follows. These figures include all of the entity's transactions for the year except for the results of several transactions related to sales made to a French customer. A separate ledger has been maintained for these transactions denominated in French francs. This ledger follows the company's trial balance.

Trial Balance—Swedish Subsidiary
December 31, 1997

	Debit	Credit
Cash	SKr 41,000	
Accounts Receivable	126,000	
Forward contract receivable (kronor)	21,000	
Deferred discount on forward contract	1,000	
Inventory	128,000	
Land	160,000	
Fixed assets	228,000	
Accumulated depreciation		SKr 98,100
Accounts payable		39,000
Notes payable		56,000
Bonds payable		125,000
Forward contract payable (French francs)		22,000
Common stock		110,000
Retained earnings, 1/1/97		194,800
Sales		350,000
Cost of goods sold	165,000	
Depreciation expense	10,900	
Salary expense	36,000	
Rent expense	12,000	
Other expenses	41,000	
Dividends paid, 7/1/97	25,000	
Totals	SKr 994,878	SKr 994,878

Ledger—Transactions in French Francs
December 31, 1997

	Debit	Credit
Cash	FF 10,000	
Accounts receivable...............................	28,000	
Fixed assets	20,000	
Accumulated depreciation		FF 4,000
Notes payable....................................		15,000
Sales		44,000
Depreciation expense..............................	4,000	
Interest expense	1,000	
Totals	FF 63,000	FF 63,000

Additional Information:

- The Swedish subsidiary began selling to the French customer at the beginning of the current year. At that time, 20,000 francs were borrowed to acquire a truck for delivery purposes. One-fourth of that debt was paid before the end of the year. Sales to France were made evenly during the period.

- The U.S. dollar exchange rates for the Swedish krona are as follows:

January 1, 1997	$.200 = 1.00 krona
Weighted-average rate for 1997	$.192 = 1.00 krona
July 1, 1997	$.190 = 1.00 krona
December 31, 1997	$1.82 = 1.00 krona

- The exchange rates applicable for the remeasurement of the French franc transactions into Swedish kronor are as follows:

January 1, 1997	1.25 kronor = 1.00 franc
Weighted-average rate for 1997	1.16 kronor = 1.00 franc
December 1, 1997	1.10 kronor = 1.00 franc
December 31, 1997	1.04 kronor = 1.00 franc

- On December 1, 1997, the Swedish subsidiary decided to hedge the net monetary asset position denominated in French francs. Therefore, the company signed a three-month forward contract to sell 20,000 French francs at a forward rate of 1.05 kronor per franc. As a result of this forward contract, 21,000 Swedish kronor were received on March 1, 1998, in exchange for the delivery of 20,000 francs. For recording purposes, the foreign contract payable (the 20,000 francs) was remeasured as 22,000 kronor based on the spot exchange rate on that date of 1.10 kronor per franc. Because the value of the remeasured obligation (SKr 22,000) exceeded the receivable (SKr 21,000), a Deferred Discount of 1,000 kronor was recorded.

- The Swedish subsidiary expended SKr 10,000 during the year for research and development. In accordance with Swedish accounting rules, this cost has been capitalized within the Fixed Assets account. This expenditure had no effect on the depreciation recognized for the year.

Required

Prepare financial statements for the year ending December 31, 1997, for the Swedish subsidiary. Translate these statements according to *SFAS 52* into U.S. dollars to facilitate the preparation of consolidated statements. The Swedish krona is the subsidiary's functional currency.

Solution

Remeasurement of Foreign Currency Balances. A portion of the Swedish subsidiary's operating results are presently stated in French francs. These balances must be remeasured into the functional currency, Swedish krona, before the translation process can begin. In remeasuring these accounts using the temporal method, the krona value of the monetary assets and liabilities are determined by using the current (C) exchange rate (1.04 kronor per franc) whereas all other accounts are remeasured at historical (H) or average (A) rates.

Remeasurement of Foreign Currency Balances

	Francs		Rate		Kronor
Sales	44,000	×	1.16 A	=	51,040
Interest expense	(1,000)	×	1.16 A	=	(1,160)
Depreciation expense	(4,000)	×	1.25 H	=	(5,000)
Income from franc transactions	39,000				44,880
Cash	10,000	×	1.04 C	=	10,400
Accounts receivable	28,000	×	1.04 C	=	29,120
Fixed assets	20,000	×	1.25 H	=	25,000
Accumulated depreciation	(4,000)	×	1.25 H	=	(5,000)
Total franc assets	54,000				59,520
Notes payable	15,000	×	1.04 C	=	15,600
Income from franc transactions	39,000		from above		44,880
	54,000				60,480
Remeasurement loss					(960)
Total					59,520

Remeasurement Loss for 1997

	Francs		Rate		Kronor
Net monetary asset balance, 1/1/97	FF –0–				SKr –0–
Increases in net monetary items:					
Operations (sales less interest expense)	43,000	×	1.16	=	49,880
Decreases in net monetary items:					
Purchased truck, 1/1/97	(20,000)	×	1.25	=	(25,000)
Net monetary assets, 12/31/97	FF 23,000				SKr 24,880
Net monetary assets, 12/31/97 at current exchange rate	FF 23,000	×	1.04	=	SKr 23,920
Remeasurement loss (gain)					SKr 960

The net monetary asset exposure (cash and accounts receivable > notes payable) and depreciation of the French franc create a remeasurement loss of SKr 960. The asset exposure was hedged, however, by creating a forward contract payable. The remeasured value of the forward contract payable at December 1, 1997, was $22,000. At December 31, 1997, the forward contract payable would be remeasured as follows:

	Francs		Rate		Kronor
Forward contract payable	20,000	×	1.04 C	=	20,800

The decrease in krona value of the forward contract payable results in a remeasurement gain of SKr 1,200. This gain is offset against the remeasurement loss related to the French franc transactions, resulting in a net gain of SKr 240. This amount must be reflected in the Swedish subsidiary's financial statements and subsequently is translated into U.S. dollars.

The remeasured figures from the French operation must be combined in some manner with the subsidiary's trial balance denominated in Swedish kronor. For example, the accounts may simply be added together on a worksheet. As an alternative, a year-end adjustment can be recorded in the accounting system of the Swedish subsidiary to add the remeasured balances for financial reporting purposes. In recording these figures, the forward contract payable also is adjusted to the current rate.

12/31/97 Adjustment	Debit	Credit
Cash	SKr 10,400	
Accounts receivable	29,120	
Fixed assets	25,000	
Depreciation expense	5,000	
Interest expense	1,160	
Forward contract payable (French francs)	1,200	
Accumulated depreciation		SKr 5,000
Notes Payable		15,600
Sales		51,040
Remeasurement gain		240

To record foreign currency transactions originally denominated in francs as well as to adjust the forward exchange contract payable from 22,000 kronor to 20,800 kronor.

Two other adjustments are necessary before the Swedish krona financial statements of the subsidiary can be translated into the parent's reporting currency. First, periodic amortization must be recognized on the SKr 1,000 discount related to the forward contract. Second, the research and development costs incurred by the Swedish entity should be reclassified as an expense as required by *SFAS 2*, "Accounting for Research and Development Costs," December 1974. After this adjustment, the Swedish subsidiary's statements are in conformity with U.S. generally accepted accounting principles.

12/31/97 Adjustments	Debit	Credit
Other expenses............................	SKr 333	
Deferred discount on forward contract......		SKr 333
To recognize one-month amortization of the deferred discount on the three-month forward contract (1,000 × 1/3).		
Other expenses............................	SKr 10,000	
Fixed assets		SKr 10,000
To adjust fixed assets and expenses to be in compliance with U.S. GAAP.		

By combining all remeasured and adjusted balances with the Swedish subsidiary's trial balance, final figures can be derived. For example, total sales for the subsidiary are SKr 401,040 (350,000 + 51,040) while cash is SKr 51,400 (41,000 + 10,400), and so on. Having established all account balances in the functional currency (Swedish krona), the subsidiary's statements now may be translated into U.S. dollars. Under the current rate method, the dollar values to be reported for income statement items are based on the average exchange rate for the current year. All assets and liabilities are based on the current exchange rate at the balance sheet date, and equity accounts are based on historical rates in effect at the date of accounting recognition.

SWEDISH SUBSIDIARY
Income Statement
For Year Ending December 31, 1997

Sales	SKr 401,040	× .192 A =	$ 77,000
Cost of goods sold	(165,000)	× .192 A =	(31,680)
Gross profit	236,040		45,320
Depreciation expense.......................	(15,900)	× .192 A =	(3,053)
Salary expense	(36,000)	× .192 A =	(6,912)
Rent expense	(12,000)	× .192 A =	(2,304)
Other expenses...........................	(51,333)*	× .192 A =	(9,856)
Interest expense	(1,160)	× .192 A =	(223)
Remeasurement gain	240	× .192 A =	46
Net income................................	SKr 119,407		$ 23,018

*The SKr 333 of other expenses related to the amortization of the deferred discount on forward contract did not occur evenly throughout the year. Because of the immaterial size of this item, however, a separate translation at a specific (historical) rate is not being made.

Statement of Retained Earnings
For Year Ending December 31, 1997

Retained earnings, 1/1/97....................	SKr 194,800	given	$ 36,100
Net income, 1997	119,887	above	23,018
Dividends paid, 7/1/97......................	(25,000)	× .190 H =	(4,750)
Retained earnings, 12/31/97	SKr 289,687		$ 54,368

Balance Sheet
December 31, 1997

Cash	SKr 51,400	× .182 C =	$ 9,355
Accounts receivable	155,120	× .182 C =	28,232
Forward contract receivable (kronor)	21,000	× .182 C =	3,822
Deferred discount on forward contract	667	× .182 C =	121
Inventory	128,000	× .182 C =	23,296
Land	160,000	× .182 C =	29,120
Fixed assets	243,000	× .182 C =	44,226
Accumulated depreciation	(103,100)	× .182 C =	(18,764)
Total	SKr 656,087		$ 119,286
Accounts payable	SKr 39,000	× .182 C =	$ 7,098
Notes payable	71,600	× .182 C =	13,031
Bonds payable	125,000	× .182 C =	22,750
Forward contract payable (francs)	20,800	× .182 C =	3,786
Common stock	110,000	given	21,000
Retained earnings	289,687	above	54,368
Cumulative translation adjustment			(2,625)
Total	SKr 656,087		$ 119,286

The cumulative translation adjustment at 12/31/97 is comprised of the beginning balance (given) plus the translation adjustment for the current year:

Cumulative Translation Adjustment

Balance, 1/1/97	$ 3,860
Translation adjustment for 1997	(6,485)
Balance, 12/31/97	$(2,625)

The negative translation adjustment for 1997 of $6,485 is calculated by considering the effect of exchange rate changes on net assets:

Translation Adjustment for 1997

Net assets, 1/1/97	SKr 304,800*	× .200 =	$60,960
Increase in net assets:			
Net income, 1997	119,887	× .192 =	23,018
Decrease in net assets:			
Dividends, 7/1/97	(25,000)	× .190 =	(4,750)
Net assets, 12/31/97	SKr 399,687†		$79,228
Net assets, 12/31/97 at current exchange rate	SKr 399,687	× .182 =	72,743
Translation adjustment, 1997—negative			$ 6,485

*Indicated by January 1, 1997, stockholders' equity balances—Common stock, SKr 110,000; Retained earnings, SKr 194,800.

†Indicated by December 31, 1997, stockholders' equity balances—Common stock, SKr 110,000; Retained earnings, SKr 289,687.

QUESTIONS

1. What are the two major issues related to the translation of foreign currency financial statements?

2. What causes balance sheet (or translation) exposure to foreign exchange risk? How does balance sheet exposure compare with transaction exposure?

3. Why might a company want to hedge its balance sheet exposure? What is the paradox associated with hedging balance sheet exposure?

4. Under FASB *SFAS 52*, how are gains and losses on forward contracts used to hedge the net investment in a foreign subsidiary reported in the consolidated financial statements?

5. What is the concept underlying the temporal method of translation? What is the concept underlying the current rate method of translation? How does balance sheet exposure differ under these two methods?

6. In translating the financial statements of a foreign subsidiary, why is the value assigned to retained earnings considered especially difficult to determine? How is this problem normally resolved?

7. What were the major criticisms of FASB *SFAS 8?*

8. Clarke Company has a subsidiary operating in a foreign country. In relation to this subsidiary, what is meant by the term *functional currency?* How is the functional currency determined?

9. A translation adjustment must be calculated and disclosed whenever financial statements of a foreign subsidiary are translated into the parent's reporting currency. How is this figure computed, and where is the amount reported in the financial statements?

10. The FASB put forth two theories about the underlying nature of a translation adjustment. What are these theories, and which one was considered correct by the FASB?

11. When is remeasurement rather than translation appropriate? How does remeasurement differ from translation?

12. Which translation method does FASB *SFAS 52* require for operations in highly inflationary countries? What is the rationale for mandating use of this method?

LIBRARY ASSIGNMENT

1. Read the following:

   "Plenty of Opportunity to Fool Around," *Forbes,* June 2, 1986.

   "Foreign Currency Translation," *Statement of Financial Accounting Standards No. 52,* FASB, paragraphs 5–10, 39–46, and 77–84.

   Write a short report addressing two questions: How could more guidance be given in the selection of a foreign subsidiary's functional currency? Should more official guidance be provided in connection with the selection of a foreign subsidiary's functional currency?

PROBLEMS

1. What is a subsidiary's functional currency?
   a. The parent's reporting currency.
   b. The currency in which transactions are denominated.
   c. The currency in which the entity primarily generates and expends cash.
   d. Always the currency of the country in which the company has its headquarters.

2. The translation process and the remeasurement process are being compared. Which of the following statements is true?
   a. The reported balance of inventory is normally the same under both methods.
   b. The reported balance of equipment is normally the same under both methods.
   c. The reported balance of sales is normally the same under both methods.
   d. The reported balance of depreciation expense is normally the same under both methods.

3. Which of the following statements is true for the translation process (as opposed to remeasurement)?
   a. A translation adjustment can affect consolidated net income.
   b. Equipment is translated at the historical exchange rate in effect at the date of its purchase.
   c. A translation adjustment is created by the change in the relative value of a subsidiary's net assets caused by currency rate fluctuations.
   d. A translation adjustment is created by the change in the relative value of a subsidiary's monetary assets and monetary liabilities caused by currency rate fluctuations.

4. A subsidiary of Byner Corporation has one asset (inventory) and no liabilities. The functional currency for this subsidiary is the peso. The inventory was acquired for

100,000 pesos when the exchange rate was $.16 = 1 peso. Consolidated statements are to be produced and the current exchange rate is $.19 = 1 peso. Which of the following statements is true for the consolidated financial statements?
- a. A remeasurement gain must be reported.
- b. A positive translation adjustment must be reported.
- c. A negative translation adjustment must be reported.
- d. A remeasurement loss must be reported.

5. At what rates should the following balance sheet accounts in foreign statements be translated into U.S. dollars?

	Accumulated Depreciation—Equipment	Equipment
a.	Current	Current
b.	Current	Average for year
c.	Historical	Current
d.	Historical	Historical

(AICPA adapted)

Questions 6 and 7 are based on the following information: Certain balance sheet accounts of a foreign subsidiary of the Rose Company have been stated in U.S. dollars as follows:

	Stated at	
	Current Rates	Historical Rates
Accounts receivable, current	$200,000	$220,000
Accounts receivable, long term	100,000	110,000
Prepaid insurance	50,000	55,000
Goodwill	80,000	85,000
	$430,000	$470,000

6. A foreign currency is the functional currency of this subsidiary. What total should be included in Rose's balance sheet for the preceding items?
- a. $430,000.
- b. $435,000.
- c. $440,000.
- d. $450,000.

7. The U.S. dollar is the functional currency of this subsidiary. What total should be included in Rose's balance sheet for the above items?
- a. $430,000.
- b. $435,000.
- c. $440,000.
- d. $450,000.

(AICPA adapted)

Questions 8 and 9 are based on the following information: A subsidiary of Salisbury, Inc., is located in a foreign country. The functional currency of this subsidiary is the schweikart (SWK). The subsidiary acquires inventory on credit on November 1, 1997, for SWK 100,000 that is sold on January 17, 1998, for SWK 130,000. The subsidiary pays for the inventory on January 31, 1998. Currency exchange rates between dollars and schweikart are as follows:

November 1, 1997	$.16 = 1 SWK
December 31, 1997	$.17 = 1 SWK
January 17, 1998	$.18 = 1 SWK
January 31, 1998	$.19 = 1 SWK
Average for 1998	$.20 = 1 SWK

8. What figure is reported for this inventory on Salisbury's consolidated balance sheet at December 31, 1997?
- a. $16,000.
- b. $17,000.
- c. $18,000.
- d. $19,000.

9. What figure is reported for cost of goods sold on Salisbury's consolidated income statement for the year ending December 31, 1998?
    a. $16,000.
    b. $17,000.
    c. $18,000.
    d. $19,000.
    e. $20,000.

10. A subsidiary of Clarke Corporation buys marketable equity securities and inventory on April 1, 1997, for 100,000 pesos each. Both these items are paid for on June 1, 1997, and are still on hand at year's end. Inventory is carried at cost under the lower-of-cost-or-market rule. Currency exchange rates are as follows:

January 1, 1997	$.15 = 1 peso
April 1, 1997	$.16 = 1 peso
June 1, 1997	$.17 = 1 peso
December 31, 1997	$.19 = 1 peso

    Assume that the peso is the subsidiary's functional currency. On a consolidated balance sheet as of December 31, 1997, what balances are reported?
    a. Marketable equity securities = $16,000 and Inventory = $16,000.
    b. Marketable equity securities = $17,000 and Inventory = $17,000.
    c. Marketable equity securities = $19,000 and Inventory = $16,000.
    d. Marketable equity securities = $19,000 and Inventory = $19,000.

11. Assume that the U.S. dollar is the subsidiary's functional currency. On a consolidated balance sheet as of December 31, 1997, what balances are reported?
    a. Marketable equity securities = $16,000 and Inventory = $16,000.
    b. Marketable equity securities = $17,000 and Inventory = $17,000.
    c. Marketable equity securities = $19,000 and Inventory = $16,000.
    d. Marketable equity securities = $19,000 and Inventory = $19,000.

12. A U.S. company's foreign subsidiary had the following amounts in foreign currency units (FCU) in 1997:

Cost of goods sold	FCU 10 million
Ending inventory	FCU 500,000
Beginning inventory	FCU 200,000

    The average exchange rate during 1997 was $.80 = FCU 1. The beginning inventory was acquired when the exchange rate was $1.00 = FCU 1. Ending inventory was acquired when the exchange rate was $.75 = FCU 1. The exchange rate at December 31, 1997, was $.70 = FCU 1. Assuming that the foreign country is highly inflationary, at what amount should the foreign subsidiary's cost of goods sold be reflected in the U.S. dollar income statement?
    a. $7,815,000.
    b. $8,040,000.
    c. $8,065,000.
    d. $8,090.000.

13. Ace Corporation starts a subsidiary in a foreign country; the subsidiary has the peso as its functional currency. On January 1, 1997, Ace buys all of the subsidiary's common stock for 20,000 pesos. On April 1, 1997, the subsidiary purchases inventory for 20,000 pesos with payment made on May 1, 1997. This inventory is sold on August 1, 1997, for 30,000 pesos, which is collected on October 1, 1997. Currency exchange rates are as follows:

January 1, 1997	$.15 = 1 peso
April 1, 1997	$.17 = 1 peso
May 1, 1997	$.18 = 1 peso
August 1, 1997	$.19 = 1 peso
October 1, 1997	$.20 = 1 peso
December 31, 1997	$.21 = 1 peso

In preparing consolidated financial statements, what translation adjustment will be reported at the end of 1997?

a. $400 positive (credit).
b. $600 positive (credit).
c. $1,400 positive (credit).
d. $1,800 positive (credit).

14. Which method of translation maintains, in the translated financial statements, the underlying valuation methods used in the foreign currency financial statements?

a. Current rate method; income statement translated at average exchange rate for the year.
b. Current rate method; income statement translated at exchange rate at the balance sheet date.
c. Temporal method.
d. Monetary/nonmonetary method.

15. The Houston Corporation operates a branch operation in a foreign country. Although this branch deals in pesos, the U.S. dollar is viewed as its functional currency. Thus, a remeasurement is necessary to produce financial information for external reporting purposes. The branch begins the year with 100,000 pesos in cash and no other assets or liabilities. However, the branch immediately uses 60,000 pesos to acquire equipment. On May 1, inventory costing 30,000 pesos is purchased for cash. This merchandise is sold on July 1 for 50,000 pesos cash. The branch transfers 10,000 pesos to the parent on October 1 and records depreciation on the equipment for the year of 6,000 pesos. Currency exchange rates are as follows:

January 1	$.16 = 1 peso
May 1	$.18 = 1 peso
July 1	$.20 = 1 peso
October 1	$.21 = 1 peso
December 31	$.22 = 1 peso
Average for the year	$.19 = 1 peso

What is the remeasurement gain to be recognized in the consolidated income statement?

a. $2,100.
b. $2,400.
c. $2,700.
d. $3,000.

16. Which of the following items is *not* remeasured using historical exchange rates under the temporal method?

a. Accumulated depreciation on equipment.
b. Cost of goods sold.
c. Marketable equity securities.
d. Retained earnings.

17. In accordance with U.S. generally accepted accounting principles, which translation combination would be appropriate for a foreign operation whose functional currency is the U.S. dollar?

	Method	Treatment of Translation Adjustment
a.	Temporal	Separate component of stockholders' equity
b.	Temporal	Gain or loss in income statement
c.	Current rate	Separate component of stockholders' equity
d.	Current rate	Gain or loss in income statement

18. A foreign subsidiary's functional currency is its local currency, which has not experienced significant inflation. The weighted-average exchange rate for the current year is the appropriate exchange rate for translating:

	Wages Expense	Wages Payable
a.	Yes	Yes
b.	Yes	No
c.	No	Yes
d.	No	No

19. The functional currency of DeZoort Inc.'s British subsidiary is the British pound. DeZoort borrowed British pounds as a partial hedge of its investment in the subsidiary. In preparing consolidated financial statements, DeZoort's negative translation adjustment on its investment in the subsidiary exceeded its foreign exchange gain on the borrowing. How should the effects of the negative translation adjustment and foreign exchange gain be reported in DeZoort's consolidated financial statements?

    a. The translation adjustment is reported separately in the stockholders' equity section of the balance sheet and the foreign exchange gain is reported in the income statement.

    b. The translation adjustment is reported in the income statement and the foreign exchange gain is deferred in the stockholders' equity section of the balance sheet.

    c. The translation adjustment less the foreign exchange gain is reported separately in the stockholders' equity section of the balance sheet.

    d. The translation adjustment less the foreign exchange gain is reported in the income statement.

    (AICPA adapted)

20. Gains from remeasuring a foreign subsidiary's financial statements from the local currency, which is not the functional currency, into the parent's currency should be reported as a(n)

    a. Deferred foreign exchange gain.

    b. Separate component of stockholders' equity.

    c. Extraordinary item, net of income taxes.

    d. Part of continuing operations.

    (AICPA adapted)

21. The foreign currency is the functional currency for a foreign subsidiary. At what exchange rate should each of the following accounts be translated:

    Rent Expense
    Dividends Paid
    Equipment
    Notes Payable
    Sales
    Depreciation Expense
    Cash
    Accumulated Depreciation
    Common Stock

22. On January 1, 1997, Dandu Corporation started a subsidiary in a foreign country. On April 1, 1997, the subsidiary purchased inventory at a cost of 120,000 local currency units (LCU). One-fourth of this inventory remained unsold at the end of 1997 while 40 percent of the liability from the purchase had not yet been paid. The exchange rates were

January 1, 1997	$1 = LCU 2.5
April 1, 1997	$1 = LCU 2.8
Average for 1997	$1 = LCU 2.7
December 31, 1997	$1 = LCU 3.0

    What should be the December 31, 1997, inventory and accounts payable balances for this foreign subsidiary as translated into U.S. dollars?

23. The following series of accounts is denominated as of December 31, 1997, in pesos. For reporting purposes, these figures need to be stated in U.S. dollars. For each balance, indicate the exchange rate that would be used if a translation is made. Then, again for each account, provide the exchange rate that would be necessary if a remeasurement is being made. The company was started in 1980. The buildings were acquired in 1982 and the patents in 1983.

	Translation	**Remeasurement**
Accounts payable.		
Accounts receivable		
Accumulated depreciation.		
Advertising expense		
Amortization expense (patents)		
Buildings		
Cash.		
Common stock		
Depreciation expense		
Dividends paid (10/1/97)		
Notes payable—due in 1999		
Patents (net)		
Salary expense		
Sales		

Exchange rates are as follows:

1980	1 peso = $.28
1982	1 peso = $.26
1983	1 peso = $.25
January 1, 1997	1 peso = $.24
April 1, 1997	1 peso = $.23
July 1, 1997	1 peso = $.22
October 1, 1997	1 peso = $.20
December 31, 1997	1 peso = $.16
Average for 1997	1 peso = $.19

24. On December 18, 1997, Stephanie Corporation acquired 100 percent of a Swiss company for Sfr 3.7 million. At the date of acquisition, the exchange rate was $.70 = Sfr 1. The acquisition price is attributable to the following assets and liabilities:

Cash	Sfr	500,000
Inventory		1,000,000
Fixed assets		3,000,000
Notes payable		(800,000)

Stephanie Corporation prepares consolidated financial statements on December 31, 1997. By that date, the Swiss franc has appreciated to $.75 = Sfr 1. Because of the year-end holidays, no transactions took place prior to consolidation.

Required

(a) Determine the translation adjustment to be reported on Stephanie's December 31, 1997, consolidated balance sheet assuming that the Swiss franc is the Swiss subsidiary's functional currency? What is the economic relevance of this translation adjustment?

(b) Determine the remeasurement gain or loss to be reported in Stephanie's 1997 consolidated income assuming that the U.S. dollar is the functional currency. What is the economic relevance of this remeasurement gain or loss?

25. The Fenwicke Company began operating a subsidiary in a foreign country on January 1, 1997, by acquiring all of the common stock for LCU 40,000. This subsidiary immediately borrowed LCU 100,000 on a five-year note with 10 percent interest payable annually beginning on January 1, 1998. A building was then purchased for LCU 140,000. This property had a 10-year anticipated life and no salvage value and is to be depreciated using the straight-line method. The building is rented for three years to a group of local doctors for LCU 5,000 per month. By year-end, payments totaling LCU 50,000 had been made. On October 1, LCU 4,000 was paid for a repair made on that date. A cash dividend of LCU 5,000 is transferred back to Fenwicke on December 31,

1997. The functional currency for the subsidiary is the LCU. Currency exchange rates are as follows:

January 1, 1997	$2.00 = LCU 1
October 1, 1997	$1.85 = LCU 1
Average for 1997	$1.90 = LCU 1
December 31, 1997	$1.80 = LCU 1

Required

Prepare an income statement, statement of retained earnings, and balance sheet for this subsidiary in LCU and then translate these amounts into U.S. dollars.

26. Refer to the information provided in problem 25. Prepare a statement of cash flows in LCU for Fenwicke's foreign subsidiary and then translate these amounts into U.S. dollars.

27. The Watson Company has a subsidiary in the country of Alonza where the local currency unit is the Kamel (KM). On December 31, 1996, the subsidiary has the following balance sheet:

Cash	KM 16,000	Notes payable (due 1998)	KM 19,000
Inventory	10,000	Common stock	20,000
Land	4,000	Retained earnings	10,000
Building	40,000		
Accumulated depreciation	(21,000)		
	KM 49,000		KM 49,000

This inventory was acquired on August 1, 1996; the land and buildings were acquired in 1984. The common stock was issued in 1978. During 1997, the following transactions took place:

1997

Feb. 1	Paid 5,000 KM on the note payable.
May 1	Sold entire inventory for 15,000 KM on account.
June 1	Sold land for 5,000 KM cash.
Aug. 1	Collected all accounts receivable.
Sept. 1	Signed long-term note to receive 6,000 KM cash.
Oct. 1	Bought inventory for 12,000 KM cash.
Nov. 1	Bought land for 4,000 KM on account.
Dec. 1	Paid dividend to parent—3,000 KM cash.
Dec. 31	Recorded depreciation for the entire year of 2,000 KM.

The exchange rates are as follows:

1978	1 KM = $.24
1984	1 KM = $.21
August 1, 1996	1 KM = $.31
December 31, 1996	1 KM = $.32
February 1, 1997	1 KM = $.33
May 1, 1997	1 KM = $.34
June 1, 1997	1 KM = $.35
August 1, 1997	1 KM = $.37
September 1, 1997	1 KM = $.38
October 1, 1997	1 KM = $.39
November 1, 1997	1 KM = $.40
December 1, 1997	1 KM = $.41
December 31, 1997	1 KM = $.42
Average for 1997	1 KM = $.37

Required

a. If this is a translation, what is the translation adjustment determined solely for 1997?

b. If this is a remeasurement, what is the transaction gain or loss determined solely for 1997?

28. Aerkion Company starts the year of 1997 with two assets: cash of 22,000 LCU (local currency units) and land that originally cost 60,000 LCU when acquired on April 4, 1994. On May 1, 1997, the company rendered services to a customer for 30,000 LCU, an amount immediately paid in cash. On October 1, 1997, the company incurred an operating expense of 18,000 LCU that was immediately paid. No other transactions occurred during the year. Currency exchange rates were as follows:

April 4, 1994	1 LCU = $.23
January 1, 1997	1 LCU = $.24
May 1, 1997	1 LCU = $.25
October 1, 1997	1 LCU = $.26
Average for 1997	1 LCU = $.27
December 31, 1997	1 LCU = $.29

Required

   a. Assume that Aerkion is a foreign subsidiary of a U.S. multinational company that uses the U.S. dollar as its reporting currency. Assume also that the LCU is the functional currency of the subsidiary. What is the translation adjustment for this subsidiary for the year 1997?

   b. Assume that Aerkion is a foreign subsidiary of a U.S. multinational company that uses the U.S. dollar as its reporting currency. Assume also that the U.S. dollar is the functional currency of the subsidiary. What is the remeasurement gain or loss for 1997?

   c. Assume that Aerkion is a foreign subsidiary of a U.S. multinational company. On the December 31, 1997, balance sheet, what is the translated value of the Land account? On a December 31, 1997, balance sheet, what is the remeasured value of the Land account?

29. Lancer, Inc., starts a subsidiary in a foreign country on January 1, 1997. The following account balances are for the year ending December 31, 1998, and are stated in kanquo (KQ), the local currency.

Sales	KQ 200,000
Inventory (bought on 3/1/98)	100,000
Equipment (bought on 1/1/97)	80,000
Rent expense	10,000
Dividends (paid on 10/1/98)	20,000
Notes receivable (to be collected in 2001)	30,000
Accumulated depreciation—Equipment	24,000
Salary payable	5,000
Depreciation expense	8,000

The following exchange rates are applicable:

January 1, 1997	$1 = 13 KQ
January 1, 1998	$1 = 18 KQ
March 1, 1998	$1 = 19 KQ
October 1, 1998	$1 = 21 KQ
December 31, 1998	$1 = 22 KQ
Average for 1997	$1 = 14 KQ
Average for 1998	$1 = 20 KQ

Lancer is preparing account balances to produce consolidated financial statements.

   a. Assuming that the kanquo is the functional currency, what exchange rate would be used to report each of these accounts in U.S. dollar consolidated financial statements?

   b. Assuming that the U.S. dollar is the functional currency, what exchange rate would be used to report each of these accounts in U.S. dollar consolidated financial statements?

30. The Board Company has a foreign subsidiary that began operations at the start of 1997 with assets of 132,000 kites (the local currency unit) and liabilities of 54,000 kites. During this initial year of operation, the subsidiary reported a profit of 26,000 kites. Two dividends were distributed; each was for 5,000 kites with one dividend paid on March 1 and the other on October 1. Applicable exchange rates are as follows:

January 1, 1997 (start of business)	$0.80 = 1 kite
March 1, 1997	$0.78 = 1 kite
Weighted-average rate for 1997	$0.77 = 1 kite
October 1, 1997	$0.76 = 1 kite
December 31, 1997	$0.75 = 1 kite

Required

a. Assume that the kite is the functional currency for this subsidiary. What translation adjustment would be reported by Board for the year 1997?

b. Assume that on October 1, 1997, Board entered into a forward exchange contract to hedge the net investment in this subsidiary. On that date, Board agreed to sell 200,000 kites in three months at a forward exchange rate of $0.76 = 1 kite. Prepare the journal entries required by this forward contract. In addition, compute the translation adjustment to be reported by Board for the year 1997 under this second set of circumstances.

31. Kingsfield starts a subsidiary operation in a foreign country on January 1, 1997. The currency in this country is the kumquat (KQ). To get this business started, Kingsfield invests 10,000 kumquats. Of this amount, 3,000 kumquats are expended immediately to acquire equipment. Later, on April 1, 1997, land also is purchased. All operational activities of the subsidiary occur at an even rate throughout the year. The currency exchange rates for this year are as follows:

January 1, 1997	KQ 1 = $1.71
April 1, 1997	KQ 1 = $1.59
June 1, 1997	KQ 1 = $1.66
Weighted average—1997	KQ 1 = $1.64
December 31, 1997	KQ 1 = $1.62

As of December 31, 1997, the subsidiary reports the following trial balance:

	Debits	Credits
Cash	KQ 8,000	
Accounts receivable	9,000	
Equipment	3,000	
Accumulated depreciation		KQ 600
Land	5,000	
Accounts payable		3,000
Notes payable (due 1999)		5,000
Common stock		10,000
Dividends paid (6/1/97)	4,000	
Sales		25,000
Salary expense	5,000	
Depreciation expense	600	
Miscellaneous expenses	9,000	
Totals	KQ 43,600	KQ 43,600

Kingsfield is a corporation based in East Lansing, Michigan, and, therefore, uses the U.S. dollar as its reporting currency.

Required

a. Assume that the functional currency of the subsidiary is the kumquat. Prepare a trial balance for the subsidiary in U.S. dollars so that consolidated financial statements can be prepared.

b. Assume that the subsidiary's functional currency is the U.S. dollar. Prepare a trial balance for the subsidiary in U.S. dollars so that consolidated financial statements can be prepared.

32. Livingston Company is a wholly owned subsidiary of Rose Corporation. Livingston operates in a foreign country with financial statements recorded in goghs (GH), the company's functional currency. Financial statements for the year of 1997 are as follows:

Income Statement
For Year Ending December 31, 1997

Sales	GH 270,000
Cost of goods sold	(155,000)
Gross profit	115,000
Less: Operating expenses	(54,000)
Gain on sale of equipment	10,000
Net income	GH 71,000

Statement of Retained Earnings
For Year Ending December 31, 1997

Retained earnings, 1/1/97	GH 216,000
Net income	71,000
Less: Dividends paid	(26,000)
Retained earnings, 12/31/97	GH 261,000

Balance Sheet
December 31, 1997

Assets

Cash	GH 44,000
Receivables	116,000
Inventory	58,000
Fixed assets (net)	339,000
Total assets	GH 557,000

Liabilities and Equities

Liabilities	GH 176,000
Common stock	120,000
Retained earnings, 12/31/97	261,000
Total liabilities and equities	GH 557,000

Additional Information:

■ The common stock was issued in 1989 when the exchange rate was $1.00 = .48 GH; fixed assets were acquired in 1990 when the rate was $1.00 = .50 GH.

■ As of January 1, 1997, the retained earnings balance was translated as $397,000.

■ The currency exchange rates for the current year are as follows:

January 1, 1997	$1.00 = .60 goghs
April 1, 1997	$1.00 = .62 goghs
September 1, 1997	$1.00 = .58 goghs
December 31, 1997	$1.00 = .65 goghs
Weighted-average rate for 1997	$1.00 = .63 goghs

■ Inventory was acquired evenly throughout the year.

■ A translation adjustment was reported on the December 31, 1996, balance sheet with a debit balance of $85,000.

■ Dividends were paid on April 1, 1997, and a piece of equipment was sold on September 1, 1997.

Required

Translate the foreign currency statements into the parent's reporting currency, the U.S. dollar.

33. The following account balances are for the Agee Company as of January 1, 1997, and again as of December 31, 1997. All figures are denominated in kroner (Kr).

	1/1/97	12/31/97
Accounts payable...............................	(18,000)	(24,000)
Accounts receivable.............................	35,000	79,000
Accumulated depreciation—buildings	(20,000)	(25,000)
Accumulated depreciation—equipment.................	–0–	(5,000)
Bonds payable—due 2002	(50,000)	(50,000)
Buildings	118,000	97,000
Cash..	35,000	8,000
Common stock	(70,000)	(80,000)
Depreciation expense	–0–	15,000
Dividends (10/1/97).............................	–0–	32,000
Equipment	–0–	30,000
Gain on sale of building..........................	–0–	(6,000)
Rent expense..................................	–0–	14,000
Retained earnings	(30,000)	(30,000)
Salary expense	–0–	20,000
Sales	–0–	(80,000)
Utilities expense	–0–	5,000

Additional Information:

- Additional shares of common stock were issued during the year on April 1, 1997. Common stock at January 1, 1997, also was sold at the start of operations in 1980.
- Buildings were purchased in 1982. One building with a book value of Kr 16,000 was sold on July 1 of the current year.
- Equipment was acquired on April 1, 1997.
- Retained earnings as of January 1, 1997, was reported as $62,319.

Relevant exchange rates were as follows:

1980	$2.40 = 1 Kr
1982	$2.20 = 1 Kr
January 1, 1997	$2.50 = 1 Kr
April 1, 1997	$2.60 = 1 Kr
July 1, 1997	$2.80 = 1 Kr
October 1, 1997	$2.90 = 1 Kr
December 31, 1997	$3.00 = 1 Kr
Average for 1997	$2.70 = 1 Kr

Required

a. If a remeasurement is being carried out, what would be the remeasurement gain or loss for 1997?

b. If a translation is being carried out, what would be the translation adjustment for 1997?

34. The Sendelbach Corporation is a U.S.-based organization with operations throughout the world. One of the company's subsidiaries is headquartered in Frankfurt. Although this wholly owned company operates primarily in Germany, some transactions are carried out through a branch in France. Therefore, the subsidiary maintains a ledger denominated in French francs (FF) as well as a general ledger in deutsche marks (DM).

As of December 31, 1997, the German subsidiary is preparing financial statements in anticipation of consolidation with the U.S. parent corporation. Both ledgers for the subsidiary are as follows:

Main Operation—Germany

	Debit	Credit
Accounts payable		DM 35,000
Accumulated depreciation		27,000
Buildings and equipment	DM 167,000	
Cash	26,000	
Common stock		50,000
Cost of goods sold	203,000	
Depreciation expense	8,000	
Dividends paid, 4/1/97	28,000	
Gain on sale of equipment, 6/1/97		5,000
Inventory	98,000	
Notes payable—due in 1999		76,000
Receivables	68,000	
Retained earnings, 1/1/97		135,540
Salary expense	26,000	
Sales		312,000
Utility expense	9,000	
Branch operation	7,540	
Totals	DM 640,540	DM 640,540

Branch Operation—France

	Debit	Credit
Accounts payable		FF 49,000
Accumulated depreciation		19,000
Building and equipment	FF 40,000	
Cash	59,000	
Depreciation expense	2,000	
Inventory (beginning—income statement)	23,000	
Inventory (ending—income statement)		28,000
Inventory (ending—balance sheet)	28,000	
Purchases	68,000	
Receivables	21,000	
Salary expense	9,000	
Sales		124,000
Main office		30,000
Totals	FF 250,000	FF 250,000

Additional Information:

- The functional currency for the German subsidiary is the deutsche mark while the reporting currency for Sendelbach is the U.S. dollar. The German and French operations are not viewed as separate accounting entities.
- The building and equipment used in the French operation were acquired in 1983 when the currency exchange rate was DM .25 = FF 1.
- Purchases should be assumed as having been made evenly throughout the fiscal year.
- Beginning inventory was acquired evenly throughout 1996; ending inventory was acquired evenly throughout 1997.
- The Main Office account found on the French records should be considered an equity account. This balance was remeasured into DM 7,540 on December 31, 1996, and no further transactions have occurred.
- Currency exchange rates applicable to the French operation are as follows:

Weighted average, 1996	DM .30 = FF 1
January 1, 1997	DM .32 = FF 1
Weighted-average rate for 1997	DM .34 = FF 1
December 31, 1997	DM .35 = FF 1

- On the December 31, 1996, consolidated balance sheet, a cumulative translation adjustment was reported with a $36,950 credit (positive) balance.
- The subsidiary's common stock was issued in 1976 when the exchange rate was $.45 = DM 1.

■ The December 31, 1996, balance of retained earnings for this subsidiary was DM 135,540, a figure that has been translated into $70,428.

■ The applicable currency exchange rates for translation purposes are as follows:

January 1, 1997	$.70 = DM 1
April 1, 1997	$.69 = DM 1
June 1, 1997	$.68 = DM 1
Weighted-average rate for 1997	$.67 = DM 1
December 31, 1997	$.65 = DM 1

Required

a. Remeasure the French operational figures from francs into deutsche marks. (Hint: back into the beginning net monetary asset or liability position.)

b. Prepare financial statements for this subsidiary in its functional currency.

c. Translate the functional currency financial statements into U.S. dollars so that Sendelbach can prepare consolidated financial statements.

35. On January 1, 1997, the Cayce Corporation purchased 100 percent of the Simbel Company at a cost of $126,000. Cayce is a U.S.-based company headquartered in Buffalo, New York, and Simbel is in Cairo, Egypt. Cayce accounts for its investment in Simbel under the cost method. Any excess of purchase price over book value is attributable to undervalued land on Simbel's books. Simbel had no retained earnings at the date of acquisition. Following are the 1998 financial statements for the two operations. Cayce's information is stated in U.S. dollars ($) while Simbel's statements are reported in Egyptian pounds (£E).

	Cayce Corporation	Simbel Company
Sales	$200,000	£E 800,000
Cost of goods sold	(93,800)	(420,000)
Salary expense	(19,000)	(74,000)
Rent expense	(7,000)	(46,000)
Other expenses	(21,000)	(59,000)
Dividend income—from Simbel	13,750	–0–
Gain on sale of fixed asset, 10/1/98	–0–	30,000
Net income	$ 72,950	£E 231,000
Retained earnings, 1/1/98	$318,000	£E 133,000
Net income	72,950	231,000
Dividends paid	(24,000)	(50,000)
Retained earnings, 12/31/98	$366,950	£E 314,000
Cash and receivables	$110,750	£E 146,000
Inventory	98,000	297,000
Prepaid expenses	30,000	–0–
Investment in Simbel (cost)	126,000	–0–
Fixed assets (net)	398,000	455,000
Total assets	$762,750	£E 898,000
Accounts payable	$ 60,800	£E 54,000
Notes payable—due in 2001	132,000	140,000
Common stock	120,000	240,000
Additional paid-in capital	83,000	150,000
Retained earnings, 12/31/98	366,950	314,000
Total liabilities and equities	$762,750	£E 898,000

Additional Information:

■ During 1997, the first year of joint operation, Simbel reported income of 163,000 pounds earned evenly throughout the year. A dividend of 30,000 pounds was paid to Cayce on June 1 of that year. The 1998 dividend paid by Simbel also was made on June 1.

■ On December 9, 1998, Simbel classified a 10,000 pound expenditure as a rent expense, although this payment related to prepayment of rent for the first few months of 1999.

■ The exchange rates between the U.S. dollar and Egyptian pound are as follows:

January 1, 1997	$.300 = 1 pound
June 1, 1997	$.290 = 1 pound
Weighted-average rate for 1997	$.288 = 1 pound
December 31, 1997	$.280 = 1 pound
June 1, 1998	$.275 = 1 pound
October 1, 1998	$.273 = 1 pound
Weighted-average rate for 1998	$.272 = 1 pound
December 31, 1998	$.270 = 1 pound

Required

Prepare consolidated financial statements for Cayce Corporation and its consolidated subsidiary. Assume that the U.S. dollar is the reporting currency of the parent company whereas the Egyptian pound is the subsidiary's functional currency.

36. Diekmann Company, a U.S.-based company, acquired a 100 percent interest in Rakona A.S. in the Czech Republic on January 1, 1997, when the exchange rate for the Czech koruna (Kčs) was $.05. The financial statements of Rakona as of December 31, 1998, two years later, are as follows:

Balance Sheet
December 31, 1998

Assets

Cash	Kčs 2,000,000
Accounts receivable (net)	3,300,000
Inventory	8,500,000
Equipment	25,000,000
Less: accumulated depreciation	(8,500,000)
Building	72,000,000
Less: accumulated depreciation	(30,300,000)
Land	6,000,000
Total assets	Kčs 78,000,000

Liabilities and Stockholders' Equity

Accounts payable	Kčs 2,500,000
Long-term debt	50,000,000
Common stock	5,000,000
Additional paid-in capital	15,000,000
Retained earnings	5,500,000
Total liabilities and stockholders' equity	Kčs 78,000,000

Statement of Income and Retained Earnings
For the Year Ending December 31, 1998

Sales	Kčs 25,000,000
Cost of goods sold	(12,000,000)
Depreciation expense—equipment	(2,500,000)
Depreciation expense—building	(1,800,000)
Research and development expense	(1,200,000)
Other expenses (including taxes)	(1,000,000)
Net income	Kčs 6,500,000
Plus: Retained earnings, 1/1/98	500,000
Less: Dividends, 1998	(1,500,000)
Retained earnings, 12/31/98	Kčs 5,500,000

Additional Information:

■ The January 1, 1998, beginning inventory of Kčs 6,000,000 was acquired on December 18, 1997, when the exchange rate was $.043. Purchases of inventory during 1998 were acquired uniformly throughout the year. The December 31, 1998, ending inventory of Kčs 8,500,000 was acquired in the latter part of 1998 when the exchange rate was $.032. All fixed assets were on the books when the subsidiary was acquired except for Kčs 5,000,000 of equipment acquired on January 3, 1998, when the exchange rate was $.036 and Kčs 12,000,000 in buildings acquired on March 5, 1998, when the exchange rate was $.034. Equipment is depreciated on a straight-line basis over 10 years. Buildings are depreciated on a straight-line basis over 40 years. A full year's depreciation is taken in the year of acquisition.

■ Dividends were declared and paid on December 15, 1998, when the exchange rate was $.031.

■ Other exchange rates are:

January 1, 1998	$.040
Average 1998	$.035
December 31, 1998	$.030

Required

Part I. Prepare U.S. dollar translated financial statements in accordance with FASB *Statement 52* at December 31, 1998, in the following three situations:

a. The Czech koruna is the functional currency. The December 31, 1997, U.S. dollar translated balance sheet reported retained earnings of $22,500. The December 31, 1997, cumulative translation adjustment was negative $202,500 (debit balance).

b. The U.S. dollar is the functional currency. The December 31, 1997, retained earnings in U.S. dollars (including a 1997 remeasurement gain) that appeared in Rakona's remeasured financial statements was $353,000.

c. The U.S. dollar is the functional currency, but Rakona has no long-term debt. Instead, Rakona has common stock of Kčs 20,000,000 and additional paid-in capital of Kčs 50,000,000. The December 31, 1997, U.S. dollar translated balance sheet reported a negative balance in retained earnings of $147,000 (including a 1997 remeasurement loss).

Part II. Explain the positive or negative sign of the translation adjustment in Part I*a* and explain why there is a remeasurement gain or loss in Parts I*b* and I*c*.

11

Worldwide Accounting Diversity and International Standards

QUESTIONS TO CONSIDER

- Why do accounting and reporting principles differ throughout the world?

- What are the major classes of accounting systems worldwide?

- What benefits are gained from establishing international accounting standards? What obstacles stand in the way of international standards?

- What progress has the European Union achieved in establishing uniform accounting standards in that region of the world?

- What progress has the International Accounting Standards Committee achieved in establishing worldwide accounting standards? How does this group enforce its standards?

- How do the accounting principles differ between Japan, the United Kingdom, Germany, the United States, and other countries? What differences are found in the structure of the financial statements produced in these countries?

- By what methods are assets valued across countries? How are consolidated financial statements prepared in various countries?

Each country has its own unique set of accounting and financial reporting rules; no two countries are alike in this regard. Considerable differences exist across countries in the accounting treatment of many items. As shown in Chapter 3, for example, goodwill is an asset and amortized to income in the United States; however, it may be a direct reduction of owners' equity in the United Kingdom. The pooling of interests method of accounting for business combinations is used in the United States when certain criteria are met; this method is not acceptable under any circumstances in Australia, France, or Mexico. For the most part, U.S. companies are not allowed to report assets at amounts greater than historical cost. Brazilian companies, on the other hand, must write up their assets on the balance sheet to inflation-adjusted amounts, and several Dutch companies report their assets on the balance sheet at current replacement cost. Numerous other differences exist across countries. In its 1994 annual report, the German automaker Daimler-Benz described 10 significant differences between U.S. and German accounting rules.[1] If Daimler-Benz had used U.S. GAAP in 1994, its net income would have been 18 percent larger than what the firm actually reported in conformity with German legal requirements and its stockholders' equity would have been 45 percent larger. In its 1994 annual report, the British beverage company Cadbury Schweppes listed eight significant differences between U.S. and U.K. GAAP.[2] If Cadbury Schweppes had used U.S. accounting rules, its 1994 net income

---

[1] The largest adjustments related to differences in accounting for pensions, financial instruments, deferred taxes, and the sale of a leasing subsidiary.

[2] The accounting differences requiring the greatest adjustments were related to goodwill and other intangibles, pensions, and deferred taxes.

would have been 15 percent smaller than what the firm actually reported in accordance with U.K. GAAP, and its shareholders' equity would have been 52 percent larger.

PROBLEMS CAUSED BY DIVERSE ACCOUNTING PRACTICES

The diversity in accounting practice across countries causes problems that can be quite serious for some parties. One problem relates to the preparation of consolidated financial statements by companies with foreign operations. Consider Coca-Cola Company that has subsidiaries in more than 100 countries around the world. Each subsidiary incorporated in the country in which it is located is required to prepare financial statements in accordance with local regulations. These regulations usually require companies to keep books in the local currency and follow local accounting principles. Thus, Coca-Cola FEMSA S.A. prepares financial statements in Mexican pesos using Mexican accounting rules and Coca-Cola Amatil Ltd. prepares financial statements in Australian dollars using Australian standards. To prepare consolidated financial statements in the United States, in addition to translating the foreign currency financial statements into U.S. dollars, the parent company must also convert the financial statements of its foreign subsidiaries into U.S. GAAP. Each foreign subsidiary must either maintain two sets of books prepared in accordance with both local and U.S. GAAP or, as is more common, make reconciliations from local GAAP to U.S. GAAP at the balance sheet date. In either case, considerable effort and cost are involved; company personnel must develop an expertise in more than one country's accounting standards.

A second problem relates to companies gaining access to foreign capital markets. If a company desires to obtain capital by selling stock or borrowing money in a foreign country, it likely is required to present a set of financial statements prepared in accordance with the accounting standards in the country in which the capital is being obtained. Consider the case of the Swedish automaker Volvo. The equity market in Sweden is so small (there are fewer than 9 million Swedes) and Volvo's capital needs are so great that Volvo has found it necessary to have its common shares listed on stock exchanges in London, Frankfurt, Paris, Zurich, Brussels, Tokyo, and on NASDAQ in the United States. To have their stock traded in the United States, foreign companies must prepare financial statements using U.S. accounting standards. This can be quite costly. To prepare for a New York Stock Exchange (NYSE) listing in 1993, the German automaker Daimler-Benz estimated it spent $60 million to initially prepare U.S. GAAP financial statements; it planned to spend $15 to 20 million each year thereafter.[3]

A third problem relates to the lack of comparability of financial statements between companies from different countries. This can significantly affect the analysis of foreign financial statements for making investment and lending decisions. In 1994 alone, U.S. investors bought nearly $50 billion in debt and equity of foreign entities while foreign investors pumped approximately $59 billion into U.S. entities through similar acquisitions.[4] In recent years there has been an explosion in mutual funds that invest in the stock of foreign companies—from 123 in 1989 to 534 at the end of 1995.[5] T. Rowe Price's New Asia Fund, for example, invests exclusively in stocks

---

[3]Allan B. Afterman, *International Accounting, Financial Reporting, and Analysis* (New York: Warren, Gorham & Lamont, 1995), pp. C1–17 and C1–22.

[4]U.S. Department of Commerce, *Survey of Current Business,* June 1995, p. 106.

[5]James L. Cochrane, James E. Shapiro, and Jean E. Tobin, "Foreign Equities and U.S. Investors: Breaking Down the Barriers Separating Supply and Demand," NYSE Working Paper 95–04, 1995.

and bonds of companies located in Asian countries other than Japan. The job of deciding which foreign company to invest in is complicated by the fact that foreign companies use different accounting rules from those used in the United States and those rules differ from country to country. It is very difficult, if not impossible, for a potential investor to directly compare the financial position and performance of a chemical company in Germany (Hoechst), the Netherlands (AKZO), and Great Britain (ICI) because these three countries have different financial accounting and reporting standards. According to Ralph E. Walters, chairman of the steering committee of the International Accounting Standards Committee, "either international investors have to be extremely knowledgeable about multiple reporting methods or they have to be willing to take greater risk."[6]

A lack of comparability of financial statements also can have an adverse effect on corporations when making foreign acquisition decisions. As a case in point, consider the recent experience of foreign investors in Eastern Europe. After the fall of the Berlin Wall in 1989, officials invited Western companies to acquire newly privatized companies in Poland, Hungary, and other countries in the former communist bloc. The concept of profit and accounting for assets in those countries under communism was so much different from accounting practice in the West that most Western investors found financial statements useless in helping them determine the most attractive acquisition targets. Many investors asked the Big 6 public accounting firms to convert financial statements to a Western basis before acquisition of a company could be seriously considered.

Because of the problems associated with worldwide accounting diversity, attempts to reduce accounting differences across countries have been ongoing for more than three decades. This process is known as *harmonization*. The ultimate goal of harmonization is to have all companies around the world follow one set of international accounting standards.

This chapter is divided into two parts. Part one presents evidence of accounting diversity, explores the reasons for accounting diversity, describes international patterns or models of accounting, and discusses and evaluates accounting harmonization efforts. Regarding harmonization, we concentrate on the effort undertaken in the European Union and on the international accounting standards developed by the International Accounting Standards Committee.

Part two provides a description of accounting principles and the accounting profession in several major countries, and examines reporting principles utilized around the world in connection with specific accounting problems such as consolidations and the valuation of assets. This coverage provides a comparison of the similarities and differences between U.S. GAAP and principles used in other areas of the world.

EVIDENCE OF ACCOUNTING DIVERSITY

Exhibit 11–1 presents the 1995 balance sheet for the British pharmaceutical company Glaxo Wellcome PLC. A quick examination of this statement shows several differences in format and terminology between the United Kingdom and the United States. Noncurrent assets in general are called fixed assets in the United Kingdom, whereas plant, property, and equipment are referred to as tangible assets. Liabilities are called creditors, and accounts receivable are debtors. Unless one is fluent in the language of British accounting, stocks might be thought to be marketable securities, when in actuality stocks are inventories. Called up share capital is the par value and share premium account is the paid-in capital in excess of par on common stock. Retained earnings are not reported separately; instead the British include them in Other reserves, and place goodwill in the Goodwill reserve rather than capitalizing it as an asset.

---

[6]Stephen H. Collins, "The Move to Globalization," *Journal of Accountancy,* March 1989, p. 82.

**Balance Sheet
December 31, 1995**

		Notes	At 31.12.95 £m
Fixed assets	Tangible assets	13	4,165
	Investments	14	96
			4,261
Current assets	Stocks	15	811
	Debtors	16	2,045
	Asset for disposal	24	150
	Investments	18	1,041
	Cash at bank	18	233
			4,280
Creditors: Amounts due within one year	Loans and overdrafts	18	3,004
	Other creditors	17	2,462
			5,466
Net current (liabilities)/assets			(1,186)
Total assets less current liabilities			3,075
Creditors: Amounts due after one year	Loans	18	1,343
	Convertible bonds	18	123
	Other creditors	17	71
			1,537
Provisions for liabilities and charges		19	1,317
Net assets		26	221
Capital and reserves	Called up share capital	22	876
	Share premium account	22	373
	Goodwill reserve	23	(5,197)
	Other reserves	23	4,039
Equity shareholders' funds			91
Equity minority interests			130
Capital employed			221

From the perspective of U.S. financial reporting, the U.K. balance sheet has an unusual structure. Rather than the U.S. norm of Assets = Liabilities + Shareholders' Equity, Glaxo's balance sheet is presented as Net Assets = Capital Employed. Listed in reverse order of liquidity, assets start with tangible assets and move down to cash. Current liabilities follow current assets to arrive at net working capital. Long-term liabilities then are listed to arrive at net assets.

All of these superficial differences would probably cause a financial analyst no problem in analyzing the company's financial statements. More important than the format and terminology differences are the differences in measurement rules employed to value assets and calculate income. Because Glaxo Wellcome's common stock is listed on the New York Stock Exchange, the company is required to be registered and file financial statements with the U.S. Securities and Exchange Commission (SEC). For foreign registrants, the SEC requires income and stockholders' equity reported under foreign GAAP to be reconciled with U.S. GAAP. Glaxo Wellcome's 1995 reconciliation to U.S. GAAP is in Exhibit 11–2. This reconciliation provides significant insight into the major differences in accounting principles between the United States and the United Kingdom. Note that although only nine items required adjustments, the aggregate effect on income and stockholders' equity was highly significant. Income under U.S. GAAP was 31 percent smaller than under U.K.

GLAXO WELLCOME PLC
Reconciliation to U.S. GAAP
December 31, 1995

Profit	to 31.12.95 £m	to 31.12.95 US$m
Profit attritutable to shareholders under U.K. GAAP	1,458	2,304
U.S. GAAP adjustments		
Purchased research and development expenditure	(400)	(632)
Amortisation of goodwill	(398)	(629)
Amortisation of intangible assets	(371)	(586)
Integration*	745	1,177
Purchased stock	(64)	(101)
Post retirement benefits other than pensions	—	—
Deferred taxation	58	91
Other	15	24
Net income under U.S. GAAP	1,043	1,648

	Pence	US$
Income per ordinary share of 25p under U.S. GAAP	31.9	0.50

Equity shareholders' funds	£m	US$m
Equity shareholders' funds under U.K. GAAP	91	141
U.S. GAAP adjustments		
Goodwill	4,877	7,559
Intangible assets	2,084	3,230
Unrealised gains on fixed asset investments:		
Prior year effect on adoption of FAS 115	20	31
Current period	196	304
Purchased stock	21	33
Business for disposal	618	958
Ordinary dividends	526	815
Deferred taxation	(273)	(423)
Other	8	12
Shareholders' equity under U.S. GAAP	8,168	12,660

*Author's note: This item refers to the costs associated with integrating the premerger Glaxo and Wellcome businesses into a single business.

GAAP and stockholders' equity under U.S. GAAP was 89 times larger than under U.K. GAAP. Return on total stockholders' equity is 1,602 percent under British GAAP, but only 13 percent under U.S. GAAP; this ratio is 123 times larger under British rules.

Magnitude of Accounting Diversity

Although it is generally assumed that accounting diversity results in significant differences in the measurement of income and equity across countries, until recently there was very little systematic empirical documentation of the effect these differences have on published financial statements. In 1993, the SEC published a survey that examincs the U.S. GAAP reconciliations made by 444 foreign entities from 36 countries.[7] The results of that survey indicate that approximately two-thirds of the foreign companies showed material differences between net income and owners' equity reported on the basis of home GAAP and U.S. GAAP. Of those with material

[7]United States Securities and Exchange Commission, *Survey of Financial Statement Reconciliations by Foreign Registrants* (Washington, D.C., 1993).

differences, net income would have been lower under U.S. GAAP for about two-thirds of the companies (higher using U.S. GAAP for about one-third). This indicates that, for the majority of foreign entities with stock listings in the United States, U.S. GAAP is more conservative than their home country GAAP. Similar results were found with regard to owners' equity. At the extremes, income was 29 times higher under U.S. GAAP for one foreign entity, and 178 times higher using British GAAP for another entity. In addition, the study found significant differences are spread relatively evenly across countries. In other words, material differences are as likely to exist for a British or Canadian company as for a company in South America, Asia, or Continental Europe.

Focusing on the U.S. GAAP reconciliations of British companies, a separate study found that all 39 companies examined reported material differences in income or equity. Over 90 percent reported lower income under U.S. GAAP and approximately 60 percent reported higher equity. The average difference in income, even after including those with higher U.S. GAAP income, was a 42 percent reduction in income when reconciling to U.S. GAAP.[8] It is clear that differences in accounting principles can have a material impact on amounts reported in financial statements.

REASONS FOR ACCOUNTING DIVERSITY

Why does each country have its own unique set of financial reporting practices? Accounting scholars have hypothesized numerous influences on a country's accounting system, including factors as varied as the nature of the political system, the stage of economic development, and the state of accounting education and research. A survey of the relevant literature identified the following five items as commonly accepted factors influencing a country's financial reporting practices: (1) legal system, (2) taxation, (3) providers of financing, (4) inflation, and (5) political and economic ties.[9]

Legal System

The two major types of legal systems used around the world are common law and codified Roman law. Common law began in England and is found primarily in the English-speaking countries of the world. Common law countries rely on a limited amount of statute law that is interpreted by the courts. Court decisions establish precedents thereby developing case law that supplements the statutes. A system of code law, followed in most non-English-speaking countries, originated in the Roman *jus civile* and was developed further in European universities during the Middle Ages. Code law countries tend to have relatively more statute or codified law governing a wider range of human activity.

What does a country's legal system have to do with accounting? Code law countries generally have a corporation law (sometimes called a commercial code or companies act) that establishes the basic legal parameters governing business enterprises. The corporation law often stipulates which financial statements must be published in accordance with a prescribed format. Additional accounting measurement and disclosure rules are included in an accounting law that has been debated and passed by the national legislature. The accounting profession tends to have little influence on the development of accounting standards. In countries with a tradition of common law,

---

[8]Vivian Periar, Ron Paterson, and Allister Wilson, *UK/US GAAP Comparison,* 2nd ed. (London: Kogan Page Limited, 1992), pp. 384–393.

[9]Gary K. Meek and Sharokh M. Saudagaran, "A Survey of Research on Financial Reporting in a Transnational Context," *Journal of Accounting Literature,* 1990, pp. 145–82.

although a corporation law laying the basic framework for accounting might exist (such as in the United Kingdom), the profession or an independent, nongovernmental body representing a variety of constituencies establishes specific accounting rules. Thus, the type of legal system in a country determines whether the primary source of accounting rules is the government or the accounting profession.

In code law countries, the accounting law is rather general; it does not provide much detail regarding specific accounting practices and may provide no guidance at all in certain areas. Germany is a good example of a code law country. The current German accounting law passed in 1985 is only 47 pages in length and is silent with regard to issues such as leases, foreign currency translation, and a cash flows statement.[10] Common law countries, where a nongovernment organization is likely to develop accounting standards, have much more detailed rules. The extreme case might be the FASB in the United States. The Board provides very specific detail in its Statements of Financial Accounting Standards about how to apply the rules and has been accused of producing a standards overload. To illustrate this point, consider the rules related to accounting for leases in the United States and Germany. In the United States, *SFAS 13* requires leases to be capitalized if any one of four very specific criteria is met. Subsequent FASB statements establish rules for specific situations such as sales with leasebacks (*SFAS 28*), sales-type leases of real estate (*SFAS 98*), and changes in leases resulting from refundings of tax-exempt debt (*SFAS 22*). In contrast, the German accounting law is silent with regard to leases. The only guidance in the law is in paragraph 285 that simply states all liabilities must be recorded. In those situations where no guidance is provided in the law, German companies must refer to other sources including tax law and opinions of the German auditing profession to decide how to do their accounting. Interestingly enough, an important source of accounting practice in Germany comes from textbooks and commentaries written by accounting academicians.

Taxation

In some countries, published financial statements form the basis for taxation, whereas in other countries, financial statements are adjusted for tax purposes and submitted to the government separately from the reports sent to stockholders. Continuing to focus on Germany, its so-called conformity principle (*Massgeblichkeitsprinzip*) requires that, in most cases, an expense also must be used in the calculation of financial statement income to be deductible for tax purposes. Well-managed German companies attempt to minimize income for tax purposes, for example, through the use of accelerated depreciation to reduce their tax liability. As a result of the conformity principle, accelerated depreciation also must be taken in the calculation of accounting income.

In the United States, on the other hand, conformity between the tax statement and financial statements is required only for the use of the LIFO inventory cost flow assumption. U.S. companies are allowed to use accelerated depreciation for tax purposes and straight-line depreciation in the financial statements. All else being equal, a U.S. company is likely to report higher income than its German counterpart.

The difference between tax and accounting income gives rise to the necessity to account for deferred income taxes, a major issue in the United States in recent years. Deferred income taxes are much less of an issue in Germany, and for many German companies do not exist at all. This is also true in other code law countries such as France and Japan.

---

[10]Jermyn Paul Brooks and Dietz Mertin, *Neues Deutsches Bilanzrecht* (Düsseldorf: IDW-Verlag GmbH, 1986).

Providers of Financing

The major providers of financing for business enterprises are family members, banks, governments, and shareholders. In those countries in which company financing is dominated by families, banks, or the state, there is less pressure for public accountability and information disclosure. Banks and the state often are represented on the board of directors and therefore are able to obtain information necessary for decision making from inside the company. As companies become more dependent on financing from the general populace through the public offering of shares of stock, the demand for more information made available outside the company becomes greater. It simply is not feasible for the company to allow the hundreds, thousands, or hundreds of thousands of shareholders access to internal accounting records. The information needs of those financial statement users can be satisfied only through extensive disclosures in accounting reports.

There also can be a difference in orientation, with stockholders more interested in profit (emphasis on the income statement) and banks more interested in solvency and liquidity (emphasis on the balance sheet). Bankers prefer companies to practice rather conservative accounting with regard to assets and liabilities. To measure the importance of stockholders as a source of financing, we consider the number of domestic companies listed on stock exchanges in a country compared to its population.

Country	Companies[11]	Population (millions)	Companies per Million	Legal System
Germany	425	81 million	5.2	Code
France	515	57 million	9.0	Code
Spain	401	39 million	10.3	Code
Japan	1,651	124 million	13.3	Code
United States	5,819	256 million	22.7	Common
United Kingdom	1,878	58 million	32.4	Common
Canada	1,049	27 million	38.9	Common
Australia	1,038	18 million	57.7	Common

Inflation

Countries with chronically high rates of inflation have been forced to adopt accounting rules that require the inflation adjustment of historical cost amounts. This has been especially true in South America, that as a region has had more inflation than any other part of the world. For example, prior to recent economic reform, Brazil regularly experienced annual inflation rates exceeding 100 percent. The high point was reached in 1993 when annual inflation was nearly 1,800 percent. Double- and triple-digit inflation rates render historical costs meaningless. This factor primarily distinguishes accounting in South America from the rest of the world.

Political and Economic Ties

Accounting is a technology that can be borrowed relatively easily from or imposed on another country. Through political and economic linkages, accounting rules have been conveyed from one country to another. For example, through previous colonialism, both England and France have transferred their accounting frameworks to a variety of countries around the world. British accounting systems can be found in countries as far flung as Australia and Zimbabwe. French accounting is prevalent in

---

[11]Christopher W. Nobes and Robert H. Parker, eds., *Comparative International Accounting*, 4th ed. (Englewood Cliffs, N.J.: Prentice Hall, 1995), p. 9.

the former French colonies of western Africa. More recently, economic ties with the United States have had an impact on accounting in Canada, Mexico, and Israel.

Correlation of Factors

Whether by coincidence or not, there is a high degree of correlation between the legal system, tax conformity, and source of financing. Common law countries separate taxation from accounting and rely more heavily on the stock market as a source of capital. Code law countries link taxation to accounting statements and rely less on financing provided by shareholders.

ACCOUNTING CLUSTERS

Given the discussion regarding factors influencing accounting practice worldwide, it should not be surprising to learn that clusters of countries share common accounting practices. One classification scheme identifies four major accounting models: British-American, Continental, South American, and Mixed Economy.[12] **British-American** describes the approach used in the United Kingdom and United States where accounting is oriented toward the decision needs of large numbers of investors and creditors. Dutch accounting is quite similar. This model is used in most of the English-speaking countries, and other countries heavily influenced by the United Kingdom or United States. Most of these countries follow a common law legal system. The **Continental** model is used by most of continental Europe and Japan. Companies in this group usually are tied quite closely to banks that serve as the primary suppliers of financing. As these are code law countries, accounting is legalistic, designed to provide information for taxation or government planning purposes. The **South American** model resembles the Continental model in its legalistic, tax, and government planning orientation. This model distinguishes itself, however, through the extensive use of adjustments for inflation. The **Mixed Economy** model describes the approach recently developed in Eastern Europe and the former Soviet Union that combines elements of the former planned economic system and the recent market economy reforms.

Concentrating on the British-American and Continental model countries, Professor Chris Nobes has developed a more refined classification scheme that shows how the financial reporting systems in 14 developed countries relate to one another. An adaptation of Nobes' classification is in Exhibit 11–3.[13]

A Hypothetical Model of Accounting Diversity

The terms *micro-based* and *macro-uniform* describe the British-American and Continental models, respectively. Each of these classes is divided into two subclasses that are further divided into families. Within the micro-based class of accounting system, there is a subclass heavily influenced by business economics and accounting theory. The Netherlands is the only country in this subclass. One manifestation of the influence of theory is that Dutch companies may use current replacement cost accounting in their primary financial statements. The other micro-based subclass is of British origin and is more pragmatic and oriented toward business practice, relying less on economic theory in the development of accounting rules. The British origin subclass can be split into two families; one dominated by the United States and one dominated

---

[12]Gerhard G. Mueller, Helen Gernon, and Gary Meek, *Accounting—An International Perspective,* 3rd ed. (Burr Ridge, Ill.: Richard D. Irwin, 1994), pp. 8–12.

[13]Source: C. W. Nobes, "A Judgemental International Classification of Financial Reporting Practices," *Journal of Business Finance and Accounting,* Spring 1983, p. 7.

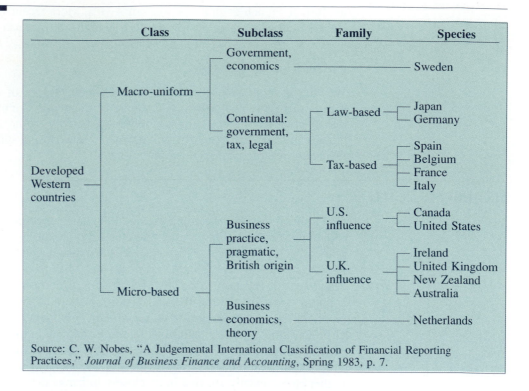

Source: C. W. Nobes, "A Judgemental International Classification of Financial Reporting Practices," *Journal of Business Finance and Accounting*, Spring 1983, p. 7.

by the United Kingdom. Nobes does not indicate how these two families differ from one another.

On the macro-uniform side of the model, a government, economics subclass has only one country, Sweden. Swedish accounting distinguishes itself from the other macro-uniform countries in its being closely aligned with national economic policies. For example, income smoothing is allowed to promote economic stability and social accounting has developed to meet macroeconomic concerns. The Continental government, tax, legal subclass contains Continental European countries divided into two families. Led by Germany, the law-based family includes Japan. The tax-based family consists of several Romance-language countries. The major difference between these families is that the accounting law is the primary determinant of accounting practice in Germany, whereas the tax law dominates in the Southern European countries.

The importance of this hierarchical model is that it shows the comparative distances between countries and could be used as a blueprint for determining where financial statement comparability is likely to be greater. For example, comparisons of financial statements between the United States and Canada (that are in the same family) are likely to be more valid than comparisons between the United States and the United Kingdom (that are not in the same family). However, the United States and the United Kingdom (which are in the same subclass) are more comparable than are the United States and the Netherlands (that are in different subclasses). Finally, comparisons between the United States and the Netherlands (that are in the same class) might be more meaningful than comparisons between the United States and any of the macro-uniform countries.

The hypothetical model in Exhibit 11–3 was empirically tested in 1993.[14] Data gathered on 100 financial reporting practices in 50 countries (including the 14 coun-

---

[14]Timothy S. Doupnik and Stephen B. Salter, "An Empirical Test of a Judgemental International Classification of Financial Reporting Practices," *Journal of International Business Studies*, First Quarter 1993, pp. 41–60.

Exhibit 11–4
Results of Cluster Analysis on
100 Financial Reporting
Practices

Micro Class			Macro Class		
Cluster 1	**Cluster 2**	**Cluster 3**	**Cluster 5**	**Cluster 7**	
Australia	Bermuda	Costa Rica	Colombia	Finland	
Botswana	Canada		Denmark	Sweden	
Hong Kong	Israel	**Cluster 4**	France		
Ireland	United States	Argentina	Italy	**Cluster 8**	
Jamaica		Brazil	Norway	Germany	
Luxembourg		Chile	Portugal		
Malaysia		Mexico	Spain	**Cluster 9**	
Namibia				Japan	
Netherlands			**Cluster 6**		
Netherlands Antilles			Belgium		
Nigeria			Egypt		
New Zealand			Liberia		
Philippines			Panama		
Papua New Guinea			Saudi Arabia		
South Africa			Thailand		
Singapore			United Arab Emirates		
Sri Lanka					
Taiwan					
Trinidad and Tobago					
United Kingdom					
Zambia					
Zimbabwe					

Source: Timothy S. Doupnik and Stephen B. Salter, "An Empirical Test of a Judgemental International Classification of Financial Reporting Practices," *Journal of International Business Studies*, First Quarter 1993, p. 53.

tries in Exhibit 11-3) were analyzed using the statistical procedure of hierarchical cluster analysis. The significant clusters arising from the analysis are in Exhibit 11–4.

The results clearly indicate two significantly different classes of accounting system being used across these countries. The major deviations from Nobes' model are that the Netherlands is in the U.K. influence group rather than in a subclass by itself; Japanese accounting is not as similar to German accounting as hypothesized; and Belgium is not in the group with France, Spain, and Italy. Indeed, considerably less similarity appears among the macro countries (as evidenced by the greater number of clusters) than among the countries comprising the micro class.

The large size of the U.K. influence cluster (Cluster 1) clearly shows the influence of British colonialism on accounting development. In contrast, Cluster 2, which includes the United States, is quite small. The emergence of Cluster 4, which includes several Latin American countries, is evidence of the importance of inflation as a factor affecting accounting practice.

The two classes of accounting reflected in Exhibit 11–4 differ significantly on 66 of the 100 financial reporting practices examined.[15] Differences exist for 41 of the 56 disclosure practices studied. In all but one case, the micro class of countries provided a higher level of disclosure than the macro class of countries. There were also significant differences for 25 of the 44 practices examined affecting income measurement. Of particular importance is the item asking whether accounting practice adhered to tax requirements. The mean level of agreement with this statement among macro countries was 72 percent, whereas it was only 45 percent among micro countries. To summarize, companies in the micro-based countries provide more extensive disclosure than do companies in the macro-uniform countries, and companies in the macro countries are more heavily influenced by taxation than are companies in the micro countries. These results are consistent with the relative importance of equity

---

[15]Doupnik and Salter, 1993, p. 56.

finance and relatively weak link between accounting and taxation in the micro countries.

Major Deviations from U.S. GAAP

The discussion thus far has explained why accounting practices might differ across countries and how different countries' accounting systems relate to one another without specifically indicating where those differences exist. Before comparing specific accounting issues across selected countries in the second part of this chapter, we look at the major areas of difference. One way of looking at this is to consider the items most frequently requiring adjustment in foreign reconciliations to U.S. GAAP. In its 1993 study, the SEC found that the ten accounting issues most commonly requiring adjustments were

- Depreciation and amortization (137).
- Deferred or capitalized costs (117).
- Deferred taxes (114).
- Pension costs (including other post-retirement benefits) (66).
- Foreign currency translation (62).
- Gain/loss on disposal of assets (48).
- Business combinations (including goodwill) (37).
- Extraordinary items, discontinued operations, and accounting changes (37).
- Employee compensation (26).
- Investments in associated entities (equity method) (23).[16]

(The amounts in parentheses indicate the number of companies reporting the specific adjustment out of a total of 286 companies with reconciling items.)

INTERNATIONAL HARMONIZATION OF FINANCIAL REPORTING

The preceding sections make clear the significant, systematic differences in accounting practices across countries. As noted in the introduction, these differences cause complications for those preparing and using financial statements. Several organizations around the world are involved in an effort to harmonize financial reporting practices.

Harmonization is the process of reducing differences in financial reporting practices across countries, thereby increasing the comparability of financial statements. Ultimately, harmonization implies development of a set of international accounting standards that would be applied in all countries.

Arguments for Harmonization

Proponents of accounting harmonization argue that comparability of financial statements worldwide is necessary for the globalization of capital markets. Financial statement comparability would make it easier for investors to evaluate potential investments in foreign securities and thereby take advantage of the risk reduction possible through international diversification. It also would simplify the evaluation by multinational companies of possible foreign takeover targets. From the other side, with harmonization, companies could gain access to all capital markets in the world with one set of financial statements. This would allow companies to lower their cost

---

[16]United States Securities and Exchange Commission, *Survey of Financial Statement Reconciliations by Foreign Registrants*, (Washington, D.C.: Government Printing Office, 1993), p. 10.

of capital and would make it easier for foreign investors to acquire the company's stock.

One set of universally accepted accounting standards would reduce the cost of preparing worldwide consolidated financial statements, and the auditing of these statements also would be simplified. Multinational companies would find it easier to transfer accounting staff to other countries. This would be true for the international auditing firms as well.

Arguments against Harmonization

The greatest obstacle to harmonization is the magnitude of the current differences between countries and the fact that the political cost of eliminating those differences would be enormous. As stated by Dennis Beresford, chairman of the FASB, "high on almost everybody's list of obstacles is nationalism. Whether out of deep-seated tradition, indifference born of economic power, or resistance to intrusion of foreign influence, some say that national entities will not bow to any international body."[17] Arriving at principles that satisfy all of the parties involved throughout the world seems an almost Herculean task.

Not only is harmonization difficult to achieve, the need for such standards is not universally accepted. As stated by Seagram's Richard Karl Goeltz: "Full harmonization of international accounting standards is probably neither practical nor truly valuable. . . . It is not clear whether significant benefits would be derived in fact. A well-developed global capital market exists already. It has evolved without uniform accounting standards."[18] Opponents of harmonization argue that it is unnecessary to force all companies worldwide to follow a common set of rules. The international capital market will force those companies that benefit from accessing the market to provide the required accounting information without harmonization.

Yet another argument against harmonization is that because of different environmental influences, differences in accounting across countries might be appropriate and necessary. For example, countries at different stages of economic development or that rely on different sources of financing perhaps should have differently oriented accounting systems.

Regardless of the arguments against harmonization, substantial effort to reduce differences in accounting practice have been ongoing for several decades. The question is no longer *whether* harmonization should be strived for, but *to what extent* can accounting practices be harmonized and *how fast*.

MAJOR HARMONIZATION EFFORTS

While numerous organizations are involved in harmonization on either a regional or worldwide basis, the two most important players in this effort have been the European Union on a regional basis and the International Accounting Standards Committee on a global basis.

European Union

The major objectives embodied in the Treaty of Rome that created the European Economic Community in 1957 (now called the European Union) was the establishment of free movement of persons, goods and services, and capital across member

---

[17]Dennis R. Beresford, "Accounting for International Operations," *CPA Journal*, October 1988, pp. 79–80.

[18]Richard Karl Goeltz, "International Accounting Harmonization: The Impossible (and Unnecessary?) Dream," *Accounting Horizons*, March 1991, pp. 85–86.

countries. To achieve a common capital market, the European Union (EU) has attempted to harmonize financial reporting practices within the community. To do this, the EU issues directives that must be incorporated into the laws of member nations. Two directives have helped harmonize accounting: The Fourth Directive, issued in 1978, deals with valuation rules, disclosure requirements, and the format of financial statements. The Seventh Directive, issued in 1983, relates to the preparation of consolidated financial statements.

The Seventh Directive requires companies to prepare consolidated financial statements and outlines the procedures for their preparation. This directive has had a significant impact on European accounting as consolidations were previously uncommon on the Continent.

The Fourth Directive provides considerable flexibility with dozens of provisions beginning with the expression, "member states may require or permit companies to"; these allow countries to choose from among acceptable alternatives. One manifestation of this flexibility is that under Dutch and British law, companies may write up assets to higher market values, whereas in Germany this is strictly forbidden. Notwithstanding this flexibility, implementation of the directives into local law has caused extensive change in accounting practice in several countries. For example, some of the changes in German accounting practice brought about by the integration of EU Directives into local law are

1. Required inclusion of notes to the financial statements.
2. Preparation of consolidated financial statements on a worldwide basis, that is, foreign subsidiaries no longer can be excluded from consolidation.
3. Elimination of unrealized intercompany losses on consolidation.
4. Use of the equity method for investments in associated companies.
5. Disclosure of comparative figures in the balance sheet and income statement.
6. Disclosure of liabilities with a maturity of less than one year, and
7. Accrual of deferred tax liabilities and pension obligations.[19]

Most of these innovations have been common practice in the United States for several decades.

Given that EU countries are in four of the nine clusters in Exhibit 11–4, the Fourth and Seventh Directives clearly have not created complete harmonization within the European Union. As an illustration of the effects of differing principles within the EU, the profits of one case study company were measured in European Currency Units using the accounting principles of various member states. The results are almost startling:

Most Likely Profit—Case Study Company

Country	ECUs (millions)
Spain	131
Germany	133
Belgium	135
Netherlands	140
France	149
Italy	174
United Kingdom[20]	192

[19]Timothy S. Doupnik, "Recent Innovations in German Accounting Practice through the Integration of EC Directives," *Advances in International Accounting,* 1992, pp. 75–103.

[20]Anthony Carey, "Harmonization: Europe Moves Forward," *Accountancy,* March 1990, pp. 92–93.

Part of the difference in profit across EU countries is the result of several important topics not covered in the directives including lease accounting, foreign currency translation, accounting changes, contingencies, income taxes, and long-term construction contracts. In 1990, the EU Commission indicated that there would be no further accounting directives. Instead, the EU Forum of standard setters was created which has considered several issues not covered in the directives. The forum has not yet issued any pronouncements, and is proving to be little more than a discussion group.

Although the EU Directives have not led to complete comparability across member nations, they have not been a complete failure as differences in financial statements are not nearly as great as they once were. In addition, the EU Directives have served as a basic framework of accounting that has been adopted by other countries in search of an accounting model. With the economic reforms in Eastern Europe since 1989, several countries in that region have found it necessary to abandon the Soviet style accounting system previously used in favor of a Western, market-oriented system. Hungary, Poland, and the Czech and Slovak Republics have all written new accounting laws primarily based on the EU directives. Each of these countries appears to be looking ahead to the day when it will apply for EU membership. This is further evidence of the influence that economic ties among countries can have on accounting practice.

INTERNATIONAL ACCOUNTING STANDARDS COMMITTEE

In hopes of eliminating the diversity of principles used throughout the world, the International Accounting Standards Committee (IASC) was formed in June 1973 by accountancy bodies in Australia, Canada, France, Germany, Japan, Mexico, the Netherlands, the United Kingdom and Ireland, and the United States. Similar in some ways to the FASB and GASB, the IASC is a private organization based in London. Governments do not belong, only accounting organizations can be members. Since 1973, the initial group has grown to more than 100 accountancy bodies representing 85 nations. From the United States, the American Institute of CPAs (AICPA) and the Institute of Management Accountants (IMA) are members.

A board consisting of representatives from 13 countries plus a representative from the International Association of Financial Analysts produces IASC accounting pronouncements. In 1995, this board consisted of representatives from eight of the founding nations (all but Mexico) plus India, Italy, Jordan, Scandinavia, and South Africa. The board normally meets three times a year for three or four days. The board also holds meetings twice a year with its consultative group made up of a wide range of parties including a member of the FASB. For any official pronouncement to be issued, at least 11 of the 14 board members must agree.

The goals of the IASC are detailed in the body's constitution:

- To formulate and publish in the public interest accounting standards to be observed in the presentation of financial statements and to promote their worldwide acceptance and observance.

- To work generally for the improvement and harmonization of regulations, accounting standards and procedures relating to the presentation of financial statements.[21]

As of January 1997, the IASC had issued 32 International Accounting Standards, some of which have been subsequently revised (see Exhibit 11–5). A conceptual framework similar in scope to that developed by the U.S. FASB also has been created. International Accounting Standards (IASs) have addressed worldwide reporting con-

---

[21]International Accounting Standards Committee Constitution, January 1983, para. 2.

	Title	Issued
IAS 1	Disclosure of Accounting Policies	1/75
IAS 2	Inventories	10/75 (revised 1993)
IAS 3	(Superceded by IAS 27 and 28)	
IAS 4	Depreciation Accounting	10/76
IAS 5	Information to Be Disclosed in Financial Statements	10/76
IAS 6	(Superceded by IAS 15)	
IAS 7	Cash Flow Statements	10/77 (revised 1992)
IAS 8	Net Profit or Loss for the Period, Fundamental Errors and Changes in Accounting Policies	2/78 (revised 1993)
IAS 9	Research and Development Costs	7/78 (revised 1993)
IAS 10	Contingencies and Events Occurring after the Balance Sheet Date	10/78
IAS 11	Construction Contracts	3/79 (revised 1993)
IAS 12	Accounting for Taxes on Income	7/79
IAS 13	Presentation of Current Assets and Current Liabilities	11/79
IAS 14	Reporting Financial Information by Segment	8/81
IAS 15	Information Reflecting the Effects of Changing Prices	11/81
IAS 16	Property, Plant and Equipment	3/82 (revised 1993)
IAS 17	Accounting for Leases	9/82
IAS 18	Revenue	12/82 (revised 1993)
IAS 19	Retirement Benefit Costs	1/83 (revised 1993)
IAS 20	Accounting for Government Grants and Disclosure of Government Assistance	4/83
IAS 21	The Effects of Changes in Foreign Exchange Rates	7/83 (revised 1993)
IAS 22	Business Combinations	11/83 (revised 1993)
IAS 23	Borrowing Costs	3/84 (revised 1993)
IAS 24	Related Party Disclosures	7/84
IAS 25	Accounting for Investments	3/86
IAS 26	Accounting and Reporting by Retirement Benefit Plans	1/87
IAS 27	Consolidated Financial Statements and Accounting for Investments in Subsidiaries	4/89
IAS 28	Accounting for Investments in Associates	4/89
IAS 29	Financial Reporting in Hyperinflationary Economies	7/89
IAS 30	Disclosures in the Financial Statements of Banks and Similar Financial Institutions	8/90
IAS 31	Financial Reporting of Interests in Joint Ventures	12/90
IAS 32	Financial Instruments: Disclosure and Presentation	3/95

Exposure Drafts Outstanding

E 49	Income Taxes
E 50	Intangible Assets
E 51	Reporting Financial Information by Segment
E 52	Earnings per Share

cerns ranging from consolidated financial statements to accounting for income taxes and disclosure of related party transactions. Because the IASC is a private body, these pronouncements cannot be enforced. Instead, the IASC has attempted to gain acceptance in a number of ways. For example, countries that do not have extensive accounting principles are urged to adopt the IASC's guidelines, thus "guaranteeing a certain level of quality and compatibility for the particular standard."[22]

---

[22]International Accounting Standards Committee, *Objectives and Procedures,* January 1983, para. 9.

Relatively few countries have formally adopted IASs as their national practice. The list of countries that had adopted IASs by 1988 follows; note that all of these are developing nations and all have a British heritage.

IAS as National Requirement		IAS as Basis for National Standard	
Cyprus	Pakistan	Egypt	Kenya
Malawi	Zimbabwe	Fiji	Nigeria
Malaysia		India	Singapore[23]

Countries that already have a system of accounting standards in place are asked to eliminate any material differences with IASC pronouncements. "No enforcement mechanism exists to assure that the standards, once issued, are followed. Rather, the accounting professional body within each country has merely signed a pledge, representing that it will use its 'best efforts' to have the standard setters in their country move to accept the international standards."[24]

As a result of this best efforts pledge, the AICPA board of directors has formally stated that if significant variances exist between international standards and U.S. GAAP, "the AICPA will urge the FASB and/or GASB to give early consideration to such differences with a view to achieving harmonization of those areas in which a significant difference exists."[25] Neither the United States, nor any other major industrial country has given formal recognition to IASC standards.

One other method historically used by the IASC to gain support has been the acceptance of alternative accounting methods. Rarely has the board selected one approach to a problem in preference to all others. To get at least 11 of the 14 board members to support a new standard, usually at least two methods (and often more) have to be allowed. For example, IAS 2, issued in 1975, allowed the use of specific identification, FIFO, LIFO, average cost, and the base stock method for valuing inventories, effectively sanctioning most of the alternative methods in worldwide use. For the same reason, both the U.S. treatment of expensing goodwill over a period of up to 40 years and the U.K. approach of writing off goodwill directly to stockholders' equity were allowed by the IASC. Although initially necessary from a political perspective perhaps, such compromise has brought the IASC under heavy criticism.

A study conducted by the IASC in 1988 found that all or most companies listed on the stock exchange in those countries in Exhibit 11–3 (except Italy and Germany) were in compliance with IASC standards.[26] Given that research has shown that these countries are following at least four significantly different models of accounting, it is obvious that IASC standards have introduced little if any comparability of financial statements across countries.

THE COMPARABILITY PROJECT

The International Organization of Securities Commissions (IOSCO) has put pressure on the IASC to reduce available options. IOSCO's membership is comprised of the stock exchange regulators in 14 developed countries and includes the U.S. SEC. IOSCO wants the IASC to reduce the number of acceptable methods to introduce real comparability across countries. Once that goal is achieved, IOSCO has stated

---

[23]International Accounting Standards Committee, *Survey of the Use and Application of International Accounting Standards*, 1988, pp. 9–14.

[24]Arthur R. Wyatt, "Seeking Credibility in a Global Economy," *New Accountant*, September 1992, p. 6.

[25]AICPA, *International Accounting and Auditing Standards*, October 1, 1988, page 11,002.

[26]International Accounting Standards Committee, *Survey of the Use and Application of International Accounting Standards*, 1988, p. 5.

that it will push securities regulators in member countries to allow financial statements of foreign registrants to be prepared in accordance with international accounting standards. "This could mean, for example, that if a French company had a simultaneous stock offering in the United States, Canada, and Japan, financial statements prepared in accordance with international standards could be used in all three nations."[27]

The IASC appears to have the opportunity to become an increasingly strong force in the world of accounting but only if it can eliminate the availability of optional methods. For this reason, the IASC embarked on a *comparability project* in 1987, the purpose of which was "to eliminate most of the choices of accounting treatment currently permitted under International Accounting Standards."[28] In January 1989, the IASC released Exposure Draft 32 entitled *Comparability of Financial Statements* which was designed to revise 12 of the committee's previous statements. For treatments permitted in previous international standards, ED32 indicated (1) preferred treatments, (2) treatments allowed as acceptable alternatives, and (3) treatments to be eliminated. Many view this project as the possible first act in making truly international accounting standards a reality.

After considering numerous comments received from interested parties worldwide, a Statement of Intent (draft standard) was released in 1990. Subsequently, 10 revised International Accounting Standards were approved in 1993 effective for accounting periods beginning on or after January 1, 1995. Some of the major revisions are included in Exhibit 11–6.

For the first time, compliance with U.S. GAAP no longer ensures that companies are also in compliance with International Accounting Standards (IASs). For example, the *SFAS 52* requirement of translating the financial statements of foreign operations in highly inflationary economies without first adjusting for inflation and the *SFAS 2* requirement that all development costs must be expensed immediately are no longer acceptable under revised IASs. In addition, amortizing goodwill over 40 years as is allowed in the United States would be inconsistent with international standards. It will be interesting to see if, over time, U.S. accounting practice moves to be in compliance once again with IASs.

The IASC's deliberations regarding LIFO demonstrate the political reality in which it must attempt to develop internationally acceptable standards. The use of LIFO is not the IASC's benchmark treatment, but it is an allowed alternative. While very popular in the United States, LIFO is not widely used in other countries and is in fact unacceptable in many. After designating LIFO as an allowed alternative in ED32, the IASC was criticized by several countries for favoring the United States. In reaction to this pressure, the IASC reconsidered its position on LIFO and subsequently eliminated LIFO as an acceptable treatment in the 1990 Statement of Intent. While appeasing several countries, this was met with negative reaction by the AICPA in the United States. Because of the importance of the United States in supporting the IASC's efforts, the IASC reversed its decision once again and IAS 2 (revised) does allow the use of LIFO when a reconciliation to FIFO or weighted average cost also is provided.

Support of Securities Exchange Regulators

To a great extent, the IASC's legitimacy as the international standard setter derives from its work being endorsed by IOSCO. IOSCO has indicated that if the IASC can develop a comprehensive set of core standards, it will endorse that core as acceptable

---

[27]Stephen H. Collins, "The SEC on Full and Fair Disclosure," *Journal of Accountancy,* January 1989, p. 84.

[28]International Accounting Standards Committee, *International Accounting Standards 1990* (London: IASC, 1990), p. 13.

Exhibit 11-6   Major Results of the IASC's Comparability Project

Issue	Benchmark Treatment	Allowed Alternative Treatment	Eliminated Treatment
IAS 2—Assignment of cost to inventories	Specific identification if possible, otherwise FIFO or weighted average cost.	LIFO.	Base stock formula.
IAS 8—Cumulative effect of a change in accounting policy	Reported as an adjustment to the opening balance of retained earnings.	Included in the determination of net profit or loss for the current period.	
IAS 9—Development costs	Recognize as asset when criteria are met, expense when criteria are not met.		Recognize as expense when capitalization criteria are met.
IAS 11—Recognition of revenue and net income on long-term construction contracts	Percentage of completion method when certain criteria met.		Completed contract method when percentage of completion criteria met.
IAS 16—Carrying value of property, plant, and equipment	Cost less any accumulated depreciation.	Fair value less any accumulated depreciation.	
IAS 18—Recognition of revenue on transactions involving the rendering of services	Percentage of completion method when criteria met.		Completed contract method when percentage of completion criteria met.
IAS 19—Retirement benefit costs	Accrued benefit valuation method.	Projected benefit valuation method.	
IAS 21—Exchange rate for translating income items of foreign entities	Rate at date of the transaction (or average rate as an approximation).		Rate at balance sheet date (current rate).
IAS 21—Subsidiaries operating in hyperinflationary economies	Restate financial statements for inflation and then translate.		Translate financial statements without prior restatement for inflation.
IAS 22—Positive goodwill	Recognize as an asset and amortize to income over its useful life. The amortization period should not exceed 5 years, unless a longer period can be justified that should not exceed 20 years.		Adjust immediately to owners' equity.
IAS 23—Borrowing costs	Recognize as part of the cost of an asset if it takes a substantial period of time to get the asset ready for sale or use.		Recognize as expense when capitalization criteria are met.

for cross-border capital raising and cross-listing of securities. As a result, Toyota Motor Corporation could list its stock on the New York Stock Exchange and General Motors Corporation could list its stock in Tokyo by filing IAS-based financial statements with the respective securities commissions. (Of course, this assumes that the securities commission in Japan and the SEC in the United States would agree to follow IOSCO's endorsement.)

In 1993, IOSCO endorsed IAS 7 "Cash Flows Statements" (revised in 1992), and in 1994 it indicated that another 14 standards (including 8 of the 10 revised in the comparability project) need no further improvement to be considered core standards. In July 1995, the IASC developed a work program that IOSCO agrees will result in a comprehensive set of core standards. IOSCO will not endorse further IASs until the IASC has completed all the core standards to IOSCO's satisfaction. Informally, 11 of the 14 IOSCO members have indicated that the current IASs are satisfactory. The three IOSCO members not yet completely satisfied are Canada, Japan, and the United States. Although IOSCO has not yet completely endorsed IASs, several stock exchanges around the world—including London, Amsterdam, and Hong Kong—currently accept IAS-based financial statements for cross-listings.

The U.S. SEC has given partial recognition to international standards. Since 1994, the SEC no longer requires reconciliation to U.S. GAAP if a foreign registrant uses the relevant IAS related to:

- Statement of cash flows.
- Amortization of goodwill.
- Translation of financial statements of subsidiaries in highly inflationary economies.
- Distinction between purchase and pooling of interests.

The FASB is sometimes criticized for not being interested in the IASC and its activities. However, there has actually been considerable cooperation between the two organizations over the years. The FASB is a member of IASC's consultative group, the only standard setter included in that group. The IASC and FASB worked together on an earnings per share project, and, these two bodies worked together with the Canadian Institute of Chartered Accountants to revise rules related to segmental reporting. The chairman of the FASB's parent organization, the Financial Accounting Foundation (FAF), has indicated that FAF will promote the development and acceptance of international standards.[29]

The FASB conducted a comparison of IASC standards with U.S. GAAP in 1996.[30] Although it is widely assumed that IAS and U.S. GAAP are generally consistent with one another, that study shows that considerable differences exist in the two sets of accounting principles.

> As some of the comparative analyses in this report show, some of the IASC standards and their U.S. GAAP counterparts do have a similar underlying approach to accounting in certain areas, and it may be possible to arrive at similar results under both standards. However, such similarity may be compromised by the existence of alternatives or the absence of implementation guidance within the standards. Either of those circumstances could lead to very different results in the financial statements.[31]

The FASB identified 218 items covered by both U.S. GAAP and IASC standards. The following table lists the degree of similarity across these items:

	Number	Percent
Similar approach and guidance	56	26%
Similar approach but different guidance	79	36
Different approach	56	26
Alternative approaches permitted	27	12
	218	100%

[29]Glenn Cheney, "Cook Defends Independence, Pushes for Global Standards," *Accounting Today,* November 25–December 15, 1996, pp. 16 and 20.

[30]Financial Accounting Standards Board. *The IASC-U.S. Comparison Project: A Report on the Similarities and Differences between IASC Standards and U.S. GAAP,* ed. Carrie Bloomer (Norwalk, Conn.: FASB, 1996).

[31]Ibid., p. 15.

VOLUNTARY ADOPTION OF INTERNATIONAL ACCOUNTING STANDARDS

A growing number of companies, especially in Europe, have adopted international standards on a voluntary basis. Many multinational companies in Finland include a set of IAS-based financial statements in their annual reports in addition to a set prepared in compliance with Finnish accounting law. In France, companies are required to follow French accounting law in preparing the parent company financial statements but may follow other rules in the consolidated statements. Many large French companies have opted to apply IASs in their consolidated financial statements. For example, the French company Saint-Gobain indicates the following in its summary of significant accounting policies:

> The Group's consolidated financial statements are prepared and presented in accordance with French law concerning consolidated financial statements dated January 3, 1985, and the related decree dated February 17, 1986.
>
> The accounting principles applied by the Group are also in accordance with international accounting principles formulated by the International Accounting Standards Committee.

Interestingly enough, a number of French companies including PSA Peugeot Citroën use U.S. GAAP in their consolidated statements.

Exploiting the flexibility allowed by their local accounting laws, several Swiss and German companies have elected to follow international standards in their consolidated statements as well. For example, the German chemical giant Hoechst AG prepared its 1995 financial statements in accordance with IASC standards:

> The 1995 Group financial statements are based on the International Accounting Standards (IAS) of the International Accounting Standards Committee (IASC) in the version valid on the balance sheet date. In order to comply with the provisions of the German Commercial Code, we make appropriate use of the existing options under the German Commercial Code and IAS, thereby permitting conformance with both sets of accounting standards.

During the 1980s, the Toronto Stock Exchange asked Canadian companies to begin referring to the use of international accounting standards in their financial statements. Although this was only a request, more than 100 companies complied. Alcan Aluminum Ltd., for example, reported that its 1995 statements were "prepared in accordance with accounting principles generally accepted in Canada. . . . They conform in all material respects with accounting principles established by the International Accounting Standards Committee."

International accounting standards have been largely ignored by companies in the United States. A study conducted by the IASC found that approximately 200 companies worldwide indicated compliance with IASs.[32] (Nearly half of the companies were in Canada and France.) Only six of these companies are in the United States, even though at the time the study was conducted, most U.S. companies could claim compliance with IASs. Beginning in the early 1980s, General Electric Company set a precedent by indicating its adherence to international accounting standards in its annual report. Its 1990 "Management Responsibility Report," contains the following disclosure: "Accounting principles used in preparing the financial statements are those that are generally accepted in the United States. These principles are consistent in most important aspects with standards issued by the International Accounting Standards Committee." For whatever reason, this statement has been absent from General Electric's annual reports since 1990.

---

[32]Allan B. Afterman, *International Accounting, Financial Reporting, and Analysis* (New York: Warren, Gorham & Lamont, 1995), pp. B1-22.

WHAT DOES THE FUTURE HOLD?

Not everyone is necessarily pleased with the progress being made by the IASC. "Now that the London-based International Accounting Standards Committee is close to rolling out universal accounting standards, some American companies are getting cold feet. That's because, looking down the road, many U.S. companies fear that standards set in London may one day replace standards currently used in the United States."[33]

If the revised IASs resulting from the comparability project can gain wide acceptance, the IASC will have made an important stride in harmonizing accounting principles throughout the world. Unfortunately, many questions remain unanswered: Will countries where the government controls the development of accounting principles have any interest in relinquishing part of that power to the IASC? Will countries with well-developed accounting principles, such as the United States, accept rules that differ from their own?

If the IASC, which meets a few times per year with virtually no staff, changes the handling of items such as development costs or goodwill amortization, will the full-time, well-staffed FASB make those same changes in U.S. GAAP just for conformity? Should the FASB make those changes? If not, how will the work of the IASC be affected? To date, such issues have not been faced.

Regardless of the future success or failure of the IASC, it is clear that the FASB is interested in harmonizing U.S. GAAP with the accounting standards of other countries. In announcing a project to address issues related to the accounting for business combinations and intangible assets, FASB chairman Dennis Beresford made the following comments:

> A great deal of disparity exists among the United States and other countries in the business combinations and intangibles areas. . . . For example, the "pooling of interests" method of accounting for combinations is widely used in the U.S., but only rarely used outside this country. Additionally, the accounting for purchased goodwill is different here from the methods employed in certain other countries. With this project, the FASB has the chance to harmonize U.S. standards with those of other countries and those of international standard setters and make financial reporting more comparable around the world.[34]

A single, universal accounting language may well become an eventual reality but at this point no one can foresee what will actually happen. International accounting standards may be desirable or even necessary; however, whether acceptance can be won for any set of principles remains to be seen.

ACCOUNTING PRINCIPLES AROUND THE WORLD

Just like food dishes and native dress, accounting principles vary from country to country. To understand each unique set of reporting standards that has evolved, one must examine the structure and development of the accounting profession in these areas. To aid your understanding of the techniques in use, the remainder of this chapter analyzes national accounting principles by presenting two types of information:

1. A discussion of the accounting profession as it is structured in several key countries, along with an introduction to the financial statements currently produced in these countries.

2. A study of several specific accounting problems and the method by which these issues have been resolved in different countries.

---

[33]Roula Khalaf, "Esperanto for Accountants," *Forbes,* March 3, 1992, pp. 50–51.

[34]"FASB to Address Business Combination Issues," FASB News Release, August 22, 1996.

THE ACCOUNTING PROFESSION AND FINANCIAL STATEMENT PRESENTATION

United Kingdom

"The United Kingdom has the oldest accounting profession in the world today, and its reputation is second to none."[35] As this quotation indicates, no discussion of world accounting principles would be complete without a study of the United Kingdom, a world leader in commerce and accounting. The legal foundation for accounting is provided by the Companies Acts, a series of legislation culminating in the Companies Act of 1989. The Companies Acts are basic commercial legislation designed to provide legal rules for U.K. corporations concerning issues dealing with management, administration, and dissolution. However, these laws also cover the issuance and content of financial statements. Prior to the 1980s, the law provided little more than a framework within which the accounting profession could set more detailed principles.[36] In 1981, the Companies Act was amended to incorporate the European Union's Fourth Directive and in 1989 it was amended to implement the Seventh Directive thereby increasing the importance of legislation in determining GAAP. Although the law prescribes some specific accounting procedures consistent with the EU directives, the law also requires companies to present a "true and fair view" of their results and financial position. This principle overrides the detailed requirements of the law. That is, if strict compliance with legislated accounting rules (or professional accounting standards) would not allow for a true and fair view to be presented, British companies should deviate from the rules. A survey of some 450 British companies in 1993 found that 10 percent used the true and fair view override.[37] The concept of true and fair view has been adopted by the EU in its accounting directives.

In the United Kingdom, professional accounting organizations are quite important—membership now nears 200,000. A person may be a chartered accountant only through membership in the Institutes of Chartered Accountants in England and Wales, of Scotland, or in Ireland. Normally, once required exams have been passed, a license to practice is available to members after two years of approved experience.

In total, six different professional groups exist with the largest being the Institute of Chartered Accountants in England and Wales. Until recently, these organizations collectively controlled the accounting standard-setting process. Together, they formally created a Consultative Committee of Accountancy Bodies. A subcommittee of this group, the Accounting Standards Committee (ASC), produced 25 Statements of Standard Accounting Practice (SSAPs) between 1971 and 1990.

The ASC was originally created "to reduce and regularize the range of permissable accounting treatments applicable to comparable transactions and situations."[38] Over the years, the ASC gradually branched into a standard-setting role. However, the committee experienced difficulty because its pronouncements had to be accepted by each of the six professional organizations before being issued. Thus, the creation of accounting standards was agonizingly slow at times.

Consequently, the Accounting Standards Board (ASB) was formed on August 1, 1990, to replace the ASC as the standard-setting organization in the United Kingdom. The ASB is an independent body styled somewhat along the lines of the FASB in the United States. The ASB issues Financial Reporting Standards (FRSs) on its own

---

[35]Geoffrey Alan Lee, "Accounting in the United Kingdom," *International Accounting* (New York: Harper & Row, 1984), p. 261.

[36]Lee H. Radebaugh and Sidney J. Gray, *International Accounting and Multinational Enterprises,* 3rd ed. (New York: John Wiley and Sons, 1993), p. 83.

[37]J. M. Samuels, R. E. Brayshaw, and J. M. Cramer, *Financial Statement Analysis in Europe* (London: Chapman and Hall, 1995), p. 361.

[38]Emile Woolf, "The ASC at the Crossroads," *Accountancy,* September 1988, p. 72.

authority. The ASB has sanctioned all of the SSAPs and has issued several FRSs including one that requires cash flow information. Any deviation from the ASB's standards must be explained and the financial effects disclosed.

A second body, the Review Panel, was created along with the ASB. The Review Panel monitors compliance with the accounting standards. This panel has the authority to seek a court order against companies producing financial statements that fail to provide a true and fair view.

Financial statements must be submitted to the shareholders at the annual meeting. A directors' report is included describing the directors' activities for the period, post balance sheet events, the business year in general, research and development activities, and a host of other information. The financial statements themselves are normally the balance sheet, the profit and loss account, and a cash flows statement. In addition, a statement of total recognized gains and losses often is presented that among other things reports the amount of translation adjustments included in stockholders' equity but not in income. In contrast to the United States, parent company financial statements also are provided along with the consolidated statements.

For the balance sheet and profit and loss account, two different formats (allowed under the EU's Fourth Directive) are available—a vertical or a horizontal presentation. Most British companies provide a vertical balance sheet; an example is that of Glaxo Wellcome PLC in Exhibit 11–1. An example of a British profit and loss account for the food products company Whitbread PLC is in Exhibit 11–7.

Exhibit 11–7
United Kingdom Income Statement

WHITBREAD PLC
Group Profit and Loss Account
Year Ended February 25, 1995

	Notes	Before Exceptional Items £m	Exceptional Items £m	Total £m
Turnover from continuing operations ..	2	2,471.8	—	2,471.8
Cost of sales....................		(1,915.4)	—	(1,915.4)
Gross profit		556.4	—	556.4
Net operating expenses		(291.8)	—	(291.8)
Operating profit from continuing operations....................	3	264.6	—	264.6
Nonoperating items				
Net profit on disposal of fixed assets in continuing operations		—	40.3	40.3
Provision for loss on the disposal of a business		—	(20.0)	(20.0)
Profit before interest		264.6	20.3	284.9
Interest........................	7	(9.5)	—	(9.5)
Profit before taxation		255.1	20.3	275.4
Taxation.......................	8	(70.0)	—	(70.0)
Profit after taxation		185.1	20.3	205.4
Equity minority interests		(0.3)	—	(0.3)
Preference dividends		(0.4)	—	(0.4)
Profit earned for ordinary shareholders	9	184.4	20.3	204.7
Ordinary dividends	10	(96.9)	—	(96.9)
Retained profit for the year	24	87.5	20.3	107.8
Earnings per share (pence)				
Basic.........................	11			42.76
Adjusted basic	11	38.52		

In the United Kingdom, the group profit and loss account is the equivalent of a consolidated income statement. The statement begins with *turnover* (the British term for net sales) followed by operating expenses, interest, and then taxes. The net profit from and loss on disposal of discontinued operations are nonoperating items and appear in a separate column. Unlike in the United States, discontinued operations are reported in the profit and loss account before taxation. Similar to the United States, British companies must report earnings per share at the bottom of the profit and loss account. Also as in the United States, reported figures tend to be highly condensed with much of the information provided in the notes to the statements. On the face of the financial statements, specific references relate the notes to particular line items.

Germany

Accounting principles in Germany are set by the national legislature (*Bundestag*). Currently, these mandatory principles are outlined in detail in the Third Book of the Commercial Code (*Handelsgesetzbuch*). Tax laws have had a significant influence on the reporting principles established by the code. In addition, as the code is silent with regard to many accounting issues, German companies refer to tax law, professional pronouncements, academic commentaries, and international accounting standards to fill in the gaps. Actual changes in the accounting laws are rare because they must be passed by the legislature. As noted earlier in this chapter, the most recent accounting law was passed in December 1985 to bring German accounting principles in line with the directives of the European Union. Although this law introduced the notion of a true and fair view into German accounting practice, application of this principle differs from that in the United Kingdom. Günter Seckler found, "It still seems to be the dominant opinion in Germany that compliance with legal requirements ensures a true and fair presentation."[39] Financial statements must be prepared in accordance with the code. If this does not result in a true and fair view, additional information must be presented in the notes to the financial statements.

As in many countries where legislated accounting rules exist, German accounting is considered quite conservative. This is true for two major reasons: One is the so-called tax conformity principle that is almost unknown in other countries. In Germany, commercial financial statements are the basis for taxation. Thus, for an item to be deducted for tax purposes, it must be recorded as an expense in calculating income in the financial statements. Companies interested in taking advantage of provisions in the tax law to reduce taxable income are required to report lower financial income as well. Two, German accounting "is greatly influenced by the German banks, because they provide the major investment and mandate the reporting requirements for many industries in Germany. . . . When individuals in other countries analyze the financial statements, they generally write up the figures because of the extreme conservatism of German policies and procedures."[40] In fact, the German Association of Financial Analysts (DVFA) has developed a standardized procedure for adjusting reported earnings to assess the real profitability of German companies. The adjustments include adding back to income special depreciation allowed for tax purposes and excess amounts transferred to provisions.

The accounting profession in Germany is well established. The *Wirtschaftsprüfer* is the equivalent of a Certified Public Accountant. A person can use this designation only after passing a series of difficult examinations and gaining six years of relevant experience. Only college graduates with degrees in economics, law, or a related

---

[39]Günter Seckler, "Germany," in *European Accounting Guide,* 2nd ed. ed. David Alexander and Simon Archer (New York: Harcourt Brace & Company, 1995), p. 227.

[40]Roger K. Doost and Karen M. Ligon, "How U.S. and European Accounting Practices Differ," *Management Accounting,* October 1986, p. 40.

subject may sit for the exams. "Because of the comprehensive requirements for entry to the profession, it is almost impossible to fulfill all of them before the age of 30, and most are 35 before they are admitted."[41] The profession's self-governing body is the *Wirtschaftsprüferkammer* that enforces strict rules on independence and ethics.

In Germany, companies must produce a balance sheet each year as well as an income statement and notes to the financial statements. Also required is a management report to discuss issues such as current business position, significant subsequent events, future prospects, and research and development activities. Many companies fulfill a disclosure requirement regarding changes in fixed assets by providing a statement of fixed assets in addition to the balance sheet and income statement. Although a statement of cash flows is not required, many of the large companies provide one voluntarily in their annual reports.

The income statement must be produced according to one of two formats. The cost of sales approach, which has grown in popularity in recent years with Germany's larger multinationals, is similar to the structure of the income statement typically found in the United States. In contrast, the type-of-cost statement is more traditional in Germany. The consolidated statement of income for Mannesmann AG for the year ending December 31, 1995, is an example of this format (see Exhibit 11–8).

In the traditional cost of sales format used in the United States, manufacturing costs (materials, labor, overhead) are included in the cost of sales line item in the income statement and administrative costs are reported in a separate line. Under this approach, the total wages and salaries paid by a company are disaggregated into two parts—manufacturing wages are reported in cost of sales and administrative wages are reported in administrative expense. The same is true for depreciation and other operating expenses. Using the type-of-cost approach, Mannesmann reports total

Exhibit 11–8
German Income Statement

MANNESMANN AG
Consolidated Profit and Loss Account
Year Ended December 31, 1995

	Notes	DM millions
Net sales	(1)	32,094
Variation in stocks of finished goods and in work in progress and other own work capitalized	(2)	830
Total operating output		32,924
Other operating income	(3)	831
Cost of materials	(4)	−18,070
Staff costs	(5)	−9,468
Depreciation of intangible and tangible assets		−1,813
Other operating expenses	(6)	−3,491
Net income from participating interests	(7)	257
Value adjustments to financial assets and investments		−14
Net interest	(8)	−245
Result of ordinary activities		911
Extraordinary results	(9)	102
Taxes on profits		−312
Net profit for the year		701
Profit attributable to minority interests		−213
Loss attributable to minority interests		45
Change in the Group's revenue reserves		−239
Profit available for distribution		294

[41]Thomas G. Evans, Martin E. Taylor, and Oscar Holzmann, *International Accounting and Reporting,* 2nd ed. (Cincinnati, Ohio: South Western Publishing, 1994), p. 41.

wages and salaries (manufacturing and administrative) in a single line titled staff costs. Similarly, total depreciation is reported in one line, as is total other operating expenses. The materials component of cost of sales is reported by Mannesmann in two parts—purchases are reported as an expense in cost of materials, and the difference between beginning and ending inventory is treated as an adjustment to sales. Although quite unique in appearance when compared to a U.S. income statement, the type-of-cost approach results in the same calculation of earnings as the cost of sales approach. One analytical limitation of this approach, however, is that it is not possible to calculate the cost of sales; therefore, gross profit cannot be determined.

Note the 1995 consolidated balance sheet for the tire manufacturer Continental AG in Exhibit 11–9. Similar to the financial reporting in the United Kingdom, the German balance sheet begins with noncurrent assets followed by current assets. The somewhat strange sounding account liquid assets includes cash and cash equivalents. Prepaid expenses are not classified as either current or noncurrent. Stockholders' equity usually appears next before the reporting of any liabilities. As with many foreign countries, reserve figures are included within stockholders' equity to record adjustments that do not affect net income similar to the U.S. treatment of unrealized gains/losses on available for sale marketable securities. Footnote disclosure indicates that Continental's consolidated reserves include the premium on issuance of stock, the offsetting of goodwill with no effect on income, foreign exchange differences

Exhibit 11–9
German Balance Sheet

CONTINENTAL AKTIENGESELLSCHAFT
Consolidated Balance Sheet
December 31, 1995

	See Note No.	DM million
Assets		
Fixed assets and investments		
Intangible assets	(1)	503.0
Property, plant, and equipment	(2)	2,876.2
Investments	(3)	105.8
		3,485.0
Current assets		
Inventories	(4)	1,504.1
Receivables and other assets	(5)	1,590.8
Marketable securities		—
Liquid assets	(6)	89.6
		3,184.5
Prepaid expenses	(7)	**33.9**
		6,703.4
Shareholders' equity and liabilities		
Shareholders' equity	(8)	
Subscribed capital		469.7
Consolidated reserves		966.6
Minority interests	(9)	200.8
Net income available for distribution		47.2
		1,684.3
Special reserves	(10)	**11.3**
Provisions	(11)	**1,832.5**
Liabilities	(12)	**3,175.3**
		6,703.4

with no effect on income, reserve for retirement benefits, and other changes. The special reserves below shareholders' equity consist of an investment grant provided by the government.

German companies do not classify obligations on the balance sheet as current and noncurrent. Instead, they classify obligations as either estimated accruals (provisions) or those having a fixed, contractual nature (liabilities). German companies have traditionally considered liabilities due within the next five years as short term. However, the 1985 accounting law requires companies to disclose in the notes the amount of liabilities due within one year; many companies also continue to indicate those liabilities due in more than five years.

Continental's provisions include estimated accruals for such items as pensions, taxes, warranties, deferred repairs, and other undetermined obligations. In addition to being extremely conservative, German companies are notorious for their use of provisions to conceal profits and create hidden reserves. In profitable years, provisions are created for items such as deferred repairs, that is, repairs the company plans to make sometime in the future, or for undetermined obligations resulting from general business risks that might occur in the future. The counterpart to the balance sheet provision is an expense or loss reported in income. In years in which profits are below expectations, provisions are released with an offsetting increase to income. This income smoothing is an acceptable practice, done within the law, and very much a part of German business culture.

One of the most dramatic examples of the use of hidden reserves was carried out by Daimler-Benz AG in 1989. In 1988, the company reported income of 1.7 billion deutschemarks (DM). Because 1989 was a bad year for automobile sales, analysts expected Daimler-Benz's 1989 income to be somewhat lower than the year before. It created quite a stir in the German business community when the company reported 1989 income as DM6.8 billion, a fourfold increase over the prior year. The notes to the 1989 financial statements provide the following explanation:

> Provisions for old-age pensions and similar obligations are actuarially computed in accordance with the tax regulation of Section 6a of the Income Tax Act, at an interest rate of 6 percent per annum. Previously, a rate of 3.5 percent was used. Using the higher interest rate resulted in higher income of about DM4.9 billion and is shown in the income statement under "Other Operating Income."

Through the selection of a low (and therefore more conservative) discount rate from a range accepted by tax law, Daimler-Benz was able to report higher expenses in years prior to 1989 and thus establish hidden reserves. The release of those reserves in 1989 through a change in the discount rate significantly affected net income. Without the change, income would have been only DM1.9 billion.

In 1992, Daimler-Benz reported net income of DM1.45 billion after creating provisions for loss contingencies of DM774 million. Otherwise, 1992 profit would have been DM2.22 billion. In 1993, reported income was DM615 million, but included the release of previous provisions of DM4.26 billion, thus masking a loss of some DM3.65 billion.

Perhaps the ultimate in income smoothing was done by the electrical equipment manufacturer AEG that reported net income of exactly zero in each of the three years—1985, 1986, and 1987. The odds of a company generating net income of zero in any given year, let alone three years in a row, without the help of income smoothing are extremely small.

Some evidence indicates that German accounting may be in the process of change:

> "It is time," said the chief executive of Germany's largest bank at a recent press conference, "for Germany to enter the civilized world." Hilmar Kopper, head of the Deutsche Bank, was referring to German companies' accounting practices, and his remarks came shortly after Daimler-Benz had announced it would be moving from the teutonic version of accounting to the Anglo-American. . . . German accounting differs from Anglo-American in a number of

important areas, not least that it makes no claim to provide a 'true and fair' view of economic reality."[42]

As noted earlier in this chapter, now a number of German companies are using the flexibility of the German accounting law to voluntarily apply international accounting standards, and there is some discussion to allow German companies to follow international standards in lieu of the law in preparing consolidated financial statements.

Japan

Japan is an increasingly dominant industrial and financial power; we will need to come to terms with that country's accounting policies. Japanese accounting in the 1990s is a product of a native medieval double entry bookkeeping system, a borrowing from German (and French) commercial legal codes in the late 19th century, and U.S.-inspired securities legislation of the postwar period.[43]

In Japan and most other code law countries, basic accounting principles are set primarily by the government. The Japanese Commercial Code requires annual audited financial statements of joint stock corporations (known as *Kabushiki Kaisha* or KK) that have stated capital of at least 500 million yen or total liabilities of 20 billion yen or more. The Securities and Exchange Law imposes a similar reporting requirement on companies listed on Japanese stock exchanges as well as companies issuing stocks and bonds in the amount of 100 million yen or more. Consequently, many Japanese companies must produce two sets of financial statements: one to fulfill the requirements of the Commercial Code and the other based on securities laws. The two sets of statements are very similar except that the securities laws require more disclosure and its requirements are more precisely defined.

The Commercial Code prescribes a few basic accounting principles (valuation of assets and liabilities, recording of deferred assets, and the like). These rules are supplemented by the *Financial Accounting Standards for Business Enterprises* developed by the Business Accounting Deliberation Council (BADC). The BADC is, therefore, the single most important source of accounting principles in Japan. The BADC is made up of individuals drawn from the government, business, education, and the accounting profession. Membership in this council is by appointment of the Ministry of Finance which, therefore, allows government control.

Financial reporting in Japan is quite heavily influenced by tax laws. Companies usually follow the tax guidelines in producing their statements unless absolutely prohibited. Fortunately, the tax laws are written so that actual differences with official accounting pronouncements are few.

The adjustment of book income to taxable income on the tax return is not allowed in principle. Therefore, the so-called two sets of books problem prevalent in the United States is rarely mentioned in Japan. When a discrepancy exists between the income tax code and other financial accounting regulations, the corporation inevitably follows the procedures endorsed by the income tax code.[44]

The Japanese Institute of Certified Public Accountants (JICPA) has not become a powerful force in establishing accounting principles. The Audit Committee of the JICPA, though, does issue papers describing preferable accounting practices.

---

[42]David Waller, "Daimler-Benz Gears Up for a Drive on the Freeway," *Financial Times,* April 29, 1993, p. 18.

[43]Christopher Nobes and Sadayoshi Maeda, "Japanese Accounts: Interpreters Needed," *Accountancy,* September 1990, p. 82.

[44]Toshio Iino and Ryoji Inouye, "Financial Accounting and Reporting in Japan," in *International Accounting,* ed. H. Peter Holzer (New York: Harper & Row, 1984), p. 377.

To become a certified public accountant in Japan, applicants must pass three examinations: the first (from which college graduates are exempted) consists of mathematics, the Japanese language, and a thesis. The second is comprised of accounting, cost accounting, auditing, management, economics, and commercial law. Passing this second test qualifies one as a Junior CPA. Then, after three years of experience, a third examination is required to become a CPA. This final test is made up of accounting practice, auditing practice, and financial analysis.

Historically, accounting has not had the importance in Japan that is found in other developed nations.

Not only do officials of Japanese companies generally ignore the stock market, they don't use complex financial information much themselves either. "Cost accounting doesn't exist," [says Daniel Maher, partner of Chuo/Coopers & Lybrand Consulting in Tokyo]. "There are more accountants in Missouri than in all of Japan." In fact, there are only about 11,000 certified public accountants in Japan, compared with some 300,000 in the United States. Instead of corporate accounting departments or professional accountants, most Japanese companies have small accounting groups attached to projects and staffed by generalists who rotated through accounting between assignments to, say, personnel and sales.[45]

Financial statements required by the Japanese Commercial Code consist of the following:

- Balance sheet.
- Income statement.
- Proposal of appropriation of profit or disposition of loss.
- Business report.

Although a statement of cash flows is not specifically required, companies must provide extensive cash flow information in supplementary information filed with the Ministry of Finance. It is not uncommon for companies to voluntarily provide a cash flows statement in their annual reports.

The Japanese balance sheet is similar in appearance to that used in the United States. Assets usually are either current or long-term, and liabilities are divided between current and noncurrent. Long-term assets usually are categorized as investments; property, plant, and equipment; and deferred charges. Differences in presentation primarily relate to differences in accounting principles. For example, as allowed by Japanese accounting principles, Nissan Motor Co. reported translation adjustments arising from consolidation of foreign operations as an asset on its March 31, 1995, balance sheet, and Kobe Steel Ltd. reported research and development expense as a deferred asset on its March 31, 1995, balance sheet. Retained earnings may show amounts that have been voluntarily reserved by corporate officials.

In addition, the stockholders' equity section reports a legal reserve required to be established. As an example, Snow Brand Milk Products Co. Ltd. reported a legal reserve of 4,290 million yen ($48 million) on its March 31, 1995 balance sheet. A note explained this balance as follows:

The Commercial Code of Japan provides for an amount equivalent to at least 10 percent of expenditures as appropriations of retained earnings to be appropriated to legal reserve until such reserve equals 25 percent of stated capital. The Commercial Code also provides that both additional paid-in capital and legal reserve are not available for dividends, but may be used to reduce a deficit by resolution of the stockholders or may be transferred to capital stock by a resolution of the Board of Directors.

[45]Paula Doe, "What's Buried Inside Japanese Annual Reports?" *Electronic Business,* February 10, 1992, p. 28.

The Japanese income statement is divided into two sections to arrive at income before income taxes: ordinary income and extraordinary (or special) items. The income statement of Mitsubishi Heavy Industries, Ltd., in Exhibit 11–10 is an example of this structure. The first part of this statement includes operating revenues and expenses as well as nonoperating items such as interest and dividend income, and interest expense. The definition of an extraordinary item is not as restrictive in Japan as it is in the United States. The extraordinary (or special) section includes items such as losses due to earthquakes that would be considered extraordinary in the United States, but also includes items that would be considered quite ordinary, such as gains from the sale of fixed assets. Moreover, extraordinary items appear on a gross basis before taxes rather than net of tax as required in the United States. Japanese companies are required to report earnings per share calculated as net income divided by the weighted average number of shares outstanding during the period. There is no requirement to present earnings per share on a fully diluted basis.

It is very common for large Japanese companies to prepare an English language version of their annual report—these are known as convenience translations. (The same is true for the larger European companies such as Mannesmann and Continental.) In their English language convenience translations, Japanese companies usually translate yen amounts into U.S. dollars for the benefit of foreign readers. Note 2 to Mitsubishi Heavy Industries' financial statements indicates how this is carried out.

> U.S. dollar amounts are included solely for convenience. These translations should not be construed as representations that the Japanese yen actually represent, or have been or could be converted into, U.S. dollars.
>
> As the amounts shown in U.S. dollars are for convenience only, the rate of ¥89.35=U.S.$1 prevailing at March 31, 1995, has been used for the purpose of presentation of the U.S. dollar amounts in the accompanying consolidated financial statements.

Because each financial statement item is translated using the same rate, no translation adjustment arises.

Differences in business environments and accounting principles can have a significant impact on the comparability of financial ratios across countries. Consider the following ratios calculated in 1983:[46]

Average Japanese and U.S. Financial Ratios for Manufacturing Companies

Country	Current Ratio	Debt Ratio	Average Collection Period	Profit Margin	Return on Assets
Japan	1.15	.84	86 days	1.3%	1.2%
United States	1.94	.47	43 days	5.4%	7.4%

Based on these ratios, it appears that the average Japanese company is less liquid, less solvent, less efficient, and less profitable than the average U.S. company. From a U.S. perspective, the average Japanese firm appears to be an unattractive potential investment teetering on the brink of bankruptcy. However, a direct comparison of these ratios can be misleading. One should consider the differences in U.S. and Japanese business environments as well as differences in accounting principles when comparing financial data from companies in these two countries.

Japan's lower current ratio arises through the extensive use of short-term debt, rolled over when it comes due, to finance fixed assets. This is preferred by both banks and borrowers as interest rates are lower than on long-term debt but can be more frequently adjusted by the banks. The higher debt ratio in Japan is evidence of

---

[46]Frederick D. S. Choi, Hisaaki Hino, Sang Kee Min, Sang Oh Nam, Junichi Ujiie, and Arthure I. Stonehill, "Analyzing Foreign Financial Statements: The Use and Misuse of International Ratio Analysis," *Journal of International Business Studies,* Spring–Summer 1983, p. 116.

Exhibit 11–10
Japanese Income Statement

MITSUBISHI HEAVY INDUSTRIES, LTD. Consolidated Statement of Income For the Year Ended March 31, 1995		
	In Millions of Yen 1995	In Thousands of U.S. Dollars (Note 2) 1995
Net sales	¥2,848,527	$31,880,547
Cost of sales............................	2,366,363	26,484,194
Reversal of deferred profit on installment sales of ships and plants (Note 5)	(181)	(2,030)
Gross profit	482,345	5,398,383
Selling, general, and administrative expenses	295,524	3,307,492
Operating income	186,821	2,090,891
Nonoperating income:		
Interest and dividend income	33,784	378,109
Gains from sales of securities	—	—
Other income	2,039	22,825
	35,823	400,934
Nonoperating expenses:		
Interest expense........................	38,866	434,987
Exchange losses on foreign currency receivables and payables	11,645	130,329
Other expenses	16,841	188,485
	67,352	733,801
Ordinary income	155,292	1,738,024
Gains from sales of fixed assets (Note 6)	(4,312)	(48,255)
Forward exchange contract profit on foreign currency debenture (Note 7).....................	(1,650)	(18,469)
Losses incurred in connection with the Great Hanshin Earthquake (Note 8)	27,025	302,459
Valuation loss on foreign currency receivables and payables caused by significant change in foreign exchange rates........................	18,323	205,070
Deduction from the acquisition cost of fixed assets	4,212	47,150
Income before income taxes	111,694	1,250,069
Income taxes (Note 10)	45,395	508,054
Income after taxes..................	66,299	742,015
Minority interests in income (loss) after taxes	818	9,151
Income from consolidated operations	65,481	732,864
Equity in earnings of unconsolidated subsidiaries and companies owned 50 percent or less	12,424	139,040
Net income	¥ 77,905	$ 871,904
Per 100 Shares of Common Stock:	**In Yen**	**In U.S. Dollars**
Net income (primary)	¥ 2,313	$ 25.89
Cash dividends	800	8.95

the importance of banks as providers of capital. After World War II, little equity capital existed and the major source of funds for rebuilding the country was government-supported bank loans. Close relationships between banks and companies have evolved to the point where banks seldom impose penalties for late interest payments or call delinquent loans, instead they postpone interest and principal payments. The longer accounts receivable collection period is due to the Japanese tradition of lifetime employment and the willingness of companies to help one another out when times are tough. Customers receive extensions on paying their accounts so they are not put in a financial bind where they might have to reduce the workforce. The survival and stability of the customer in turn allows the supplier to maintain a stable level of production and employment. The smaller profit margin and return on assets results from both the environment and conservative accounting practices. Gross margins are smaller because of the highly competitive export markets in which Japanese companies tend to operate. Japanese managers are not as concerned with short-term profits, partly because of greater job security, and prefer to focus their attention on sales growth and market share rather than net income. The negative impact these environmental factors have on profitability is exacerbated by conservative accounting partly due to the linkage with taxation.

THE HANDLING OF SPECIFIC ACCOUNTING PROBLEMS AROUND THE WORLD

The final section of this chapter examines several specific financial reporting issues from the perspective of individual countries as well as the current international accounting standards. We make no attempt to describe the accounting principles of every nation. Instead, we present a cross-section of countries to indicate the range of possible treatments that have developed throughout the world. These countries are the United Kingdom, France, and Germany in Europe; Japan and Korea in Asia; and Canada, Mexico, and Brazil in the Americas. Each of these countries is a major location of direct foreign investment by U.S. corporations.

Reported Value of Assets

United Kingdom In the United Kingdom, companies are free to choose the method by which they value assets. Although historical cost can serve as the basis, they may report some (or all) accounts at a current value. The method of current valuation depends on the type of asset. They can state intangible assets, tangible fixed assets, inventory, and short-term investments at their current cost. Current cost is the lower of replacement cost or net realizable value. Market value is used for long-term investments and serves as an allowed alternative for tangible fixed assets. If revaluation occurs, any accumulated depreciation is usually eliminated with the reported balance then being adjusted to the new basis. The change in the asset's value creates a "revaluation reserve" that is reported in the capital and reserves section of the balance sheet. Subsequent depreciation is based on the revalued figures. If assets are revalued, companies must indicate what the historical cost profit would have been. Whitbread PLC's calculation of historical cost profit for the year ended February 25, 1995, is as follows:

	£m
Reported profit before taxation	275.4
Realisation of revaluation gains/(deficits)	37.7
Difference between the historical cost depreciation charge and the actual depreciation charge calculated on the revalued amount	(3.6)
Historical cost profit before taxation	309.5

France Although historical cost is the basis for reporting, revaluing property, plant, and equipment as well as inventory to current value has been permitted in France since 1984. If revaluation occurs, it must apply to all applicable assets. To record the change, a separate reserve balance must be established within stockholders' equity. Revaluation tends to be infrequent because increases in value are taxed (although the extra depreciation is subsequently allowed as a tax deduction). The revaluation of intangibles is not permitted. Occasional tax-free revaluations are allowed or required by the government when inflation rates are high. Such revaluations occurred in 1945, 1959, and 1976.

Germany   Accountants use historical cost as the basis for reporting assets. Following a conservative approach, upward revaluations of assets are not allowed but provisions for extraordinary depreciation are required if a permanent impairment of value is anticipated.

Japan   The Japanese approach to reporting assets resembles the procedures used in the United States. Current assets appear at cost unless market value is significantly less and recovery is not expected. Unlike the United States, marketable securities are not allowed to be written up in value. The reporting of fixed assets is based on historical cost unless a permanent impairment of value has occurred.

Korea   Korean companies utilize historical cost. Revaluation to market value is allowed if the Bank of Korea wholesale price index has risen 25 percent or more since the date of an asset's acquisition or previous revaluation. Such adjustments are optional but can be made only on the first day of the business year. A company that records a revaluation through an increase in a capital reserve pays a 3 percent tax.

Canada   Historical cost is capitalized and amortized over the useful life of the asset. Prior to 1990, Canadian companies could write assets up to an appraised value above cost. The procedure was rarely used and now has been eliminated.

Mexico   Inventories and fixed assets are reported initially at historical cost and then restated to current values at the balance sheet date. Public companies must restate these assets to current replacement cost and use that figure for calculating cost of sales and depreciation. Nonpublic companies may restate using replacement cost or a consumer price index.

Brazil   Publicly traded companies must prepare financial statements in units of constant purchasing power. They adjust inventories, investments, and fixed assets upward for inflation on each balance sheet date and discount receivables to their present value. They base the cost of goods sold and depreciation on the inflation-adjusted values of assets. Nonpublic companies are not allowed to restate inventories.

International Accounting Standards   Under IAS 16, the benchmark treatment for property, plant, and equipment is to report it at historical cost less accumulated depreciation. The allowed alternative treatment is to revalue property, plant, and equipment at its fair value. If assets are revalued, an entire class must be adjusted or some systematic approach must be applied; assets cannot be revalued selectively. Any reduction in value is recorded as a decrease in net income, whereas an increase creates a revaluation surplus to be shown within the shareholders' equity section of the balance sheet.

Business Combinations and Consolidation Accounting

United Kingdom   All subsidiaries are consolidated unless (1) control is only temporary, (2) restrictions hinder the parent's ability to exercise its rights, or (3) the subsidiary's activities are so dissimilar that consolidation would be misleading. Rules for pooling of interests or merger accounting are more lenient in the United Kingdom than in the United States. A company that makes an offer for all outstanding shares and obtains at least 90 percent can use pooling of interests accounting. Otherwise, the combination is a purchase or acquisition.

France   Consolidation of financial statements has been required only since 1986, although voluntary preparation has been common for some time. Purchase accounting in France is similar to that used in the United States; however, control is assumed if 40 percent or more of a company's voting stock is held and no other stockholder owns more. The pooling of interests method is not considered acceptable. A subsidiary need not be consolidated if restrictions hinder the parent's control, the shares are held for resale, or the subsidiary's operations are so dissimilar to those of the parent that consolidated statements would be misleading. In addition, subsidiaries not significant in relation to the group as a whole and subsidiaries whose financial statements are not produced in time for inclusion in the consolidated accounts are accounted for by the cost method.

Germany   Historically, large companies (defined by size of assets, sales, and employees) had to consolidate all domestic subsidiaries but could omit foreign ones. Beginning in 1990, the size limit was reduced significantly for preparing consolidated statements. In addition, after that date, all foreign subsidiaries had to be included in the consolidated figures. The purchase method predominates, but the pooling of interests method may be used if 90 percent of a subsidiary's voting stock is exchanged for new shares of the parent. However, income figures are not consolidated retroactively when this method is applied. Reasons for excluding a subsidiary from consolidation are similar to those in France.

Japan   Acquisition and mergers are so rare in Japan that consolidation accounting has not been well developed. As a result, until 1992, firms produced parent company statements rather than consolidated statements. Mergers are accomplished through an exchange of stocks and are usually recorded by the pooling of interests method. However, if one company is clearly in a subsidiary position, purchase accounting is used. For a pooling, income statement figures are not combined retroactively as is the practice in the United States.

Korea   Unaudited consolidated statements are supplements to the parent company statements. On its own statements, the parent records all subsidiaries using the cost method. In preparing consolidated statements, companies use the purchase method unless any relevant regulation requires the pooling of interests method.

Canada   Use of the pooling of interests method is very rare in Canada; it is only considered appropriate if the acquiring party cannot be identified. The purchase method applies to all other business combinations. Consolidation is required unless control of a subsidiary is seriously impaired, control is temporary, or the activities of the subsidiary are considered to be dissimilar to that of the remainder of the combination.

Mexico   All subsidiaries that are more than 50 percent controlled must be consolidated unless the subsidiary is bankrupt or, for foreign subsidiaries, foreign exchange controls limit the payment of dividends to the parent. In addition, a company that is 50 percent or less owned can be considered a subsidiary if the parent exercises control. Only the purchase method is appropriate.

Brazil   Companies must prepare consolidated financial statements if their subsidiaries make up more than 30 percent of total equity. Controlled subsidiaries must be consolidated unless control is temporary, the subsidiary is bankrupt, or the subsidiary's operations are dissimilar to those of the parent. Control is assumed to exist when more than 50 percent of voting shares are owned, either directly or indirectly.

International Accounting Standards   IAS 22 requires use of the purchase method for a business combination except in the rare case of a uniting of interests when an acquirer cannot be identified. In that situation, the pooling of interests method is appropriate. According to IAS 27, all subsidiaries, both foreign and domestic, should be consolidated unless control is temporary because the subsidiary is to be disposed of in the near future or severe long-term restrictions impair control.

Accounting for Goodwill

United Kingdom   Certainly one of the most controversial accounting rules in the United Kingdom is the handling of purchased goodwill. Although the amount is computed in the same manner as in the United States, goodwill traditionally has been written off immediately against an equity reserve. This can have a significant impact on the amount of stockholders' equity reported in the balance sheet as demonstrated in Exhibit 11–1 where Glaxo Wellcome, a company with total reported assets of £8,541 million, reports shareholders' funds of only £91 million. U.K. accounting rules allow the company to record goodwill as an asset and then amortize the cost over up to 40 years. However, this treatment does not appear to be widely used.

France   Firms capitalize goodwill and amortize it as an expense generally over 5 to 20 years although French law does not specify a maximum amortization period.

Germany   Goodwill may be capitalized as an asset and amortized over five years (including the year of acquisition) or the period expected to be benefited. For tax purposes, a life of 15 years is used. Alternatively, goodwill may be written off immediately to an equity account.

Japan   Computation of goodwill is similar to that in the United States. Accountants charge the amount of goodwill directly to income if the amount is not considered significant. If capitalized, goodwill is amortized over up to five years unless some other period of time can be justified.

Korea   Reported on the balance sheet as an intangible asset, goodwill is amortized to income over a five-year period. To the extent that the excess of purchase price over fair market value of acquired net assets does not represent goodwill it should be recorded as an expense immediately.

Canada   The treatment of positive goodwill is similar to that used in the United States, but negative goodwill is not recognized.

Mexico   Goodwill is recognized as an asset and amortized over a reasonable period not exceeding 20 years. Similar to Korea, any excess of purchase price that cannot be considered to be goodwill should be expensed immediately.

Brazil   The excess of cost over fair market value of net assets is recognized as an asset—goodwill. Unlike other countries, in Brazil the cost of goodwill must be divided into that portion attributable to unrecorded intangible assets, such as customer lists, and that portion attributable to future profitability. Firms account for and amortize the two components of goodwill separately over appropriate time periods. They amortize that portion attributable to future profitability over the time horizon used in making future profit projections and the portion attributable to intangible assets over the expected period of use.

International Accounting Standards   The recent revision to IAS 22 now requires that goodwill be recognized as an asset and amortized on a straight-line basis over its useful life. The amortization period should not exceed five years, unless a longer period can be justified; then the amortization period should not exceed 20 years. The previous option of an immediate write off to equity is no longer acceptable.

Translation of Foreign Currency Financial Statements

United Kingdom   Companies normally use the current rate method with translation adjustments taken to reserves. Income items may be translated using either the average rate or the current rate at the balance sheet date. If the business activities of the foreign operation are closely aligned with those of the parent, the temporal method is used with a translation gain or loss reported in income. Although the concept of a functional currency is not formally used, British translation rules are very similar to those in the United States. The major difference is the optional use of the current rate for translating income when using the current rate method. Another deviation is the recommendation that financial statements of subsidiaries in hyperinflationary countries be restated for inflation and then translated using the current rate method.

France   French accounting rules specify no particular translation method. Majority practice is to use the current rate method, using the average exchange rate to translate income items, with translation adjustments taken to equity.

Germany   As in France, the Commercial Code specifies no method. Moreover, there appears to be no prevalent practice. Accountants use a variety of methods and deal with translation adjustments in different ways. One conservative variation is to report negative translation adjustments in income and positive translation adjustments in stockholders' equity.

Japan   Japanese translation rules are much different from those in the United States. These rules stipulate assets carried at historical cost, noncurrent liabilities, and equity accounts must be translated at historical rates. Assets carried at current value and current liabilities are translated at current rates. Revenues and expenses are translated at average rates except for expenses related to assets carried at historical cost that are translated at historical rates. Translation adjustments are reported as assets (negative) or liabilities (positive) in the consolidated balance sheet. Actual compliance with these rules is limited.

Korea   Firms use the current rate method to translate the financial statements of foreign subsidiaries. They use average exchange rates to translate income.

Canada   Translation rules in Canada are very similar to those in the United States. The major difference is that when the temporal method is used, the translation adjustment related to long-term monetary items may be deferred and amortized to income over the life of the item.

Mexico   No regulations pertain to the translation of foreign currency financial statements. Many companies follow the U.S. rule, *SFAS 52;* where this rule is not followed, practice varies considerably.

Brazil   Firms use the current rate method and recognize translation gains and losses in the income statement.

International Accounting Standards.   Foreign subsidiaries fall into two classes: those that are an integral part of the parent's operations (foreign operations) and those that are self-sustaining (foreign entities). Whether a subsidiary is a foreign operation or a foreign entity is determined by the currency in which the subsidiary makes sales, incurs expenses, and obtains finance, as well as whether the subsidiary is relatively autonomous or has few transactions with the parent. Foreign entities should use the current rate method with income statement items translated at the actual or average exchange rate. Firms should adjust the financial statements of foreign entities in hyperinflationary environments for inflation prior to translation, and use the current rate for translating the income statement. For foreign operations, they should use the temporal method with translation gains and losses reported in income.

Inventory Valuation

United Kingdom Inventory is carried at the lower of cost or net realizable value. FIFO, average cost, or any similar cost flow assumption may be used. LIFO is not acceptable for tax purposes, and therefore, its application is rare.

France Inventory is carried at the lower of cost or either realizable value or replacement cost. FIFO and averaging are the only methods allowed for statutory reporting purposes. LIFO is allowed for consolidated financial statements.

Germany Inventory is carried at the lower of cost or market, where market is replacement cost for materials and net realizable value for work in process and finished goods. Specific identification is preferred; however, if not possible, the moving average method is recommended. FIFO and LIFO also are allowed.

Japan Inventory is reported at the lower of cost or market. Market value is usually the repurchase price. FIFO, LIFO, average cost, specific identification, and latest purchase price are all acceptable costing methods.

Korea Firms value inventories at the lower of cost or market. Specific identification, FIFO, LIFO, average cost, or a retail pricing method are all acceptable for determining cost. Market value is based on a price survey index published by a reputable price survey institute, or net realizable value if an index is not available.

Canada Inventory is carried at the lower of cost or market. Market value can be determined by any appropriate method. FIFO, LIFO, and averaging are all acceptable by Canadian accounting standards. The reporting entity selects the method that provides the fairest matching of costs. As in the United Kingdom, LIFO is not accepted for tax purposes so its use is limited.

Mexico Inventory is reported on the balance sheet at the lower of restated value and realizable value. LIFO, FIFO, average cost, specific identification, and last purchase price are all acceptable methods.

Brazil FIFO, LIFO, average cost, and specific identification are all acceptable cost flow assumptions. Because it is not acceptable for tax purposes, LIFO is rarely used. Inventories are reported at the lower of cost or market (lower of inflation-adjusted cost or market for public companies). Market is defined differently for various types of inventory—replacement cost for materials and net realizable value for work in process and finished goods.

International Accounting Standards IAS 2 (as revised in 1993) recommends that inventories be carried at the lower of cost or net realizable value. Specific identification should be used for items that are not ordinarily interchangeable. For other items, the benchmark treatment is either FIFO or weighted average cost. However, LIFO is also sanctioned as an allowed alternative treatment.

Reporting Accounting Changes

United Kingdom   Changes are permitted only if the new method can be justified as preferable; these changes are handled retroactively. Thus, no cumulative effect of an accounting change is included in the current year's figures. Instead, firms adjust past balances to reflect the impact of the change in method.

France   Generally, a company recognizes the cumulative effect of a change in current income as an exceptional item. When the accounting change is mandated by a change in statutory requirements, however, it treats the effect as a prior period adjustment with adjustments being made to opening balances.

Germany   Changes in general measurement and valuation principles are allowed only in justifiable, exceptional situations. An exception to this is an accounting change made to realize income tax savings; to qualify for tax purposes, the change also must be reflected in the financial statements. The cumulative effect of an accounting change is reported in current income. Retroactive restatement is not allowed. The extent to which income was affected by accounting changes made solely for tax savings also must be disclosed.

Japan   In Japan, accounting changes are not made except for good reason and tend to be rare. When made, a retroactive restatement is not allowed and the cumulative effect is not recognized. The effect of the change is limited to the change in the current year's income from applying the new principle.

Korea   Changes in accounting principles are applied prospectively so that neither a retroactive restatement nor a cumulative effect adjustment is needed. Such changes can be made only if they make the statements more reliable or if they are mandated by a new accounting principle.

Canada   Accounting for a change in method is retroactive and, thus, similar to the approach used in the United Kingdom. Current recognition is appropriate, though, if necessary data cannot be gathered for restatement purposes. In contrast to the United Kingdom, a new method does not have to be preferable; changes are allowed as long as the method being adopted is a generally accepted accounting principle.

Mexico   Similar to Japan and Korea, the effect of an accounting change is recognized prospectively beginning with the current year's income.

Brazil   Accounting changes are allowed and need not be justified as being preferable to the previous principle used. The cumulative effect of an accounting change is handled as a prior period adjustment by adjusting the opening balance in retained earnings.

International Accounting Standards   IAS 8 (as revised in 1993) indicates that accounting changes should be made only if required by law or by an accounting standard setting body or if the change would result in a more appropriate presentation of financial information. Firms should apply the change retrospectively with the cumulative effect of the change treated as an adjustment to the opening balance in retained earnings. As an allowed alternative, they may include the cumulative effect in the calculation of the current period's income. Comparative information should be restated unless this is impracticable. If the amount of the adjustment to the beginning balance in retained earnings cannot be reasonably determined, firms should apply the accounting change prospectively.

Which Accounting Method Really Is Appropriate?

In this era of rapidly changing technology, research and development expenditures are one of the most important factors in the future success of many companies. Organizations that spend too little on R&D risk being left behind by the competition. Conversely, companies that spend too much may waste money or not be able to make efficient use of the results.

In the United States, all research and development expenditures are expensed as incurred. Germany and Mexico use this same treatment. However, expensing all research and development costs is not an approach used in much of the world. Firms in the United Kingdom can capitalize development costs if a clearly defined project exists, the expenditure is separately identifiable, future revenues are expected to be greater than the capitalized cost, the company has the ability to complete the project, and the outcome has been assessed with reasonable certainty. Similarly, Canadian companies must capitalize development costs when certain criteria are met. Japanese accounting allows both research and development costs to be capitalized if the research is directed toward new goods or techniques, development of markets, or exploitation of resources. Korean businesses capitalize their research and development costs when they are incurred in relation to a specific product or technology, when costs can be separately identified, and when the recovery of costs is reasonably expected. France and Brazil also allow research and development costs to be capitalized under certain conditions.

Should any portion of research and development costs be capitalized? Is the expensing of all research and development expenditures the best method of reporting these vital costs? Is the U.S. system necessarily the best approach? Which approach provides the best representation of the company's activities?

Other Accounting Issues

Lease Capitalization There is no consensus among the eight countries regarding the capitalization of leases. The United Kingdom, Korea, Canada, and Mexico require capitalization when specified criteria are met. This is also the treatment required in IAS 17. In contrast, all leases are accounted for as operating leases in Japan and Brazil. In France, only operating lease accounting is allowed in the statutory accounts; lease capitalization is optional for consolidated financial statements. Lease accounting in Germany depends on complex tax rules.

Long-Term Contracts IAS 11 (revised in 1993) requires use of the percentage of completion method for long-term construction contracts when certain criteria are met. Similar procedures are followed in the United Kingdom, Canada, Mexico, and Brazil. In France, Japan, and Korea, firms may use the percentage of completion method when criteria are met, but the method is not required. Although not specifically disallowed, the percentage of completion method is almost never used in Germany.

Interest Capitalization The benchmark treatment recognized in IAS 23 is that all interest should be expensed immediately. Capitalization of interest directly attributable to the acquisition, construction, or production of a qualifying asset is an allowed alternative treatment. Brazil and Japan follow the benchmark treatment, requiring all interest to be expensed. The other countries allow for interest capitalization with the method and conditions under which interest may be capitalized varying from country to country.

Income Taxes The international standard (IAS 12) allows use of either the deferred or liability method in accounting for differences between accounting and taxable income (deferred income taxes). Companies in France may choose between these two methods. The deferred method is preferred in Canada, whereas the liability method is used in the United Kingdom, Germany, Mexico, and Brazil. Deferred taxes are not recognized in Japan or Korea.

Investments in Associates   IAS 28 requires the use of the equity method for accounting for investments in associated companies. An associate is an enterprise in which the investor has significant influence. Significant influence is presumed when the investor holds, directly or indirectly, 20 percent or more of the voting power of the investee. Similar rules exist in each of the eight countries under examination. The only exceptions are that, in Mexico, significant influence is presumed on 10 percent ownership and, in Brazil, the equity method must be used with only 10 percent ownership if administrative influence exists.

SUMMARY

1. The world is rapidly developing a global economy with numerous multinational corporations. U.S. companies are expanding into other countries while foreign investors are acquiring businesses in the United States. Thus, a knowledge of the accounting principles applied throughout the world is necessary to be an efficient decision maker, especially when dealing with international capital markets. The wide diversity of these accounting principles can make the understanding of reported financial information as well as the comparison of companies a difficult task.

2. Accounting rules differ significantly across countries partially because of environmental factors such as the type of legal system followed in the country, the importance of equity as a source of capital, and the extent to which accounting statements serve as the basis for taxation. The two major classes of accounting systems in the world are the macro-uniform and the micro-based classes. Each class is comprised of several families, the largest of which is heavily influenced by accounting development in the United Kingdom.

3. The International Accounting Standards Committee was formed in 1973 to develop a set of accounting principles universally applicable in all countries. The IASC includes more than 100 member organizations from around the world and had produced 32 International Accounting Standards by January 1997. As a private organization, the IASC cannot legally enforce these pronouncements. Instead, member organizations pledge to work toward adoption of these standards in their respective countries. The IASC has recently revised several existing standards as a part of its comparability project. This effort is endorsed by the International Organization of Securities Commissions, and several major multinational companies have adopted IASs in preparing their financial statements.

4. The accounting standards in Japan, Germany, and other macro-uniform countries are based on government regulation and are quite conservative. Financial institutions and tax authorities are considered the primary users of published financial data. In the United Kingdom, a micro-based country, individual investors are the main users of statements. Accounting standards are set by the accounting profession and measurement rules are less conservative. The financial statements of each of these countries exhibit a number of unique characteristics when viewed from the perspective of a U.S. company. For example, the profit and loss statement in Japan labels a wide variety of transactions as extraordinary (or special). In both Germany and the United Kingdom, the balance sheet begins with fixed assets.

5. Accounting principles throughout the world often differ from those applied in the United States. For example, although the recording of assets such as inventory, land, buildings, and equipment is based on historical cost in the United States, some countries allow companies to adjust these balances to higher values. This procedure can be carried out using inflation indices (as in Brazil) or by determining current values (as in the United Kingdom). In addition, goodwill resulting from the purchase of another company may be charged to stockholders' equity (as in the United Kingdom) or written off over a period as short as 5 years (Germany) or as long as 40 years (the United States). Other areas in which significant differences exist include use of the pooling of interests method, translation of foreign currency financial statements, accounting changes, lease accounting, interest capitalization, and accounting for investments in associates.

COMPREHENSIVE ILLUSTRATION

Problem

(Estimated Time: 20 to 30 minutes)

Part A

A company is preparing financial statements for the year ending December 31, 1997. To arrive at final figures, the company must account for goodwill of $1 million resulting from the acquisition of a subsidiary on January 1. The company wants to report the minimum amount of expense each year and can justify an almost unlimited life for the intangible benefits of the business combination from which the goodwill was derived.

What expense should be reported if the company is preparing statements under the accounting rules and principles of each of the following:

United Kingdom.

France.

Germany.

Japan.

Canada.

United States.

International Accounting Standards Committee.

Part B

A company plans to switch from one accounting principle to another at the beginning of 1998 and can justify this decision. Application of the new method would have increased net income in past years by $300,000 while raising net income in 1998 by $100,000.

What is the impact on current net income if the company is preparing statements under the accounting rules and principles of each of the following:

United Kingdom.

France.

Korea.

Canada.

Mexico.

United States.

International Accounting Standards Committee.

Part C

A company owns a piece of land that cost $400,000 when acquired in 1987. At the end of 1997, the land has a fair market value of $760,000, and during the period 1987–1997 prices have increased in general due to inflation by 150 percent.

What figure should be reported for this asset if the company is preparing statements under the accounting rules and principles of each of the following:

United Kingdom.

France.

Germany.

Japan.

Korea.

Canada.

Brazil.

United States.

International Accounting Standards Committee.

Solution

Part A

United Kingdom   Goodwill can be written off directly to stockholders' equity so that expense recognition is not necessary. This approach is popular because no expense is recorded. Thus, a maximum amount of net income is always reported.

France Firms use a 5- to 20-year period as the life for goodwill. Since the minimum expense is desired, a 20-year period would be chosen to arrive at an expense of $50,000 each year.

Germany As in the United Kingdom, goodwill may be written off directly to stockholders' equity with no impact on income. If this option is elected, no expense would be reported in 1997 or subsequent years.

Japan A five-year period is the normal amortization when this intangible asset is encountered. Thus, an expense of $200,000 is appropriate for 1997. A longer life may be used but only if that period of time can be justified.

Canada A period of up to 40 years can be used for amortization purposes so that the minimum expense for 1997 is $25,000.

United States As with Canada, a 40-year period is maximum. In this example, the expense to be recognized over that period is $25,000 per year.

International Accounting Standards The IASC recommends a five-year amortization period that, if justified, can be extended to 20 years. The minimum amount of amortization expense would be $50,000.

Part B

United Kingdom In reporting this change in accounting principle, previous years' income and the beginning balance in retained earnings would be increased by $300,000 while current income would rise by $100,000. Retroactive adjustment is utilized in the United Kingdom for accounting changes.

France In addition to the increase in 1998 income of $100,000, an exceptional gain of $300,000 also would be reported in 1998; the total impact would be $400,000.

Korea The effect on the prior years would be left as is. Proper accounting would be limited to the effect on the current year; this change would increase 1998 net income by $100,000.

Canada As with the United Kingdom, the impact on past years would not affect the 1998 income. A $300,000 retroactive restatement is made to adjust all historical figures to the newly selected method. For 1998, only the $100,000 increase in net income is recognized.

Mexico The entire $400,000 impact is recorded within the current period. For legal reasons, a retroactive change in the reported figures for the past years is not allowed.

United States For most accounting changes, firms would adjust the affected income account (or accounts) for the $100,000 so that no special treatment is required in the current operating figures. However, the $300,000 increase in past years' income is shown, net of taxes, at the bottom of the current income statement as a cumulative effect of an accounting change. Thus, similar to France and Mexico, the entire $400,000 is reported in current income. A few changes, such as a switch from LIFO, are handled through retroactive restatement rather than by the calculation and reporting of a cumulative effect.

International Accounting Standards Accounting changes are allowed if required by official or legal accounting pronouncements or to achieve a more appropriate presentation. The effect on the current year ($100,000) and on past years ($300,000) must be calculated and disclosed. The preferred treatment is to adjust the beginning balance of retained earnings by $300,000; alternatively, reporting the $300,000 retroactive adjustment in current income also is allowed.

Part C

United Kingdom The reporting entity has the option of using either the $400,000 historical cost to report the land or adjusting this asset to its $760,000 market value.

France   The $400,000 historical cost would be the basis for reporting; however, the company is allowed to adjust the value upward to $760,000 if all applicable assets are revalued. Since this increment is taxable, companies rarely avail themselves of the opportunity for such increases. When inflation is severe, the government also may allow (or mandate) a tax-free write-up to fair market value.

Germany   In the conservative German system, the $400,000 historical cost would be retained.

Japan   In Japan, the historical cost of $400,000 would be utilized unless a permanent impairment of value had occurred.

Korea   Historical cost is used unless the effects of inflation have been extreme. If the inflation rate since acquisition (as measured by the Bank of Korea wholesale price index) has been 25 percent or more, an adjustment to fair market value is allowed, although not required.

Canada   Historical cost figures of $400,000 are retained.

Brazil   Because of the high inflation rate, the historical cost of $400,000 is restated using a government inflation index. Assuming 150 percent inflation, the new figure is $600,000.

United States   The historical cost of $400,000 is appropriate for U.S. companies. Any permanent impairment of value requires a downward adjustment.

International Accounting Standards   The benchmark treatment is historical cost of $400,000. As an alternative, the asset may be written up to the fair value of $760,000. The increase in value would be reflected in a reserve account in stockholders' equity.

QUESTIONS

1. Why would the knowledge of accounting principles used throughout the world be important to a businessperson in the United States?
2. Since a multitude of different sets of accounting principles exist in the world, which sets of principles are applicable to a particular company?
3. Why have international accounting standards been developed?
4. Why has the ability to make comparisons between companies in different countries become important in recent years?
5. What factors contribute to the diversity of accounting principles worldwide?
6. What are the major classes of accounting systems used throughout the world? What are the major influences on these different accounting systems?
7. What major accounting families comprise the macro-uniform class of accounting system? What families make up the micro-based class?
8. What arguments can be made in favor of international harmonization? What arguments can be made against it?
9. What are the Fourth and Seventh Directives?
10. What groups compose the membership of the International Accounting Standards Committee?
11. What are the goals of the IASC?
12. Why is the IASC not able to enforce the accounting standards that it issues?
13. Over the years, how has the IASC attempted to gain acceptance of the international standards that it has produced?
14. What problems has the IASC encountered in trying to gain acceptance for the international standards that have been issued?
15. How do the work of the IASC and the harmonization efforts of the European Union differ?
16. Why were several of the original standards issued by the IASC revised in 1993?
17. Why has interest in international accounting standards increased in recent years?

18. What impact would the acceptance of international accounting standards by the regulators of the global capital markets have?

19. What is the basis for the accounting principles used in the United Kingdom, Japan, and Germany?

20. How does a balance sheet prepared for a U.K. company differ from that produced by a U.S. company?

21. Why is the net income figure computed by a German company often assumed to be understated?

22. How does an income statement produced by a Japanese company differ from that produced by a U.S. company?

23. In the United States, historical cost is the basis for valuing assets, especially inventory, land, buildings, and equipment. What other valuation methods are utilized in countries around the world?

24. How is the pooling of interests method applied in countries around the world?

25. How do companies in the United Kingdom usually account for goodwill? Why is this approach considered controversial?

26. How are the financial statements of foreign subsidiaries translated in different countries around the world?

27. How are research and development costs recorded around the world?

LIBRARY ASSIGNMENTS

1. Obtain the financial statements for a foreign company such as Volkswagen (Germany), Michelin (France), Grand Metropolitan (UK), Nestlé (Switzerland), Toyota (Japan), Electrolux (Sweden), or The News Corporation (Australia). List five major differences between the statements of a foreign company and the statements of a U.S. corporation.

2. Read the following articles and any other published information concerning international accounting standards and the IASC:

    "International Accounting Standards: Are They Coming to America?" *CPA Journal*, October 1992.

    "The International Harmonization of Accounting: In Search of Influence," *International Journal of Accounting* 27, no. 3, 1992.

    "The Growing Importance of International Accounting Standards," *Journal of Accountancy*, September 1991.

    "Is GAAP the Gap to International Markets?" *Management Accounting*, August 1990.

    "Commentary—Internationalization of Accounting Standards," *Accounting Horizons*, March 1990.

    "International Accounting Standards: A New Perspective," *Accounting Horizons*, September 1989.

    "The Move to Globalization," *Journal of Accountancy*, March 1989.

    "Calling All National Standards Setters," *Accountancy*, February 1988.

    "An Appraisal of the International Accounting Standards Committee," *CPA Journal*, May 1986.

    Write a report describing the activities of the International Accounting Standards Committee to date and discussing this group's chances of future success, especially in the United States.

PROBLEMS

1. Which of the following is not a reason for establishing international accounting standards?
    a. Some countries do not have the resources to develop accounting standards on their own.
    b. Comparability is needed between companies operating in different areas of the world.

      c. Some of the accounting principles allowed in various countries report markedly different results for similar transactions.

      d. Demand in the United States is heavy for an alternative to U.S. generally accepted accounting principles.

2. The International Accounting Standards Committee (IASC) was formed by representatives of several different

      a. Government agencies.

      b. Accountancy bodies.

      c. Legislative organizations.

      d. Academic organizations.

3. The goal of the IASC is to

      a. Formulate and publish accounting standards as well as harmonize accounting standards.

      b. Establish a quality review process for all international financial statements.

      c. Promote adequate reporting disclosure so that unique accounting standards can continue to be employed around the world.

      d. Require that all financial standards be consistent with the standards used in the United States because of its central role in the capital markets of the world.

4. Why does the IASC currently have only limited powers?

      a. The IASC is a private organization and, thus, cannot enforce the use of its official pronouncements.

      b. The IASC has always refused to mandate that its pronouncements must be followed.

      c. International capital markets establish and use their own accounting principles that must be followed in all cases.

      d. The IASC is a new organization that has not yet had time to exert significant influence in the world of accounting.

5. How does the macro-uniform class differ from the micro-based class of accounting system?

      a. The micro-based class is more heavily influenced by taxation.

      b. In the macro-uniform class, accounting rules tend to be set by the government.

      c. The macro-uniform class consists primarily of countries in the U.S.-influence and U.K.-influence accounting families.

      d. The micro-based class provides lower levels of disclosure in financial statements than the macro-uniform class.

6. The IASC

      a. Held its first meeting in 1911.

      b. Is composed of representatives of various governmental accounting bodies.

      c. Began with 84 member organizations.

      d. Was formed in 1973.

7. Which of the following countries is not in the micro-based class of accounting systems?

      a. Hong Kong.

      b. Spain.

      c. Australia.

      d. Canada.

8. According to critics, what is the major problem with the original standards produced by the IASC?

      a. Too many popular methods have been eliminated.

      b. Too many optional methods have remained.

      c. The IASC has failed to examine and report on key accounting issues.

      d. The pronouncements tend to be too similar to U.S. GAAP.

9. Why would some German companies probably prefer to follow the accounting standards of the IASC?

      a. German accounting principles are extremely complicated so that appropriate financial statements can be difficult to produce.

      b. The Germans have tended to follow U.S. generally accepted accounting principles rather than develop their own accounting principles.

      c. The use of IASC standards allows German companies to be more fairly compared with companies from other countries.

      d. The Germans have virtually no accounting principles so that comparison between companies within the country is virtually impossible.

10. Why have international accounting principles become a topic of special interest in recent times?

    a. The development of international capital markets and the continued consolidation of the European Community have created a need for comparable information from companies located around the world.

    b. The Financial Accounting Standards Board recently has asked the IASC to develop solutions to several specific accounting issues, including earnings per share.

    c. Most multinational companies have switched to international accounting standards rather than continuing to use national standards.

    d. A number of IASC pronouncements have forced the FASB to change several significant American accounting principles.

11. What attempt has been made by the IASC to gain greater acceptance of international accounting standards?

    a. Rules are being mandated now for individual countries.

    b. An attempt is being made to provide more flexibility within the international standards.

    c. The IASC is developing a new system of accounting principles to be applied according to the size of the organization.

    d. Optional methods have been eliminated.

12. Japanese accounting principles are

    a. Promulgated by the Japanese Institute of Certified Public Accountants.

    b. Established by the government.

    c. Quite liberal in nature.

    d. Similar in most respects to international accounting standards.

13. In Japan, extraordinary items are

    a. Never reported.

    b. More limited than in the United States.

    c. Items not necessarily considered extraordinary in the United States.

    d. Unusual and infrequent.

14. In the United Kingdom, a balance sheet

    a. Begins with fixed assets and then reports current assets less current liabilities.

    b. Is not required except for companies of a specific size.

    c. Begins with stockholders' equity.

    d. Is similar to a balance sheet that would be produced by a U.S. company.

15. In the United Kingdom, one encounters Stocks and Debtors accounts. What do these balances represent?

	Stocks	Debtors
a.	Investments	Minority interest
b.	Treasury stock	Notes payable
c.	Capital stock	Notes receivable
d.	Inventory	Receivables

16. In the financial reporting utilized in the United Kingdom, to what does the term *turnover* refer?

    a. Net sales.

    b. Age of inventory.

    c. Length of time needed to collect accounts receivable.

    d. Profit as a percentage of net assets.

17. In German accounting, hidden reserves are

    a. Assets invested for specified future use.

    b. Created to be able to smooth income from one period to the next.

    c. Equity balances used to record adjustments not included in computing net income.

    d. Annual adjustments to net income caused by the effects of inflation.

18. Which of the following does *not* help to explain why Japanese profitability ratios are lower than in the United States?

    a. Japanese companies are not as concerned about generating profit.

    b. Japanese accounting rules are more conservative.

    c. Japanese companies tend to borrow short term to finance asset acquisitions.

    d. Japanese companies rely more heavily on debt than on equity financing.

19. How do Japanese and United Kingdom accounting principles differ in the valuation of assets?
    a. In the United Kingdom, all assets are based on historical cost, while in Japan market value is always used.
    b. Both countries revalue assets. In the United Kingdom, current cost is required, while in Japan market value is appropriate.
    c. In the United Kingdom, revaluation is permitted but in Japan historical cost is appropriate unless a permanent impairment of value has occurred.
    d. In the United Kingdom, assets always are recorded at net present value, whereas in Japan current cost must be used.

20. Which of the following is a major influence on German financial reporting?
    a. Financial analysts and investors in equity securities.
    b. The Securities Transactions Committee.
    c. German banks because they provide a major portion of the financial capital.
    d. The International Accounting Standards Committee.

21. Which of the following is true for the German type-of-cost format income statement?
    a. All income items other than revenues from the sale of inventory are labeled as extraordinary gains and losses.
    b. Changes in inventory levels are reported as adjustments to sales.
    c. Cost of goods sold is shown prior to revenues.
    d. Income taxes are not viewed as expenses.

22. Why is the revaluation of assets rare in France?
    a. Inflation is low.
    b. Revaluation gains are taxed by the government.
    c. Revaluations can be made only with specific types of objective proof.
    d. Accounting principles are extremely conservative in France.

23. What basis is used for valuing assets in Brazil?
    a. Historical cost.
    b. Lower of cost or market.
    c. Current market value.
    d. Historical cost adjusted for general inflation.

24. In Mexico, business combinations usually are reported through:
    a. Consolidated statements including only domestic companies.
    b. Consolidated statements including subsidiaries in which more than 50 percent of the voting stock is held.
    c. Consolidated statements using the pooling of interests method only.
    d. Parent company statements only.

25. Goodwill
    a. Can be amortized over a 50-year period in Germany.
    b. Can be written off directly to stockholders' equity in the United Kingdom.
    c. Is accounted for in the same manner in Japan as in the United States.
    d. Is expensed immediately in Canada.

26. LIFO
    a. Is a preferred method according to international accounting standards.
    b. Is required in Japan.
    c. Is an allowed method in Canada.
    d. Is the predominant method used in the United Kingdom because of the rate of inflation.

27. In reporting research and development costs:
    a. Most countries capitalize research costs but expense development costs when incurred.
    b. Some countries capitalize some portion of development costs.
    c. Usually only one approach is found throughout the world.
    d. Most countries record all research and development costs as expenses when incurred.

28. Answer the following questions about the IASC:
    a. What factors have tended to prevent the acceptance of the IASC's international accounting standards?
    b. What is the present composition of the IASC?

c. What are the goals of the IASC?

d. What was the IASC's comparability project? What was its objective? What is the outcome of the project?

e. What evidence is there that IASC standards are becoming acceptable around the world?

29. A multinational company is planning to raise a significant amount of capital funds by issuing stocks and bonds in the United States, the United Kingdom, Japan, and France. What impact might the IASC's international accounting standards have on the reporting of this company?

30. A financial advisor is investigating two companies as possible investment recommendations. One of the companies is headquartered in Japan while the other operates in the United Kingdom. In comparing the financial statements of these two organizations, what aspects of the national accounting principles (and business practices) should the investor consider?

31. A German company reports a net income figure that is to be compared with that of a counterpart company in the United States. What factors should be considered in making this evaluation?

32. Chapter 11, as well as several previous chapters, describes a number of techniques used to account for goodwill. List the possible methods for reporting and amortizing this intangible asset. Which method actually provides the fairest presentation of the consolidated company's financial operations and position?

33. In what situations do the countries of the world allow some portion of research and development expenditures to be capitalized?

34. Compare and contrast a balance sheet produced by a German company with a balance sheet developed by a British company.

35. Compare and contrast an income statement prepared by a Germany company with an income statement prepared by a Japanese company.

C H A P T E R

Reporting Disaggregated Information

12

QUESTIONS TO CONSIDER

- The consolidation process brings together the many, varied components of a business combination to form a single set of financial statements. How can a reader of such statements evaluate the results and prospects of the individual segments that make up the organization?

- How are the operating segments of a company identified, and how is the significance of each of these units determined?

- What information must a company disclose in its financial statements about its various operating segments?

- What information must a company disclose about its products and services, and about its operations in foreign countries?

- What guidance has the FASB provided to reporting entities concerning disclosure of major customers?

As one of the largest industrial firms in the United States, Philip Morris Companies Inc. reported consolidated operating revenues of $69.2 billion in 1996.[1] Philip Morris is well-known as a cigarette manufacturer; it is less well-known as a maker of beer and food products. How much of the company's consolidated revenues was generated from these different lines of business? Knowing this could be very useful to potential investors as opportunities for future growth and profitability in these different industries could differ significantly.

To comply with U.S. GAAP, Philip Morris disaggregated its 1996 consolidated operating revenues and reported that the company's revenues were generated from these different ventures: approximately $36.5 billion came from tobacco, $27.9 billion from food, $4.3 billion from beer, and $378 million from financial services and real estate. Additional information disclosed by Philip Morris indicated that $38.5 billion of the 1996 consolidated operating revenues were generated in the United States, $24.2 billion in Europe, and $6.5 billion in other parts of the world.[2] Such information, describing the various components of Philip Morris' operations (both by line of business and by geographic area), often can be more useful to an analyst than the single sales figure reported in the consolidated income statement. "All investors like segment reporting—separate financials for each division—because it enables them to analyze how well each part of a corporation is doing."[3] This chapter examines the specific requirements for disaggregating financial statement information required by the

---

[1]Philip Morris Companies Inc., 1996 Annual Report, p. 34.
[2]Philip Morris Companies Inc., 1996 Annual Report, p. 41.
[3]Robert A. Parker, "How Do You Play the New Annual Report Game?"*Communication World*, September 1990, p. 26.

FASB. New rules for reporting segment information were approved in 1997. Before examining those rules, we trace the history of segment reporting in the United States to better explain the importance of disaggregated information for financial analysts.

DISAGGREGATED INFORMATION—HISTORICAL PERSPECTIVE

To facilitate the analysis and evaluation of financial data, in the 1960s several groups began to push the accounting profession to require disclosure of disaggregated figures such as those reported by Philip Morris. Not surprisingly, the timing of this movement corresponded with a period of significant corporate merger and acquisition activity. As business organizations expanded through ever-widening diversification, financial statement analysis became increasingly difficult. The broadening of an enterprise's activities into different products, industries, or geographic areas complicates the analysis of conditions, trends, and ratios and, therefore, the ability to predict. The various industry segments or geographic areas of operations of an enterprise may have different rates of profitability, degrees and types of risk, and opportunities for growth.

Because of the increasingly diverse activities of many organizations, disclosure of additional information was sought to help the readers of financial statements. The identity of the significant elements of an entity's operations was viewed as an important complement to consolidated totals. Thus, such organizations as the Financial Analysts Federation and the Financial Executives Institute provided support for the inclusion of data describing the major components (or segments) of an enterprise as a means of enhancing the informational content of corporate financial statements.

As a result of the demand for disaggregated information, a number of official steps have been taken since the 1960s to encourage or mandate such presentation within financial statements. During this period, the Accounting Principles Board (APB) and the New York Stock Exchange both urged companies to present such data voluntarily. The Securities and Exchange Commission as well as the Federal Trade Commission required the reporting of certain line-of-business information within documents filed with those bodies.

Because of the cost to generate this data and the fear that confidential information would be disclosed to competitors, however, not all reporting corporations agreed with these requirements. "Segment reporting came into being after a vicious battle waged between the Federal Trade Commission and big corporations in the mid-1970s. The corporations fought the FTC's demands for income statements and balance sheets on each of their different lines of business all the way to the Supreme Court, and they lost."[4]

The move toward dissemination of disaggregated information culminated in December 1976 with the release by the FASB of *SFAS 14*, "Financial Reporting for Segments of a Business Enterprise." This pronouncement established guidelines for the presentation within corporate financial statements of information to describe the various segments that constitute each reporting entity.

FASB STATEMENT 14

Specifically, *Statement 14* required financial information to be presented portraying as many as four distinct aspects of a company's operations.

---

[4]Dana Wechsler and Katarzyna Wandycz, " 'An Innate Fear of Disclosure,' " *Forbes*, February 5, 1990.

1. *Industry segments.* A company was required to disclose for each reportable industry segment:

   Revenues.
   Operating profit or loss.
   Identifiable assets.
   Aggregate amount of depreciation, depletion, and amortization expense.
   Capital expenditures.
   Equity in the net income from an investment in the net assets of equity investees.

2. *Domestic and foreign operations.* A company had to disclose for domestic operations as well as for operations in each significant foreign geographic area:

   Revenues.
   Operating profit or loss.
   Identifiable assets.

3. *Export sales.* A company reported for domestic operations the amount of revenue derived from exporting products to unaffiliated customers in foreign countries.

4. *Major customers.* A company was required to disclose the amount of revenue derived from sales to each major customer.

Most companies made this information available within the notes to the financial statements. Companies also were allowed to report segment data in the body of the statements or as a separate schedule attached to the financial statements. In addition, some companies, such as the Colgate-Palmolive Company, provided this information in Management's Discussion and Analysis.

As an illustration of the industry segment disclosures required, a note to the 1996 financial statements of General Electric Company indicated that total consolidated revenues of $79.18 billion were generated by the following separately identifiable industry segments (in millions):

GE	
Aircraft engines	$ 6,302
Appliances	6,375
Broadcasting	5,232
Industrial products and systems	10,412
Materials	6,509
Power generation	7,257
Technical products and services	4,692
All other	3,108
Corporate items and eliminations	(322)
Total GE	49,565
GECS	
Financing	23,742
Specialty insurance	8,966
All other	5
Total GECS	32,713
Eliminations	(3,099)
Consolidated revenues	$79,179

The information reported by General Electric went on to give the operating profit, assets, depreciation and amortization, and the total amount of capital expenditures for each of these segments.

The 1996 annual report of the Hewlett-Packard Company disclosed the following information about its operations in several different geographic areas (in millions):

	Net Revenues	Earnings from Operations	Identifiable Assets
United States	$24,304	$2,470	$14,321
Europe	14,895	769	7,991
Japan, Other Asia Pacific, Canada, Latin America	13,597	1,173	7,200

Data describing industry segments and foreign operations was not the only disaggregated information to be disclosed based on the standards set by *SFAS 14*. As required by this same pronouncement, the financial statements of Caterpillar Inc. reported that $5.13 billion of its 1995 sales came from exporting products to customers outside of the United States (the largest amount was $1.527 billion to the Asia/Pacific area). The toy manufacturer Hasbro, Inc., also complied with *Statement 14* by disclosing "sales to the Company's two largest customers, Toys R Us, Inc., and Wal-Mart Stores, Inc., amounted to 21 percent and 12 percent, respectively, of consolidated net revenues during each year of 1995 and 1994 and 20 percent and 11 percent, respectively, in 1993."

USEFULNESS OF DISAGGREGATED FINANCIAL INFORMATION

As can be seen from these illustrations, *SFAS 14* had a significant impact on the financial reporting process. The goal of reporting segment information is to enhance the usefulness of a corporation's financial statements. With disaggregation, the past and present operational success of each corporate component can be analyzed on an ongoing basis. Lockheed Martin, as an example, disclosed an overall decrease of $53 million in its revenues between 1994 and 1995. However, during that time, three of its five industry segments actually had an increase in revenues totaling more than $1,180 million. Although of significant interest to anyone evaluating the company, this information is not evident from the single revenue figure presented on the consolidated income statement.

Just as important, segment data can assist analysts in predicting the effects of future changes in an organization's environment. For example, if a recession is anticipated for textile manufacturing, the degree of a company's involvement in that industry is vital information to a present or potential investor. Similarly, data describing operations in a particular area of the world is of immediate interest if political turbulence becomes prevalent there.

In its 1993 position paper entitled *Financial Reporting in the 1990s and Beyond*, the Association for Investment Management and Research (formerly the Financial Analysts Federation) left no doubt as to the importance of segment reporting:

> It is vital, essential, fundamental, indispensable, and integral to the investment analysis process. Analysts need to know and understand how the various components of a multifaceted enterprise behave economically. One weak member of the group is analogous to a section of blight on a piece of fruit; it has the potential to spread rot over the entirety. Even in the absence of weakness, different segments will generate dissimilar streams of cash flows to which are attached disparate risks and which bring about unique values. Thus, without disaggregation, there is no sensible way to predict the overall amounts, timing, or risks of a complete enterprise's cash flows. There is little dispute over the analytic usefulness of disaggregated financial data (pages 59 and 60).

A substantial body of academic research has empirically investigated the usefulness of *SFAS 14* disclosures. Some of the major findings are

■ Industry segment data improve analysts' accuracy in predicting consolidated sales and earnings; this is true for both large and small firms.

- The availability of industry segment data leads to greater consensus among analysts regarding their forecasts of sales and earnings.
- Segment *revenue* data (both industry and geographic) appear to be more useful than segment *earnings* data in making forecasts.
- The initial disclosure of geographic area data was used by stock market participants in assessing the riskiness of companies with foreign operations.[5]

When considered as a whole, the extant research clearly indicates that *SFAS 14* segment data have been useful to investors and creditors in evaluating the risk and return associated with investment or lending alternatives.

Notwithstanding the fact that in complying with *SFAS 14* companies provided information useful to external users of financial statements, financial analysts have consistently requested that information be disaggregated to a much greater degree than was done in practice. In its 1993 position paper referred to earlier, the AIMR indicated that "There is no disagreement among AIMR members that segment information is totally vital to their work. There also is general agreement among them that the current segment reporting standard, *Financial Accounting Standard No. 14*, is inadequate."[6]

One area of concern was the flexibility with which industry segments could be identified. *Statement 14* (par. 10[a]) defined an industry segment as a "component of an enterprise engaged in providing a product or service or a group of related products and services primarily to unaffiliated customers (i.e., customers outside the enterprise) for a profit." Although this definition seems reasonable, problems often are encountered in actual application. An industry segment can be viewed as a very broad classification encompassing many, varied products and services only slightly related by nature. Conversely, a company may narrowly define its industry segments by including only closely related products or services within each segment. For example, a company producing baseball bats in one manufacturing plant and pool cues in a separate facility can properly view these operations as lying entirely within a single industry: production of sporting goods. Alternatively, this same enterprise may perceive these products as basically unrelated, therefore indicating the existence of two segments: the production of baseball bats and the production of pool cues.

One problem with this flexibility is where management determines that the company has a "dominant industry segment." *SFAS 14* provided that where a single segment made up more than 90 percent of a company's revenues, operating profit or loss, and identifiable assets, industry segment disclosures were not required. As an example, McDonald's Corporation, one of the largest corporations in the world, reported in its 1996 annual report that the company "operates exclusively in the food service industry," and thereby avoided providing industry segment information.[7]

Despite the apparent diversity of U.S. businesses, companies with dominant industry segments have been very common. In a survey of 600 companies, the AICPA's *Accounting Trends and Techniques* found that only 350 of these organizations reported industry segment revenues in their 1994 annual report.[8] The remainder must have viewed themselves as operating primarily in only one industry.

The AIMR's position paper criticized the FASB's approach as follows:

FAS 14 requires disclosure of line-of-business information classified by "industry segment." Its definition of segment is necessarily imprecise, recognizing that there are numerous practi-

[5]For an extensive review of the relevant literature, see Paul Pacter, *Reporting Disaggregated Information* (Stamford, CT: FASB, February 1993), pp. 131–202.

[6]Association for Investment Management and Research, *Financial Reporting in the 1990s and Beyond* (Charlottesville, VA: AIMR, 1993), page 5.

[7]McDonald's Corporation, 1996 Annual Report, p. 39.

[8]American Institute of Certified Public Accountants, *Accounting Trends and Techniques—1995*, 49th ed. (New York: AICPA, 1995), p. 17.

cal problems in applying that definition to different business entities operating under disparate circumstances. That weakness in *FAS 14* has been exploited by many enterprises to suit their own financial reporting purposes. As a result, we have seen one of the ten largest firms in the country report all of its operations as being in a single, very broadly defined industry segment. (page 60)

The AICPA's Special Committee on Financial Reporting, which published *Improving Business Reporting—A Customer Focus* in 1994, echoed this sentiment by stating that "[users] believe that many companies define industry segments too broadly for business reporting and thus report on too few industry segments."[9]

Both the AIMR and the AICPA's special committee recommended that segment reporting be aligned with internal reporting with segments defined on the basis of how an enterprise is organized and managed. Segments based on an enterprise's internal organization structure would have four advantages:

1. Knowledge of an enterprise's organization structure is valuable because it reflects the risks and opportunities believed to be important by management.

2. The ability to see the company the way it is viewed by management improves an analyst's ability to predict management actions that can significantly affect future cash flows.

3. Because segment information already is generated for management's use on the basis of the company's internal structure, the incremental cost of providing that information externally should be minimal.

4. Segments based on an existing internal structure should be less subjective than segments based on the term *industry*.[10]

Other recommendations for improving segment reporting made by the AIMR include:

- Disclose segment information in interim financial statements.
- Disclose revenues and profit by product or service line, even if the company is deemed to operate in only one industry.
- Provide additional guidance as to how segments should be identified with the objectives to (1) disaggregate the company into more segments, (2) enhance the comparability of segments across companies, and (3) make segments consistent with the segmentation used by management in making decisions.
- Disclose more information—such as cash flows, liabilities, net assets, cost of goods sold, and interest expense.
- Disclose what is in segments designated as "other."
- Provide more descriptive information about the segments.

In 1992, at the request of the AIMR, the AICPA Special Committee on Financial Reporting, and others, the FASB and the Accounting Standards Board (AcSB) in Canada decided to jointly reconsider segmental reporting with the objective of developing common standards that would apply in both the United States and Canada. After several years of study, in January 1996, the FASB issued an Exposure Draft for a Proposed Statement of Financial Accounting Standards entitled "Reporting Disaggregated Information about a Business Enterprise." The AcSB also issued an exposure draft identical in its applicable requirements to the FASB's proposed statement. In addition, the IASC issued an Exposure Draft on this topic which, while not identical, is similar to the FASB's. Members of both the FASB and the AcSB participated in IASC meetings on segment reporting to exchange views.

---

[9]American Institute of Certified Public Accountants, *Improving Business Reporting—A Customer Focus* (New York: AICPA, 1994), p. 69.

[10]FASB, Proposed Statement of Financial Accounting Standards, "Reporting Disaggregated Information about a Business Enterprise," 1996, para. 66–67.

Does IBM Really Have Only One Industry Segment?

Not all corporations have readily embraced segment reporting. All disclosure has a cost; gathering and monitoring information for each segment may not be cheap. In addition, some companies fear that such data could be useful to their competitors. One solution is to define the company as having only one segment so that disaggregation is not required. With the very flexible guidelines established in *SFAS 14* for identifying segments, many companies are able to avoid presenting segment information in this manner (see footnote 9 in this chapter).

Consider IBM. As befits its size, the $63 billion (estimated 1989 sales) computer company is in several lines of business, including personal computers, mainframes, electronic mail systems and semiconductors (IBM's semiconductor facilities rank among the world's largest). How is each of these segments doing? That's hard to say. IBM reports figures for a grand total of one segment, called "information-processing systems, software, communications systems and other products and services." . . . Does anybody care? They should. Says Eugene Glazer, technology analyst at Dean Witter Reynolds: "Investors need to know how a company is doing in each major business. Maybe one business is so dominant and earning such huge profits that it's masking errors in other businesses."[11]

To be fair, although IBM indicates that a single segment "represents more than 90 percent of consolidated revenue, operating profit, and identifiable assets," it nevertheless voluntarily disaggregates revenues "by classes of similar products or services within the information technology segment." However, data on operating profit, assets, depreciation, and capital expenditures are not similarly disaggregated. Should the FASB tighten up its rules on defining segments to ensure that all companies present appropriately disaggregated information?

In June 1997, *FASB Statement 131*, "Disclosures about Segments of an Enterprise and Related Information," was approved. Effective for fiscal years beginning after December 15, 1997, this statement makes substantial changes to the segment disclosures required to be provided by U.S. companies. There is a significant change in *how reportable segments are determined*, as well as in the *amount and types of information* to be provided.

FASB STATEMENT 131

According to *SFAS 131*, the objective of segment reporting is to provide information about the different business activities in which an enterprise engages and the different economic environments in which it operates to help users of financial statements:

- Better understand the enterprise's performance.
- Better assess its prospects for future net cash flows.
- Make more informed judgments about the enterprise as a whole (para. 3).

The Management Approach

To achieve this objective, *SFAS 131* has adopted the so-called management approach for determining segments. The management approach is based on the way that management disaggregates the enterprise for making operating decisions. These disaggregated components are *operating segments*, which will be evident from the enterprise's organization structure. More specifically, an operating segment is a component of an enterprise:

- That engages in business activities from which it earns revenues and incurs expenses.
- Whose operating results are regularly reviewed by the chief operating decision maker to assess performance and make resource allocation decisions.
- For which discrete financial information is available.

[11]Wechsler and Wandycz, " 'An Innate Fear of Disclosure,' " p. 126.

An organizational unit can be an operating segment even if all of its revenue or expense results from transactions with other segments as might be the case in a vertically integrated company. However, not all parts of a company will necessarily be included in an operating segment. For example, a research and development unit that incurs expenses but does not earn revenues would not be an operating segment. Similarly, corporate headquarters might not earn revenues or might earn revenues that are only incidental to the activities of the enterprise and therefore would not be considered an operating segment.

For many companies, only one set of organizational units qualifies as operating segments. In some companies, however, business activities are disaggregated in more than one way and multiple sets of reports are used by the chief operating decision maker. For example, a company might generate reports by geographic region *and* by product line. In those cases, two additional criteria must be considered to identify operating segments:

1. An operating segment has a segment manager who is directly accountable to the chief operating decision maker for its financial performance. If more than one set of organizational units exists, but there is only one set for which segment managers are held responsible, that set constitutes the operating segments.

2. If segment managers exist for two or more overlapping sets of organizational units (as in a matrix form of organization), the nature of the business activities must be considered, and the organizational units based on products and services constitute the operating segments. For example, if certain managers are responsible for different product lines and other managers are responsible for different geographic areas, the enterprise components based on products would constitute the operating segments.

DETERMINING REPORTABLE OPERATING SEGMENTS

After a company has identified its operating segments based on its internal reporting system, management must decide which of these segments should be reported separately. Generally, information must be reported separately for each operating segment that meets one or more quantitative thresholds established in *SFAS 131. However, if two or more operating segments have essentially the same business activities in essentially the same economic environments, information for those individual segments may be combined.* "For example, a retail chain may have 10 stores that individually meet the definition of an operating segment, but each store is essentially the same as the others."[12] In that case, the Board believes that the benefit to be derived from separately reporting each operating segment would not justify the cost of disclosure. In determining whether business activities and environments are similar, management must consider these aggregation criteria:

1. The nature of the products and services provided by each operating segment.
2. The nature of the production process.
3. The type or class of customer.
4. The distribution methods.
5. If applicable, the nature of the regulatory environment.

Segments must be similar in each and every one of these areas to be combined. However, aggregation of similar segments is not required.

---

[12]*FASB Statement 131*, "Disclosures about Segments of an Enterprise and Related Information," June 1997, para. 73.

Quantitative Thresholds

After determining whether any segments are to be aggregated, management next must determine which of its operating segments are significant enough to justify separate disclosure. In *Statement 131*, the FASB decided to retain the three tests introduced in *SFAS 14* for identifying operating segments for which separate disclosure is required:

- A revenue test.
- A profit or loss test.
- An asset test.

An operating segment needs to satisfy only one of these tests to be considered of significant size to necessitate separate disclosure.

To apply these three tests, a segment's revenues, profit or loss, and assets must be determined. *SFAS 131* does not stipulate a specific measure of profit or loss, such as operating profit or income before taxes, to be used in applying these tests. Instead, the measure of profit used by the chief operating decision maker in evaluating operating segments is to be used. An operating segment is considered to be significant if it meets any one of the following tests:

1. *Revenue test.* Segment revenues, both external and intersegment, are 10 percent or more of the combined revenue, internal and external, of all reported operating segments.
2. *Profit or loss test.* Segment profit or loss is 10 percent or more of the greater (in absolute terms) of the combined reported profit of all profitable segments or the combined reported loss of all segments incurring a loss.
3. *Asset test.* Segment assets are 10 percent or more of the combined assets of all operating segments.

Application of the revenue and asset tests would seem to pose few problems. In contrast, the profit or loss test is more complicated and warrants illustration. For this purpose, assume that the Durham Company has five separate operating segments with the following profits or losses:

Durham Company Segments—Profits and Losses

Soft drinks	$1,700,000
Wine.	(600,000)
Food products	240,000
Paper packaging.	880,000
Recreation parks	(130,000)
Net operating profit	$2,090,000

Three of these industry segments (soft drinks, food products, and paper packaging) report profits that total $2,820,000. The two remaining segments have losses for the year in the amount of $730,000.

Profits		Losses	
Soft drinks	$1,700,000	Wine	$600,000
Food products	240,000	Recreation parks	130,000
Paper packaging	880,000		
Total.	$2,820,000	Total	$730,000

Consequently, $2,820,000 serves as the basis for the profit or loss test because that figure is greater in absolute terms than $730,000. Based on the 10 percent threshold, any operating segment with either a profit *or loss* of more than $282,000 (10% × $2,820,000) is considered material and, thus, must be disclosed separately. According to this one test, the soft drink and paper packaging segments (with operating profits of $1.7 million and $880,000, respectively) are both judged to be reportable as is the wine segment, despite having a loss of $600,000.

Operating segments that do not meet any of the quantitative thresholds may be combined to produce a reportable segment if they share a *majority* of the aggregation criteria listed earlier. For Durham Company, the food products and recreation parks operating segments would not meet any of the aggregation criteria. Operating segments that are not individually significant and that cannot be aggregated with other segments are combined and disclosed in an *all other* category. The sources of the revenues included in the All Other category must be disclosed.

TESTING PROCEDURES—COMPLETE ILLUSTRATION

To provide a comprehensive example of all three of these testing procedures, assume that the Atkinson Company is a large business combination comprised of six operating segments: automotive, furniture, textbook, motion picture, appliance, and finance. Complete information about each of these segments, as reported internally to the chief operating decision maker, appears in Exhibit 12–1.

The Revenue Test.   In applying the revenue test to the operating segments of the Atkinson Company, the combined revenue of all segments must be determined:

Operating Segment	Total Revenues
Automotive	$41.6
Furniture	9.0
Textbook	6.8
Motion picture	22.8
Appliance	5.3
Finance	12.3
Combined total	$97.8

Exhibit 12–1   Reportable Segment Testing

ATKINSON COMPANY						
	Automotive	**Furniture**	**Textbook**	**Motion Picture**	**Appliance**	**Finance**
Revenues:						
Sales to outsiders	$32.6*	$6.9	$6.6	$22.2	$3.1	–0–
Intersegment transfers	6.6	1.2	–0–	–0–	1.9	–0–
Interest revenue—outsiders	2.4	.9	.2	.6	.3	8.7
Interest revenue—intersegment loans	–0–	–0–	–0–	–0–	–0–	3.6
Total revenues	$41.6	$9.0	$6.8	$22.8	$5.3	$12.3
Expenses:						
Operating expenses—outsiders	$17.1	$3.6	$7.3	$24.0	$3.6	$ 2.3
Operating expenses—intersegment transfers	4.8	1.0	–0–	–0–	.8	.8
Interest expense	2.1	1.0	2.2	4.6	–0–	6.1
Income taxes	6.6	1.4	(1.5)	(3.1)	.4	.1
Total expenses	$30.6	$7.0	$8.0	$25.5	$4.0	$ 9.3
Assets:						
Tangible	$ 9.6	$1.1	$ .8	$10.9	$ .9	$ 9.2
Intangible	1.8	.2	.7	3.6	.1	–0–
Intersegment loans	–0–	–0–	–0–	–0–	–0–	5.4
Total assets	$11.4	$1.3	$1.5	$14.5	$1.0	$14.6

*All figures in millions.

Because these six segments have total revenues of $97.8 million, that figure is used in applying the revenue test. Based on the 10 percent significance level, any segment with revenues of more than $9.78 million qualifies for required disclosure. Accordingly, the automotive, the motion picture, and finance segments all have satisfied this particular criterion. Appropriate disaggregated information, therefore, must be presented within Atkinson's financial statements for each of these three operating segments.

The Profit or Loss Test. The profit or loss for each operating segment is determined by subtracting segment expenses from total segment revenues. *SFAS 131* does not require common costs to be allocated to individual segments to determine segment profit or loss if this is not normally done for internal purposes. For example, an enterprise that accounts for pension expense only on a consolidated basis is not required to allocate pension expense to each operating segment. Any allocations that are made must be done on a reasonable basis. Moreover, segment profit or loss does not have to be calculated in accordance with generally accepted accounting principles if the measure reported internally is calculated on another basis. To assist the readers of financial statements in understanding segment disclosures, *SFAS 131* does require disclosure of any differences in the basis of measurement between segment and consolidated amounts.

Each operating segment's profit or loss is calculated as follows:

Operating Segment	Total Revenues	Total Expenses	Profit	Loss
Automotive	$41.6*	$30.6	$11.0	–0–
Furniture	9.0	7.0	2.0	–0–
Textbook	6.8	8.0	–0–	$ 1.2
Motion picture	22.8	25.5	–0–	2.7
Appliance	5.3	4.0	1.3	–0–
Finance	12.3	9.3	3.0	–0–
Totals	$97.8	$84.4	$19.3	$ 3.9

*All figures are in millions.

The $19.3 million total (the four profit figures) is greater in an absolute sense than the $3.9 million in losses. Therefore, this larger balance serves as the basis for the second quantitative test. Because the FASB has again established a 10 percent criterion, either a profit or loss of $1.93 million or more qualifies a segment for disaggregation. According to the income totals just calculated, the automotive, furniture, motion picture, and finance segments of the Atkinson Company are large enough to warrant separate disclosure.

The Asset Test. The final test designed by the FASB is based on the operating segments' combined total assets:

Operating Segment	Assets
Automotive	$11.4
Furniture	1.3
Textbook	1.5
Motion picture	14.5
Appliance	1.0
Finance	14.6
Combined total	$44.3

Because 10 percent of the combined total equals $4.43 million, any segment holding at least that amount of assets is viewed as a reportable segment. Consequently, according to this final significance test, the automotive, motion picture, and finance segments are each considered of sufficient size to require disaggregation. The three remaining segments do not have sufficient assets to pass this particular test.

Analysis of Test Results.　A summary of all three significance tests as applied to the Atkinson Company is as follows:

Operating Segments	Revenue Test	Profit or Loss Test	Asset Test
Automotive..............	✔	✔	✔
Furniture		✔	
Textbook			
Motion picture	✔	✔	✔
Appliance...............			
Finance	✔	✔	✔

Four of this company's operating segments (automotive, furniture, motion picture, and finance) have been determined to be separately reportable. Because neither the appliance nor the textbook segments have met any of these three tests, disaggregated information describing their *individual* operations is not required. However, the financial data accumulated from these two nonsignificant segments still has to be presented. The figures can be combined and disclosed as aggregate amounts in an All Other category with appropriate disclosure of the source of revenues.

OTHER GUIDELINES

Several other FASB guidelines apply to the disclosure of operating segment information. These rules are designed to ensure that the disaggregated data is consistent from year to year and relevant to the needs of financial statement users. For example, any operating segment that has been reportable in the past and is judged by management to be of continuing significance should be disclosed separately in the current statements regardless of the outcome of the testing process. This degree of flexibility is included within the rules to assure the ongoing usefulness of the disaggregated information, especially for comparison purposes.

In a similar manner, if an operating segment newly qualifies for disclosure in the current year, prior period segment data presented for comparative purposes must be restated to reflect the newly reportable segment as a separate segment. Once again, the comparability of information has been given high priority in setting the standards for disclosure.

One final issue raised by *SFAS 131* concerns the number of operating segments that should be disclosed. To enhance the value of the disaggregated information, a substantial portion of a company's operations should be presented individually. Thus, the FASB has stated that a sufficient number of segments is presumed to be included only if their combined sales to unaffiliated customers is at least 75 percent of total company sales made to outsiders. If this lower limit is not achieved, additional segments must be disclosed separately despite their failure to satisfy even one of the three quantitative thresholds.

As an illustration, assume that the Brendan Corporation has identified seven industry segments that have generated revenues as follows (in millions):

Operating Segments	Sales to Unaffiliated Customers	Intersegment Transfers	Segment Revenues (and percent of total)
Housewares	$ 5.5	$ 1.6	$ 7.1　(9.3%)
Toys.......................	6.2	–0–	6.2　(8.1%)
Pottery	3.4	7.9	11.3 (14.8%) ✔
Lumber	6.6	10.4	17.0 (22.3%) ✔
Lawn mowers	7.2	–0–	7.2　(9.4%)
Appliances	2.1	6.2	8.3 (10.9%) ✔
Construction	19.2	–0–	19.2 (25.2%) ✔
Totals.....................	$50.2	$26.1	$76.3　(100%)

Based on the 10 percent revenue test, four of these segments are reportable (because each has total revenues of more than $7.63 million): pottery, lumber, appliances, and construction. Assuming that none of the other segments qualify as significant in either of the two remaining tests, disclosure of disaggregated data is required only for these four segments. However, the FASB's 75 percent rule has not been met; the reportable segments generate just 62.4 percent of the company's total sales to unrelated parties (in millions):

Reportable Segments	Sales to Unaffiliated Customers
Pottery	$ 3.4
Lumber	6.6
Appliances	2.1
Construction	19.2
Total	$31.3

Information being disaggregated: $31.3 million/$50.2 million = 62.4%.

To satisfy the 75 percent requirement, Brendan Corporation must also include the lawn mower segment within the disaggregated data being presented. With the addition of this nonsignificant segment, sales to outside parties of $38.5 million ($31.3 + $7.2) now are disclosed. This figure amounts to 76.7 percent of the company total ($38.5 million/$50.2 million). The two remaining segments—housewares and toys—could still be included separately within the disaggregated data; disclosure is not prohibited. However, information for these two segments would probably be combined and reported as aggregate figures.

One final aspect of these reporting requirements should be mentioned. Some companies might be organized in such a fashion that there exists a relatively large number of operating segments. The FASB suggests there may be a practical limit to the number of operating segments that should be reported separately. Beyond that limit, the information becomes too detailed to be of use. *SFAS 131* (para. 24) indicates that "Although no precise limit has been determined, as the number of segments that are reportable . . . increases above 10, the enterprise should consider whether a practical limit has been reached."

INFORMATION TO BE DISCLOSED BY OPERATING SEGMENT

Consistent with requests from the financial analyst community, *SFAS 131* has significantly expanded the amount of information to be disclosed for each operating segment:

1. *General information* about the operating segment:

   - Factors used to identify operating segments.
   - Types of products and services from which each operating segment derives its revenues.

2. *Segment profit or loss* and the following revenues and expenses included in segment profit or loss:

   - Revenues from external customers.
   - Revenues from transactions with other operating segments.
   - Interest revenue and interest expense (reported separately); net interest revenue may be reported for finance segments if this measure is used internally for evaluation.
   - Depreciation, depletion, and amortization expense.
   - Other significant noncash items included in segment profit or loss.
   - Unusual items (discontinued operations and extraordinary items).
   - Income tax expense or benefit.

3. *Total segment assets* and the following related items:

- Investment in equity method affiliates.
- Expenditures for additions to long-lived assets.

Although requested by the AIMR, the FASB does not specifically require cash flow information to be reported for each operating segment because this information often is not generated by segment for internal reporting purposes. The requirement to disclose noncash items other than depreciation is an attempt to provide information that might enhance users' ability to estimate cash flow from operations.

SFAS 131 need not be applied to immaterial items. For example, some segments do not have material amounts of interest revenue and expense, and therefore disclosure of these items of information would not be necessary. In addition, if an item of information is not generated by the internal financial reporting system on a segment basis, that item need not be disclosed. This is consistent with the FASB's desire that segment reporting creates as little additional cost to an enterprise as possible.

To demonstrate how the operating segment information might be disclosed, let us return to the Atkinson Company example referred to earlier in this chapter. Application of the quantitative threshold tests resulted in four separately reportable segments (automotive, furniture, motion picture, and finance). The nonsignificant operating segments (textbook and appliance) are combined in an All Other category. Exhibit 12–2 shows the operating segment disclosures included in the Atkinson Company's financial statements.

In addition to information provided in Exhibit 12–1, information on depreciation and amortization, other significant noncash items, and expenditures for long-lived segment assets has been gathered for each operating segment to comply with the disclosure requirements. Only the automotive segment has other significant noncash items, and none of the segments has equity method investments. Atkinson Company had no unusual items during the year.

To determine whether a sufficient number of segments is included, the ratio of combined sales to unaffiliated customers for the separately reported operating segments must be compared with total company sales made to outsiders. The combined amount of revenues from external customers disclosed for the automotive, furniture, motion picture, and finance segments is $61.7 million. Total revenues from external customers is $71.4 million:

$$\$61.7 \text{ million}/\$71.4 \text{ million} = 86.4\%.$$

Exhibit 1 2 – 2   Operating Segment Disclosures

ATKINSON COMPANY					
			Operating Segment		
	Automotive	**Furniture**	**Motion Picture**	**Finance**	**All Other**
Revenues from external customers	$32.6*	$6.9	$22.2	$ —	$ 9.7
Intersegment revenues	6.6	1.2	—	—	1.9
Segment profit (loss)	11.0	2.0	(2.7)	3.0	.1
Interest revenue	2.4	.9	—	—	.2
Interest expense	2.1	1.0	4.6	—	2.2
Net interest revenue	—	—	—	6.2	—
Depreciation and amortization	2.7	1.5	2.4	.9	.4
Other significant noncash items:					
Cost in excess of billings on long-term contracts	.8	—	—	—	—
Income tax expense (benefit)	6.6	1.4	(3.1)	.1	(1.1)
Segment assets	11.4	1.3	14.5	14.6	2.5
Expenditures for segment assets	3.5	.4	3.7	1.7	1.3
All figures in millions.					

Because 86.4 percent exceeds the lower limit of 75 percent imposed by the FASB, the level of disaggregation reported by Atkinson Company is adequate.

Reconciliations to Consolidated Totals

As noted earlier, *SFAS 131* does not require that disaggregated information be provided in accordance with generally accepted accounting principles. Instead, information is to be provided as it is prepared by the company's internal reporting system even if not based on GAAP. "Preparing segment information in accordance with the generally accepted accounting principles used at the consolidated level would be difficult because some generally accepted accounting principles are not intended to apply at a segment level" (*SFAS 131*, para 84). Examples are the accounting for inventory on a LIFO basis when inventory pools include items in more than one segment, accounting for companywide pension plans, and accounting for purchased goodwill. Accordingly, allocation of these items to individual operating segments is not required.

However, the total of the reportable segments' revenues must be reconciled to consolidated revenues and the total of reportable segments' profit or loss must be reconciled to income before tax for the company as a whole. Adjustments and eliminations that have been made to develop enterprise financial statements in compliance with generally accepted accounting principles must be identified. Examples would be the elimination of intersegment revenues and an adjustment for companywide pension expense. The same is true for reconciliation of total segments' assets to the enterprise's total assets.

In addition, in reconciling the total of segments' revenues, profit or loss, and assets to the enterprise totals, the aggregate amount of revenues, profit or loss, and assets from immaterial operating segments must be disclosed. The company also must disclose assets, revenues, expenses, gains, losses, interest expense, and depreciation, depletion, and amortization expense for components of the enterprise that are not operating segments. This would include, for example, assets and expenses associated with corporate headquarters. An example of how these reconciliations might be made by Atkinson Company is presented in Exhibit 12–3.

E x h i b i t 1 2 – 3
Reconciliation of Segment Results to Consolidated Totals

ATKINSON COMPANY	
Revenues	
Total segment revenues	$ 97.8*
Elimination of intersegment revenues	(13.3)
Total consolidated revenues	$ 84.5
Profit or Loss	
Total segment profit or loss	$ 13.4
Total segment income taxes	3.9
Total segment profit before income taxes	$ 17.3
Elimination of intersegment profits	(2.3)
Unallocated amounts:	
Litigation settlement received	3.6
Other corporate expenses	(2.7)
Adjustment to pension expense in consolidation	(.8)
Consolidated income before income taxes	$ 15.1
Assets	
Total for reported segments	$ 44.3
Elimination of intersegment loans	(5.4)
Goodwill not allocated to segments	3.2
Other unallocated amounts	2.6
Total consolidated assets	$ 44.7

*All figures in millions.

There are three adjustments that Atkinson Company must make in reconciling segment results with consolidated totals. The first adjustment is the elimination of intercompany revenues, profit or loss, and assets that are not included in consolidated totals. The elimination of intersegment revenues includes intersegment transfers amounting to $9.7 million plus $3.6 million of intersegment interest revenue generated by the finance segment. The second adjustment relates to corporate items that have not been allocated to the operating segments. These include purchased goodwill, a litigation settlement received by the company, and corporate headquarters expenses and assets. The third adjustment reconciles differences in segment accounting practices from accounting practices used in the consolidated financial statements. The only adjustment of this nature made by Atkinson Company is related to the accounting for pension expense. Individual operating segments measure pension expense based on cash payments made to the pension plan. Because GAAP requires pension expense to be measured on an accrual basis, an adjustment for the amount of pension expense to be recognized in the consolidated statements is necessary.

In addition to the operating segment disclosures and reconciliation of segment results to consolidated totals, companies also must provide an explanation of the measurement of segment profit or loss and segment assets. This explanation should include a description of any differences in measuring segment profit or loss and consolidated income before tax, any differences in measuring segment assets and consolidated assets, and any differences in measuring segment profit or loss and segment assets. An example of this last item would be where depreciation expense is allocated to segments but the related depreciable assets are not. The basis of accounting for intersegment transactions also must be described.

INTERIM REPORTING

The management approach should result in less costly disclosure because this information, by definition, already is collected by management. Since the information is readily available, *Statement 131* also requires segment disclosures to be made in interim reports. This was one of the major recommendations made by the AIMR for improving segment reporting. The following items of information are required to be included in interim reports for each operating segment:

- Revenues from external customers.
- Intersegment revenues.
- Segment profit or loss.
- Total assets, if there has been a material change from the last annual report.

In addition, total segments' profit or loss must be reconciled to the enterprise's total income before taxes, and any change from the last annual report in the basis of measurement of segment profit or loss must be disclosed. Requiring only a few items of information in interim reports is a compromise between the desire of users to have the same information as is provided in annual financial statements and the cost to preparers who must report the information.

The FASB does not require segment information to be provided in interim financial statements until the second year that a company applies *SFAS 131*. Without a full set of segment information in an annual report to compare with, the Board believes that segment information in interim reports would be less meaningful.

ENTERPRISEWIDE DISCLOSURES

Information about Products and Services

The FASB recognizes that some enterprises are not organized along product or service lines. For example, some enterprises are organized by geographic areas. Moreover, some enterprises may have only one operating segment yet provide a range of different products and services. To provide some comparability between enterprises, *SFAS 131* requires *disclosure of revenues derived from transactions with external customers from each product or service* if operating segments have not been determined based on differences in products or services. An enterprise with only one operating segment also would have to disclose revenues from external customers on the basis of product or service. However, providing this information is not required if impracticable, that is, the information is not available and the cost to develop it would be excessive.

Information about Geographic Areas

In addition, the following two items of information must be reported *(1) for the domestic country, (2) for all foreign countries in which the enterprise derives revenues or holds assets, and (3) for each foreign country in which a material amount of revenues is derived or assets are held:*

- Revenues from external customers.
- Long-lived assets.

Geographic area information must be disclosed even if the company has only one operating segment and therefore does not otherwise provide segment information. The previous requirement under *SFAS 14* to disclose *profit or loss* by geographic area no longer exists.

Note that the FASB requires companies to disclose information for *each material country*. Requiring disclosure at the country level is a significant change from *SFAS 14*. The FASB believes reporting information about individual countries rather than larger areas has two benefits. First, it reduces the burden on preparers of financial statements as most operating segments are likely to have material operations in only a few countries. Second, the information is easier to interpret and therefore more useful because individual countries within a geographic area often experience very different rates of economic growth and economic conditions.

Although the FASB considered using a 10 percent rule for determining when a country is material, ultimately it decided to leave this determination to management's judgment. In determining materiality, management should apply the concept that an item is material if its omission could change a user's decision about the enterprise as a whole. The FASB does not provide more specific guidance on this issue.

Information about Major Customers

One final but important disclosure requirement originally established by *SFAS 14* has been retained in *Statement 131*. A reporting entity must indicate its reliance on any major customer. *Presentation of this information is required whenever 10 percent or more of a company's revenues are derived from a single customer.* The existence of all major customers must be disclosed along with the related amount of revenues and the identity of the operating segment earning the revenues. Interestingly enough, the company need not reveal the identity of the customer.

An example of how this information has been disclosed under *SFAS 14* can be found in the 1996 annual report for the Briggs & Stratton Corporation. Note 4 to the financial statements indicated that significant sales had been made to three "major engine customers that exceeded 10 percent of total Company net sales. The sales to these customers are summarized below (in thousands of dollars and percent of total Company sales):"

Customer	1996 Sales	1996 Percent	1995 Sales	1995 Percent	1994 Sales	1994 Percent
A	$267,257	21%	$237,241	18%	$234,363	18%
B	177,314	14	155,072	12	148,091	12
C	163,065	13	189,916	14	149,397	12
	$607,636	48%	$582,229	44%	$531,851	42%

Of 600 companies surveyed in *Accounting Trends and Techniques*, 170 indicated the existence of a major customer in their 1994 annual report.[13]

Statement 131 indicates that major customer disclosures are required even if a company operates only in one segment and therefore does not provide segment information. Also, to avoid any confusion, "a group of entities under common control shall be considered as a single customer, and the federal government, a state government, a local government (for example, a county or municipality), or a foreign government shall each be considered as a single customer" (*SFAS 131*, para. 39).

In addition to requiring information about major customers, *SFAS 14* also required information about export sales. Providing information on export sales, however, is no longer necessary under *Statement 131*.

SUMMARY

1. The consolidation of information from many, varied companies into a set of consolidated financial statements tends to camouflage the characteristics of the individual components. Consequently, during the 1960s, several groups made a strong push to require that disaggregated information be included as an integral part of financial reporting to provide a means for analyzing the components of a business combination.

2. The move toward dissemination of disaggregated information culminated in 1976 with the release by the FASB of *Statement 14*, "Financial Reporting for Segments of a Business Enterprise." This pronouncement established guidelines for the required presentation of information describing the various segments that make up a reporting entity. *SFAS 14* required disclosure of information on as many as four distinct aspects of a company's operations: industry segments, geographic segments, export sales, and sales to major customers.

3. Over the years since *SFAS 14* was introduced, financial analysts consistently requested that financial statements be disaggregated to a much greater degree than was done in practice. In direct response to the criticisms and suggestions made by the financial analyst community, the FASB issued a new standard for segment reporting in 1997— *SFAS 131*.

4. *SFAS 131* adopts a so-called management approach in which operating segments are based on a company's organization structure and internal reporting system. The management approach should enhance the usefulness of segment information as it highlights the risks and opportunities that management believes are important and allows the analyst to see the company through the eyes of management. This approach also has the advantage of reducing the cost of providing segment information because that information already is being produced for internal use.

5. Once operating segments have been identified, a company must determine which of these segments is of significant magnitude to warrant separate disclosure. *SFAS 131* created three quantitative threshold tests to be applied to identify reportable segments: a revenue test, a profit or loss test, and an asset test. A segment need satisfy only one of these tests to be considered of sufficient size to necessitate disclosure. Each test is based on identifying segments that meet a 10 percent minimum of the related combined total. The profit and loss test has a 10 percent criterion based on the greater (in an absolute sense) of the total profit from all segments with profits or the total loss from all segments with losses.

---

[13]AICPA, *Accounting Trends and Techniques—1995*, p. 17.

6. For each reportable operating segment, several types of information must be reported: selected revenues, profit or loss, selected expenses, assets, capital expenditures, and equity method investment and income. Revenues from external customers must be reported separately from intersegment revenues. In addition, the types of products and services from which each segment derives its revenues must be disclosed.

7. *SFAS 131* establishes a set of parameters for the number of segments that should be reported by an enterprise. As a minimum, the separately disclosed units must generate at least 75 percent of the total sales made to unaffiliated parties. For an upper limit, the pronouncement suggests that the disclosure of more than 10 industry segments reduces the usefulness of the information.

8. Companies are required to reconcile the total of all segments' revenues, profit or loss, and assets to the consolidated totals. The major reconciliation adjustments relate to intercompany revenues, profit or loss, and assets eliminated in consolidation; revenues, profit or loss, and assets that have not been allocated to individual operating segments; and differences in accounting methods used by segments and in preparing consolidated financial statements.

9. At financial analysts' request, the FASB requires certain items of information to be disclosed in interim reports. Specifically, revenues from outside customers, intersegment revenues, and segment profit or loss must be disclosed in interim reports for each operating segment. In addition, total assets must be reported by segment if there has been a material change since the last annual report.

10. *SFAS 131* requires several enterprisewide disclosures. If an enterprise does not define operating segments internally on a product line basis or has only one operating segment, disclosure of revenues derived from each product or service is required.

11. In addition, revenues from external customers and long-lived assets must be reported for the domestic country, for each foreign country in which a material amount of revenues is generated or assets are held, and for all foreign countries in total. *SFAS 131* does not provide any threshold tests for determining when operations in a foreign country are material.

12. Disclosure of one other type of information is required by *SFAS 131*. The reporting entity must indicate the existence of major customers whenever 10 percent or more of consolidated revenues are derived from a single unaffiliated party.

COMPREHENSIVE ILLUSTRATION

Problem

(Estimated Time: 25 to 40 Minutes) The Battey Corporation, an enterprise located in the United States, manufactures several different products: natural fibers, synthetic fibers, leather, plastics, and wood. The company is organized into five operating divisions based on these different products. The company has developed a number of subsidiaries that carry on operations throughout the world. At the end of 1998, as part of the internal reporting process the following revenues, profits, and assets (in millions) were reported to the chief operating decision maker:

Revenues by Operating Segment	United States	Canada	Mexico	France	Italy	Brazil
Natural fibers						
Sales to external customers	$1,739	—	$342	$606	—	$1,171
Intersegment sales	—	—	—	—	—	146
Synthetic fibers						
Sales to external customers	290	116	—	—	—	37
Intersegment sales	12	5	—	—	—	—
Leather						
Sales to external customers	230	—	57	—	278	55
Intersegment sales	22	—	9	—	34	9
Plastics						
Sales to external customers	748	286	—	83	92	528
Intersegment sales	21	12	—	—	—	72
Wood						
Sales to external customers	116	22	—	—	—	149
Intersegment sales	17	3	—	—	—	28

Operating Profit or Loss by Operating Segment	United States	Canada	Mexico	France	Italy	Brazil
Natural fibers	$ 526	—	$ 92	$146	—	$ 404
Synthetic fibers	21	8	—	—	—	10
Leather	70	—	27	—	94	24
Plastics	182	74	—	18	24	68
Wood	18	5	—	—	—	37

Assets by Operating Segment	United States	Canada	Mexico	France	Italy	Brazil
Natural fibers	$1,005	—	$223	$296	—	$ 817
Synthetic fibers	163	50	—	—	—	74
Leather	146	—	41	—	150	38
Plastics	425	173	—	54	58	327
Wood	66	19	—	—	—	143

Required

a. Determine the operating segments that should be reported separately in Battey's 1998 financial statements using the criteria established in *SFAS 131*.

b. Determine the geographic areas for which revenues should be reported separately in Battey's 1998 financial statements. Assume that Battey has elected to define a material country as one in which sales to external customers are 10 percent or more of consolidated sales.

c. Determine the volume of revenues that has to be generated from a single customer to necessitate disclosure of a major customer under *SFAS 131*.

Solution

a. Battey Corporation determines its reportable operating segments by following the three-step process established in *SFAS 131*. First, operating segments are identified. Second, aggregation criteria are examined to determine whether any operating segments may be combined. Third, reportable operating segments are determined by applying the three quantitative threshold tests.

Identification of Operating Segments. Battey's internal reporting system provides information to the chief operating decision maker by operating division and by country. Either of these components conceivably could be identified as operating segments for segment reporting purposes. However, in this type of situation, *SFAS 131* stipulates that the components based on products and services constitute the operating segments. Thus, the five operating divisions are identified as Battey's operating segments.

Aggregation Criteria. The aggregation criteria included in *SFAS 131* are examined next to determine whether any operating segments can be combined. Management determines the economic characteristics of the Natural Fibers and Synthetic Fibers operating divisions to be very similar. In addition, there is considerable similarity with regard to the nature of the product, production process, customers, and distribution methods in these two divisions. Because each of *SFAS 131*'s aggregation criteria are met, Battey elects to combine these two segments into a single Fibers category.

Quantitative Threshold Tests. Determination of Battey's reportable operating segments is dependent on the three materiality tests described in this chapter. The revenue test can be performed directly from the information provided. Any operating segment with total revenues (including intersegment sales) equal to 10 percent or more of combined revenue (internal and external) must be reported separately:

Revenue Test (in millions)

Operating Segments	Total Revenues (including intersegment)	
Fibers	$4,464	60.8%
Leather	694	9.5
Plastics	1,842	25.1
Wood	335	4.6
Total combined revenues	$7,335	100.0%

Reportable segments—fibers and plastics.

The profit or loss test can be carried out next. Any operating segment with profit or loss equal to 10 percent or more of the greater, in absolute amount, of combined segment profit (for those segments with a profit) or combined segment loss (for those segments with a loss) must be reported separately. Because each of Battey's operating segments generated a profit in 1998, this test can be applied by determining the total combined profit:

Profit or Loss Test (in millions)

Operating Segments	Total Profit or Loss	
Fibers	$1,207	65.3%
Leather	215	11.6
Plastics	366	19.8
Wood	60	3.2
Total combined segment profit	$1,848	100.0%

Reportable segments—fibers, leather, and plastics.

Lastly, the asset test is performed:

Asset Test (in millions)

Operating Segments	Total Assets	
Fibers	$2,628	61.6%
Leather	375	8.8
Plastics	1,037	24.3
Wood	228	5.3
Total combined segment assets	$4,268	100.0%

Reportable segments—fibers and plastics.

Based on these three tests, information about the fibers, leather, and plastics operating segments must be reported separately. Information on the immaterial wood segment need not be reported. However, the revenues, profit, and assets of this segment would be included in reconciliations to consolidated totals.

b. Battey must report revenues from external customers for the United States, for all foreign countries, and for each foreign country in which the company generates a material amount of revenues. *SFAS 131* provides no quantitative tests for determining when a foreign country is material; this is left to management's judgment. Battey has decided to define materiality as sales to external customers equal to 10 percent or more of consolidated revenues. This was one of two criteria established in *SFAS 14* for determining significant geographic areas.

Revenue Test (in millions)

Country	Sales to External Customers	
United States	$3,123	45.0%
Canada	424	6.1
Mexico	399	5.8
France	689	9.9
Italy	370	5.3
Brazil	1,940	27.9
Total consolidated revenues	$6,945	100.0%

Using this criterion, Battey would report the United States and Brazil separately, and the remaining countries would be combined into an All Other category. Alternatively, if Battey had established a materiality threshold of 5 percent, each of the foreign countries in which the company generates revenues would be reported separately. Once again, determination of materiality is left to management's judgment.

c. The significance test for disclosure of a major customer is 10 percent of consolidated revenues. Under the guidelines of *SFAS 131*, Battey must report the existence of any major customer from which $694.5 million or more in revenues were generated during 1998.

QUESTIONS

1. How does the consolidation process tend to disguise information needed to analyze the financial operations of a diversified organization?

2. What is disaggregated financial information?

3. *SFAS 14* required many companies to present disaggregated information about several different aspects of current operations. What were the various types of segments that may have required disclosure?

4. What was *SFAS 14*'s dominant industry segment rule and what problem could this rule generate?

5. According to the FASB, what is the major objective of segment reporting?

6. *SFAS 131*'s management approach requires firms to define segments on the basis of the firm's internal organization structure. What are the advantages in defining segments on this basis?

7. What is an operating segment?

8. How are operating segments determined when business activities are disaggregated in more than one way and multiple sets of reports are used by the chief operating decision maker?

9. Describe the three tests for identifying reportable operating segments.

10. What information must an enterprise report for each of its material operating segments?

11. Under what conditions must an enterprise provide information about products and services?

12. Under what conditions must an enterprise provide information about geographic areas?

13. What information must an enterprise report by geographic area?

14. To satisfy *SFAS 131*'s geographic area disclosure requirements, what is the minimum and maximum number of countries for which information should be reported separately?

15. Under what conditions should a company disclose the amount of sales from a major customer?

16. According to *SFAS 131*, what type of segment information must be provided in interim financial statements?

LIBRARY ASSIGNMENTS

1. Locate the latest annual reports for two companies generally considered to be competitors. Based solely on the segment information, write a report describing and evaluating the two companies. Possible companies include:

   Chemical: DuPont, Dow Chemical, Monsanto, Union Carbide
   Pharmaceutical: Merck, Schering-Plough, Pfizer, Eli Lilly
   Computer: IBM, Hewlett-Packard, Digital Equipment, Apple Computer, Compaq
   Food Products: Heinz, Quaker Oats, Sara Lee, Campbell Soup
   Automobile: Chrysler, Ford, General Motors
   Beverage: Coca-Cola, PepsiCo
   Petroleum: Chevron, Exxon, Mobil Oil, Texaco

2. Read the following as well as any other published information on the reporting of segment information:

   " 'An Innate Fear of Disclosure,' " *Forbes*, February 5, 1990.
   "How Much Is Known?" *The Woman CPA*, October 1989.

   Write a report discussing whether the FASB should change the method by which segments of a business are identified to remove some of the flexibility that is currently allowed.

PROBLEMS

1. Which of the following is not considered by the FASB to be an objective of segment reporting?
   a. It helps users better understand the enterprise's performance.
   b. It helps users better assess the enterprise's prospects for future cash flows.
   c. It helps users make more informed judgments about the enterprise as a whole.
   d. It helps users make comparisons between a segment of one enterprise and a similar segment of another enterprise.

2. Under *SFAS 131*, which of the following items of information would Most Company not be required to disclose, even if it were material in amount?
   a. Revenues generated from sales of its Consumer Products line of goods.
   b. Revenues generated by its Japanese subsidiary.
   c. Revenues generated from export sales.
   d. Revenues generated from sales to Wal-Mart.

3. Which of the following operating segment disclosures is not required by *SFAS 131*?
   a. Liabilities.
   b. Interest expense.
   c. Intersegment sales.
   d. Unusual items (extraordinary items and discontinued operations).

4. In determining whether a particular operating segment is of significant size to warrant disclosure, which of the following statements is true?
   a. Three tests are applied and all three must be met.
   b. Four tests are applied but only one must be met.
   c. Three tests are applied but only one must be met.
   d. Four tests are applied and all four must be met.

5. Which of the following statements would not be true under *SFAS 131*?
   a. Operating segments can be determined by looking at a company's organization chart.
   b. Companies may combine individual foreign countries into geographic areas for purposes of complying with the geographic area disclosure requirements.
   c. If operating segments are defined by product lines, companies must provide revenue and asset information for the domestic country and each material foreign country.
   d. Companies must disclose total assets, investment in equity method affiliates, and total expenditures for long-lived assets by operating segment.

6. Which of the following is not necessarily true for an operating segment?
   a. An operating segment earns revenues and incurs expenses.
   b. An operating segment is regularly reviewed by the chief operating decision maker to assess performance and make resource allocation decisions.
   c. Discrete financial information generated by the internal accounting system is available for an operating segment.
   d. An operating segment regularly generates a profit from its normal, ongoing operations.

7. Which of the following is a criterion for determining whether an operating segment is separately reportable?
   a. Segment liabilities are 10 percent or more of consolidated liabilities.
   b. Segment profit or loss is 10 percent or more of consolidated net income.
   c. Segment assets are 10 percent or more of combined segment assets.
   d. Segment revenues from external sales are 5 percent or more of combined segment revenues from external sales.

8. Which of the following items is required to be disclosed by geographic area?
   a. Total assets.
   b. Revenues from external customers.
   c. Profit or loss.
   d. Capital expenditures.

9. According to *SFAS 131*, which of the following would be an acceptable grouping of countries for providing information by geographic area?
   a. United States, Mexico, Japan, Spain, All Other Countries.
   b. United States, Canada and Mexico, Germany, Italy.

     c. United States, Taiwan, Japan, Europe.

     d. Canada, Germany, France, All Other Countries.

10. Which of the following statements is true?

     a. *SFAS 131* does not require segment information to be reported in accordance with generally accepted accounting principles.

     b. *SFAS 131* does not require a reconciliation of segment assets to consolidated assets.

     c. *SFAS 131* requires geographic area information to be disclosed in interim financial statements.

     d. *SFAS 131* requires disclosure of the identity of a major customer.

11. Which of the following items is not required to be reported in interim financial statements for each material operating segment?

     a. Revenues from external customers.

     b. Intersegment revenues.

     c. Segment assets.

     d. Segment profit or loss.

12. The Plume Company has a paper products operating segment. Which of the following items does Plume not have to report for this segment?

     a. Interest expense.

     b. Research and development expense.

     c. Depreciation and amortization expense.

     d. Interest income.

13. The Estilo Company has three operating segments with the following information:

	Paper	Pencils	Hats
Sales to outsiders	$8,000	$4,000	$6,000
Intersegment transfers	600	1,000	1,400

In addition, revenues generated at corporate headquarters are $1,000.

    What is the minimum amount of revenue that each of these segments must have to be considered separately reportable?

     a. $1,800.

     b. $1,900.

     c. $2,000.

     d. $2,100.

14. The Carson Company has four separate operating segments:

	Apples	Oranges	Pears	Peaches
Sales to outsiders	$123,000	$81,000	$95,000	$77,000
Intersegment transfers	31,000	26,000	13,000	18,000

What amount of revenues must be generated from one customer before that party must be identified as a major customer?

     a. $37,600.

     b. $41,200.

     c. $46,400.

     d. $56,400.

15. The Jarvis Corporation has six different operating segments reporting the following operating profit and loss figures:

K	$ 80,000 loss	N	$440,000 profit
L	140,000 profit	O	90,000 profit
M	940,000 loss	P	100,000 profit

Which of the following statements is not true?

     a. K is not a reportable segment based on this one test.

     b. L is a reportable segment based on this test.

     c. O is not a reportable segment based on this one test.

     d. P is a reportable segment based on this test.

16. Quatro Corp. is engaged solely in manufacturing operations. The following data pertain to the operating segments for the year 1999:

Operating Segment	Total Revenues	Profit	Assets at 12/31/99
A.............	$10,000,000	$1,750,000	$20,000,000
B.............	8,000,000	1,400,000	17,500,000
C.............	6,000,000	1,200,000	12,500,000
D.............	3,000,000	550,000	7,500,000
E.............	4,250,000	675,000	7,000,000
F.............	1,500,000	225,000	3,000,000
	$32,750,000	$5,800,000	$67,500,000

In its segment information for 1999, how many reportable segments does Quatro have?

a. Three.
b. Four.
c. Five.
d. Six.

(AICPA adapted)

17. What is the minimum number of operating segments that must be separately reported?
   a. Ten.
   b. Segments with at least 75 percent of revenues as measured by the revenue test.
   c. At least 75 percent of the segments must be separately reported.
   d. Segments with at least 75 percent of the revenues generated from outside parties.

18. The Medford Company has seven operating segments but only four (G, H, I, and J) are of significant size to warrant separate disclosure. Segments K, L, and M are not large enough. As a whole, these segments have revenues generated from outside parties of $710,000 ($520,000 + $190,000). In addition, the segments had $260,000 in intersegment transfers ($220,000 + $40,000).

	Outside Sales	Intersegment Sales
G	$120,000	$ 80,000
H	150,000	50,000
I.............	160,000	20,000
J.............	90,000	70,000
Totals	$520,000	$220,000

	Outside Sales	Intersegment Sales
K	$ 60,000	–0–
L	70,000	$ 20,000
M...........	60,000	20,000
Totals	$190,000	$ 40,000

Which of the following statements is true?
   a. A sufficient number of segments is being reported because those segments have $740,000 in revenues out of a total of $970,000 for the company as a whole.
   b. Not enough segments are being reported because those segments have $520,000 in outside sales out of a total of $710,000 for the company as a whole.
   c. Not enough segments are being reported because those segments have $740,000 in revenues out of a total of $970,000 for the company as a whole.
   d. A sufficient number of segments is being reported because those segments have $520,000 in outside sales out of a total of $710,000 for the company as a whole.

19. What information should a company present about revenues by geographic area?
   a. Disclose separately the amount of sales to unaffiliated customers and the amount of intracompany sales between geographic areas.
   b. Disclose as a combined amount sales to unaffiliated customers and intracompany sales between geographic areas.
   c. Disclose separately the amount of sales to unaffiliated customers but not the amount of intracompany sales between geographic areas.
   d. No disclosure of revenues from foreign operations need be reported.

(AICPA adapted)

20. The Fireside Corporation is organized into four operating segments. The following segment information was generated by the internal reporting system in 1998:

	Revenues from Outsiders	Intersegment Transfers	Operating Expenses
Cards	$1,200,000	$100,000	$ 900,000
Calendars	900,000	200,000	1,350,000
Clothing	1,000,000	—	700,000
Books	800,000	50,000	770,000

Additional operating expenses (of a general nature) incurred by the company amounted to $700,000.

What is the profit or loss of each of these segments? Carry out the profit or loss test to determine which of these segments is separately reportable.

21. The Ecru Company has identified five industry segments: plastics, metals, lumber, paper, and finance. Each of these segments has been consolidated appropriately by the company in producing its annual financial statements. Information describing each segment is presented here (in thousands):

	Plastics	Metals	Lumber	Paper	Finance
Sales to outside parties	$6,319	$2,144	$636	$347	–0–
Intersegment transfers	106	131	96	108	–0–
Interest income from outside parties	–0–	19	6	–0–	$ 27
Interest income from intersegment loans	–0–	–0–	–0–	–0–	159
Operating expenses	3,914	1,612	916	579	16
Interest expense	61	16	51	31	87
Tangible assets	1,291	2,986	314	561	104
Intangible assets	72	361	–0–	48	–0–
Intersegment loans	–0–	–0–	–0–	–0–	664

In addition, Ecru has $1,250,000 in common expenses that are not allocated to the various segments.

Required

Perform the testing procedures designed by the FASB to determine the reportable operating segments of the Ecru Company.

22. Following is financial information describing the six operating segments that make up Fairfield, Inc. (in thousands):

	Segments					
	Red	Blue	Green	Pink	Black	White
Sales to outside parties	$1,811	$812	$514	$309	$121	$ 99
Intersegment revenues	16	91	109	–0–	16	302
Salary expense	614	379	402	312	317	62
Rent expense	139	166	81	91	42	31
Interest expense	65	59	82	49	14	5
Income tax expense (savings)	141	87	61	(86)	(64)	–0–

The following questions should be considered independently. Unless specified, none of the six segments has primarily a financial nature.

Required

a. What minimum amount of revenue must be generated by any one segment to be of significant size to require disaggregated disclosure?
b. If only Red, Blue, and Green are of sufficient size to necessitate separate disclosure, is Fairfield disclosing disaggregated data for enough segments?
c. What volume of revenues must be generated from a single client to necessitate disclosing the existence of a major customer?
d. If these six segments each has a profit or loss (in thousands) as follows, which is of significant size to warrant separate disclosure?

Red	$1,074	Pink	$ (94)
Blue	449	Black	(222)
Green	140	White	308

23. The Mason Company has prepared consolidated financial statements for the current year and is now gathering information in connection with the following five operating segments it has identified.

    Determine the reportable segments by carrying out each of the applicable tests. Also describe the procedure utilized to ensure that a sufficient number of segments is being separately disclosed. (Figures are in thousands.)

	Company Total	Books	Computers	Maps	Travel	Finance
Sales to outside parties...	$1,547	$121	$ 696	$416	$314	–0–
Intersegment sales	421	24	240	39	118	–0–
Interest income—external	97	60	–0–	–0–	–0–	$ 37
Interest income— intersegment loans	147	–0–	–0–	–0–	–0–	147
Assets..............	3,398	206	1,378	248	326	1,240
Operating expenses	1,460	115	818	304	190	33
Expenses—intersegment sales	198	70	51	31	46	–0–
Interest expense—external	107	–0–	–0–	–0–	–0–	107
Interest expense— intersegment loans	177	21	71	38	47	–0–
Income tax expense (savings)	21	12	(41)	27	31	(8)
General corporate expenses	55					
Unallocated operating costs	80					

24. In the past, the Slatter Corporation has operated primarily in the United States. However, a few years ago, the company opened a plant in Spain to produce merchandise that is sold within that country. This foreign operation has been so successful that during the past 24 months, the company also started a manufacturing plant in Italy as well as another in Greece. Financial information for each of these facilities follows:

	Spain	Italy	Greece
Sales	$395,000	$272,000	$463,000
Intersegment transfers	–0–	–0–	62,000
Operating expenses	172,000	206,000	190,000
Interest expense.......................	16,000	29,000	19,000
Income taxes........................	67,000	19,000	34,000
Long-lived assets	191,000	106,000	72,000

The company's domestic (U.S.) operations reported the following information for the current year:

Sales to unaffiliated customers....................	$4,610,000
Intersegment transfers...........................	427,000
Operating expenses	2,410,000
Interest expense	136,000
Income taxes	819,000
Long-lived assets	1,894,000

Slatter has adopted the following criteria for determining the materiality of an individual foreign country: (1) sales to unaffiliated customers within a country are 10 percent or more of consolidated sales, or (2) long-lived assets within a country are 10 percent or more of consolidated long-lived assets.

Required

Apply the materiality tests adopted by Slatter to determine those countries to be reported separately.

25. The following information was extracted from Note 11 (Segment Reporting) in Philip Morris Companies Inc. 1995 annual report:

Data by Segment

| | December 31 | | |
(in millions)	1995	1994	1993
Operating revenues:			
Tobacco	$32,316	$28,671	$25,973
Food	29,074	31,669	30,372
Beer	4,304	4,297	4,154
Financial services and real estate	377	488	402
Total operating revenues	$66,071	$65,125	$60,901
Operating profit:			
Tobacco	$ 7,177	$ 6,162	$ 4,910
Food	3,188	3,108	2,608
Beer	444	413	215
Financial services and real estate	164	208	249
Total operating profit	10,973	9,891	7,982
Unallocated corporate expenses	447	442	395
Operating income	$10,526	$ 9,449	$ 7,587
Identifiable assets:			
Tobacco	$11,196	$ 9,926	$ 9,523
Food	33,447	34,822	33,253
Beer	1,751	1,706	1,706
Financial services and real estate	5,632	5,193	5,659
Total identifiable assets	52,026	51,647	50,141
Other assets	1,785	1,002	1,064
Total assets	$53,811	$52,649	$51,205

In addition, Note 15 (Contingencies) to the consolidated financial statements consists of five pages of information on legal proceedings against the company, primarily class-action lawsuits filed in the United States related to diseases allegedly caused by cigarette smoking.

Required

1. Calculate the following for each industry segment:

    Percentage of total operating profit; 1995.
    Percentage growth in operating profit; 1994 to 1995.
    Operating profit as a percentage of operating revenues; 1995.
    Operating profit as a percentage of identifiable assets; 1995.

2. What do these ratios tell you about the importance of the various industry segments to Philip Morris' overall profitability? How might Note 15 factor into an assessment of the company's future prospects?

26. In complying with the geographic area requirements of *SFAS 14* in its 1995 annual report, the Coca-Cola Company disclosed the following (in millions):

	United States	Africa	Greater Europe	Latin America	Middle and Far East and Canada	Corporate	Consolidated
1995							
Net operating revenues	$5,261	$595	$6,025	$1,920	$4,162	$ 55	$18,018
Operating income	840	206	1,300	767	1,437	(488)	4,092
Identifiable operating assets	3,384	348	4,301	1,294	1,539	1,461*	12,327
1994							
Net operating revenues	$5,092	$522	$5,047	$1,928	$3,551	$ 41	$16,181
Operating income	869	182	1,173	713	1,208	(429)	3,716
Identifiable operating assets	2,991	357	3,958	1,164	1,437	1,456*	11,363
1993							
Net operating revenues	$4,586	$255	$4,456	$1,683	$2,957	$ 26	$13,963
Operating income	782	152	1,029	582	1,005	(442)	3,108
Identifiable operating assets	2,682	153	3,287	1,220	1,184	1,280*	9,806

*Corporate identifiable operating assets are composed principally of marketable securities, finance subsidiary receivables and fixed assets.

Required

1. Calculate the following ratios for each geographic area in which Coca-Cola operates:

   Percentage growth in net operating revenues; 1994–1995.

   Percentage of total net operating revenues (excluding Corporate); 1995.

   Operating income as a percentage of operating revenues (profit margin); 1995.

2. Is there any particular area of the world in which you believe Coca-Cola should attempt to expand its operations to increase operating revenues and operating income?

3. Is there any additional information you would like to have in answering question 2?

13

Accounting for Legal Reorganizations and Liquidations

QUESTIONS TO CONSIDER

- What is the difference between a voluntary and an involuntary bankruptcy petition?

- How does the liquidation of an insolvent company (a Chapter 7 bankruptcy) differ from a reorganization (a Chapter 11 bankruptcy)?

- Why would the creditors of an insolvent company allow it to reorganize rather than attempt to force a liquidation of its assets?

- What assistance can be provided to an insolvent company by an accountant?

- What provisions are frequently found in a bankruptcy reorganization plan?

- What financial reporting is made for a company while it is going through reorganization?

- What financial reporting is made for a company that successfully leaves bankruptcy reorganization?

- If an insolvent company is liquidated, what distribution is made of the assets that result? How is a fair and equitable settlement produced?

- In bankruptcy cases, what is meant by terms such as *debtor in possession*, *cram down*, and *order for relief*?

One common thread that runs through a significant portion of this textbook is the accounting for an organization when viewed as a whole.[1] Chapters 2 through 7, for example, examine the consolidation of financial information generated by two or more companies that have been united in a business combination. Although the handling of specific accounts was included in that coverage, the primary emphasis was placed on reporting these companies as a single economic entity.

Likewise, the analysis of foreign currency translation demonstrated the procedures to be used in consolidating the financial position and operating results of a subsidiary operating anywhere in the world. Chapter 12 presented disaggregation reporting requirements that were created as another means of disclosing complete information to describe an entity. Once again, in both cases, the accounting goal was to convey data about the entire operation.

Continuing with this theme, subsequent chapters present the specialized accounting procedures utilized in reporting to the SEC as well as by partnerships, state and local government units, not-for-profit organizations, estates, and trusts.

The method by which financial data are accumulated and disclosed to describe an organization is not a rigid structure. Accounting is adaptable; its development in specific circumstances is influenced by several factors: the purpose of the information, the nature of the organization, the environment in which the entity operates,

---

[1]Intermediate accounting, in contrast, tends to examine the reporting of specific assets and liabilities such as leases, pensions, and bonds.

and so on. Thus, to report a business combination, a foreign subsidiary, an industry segment, a partnership, a government unit, an estate, or a not-for-profit organization, accountants must develop unique reporting techniques that meet particular needs and problems.

Chapter 13 extends this coverage by presenting the accounting procedures required in bankruptcy cases. A financially troubled company as well as its owners and creditors all face the prospect of incurring significant losses. Thus, the accountant must adapt financial reporting to meet many and varied informational needs. The increase in the number of failed businesses in recent years has made this accounting process especially important.

ACCOUNTING FOR LEGAL REORGANIZATIONS AND LIQUIDATIONS

Centuries ago in Italy the bankrupt merchant would be forced into an odd form of pillory. He would have the table he did business at in the town square broken. At least one source says the word *bankruptcy* derives from the Italian words for this practice, which translate to *broken bench.*[2]

A basic assumption of accounting is that a business is considered a *going concern* unless evidence to the contrary is discovered. As a result, assets such as inventory, land, buildings, and equipment are reported based on historical cost rather than net realizable value. Unfortunately, not all companies prove to be going concerns. In 1994 alone, 71,520 businesses failed in the United States.[3] A list of organizations beginning bankruptcy proceedings during recent years contains some of the best-known corporate names in America:

Wang Laboratories
Phar-Mor, Inc.
Savin Corporation
Drexel Burnham Lambert Group
Orion Pictures
Presidential Airlines
Kaiser Steel Corporation
Grand Union
Ben Franklin Retail Stores
Best Products
Dow Corning
Fruehauf Trailer
Bradlees
Italian Oven[4]

---

[2]"In Pursuit of a Balanced Bankruptcy Law," *ABA Banking Journal,* May 1993, p. 50.

[3]Department of Commerce, *Statistical Abstract of the United States 1996* (Washington, D.C.: Government Printing Office, 1996), p. 543.

[4]The author (JH) is personally aware of the trauma associated with bankruptcy because he owned several hundred shares of both Presidential Airlines and Kaiser Steel at the time each company filed for bankruptcy. The demise of these two companies may be taken as an indication of the author's astute investment expertise.

What happens to these businesses after they fail? Who gets the assets? Are the creditors protected? How does the accountant reflect the economic plight of the company?

Virtually all businesses undergo financial difficulties at various times. Economic downturns, poor product performance, or litigation losses can create cash flow difficulties for even the best-managed organizations. Most companies take remedial actions and work to return their operations to normal profitability. However, as the preceding list indicates, not all companies are able to solve their monetary difficulties. If problems persist, a company can eventually become *insolvent,* unable to pay debts as the obligations come due. When creditors are not paid, they obviously attempt to protect their financial interests in hopes of reducing the possibility of loss. They may seek recovery from the distressed company in several ways: repossession of assets, the filing of lawsuits, foreclosure on loans, and so on. An insolvent company can literally become besieged by its creditors.

If left unchecked, pandemonium would be the possible outcome of a company's insolvency. As a result, some of the creditors and stockholders as well as the company itself could find themselves treated unfairly. One party might be able to collect in full while another is left with a total loss. *Thus, bankruptcy laws have been established in the United States to structure this process, provide protection for all parties, and ensure fair and equitable treatment.*

Although a complete coverage of bankruptcy statutes is more appropriate for a business law textbook, significant aspects of this process directly involve accountants. "In many small business situations, the company accountant is the sole outside financial advisor and the first to recognize that the deteriorating financial picture mandates consideration of bankruptcy in one form or another. In many such situations, the accountant's role in convincing management that a timely reorganization under the bankruptcy law is the sole means of salvaging any part of the business may be critical."[5]

Bankruptcy Reform Act of 1978

> Over the ages debtors who found themselves unable to meet obligations were dealt with harshly. Not only were all their assets taken from them, but they were given little or no relief through legal forgiveness of debts. Many of them ended up in debtors' prisons with all means of rehabilitation removed. A large number of the early settlers in this country left their homelands to escape such a fate.[6]

Based on an original provision of the U.S. Constitution, all bankruptcy laws in this country must be created by Congress. However, virtually no federal bankruptcy laws were actually passed until the Bankruptcy Act of 1898 (which was subsequently revised in 1938 by the Chandler Act). Later, following a decade of study and debate by Congress, these laws were replaced with the Bankruptcy Reform Act of 1978. Congress subsequently revised and updated that act by passing the Bankruptcy Reform Act of 1994. Today, this legislation provides the legal structure for most bankruptcy proceedings.[7] *To this end, it strives to achieve two goals in connection with insolvency cases: (1) the fair distribution of assets to creditors and (2) the discharge of an honest debtor from debt.*

---

[5]John K. Pearson, "The Role of the Accountant in Business Bankruptcies," *The National Public Accountant,* November 1982, p. 22.

[6]Homer A. Bonhiver, *The Expanded Role of the Accountant under the 1978 Bankruptcy Code* (New York: Deloitte Haskins & Sells, 1980), p. 7.

[7]The Bankruptcy Reform Act applies to corporations, partnerships, and individuals. However, certain types of companies are excluded from portions or even all of its provisions because other laws are applicable. Such organizations include insurance companies, banks, railroads, and stockbrokers.

Voluntary and Involuntary Petitions When insolvency occurs, any interested party has the right to seek protection under the Bankruptcy Reform Act.[8] Thus, the company itself can file a petition with the court to begin bankruptcy proceedings. If the company is the instigator, the process is referred to as a *voluntary* bankruptcy. In such cases, the company's petition has to be accompanied by exhibits listing all debts as well as assets (reported at fair market value). Company officials also must respond to questions concerning various aspects of the business's affairs. Such questions include:

- When did the business commence?
- In whose possession are the books of account and records?
- When was the last inventory of property taken?

Creditors also may seek to force a debtor into bankruptcy (known as an *involuntary* bankruptcy) in hopes of reducing their potential losses. To avoid nuisance actions, bankruptcy laws regulate the filing of involuntary petitions. Where a company has 12 or more unsecured creditors, at least 3 have to sign the petition. In addition, the creditors that sign must have unsecured debts of at least $10,000. If fewer than 12 unsecured creditors exist, only a single signer is required but the $10,000 minimum debt limit remains. Zale Corporation's creditors provide an example of the former situation. "Three Zale Corporation bondholders filed an involuntary bankruptcy law petition against the troubled jewelry chain yesterday, two days after it declared a moratorium on all payments to banks, bondholders and suppliers. Whether Zale, the nation's largest jewelry chain, will fight the petition remains to be seen."[9]

Neither a voluntary nor an involuntary petition automatically creates a bankruptcy case. Voluntary petitions are rejected by the court if the action is considered detrimental to the creditors. Involuntary petitions also can be rejected unless evidence exists to indicate that the debtor is not actually able to meet obligations as they come due. Merely being slow to pay is not sufficient. The debtor may well fight an involuntary petition fearing that it will taint its reputation in the business community.

If the petition is accepted by the court, an *order for relief* is granted. This order halts all actions against the debtor, thus providing time for the various parties involved to develop a course of action. In addition, the company comes under the authority of the bankruptcy court so that any distributions must be made in a fair manner. "To prevent creditors from seizing whatever is handy once the bankruptcy is filed, the Bankruptcy Code provides for an automatic stay or injunction that prohibits actions by creditors to collect debts from the debtor or the debtor's property without the court's permission. The automatic stay bars any creditor (including governmental creditors such as the Internal Revenue Service) from taking any action against the debtor or the debtor's property."[10]

Classification of Creditors Following the issuance of an order for relief, each creditor's view of a bankruptcy case is obviously influenced by the possible risk of loss. However, many creditors may have already obtained some measure of security for themselves. At the time a debt is created, the parties can agree that a mortgage lien or security interest will be attached to specified assets (known as *collateral*) owned by the debtor. Such action is most likely when the amounts involved are great

---

[8]As is discussed later in this chapter, insolvency (not being able to pay debts as they come due) is not necessary for the filing of a bankruptcy petition. Such companies as the Manville Corporation, Texaco, and A. H. Robins have filed for protection under the Bankruptcy Reform Act in hopes of settling massive litigation claims.

[9]"Dissident Bondholders File Petition to Force Zale into Bankruptcy," *The Wall Street Journal,* January 2, 1992, p. A4.

[10]Pearson, "The Role of the Accountant," p. 24.

or the debtor is experiencing financial difficulty. In the event that the liability is not paid when due, the creditor has the right to force the sale (or, in some cases, the return) of the pledged property with the proceeds being used to satisfy all or part of the obligation. Thus, in bankruptcy proceedings, a secured creditor is in a much less vulnerable position than an unsecured creditor.

Because of the possible presence of liens, all loans and other liabilities are reported to the court according to their degree of protection against loss. Hence, some debts are identified as *fully secured* to indicate that the net realizable value of the collateral exceeds the amount of the obligation. Despite the debtor's insolvency, these creditors will not suffer loss; they are completely protected by the pledged property. Any money received from the asset that is in excess of the balance of the debt is used to pay unsecured creditors.

Conversely, if a liability is labeled as *partially secured,* the value of the collateral covers only a portion of the obligation. The remainder is considered unsecured so that the creditor risks losing some or all of this additional amount. As an example, a bank might have a $90,000 loan due from an insolvent party protected by a lien attached to land valued at $64,000. This debt is only partially secured; $26,000 of the balance would not be satisfied by the asset so that this portion must be reported to the court as unsecured.

All other liabilities are unsecured; these creditors have no legal right to any specific assets of the debtor. They are only entitled to share in any funds that remain after all secured claims have been settled. Obviously, unsecured creditors are in a precarious position. Unless a debtor's assets greatly exceed secured liabilities (which is unlikely in most insolvency cases), significant losses can be expected if liquidation is necessary. Hence, one of the most important aspects of the bankruptcy laws is the ranking of unsecured claims. Only in this manner is a systematic distribution of any remaining assets possible.

The Bankruptcy Reform Act does identify several types of unsecured liabilities that have priority and must be paid before other unsecured debts are settled. *These obligations are ranked with each level having to be satisfied in full before any payment is made to the next.*

Unsecured Liabilities Having Priority[11]

1. Claims for administrative expenses such as the costs of preserving and liquidating the estate. All trustee expenses are included in this category as well as the costs of outside attorneys, accountants, or other consultants. Without this high-priority ranking, insolvent companies would have extreme problems convincing qualified individuals to serve in these essential positions. However, in recent years, the amounts assessed for such services have come under fire from many critics: "The 26 firms involved in the Eastern Air Lines Inc. bankruptcy in 1989 charged close to $86 million in fees."[12] "After six years in Chapter 11 bankruptcy-court proceedings, the documents show, the trustee of (Finley Kumble's) estate collected $60 million in cash for the creditors. But some $48 million, or 80 percent, has been spent just on operating and administering the bankruptcy case."[13]

2. Obligations arising between the date that a petition is filed with the bankruptcy court and the appointment of a trustee or the issuance of an order

---

[11]Only the most significant unsecured liabilities that are given priority are included here. For a complete list, please check a current business law textbook.

[12]Ronald Glover, Kathleen Kerwin, and Lisa Driscoll, "There's Plenty for All at the Bankruptcy Banquet," *Business Week,* November 4, 1991, p. 124.

[13]Amy Stevens, "Finley Kumble's Creditors Left Wanting but Bankruptcy Pros Collect Their Fees," *The Wall Street Journal,* April 8, 1994, p. B1.

What Do We Do Now?

The Toledo Shirt Company manufactures men's shirts sold to department stores and other outlets throughout Ohio, Illinois, and Indiana. For the past 14 years, one of the Toledo's major customers has been Abraham and Sons, a chain of nine stores selling men's clothing. Unfortunately, 18 months ago, Mr. Abraham retired and his two sons took complete control of the organization. Since that time, they have invested enormous sums of money in an attempt to expand each store by selling women's clothing. Success in this new market has been difficult; Abraham and Sons is not known for selling women's clothing and no one in the company has much expertise in the area.

Approximately seven months ago, James Thurber, the chief financial officer of the Toledo Shirt Company, began to notice that it was taking longer than usual to collect payments from Abraham and Sons. Instead of the normal 30 days, the retailer was taking at least 45 days—and frequently longer—to pay each invoice. Because of the amount of money involved, Thurber began to monitor the balance each day. When the age of the receivable ($71,000) hit 65 days, he placed a call to Abraham and Sons. The treasurer assured him that the company was merely having seasonal cash flow problems but that payments would soon be back on a normal schedule.

Thurber was still concerned and shortly thereafter placed Abraham and Sons on a "cash and carry" basis; no sales were to be made unless cash was collected in advance. The company's treasurer immediately called Thurber to complain bitterly. "We have been one of your best customers for well over a decade but now that we have gotten into a bit of trouble you stab us in the back. When we straighten things out here, we will remember this. We can get our shirts from someone else. Our expansions are now complete; we have hired an expert to help us market women's clothing. We can see the light at the end of the tunnel. Abraham and Sons will soon be more profitable than ever." In hopes of appeasing the customer while still protecting his own position, Thurber agreed to sell merchandise to Abraham and Sons on a very limited credit basis.

A few days later, Thurber received a disturbing phone call from a vice president with another clothing manufacturer. "We've got to force Abraham and Sons into bankruptcy immediately to protect ourselves. Those guys are running the company straight into the ground. They owe me $38,000 and I can only hope to collect a small portion of it now. I need two other creditors to sign the petition and I want Toledo Shirt to be one of them. Abraham and Sons has already mortgaged all of its buildings and equipment so we can't get anything from those assets. Inventory stocks are dwindling and sales have disappeared since they've tried to change the image of their stores. We can still get some of our money but if we wait much longer nothing will be left but the bones."

Should the Toledo Shirt Company be loyal to a good customer or start the bankruptcy process to protect itself? What actions should Thurber take?

for relief. In voluntary cases, such claims are quite rare since an order for relief is usually entered at the time the petition is filed. This provision is important, however, in helping the debtor to continue operations if an involuntary petition is presented but no legal action is immediately taken. Without this ranking, suppliers would stop supplying merchandise to the debtor until the matter was resolved. The debtor can continue to buy goods and stay in business while resisting an involuntary petition.

3. Employee claims for wages earned during the 90 days preceding the filing of a petition. The amount of this priority is limited, though, to $4,000 per individual. This priority ranking does not include officers' salaries. It is designed to prevent employees from being penalized by the company's problems and also encourages them to continue working until the bankruptcy issue is settled.

4. Employee claims for contributions to benefit plans earned during the 180 days preceding the filing of a petition. Once again, a limit of $4,000 per individual (reduced by certain specified payments) is enforced.

5. Claims for the return of deposits made by customers to acquire property or services which were never delivered or provided by the debtor. The priority

figure, in this case, is limited to $1,800. These claimants did not intend to be creditors; they were merely trying to make a purchase.

6. Government claims for unpaid taxes.

All other obligations of an insolvent company are classified as general unsecured claims that can be repaid only after the creditors with priority have been satisfied. *If the funds that remain for the general unsecured debts are not sufficient to settle all claims, the available money must be divided proportionally.*

Liquidation versus Reorganization The most important decision in any bankruptcy filing (either voluntary or involuntary) is the method by which the debtor will be discharged from its obligations. One obvious option is to liquidate the company's assets with the proceeds being distributed to creditors based on their secured positions and the priority ranking system just outlined. However, a very important alternative to liquidation does exist. The debtor company may survive insolvency and continue operations if a proposal for reorganization is accepted by the parties involved.

> There are many reasons why a business gets sick, but they don't necessarily mean it should be destroyed. Hundreds of thousands of businesses that at one time or another had financial difficulties survive today as the result of Chapter 11 proceedings. They continue to contribute to employment, to tax revenues, to overall growth. It's counterproductive to destroy the business value of an asset by liquidating it and paying it out in a Chapter 7 if that company shows signs of being able to recover in a reorganization.[14]

Under most reorganization plans, the creditors agree to absorb a partial loss rather than force the insolvent company to liquidate. Before accepting such an arrangement, the creditors (as well as the bankruptcy court) must be convinced that a greater return will be achieved by helping to rehabilitate the debtor. Often, as an example, payment of a specified percentage of the debt is promised to the creditors but usually only at some future date. One benefit associated with reorganizations is that the creditor may be able to retain the insolvent company as a customer. In many cases, continuation of this relationship is an important concern if the debtor has historically been a good client. Furthermore, the priority ranking system often leaves the general unsecured creditors with very little to lose in trying to avoid a liquidation.

Legal guidelines for the liquidation of a debtor are contained in Chapter 7 of Title I of the Bankruptcy Reform Act while Chapter 11 describes the reorganization process. Consequently, the proceedings have come to be referred to as a "Chapter 7 bankruptcy" (liquidation) or a "Chapter 11 bankruptcy" (reorganization). Accountants face two entirely different reporting situations depending on the type of bankruptcy encountered. However, in both cases, sufficient data must be obtained and reported to keep all parties adequately informed about the events as they occur.

Statement of Financial Affairs

Normally, at the start of bankruptcy proceedings, a statement of financial affairs is prepared for the debtor.[15] This schedule provides information about the current financial position of the company and helps all of the parties as they consider what actions to take. This statement is especially important in assisting the unsecured creditors as

---

[14]James A. Goodman as interviewed by Robert A. Mamis, "Why Bankruptcy Works," *Inc.,* October 1996, p. 39.

[15]The questionnaire completed by the insolvent company at the beginning of the bankruptcy proceedings is referred to as a statement of affairs. Although the titles are similar, the schedule of assets and liabilities discussed here is quite different from the legal questionnaire.

576   Chapter 13

DISCUSSION QUESTION

How Much Is That Building Really Worth?

Viron, Inc., was created in 1996 to recycle plastic products and manufacture a variety of new items. The actual production process was quite complex in that the old plastic had to be divided into categories and then reclaimed based on the composition. New products were made based on the type of plastic available and the market demand.

In December 1996, the company spent $2.3 million to construct a building for manufacturing purposes. The facility was designed specifically to meet the needs of Viron. The building was constructed near Gaffney, South Carolina, to take advantage of a large labor force available because of high unemployment in the area.

Unfortunately, the company was not able to generate revenues quickly enough to reach a break-even point and was forced to file for bankruptcy. An accountant has been hired to produce a statement of financial affairs to aid the parties in deciding whether to liquidate or reorganize.

In producing the statement of financial affairs, the accountant needed to establish a liquidation value for the building that was the company's largest asset. A real estate appraiser was brought in who made the following comments about the building: "The building is well made and practically new. It is clearly worth over $2 million. However, I doubt that anyone is going to pay that much for it. We don't get a lot of new industry in this area, so not many companies buy large buildings. Even if a company did buy the building, it would have to spend a significant amount of money for conversion purposes. Unless a company just wanted to recycle plastics, the building would have to be completely adapted to any other purpose. To tell you the truth, I am not sure it can be sold at any price. Of course, if someone wants to recycle plastics, it just might bring $2 million."

In producing the statement of financial affairs, how should the accountant report this building?

they decide whether to push for reorganization or liquidation. The debtor's assets and liabilities are reported according to the classifications relevant to a liquidation. Consequently, assets are labeled as:

1. Pledged with fully secured creditors.
2. Pledged with partially secured creditors.
3. Available for priority liabilities and unsecured creditors (often referred to as *free assets*).

The debts of the company are then listed in a parallel fashion as:

1. Liabilities with priority.
2. Fully secured creditors.
3. Partially secured creditors.
4. Unsecured creditors.

Stockholders are included in this final group.

The statement of financial affairs is produced under the assumption that liquidation will occur. Thus, historical cost figures are not relevant. The various parties to the bankruptcy desire information that reflects (1) the net realizable value of the debtor's assets and (2) the ultimate application of these proceeds to specific liabilities. Based on this data, both creditors and stockholders are able to estimate the monetary resources that will be available after all secured claims and priority liabilities have been settled. By comparing this total with the amount of unsecured liabilities, any member of these groups can approximate the potential loss that is being faced.

The information found in a statement of financial affairs can affect the outcome of the bankruptcy. If, for example, the statement indicates that unsecured creditors are destined to suffer a material loss in a liquidation, this group will probably favor reorganizing the company in hopes of averting such a consequence. Conversely, if the statement shows that all creditors will be paid in full and that a distribution to the stockholders is also possible, liquidation becomes a much more viable option. Thus, all parties involved with an insolvent company should consult a statement of financial affairs before deciding on the fate of the operation.

Statement of Financial Affairs Illustrated

To demonstrate the preparation of this statement, assume that the Chaplin Company has experienced severe financial difficulties in recent times and is currently insolvent. A voluntary bankruptcy petition will soon be filed and company officials are trying to decide whether to seek liquidation or reorganization. Consequently, they have asked their accountant to produce a statement of financial affairs to assist them in formulating an appropriate strategy. A current balance sheet for Chaplin, prepared as if the company were a going concern, is presented in Exhibit 13–1.

Prior to the creation of a statement of financial affairs, additional data must be ascertained concerning the insolvent company and its assets and liabilities. Hence, in this illustration, the following information has been accumulated about the Chaplin Company:

- The investment reported on the balance sheet has appreciated in value since being acquired and is now worth $20,000. Dividends of $500 are currently due from this investment, although the revenue has not yet been recognized by Chaplin.

- Officials estimate that $12,000 of the company's accounts receivable can still be collected despite the bankruptcy proceedings.

- By spending $5,000 for repairs and marketing, the inventory currently held by Chaplin can be sold for $50,000.

Exhibit 13–1
Financial Position Prior to Bankruptcy Petition

CHAPLIN COMPANY
Balance Sheet
June 30, 1998
Assets

Current assets:		
Cash	$ 2,000	
Investment (equity method)	15,000	
Accounts receivable (net)	23,000	
Inventory	41,000	
Prepaid expenses	3,000	$84,000
Land, building, equipment, and other assets:		
Land	100,000	
Building (net)	110,000	
Equipment (net)	80,000	
Intangible assets	15,000	305,000
Total assets		$389,000

Liabilities and Stockholders' Equity

Current liabilities:		
Notes payable (secured by inventory)	$ 75,000	
Accounts payable	60,000	
Accrued expenses	18,000	$153,000
Long-term liabilities:		
Notes payable (secured by lien on land and buildings)		200,000
Stockholders' equity:		
Common stock	100,000	
Retained earnings (deficit)	(64,000)	36,000
Total liabilities and stockholders' equity		$389,000

- A refund of $1,000 will be received from the various prepaid expenses but the company's intangible assets have no resale value.
- The land and building are in an excellent location and can be sold for a figure 10 percent more than book value. However, the equipment was specially designed for Chaplin. Company officials anticipate having trouble finding a buyer unless the price is reduced considerably. Hence, they expect to receive only 40 percent of current book value for these assets.
- Administrative costs of $21,500 are projected if liquidation of the company does occur.
- Accrued expenses include salaries of $13,000. Of this figure, one person is owed a total of $5,000 but that individual is the only employee due an amount in excess of $4,000. Payroll taxes withheld from wages but not yet paid to the government total $3,000. However, company records currently show only a $1,000 portion of this liability.
- Interest of $5,000 on the company's long-term liabilities has not been accrued for the first six months of 1998.

From this information, the statement of financial affairs presented in Exhibit 13–2 for the Chaplin Company can be prepared. Several aspects of this statement should be specifically noted:

1. The current and long-term distinctions usually applied to assets and liabilities are omitted. Since the company is on the verge of going out of business, such classifications are meaningless. Instead, the statement is designed to separate the secured and unsecured balances.

2. Book values are included on the left side of the schedule but only for informational purposes. These figures are not relevant in a bankruptcy. *All assets are reported at net realizable value, whereas liabilities are shown at the amount required for settlement.*

3. The dividend receivable and the interest payable are both included in Exhibit 13–2, although neither has been recorded on the balance sheet. The payroll tax liability also is reported at the amount presently owed by the company. Since these balances represent future cash flows, currently updated figures must be disclosed within the statement of financial affairs.

4. Liabilities having priority are individually identified within the liability section (point A). Because these claims will be paid before other unsecured creditors, the $36,500 total also is subtracted directly from the free assets (point B). Although not yet incurred, estimated administrative costs are included in this category since such expenses will be necessary for a liquidation. Salaries payable are also considered priority liabilities. However, the $1,000 owed to an employee in excess of the individual $4,000 limit is separated as an unsecured claim (point C).

5. According to this statement, if liquidation occurs, Chaplin expects to have only $57,000 in free assets remaining after settling all liabilities with priority (point D). Unfortunately, the liability section shows unsecured claims with a total of $95,000. These creditors, therefore, face a $38,000 loss ($95,000 − $57,000) if the company is liquidated (point E). This final distribution is often stated in a percentage form:

$$\frac{\text{Free assets}}{\text{Unsecured claims}} = \frac{\$57,000}{\$95,000} = 60\%$$

Thus, unsecured creditors can anticipate receiving only 60 percent of their claims. An individual, for example, who is owed $400 by this company should anticipate collecting only $240 ($400 × 60%) following liquidation.

Exhibit 13-2

CHAPLIN COMPANY
Statement of Financial Affairs
June 30, 1998

Book Values				Available for Unsecured Creditors
	Assets			
	Pledged with fully secured creditors:			
$210,000	Land and building	$ 231,000		
	Less: Notes payable (long term)	(200,000)		
	Interest payable	(5,000)		$26,000
	Pledged with partially secured creditors:			
41,000	Inventory	$ 45,000		
	Less: Notes payable (current)	(75,000)		–0–
	Free assets:			
2,000	Cash			2,000
15,000	Investment in marketable securities			20,000
–0–	Dividends receivable			500
23,000	Accounts receivable			12,000
3,000	Prepaid expenses			1,000
80,000	Equipment			32,000
15,000	Intangible assets			–0–
	Total available to pay liabilities with priority and unsecured creditors			93,500
	Less: Liabilities with priority (see Ⓐ)			(36,500) Ⓑ
	Available for unsecured creditors			57,000 Ⓓ
	Estimated deficiency			38,000 Ⓔ
$389,000				$95,000

Book Values				Unsecured— Nonpriority Liabilities
	Liabilities and Stockholders' Equity			
	Liabilities with priority:			
–0–	Administrative expenses (estimated)	$ 21,500		
$ 13,000	Salaries payable (accrued expenses)	12,000		$1,000 Ⓒ
1,000	Payroll taxes payable (accrued expenses)	3,000		
	Total	$ 36,500 Ⓐ		
	Fully secured creditors:			
200,000	Notes payable	200,000		
–0–	Interest payable	5,000		
	Less: Land and building	(231,000)		–0–
	Partially secured creditors:			
75,000	Notes payable	75,000		
	Less: Inventory	(45,000)		30,000
	Unsecured creditors:			
60,000	Accounts payable			60,000
4,000	Accrued expenses (other than salaries and payroll taxes)			4,000
36,000	Stockholders' equity			
$389,000				$95,000

6. If the statement of financial affairs had shown the company with more free assets (after subtracting liabilities with priority) than unsecured claims, all creditors could expect to be paid in full with any excess money going to Chaplin's stockholders.

LIQUIDATION—A CHAPTER 7 BANKRUPTCY

When an insolvent company is to be liquidated, the process is regulated by the provisions found in Chapter 7 of the Bankruptcy Reform Act. This set of laws was written to provide an orderly and equitable structure for the selling of assets and payment of debts. To this end, several events occur after an order for relief has been entered by the court in either a voluntary or involuntary liquidation case.

First, an interim trustee is appointed by the court to oversee the company and its liquidation. This individual is charged with preserving the assets and preventing loss of the estate. Thus, creditors are protected from any detrimental actions that might be undertaken by the management, the ownership, or any of the other creditors. The interim trustee (as well as the permanent trustee if one is subsequently selected by the creditors) must carry out a number of tasks shortly after being appointed. These functions would include (but not be limited to) the following:

■ Changing locks and moving all assets and records to locations controlled by the trustee.

■ Posting notices that all assets of the business are now in the possession of the U.S. trustee and that tampering with or removing any contents is a violation of federal laws.

■ Notifying the post office that all mail for the company is to be sent to the trustee.

■ Opening a new bank account in the name of the trustee, and notifying banks that no withdrawals of the company's money are allowed except by the trustee.

■ Compiling all financial records and placing them in the custody of the trustee's own accountant.

■ Obtaining possession of any corporate records including minute books and other official documents.[16]

The court then calls for a meeting of all creditors who have appropriately filed a proof of claim against the debtor. This group may choose to elect a permanent trustee to replace the person temporarily appointed by the court. A majority (in number as well as in dollars due from the company) of the unsecured, nonpriority creditors must agree to this new trustee. If a decision cannot be reached by the creditors, the interim trustee is retained.

As a further action taken to ensure fairness, a committee of between 3 and 11 unsecured creditors is selected to help protect the group's interests. This committee of creditors:

■ Consults with the trustee regarding the administration of the estate.

■ Makes recommendations to the trustee regarding the performance of the trustee's duties.

■ Submits to the court any questions affecting the administration of the estate.[17]

Role of the Trustee

In the liquidation of any company, the trustee is a central figure. This individual must recover all property belonging to the insolvent company, preserve the estate from any further deterioration, liquidate noncash assets, and make distributions to the proper claimants. Additionally, the trustee may even need to continue operating the company to complete business activities that were in progress when the order for relief

---

[16]Bonhiver, *The Expanded Role of the Accountant,* pp. 50–51.

[17]Ibid., p. 26.

was entered. To accomplish such a multitude of objectives, this individual holds wide-ranging authority in bankruptcy matters. For example, the trustee has the right to appoint attorneys, accountants, consultants, and other outside professionals as needed to provide assistance.

The trustee can also void any transfer of property (known as a *preference*) made by the debtor within 90 days *prior* to the filing of the bankruptcy petition if the company was already insolvent at the time. These payments must then be returned by the recipient and be included within the debtor's free assets.[18] For example,

> Drexel Burnham Lambert Group Inc. made more than $600 million in payments that may be recoverable under bankruptcy law because the transactions occurred during the three months immediately prior to the company's bankruptcy-court filing. The payments were disclosed in the company's statement of financial affairs, . . . such payments, with certain exceptions, can be recovered if it is shown that a company gave preference to some creditors and if the debtor was insolvent at the time.[19]

This rule is intended to prevent one party from gaining advantage over another in the sometimes hectic period just before a bankruptcy petition is filed. Return of the asset is not necessary, however, if the transfer was for no more than would have been paid to this party in a liquidation.

Not surprisingly, the trustee must make a proper recording of all activities and report them periodically to the court and other interested parties. For this purpose, the trustee can either establish a separate set of financial records or simply use the accounting system of the insolvent company. To reflect the stewardship responsibility being accepted, trustees frequently prefer to start their own independent record-keeping system, especially in cases where liquidation is to occur.

Interestingly, the actual reporting rules created by the Bankruptcy Reform Act are quite general: "Each trustee, examiner, and debtor-in-possession is required to file 'such reports as are necessary or as the court orders.' . . . In the past there have been no specific guidelines or forms used in the preparation of these reports."[20] Consequently, a wide variety of statements and reports may be encountered in liquidations. However, *a statement of realization and liquidation* is commonly used by the trustee to report the major aspects of the liquidation process. This statement is designed to convey the following information:

- The account balances reported by the company at the date on which the order for relief was filed.
- The cash receipts generated by the sale of the debtor's property.
- The cash disbursements made by the trustee to wind up the affairs of the business and to pay the secured creditors.
- Any other transactions of the company such as the write off of assets and the recognition of unrecorded liabilities.

Any cash that remains after this series of events is paid to the unsecured creditors with the priority claims being settled first.

---

[18]The 90-day limit is extended to one year if the transfer is made to an inside party such as an officer or a director or an affiliated company. The one-year limit also applies to any transfer made by the debtor with the intent to defraud another party.

[19]Wade Lambert, "Drexel Payments of Over $600 Million Before Chapter 11 May Be Recoverable," *The Wall Street Journal*, May 7, 1990, p. A3.

[20]In a reorganization, the ownership usually remains in possession of the company. This group is allowed to continue operating the business and is referred to as a debtor in possession. To monitor the debtor in possession's activities, the court has the right to appoint an examiner. This individual investigates the business so that reports and recommendations can be made to the courts. (See, for example, "The CPA's Role as Bankruptcy Examiner," *CPA Journal*, September 1991, pp. 42–50.) Quote from Bonhiver, *The Expanded Role of the Accountant*, p. 69.

Statement of Realization and Liquidation Illustrated

To demonstrate the production of a statement of realization and liquidation, the information previously presented for the Chaplin Company is once again utilized. Assume that company officials have decided to liquidate the business, a procedure regulated by Chapter 7 of the Bankruptcy Reform Act. An interim trustee is appointed by the court and then confirmed by the creditors to oversee the liquidation of assets and distribution of cash. A creditors' committee is also formed to ensure a fair and impartial distribution.

The dollar amounts resulting from this liquidation do not necessarily agree with the balances used in creating the statement of financial affairs in Exhibit 13–2. The previous statement was based on projected sales and other estimations, whereas a statement of realization and liquidation reports the actual transactions and other events as they occur. Consequently, discrepancies should be expected. The following transactions occur in liquidating this company:

Liquidation of Chaplin Company

1998

July 1   The accounting records shown in Exhibit 13–1 are adjusted to correct balances as of June 30, 1998, the date on which the order for relief was entered. Hence, the dividends receivable, interest payable, and additional payroll tax liability are recognized.

July 23   The trustee expends $7,000 to dispose of the company's inventory at a negotiated price of $51,000. The net cash results are applied to the notes payable for which the inventory had served as partial security.

July 29   Collection is made of the $500 cash dividend accrued as of June 30. The related investments (being reported at $15,000) are then sold for $19,600.

Aug. 17   Accounts receivable of $16,000 are collected. The remaining balances are written off as bad debts.

Aug. 30   The trustee determines that no refund is available from any of the company's prepaid expenses. The intangible assets also are removed from the financial records because they have no cash value.

Sept. 25   The land and building are sold for $208,000 with $205,000 of this money being immediately used by the trustee to pay off the secured creditors.

Oct. 9   After an extended search for a buyer, the equipment is sold for $42,000 in cash.

Nov. 1   An invoice of $24,900 is received for various administrative expenses incurred in liquidating the company. The trustee also reclassifies the remaining partially secured liabilities as unsecured.

Nov. 9   Since the noncash assets have now been converted into cash and all secured claims settled, the trustee begins to plan for the distribution of any remaining funds. The liabilities with priority are to be paid first. The excess will then be applied to the claims of unsecured nonpriority creditors.

The actual structure used in producing a statement of realization and liquidation can vary significantly. One popular form presents the various account groups on a horizontal plane with the liquidating transactions shown vertically. In this manner, accountants are able to record the events as they occur as well as the effect on each account classification. Exhibit 13–3 has been constructed in this style to display the liquidation of the Chaplin Company.

Exhibit 13–3   Final Statement

CHAPLIN COMPANY
Statement of Realization and Liquidation
June 30, 1998 to November 9, 1998

Date		Cash	Noncash Assets	Liabilities with Priority	Fully Secured Creditors	Partially Secured Creditors	Unsecured— Nonpriority Liabilities	Stockholders' Equity (Deficit)
6/30/98	Book balances	$ 2,000	$387,000	$13,000*	$200,000	$ 75,000	$65,000†	$ 36,000
7/1/98	Adjustments for dividends, interest, and payroll taxes		500	2,000	5,000			(6,500)
7/1/98	Adjusted book balances	2,000	387,500	15,000	205,000	75,000	65,000	29,500
7/23/98	Inventory sold—recorded net of disposal costs	44,000	(41,000)					3,000
7/23/98	Proceeds from inventory paid to secured creditors	(44,000)				(44,000)		
7/29/98	Investments sold and dividends received	20,100	(15,500)					4,600
8/17/98	Receivables collected with remainder written off	16,000	(23,000)					(7,000)
8/30/98	Intangible assets and prepaid expenses written off		(18,000)					(18,000)
9/25/98	Land and building sold	208,000	(210,000)					(2,000)
9/25/98	Proceeds from land and building paid to secured creditors	(205,000)			(205,000)			
10/9/98	Equipment sold	42,000	(80,000)					(38,000)
11/1/98	Administrative expenses accrued			24,900				(24,900)
11/1/98	Excess of partially secured liabilities reclassified as an unsecured claim					(31,000)	31,000	
11/9/98	Final balances remaining for unsecured creditors	$ 83,100	-0-	$39,900	-0-	-0-	$96,000	$(52,800)

*Includes salary payable of $12,000 (amount due employees but limited to $4,000 per individual) and $1,000 in payroll taxes owed to the government.
†Accounts payable plus accrued expenses other than salary payable (within $4,000 per person limitation) and payroll tax liability.

As can be seen from this exhibit, many aspects of the statement of realization and liquidation are no more than mechanical bookkeeping procedures used to record the liquidating transactions: inventory is sold at a profit, creditors are paid, receivables and dividends are collected, and so forth. Probably the most significant information presented in this statement is the measurement and classification of the insolvent company's liabilities. In the same manner as the statement of financial affairs, both fully and partially secured claims are reported separately from liabilities with priority and unsecured nonpriority claims.

For the Chaplin Company, Exhibit 13–3 discloses that $135,900 in debts remain as of November 9 ($39,900 in priority claims and $96,000 in unsecured nonpriority liabilities). Unfortunately, after satisfying all of the secured liabilities, only $83,100 in cash is retained by the company. The trustee must first use this money to pay the three liabilities with priority according to the following ranking:

Administrative expenses	$24,900
Salaries payable (within the $4,000 per person limitation)	12,000
Payroll taxes payable	3,000
Total	$39,900

These disbursements leave the company with $43,200 ($83,100 − $39,900) in cash but $96,000 in unsecured liabilities. Consequently, the remaining creditors are able to collect only 45 percent of their claims against the Chaplin Company:

$$\frac{\$43,200}{\$96,000} = 45 \text{ percent}$$

Because all liabilities have not been paid in full, the stockholders receive nothing from the liquidation process.

Interestingly, the unsecured nonpriority creditors are receiving a smaller percentage of their claims than the 60 percent figure projected in the statement of financial affairs (produced in Exhibit 13–2). Although this earlier statement plays an important role in bankruptcy proceedings, its accuracy is limited by the preparer's ability to foretell future events.

REORGANIZATION—A CHAPTER 11 BANKRUPTCY

Reorganization under the federal Bankruptcy Code is a way to salvage a company, not liquidate it. While it's true that the original owners of a company rescued in this way are often left without anything, others whose livelihoods depend on the company's fortunes may come out with their interests intact. The company's creditors, for example, may take over as the new owners. Its suppliers still may count on the company as a customer. Its customers still may count on the company as a supplier. And perhaps most important, many of its employees may be able to keep the jobs that otherwise would have been sacrificed in a liquidation.[21]

For the year ending June 30, 1992, approximately 24,000 petitions (both voluntary and involuntary) were filed in the United States to reorganize insolvent corporations based on Chapter 11 of the Bankruptcy Reform Act.[22] These reorganizations made up about 25 percent of all bankruptcies. In such cases, an attempt is being made to salvage the company so that operations can continue. Although this legal procedure offers the company some hope of survival, reorganization is certainly not a guarantee of future prosperity. Most companies that attempt to reorganize eventually are liquidated. In practice, though, reorganization appears to be biased in favor of large

[21]John Robbins, Al Goll, and Paul Rosenfield, "Accounting for Companies in Chapter 11 Reorganization," *Journal of Accountancy,* January 1991, p. 75.

[22]Michael Selz, "For Many Small Businesses, Chapter 11 Closes the Book," *The Wall Street Journal,* November 4, 1992, p. B2.

organizations. One expert estimates that 90 percent of big corporations that attempt to reorganize emerge as functioning entities while fewer than 20 percent of smaller companies survive.[23]

Many reorganizations may actually fail because the debtor struggles too long before filing a petition:

> Seeking bankruptcy because disaster looms—not after it has arrived—helps (gives the corporation time and provides equality of treatment). . . . Once a company files under the bankruptcy laws, suppliers are likely to demand cash on delivery. So management that moves before liquid assets are depleted has a better chance of making a go of reorganization.[24]

Obviously, the activities and events surrounding a reorganization differ significantly from a liquidation. One important distinction is that control over the company is normally retained by the ownership (referred to as a *debtor in possession*). However, if fraud or gross mismanagement can be proven, the court has the authority to appoint an independent trustee to assume control. For example, a trustee was brought in to take over Eastern Airlines after the bankruptcy judge found the management of Eastern and its parent to be "unfit" to operate the airline.[25] Unless replaced, the debtor in possession continues to operate the company and has the primary responsibility for developing an acceptable plan of reorganization.

While a reorganization is in process, the owners and managers are legally required to preserve the company's estate as of the date that the order for relief is entered. In this way, the bankruptcy regulations seek to reduce the losses that may have to be absorbed by creditors and stockholders when either reorganization or liquidation eventually occurs. For this reason, a newsletter distributed by the A. H. Robins Company to employees a few days after the corporation filed for Chapter 11 protection specified that "the company cannot pay any creditor or supplier for goods delivered or services rendered before August 21, 1985. The company is prohibited from making such payments unless there is a special court order. Monthly bills will have to be prorated to assure all creditors are treated the same."[26]

The Plan for Reorganization

> The plan is the heart of every Chapter 11 reorganization. The provisions of the plan specify the treatment of all creditors and equity holders upon its approval by the Bankruptcy Court. Moreover, the plan shapes the financial structure of the entity that emerges.[27]

The most intriguing aspect of a Chapter 11 bankruptcy is the plan developed to rescue the company from insolvency. Initially, proposals can be filed with the court only by the debtor in possession. However, if a plan for reorganization is not put forth within 120 days of the order for relief or accepted within 180 days (unless an extension is granted by the court), any interested party has the right to prepare and file a proposal. Creditors of Revco D. S. Inc. had the interesting quandary of choosing between three different reorganization plans: one backed by the company's management, one proposed by Rite Aid Corporation, and one submitted by Jack Eckerd Corporation.[28]

[23]Ibid.

[24]Daniel B. Moskowitz and Mark Ivey, "You Don't Have to Be Broke to Need Chapter 11," *Business Week*, April 27, 1987, p. 108.

[25]Carolyn Phillips, "Marty Shugrue Has Background Needed to Save Eastern Air," *The Wall Street Journal*, April 20, 1990, p. A6.

[26]Thomas R. Morris, "Some Questions Went Unasked," *Richmond Times-Dispatch*, May 18, 1986, p. B1.

[27]AICPA Statement of Position 90–7, *Financial Reporting by Entities in Reorganization Under the Bankruptcy Code*, November 19, 1990, par. 3.

[28]Gabriella Stern, "Timing of Revco Status Change Stays Uncertain," *The Wall Street Journal*, January 6, 1992, p. A3.

A reorganization plan may contain an unlimited number of provisions: proposed changes in the company, additional financing arrangements, alterations in the debt structure, and the like.[29] Regardless of the specific contents, the intent of all such plans is to provide a feasible long-term solution to the company's monetary difficulties. However, to gain acceptance by the parties involved, convincing evidence must be presented that the plan will enable the business to emerge from bankruptcy as a viable going concern. Although a definitive list of elements that could be included in a reorganization proposal is not possible, some of the most common are

1. *Plans proposing changes in the company's operations.* In hopes of improving liquidity, officials may decide to introduce new product lines or sell off unprofitable assets or even entire businesses. The closing of failing operations is especially common. A debtor in possession bears the burden of proving that the problems that led to insolvency can be eliminated and then avoided in the future. As an example, before emerging from Chapter 11 reorganization, House of Fabrics Inc. made a number of significant business changes:

> Since it opted to reorganize under bankruptcy court protection, the company, among other things, has closed more than 200 stores, reduced debt, secured a new three-year $60 million credit facility and disposed of surplus real estate. Earlier this week, the retail fabric and craft store operator announced the addition of three new board members.[30]

2. *Plans for generating additional monetary resources.* Companies faced with insolvency must develop new sources of cash, often in a short time period. Loans and the sale of both common and preferred stocks are frequently negotiated during reorganization to provide funding for the continuation of the business. For example, as part of the initial reorganization plan put forth by Orion Pictures, its majority owner, Metromedia Company, agreed to invest $15 million in cash. Without the willingness of the owners to back the company, creditors would probably be hesitant about agreeing to a reorganization.

3. *Plans for changes in the management of the company.* Frequently, a financial crisis is blamed on poor management. In that situation, proposing to reorganize a company with the management team intact is probably not a practical suggestion. Therefore, many plans include the hiring of new individuals to implement the reorganization and run important aspects of the company. These changes may even affect the board of directors elected by the stockholders to oversee the company and its operations: "Manville Corporation agreed to let creditors have the final say in any board appointments, eliminating the last major obstacle in gaining approval of its 3½ year bankruptcy-law reorganization."[31]

4. *Plans to settle the debts of the company that existed when the order for relief was entered.* No element of a reorganization plan is more important than the proposal for satisfying the various creditors of the company. In most cases, their agreement is necessary before the court will confirm any plan of reorganization. The actual proposal to settle these debts may take one of several forms:

■   Assets can be transferred to creditors who accept this payment in exchange for extinguishing a specified amount of debt. The book value of the liability being canceled is usually greater than the fair market value of the assets rendered.

---

[29]See, for example, "When Will Somebody—Anybody—Rescue Battered Allegheny?" *The Wall Street Journal,* April 19, 1990, p. A1.

[30]"Bankruptcy Period Ends; Stock to Resume Trading," *The Wall Street Journal,* August 1, 1996, p. B4.

[31]Cynthia F. Mitchell, "Manville Is Said to Have Agreed to Let Creditors Decide Board Appointments," *The Wall Street Journal,* April 25, 1986, p. 5.

- An equity interest (such as common stock, preferred stock, or stock rights) can be conveyed to creditors to settle an outstanding debt.
- The terms of the outstanding liabilities can be modified: maturity dates extended, interest rates lowered, face values reduced, accrued interest forgiven, and so on.

Acceptance and Confirmation of Reorganization Plan

The creation of a plan for reorganization does not guarantee its implementation. The Bankruptcy Reform Act specifies that a plan must be voted on by both the company's creditors and stockholders before being confirmed by the court. *To be accepted, each class of creditors must vote for the plan.* Acceptance requires the approval of two-thirds in dollar amount and more than one-half in the number of claims that cast votes. A separate vote is also required of each class of shareholders. For approval, at least two-thirds (measured by the number of shares held) of the owners who vote must agree to the proposed reorganization. Convincing all parties to support any specific plan is not an easy task since agreement often means the acceptance of a significant loss. However, any class of creditors that is not damaged by a reorganization is assumed to have accepted the plan without the necessity of a vote.

Although creditor and stockholder approval may be gained, confirmation by the court is still required. The court reviews the proposal and can reject the reorganization plan if a claimant (who did not vote for acceptance) would receive more through liquidation. The court also has the authority to confirm a reorganization plan that was not accepted by a particular class of creditors or stockholders. This provision is referred to as a *cram down*; it occurs when the court determines that the plan is fair and equitable. As an alternative, the court may convert a Chapter 11 reorganization into a Chapter 7 liquidation at any time if the development of an acceptable plan does not appear to be possible.

Financial Reporting during Reorganization

Developing and gaining approval for a reorganization plan can take years. During that period, the company continues operating under the assumption that it is eventually going to emerge from the bankruptcy proceedings. In the past, official accounting literature has provided virtually no guidance for the financial statements to be prepared by a company while in reorganization. However, the increased volume of companies (especially larger organizations) going through reorganization during the 1980s emphasized the need for some type of guidelines to be established.

Finally, in 1990, the AICPA Task Force on Financial Reporting by Entities in Reorganization Under the Bankruptcy Code issued Statement of Position 90–7 (*Financial Reporting by Entities in Reorganization Under the Bankruptcy Code*) (referred to as SOP 90–7). This pronouncement provides standards for the preparation of financial statements at two times:

1. During the period when a company is going through reorganization.
2. At the point that the company emerges from reorganization.

While going through reorganization, the company faces several specific accounting questions:

- Should the income effects resulting from operating activities be differentiated from transactions connected solely with the reorganization process?
- How should liabilities be reported? Since some of the debts may not be paid for years and then may require payment of an amount considerably less than face value, how should this information be conveyed?
- Does reorganization necessitate a change in the reporting basis of the company's assets?

The Income Statement during Reorganization   According to SOP 90–7, any gains, losses, revenues, and expenses resulting from the reorganization of the business should be reported separately. Such items are placed on the income statement before any income tax expense or benefits.[32]

Reorganization items would include any gains and losses on the sale of assets necessitated by the reorganization. In addition, as mentioned previously, enormous amounts of professional fees may be incurred. Historically, these items could be handled by any one of several different methods. SOP 90–7 requires that these costs be expensed as incurred.

> What's the proper way to account for lawyers' and investment bankers' fees that can run to millions monthly for large cases like LTV? It makes sense to expense them along the way— and that's what the new rules call for. In the past, some clever companies capitalized the fees on the theory that part of the work would benefit the company as a going concern.[33]

Interest expense and interest revenue were also discussed in SOP 90–7. During reorganization, interest expense usually does not accrue on debts owed at the date on which the order for relief is granted. The amount of liability on that date is frozen. Thus, recognition of interest is only necessary if payment will be made during the proceeding (for example, on debts incurred during the bankruptcy) or if the interest will probably be an allowed claim (for example, if the amount was owed but unrecorded prior to the granting of the order for relief). Any interest expense that is recognized is not really a result of the reorganization process and should not be separately reported as a reorganization item.

In contrast, interest revenue can increase to a quite substantial amount during reorganization. Because the company is not forced to pay the debts incurred prior to the date of the order for relief, cash reserves tend to grow and the resulting interest can become a significant source of income. *Any interest revenue that would not have been earned except for the proceeding is reported separately as a reorganization item.*

For example, the 1994 income statement for Columbia Gas System, Inc., reported a reduction in net income of $12.3 million from reorganization items. This figure included interest revenue of $63.4 million, and professional fees and other related adjustments of $35.4 million. A related footnote explains that the company has "earned income on cash accumulated from the suspension of payments related to prepetition liabilities, incurred expenses associated with professional fees and other related services and, in 1994, reflected adjustments to producer claim levels."

To illustrate, assume that the Crawford Corporation files a voluntary bankruptcy petition and is granted an order for relief on January 1, 1998. Thereafter, the ownership and management of the company begins to (1) work on a reorganization plan and (2) rehabilitate the company. Several branch operations are closed and accountants, lawyers, and other professionals are hired to assist in the reorganization. At the end of 1998, the bankruptcy is still in progress. The company prepares the income statement shown in Exhibit 13–4 so that the reader can distinguish the results of operating activities from the reorganization items.

The Balance Sheet during Reorganization   A new entity is not created when a company moves into reorganization. Therefore, traditional generally accepted accounting principles continue to apply. Assets, for example, should still be reported at their book values. However, many of the liabilities are likely to be reduced as part of the final reorganization plan. In addition, because of the order for relief, the current/noncurrent classification system is no longer applicable; payments may be delayed for years.

---

[32]In a similar manner, the statement of cash flows should be constructed so that reorganization items are shown separately within the operating, investing, and financing categories.

[33]Laura Jereski, "Starting Fresh," *Forbes,* April 15, 1991, p. 105.

CRAWFORD CORPORATION
(Debtor-in-Possession)
Income Statement
For Year Ended December 31, 1998

Revenues:		
Sales		$ 650,000
Cost and expenses:		
Cost of goods sold.	$ 346,000	
General and administrative expenses	165,000	
Selling expenses	86,000	
Interest expense.	4,000	601,000
Earnings before reorganization items and tax effects		49,000
Reorganization items:		
Loss on closing of branches	(86,000)	
Professional fees	(75,000)	
Interest revenue	26,000	(135,000)
Loss before income tax benefit		(86,000)
Income tax benefit		18,800
Net loss		(67,200)
Loss per common share		$ (.56)

Thus, in reporting the liabilities of a company being reorganized, debts subject to compromise (reduction by the court through acceptance of a reorganization plan) must be disclosed separately. Unsecured and partially secured obligations existing as of the granting of the order for relief fall into this category. Fully secured liabilities and all debts incurred since that date are not subject to compromise and must be reported in a normal manner as either a current or noncurrent liability.

According to SOP 90–7 (par. 24), liabilities subject to compromise "should be reported on the basis of the expected amount of the allowed claims . . . as opposed to the amounts for which those allowed claims may be settled." Thus, the company does not attempt to anticipate the payment required by a final plan but simply discloses the amount of these claims.

The liability section of a company during this reorganization period would appear as follows:

Liabilities Not Subject to Compromise		
Current liabilities:		
Short-term note payable	$ 62,000	
Accounts payable	86,000	
Accrued expenses and other liabilities	13,000	$161,000
Long-term liabilities: note payable.		40,000
Liabilities not subject to compromise		$201,000
Liabilities Subject to Compromise		
Prior tax claims	$ 77,000	
Notes payable	100,000	
Trade and other miscellaneous claims	133,000	310,000
Total liabilities		$511,000

Financial Reporting for Companies Emerging from Reorganization

Is a company that successfully leaves Chapter 11 status considered a new entity so that current values should be assigned to its asset and liability accounts (referred to as fresh start reporting)? Or, is the company simply a continuation of the organization that entered bankruptcy so that historical figures are still applicable? SOP 90–7 holds that these accounts should be adjusted to current value if two criteria are met (par. 36):

590   Chapter 13

- The reorganization (or market) value of the assets of the emerging company is less than the total of the allowed claims as of the date of the order for relief plus the liabilities incurred subsequently.
- The original owners of the voting stock are left with less than 50 percent of the voting stock of the company when it emerges from bankruptcy.

Meeting the first criterion shows that the old company could not have continued in business as a going concern. The second criterion indicates that control of the company has changed.

These two criteria are met in many, if not most, Chapter 11 bankruptcies. Consequently, the entity is reported as if it were a brand new business. For example, in financial statements for the year ending February 1, 1992, Carter Hawley Hale Stores, Inc., reported that "on confirmation of a plan of reorganization, the Company expects to utilize 'fresh start accounting' in accordance with the guidelines for accounting for emergence from bankruptcy. Fresh start accounting is expected to result in a restatement of Company assets to reflect current values."

In applying fresh start accounting, the reorganization value of the entity that emerges from bankruptcy must first be determined. According to paragraph 9 of SOP 90–7, "reorganization value generally approximates fair value of the entity before considering liabilities and approximates the amount a willing buyer would pay for the assets of the entity immediately after the restructuring . . . generally it is determined by discounting future cash flows for the reconstituted business that will emerge." This total value is then assigned to the specific tangible and intangible assets of the company in the same way as in a purchase combination.

If the reorganization value for the company is greater than the amounts assigned to these specific assets, an account akin to goodwill is recognized. For example, following reorganization, the balance sheet of Doskocil Companies reported an intangible asset, "reorganization value in excess of amounts allocable to identifiable assets, net of accumulated depreciation," as of December 31, 1994, of $82.6 million (out of total assets of $457.7 million). This balance can be amortized to expense over a period of up to 40 years. However, to avoid the extended write offs that have been common with goodwill, SOP 90–7 (par. 38) does state that factors usually indicate "a useful life of substantially less than forty years."

To illustrate, assume that a company has a reorganization value of $280,000 but only two specific assets. Land (with a book value of $90,000) is worth $150,000 and a building (with a book value of $78,000) is valued at $100,000. If the criteria for fresh start accounting are met, this company would emerge from bankruptcy with these assets recorded at their market values of $150,000 and $100,000 rather than the historical book values. In addition, the excess $30,000 ($280,000 − $250,000) would be assigned to this new intangible asset account.

The reporting of liabilities following a reorganization also creates a concern because many of these balances will be reduced and the payment period extended. SOP 90–7 requires that all liabilities (except for deferred income taxes which should be accounted for according to the provisions of FASB *Statement 109*) must be reported at the present value of the future cash payments.

To make the necessary asset adjustments to fresh start accounting, additional paid-in capital is normally increased or decreased. However, any write-down of a liability creates a recognized gain. Finally, because the company is viewed as a new entity, it must leave reorganization with a zero balance in retained earnings.

Fresh Start Accounting Illustrated

Assume that a company has the following trial balance just prior to emerging from bankruptcy:

	Debit	Credit
Current assets	$ 50,000	
Land	100,000	
Buildings	400,000	
Equipment	250,000	
Accounts payable (incurred since the order for relief was granted)		$ 100,000
Liabilities when the order for relief was granted:		
Accounts payable.................................		60,000
Accrued expenses		50,000
Note payable (due in 3 years)		300,000
Bonds payable (due in 5 years)		600,000
Common stock (50,000 shares with a $1 par value)		50,000
Additional paid-in capital		40,000
Retained earnings (deficit)	400,000	
Totals	$1,200,000	$1,200,000

Other Information:

- *Assets.* The company's land has a market value of $120,000; the building is worth $500,000. Other assets are worth their book values. The reorganization value of the company's assets is assumed to be $1,000,000 based on discounted future cash flows.

- *Liabilities.* The $100,000 of accounts payable incurred since the order for relief was granted must be paid in full as the individual balances come due. The accounts payable and accrued expenses that were owed when the order for relief was granted will be converted into one-year notes payable of $70,000, paying interest of 10 percent. The $300,000 note payable on the trial balance will be converted into a 10-year, 8 percent note of $100,000. These creditors also get 20,000 shares of stock that is to be turned in to the company by the common stockholders. Finally, the $600,000 bonds payable would be converted into eight-year, 9 percent notes totaling $430,000. The bondholders also get 15,000 shares of common stock turned in by the current owners.

- *Stockholders' Equity.* The owners of the common stock will return 70 percent of their stock (35,000 shares) to the company to be issued as specified above. The reorganization value of the assets is $1,000,000 and the debts of the company after the proceeding total $700,000 ($100,000 + $70,000 + $100,000 + $430,000). Thus, stockholders' equity must be the $300,000 difference. Since shares with a $50,000 par value would still be outstanding, additional paid-in capital is adjusted to $250,000.

In accounting for this reorganization, the initial question to be resolved is whether fresh start accounting is appropriate. The first criterion is met since the reorganization value of the assets ($1,000,000) is less than the sum of all postpetition liabilities ($100,000 accounts payable) and allowed claims (the $1,010,000 total of liabilities remaining from the date of the order for relief before any write-down). The second criterion is also met since the original stockholders receive less than 50 percent of the shares after the plan takes effect. At that point, they will have only 15,000 of the 50,000 outstanding shares.

Because fresh start accounting is appropriate, the assets must be adjusted to market value. In addition, an intangible asset is recognized for the $80,000 reorganization value of the company in excess of the value assigned to specific assets. The reorganization value is $1 million, but the market value of the assets is only $920,000 (current assets $50,000, land $120,000 [adjusted], buildings $500,000 [adjusted], and equipment $250,000). Since the accounts are already recorded at book value, adjustment is only necessary when market value differs from this book value:

Land	20,000	
Buildings	100,000	
Reorganization Value in Excess of Amount Allocable		
to Identifiable Assets	80,000	
Additional Paid-In Capital		200,000
To adjust asset accounts to fresh start accounting and to		
recognize excess value as an intangible asset subject to		
amortization.		

Next, the 35,000 shares of common stock returned to the company by the original owners should be recorded:

Common Stock	35,000	
Additional Paid-In Capital		35,000
To record shares of common stock returned to the company by		
owners as part of the reorganization agreement.		

The liability accounts on the records at the date of the order for relief must now be adjusted for the provisions of the bankruptcy reorganization plan. Because all of the new debts bear a reasonable interest rate, present value computations are not necessary. The first entry is a straight conversion with a gain recorded for the difference between the old debt and the new.

Accounts Payable	60,000	
Accrued Expenses	50,000	
Notes Payable (1 year)		70,000
Gain on Debt Discharge		40,000
To convert liabilities to a one-year note as per reorganization plan.		

The other two debt entries require a computation for the amount to be assigned to additional paid-in capital. The assumed total APIC for the company as computed earlier is $250,000. Since the holders of the notes receive 20,000 shares of stock (or 40 percent of the 50,000 share total), this stock is assigned additional paid-in capital of $100,000 (40 percent). The holders of the bonds are to get 15,000 shares (30 percent of the company total). Hence, additional paid-in capital of $75,000 (30 percent) is recorded.

Note Payable (3 years)	300,000	
Note Payable (10 years)		100,000
Common Stock (par value of 20,000 shares)		20,000
Additional Paid-In Capital (40 percent of company total) . . .		100,000
Gain on Debt Discharge		80,000
To record exchange with gain recorded for difference between		
book value of old note and the amount recorded for new note		
and shares of stock.		

Bonds Payable	600,000	
Notes Payable (8 years)		430,000
Common Stock (par value of 15,000 shares)		15,000
Additional Paid-In Capital (30 percent of company total) . . .		75,000
Gain on Debt Discharge		80,000
To record exchange with gain recorded for difference between		
book value of old bonds and the amount recorded for new notes		
and shares of stock.		

Additional Paid-In Capital now has a balance of $450,000 ($40,000 beginning balance plus $200,000 for adjusting assets plus $35,000 for shares returned by owners plus $100,000 because of shares issued for note and $75,000 because of shares issued for bonds). Therefore, this balance is $200,000 more than the amount to be reported as established through the provisions of the reorganization agreement. In addition, the Gain on Debt Discharge account has a balance of $200,000 ($40,000 + $80,000 + $80,000), a figure that must be closed out. Adjusting and closing these

DISCUSSION QUESTION

Is This the Real Purpose of the Bankruptcy Laws?

Insolvency is not a necessary condition for bankruptcy. Moreover, a firm may petition the court for protection under Chapter 11 even though it is not insolvent. If the business can demonstrate real financial trouble, the court will generally not dismiss the petition. In recent years, Chapter 11 has been looked upon as a safe harbor for gaining time to restructure the business and to head off more serious financial problems. *For example, when Johns Manville filed a petition under Chapter 11, it was a profitable, financially sound company. Yet, it faced numerous lawsuits for damages resulting from asbestos products it sold. Reorganization helped Johns Manville deal with its financial problems.*[34] (emphasis added)

During recent years, the filing of a voluntary Chapter 11 bankruptcy petition has become a tool sometimes used by companies to settle significant financial problems. Just as Johns Manville reorganized to settle the claims of asbestos victims, A. H. Robins followed a similar path to resolve thousands of lawsuits stemming from injuries resulting from the Dalkon Shield intrauterine device. The Wilson Foods Corporation managed to reduce union wages by filing under Chapter 11 as did Continental Airlines Corporation.

Not surprisingly, seeking protection under Chapter 11 to force a bargained resolution of a financial difficulty is a controversial legal maneuver. Creditors and claimants often argue that this procedure is used to avoid responsibility while the companies counter that bankruptcy can become the only realistic means of achieving any settlement.

Should companies be allowed to use the provisions of Chapter 11 in this manner?

accounts eliminates the deficit in retained earnings so that the emerging company has no balance in this equity account.

Additional Paid-In Capital	200,000	
Gain on Debt Discharge	200,000	
Retained Earnings (Deficit)		400,000
To adjust Additional Paid-In Capital balance to correct amount, close out Gain account, and eliminate deficit balance.		

After posting these entries, this company emerges from bankruptcy with

1. Its assets at fair market value.
2. Its debts equal to the present value of the future cash payments (except for any deferred income taxes).
3. No deficit balance.

	Debit	Credit
Current assets	$ 50,000	
Land	120,000	
Buildings	500,000	
Equipment	250,000	
Reorganization value in excess of amounts allocable to identifiable assets	80,000	
Accounts payable		$ 100,000
Note payable (due in 1 year)		70,000
Note payable (due in 10 years)		100,000
Notes payable (due in 8 years)		430,000
Common stock (50,000 shares with a $1 par value)		50,000
Additional paid-in capital		250,000
Retained earnings	–0–	–0–
Totals	$1,000,000	$1,000,000

---

[34]Paul J. Corr and Donald D. Bourque, "Managing in a Reorganization," *Management Accounting,* January 1988, p. 34.

SUMMARY

1. Every year a significant number of businesses in the United States become insolvent, unable to pay debts as they come due. Since creditors as well as owners hold financial interests in each failed company, bankruptcy laws have been written to provide protection for all parties. The Bankruptcy Reform Act of 1978 (as amended) currently serves as the primary structure for these legal proceedings. This act was designed to ensure a fair distribution of all remaining properties while discharging the obligations of an honest debtor.

2. Bankruptcy proceedings can be instigated voluntarily by the insolvent debtor or involuntarily by a group of creditors. In either case, an order for relief is usually granted by the court to halt all actions against the debtor. Some creditors may have already gained protection for themselves by having a mortgage lien or security interest attached to specific assets. A creditor is considered fully secured if the value of any collateral exceeds the related debt balance but is only partially secured if the obligation is larger. All other liabilities are unsecured; these creditors have legal rights but not to any specific assets of the debtor. The Bankruptcy Reform Act does list several types of unsecured liabilities (including administrative expenses and government claims for unpaid taxes) that have priority and must be paid before other unsecured debts are settled.

3. The parties involved in a bankruptcy want, and need, to be informed of the possible outcome, especially if liquidation is being considered. Thus, a Statement of Financial Affairs can be prepared for an insolvent company. This document lists the net realizable value of all remaining assets along with an indication of any property pledged to specific creditors. In addition, the liabilities of the business are segregated and disclosed within four classifications: fully secured, partially secured, unsecured with priority, and unsecured. Prior to the filing of a bankruptcy petition, this information can help the parties in deciding whether either liquidation or reorganization is the best course of action. However, this statement should be viewed as a projection since many of the reported values are merely estimations.

4. If the assets of the insolvent company will be liquidated to satisfy obligations (a Chapter 7 bankruptcy), a trustee is appointed to oversee the process. This individual must recover all property belonging to the company, liquidate noncash assets, possibly continue running operations to complete any business in progress, and make appropriate payments. To convey information about these events and transactions, a Statement of Realization and Liquidation is commonly prepared by the trustee. This statement provides a current report of all account balances as well as transactions to date.

5. Liquidation is not the only alternative available to an insolvent business. The company may seek to survive by developing a reorganization plan (a Chapter 11 bankruptcy). Reorganization is possible only if the plan is accepted by creditors, shareholders, and the court. While a reorganization is in process, the owners and management must preserve the company's estate as of the date on which the order of relief was entered. Although the ownership has the initial opportunity for creating a proposal for action, any interested party has the right to file a reorganization plan after a period of time.

6. Reorganization plans usually contain a number of provisions for modifying operations, generating new financing by equity or debt, and settling the liabilities existing when the order for relief was entered. To be accepted, each class of creditors and shareholders has to support the agreement. Thereafter, the reorganization plan must be confirmed by the court.

7. During reorganization, a company reports its liabilities as being subject to compromise or not subject to compromise. The first category includes all unsecured and partially secured debts that existed on the day the order for relief was granted. The balance to be reported is the expected amount of allowed claims rather than the estimated amount of settlement. Liabilities not subject to compromise are those debts fully secured or incurred following the granting of the order for relief.

8. An income statement prepared during the period of reorganization should disclose operating activities separately from reorganization items. Professional fees associated with the reorganization such as lawyers' charges are reorganization items that are expensed as

incurred. Any interest revenue earned during this period because of an increase in the company's cash reserves should also be reported as a reorganization item.

9. Many companies that emerge from reorganization proceedings must apply fresh start accounting. Assets are recorded at fair market value and an intangible asset, "reorganization value in excess of amounts allocable to identifiable assets," might also be necessary. Liabilities (except for deferred income taxes) are reported at the present value of required cash flows. Retained earnings (or a deficit) is eliminated. Additional paid-in capital is adjusted to keep the balance sheet in equilibrium.

COMPREHENSIVE ILLUSTRATION

Problem

(Estimated Time: 50 to 65 Minutes) The Roth Company is insolvent and in the process of filing for relief under the provisions of the Bankruptcy Reform Act of 1978. Roth has no cash and the company's balance sheet currently shows accounts payable of $48,000. An additional $8,000 is owed in connection with various expenses but these amounts have not yet been recorded. The company's assets with an indication of both book value and anticipated net realizable value follow:

	Book Value	Expected Net Realizable Value
Accounts receivable	$ 31,000	$ 9,000
Inventory	48,000	36,000
Investments	10,000	18,000
Land	80,000	75,000
Buildings	90,000	60,000
Accumulated depreciation	(38,000)	
Equipment	110,000	20,000
Accumulated depreciation	(61,000)	
Other assets	5,000	–0–
Totals	$275,000	$218,000

Roth has three notes payable, each with a different maturity date:

■ Note one due in 5 years—$120,000 secured by a mortgage lien on Roth's land and buildings.
■ Note two due in 8 years—$30,000 secured by Roth's investments.
■ Note three due in 10 years—$35,000 unsecured.

Of the accounts payable owed by Roth, $10,000 represents salaries to employees. However, no individual is entitled to receive more than $1,300. An additional $3,000 is included in this liability figure that is due to the U.S. government in connection with taxes.

The stockholders' equity balance reported by the company at the current date is $42,000: common stock of $140,000 and a deficit of $98,000. If the company is liquidated, administrative expenses of approximately $20,000 will be incurred.

Required:

a. Prepare a statement of financial affairs for Roth to indicate the expected availability of funds if the company is liquidated.
b. Assume that Roth owes Philip, Inc., a total of $2,000. This liability is unsecured. If Roth is liquidated, what amount of money can Philip expect to receive?
c. What amount will be paid on note 2 if Roth is liquidated?
d. Assume that Roth is immediately reorganized. The company has a reorganization value of $230,000, and the net realizable value is to be the assigned value for each asset. The accounts payable and accrued expenses are reduced to $20,000. Note one is reduced to a $30,000 note due in four years with a 7 percent annual interest rate. This creditor also receives half of the outstanding stock of the company from the owners. Note two is reduced to a $12,000 note due in five years with an 8 percent annual interest rate. This creditor also receives 10 percent of the outstanding stock of the company from the

owners. Note three is reduced to $5,000 due in three years with a 9 percent annual
interest rate.

Prepare a trial balance for this company after it emerges from bankruptcy.

Solution

a. To develop a statement of financial affairs for this company, the following preliminary
actions must be taken:

■ The $8,000 in unrecorded accounts payable must be entered into the company's
accounting records. Since these debts were incurred in connection with expenses, the
deficit is increased by a corresponding amount.

■ The unsecured liabilities that have priority are identified:

Administrative costs (estimated)	$20,000
Salary payable	10,000
Amount due to government for taxes	3,000
Total liabilities with priority	$33,000

■ The secured claims should be appropriately classified:

Note one is fully secured because Roth's land and buildings can be sold for an amount in
excess of the $120,000 balance.

Note two is only partially secured because Roth's investments are worth less than $30,000.

With this information, the statement of financial affairs in Exhibit 13–5 can be produced.

b. Based on the information provided by the statement of financial affairs, Philip, Inc.,
should receive 52.2 percent of its $2,000 unsecured claim or $1,044. Roth anticipates
having $47,000 in free assets remaining at the end of the liquidation. This amount must
be distributed to unsecured creditors with total claims of $90,000. Therefore, only 52.2
percent of each obligation can be paid:

$$\frac{\$47,000}{\$90,000} = 52.2 \text{ percent (rounded)}$$

c. The $30,000 note payable is partially secured by Roth's investments, an asset having a
net realizable value of only $18,000. The remaining $12,000 is an unsecured claim which
(as computed in requirement b.) will be paid 52.2 percent of face value. Thus, the holder
of this note can expect to receive $24,264:

Net realizable value of investments	$18,000
Payment on $12,000 unsecured claim (52.2 percent)	6,264
Amount to be received	$24,264

d. Fresh start accounting is appropriate. The reorganization value of $230,000 is less than
the $241,000 total amount of claims (no liabilities after the issuance of the order for relief
are indicated).

Accounts payable	$ 48,000
Accrued expenses	8,000
Note one	120,000
Note two	30,000
Note three	35,000
Total claims	$241,000

In addition, the original owners of the stock retain only 40 percent of the shares after the
company leaves the bankruptcy proceeding.

The company's assets are assigned values equal to their net realizable value based on the
information provided. Since the reorganization value of $230,000 is $12,000 in excess of the total
net realizable value of $218,000, an intangible asset is recognized for that amount.

The liabilities are each adjusted to the newly agreed-on amounts. Present value computations
are not required because a reasonable interest rate is included in each case. These debts now total
$67,000 ($20,000 + $30,000 + $12,000 + $5,000).

Because the reorganization value is $230,000, stockholders' equity must be $163,000
($230,000 − $67,000). The number of outstanding shares of common stock has not changed so

Exhibit 13–5

ROTH COMPANY
Statement of Financial Affairs

Book Values			Available for Unsecured Creditors
	Assets		
	Pledged with fully secured creditors:		
$132,000	Land and buildings	$ 135,000	
	Less: Note payable	(120,000)	$ 15,000
	Pledged with partially secured creditors:		
10,000	Investments	18,000	
	Less: Note payable	(30,000)	–0–
	Free assets:		
31,000	Accounts receivable		9,000
48,000	Inventory		36,000
49,000	Equipment		20,000
5,000	Intangible assets		–0–
	Total available for liabilities with priority and unsecured creditors		80,000
	Less: Liabilities with priority (listed opposite)		(33,000)
	Available for unsecured creditors		47,000
	Estimated deficiency		43,000
$275,000			$ 90,000

Book Values			Unsecured— Nonpriority Liabilities
	Liabilities and Stockholders' Equity		
	Liabilities with priority:		
–0–	Administrative expenses (estimated)	$ 20,000	
	Accounts payable:		
$ 10,000	Salaries payable	10,000	
3,000	Taxes payable	3,000	
	Total	$ 33,000	
	Fully secured creditors:		
120,000	Note payable	120,000	
	Less: Land and buildings	(135,000)	–0–
	Partially secured creditors:		
30,000	Note payable	30,000	
	Less: Investments	(18,000)	$ 12,000
	Unsecured creditors:		
35,000	Note payable		35,000
43,000	Accounts payable (other than salaries and taxes, although unrecorded liabilities have been included)		43,000
34,000	Stockholders' equity (adjusted for unrecorded liabilities)		–0–
$275,000			$ 90,000

that account retains its balance of $140,000. The other $23,000 of stockholders' equity is re-corded as additional paid-in capital.

	Debit	Credit
Accounts receivable.	$ 9,000	
Inventory	36,000	
Investments	18,000	
Land	75,000	
Buildings	60,000	
Equipment	20,000	
Reorganization value in excess of amounts allocable to identifiable assets	12,000	
Accounts payable and accrued expenses		$ 20,000
Note payable one		30,000
Note payable two		12,000
Note payable three		5,000
Common stock		140,000
Additional paid-in capital		23,000
Totals	$230,000	$230,000

QUESTIONS

1. What is meant by the term *insolvent?*
2. At present, what federal legislation governs most bankruptcy proceedings?
3. What are the primary objectives of a bankruptcy proceeding?
4. A bankruptcy case may begin with either a voluntary or an involuntary petition. What is the difference? What are the requirements for an involuntary petition?
5. An order for relief is entered by a bankruptcy court. How does this action affect an insolvent company and its creditors?
6. What is the difference in fully secured liabilities, partially secured liabilities, and unsecured liabilities?
7. In a bankruptcy proceeding, what is the significance of a liability with priority? What are the six general categories of liabilities that have priority in a liquidation?
8. Why are the administrative expenses incurred during a liquidation classified as liabilities having priority?
9. What is the difference between a Chapter 7 bankruptcy and a Chapter 11 bankruptcy?
10. Why might unsecured creditors favor reorganizing an insolvent company rather than forcing it into liquidation?
11. What is the purpose of a statement of financial affairs? Why might this statement be prepared before a bankruptcy petition is filed?
12. In the liquidation of a company, what actions are performed by the trustee?
13. A trustee for a company that is being liquidated voids a preference transfer. What has happened, and why was this action taken by the trustee?
14. A statement of realization and liquidation is prepared for a company that is being liquidated. What information can be ascertained from this statement?
15. What is meant by the term *debtor in possession?*
16. Who can develop reorganization plans in a Chapter 11 bankruptcy?
17. What types of proposals might be found in a reorganization plan?
18. Under normal conditions, how does a reorganization plan become effective?
19. In a bankruptcy proceeding, what is a *cram down?*
20. While a company goes through reorganization, how should its liabilities be reported?
21. During reorganization, how should a company's income statement be structured?
22. What accounting is made of the professional fees incurred during a reorganization?
23. What is meant by *fresh start accounting?*
24. Under what conditions is fresh start accounting used by a company emerging from a bankruptcy reorganization?

25. When fresh start accounting is utilized, how are a company's assets reported? How are its liabilities reported?

26. How is a "reorganization value in excess of amounts allocable to identifiable assets" account computed? Where is this balance reported? What happens to the balance?

LIBRARY ASSIGNMENTS

1. Locate *The Wall Street Journal General Index* for a recent year. Under the heading, "Bankruptcies" identify one company that has recently completed bankruptcy proceedings. Then, in *The Wall Street Journal Corporate Index,* under the name of this company, locate articles that describe the various stages of the process from beginning through resolution. Write a report to answer the following questions:

   - Was the bankruptcy voluntary or involuntary?
   - What events led up to the filing of the bankruptcy petition?
   - What actions did the company take to bring the matter to a final resolution?
   - Did the bankruptcy end in liquidation or reorganization?
   - What were the significant provisions of the liquidation or the reorganization plan?
   - What losses, if any, were the creditors forced to suffer?

2. Read the following as well as any other published articles describing the work of the accountant in bankruptcy cases:

   "Managing in a Reorganization," *Management Accounting,* January 1988.
   "What to Do When Chapter 11 Threatens," *Journal of Accountancy,* May 1993.
   "Accounting Services in Insolvency and Bankruptcy," *Connecticut CPA Quarterly,* December 1987.
   "Management Accounting—How a Workout Specialist Operates," *Journal of Accountancy,* January 1992.
   "What a CPA Should Know Before a Business Fails," *Journal of Accountancy,* June 1991.
   "The CPA's Role as Bankruptcy Examiner," *CPA Journal,* September 1991.
   "What Accountants Need to Know About the Bankruptcy Valuation Process," *Ohio CPA Journal,* June 1992.

   Write a report describing the services that can be performed by an accountant during a corporate bankruptcy. Include activities to be carried out prior to the filing of a petition as well as any functions thereafter.

3. Read the following as well as any other published articles concerning possible changes in the bankruptcy laws pertaining to Chapter 11 reorganizations:

   "The Untenable Case for Chapter 11," *Yale Law Journal,* March 1992.
   "Bankruptcy Lawyers Dispute Call for Scrapping Chapter 11 Process," *The Wall Street Journal,* March 19, 1992, p. B5.
   "The Bankruptcy Game," *Time,* May 18, 1992.
   "Pulling a Company through Chapter 11 Is a Risky Business as Hurdles Abound," *The Wall Street Journal,* January 16, 1990, p. A10.
   "Blimey! CPAs!" *Forbes,* March 15, 1992.
   "For Many Small Businesses, Chapter 11 Closes the Book," *The Wall Street Journal,* November 4, 1992, p. B2.

   Write a report describing possible problems with the current laws as they pertain to the reorganization process and changes in these laws that might be justified.

PROBLEMS

1. What are the objectives of the bankruptcy laws in the United States?
   a. Provide relief for the court system in this country and ensure that all debtors are treated the same.
   b. Distribute assets fairly and discharge honest debtors from their obligations.
   c. Protect the economy and stimulate growth.
   d. Prevent insolvency and protect shareholders.

2. In a bankruptcy, which of the following statements is true?
   a. An order for relief only results from a voluntary petition.
   b. Creditors entering an involuntary petition must have debts totaling at least $20,000.
   c. Secured notes payable are considered liabilities with priority on a statement of affairs.
   d. A liquidation is referred to as a Chapter 7 bankruptcy, whereas a reorganization is a Chapter 11 bankruptcy.

3. In the reporting of a liquidation, assets are shown at:
   a. Present value calculated using an appropriate effective rate.
   b. Net realizable value.
   c. Historical cost.
   d. Book value.

4. An involuntary bankruptcy petition must be filed by:
   a. The insolvent company's attorney.
   b. The holders of the insolvent company's debenture bonds.
   c. Unsecured creditors with total debts of at least $10,000.
   d. The management of the company.

5. An order for relief:
   a. Prohibits creditors from taking action to collect from an insolvent company without court approval.
   b. Calls for the immediate distribution of free assets to unsecured creditors.
   c. Can only be entered in an involuntary bankruptcy proceeding.
   d. Gives an insolvent company time to file a voluntary bankruptcy petition.

6. Which of the following is not a liability that has priority in a liquidation?
   a. Administrative expenses incurred in the liquidation.
   b. Salary payable of $800 per person owed to 26 employees.
   c. Payroll taxes due to the federal government.
   d. Advertising expense incurred before the company became insolvent.

7. Which of the following is the minimum limitation necessary for the filing of an involuntary bankruptcy petition?
   a. The signature of 12 creditors to whom the debtor owes at least $3,000 in unsecured debt.
   b. The signature of six creditors to whom the debtor owes at least $20,000 in unsecured debt.
   c. The signature of three creditors to whom the debtor owes at least $10,000 in unsecured debt.
   d. The signature of nine creditors to whom the debtor owes at least $25,000 in unsecured debt.

8. On a statement of financial affairs, how are liabilities classified?
   a. Current and noncurrent.
   b. Secured and unsecured.
   c. Monetary and nonmonetary.
   d. Historic and futuristic.

9. What is a debtor in possession?
   a. The holder of a note receivable issued by an insolvent company prior to the granting of an order for relief.
   b. A fully secured creditor.
   c. The ownership of an insolvent company that continues in control of the organization during a bankruptcy reorganization.
   d. The stockholders in a Chapter 7 bankruptcy.

10. How are anticipated administrative expenses reported on a statement of financial affairs?
    a. As a footnote until actually incurred.
    b. As a liability with priority.
    c. As a partially secured liability.
    d. As an unsecured liability.

11. Just prior to filing a voluntary Chapter 7 bankruptcy petition, Haynes Company pays a supplier $1,000 to satisfy an unsecured claim. Haynes was insolvent at the time. Subsequently, the trustee appointed to oversee this liquidation forces the return of this $1,000. Which of the following is correct?

    a. A preference transfer has been voided.
    b. All transactions prior to a voluntary bankruptcy proceeding must be nullified.
    c. The supplier should sue for the return of this money.
    d. The $1,000 claim becomes a liability with priority.

12. Which of the following is not an expected function of a bankruptcy trustee?
    a. The filing of a plan of reorganization.
    b. Recovery of all property belonging to a company.
    c. Liquidation of noncash assets.
    d. The distribution of assets to the proper claimants.

13. What is an inherent limitation of the statement of financial affairs?
    a. Many of the amounts reported are only estimations that might prove to be inaccurate.
    b. The statement is only applicable to a Chapter 11 bankruptcy.
    c. The statement covers only a short time, whereas a bankruptcy may last much longer.
    d. The figures on the statement vary between a voluntary and an involuntary bankruptcy.

14. What is a cram down?
    a. An agreement about the total amount of money to be reserved to pay creditors who have priority.
    b. The confirmation by the bankruptcy court of a reorganization even though it was not accepted by a class of creditors or stockholders.
    c. The filing of an involuntary bankruptcy petition, especially by the holders of partially secured debts.
    d. The decision made by the court as to whether a particular creditor has priority.

15. On a balance sheet prepared for a company during its reorganization, how are liabilities reported?
    a. As current and long term.
    b. As monetary and nonmonetary.
    c. As subject to compromise and not subject to compromise.
    d. As equity related and debt related.

16. On a balance sheet prepared for a company during its reorganization, at what balance are liabilities reported?
    a. At the expected amount of the allowed claims.
    b. At the present value of the expected future cash flows.
    c. At the expected amount of the settlement.
    d. At the amount of the anticipated final payment.

17. Which of the following is not a reorganization item for purposes of reporting a company's income statement during a Chapter 11 bankruptcy?
    a. Professional fees.
    b. Interest income.
    c. Interest expense.
    d. Gains and losses on closing facilities.

18. What accounting is made for professional fees incurred during a bankruptcy reorganization?
    a. They must be expensed immediately.
    b. They must be capitalized and written off over 40 years or less.
    c. They must be capitalized until the company emerges from the reorganization.
    d. They are either expensed or capitalized depending on the nature of the expenditure.

19. Which of the following is necessary for a company to use fresh start accounting?
    a. The original owners must hold at least 50 percent of the stock of the company when it emerges from bankruptcy.
    b. The reorganization value of the company must exceed the value of all assets.
    c. The reorganization value of the company must exceed the value of all liabilities.
    d. The original owners must hold less than 50 percent of the stock of the company when it emerges from bankruptcy.

20. If the reorganization value of a company emerging from bankruptcy is larger than the values that can be assigned to specific assets, what accounting is made of the difference?
    a. Because of conservatism, the difference is simply ignored.
    b. The difference is expensed immediately.

    c. The difference is capitalized as an intangible asset.

    d. The difference is recorded as a professional fee.

21. For a company emerging from bankruptcy, how are its liabilities (other than deferred income taxes) reported?

    a. At their historical value.

    b. At zero because of fresh start accounting.

    c. At the present value of the future cash flows.

    d. At the negotiated value less all professional fees incurred in the reorganization.

22. A company is to be liquidated and has the following liabilities:

Income taxes	$ 8,000
Notes payable (secured by land)	120,000
Accounts payable	83,000
Salary payable (evenly divided between two employees)	6,000
Bonds payable	70,000
Administrative expenses for liquidation	20,000

The company has the following assets:

	Book Value	Fair Market Value
Current assets	$ 80,000	$ 33,000
Land	100,000	90,000
Buildings and equipment	100,000	110,000

How much money will the holders of the notes payable collect following the liquidation?

23. The Xavier Company is going through a Chapter 7 bankruptcy. All assets have been liquidated and the company retains only $12,000 in free cash. The following debts, totaling $27,000, remain:

Government claims to unpaid taxes	$5,000
Salary during last month owed to Mr. Key (not an officer)	7,000
Administrative expenses	3,000
Salary during last month owed to Ms. Rankin (not an officer)	5,000
Unsecured accounts payable	7,000

For each of these debts, indicate how much money will be paid to the creditor.

24. Ataway Company has had severe financial difficulties and is considering the possibility of filing a bankruptcy petition. At this time, the company has the following assets (stated at net realizable value) and liabilities.

Assets (pledged against debts of $70,000)	$116,000
Assets (pledged against debts of $130,000)	50,000
Other assets	80,000
Liabilities with priority	42,000
Unsecured creditors	200,000

In a liquidation, how much money would be paid on the partially secured debt?

25. The Chesterfield Company has cash of $50,000, inventory worth $90,000, and a building worth $130,000. Unfortunately, the company also has accounts payable of $180,000, a note payable of $80,000 (secured by the inventory), liabilities with priority of $20,000, a bond payable of $150,000 (secured by the building). In a Chapter 7 bankruptcy, how much money will the holders of the bond expect to receive?

26. The Mondesto Company has the following:

Unsecured creditors	$230,000
Liabilities with priority	110,000
Secured liabilities:	
Debt one, $210,000; value of pledged asset	180,000
Debt two, $170,000; value of pledged asset	100,000
Debt three, $120,000; value of pledged asset	140,000

The company also has a number of other assets that are not pledged in any way. The creditors holding debt two want to receive at least $142,000. For how much do these free assets have to be sold so that debt two would receive exactly $142,000?

27. A statement of financial affairs created for an insolvent corporation that is beginning the process of liquidation discloses the following data (assets are shown at net realizable values):

Assets pledged with fully secured creditors	$200,000
Fully secured liabilities	150,000
Assets pledged with partially secured creditors	380,000
Partially secured liabilities	490,000
Free assets	300,000
Unsecured liabilities with priority	160,000
Unsecured liabilities	500,000

Required:

a. This company owes $3,000 to an unsecured creditor (without priority). How much money can this creditor expect to collect?

b. This company owes $100,000 to a bank on a note payable that is secured by a security interest attached to property with an estimated net realizable value of $80,000. How much money can this bank expect to collect?

28. A company preparing for a Chapter 7 liquidation has the following.

Liabilities:

■ Note payable A of $90,000 secured by land having a book value of $50,000 and a fair market value of $70,000.

■ Note payable B of $120,000 secured by a building having a book value of $60,000 and a fair market value of $40,000.

■ Note payable C of $60,000, unsecured.

■ Administrative expenses payable of $20,000.

■ Accounts payable of $120,000.

■ Income taxes payable of $30,000.

Other assets:

■ Cash $10,000.

■ Inventory $100,000, but with fair market value of $60,000.

■ Equipment $90,000, but with fair market value of $50,000.

How much will each of the company's liabilities be paid after liquidation?

29. The Olds Company declares Chapter 7 bankruptcy. Here are the accounts at that time; administrative expenses are estimated to be $12,000.

Cash	$ 24,000	
Accounts receivable	60,000	(worth $28,000)
Inventory	70,000	(worth $56,000)
Land (secures note A)	200,000	(worth $160,000)
Building (secures bonds)	400,000	(worth $320,000)
Equipment	120,000	(worth unknown)
Accounts payable	180,000	
Taxes payable to government	20,000	
Note payable A	170,000	
Note payable B	250,000	
Bonds payable	300,000	

The holders of note payable B want to collect at least $125,000. To achieve that goal, how much does the company have to receive in the liquidation of its equipment?

30. A company is going through a Chapter 7 bankruptcy and has the following account balances:

Cash	$ 30,000
Receivables (30 percent collectible)	50,000
Inventory (worth $39,000)	90,000
Land (worth $120,000) (secures note payable)	100,000
Buildings (worth $180,000) (secures bonds payable)	200,000

Salary payable (7 workers owed equal amounts for last 5 weeks)	10,000
Accounts payable	90,000
Note payable (secured by land).......................................	110,000
Bonds payable (secured by building)	300,000
Common stock	100,000
Retained earnings	(140,000)

How much will be paid on each of the following:

Salary payable
Accounts payable
Note payable
Bonds payable

31. The Pumpkin Company is going through bankruptcy reorganization. It has a note payable for $200,000 that was incurred prior to the order for relief. The company believes that the note will be settled for $60,000 in cash. It is also possible that the creditor will take a piece of land instead that cost the company $50,000 but is worth $72,000. On a balance sheet during the reorganization period, how will this debt be reported?

32. Under fresh start accounting, a company is coming out of reorganization with the following accounts:

	Book Value	Fair Market Value
Receivables	$ 80,000	$ 90,000
Inventory.......................	200,000	210,000
Buildings.......................	300,000	400,000
Liabilities	300,000	300,000
Common Stock	330,000	
Additional paid-in capital	20,000	
Retained earnings (Deficit)	(70,000)	

The company's assets have a reorganization value of $760,000. The owners of the company before the organization have transferred 80 percent of the outstanding stock to the creditors.

Required:

Prepare the journal entry that is necessary to adjust the company's records to fresh start accounting.

33. The Addison Corporation is currently going through a Chapter 11 bankruptcy. The company has the following account balances. Prepare an income statement for this organization. The effective tax rate is 20 percent (realization of any tax benefits is anticipated).

	Debit	Credit
Advertising expense	$ 24,000	
Cost of goods sold	211,000	
Depreciation expense	22,000	
Interest expense	4,000	
Interest revenue		$ 32,000
Loss on closing of branch..........	109,000	
Professional fees	71,000	
Rent expense.....................	16,000	
Revenues		467,000
Salary expense...................	70,000	

34. The Kansas City Corporation holds three assets when it comes out of Chapter 11 bankruptcy:

	Book Value	Market Value
Inventory	$ 86,000	$ 50,000
Land and buildings	250,000	400,000
Equipment	123,000	110,000

The company has a reorganization value of $600,000.

Required:

    a. Describe the rules for applying fresh start accounting to the Kansas City Corporation.

    b. If fresh start accounting is appropriate, how will the assets of this company be reported?

    c. If a "reorganization value in excess of amounts allocable to identifiable assets" account is recognized, where should it be reported? What happens to this balance?

35. The Jaez Corporation is in the process of going through a reorganization. As of December 31, 1998, the company's accountant has determined the following information although the company is still several months away from emerging from the bankruptcy proceeding. Prepare a balance sheet in appropriate form.

	Book Value	Market Value
Assets		
Cash	$ 23,000	$ 23,000
Inventory	45,000	47,000
Land	140,000	210,000
Buildings	220,000	260,000
Equipment	154,000	157,000

	Allowed Claims	Expected Settlement
Liabilities as of the date of the order for relief		
Accounts payable	$ 123,000	$ 20,000
Accrued expenses	30,000	4,000
Income taxes payable	22,000	18,000
Note payable (due 2001, secured by land)	100,000	100,000
Note payable (due 2003)	170,000	80,000
Liabilities since the date of the order for relief		
Accounts payable	$ 60,000	
Note payable (due 2000)	100,000	
Stockholders' equity		
Common stock	$ 200,000	
Deficit	(223,000)	

36. The Ristoni Company is in the process of emerging from a Chapter 11 bankruptcy. The company will apply fresh start accounting as of December 31, 1998. The company currently has 30,000 shares of common stock outstanding with a $240,000 par value. As part of the reorganization, the owners will contribute 18,000 shares of this stock back to the company. A deficit balance of $330,000 also is being reported.

    The company has the following asset accounts:

	Book Value	Market Value
Accounts receivable	$100,000	$ 80,000
Inventory	112,000	90,000
Land and buildings	420,000	500,000
Equipment	78,000	65,000

    The company's liabilities will be settled as follows. Assume that all notes will be issued at reasonable interest rates.

- Accounts payable of $80,000 will be settled with a note for $5,000. These creditors will also get 1,000 shares of the stock contributed by the owners.
- Accrued expenses of $35,000 will be settled with a note for $4,000.
- Note payable (due 2002) of $100,000 was fully secured and has not been renegotiated.
- Note payable (due 1998) of $200,000 will be settled with a note for $50,000 and 10,000 shares of the stock contributed by the owners.
- Note payable (due 1999) of $185,000 will be settled with a note for $71,000 and 7,000 shares of the stock contributed by the owners.
- Note payable (due 2000) of $200,000 will be settled with a note for $110,000.

    The company has a reorganization value of $780,000.

Required:

Prepare all of the journal entries for Ristoni so that the company can emerge from the bankruptcy proceeding.

37. The Smith Corporation has gone through bankruptcy and is ready to emerge as a reorganized entity on December 31, 1998. On this date, the company has the following assets (market value is based on the discounted future cash flows that are anticipated):

	Book Value	Market Value
Accounts receivable	$ 20,000	$ 18,000
Inventory	143,000	111,000
Land and buildings	250,000	278,000
Machinery	144,000	121,000
Patents	100,000	125,000

The company has a reorganization value of $800,000.

The company has 50,000 shares of $10 par value common stock outstanding. A deficit retained earnings balance of $670,000 also is reported. The owners will distribute 30,000 shares of this stock as part of the reorganization plan.

The company's liabilities will be settled as follows:

- Accounts payable (existing at the date on which the order for relief was granted) of $180,000 will be settled with an 8 percent, two-year note for $35,000.
- Accounts payable (incurred since the date on which the order for relief was granted) of $97,000 will be paid in the regular course of business.
- Note payable—First Metropolitan Bank of $200,000 will be settled with an 8 percent, five-year note for $50,000 and 15,000 shares of the stock contributed by the owners.
- Note payable—Northwestern Bank of Tulsa of $350,000 will be settled with a 7 percent, eight-year note for $100,000 and 15,000 shares of the stock contributed by the owners.

Required:

a. How does the accountant for Smith Corporation know that fresh start accounting must be utilized?
b. Prepare a balance sheet for the Smith Corporation upon its emergence from reorganization.

38. Ambrose Corporation reports the following information:

	Book Value	Liquidation Value
Assets pledged with fully secured creditors	$220,000	$245,000
Assets pledged with partially secured creditors	111,000	103,000
Other assets	140,000	81,000
Liabilities with priority	36,000	
Fully secured liabilities	200,000	
Partially secured liabilities	180,000	
Unsecured liabilities.	283,000	

In liquidation, what amount of cash should each class of the liabilities expect to collect?

39. The following balance sheet has been prepared by the accountant for the Limestone Company as of June 3, 1998, the date on which the company is to file a voluntary petition of bankruptcy.

LIMESTONE COMPANY
Balance Sheet
June 3, 1998

Assets

Cash	$ 3,000
Accounts receivable (net)	65,000
Inventory	88,000
Land	100,000
Buildings (net)	300,000
Equipment (net)	180,000
Total assets	$736,000

Liabilities and Equities

Accounts payable	$ 98,000
Notes payable—current	
(secured by equipment)	250,000
Notes payable—long term	
(secured by land and buildings)	190,000
Common stock	120,000
Retained earnings	78,000
Total liabilities and equities	$736,000

Additional Information:

- If the company is liquidated, administrative expenses estimated at $18,000 are expected to be incurred.
- The accounts payable figure includes $10,000 in wages earned by the company's 12 employees during May. No one earned more than $1,300.
- Taxes of $14,000 owed to the U.S. government have not been included in the liabilities.
- Company officials estimate that 40 percent of the accounts receivable will be collected in a liquidation and that the inventory can be disposed of for $80,000. The land and buildings are to be sold together for approximately $310,000; the equipment should bring $130,000 at auction.

Required:

Prepare a statement of financial affairs for the Limestone Company as of June 3, 1998.

40. Creditors of Jones Corporation are considering petitioning the courts to force the company into Chapter 7 bankruptcy. The following information has been determined. Administrative expenses in connection with the liquidation are estimated to be $22,000. Indicate the amount of money that each class of creditors can anticipate receiving.

	Book Value	Net Realizable Value
Cash	$ 6,000	$ 6,000
Accounts receivable	32,000	18,000
Inventory	45,000	31,000
Supplies	3,000	–0–
Investments	2,000	8,000
Land	60,000	72,000
Buildings	90,000	68,000
Equipment	50,000	35,000
Notes payable (secured by land)	65,000	
Notes payable (secured by buildings)	78,000	
Bonds payable (secured by equipment)	115,000	
Accounts payable	70,000	
Salary payable (two weeks' salary for the 20		
employees)	6,000	
Taxes payable	10,000	

41. The Anteium Company owes $80,000 on a note payable that is currently due. The note is held by a local bank and is secured by a mortgage lien attached to three acres of land worth $48,000. The land originally cost Anteium $31,000 when acquired several years ago. The only other account balances for this company are investments of $20,000 (but worth $25,000), accounts payable of $20,000, common stock of $40,000, and a deficit of $89,000. Anteium is insolvent and attempting to arrange a reorganization so that the business can continue to operate. The reorganization value of the company is $82,000.

Each of the following should be viewed as independent situations:

- *a.* On a statement of financial affairs, how would this note be reported? How would the land be shown?
- *b.* Assume that Anteium develops an acceptable reorganization plan. Sixty percent of the common stock is transferred to the bank to settle that particular obligation. A 7 percent, three-year note payable for $5,000 is used to settle the accounts payable. How would Anteium record the reorganization?
- *c.* Assume that Anteium is liquidated. The land and investments are sold for $50,000 and $26,000, respectively. Administrative expenses amount to $11,000. How much will the various parties collect?

42. The following balance sheet has been produced for the Litz Corporation as of August 8, 1998, the date on which the company is to begin selling assets as part of a corporate liquidation.

LITZ CORPORATION
Balance Sheet
August 8, 1998

Assets

Cash	$ 16,000
Accounts receivable (net)	82,000
Investments	32,000
Inventory (net realizable value is expected to approximate cost)	69,000
Land	30,000
Buildings (net)	340,000
Equipment (net)	210,000
Total assets	$779,000

Liabilities and Equities

Accounts payable	$150,000
Notes payable—current (secured by inventory)	132,000
Notes payable—long term (secured by land and buildings [valued at $300,000])	259,000
Common stock	135,000
Retained earnings	103,000
Total liabilities and equities	$779,000

The following events occur during the liquidation process:

- The investments are sold for $39,000.
- The inventory is sold at auction for $48,000.
- The money derived from the inventory is applied against the short-term notes payable.
- Administrative expenses of $15,000 are incurred in connection with the liquidation.
- The land and buildings are sold for $315,000. The long-term notes payable are paid.
- The accountant determines that $34,000 of the accounts payable are liabilities with priority.
- The company's equipment is sold for $84,000.
- Accounts receivable of $34,000 are collected. The remainder of the receivables are considered uncollectible.
- The administrative expenses are paid.

Required:

    a. Prepare a statement of realization and liquidation for the period just described.
    b. What percentage of their claims should the unsecured creditors receive?

43. The following balance sheet has been prepared by the accountant of the Becket Corporation as of November 10, 1998, the date on which the company is to release a plan for reorganizing operations under Chapter 11 of the Bankruptcy Reform Act.

BECKET CORPORATION
Balance Sheet
November 10, 1998

Assets

Cash	$ 12,000
Accounts receivable (net)	61,000
Investments	26,000
Inventory (net realizable value is expected to approximate 80% of cost)	80,000
Land	57,000
Buildings (net)	248,000
Equipment (net)	117,000
Total assets	$ 601,000

Liabilities and Equities

Accounts payable	$ 129,000
Notes payable—current (secured by equipment)	220,000
Notes payable—(due in 2001)	
(secured by land and buildings)	325,000
Common stock ($10 par value)	60,000
Retained earnings (deficit)	(133,000)
Total liabilities and equities	$ 601,000

The company presented the following proposal:
1. The reorganization value of the company's assets just prior to emerging from bankruptcy is set at $650,000.
2. Accounts receivable of $20,000 are written off as uncollectible. Investments are worth $40,000, land is worth $80,000, the buildings are worth $300,000, and the equipment is worth $86,000.
3. An outside investor has been found who will buy 7,000 shares of common stock at $11 per share.
4. The company's investments are to be sold for $40,000 in cash with the proceeds going to the holders of the current note payable. The remainder of these short-term notes will be converted into $130,000 of notes due in 2002 and paying 10 percent annual cash interest.
5. All accounts payable will be exchanged for $40,000 in notes payable due in 1999 and paying 8 percent annual interest.
6. Title to land costing $20,000 but worth $50,000 will be transferred to the holders of the note payable due in 2001. In addition, these creditors will receive $180,000 in notes payable (paying 10 percent annual interest) coming due in 2001. These creditors also are issued 3,000 shares of previously unissued common stock.

Required:

Prepare journal entries for Becket to record the transactions as put forth in this reorganization plan.

44. The Oregon Corporation has filed a voluntary petition to reorganize the company under Chapter 11 of the Bankruptcy Reform Act. The creditors are considering an attempt to force liquidation. The company currently holds cash of $6,000 and accounts receivable of $25,000. In addition, the company owns four pieces of land. The first two (labeled A and B) cost $8,000 each. Plots C and D cost the company $20,000 and $25,000, respectively. A mortgage lien is attached to each parcel of land as security for four different notes payable of $15,000 apiece. Presently, the land can be sold for:

Plot A	$16,000
Plot B	$11,000
Plot C	$14,000
Plot D	$27,000

Another $25,000 note payable is unsecured. Accounts payable at this time total $32,000. Of this amount, $12,000 is salary owed to the company's workers. No employee is due more than $1,800.

The company expects to collect $12,000 from the accounts receivable if liquidation becomes necessary. Administrative expenses required for liquidation are anticipated to be $16,000.

Required:

a. Prepare a statement of financial affairs for the Oregon Corporation.
b. If the company is liquidated, how much cash would be paid on the note payable secured by plot B?
c. If the company is liquidated, how much cash would be paid on the note payable that is unsecured?
d. If the company is liquidated and plot D is sold for $30,000, how much cash would be paid on the note payable secured by plot B?

45. Lynch, Inc., is a hardware store operating in Boulder, Colorado. Management has recently made some poor inventory acquisitions that have loaded the store with unsalable merchandise. Because of the drop in revenues, the company is now insolvent.

The entire inventory can be sold for only $33,000. Following is a trial balance as of March 14, 1998, the day the company files for a Chapter 7 liquidation.

	Debit	Credit
Accounts payable		$ 33,000
Accounts receivable	$ 25,000	
Accumulated depreciation, building		50,000
Accumulated depreciation, equipment		16,000
Additional paid-in capital		8,000
Advertising payable		4,000
Building	80,000	
Cash	1,000	
Common stock		50,000
Equipment	30,000	
Inventory	100,000	
Investments	15,000	
Land	10,000	
Note payable—Colorado Savings and Loan (secured by lien on land and building)		70,000
Note payable—First National Bank (secured by equipment)		150,000
Payroll taxes payable		1,000
Retained earnings (deficit)	126,000	
Salary payable		5,000
Totals	$387,000	$387,000

Company officials believe that 60 percent of the accounts receivable can be collected if the company is liquidated. The building and land have a market value of $75,000, while the equipment is worth $19,000. The investments represent shares of a nationally traded company that can be sold at the current time for $21,000. Administrative expenses necessary to carry out a liquidation would approximate $16,000.

Required:

Prepare a statement of financial affairs for Lynch, Inc., as of March 14, 1998.

46. Use the trial balance presented for Lynch, Inc., in problem 45. Assume that the company will be liquidated and the following transactions occur:

- Accounts receivable of $18,000 are collected.
- All of the company's inventory is sold for $40,000.
- Additional accounts payable of $10,000 incurred for various expenses such as utilities and maintenance are discovered.
- The land and building are sold for $71,000.
- The note payable due to the Colorado Savings and Loan is paid.
- The equipment is sold at auction for only $11,000 with the proceeds applied to the note owed to the First National Bank.
- The investments are sold for $21,000.
- Administrative expenses total $20,000 as of July 23, 1998, but no payment has yet been made.

Required:

a. Prepare a statement of realization and liquidation for the period from March 14, 1998, through July 23, 1998.

b. How much cash would be paid to an unsecured, nonpriority creditor who is owed a total of $1,000 by Lynch, Inc.?

47. The Holmes Corporation has filed a voluntary petition with the bankruptcy court in hopes of reorganizing the company. A statement of financial affairs has been prepared for Holmes showing the following debts:

Liabilities with priority:
Salary payable . . . . $ 18,000
Fully secured creditors:
Notes payable (secured by land and
buildings valued at $84,000)   70,000
Partially secured creditors:
Notes payable (secured by inventory
valued at $30,000)   140,000
Unsecured creditors:
Notes payable   50,000
Accounts payable   10,000
Accrued expenses   4,000

The company has 10,000 shares of common stock outstanding with a par value of $5 per share. In addition, the company is currently reporting a deficit balance of $132,000.

Company officials have proposed the following reorganization plan:

- The company's assets have a total book value of $210,000, an amount considered to be equal to fair market value. The reorganization value of the assets as a whole, though, is set at $225,000.
- Employees will receive a one-year note in lieu of all salaries owed. Interest will be 10 percent, a normal rate for this type of liability.
- The fully secured note will have all future interest dropped from a 15 percent rate, which is now unrealistic, to a 10 percent rate.
- The partially secured note payable will be satisfied by the signing of a new six-year $30,000 note paying 10 percent annual interest. In addition, this creditor will receive 5,000 new shares of Holmes' common stock.
- An outside investor has been enlisted to buy 6,000 new shares of common stock at $6 per share.
- The unsecured creditors will be offered 20 cents on the dollar to settle the remaining liabilities.

If this plan of reorganization is accepted and becomes effective, what journal entries would be recorded by the Holmes Corporation?

14

Partnerships: Formation and Operation

- Why are some businesses legally organized as partnerships rather than as corporations?

- Why do the equity accounts of a partnership differ from those of a corporation? How do these accounts differ?

- If a partner brings an intangible attribute (such as a business expertise or an established clientele) to a partnership, how is this contribution valued and recorded?

- How is the annual net income that is earned by a partnership allocated among the individual capital accounts maintained for each partner?

- If a partner withdraws from a partnership and receives more cash than is recorded in the appropriate capital account, what accounting does the business make of the excess payment?

A reader of college accounting textbooks might well come to the conclusion that business activity is carried out exclusively by corporations. Because most large companies are legally incorporated, a vast majority of textbook references and illustrations concern corporate organizations. Contrary to the perception being relayed, partnerships (as well as sole proprietorships) make up a vital element of the business community. Based on the filing of income tax returns, more than 1.4 million partnerships were estimated to be in existence in the United States in 1993 (as compared to nearly 4 million corporations). One author makes a very important assessment of the significance of partnerships to the economy: "One-quarter of all start-ups begin as partnerships."[1]

The Partnership form is found in a wide range of business activities, from small local operations to worldwide enterprises. Examples found in the American economy include:

- Individual proprietors often join together in the formation of a partnership as a means of reducing expenses, expanding services, and adding increased expertise.

- Partnerships are a common means by which friends and relatives can create and organize a business endeavor.

- Doctors, lawyers, and other professionals have historically formed partnerships because of legal prohibitions against the incorporation of their practices. Although some states now permit such organizations to become professional corporations, operating as a partnership or sole proprietorship is still necessary in many areas.

---

[1]Nick Kochan, "Two Is Company," *Director,* August 1996, p. 42.

Over the years, some partnerships have grown to enormous sizes. Connell Limited Partnership, for example, recycles and manufactures metal products; in 1996 it had revenues of $1.26 billion.[2] An announcement of the merger of Deloitte Haskins & Sells and Touche Ross stated that the combined organization would have 5,470 partners. "The new international firm will have 1989 worldwide revenue in excess of $4 billion, will employ 65,000 people and will be one of the world's largest accounting and consulting firms, with a leading position in substantially all major U.S. and international markets."[3]

Certainly some of the most successful organizations in business today are partnerships. "Winning teams include Hanson's James Hanson and Gordon White, the Body Shop's Anita and Gordon Roddick, the partners of the U.S. investment bank Goldman Sachs, and in a different way, the partners of the country's largest law and accounting firms."[4]

PARTNERSHIPS—ADVANTAGES AND DISADVANTAGES

The popularity of the partnership format is based on several advantages inherent to this type of organization. An analysis of these attributes explains why more than 1.4 million enterprises in the United States are partnerships rather than corporations.

One of the most common motives is the ease of formation. Only an oral agreement is necessary to create a legally binding partnership. In contrast, depending on specific state laws, incorporation requires the filing of a formal application along with the completion of various other forms and documents. Operators of small businesses may find the convenience involved in creating a partnership to be an especially appealing characteristic.

Other justifications for structuring a business as a partnership can be discovered within the tax laws.

> The partnership form of business has become increasingly popular in the United States, and it may account for a significant portion of new business formation in the future. One reason for the burgeoning of partnerships is that this form of business offers many of the risk-sharing opportunities of the corporate form without the burden of corporate income taxation.[5]

Although a detailed investigation of taxation rules and regulations goes beyond the scope of this textbook, a few aspects are quite relevant to the current discussion. One area of the law warrants particular attention: the method by which partnerships are taxed. Although an informational tax return must be filed on an annual basis, *the partnership itself pays no income taxes*. For taxation purposes, the government does not view a partnership as an entity apart from its owners.

Partnership revenue and expense items (as defined by the tax laws) must be assigned directly to the individual partners with the income taxes being paid by them. By passing income balances through to the partners in this manner, double-taxation of profits that are earned by the business and then distributed to the owners is

---

[2]Steve Kichen, Tina Russo McCarthy, and Peter Newcomb, "The Private 500," *Forbes,* December 2, 1996, p. 166.

[3]*DH & S Review,* July 17, 1989, pp. 1–2.

[4]Kochan, p. 42.

[5]Harry Watson, "An Analysis of the Formation and Behavior of Partnerships," *Public Finance Quarterly,* July 1989, p. 281.

avoided.[6] In a corporation, income is taxed twice: when earned and again when conveyed as a dividend. A partnership's income is only taxed at the time that it is initially earned by the business.

As an illustration, assume that a business earns $100. After paying any income taxes, the remainder is immediately conveyed to its owners. A tax rate of 30 percent is assumed for both individuals and corporations. As the following table shows, if this business is a partnership rather than a corporation, the owners are left with $21 more expendable income, which is 21 percent of the business income. This difference, though, does narrow as tax rates are lowered. Thus, the decrease in federal income tax rates during the 1980s reduced, somewhat, the tax appeal of partnerships.

	Partnership	Corporation
Income before income taxes	$100	$100
Income taxes paid by business (30%)	–0–	(30)
Income distributed to owners	$100	$ 70
Income taxes paid by owners (30%)	(30)	(21)
Expendable income	$ 70	$ 49

The advantage of single taxation has led some larger companies in recent years to convert to the partnership form: The Boston Celtics and Motel 6 are just two examples of corporations that converted to partnerships to maximize after-tax returns to investors.[7]

Historically, another tax advantage was available to owners who invested in a partnership, although the potential benefits have been greatly reduced by changes in the tax laws. In the past, partnerships could be designed specifically to serve as tax shelters. The investor would acquire an interest but would not participate in the business. These investments were created, especially in certain industries, to produce immediate tax losses or write-offs in exchange for possible profits in the future. The losses were then used to offset the partner's current taxable income, thereby deferring taxes and conserving cash flows. The subsequent income that resulted from the partnership frequently was spread over a number of years so that the taxpayer maintained taxable income levels within lower tax rate brackets.[8]

However, such passive activity losses (where the taxpayer does not materially participate in the actual business activities) are now only allowed for tax purposes as a reduction to offset other passive activity profits. In most cases, these losses can no longer be used to reduce earned income such as salaries. Thus, unless a taxpayer has significant passive activity income (from rents, for example), little or no tax advantage comes from this type of investment.

The partnership form of business also has certain significant disadvantages. Perhaps the most severe problem is the unlimited liability automatically incurred by each partner. Partnership law specifies that any partner can be held personally liable for *all* debts of the business. The potential risk is especially significant when coupled with the concept of *mutual agency*. This legal term refers to the right that each partner has to incur liabilities in the name of the partnership. Consequently, partners

---

[6] Generally, the same tax advantages enjoyed by a partnership also are available to companies that qualify as S corporations. Certain restrictions, however, are placed on the usage of S corporation status by the tax laws. For example, the business can have only one class of stock and is limited to 75 stockholders. All owners must be individuals, estates, certain tax-exempt entities, or certain types of trusts.

[7] Keith Wishon and Robert P. Roche, "Making the Switch: Corporation to Partnership," *Journal of Accountancy,* March 1987, p. 90.

[8] The losses of a corporation have never provided this same benefit to stockholders. Since corporations are taxed as separate entities, a loss cannot carry through as a direct reduction in the taxable income of the company's owners.

acting within the normal scope of the business have the power to obligate the company for any amount. If the partnership fails to pay these debts, creditors can seek satisfactory remuneration from any partner that they choose.

> Partners are jointly and severally liable for the firm's obligations. As an example, if a bank had made a $10 million loan to the partnership that it could not pay, and the bank obtained a judgment against the partnership, the bank could attempt to attach the assets of any particular partner in the firm. The bank could pick and choose the partners it wished to proceed against in order to satisfy the judgment. If a partner ended up paying more than his or her share, he or she would have a right to recover from the other partners.[9]

This problem is more than just a theoretical concern. As noted in *The Wall Street Journal*,

> At least 10 partners of Laventhol & Horwath, a major accounting firm that collapsed two years ago, have filed for personal bankruptcy. They are trying to protect their savings and their homes because partners and principals of the now-defunct firm owe creditors $47.3 million.[10]

Because of the potential liability, partnerships often experience difficulty in attracting large amounts of ownership capital. Possible investors frequently avoid entering into a partnership unless they are able to participate directly in the day-to-day operations of the business. Thus, absentee ownership, which is so prevalent in corporations, is not particularly common in many partnerships.

The fear engendered by unlimited liability is relieved in some cases by the creation of a *limited partnership*. In such organizations, a number of limited partners invest money as owners but are not allowed to participate in the management of the company. These partners can still incur a loss, but the amount is restricted legally to that which each has contributed. To protect the creditors of a limited partnership, one or more general partners must be designated to assume responsibility for all obligations created in the name of the business.

Buckeye Partners, L.P. (revenues of $186 million) is an example of a limited partnership that trades on the New York Stock Exchange. According to Buckeye's December 31, 1994, balance sheet, capital of $2.5 million is reported for the company's general partners whereas the same balance for the limited partners shows a total of $243.5 million.

Such legal concepts as unlimited liability and mutual agency describe partnership characteristics that have been defined and interpreted over a great number of years. To provide consistent application across state lines in regard to these terms as well as many other legal aspects of a partnership, the Uniform Partnership Act (UPA) was created. This act, which was first proposed in 1914 and has now been adopted by all states in some form, establishes uniform standards in such areas as the nature of a partnership, the relationship of the partners to outside parties, and the dissolution of the partnership. For example, the most common legal definition of a partnership is provided by Section 6 of the act: "an association of two or more persons to carry on a business as co-owners for profit."

PARTNERSHIP ACCOUNTING—CAPITAL ACCOUNTS

Despite legal distinctions, questions should be raised before proceeding as to the need for an entirely separate study of partnership accounting.

- Does an association of two or more persons require accounting procedures significantly different from those of a corporation?
- Is proper accounting dependent on the legal form of an organization?

---

[9]An interview with Leslie D. Corwin, Esq., "What's a Partner to Do?" *The CPA Journal,* April 1991, p. 22.

[10]Lee Berton and Joann S. Lublin, "Partnership Structure Is Called in Question as Liability Risk Rises," *The Wall Street Journal,* June 10, 1992, p. A9.

The answer to these questions is both yes and no. Accounting procedures are normally standardized for assets, liabilities, revenues, and expenses regardless of the legal form of a business. *Partnership accounting, though, does exhibit unique aspects that warrant study, but they lie primarily in the handling of the partners' capital accounts.*

The stockholders' equity accounts of a corporation do not correspond directly with the capital balances found in a partnership's financial records. The various equity accounts reported by an incorporated enterprise display a greater degree of structuring: they are more precisely defined. These characteristics reflect the wide variety of equity transactions that can occur in a corporation as well as the influence of state and federal laws. Government regulation has had an effect on the accounting for corporate equity transactions in that extensive disclosure is required to protect stockholders and other outside parties.

To provide adequate information as well as to meet legal requirements, corporate accounting must provide details about numerous possible equity transactions and account balances. For example, the amount of a corporation's paid-in capital is shown separately from earned capital; the par value of each class of stock is disclosed; treasury stock, stock options, stock dividends, and other capital transactions are reported based on prescribed accounting principles.

In comparison, partnerships provide only a limited amount of equity disclosure primarily in the form of individual capital accounts that are accumulated for every partner or every class of partners. These balances measure each partner or group's interest in the book value of the net assets of the business. Thus, the equity section of a partnership balance sheet is comprised solely of capital accounts that can be affected by many different events: contributions from partners as well as distributions to them, earnings, and any other equity transactions.

However, no differentiation is drawn in the reporting of a partnership between the various sources of ownership capital. Disclosing the composition of the capital balances has not been judged necessary because partnerships have historically tended to be small with equity transactions that were rarely complex. Additionally, absentee ownership is not common, a factor that minimizes both the need for government regulation as well as the outside interest in detailed information about the capital balances.

Articles of Partnership

Because the demand for information about capital balances is limited, accounting principles specific to partnerships are based primarily on traditional approaches that have evolved over the years rather than on official pronouncements. These procedures attempt to mirror the relationship between the partners and their business especially as defined by the partnership agreement. This legal covenant, which may be either oral or written, is often referred to as the Articles of Partnership and forms the central governance for the operation of a partnership. The financial arrangements spelled out in this contract establish guidelines for the various capital transactions. Therefore, the Articles of Partnership, rather than laws or official rules, provide much of the underlying basis for partnership accounting.

Since the Articles of Partnership is a negotiated agreement created by the partners, an unlimited number of variations can be encountered in practice. Partners' rights and responsibilities frequently differ from business to business. Consequently, accountants often are hired in an advisory capacity to participate in the creation of this document to assure the equitable treatment of all parties. Although the Articles of Partnership may contain a number of provisions, an explicit understanding should always be reached in regard to the following:

- Name and address of each partner.
- Business location.

- Description of the nature of the business.
- Rights and responsibilities of each partner.
- Initial contribution to be made by each partner along with the method to be used for valuation.
- Specific method by which profits and losses are to be allocated.
- Periodic withdrawal of assets by each partner.
- Procedure for admitting new partners.
- Method for arbitrating partnership disputes.
- Life insurance provisions enabling remaining partners to acquire the interest of any deceased partner.
- Method for settling a partner's share in the business upon withdrawal, retirement, or death.[11]

Despite the importance of the Articles of Partnership, an unusual number of partnerships fail to produce this needed document.

> "You'd be surprised at the number of American law firms that operate without partnership agreements or [use] agreements that are out of date," says Ward Bower of Altman & Weil, a consulting firm that specializes in law-firm management. "Lawyers," he adds, "will sign agreements they'd never let their clients sign."[12]
>
> But despite 20 years of advice on the value of partnership agreements, the reality is that, in the majority of cases, well-structured agreements are the exception, rather than the rule, in practice units.[13]

Accounting for Capital Contributions

Several types of capital transactions occur in a partnership: allocation of profits and losses, retirement of a current partner, admission of a new partner, and so on. The initial transaction, however, is the contribution made by the partners to begin the business. In the simplest situation, the partners invest only cash amounts. For example, assume that Carter and Green form a business to be operated as a partnership. Carter contributes $50,000 in cash whereas Green invests $20,000. The initial journal entry to record the creation of this partnership is as follows:

Cash	70,000	
Carter, Capital		50,000
Green, Capital		20,000
To record cash contributed to start new partnership.		

Complications have been avoided in this first illustration by the assumption that only cash was invested. Often, though, one or more of the partners transfers noncash assets such as inventory, land, equipment, or a building to the business. Although fair market value is used to record these assets, a case could be developed for initially valuing any contributed asset at the partner's current book value. According to the concept of unlimited liability (as well as present tax laws), a partnership does not exist as an entity apart from its owners. A logical extension of the idea is that the investment

---

[11]A complete discussion of the provisions to be included in a partnership agreement can be found in "Partnership Agreements: Realities into Formalities," in the September 1986 issue of the *Journal of Accountancy* and "The Importance of Partnership Agreements," in the January 1994 issue of the *Journal of Accountancy*.

[12]Christi Harlan, "Lawyers Find it Difficult to Break Up Partnerships," *The Wall Street Journal*, October 6, 1988, p. B1.

[13]Herman J. Lowe, "Partnership Agreements: Realities into Formalities," *Journal of Accountancy*, September 1986, p. 158.

What Kind of Business Is This?

After graduating from college, Shelley Williams held several different jobs but found that she did not enjoy working for other people. Finally, she and Yvonne Hargrove, her college roommate, decided to start a business of their own. They rented a small building and opened a florist shop selling cut flowers such as roses and chrysanthemums that they bought from a local greenhouse.

Williams and Hargrove agreed to share profits and losses equally, although they also decided to take no money from the operation for at least four months. No other arrangements were made but the business did reasonably well and, after the first four months had passed, each began to draw out $250 in cash every week.

At year's end, they took their financial records to a local accountant so that they could get their income tax returns completed. He informed them that they had been operating as a partnership and that they should draw up an official Articles of Partnership or consider becoming an incorporated entity. They confessed that they had never really considered the issue and asked for his advice on the matter.

What advice should the accountant give to his clients?

---

of an asset is not a transaction occurring between two independent parties such as would warrant revaluation. This contention holds that the semblance of an arm's-length transaction is necessary to justify a change in the book value of any account.

Although retaining the recorded value for assets contributed to a partnership may seem reasonable, this method of valuation proves to be inequitable to any partner investing appreciated property. A $50,000 capital balance always results from a cash investment of that amount but the recording of other assets would be entirely dependent on the partner's original book value.

Should a partner, for example, who contributes a building having a recorded value of $18,000 but a fair market value of $50,000 be credited with only an $18,000 interest in the partnership? Since $50,000 in cash and $50,000 in appreciated property are equivalent contributions, a $32,000 difference in the partners' capital balances cannot be justified. To prevent such inequities, each item transferred to a partnership is initially recorded for external reporting purposes at current value.[14]

Requiring revaluation of contributed assets can, however, be advocated for reasons other than just the fair treatment of all partners. Despite some evidence to the contrary, a partnership can be viewed legitimately as an entity standing apart from its owners. As an example, a partnership maintains legal ownership of its assets and (depending on state law) can instigate lawsuits. For this reason, accounting practice has traditionally held that the contribution of assets (and liabilities) to a partnership is an exchange between two separately identifiable parties that should be recorded based on fair market values.

The determination of an appropriate valuation for each capital balance is more than just an accounting exercise. Over the life of a partnership, these figures serve in a number of important capacities:

1. The totals in the individual accounts often influence the assignment of profits and losses to the partners.

2. The capital account balance is usually a factor in determining the final distribution that will be received by a partner at the time of withdrawal or retirement.

3. Ending capital balances indicate the allocation to be made of any assets that remain following the liquidation of a partnership.

---

[14]For federal income tax purposes, the $18,000 book value is retained as the basis for this building, even after transfer to the partnership. Within the tax laws, no difference is seen between partners and their partnership.

To demonstrate the accounting for these capital balances, assume that Carter invests $50,000 in cash to begin the previously discussed partnership while Green contributes the following assets:

	Book Value to Green	Fair Market Value
Inventory	$ 9,000	$10,000
Land	14,000	11,000
Building	32,000	46,000
Totals	$55,000	$67,000

As an added factor, Green's building is encumbered by a $23,600 mortgage that the partnership has agreed to assume.

Based on the applicable values of these accounts, Green's net investment is equal to $43,400 ($67,000 less $23,600). The following journal entry records the formation of the partnership created by these contributions:

Cash	50,000	
Inventory	10,000	
Land	11,000	
Building.	46,000	
Mortgage Payable		23,600
Carter, Capital		50,000
Green, Capital		43,400

   To record properties contributed to start partnership. Assets and liabilities are recorded at fair market value.

One further point should be made before leaving this illustration. Although Green has contributed inventory, land, and a building, this partner holds no further right to these individual assets; they now belong to the partnership. The $43,400 capital balance represents an ownership interest in the business as a whole but does not constitute a specific claim. Having transferred title to the partnership, Green has no more right to these assets than does Carter.

Intangible Contributions   In forming a partnership, the contributions made to one or more of the partners may go beyond assets and liabilities. A doctor, for example, can bring a particular line of expertise to a partnership while a practicing dentist might have already developed an established clientele. These attributes, as well as many others, are frequently as valuable to a partnership as cash and fixed assets. *Hence, formal accounting recognition of such special contributions may be appropriately included as a provision of any partnership agreement.*

To illustrate, assume that James and Joyce plan to open an advertising agency and decide to organize the endeavor as a partnership. James contributes cash of $70,000 whereas Joyce invests only $10,000. Joyce, however, is an accomplished graphic artist, a skill that is considered especially valuable to this business. Therefore, in producing the Articles of Partnership, the partners agree to start the business with equal capital balances. Often such decisions result only after long, and sometimes heated, negotiations. Because the value assigned to an intangible contribution such as artistic talent is arbitrary at best, proper reporting depends on the ability of the partners to arrive at an equitable arrangement.

In recording this agreement, James and Joyce have two options available: (1) the bonus method and (2) the goodwill method. Each of these approaches achieves the desired result of establishing equal capital account balances. Recorded figures, however, can vary significantly depending on the procedure selected. Thus, the partners should reach an understanding prior to beginning business operations as to the method to be used. The accountant can help avoid conflicts in this area by assisting the partners in evaluating the impact created by each of these two alternatives.

I. ***The Bonus Method*** The bonus method assumes that a specialization such as Joyce's artistic abilities does *not* constitute a recordable partnership asset with a measurable cost. Hence, this approach recognizes only the assets that are physically transferred to the business (such as cash, patents, inventory, etc.). Although total partnership capital is determined by these contributions, the establishment of specific capital balances is viewed as an independent process based solely on the agreement of the partners. Since the initial equity figures are the result of negotiation, they do not need to correspond directly with the individual investments.

James and Joyce have contributed a total of $80,000 in identifiable assets to their partnership and have decided on equal capital balances. According to the bonus method, this agreement is fulfilled simply by splitting the $80,000 figure evenly between the two partners. The following entry records the formation of this partnership under this assumption:

Cash	80,000	
James, Capital		40,000
Joyce, Capital		40,000
To record cash contributions with bonus to Joyce because of		
artistic abilities.		

Joyce received a capital bonus here of $30,000 (the recorded capital balance in excess of the $10,000 cash contribution) from James in recognition of the artistic abilities she brought into the business.

II. ***The Goodwill Method*** The goodwill method is based on the assumption that an implied value can be mathematically calculated and recorded for any intangible contribution. In the present illustration, Joyce invested $60,000 less cash than James but receives an equal amount of capital according to the partnership agreement. Proponents of the goodwill method argue that Joyce's artistic talent has an apparent value of $60,000, a figure that should be included as part of this partner's capital investment. If not recorded, Joyce's primary contribution to the business is completely ignored within the accounting records.

Cash	80,000	
Goodwill	60,000	
James, Capital		70,000
Joyce, Capital		70,000
To record cash contributions with goodwill attributed to Joyce in		
recognition of artistic abilities.		

Comparison of Methods Both of these approaches achieve the intent of the partnership agreement: equal capital balances are recorded despite a difference in the partners' cash contributions. The bonus method allocates the $80,000 invested capital according to the percentages designated by the partners, whereas the goodwill method capitalizes the implied value of Joyce's intangible contribution.

Although nothing prohibits the use of either technique, the recognition of goodwill poses definite theoretical problems. In previous discussions of both the equity method (Chapter 1) and purchase consolidations (Chapter 2), goodwill was also recorded but only as a result of an acquisition made by the reporting entity. Consequently, this asset had a historical cost in the traditional accounting sense. Partnership goodwill has no such cost; the business recognizes an asset even though no funds have been spent.

The partnership of James and Joyce, for example, is able to record $60,000 in goodwill without any expenditure. Furthermore, the value attributed to this asset is based solely on a negotiated agreement between the partners; the $60,000 balance has no objectively verifiable basis. Thus, although partnership goodwill is sometimes encountered in actual practice, this "asset" should be viewed with a strong degree of professional skepticism.

Additional Capital Contributions and Withdrawals

Subsequent to the formation of a partnership, the owners may choose to contribute additional capital amounts. These investments can be made to stimulate expansion or to assist the business in overcoming working capital shortages or other problems. Regardless of the reason, the contribution is again recorded as an increment in the partner's capital account based on fair market value. For example, in the previous illustration, assume that James decides to invest another $5,000 cash in the partnership to help finance the purchase of new office furnishings. The partner's capital account balance is immediately increased by this amount to reflect the transfer being made to the partnership.

The partners also may reverse this process by withdrawing assets from the business for their own personal use. For example, one partnership, Andersons, reported in its December 31, 1994, financial statements partner withdrawals for the year of $1,759,072 as well as increases in invested capital of $733,675. To protect the interests of the other partners, the amount and timing of such withdrawals should be clearly specified in the Articles of Partnership.

In many instances, withdrawals are allowed on a regular periodic basis as a reward for ownership or as compensation for work done in the business. Often such distributions are recorded initially in a separate drawing account that is closed into the individual partner's capital account at year's end. Assume, for illustration purposes, that James and Joyce take out $1,200 and $1,500, respectively, from their business. The journal entry to record these payments is as follows:

James, Drawing	1,200	
Joyce, Drawing	1,500	
Cash		2,700

To record withdrawal of cash by partners.

Larger amounts might also be withdrawn from a partnership on occasion. A partner may have a special need for money or just desire to reduce the basic investment that has been made in the business. Such transactions are usually sporadic occurrences and in amounts significantly greater than the partner's periodic drawing. Prior approval by the other partners may be required by the Articles of Partnership.

Allocation of Income

At the end of each fiscal period, partnership revenues and expenses are closed out with the resulting net income or loss being reclassified to the partners' capital accounts. Since a separate equity balance is maintained for each partner, a method must be devised for this assignment of annual income. Because of the importance of the process, the procedure established by the partners should always be stipulated in the Articles of Partnership. If no arrangement has been specified, state partnership law normally holds that all partners share equally in any income or loss earned by the business. If an agreement has been set forth specifying only the allocation of profits, any subsequent losses must be divided in that same manner.

Actual procedures for allocating profits and losses can range from the simple to the elaborate.[15] Partnerships can avoid all complications by assigning net income on an equal basis among all partners. Other organizations attempt to devise plans that reward such factors as the expertise of the individuals or the amount of time that each

[15]See, for example, "Profit Allocation in CPA Firm Partnership Agreements," in the March 1986 issue of the *Journal of Accountancy*, pp. 91–95; "Paying Partners: A Challenge for the 1990s," in the June 1989 issue of the *Journal of Accountancy*, pp. 117—22; or "Selecting the Best Partner Compensation Method," in the December 1991 issue of the *Journal of Accountancy*, pp. 40–44.

DISCUSSION QUESTION

How Will the Profits Be Split?

James J. Dewars has been the sole owner of a small CPA firm for the past 20 years. Now 52 years old, Dewars is concerned about the continuation of his practice after he retires. He would like to begin taking more time off now although he wants to remain active in the firm for at least another 8 to 10 years. He has worked hard over the decades to build up the practice so that he presently makes a profit of $130,000 annually.

Lewis Huffman has been working for Dewars for the past four years. He now earns a salary of $40,000 per year. He is a very dedicated employee who generally works 52–60 hours per week. In the past, Dewars has been in charge of the bigger, more profitable audit clients whereas Huffman, with less experience, worked with the smaller clients. Both Dewars and Huffman do some tax work although that segment of the business has never been emphasized.

Sally Scriba has been working for the past seven years with another CPA firm as a tax specialist. She has no auditing experience but has a great reputation in tax planning and preparation. She currently has an annual salary of $60,000.

Dewars, Huffman, and Scriba are negotiating the creation of a new CPA firm as a partnership. Dewars plans to reduce his time in this firm although he will continue to work with many of the clients that he has served for the past two decades. Huffman will begin to take over some of the major audit jobs. Scriba will start and develop an extensive tax practice for the firm.

Because of the changes in the firm, the three potential partners anticipate earning a total net income in the first year of operations of between $130,000 and $190,000. Thereafter, they hope that profits will increase at the rate of 10 to 20 percent annually for the next five years or so.

How should this partnership allocate its future net income to the partners?

works. Some agreements also consider the capital invested in the business as an element that should be recognized within the allocation process.

To serve as an initial illustration, assume that Tinker, Evers, and Chance form a partnership by investing cash of $120,000, $90,000, and $75,000, respectively. The Articles of Partnership are drawn up to specify that Evers will be allotted 40 percent of all profits and losses because of previous business experience while Tinker and Chance are to divide the remaining 60 percent equally. This agreement also stipulates that each partner is allowed to withdraw $10,000 in cash annually from the business. The amount of this withdrawal is not directly dependent on the method utilized for income allocation. *From an accounting perspective, the assignment of income and the setting of withdrawal limits are two separate decisions.*

At the end of the first year of operations, the partnership reports net income of $60,000. To reflect the changes made in the partners' capital balances, the closing process consists of the following two journal entries. The assumption is made here that each partner has taken the allowed amount of drawing during the year. In addition, all revenues and expenses have been closed into an Income Summary account.

Tinker, Capital	10,000	
Evers, Capital	10,000	
Chance, Capital	10,000	
Tinker, Drawing		10,000
Evers, Drawing		10,000
Chance, Drawing		10,000

To close out drawing accounts of the three partners.

Income Summary	60,000	
Tinker, Capital (30%)		18,000
Evers, Capital (40%)		24,000
Chance, Capital (30%)		18,000

To allocate net income based on partnership agreement.

Statement of Partners' Capital. Since no Retained Earnings balance is separately disclosed by a partnership, the statement of retained earnings reported by a corporation is replaced by a statement of partners' capital. The following financial statement is based on the data presented for the partnership of Tinker, Evers, and Chance. The changes made during the year in the individual capital accounts are outlined along with totals representing the partnership as a whole.

TINKER, EVERS, AND CHANCE
Statement of Partners' Capital
For Year Ending December 31, Year 1

	Tinker, Capital	Evers, Capital	Chance, Capital	Totals
Capital balances beginning of year	$120,000	$ 90,000	$ 75,000	$285,000
Allocation of net income	18,000	24,000	18,000	60,000
Drawings	(10,000)	(10,000)	(10,000)	(30,000)
Capital balances end of year	$128,000	$104,000	$ 83,000	$315,000

Alternative Allocation Techniques—Example One   Assigning net income based on a ratio may be simple, but this approach is not necessarily equitable to all partners. For example, assume that Tinker does not participate in the operations of the partnership but is the contributor of the largest amount of capital. Evers and Chance both work full time in the business, but Evers has considerably more experience in this line of work.

Under these circumstances, no single ratio would properly reflect the various contributions being made by each of the partners. Indeed, an unlimited number of alternative allocation plans could be devised in hopes of achieving fair treatment for all parties. For example, because of the different levels of capital being invested, consideration should be given to the inclusion of interest within the allocation process. A compensation allowance is also a possibility, usually in an amount corresponding to the number of hours worked or the level of a partner's business expertise.

To demonstrate one possible option, assume that Tinker, Evers, and Chance begin their partnership based on the facts presented originally except that they arrive at a more detailed method of allocating profits and losses. After considerable negotiations, an Articles of Partnership agreement is drawn up that credits each partner annually for interest in an amount equal to 10 percent of the beginning capital balance for the year. Evers and Chance also will be allotted $15,000 apiece as a compensation allowance in recognition of their participation in daily operations. Any remaining profit or loss will be split 4:3:3, with the largest share going to Evers because of the work experience that this partner brings to the business. As with any appropriate allocation, this pattern is an attempt to be fair to all three of the partners.

Under this arrangement, the $60,000 net income earned by the partnership in the first year of operation would be prorated as follows. The sequential alignment of the various provisions is irrelevant except that the ratio, which is used to divide the remaining profit or loss, must be calculated last.

	Tinker	Evers	Chance	Totals
Interest (10% of beginning capital)	$12,000	$ 9,000	$ 7,500	$28,500
Compensation allowance	–0–	15,000	15,000	30,000
Remaining income:				
$60,000				
(28,500)				
(30,000)				
$ 1,500	450 (30%)	600 (40%)	450 (30%)	1,500
Totals	$12,450	$24,600	$22,950	$60,000

For the partnership of Tinker, Evers, and Chance, the allocations just calculated lead to the following closing entry:

Income Summary	60,000	
Tinker, Capital		12,450
Evers, Capital		24,600
Chance, Capital		22,950

    To allocate income for the year to the individual partners based on partnership agreement.

Alternative Allocation Techniques—Example Two As indicated by the preceding illustration, the assignment process is no more than a series of mechanical steps reflecting the change in each partner's capital balance resulting from the provisions of the partnership agreement. The number of different allocation procedures that could be employed is limited solely by the imagination of the partners. Although interest, compensation allowances, and various ratios are the predominant factors encountered in practice, other possibilities do exist. Therefore, another approach to the allocation process is presented to further illustrate some of the variations that can be utilized. A two-person partnership is used here to simplify the computations.

Assume that Webber and Rice formed a partnership in 1987 to operate a bookstore. Webber contributed the initial capital while Rice managed the business. With the assistance of their accountant, they wrote an Articles of Partnership agreement that contains the following provisions:

1. Each partner is allowed to draw $1,000 in cash from the business every month. Any withdrawal in excess of that figure will be accounted for as a direct reduction to the partner's capital balance.
2. Partnership profits and losses will be allocated each year according to the following plan:
   a. Interest of 15 percent will be accrued by each partner based on the monthly average capital balance for the year (calculated without regard for normal drawings or current income).
   b. As a reward for operating the business, Rice is to receive credit for a bonus equal to 20 percent of the year's net income. However, no bonus is earned if the partnership reports a net loss.
   c. Any remaining profit or loss will be divided equally between the two partners.

Assume that Webber and Rice subsequently begin the year of 1998 with capital balances of $150,000 and $30,000, respectively. On April 1 of that year, Webber invests an additional $8,000 cash in the business, while on July 1, Rice withdraws $6,000 in excess of the specified drawing allowance. Assume further that the partnership reports income of $30,000 for 1998.

Because the interest factor established in this allocation plan is based on a monthly average figure, the amount to be credited to each partner has to be determined by means of a preliminary calculation:

Webber—Interest Allocation

Beginning balance:	$150,000 × 3 months =	$ 450,000
Balance, 4/1/98:	$158,000 × 9 months =	1,422,000
		1,872,000
	×	$\frac{1}{12}$
Monthly average capital balance		156,000
Interest rate	×	15%
Interest credited to Webber		$ 23,400

Rice—Interest Allocation

Beginning balance:	$30,000 × 6 months =	$	180,000
Balance, 7/1/98:	$24,000 × 6 months =		144,000
			324,000
		×	1/12
Monthly average capital balance			27,000
Interest rate		×	15%
Interest credited to Rice	$		4,050

Following this initial computation, the actual assignment of income can proceed according to the provisions specified in the partnership agreement. The stipulations drawn up by Webber and Rice must be followed exactly, even though the business's $30,000 profit in 1998 is not sufficient to cover both the interest and the bonus. Income allocation is a mechanical process that should always be carried out as stated in the Articles of Partnership without regard for the specific level of income or loss.

Based on the plan that was created, Webber's capital increases by $21,675 during 1998 while Rice is assigned only $8,325:

	Webber	Rice	Totals
Interest (above)	$23,400	$4,050	$27,450
Bonus (20% × $30,000)	–0–	6,000	6,000
Remaining income (loss):			
$30,000			
(27,450)			
(6,000)			
$(3,450)	(1,725) (50%)	(1,725) (50%)	(3,450)
Totals	$21,675	$8,325	$30,000

ACCOUNTING FOR PARTNERSHIP DISSOLUTION

In many partnerships, capital transactions are limited almost exclusively to contributions, drawings, and profit and loss allocations. Normally, though, over any extended period, changes occur in the members who make up a partnership. Employees may be promoted into the partnership or new owners brought in from outside the organization to add capital or expertise to the business. Current partners eventually retire, die, or simply elect to leave the partnership. Large operations may even experience such changes on a routine basis. One international accounting firm has estimated that 50 to 70 partners leave the organization each year for a variety of reasons. That, apparently, is not an isolated situation; "major accounting firms have gotten rid of between 5 percent and 14 percent of their partners over the past 18 months."[16]

Regardless of the nature or the frequency of the event, any alteration in the specific individuals composing a partnership automatically leads to legal dissolution. In many instances, the break up is merely a prerequisite to the formation of a new partnership. For example, if Abernethy and Chapman decide to allow Miller to become a partner in their business, the legally recognized partnership of Abernethy and Chapman has to be dissolved first. The business property as well as the right to future profits can then be conveyed to the newly formed partnership of Abernethy, Chapman, and Miller. The change is a legal change. Actual operations of the business would probably continue unimpeded by this alteration in ownership.

Conversely, should the partners so choose, dissolution can be a preliminary step in the termination and liquidation of the business. The death of a partner, lack of sufficient profits, or internal management differences may lead the partners to the

---

[16]Berton and Lublin, p. A9.

break up of the partnership business. Under this circumstance, partnership properties are sold, debts paid, and any remaining assets distributed to the individual partners. Thus, in liquidations (which are analyzed in detail in the next chapter) both the partnership and the business cease to exist.

Dissolution—Admission of a New Partner

One of the most prevalent changes in the makeup of a partnership is the addition of a new partner. An employee may have worked for years to gain this opportunity or a prospective partner might offer new investment capital or business experience necessary for future business success. An individual can gain admittance to a partnership in one of two ways: (1) by purchasing an ownership interest from a current partner or (2) by contributing assets directly to the business.

In recording either transaction, the accountant has the option, once again, of retaining the book value for all partnership assets and liabilities (as exemplified by the bonus method) or revaluing these accounts to their present market values (the goodwill method). Although both are acceptable, the decision as to a theoretical preference between the bonus and goodwill methods hinges on one single question: *Should the dissolved partnership and the newly formed partnership be viewed as two separate reporting entities?*

If the new partnership is merely an extension of the old, no basis exists for restatement. The transfer of ownership is only a change in a legal sense and has no direct impact on business assets and liabilities. However, if the continuation of the business represents a legitimate transfer of property from one partnership to another, revaluation of all accounts and recognition of goodwill can be justified.

Because both approaches are encountered in practice, each is presented in this textbook. However, the concerns previously discussed in connection with partnership goodwill still exist: recognition is not based on historical cost and no objective verification can be made of the amount being capitalized. One alternative revaluation approach has been devised that attempts to circumvent the problems involved with partnership goodwill. This hybrid method revalues all partnership assets and liabilities to fair market value without any corresponding recognition being made of goodwill.

Admission through Purchase of a Current Interest   As mentioned, one method of gaining admittance to a partnership is by the purchase of a current interest. One or more partners may choose to sell their portion of the business to an outside party. This type transaction is most common in operations that rely primarily on monetary capital rather than on the business expertise of the partners.

In making a transfer of ownership, a partner can actually convey only three rights:

1. *The right of co-ownership in the business property.* This right justifies the partner's periodic drawings from the business as well as the distribution settlement paid at liquidation or at the time of a partner's withdrawal.
2. *The right to share in profits and losses as specified in the Articles of Partnership.*
3. *The right to participate in the management of the business.*

Unless restricted by the Articles of Partnership, every partner has the power to sell or assign the first two of these partnership rights at any time. Their transfer poses no threat of financial harm to the remaining partners. In contrast, partnership law states that the right to participate in the management of the business can only be conveyed with the consent of all partners. This particular right is considered essential to the future earning power of the enterprise as well as the maintenance of business assets. Therefore, current partners are protected from the intrusion of parties who might be considered detrimental to the management of the company.

As an illustration, assume that Scott, Thompson, and York formed a partnership several years ago. Subsequently, York decides to leave the partnership and offers to sell his interest to Morgan. Although York may transfer the right of property ownership as well as the specified share of future profits and losses, Morgan is not automatically admitted into the partnership. York legally remains a partner until such time as both Scott and Thompson agree to allow Morgan to participate in the management of the business.

To demonstrate the accounting procedures applicable to the transfer of a partnership interest, assume that the following information is available relating to the partnership of Scott, Thompson, and York:

Partner	Capital Balance	Profit and Loss Ratio
Scott	$ 50,000	20%
Thompson	30,000	50
York	20,000	30
Total capital	$100,000	

In this example, the relationship of the capital accounts to one another does not correspond with the partners' profit and loss ratio. Capital balances are historical cost figures. They result from contributions and withdrawals made throughout the life of the business as well as from the allocation of partnership income. Therefore, any correlation between a partner's recorded capital at a particular point in time and the profit and loss percentage would probably be coincidental. Scott, for example, has 50 percent of the current partnership capital ($50,000/$100,000), although entitled to only a 20 percent allocation of income.

Instead of York selling his interest to Morgan, assume that each of these three partners elects to transfer a 20 percent interest to Morgan for a total payment of $30,000. According to the sales contract, *the money is to be paid directly to the owners*. One approach to the recording of this transaction is that, since Morgan's purchase is carried out between the individual parties, the acquisition has no impact on the assets and liabilities held by the partnership. Because the business is not involved, the transfer of ownership requires a simple reclassification without any accompanying revaluation. Book value is retained. This approach is similar to the bonus method; only a legal change in ownership is occurring so that neither revaluation of assets or liabilities nor goodwill is appropriate.

Book Value Approach

Scott, Capital (20% of capital balance)	10,000	
Thompson, Capital (20%)	6,000	
York, Capital (20%)	4,000	
Morgan, Capital (20% of total)		20,000

Reclassification of capital to reflect Morgan's acquisition. Money paid directly to partners.

An alternative for recording this acquisition by Morgan does exist that relies on a different perspective of the new partner's admission. Legally, the partnership of Scott, Thompson, and York is transferring all assets and liabilities to the partnership of Scott, Thompson, York, and Morgan. Therefore, according to the logic underlying the goodwill method, a transaction is occurring between two separate reporting entities, an event that necessitates the complete revaluation of all assets and liabilities.

Since Morgan is paying $30,000 for a 20 percent interest in the partnership, the implied value of the business as a whole is $150,000 ($30,000/20%). However, the current book value is only $100,000; thus, a $50,000 upward revaluation is indicated. This adjustment is reflected by restating specific partnership asset and liability accounts to market value with any remaining balance being recorded as goodwill. After the implied value of the partnership is established, the reclassification can be recorded based on the new capital balances.

Goodwill (Revaluation) Approach

Goodwill (or specific accounts)	50,000	
Scott, Capital (20% of goodwill)		10,000
Thompson, Capital (50%)		25,000
York, Capital (30%)		15,000

Recognition of goodwill based on size of Morgan's purchase price.

Scott, Capital (20% of new capital balance)	12,000	
Thompson, Capital (20%)	11,000	
York, Capital (20%)	7,000	
Morgan, Capital (20% of new total)		30,000

Reclassification of capital to reflect Morgan's acquisition. Money paid directly to partners.

As can be seen here, the $50,000 revaluation is credited to the original partners based on the profit and loss ratio rather than on their percentages of capital. Recognition of goodwill (or an increase in the book value of specific accounts) indicates that unrecorded gains have accrued to the business during the previous years of operation. Therefore, the equitable treatment is to allocate this increment among the partners according to their profit and loss percentages.

Admission by a Contribution Made to the Partnership　Entrance into a partnership is not obtained solely by the purchase of a current partner's interest. An outsider may be admitted to the ownership by contributing cash or other assets directly to the business rather than to the partners. For example, assume that King and Wilson maintain a partnership and presently report capital balances of $80,000 and $20,000, respectively. According to the Articles of Partnership, King is entitled to 60 percent of all profits and losses with the remaining 40 percent credited to Wilson. By agreement of the partners, Simpson is now being allowed to enter the partnership for a payment of $20,000 *with this money going into the business.* Based on negotiations that preceded the acquisition, all parties have agreed that Simpson receives an initial 10 percent interest in partnership property.

Bonus Credited to Original Partners　The bonus (or no revaluation) method maintains the same recorded value for all partnership assets and liabilities despite Simpson's admittance. The capital balance for this new partner is simply set at the appropriate 10 percent level based on the book value of the partnership taken as a whole (after the payment is recorded). Since $20,000 is currently being invested, total reported capital increases to $120,000. Thus, Simpson's 10 percent interest is computed as $12,000. *The $8,000 difference between the amount contributed and this allotted capital balance is viewed as a bonus.* Since Simpson is willing to accept a capital balance that is less than the investment being made, this bonus is attributed to the original partners (based on their profit and loss ratio). Because of the nature of the transaction, no need is perceived for recognizing goodwill or revaluing any of the assets or liabilities.

Cash	20,000	
Simpson, Capital (10% of total capital)		12,000
King, Capital (60% of bonus)		4,800
Wilson, Capital (40% of bonus)		3,200

To record Simpson's entrance into partnership with $8,000 extra payment recorded as bonus to original partners.

Goodwill Credited to Original Partners　The goodwill method views Simpson's payment as evidence that the partnership as a whole possesses an actual value of

$200,000 ($20,000/10 percent). Since, even with the new partner's investment, only $120,000 in net assets is being reported, a valuation adjustment of $80,000 is implied.[17] Over the previous years, unrecorded gains have apparently accrued to the business. This $80,000 figure might reflect the need to revalue specific accounts such as inventory or equipment, although the entire amount, or some portion, may simply be recorded as goodwill.

Goodwill (or specific accounts)	80,000	
King, Capital (60% of goodwill)		48,000
Wilson, Capital (40%)		32,000
To recognize goodwill based on Simpson's purchase price.		
Cash	20,000	
Simpson, Capital		20,000
To record Simpson's admission into partnership.		

Comparison of Bonus Method and Goodwill Method   Completely different capital balances (as well as asset and liability figures) result from these two approaches. In both cases, though, the new partner is properly credited with 10 percent of total partnership capital.

	Bonus Method	Goodwill Method
Assets less liabilities (as reported)	$100,000	$100,000
Simpson's contribution......................	20,000	20,000
Goodwill	–0–	80,000
Total......................................	$120,000	$200,000
Simpson's capital.........................	$ 12,000	$ 20,000

Because Simpson contributed an amount greater than 10 percent of the resulting book value of the partnership, this business is perceived as being worth more than the recorded accounts presently indicate. Therefore, the bonus in the first instance and the goodwill in the second were both assumed as accruing to the two original partners. Such a presumption is not unusual in an established business, especially if profitable operations have been developed over a number of years.

Hybrid Method of Recording Admission of New Partner   One other approach to the admission of Simpson can be devised. Assume that the assets and liabilities of the King and Wilson partnership have a book value of $100,000 as stated earlier. Also assume that a piece of land held by the business is actually worth $30,000 more than its currently recorded book value. Thus, the identifiable assets of the partnership are worth $130,000. Simpson pays $20,000 for a 10 percent interest.

In this approach, the identifiable assets (such as land) are revalued but no goodwill is recognized.

Land	30,000	
King, Capital (60% of revaluation)		18,000
Wilson, Capital (40%)		12,000
To record current market value of land in preparation for admission		
of new partner.		

The admission of Simpson and the payment of $20,000 brings the total capital balance to $150,000. Because Simpson is acquiring a 10 percent interest, a capital balance of $15,000 is recorded. The extra $5,000 payment ($20,000 − $15,000) is attributed as a bonus to the original partners.

---

[17]Since the $20,000 is being put into the business in this example, total capital to be used in the goodwill computation has increased to $120,000. If, as in the previous illustration, payment had been made directly to the partners, the original capital of $100,000 is retained in determining goodwill.

Cash	20,000	
Simpson, Capital (10% of total capital)		15,000
King, Capital (60% of bonus)		3,000
Wilson, Capital (40% of bonus)		2,000
To record entrance of Simpson into partnership and bonus assigned		
to original partners.		

Bonus or Goodwill Credited to New Partner   As previously discussed, Simpson also may be contributing some attribute other than tangible assets to this partnership. Therefore, the Articles of Partnership may be written to credit the new partner rather than the original partners, with either a bonus or goodwill. Because of an excellent professional reputation, valuable business contacts, or myriad other possible factors, Simpson might be able to negotiate a beginning capital balance in excess of the $20,000 cash contribution. This same circumstance may also result if the business is desperate for new capital and is willing to offer favorable terms as an enticement to the potential partner.

To illustrate, assume that Simpson receives a 20 percent interest in the preceding partnership (rather than the originally stated 10 percent) in exchange for the $20,000 cash investment. The specific rationale for the higher ownership percentage need not be identified.

The bonus method sets Simpson's initial capital at $24,000 (20 percent of the $120,000 book value). To achieve this balance, a capital bonus of $4,000 must be credited to Simpson by the present partners:

Cash	20,000	
King, Capital (60% of bonus)	2,400	
Wilson, Capital (40% of bonus)	1,600	
Simpson, Capital		24,000
To record Simpson's entrance into partnership with reduced		
payment reported as a bonus from original partners.		

If goodwill rather than a bonus is attributed to the *entering partner,* a mathematical problem arises in determining the implicit value of the business as a whole. In the current illustration, Simpson paid $20,000 for a 20 percent interest. Therefore, the value of the company is calculated as only $100,000 ($20,000/20 percent), a figure that is less than the $120,000 in net assets being reported after the new contribution. Negative goodwill appears to exist. One possibility is that individual partnership assets are overvalued and require reduction. As an alternative, the cash contribution might not be an accurate representation of the new partner's investment. Simpson could be bringing an intangible contribution (goodwill) to the business along with the $20,000. This additional amount can be determined only algebraically:

$$\text{Simpson's capital} = 20 \text{ percent of partnership capital}$$

Therefore

$$\$20,000 + \text{Goodwill} = .20\ (\$100,000 + \$20,000 + \text{Goodwill})$$
$$\$20,000 + \text{Goodwill} = \$20,000 + \$4,000 + .20\ \text{Goodwill}$$
$$.80\ \text{Goodwill} = \$4,000$$
$$\text{Goodwill} = \$5,000$$

If the partners determine that Simpson is, indeed, making an intangible contribution (a particular skill, for example, or a developed clientele), Simpson should be credited with a $25,000 capital investment: $20,000 cash and $5,000 goodwill. When added to the original $100,000 in net assets reported by the partnership, this contribution raises the total capital for the business to $125,000. As specified by the purchase agreement, Simpson's interest now represents a 20 percent share of the partnership ($25,000/$125,000).

Recognizing $5,000 in goodwill has established the proper relationship between the new partner and the partnership. Therefore, the following journal entry should be recorded to reflect this transaction:

Cash	20,000	
Goodwill	5,000	
Simpson, Capital		25,000

To record Simpson's entrance into partnership with goodwill attributed to this new partner.

Dissolution—Withdrawal by a Partner

Admission of a new partner is not the only method by which a partnership can undergo a change in composition. Over the life of the business, partners occasionally leave the organization. Death or retirement can occur, or a partner may simply elect to withdraw from the partnership. The Articles of Partnership also can allow for the expulsion of a partner under certain conditions.

Once again, any change in membership legally dissolves the partnership, although the business's operations usually continue uninterrupted under the ownership of the remaining partners. Regardless of the reason for dissolution, some method of establishing an equitable settlement of the withdrawing partner's interest in the business is necessary. Often, the partner (or the partner's estate) may simply sell the interest to an outside party, with approval, or to one or more of the remaining partners. As an alternative, cash or other assets can be distributed from the business as a means of settling a partner's right of co-ownership. Consequently, life insurance policies are held by many partnerships solely to provide adequate cash to liquidate a partner's interest upon death.

Whether withdrawal is caused by death or some other reason, a final distribution will not necessarily equal the book value of the partner's capital account. A capital balance is only a recording of historical transactions and rarely represents the true value inherent in a business. Instead, payment is frequently based on the value of the partner's interest as ascertained by either negotiation or appraisal. Since the determination of a settlement can be derived in many ways, the Articles of Partnership should contain exact provisions regulating this procedure.

The withdrawal of an individual partner and the resulting distribution of partnership property can, again, be accounted for by either the bonus (no revaluation) method or the goodwill (revaluation) method. However, once again, a hybrid option is available.

As in earlier illustrations, if a bonus is recorded, the amount can be attributed to either of the parties involved: the withdrawing partner or the remaining partners. Conversely, any revaluation of partnership property (as well as the establishment of a goodwill balance) is allocated among all partners in recognition of possible unrecorded gains. As before, the hybrid approach restates assets and liabilities to fair market value but makes no recording of goodwill. In this last alternative, the legal change in ownership is reflected but the theoretical problems associated with partnership goodwill are avoided.

Accounting for the Withdrawal of a Partner—Illustration   To demonstrate the various approaches that can be taken to account for a partner's withdrawal, assume that the partnership of Duncan, Smith, and Windsor has been in existence for a number of years. At the present time, the partners have the following capital balances as well as the indicated profit and loss percentages:

Partner	Capital Balance	Profit and Loss Ratio
Duncan	$ 70,000	50%
Smith	20,000	30%
Windsor	10,000	20%
Total capital	$100,000	

Windsor decides to withdraw from the partnership but Duncan and Smith plan to continue operating the business. As per the original partnership agreement, a final settlement distribution for Windsor is computed based on the following specified provisions:

1. An appraisal will be made by an independent expert to determine the estimated fair market value of the business.
2. Any individual who leaves the partnership is to receive cash or other assets equal to that partner's current capital balance after recording an appropriate share of any adjustment indicated by the previous valuation. The allocation of unrecorded gains and losses is based on the normal profit and loss ratio.

Following Windsor's decision to withdraw from the partnership, an immediate appraisal is made of the business and its property. Total fair market value is estimated at $180,000, a figure $80,000 in excess of book value. According to this valuation, land held by the partnership is currently worth $50,000 more than its original cost. In addition, $30,000 in goodwill is attributed to the partnership based on the value of the business as a going concern. *Therefore, Windsor is paid $26,000 on leaving the partnership: the original $10,000 capital balance plus a 20 percent share of this $80,000 increment.* The amount of payment is not in dispute, only the method of recording the withdrawal is in question.

Bonus Method Applied   If the bonus method is used by the partnership to record this transaction, the extra $16,000 paid to Windsor is simply recorded as a decrease in the remaining partners' capital accounts. Historically, Duncan and Smith have been credited with 50 percent and 30 percent of all profits and losses, respectively. This same relative ratio is used now to allocate the reduction between these two remaining partners on a ⅝ and ⅜ basis:

Bonus Method

Windsor, Capital (to remove account balance)	10,000	
Duncan, Capital (⅝ of excess distribution)	10,000	
Smith, Capital (⅜ of excess distribution)	6,000	
Cash		26,000

To record Windsor's withdrawal with $16,000 excess distribution taken from remaining partners.

Goodwill Method Applied   This same transaction can also be accounted for by means of the goodwill (or revaluation) approach. The appraisal indicates that land is undervalued on the partnership's records by $50,000 and that goodwill of $30,000 has apparently accrued to the business over the years. The first of the following entries recognizes these valuations. This adjustment properly equates Windsor's capital balance with the $26,000 cash distribution. Windsor's equity balance is merely removed in the second entry at the time of payment.

Goodwill Method

Land	50,000	
Goodwill	30,000	
Duncan, Capital (50%)		40,000
Smith, Capital (30%)		24,000
Windsor, Capital (20%)		16,000

Recognition of land value and goodwill as a preliminary step to Windsor's withdrawal.

Windsor, Capital (to remove account balance)	26,000	
Cash		26,000

Cash distribution made to Windsor in settlement of partnership interest.

The implied value of a partnership as a whole cannot be determined directly from the amount distributed to a withdrawing partner. For example, paying Windsor $26,000 did not indicate that total capital should be $130,000 ($26,000/20%). This computation is appropriate only when (1) a new partner is admitted or (2) the percentage of capital is the same as the profit and loss ratio. Instead, the $26,000 payment here necessitates a $16,000 increase being made to Windsor's reported capital ($26,000 – $10,000). Because Windsor is entitled to 20 percent of profits and losses, a total revaluation of $80,000 is required ($16,000/20%) to arrive at this appropriate equity balance.

Hybrid Method Applied   As indicated previously, a hybrid approach also can be adopted to record a partner's withdrawal. Asset and liability revaluations are still recognized but goodwill is ignored. A bonus must be recorded to reconcile the partner's adjusted capital balance with the final distribution.

In the current illustration, for example, no goodwill is recorded. However, the book value of the land is increased by $50,000 in recognition of present worth. This adjustment increases Windsor's capital balance to $20,000, a figure that is still less than the $26,000 distribution. The $6,000 difference is recorded as a bonus taken from the remaining two partners according to their relative profit and loss ratio.

Hybrid Method

Land	50,000	
Duncan, Capital (50%)		25,000
Smith, Capital (30%)		15,000
Windsor, Capital (20%)		10,000

To adjust land account to fair market value as a preliminary step in Windsor's withdrawal.

Windsor, Capital (to remove account balances)	20,000	
Duncan, Capital (⅝ of bonus)	3,750	
Smith, Capital (⅜ of bonus)	2,250	
Cash		26,000

Final distribution made to Windsor with $6,000 bonus taken from remaining partners.

SUMMARY

1. A partnership is defined as "an association of two or more persons to carry on a business as co-owners for profit." This form of business organization exists throughout the American economy ranging in size from small, part-time operations to international enterprises. The partnership format is popular for many reasons, including the ease of creation and the avoidance of the double taxation that is inherent in corporate ownership. However, the unlimited liability incurred by each general partner normally restricts the growth potential of most partnerships. Thus, although the quantity of partnerships in the United States is great, their size tends to be small.

2. The unique elements of partnership accounting are found primarily in the capital accounts that are accumulated for each partner. The basis for recording these balances is the Articles of Partnership, a document that should be established as a prerequisite to the formation of any partnership. One of the principal provisions of this agreement is the initial investment to be made by each partner. Noncash contributions such as inventory or land are entered into the partnership's accounting records at fair market value.

3. In forming a partnership, the contributions made by the partners need not be limited to tangible assets. A particular line of expertise possessed by a partner or an established clientele are attributes that can have a significant value to a partnership. Two methods of recording this type of investment are found in practice. Under the bonus method, only identifiable assets are recognized. The capital accounts are then aligned to indicate the balances negotiated by the partners. According to the goodwill approach, all contributions

(even those of a nebulous nature such as an expertise) are valued and recorded, often as goodwill.

4. Another accounting issue to be resolved in forming a partnership is the allocation of annual net income. In closing out the revenue and expense accounts at the end of each period, some assignment must be made to the individual capital balances. Although an equal division can be used to allocate the profit or loss, partners frequently devise unique plans in an attempt to be equitable. Such factors as time worked, expertise, and invested capital should be considered in creating an allocation procedure.

5. Over time, changes occur in the makeup of a partnership because of the death or retirement of the individuals or the admission of new partners. Such changes dissolve the existing partnership, although the business frequently continues uninterrupted through a newly formed partnership. If, for example, a new partner is admitted by the acquisition of a present interest, the capital balances can simply be reclassified to reflect the change in ownership. As an alternative, the purchase price may be viewed as evidence of the underlying value of the organization as a whole. Based on this calculation, asset and liability balances are adjusted to market value, and any residual goodwill is recognized.

6. Admission into an existing partnership also can be achieved by a direct capital contribution to the business. Because of negotiations between the parties, the amount invested will not always agree with the beginning capital balance attributed to the new partner. The bonus method resolves this conflict by simply reclassifying the various capital accounts to align the balances with specified totals and percentages. Revaluation of assets and liabilities is not carried out under this approach. Conversely, according to the goodwill method, all accounts are adjusted first to fair market value. The price paid by the new partner is used to compute an implied value for the partnership, and any excess over market value is recorded as goodwill.

7. The composition of a partnership also can undergo changes because of the death or retirement of a partner. Individuals may decide to simply withdraw. Such changes legally dissolve the partnership, although business operations frequently continue under the ownership of the remaining partners. In compensating the departing partner, the final asset distribution may differ from the ending capital balance. This disparity can, once again, be accounted for by means of the bonus method, which adjusts the remaining capital accounts to absorb the bonus being paid. The goodwill approach also can be applied wherein all assets and liabilities are restated to fair market value with any goodwill being recognized. Finally, a hybrid method revalues the assets and liabilities but ignores goodwill. Under this last approach, any amount paid to the departing partner in excess of the newly adjusted capital balance is accounted for by means of the bonus method.

COMPREHENSIVE ILLUSTRATION

Problem

(*Estimated Time: 30 to 40 Minutes*) Heyman and Mullins begin a partnership on January 1, 1998. Heyman invests $40,000 cash as well as inventory costing $15,000 but with a current appraised value of only $12,000. Mullins contributes a building with a $40,000 book value and a $48,000 fair market value. The partnership also accepts responsibility for a $10,000 note payable owed in connection with this building.

The partners agree to begin operations with equal capital balances. The Articles of Partnership also provide that at the end of each year profits and losses are allocated as follows:

1. For managing the business, Heyman is credited with a bonus of 10 percent of partnership income after subtracting the bonus. No bonus is accrued if the partnership records a loss.

2. Both partners are entitled to interest equal to 10 percent of the average monthly capital balance for the year without regard for the income or drawings of that year.

3. Any remaining profit or loss is divided 60 percent to Heyman and 40 percent to Mullins.

4. Each partner is allowed to withdraw $800 per month in cash from the business.

On October 1, 1998, Heyman invests an additional $12,000 cash in the business. For 1998, the partnership reports income of $33,000.

Lewis, an employee, is allowed to join the partnership on January 1, 1999. The new partner invests $66,000 directly into the business for a one-third interest in the partnership property. The revised partnership agreement still allows for both the bonus to Heyman as well as the 10 percent interest, but all remaining profits and losses are now split 40 percent each to Heyman and Lewis with the remaining 20 percent to Mullins. Lewis is also entitled to $800 per month in drawings.

Mullins chooses to withdraw from the partnership a few years later. After negotiations, all parties agree that Mullins should be paid a $90,000 settlement. The capital balances on that date were as follows:

$$
\begin{array}{lr}
\text{Heyman, capital} & \$88,000 \\
\text{Mullins, capital} & 78,000 \\
\text{Lewis, capital} & 72,000
\end{array}
$$

Required

a. Assuming that the bonus method is used exclusively by this partnership, make all necessary journal entries. Entries for the monthly drawings of the partners are not required.

b. Assuming that the goodwill method is used exclusively by this partnership, make all necessary journal entries. Again, entries for the monthly drawings are not required.

Solution

a. **Bonus Method**

1998

Jan. 1   All contributed property is recorded at fair market value. Under the bonus method, total capital is then divided as specified between the partners.

Cash	40,000	
Inventory	12,000	
Building	48,000	
Note Payable		10,000
Heyman, Capital (50%)		45,000
Mullins, Capital (50%)		45,000

To record initial contributions to partnership along with equal capital balances.

Oct. 1

Cash	12,000	
Heyman, Capital		12,000

To record additional investment by partner.

Dec. 31   Both the bonus assigned to Heyman and the interest accrual must be computed as preliminary steps in the income allocation process. Since the bonus is based on income after subtracting the bonus, the amount must be calculated algebraically:

$$
\begin{aligned}
\text{Bonus} &= .10\,(\$33,000 - \text{Bonus}) \\
\text{Bonus} &= \$3,300 - .10\ \text{Bonus} \\
1.10\ \text{Bonus} &= \$3,300 \\
\text{Bonus} &= \$3,000
\end{aligned}
$$

According to the partnership agreement, the interest allocation is based on a monthly average figure. Mullins's capital balance of $45,000 did not change during the year; therefore $4,500 (10 percent) is the appropriate interest accrual for that partner. However, because of the October 1, 1998, contribution, Heyman's interest must be determined as follows:

Beginning balance:	$45,000 × 9 months =	$405,000
New balance:	$57,000 × 3 months =	171,000
		576,000
		× 1/12
Monthly average—capital balance		48,000
Interest rate		× 10%
Interest credited to Heyman		$ 4,800

Following the bonus and interest computations, the $33,000 income earned by the business in 1998 can be allocated according to the previously specified arrangement:

	Heyman	Mullins	Totals
Bonus (above)	$ 3,000	–0–	$ 3,000
Interest (above)	4,800	$ 4,500	9,300
Remaining income:			
$33,000			
(3,000)			
(9,300)			
$20,700	12,420 (60%)	8,280 (40%)	20,700
Income allocation	$20,220	$12,780	$33,000

Thus, the partnership's closing entries for the year of 1998 would be recorded as follows:

Heyman, Capital	9,600	
Mullins, Capital	9,600	
Heyman, Drawing		9,600
Mullins, Drawing		9,600

    To close out $800 per month drawing accounts for the year of 1998.

Income Summary	33,000	
Heyman, Capital		20,220
Mullins, Capital		12,780

    To close out profit for year to capital accounts as computed above.

At the end of this initial year of operation, the partners' capital accounts hold the following balances:

	Heyman	Mullins	Totals
Beginning balance	$45,000	$45,000	$ 90,000
Additional investment	12,000	–0–	12,000
Drawing	(9,600)	(9,600)	(19,200)
Net income (above)	20,220	12,780	33,000
Total capital	$67,620	$48,180	$115,800

1999

Jan. 1

Lewis contributed $66,000 to the business for a one-third interest in the partnership property. Combined with the $115,800 balance computed above, the partnership now has total capital of $181,800. Since no revaluation is recorded under the bonus approach, a one-third interest in the partnership equals $60,600 ($181,800 × ⅓). Lewis has invested $5,400 in excess of this amount, a balance viewed as a bonus accruing to the original partners:

Cash	66,000	
Lewis, Capital		60,600
Heyman, Capital (60% of bonus)		3,240
Mullins, Capital (40% of bonus)		2,160

    To record Lewis's entrance into partnership with bonus to original partners.

Several years later

The final event in this illustration is Mullins's withdrawal from the partnership. Although a capital balance of only $78,000 is reported for this partner, the final distribution is set at $90,000. The extra $12,000 payment represents a bonus assigned to Mullins, an amount that decreases the capital of the remaining two partners. Since Heyman and Lewis have previously accrued equal 40 percent shares of all profits and losses, the reduction is split evenly between the two.

Mullins, Capital	78,000	
Heyman, Capital (½ of bonus payment)	6,000	
Lewis, Capital (½ of bonus payment)	6,000	
Cash		90,000

Withdrawal of Mullins with bonus taken from
remaining partners.

b. Goodwill Method

1998

Jan. 1   The fair market value of Heyman's contribution is $52,000, whereas Mullins is investing only a net $38,000 (the value of the building less the accompanying debt). Because the capital accounts are initially to be equal, Mullins is presumed to be contributing goodwill of $14,000.

Cash	40,000	
Inventory	12,000	
Building	48,000	
Goodwill	14,000	
Note payable		10,000
Heyman, Capital		52,000
Mullins, Capital		52,000

Creation of partnership with goodwill attributed to Mullins.

Oct. 1

| Cash . . . . | 12,000 | |
| Heyman, Capital . . . . | | 12,000 |

To record additional contribution by partner.

Dec. 31   Although Heyman's bonus is still $3,000 as derived in requirement *a*, the interest accruals must be recalculated because the capital balances are different. Mullins's capital for the entire year was $52,000; thus, interest of $5,200 (10 percent) is appropriate. However, Heyman's balance changed during the year so that a monthly average must be determined as a basis for computing interest:

Beginning balance:	$52,000 × 9 months =	$468,000
New balance:	$64,000 × 3 months =	192,000
		660,000
		× 1/12
Monthly average—capital balance		55,000
Interest rate		× 10%
Interest credited to Heyman		$ 5,500

Consequently, the $33,000 partnership income reported for 1998 is allocated as follows:

	Heyman	Mullins	Totals
Bonus (above)	$ 3,000	–0–	$ 3,000
Interest (above)	5,500	$ 5,200	10,700
Remaining income:			
$33,000			
(3,000)			
(10,700)			
$19,300	11,580 (60%)	7,720 (40%)	19,300
Income allocation	$20,080	$12,920	$33,000

The 1998 closing entries made under the goodwill approach would be as follows:

Heyman, Capital	9,600	
Mullins, Capital	9,600	
Heyman, Drawing		9,600
Mullins, Drawing		9,600

To close out drawing accounts for the year.

Income Summary	33,000	
Heyman, Capital		20,080
Mullins, Capital		12,920

To assign 1998 profits per allocation determined above.

After the closing process, the capital balances are composed of the following items:

	Heyman	Mullins	Totals
Beginning balance	$52,000	$52,000	$104,000
Additional investment.............	12,000	–0–	12,000
Drawing	(9,600)	(9,600)	(19,200)
Net income	20,080	12,920	33,000
Total capital..................	$74,480	$55,320	$129,800

1999

Jan. 1   Lewis's investment of $66,000 for a one-third interest in the partnership property implies that the business as a whole is worth $198,000 ($66,000 divided by 1/3). After adding Lewis's contribution to the present capital balance of $129,800, the business reports total net assets of only $195,800. Thus, a $2,200 gain in value ($198,000 − $195,800) is indicated and will be recognized at this time. Assuming that all partnership assets and liabilities are appropriately valued, this entire balance is attributed to goodwill.

Goodwill	2,200	
Heyman, Capital (60%).................		1,320
Mullins, Capital (40%)		880

To recognize goodwill based on Lewis's acquisition price.

Cash	66,000	
Lewis, Capital		66,000

Admission of Lewis to the partnership.

Several years later   To conclude this illustration, Mullins's withdrawal must be recorded. This partner is to receive a distribution that is $12,000 greater than the corresponding capital balance of $78,000. Since Mullins is entitled to a 20 percent share of profits and losses, the additional $12,000 payment indicates that the partnership as a whole is undervalued by $60,000 ($12,000/20%). Only in that circumstance would the extra payment to Mullins be justified. Therefore, once again, goodwill is recognized with the final distribution then being made.

Goodwill	60,000	
Heyman, Capital (40%).................		24,000
Mullins, Capital (20%)		12,000
Lewis, Capital (40%)		24,000

Recognition of goodwill based on withdrawal amount paid to Mullins.

Mullins, Capital	90,000	
Cash		90,000

Money distributed to partner.

QUESTIONS

1. What are the advantages of operating a business as a partnership rather than as a corporation? What are the disadvantages?

2. How does partnership accounting differ from corporate accounting?

3. What information is conveyed by the capital accounts found in partnership accounting?

4. What is an Articles of Partnership agreement, and what information should this document contain?

5. What valuation should be recorded for noncash assets transferred to a partnership by one of the partners?

6. If a partner is contributing attributes to a partnership such as an established clientele or a particular expertise, what two methods can be applied to record the contribution? Describe each of these methods.

7. What is the purpose of a drawing account in a partnership's financial records?

8. At what point in the accounting process does the allocation of partnership income become significant?

9. What provisions can be used in a partnership agreement to establish an equitable allocation of income among all partners?

10. If no agreement exists in a partnership as to the allocation of income, what method is appropriate?

11. What is a partnership dissolution? Does dissolution automatically necessitate the cessation of business and the liquidation of partnership assets?

12. By what methods can a new partner gain admittance into a partnership?

13. When a partner sells an ownership interest in a partnership, what rights are conveyed to the new owner?

14. A new partner enters a partnership and goodwill is calculated and credited to the original partners. How is the specific amount of goodwill assigned to these partners?

15. Under what circumstance might goodwill be allocated to a new partner entering a partnership?

16. When a partner withdraws from a partnership, why is the final distribution often based on the appraised value of the business rather than on the book value of the capital account balance?

LIBRARY ASSIGNMENTS

1. Read the following as well as any other published materials describing the creation of a partnership:

> "How to Choose the Right Form of Doing Business," *Management Accounting,* January 1985.
> "Helping Clients Choose the Legal Form for a Small Business," *The Practical Accountant,* October 1990.
> "Should You Convert Your Practice to a Limited Liability Company?" *Law Practice Management,* September 1996.
> "Choosing a Business Entity in the 1990s," *Pennsylvania CPA Journal,* August 1995.
> "Selecting a Form of Business," *The CPA Journal,* April 1997.
> "Making the Switch: Corporation to Partnership," *Journal of Accountancy,* March 1987.

Write a report discussing the issues to be considered in deciding whether a partnership or some other legal form is preferable.

2. Read the following as well as any other published materials discussing the legal liability faced by partners:

> "Partnership Structure Is Called in Question as Liability Risk Rises," *The Wall Street Journal,* June 10, 1992.
> "What's a Partner to Do?" *The CPA Journal,* April 1991.

"Big 6 Firms Consider Incorporation," *World Accounting Report,* August 1994.

"Goldman Chooses Limited Liability for New Structure," *The Wall Street Journal,* May 22, 1996.

Write a report discussing whether the potential liability of partners should be limited in some manner.

PROBLEMS

1. Which of the following is not a reason for the popularity of partnerships as a legal form for businesses?
   a. Partnerships need only be formed by an oral agreement.
   b. Partnerships can more easily generate significant amounts of capital.
   c. Partnerships avoid the double-taxation of income that is found in corporations.
   d. In some cases, losses may be used to offset gains for tax purposes.

2. How does partnership accounting differ from corporate accounting?
   a. The matching principle is not considered appropriate for partnership accounting.
   b. Revenues are recognized at a different time by a partnership than is appropriate for a corporation.
   c. Individual capital accounts replace the contributed capital and retained earnings balances found in corporate accounting.
   d. All assets are reported by partnerships at fair market value as of the latest balance sheet date.

3. Pat, Jean Lou, and Diane are partners with capital balances of $50,000, $30,000, and $20,000, respectively. These three partners share profits and losses equally. For an investment of $50,000 cash (being paid to the business), MaryAnn is to be admitted as a partner with a one-fourth interest in capital and profits. Based on this information, the amount of MaryAnn's investment can best be justified by which of the following?
   a. MaryAnn will receive a bonus from the other partners upon her admission to the partnership.
   b. Assets of the partnership were overvalued immediately prior to MaryAnn's investment.
   c. The book value of the partnership's net assets was less than the fair value immediately prior to MaryAnn's investment.
   d. MaryAnn is apparently bringing goodwill into the partnership, and her capital account will be credited for the appropriate amount.

   (AICPA adapted)

4. A partnership has the following capital balances:

Albert (50% of gains and losses)	$ 80,000
Barrymore (20%)	60,000
Candroth (30%)	140,000

   Danville is going to invest $70,000 into the business to acquire a 30 percent ownership interest. Goodwill is to be recorded. What will be Danville's beginning capital balance?
   a. $70,000.
   b. $90,000.
   c. $105,000.
   d. $120,000.

5. A partnership has the following capital balances:

Elgin (40% of gains and losses)	$100,000
Jethro (30%)	200,000
Foy (30%)	300,000

   Oscar is going to pay a total of $200,000 to these three partners to acquire a 25 percent ownership interest from each. Goodwill is to be recorded. What will be Jethro's capital balance after the transaction?
   a. $150,000.
   b. $175,000.
   c. $195,000.
   d. $200,000.

6. Bolcar has a capital balance of $110,000 with Neary having a $40,000 balance. These two partners share profits and losses 70 percent (Bolcar) and 30 percent (Neary). Kansas invests $50,000 in cash into the partnership for a 30 percent ownership. The bonus method will be used. What is Neary's capital balance after Kansas's investment?
 - a. $35,000.
 - b. $37,000.
 - c. $40,000.
 - d. $43,000.

7. Bishop has a capital balance in a local partnership of $120,000 with Cotton having a $90,000 balance. These two partners share profits and losses by a ratio of 60 percent to Bishop and 40 percent to Cotton. Lovett invests $60,000 in cash into the partnership for a 20 percent ownership. The goodwill method will be used. What is Cotton's capital balance after this new investment?
 - a. $99,600.
 - b. $102,000.
 - c. $112,000.
 - d. $126,000.

8. Messalina has a capital balance of $210,000 with Romulus having a $140,000 balance. These two partners share profits and losses 60 percent (Messalina) and 40 percent (Romulus). Claudius invests $100,000 in cash into the partnership for a 20 percent ownership. The bonus method will be used. What are the capital balances for Messalina, Romulus, and Claudius after this investment is recorded?
 - a. $216,000, $144,000, $90,000.
 - b. $218,000, $142,000, $88,000.
 - c. $222,000, $148,000, $80,000.
 - d. $240,000, $160,000, $100,000.

9. A partnership begins 1998 with the following capital balances:

Arthur, Capital	$ 60,000
Baxter, Capital	80,000
Cartwright, Capital	100,000

The Articles of Partnership stipulate that profits and losses be assigned in the following manner:
 - Each partner is allocated interest equal to 10 percent of the beginning capital balance.
 - Baxter is allocated compensation of $20,000 per year.
 - Any remaining profits and losses are allocated on a 3:3:4 basis, respectively.
 - Each partner is allowed to withdraw up to $5,000 cash per year.

Assuming that the net income for 1998 is $50,000 and that each partner withdraws the maximum amount allowed, what is the balance in Cartwright's Capital account at the end of that year?
 - a. $105,800.
 - b. $106,200.
 - c. $106,900.
 - d. $107,400.

10. A partnership begins its first year of operations with the following capital balances:

Winston, Capital	$110,000
Durham, Capital	80,000
Salem, Capital	110,000

According to the Articles of Partnership, all profits will be assigned as follows:
 - Winston will be awarded an annual salary of $20,000 with $10,000 assigned to Salem.
 - The partners will be attributed with interest equal to 10 percent of the capital balance as of the first day of the year.
 - The remainder will be assigned on a 5:2:3 basis, respectively.
 - Each partner is allowed to withdraw up to $10,000 per year.

Assume that the net loss for the first year of operations is $20,000 with net income of $40,000 in the subsequent year. Assume further that each partner withdraws the maximum amount from the business each period. What is the balance in Winston's Capital account at the end of the second year?

- *a.* $102,600.
- *b.* $104,400.
- *c.* $108,600.
- *d.* $109,200.

11. A partnership has the following capital balances:

Allen, Capital	$ 60,000
Burns, Capital	30,000
Costello, Capital	90,000

Profits and losses are split as follows: Allen (20%), Burns (30%), and Costello (50%). Costello wants to leave the partnership and is paid $100,000 from the business based on provisions in the Articles of Partnership. If the partnership uses the bonus method, what is the balance of Burns's Capital account after Costello withdraws?

- *a.* $24,000.
- *b.* $27,000.
- *c.* $33,000.
- *d.* $36,000.

12. As of December 31, 1998, the Cisco partnership has the following capital balances:

Montana, Capital	$130,000
Rice, Capital	110,000
Craig, Capital	80,000
Taylor, Capital	70,000

Profits and losses are split on a 3:3:2:2 basis, respectively. Craig decides to leave the partnership and is paid $90,000 from the business based on their original contractual agreement. If the goodwill method is to be applied, what is the balance of Montana's Capital account after Craig withdraws?

- *a.* $133,000.
- *b.* $137,500.
- *c.* $140,000.
- *d.* $145,000.

Problems 13 and 14 are independent problems based on the following capital account balances:

William (40% of gains and losses)	$220,000
Jennings (40%)	160,000
Bryan (20%)	110,000

13. Darrow invests $270,000 in cash for a 30 percent ownership interest. The money goes to the original partners. Goodwill is to be recorded. How much goodwill should be recognized, and what is Darrow's beginning capital balance?

- *a.* $410,000 and $270,000.
- *b.* $140,000 and $270,000.
- *c.* $140,000 and $189,000.
- *d.* $410,000 and $189,000.

14. Darrow invests $250,000 in cash for a 30 percent ownership interest. The money goes to the business. No goodwill or other revaluation is to be recorded. After the transaction, what is Jennings's capital balance?

- *a.* $160,000.
- *b.* $168,000.
- *c.* $170,200.
- *d.* $171,200.

15. Lear is to become a partner in the WS partnership by paying $80,000 in cash to the business. At present, Hamlet has a capital balance of $70,000 while MacBeth reports a total of only $40,000. Hamlet and MacBeth share profits on a 7:3 basis. Lear is acquiring 40 percent of the new partnership.

    a. If the goodwill method is applied, what will the three capital balances be following the payment by Lear?

    b. If the bonus method is applied, what will the three capital balances be following the payment by Lear?

16. The AKS partnership has the following capital balances at the beginning of the current year:

Arond (40% of profits and losses)	$80,000
Kant (40%)	70,000
Selvin (20%)	60,000

Required

    a. If Tronsty invests $60,000 in cash into the business for a 20 percent interest, what journal entry is recorded? Assume the bonus method is in use.

    b. If Tronsty invests $50,000 in cash into the business for a 20 percent interest, what journal entry is recorded? Assume the bonus method is in use.

    c. If Tronsty invests $55,000 in cash into the business for a 20 percent interest, what journal entry is recorded? Assume the goodwill method is in use.

17. A partnership has the following account balances: Cash $50,000; Other Assets $600,000; Liabilities $240,000; Nixon, Capital (50% of profits and losses) $200,000; Hoover, Capital (20%) $120,000; Polk, Capital (30%) $90,000. Each of the following questions should be viewed as an independent situation:

    a. Grant invests $80,000 into the partnership for an 18 percent capital interest. Goodwill is to be recognized. What are the capital accounts thereafter?

    b. Grant invests $100,000 into the partnership to get a 20 percent capital balance. Goodwill is not to be recorded. What are the capital accounts thereafter?

18. The C-P partnership has the following capital account balances on January 1, 1998:

Com, Capital	$150,000
Pack, Capital	110,000

    Com is allocated 60 percent of all profits and losses with the remaining 40 percent assigned to Pack after interest of 10 percent is given to each partner based on beginning capital balances.

    On January 1, 1998, Hal invests $76,000 cash for a 20 percent interest in the partnership. This transaction is recorded by the goodwill method. After this transaction, 10 percent interest is still to go to each partner. Profits and losses will then be split as follows: Com (50%), Pack (30%), and Hal (20%). In 1998, the partnership reports a net income of $36,000.

Required:

    a. Prepare the journal entry to record Hal's entrance into the partnership on January 1, 1998.

    b. Determine the allocation of income at the end of 1998.

19. The partnership agreement of Jones, King, and Lane provides for the annual allocation of the business's profit or loss in the following sequence:

- Jones, the managing partner, receives a bonus equal to 20 percent of the business's profit.
- Each partner receives 15 percent interest on average capital investment.
- Any residual profit or loss is divided equally.

    The average capital investments for 1998 were

Jones	$100,000
King	200,000
Lane	300,000

    How much of the $90,000 partnership profit for 1998 should be assigned to each partner?

(AICPA adapted)

20. Purkerson, Smith, and Traynor have operated a bookstore for a number of years as a partnership. At the beginning of 1998, capital balances were as follows:

Purkerson	. . . .	$60,000
Smith	. . . .	40,000
Traynor	. . . .	20,000

Because of a cash shortage, Purkerson invests an additional $8,000 in the business on April 1, 1998.

Each partner is allowed to withdraw $1,000 cash each month.

The partners have used the same method of allocating profits and losses since the business's inception:

- Each partner is given the following compensation allowance for work done in the business: Purkerson, $18,000; Smith, $25,000; and Traynor, $8,000.
- Each partner is credited with interest equal to 10 percent of the average monthly capital balance for the year without regard for normal drawings.
- Any remaining profit or loss is allocated 4:2:4 to Purkerson, Smith, and Traynor, respectively.

The net income for 1998 is $23,600. Each partner withdraws the allotted amount each month. What are the ending capital balances for 1998?

21. On January 1, 1998, the dental partnership of Left, Center, and Right was formed when the partners contributed $20,000, $60,000, and $50,000, respectively. Over the next three years, the business reported net income and (loss) as follows:

1998	. . . .	($30,000)
1999	. . . .	$20,000
2000	. . . .	$40,000

During this period, each partner withdrew cash of $10,000 per year. Right invested an additional $12,000 in cash on February 9, 1999.

At the time that the partnership was created, the three partners agreed to allocate all profits and losses according to a specified plan written as follows:

- Each partner is entitled to interest computed at the rate of 12 percent per year based on the individual capital balances at the beginning of that year.
- Because of prior work experience, Left is entitled to an annual salary allowance of $12,000 while Center is credited with $8,000 per year.
- Any remaining profit will be split as follows: Left, 20 percent; Center, 40 percent; and Right, 40 percent. If a loss remains, the balance will be allocated: Left, 30 percent; Center, 50 percent; and Right, 20 percent.

Required:

Determine the ending capital balance for each partner as of the end of each of these three years.

22. The HELP partnership has the following capital balances as of December 31, 1998:

Lennon	. . . .	$230,000
McCartney	. . . .	190,000
Harrison	. . . .	160,000
Starr	. . . .	140,000
Total capital	. . . .	$720,000

Answer each of the following independent questions:

a. Assume the partners share profits and losses 3:3:2:2, respectively. Harrison retires and is paid $190,000 based on the terms of the original partnership agreement. If the goodwill method is in use, what is the capital balance of the remaining three partners?

b. Assume the partners share profits and losses 4:3:2:1, respectively. Lennon retires and is paid $280,000 based on the terms of the original partnership agreement. If the bonus method is in use, what is the capital balance of the remaining three partners?

23. In the early part of 1999, the partners of Page, Childers, and Smith went to a local accountant seeking assistance. They had begun a new business in 1998 but had never previously used the services of an accountant.

Page and Childers began the partnership by contributing $80,000 and $30,000 in cash, respectively. Page was to work occasionally at the business whereas Childers would be employed full time. They decided that year-end profits and losses should be assigned as follows:

- Each partner was to be allocated 10 percent interest computed on the beginning capital balances for the period.
- A compensation allowance of $5,000 was to go to Page with a $20,000 amount assigned to Childers.
- Any remaining income would be split on a 4:6 basis to Page and Childers, respectively.

In 1998, revenues totaled $90,000 with expenses reported as $64,000 (not including the compensation allowance assigned to the partners). Page withdrew cash of $8,000 during the year while Childers took out $11,000. In addition, $5,000 for repairs made to Page's home was paid by the business and charged to repair expense.

On January 1, 1999, a 20 percent interest in the partnership was sold to Smith for $43,000 cash. This money was contributed to the business with the bonus method used for accounting purposes.

Answer the following questions:

a. Why was the original profit and loss allocation, as just outlined, designed by the partners?
b. Why did the drawings for 1998 not agree with the compensation allowances provided for in the partnership agreement?
c. What journal entries should have been recorded by the partnership on December 31, 1998?
d. What journal entry should have been recorded by the partnership on January 1, 1999?

24. Following is the current balance sheet for a local partnership of doctors:

Cash and current		Liabilities	$ 40,000
assets	$ 30,000	A, capital	20,000
Land	180,000	B, capital	40,000
Building and		C, capital	90,000
equipment	100,000	D, capital	120,000
Totals	$310,000		$310,000

The following questions represent independent situations:

a. E is going to invest enough money into this partnership to receive a 25 percent interest. No goodwill or bonus is to be recorded. How much should E invest?
b. E contributes $36,000 in cash to the business to receive a 10 percent interest in the partnership. Goodwill is to be recorded. Profits and losses have previously been split according to the following percentages: A, 30%; B, 10%; C, 40%; and D, 20%. After E makes this investment, what are the individual capital balances?
c. E contributes $42,000 in cash to the business to receive a 20 percent interest in the partnership. Goodwill is to be recorded. The four original partners share all profits and losses equally. After E makes this investment, what are the individual capital balances?
d. E contributes $55,000 in cash to the business to receive a 20 percent interest in the partnership. No goodwill or other asset revaluation is to be recorded. Profits and losses have previously been split according to the following percentages: A, 10%; B, 30%; C, 20%; and D, 40%. After E makes this investment, what are the individual capital balances?
e. C retires from the partnership and, as per the original partnership agreement, is to receive cash equal to 125 percent of her final capital balance. No goodwill or other asset revaluation is to be recognized. All partners share profits and losses equally. After the withdrawal, what are the individual capital balances of the remaining partners?

25. Partnership agreements usually specify a profit and loss ratio. They may also provide such additional features as salaries, bonuses, and interest allowances on invested capital.

Required

a. What is the objective of profit and loss sharing arrangements? Why may other features be needed in addition to a profit and loss ratio?

    b. Discuss the arguments for recording salary and bonus allowances to partners as expenses of the business.

    c. Discuss the arguments against treating partnership salary and bonus allowances as expenses.

    d. In addition to other profit and loss sharing features, a partnership agreement might state that "interest is to be allowed on invested capital." List the additional provisions that should be included in the partnership agreement so that "interest to be allowed on invested capital" can be computed.

(AICPA adapted)

26. Boswell and Johnson form a partnership on May 1, 1998. Boswell contributes cash of $50,000; Johnson conveys title to the following properties to the partnership:

	Book Value	Fair Market Value
Land	$15,000	$28,000
Building and equipment	35,000	36,000

    The partners agree to start their partnership with equal capital balances. No goodwill is to be recognized.

    According to the Articles of Partnership written by the partners, profits and losses are allocated based on the following formula:

- Boswell receives a compensation allowance of $1,000 per month.
- All remaining profits and losses are split 60:40 to Johnson and Boswell, respectively.
- Annual cash drawings of $5,000 can be made by each partner beginning in 1999.

Net income of $11,000 is earned by the business during 1998.

    Walpole is invited to join the partnership on January 1, 1999. Because of Walpole's business reputation and financial expertise, she is given a 40 percent interest for $54,000 cash. The bonus approach is used to record this investment, made directly to the business. The Articles of Partnership are amended to give Walpole a $2,000 compensation allowance per month and an annual cash drawing of $10,000. Remaining profits are now allocated:

Johnson	48%
Boswell	12%
Walpole	40%

    All drawings are taken by the partners during 1999. At the end of that year, the partnership reports an earned net income of $28,000.

    On January 1, 2000, Pope (previously a partnership employee) is admitted into the partnership. Each partner transfers 10 percent to Pope. Pope makes the following payments directly to the partners:

To Johnson	$5,672
To Boswell	7,880
To Pope	8,688

    Once again, the Articles of Partnership must be amended to allow for the entrance of the new partner. This change entitles Pope to a compensation allowance of $800 per month and an annual drawing of $4,000. Profits and losses are now assigned.

Johnson	40.5%
Boswell	13.5%
Walpole	36.0%
Pope	10.0%

    For the year of 2000, the partnership earned a profit of $46,000, and each partner withdrew the allowed amount of cash.

Required

Determine the capital balances for the individual partners as of the end of each year: 1998 through 2000.

27. Gray, Stone, and Lawson open an accounting practice on January 1, 1998, in San Diego, California. The business is to be operated as a partnership with Gray and Stone serving as the senior partners because of their years of experience. To establish the business,

Gray, Stone, and Lawson contribute cash and other properties valued at $210,000, $180,000, and $90,000, respectively. A partnership agreement is drawn up that carries the following stipulations:

a. Personal drawings are allowed annually up to an amount equal to 10 percent of the beginning capital balance for the year.

b. Profits and losses are allocated according to the following plan:

(1) A salary allowance is credited to each partner in an amount equal to $8 per billable hour worked by that individual during the year.

(2) Interest is credited to the partners' capital accounts at the rate of 12 percent of the average monthly balance for the year (computed without regard for current income or drawings).

(3) An annual bonus is to be credited to Gray and Stone. Each bonus is to be 10 percent of net income after subtracting the bonus, the salary allowance, and the interest. Also included in the agreement is the provision that the bonus cannot be a negative amount.

(4) Any remaining partnership profit or loss is to be divided evenly among all partners.

Because of monetary problems encountered in getting the business started, Gray invests an additional $9,100 on May 1, 1998. On January 1, 1999, the partners allow Monet to buy into the partnership. Monet contributes cash directly to the business in an amount equal to a 25 percent interest in the book value of the partnership property subsequent to this contribution. The partnership agreement as to splitting profits and losses is not altered at the time of Monet's entrance into the firm; the general provisions continue to be applicable.

The billable hours for the partners during the first three years of operation are as follows:

	1998	1999	2000
Gray	1,710	1,800	1,880
Stone	1,440	1,500	1,620
Lawson	1,300	1,380	1,310
Monet	–0–	1,190	1,580

The partnership reports net income for 1998 through 2000 as follows:

1998	$ 65,000
1999	(20,400)
2000	152,800

Each partner withdraws the maximum allowable amount each year.

Required

a. Determine the allocation of income for each of these three years (to the nearest dollar).

b. Prepare in appropriate form a statement of partners' capital for the year ending December 31, 1998.

28. A partnership of attorneys in the St. Louis, Missouri, area has the following balance sheet accounts as of January 1, 1999:

Assets	$320,000	Liabilities	$120,000
		Athos, capital	80,000
		Porthos, capital	70,000
		Aramis, capital	50,000

According to the Articles of Partnership, Athos is to receive an allocation of 50 percent of all partnership profits and losses while Porthos gets 30 percent and Aramis 20 percent. The book value of each asset and liability should be considered an accurate representation of fair market value.

Required

For each of the following *independent* situations, prepare the journal entry or entries to be recorded by the partnership. (Round to nearest dollar.)

a. Porthos, with permission of the other partners, decides to sell half of his partnership interest to D'Artagnan for $50,000 in cash. No asset revaluation or goodwill is to be recorded by the partnership.

[handwritten: record goodwill]

[handwritten: gw=50000]

[handwritten: private transaction — credit to D cap 25000]

b. All three of the present partners agree to sell 10 percent of each partnership interest to D'Artagnan for a total cash payment of $25,000. Each partner receives a negotiated portion of this amount. Goodwill is being recorded as a result of the transaction.

[handwritten: Aramis increase 1400]

c. D'Artagnan is allowed to become a partner with a 10 percent ownership interest by contributing $30,000 in cash directly into the business. The bonus method is used to record this admission. *[handwritten: old partner]*

[handwritten: revalue old partner]

d. Use the same facts as in requirement *c*, except that the entrance into the partnership is recorded by the goodwill method. *[handwritten: gw= 70000]* *[handwritten: Aramis increase 14000]*

e. D'Artagnan is allowed to become a partner with a 10 percent ownership interest by contributing $12,222 in cash directly to the business. The goodwill method is used to record this transaction. *[handwritten: gw= 10000]* *[handwritten: algebra   original invest + gw]*

[handwritten: retirement — Aramis increase by 16000]

f. Aramis decides to retire and leave the partnership. An independent appraisal of the business and its assets indicates a current fair market value of $280,000. Goodwill is to be recorded. Aramis will then be given the exact amount of cash that will close out his capital account. *[handwritten: gw= 80000]*

29. Steve Reese is a well-known interior designer in Fort Worth, Texas. He wants to start his own business and convinces Rob O'Donnell, a local merchant, to contribute the capital to form a partnership. On January 1, 1998, O'Donnell invests a building worth $52,000 and equipment valued at $16,000 as well as $12,000 in cash. Although Reese makes no tangible contribution to the partnership, he will operate the business and be an equal partner in the beginning capital balances.

To entice O'Donnell to join this partnership, Reese draws up the following agreement:

- O'Donnell will be credited annually with interest equal to 20 percent of the beginning capital balance for the year.
- O'Donnell will also have added to his capital account 15 percent of partnership income each year (without regard for the preceding interest figure) or $4,000, whichever is greater. All remaining income is credited to Reese.
- Neither partner is allowed to withdraw funds from the partnership during 1998. Thereafter, they can each draw out $5,000 annually or 20 percent of the beginning capital balance for the year, whichever is greater.

A net loss of $10,000 is reported by the partnership during the first year of its operation. On January 1, 1999, Terri Dunn becomes a third partner in this business by contributing $15,000 cash to the partnership. Dunn receives a 20 percent share of the business's capital. The profit and loss agreement is altered as follows:

- O'Donnell is still entitled to (1) interest on his beginning capital balance as well as (2) the share of partnership income just specified.
- Any remaining profit or loss will be split on a 6:4 basis between Reese and Dunn, respectively.

Partnership income for 1999 is reported as $44,000. Each partner withdraws the full amount that is allowed.

On January 1, 2000, Dunn falls ill and sells her interest in the partnership (with the consent of the other two partners) to Judy Postner. Postner pays $46,000 directly to Dunn. Net income for 2000 is $61,000 with the partners again taking their full drawing allowance.

On January 1, 2001, Postner elects to withdraw from the business for personal reasons. The Articles of Partnership contain a provision stating that any partner may leave the partnership at any time and is entitled to receive cash in an amount equal to the recorded capital balance at that time plus 10 percent.

Required

a. Prepare journal entries to record the preceding transactions on the assumption that the bonus (or no revaluation) method is used. Drawings need not be recorded, although the balances should be included in the closing entries.

b. Prepare journal entries to record the previous transactions on the assumption that the goodwill (or revaluation) method is used. Drawings need not be recorded, although the balances should be included in the closing entries.

(Round all amounts off to the nearest dollar.)

CHAPTER

15

Partnerships: Termination and Liquidation

QUESTIONS TO CONSIDER

- Under what conditions would a partnership be liquidated?

- What information should an accountant report to reflect the liquidation of a partnership?

- In a partnership liquidation, what happens if one or more partners reports a deficit capital balance?

- How are any remaining assets distributed if a partnership or one of its partners becomes insolvent?

- What are safe capital balances and how are they determined?

- How does the accountant determine which partners receive cash during a partnership liquidation?

Termination of business activities followed by the liquidation of partnership property can take place for a variety of reasons, both legal and personal.

I'm spending a great deal of time helping physician clients patch up partnership disputes and pull together. That is until I run up against a group where personalities, philosophies, or work styles are truly irreconcilable. In these cases, the best solution is a split. . . . Once the doctors know they want to split, they can meet to discuss their problems. While these sessions are often stormy, in the end the doctors usually find themselves agreeing for once. Their consensus? They'll each benefit more from going their separate ways than enduring a situation that's not working. Still, there's no denying that severing any partnership is emotionally wrenching.[1]

These sentiments, expressed by a financial consultant in the medical management field, indicate the potential frailty of a partnership. Although a business organized in this manner can exist indefinitely through periodic changes within the ownership, the actual cessation of operations is not an uncommon occurrence. As indicated by the preceding quotation, the partners may simply be incompatible and choose to cease operations. The same outcome might result if profit figures fail to reach projected levels. "In the best of times, partnerships are fragile. But in the current recession, the breakup rate has worsened as cost-cutting and other pressures heighten tensions between partners."[2]

The death of a partner is another event that dissolves a partnership and frequently leads to the termination of business operations. Rather than continuing under a new partnership arrangement, the remaining owners may discover that liquidation is necessary to settle the

---

[1]Leif C. Beck, "When a Group Is Better Off Splitting Up," *Medical Economics,* March 5, 1984, p. 183.

[2]Sue Shellenbarger, "Cutting Losses When Partners Face a Breakup," *The Wall Street Journal,* May 21, 1991, p. B1.

651

claims of the deceased partner's estate. A similar action may be required if one or more of the partners elects to change careers or retire. Under that circumstance, liquidation is often the most convenient method for winding up the financial affairs of the business.

As a final possibility, a partnership can be legally forced into selling its noncash assets by the bankruptcy of the business or even that of an individual partner. Laventhol & Horwath, the seventh largest public accounting firm in the United States, filed for bankruptcy protection in 1990 after the firm came under intense financial pressure from numerous lawsuits. "Laventhol said that at least 100 lawsuits are pending in state and federal courts. Bankruptcy court protection 'is absolutely necessary in order to protect the debtor and its creditors from the devastating results a destructive race for assets will cause' the firm said."[3]

The bankruptcy of Laventhol & Horwath was not an isolated incident.

> Law firms are going out of business at a steady clip, and a few major accounting firms have collapsed in recent years. "At least a dozen [major law] firms have failed in the past three or four years," figures Bradford W. Hildebrandt, chairman of a legal consulting firm in Somerville, N.J. "In the next year or two, there could be another half-dozen."[4]

TERMINATION AND LIQUIDATION—PROTECTING THE INTERESTS OF ALL PARTIES

As discussed in Chapter 13, accounting for the termination and liquidation of a business can prove to be a delicate task. Losses, especially in bankruptcy cases, are commonly incurred. Thus, both creditors and owners demand continuous accounting information that enables them to monitor and assess their financial risks. In generating this data for a partnership, the accountant must record:

- The conversion of partnership assets into cash.
- The allocation of the resulting gains and losses.
- The payment of liabilities and expenses.
- The distribution of any remaining assets to the partners based on their final capital balances.

Beyond the goal of merely reporting these transactions, the accountant must work to ensure the equitable treatment of all parties involved in the liquidation. The accounting records, for example, serve as the basis for allocating available assets to creditors as well as to the individual partners. If assets are limited, the accountant also may have to make recommendations as to the appropriate method for distributing any remaining funds. Protecting the interests of the partnership creditors is an especially significant duty since the Uniform Partnership Act specifies that they have first priority to the assets held by the business at the time of dissolution. The accountant's desire for an equitable settlement is enhanced, no doubt, in that any party to a liquidation who is not treated fairly can seek legal recovery from the responsible party.

Not only the creditors but also the partners themselves have a great interest in the financial data produced during the period of liquidation. They must be concerned, for

---

[3]Peter Pae, "Laventhol Bankruptcy Filing Indicates Liabilities May Be as Much as $2 Billion," *The Wall Street Journal,* November 23, 1990, p. A4.

[4]Lee Berton and Joann S. Lublin, "Partnership Structure Is Called in Question as Liability Risk Rises," *The Wall Street Journal,* June 10, 1992, p. A9.

example, about the possibility of incurring substantial monetary losses. The potential for loss is especially significant because of the unlimited liability to which the partners are exposed.

As long as a partnership can meet all obligations, a partner's risk is normally no greater than that of a corporate stockholder. However, should the partnership become insolvent, each partner faces the possibility of having to satisfy *all* remaining obligations personally. Although any partner suffering more than a proportionate share of these losses can seek legal retribution from the remaining owners, this process is not always an effective remedy. The other partners may themselves be insolvent, or anticipated legal costs might discourage the damaged party from seeking recovery. Therefore, each partner usually has a keen interest in monitoring the progress of a liquidation as it transpires.

> When a company files for bankruptcy court protection, its creditors are permitted only to make claims against the corporation, rather than against its shareholders. But when partnerships such as Laventhol file, creditors can sue individual partners in an effort to recover their money. Bankruptcy law experts say that Laventhol's creditors, which include banks, landlords, suppliers, and plaintiffs in litigation, are expected to try to recover money from partners, as well as from the partnership, if Laventhol is unable to satisfy their claims with its remaining assets."[5]

Termination and Liquidation Procedures Illustrated

The procedures involved in terminating and liquidating a partnership are basically mechanical. Partnership assets are converted into cash that is used to pay business obligations as well as liquidation expenses. *Any remaining assets are then distributed to the individual partners based on their final capital balances.* As no further ledger accounts exist, the partnership's books are permanently closed. If each partner has a large enough capital balance to absorb all liquidation losses, the accountant should experience little difficulty in recording this series of transactions.

To illustrate the typical process, assume that Morgan and Houseman have been operating an antique business as a partnership for a number of years. On May 1, 1998, the partners decide to terminate business activities, liquidate all noncash assets, and dissolve their partnership. Although a specific explanation for this action is not given, any number of reasons might exist. The partners, for example, could have come to a disagreement so that they no longer believe they can work together. As an alternative possibility, business profits may have been inadequate to warrant the continuing investment of their time and capital.

Following is a balance sheet for the partnership of Morgan and Houseman as of the termination date. The revenue, expense, and drawing accounts have been closed out as a preliminary step in terminating the business. A separate reporting will subsequently be made of the gains and losses that occur during the final winding-down process.

MORGAN AND HOUSEMAN
Balance Sheet
May 1, 1998

Assets		Liabilities and Capital	
Cash	$ 45,000	Liabilities	$ 32,000
Accounts receivable	12,000	Morgan, capital	50,000
Inventory	22,000	Houseman, capital	38,000
Land, building, and equipment (net)	41,000		
		Total liabilities and	
Total assets	$120,000	capital	$120,000

---
[5]Laurie P. Cohen, "Laventhol Partners Face Long Process that Could End in Personal Bankruptcy," *The Wall Street Journal*, November 20, 1990, p. B5.

The assumption is made here that the liquidation of Morgan and Houseman proceeds in an orderly fashion through the following events:

1998

June 1   The inventory is sold at auction for $15,000. Morgan and Houseman allocate all profits and losses on a 6:4 basis, respectively.

July 15   Of the total accounts receivable, $9,000 is collected with the remainder being written off as bad debts.

Aug. 20   The fixed assets are sold for a total of $29,000.

Aug. 25   All partnership liabilities are paid.

Sept. 10 A total of $3,000 in liquidation expenses is paid to cover costs such as accounting and legal fees as well as the commissions incurred in disposing of partnership property.

Oct. 15   All remaining cash is distributed to the owners based on their final capital account balances.

As can be seen, the partnership of Morgan and Houseman incurs a number of losses in liquidating this property. Such losses are almost anticipated because the need for immediate sale is usually held as a high priority in a liquidation. Furthermore, a portion of the assets used by any business, such as equipment and buildings, may have a utility that is strictly limited to a particular type of operation. If the property is not easily adaptable, disposal at any reasonable price often proves to be a problem.

To record the liquidation of Morgan and Houseman, the following journal entries would be made. Rather than report specific income and expense balances, gains and losses are traditionally recorded directly to the partners' capital accounts. Since operations have ceased, determination of a separate net income figure for this period would provide little informational value. *Instead, a primary concern of the parties involved in any liquidation is the continuing changes in each partner's capital balance.*

6/1/98	Cash...	15,000	
	Morgan, Capital (60% of loss)	4,200	
	Houseman, Capital (40% of loss)	2,800	
	Inventory		22,000
	To record sale of partnership inventory at a $7,000 loss.		
7/15/98	Cash...	9,000	
	Morgan, Capital	1,800	
	Houseman, Capital..............................	1,200	
	Accounts Receivable		12,000
	To record collection of accounts receivable with write-off of remaining $3,000 in accounts as bad debts.		
8/20/98	Cash...	29,000	
	Morgan, Capital	7,200	
	Houseman, Capital..............................	4,800	
	Land, Building, and Equipment (net)		41,000
	To record sale of fixed assets and allocation of $12,000 loss.		
8/25/98	Liabilities	32,000	
	Cash		32,000
	Payment made to settle the liabilities of the partnership.		
9/10/98	Morgan, Capital	1,800	
	Houseman, Capital.............................	1,200	
	Cash		3,000
	To pay liquidation expenses with the amounts recorded as direct reductions to the partners' capital accounts.		

After liquidating the partnership assets and paying off all obligations, the cash that remains can be divided between Morgan and Houseman personally. The following schedule is utilized to determine the partners' ending capital account balances and, thus, the appropriate distribution for this final payment.

Cash and Capital Account Balances*

	Cash	Morgan, Capital	Houseman, Capital
Beginning balances	$ 45,000	$50,000	$38,000
Sold inventory	15,000	(4,200)	(2,800)
Collected accounts receivable	9,000	(1,800)	(1,200)
Sold fixed assets	29,000	(7,200)	(4,800)
Paid liabilities	(32,000)	–0–	–0–
Paid liquidation expenses	(3,000)	(1,800)	(1,200)
Final totals	$ 63,000	$35,000	$28,000

*Because of the presence of other assets as well as liabilities, the Cash and Capital accounts will not be in agreement until the end of the liquidation process.

After the ending capital balances have been calculated, the remaining cash can be distributed to the partners to close out the financial records of the partnership:

10/15/98	Morgan, Capital	35,000	
	Houseman, Capital	28,000	
	Cash		63,000
	To distribute cash to partners in accordance with final capital balances.		

Schedule of Liquidation

Liquidation may take a considerable length of time to complete. Because the various parties involved need continually updated financial information, the accountant should produce frequent reports summarizing the transactions as they occur. Consequently, a statement (often referred to as the schedule of liquidation) can be prepared at periodic intervals to disclose:

- Transactions to date.
- Property still being held by the partnership.
- Liabilities remaining to be paid.
- Current cash and capital balances.

Although the preceding Morgan and Houseman example has been condensed into a few events occurring during a brief period of time, partnership liquidations usually require numerous transactions that transpire over months and, perhaps, even years. By receiving frequent schedules of liquidation, both the creditors and the partners are able to stay apprised of the results of this lengthy process.

Exhibit 15–1 presents the final schedule of liquidation for the partnership of Morgan and Houseman. Previous statements would have been distributed by the accountant at each important juncture of this liquidation to meet the informational needs of the parties involved. The example produced here demonstrates the stair-step approach incorporated in preparing a schedule of liquidation. The effects of each transaction (or group of transactions) are outlined in a horizontal fashion so that current account balances as well as all prior transactions are evident. This structuring also facilitates the preparation of future statements: a new layer summarizing recent events can simply be added to the bottom each time that a new schedule is to be produced.

Exhibit 15-1

MORGAN AND HOUSEMAN
Schedule of Partnership Liquidation
Final Balances

	Cash	Noncash Assets	Liabilities	Morgan, Capital (60%)	Houseman, Capital (40%)
Beginning balances, 5/1/98	$ 45,000	$ 75,000	$ 32,000	$ 50,000	$ 38,000
Sold inventory, 6/1/98	15,000	(22,000)		(4,200)	(2,800)
Updated balances	60,000	53,000	32,000	45,800	35,200
Collected receivables, 7/15/98	9,000	(12,000)		(1,800)	(1,200)
Updated balances	69,000	41,000	32,000	44,000	34,000
Sold fixed assets, 8/20/98	29,000	(41,000)		(7,200)	(4,800)
Updated balances	98,000	–0–	32,000	36,800	29,200
Paid liabilities, 8/25/98	(32,000)		(32,000)		
Updated balances	66,000	–0–	–0–	36,800	29,200
Paid liquidation expenses, 9/10/98	(3,000)			(1,800)	(1,200)
Updated balances	63,000	–0–	–0–	35,000	28,000
Distributed remaining cash, 10/15/98	(63,000)			(35,000)	(28,000)
Closing balances	–0–	–0–	–0–	–0–	–0–

Deficit Capital Balance—Contribution Made by Partner

In Exhibit 15–1, the liquidation process ended with all partners continuing to report positive capital balances. Thus, Morgan and Houseman were both able to share in the $63,000 cash that remained. Unfortunately, such an outcome is not always assured. At the end of a liquidation, one or more partners may be reporting a negative capital account. Or, the partnership may not even be able to generate enough cash to satisfy all of the claims of its creditors. Such deficits are most likely to occur when the partnership is already insolvent at the start of the liquidation or when the disposal of noncash assets results in material losses. Under these circumstances, the accounting procedures to be applied depend on legal regulations as well as the individual actions of the partners.

As an example, assume that the partnership of Holland, Dozier, and Ross was dissolved at the beginning of the current year. Business activities were terminated and all noncash assets were subsequently converted into cash. During the liquidation process, the partnership incurred a number of large losses that have been allocated to the partners' capital accounts on a 4:4:2 basis, respectively. A portion of the resulting cash is then used to pay all partnership liabilities and liquidation expenses.

Following these transactions, only the following four account balances remain open within the partnership's records:

Cash	$20,000	Holland, Capital	$(6,000)
		Dozier, Capital	15,000
		Ross, Capital	11,000
		Total	$20,000

Holland is now reporting a negative capital balance of $6,000; the assigned share of partnership losses has exceeded this partner's net contribution. In such cases, the Uniform Partnership Act (Section 18[a]) stipulates that the partner "must contribute toward the losses, whether of capital or otherwise, sustained by the partnership according to his share in the profits." Therefore, Holland is legally required to convey an additional $6,000 to the partnership at this time to eliminate the deficit balance. This contribution raises the cash balance to $26,000 so that a complete distribution can be made to Dozier ($15,000) and Ross ($11,000) in line with their capital accounts. The journal entry for this final payment closes out the partnership records.

Cash	6,000	
Holland, Capital		6,000

To record contribution made by Holland to extinguish negative
capital balance.

Dozier, Capital	15,000	
Ross, Capital	11,000	
Cash		26,000

To distribute remaining cash to partners in accordance with their
ending capital balances.

Deficit Capital Balance—Loss to Remaining Partners

An alternative scenario can easily be conceived for the previous partnership liquidation. Although Holland's capital account shows a $6,000 deficit balance, this partner may resist any attempt to force an additional investment, especially since the business is in the process of being terminated. The possibility of such recalcitrance is enhanced if the individual is having personal financial difficulties. Thus, the remaining partners may eventually have to resort to formal litigation to gain Holland's contribution. Until that legal action is concluded, the partnership records remain open, although inactive.

Distribution of Safe Payments   While awaiting the final resolution of this matter, no compelling reason exists for the partnership to continue holding $20,000 in cash. These funds will eventually be paid to Dozier and Ross regardless of any action taken by Holland. Thus, an immediate transfer should be made to these two partners to allow them the use of their money. However, since Dozier has a $15,000 capital account balance while Ross currently reports $11,000, a complete distribution is not possible. A method must be devised, therefore, to allow for a fair allocation of the available $20,000.

To ensure the equitable treatment of all parties, this initial distribution is based on the assumption that the $6,000 capital deficit will prove to be a total loss to the partnership. Holland may, for example, be completely insolvent so that no further payment will ever be forthcoming. By making this conservative presumption, the accountant is able to calculate the lowest possible amounts (or safe balances) that Dozier and Ross must retain in their capital accounts to be able to absorb all future losses.

Should Holland's $6,000 deficit (or any portion of it) prove uncollectible, the loss will be written off against the capital accounts of Dozier and Ross. Allocation of this amount is based on the relative profit and loss ratio specified in the Articles of Partnership. According to the information provided in this illustration, Dozier and Ross are credited with 40 percent and 20 percent of all partnership income, respectively. This 40:20 ratio equates to a 2:1 relationship (or $\frac{2}{3}$:$\frac{1}{3}$) between the two. Thus, if no part of the $6,000 deficit balance is ever recovered from Holland, $4,000 (two-thirds) of the loss will be assigned to Dozier and $2,000 (one-third) to Ross.

Allocation of Potential $6,000 Loss

Dozier . . . . $\frac{2}{3}$ of $(6,000) = $(4,000)
Ross . . . . $\frac{1}{3}$ of $(6,000) = $(2,000)

These amounts represent the maximum potential reductions that might still be incurred by the two remaining partners. Depending on Holland's actions, Dozier could be forced to absorb an additional loss of $4,000 while Ross's capital account may decrease by as much as $2,000. These balances must, therefore, remain in the respective capital accounts until the issue is resolved. Hence, Dozier is entitled to receive $11,000 at the present time; this distribution reduces the applicable capital account from $15,000 to the minimum $4,000 level. Likewise, a $9,000 payment to Ross decreases the $11,000 capital balance to the $2,000 limit. These $11,000 and $9,000 figures represent safe payments that can be distributed to the partners without fear of new deficits being created subsequently.

Dozier, Capital	11,000	
Ross, Capital	9,000	
Cash		20,000

To distribute cash to Dozier and Ross based on safe capital balances, using the assumption that Holland will not contribute further to the partnership.

After this $20,000 in cash has been distributed, only a few other events can possibly occur during the remaining life of the partnership. Holland, either voluntarily or through legal persuasion, may contribute the entire $6,000 needed to eradicate the capital deficit. In that situation, the money should be immediately turned over to Dozier ($4,000) and Ross ($2,000) based on their remaining capital balances. The partnership records are effectively closed by this final distribution.

A second possibility is that Dozier and Ross may be unable to recover any part of the deficit from Holland. These two remaining partners must then absorb the $6,000 loss themselves. Since safe capital balances have been maintained, recording a complete default by Holland serves to close out the partnership books.

Dozier, Capital (⅔ of loss).	˙ 4,000	
Ross, Capital (⅓ of loss)	2,000	
Holland, Capital		6,000

To allocate deficit capital balance of insolvent partner.

Deficit Is Partly Collectible   One other ending to this partnership liquidation is conceivable. A portion of the $6,000 may be recovered from Holland although the remainder proves to be uncollectible. This partner may become bankrupt or the other partners might simply give up trying to collect. The partners could also negotiate this settlement to avoid protracted legal actions.

To illustrate, assume that Holland manages to contribute $3,600 to the partnership but subsequently files for relief under the provisions of the bankruptcy laws. In a later legal arrangement, $1,000 additional cash goes to the partnership, but the final $1,400 will never be collected. This series of events creates the following effects within the liquidation process:

1. The initial $3,600 contribution is distributed to Dozier and Ross based on a new computation of their safe capital balances.
2. The $1,400 default is charged against the two positive capital balances in accordance with the relative profit and loss ratio.
3. The final $1,000 contribution is then paid to Dozier and Ross in amounts equal to their ending capital accounts, a transaction that closes the partnership's financial records.

The distribution of the first $3,600 depends on a recalculation of the minimum capital balances that Dozier and Ross must maintain to absorb all potential losses. Each of these computations is produced because of a basic realization: Holland's remaining deficit balance ($2,400 at this time) could prove to be a total loss. This approach guarantees that the other two partners will continue to report adequate capital until the liquidation is ultimately resolved.

	Current Capital	Allocation of Potential Loss	Safe Capital Payments
Dozier.............	$4,000	⅔ of $(2,400) = $(1,600)	$2,400
Ross	2,000	⅓ of $(2,400) = $ (800)	1,200

Thus, the $3,600 in cash that is now available is distributed immediately to Dozier and Ross based on their safe balances.

Cash	3,600	
Holland, Capital		3,600

Dozier, Capital	2,400	
Ross, Capital	1,200	
Cash..		3,600

To record capital contribution by Holland and subsequent distribution of funds to Dozier and Ross based on safe capital balances.

After recording this $3,600 contribution from Holland and the subsequent disbursement, the capital accounts for the partnership stay open, registering the following individual balances:

Holland, Capital (deficit) .... $(2,400)
Dozier, Capital (safe balance) 1,600
Ross, Capital (safe balance) 800

These accounts continue to remain on the partnership books until the final resolution of Holland's obligation.

In this illustration, the $1,000 legal settlement and the remaining $1,400 loss ultimately allow the parties to close out the records:

Cash	1,000	
Dozier, Capital (⅔ of loss)...........................	933	
Ross, Capital (⅓ of loss)	467	
Holland, Capital		2,400

To record final $1,000 cash settlement of Holland's interest and resulting $1,400 loss.

Dozier, Capital	667	
Ross, Capital	333	
Cash..		1,000

To distribute final cash balance based upon remaining capital account totals.

Marshaling of Assets

In the previous example, one partner (Holland) became insolvent during the liquidation process. Personal bankruptcy is not uncommon and raises questions as to the legal right that damaged partners have to proceed against an insolvent partner. *More specifically, is a deficit capital balance the legal equivalent of any other personal liability? Do partners who must absorb additional losses have the same rights against their partners as other creditors?*

Addressing this issue, the Uniform Partnership Act (Section 40[i]) stipulates that:

Where a partner has become bankrupt or his estate is insolvent the claims against his separate property shall rank in the following order:
   (I) Those owing to separate creditors,
   (II) Those owing to partnership creditors,
   (III) Those owing to partners by way of contribution.

This ranking of the claims against an individual is normally referred to as the marshaling of assets and allows for an orderly distribution of property in bankruptcy cases. It clearly shows that partners rank last in collecting from a bankrupt partner.

To demonstrate the effects created by this legal doctrine, assume that Stone is a partner in a business that is undergoing final liquidation. The partnership is insolvent: all assets have been expended but liabilities of $15,000 still remain. Stone is also personally insolvent. The assets currently held by this individual cannot satisfy all obligations:

Personal assets	$50,000
Personal liabilities	40,000
Deficit capital balance—partnership	19,000

Under these circumstances, the ranking established by the Uniform Partnership Act becomes extremely important. Stone does hold $50,000 in assets. However, since these assets are limited, recovery by the various parties is dependent on the pattern of distribution. According to the marshaling of assets doctrine, Stone's own creditors have first priority. After these claims have been satisfied, remaining assets should be used to remunerate any partnership creditors who have sought recovery directly from Stone.

As indicated, remaining partnership debts are $15,000 and these creditors may seek to collect from Stone. Only then, after personal creditors as well as partnership creditors are paid, can the other partners lay claim to the residual portion of Stone's assets. Obviously, because of this individual's financial condition, the chances are not good that these partners will be able to recover all or even a significant portion of the $19,000 deficit capital balance. By ranking last on this priority list, partners are forced to accept whatever assets remain.

To analyze and understand the possible effects created by the marshaling of assets concept, a variety of other situations can be considered. Assume, as an alternative to the previous example, that Stone failed to have sufficient property to satisfy even personal creditors: Stone holds $50,000 in assets but $90,000 in personal liabilities. Because of the volume of these debts, neither the partnership creditors nor the other partners are able to recoup any money from this partner. All of the personal assets must be used to pay Stone's own obligations. Even with preferential treatment, the personal creditors still face a $40,000 shortfall because of the limited quantity of available assets. This potential loss raises another legal question: can Stone's personal creditors seek recovery of the $40,000 directly from the partnership?

In response to this issue, the marshaling of assets doctrine specifies that personal creditors can, indeed, claim a partner's share of partnership assets. However, recovery of all, or even a portion, of the $40,000 is only possible if two specific criteria are met:

1. Payment of all partnership debts must be assured.
2. The insolvent partner has to have a positive capital balance.

Even if both of these conditions are met, personal creditors have no right to receive more than the total of that partner's capital balance nor more than the amount of the debt.

This priority ranking of claims provides legal guidance in insolvency cases. For a more complete demonstration of the marshaling of assets principle, three additional examples follow. Each presents the legal and accounting responses to a specific partnership liquidation problem. In the first two illustrations, one or more of the partners are personally insolvent. The third analyzes the marshaling of assets in connection with an insolvent partnership.

Insolvency—Example One   The following balance sheet has been produced for the Able, Baker, Cannon, and Duke partnership. Profit and loss percentages are also included.

Cash	$ 30,000	Liabilities.................	$ 80,000
Noncash assets	150,000	Able, capital (40%)..........	15,000
		Baker, capital (30%)	40,000
		Cannon, capital (20%)........	30,000
		Duke, capital (10%)	15,000
		Total liabilities and	
Total assets	$180,000	capital	$180,000

Baker is insolvent, and personal creditors have filed a $30,000 claim against this partner's share of partnership property. The litigation has forced the partnership to begin liquidation to settle Baker's interest. As shown in the balance sheet, the partnership has $30,000 in cash and Baker has a capital balance of $40,000.

Assume, in this example, that the noncash assets (with a book value of $150,000) subsequently are sold for $100,000 with the partnership's liabilities ($80,000) then being paid. These two actions increase the cash balance by $20,000 to a $50,000 figure. No other assets or liabilities exist. The adjusted capital accounts for each partner follow. Other than Baker, all partners are personally solvent.

	Able, Capital	Baker, Capital	Cannon, Capital	Duke, Capital
Beginning balances	$ 15,000	$ 40,000	$ 30,000	$ 15,000
$50,000 loss on liquidating of assets	(20,000) (40%)	(15,000) (30%)	(10,000) (20%)	(5,000) (10%)
Capital balances ...	$ (5,000)	$ 25,000	$ 20,000	$ 10,000

An additional contribution of $5,000 should be forthcoming from Able to eradicate the single negative capital balance. This investment raises the partnership's cash to $55,000 and permits a final distribution to Cannon ($20,000), Duke ($10,000), and *Baker's creditors* ($25,000). The liquidation losses have reduced Baker's capital account below the $30,000 level; therefore, this partner's personal creditors are unable to recover the entire amount of their claims. Despite the remaining $5,000 debt, they have no further legal recourse here; no right of recovery exists against the other partners once the capital account has been depleted.

Baker will receive nothing from this liquidation settlement because the personal obligations have not been completely satisfied. In contrast, if the final capital balance had been in excess of $30,000, Baker would have been entitled to any residual amount after all of the personal liabilities were extinguished.

Insolvency—Example Two   The following balance sheet for the partnership of Morris, Newton, Olsen, and Prince also contains the applicable profit and loss percentages. Both Morris and Prince are personally insolvent. Morris's creditors have brought an $8,000 claim against the partnership's assets while $15,000 is being sought by Prince's creditors. These claims have forced the partnership to terminate operations so that the business property can be liquidated. The question is again raised as to which partner is entitled to any cash balance that remains.

Cash	$ 10,000	Liabilities.................	$ 70,000
Noncash assets	140,000	Morris, capital (40%)	15,000
		Newton, capital (20%)........	10,000
		Olsen, capital (20%)	23,000
		Prince, capital (20%).........	32,000
		Total liabilities and	
Total assets	$150,000	capital	$150,000

The noncash assets are sold for a total of $80,000 and all liabilities paid. The partnership's accounting system records these two events as follows:

Cash	80,000			
Morris, Capital (40% of loss).......................	24,000			
Newton, Capital (20% of loss)......................	12,000			
Olsen, Capital (20% of loss)	12,000			
Prince, Capital (20% of loss)	12,000			
Noncash Assets (or specific accounts)		140,000		

To record sale of noncash assets and allocation of resulting
$60,000 loss.

Liabilities..	70,000	
Cash		70,000

To extinguish partnership obligations.

Because of these two transactions, the partnership's cash has risen from $10,000 to $20,000.

After the allocation of this loss, the capital accounts for Morris and Newton report deficit balances of $9,000 ($15,000 − $24,000) and $2,000 ($10,000 − $12,000), respectively. Although Newton is solvent and would be expected to compensate the partnership, Morris's personal financial condition does not allow for any further contribution. The $9,000 deficit must, therefore, be absorbed by Newton, Olsen, and Prince. Because these three partners have historically shared profits evenly (20:20:20), they continue to do so in recording this additional capital loss.

Newton, Capital (⅓ of loss)	3,000	
Olsen, Capital (⅓ of loss)	3,000	
Prince, Capital (⅓ of loss)	3,000	
Morris, Capital		9,000

To write off deficit capital balance of insolvent partner.

This last allocation increases Newton's deficit to a $5,000 balance ($2,000 + $3,000), an amount which the partner should now contribute in accordance with partnership law.

Cash	5,000	
Newton, Capital..................................		5,000

To record contribution necessitated by negative capital balance.

Following this series of transactions, only the cash balance (now $25,000) as well as the capital accounts of Olsen and Prince remain open within the partnership records:

	Cash	Morris, Capital	Newton, Capital	Olsen, Capital	Prince, Capital
Beginning balances	$ 10,000	$ 15,000	$ 10,000	$ 23,000	$ 32,000
Sold assets	80,000	(24,000)	(12,000)	(12,000)	(12,000)
Paid liabilities	(70,000)	–0–	–0–	–0–	–0–
Default by Morris	–0–	9,000	(3,000)	(3,000)	(3,000)
Contribution by Newton.......	5,000	–0–	5,000	–0–	–0–
Current balances	$ 25,000	–0–	–0–	$ 8,000	$ 17,000

Although $8,000 of the partnership's remaining cash goes directly to Olsen, the $17,000 attributed to Prince is first subjected to the claims of the partner's personal creditors. Because of their claims, $15,000 of this amount must be used to satisfy these obligations, with only the final $2,000 being paid to Prince.

Insolvency—Example Three The two previous illustrations have analyzed liquidations in which one or more of the partners has been personally insolvent. Another possibility is that the partnership itself may come to meet this same fate. In an active partnership, insolvency can occur if losses or drawings deplete the working capital of the operation. A bankruptcy petition may follow if debts cannot be met as they come due. Liquidation of business assets might be necessary unless additional capital is quickly generated. Even a financially sound partnership may become insolvent if material losses are incurred during a voluntary liquidation.

To serve as a basis for examining the accounting and legal ramifications of an insolvent partnership, assume that the law firm of Keller, Lewis, Monroe, and Norris is in the final stages of liquidation. All noncash assets have been sold, and available cash has been used to pay a portion of the business's liabilities. Following these transactions, the following account balances remain open within the partnership's records. The four partners in this endeavor share profits and losses equally.

Liabilities	$ 20,000
Keller, capital	(30,000)
Lewis, capital	(5,000)
Monroe, capital	5,000
Norris, capital	10,000

Note: Parentheses indicate deficit.

This partnership is insolvent; it continues to owe creditors $20,000, even after liquidation and distribution of all assets. However, additional money should be forthcoming from two of the partners. Because of their deficit capital accounts, Keller and Lewis are legally required to contribute an additional $30,000 and $5,000, respectively, to the business. With these newly available funds, the partnership will be able to pay all $20,000 of its remaining liabilities as well as make cash distributions to Monroe ($5,000) and Norris ($10,000) in accordance with their capital account balances. The partnership books would be closed by this final payment.

Once again, the possibility exists that a partner who is reporting a negative capital balance will not step forward to make a further investment. Assume, for example, that Keller is personally insolvent and cannot contribute, whereas Lewis simply refuses to supply additional funds in hopes of avoiding the obligation. *At this point, the remaining creditors may instigate legal recovery proceedings against any or all of the partners regardless of their capital balances.* Any action, however, against the insolvent partner may prove to be a futile effort because of the marshaling of assets principle.

Predicting the exact outcome of litigation is rarely possible. Thus, the assumption is made that Norris is forced to contribute $20,000 cash to make up the entire deficit. The following journal entries would then be required for this partnership:

Cash	20,000	
Norris, Capital		20,000
Liabilities	20,000	
Cash		20,000

To record capital contribution by Norris made to pay remaining partnership creditors.

After all liabilities have been settled, the partners who still maintain positive capital accounts can demand remuneration from any partner with a negative balance. Despite this legal obligation, the chances of a significant recovery from the insolvent Keller, especially under the marshaling of assets doctrine, is not likely. Thus, the partners may choose to write off this deficit to move toward closing the partnership's financial records. Legal recovery proceedings can still continue against Keller regardless of the accounting treatment. As equal partners, the $30,000 loss is absorbed evenly by Lewis, Monroe, and Norris.

Lewis, Capital (⅓ of loss)	10,000	
Monroe, Capital (⅓ of loss)	10,000	
Norris, Capital (⅓ of loss)	10,000	
Keller, Capital		30,000

To write off deficit capital balance of insolvent partner.

What Happens if a Partner Becomes Insolvent?

In 1987, three dentists—Ben Rogers, Judy Wilkinson, and Henry Walker—formed a partnership to open a practice in Toledo, Ohio. The primary purpose of the partnership was to reduce expenses since the partners could share building and equipment costs, supplies, and the services of a clerical staff. They each contributed $50,000 in cash and, with the help of a bank loan, constructed a building and acquired furniture, fixtures, and equipment. Because the partners maintained their own separate clients, annual net income has been allocated as follows: each partner receives the specific amount of revenues that he or she generated during the period less one-third of all expenses. From the beginning, the partners did not anticipate expansion of the practice; consequently, they could withdraw cash each year up to 90 percent of their share of income for the period.

The partnership had been profitable for a number of years. Over the years, Rogers used much of his income to speculate in real estate in the Toledo area. By 1998, he spent less time with the dental practice so that he could concentrate on his investments. Unfortunately, a number of these deals proved to be bad decisions and he incurred significant losses. On November 8, 1998, while Rogers was out of town, a $97,000 claim was filed by his personal creditors against the partnership assets. Unbeknownst to Wilkinson and Walker, Rogers had become insolvent.

Wilkinson and Walker hurriedly held a meeting to discuss the problem since Rogers could not be located. Rogers's capital account was currently at $105,000, but the partnership had only $19,000 in cash and liquid assets. The partners estimate that Rogers's equipment had been used for a number of years and could be sold for relatively little. In contrast, the building has appreciated in value and the claim could be satisfied by selling the property. However, this action would have a tremendously adverse impact on the dental practice of the remaining two partners.

What alternatives are available to Wilkinson and Walker, and what are the advantages and disadvantages of each?

The partners' capital accounts now hold the following balances:

	Keller, Capital	Lewis, Capital	Monroe, Capital	Norris, Capital
Beginning balances	$(30,000)	$ (5,000)	$ 5,000	$ 10,000
Capital contribution	–0–	–0–	–0–	20,000
Write-off of deficit balance	30,000	(10,000)	(10,000)	(10,000)
Current balances	–0–	$(15,000)	$ (5,000)	$ 20,000

Both Lewis and Monroe now have a legal obligation to reimburse the partnership to offset their deficit capital balances. Upon their payment of $15,000 and $5,000, respectively, the entire $20,000 will be distributed to Norris (the only partner with a positive balance) and the partnership's books will be closed. Should either Lewis or Monroe fail to make the appropriate contribution, the additional loss must be allocated between the two remaining partners.

Preliminary Distribution of Partnership Assets

In all of the illustrations analyzed in this chapter, distributions have been made to the partners only after all assets were sold and all liabilities paid. As previously mentioned, a liquidation may take an extended time to complete. During this lengthy process, the partnership need not retain those assets that will eventually be disbursed to the partners. If the business is safely solvent, waiting until all affairs have been settled before transferring property to the owners is not warranted. The partners should be allowed to make use of their own funds at the earliest possible time. *The objective in making any type of preliminary distribution is to assure that enough capital is maintained by the partnership to absorb all future losses.* Any capital in excess of this maximum requirement is a safe balance, an amount that can be immediately conveyed to the partner. To determine safe capital balances at any time, the accountant simply assumes that all subsequent events will result in maximum losses: no cash will be received in liquidating remaining noncash assets and each partner is personally insolvent. Any positive capital balance that would remain even after inclusion of all potential losses should be paid to the partner without delay. Although the assumption that no further funds will be generated may be unrealistic, it does ensure that negative capital balances are not created by premature payments being made to any of the partners.

Preliminary Distribution Illustrated

To demonstrate the computation of safe capital distributions, assume that a liquidating partnership reports the following balance sheet:

Cash	$ 60,000	Liabilities	$ 40,000
Noncash assets	140,000	Mason, loan	20,000
		Mason, capital (50%)	60,000
		Lee, capital (30%)	30,000
		Dixon, capital (20%)	50,000
		Total liabilities and	
Total assets	$200,000	capital	$200,000

Assume further that the partners estimate that $6,000 will be the maximum expense incurred in carrying out this liquidation. Consequently, the partnership needs only $46,000 to meet all obligations: $40,000 to satisfy partnership liabilities and $6,000 for these final expenses. Since $60,000 in cash is being held, the partnership can transfer the extra $14,000 to the partners immediately without fear of injuring any of the participants in the liquidation. However, the appropriate allocation of this money is not readily apparent; therefore, safe capital balances must be computed to guide the actual distribution.

Before the allocation of this $14,000 is demonstrated, the appropriate handling of a partner's loan balance should be examined. According to the balance sheet, Mason has contributed $20,000 to the business at some point in the past, an amount that was considered a loan rather than additional capital. Perhaps the partnership was in desperate need of funds and could only generate new financing by accepting a high interest rate loan. Regardless of the reason, the question remains as to the status of this account: Is the $20,000 to be viewed as a liability to the partner or as a capital balance? The answer becomes especially significant during the liquidation process since available funds often are limited. In this regard, the Uniform Partnership Act (Section 40[b]) stipulates that loans to partners rank behind obligations to outside creditors in order of payment but ahead of the partners' capital balances.

Although this legal provision indicates that the debt to Mason must be repaid entirely before any distribution of capital can be made to the other partners, actual accounting practice seems to have taken a different view. "In preparing predistribution schedules, accountants typically offset partners' loans with the partners' capital accounts and then distribute funds accordingly."[6] In other words, the loan is merged in with the partner's capital account balance at the beginning of liquidation. Thus, appropriate handling of a loan from a partner is not entirely certain.

To illustrate the potential problem with this conflict, assume that a partnership has $20,000 in cash left after liquidation. Partner A has a positive capital balance of $20,000 whereas Partner B has a negative capital of $20,000. In addition, Partner B has previously loaned the partnership $20,000. If Partner B is insolvent,[7] a distribution problem arises. If the provisions of the UPA are followed literally, the $20,000

---

[6]Robert E. Whitis and Jeffrey R. Pittman, "Inconsistencies Between Accounting Practices and Statutory Law in Partnership Liquidations," *Accounting Educators' Journal,* Fall 1996, p. 99.

[7]The same problem should not exist if the partner is solvent. The partner is legally required to contribute enough funds to delete any capital deficit. Thus, in this case, Partner B would receive the $20,000 loan repayment but then has to contribute $20,000 because of the negative capital balance. That cash amount would go to Partner A because of that partner's positive capital balance.

cash should be given to Partner B (probably to the creditors of Partner B). Because Partner B is insolvent, no more assets can be expected from this individual. Thus, Partner A has to absorb the entire $20,000 deficit capital balance and will get no portion of the $20,000 in cash that is held by the business.

However, despite the UPA, common practice appears to be that the loan from Partner B will be used to offset that partner's negative capital balance. Using that approach, Partner B is left with a zero capital balance so that the entire $20,000 goes to Partner A; the creditors of Partner B get nothing. Thus, when a loan comes from a partner who later becomes insolvent and also reports a negative capital balance, the handling of the loan becomes significant. Unfortunately, further legal guidance does not exist at this time because "no reported state or federal opinion has directly ruled on the right of offset of potential capital deficits."[8]

In this textbook, in order to follow common practice, a loan from a partner will always be accounted for in liquidation as if the balance were a component of the partner's capital. By this offset, the accountant can reduce the amount accumulated as a negative capital balance for any insolvent partner. Any such loan can be transferred into the corresponding capital account at the start of the liquidation process. Similarly, any loans due from a partner should be shown as a reduction in the appropriate capital balance.

Proposed Schedule of Liquidation   Returning to the current illustration, the accountant needs to determine an equitable distribution for the $14,000 cash presently available. To structure this computation, a proposed schedule of liquidation is developed *based on the underlying assumption that all future events will result in total losses*. In Exhibit 15–2, this statement is presented for the Mason, Lee, and Dixon partnership. To expedite coverage, the $20,000 loan has already been transferred into Mason's capital account. Thus, regardless of whether this partner arrives at a deficit or a safe capital balance, the loan figure already will have been included.

In producing Exhibit 15–2, complete losses ($140,000) are forecast in connection with the disposition of all noncash assets, and liquidation expenses are anticipated at maximum amounts ($6,000). Following the projected payment of liabilities, any

Exhibit 15–2

	Cash	Noncash Assets	Liabilities	Mason, Capital (50%)	Lee, Capital (30%)	Dixon, Capital (20%)
MASON, LEE, AND DIXON — Proposed Schedule of Liquidation—Initial Safe Capital Balances						
Beginning balances..............	$ 60,000	$ 140,000	$ 40,000	$ 80,000	$ 30,000	$ 50,000
Maximum loss on noncash assets......	–0–	(140,000)	–0–	(70,000)	(42,000)	(28,000)
Maximum liquidation expenses	(6,000)	–0–	–0–	(3,000)	(1,800)	(1,200)
Payment of liabilities	(40,000)	–0–	(40,000)	–0–	–0–	–0–
Potential balances	14,000	–0–	–0–	7,000	(13,800)	20,800
Assume Lee to be insolvent	–0–	–0–	–0–	(9,857) (⁵⁄₇)	13,800	(3,943) (²⁄₇)
Potential balances	14,000	–0–	–0–	(2,857)	–0–	16,857
Assume Mason to be insolvent	–0–	–0–	–0–	2,857	–0–	(2,857)
Safe balances	$ 14,000	–0–	–0–	–0–	–0–	$ 14,000

[8]Robert E. Whitis and Jeffrey R. Pittman, "Inconsistencies Between Accounting Practices and Statutory Law in Partnership Liquidations," *Accounting Educators' Journal,* Fall 1996, p. 93.

partner reporting a negative capital account is assumed to be personally insolvent. These potential deficit balances are written off with the losses being assigned to the remaining solvent partners based on their relative profit and loss ratio. Lee, with a negative $13,800, is eliminated first. This allocation creates a deficit of $2,857 for Mason, an amount that must be absorbed solely by Dixon. After this series of maximum losses has been simulated, any positive capital balance that still remains is considered safe; a cash distribution of that amount can be made to the specific partners.

Exhibit 15–2 indicates that only Dixon has a large enough capital balance at the present time to absorb all possible future losses. Thus, the entire $14,000 can be distributed to this partner with no fear that the capital account will ever report a deficit. Based on current practice, Mason, despite having made a $20,000 loan to the partnership, is entitled to no part of this initial distribution. The loan is of insufficient size to prevent potential deficits from occurring in Mason's capital account.

One series of computations found in this proposed schedule of liquidation merits additional attention. The simulated losses initially create a $13,800 negative balance in Lee's capital account while the other two partners continue to report positive figures. Lee's projected deficit must then be absorbed by Mason and Dixon according to their relative profit and loss percentages. Previously, Mason has been allocated 50 percent of net income with 20 percent recorded to Dixon. These figures equate to a $50/70:20/70$ or a $5/7:2/7$ ratio. Based on this realigned relationship, the $13,800 deficit is allocated between Mason ($5/7$ or $9,857) and Dixon ($2/7$ or $3,943), reducing Mason's own capital account to a negative balance as shown in Exhibit 15–2.

Continuing with the assumption that maximum losses occur in all cases, Mason's $2,857 deficit is accounted for as if that partner were also personally insolvent. Therefore, the entire negative balance is assigned to Dixon, the only partner still retaining a positive capital account. Since all potential losses have been recognized at this point, the remaining $14,000 capital is a safe balance that should be paid to this partner. Even after the money is distributed, Dixon's capital account will still be large enough to absorb all future losses.

Liquidation in Installments   In practice, maximum liquidation losses are not likely to occur to any business. Thus, at various points during this process, additional cash amounts usually become available as partnership property is sold. If the assets are disposed of in a piecemeal fashion, cash may actually flow into the company on a regular basis for an extended period of time. As needed, updated safe capital schedules have to be developed to dictate the recipients of newly available funds. Because numerous capital distributions may be required, this process is often referred to as a *liquidation made in installments.*

To illustrate, assume that the partnership of Mason, Lee, and Dixon actually undergoes the following events in connection with its liquidation:

- As indicated by the schedule of liquidation in Exhibit 15–2, Dixon receives $14,000 in cash as a preliminary capital distribution.
- Noncash assets with a book value of $50,000 are sold for $20,000.
- All $40,000 in liabilities are settled.
- Liquidation expenses of $2,000 are paid; the partners now believe that only a maximum of $3,000 more will be expended in this manner. The original estimation of $6,000 was apparently too high.

As a result of these transactions, the partnership has an additional $21,000 in cash that is now available for distribution to the partners: $20,000 received from the sale of noncash assets and another $1,000 because of the reduced estimation of liquidation expenses. Once again, the accountant must assume maximum future losses as a means of determining the appropriate distribution of these funds. A second proposed

E x h i b i t   1 5 – 3   Liquidation for Installments

MASON, LEE, AND DIXON
Proposed Schedule of Liquidation—Subsequent
Safe Capital Balances

	Cash	Noncash Assets	Liabilities	Mason, Capital (50%)	Lee, Capital (30%)	Dixon, Capital (20%)
Beginning balances................	$ 60,000	$ 140,000	$ 40,000	$ 80,000	$ 30,000	$ 50,000
Capital distribution—safe balances.....	(14,000)	–0–	–0–	–0–	–0–	(14,000)
Disposal of noncash assets	20,000	(50,000)	–0–	(15,000)	(9,000)	(6,000)
Liabilities paid...................	(40,000)	–0–	(40,000)	–0–	–0–	–0–
Liquidation expenses	(2,000)	–0–	–0–	(1,000)	(600)	(400)
Current balances	24,000	90,000	–0–	64,000	20,400	29,600
Maximum loss on remaining noncash assets........................	–0–	(90,000)	–0–	(45,000)	(27,000)	(18,000)
Maximum liquidation expenses	(3,000)	–0–	–0–	(1,500)	(900)	(600)
Potential balances	21,000	–0–	–0–	17,500	(7,500)	11,000
Assume Lee to be insolvent	–0–	–0–	–0–	(5,357) (5/7)	(7,500)	(2,143) (2/7)
Safe balances—current	$ 21,000	–0–	–0–	$ 12,143	–0–	$ 8,857

schedule of liquidation is produced in Exhibit 15–3, indicating that $12,143 of this amount should go to Mason with the remaining $8,857 to Dixon. To facilitate a better visual understanding, actual transactions are recorded first on this schedule, followed by the assumed losses. *A dotted line separates the real from the potential occurrences.*

Predistribution Plan

The liquidation of a partnership can require numerous transactions occurring over a lengthy time. The continual production of proposed schedules of liquidation may become a burdensome chore. Two separate statements already have been required in the previous illustration, and the partnership still possesses $90,000 in noncash assets awaiting conversion. *Therefore, at the start of a liquidation, most accountants produce a single predistribution plan to serve as a guideline for all future payments.* Thereafter, whenever cash becomes available, this plan indicates the appropriate recipients without the necessity of drawing up ever-changing proposed schedules of liquidation.

A predistribution plan is developed by simulating a series of losses that are each just large enough to eliminate, one at a time, all of the partners' claims to cash. This approach recognizes that the individual capital accounts exhibit differing degrees of sensitivity to losses. These accounts possess varying balances and may be charged with losses at different rates. Consequently, a predistribution plan is based on calculating the losses (the "maximum loss allowable") that would eliminate each of these capital balances in a sequential pattern. This series of absorbed losses then forms the basis for the predistribution plan.

To demonstrate the creation of a predistribution plan, assume that the following partnership is to be liquidated:

Cash	–0–	Liabilities................	$100,000
Noncash assets	$221,000	Rubens, capital (50%)	30,000
		Smith, capital (20%)	40,000
		Trice, capital (30%)	51,000
Total assets..............	$221,000	Total liabilities and capital	$221,000

The partnership capital reported by this organization totals $121,000. However, the individual balances for the partners range from $30,000 to $51,000 while profits and losses are assigned according to three different percentages. Thus, each partner's current capital balance would be reduced to zero by differing losses. *As a prerequisite to developing a predistribution plan, the sensitivity to losses exhibited by each of these capital accounts must be measured.*

Partner	Capital Balance/ Loss Allocation	Maximum Loss that Can Be Absorbed
Rubens	$30,000/50%	$ 60,000 ✔
Smith..........	40,000/20%	200,000
Trice	51,000/30%	170,000

Rubens is the partner in the most vulnerable position at the present time. Based on a 50 percent share of income, a loss of only $60,000 is needed to reduce this partner's capital account to a zero balance. If the partnership does incur a loss of this amount, Rubens can no longer hope to recover any funds from the liquidation process. Thus, the potential effects of this loss (referred to as a Step 1 loss) is simulated through the following schedule:

	Rubens, Capital	Smith, Capital	Trice, Capital
Beginning balances	$ 30,000	$ 40,000	$ 51,000
Assumed $60,000 loss	(30,000) (50%)	(12,000) (20%)	(18,000) (30%)
Step 1 balances	–0–	$ 28,000	$ 33,000

As previously discussed, the predistribution plan is based on describing the series of losses that would eliminate each partner's capital in turn and, thus, all claims to cash. In the previous Step 1 schedule, the $60,000 loss did reduce Ruben's capital account to zero. Assuming, as a precautionary step, that Rubens is personally insolvent, all further losses would have to be allocated between Smith and Trice. Since these two partners have previously shared partnership profits and losses on a 20 percent and 30 percent basis, a $^{20}/_{50}$:$^{30}/_{50}$ relationship exists between them (or 40%:60%). Therefore, these realigned percentages must now be utilized in calculating a Step 2 loss, the amount large enough to exclude one of these two remaining partners from sharing in any future cash distributions.

Partner	Capital Balance/ Loss Allocation	Maximum Loss that Can Be Absorbed
Smith..........	$28,000/40%	$ 70,000
Trice	33,000/60%	55,000 ✔

Since Rubens's capital balance already has been eliminated, Trice is now in the most vulnerable position: only a $55,000 Step 2 loss is needed to reduce this partner's capital account to a zero balance.

	Rubens, Capital	Smith, Capital	Trice, Capital
Beginning balances	$ 30,000	$ 40,000	$ 51,000
Assumed $60,000 loss	(30,000) (50%)	(12,000) (20%)	(18,000) (30%)
Step 1 balances	–0–	28,000	33,000
Assumed $55,000 loss	–0–	(22,000) (40%)	(33,000) (60%)
Step 2 balances	–0–	$ 6,000	–0–

According to this second schedule, a total loss of $115,000 ($60,000 from Step 1 plus $55,000 from Step 2) would leave capital of only $6,000, a balance attributed entirely to Smith. At this final point in the simulation, an additional loss of this amount also ends Smith's right to receive any funds from the liquidation process.

Having the sole positive capital account remaining, this partner would have to absorb the entire amount of the final loss.

	Rubens, Capital	Smith, Capital	Trice, Capital
Beginning balances	$ 30,000	$ 40,000	$ 51,000
Assumed $60,000 loss	(30,000) (50%)	(12,000) (20%)	(18,000) (30%)
Step 1 balances	–0–	28,000	33,000
Assumed $55,000 loss	–0–	(22,000) (40%)	(33,000) (60%)
Step 2 balances	–0–	6,000	–0–
Assumed $6,000 loss	–0–	(6,000) (100%)	–0–
Final balances	–0–	–0–	–0–

Once each partner's capital account has been reduced to zero through this series of simulated losses, a predistribution plan for the liquidation can be devised. *This procedure requires working backward through the final schedule above, determining the effects that will result if the assumed losses do not occur.* Without these losses, cash becomes available for the partners; therefore, a direct relationship exists between the volume of losses and the distribution pattern. The last $6,000 loss, for example, is to be absorbed entirely by Smith. Should that loss fail to materialize, Smith is left with a positive safe capital balance of this amount. Thus, as cash becomes available, the first $6,000 received (in excess of partnership obligations and anticipated liquidation expenses) should be distributed solely to Smith.

In a similar manner, the preceding $55,000 Step 2 loss was divided between Smith and Trice on a 4:6 basis. Again, if such losses do not occur, these balances need not be retained to protect the partnership against capital deficits. Therefore, after Smith has received the initial $6,000, any further cash that becomes available (up to an additional $55,000) will be split between Smith (40 percent) and Trice (60 percent). For example, if exactly $61,000 in cash is held by the partnership in excess of liabilities and possible liquidation expenses, the following distribution should be made:

	Rubens	Smith	Trice
First $6,000	–0–	$ 6,000	–0–
Next $55,000	–0–	22,000 (40%)	$33,000 (60%)
Cash distribution	–0–	$28,000	$33,000

The predistribution plan can be completed by including the Step 1 loss, an amount that was to be absorbed by the partners on a 5:2:3 basis. Thus, all money that becomes available to the partners after the initial $61,000 is to be distributed according to the original profit and loss ratio. At this point in the liquidation, enough cash would have been generated to ensure that each partner has a safe capital balance: no possibility exists that a future deficit can occur. Any further increases in the projected capital balances will be allocated by the 5:2:3 allocation pattern. *For this reason, once all partners have begun to receive a portion of the cash disbursements, any remaining funds are divided based on the original profit and loss percentages.*

To inform all parties of the order by which available cash will be disbursed, the predistribution plan should be formally prepared in a schedule format prior to beginning liquidation. Following is the predistribution plan for the partnership of Rubens, Smith, and Trice. To complete this illustration, liquidation expenses of $12,000 have been estimated. Since these expenses have the same effect on the capital accounts as losses, they do not change the sequential pattern by which assets eventually will be distributed.

RUBENS, SMITH, AND TRICE
Predistribution Plan

Available Cash		Recipient
First	$112,000	Creditors ($100,000) and liquidation expenses (estimated at $12,000)
Next	6,000	Smith
Next	55,000	Smith (40%) and Trice (60%)
All further cash balances		Rubens (50%), Smith (20%), and Trice (30%)

SUMMARY

1. Although a partnership can exist indefinitely through the periodic admission of new partners, termination of business activities and liquidation of property may take place for a number of reasons. A partner's death or retirement can trigger this process as well as the insolvency of a partner or even the partnership itself. Because of the risk that large losses will be incurred during liquidation, all parties usually seek frequent and timely information describing ongoing developments. The accountant is expected to furnish this data while also working to ensure the equitable treatment of all parties.

2. The liquidation process entails (a) converting partnership property into cash, (b) paying off liabilities and liquidation expenses, and (c) conveying any remaining property to the partners based on their final capital balances. As a means of reporting these transactions, a schedule of liquidation should be produced at periodic intervals. This statement discloses all recent transactions, the assets and liabilities still being held, and the current capital balances. Distribution of this schedule on a regular basis allows the various parties involved in the liquidation to monitor the progress being made.

3. During a liquidation, negative capital balances can arise for one or more of the partners, especially if material losses are incurred in disposing of partnership property. In such cases, the specific partner or partners should contribute enough additional assets to eliminate their deficits. If payment is slow in coming, any cash still held by the partnership can be immediately divided among the partners that have safe capital balances. A safe balance is the amount of capital that would remain even if maximum future losses occur: noncash assets are lost in total and all partners with deficits fail to fulfill their legal obligations. In making these computations, negative capital balances are absorbed by the remaining partners based on their relative profit and loss ratio.

4. To enable an orderly and fair distribution during liquidation, the Uniform Partnership Act establishes a priority listing for all claims, a ranking referred to as the *marshaling of assets*. This principle states that partners with positive capital balances can recover losses from a partner reporting a deficit but only after adequate protection has been ensured for that individual's creditors as well as the partnership's creditors. The act also specifies that a partner's personal creditors can seek recovery of losses from the partnership to the extent of that person's capital balance after protection of partnership creditors is assured.

5. The actual liquidation of a partnership can take an extended period to complete. Oftentimes, cash is generated during the early stages of this process in excess of the amount needed to cover liabilities and liquidation expenses. The accountant should propose a fair and immediate distribution of these available funds. A proposed schedule of liquidation can be created as a guide for such cash distributions. This statement is based on a *simulated* series of transactions: sale of all noncash assets, payment of liquidation expenses, and so on. At every point, maximum losses are assumed: noncash assets have no resale value, liquidation expenses are set at the maximum level, and all partners are personally insolvent. Any safe capital balance that would remain after incurring such losses represents a distribution that can be made at the present time. Even after this payment, the capital account will still be large enough to absorb all potential losses.

6. The liquidation of a partnership can require numerous transactions occurring over a lengthy time. Thus, the accountant may discover that the continual production of

proposed schedules of liquidation becomes a burdensome chore. For this reason, a single predistribution plan is usually produced at the start of the liquidation process. This plan serves as a definitive guideline for all payments to be made to the partners. To create this plan, a series of losses is simulated with each one, in turn, exactly eliminating the capital balance of a partner. After all capital accounts have been reduced to zero through these assumed losses, the predistribution plan is devised by working backward through the series. In effect, the accountant is measuring the cash that will become available if such losses do not occur.

COMPREHENSIVE ILLUSTRATION

Problem

(Estimated Time: 30 to 40 Minutes) For the past several years, the partnership of Andrews, Caso, Quinn, and Sheridan has operated a local department store. Based on the provisions of the original Articles of Partnership, all profits and losses have been allocated on a 4:3:2:1 ratio, respectively. Recently, both Caso and Quinn have undergone personal financial problems, and as a result, each of these individuals is now insolvent. Caso's creditors have filed a $20,000 claim against the partnership's assets while $22,000 is being sought to repay Quinn's personal debts. To satisfy these legal obligations, the partnership property must be liquidated. The partners estimate that they will incur $12,000 in expenses in disposing of all noncash assets.

At the time that active operations cease and the liquidation is begun, the following balance sheet is produced for this partnership. All measurement accounts have been closed out to arrive at the current capital balances.

Cash	$ 20,000	Liabilities	$140,000
Noncash assets	280,000	Caso, loan	10,000
		Andrews, capital (40%)	76,000
		Caso, capital (30%)	14,000
		Quinn, capital (20%)	51,000
		Sheridan, capital (10%)	9,000
Total assets	$300,000	Total liabilities and capital	$300,000

During the lengthy liquidation process, the following transactions take place:

- Noncash assets with a book value of $190,000 are sold for $140,000 cash.
- Liquidation expenses of $14,000 are paid.
- Safe capital distributions are made to the partners.
- Payment is made of all business liabilities.
- The remaining noncash assets are sold for $10,000.
- Deficit capital balances for any insolvent partners are deemed to be uncollectible.
- Appropriate cash contributions are received from any solvent partner who is reporting a negative capital balance.
- Final cash distributions are made.

Required

a. Using the information that is available prior to the start of the liquidation process, develop a predistribution plan for this partnership.
b. Prepare journal entries to record the actual liquidation transactions.

Solution

a. This partnership begins the liquidation process with capital amounting to $160,000. This total includes the $10,000 loan from Caso since the liability must be retained as a possible offset against any eventual deficit capital balance. Therefore, the predistribution plan is based on the assumption that $160,000 in losses will be incurred, entirely eliminating all partnership capital. As discussed in this chapter, these simulated losses are arranged in a series so that each capital account is sequentially reduced to a zero balance.

At the start of the liquidation, Caso's capital position is the most vulnerable.

Partner	Capital Balance/ Loss Allocation	Maximum Loss that Can Be Absorbed
Andrews	$76,000/40%	$190,000
Caso	24,000/30%	80,000 ✔
Quinn	51,000/20%	255,000
Sheridan	9,000/10%	90,000

As indicated by this schedule, an $80,000 loss would eradicate both Caso's $14,000 capital balance and the $10,000 loan. Therefore, to start the development of a predistribution plan, this loss is assumed to have occurred.

	Andrews, Capital	Caso, Loan and Capital	Quinn, Capital	Sheridan, Capital
Beginning balances	$ 76,000	$ 24,000	$ 51,000	$ 9,000
Assumed $80,000 loss	(32,000) (40%)	(24,000) (30%)	(16,000) (20%)	(8,000) (10%)
Step 1 balances	$ 44,000	–0–	$ 35,000	$ 1,000

With Caso's capital account eliminated, further losses are to be split among the remaining partners in the ratio of 4:2:1 (or $\frac{4}{7}$:$\frac{2}{7}$:$\frac{1}{7}$). As only an additional $7,000 loss (the $1,000 capital divided by $\frac{1}{7}$) is now needed to reduce Sheridan's account to zero, this partner is in the second most vulnerable position.

	Andrews	Caso	Quinn	Sheridan
Step 1 balances (above)	$44,000	–0–	$35,000	$ 1,000
Assumed $7,000 loss	(4,000) ($\frac{4}{7}$)	–0–	(2,000) ($\frac{2}{7}$)	(1,000) ($\frac{1}{7}$)
Step 2 balances	$40,000	–0–	$33,000	–0–

Following these two simulated losses, only Andrews and Quinn continue to report positive capital balances. Thus, they divide further losses on a 4:2 basis or 66⅔%:33⅓%. Based on these realigned percentages, Andrews's position has become the most vulnerable. A further loss of $60,000 ($40,000/66⅔%) reduces this partner's remaining capital to zero whereas a $99,000 loss ($33,000/33⅓%) is required to eliminate Quinn's balance.

	Andrews	Caso	Quinn	Sheridan
Step 2 balances (above)	$ 40,000	–0–	$ 33,000	–0–
Assumed $60,000 loss	(40,000) (66⅔%)	–0–	(20,000) (33⅓%)	–0–
Step 3 balances	–0–	–0–	$ 13,000	–0–

The final $13,000 capital balance belongs to Quinn; an additional loss of this amount is necessary to remove the last element of partnership capital.

Based on the results of this series of simulated losses, a predistribution plan can be created. However, the $140,000 in liabilities owed by the partnership still have first priority to available cash. Additionally, $12,000 must be retained to cover the anticipated liquidation expenses.

ANDREWS, CASO, QUINN, AND SHERIDAN
Predistribution Plan

Available Cash		Recipient
First	$152,000	Creditors and anticipated liquidation expenses
Next	13,000	Quinn
Next	60,000	Andrews (66⅔%) and Quinn (33⅓%)
Next	7,000	Andrews ($\frac{4}{7}$), Quinn ($\frac{2}{7}$), and Sheridan ($\frac{1}{7}$)
All further cash		Andrews (40%), Caso (30%), Quinn (20%), and Sheridan (10%)

Because of their insolvency, initial payments to Caso ($20,000) and Quinn ($22,000) may actually go to their personal creditors.

b. Journal entries for the liquidation:

Caso, Loan	10,000	
Caso, Capital		10,000

To offset loan against capital balance in anticipation of liquidation.

Cash	140,000	
Andrews, Capital (40% of loss)	20,000	
Caso, Capital (30% of loss)	15,000	
Quinn, Capital (20% of loss)	10,000	
Sheridan, Capital (10% of loss)	5,000	
Noncash Assets		190,000

To record sale of noncash assets and allocation of $50,000 loss.

Andrews, Capital (40%)	5,600	
Caso, Capital (30%)	4,200	
Quinn, Capital (20%)	2,800	
Sheridan, Capital (10%)	1,400	
Cash.......................................		14,000

Payment of liquidation expenses.

■ The partnership is now holding $146,000 in cash, $6,000 more than is needed to satisfy all liabilities and estimated expenses. According to the predistribution plan drawn up in requirement *a*, this entire amount can be safely distributed to Quinn (or to Quinn's creditors).

Quinn, Capital	6,000	
Cash.......................................		6,000

To distribute available cash based on safe capital balance.

Liabilities.....................................	140,000	
Cash.......................................		140,000

To extinguish all partnership debts.

Cash	10,000	
Andrews, Capital (40% of loss)	32,000	
Caso, Capital (30% of loss)	24,000	
Quinn, Capital (20% of loss)	16,000	
Sheridan, Capital (10% of loss)	8,000	
Noncash Assets		90,000

To record sale of remaining noncash assets and allocation of $80,000 loss.

■ At this point in the liquidation, only the cash and the capital accounts remain open on the partnership books.

	Cash	Andrews, Capital	Caso, Capital	Quinn, Capital	Sheridan, Capital
Beginning balances	$ 20,000	$ 76,000	$ 14,000	$ 51,000	$ 9,000
Loan offset	–0–	–0–	10,000	–0–	–0–
Sale of noncash assets	140,000	(20,000)	(15,000)	(10,000)	(5,000)
Liquidation expenses	(14,000)	(5,600)	(4,200)	(2,800)	(1,400)
Cash distribution	(6,000)	–0–	–0–	(6,000)	–0–
Payment of liabilities........	(140,000)	–0–	–0–	–0–	–0–
Sale of noncash assets	10,000	(32,000)	(24,000)	(16,000)	(8,000)
Current balances	$ 10,000	$ 18,400	$(19,200)	$ 16,200	$(5,400)

Because Caso is personally insolvent, the $19,200 deficit balance will not be repaid and must be absorbed by the remaining three partners on a 4:2:1 basis.

Andrews, Capital (⁴/₇ of loss)	10,971	
Quinn, Capital (²/₇ of loss)	5,486	
Sheridan, Capital (¹/₇ of loss)	2,743	
Caso, Capital		19,200

To write-off deficit capital balance of insolvent partner.

■ This last allocation decreases Sheridan's capital account to a $8,143 negative total. Since this partner is personally solvent, that amount should be contributed to the partnership in accordance with regulations of the Uniform Partnership Act.

Cash   8,143
    Sheridan, Capital   8,143
    To record contribution made to eliminate deficit capital balance.

■ Sheridan's contribution brings the final cash total for the partnership to $18,143. This amount is distributed to the two partners who continue to maintain positive capital balances: Andrews and Quinn (or Quinn's creditors).

	Andrews, Capital	Quinn, Capital
Balances above	$18,400	$16,200
Caso default	(10,971)	(5,486)
Final balances	$ 7,429	$10,714
Andrews, Capital.	7,429	
Quinn, Capital	10,714	
Cash		18,143

    To distribute remaining cash according to final capital balances.

QUESTIONS

1. What is the difference between the dissolution of a partnership and the liquidation of partnership property?
2. Why would the members of a partnership elect to terminate business operations and liquidate all noncash assets?
3. Why are liquidation gains and losses usually recorded as direct adjustments to the partners' capital accounts?
4. After liquidating all property and paying partnership obligations, on what basis is the remaining cash allocated among the partners?
5. What is the purpose of a schedule of liquidation? What information does this statement convey to its readers?
6. According to the Uniform Partnership Act, what events should legally occur if a partner incurs a negative capital balance during the liquidation process?
7. How are safe capital balances computed when preliminary distributions of cash are to be made during a partnership liquidation?
8. What is the purpose of the marshaling of assets doctrine? What does this doctrine specifically state?
9. A partner is personally insolvent. Can this partner's creditors lay claim to partnership assets?
10. How do loans from partners affect the distribution of assets in a partnership liquidation? What alternatives can affect the handling of such loans?
11. What is the purpose of a proposed schedule of liquidation, and how is it developed?
12. How is a predistribution plan created for a partnership liquidation?

LIBRARY ASSIGNMENTS

1. Read the following as well as any other published articles on partnership liquidation:
    "Partnerships: If There's a Beginning . . . There's an End," *National Public Accountant,* April 1992.
    "Breaking Up Is Hard to Do," *Nation's Business,* July 1988.

"Reconcilable Differences," *Inc.*, April 1991.

"Cutting Losses When Partners Face a Breakup," *The Wall Street Journal*, May 21, 1991, p. B1.

"When a Group Is Better Off Splitting Up," *Medical Economics*, March 5, 1984.

Write a short report describing various situations that lead to the dissolution of a partnership.

2. Read the following as well as any other published articles on the bankruptcy of the partnership of Laventhol & Horwath:

"Laventhol Says It Plans to File for Chapter 11," *The Wall Street Journal*, November 20, 1990, p. A3.

"Laventhol Partners Face Long Process that Could End in Personal Bankruptcy," *The Wall Street Journal*, November 20, 1990, p. B5.

"Laventhol Bankruptcy Filing Indicates Liabilities May Be as Much as $2 Billion," *The Wall Street Journal*, November 23, 1990, p. A4.

Write a report describing the potential liabilities incurred by the members of a partnership.

PROBLEMS

1. If a partnership is liquidated, how is the final allocation of business assets made to the partners?
   a. Equally.
   b. According to the profit and loss ratio.
   c. According to the final capital account balances.
   d. According to the initial investment made by each of the partners.

2. Which of the following statements is true concerning the accounting that is made for a partnership going through liquidation?
   a. Gains and losses are reported directly as increases and decreases in the appropriate capital account.
   b. A separate income statement is created just to measure the profit or loss generated during liquidation.
   c. Since gains and losses rarely occur during liquidation, no special accounting treatment is warranted.
   d. Within a liquidation, all gains and losses are divided equally among the partners.

3. During a liquidation, a partner's capital account balance drops below zero. What *should* happen?
   a. The other partners should file a legal suit against the partner with the deficit balance.
   b. The partner with the highest capital balance should contribute sufficient assets to eliminate the deficit.
   c. The deficit balance should be removed from the accounting records with only the remaining partners sharing in future gains and losses.
   d. The partner with a deficit should contribute enough assets to offset the deficit balance.

4. What is the marshaling of assets?
   a. A listing of all partnership assets that is prepared whenever a formal accounting is to be made.
   b. A ranking of claims to be paid when a partner has become insolvent.
   c. The method by which a retiring partner's share of partnership is determined.
   d. The gathering of partnership assets just prior to the commencement of the liquidation process.

5. A local partnership is in the process of liquidating and is currently reporting the following capital balances:

Angela, capital (50% share of all profits and losses) $19,000
Woodrow, capital (30%) 18,000
Cassidy, capital (20%) . . . . (12,000)

Cassidy has indicated that the $12,000 deficit will be covered by a forthcoming contribution. However, the two remaining partners have asked to receive the $25,000 in cash that is presently available. How much of this money should each partner be given?

a. Angela, $13,000; Woodrow, $12,000.
b. Angela, $11,500; Woodrow, $13,500.
c. Angela, $12,000; Woodrow, $13,000.
d. Angela, $12,500; Woodrow, $12,500.

6. A local partnership is considering the possibility of liquidation because one of the partners (Bell) is insolvent. Capital balances at the current time are as follows. Profits and losses are divided on a 4:3:2:1 basis, respectively.

Bell, capital	$50,000
Hardy, capital	56,000
Dennard, capital	14,000
Suddath, capital	80,000

Bell's creditors have filed a $21,000 claim against the partnership's assets. The partnership currently holds assets reported at $300,000 and liabilities of $100,000. If the assets can be sold for $190,000, what is the minimum amount that Bell's creditors would receive?

a. –0–.
b. $2,000.
c. $2,800.
d. $6,000.

7. What is a predistribution plan?

a. A guideline for the cash distributions made to partners during a liquidation.
b. A list of the procedures to be performed during a liquidation.
c. A determination of the final cash distribution to be made to the partners on the settlement date.
d. A detailed list of the transactions that will transpire in the reorganization of a partnership.

8. A partnership has the following balance sheet just before final liquidation is to begin:

Cash	$ 26,000	Liabilities	$ 50,000
Inventory	31,000	Art, capital (40% of	
Other assets	62,000	profits and losses)	18,000
		Raymond, capital (30%)	25,000
		Darby, capital (30%)	26,000
Total	$119,000	Total	$119,000

Liquidation expenses are estimated to be $12,000. The other assets are sold for $40,000. What distribution can be made to the partners?

a. –0– to Art, $1,500 to Raymond, $2,500 to Darby.
b. $1,333 to Art, $1,333 to Raymond, $1,334 to Darby.
c. –0– to Art, $1,200 to Raymond, $2,800 to Darby.
d. $600 to Art, $1,200 to Raymond, $2,200 to Darby.

9. A partnership has the following capital balances: A (20% of profits and losses) = $100,000; B (30% of profits and losses) = $120,000; C (50% of profits and losses) = $180,000. If the partnership is to be liquidated and $30,000 becomes immediately available, who gets that money?

a. $6,000 to A, $9,000 to B, $15,000 to C.
b. $22,000 to A, $3,000 to B, $5,000 to C.
c. $22,000 to A, $8,000 to B, –0– to C.
d. $24,000 to A, $6,000 to B, –0– to C.

10. A partnership is currently holding $400,000 in assets and $234,000 in liabilities. The partnership is to be liquidated and $20,000 is the best estimation of the expenses that will be incurred during this process. The four partners share profits and losses on a 4:3:1:2 basis, respectively. Capital balances at the start of the liquidation are as follows:

Kevin, capital	$59,000
Michael, capital	39,000
Brendan, capital	34,000
Jonathan, capital	34,000

The partners realize that Brendan will be the first partner to start receiving cash. How much cash will Brendan receive before any of the other partners collect any cash?
- a. $12,250.
- b. $14,750.
- c. $17,000.
- d. $19,500.

11. Carney, Pierce, Menton, and Hoehn are partners who share profits and losses on a 4:3:2:1 basis, respectively. They are presently beginning to liquidate the business. At the start of this process, capital balances are as follows:

Carney, capital	$60,000
Pierce, capital	27,000
Menton, capital	43,000
Hoehn, capital	20,000

Which of the following statements is true?
- a. The first available $2,000 will go to Hoehn.
- b. Carney will be the last partner to receive any available cash.
- c. The first available $3,000 will go to Menton.
- d. Carney will collect a portion of any available cash prior to Hoehn receiving money.

12. A partnership has gone through liquidation and now reports the following account balances:

Cash	$16,000
Loan from Jones	3,000
Wayman, capital	(2,000) (deficit)
Jones, capital	(5,000) (deficit)
Fuller, capital	13,000
Rogers, capital	7,000

Profits and losses are allocated on the following basis: Wayman, 30 percent; Jones, 20 percent; Fuller, 30 percent; and Rogers, 20 percent. Which of the following events should occur now?
- a. Jones should receive $3,000 cash because of the loan balance.
- b. Fuller should receive $11,800 and Rogers $6,200.
- c. Fuller should receive $10,600 and Rogers $5,400.
- d. Jones should receive $3,000, Fuller $8,800, and Rogers $4,200.

13. A partnership has the following account balances: Cash, $70,000; Other Assets, $540,000; Liabilities, $260,000; Nixon (50% of profits and losses), $170,000; Cleveland (30%), $110,000; Pierce (20%), $70,000. The company liquidates and $8,000 becomes available to the partners. Who gets the $8,000?

14. A local partnership has only two assets (cash of $10,000 and land with a cost of $35,000). All liabilities have been paid and the following capital balances are currently being recorded. The partners share profits and losses on a 4:3:3 basis, respectively. All partners are insolvent.

Brown, capital	$25,000
Fish, capital	15,000
Stone, capital	5,000

Required
- a. If the land is sold for $25,000, how much cash does each of the partners receive in a final settlement?
- b. If the land is sold for $15,000, how much cash does each of the partners receive in a final settlement?
- c. If the land is sold for $5,000, how much cash does each of the partners receive in a final settlement?

b4
class

15. A local dental partnership has been liquidated and the final capital balances are as follows:

Atkinson, capital (40% of all profits and losses)	$60,000
Kaporale, capital (30%)	20,000
Dennsmore, capital (20%)	(30,000)
Rasputin, capital (10%)	(50,000)

If Rasputin contributes additional cash to partnership of $20,000, what should happen to that money?

16. A partnership currently holds three assets: cash, $10,000 book value; land, $35,000; and a building, $50,000. The partners anticipate that expenses required to liquidate their partnership will amount to $5,000. Capital balances are as follows:

Ace, capital	$25,000
Ball, capital	28,000
Eaton, capital	20,000
Lake, capital	22,000

The partners share profits and losses as follows: Ace (30%), Ball (30%), Eaton (20%), and Lake (20%). If a preliminary distribution of cash is to be made, how much will each of these partners receive?

B4
class

17. The following condensed balance sheet is for the partnership of Hardwick, Saunders, and Ferris, who share profits and losses in the ratio of 4:3:3 respectively:

Acct Rec

Cash	$ 90,000	Accounts payable	$210,000
Other assets	820,000	Ferris, loan *Acct pay*	40,000
Hardwick, loan	30,000	Hardwick, capital	300,000
		Saunders, capital	200,000
		Ferris, capital	190,000
		Total liabilities and	
Total assets	$940,000	capital	$940,000

492,000 Loss to absorb assume

The partners decide to liquidate the partnership. Forty percent of the other assets are sold for $200,000. Prepare a proposed schedule of liquidation.

18. The following condensed balance sheet is for the partnership of Miller, Tyson, and Watson, who share profits and losses in the ratio of 6:2:2 respectively:

Cash	$ 40,000	Liabilities	$ 70,000
Other assets	140,000	Miller, capital	50,000
		Tyson, capital	50,000
		Watson, capital	10,000
		Total liabilities and	
Total assets	$180,000	capital	$180,000

For how much money do the other assets have to be sold so that each partner receives some amount of cash in a liquidation?

19. A partnership's balance sheet is as follows:

Cash	$ 60,000	Liabilities	$ 50,000
Noncash assets	120,000	Babb, capital	60,000
		Whitaker, capital	20,000
		Edwards, capital	50,000
		Total liabilities and	
Total assets	$180,000	capital	$180,000

Babb, Whitaker, and Edwards share profits and losses in the ratio of 4:2:4, respectively. This business is to be terminated and the partners estimate that $8,000 in liquidation expenses will be incurred. How should the $2,000 in safe cash that is presently held be disbursed?

20. A partnership has liquidated all assets but still reports the following account balances:

Loan from White	$ 6,000
Black, capital	3,000
White, capital	(9,000) (deficit)
Green, capital	(3,000) (deficit)
Brown, capital	15,000
Blue, capital	(12,000) (deficit)

The partners split profits and losses as follows: Black, 30 percent; White, 30 percent; Green, 10 percent; Brown, 20 percent; and Blue, 10 percent.

Assuming that all partners are personally insolvent except for Green and Brown, how much cash must Green now contribute to this partnership?

21. The following balance sheet is for a local partnership in which the partners have become very unhappy with each other. To avoid further conflict, they have decided to cease operations and sell all assets. Using this data, answer the following questions. Each question should be viewed as an independent situation.

Cash	$ 40,000	Liabilities	$ 30,000
Land	130,000	Adams, capital	80,000
Building	120,000	Baker, capital	30,000
		Carvil, capital	60,000
		Dobbs, capital	90,000
		Total liabilities and	
Total assets	$290,000	capital	$290,000

Required

a. The partnership is to be liquidated and the $10,000 cash that exceeds the partnership liabilities is to be disbursed immediately. If profits and losses are allocated on a 2:3:3:2 basis, respectively, how will the $10,000 be divided?

b. The partnership is to be liquidated and the $10,000 cash that exceeds the partnership liabilities is to be disbursed immediately. If profits and losses are allocated on a 2:2:3:3 basis, respectively, how will the $10,000 be divided?

c. The partnership is to be liquidated. The building is immediately sold for $70,000 to give total cash of $110,000. The liabilities are then paid leaving a cash balance of $80,000. This cash is to be distributed to the partners. How much of this money will each partner get if profits and losses are allocated on a 1:3:3:3 basis, respectively?

d. The partnership is to be liquidated. Assume that profits and losses are allocated on a 1:3:4:2 basis, respectively. How much money must be received from selling the land and building to assure that Carvil receives a portion?

22. The partnership of Larson, Norris, Spencer, and Harrison has decided to terminate operations and liquidate all business property. During this process, the partners expect to incur $8,000 in liquidation expenses. All of the partners are currently solvent.

The balance sheet reported by this partnership at the time that the liquidation commenced follows. The percentages indicate the allocation of profits and losses to each of the four partners.

Cash	$ 28,250	Liabilities	$ 47,000
Accounts receivable	44,000	Larson, capital (20%)	15,000
Inventory	39,000	Norris, capital (30%)	60,000
Land and buildings	23,000	Spencer, capital (20%)	75,000
Equipment	104,000	Harrison, capital (30%)	41,250
		Total liabilities and	
Total assets	$238,250	capital	$238,250

Required

Based on the information that has been provided, prepare a predistribution plan for the liquidation of this partnership.

23. The following partnership is being liquidated beginning on July 13, 1998:

Cash....................	$ 36,000	Liabilities	$ 50,000
Noncash assets	174,000	Able, loan	10,000
		Able, capital (20%)	40,000
		Moon, capital (30%)........	60,000
		Yerkl, capital (50%)	50,000

Required

a. Liquidation expenses are estimated to be $12,000. Prepare a predistribution schedule to guide the distribution of cash.

b. Assume assets costing $28,000 are sold for $40,000. How is the available cash to be divided?

24. A local partnership is to be liquidated. Commissions and other liquidation expenses are expected to total $19,000. The business's balance sheet prior to the commencement of liquidation is as follows:

Cash....................	$ 27,000	Liabilities	$ 40,000
Noncash assets	254,000	Simpson, capital (20%)......	18,000
		Hart, capital (40%).........	40,000
		Bobb, capital (20%)	48,000
		Reidl, capital (20%)	135,000
		Total liabilities and	
Total Assets	$281,000	capital	$281,000

Prepare a predistribution schedule for this partnership.

25. The following information concerns two different partnerships. These problems should be viewed as independent situations.

Part A

The partnership of Ross, Milburn, and Thomas has the following account balances:

Cash....................	$ 36,000	Liabilities	$17,000
Noncash assets	100,000	Ross, capital	69,000
		Milburn, capital	(8,000) (deficit)
		Thomas, capital	58,000

This partnership is in the process of being liquidated. Ross and Milburn are each entitled to 40 percent of all profits and losses with the remaining 20 percent to Thomas.

a. What is the maximum amount that Milburn might have to contribute to this partnership because of the deficit capital balance?

b. How should the $19,000 cash that is presently available in excess of liabilities be distributed?

c. If the noncash assets are sold for a total of $41,000, what is the minimum amount of cash that could be received by Thomas?

Part B

The partnership of Sampson, Klingon, Carton, and Romulan is being liquidated and currently holds cash of $9,000 but no other assets. Liabilities amount to $24,000. The capital balances are as follows:

Sampson	$ 9,000
Klingon	(17,000)
Carton	5,000
Romulan	(12,000)

Profits and losses are allocated on the following basis: Sampson, 40 percent, Klingon, 20 percent, Carton, 30 percent, and Romulan, 10 percent.

a. If both Klingon and Romulan are personally insolvent, how much money does Carton have to contribute to this partnership?

b. If only Romulan is personally insolvent, how much money does Klingon have to contribute? How will these funds be disbursed?

c. If only Klingon is personally insolvent, how much money should Sampson receive from the liquidation?

26. March, April, and May have been in partnership for a number of years. Recently, the partners have each become personally insolvent and, thus, have decided to liquidate the business in hopes of remedying their personal financial problems. The partners allocate all profits and losses on a 2:3:1 basis, respectively. As of September 1, 1998, the partnership balance sheet is as follows:

Cash	$ 11,000	Liabilities	$ 61,000	
Accounts receivable	84,000	March, capital	25,000	
Inventory	74,000	April, capital	75,000	
Land, building, and equipment		May, capital	46,000	
(net)	38,000			
		Total liabilities and		
Total assets	$207,000	capital	$207,000	

Prepare journal entries for the following transactions:

- Sold all of the inventory for $56,000 cash.
- Paid $7,500 in liquidation expenses.
- Paid $40,000 of the partnership's liabilities.
- Collected $45,000 of the accounts receivable.
- Safe cash balances are distributed; no further liquidation expenses are anticipated by the partners.
- The remaining accounts receivable are sold for 30 percent of face value.
- The land, building, and equipment are sold for $17,000.
- All remaining liabilities of the partnership are paid.
- The cash held by the business is distributed to the partners.

27. The partnership of W, X, Y, and Z has the following balance sheet:

Cash	$ 30,000	Liabilities	$ 42,000
Other assets	220,000	W, capital (50% of profits	
		and losses)	60,000
		X, capital (30%)	78,000
		Y, capital (10%)	40,000
		Z, capital (10%)	30,000

Z is personally insolvent and one of his creditors is considering suing the partnership for the $5,000 that is currently due. The creditor realizes that liquidation may result from this litigation and does not wish to force such an extreme action unless reasonably assured of getting the money that is due. If the other assets are sold, how much money must be received by the partnership to ensure that $5,000 would become available from Z's portion of the business? Liquidation expenses are expected to be $15,000.

28. On January 1, 1998, the partners of Van, Bakel, and Cox (who share profits and losses in the ratio of 5:3:2, respectively) decide to liquidate their partnership. The trial balance at this date is as follows:

	Debit	Credit
Cash	$ 18,000	
Accounts receivable	66,000	
Inventory	52,000	
Machinery and equipment, net	189,000	
Van, loan	30,000	
Accounts payable		$ 53,000
Bakel, loan		20,000
Van, capital		118,000
Bakel, capital		90,000
Cox, capital		74,000
Totals	$355,000	$355,000

The partners plan a program of piecemeal conversion of the business's assets to minimize liquidation losses. All available cash, less an amount retained to provide for future expenses, is to be distributed to the partners at the end of each month. A summary of the liquidation transactions is as follows:

1998

January ■ $51,000 is collected on the accounts receivable; the balance is deemed *actual*
uncollectible.
■ $38,000 is received for the entire inventory. *actual*
■ $2,000 in liquidation expenses are paid. *actual*
■ $50,000 is paid to the outside creditors, after offsetting a $3,000 credit *actual*
memorandum received by the partnership on January 11, 1998.
potential ■ $10,000 cash is retained in the business at the end of January to cover any
unrecorded liabilities and anticipated expenses. The remainder is distributed
to the partners.

February ■ $3,000 in liquidation expenses are paid. *actual*
■ $6,000 cash is retained in the business at the end of the month to cover
unrecorded liabilities and anticipated expenses. *potential*

March ■ $146,000 is received on the sale of all machinery and equipment.
actual ■ $5,000 in final liquidation expenses are paid.
■ No cash is retained in the business.

Required

Prepare a schedule to compute the safe installment payments made to the partners at the end
of each of these three months.

(AICPA adapted)

29. Following are a series of independent cases. In each situation, indicate the cash
distribution to be made at the end of the liquidation process. *Unless otherwise stated,
assume that all solvent partners will reimburse the partnership for their deficit capital
balances.*

Part A

The following accounts are presently being reported by the Simon, Haynes, and Jackson
partnership:

Cash	$30,000
Liabilities	22,000
Haynes, loan	10,000
Simon, capital (40%)	16,000
Haynes, capital (20%)	(6,000)
Jackson, capital (40%)	(12,000)

Jackson is personally insolvent and can contribute only an additional $3,000 to the
partnership. Simon is also insolvent and has no available funds.

Part B

Hough, Luck, and Cummings operate a local accounting firm as a partnership. After
working together for several years, they have decided to liquidate the partnership's
property. The partners have prepared the following balance sheet:

Cash	$ 20,000	Liabilities	$ 40,000
Hough, loan	8,000	Luck, loan	10,000
Noncash assets	162,000	Hough, capital (50%)	90,000
		Luck, capital (40%)	30,000
		Cummings, capital (10%)	20,000
		Total liabilities and	
Total assets	$190,000	capital	$190,000

The noncash assets are sold for $80,000, with $21,000 of this amount being used to
pay liquidation expenses. All three of these partners are personally insolvent.

Part C

Use the same information as in part B, except assume that the profits and losses are split
2:4:4 to Hough, Luck, and Cummings, respectively, and that liquidation expenses are
only $6,000.

Part D

Following the liquidation of all noncash assets, the partnership of Redmond, Ledbetter, Watson, and Sandridge has the following account balances:

Liabilities	$28,000
Redmond, loan	5,000
Redmond, capital (20%)	(21,000)
Ledbetter, capital (10%)	(30,000)
Watson, capital (30%)	3,000
Sandridge, capital (40%)	15,000

Redmond is personally insolvent.

30. The partnership of Frick, Wilson, and Clarke has elected to cease all operations and liquidate its business property. A balance sheet drawn up at this time shows the following account balances:

Cash....................	$ 48,000	Liabilities	$ 35,000
Noncash assets	177,000	Frick, capital (60%)	101,000
		Wilson, capital (20%)	28,000
		Clarke, capital (20%)	61,000
		Total liabilities and	
Total assets	$225,000	capital	$225,000

The following transactions occur in liquidating this business:

- Safe capital balances are immediately distributed to the partners. Liquidation expenses of $9,000 are estimated as a basis for this computation.
- Noncash assets with a book value of $80,000 are sold for $48,000.
- All liabilities are paid.
- Safe capital balances are again distributed.
- Remaining noncash assets are sold for $44,000.
- Liquidation expenses of $7,000 are paid.
- Remaining cash is distributed to the partners and the financial records of the business permanently closed.

Required

Produce a final schedule of liquidation for this partnership.

31. **Part A**

The partnership of Wingler, Norris, Rodgers, and Guthrie was formed several years ago as a local architectural firm. Several of the partners have recently undergone personal financial problems and decided to terminate operations and liquidate the business. The following balance sheet is drawn up as a guideline for this process:

Cash....................	$ 15,000	Liabilities	$ 74,000
Accounts receivable	82,000	Rodgers, loan	35,000
Inventory	101,000	Wingler, capital (30%)	120,000
Land....................	85,000	Norris, capital (10%)	88,000
Building and equipment (net)	168,000	Rodgers, capital (20%)	74,000
		Guthrie, capital (40%)	60,000
		Total liabilities and	
Total assets	$451,000	capital	$451,000

At the time the liquidation commences, expenses of $16,000 are anticipated as being necessary to dispose of all property.

Required

Prepare a predistribution plan for this partnership.

Part B

The following transactions transpire during the liquidation of the Wingler, Norris, Rodgers, and Guthrie partnership:

- Of the total accounts receivable, 80 percent are collected with the rest judged as uncollectible.

- The land, building, and equipment are sold for $150,000.
- Safe capital distributions are made.
- Guthrie becomes personally insolvent. No further contributions will be forthcoming from this partner.
- All liabilities are paid.
- All inventory is sold for $71,000.
- Safe capital distributions are again made.
- Liquidation expenses of $11,000 are paid.
- Final cash disbursements are made to the partners based on the assumption that all partners other than Guthrie are personally solvent.

Required

Prepare journal entries to record these liquidation transactions.

Accounting for State and Local Governments (Part One)

QUESTIONS TO CONSIDER

- Why is the accounting for state and local governments significantly different than that used by profit-oriented businesses?

- Who are the users of the financial data produced by state and local government units, and why is such a wide variety of informational needs encountered?

- What is fund accounting, and why is it utilized by state and local governments?

- Why is budgetary control considered so important in a government? In what ways is budgetary control established in the accounting system?

- How has the Governmental Accounting Standards Board affected the financial reporting of state and local governments?

- Why are encumbrances recorded by a government?

- When are revenues and expenditures recognized by a government?

- The June 30, 1995, balance sheet produced for the city of Los Angeles, California, disclosed a reserve for encumbrances totaling approximately $490 million.

- At that same date, the city of Toccoa, Georgia, with a population of only 8,000, issued a statement of revenues, expenditures, and changes in fund balance composed of four separate columns and an accompanying balance sheet with eight columns.

- In 1991, Washington, D.C., eliminated an accumulated General Fund deficit of approximately $330 million by issuing General Fund Recovery Bonds.

The accounting curriculum offered at many colleges primarily provides students with an understanding of the financial reporting procedures appropriate for profit-oriented enterprises. In most accounting courses, virtually every issue is analyzed in terms of the potential impact on net income and earnings per share. Textbooks contribute to this emphasis by examining numerous authoritative pronouncements that establish rigid guidelines for the recognition of revenues and expenses. Consequently, the calculation of the bottom-line figure may appear to be the ultimate objective of all accounting.

For this reason, students are frequently surprised to discover that the basic structure of financial accounting is altered dramatically when the profit motive is removed. Many accounting principles applied by city governments vary from the principles used by Exxon Corporation. The existence of different generally accepted accounting principles is especially significant because one-third of the economic activity in the United States is conducted by nonbusiness organizations.[1] Thus, despite the apparently obscured role of governments and not-for-profit organizations within many accounting courses, coverage is no less important than that provided for profit-oriented businesses.

As indicated by these data for Los Angeles, Toccoa, and Washington, the reporting process for state and local governments exhibits many unique characteristics. A governmental balance sheet, as an example, usually displays numerous columns while both actual and budgetary balances are presented for many of the government's revenues and expenditures. Even the accounting terminology may appear initially to resemble a foreign language. In reporting on state and local governments, such alien terms as *fund accounting, encumbrances, nonexpendable trust funds, special revenue funds,* and *appropriations* are all quite commonplace.

Despite many special features, the accounting process applicable to state and local governments is no different in one important respect from any other type of accounting: *the overall objective is to satisfy the needs of financial statement users.* The procedures and terminology deviate from for-profit reporting primarily because the informational requirements of these users are different. Thus, the composition of published financial statements has evolved to conform to these perceived needs.

Historically, the development of governmental accounting standards has proceeded more slowly than that of profit-oriented financial reporting. However, the recent work of the Governmental Accounting Standards Board has pushed government accounting into a highly evolutionary stage. Significant changes in both accounting and reporting have been mandated in recent years with other steps proposed.

Consequently, much discussion continues as to whether user needs are being met by current financial reporting. If not, what changes are needed? Questions are constantly raised and discussed about the propriety of many common practices found in governmental accounting as well as proposed improvements. Thus, controversy still surrounds many elements of the reporting process demonstrated herein.

Chapters 16 and 17 provide an introduction to the accounting for state and local governments (cities, towns, school districts, counties, states, and the like). However, for many aspects of this coverage, current standards as well as proposals for future financial reporting are presented.

---

[1]Robert N. Anthony, ''Making Sense of Nonbusiness Accounting,'' *Harvard Business Review,* May–June 1980, p. 84.

INTRODUCTION TO THE ACCOUNTING FOR STATE AND LOCAL GOVERNMENTS

In this country, literally thousands of state and local government reporting entities touch the lives of the citizenry on a daily basis. Income and sales taxes are collected, property taxes are assessed, schools are operated, fire departments are maintained, garbage is collected, and roads are paved. Actions of one or more governments affect every individual. Accounting for a government is not merely a matching of expenses with revenues so that net income can be determined. For many governments, deficit spending has become a troubling practice. The allocation of resources between such worthy causes as education, police, welfare, and the environment creates heated debate. Some services have had to be curtailed. In recent times, citizens have come to realize that additional oversight is needed so that governments live within their means while still making the best use of available funding.

Over the years, a number of attempts have been made to establish generally accepted accounting principles for state and local governments. The American Institute of Certified Public Accountants (AICPA) and the National Council on Governmental Accounting (NCGA) made some significant strides during previous decades in establishing sound accounting principles.[2] In June of 1984, the Governmental Accounting Standards Board (GASB) became the public sector counterpart of the Financial Accounting Standards Board. The GASB holds the primary responsibility in the United States for setting authoritative accounting standards for state and local government units.

In the same manner as the Financial Accounting Standards Board, the GASB is an independent body functioning under the oversight of the Financial Accounting Foundation. Thus, a formal mechanism is in place to continue the development of governmental accounting. Since its creation, the GASB has produced a number of governmental accounting standards as well as technical bulletins, interpretations, and a concepts statement. In 1997, GASB produced a codification of authoritative pronouncements as a guideline for reporting purposes. In 1997 the GASB proposed changes in governmental reporting that, if adopted, will dramatically change the way governments measure and report their operations.

Governmental Accounting—User Needs

The unique aspects of governmental accounting are a direct result of the perceived needs of financial statement users. Identification of these informational requirements is, therefore, a logical first step in the study of the accounting principles applied by state and local governments. Specific procedures utilized in the reporting process can be understood best as an outgrowth of these needs. Often, though, user expectations are complex and even contradictory. The taxpayer, the government employee, the bondholder, and the public official may each be seeking distinctly different types of financial information about a governmental unit.

> My own reflection on the subject leads me to the conviction that appropriate and adequate accounting for state and local governmental units involves a far more complex set of interrela-

[2] The NCGA was a quasi-independent agency of the Government Finance Officers Association. The NCGA held authority for state and local government accounting from 1973 through 1984. The National Committee on Municipal Accounting had this responsibility from 1934 until 1941 while the National Committee on Governmental Accounting established government accounting principles from 1949 through 1954 and again from 1967 until 1973. During several periods, no group held responsibility for the development of governmental accounting. For an overview of the history of governmental accounting standards and the creation of the GASB, see "The Evolution of Governmental Accounting Standard Setting," by David R. Bean published in the December 1984 issue of *Governmental Finance*.

tionships, to be reported to a more diverse set of users with a greater variety of interests and needs, than exists in business accounting and reporting.[3]

In its *Concepts Statement No. 1,* "Objectives of Financial Reporting," the GASB recognized this same problem by identifying three groups of primary users of external state and local governmental financial reports: the citizenry, legislative and oversight bodies, and creditors and investors. The needs and interests of each of these groups were then described:

Citizenry—Want to evaluate the likelihood of tax or service fee increases, to determine the sources and uses of resources, to forecast revenues in order to influence spending decisions, to ensure that resources were used in accordance with appropriations, to assess financial condition, and to compare budgeted to actual results.

Legislative and oversight bodies—Want to assess the overall financial condition when developing budgets and program recommendations, to monitor operating results to assure compliance with mandates, to determine the reasonableness of fees and the need for tax changes, and to ascertain the ability to finance new programs and capital needs.

Investors and creditors—Want to know the amount of available and likely future financial resources, to measure the debt position and the ability to service that debt, and to review operating results and cash flow data.[4]

Thus, a significant obstacle is encountered in the quest for fair governmental reporting: user needs are so broad that no one set of financial statements or accounting principles can possibly satisfy all expectations. How can voters, bondholders, city officials, and the other users of the financial statements provided by state and local governments all receive the information that is needed? The question of satisfying a wide variety of user needs is a constant theme in discussions of state and local government accounting.

Accountability and Governmental Accounting

Despite the variety of users, one aspect of governmental reporting has remained constant over the years: the goal of making the government accountable to the public. Because of the essential role of democracy within American society, governmental accounting principles always have attempted to provide a vehicle for evaluating the actions of the government. Citizens should be aware of the means used by officials to raise money and the allocations made of these scarce resources. Voters must evaluate the wisdom, as well as the honesty, of the members of government. Since most voters are also taxpayers, they naturally exhibit special interest in the results obtained from their involuntary contributions, such as taxes. *Because elected and appointed officials hold authority over the public's money, governmental reporting has traditionally stressed this stewardship responsibility.*

Accountability is the cornerstone of all financial reporting in government. . . . Accountability requires governments to answer to the citizenry—to justify the raising of public resources and the purposes for which they are used. Governmental accountability is based on the belief that the citizenry has a "right to know," a right to receive openly declared facts that may lead to public debate by the citizens and their elected representatives.[5]

For this reason, primary accounting emphasis has traditionally been directed toward measuring and identifying the public funds generated and expended by each of a government's diverse activities. To meet this objective, the financial statements attempt to answer three questions:

---

[3]Robert K. Mautz, "Financial Reporting: Should Government Emulate Business?" *Journal of Accountancy,* August 1981, p. 53.

[4]*GASB Concepts Statement No. 1,* "Objectives of Financial Reporting," May 1987, para. 33–37.

[5]*GASB Concepts Statement No. 1,* para. 56.

- Where did the financial resources come from?
- Where did the financial resources go?
- What amount of financial resources is presently held?

Obviously, stressing government accountability is an approach to accounting that is not capable of meeting all user needs; thus, many conventional reporting objectives long have been ignored. As just one example, little information has historically been required of a state or local government that would allow an assessment of projected cash flows. Not surprisingly, investors and creditors have frequently been sharp critics of governmental accounting. "When cities get into financial trouble, few citizens know about it until the day the interest can't be met or the teachers paid. . . . Had the books been kept like any decent corporation's that could never have happened."[6]

Although accountability is a central concern, other user needs must be addressed. The debate will continue for many years concerning the future evolution of accounting principles for state and local government units. However, regardless of the actions of the GASB or other bodies, accountability will undoubtedly remain a primary priority for the financial reports issued by state and local government units. The need to oversee and control elected officials simply must play a central role in the development of government accounting standards.

Control of Public Funds

The attempt to establish financial control over public funds goes beyond the mere monitoring of financial resources. Over the years, a set of procedures has been created to report the financial affairs of the vast array of functions carried out by state and local government units. This process is especially important since public officials often hold authority over sums of money that can be staggering in size. The city of Los Angeles, California, for example, reported revenues of more than $8 billion for the year ending June 30, 1995. Such funds are accumulated through charges and taxes. Although laws require the appropriate utilization of such monies, compliance is not always easy for the average citizen to ascertain.

Stressing accountability and the stewardship role played by government officials is in diametric contrast to a profit-oriented business where stockholders contribute capital voluntarily and then elect a board of directors to monitor operating and financial activities. Board members along with stockholders and other interested parties have access to accounting data, such as net income, earnings per share, and return on investment, which allows an assessment to be made of management's utilization of the resources provided. In a government, though, oversight and computed measures of success are more difficult to achieve. For example, neither net income nor earnings per share can measure the performance of a fire department.

Because of the citizens' desire to monitor elected officials, governmental accounting has developed its own specialized control procedures. Budgets, for example, must be legally adopted by a government's legislative body to indicate anticipated revenues and approved expenditures. To highlight these projections, many of the budget figures are physically entered into the government's accounting records and then presented as a component of the annual financial statements. In this manner, comparisons can be drawn between the expected activity for each specific function and actual revenue and expenditure figures.

Additional control over government spending is achieved by recording purchase commitments (commonly referred to as *encumbrances*). The acquisition of a fax machine, for example, is formally journalized as an encumbrance at the time the item

---

[6]Richard Greene, "You Can't Fight City Hall—If You Can't Understand It," *Forbes*, March 3, 1980, p. 92.

is ordered rather than when the title transfers. By measuring both expended as well as committed funds, the entity is less likely to overspend available resources. Unfortunately, neither budgetary entries nor encumbrances have proven to be totally successful in eliminating the possibility of excessive government spending.

Reporting Diverse Governmental Activities—Fund Accounting

Beyond the goal of establishing accountability and fiscal control, the accountant also faces the challenge of reporting the diverse array of activities within most government units. Because no common profit motive exists to tie all of these functions and services together, traditional consolidated balances have been omitted. Combining operating results from the city zoo, the fire department, the motor pool, the water system, and the like would provide figures of questionable utility.[7] Historically, an underlying assumption of government accounting is that most statement users prefer information segregated by function so that each activity can be assessed individually. Hence, the accounting process is constructed to accumulate separate data to describe the financial affairs of every activity (library, school system, police department, road construction, etc.). Then revenues, expenditures, financial resources, and the like can be reported for each specific function.

The diversity inherent in most state or local government units mandates that a single set of accounting records simply is not sufficient to monitor all activities. Therefore, financial transactions and adjustments are recorded in quasi-independent bookkeeping systems referred to as funds. *Each fund is a self-balancing set of accounts used to record data generated by an identifiable government function. All of these funds taken together make up the government's financial reporting system.* Accounting for an entity as a group of funds is probably the single most unique element of governmental accounting.

> The diverse nature of governmental operations and the necessity of assuring legal compliance preclude recording and summarizing all governmental financial transactions and balances in a single accounting entity. Unlike a private business, which is accounted for as a single entity, a governmental unit is accounted for through several separate fund and account group entities, each accounting for designated assets, liabilities, and equity or other balances.[8]

Although a single list of separately reportable functions of a state or local government is not possible, the following commonly are encountered:

Public safety	Judicial system
Highway maintenance	Debt repayment
Sanitation	Bridge construction
Health	Water and sewer system
Welfare	Municipal swimming pool
Culture and recreation	Data processing center
Education	Endowment funds
Parks	Employee pensions

[7]Failure to consolidate the financial statements of a state or government unit often has been criticized, especially by individuals seeking statements more in line with business-oriented accounting. "When those accustomed to business financial statements try to read the financial statements of a nonbusiness organization, however, they find themselves in a different world. Instead of a report on the entity as a whole, they find fragmented data, presented in columns on a single statement, or in a succession of separate statements, each of which deals with a piece of the organization." (Robert N. Anthony, "Making Sense of Nonbusiness Accounting," *Harvard Business Review,* May–June 1980, p. 83.)

[8]*Codification of Governmental Accounting and Financial Reporting Standards* (Norwalk, Conn.: Governmental Accounting Standards Board, 1992), sec. 1300.101.

The actual number of funds in use depends on the extent of services being offered by the government and the grouping of related activities. For example, separate funds may be set up for a high school and its athletic programs or all of these activities may be combined into a single fund.

> The general rule is to establish the minimum number of separate funds consistent with legal specifications and operational requirements. . . . Using too many funds causes inflexibility and undue complexity . . . and is best avoided in the interest of efficient and economical financial administration.[9]

If a government had to account only for service activities such as police and fire protection, reporting problems could be minimized. Although establishing separate funds would still be necessary for the individual functions, accounting procedures could be similar in each case, if not identical. Within these various funds, the emphasis would be placed on control and accountability through the reporting of revenues and expenditures relating to the specified service.

However, many government operations (such as municipal golf courses, toll roads, convention centers, and airports) attempt to generate revenues rather than simply serve the populace. Because this goal parallels that held by business-type enterprises, traditional government accounting procedures are not appropriate to these functions. In effect, a municipality cannot report the activities of a police department and a golf course by using the same accounting principles; the objectives are simply too diverse.

To add to the accountant's difficulty, a third distinct type of government function (beyond service activities and revenue generating enterprises) also can be identified. State and local governments frequently serve in a trustee capacity, holding money or other assets to be used for a particular purpose. Employee pension funds, for example, often are maintained so that government workers can receive benefits after their retirement.

A similar trustee role is served if the government administers any property that has been received through donation. In some instances, the government intends to do no more than ensure an appropriate utilization of the gift. Therefore, the receipt and its ultimate use are accounted for jointly as a service activity. Money given to a school district to buy equipment falls into this category. At other times, though, the trustee capacity takes on a distinct business appearance. Assets (such as rental property, for example) can be donated to a government with the stipulation that only subsequently earned income is to be spent. To satisfy this provision, income measurement becomes a primary objective in fulfilling the government's fiduciary role.

Fund Accounting Classifications

Because of the large number of activities carried out by many government units, designing distinct accounting procedures for each fund is neither feasible nor desirable. Instead, to facilitate the reporting process, a grouping system has been devised with all funds being placed into one of three broad classifications:

- *Governmental funds*—account for "those activities of a government that are carried out primarily to provide services to citizens and that are financed primarily through taxes and intergovernmental revenues."[10] A police department would be reported within the governmental funds.
- *Proprietary funds*—account for "a government's ongoing organizations and activities that are similar to those often found in the private sector."[11] This

---

[9]GASB Cod. sec. 1100.108.

[10]*GASB Statement No. 11*, par. 3h.

[11]GASB Cod. sec. 1300.102b.

fund type normally encompasses operations where a user charge is assessed. A toll road would be reported within the proprietary funds.

■ *Fiduciary funds*—account for monies held by the government in a trustee capacity. Assets held for a pension plan would be reported within the fiduciary funds.

A fourth category referred to as *account groups* also exists in connection with the governmental funds to provide a listing of both general fixed assets and long-term debts. These account groups provide control and accountability over these assets and liabilities. Since resources are neither received nor expended by the account groups, they are not viewed as funds in the definitional sense. However, these two groups play an integral role in the government's reporting system.

Governmental Funds   In most state or municipal accounting systems, the governmental funds tend to dominate because a service orientation usually prevails. For reporting purposes, individual records are maintained for every distinct function: public safety, libraries, construction of a town hall, and so on. In each of these governmental funds, financial resources are accumulated and expended to achieve one or more desired public goals.

To provide better reported information and control as well as to allow for the development of more precise accounting principles, the governmental funds are subdivided into four categories: the General Fund, Special Revenue Funds, Capital Projects Funds, and Debt Service Funds. Although the basic accounting objectives are the same for each of these fund types, actual procedures may vary depending on the nature of the service. Thus, this classification system allows specific accounting guidelines to be directed toward each fund type while providing an overall structure for financial reporting purposes.

The General Fund   The GASB's definition of the General Fund appears to be somewhat understated: "to account for all financial resources except those required to be accounted for in another fund."[12] This description seems to imply that the General Fund records only miscellaneous revenues and expenditures when, in actuality, this fund type accounts for many of a government's most important services. Whereas the other governmental funds report specific events or projects, the General Fund records a broad range of ongoing activities. For example, the financial statements for the city of Atlanta, Georgia, disclose seven major areas of current expenditures within the General Fund: general government, police, fire, corrections, public works, parks and recreation, and employee benefits. Expenditures recorded in the General Fund of this city made up 60 percent of the total for all of the governmental funds during 1994.

Special Revenue Funds   Special revenue funds account for revenues that have been legally restricted as to expenditure. These financial resources must be spent in a specified fashion. Saint Paul, Minnesota, for example, reported approximately $38 million of revenues within special revenue funds during the 1995 fiscal year. This money was generated from sources as diverse as cable television franchising fees, rent received from the use of Municipal Stadium, administration fees for charitable gambling, grants used for police training, and the sale of zoo animals. The Special Revenue Funds category accounts for these monies because *legal restrictions had been attached to the revenue to require that expenditure be limited to specific purposes.* As an example, the city council of Saint Paul had specified that any money collected from the sale of zoo animals had to be spent to acquire new animals. Thus,

---

[12]GASB Cod. sec. 1300.104.

any resources received from this source are monitored by inclusion in the special revenue funds until properly expended.

Capital Projects Funds   As the title implies, this fund type accounts for costs incurred in acquiring or constructing major government facilities such as bridges, high schools, roads, or municipal office complexes. Funding for these projects is normally derived from grants, the sale of bonds, or is transferred from general revenues. The actual asset is not recorded here but merely the money to finance the purchase or construction along with the actual expenditure. For example, Gwinette County, Georgia, collected approximately $69 million in 1995 from a 1 percent local option tax to be used for road improvements.

Debt Service Funds   These funds record monies accumulated to pay long-term liabilities and interest as they come due.[13] However, this fund type does not account for a government's long-term debt. Rather, debt service funds monitor the financial resources currently available to satisfy long-term liabilities and also record the eventual payment. Thus, on June 30, 1994, the city of Phoenix, Arizona, reported more than $135 million of cash and investments in its debt service funds but not one dollar of accompanying long-term debt. This same fund reported the expenditure of $94 million during the previous year to cover principal and interest payments.

Proprietary Funds   The proprietary funds account for ongoing activities similar to those found in the business world. To facilitate financial reporting, the proprietary funds are broken down into two major divisions:

Enterprise Funds   Any government operation that is financed, at least in part, by outside user charges may be classified as an Enterprise Fund if the government intends to measure profit or loss from the fund. A municipality, for example, may generate revenues from the use of a public swimming pool, golf course, airport, water and sewage service, and the like. As an illustration, the city of Chicago, Illinois, reports the operation of O'Hare International Airport within its enterprise funds. In some cases, though, heavily subsidized activities such as mass transit may be viewed as either governmental funds or proprietary funds.

Because customers are assessed direct fees, enterprise fund activities resemble businesses. Not surprisingly, the accounting process parallels that found in for-profit reporting. The funds use accrual basis accounting with a focus on economic, not just current financial, resources.

Internal Service Funds   This second proprietary fund accounts for any operation that provides services to another department or agency within the government on a cost-reimbursement basis. As with Enterprise Funds, fees are charged but the service is performed for the benefit of the government rather than for outside users. The city of Richmond, Virginia, for example, lists eight operations in its 1995 financial statements that are accounted for as separate internal service funds:

Warehouse—provides office supplies.
Automotive maintenance—provides for repairs and maintenance of city-owned vehicles.
Central duplicating service—provides copying services.
Telecommunications—provides telephone and other communication services.

---

[13] Some state and local governments choose to maintain assets for debt service within the General Fund rather than in a separate category. This approach is acceptable, especially if the amounts are relatively small.

Central postage service—provides mailroom services.

Automotive leased equipment—owns and leases vehicles to other departments and agencies.

Public works stores—provides supplies of a bulk nature such as sand, bricks, and construction materials.

Richmond school board warehouse—provides supplies for the public schools.

Fiduciary Funds   The final classification, the fiduciary funds (also referred to as Trust and Agency Funds), accounts for assets held in a trustee capacity. Four distinct types of fiduciary funds can exist within a government's accounting system:

Expendable Trust Funds   The first type accounts for resources donated to a government for a specified purpose where both the principal and any future earnings may be spent. A certificate of deposit given to a city to build a tennis court, for example, falls into this category because both the gift and subsequent income can be used for the designated project. As an illustration, the city of Saint Paul, Minnesota, reported 11 separate expendable trust funds as of December 31, 1995, holding over $300,000. These resources had been given by various groups and individuals in hopes of accomplishing a number of community goals. For example, a former library employee left a portion of her estate to support the city's library system, and a family donated money for the construction of a Japanese garden.

Governments are warned, however, not to overuse this designation. "Governments often classify activities as Expendable Trust Funds when they could be accounted for as easily in either the General Fund or in a Special Revenue Fund. If a formal trust agreement is not established, the trust fund classification should not be used."[14]

Nonexpendable Trust Funds   Because the second type of fiduciary fund monitors resources donated to a government for a specific project where only the subsequent earnings may be expended, the principal of such funds must be left intact. This fund type would be utilized, as an example, to record a monetary gift made to a library with the provision that all income derived from this principal be spent on the purchase of books. In fact, the city of Walla Walla, Washington, has four nonexpendable trust funds including the Eyraud Endowment, a donation made with the stipulation that the income must be spent for children's books and sports reference books for the city's library.

Pension Trust Funds   The third type accounts for an employee retirement system. Because of the need to provide adequate benefits for government workers, this fund type can grow to be quite large. The state of Alaska, as an example, reported assets of more than $9.8 billion in its pension trust fund at the end of 1996.

Agency Funds   The fourth type records any resources held by a government as an agent for individuals or other government units. Taxes and tolls, for example, are occasionally collected by one body on behalf of another. To ensure safety and control, this money should be separately maintained in an Agency Fund until transferred to the proper authority.

The GASB provides specific accounting guidance for the reporting of these four fiduciary funds: "Expendable trust funds are accounted for in essentially the same manner as governmental funds. Nonexpendable trust funds and pension trust funds

---

[14]Paul E. Glick, *Fund Structure Including Interfund Transactions* (Chicago: Government Finance Officers Association, 1987), p. 12.

are accounted for in essentially the same manner as proprietary funds. Agency funds are purely custodial (assets equal liabilities) and thus do not involve measurement of results of operations."[15]

By using more than one accounting approach, governments recognize the essential differences among the various Trust and Agency Funds. Determination of income is important in both Nonexpendable Trust Funds and Pension Trust Funds; therefore, financial reporting (like that of Enterprise Funds and Internal Service Funds) resembles that of for-profit businesses. In contrast, since all resources can be spent in an Expendable Trust Fund, computation of net income is not necessary. Consequently, governmental fund accounting principles are utilized. Agency Funds normally have only two transactions (the creation of a liability and its payment) so that specific accounting procedures are not required.

Coverage of Fund Accounting Procedures   The formal classification system just described is extremely useful in the financial reporting of a state or local government. However, an understanding of appropriate accounting procedures can best be achieved by labeling each fund type as either a governmental-type or a business-type:

Governmental-Type Funds	Business-Type Funds
Governmental funds:	Proprietary funds:
General Fund	Enterprise Funds
Special Revenue Funds	Internal Service Funds
Capital Projects Funds	
Debt Service Funds	Fiduciary funds:
	Nonexpendable Trust Funds
Fiduciary funds:	Pension Trust Funds
Expendable Trust Funds	

The reporting process utilized by the five government-type funds is examined in this chapter while the four business-type funds are analyzed in Chapter 17. Also presented there are accounting procedures used in the remaining fund category, the Agency Funds, although they are limited to recording an asset inflow and its subsequent disbursement.

ACCOUNTING FOR GOVERNMENTAL-TYPE FUNDS

The remainder of this chapter presents many of the unique aspects of the accounting process utilized within the governmental-type funds: the General Fund, Special Revenue Funds, Capital Projects Funds, Debt Service Funds, and Expendable Trust Funds. The reporting principles for these funds have been developed without an underlying profit motive. Thus, the distinguishing features described here often fail to correspond to procedures traditionally associated with the financial accounting utilized by for-profit businesses.

For organizational purposes, coverage of governmental-type funds includes the following discussions, events, and transactions:

■ The importance of budgets and the recording of budgetary entries.
■ The purpose of, and accounting for, encumbrances.
■ The recognition of expenditures for operations and capital additions.
■ The recognition of revenues.
■ The sale of bonds: capital debt and operating debt.
■ The accounting for special assessment of taxes.
■ The recording of interfund transactions.
■ The reporting of fund equity.

---

[15]GASB Cod. sec. 1300.102.

Each of these elements is an important aspect of the accounting process for the governmental-type funds of a state or local government. Knowledge of the reporting of each of these elements is an essential beginning step in understanding governmental accounting.

The Importance of Budgets and the Recording of Budgetary Entries

"Financing is an important part of the governmental environment, particularly for governmental-type activities. For those activities, the budget is the primary method of directing and controlling the financial process."[16] In a chronological sense, the first significant accounting procedure encountered in a state or locality is the recording of budgetary entries. To enhance accountability, government officials normally are required to adopt an annual budget for each separate activity to anticipate the inflow of financial resources and establish approved expenditure levels. In its "Objectives of Financial Reporting," the GASB indicates that the budget serves these important purposes:

1. Expresses public policy. If, for example, more money is budgeted for child care and less for the environment, the citizens are made aware of the decision that has been made to allocate limited government resources.

2. Serves as an expression of financial intent for the upcoming fiscal year. The budget presents the financial plan for the government for the period.

3. Provides control because spending limitations are established.

4. Offers a means of evaluating performance by allowing a comparison between actual results and the levels of funding found in the budget.

The GASB even states that "many believe the budget is the most significant financial document produced by a government unit."[17]

Once a budget has been produced and enacted into law, formal accounting recognition is frequently required as a means of enhancing the benefits just described. In this way, the public is given the opportunity to learn of the expected amounts to be received and the expenditures to be made with these financial resources. Since the General Fund and the Special Revenue Funds account for a wide range of ongoing service activities, reporting both revenue projections as well as compliance with spending limitations is considered essential for government accountability. Therefore, the approved budget figures for these two fund types formally are entered into the accounting records at the start of each fiscal year. Citizens can then draw comparisons between actual and budgeted figures at any interim point during the period.

As an illustration, assume that a city enacts a motel excise tax to promote tourism and conventions. Because the funding is legally restricted for this specified purpose, a separate Special Revenue Fund is established. Assume further that for the 1998 fiscal year an estimation is made that $412,000 in revenues will be generated by the tax. Based on this projection, the city council authorizes the expenditure of $400,000 (referred to as an *appropriation*) for programs during the current year. The $12,000 difference between the anticipated inflow and this appropriation is a budgeted surplus to be accumulated by the government in case the levy proves to be too small or for use in future years. To highlight the council's action, the following journal entry is included in the accounting records of this fund:

Special Revenue Fund (beginning of year)

Estimated Revenues—Tax Levy	412,000	
Appropriations—Tourism and Convention Promotions		400,000
(Budgetary) Fund Balance		12,000
To record annual budget for tax levy to support tourism.		

---

[16]*GASB Statement No. 11,* para. 9.

[17]*GASB Concepts Statement No. 1,* para. 19.

This entry indicates the source of the funding (the tax revenue) as well as the approved amount of expenditures. The Fund Balance account indicates the presence of an anticipated surplus (or, in some cases, a shortage) projected for the period. Each of these figures remains within the records of this Special Revenue Fund for the entire year to allow for planning and control. Citizens can see how much is to be spent for these programs and the source of this funding.

As is discussed in the next chapter, one of the financial statements produced for a state or locality is the "Statement of Revenues, Expenditures, and Changes in Fund Balance—Budget and Actual." Thus, the budget figures are not simply left on the financial records for the year and then forgotten. For each of the funds that formally records a budget, the actual amounts for the period as well as the budgeted numbers are presented side by side for comparison purposes. In 1994, as an example, the financial statements for the city of Denver, Colorado, reported that $352,440,000 in taxes were anticipated within the General Fund's budget but $352,880,000 was actually recognized. In that same statement, an appropriation of $221,173,000 was shown for public safety but only $220,920,000 had actually been expended.

Because of the numerous activities encompassed by the General Fund (or any other fund), the accounting system may utilize subsidiary ledgers so that each balance can be identified separately by specific function. For example, the overall budget for the General Fund could include revenue projections and approved spending limitations for scores of diverse activities such as the school system, garbage collection, and the fire department. To facilitate the recording process, control accounts can be maintained in the general ledger with balances that are explained elsewhere in the system using individual subsidiary ledgers.

As an illustration, assume that a city estimates all General Fund revenues for the current year will equal $1,640,000 while spending levels of $1,180,000 have been set by the city council. Transfers to other funds (referred to as an other financing use since the money does not leave the government) totaling $400,000 have also been approved. These budgeted totals are entered into the General Fund. Simultaneously, separate subsidiary ledgers record detailed information to list the actual source of anticipated revenues (such as property taxes, income taxes, sales taxes, tolls, licenses, and the like) and the individual appropriations and approved transfers. The accounting system is accumulating information both in total and by separate functions.

General Fund (beginning of year)

Estimated Revenues Control	1,640,000	
Appropriations Control		1,180,000
Estimated Other Financing Uses—Operating Transfers Out		400,000
(Budgetary) Fund Balance		60,000

    To record legally adopted operating budget for the General
    Fund with separate subsidiary ledger accounts used by the
    government to explain individual revenues and
    appropriations.

The budget figures remain in the accounting records for informational purposes throughout the period. They are ultimately removed at the end of the fiscal year through a simple reversal of the original entry:

General Fund (closing entry)

Appropriations Control	1,180,000	
Estimated Other Financing Uses—Operating Transfers Out....	400,000	
(Budgetary) Fund Balance	60,000	
Estimated Revenues Control		1,640,000

    To remove budgetary entry.

In this manner, budgetary entries create no permanent impact on the accounting system but still serve in a control capacity throughout the year.

As mentioned previously, the reporting procedures used in each of the government-type funds are similar but not necessarily identical. Budgetary entries provide a good example of the differences in accounting for the individual fund types. *Within the General Fund, Special Revenue Funds, and Expendable Trust Funds, annual budgets are always recorded.* The volume of transactions as well as the variety of activities monitored within these three fund types can strain the government's ability to establish fiscal control. Recording the annual budget within the bookkeeping system is viewed as an appropriate strategy for enhancing planning, public awareness, and accountability.

In other governmental-type funds, budgets need not be recorded if oversight can be established by alternative means. Formal budgetary entries, for example, are normally omitted from Debt Service Funds. All activities of this particular fund type (accumulation of financial resources and payment of long-term debts and interest) are governed by contractual provision. Budget entries would provide little additional control or other informational value; thus, accounting recognition is not warranted.

Conversely, the recording of a budget is optional in reporting Capital Projects Funds. This fund type accounts for the construction and acquisition of projects that in some instances consist of no more than a simple contractual arrangement. A city, as an example, might hire an independent contractor to construct a sidewalk. In such cases, a signed contract usually sets the legal level of expenditure; thus, a budgetary entry is not necessary. However, if the government unit is building a major facility (such as a fire station) or if a number of contractors are involved in a single project, the inclusion of budgetary entries is recommended to accentuate planning and control.

Encumbrances

Governmental accounting demonstrates many unique aspects from separate account groups to fund accounting and budgetary entries. All are basic to the reporting process used by the governmental-type funds. One additional budgetary procedure that plays a central role in this system is the recording of monetary commitments referred to as *encumbrances. In diametric contrast to for-profit accounting, purchase commitments and contracts are recorded in the governmental funds prior to becoming legal liabilities.* Encumbrance accounting is appropriate in any governmental-type fund. Maintaining a record of these encumbrances provides an additional means of controlling fund spending. At any point during the fiscal year, information on both expended and committed funds is available. "An encumbrance accounting system acts as an early warning device. By controlling expenditure commitments, the government significantly reduces the opportunity to overexpend an appropriation."[18]

To illustrate, assume that a city orders $18,000 in supplies for ongoing General Fund activities. A for-profit business would make no entry at this point. However, this amount of the city's financial resources is now committed even though no formal liability exists until the supplies are received. Therefore, the following journal entry creates a record of this order and any other orders, contracts, and commitments that are currently outstanding:

General Fund

Encumbrances Control 18,000
      Fund Balance—Reserved for Encumbrances 18,000
        To record order placed for supplies.

The Encumbrances account records the commitment that has been incurred while "Fund Balance—Reserved for Encumbrances" is an equity-type balance indicating the amount of the city's assets required to fulfill future obligations.

---

[18]Government Finance Officers Association, *Governmental Accounting, Auditing, and Financial Reporting* (Chicago: 1988), p. 17.

When the preceding items are received, the commitment is replaced by a legal liability. Hence, the encumbrance is removed from the accounting records and an Inventory of Supplies account (or an Expenditure account if the purchases method rather than the consumption method is in use) is recognized. Often, because of sales taxes, freight costs, or other price adjustments, the actual invoice total differs from the estimated figure recorded at the time the order was processed. For this reason, the expenditure does not necessarily agree with the corresponding encumbrance. Assume, for illustration purposes, that the supplies received here are accompanied by an invoice for $18,160.

General Fund

Fund Balance—Reserved for Encumbrances	18,000	
Encumbrances Control		18,000
To remove encumbrance for supplies that have now been received.		
Inventory of Supplies (or Expenditures—Supplies)	18,160	
Vouchers Payable		18,160
To record the receipt of supplies and the accompanying liability.		

The Fund Balance—Reserved for Encumbrances account appears as an equity on the balance sheet to indicate that financial resources currently being held already are committed. As an example, the city of Atlanta, Georgia, reported the following Fund Balance—Reserved for Encumbrances figures in its December 31, 1995, balance sheet:

General Fund	$ 19,948,000
Capital Projects Funds	150,300,000
Expendable Trust Funds	3,744,000

This indicates that $19,948,000 of the net assets of the General Fund are unavailable for future appropriation because the city has outstanding commitments totaling this amount. Additionally, the city has outstanding commitments of $150,300,000 and $3,744,000 related to capital projects and expendable trusts, respectively.

Recognition of Expenditures for Operation and Capital Additions

Although budgetary entries are unique, their impact on the accounting process is somewhat limited because they do not directly affect a fund's financial results for the period. Conversely, the method by which a state or locality records the receipt and disbursement of resources can significantly alter the entire complexion of the reported data. For example, in the governmental-type funds, a primary emphasis is on the measurement of changes in current financial resources. *Therefore, neither expenses nor capital assets are recorded.*

Instead, an Expenditures account reflects any outflow or reduction of net financial resources from the acquisition of a good or service (or some other utility). A subsidiary ledger (or a system of separate accounts) normally identifies the exact reason for each change, but the actual decrease is recorded as an expenditure whether it is for rent, a fire truck, salaries, or a computer. Spending $1,000 for electricity for the past three months is an expenditure of a fund's financial resources in exactly the same way that buying a $70,000 ambulance is.

Expenditures—Electricity	1,000	
Voucher (or Accounts) Payable		1,000
To record charges covering the past three months.		
Expenditures—Ambulance	70,000	
Voucher (or Accounts) Payable		70,000
To record acquisition of new ambulance.		

Within the government-type funds, expenditures (and revenues) are recognized on the *modified accrual basis* of accounting. For expenditures, modified accrual accounting requires recognition to be made when a liability is created. "The measurement focus of governmental fund accounting is on *expenditures*—decreases in net financial resources—rather than expenses. Most expenditures and transfers out are measurable and should be recorded when the related liability is incurred."[19]

The recording of expenditures rather than expenses and capital assets is one of the most distinctive characteristics of governmental accounting. A for-profit business enterprise that purchases a building or a machine capitalizes all related costs and then recognizes depreciation expense during each year of the asset's useful life. This depreciation is a factor in the computation of the organization's annual net income.

In contrast, a government-type fund records the entire cost of all buildings, machines, and other capital assets as expenditures. The outflow of current financial resources is important. No income figure is computed for these funds; thus, the computation and recording of subsequent depreciation is not relevant to the reporting process and is omitted entirely.

Expenditures are measurement accounts closed out at the end of each fiscal year. Since the financial resources have been reduced, the impact on the fund is recognized immediately. In the governmental-type funds, the amount of financial resources being utilized is the important information. This approach is clearly designed to assist the government unit in establishing accountability over current spending levels. For example, the city of Buffalo, New York, reported in its 1990 financial statements the expenditure of more than $650,000 for the acquisition of fire-fighting vehicles and another $384,000 for fire prevention services. Although one item was an asset and the other an expense, the city showed both as expenditures in the current period.

The general ledger system is designed to record expenditures in a manner that meets the information needs of the government and the financial statement users. Within a given fund, expenditures may be recorded by:

Function—such as public safety or recreation.

Department—such as police, fire, and parks.

Activity—which include different functions within a department, such as fire extinguishment and fire inspections.

Character—which include current operating expenditures, capital outlay, and debt service.

Object—which detail inputs such as salaries and supplies.

Additionally, expenditures may be reported by programs. Programs differ from these classifications in that programs often involve more than one department. Public safety programs, for example, might include the police, fire, health, and other departments.

General Fixed Assets Account Group   One interesting result of measuring and reporting expenditures is that the records of the governmental-type funds contain virtually no assets other than financial resources such as cash, receivables, and investments. All capital assets such as buildings, equipment, vehicles, and the like have been recorded as expenditures at the time of purchase and then closed out at the end of the fiscal period. Despite the desire to focus on spending, proper control cannot be served without some recording of the government's capital assets. Thus, a separate General Fixed Assets Account Group lists the ownership of these assets as well as any capitalized leased property.

---

[19]GASB Cod. sec. 1600.117.

The primary purposes for governmental fund accounting are to reflect its revenues and expenditures—the sources and uses of its financial resources—and its assets, the related liabilities, and the net financial resources available for subsequent appropriation and expenditure. These objectives can most readily be achieved by excluding general fixed assets from the governmental fund accounts and recording them in a separate General Fixed Assets Account Group.[20]

This segregation allows the governmental-type funds to focus on expendable financial resources.

The use of a separate General Fixed Assets Account Group necessitates that acquisitions actually be recorded twice. To illustrate, assume that $160,000 from a city's General Fund is used to purchase a fire truck. This expenditure is recognized in the General Fund whereas the asset itself is concurrently recorded in the General Fixed Assets Account Group. The second entry includes not only the cost and identity of the asset but also the source of funding (such as general obligation bonds, capital projects funds, gifts, and so forth). This Investment in General Fixed Assets designation is a balancing figure that reports the various sources used to acquire capital assets and appears as an *Other Credit* in the equity section of the government's balance sheet.

Although the cost of this asset is appropriately recorded here, fair market value would be used for any donated assets.

General Fund

Expenditures—Capital Assets	160,000	
Vouchers Payable		160,000
To record acquisition of fire truck.		

General Fixed Assets Account Group

Machinery and Equipment	160,000	
Investment in General Fixed Assets—General Fund Revenues		160,000
To record acquisition of fire truck.		

If this fire truck is ever disposed of through trade, sale, retirement, or accident, removal from the General Fixed Assets Account Group is made by reversing this original entry.

One variation of the accounting process for capital assets is encountered in connection with construction projects. If work on any job extends into more than one fiscal period, a Construction in Progress account must be set up in the General Fixed Assets Account Group to record all costs incurred prior to completion. At the time the asset eventually becomes usable, the final balance is simply reclassified into a permanent account. The actual expenditure also must be reported. For construction projects, the decrease in financial resources would normally be recorded in the Capital Projects Funds.

The recording of some construction projects as assets within the General Fixed Asset Account Group has been questioned. A street or a sidewalk, for example, cannot be sold and has no future value apart from the services they provide. Thus, while traditional capital assets such as schools, town halls, trucks, and machinery always are recognized in the General Fixed Assets Account Group, states and localities are allowed the option of "reporting public domain or 'infrastructure' fixed assets—roads, bridges, curbs and gutters, streets and sidewalks, drainage systems, lighting systems, and similar assets that are immovable and of value only to the governmental unit."[21] Some government units meticulously record such infrastructure items whereas others do not.[22]

---

[20]GASB Cod. sec. 1400.107.

[21]GASB Cod. sec. 1400.109.

[22]There is a current proposal outstanding by the GASB to require recording infrastructure assets.

DISCUSSION QUESTION

Is It an Asset or a Liability?

In the August 1989 issue of the *Journal of Accountancy,* R. K. Mautz discusses the unique reporting needs of governments and not-for-profit organizations (such as charities) in "Not-For-Profit Financial Reporting: Another View." As an illustration of their accounting problems, Mautz examines the method by which a city should record a newly constructed high school building. Conventional business wisdom would say that such a property represents an asset of the government. Thus, the cost should be capitalized and then depreciated over an estimated useful life. However, in paragraph 26 of FASB *Concepts Statement No. 6,* an essential characteristic of an asset is "a probable future benefit . . . to contribute directly or indirectly to future cash inflows."

Mautz reasons that the school building cannot be considered an asset since it provides no net contribution to cash inflows. In truth, a high school requires the government to make significant cash outflows for maintenance, repairs, utilities, salaries, and the like. Public educational facilities (as well as most of the other properties of a government such as a fire station or municipal building) are acquired with the understanding that net cash outflows will result.

Consequently, Mautz considers whether the construction of a high school is not actually the incurrence of a liability since the government is taking on an obligation that will necessitate future cash payments. This idea also is rejected, once again based on the guidance of *Concepts Statement No. 6* (paragraph 36), because the cash outflow is not required at a "specified or determinable date, on occurrence of a specified event, or on demand."

Is a high school building an asset or is it a liability? If it is neither, how should the cost be recorded? Can a government be accounted for in the same manner as a for-profit enterprise?

Depreciation Expense   Because of the absence of capital assets, depreciation expense is not recorded within any of the government-type funds. Although accumulated depreciation totals may be disclosed in the General Fixed Assets Account Group, recognition of an expense is inconsistent with the goal of maintaining control over financial resources that is emphasized throughout these funds. Additionally, depreciation figures are not considered relevant to the reporting process since net income is not being calculated.

> Expenditures, not expenses, are measured in governmental fund accounting. To record depreciation expense in governmental funds would inappropriately mix two fundamentally different measurements, expenses and expenditures. General fixed asset acquisitions *require* the use of governmental fund financial resources and are recorded as expenditures. General fixed asset sale proceeds *provide* governmental fund financial resources. Depreciation expense is neither a source nor a use of governmental fund financial resources, and thus is not properly recorded in the accounts of such funds. . . . Recording accumulated depreciation in the General Fixed Assets Account Group is optional. Where it is recorded, the entry should increase the Accumulated Depreciation account(s) and decrease the Investment in General Fixed Assets account(s).[23]

Supplies and Prepaid Items   Traditionally, supplies and prepaid items have been recorded as expenditures at the point in time that a liability is created. No asset is initially recorded because neither supplies nor prepaid items (such as rent or insurance) can be expended. For reporting purposes, though, materials or prepayments that remain at year's end must be entered into the accounting records as assets prior to production of financial statements. This adjustment is created by utilizing an equity balance with a title such as Fund Balance Reserved for Inventory of Supplies (or Prepaid Items). This account indicates an asset is present that is not available for spending purposes.

---

[23]GASB Cod. sec. 1400.116–118.

This traditional approach, referred to as the *purchases method,* is based on the modified accrual method of accounting. The expenditure is recorded when the liability is first incurred. Some governments choose to measure supplies expenditures on an alternative method, the *consumption method.*

The consumption method parallels the process that would be applied by a for-profit business. Any supplies or prepayments are recorded as assets when acquired. Subsequently, as the items are consumed by usage or over time, the cost is reclassified into an Expenditures account. Therefore, under this approach, the expenditure is matched with the period of specific usage.

As an illustration, assume that $20,000 in supplies are purchased by a municipality for various General Fund activities. During the remainder of the period, $18,000 of this amount is used so that only $2,000 remains at year's end. These events could be recorded through either of the following sets of entries:

Consumption Method

Inventory of Supplies	20,000	
Vouchers Payable		20,000
To record purchase of supplies for various ongoing activities.		
Expenditures—Control	18,000	
Inventory of Supplies		18,000
To record consumption of supplies during period.		

Purchases Method

Expenditures—Supplies	20,000	
Vouchers Payable		20,000
To record purchase of supplies for various ongoing activities.		
Inventory of Supplies	2,000	
Fund Balance—Reserved for Inventory of Supplies		2,000
To record supplies remaining at year's end.		

Recognition of Revenues

As with expenditures, revenues are recognized in governmental-type funds on the modified accrual basis of accounting. Under modified accrual accounting, revenues should be reported within the governmental-type funds in the time period in which they become both *measurable* and *available.*

- The *measurable* criterion requires that the revenue must be subject to reasonable estimation.
- *Available* is defined as "collectible within the current period or soon enough thereafter to be used to pay liabilities of the current period."[24]

Revenues from fines and forfeitures, as an example, generally are not subject to reasonable estimation until received; thus, recognition is delayed until cash is physically collected. Conversely, property taxes—the largest source of revenue for many municipalities—are normally recognized under modified accrual accounting as soon as the tax is levied since the probable amount to be received during the current period can usually be anticipated at that point.

Specific guidance for recognition is provided next by looking at the individual sources of government revenues.

---

[24]GASB Cod. sec. 1600.106.

Property Taxes   Under modified accrual accounting, revenues are recognized when they become measurable and available.

For illustrative purposes, assume that Ginsburg County levies $400,000 in property taxes on May 1, 1998. The government estimates that $20,000 will go unpaid.

May 1, 1998 Entry

Property Tax Receivable (amount levied)	400,000	
Revenue—Property Taxes		380,000
Allowance for Uncollectible Taxes		20,000
To recognize property tax levy made in 1998.		

Although not shown here, the collection of the taxes and the write-off of any accounts would be normal entries.

Because the $20,000 estimated uncollectible portion is not expected to be *available* in the period to finance expenditures, it is deducted from the amount recognized as revenue. For purposes of revenue recognition, the term, available, is defined as "collectible within the current period or soon enough thereafter to be used to pay liabilities of the current period."[25] Clearly, this definition requires judgment on the part of government officials. Taxes that are levied but will not be collected until a year later may be more properly classified as *deferred revenue* if they are not expected to be available to pay current period liabilities. Assume the same facts as the above example except that $95,000 of the collectible receivables are due in the following year and are not expected to be received soon enough to be used to pay liabilities of the current period. In that case the appropriate journal entry would be:

May 1, 1998 Entry

Property Tax Revenue (amount levied)	400,000	
Revenue—Property Taxes		285,000
Deferred Revenue		95,000
Allowance for Uncollectible Taxes		20,000
To recognize tax levy made in 1998.		

Income Taxes, Sales Taxes, Fines, Fees, and Licenses   *GASB Statement No. 22*, "Accounting for Taxpayer-Assessed Tax Revenues in Governmental Funds," requires sales and income taxes to be recognized in the accounting period in which they become susceptible to accrual. That is, when they become both measurable and available to finance expenditures of the fiscal period. For example, a government's claim to sales taxes is established when a business makes a taxable sale and its claim to income taxes is established when a citizen or business earns taxable income. In contrast, many of the revenues anticipated by a state or locality will not meet the current criteria of being measurable and available until physically collected. For this reason, recognition of resource inflows such as parking fees, traffic court fines, and business licenses are normally delayed until cash is received. The amounts usually cannot be estimated in advance and are not available to satisfy current obligations until collected. For that reason, many individuals incorrectly believe that governmental accounting is a cash-based reporting system.

Grants and Entitlements   A common source of revenues for many governments is grants and entitlements, monies transferred from one government to another to meet a specified purpose or because of a particular law. *Statement No. 2* of the National Council on Governmental Accounting, "Grant, Entitlement, and Shared Revenue Accounting by State and Local Governments" (March 1979), addressed recognition of these resources.

---

[25]GASB Codification Sec. 1600.106

Grants and entitlements may take many forms. A state could convey money to a city to provide financing for the acquisition of new emergency medical equipment or to assist in feeding the hungry and homeless. The federal government might transfer funds to a county for road construction. The amounts involved can be significant. In 1995, Los Angeles, California, reported grant revenues within its Special Revenue Funds in excess of $650 million from various federal, state, and private agencies.

When grants and entitlements are received, legal restrictions often are attached to ensure that the funds are expended for the proposed purpose. Therefore, if the money is given for an operating project, the Special Revenue Funds category usually is applicable because the money is designated for a specific purpose or expenditure. Conversely, if the funds are given for construction or acquisition of fixed assets, recording is made in the Capital Projects Funds.

Revenue recognition for such items frequently must be delayed beyond the time of receipt. In many cases, proper expenditure is required of the government to keep the funding. *Consequently, the revenues should not be recognized until the money is appropriately spent.* Proper expenditure is necessary to earn the resources. Thus, if stipulations are included, a Deferred Revenue account is established as a liability with this balance being reclassified as a revenue at the time the required expenditure is made.

For example, at June 30, 1990, the city of Norfolk, Virginia, explains a $3 million Deferred Revenue liability found within its Special Revenue Funds as follows:

> This represents a liability incurred by the City for monies accepted from a grantor using an advancement method for payments. The liability is reduced and revenue recorded when expenditures are made in accordance with grantor's requirements. If expenditures are not made, the funds will revert back to the grantor.[26]

Assume that the city of Redlands, as an illustration, collects $300,000 on September 1, 1998, from the federal government to supplement the salaries of kindergarten teachers. The money is held for a short time and $100,000 is spent on October 1, 1998, for the designated purpose. The city should record these events through the following entries:

Special Revenue Fund
September 1, 1998

Cash	300,000	
Deferred Revenues		300,000

Receipt of grant from the federal government to supplement the salaries of kindergarten teachers.

Special Revenue Fund
October 1, 1998

Expenditures—Teachers' Salaries	100,000	
Cash		100,000

Grant money used to supplement salaries of city's kindergarten teachers.

Deferred Revenue	100,000	
Revenues—Federal Grant		100,000

To record recognition of revenue in connection with the appropriate expenditure of federal grant.

GASB Statement No. 24, "Accounting and Financial Reporting for Certain Grants and Other Financial Assistance," requires governments to record pass-through grants of cash or food stamps as both revenues and expenditures. Pass-through grants received by state governments from the federal government include: Food Stamps, Aid to Families with Dependent Children, and Commodities Programs. Generally, these

---

[26]Note 20 of the city's comprehensive annual financial report.

are recognized in the General or Special Revenue Funds. Prior to this standard, many governments recorded assets received under such assistance programs in Agency Funds.

Issuance of Bonds

Although not a revenue, the issuance of bonds serves as a major source of funding for many state and local governments. Proceeds from such sales may be used for many purposes, including general financing and a wide variety of construction projects. In 1994, the city of Phoenix, Arizona, issued $90 million in bonds to finance a number of capital projects, including a library, science museum, and museum of history.

Since the proceeds of a bond have to be repaid, no revenues are recognized. However, the inflow of financial resources into a specific fund must be recorded in some manner. Assume, for example, that the town of Ruark sells $5 million in general obligation bonds to finance the construction of a new school building. Because of the purpose of this action, a Capital Projects Fund is designated to receive the cash. To emphasize that this money is not derived from a revenue, a special designation, *Other Financing Sources,* is utilized. Thus, the following entry would be appropriate to record the sale:

Capital Projects Fund

Cash	5,000,000	
Other Financing Sources—Bond Proceeds		5,000,000
To record issuance of bond to finance construction project.		

Although an inflow of cash into this fund has taken place, no revenue has been generated. However, in the same manner as a revenue, Other Financing Sources is a measurement account that is closed out at the end of the year. Furthermore, a subsidiary ledger is apparently not in use since the account title is specific: Other Financing Sources—Bond Proceeds.

General Long-Term Debt Account Group   As shown in the previous entry, the $5 million liability is completely omitted from the Capital Projects Funds. Since the governmental-type funds stress accounting for the inflows and outflows of financial resources, recognition of long-term debts in these funds has traditionally been considered inappropriate. Despite this objective, some record of these obligations is essential to the fair presentation of the government's financial position. As with general fixed assets, a separate account group (*General Long-Term Debt Account Group*) is established to perform the sole function of listing the noncurrent liabilities of the governmental-type funds. Therefore, to record the bond just issued, a second entry is needed:

General Long-Term Debt Account Group

Amount to Be Provided for Payment of Bonds	5,000,000	
Bonds Payable		5,000,000
To record issuance of bonds for new school construction.		

The Amount to Be Provided account in this entry would appear as an *Other Debit* in the asset section of the combined balance sheet of the government. This balance discloses the amount of cash to be generated by the government in the future to extinguish the principal of the debt. Over time, as resources are accumulated within the Debt Service Funds for this purpose, the Amount to Be Provided figure would be reclassified into an Amount Available in Debt Service Funds account. For example, as of June 30, 1996, the city of Las Vegas, Nevada, reported total debt of $138,689,000 in its General Long-Term Debt Account Group. However, at that time, the city was already holding net assets of $12,090,000 in its Debt Service Fund to be used for future repayment purposes. Thus, as an Other Debit in the balance sheet of the General Long-Term Debt Account Group, the city reported two balances:

Amount available in debt service funds	$ 12,090,000
Amount to be provided for retirement of long-term debt	126,599,000
Total	$138,689,000

To illustrate further, assume that following a bond issue of $5 million, the town of Ruark begins to set money aside for eventual payment. Thus, $600,000 is transferred from the General Fund to the Debt Service Funds, an amount that will be used to pay the debt when due. If these funds remain in the Debt Service Fund at the balance sheet date, the government records the following adjustment in the General Long-Term Debt Account Group. No expenditure is recorded nor is the liability reduced because payment has not been made.

General Long-Term Debt Account Group

Amount Available in Debt Service Fund	600,000	
Amount to be Provided		600,000
To indicate that resources of this amount have been set aside to extinguish bonds.		

Payment of Long-Term Liabilities

Expenditures to recognize payment of long-term debt and related interest are recorded in the Debt Service Funds only when due. Thus, interest for an entire year that is due on January 15, 1998, is recorded in total as an expenditure on that date; no impact is recognized in 1997. This approach has been used so that the expenditure is reported in the same time period as the appropriation for the expenditure. The rationale for not accruing interest is that current resources need not be appropriated for interest that is not yet legally due. However, matured interest payable is recorded as an expenditure and liability of the Debt Service Fund.

The following entries illustrate the current process. This example assumes that cash previously has been set aside in the Debt Service Funds to settle a bond coming due. Of the total amount, $600,000 is to satisfy the principal with $40,000 serving as the interest payment for the period. Two entries are necessary: one to record the expenditures and the other to remove the debt.

Debt Service Funds

Expenditures—Bond Principal	600,000	
Expenditures—Interest	40,000	
Cash		640,000
To pay bonds and interest that are currently due.		

General Long-Term Debt Account Group

Bonds Payable	600,000	
Amount Available in Debt Service Funds		600,000
To remove debt that is extinguished with funds held in the Debt Service Funds.		

Special Assessments

Governments frequently provide improvements or services that directly benefit a particular property and assess the costs (in whole or part) to the owner. In many cases, the owners actually petition the government to initiate such projects because of the enhancement of property values. Paving streets, laying water and sewage lines, and the construction of curbing and sidewalks are typical examples. To finance the work being done, the government usually issues debt while concurrently placing a lien on the property to ensure reimbursement. Payment by the owners often is made in installments, sometimes stretching over several years. If public property also is benefited or if the governing body so chooses, a portion of the cost may be absorbed by the state or locality.

Prior to 1987, these activities were accounted for within a separate governmental fund type, the Special Assessments Fund. However, the GASB now requires, in most cases, that these construction costs be recorded in the Capital Projects Fund with the debt shown in the General Long-Term Debt account group. The assessment of the owners is entered as a receivable within the Debt Service Funds.

To illustrate, assume that a sidewalk is to be added to a neighborhood by a city government at a cost of $15,000. Bonds are to be sold for this amount with repayment to be made over three years using money collected from the owners. Although the city will not pay this debt, the government has agreed to be secondarily liable if any defaults occur.[27] The actual assessment is not made until after the construction is completed. The following entries reflect these various events:

Capital Projects Fund

Cash	15,000	
Other Financing Sources—Special Assessment Bonds		15,000

To record issuance of bond with proceeds to be used to construct a sidewalk. Assessment of property owners will provide the payment for this liability.

General Long-Term Debt Account Group

Amount to Be Provided from Special Assessments	15,000	
Special Assessment Debt with Government Commitment		15,000

To record issuance of bond with money used in construction of a sidewalk.

Capital Projects Fund

Expenditures—Sidewalk	15,000	
Contracts Payable		15,000

To record completion of a sidewalk.

Debt Service Funds

Special Assessments Receivable	15,000	
Deferred Revenues—Special Assessments		15,000

To record levy for construction work done in connection with a sidewalk with costs to be paid by owners being benefited. As collections are made, deferred revenues will be reclassified as revenues.

General Fixed Assets Account Group
(optional entry for infrastructure)

Improvements Other than Buildings	15,000	
Investment in General Fixed Assets—Special Assessments		15,000

To record construction costs of a sidewalk.

Several aspects of these entries should be noted:

■ The debt is recorded by the city although the amount is anticipated to be paid in full by the owners rather than the government. To disclose the city's responsibility for possible defaults, the entire debt is included in the General Long-Term Debt Account Group. However, if the government could in no way be held liable, this obligation would be omitted. In that circumstance, subsequent payments by the owners are funneled through an Agency Fund to extinguish the debt with no other recording required.

---

[27]In the event that the government assumes no liability (primary or secondary) for special assessment debt, GASB standards require the collection and payments of special assessment taxes to be accounted for in an Agency Fund.

- The asset is included at cost within the General Fixed Asset Account Group although no government funds were actually required. However, as an infrastructure item, this recording is optional.

Interfund Transactions

Interfund transactions are commonly used within most government units as a means of directing sufficient resources to all activities and functions. Monetary transfers made from the General Fund are especially prevalent since many government revenues are initially accumulated in this fund. Such transactions should be recorded in both funds simultaneously at the time of authorization. However, the specific method of accounting for these transfers is based on the nature of the transfer.

Operating Transfers The most common intercompany transactions are *operating transfers* that are used primarily within the governmental-type funds to ensure adequate financing of budgeted expenditures. A county might transfer unrestricted funds, for example, to debt service to ensure that future obligations can be paid. A city council could vote to transfer $800,000 from the General Fund to the Capital Projects Funds to cover a portion of the cost of a new school building. In this second scenario, the following entries would be recorded:

General Fund

Other Financing Uses—Operating Transfers Out—		
Capital Projects Fund	800,000	
Due to Capital Projects Fund		800,000
Transfer is authorized for school construction.		

Capital Projects Funds

Due from General Fund	800,000	
Other Financing Source—Operating Transfers In—		
General Fund		800,000
Transfer is to be received for school construction.		

The *Other Financing Uses/Sources* designations are appropriate here; monetary resources are being moved into and out of these funds although neither revenues nor expenditures have been earned or incurred. These balances are eventually reported by the funds in the Statement of Revenues, Expenditures, and Changes in Fund Balances. Both accounts are then closed out at the end of the current year. The *Due to/Due from* accounts are the equivalent of interfund payable and receivable balances.

When the actual transfer occurs, the following entries result:

General Fund

Due to Capital Projects Fund	800,000	
Cash		800,000
To transfer cash to Capital Projects Fund.		

Capital Projects Fund

Cash	800,000	
Due from General Fund		800,000
Receipt of transfer from General Fund.		

Residual Equity Transfers Not all monetary transfers are for operating purposes; nonrecurring or nonroutine transfers may also occur. In some instances, money is transferred from the General Fund to create a Proprietary Fund, either an Enterprise Fund or Internal Service Fund. For example, on July 1, 1989, the city of Wilmington, Delaware, transferred $990,877 as initial funding for the Wilmington Homeownership Fund, an enterprise fund created to offer home ownership to low-to-moderate income families.

Because of the business-type nature of proprietary funds, government financing resembles a contribution of capital more than an operating transfer. Thus, the following entries are required if a city transfers $310,000 from its General Fund for the purpose of creating a print shop to assist the rest of the government. Since the print shop provides services within the government for a fee, an Internal Service Fund is being formed. The following chapter covers accounting procedures for this type of Proprietary Fund in more detail.

General Fund

Residual Equity Transfer Out—Print Shop	310,000	
Cash		310,000

To record transfer made to begin a print shop serving all areas of the city government.

Internal Service Fund

Cash	310,000	
Contributed Capital—Government		310,000

To record transfer providing initial funding for print shop.

As with the operating transfer, the *Residual Equity Transfer Out* account also appears within the Statement of Revenues, Expenditures, and Changes in Fund Balances. However, as can be seen in Exhibit 16–1 at the end of this chapter, this type of transfer is shown as a direct decrease in the fund balance of the General Fund rather than as an other financing use. The Contributed Capital account on the Internal Service Fund is equivalent to a paid-in-equity account and is not included in the determination of retained earnings.

Quasi-External Transactions   Some transfers made within a government actually replace revenues and expenditures. For example, a payment made by a city to its own print shop (or any other Internal Service Fund or Enterprise Fund) for services or materials is treated as the equivalent of a transaction with an outside party. To avoid confusion in reporting, such transfers are recorded as revenues and expenditures just as if the transaction had occurred with an unrelated party. No differentiation is made.

Assuming that the print shop (or the motor pool or the data processing center) does a $20,000 project for the General Fund, the following recording is appropriate:

General Fund

Expenditures—Printing	20,000	
Cash		20,000

To pay for printing work done for the city by its print shop.

Internal Service Fund

Cash	20,000	
Revenues—Printing		20,000

To recognize revenue generated by work done for city's General Fund.

Fund Equity

Fund balance is the component of fund equity that reports the excess or deficiency of a fund's current assets relative to its current liabilities. . . . Unreserved fund balance is that portion of fund balance that is appropriate for expenditures and is not legally segregated for specific future use.[28]

---

[28]GASB, "Preliminary Views—Implementation of *GASB Statement No. 11*, 'Measurement Focus and Basis of Accounting—Governmental Fund Operating Statements,' " April 30, 1992, paragraph 27.

In a for-profit corporation, the equity section of the balance sheet is presented according to the sources of the business's net assets: paid-in capital and earned capital. Conversely, the governmental-type funds of a state or locality use equity accounts to disclose the availability of resources for future spending purposes. As an example, this chapter has examined the Fund Balance—Reserved for Inventory of Supplies, an equity balance indicating that assets are being held as supplies so expenditure is not possible. Likewise, the Fund Balance—Reserved for Encumbrances reports commitments already made for the subsequent expenditure of the fund's resources.

Fund Balance—Unreserved, Undesignated Governmental-type funds also possess current assets that have not been designated for a specific expenditure. For example, a General Fund holding $90,000 in cash, receivables, and investments but only $50,000 in monetary obligations (and no commitments) has $40,000 in unrestricted net assets. These resources are available for immediate expenditure. To disclose this surplus, an equity account entitled *Fund Balance—Unreserved, Undesignated* is maintained on the balance sheet. The total in this account is actually created as a result of absorbing revenues, expenditures, other financing sources and uses, and residual equity transfers within the annual closing process.

Fund Balances—Illustrated To provide a demonstration, assume that the city of Morganton had $175,000 in unrestricted net current assets (and no encumbrances) in the General Fund on July 1, 1998, the beginning of the fiscal year. During the next 12 months, the following events transpire:

Financial Resource Inflows:
Revenues (property taxes, licenses, etc.)	$600,000
Other financing sources	
Bond proceeds—capital acquisitions	200,000
Operating transfers in	100,000
	$900,000

Financial Resource Outflows:
Expenditures (trucks, salary, etc.)	$533,000
Other financing uses (transfers out)	200,000
Residual equity transfer	85,000
	$818,000

In addition, assume that $20,000 in commitments outstanding will be honored in the next fiscal period. At year's end, the following closing entries are required:[29]

General Fund
(closing entries)

Revenues	600,000	
Other Financing Sources—Bond Proceeds	200,000	
Other Financing Sources—Operating Transfers In	100,000	
Expenditures		533,000
Other Financing Sources—Operating Transfers Out		200,000
Residual Equity Transfer		85,000
Encumbrances		20,000
Fund Balance—Unreserved, Undesignated		62,000

To close out current period inflows and outflows of financial resources.

Based on the information provided, an illustration of a condensed statement of revenues, expenditures, and changes in fund balance can be constructed for this municipality as shown in Exhibit 16–1. In addition, a typical balance sheet (also

[29]As illustrated previously, budgetary entries also are closed out at year-end.

CITY OF MORGANTON
General Fund
Statement of Revenues, Expenditures, and
Changes in Fund Balance (Condensed)
Year Ended June 30, 1999

Revenues		$ 600,000
Expenditures		(533,000)
Excess of revenues over expenditures		$ 67,000
Other financing sources (uses):		
Bond proceeds—Capital debt	$ 200,000	
Operating transfers in	100,000	
Operating transfers out	(200,000)	
Total other financing sources (uses)		100,000
Excess of revenues and other financing sources over expenditures and other financing uses		$ 167,000
Unreserved fund balance, July 1, 1998		175,000
Residual equity transfers out		(85,000)
Less: Increase in reserve for encumbrances		(20,000)
Unreserved fund balance, June 30, 1999		$ 237,000

CITY OF MORGANTON
General Fund
Balance Sheet (Condensed)
June 30, 1999

Assets

Cash	$ 61,900
Investments	105,000
Receivables (net of allowances):	
Taxes	184,000
Accounts	48,850
Due from other funds	26,000
Total assets	$ 425,750

Liabilities

Vouchers payable	$ 125,930
Contracts payable	16,720
Due to other funds	26,100
Total liabilities	$ 168,750

Equity
Fund balances:

Reserved for encumbrances	$ 20,000
Unreserved, undesignated	237,000
Total fund balances	257,000
Total liabilities and equity	$ 425,750

condensed) is included. The individual current asset and current liability balances are presented for illustration purposes only and do not reflect the specific transactions indicated earlier.[30]

Encumbrances Outstanding at Year's End   The balance sheet at June 30, 1999, includes outstanding commitments, totaling $20,000 (Fund balances: Reserved for encumbrances). The reserve for encumbrances appearing on the June 30, 1999, bal-

[30]More complete governmental financial statements are examined in the following chapter. As is discussed in more detail at that time, an additional statement also must be presented for the governmental-type funds that adopt budgets, disclosing both budgeted and actual figures for revenues, expenditures, and other changes in fund balance.

ance sheet should be reclassified to Reserved for Encumbrances—Prior Year at the beginning of the 1999–2000 fiscal year.

General Fund
(Fiscal year 1999–2000)

July 1, 1999

Reserve for Encumbrances	20,000	
Reserve for Encumbrances—Prior Year		20,000

    To reclassify encumbrances outstanding at year-end June 30, 1999, as prior year reserve for encumbrances.

Since the associated encumbrance was closed to Unreserved, Undesignated Fund Balance at June 30, 1999, a different treatment is required when the commitment becomes a liability. When the goods or services are received, the expenditure should be labeled to identify the outflow with the decisions of the previous fiscal period. Assume the items received have an invoice amount of $19,500, the entry to record the expenditure is as follows:

General Fund
(Fiscal year 1999–2000)

July 1999

Expenditures—Fiscal Year 1998–99	19,500	
Vouchers (or Accounts) Payable		19,500

    To record expenditure for items ordered in previous fiscal period.

The expenditure of $19,500 is identified with the previous fiscal year (1998–99) and referred to as a prior year expenditure. The prior year expenditure and reserve for encumbrances are closed to Unreserved Fund Balance as follows:

General Fund
Closing entry
June 30, 2000

Reserve for Encumbrances—Prior year	20,000	
Expenditures—Fiscal Year 1998–99		19,500
Unreserved Fund Balance		500

The increase in unreserved fund balance indicates that $500 of the net assets of the General Fund, which had been reserved previously for outstanding commitments, are now available for current year expenditures.

SUMMARY

1. The accounting procedures utilized by state and local governments vary in many significant respects from the reporting process employed by profit-oriented businesses. These differences originated because the informational requirements of financial statement users are assumed to change when the profit motive is removed. Furthermore, varying needs are encountered among the users of government accounting data. The voter, the taxpayer, the city official, and the bond investor all seek specific types of information. Since 1984, the Governmental Accounting Standards Board (GASB) has been in charge of developing accounting principles to satisfy the unique needs of the users of governmental financial statements.

2. Accountability is the major emphasis in state and local government financial reporting. The accounting principles and procedures are designed to assist in controlling financial operations as well as the government officials who serve as stewards over public funds. The reporting process also must be capable of accounting for the wide range of activities often encountered in a governmental unit (such as the police department, ambulance service, zoo, motor pool, municipal golf course, trash collection, and the like). Because income determination is not important to most of these activities, many features of governmental accounting vary significantly from the procedures traditionally associated with for-profit enterprises.

3. One of the most unique aspects of government financial reporting is the use of fund accounting. Each of the distinct functions of a state or locality is recorded in an individual, self-balancing reporting system referred to as a fund. Because of the broad range of possible activities, specific accounting procedures have been designed for the various funds. For a state or local government, ten fund types are identified that are grouped within three general categories: (1) Governmental Funds (the General Fund, Special Revenue Funds, Capital Projects Funds, and Debt Service Funds); (2) Proprietary Funds (Enterprise Funds and Internal Service Funds); and (3) Fiduciary Funds (Expendable Trust Funds, Nonexpendable Trust Funds, Pension Trust Funds, and Agency Funds). In addition, two account groups are utilized in connection with the governmental funds: General Fixed Assets Account Group and General Long-Term Debt Account Group.

4. Five of the funds (the four Governmental Funds plus the Expendable Trust Fund) are primarily service-oriented and are referred to as governmental-type funds. These funds utilize many of the unusual accounting procedures traditionally associated with governmental reporting. For example, budgetary entries are required in the General Fund, Special Revenue Funds, and Expendable Trust Funds while being optional in the Debt Service Funds and Capital Projects Funds. Annual financial budgets are adopted for each fund (to promote financial planning and control) and are entered directly into the accounting records by means of a journal entry. Comparisons can then be drawn at any time during the period between actual and budgeted figures. At year's end, both amounts are reported in the Statement of Revenues, Expenditures, and Changes in Fund Balances—Budget and Actual.

5. An additional procedure that plays an essential budgetary role in the governmental-type fund for a state or local government accounting system is the recording of monetary commitments known as encumbrances. The reporting of encumbrances is intended to help prevent the overspending of a fund's resources. An Encumbrances account balance is established at the time that a purchase order is approved or a contract signed. This account balance is eventually removed when a formal liability is incurred.

6. Another significant aspect of the accounting process found in state and local government units is the recognition of expenditures. To assist in maintaining control over spending, governmental-type funds focus on recording expenditures rather than either expenses or asset acquisitions. This approach is designed to help monitor the uses made by a government of its financial resources. Thus, spending is recorded in this manner whether it is for buildings, equipment, or traditional expenses such as rents and salaries. Modified accrual accounting is used for recognition purposes. Under this approach, each expenditure is entered into the records at the time a liability is incurred.

7. Despite the emphasis on reporting expenditures, some permanent recording of fixed asset acquisitions is still considered necessary. Consequently, long-lived assets purchased by any of the governmental-type funds are listed separately in a General Fixed Assets Account Group. Since depreciation is not an expenditure, its recording is omitted entirely from these funds.

8. Modified accrual accounting requires that revenues be recognized in the period in which they become both measurable and available. Thus, property, sales, and income taxes usually are accrued when assessed but many other revenues are recognized only when cash is received.

9. Several other aspects of the governmental accounting process that warrant special attention because of unique reporting requirements include the sale of bonds, interfund transactions, and the recording of commitments. The issuance of bonds is an especially important procedure since state and local governments often raise considerable amounts of their resources in this manner. At the time of sale, the appropriate fund records the inflow of cash as an Other Financing Source. Concurrently, the liability is listed separately in the General Long-Term Debt Account Group.

10. Because of the need to provide sufficient monetary resources to all appropriate functions, interfund transactions are common within most government units. Three different types are identified: (1) operating transfers designed to direct money to the various governmental funds, (2) residual equity transfers made to create or finance proprietary

activities, and (3) quasi-external transactions used to pay for services performed within the government for a fee.

COMPREHENSIVE ILLUSTRATION

Problem

(*Estimated Time: 30 to 55 minutes*) The town of Drexel, North Carolina, has the following financial transactions occur during the 1998 fiscal year. Prepare journal entries for these events indicating the appropriate fund(s) or group of accounts in each case. Closing entries are not required.

1. The town council adopts a budget estimating general revenues of $740,000 and establishing approved expenditures of $610,000 and operating transfers out of $100,000. A surplus of $30,000 is projected. The council also agrees that an additional $8,000 in anticipated parking meter receipts is to be used to send needy children to summer camp.

2. Property taxes of $700,000 are levied for 1998. Based on past experience, 2 percent are estimated as uncollectible.

3. Three new police cars are ordered at an approximate cost of $96,000.

4. A transfer of $50,000 is made from the General Fund to a Debt Service Fund. This money, along with $28,000 already in the Debt Service Fund, is used to pay a $70,000 bond payable that comes due plus accrued interest.

5. The town council approves construction of a $850,000 town hall. Of this amount, $700,000 will be raised by a bond issue with the remainder coming from a state grant that has already been approved (although not yet received) and must be spent for this building and its furnishings.

6. The town sells the bonds mentioned in (5) for $700,000.

7. Parking meter revenues of $6,600 are collected and immediately used to send deserving children to camp.

8. Property tax collections amount to $660,000.

9. A contract to build the new town hall at a cost of $828,000 is signed and the commitment is recorded.

10. The town agrees to put curbing on several local streets at a cost of $80,000. Ten percent of this money will come from the General Fund with the remainder to be charged to the property owners being benefited. The town will be secondarily liable for the entire amount.

11. The three new police cars arrive at an actual cost of $95,000.

12. An invoice for the work to date of $120,000 is received from the contractor in connection with the new town hall. Five percent is retained to ensure completion of the contract with the remainder to be paid by the town in 60 days.

13. Bonds of $72,000 are sold to finance the curbing project.

14. Licenses and fees of $18,000 are collected by the town. No previous recording had been made.

15. The state pays the $150,000 grant described in (5) in connection with the town hall. Of this total, $20,000 is spent immediately to acquire furniture for the facility.

16. The town issues an $80,000 two-year bond to finance ongoing operating activities.

Solution

The following entries should be recorded within the accounting system of the town of Drexel. In some cases, the entries are optional and are so identified.

	General Fund		
1.			
Estimated Revenues Control		740,000	
Appropriations Control			610,000
Estimated Other Financing			
Uses—Operating Transfers Out			100,000
(Budgetary) Fund Balance			30,000
To record 1998 budget.			

Special Revenue Fund

Estimated Revenues—Parking Meter Receipts	8,000	
Appropriations—Summer Camp.		8,000

To record 1998 budget for parking meter revenues and related expenditures.

2.　　　　　　　　**General Fund**

Taxes Receivable—Current.	700,000	
Allowance for Uncollectible Taxes (2%)		14,000
Revenues Control (95%)		686,000

To record property tax levy.

3.　　　　　　　　**General Fund**

Encumbrances Control	96,000	
Budgetary Fund Balance—Reserved for		
Encumbrances.		96,000

Police cars ordered.

4.　　　　　　　　**General Fund**

Other Financing Uses—Operating Transfer Out	50,000	
Cash		50,000

Transfer made to Debt Service Fund.

Debt Service Fund

Cash	50,000	
Other Financing Sources—Operating		
Transfer In		50,000

Transfer received from General Fund.

Expenditures Control	78,000	
Cash		78,000

Payment of bond principal ($70,000) and interest ($8,000).

General Long-Term Debt Account Group

Bonds Payable	70,000	
Amount Available in Debt Service Funds		28,000
Amount to Be Provided		42,000

To remove extinguished debt.

5.　　　　　　　　**Capital Projects Fund**

Estimated Revenues—State Grant	150,000	
Estimated Other Financing		
Sources—Bond Proceeds	700,000	
Appropriations—Construction of Town Hall		850,000

Optional entry to record construction budget.

Due from State	150,000	
Deferred Revenues—State Grant		150,000

To accrue approved grant from state. Revenue will be earned by making appropriate expenditure.

6.　　　　　　　　**Capital Projects Fund**

Cash	700,000	
Other Financing Sources—Bond Proceeds.		700,000

To record receipt from bond issue.

General Long-Term Debt Account Group

Amount to Be Provided	700,000	
Bonds Payable		700,000

To record receipt from bond issue.

7.　　　　　　　　**Special Revenue Fund**

Cash	6,600	
Revenues—Parking Meter Receipts		6,600

To record parking meter revenues.

Expenditures—Children to Camp	6,600	
Cash		6,600

Money is spent to send children to camp.

8.   **General Fund**

Cash 660,000
    Taxes Receivable—Current   660,000
Property tax collections.

9.   **Capital Projects Fund**

Encumbrances—Town Hall Construction 828,000
    Reserved for Encumbrances.......................   828,000
Contract signed to construct town hall.

10.   **Capital Projects Fund**

Estimated Revenues—Special Assessments 72,000
Estimated Other Financing Sources—
    Operating Transfers In 8,000
    Appropriations—Curbing.........................   80,000
Optional entry to record budget for curbing project with 10
percent payable from General Fund.

Due from General Fund............................. 8,000
    Other Financing Sources—Operating Transfer In   8,000
To accrue interfund transfer that has been authorized.

                                                 General Fund

Other Financing Uses—Operating Transfers Out 8,000
    Due to Capital Projects Fund......................   8,000
To record authorized transfer.

11.   **General Fund**

Reserved for Encumbrances 96,000
    Encumbrances Control   96,000
To remove encumbrance on police cars.

Expenditures Control 95,000
    Vouchers Payable   95,000
To record actual invoice price for police cars.

                                       General Fixed Assets Account Group

Machinery and Equipment 95,000
    Investment in General Fixed Assets—
      General Fund   95,000
To record acquisition of police cars.

12.   **Capital Projects Fund**

Reserved for Encumbrances 120,000
    Encumbrances—Town Hall Construction   120,000
To cancel portion of encumbrance.

Expenditures—Town Hall Construction 120,000
    Contracts Payable...............................   114,000
    Contracts Payable—Retained
      Percentage (5%)   6,000
To establish liability for town hall construction.

                                       General Fixed Assets Account Group

Construction in Progress 120,000
    Investments in General Fixed Assets—
      Capital Projects Funds.........................   120,000
To record cost to date of construction of town hall.

13.   **Capital Projects Fund**

Cash 72,000
    Other Financing Sources—
      Special Assessment Bonds   72,000
To record cash received from issuance of special assessments
bonds.

General Long-Term Debt Account Group

Amount to Be Provided from Special Assessments	72,000	
Special Assessment Bond with Government Commitment		72,000
To record outstanding bonds.		

14.   **General Fund**

Cash	18,000	
Revenue Control		18,000
Collection of licenses and fees.		

15.   **Capital Projects Fund**

Cash	150,000	
Due from State		150,000
Grant is collected from state government for town hall and furnishings.		
Expenditures—Furniture	20,000	
Cash		20,000
Part of state grant is spent to furnish new town hall.		
Deferred Revenues—State Grant	20,000	
Revenues—State Grant		20,000
To recognize revenue in connection with state grant properly spent.		

General Fixed Asset Account Group

Furniture	20,000	
Investment in General Fixed Assets—State Grant		20,000
To record cost of furniture for town hall.		

16.   **General Fund**

Cash	80,000	
Other Financing Sources—Bond Proceeds		80,000
Sold bond to finance ongoing activities.		

General Long-Term Debt Account Group

Amount to Be Provided	80,000	
Bond Payable		80,000
To record two-year bond that was issued to finance ongoing activities.		

QUESTIONS

1. Identify the different users of the financial statements of state and local governments. How do their informational requirements vary?

2. What is the primary reporting emphasis in governmental accounting? Why has this emphasis been adopted?

3. Why are consolidated financial statements not considered appropriate for a government reporting unit?

4. What is a fund? Why are governmental accounting records broken down into individual funds?

5. Why are differing accounting methods used by the various funds of a state or local government?

6. What are the three broad classifications into which all funds can be categorized? What are the identifying characteristics of each of these fund types?

7. What is an account group? Why is an account group not considered a fund?

8. What are the four fund types that fall within the governmental funds? What activities are accounted for by each of these funds?

9. Which two major fund types are within proprietary funds? What activities are accounted for by each?

10. What is the difference between an Expendable Trust Fund and a Nonexpendable Trust Fund?

11. All of the funds of a state or local government (except for the Agency Funds) can be viewed as either governmental-type or business-type. What is the difference in accounting emphasis between these two groups?

12. Why are budgets formally recorded in the accounting records of some governmental funds? Which of the fund types record budgetary entries?

13. What is an appropriation?

14. Why does the accounting process that is utilized by governmental-type funds emphasize expenditures rather than expenses?

15. Under modified accrual accounting, when should expenditures be recorded? Under accrual accounting, when should expenditures be recorded?

16. Since the governmental-type funds record expenditures, how are fixed assets reported?

17. Why is depreciation expense not recognized in the governmental-type funds?

18. Under modified accrual accounting, when should revenues be recognized? Under accrual accounting, when should revenues be recognized?

19. When is the Other Financing Sources designation considered to be appropriate? When is the Other Financing Uses designation used?

20. What is the traditional method of recording the long-term liabilities issued by the governmental-type funds?

21. Describe the revenue recognition process in connection with grants.

22. What are the three types of interfund transactions? How should each be recorded?

23. What is the purpose of an encumbrance? When is an encumbrance recorded?

24. What accounting is made for encumbrances that remain outstanding at the end of a fiscal year?

25. What is a special assessment, and how are special assessments accounted for by a state or local government?

26. What are the two ways to account for the supplies bought and used by governmental-type funds?

27. What account balances are closed out annually in a governmental-type fund? Into what account are these balances closed?

LIBRARY ASSIGNMENTS

1. Read the following articles and any other published information discussing the unique features of not-for-profit accounting:

   "Orange County Crisis," *The Wall Street Journal,* December 8, 1994, p. A1, A12.

   Balance Budget Requirements: State Experiences and Implications for the Federal Government, United States General Accounting Office, 1993, GAO: AFMD-93-58BR.

   "Making Sense of Nonbusiness Accounting," *Harvard Business Review,* May–June 1980.

   "Advantages of Fund Accounting in 'Nonprofits,' " *Harvard Business Review,* May–June 1980.

   "Financial Reporting: Should Government Emulate Business?" *Journal of Accountancy,* August 1981.

   "Monuments, Mistakes, and Opportunities," *Accounting Horizons,* June 1988.

   "The Nature of Public Assets: A Response to Mautz," *Accounting Horizons,* June 1990.

   "Not-for-Profit Financial Reporting: Another View," *Journal of Accountancy,* August 1989.

   In this last article, the following question is raised: Are not-for-profit organizations truly so different from for-profit entities that an entirely different reporting system is necessary? Write a short report to address this issue.

2. Obtain a copy of the latest comprehensive annual financial report of a state or local government. If one is not available in the library, request a copy, either by telephone or mail, from the Director of Finance of the governmental unit. Write a report to answer the following questions:

    ■ How many separate fund types are presented in the balance sheet?
    ■ What types of assets are found in the General Fund?
    ■ For the General Fund, what amount is shown as the Fund Balance—Unreserved, Undesignated?
    ■ What is the total reported balance of assets in the General Fixed Asset Account Group?
    ■ What types of activities are reported within the Special Revenue Funds?
    ■ What is the total amount of debt reported in the General Long-Term Debt Account Group?
    ■ Does the General Fund show a year-end total for Fund Balance—Reserved for Encumbrances? If so, what is this balance?
    ■ What amount of total revenues and expenditures are reported for the General Fund?
    ■ Were General Fund revenues greater or less than the budgeted figure?
    ■ What other financing sources and uses are listed for the General Fund?
    ■ Are any residual equity transfers listed?
    ■ If the government has Expendable Trust Funds, what specific funds are included under this category?

PROBLEMS

1. What is the underlying reason a governmental unit uses separate funds to account for various transactions?
    a. Governmental units are so large that accounting for all transactions as a single unit would be unduly cumbersome
    b. Because of the diverse nature of the services offered and legal provisions regarding activities of a governmental unit, activities must be segregated by functional nature.
    c. Generally accepted accounting principles require that all not-for-profit entities report on a funds basis.
    d. Many activities carried on by governmental units are short-lived so that inclusion in a general set of accounts could cause undue probability of error or omission.

    (AICPA adapted)

2. Which of the following is not a Governmental Fund?
    a. Special Revenue Fund.
    b. Internal Service Fund.
    c. Capital Projects Fund.
    d. Debt Service Fund.

3. What is the purpose of a Special Revenue Fund?
    a. To account for revenues legally restricted as to expenditure.
    b. To account for ongoing activities.
    c. To account for gifts where only subsequently earned income can be expended.
    d. To account for the cost of long-lived assets bought with designated funds.

4. What is the purpose of Enterprise Funds?
    a. To account for operations that provide services to other departments within a government.
    b. To account for asset transfers.
    c. To account for ongoing activities such as the police and fire departments.
    d. To account for operations financed in whole or in part by outside user charges.

5. How do Expendable Trust Funds differ from Nonexpendable Trust Funds?
    a. Expendable Trust Funds account for monies that have already been spent whereas Nonexpendable Trust Funds account for monies to be spent.
    b. Expendable Trust Funds account for gifts where the entire amount can be spent whereas Nonexpendable Trust Funds account for gifts where only subsequently earned income can be spent.

     c. Expendable Trust Funds account for monies that can be spent at any time whereas Nonexpendable Trust Funds account for monies that can only be spent after the passage of a specified time.

     d. Expendable Trust Funds account for monies that must be spent for operating activities whereas Nonexpendable Trust Funds account for monies that must be spent for fixed assets.

6. Which of the following statements is true concerning the recording of a budget?
     a. At the beginning of the year, Appropriations is debited.
     b. A debit to the Budgetary Fund Balance account indicates an expected surplus.
     c. At the beginning of the year, Estimated Revenues is debited.
     d. At the end of the year, Appropriations is credited.

7. Which of the following funds does not always record a budgetary entry?
     a. Debt Service Funds.
     b. Expendable Trust Funds.
     c. Special Revenue Funds.
     d. General Fund.

8. When fixed assets purchased from General Fund revenues were received, the appropriate journal entry was made in the General Fixed Assets Account Group. What account, if any, should have been debited in the General Fund?
     a. No journal entry should have been made in the General Fund.
     b. Expenditures.
     c. Fixed assets.
     d. Encumbrances.

(AICPA adapted)

9. A police department is acquiring a new car that is being accounted for within the General Fund. What recording should be made?
     a. As a vehicle within the General Fund.
     b. As an expenditure within the General Fixed Assets Account Group.
     c. As a vehicle within the General Fund and as an expenditure within the General Fixed Assets Account Group.
     d. As an expenditure within the General Fund and as a vehicle within the General Fixed Assets Account Group.

10. Machinery is acquired for the fire department using monies from the General Fund. Which of the following is true?
     a. Depreciation expense is not recognized although the reporting of accumulated depreciation within the General Fixed Assets Account Group is allowed.
     b. Depreciation is recorded but only if the machinery is recorded within the General Fund.
     c. The machinery's reported balance is adjusted each year to its market value.
     d. Depreciation expense is allowed but only if no Expenditure has been recorded.

11. A city acquires supplies and is using the consumption method of recording. Which of the following statements is true?
     a. An Expenditures account was debited at the time of receipt.
     b. An expense is recorded as the supplies are consumed.
     c. An Inventory account is debited at the time of the acquisition.
     d. The supplies are recorded within the General Fixed Assets Account Group.

12. According to modified accrual accounting, when should revenues be recognized?
     a. When earned and collected.
     b. When earned and collection is reasonably assured.
     c. When measurable and available.
     d. When the underlying transaction has taken place and a demand for the money has been made.

13. Fund accounting is used by governmental units with resources that must be
     a. Composed of cash or cash equivalents.
     b. Incorporated into combined or combining financial statements.
     c. Segregated for the purpose of carrying on specific activities or attaining certain objectives.
     d. Segregated physically according to various objectives.

(AICPA adapted)

14. In preparing combined financial statements for a governmental entity, interfund receivables and payables should be
    a. Reported as reservations of fund balance.
    b. Reported as additions to or reductions from the unrestricted fund balance.
    c. Reported as amounts due to and due from other funds.
    d. Eliminated.

    (AICPA adapted)

15. The expenditure element "salaries and wages" is an example of which type of classification?
    a. Object.
    b. Program.
    c. Function.
    d. Activity.

    (AICPA adapted)

16. During the year ending December 31, 1998, Leyland City received a state grant of $500,000 to finance the purchase of buses, and an additional grant of $100,000 to aid in the financing of bus operations. Only $300,000 of the capital grant was used in 1998 for the purchase of buses although the entire operating grant of $100,000 was spent during the year.

    If Leyland's bus transportation system is accounted for as part of the General Fund, how much should Leyland report as revenues for this year?
    a. $100,000.
    b. $300,000.
    c. $400,000.
    d. $500,000.

    (AICPA adapted)

17. A city receives a state grant that must be spent to remove litter. When is the revenue recognized?
    a. When received.
    b. When appropriately spent.
    c. When measurable and available.
    d. When earned.

18. A city issues a five-year bond to finance the construction of a new government building. Which of the following statements is not true?
    a. An Amount to be Provided account appears in the General Long-Term Debt Account Group.
    b. The bond appears in a Debt Service Fund.
    c. The cash is recorded in a Capital Projects Fund.
    d. An Other Financing Source account appears in the Capital Projects Fund.

19. Money is transferred from the General Fund to the Capital Projects Funds to provide financing for a new construction project. This transaction is an example of
    a. An operating transfer.
    b. A residual equity transfer.
    c. A capital contribution.
    d. A quasi-external transaction.

20. When is the Other Financing Source designation used?
    a. For revenues other than property taxes.
    b. For bond proceeds and transfers-in.
    c. For interest and other investment income.
    d. For quasi-external transactions.

21. What is a residual equity transfer?
    a. A transfer by a government of money to provide permanent financing for a Proprietary Fund.
    b. A transfer that increases the Fund Balance of the General Fund.
    c. A transfer of the remaining book value of a fixed asset.
    d. A transfer of any funds remaining after a project has been entirely completed.

22. Which of the following is an example of a quasi-external transaction of a city?

    a. Money is transferred from the General Fund to the Capital Projects Fund.

    b. A transfer is made to start an Enterprise Fund.

    c. The General Fund pays the city print shop for work done.

    d. A building is acquired with the proceeds of a bond.

23. A city constructs a special assessment project (a sidewalk) for which it is secondarily liable. Bonds of $90,000 are issued. Another $10,000 is authorized and transferred out of the General Fund. The sidewalk is built for $100,000. The citizens are billed for $90,000. They pay this amount and the debt is paid off. Where is the $100,000 expenditure recorded?
    a. No recording is made by the city.
    b. Agency Fund.
    c. General Fund.
    d. Capital Projects Fund.

24. Work is done by a city as a special assessment. Curbing is constructed in a new neighborhood. Under what condition should this activity be recorded in an Agency Fund?
    a. Never; the work is reported in the Capital Projects Funds.
    b. Only if the city is secondarily liable for any debt incurred to finance construction costs.
    c. Only if the city is in no way liable for the costs of the construction.
    d. In all cases.

25. When is an encumbrance first recorded?
    a. At the time the budget is passed.
    b. When the appropriation is made.
    c. When a purchase commitment is made.
    d. When an acquired asset is received.

26. An encumbrance is outstanding at the end of a city's fiscal year. The encumbrance will still be honored in the next period. How is this information reported in the first year?
    a. All encumbrance balances are removed but a fund balance amount is reclassified to disclose the commitment.
    b. If the encumbrance is to be honored, nothing is done at the end of the first period.
    c. Since the encumbrance is to be honored, the amount is reclassified as a liability.
    d. Since the financial impact will be in the following period, no disclosure is necessary.

27. When supplies ordered by a governmental unit are received at an actual price less than the estimated price on the purchase order, the Encumbrance account is:
    a. Credited for the estimated price on the purchase order.
    b. Credited for the actual price for the supplies received.
    c. Debited for the estimated price on the purchase order.
    d. Debited for the actual price for the supplies received.

    (AICPA)

28. Which of the following account balances found in the General Fund is not closed out at the end of the fiscal period?
    a. Due to Capital Projects Fund.
    b. Other Financing Sources—Bond Proceeds.
    c. Expenditures Control.
    d. Residual Equity Transfer.

29. The board of commissioners of the city of Hartmoore adopted a General Fund budget for the year ending June 30, 1999, which indicated revenues of $1,000,000, bond proceeds of $400,000, appropriations of $900,000, and operating transfers out of $300,000. If this budget is formally integrated into the accounting records, what is the required journal entry at the beginning of the year? What later entry is required?

30. A city orders a new computer at an anticipated cost of $88,000. It is received with an actual cost of $89,400. Payment is subsequently made. Give all of the required journal entries and identify the type of fund or account group in which each entry is recorded.

31. Cash of $90,000 is transferred from a city's general fund to start construction on a police station. A bond of $830,000 is issued at face value. The police station is built for $920,000. Prepare all necessary journal entries for these transactions and identify the

type of fund or account group in which each entry is recorded. Assume that the commitment is not recorded by the city.

32. On December 31, 1998, the city of Crawford paid $3.8 million for the total cost of a new fire station built during the year. To finance the project, $3 million in bonds were issued at face value with the remaining $800,000 transferred from the General Fund. What journal entries should be recorded by the Capital Projects Fund? What other journal entries should be made within Crawford's accounting system?

33. The following balances are found in the accounting system for Burwood Village's parks and recreation department at March 31, 1999:

> Appropriations—supplies $7,500
> Expenditures—supplies 4,500
> Encumbrances—supplies ordered 750

A request has been made for additional baseball bats. How much does the department have available for this purchase?

(AICPA adapted)

34. The following data relates to Lely Township:

> Cost of printing and binding equipment used for servicing
>   all of Lely's departments on a cost-reimbursement basis $100,000
> Cost of equipment used for supplying water to Lely's
>   residents   900,000
> Receivables for completed sidewalks to be paid in
>   installments by affected property owners (the town is
>   secondarily liable)   950,000
> Cash received from federal government which must be
>   used for highway maintenance   995,000

How much of these assets should be reported in a Special Revenue Fund? How much of these assets should be accounted for in an Internal Service Fund? How much of these assets should be accounted for in an Enterprise Fund?

(AICPA adapted)

35. A local government incurs the following transactions during the current fiscal period. Prepare journal entries without dollar amounts. Indicate the fund type or account group in which each entry is being recorded.
    a. Budget is passed for the police department, ambulance service, and other ongoing activities. Funding is from property taxes, transfers, and bond proceeds. All monetary outflows will be for expenses and fixed assets. A deficit is projected.
    b. A bond is issued at face value to fund the construction of a new municipal building.
    c. A computer is ordered to be used by the tax department.
    d. The computer is received.
    e. The invoice for the computer is paid.
    f. City council agrees to transfer money from General Fund as partial payment for a special assessments project. This money has not yet been transferred. The city will be secondarily liable for any money borrowed for this work.
    g. City council creates a motor pool to service all government vehicles. Money is transferred from General Fund to provide permanent financing for this facility.
    h. Property taxes are levied. Although officials believe that most of these taxes should be collected during the current period, a portion will be received during the subsequent year with a small percentage estimated to be uncollectible. Modified accrual accounting is being used.
    i. Grant money is collected from the state to be spent as a supplement to the salaries of the police force. No entry has previously been recorded.
    j. A portion of the grant money in (i) is properly spent.

36. Make journal entries for the governmental funds of the city of Pudding to record the following transactions. Indicate the fund or account group in which each entry is being made.
    a. Ordered a new truck for the sanitation department at a cost of $94,000.
    b. The city print shop did work for the school system (but has not yet been paid). The printing was charged out at $1,200.

  c. A $700,000 bond was issued to build a new road.

  d. Cash of $20,000 is transferred from the General Fund to provide permanent financing for a municipal swimming pool that will be viewed as an Enterprise Fund.

  e. The truck ordered in (*a*) is received at an actual cost of $96,000. Payment is not made at this time.

  f. Cash of $32,000 is transferred from the General Fund to a Capital Projects Fund.

  g. A state grant of $30,000 is received that must be spent to promote recycling.

  h. The first $5,000 of the state grant received in (*g*) is appropriately expended.

37. Prepare journal entries for a state or local government to record the following transactions. Indicate the funds or account groups involved. Only entries in the governmental-type funds need be recorded.

  a. A $300,000 bond is sold at face value by the government to finance construction of a warehouse.

  b. A $400,000 contract is signed for construction of the warehouse.

  c. A $20,000 transfer of unrestricted funds was made for the eventual payment of the debt in (*a*).

  d. Equipment for the fire department is received with a cost of $12,000. When ordered, an anticipated cost of $11,800 had been recorded.

  e. Supplies to be used in the schools are bought for $2,000 cash. The consumption method is being used.

  f. A state grant of $5,000 is received to supplement police salaries.

  g. Property tax assessments are mailed to citizens of the government. The total assessment is $600,000 although officials anticipate that 4 percent will never be collected and another 5 percent will not be received for several years. Modified accrual accounting is to be used.

38. The following trial balances are for the governmental funds of the city of Copeland prepared from the current accounting records:

General Fund

	Debit	Credit
Cash	$ 19,000	
Taxes receivable	112,000	
Allowance for uncollectible taxes		$ 2,000
Vouchers payable		24,000
Due to debt service fund		10,000
Deferred revenues		16,000
Budgetary fund balance—Reserved for encumbrances		9,000
Fund balance—Unreserved, undesignated		103,000
Revenues control		176,000
Expenditures control	110,000	
Other financing uses control	90,000	
Encumbrances control	9,000	
Estimated revenues control	190,000	
Appropriations control		171,000
Budgetary fund balance		19,000
Totals	$530,000	$530,000

Debt Service Fund

	Debit	Credit
Cash	$ 8,000	
Investments	51,000	
Taxes receivable	11,000	
Due from general fund	10,000	
Fund balance—Designated for debt service		45,000
Revenues control		20,000
Other financing sources—Operating transfers in		90,000
Expenditures control	75,000	
Totals	$155,000	$155,000

Capital Projects Fund

	Debit	Credit
Cash	$ 70,000	
Special assessments receivable	90,000	
Contracts payable		$ 50,000
Deferred revenues		90,000
Budgetary fund balance—Reserved for encumbrances		16,000
Fund balance—Unreserved, undesignated		–0–
Other financing sources		150,000
Expenditures control	130,000	
Encumbrances	16,000	
Estimated other financing sources	150,000	
Appropriations		150,000
Totals	$456,000	$456,000

Special Revenue Fund

	Debit	Credit
Cash	$ 14,000	
Taxes receivable	41,000	
Inventory of supplies	4,000	
Vouchers payable		$ 25,000
Deferred revenues		3,000
Fund balance—Reserved for inventory of supplies		4,000
Budgetary fund balance—Reserved for encumbrances		3,000
Fund balance—Unreserved, undesignated		19,000
Revenues control		56,000
Expenditures control	48,000	
Encumbrances	3,000	
Estimated revenues	75,000	
Appropriations		60,000
Budgetary fund balance		15,000
Totals	$185,000	$185,000

Required:

Based on the information presented for each of these governmental funds, answer the following questions:

 a. How much more money can be expended or committed by the General Fund during the remainder of the current year?

 b. Which closing entries would be necessary for the General Fund?

 c. Deferred revenues appear in three of these trial balances. What possible explanations exist for these balances?

 d. Why does the Capital Projects Fund have no construction or fixed asset accounts?

 e. What does the $150,000 Appropriations balance found in the Capital Projects Fund represent?

 f. Several of the funds have balances for Encumbrances and Budgetary Fund Balance—Reserved for Encumbrance. How will these amounts be accounted for at the end of the fiscal year?

 g. Why does the Fund Balance—Unreserved, Undesignated account in the Capital Projects Fund have a zero balance?

 h. What are possible explanations for the $150,000 Other Financing Sources balance found in the Capital Projects Fund?

 i. What does the $75,000 balance in the Expenditures Control account of the Debt Service Fund represent?

 j. What is the purpose of the Special Assessments Receivable found in the Capital Projects Fund?

 k. In the Special Revenue Fund, what is the purpose of the Fund Balance—Reserved for Inventory of Supplies account?

 l. Why does the Debt Service Fund not have budgetary account balances?

39. Following are descriptions of transactions and other financial events for the city of Tetris for the year ending December 31, 1999. Not all transactions have been included here.

Only the General Fund formally records a budget. No encumbrances were carried over from 1998.

Paid salary for police officers	$ 21,000
Government grant is received to pay ambulance drivers	40,000
Estimated revenues	232,000
Invoices were received for rent on equipment used by fire department	
during last four months of the year	3,000
Paid for newly constructed city hall	1,044,000
Commitment made to acquire new ambulance	111,000
Cash received from bonds sold for construction purposes	300,000
Order placed for new sanitation truck	69,000
Paid salary of ambulance drivers—money derived from state government	
grant given for that purpose	24,000
Paid for supplies for school system	16,000
Transfer made by General Fund to eventually pay off a long-term debt . . .	33,000
Received but did not pay for a new ambulance	120,000
Property tax receivables were levied. City anticipates that 95 percent	
will be collected and 5 percent will be bad	200,000
Acquired and paid for new school bus	40,000
Cash received from business taxes and parking meters (not previously	
accrued)	14,000
Appropriations	225,000

The following questions are independent although each is based on the preceding information. When making journal entries, indicate the fund.

a. What is the balance in the Budgetary Fund Balance account for the year and is it a debit or credit?

b. Assume that 60 percent of the school supplies are used during the year so that 40 percent remain. If the consumption method is being applied, how is the recording handled?

c. The sanitation truck that was ordered was not received prior to the end of the year. The commitment will be honored in the subsequent year when the truck arrives. What journal entries are needed at the end of 1999?

d. Assume the ambulance was received on December 31, 1999. Provide all necessary journal entries on that date.

e. Give all journal entries that should have been made when the $33,000 transfer was made to eventually pay off a long-term debt.

f. What amount of revenue would be recognized for the period? Explain the makeup of this total.

g. What deferred revenue figures would appear in this city's balance sheet?

h. What are the total expenditures? Explain the makeup of this total.

i. What journal entries were prepared when the bonds were issued?

40. Zuraw County is located in the western part of the state. At the beginning of the current fiscal year, the county's accountant retired. Government officials of Zuraw County were unable to fill this accounting vacancy for a number of months. When a qualified individual finally was hired for the job, a current trial balance for the General Fund was prepared:

	Debit	Credit
Cash	$ 56,000	
Due from capital projects fund	50,000	
Vouchers payable		$ 31,000
Deferred revenues		18,000
Budgetary fund balance—Reserved for encumbrances		9,000
Fund balance—Unreserved, undesignated		17,000
Revenues control		330,000
Expenditures control	264,000	
Truck	16,000	
Encumbrances control	9,000	
Estimated revenues	390,000	
Appropriations		350,000
Budgetary fund balance		30,000
Totals	$785,000	$785,000

Upon investigation, the new accountant discovered that the following events had occurred during the time that Zuraw County was without an accountant:

- The property tax levy for the current year was never entered into the financial records. Instead, the county recorded all cash collections as revenues when received. The original assessment was $400,000. Of that amount, $300,000 has been received to date with $90,000 more expected by the end of the year with the remaining $10,000 judged to be uncollectible. Receivables of $18,000 carried over from the previous year were also collected during the period and credited to taxes receivable. Modified accrual accounting is used.

- A new truck was acquired for $16,000 in cash during the year. The only entry relating to this acquisition was made in the General Fund.

- During the year, the county followed the policy of recording encumbrances for all purchase commitments. At the time a legal liability was incurred, the original encumbrance was eliminated based on the final invoice price. For the current period, $175,000 in encumbrances have been recorded. Subsequently, related expenditures of $166,000 were journalized, although the original encumbrances for these acquisitions totaled only $162,400.

- A transfer of $50,000 was made to the Capital Projects Fund during the year as permanent financing for a new city hall. This amount was recorded in the Capital Projects Fund as a credit to the Fund Balance—Unreserved, Undesignated account.

- County officials had estimated that $10,000 would be collected from parking meters and other miscellaneous revenues. This figure was debited to Estimated Revenues at the beginning of the period and credited to the Fund Balance—Unreserved, Undesignated account.

- The General Fund owes $5,000 to the Capital Projects Fund as the county's portion of the cost of a sidewalk construction project.

Required:

Prepare the correcting entries for Zuraw County needed to adjust the records of the General Fund as well as any other fund.

41.   Chesterfield County incurred the following list of transactions. Record these transactions indicating, in each case, the fund type or account group in which the entry is recorded.

  a.   A budget is passed for all ongoing activities. Revenue is anticipated to be $834,000 with approved spending of $540,000 and operating transfers out of $242,000.

  b.   A contract is signed with a construction company to build a new central office building for the government at a cost of $8 million. A budget for this project has previously been recorded.

  c.   Bonds are sold for $8 million (face value) to finance construction of the new office building.

  d.   The new building is completed. An invoice is received and paid.

  e.   Previously unrestricted cash of $1 million is set aside to begin paying the bonds issued in (*c*).

  f.   A portion of the bonds come due and $1 million is paid. Of this total, $100,000 represents interest. The interest had not been previously accrued.

  g.   Property tax levies are assessed to the citizens. Total billing for this tax is $800,000. Ninety percent is assumed to be collectible in this period with receipt of an additional 6 percent during subsequent periods, but in time to be available to pay current period liabilities. The remainder is expected to be uncollectible.

  h.   Cash of $120,000 is received from a toll road. Legally, 80 percent of this money has to be spent on highway maintenance. The remainder is held until the end of the year and then transferred to the state.

  i.   Investments valued at $300,000 are received by the county as a donation from a grateful citizen. Income from these investments must be used to beautify local parks.

42.   The following trial balance is taken from the General Fund of the city of Jennings for the year ending December 31, 1998. Prepare a condensed statement of revenues, expenditures, and changes in fund balance and also prepare a condensed balance sheet.

	Debit	Credit
Budgetary fund balance—Reserved for encumbrances		$ 90,000
Cash	$ 30,000	
Contracts payable		90,000
Deferred revenues		40,000
Due from capital projects funds	60,000	
Due to debt service funds		40,000
Encumbrances	90,000	
Expenditures	420,000	
Fund balance—Unreserved, undesignated		170,000
Investments	410,000	
Residual equity transfer	70,000	
Revenues		740,000
Other financing sources—Bond proceeds		300,000
Other financing sources—Transfers in		50,000
Other financing uses—Transfers out	400,000	
Taxes receivable	220,000	
Vouchers payable		180,000
Totals	$1,700,000	$1,700,000

43. In a special election held on May 1, 1998, the citizens of the city of Nicknar voted to approve a $10 million issue of 6 percent bonds maturing in 2018. The proceeds of this sale will help finance the construction of a new civic center. The total cost of the project was estimated at $15 million. The remaining $5 million will be funded by a state grant that has been approved but not yet received. The grant can be used only for this specific construction.

A Capital Projects Fund was established to account for the project. The budget authorization has previously been recorded in a memorandum entry. The following transactions occurred during the fiscal year beginning July 1, 1998, and ending June 30, 1999:

- On July 1, the General Fund loaned $500,000 to this project to defray engineering costs and other initial expenses.
- Preliminary engineering and planning costs of $320,000 were paid to Akron Engineering Company. No encumbrance had been recorded for this cost.
- On December 1, the bonds were sold at 101. The premium on these bonds was transferred to the Debt Service Funds to be used for eventual repayment purposes.
- On March 15, a contract for $12 million was entered into with Candu Construction Company for the major part of the building project.
- Orders were placed for materials estimated to cost $55,000.
- On April 1, a partial payment of $2.5 million was received from the state. This money can be spent only after the city has expended $7 million of its own funds.
- The previously ordered materials were received at a cost of $51,000 and paid.
- On June 15, an invoice for $2 million was received from Candu Construction for work done to date on the project. As per the terms of the contract, the city will withhold 6 percent of any billing until the building is completed and pay the remainder at the end of 30 days.
- The General Fund was repaid the $500,000 previously loaned.

Required:

Based on the preceding transactions:

a. Prepare journal entries to record the transactions for this capital projects fund for the period July 1, 1998, through June 30, 1999. Include the appropriate closing entries at June 30, 1999.

b. Prepare a balance sheet for this fund as of June 30, 1999.

(AICPA adapted)

44. Following are a series of events undergone by Dawn Village. Prepare the appropriate journal entries for these transactions indicating the specific fund type or account group within which each entry is being recorded.

- A formal budget is adopted for the village. Revenues of $385,000 are predicted. Of this total, $360,000 has been assigned to the General Fund and $25,000 to Special

Revenues Funds. Approved expenditures are set at $370,000: General Fund—$345,000 and Special Revenues Funds—$25,000.

- A new police car is received at an invoice cost of $41,900. A $42,500 encumbrance had been recorded previously by the village.
- A $100,000 grant is received by the village to be used for trash removal.
- Property taxes of $350,000 are levied by the village. Of this amount, 85 percent collection is expected during the current year with 10 percent anticipated during subsequent periods but not in time to be available for payment of current year liabilities. The remainder will probably be uncollectible. The first $25,000 portion of this levy that is collected is for the Special Revenues Fund.
- $69,000 of the grant money is spent for trash removal.
- A special assessments project costing $90,000 is approved; a section of a local road is to be repaved. The village provides the initial support by putting up 10 percent of this cost (from the General Fund). Residents who will benefit from this project will contribute the remaining 90 percent at the time of completion. The county issues a $80,000 bond payable at face value to help finance the work. The transfer is also made at this time.
- The village collects cash of $112,000. Of this amount, $100,000 is from property taxes while the remainder comes from fines, licenses, and the like that had not previously been accrued. Property tax receivables of $5,000 were judged to be uncollectible.
- The village orders a new computer at an estimated cost of $46,250.
- A total of $70,000 is transferred from the General Fund to the Capital Projects Fund as the initial funding in anticipation of building a new fire station.
- The village pays $60,000 from the General Fund. Salaries for government employees accounted for $13,000 of this total with the rest being paid for the computer which arrived two weeks before.
- A bond payable of $900,000 was issued for $893,000 to finance construction of a new fire station. A contract for $839,000 is then signed with the contractor who will build the new facility.
- A first payment of $87,000 is made on the new fire station based on the current degree of completion.

45. The following trial balance is for the General Fund of the city of Torndup at December 31, 1998. The city plans to honor all remaining commitments during 1999. Prepare a condensed statement of revenues, expenditures, and changes in fund balance as well as a condensed balance sheet.

	Debit	Credit
Accounts payable		$ 4,000
Accounts receivable	$ 32,000	
Allowance for doubtful accounts—Taxes		6,000
Budgetary fund balance—Reserved for encumbrances		30,000
Cash	18,000	
Deferred revenues		8,000
Encumbrances control	30,000	
Expenditures control	370,000	
Fund balance—Unreserved, undesignated (1/1/98)		170,000
Investments	117,000	
Other financing sources—Bond proceeds		72,000
Other financing sources—Operating transfers in		5,000
Other financing uses—Operating transfers out	80,000	
Residual equity transfers	20,000	
Revenues control		440,000
Taxes receivable	91,000	
Vouchers payable		23,000
Totals	$758,000	$758,000

17

Accounting for State and Local Governments (Part Two)

- In what ways does the accounting process used by the proprietary-type activities of a state or local government differ from the procedures applied to governmental-type funds?

- How are proprietary and fiduciary funds reported within the financial statements of a government?

- What controversies surround the reporting of Internal Service Funds?

- How is the reporting unit defined for a state or local government? What activities are included within the financial reporting of most governments?

- What is the difference in the primary government and its component units? How has *GASB Statement No. 14* affected the composition of governmental financial statements?

- What financial statements and other information are presented in the comprehensive annual financial report of a state or locality?

Chapter 16 introduced the accounting procedures utilized by state and local government organizations. To initiate this coverage, the reporting process applied to governmental-type funds (such as the General Fund and Special Revenue Funds) was analyzed in detail. Budgetary entries, expenditures, encumbrances, transfers, fund balances, and other unique aspects of governmental reporting were examined at that time. However, governmental accounting is not limited to the procedures previously illustrated. Consequently, the current chapter expands on this introductory material.

Chapter 17 analyzes four additional aspects of state and local government reporting:

- The first section presents appropriate financial accounting for the various proprietary and fiduciary activities of state and local government units. Included are overviews of both the functioning and the reporting of funds such as the Enterprise Funds, Internal Service Funds, and Nonexpendable Trust Funds.

- The second section describes the identification of the specific reporting unit encompassed by the financial statements of a government. The GASB has recently looked at this issue and set forth guidelines for the activities that should be included within the financial statements of a state or local government.

- The third section completes coverage of governmental accounting with a discussion of the comprehensive annual financial report utilized by these entities for external reporting purposes.

■ The fourth section describes changes to governmental financial statements that had

   been proposed by the GASB at the time this text was published.

PROPRIETARY- AND FIDUCIARY-TYPE FUNDS

The 1994 financial statements published by the city of Denver, Colorado, indicate the ownership and operation of a hospital, an airport, a stadium, a golf course, and a water treatment plant. According to the financial statements for Grand Forks, North Dakota, that city maintains a motor pool to service city-owned vehicles as well as a centralized purchasing department and a data processing center, both of which assist various government operations. Although these activities are not unusual for a government, their functions are markedly different from those of a police or fire department. A stadium, parking garage, and water utility do serve the public but only for a specified charge. A motor pool or data processing center also offers services but to the government itself; even then, monetary fees are still assessed.

As previously discussed, the operations of most state and local governments include a broad range of activities accounted for in governmental funds, proprietary funds, and fiduciary funds. Such internal diversity has always complicated the accounting and reporting process. While service-oriented activities utilize one approach to financial reporting, the proprietary funds and certain of the fiduciary funds are fundamentally different in nature and require alternative means of accounting.

The previous chapter examined the governmental-type funds. Coverage of the reporting procedures employed in the five remaining fund categories (Enterprise Funds, Internal Service Funds, Pension Trust Funds, Nonexpendable Trust Funds, and Agency Funds) has been deferred until the current chapter to avoid possible confusion. The dissimilarities between these two accounting approaches are more easily understood when introduced separately.

Exhibit 17–1 presents an overview of several of the major differences between governmental-type and proprietary-type funds.

Objective—Income Determination

The primary emphasis underlying the accounting for proprietary-type funds (except for Agency Funds) stresses income determination rather than the flow of current financial resources. In the Enterprise Funds and Internal Service Funds, operating costs are recovered, at least partially, through user charges rather than from property taxes or other government revenues. Because of the functional similarity with commercial endeavors, the operational efficiency of these activities is reflected by the computation of an earned income figure. "The generally accepted accounting principles here are those applicable to similar businesses in the private sector; and the measurement focus is on determination of net income, financial position, and changes in financial position."[1]

The two remaining funds (Pension Trust Funds and Nonexpendable Trust Funds) are fiduciary in nature; assets are held by the government to be used for stipulated purposes. Income also is calculated for these funds as a means of measuring the effective utilization of the resources on hand. For the Nonexpendable Trust Funds, this computation also indicates the amount of resources that can be expended for the designated purpose.

---

[1]*Codification of Governmental Accounting and Financial Reporting Standards* (Norwalk, Conn.: Governmental Accounting Standards Board, 1992), sec. 1300.102b.

	Governmental-Type Funds*	**Proprietary-Type Funds†**
Accounting emphasis	Accountability.	Measurement of net income.
Measurement focus	Flow of current financial resources.	Change in economic resources.
Basis of accounting	Modified accrual accounting.	Accrual accounting.
Budgets	Recorded in most funds.	Adopted but not recorded in the accounting system.
Encumbrances	Recorded in most funds at the time a purchase commitment or contract is made.	Not recorded.
Outflow of financial resources	Recorded as expenditures.	Recorded as assets or expenses.
Depreciation	Not reported.	Reported as an expense each period.
Recognition of revenues	When measurable and available.	When earning process is substantially completed.
Fixed assets and long-term debt	Recorded in separate account groups.	Recorded within the individual funds.
Equity accounts	Fund balances.	Most funds report contributed capital and retained capital.

*The governmental-type funds are the General Fund, Special Revenue Funds, Debt Service Funds, Capital Projects Funds, and Expendable Trust Funds.

†The proprietary-type funds are the Enterprise Funds, Internal Service Funds, Nonexpendable Trust Funds, and Pension Trust Funds. The Agency Funds record only the creation and settlement of liabilities.

Because profitability determination, rather than accountability, is underscored in these four fund categories, the following characteristics are applicable:

■ Budgetary entries are never recorded. Although budgets always should be adopted by the proprietary-type funds, physically entering the amounts into the financial records provides little benefit. Expenditure levels for the fiduciary funds, as an example, are regulated by contract or agreement; the inclusion of budgetary entries neither reinforces nor changes those stipulations. In the proprietary funds, "the demand for the goods and services provided largely determines the appropriate level of revenues and expenses. . . . Thus, as in commercial accounting, flexible budgets—prepared for several levels of possible activity—typically are better for proprietary fund planning, control, and evaluation purposes than are fixed budgets. . . . Thus, integration of fixed dollar budgetary accounts usually is neither necessary nor appropriate in proprietary fund accounting systems."[2]

■ Accrual accounting—and not modified accrual accounting—has historically served as the basis for recognizing revenues and expenses. Since income calculation rather than accountability for financial resources is being stressed in these funds, all revenue and expense figures are recorded in the same manner and time period as in for-profit accounting. Depreciation expense, as an example, is recognized to allocate the cost of fixed assets over their useful lives. By the same rationale, revenues are only recognized when the earning process is substantially complete. Because of this change in emphasis, encumbrances are never recorded by the proprietary-type funds and

---

[2]GASB Cod. sec. 1700.120–122.

acquisitions are either capitalized or expensed instead of being reported as expenditures.

■ Fixed assets and long-term debts are entered directly into the individual funds rather than being maintained in separate account groups. *Consequently, these proprietary-type funds stand by themselves in presenting the financial activities of specific government activities.* In addition, since the presence of these assets and liabilities permits the recognition of depreciation expense and interest accruals, net income calculation is possible. Once again, as with most aspects of these funds, a parallel to commercial accounting is evident.

GASB Statement No. 20, "Accounting and Financial Reporting for Proprietary Funds and Other Governmental Entities that Use Proprietary Fund Accounting," requires that proprietary activities use GASB standards. *Statement No. 20* allows the use of FASB standards that are not in conflict with GASB standards. Presently the GASB has issued standards for pensions, investments, and the statement of cash flows that differ from FASB standards. Proprietary funds should report using GASB standards for these items, but may use FASB standards for issues, such as contingent liabilities (*FASB Statement No. 5*), where no GASB standard exists.

Enterprise Funds

As previously indicated, state and local governments use Enterprise Funds to account for operations financed at least partially through outside user charges. Swimming pools, water utilities, municipal airports, amusement parks, and the like all fall under this heading. One survey found that 80 percent of local governmental units report at least one Enterprise Fund.[3] The city of Clearwater, Florida, operates a yacht basin; the city of Hartford, Connecticut, has a civic center; the city of Roanoke, Virginia, owns a bus service; the city of Walla Walla, Washington, maintains a cemetery.

Deciding whether an operation is an Enterprise Fund or part of the General Fund as an ongoing activity is not always easy. Should a municipal swimming pool that is 80 percent funded by the government and only 20 percent by users be considered an Enterprise Fund? No exact answer exists. The GASB permits subjectivity by allowing governments to use this fund type whenever income determination is considered appropriate:

> Enterprise funds—to account for operations (*a*) that are financed and operated in a manner similar to private business enterprises—where the intent of the governing body is that the costs (expenses, including depreciation) of providing goods or services to the general public on a continuing basis be financed or recovered primarily through user charges; or (*b*) where the governing body has decided that periodic determination of revenues earned, expenses incurred, and/or net income is appropriate for capital maintenance, public policy, management control, accountability, or other purposes.[4]

In the past, 50 percent of the costs of an activity had to be recovered from user charges before the Enterprise Funds designation was considered applicable. Now this fund type is appropriate either when user charges are the primary means of recovery or at the discretion of the governing body. Consequently, one state or locality might account for an ongoing function (such as a bus service operating at a significant loss) within the General Fund whereas another government could classify this same activity as an Enterprise Fund.

A number of factors are considered in deciding what activities are appropriately accounted for in enterprise funds. Some enterprise funds are clearly established to

---

[3]*Local Governmental Accounting Trends & Techniques,* 4th ed. (New York: American Institute of Certified Public Accountants, 1991), p. 3–1.

[4]GASB Cod. sec. 1300.104.

generate net income; frequently, these profits support other government operations. For example, the Georgia State Lottery Corporation reported net income of $370 million on sales of $1 billion for the year ended June 30, 1994. Of these profits, $363 million were transferred out of the fund during the year to support educational programs.

Financing decisions also may influence the decision to report an activity in an enterprise fund. In 1993, almost $300 billion of municipal bonds were offered by more than 10,000 governmental issuers; 69 percent of these bonds were revenue bonds.[5] While general obligation bonds are secured by the taxing authority of the government, revenue bonds rely on the earnings of a specific government activity to provide interest and principal payments. For example, a city might issue revenue bonds to finance construction of a new water treatment plant or airport terminal. The revenues generated through fees associated with the water and airport services will be used to make payments to the bondholders. Because revenue bonds are obligations of an identifiable activity of the government and are not obligations of the government as a whole, they are most appropriately accounted for in an enterprise fund. This is because the bondholders will want to see whether the activity is generating sufficient income and cash flows to enable the government to make interest and principal payments as they come due.

The accounting process for an Enterprise Fund parallels that of a profit-oriented company; thus, a complete overview here is unwarranted. In Exhibit 17–2, the financial statements for Atlanta's Department of Aviation (i.e., Hartsfield Airport) disclose information similar to that of a corporation. Little resemblance can be found to the governmental accounting procedures introduced in Chapter 16.

The financial statements for Hartsfield Airport could pass for those of a for-profit business operation. Both revenues and expenses are reported for this fund, including nearly $36 million in depreciation and amortization. A net income figure of approximately $54 million is reported. The asset section of the balance sheet shows more than $1.7 billion in property and equipment. Liabilities disclose both current and noncurrent balances. Contributed capital and retained earnings figures also are reported.

A few of the accounting procedures utilized in Enterprise Funds, however, are unique. For example, normally capital stock is not issued by an Enterprise Fund for financing purposes. Contributed capital (more than $300 million for Hartsfield Airport) comes from residual equity transfers made within the government itself or from outside grants or other sources. To illustrate this aspect of Enterprise Fund accounting, assume a city makes a residual equity transfer of $400,000 from the General Fund to begin a local bus system. Assume further that this amount is matched with a $200,000 grant for the same purpose from the state government.

Because charges are assessed to those individuals who ride the buses, the city creates an Enterprise Fund to account for this operation. Within this fund, these two initial contributions are recorded as follows:

Enterprise Fund

Cash	600,000	
Contributed Capital—Governmental		400,000
Contributed Capital—Intergovernmental		200,000

To record residual equity transfer from the General Fund and state grant received to start a local bus system.

These equity accounts represent the source of the beginning capital for this particular operation in the same way that the capital stock accounts of Ford Motor Company indicate the amounts invested by the company's stockholders.

---

[5]R. Sipf, *How Municipal Bonds Work* (New York: New York Institute of Finance, 1995).

Chapter 17

Exhibit 17-2
Financial Statements for an
Enterprise Fund

CITY OF ATLANTA, GEORGIA
Department of Aviation
Statements of Revenues, Expenses, and Changes in Fund Equity
Year Ended December 31, 1995
(in thousands)

Operating Revenues:	
Charges for services—landing fees	$ 24,867
Rentals and concessions:	
Terminal and maintenance, buildings, and other rentals	49,934
Parking, car rental, and other concessions	83,001
Total rentals and concessions	132,935
Other	12,048
Total operating revenues	169,850
Operating Expenses:	
Salaries and employee benefits	25,255
Utilities	2,401
Materials and supplies	1,784
Repairs, maintenance, and other contractual services	16,063
General services	6,443
Depreciation	41,375
Other	1,503
Total operating expenses	94,824
Operating Income	75,026
Nonoperating Revenues (Expenses):	
Interest on long-term debt, net of amounts capitalized	(44,425)
Investment income, net of amounts capitalized	11,080
Gain on disposal of assets	—
Total nonoperating expenses	(33,345)
Net income	41,681
Fund equity—Beginning of year	801,784
Contributions from U.S. Government	14,802
Fund equity—End of year	$858,267

Another reporting complexity encountered in connection with some Enterprise Funds is the legal restriction of cash or other assets. As can be seen from its statements, Hartsfield Airport reported more than $476 million in restricted assets. Many reasons might exist for holding these amounts. Public utilities, as an example, often collect deposits from customers that must be returned when service is discontinued. Local laws may require that these monetary amounts be formally segregated in the accounting records to assure safekeeping.

Similar restrictions often result from contractual provisions included in bond agreements. Bond indentures frequently stipulate that moneys collected from issuing debt be separated and spent only for the intended purposes. Money raised, for example, to build a new hangar must be used to build the new hangar and not diverted to other projects. Furthermore, the indenture may require that specified amounts of cash must be set aside each year to ensure the availability of funds to extinguish the debt when due.

Regardless of the reason for the restriction, the asset balances are identified and usually invested until time for disbursement. The restriction of such assets is recorded directly within the Enterprise Fund. A typical entry for this purpose would be as follows:

Exhibit 17–2
(*continued*)

CITY OF ATLANTA, GEORGIA
Department of Aviation
Balance Sheet
December 31, 1995
(in thousands)

Assets

Current Assets:
Receivables:

Accounts	$ 14,384
Less allowance for doubtful accounts	(2,500)
Total receivables	11,884
Materials and supplies	658
Due from other funds	—
Prepaid insurance	604
Total current assets	13,146

Restricted Assets:

Cash and cash equivalents	3,530
Cash held by fiscal agent	41,896
Investments	197,793
Investment in Pooled Investment Fund	227,864
Accrued interest receivable	3,803
Grants receivable from U.S. Government	1,296
Total restricted assets	476,182

Property and Equipment—At cost:

Land	101,607
Land purchased for noise abatement	272,496
Runways, taxiways, and other land improvements	427,261
Terminals and maintenance buildings	898,438
Other property and equipment	38,981
Construction-in-progress:	
Buildings and other structures	62,813
Runways, taxiways, and other land improvements	42,240
	1,843,836
Less accumulated depreciation	(545,521)
Property and equipment, net	1,298,315
Other Assets	2,482
Total assets	$1,790,125

Enterprise Fund

Restricted Cash (or Investments)—Bond Debt Service	90,000
Restricted Cash (or Investments)—Customer Deposits	10,000
Restricted Cash (or Investments)—Bond Proceeds	200,000
Cash	300,000

To classify various cash balances into restricted asset accounts as required by bond indenture and by local laws.

Internal Service Funds

Not surprisingly, Internal Service Funds and Enterprise Funds utilize very similar accounting procedures. The functions of these two proprietary-fund types are analogous; therefore, significant variations in reporting techniques are not justified. In both cases, charges are assessed for services being rendered. However, for Internal Service Funds, the users are internal departments or agencies within the government, rather than the public in general. A central print shop that provides services for an entire city government and a county's data processing center would both fall under this heading. Typical Internal Service Funds are as follows:

Exhibit 17–2
(*continued*)

CITY OF ATLANTA, GEORGIA
Department of Aviation
Balance Sheet
December 31, 1995
(in thousands)

Liabilities and Fund Equity

Current Liabilities:		
Accounts payable	$	1,619
Claims payable		2,875
Accrued salaries and vacation pay		2,311
Deferred revenue		197
Due to other funds		525
Total current liabilities		7,527
Liabilities Payable from Restricted Assets:		
Accounts payable		23,448
Contract retentions		2,120
Current maturities of long-term debt		14,575
Accrued interest payable		27,447
Total liabilities payable from restricted assets		67,590
Long-Term Liabilities:		
Long-term debt, excluding current maturities		854,527
Deferred pension costs		1,096
Accrued workers' compensation		1,118
Total long-term liabilities		856,741
Total liabilities		931,858
Fund Equity:		
Prior to 1974		84,777
Contributed capital		319,101
Retained earnings—reserved		359,524
Retained earnings—unreserved		94,865
Total fund equity		858,267
Total liabilities and fund equity		$1,790,125

New Haven, Connecticut	Printing and duplicating
Atlanta, Georgia	Automotive services
Norfolk, Virginia	Storehouse for materials
St. Paul, Minnesota	Manufacturing plant for asphalt

The use of Internal Service Funds appears to have become especially popular during recent years. One report found that only 16 percent of local governments reported Internal Service Funds in 1986 whereas 42 percent did just three years later in 1989.[6] In many areas, the range of government activities has increased in hopes of offering better services while reducing costs. Creating a motor pool, for example, may be cheaper than using outside mechanics. The city of St. Paul, Minnesota, lists 11 different Internal Service Funds in its 1995 annual report. Separate Internal Service Funds are formed for these individual functions for several reasons; they

- Provide the ability to account for each activity.
- Assist in costing and pricing decisions.
- Allow for the allocation of government overhead.[7]

---

[6]*Local Governmental Accounting Trends & Techniques,* p. 3–1.

[7]*Governmental Accounting, Auditing and Financial Reporting* (Chicago: Government Finance Officers Association, 1988), p. 73.

Exhibit 17–2
(*concluded*)

CITY OF ATLANTA, GEORGIA
Department of Aviation
Statement of Cash Flows
Year Ended December 31, 1995
(in thousands)

Operating Activities:

Operating income	$ 75,026
Adjustments to reconcile operating income to net cash provided by operating activities:	
Depreciation	41,375
Amortization of bond discount	1,945
Amortization and accretion of investments	7,979
Provision for uncollectible accounts	376
Changes in assets and liabilities:	
Accounts receivable	(2,393)
Other receivables	(596)
Material and supplies	185
Prepaid expenses and other assets	39
Accounts payable and accrued expenses	14,435
Net cash provided by operating activities	138,371

Investing Activities:

Interest and dividends on investments	11,080
Proceeds from nonpooled investment sales	7,327,879
Purchases of nonpooled investments	(7,316,973)
Change in pooled investments	2,572
Change in accrued interest receivable	(235)
Net cash provided by (used in) investing activities	24,323

Capital and Related Financing Activities:

Capital contributions	14,802
Repayments of debt	(11,710)
Acquisition, construction, and improvement of capital assets	(120,117)
Proceeds from sale of capital assets	—
Interest paid on revenue bonds	(48,834)
Proceeds from bond issuance	—
Payment to trust in connection with extinguishment of debt	—
Change in contract retention	338
Net cash used in capital and related financing activities	(165,521)
Net decrease in cash and cash equivalents	(2,827)
Cash and cash equivalents—Beginning of year	48,253
Cash and cash equivalents—End of year	$ 45,426

Exhibit 17–3 contains the 1996 financial statements for fleet maintenance (an Internal Service Fund) of the city of Athens-Clarke County, Georgia. As with Enterprise Funds, the statements are similar to those of a for-profit operation; property, plant, and equipment are reported as well as long-term debt, contributed capital, retained earnings, and depreciation expense. (The statement of cash flows has been omitted since it is based on information provided by these remaining statements.)

Although these financial statements resemble those of an Enterprise Fund, no restricted assets are indicated. Generally, Internal Service Funds do not offer services directly to the public; thus, the presence of customer deposits would not be anticipated. Furthermore, contractual restrictions resulting from bond obligations are not nearly as common. The capital outlays required to support Internal Service Fund activities are normally less costly than those needed by many Enterprise Funds. A subway system or water utility costs many times more than a motor pool or print shop. Therefore, a significant portion of the funding of Internal Service Funds often

Exhibit 17–3
Financial Statements for an
Internal Service Fund

ATHENS-CLARKE COUNTY, GEORGIA
Fleet Management Internal Service Fund
Statement of Revenues, Expenses, and Changes in Retained Earnings
For the fiscal year ended June 30, 1996

Operating revenues:	
Charges for services	$1,986,936
Operating Expenses:	
Personal services	666,409
Contractual services	1,255
Facilities operating	28,109
Education and training	1,029
Vehicle/equipment	1,023,800
Rental/lease	285
Supplies and materials	23,603
Noncapital	6,299
Depreciation	18,292
Indirect	27,223
Total operating expenses	1,796,304
Operating Income	190,632
Nonoperating revenues (expenses):	
Interest	29,984
Other	1,823
Net loss on disposition of fixed assets	—
Total nonoperating revenues (expenses)	31,807
Net income	222,439
Retained earnings at beginning of year	352,519
Retained earnings at end of year	$ 574,958

Balance Sheet
June 30, 1996

Assets

Current Assets:	
Cash	$ 78,540
Investments	691,578
Receivables:	
Accounts	2,456
Intragovernmental	168
Inventory	99,261
Total current assets	872,003
Property, Plant and Equipment:	588,389
Less accumulated depreciation	(147,684)
Net property, plant and equipment	440,705
Total assets	$1,312,708

Liabilities and Fund Equity

Current Liabilities:	
Accounts payable	$ 60,894
Accrued liabilities	24,073
Compensated absences payable	33,748
Total current liabilities	118,715
Fund Equity:	
Contributed capital: Athens-Clarke County	619,035
Retained earnings—unreserved	574,958
Total fund equity	1,193,993
Total liabilities and fund equity	$1,312,708

DISCUSSION QUESTION

Should Internal Service Funds Be Abolished?

If a city's school system decides to open a garage to service its buses, the activity is recorded as a part of this system. Acquisition of the building and equipment would be reported as expenditures within the General Fund or Special Revenue Funds (depending on the method used to monitor the school system). The assets themselves are listed in the General Fixed Assets Account Group. No depreciation is recorded. Cash inflows from issuing any long-term debt used to purchase the building and equipment are reported as Other Financing Sources in the appropriate governmental-type fund. This debt then is included in the General Long-Term Debt Account Group.

However, if the city created this same garage to service vehicles for several different activities (the school system, the police force, the ambulance service, and the like), it probably would report the garage as an Internal Service Fund. Thus, the garage maintains its own building and equipment as well as the long-term debt needed for financing. No expenditures are recorded by the fund but depreciation and other expenses are now appropriately reported.

Some question the validity of making such a radical change in accounting principles to account for activities providing services solely for governmental-type funds. For instance, David L. Falk and Michael H. Granof assert:

> The weakest component of the accounting system that is generally accepted for state and local governments is the internal service fund—a fund used to account for the financing of goods or services provided by one department or agency to other departments, agencies or units. So flawed is this, that allowed to stand, it weakens the persuasiveness of arguments that government should be accounted for by a model separate from business.[8]

Although Falk and Granof acknowledge that Internal Service Funds should be maintained for internal reporting purposes to promote efficiency and facilitate sharing of costs, they hold that the individual transactions and accounts should be returned to the appropriate governmental-type funds for external reporting.

Several faults have been attributed to the current reporting of Internal Service Funds:

- No consistency exists between reporting units. Some governments make wide use of Internal Service Funds; others do not utilize them—the same activities are recorded within the governmental-type funds.
- Fixed assets that should be reported as expenditures by the governmental-type funds are capitalized. Thus, the expenditures of the reporting unit may be understated.
- The government is able to remove some of its general obligation debts from the General Long-Term Debt Account Group.
- Governments can create surpluses or deficits within Internal Service Funds to manipulate fund balances. For example, price increases for intragovernmental services could be used to reduce the financial resources available in the General Fund to justify a tax increase.

  In Madison, Wisconsin, a suit brought by taxpayers underscores the policy dilemma which results from the accumulation of assets which are legally unrestricted in restricted funds. The suit charged that the city's "Nonlapsing Building Reserve Fund" was being used as a vehicle to maintain an illicit surplus which should instead be used to reduce taxes. Although the taxpayers were unsuccessful in their action, the litigation nevertheless pointed to the potential use of Internal Service Funds to undermine policy as understood by a community's citizens.[9]

- Depreciation becomes an expenditure through transfer pricing. If a garage, for example, has depreciation of $100 as its only expense, a charge of that amount to a General Fund for a repair would be recorded as an expenditure. Depreciation has effectively become an expenditure to the governmental-type fund.

Should Internal Service Funds continue to be included by state and local governments for external reporting purposes?

---

[8]David L. Falk and Michael H. Granof, "Internal Service Funds Are beyond Salvation," *Accounting Horizons,* June 1990, p. 58.

[9]Ibid., p. 63.

is provided by transfers from within the government. Sinking funds or restricted assets are rarely necessary to service the debts of these operations.

As shown in the balance sheet figures in Exhibit 17–3, Internal Service Funds frequently report intragovernmental receivables (frequently labeled "Due from") to indicate transactions within the government. Since these operations utilize accrual accounting, such balances are established as a result of revenue and expense recognition. If work is done for another unit of the government, a "Due from . . ." account records and reports the intragovernmental receivable.

To illustrate, assume that a government print shop prepares $3,000 in materials for one of the ongoing activities (for example, the police or fire department) accounted for within the General Fund. Because of the nature of the work performed, the print shop is accounted for as an Internal Service Fund. As discussed in the previous chapter, this transfer of funds is known as a quasi-external transaction because the interaction is the same as that between two unrelated parties. Thus, the charge for the service being carried out is not recorded as a transfer but as a regular business transaction.

The following journal entries would be appropriate at the time this work is completed:

Internal Service Fund

Due from Other Funds—General Fund	3,000	
Operating Revenues—Charges for Services		3,000
To record completion of printing work for a General Fund activity.		

General Fund

Expenditures Control	3,000	
Due to Other Funds—Internal Service Funds		3,000
To record work done by the print shop.		

Both the receivable and the payable remain in the financial accounts of these fund types until the money is actually transferred. At that time, the $3,000 "Due from . . ." and "Due to . . ." balances are eliminated.

Pension Trust Funds

Pension Trust Funds are fiduciary in nature rather than proprietary; money is held by the government to provide employees with retirement benefits. The major activities of such funds include collecting and investing monetary amounts as well as paying out benefits to appropriate recipients. Such trusts are common and can become huge. The city of Chicago, Illinois, for example, maintains pension trusts with total assets of more than $4.3 billion for four different groups: municipal employees, laborers, police officers, and firefighters.

Three of the four largest pension funds in the United States as of 1989 were created by state or local governments:

California Public Employees	$54.0 billion in assets
New York City Employees	$45.4 billion
New York State and Local Employees	$44.2 billion[10]

Funding for such pension trusts comes primarily from the government (as the employer) although employees themselves may add extra amounts if the plan is contributory. All cash balances then are invested by the trust with subsequently earned income added to the retirement benefits accruing to each employee. Because of the importance of maximizing the earnings produced by the assets being held, the

---

[10]James A. White, "Giant Pension Funds' Explosive Growth Concentrates Economic Assets and Power," *The Wall Street Journal,* June 28, 1990, p. C1.

accounting emphasis is placed on income determination again rather than on resource control. However, a significant degree of control is inherent in Pension Trust Funds because both contribution and expenditure levels are established by contractual agreement or actuarial estimation.

Assets can come into a Pension Trust Fund from (1) contributions or (2) earned income. The major expense is the pension benefits that are distributed. For example, in the municipal pension fund of the city of Los Angeles, California, for the year ending June 30, 1995, operating revenues were derived from just three sources:

Employer's contributions	$631 million
Employees' contributions	109 million
Investment income	735 million

At the same time, 95 percent of the operating expenses for this fund were made up of $770 million in pension benefits.

To illustrate the accounting procedures, assume that the city of Jung maintains a pension plan for its government employees. Typical transactions for this fund include:

■ The city contributes $44,000 in cash to the pension trust fund based on a contractual agreement with its employees.

■ Employees voluntarily contribute $9,000 to their pensions.

■ Investments acquired in previous years earn interest of $7,000.

To record these three increases in cash, the following entry is appropriate:

Pension Trust Fund

Cash	60,000	
Operating Revenues—Employer Contribution		44,000
Operating Revenues—Employee Contribution		9,000
Operating Revenues—Interest		7,000

To record revenue for the period by the pension trust fund.

As indicated, the number of different expenses incurred by a Pension Trust Fund is also rather limited. Some administrative and other miscellaneous expenses are periodically incurred in connection with maintaining the trust. However, the major cost is the normal benefits paid out to retired or other qualified individuals based on their pension agreement. Assuming that the city's pension pays $2,000 in expenses and distributes $14,000 to members, the following journal entry is required:

Pension Trust Fund

Operating Expenses—Administrative	2,000	
Operating Expenses—Employee Benefits	14,000	
Cash		16,000

Payments made by the pension trust fund during the current period.

Nonexpendable Trust Funds

The final fund category requiring income determination is the Nonexpendable Trust Funds. As discussed in the previous chapter, these trust funds account for assets donated to a government with the stipulation that all subsequently derived income be used for a designated purpose. The principal itself, however, must be kept intact to continue generating earnings. The city of Richmond, Virginia, for example, currently maintains four Nonexpendable Trust Funds to account for donations made to support:

Cemetery maintenance.

Scholarships and prizes for local students.

Public library.

Specific memorial purposes.

Although most gifts to a government are relatively small, some can be of significant size. On June 30, 1996, the state of Alaska reported more than $17.7 billion in assets in its Nonexpendable Trust Funds.

To ensure that the legal provisions attached to each gift are followed, determination of net income is essential. This figure sets the amount to be spent for the specified purpose. In practice, the government unit actually may opt to establish two separate accounting funds: one to maintain a record of the original gift with a second to monitor net income and its ultimate disposition. Although not required, protection of the principal is more easily assured when two funds are utilized.

As an illustration of the procedures to account for Nonexpendable Trust Funds, assume that two pieces of rental property are given to a city by a citizen with the provision that all future income be used for maintenance of the local cemetery. These donated assets are appraised at a value of $140,000 and the following journal entry is made:

Nonexpendable Trust Fund

Buildings	140,000	
Fund Balance—Reserved for Cemetery Maintenance		140,000

To record fair market value of rental property given with the specification that all income is to be used for cemetery maintenance.

During the remainder of the current fiscal year, these properties are rented to various tenants and revenues of $16,000 are earned and subsequently collected. As with all of the proprietary-type funds, accrual accounting is utilized in the recording process.

Nonexpendable Trust Fund

Rent Receivable	16,000	
Operating Revenues		16,000

To accrue rental income for current period.

Cash	16,000	
Rent Receivable		16,000

Collection of rents (following earlier accrual).

To maintain this property, the city incurs and pays a variety of maintenance expenses totaling $4,400. In addition, $7,000 in depreciation is computed for the period.

Nonexpendable Trust Fund

Operating Expenses—Maintenance	4,400	
Operating Expenses—Depreciation	7,000	
Cash		4,400
Accumulated Depreciation—Buildings		7,000

To recognize expenses associated with rental property including depreciation.

At the end of this year, net income of $4,600 is indicated ($16,000 in revenues less total expenses of $11,400). According to the terms of the gift, this balance should now be spent for the designated objective: cemetery maintenance. Frequently, the city will transfer the money to another fund to be used for the appropriate purpose. Overspending can be prevented in this manner:

Nonexpendable Trust Fund

Operating Transfer-Out—Income Earned	4,600	
Cash		4,600

To record transfer of net income balance to separate Expendable Trust Fund to be used for specified purpose.

Expendable Trust Fund

Cash	4,600	
Other Financing Sources—Trust Income (Transferred)		4,600

To record income on gifts donated to the city with the stipulation that all earnings will be used for cemetery maintenance.

Agency Funds

State and local governments use one additional fund category; however, this fund records neither a governmental-type service activity nor a proprietary-type operation. Agency Funds account solely for monies held by a government that it must eventually convey to an outside party. The city of Saint Paul, Minnesota, for example, maintains 9 Agency Funds that monitor assets received from a variety of sources including payroll taxes, Social Security taxes, money withheld from employees for U.S. savings bonds, and birth certificate surcharges that must be remitted to the state of Minnesota.

Periodically, the city transfers each of these amounts to the proper authorities. Until remitted, the balances are maintained within an Agency Fund for control purposes. Classified as a fiduciary fund, the reporting procedures are primarily designed to establish a formal record of the amounts being held at any point in time. Agency Funds have no equity, revenues, or expenses. They report only assets (usually cash or investments) and the related liabilities.

To illustrate, assume that Keith County collects a toll from each car that uses one of the local highways. Because the original cost of constructing this road was financed in part by the adjacent city of Simmons, a portion of all toll receipts is separated and shared with this city government. The following two entries would be made by the county in connection with the receipt and conveyance of this money. Assume that the county has collected $108,000 from this toll that must be given to the city of Simmons.

Agency Fund (Keith County)
Time of Collection

Cash	108,000	
Due to City of Simmons		108,000

To record portion of toll receipts that must be paid to the city.

Time of Payment

Due to City of Simmons	108,000	
Cash		108,000

To transfer tolls (accumulated by county) to the city of Simmons.

DEFINING THE REPORTING ENTITY

Although gathering and maintaining financial information is a vital step in governmental accounting, the reporting of this data to the public is equally important.

> Governmental accountability is based on the belief that the citizenry has a "right to know," a right to receive openly declared facts that may lead to public debate by the citizens and their elected representatives. Financial reporting plays a major role in fulfilling government's duty to be publicly accountable in a democratic society.[11]

In producing financial statements, a state or locality often encounters a unique problem: the determination of the specific functions to be included. Except in rare cases, a business enterprise such as Xerox or IBM simply consolidates all corporations over which control has been achieved. A state or locality, however, may interact with a number of departments, agencies, boards, institutes, commissions, and the like that have only a moderate relationship with the government. Should all of these activities be included as separate funds within the comprehensive annual financial report of the government? If not, what reporting is required?

An almost unlimited number of examples could be presented of the types of functions that create problems for government officials attempting to define the entity

---

[11]GASB Cod. sec. 100.156.

to be reported. Separate organizations such as turnpike commissions, port authorities, public housing authorities, and downtown development boards have become commonplace in recent years. These are not proprietary-type activities of the government, such as water and sewer enterprise funds, but are legally separate from the governments that created them. Creating separate organizations allows such groups to focus on specified issues or problems and sometimes provides better efficiency because of their corporate-style structure. In addition, capital markets may be more receptive to debt issued by these groups. Examples of separate organizations include the following:

■ A museum is built on city land but operates as a nonprofit corporation funded by citizen contributions. Half of the board of directors is appointed by these donors with the remainder named by the city. The property is leased from the city for $1 per year. A special tax is levied and collected by the city to help maintain the grounds and building. Should the museum be reported within the city's financial statements?

■ The state establishes a school system within a city. The school board is elected by the public and, thus, is not under the control of city officials. Property taxes are levied by the city and then distributed to the school for funding purposes. For this reason, the school budget must be approved by city officials. Should the school system be reported as part of the city?

Because of the extremely wide variety of possible activities and functions, determining the components that make up a state or locality is not always an easy task. Thus, in June 1991, the GASB issued its *Statement No. 14,* "The Financial Reporting Entity." This pronouncement provides guidance to assist governments in identifying the reporting entity. According to the Board, the major criterion for inclusion in a government's comprehensive annual financial report is financial accountability:

> Financial reporting based on accountability should enable the financial statement reader to focus on the body of organizations that are related by a common thread of accountability to the constituent citizenry. . . . Elected officials are accountable to those citizens for their public policy decisions, regardless of whether these decisions are carried out directly by the elected officials through the operations of the primary government or by their designees through the operations of specially created organizations.[12]

The Primary Government

In defining the overall reporting entity, *GASB Statement No. 14* indicates that the primary government must first be identified. According to this official pronouncement, the primary government is any government (and all of its funds, organizations, agencies, offices, and departments that are not legally separate) meeting the following three criteria:

■ Has a separately elected governing body.
■ Is legally separate.
■ Is fiscally independent of other state and local governments.

The GASB provides additional guidance for judging the last two of these criteria, legal separation and fiscal independence. The legal separation of a government is demonstrated by having corporate powers such as the right to sue and be sued in its own name and the right to buy, sell, and lease property in its own name.

A city has such powers; its police department does not. The fiscal independence of a government is indicated by having the authority to do all three of the following:

---

[12]GASB, *Statement No. 14,* "The Financial Reporting Entity," June 1991, par. 2 and 8.

- Determine its own budget without having to present the figures to any other government for approval or modification.
- Levy taxes or set rate fees without having to seek approval by another government.
- Issue bonded debt without the need for approval by another government.

A city is fiscally independent because it meets these criteria; a fire department normally is not.

Consequently, any organization that has an elected governing body, is legally separate, and is fiscally independent is a primary government. Any activity that is not legally separate from this government must be included within its financial statements.

Component Units

Many activities are legally separate from a primary government but are so closely connected that complete omission from the statements of the primary government cannot be justified. The elected officials of the primary government are still financially accountable for these separate organizations. Such entities are referred to as *component units* of the primary government.

GASB Statement No. 14 specifies two methods for identifying a separate organization as a component unit of a primary government. In the first set of criteria, officials of the primary government must appoint a voting majority of the governing board of the separate organization. Additionally, either the primary government must be able to impose its will on this board, or the separate organization must provide a financial benefit to or impose a financial burden on the primary government. For example, a commission to oversee off-track betting might be a separate legal entity. However, if the state (the primary government) appoints a voting majority of the membership and benefits from the revenues generated, the commission is considered a component unit of the state for financial reporting purposes.

The second method established by *Statement No. 14* for identifying component units is more general: "the primary government may be financially accountable if an organization is *fiscally dependent* on the primary government regardless of whether the organization has (1) a separately governing board, (2) a governing board appointed by a higher level of government, or (3) a jointly appointed board." (paragraph 21b; emphasis added)

To apply the criteria of either method to the determination of a component unit, several terms need to be clarified:

A Voting Majority of the Governing Board The authority to elect a voting majority must be substantive. If, for example, the primary government simply confirms the choices of another party, financial accountability is not created. Furthermore, *GASB Statement No. 14* states that this criterion is not met if the primary government selects the governing body from a limited slate of candidates (such as three individuals from an approved list of five). Thus, the primary government actually must appoint a voting majority of the board before the organization can be viewed as a component unit.

Imposition of the Primary Government's Will on the Governing Board Such power is indicated if the government can significantly influence the programs, projects, activities, or the level of services provided by the organization. This degree of influence is present if the primary government can remove an appointed board member at will, modify or approve budgets, override decisions of the board, modify or approve rate or fee changes, and hire or dismiss the individuals responsible for day-to-day operations.

Financial Benefit or Financial Burden on the Primary Government   According to *GASB Statement No. 14,* a financial connection between the organization and the government exists if any of the following are met:

- The government is entitled to the organization's resources.
- The government is legally obligated to finance any deficits or provide financial support.
- The government is responsible in some manner for the debts of the organization.

Fiscal Dependence on the Primary Government   As indicated previously, financial dependency exists if the organization cannot do one of the following three actions:

- Adopt its own budget.
- Levy taxes or set rates or charges for its services.
- Issue bonded debt without approval.

Inclusion also is warranted if exclusion would render the financial statements incomplete.

> This provision was written with organizations like the Municipal Assistance Corporation of New York (MAC) in mind. MAC was created in 1975 as a financing mechanism for the city. Under the *GASB Statement 14* definition of financial accountability, the MAC would not qualify for inclusion in New York City's entity because the state appoints the MAC's board. But the MAC is so inextricably linked to New York City's finances that its exclusion would render the city's financial statements misleading.[13]

The Financial Reporting of a Primary Government and Its Component Units

As demonstrated in the appendix at the end of this chapter, the various funds of the primary government (the General Revenue, Special Revenue Funds, etc.) are all reported within the general purpose financial statements. However, any component units also must be included in these same statements. The financial figures must be clearly separated so that the operations and financial position of the primary government can be distinguished from these other activities. Therefore, figures for component units are presented in separate columns (to the right) from those presented for the primary government. The component units may be combined into a single column or presented according to the specific activities. As another alternative, separate columns may be created for governmental and proprietary organizations.

GASB Statement No. 14 does allow the primary government to include certain component units as if they were part of the government (a process referred to as *blending*). Although these organizations are legally separate, they are so intertwined with the primary government that their inclusion is necessary for the appropriate presentation of the primary government's financial information.

One other aspect of the reporting process to be noted: *GASB Statement No. 14* also identifies the possible existence of *related organizations*. In such cases, the primary government is accountable because it appoints a voting majority of the governing board. However, financial accountability does not exist. Fiscal dependency is not present and the primary government cannot impose its will on the board or gather financial benefits or burdens from the relationship. Without financial accountability,

---

[13]Barbara A. Chaney, "The Governmental Financial Reporting Entity: Inclusion and Display," *The CPA Journal,* January 1993, p. 42.

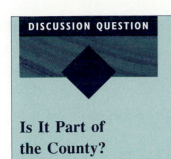

Is It Part of the County?

Harland County is in a financially distressed portion of Missouri. In hopes of enticing business to this area, the state legislature appropriated $3 million to start an industrial development commission. The federal government provided an additional $1 million. The state appointed 15 individuals to a board to oversee the operations of this commission while county officials named 5 members. The commission began operations by raising funds from local citizens and businesses. It received an extra $700,000 in donations and pledges. The county provided clerical assistance and allowed the commission to use one floor of the county office building for its headquarters. The commission's budget must be approved by the county government.

During the current period, the commission spent $2.4 million and produced financial statements. Notable success was achieved as several large manufacturing companies have begun to explore the possibility of opening plants in the county.

Harland County is presently beginning the process of producing a comprehensive annual financial report. Should the revenues, expenditures, assets, and liabilities of the industrial development commission be included? Is it part of the county's primary government, a component unit, or a related organization?

Is the industrial development commission a component unit of the state of Missouri? How should its activities be presented in the state's comprehensive annual financial report?

the organization does not qualify as a component unit to be included in the financial reporting. Instead, because of the ability to appoint a voting majority of the governing board, the primary government must disclose in notes to its financial statements the nature of the accountability for such related organizations.

ACCOUNTING FOR STATE AND LOCAL GOVERNMENTS—EXTERNAL REPORTING PROCESS

The final aspect of governmental accounting is the financial reporting process. Because so many diverse fund types exist within state and local governments, the amount and variety of data to be presented could become overwhelming to readers. To alleviate this problem, governments present information about a state or locality to the public in the form of a comprehensive annual financial report, frequently referred to as CAFR. The CAFR provides both a general perspective of every fund type and additional detailed data concerning individual funds. Readers can learn as much or as little as they desire. The structure of the CAFR includes:

- *General purpose financial statements*—to provide an overview of the financial position and operations of all fund types and account groups.
- *Combining statements by fund type*—to present financial data generated by the individual funds making up a fund type. For example, if four separate funds compose the Special Revenue Funds, financial statements for each would be included in this section of the CAFR. The city and county of San Francisco, California, as an illustration, presents financial information in this section about each of its 17 Special Revenue Funds.
- *Individual fund and account group statements*—to disclose more detailed information where needed about specific funds and account groups. If, for example, one of the Special Revenue Funds requires additional reporting, this information is presented here.
- *Schedules and statistical tables*—to demonstrate legal and contractual compliance and present other useful information. This section frequently contains information of a nonfinancial nature, such as number of police officers and miles of road.

The inclusion of schedules allows a government considerable latitude in the types of additional information that can be disclosed. For example, the 1995 comprehensive annual financial report for the city of Atlanta, Georgia, included numerous supplemental statements and schedules, such as:

Assessed and estimated value of all taxable property.

Property tax levies and collections.

Property values, construction, and bank deposits.

Ratio of bonded debt to assessed value and bonded debt per capita.

Principal taxpayers.

Property tax rates.

Because of the layered construction of the CAFR, readers have the option of either reviewing the entire financial picture of the government unit or getting very specific information about a particular activity. The CAFR often is compared to a pyramid with the general purpose financial statements at the top.

Obviously, unless a government unit is quite small, the comprehensive annual financial report just outlined frequently contains a massive amount of material. As an example, the 1995 comprehensive annual financial report for the city of Saint Paul, Minnesota, contains 244 pages of statements, schedules, notes, and statistics. The 1994 CAFR for the city of Toccoa, Georgia (total assets of $310,000) had 95 pages. By comparison, the 1994 Annual Report of General Electric Company (total assets of $194 billion) had only 64 pages.

Realizing that not all financial report users are interested in this extended volume of information, governments are allowed to issue just the general purpose financial statements by themselves "for inclusion in official statements for bond offerings and for widespread distribution to users requiring less detailed information about the government unit's finances than is contained in the CAFR."[14] In this way, adequate data are provided to these users without overburdening them with excessive amounts of material. Financial information concerning individual funds and fund types is not viewed as particularly relevant in such cases and is, therefore, omitted.

General Purpose Financial Statements

Five separate statements (as well as their accompanying notes and supplemental information) make up the general purpose financial statements produced by a government unit. Since these statements not only are included in the comprehensive annual financial report but also may be presented alone, they are central to the entire reporting process. To assist in visualizing their construction, the appendix to this chapter contains complete illustrations. These five general purpose financial statements are as follows:

1. *Combined balance sheet—all fund types and account groups.* Balance sheets for each fund type (General Fund, Capital Projects Funds, Enterprise Funds, etc.) as well as the two account groups are presented together in a columnar format. Summation figures for the governmental unit as a whole are optional but, if included, must be labeled as "memorandum only" because no actual consolidation of the financial information takes place (such as elimination of intragovernmental receivables and payables). Based on the requirements of *GASB Statement No. 14,* the balance sheets for any component units should also be included, normally to the right of the primary government information. These additional activities may be combined into a single column, divided into governmental and proprietary figures, or presented by specific function.

2. *Combined statement of revenues, expenditures, and changes in fund balances—all governmental fund types.* The statement provides a detailed listing of all revenues and expenditures of the governmental-type funds (the four governmental funds as well as any Expendable Trust Funds). "Other financing

---

[14]GASB Cod. sec. 2200.102.

sources and uses" (such as bond proceeds and interfund transfers) are also disclosed in this statement as are residual equity transfers. Based on the changes created by these monetary inflows and outflows, a final fund balance total is computed for each of these fund types. Information describing any component units similar in nature to the governmental-type funds also is included.

3. *Combined statement of revenues, expenditures, and changes in fund balances—budget and actual.* Once again, revenues, expenditures, other financing sources/uses, and changes in fund balances are disclosed. However, in this instance, both actual and budgetary figures are reported with the data structured in columns for comparison purposes. This statement is appropriate for any fund type (such as the General Fund and the Special Revenue Funds) that records budgetary entries. Many governments report encumbrances outstanding as equivalent to actual expenditures in the preparation of this statement. The justification for this treatment is that financial commitments as well as expenditures should be compared to the budget in the period in which the commitment was created. As a result, expenditures reported for a given department in the *statement of revenues, expenditures, and changes in fund balances—budget and actual* may not agree with expenditures reported in the *statement of revenues, expenditures, and changes in fund balances—all governmental fund types,* described in 2 above.

4. *Combined statement of revenues, expenses, and changes in retained earnings (or equity)—all proprietary fund types.* As the equivalent of the income statement found in for-profit accounting, this statement is developed solely for the business-type activities: Enterprise Funds, Internal Service Funds, Pension Trust Funds, and Nonexpendable Trust Funds. Net income is calculated and disclosed for each of these fund types along with the revenues and expenses that constitute this figure. Any component unit that is the equivalent of a proprietary-type organization is also reported in this manner.

5. *Combined statement of cash flows—all proprietary fund types.* Because of the recent renewed emphasis on monitoring changes in cash, a statement of cash flows is now required for the proprietary-type funds (as well as similar component units). However, this statement's format varies somewhat from that utilized by for-business enterprises. Cash flows are disclosed for four activities rather than just three: operating, noncapital financing, capital financing, and investing.[15]

PROPOSALS FOR CHANGES IN GOVERNMENTAL FINANCIAL REPORTS

Since its inception in 1984, the GASB has devoted considerable effort to improving deficiencies in governmental financial reports. The Board's most aggressive action came in 1990 with the release of *Statement 11,* "Measurement Focus and Basis of Accounting—Governmental Fund Operating Statements." This pronouncement was designed to fundamentally change the emphasis of state and local government accounting to an approach more akin to that used by private sector businesses. It required revenues to be accrued and would likely have required debt issued to finance operations to be recognized by the general fund, regardless of whether it was short or long-term.

GASB 11 proved to be very controversial. The standard specifically prohibited early implementation and its implementation was indefinitely postponed by *GASB Statement 17,* "Measurement Focus and Basis of Accounting—Governmental Fund Operating Statements: Amendment of the Effective Dates of GASB Statement no. 11 and Related Statements." As a result, no governments have implemented the stan-

---

[15]GASB, *Statement No. 9,* "Reporting Cash Flows of Proprietary and Nonexpendable Trust Funds and Governmental Entities that Use Proprietary Fund Accounting" (Norwalk, Conn.: GASB, 1989).

dard and it seems unlikely that any ever will. Unable to gain acceptance for *Statement 11,* the GASB reopened its reporting model project.

In January 1997 the GASB issued an Exposure Draft, "Basic Financial Statements—and Management's Discussion and Analysis—for State and Local Governments." If adopted by the Board, the proposed statement would be effective for fiscal years ending in 2001. The exposure draft calls for a dual perspective display of the financial position and results of operations for state and local governments as well as a management discussion and analysis.

Under the proposal, governments would provide financial statement from both *fund* and *entitywide* perspectives. In the fund perspective statements, governments would continue to present separate financial statements for each fund category. The proposal does not change the focus of accounting at the fund level. Governmental funds would continue to emphasize fiscal accountability and report the flow of financial resources using the modified accrual basis of accounting. Proprietary and fiduciary funds would continue to emphasize changes in economic resources measured on the accrual basis of accounting; thus, there would be relatively little change in the journal entries necessary to record the activities of the funds.[16]

Changes in the Fund Perspective Financial Statements

Although the recording of transactions is relatively unchanged, the proposed standard makes significant changes in the fund categories and fund financial statements. These changes include:

1. Activities currently reported in expendable trust funds would be accounted for in special revenue funds.
2. Activities currently reported in nonexpendable trust funds would be accounted for in a new fund category, *permanent funds.*
3. Governments would no longer report account groups on the fund perspective financial statements. General fixed assets and general long-term debt would be reported only at the entitywide perspective financial statements.
4. The budgetary comparison statements would include both the original budget and the adjusted budget. Currently only the adjusted budget is presented. Since governments pass budget adjustments to increase expenditure levels, few unfavorable variances appear.
5. The guidelines regarding when an activity should be accounted for in an enterprise fund are refined.
6. Transfers should be reported in enterprise funds as a change in fund equity (below the net income line), not in the determination of net income.

Entitywide Perspective Financial Statements

Although the changes proposed in the fund perspective statements are relatively minor, the entitywide perspective statements represent a significant change in governmental reporting. The purpose of the entitywide financial statements is to provide a comprehensive view of a government's operations. Critics argue that current government financial reports are overly complex and prevent citizens from obtaining a clear picture of the government's performance.[17] Presently it is very difficult to determine whether the government is raising sufficient revenue to pay the long-term costs

---

[16]One exception to this is that capital contributions to an enterprise fund would be reported as nonoperating revenue rather than contributed capital.

[17]S. Davidson, D. Green, W. Hellerstein, A. Madansky, and R. Weil, *Financial Reporting by State and Local Government Units* (Chicago: Center for Management of Public and Nonprofit Enterprise, University of Chicago, 1977).

of governmental operations, including the cost of replacing fixed assets. This makes it very difficult for citizens to determine the likelihood of future tax increases or spending cuts.

These entity-perspective statements could prove useful in assessing interperiod equity. *Interperiod equity* is a term used by the GASB to indicate the extent to which current period revenues are sufficient to pay for current period services. Present governmental accounting practices are designed to measure the flow of current financial resources, but are inadequate for assessing interperiod equity. This weakness is most apparent when one considers the effect of issuing long-term debt for operating purposes. Because bond proceeds are shown as other financing sources, long-term debt issues have the effect of increasing fund balance. In 1991, Washington, D.C., eliminated an accumulated general fund deficit of $330 million by issuing bonds. Even though the general fund deficit was eliminated, it is clear that the government had not been balancing revenues and expenditures. The accumulated deficit had simply changed form (from deficit fund balance to bonds payable) and moved from the balance sheet of the general fund to the general long-term debt account group.

The proposed entitywide financial statements present a comprehensive overview of the government. The statements include all economic resources (including infrastructure and other capital assets) and obligations (including long-term debt). The accrual basis of accounting measures changes in these resources and obligations. Examples of the entitywide financial statements appear in Exhibit 17–4.

A statement of net assets replaces the combined balance sheet. Note that the format of the statement is assets minus liabilities equals net assets; hence, the term *balance sheet* is inappropriate. Separate columns are presented for governmental activities and business activities. Additional columns would report component unit information. Although internal service funds and *permanent* funds used the accrual basis of accounting, they are included in the governmental activity column. Assets held in pension trusts are not included in the statement because the assets are not available for the government's use. The governmental activities column of the statement of net assets includes general fixed assets as well as general long-term debt, items previously reported in account groups.

Current year operations are reported in the statement of activities. The statement provides an overview of the government on a program basis. Charges associated with specific programs are deducted from the expenses to indicate the extent to which each program relies on or contributes to tax revenues. For example, charges by the city of Harris Shoals recreation department exceed departmental expenses by $50,000. In contrast, the public safety department's expenses exceed charges and grants by $2,000,000. The net expense reported by the public safety department must be paid for through tax revenues. Revenues that cannot be attributed to a specific activity, such as property taxes, are reported in the general revenue section.

The entitywide statements reflect the accrual basis of accounting; therefore, the expenses reported for each department include accruals and depreciation. Accrued interest, not yet currently payable, is recorded as interest expense. Revenues derived from other funds, such as charges by internal service funds, are eliminated in a manner similar to the elimination of intercompany sales between parent and subsidiary corporations.

The proposed statement also requires that a management discussion and analysis accompany the financial statements. Among the items to be discussed are differences between the fund perspective and entitywide perspective financial statements. Differences arise because the entitywide financial statements use the accrual basis of accounting while the governmental-type funds use the modified accrual basis. Exhibit 17–5 illustrates typical reconciling items between the fund perspective and entitywide perspective financial statements. Note that reconciliations between the enterprise funds and the business-type activities columns of the entitywide statements are not necessary because both report on the accrual basis.

Exhibit 17–4   Entitywide Perspective Financial Statements (Accrual Basis of Accounting—Economic Resources Focus)

CITY OF HARRIS SHOALS
Statement of Net Assets
June 30, 2001

	Governmental Activities	Business-Type Activities	Total
Assets:			
Cash and equivalents	$ 1,100,000	$ 700,000	$ 1,800,000
Investments	2,500,000	—	2,500,000
Receivables	1,500,000	3,400,000	4,900,000
Inventories	500,000	600,000	1,100,000
Capital assets	16,000,000	14,000,000	30,000,000
Total assets	21,600,000	18,700,000	40,300,000
Liabilities:			
Accounts payable	880,000	500,000	1,380,000
Accrued interest	20,000	—	20,000
Bonds payable	9,000,000	8,100,000	17,100,000
Total liabilities	9,900,000	8,600,000	18,500,000
Net Assets:			
Invested in capital assets, net of related debt	9,700,000	7,900,000	17,600,000
Restricted for:			
Capital projects	1,600,000	—	1,600,000
Debt service	800,000	700,000	1,500,000
Unrestricted	(400,000)	1,500,000	1,100,000
Total net assets	$11,700,000	$10,100,000	$21,800,000

CITY OF HARRIS SHOALS
Statement of Activities
For the year ending June 30, 2001

		Program Revenues		Net (Expense) Revenue		
Functions/programs	Expenses	Charges for Services	Grants and Contributions	Governmental Activities	Business-Type Activities	Total
General government	$ 950,000	$ 310,000	$ 80,000	$ (560,000)		$ (560,000)
Public safety	3,300,000	200,000	1,100,000	(2,000,000)		(2,000,000)
Interest on bonds	560,000			(560,000)		(560,000)
Recreation	600,000	650,000	—	50,000		50,000
Water and sewer	750,000	885,000	100,000		235,000	235,000
Total	$6,160,000	$2,045,000	$1,280,000	$ (3,070,000)	$ 235,000	$ (2,835,000)
General revenues:						
Property taxes				$ 2,800,000		$ 2,800,000
Interest income				200,000	$ 135,000	335,000
Total general revenues				3,000,000	135,000	3,135,000
Excess (deficiency) of revenues over expenses				(70,000)	370,000	300,000
Transfers				100,000	(100,000)	—
Change in net assets				30,000	270,000	300,000
Net assets beginning				11,670,000	9,830,000	21,500,000
Net assets ending				$11,700,000	$10,100,000	$21,800,000

Since its inception in 1984, the Governmental Accounting Standards Board has been considering what should be included in the basic set of financial statements for governments. An earlier attempt to redefine the measurement focus and basis of accounting for government operations failed to gain support and was indefinitely

Exhibit 17-5
Reconciliation of Fund
Perspective Statements to
Entitywide Perspective
Statements

Part A: Reconciliation of Fund Balances to Net Assets at the Entitywide Perspective	
Fund balance of governmental-type funds:	
General Fund	$ 350,000
Special Revenue Funds	500,000
Debt Service Funds	1,620,000
Capital Projects Funds	800,000
Net assets of proprietary-type funds not reported as business-type activities	
Internal Service Funds	900,000
(includes $450,000 of fixed assets)	
Permanent Funds	1,000,000
Fixed assets used in general government operations not reported in the funds because they are not current financial resources	15,550,000
Long-term liabilities not reported in the funds because they are not currently payable	(9,000,000)
Accrued interest on long-term liabilities not currently payable	(20,000)
Net assets of governmental activities at the entitywide perspective	$11,700,000

Part B: Reconciliation of Change in Fund Balances to Change in Net Assets at the Entitywide Perspective	
Change in fund balance of governmental-type funds:	
General Fund	(120,000)
Special Revenue Funds	100,000
Debt Service Funds	0
Capital Projects Funds	720,000
Acquisition of general fixed assets reported as expenditures in the governmental-type funds	1,550,000
Bond proceeds shown as other financing sources in the governmental funds	(1,000,000)
Depreciation on general fixed assets	(1,200,000)
Interest accrued on general obligation bonds not currently payable	(20,000)
Change in net assets of governmental activities at the entitywide perspective	$ 30,000

delayed. The current proposal may be less controversial because it retains the traditional fund perspective statements. The Board believes that the proposed changes will result in financial reports proving useful for individual citizens.

The changes described in this section are only a proposal issued by the GASB. A comment period follows the issuance of an exposure draft during which interested individuals or organizations may express an opinion and provide suggestions for improving the proposal. It is important to recognize that the final statement, if passed, may look considerably different than the proposal described in this section.

SUMMARY

1. The previous chapter examined the procedures that state and local governments use in accounting for governmental-type activities. However, the operations of many governments often extend beyond providing services to the public. Proprietary-type functions require a different approach to financial reporting. More specifically, accounting for four government funds (Enterprise Funds, Internal Service Funds, Pension Trust Funds, and Nonexpendable Trust Funds) emphasizes income determination. The procedures utilized by these funds parallel the methods found in for-profit accounting. In these specific funds, neither budgetary entries nor encumbrances are recorded. Accrual accounting is appropriate. Fixed assets and long-term debts are entered directly into the specific funds. Depreciation is calculated and recognized each period.

2. Enterprise Funds and Internal Service Funds are both proprietary in nature. The various activities recorded in these fund types are financed, at least in part, by user charges. More specifically, Enterprise Funds account for activities where public customers pay for the

use of such facilities as municipal swimming pools, toll roads, bus services, and golf courses. Internal Service Funds provide services (data processing or printing, for example) for the benefit of departments and agencies within the government. Other than the absence of capital stock accounts, these two fund types are basically accounted for in the same manner as a commercial activity.

3. Pension Trust Funds and Nonexpendable Trust Funds are fiduciary rather than proprietary; cash or other assets are conveyed to the government to be held for a particular purpose. In Pension Trust Funds, the money provides retirement benefits for public employees. Computation of net income is necessary as a means of measuring the effective utilization of the available resources. Nonexpendable Trust Funds maintain control over donations made to the government with the stipulation that only the resulting income can be expended (usually for a specified purpose). Once again, the computation of annual net income is considered to be the primary accounting objective to determine the amount available for spending purposes.

4. In preparing financial statements, a state or locality must identify all agencies, commissions, and other activities that should be included. The main consideration for inclusion is financial accountability. The primary government is first determined: an entity that is legally separate, has an elected governing board, and is fiscally independent. Once identified, any activity that is not legally separate should be included in the financial reporting process of the primary government.

5. A primary government must also report any component units that are legally separate but so closely connected that omission cannot be justified. A component unit has a voting majority of its governing board appointed by the primary government. In addition, the primary government must be able to impose its will on the board or the component unit must provide a financial benefit or impose a financial burden on the primary government. As an alternative, the outside organization is considered to be a component unit if it is fiscally dependent on the primary government. Component units are reported to the right of the primary government in the entity's financial statements.

6. The external financial reporting of a state or locality takes the form of a comprehensive annual financial report (CAFR). This document includes general purpose financial statements for the government as a whole supplemented by individual statements for each fund type and account group. Schedules and statistics also may be included to demonstrate compliance with legal regulations or to provide more detailed information about a specific function.

COMPREHENSIVE ILLUSTRATION

Problem

(Estimated Time: 20 to 25 Minutes) The city of Edison created a water utility to provide services to local residents. The following transactions occurred in connection with the project. Record the appropriate journal entries for this utility. Entries for other funds may be omitted.

1. Cash of $300,000 was transferred from the city's General Fund as initial financing for the utility. This balance was regarded as permanent funding. An additional $225,000 was loaned by the General Fund to the utility.
2. A $560,000 bond payable was issued at face value to provide the additional capital needed for the operations of this utility.
3. A $790,000 building was constructed and payment was made. The facility houses the water utility, both the administrative offices and the operations.
4. As a preliminary step in acquiring services from the city, customers pay a total of $110,000 to the utility in refundable deposits. For control purposes, this amount will be segregated in the utility's accounting records.
5. The first series of invoices was mailed to customers with charges totaling $225,000.
6. The utility pays the following expenses:

Salaries	$48,000
Utilities	12,000
Maintenance	31,000

An additional $21,000 in salaries was owed at the end of the fiscal period. Depreciation expense of $13,000 has been calculated.

7. A total of $40,000 was paid on the bonds payable with $21,000 of this amount representing interest for the period.
8. Closing entries were recorded by the utility.

Solution

Since this utility should be accounted for as an Enterprise Fund, the following journal entries are appropriate:

```
1.  Cash ............................................  525,000
        Contributed Capital—Governmental ..................          300,000
        Due to General Fund ...............................          225,000
    To record initial transfers made to start water utility project.

2.  Cash ............................................  560,000
        Bonds Payable .....................................          560,000
    Proceeds received from bonds issued to finance water
    utility.

3.  Building ........................................  790,000
        Cash ..............................................          790,000
    Building construction costs incurred by water utility.

4.  Restricted Cash—Customers' Deposits ............  110,000
        Customers' Deposits Payable .......................          110,000
    To record refundable deposits received from utility
    customers.

5.  Accounts Receivable .............................  225,000
        Utility Revenues ..................................          225,000
    To accrue income for period.

6.  Salary Expense ..................................   69,000
    Utilities Expense ...............................   12,000
    Maintenance Expense .............................   31,000
    Depreciation Expense ............................   13,000
        Cash ..............................................           91,000
        Salary Payable ....................................           21,000
        Accumulated Depreciation ..........................           13,000
    To record expenses for current fiscal period.

7.  Bonds Payable ...................................   19,000
    Interest Expense ................................   21,000
        Cash ..............................................           40,000
    Payment made on bond interest and principal.

8.  Utility Revenues ................................  225,000
        Retained Earnings .................................          225,000
    To close out revenues for the period.
    Retained Earnings ...............................  146,000
        Salary Expense ....................................           69,000
        Utilities Expense .................................           12,000
        Maintenance Expense ...............................           31,000
        Depreciation Expense ..............................           13,000
        Interest Expense ..................................           21,000
    To close out water utility's expenses.
```

APPENDIX

General-Purpose Financial Statements— State or Local Government

The next several pages contain examples of the general-purpose financial statements prepared by a state or local government unit. In reading these statements, assume that the primary government has several component units. Some of these components are similar to governmental funds whereas the others are proprietary in nature.

For adequate disclosure and fair presentation, a Summary of Significant Accounting Policies and other appropriate notes to the financial statements also must be included. This information has been omitted here. Note that the total columns presented in these statements are optional.

Exhibit 17-6

CITY OF RAPHAEL
Combined Balance Sheet—All Fund Types and Account Groups
December 31, 1998

	Governmental Fund Types				Proprietary Fund Types	
	General	Special Revenue	Debt Service	Capital Projects	Enterprises	Internal Service
Assets and Other Debits						
Assets:						
Cash	$255,029	$101,385	$ 10,889	$ 666,285	$ 279,296	$ 29,700
Investments	65,000	37,200	197,638	—	—	—
Receivables (net of allowances for uncollectibles):						
Taxes, including interest, penalties, and liens	61,821	2,525	3,528	—	—	—
Accounts	8,300	3,300	—	100	26,480	—
Special assessments	—	—	—	646,385	—	—
Due from other funds	12,000	—	—	—	2,000	12,000
Due from other governments	85,000	75,260	—	640,000	—	—
Inventory, at cost	7,200	5,190	—	—	23,030	40,000
Prepaid expenses	—	—	—	—	1,200	—
Restricted assets—cash	—	—	—	—	306,753	—
Fixed assets (net, where applicable, of accumulated depreciation)	—	—	—	—	5,769,759	103,100
Other Debits:						
Amount available in debt service funds	—	—	—	—	—	—
Amount to be provided for retirement of general long-term debt	—	—	—	—	—	—
Total assets	$494,350	$224,860	$212,055	$1,952,770	$6,408,518	$184,800
Liabilities, Equity, and Other Credits						
Liabilities:						
Vouchers and accounts payable	$118,261	$ 32,454	$ —	$ 49,600	$ 116,471	$ 15,000
Contracts payable	46,900	20,300	—	166,000	26,107	—
Accrued general obligation interest	—	—	—	—	14,000	—
Other accrued expenses including compensated absences	10,700	—	—	—	2,870	—
Payable from restricted assets:						
Deposits	—	—	—	—	176,948	—
Due to:						
Other taxing units	—	—	—	—	—	55,000
Other funds	24,189	2,000	—	1,000	—	10,000
Deferred revenues	15,000	1,396	1,845	—	—	—
General obligation bonds payable	—	—	—	—	700,000	—
Revenue bonds payable	—	—	—	—	1,798,000	—
Special assessment bonds payable, with government commitment	—	—	—	—	—	—
Total liabilities	215,050	56,150	1,845	216,600	2,834,396	80,000
Equity and Other Credits:						
Contributed capital	—	—	—	—	1,406,766	95,000
Investment in general fixed assets	—	—	—	—	—	—
Retained earnings	—	—	—	—	2,167,356	9,800
Fund balance:						
Reserved for encumbrances	38,000	46,500	—	1,725,070	—	—
Reserved for inventory	7,200	5,190	—	—	—	—
Reserved for loans	—	—	—	—	—	—
Reserved for endowments	—	—	—	—	—	—
Reserved for employees' retirement system	—	—	—	—	—	—
Reserved for debt service	46,070	—	210,210	—	—	—
Unreserved, undesignated	188,030	117,020	—	11,100	—	—
Total equity and other credits	279,300	168,710	210,210	1,736,170	3,574,122	104,800
Total liabilities, equity, and other credits	$494,350	$224,860	$212,055	$1,952,770	$6,408,518	$184,800

The notes to the financial statements are an integral part of this statement.

| Fiduciary Fund Type | Account Groups | | Total Primary Government | Component Units | | Total Reporting Entity |
Trust and Agency	General Fixed Assets	General Long-Term Debt	(memorandum only)	Governmental	Proprietary	(memorandum only)
$ 216,701	$ —	$ —	$ 1,559,285	$ 36,497	$185,044	$ 1,780,826
1,239,260	—	—	1,539,098	27,312	99,609	1,666,019
617,666	—	—	685,540	—	—	685,540
—	—	—	38,180	—	—	38,180
—	—	—	646,385	—	—	646,385
11,189	—	—	37,189	—	—	37,189
—	—	—	800,260	55,000	38,765	894,025
—	—	—	75,420	6,245	116,740	198,405
—	—	—	1,200	—	8,200	9,400
—	—	—	306,753	—	—	306,753
—	6,913,250	—	12,786,109	—	344,520	13,130,629
—	—	210,210	210,210	—	—	210,210
—	—	1,489,790	1,489,790	—	—	1,489,790
$2,084,816	$6,913,250	$1,700,000	$20,175,419	$125,054	$792,878	$21,093,351
$ 5,200	$ —	$ —	$ 336,986	$ 17,441	$114,494	$ 468,921
—	—	—	259,307	—	56,000	315,307
—	—	—	14,000	—	13,111	27,111
4,700	—	—	18,270	4,400	21,475	44,145
—	—	—	176,948	—	—	176,948
680,800	—	—	735,800	—	—	735,800
—	—	—	37,189	24,500	66,575	128,264
—	—	—	18,241	3,112	—	21,353
—	—	1,145,000	1,845,000	—	375,000	2,220,000
—	—	—	1,798,000	—	—	1,798,000
—	—	555,000	555,000	—	—	555,000
690,700	—	1,700,000	5,794,741	49,453	646,655	6,490,849
—	—	—	1,501,766	—	80,000	1,581,766
—	6,913,250	—	6,913,250	—	—	6,913,250
—	—	—	2,177,156	—	66,223	2,243,379
—	—	—	1,809,570	6,900	—	1,816,470
—	—	—	12,390	6,245	—	18,635
50,050	—	—	50,050	—	—	50,050
160,865	—	—	160,865	—	—	160,865
1,183,201	—	—	1,183,201	—	—	1,183,201
—	—	—	256,280	—	—	256,280
—	—	—	316,150	62,456	—	378,606
1,394,116	6,913,250	—	14,380,678	75,601	146,223	14,602,502
$2,084,816	$6,913,250	$1,700,000	$20,175,419	$125,054	$792,878	$21,093,351

Exhibit 17-7

CITY OF RAPHAEL
Combined Statement of Revenues, Expenditures, and Changes in Fund Balances—
All Governmental Fund Types and Expendable Trust Funds
For the Fiscal Year Ended December 31, 1998

	Governmental Fund Types				Fiduciary Fund Type	Total Primary Government (memorandum only)	Component Units Governmental	Total Reporting Entity (memorandum only)
	General	Special Revenue	Debt Service	Capital Projects	Expendable Trust			
Revenues:								
Taxes	$ 881,300	$ 189,300	$ 79,177	$ —	$ —	$1,149,777	—	$1,149,777
Special assessments levied	—	—	240,000	—	—	240,000	—	240,000
Licenses and permits	103,000	—	—	—	—	103,000	39,000	142,000
Intergovernmental revenues	186,500	831,100	41,500	1,250,000	—	2,309,100	200,000	2,509,100
Charges for services	91,000	79,100	—	—	—	170,100	17,400	187,500
Fines and forfeits	33,200	—	—	—	—	33,200	—	33,200
Miscellaneous revenues	19,500	71,625	36,235	3,750	200	131,310	26,045	157,355
Total revenues	1,314,500	1,171,125	396,912	1,253,750	200	4,136,487	282,445	4,418,932
Expenditures:								
Current:								
General government	121,805	—	—	—	—	121,805	—	121,805
Public safety	258,395	480,000	—	—	—	738,395	21,490	759,885
Highways and streets	85,400	417,000	—	—	—	502,400	—	502,400
Sanitation	56,250	—	—	—	—	56,250	—	56,250

Health	44,500	—	—	—	—	44,500	54,908	99,408
Welfare	46,800	—	—	—	—	46,800	46,361	93,161
Culture and recreation	40,900	256,450	—	—	—	297,350	119,440	416,790
Education	509,150	—	—	—	2,420	511,570	22,500	534,070
Capital outlay	—	—	—	1,625,500	—	1,625,500	—	1,625,500
Debt service:								
Principal retirement	—	—	373,100	—	—	373,100	—	373,100
Interest and fiscal charges	—	—	68,420	—	—	68,420	—	68,420
Total expenditures	1,163,200	1,153,450	441,520	1,625,500	2,420	4,386,090	264,699	4,650,789
Excess (deficiency) of revenues over (under) expenditures	151,300	17,675	(44,608)	(371,750)	(2,220)	(249,603)	17,746	(231,857)
Other financing sources (uses):								
Proceeds of general obligation bonds	—	—	—	900,000	—	900,000	—	900,000
Operating transfers in	—	—	10,000	64,500	2,530	77,030	—	77,030
Operating transfers out	(74,500)	—	—	—	—	(74,500)	—	(74,500)
Total other financing sources (uses)	(74,500)	—	10,000	964,500	2,530	902,530	—	902,530
Excess of revenues and other sources over (under) expenditures and other uses	76,800	17,675	(34,608)	592,750	310	652,927	17,746	670,673
Fund balances—January 1	242,500	151,035	244,818	1,143,420	26,555	1,808,328	57,855	1,866,183
Residual equity transfer out	(40,000)	—	—	—	—	(40,000)	—	(40,000)
Fund balances—December 31	$ 279,300	$ 168,710	$ 210,210	$1,736,170	$26,865	$2,421,255	$ 75,601	$2,496,856

The notes to the financial statements are an integral part of this statement.

Exhibit 17–8

CITY OF RAPHAEL
Combined Statement of Revenues, Expenditures, and
Changes in Fund Balances—Budget and Actual—
General and Special Revenue Fund Types
For the Fiscal Year Ended December 31, 1998

	General Fund		
	Budget	**Actual**	**Variance— Favorable (Unfavorable)**
Revenues:			
Taxes	$ 882,500	$ 881,300	$ (1,200)
Licenses and permits	125,500	103,000	(22,500)
Intergovernmental revenues	200,000	186,500	(13,500)
Charges for services	90,000	91,000	1,000
Fines and forfeits	32,500	33,200	700
Miscellaneous revenues	19,500	19,500	—
Total revenues	1,350,000	1,314,500	(35,500)
Expenditures:			
Current:			
General government	129,000	121,805	7,195
Public safety	277,300	258,395	18,905
Highways and streets	84,500	85,400	(900)
Sanitation	50,000	56,250	(6,250)
Health	47,750	44,500	3,250
Welfare	51,000	46,800	4,200
Culture and recreation	44,500	40,900	3,600
Education	541,450	509,150	32,300
Total expenditures	1,225,500	1,163,200	62,300
Excess (deficiency) of revenues over (under) expenditures	124,500	151,300	26,800
Other financing sources (uses):			
Operating transfers out	(74,500)	(74,500)	—
Excess (deficiency) of revenues over (under) expenditures and other uses	50,000	76,800	26,800
Fund balances—January 1	242,500	242,500	—
Residual equity transfer out	(40,000)	(40,000)	—
Fund balances—December 31	$ 252,500	$ 279,300	$ 26,800

The notes to the financial statements are an integral part of this statement.

	Special Revenue Funds			Totals (Memorandum Only)		
	Budget	Actual	Variance—Favorable (Unfavorable)	Budget	Actual	Variance—Favorable (Unfavorable)
	$ 189,500	$ 189,300	$ (200)	$1,072,000	$1,070,600	$ (1,400)
	—	—	—	125,500	103,000	(22,500)
	837,600	831,100	(6,500)	1,037,600	1,017,600	(20,000)
	78,000	79,100	1,100	168,000	170,100	2,100
	—	—	—	32,500	33,200	700
	81,475	71,625	(9,850)	100,975	91,125	(9,850)
	1,186,575	1,171,125	(15,450)	2,536,575	2,485,625	(50,950)
	—	—	—	129,000	121,805	7,195
	494,500	480,000	14,500	771,800	738,395	33,405
	436,000	417,000	19,000	520,500	502,400	18,100
	—	—	—	50,000	56,250	(6,250)
	—	—	—	47,750	44,500	3,250
	—	—	—	51,000	46,800	4,200
	272,000	256,450	15,550	316,500	297,350	19,150
	—	—	—	541,450	509,150	32,300
	1,202,500	1,153,450	49,050	2,428,000	2,316,650	111,350
	(15,925)	17,675	33,600	108,575	168,975	60,400
	—	—	—	(74,500)	(74,500)	—
	(15,925)	17,675	33,600	34,075	94,475	60,400
	151,035	151,035	—	393,535	393,535	—
	—	—	—	(40,000)	(40,000)	—
	$ 135,110	$ 168,710	$ 33,600	$ 387,610	$ 448,010	$ 60,400

E x h i b i t 1 7 – 9

CITY OF RAPHAEL
Combined Statement of Revenues, Expenses, and Changes in
Retained Earnings/Fund Balances—All Proprietary Fund Types
and Similar Trust Funds
For the Fiscal Year Ended December 31, 1998

	Proprietary Fund Types		Fiduciary Fund Types		Totals Primary (memorandum only)	Component Units Proprietary	Total Reporting Entity (memorandum only)
	Enterprise	Internal Service	Nonexpendable Trust	Pension Trust			
Operating revenues:							
Charges for services	$ 672,150	$88,000	$ —	$ —	$ 760,150	$186,315	$ 946,465
Interest			2,480	28,460	30,940	16,010	46,950
Contributions				160,686	160,686	—	160,686
Total operating revenues	672,150	88,000	2,480	189,146	951,776	202,325	1,154,101
Operating expenses:							
Cost of sales and services	247,450	32,500	—	—	279,950	149,633	429,583
Contractual services	75,330	400	—	—	75,730		75,730
Supplies	20,310	1,900	—	—	22,210	11,442	33,652
Materials	50,940	44,000	—	—	94,940	1,088	96,028
Heat, light, and power	26,050	1,500	—	—	27,550	990	28,540
Depreciation	144,100	4,450	—	—	148,550	6,496	155,046
Benefit payments				21,000	21,000		21,000
Refunds				25,745	25,745		25,745
Total operating expenses	564,180	84,750		46,745	695,675	169,649	865,324
Operating income	107,970	3,250	2,480	142,401	256,101	32,676	288,777
Nonoperating revenues (expenses):							
Grants and gifts	55,000		45,000		100,000		100,000
Interest revenue	3,830				3,830		3,830
Other	5,000				5,000		5,000
Interest expense and fiscal charges	(92,988)				(92,988)	(15,410)	(108,398)
Total nonoperating revenues (expenses)	(29,158)		45,000		15,842	(15,410)	432
Income before operating transfers	78,812	3,250	47,480	142,401	271,943	17,266	289,209
Operating transfers in (out)			(2,530)		(2,530)		(2,530)
Net income	78,812	3,250	44,950	142,401	269,413	17,266	286,679
Retained earnings/fund balances—January 1	2,088,544	6,550	139,100	1,040,800	3,274,994	48,957	3,323,951
Retained earnings/fund balances—December 31	$2,167,356	$ 9,800	$184,050	$1,183,201	$3,544,407	$ 66,223	$3,610,630

The notes to the financial statements are an integral part of this statement.

Exhibit 17–10

CITY OF RAPHAEL
Combined Statement of Cash Flows
All Proprietary Fund Types and Nonexpendable Trust Fund
For the Fiscal Year Ended December 31, 1998

	Proprietary Fund Types		Nonexpendable Trust Fund	Total Primary Government (memorandum only)	Component Units Proprietary	Total Reporting Entity (memorandum only)
	Enterprise	Internal Service				
Cash flows from operating activities:*						
Cash from customers	$ 661,440	$ 89,160	$ —	$ 750,600	$ 183,405	$ 934,005
Interest received	—	—	2,480	2,480	15,310	17,790
Cash paid to suppliers	(86,100)	(62,970)	—	(149,070)	(140,945)	(290,015)
Cash paid to employees	(310,380)	(13,760)	—	(324,140)	(12,866)	(337,006)
Cash paid for other operating expenses	(39,640)	(5,494)	—	(45,134)	(9,451)	(54,585)
Net cash provided (used) by operating activities	225,320	6,936	2,480	234,736	35,453	270,189
Cash flows from noncapital financing activities:						
Grants and gifts	—	—	45,000	45,000	—	45,000
Operating transfers out	—	—	(2,530)	(2,530)	—	(2,530)
Net cash provided (used) by noncapital financing activities	—	—	42,470	42,470	—	42,470
Cash flows from capital and related financing activities:						
Proceeds from issuance of long-term debt	443,449	—	—	443,449	121,000	564,449
Principal payments—long-term debt	(325,000)	—	—	(325,000)	(25,000)	(350,000)
Proceeds from sale of fixed assets	11,400	—	—	11,400	—	11,400
Purchase of fixed assets	(306,921)	(22,000)	—	(328,921)	(98,450)	(427,371)
Net cash provided (used) by capital and related financing activities	(177,072)	(22,000)	—	(199,072)	(2,450)	(201,522)
Cash flows from investing activities:						
Proceeds from sale of investments	26,100	—	11,000	37,100	—	37,100
Purchase of investments	—	—	(48,800)	(48,800)	(10,000)	(58,800)
Net cash provided (used) by investing activities	26,100	—	(37,800)	(11,700)	(10,000)	(21,700)
Net increase (decrease) in cash	74,348	(15,064)	7,150	66,434	23,003	89,437
Cash, January 1	204,948	44,764	9,290	259,002	162,041	421,043
Cash, December 31	$ 279,296	$ 29,700	$ 16,440	$ 325,436	$ 185,044	$ 510,480

The notes to the financial statements are an integral part of this statement.

* Since the direct approach of deriving cash from operating activities is being used here, a reconciliation of net cash flows from operating activities to net income should also be included.

QUESTIONS

1. What is the primary emphasis in accounting for the proprietary-type funds of a state or local government?
2. What characteristics of accounting for proprietary-type funds are unique from the reporting procedures identified in the previous chapter for the governmental-type funds?
3. Why is accrual accounting rather than modified accrual accounting considered appropriate for the proprietary-type funds of a state or local government unit?
4. How are commitments accounted for in an Enterprise Fund? Why?
5. Give examples of government operations appropriately classified as Enterprise Funds. Give examples of government operations appropriately classified as Internal Service Funds.
6. Describe the controversies that surround the recording of Internal Service Funds for external reporting purposes.
7. What are "Due to" and "Due from" accounts and how are they reported?
8. Why do some Enterprise Funds have restricted asset accounts?
9. Why is income determination emphasized in a Pension Trust Fund?
10. What is the accounting objective for a Nonexpendable Trust Fund? Why?
11. What is the difference between a Nonexpendable Trust Fund and an Expendable Trust Fund?
12. What is the purpose of Agency Funds? What transactions are recorded in Agency Funds?
13. How is the presence of a primary government identified?
14. How can a government demonstrate its fiscal independence?
15. How does a primary government determine its component units?
16. How does a primary government report the financial positions and operations of its component units?
17. What is meant by blended component units?
18. In government reporting, what is a related organization and how is a related organization reported by a primary government?
19. What items are included in the comprehensive annual financial report produced for a state or local government?
20. When may a government unit issue only general purpose financial statements rather than a comprehensive annual financial report?
21. What specific financial statements make up the general purpose financial statements of a state or local government?

LIBRARY ASSIGNMENTS

1. Read the following articles and any other published information discussing the history of governmental accounting:
   "Capital Accounts of a Municipality," *The Journal of Accountancy,* October 1918.
   "Governmental Sinking Funds, Serial Bonds and Depreciation Reserves," *The Journal of Accountancy,* October 1918.
   "25 Years of State and Local Governmental Financial Reporting—An Accounting Standards Perspective," *Government Accountants Journal,* Fall 1992.
   Write a short paper discussing the changes in governmental accounting during the 20th century.
2. Read the following article:
   "Internal Service Funds Are beyond Salvation," *Accounting Horizons,* June 1990.
   Write a short paper discussing whether Internal Service Funds should be eliminated from the external reporting of a state or local government unit.
3. Read the following:

"Statement No. 14 of the Governmental Accounting Standards Board—The Financial Reporting Entity," *Journal of Accountancy,* November 1991.

"The Governmental Financial Reporting Entity: Inclusion and Display," *The CPA Journal,* January 1993.

"The GASB's Proposed Statement on the Governmental Financial Reporting Model," *The CPA Journal,* April 1997.

"The New Government Reporting Model: Is It a *Field of Dreams?*" *Accounting Horizons,* September 1997.

Write a report describing the changes made by the GASB in defining the reporting entity of a government unit. Discuss the identification of component units and their reporting.

PROBLEMS

1. Which of the following statements is not true of the proprietary-type funds of a state or local government unit?
   a. The basis of accounting is accrual accounting.
   b. Depreciation expense is recorded each period.
   c. Budgetary entries are recorded by most but not all of these funds.
   d. Fixed assets are recorded within the individual funds.

2. Which of the following accounts would not be recorded by an Enterprise Fund?
   a. Encumbrances.
   b. Buildings.
   c. Notes payable.
   d. Contributed capital.

3. What is the purpose of Nonexpendable Trust Fund?
   a. To account for monetary gifts that must be used for fixed assets.
   b. To account for monetary gifts that cannot be spent until the end of a specified period of time.
   c. To account for a gift where only the subsequently earned income can be spent.
   d. To account for a gift where the money must be used to reduce a government's debts rather than to buy assets.

4. A city's municipal airport charges a customer for rental space. When is the revenue recognized?
   a. When received.
   b. When appropriately spent.
   c. When measurable and available.
   d. When the earning process is substantially completed.

5. Fixed assets owned by a city-owned utility are accounted for in which of the following?

	Enterprise Fund	General Fixed Assets Account Group
a.	No	No
b.	No	Yes
c.	Yes	No
d.	Yes	Yes

(AICPA adapted)

6. If a pension trust fund pays out benefits to a retired city employee, what account balance is directly affected?
   a. Operating expenses.
   b. Fund balance.
   c. Pension liability.
   d. Membership contribution.

7. Money that must be turned over to the state government is collected by a city periodically. While the money is being held by the city, within which fund should it be recorded?

       a. General Fund.

       b. Agency Fund.

       c. Special Revenue Fund.

       d. Expendable Trust Fund.

8. Lake City operates a centralized data processing center through an Internal Service Fund, to provide data processing services to Lake's other governmental units. In 1998, this Internal Service Fund billed Lake's police department $100,000 for data processing services. How should the Internal Service Fund record this billing?

	Debit	Credit
a. Memorandum entry only	—	—
b. Due from police department	100,000	
Data processing expenses		100,000
c. Intragovernmental transfers	100,000	
Interfund exchanges		100,000
d. Due from police department	100,000	
Operating revenue		100,000

(AICPA adapted)

9. Which of the following is not a criterion for identifying a primary government?

    a. A separately elected governing board.

    b. Identifiable geographical boundaries.

    c. Legal separation such as being able to sue and be sued.

    d. Fiscal independence.

10. Which of the following is not a criterion for determining the fiscal independence of a government entity?

    a. The right to buy, sell, or lease property in the entity's name without the approval of another government.

    b. Determining the budget for the entity without the approval of any other body.

    c. Being able to levy taxes without having to seek approval of another government unit.

    d. Issuing bonds without the need for approval by another government.

11. What is a component unit?

    a. An Internal Service Fund.

    b. An activity that is legally separate from a primary government but must still be reported within the government's financial statements.

    c. Any fund type included in a primary government's financial statements.

    d. An account group of a governmental fund.

12. Which of the following would not indicate that a primary government has the ability to impose its will on a component unit?

    a. Being able to modify the component unit's budgets.

    b. Being able to appoint more than 21 percent of the members of the component unit's governing board.

    c. Hiring the individuals who operate the component unit on a daily basis.

    d. Overriding decisions of the governing board of the component unit.

13. Which of the following is not a general purpose financial statement of a state or local government?

    a. Combined balance sheet—all fund types and account groups.

    b. Combined income statement—all fund types and account groups.

    c. Combined statement of revenues, expenditures, and changes in fund balance—budget and actual.

    d. Combined statement of revenues, expenses, and changes in retained earnings—all proprietary fund types.

14. In the comprehensive annual financial report (CAFR) of a governmental unit, the account groups are included in

    a. Both the combined balance sheet and the combined statement of revenues, expenditures, and changes in fund balances.

    b. The combined statement of revenues, expenditures, and changes in fund balances, but not the combined balance sheet.

    c. The combined balance sheet but not the combined statement of revenues, expenditures, and changes in fund balances.

    d. Neither the combined balance sheet nor the combined statement of revenues, expenditures, and changes in fund balances.

(AICPA)

15. Which of the following would be included in the Combined Statement of Revenues, Expenditures, and Changes in Fund Balances—Budget and Actual in the comprehensive annual financial report (CAFR) of a governmental unit?

	Enterprise Fund	General Fixed Asset Account Group
a.	Yes	Yes
b.	Yes	No
c.	No	Yes
d.	No	No

(AICPA)

16. Which of the following accounts would be included in the fund equity section of the combined balance sheet of a governmental unit for the general fixed asset account group?

	Investment in General Fixed Assets	Fund Balance Reserved for Encumbrances
a.	Yes	Yes
b.	Yes	No
c.	No	No
d.	No	Yes

(AICPA)

17. The comprehensive annual financial report (CAFR) of a governmental unit should contain a Combined Statement of Revenues, Expenses, and Changes in Retained Earnings for

	Account Groups	Governmental Funds
a.	Yes	Yes
b.	Yes	No
c.	No	No
d.	No	Yes

(AICPA)

18. A city received the following: a state government grant of $100,000 to be used for a specific project, a gift from a citizen of $20,000 cash where only the subsequent income can be spent, property tax revenues of $530,000, bond proceeds of $240,000 for construction of a building for the data processing operation that services the entire city government. In which funds should each of these cash receipts be recorded?

	Grant	Gift	Tax	Bond
a.	Expendable Trust	Nonexpendable Trust	General Fund	General Fund
b.	Special Revenue	General Fund	Capital Projects	Debt Service
c.	Special Revenue	Nonexpendable Trust	General Fund	Internal Service
d.	General Fund	Expendable Trust	Special Revenue	Debt Service

19. What is the basic criterion used to determine the reporting entity for a governmental unit?

    a. Special financing arrangement.

    b. Geographic boundaries.

    c. Scope of public services.

    d. Financial accountability.

(AICPA adapted)

20. Which event(s) should be included in a statement of cash flows for a governmental entity?

    I.   Cash inflow from issuing bonds to finance city hall construction

    II. Cash outflow from a city utility representing payments in lieu of property taxes

        a. I only.

        b. II only.

        c. Both I and II.

        d. Neither I nor II.

    (AICPA adapted)

21. Fish Road property owners in Sea County are responsible for special assessment debt that arose from a storm sewer project. If the property owners default, Sea has no obligation regarding debt service, although it does bill property owners for assessments and uses the moneys it collects to pay debt holders. What fund type should Sea use to account for these collection and servicing activities?

    a. Agency.

    b. Debt service.

    c. Expendable trust funds.

    d. Capital projects.

    (AICPA adapted)

22. Tuston Township issued the following bonds during the year ended June 30, 1998:

    Bonds issued for the garbage collection enterprise fund that will
        service the debt $700,000

    Revenue bonds to be repaid from admission fees collected by the
        township zoo enterprise fund 500,000

    What amount of these bonds should be accounted for in Tuston's general long-term debt account group?

    a. $1,200,000

    b. $700,000

    c. $500,000

    d. $0

    (AICPA adapted)

23. The city of Francois, Texas, has begun the process of producing its comprehensive annual financial report (CAFR). Within the city, several organizations are related to the government. The city's accountant is trying to decide how these organizations should be included in the reporting process.

    a. What is the major criterion for inclusion in a government's CAFR?

    b. How is a primary government unit identified?

    c. How is the legal separation of a government unit evaluated?

    d. How is the fiscal independence of a government unit evaluated?

    e. What is a component unit and how are the financial position and operations of a component unit reported by a primary government?

    f. How does a primary government prove that it can impose its will on a component unit?

    g. What is meant by the blending of a component unit?

    h. What is a related organization and how does a primary government report its related organizations?

24. The city of Walkup incurred the following debts at face value on July 1, 1998:

    ■ Bonds totaling $600,000 were issued to construct locker rooms for the city's swimming pool. The interest rate was 8 percent per year. Repayment was to be made from admission charged to the swimmers.

    ■ A $50,000 note was signed with a bank to buy equipment for the city's print shop. The interest rate was 9 percent per year. Repayment was to be made from surplus amounts generated by the charges assessed by the print shop.

    In both cases, the money was received and appropriately expended. On July 1, 1999, a $70,000 payment was made on the bonds that included the interest to date. An $8,000 payment made on the note on April 1, 1999, also included the interest to date.

    Make all necessary journal entries for 1998 and 1999 and indicate the appropriate fund types. The city has a calendar year.

25. The city of Mexvell operated a motor pool serving all city-owned vehicles. The motor pool bought a new garage by paying $22,000 cash and signing a note with the local bank for $215,000. Subsequently, the motor pool did work for the police department at a cost of $13,000, which has not yet been paid. Depreciation on the garage amounted to $15,000. The first $9,000 payment made on the note included $3,700 in interest.

Give all of the entries for these transactions including the fund type or account group in which each entry would be recorded.

26. Hawkins County decided to create a sanitation service and offer it to the public for a fee. As a result, county officials planned to account for this activity within an Enterprise Fund. To begin the operations, $55,000 of previously unrestricted funds were transferred on February 1, 1998, as permanent financing. An additional $158,000 was borrowed from a local bank on March 1, 1998. The debt had a 10 percent annual interest rate. A truck was ordered from a local dealer on June 1, 1998, at an anticipated cost of $98,000. The truck was received on July 1, 1998, with an actual cost of $102,000. The truck had a $12,000 salvage value and an expected life of 10 years (assume straight-line depreciation was used). Rental space to house the truck was located at a charge of $100 per month. Rent for the first 15 months of operation was paid on June 30, 1998. During the last six months of the year, citizens were charged $15,000 for services rendered and actually paid $13,000. The remaining accounts were assumed to be collectible.

Required:

    a. Make all journal entries for this activity including any adjusting entries needed at December 31, 1998. Only entries within the Enterprise Fund are required.

    b. Prepare financial statements for this operation.

27. The following transactions are for the city of Jamin. For each, prepare all needed journal entries including an identification of the fund types.

    a. The city collected $13,000 from parking meters that must be transferred to the county government.

    b. The city transferred $21,000 into a Pension Trust Fund. Of this amount, $15,000 was contributed by the city with the remainder coming from the employees.

    c. Investments valued at $55,000 were donated to the city with the stipulation that subsequent dividend income be used to plant trees in the downtown area.

    d. Unrestricted funds totaling $23,000 were transferred to begin a print shop to service the entire city government.

    e. The city motor pool did work for the fire department at a cost of $13,000. This money has not yet been paid.

    f. The money collected in (*a*) was paid to the county.

    g. The investments received in (*c*) generated $8,000 in dividends. The agent holding these investments charged a commission of $1,000 and mailed the remaining $7,000 to the city.

    h. The $7,000 profit in (*g*) was reclassified into an Expendable Trust Fund.

    i. The print shop in (*d*) bought a building at a cost of $130,000, paid $21,000 immediately and signed a note for the remainder.

28. The following transactions are for the city of Lights. For each, prepare all necessary journal entries including an identification of the funds or account groups involved.

    a. The city council transferred $44,000 from the General Fund as permanent financing to create a print shop to service the needs of the various agencies and branches of the government.

    b. The print shop ordered printing equipment for an estimated cost of $22,000 along with approximately $4,000 in supplies.

    c. The city's golf course issued $500,000 in bonds at a price of $512,000 to finance the construction of a new club house.

    d. The printing equipment and supplies ordered in (*b*) were received by the government with an actual cost of $23,500 and $3,800, respectively. Payment will be made in 30 days.

    e. The city collected $14,600 in tolls from the roads in the area. Of this total, 90 percent must be spent by the city for highway maintenance. The remaining 10 percent will be held until the end of the year and then turned over to the state government.

f. The print shop did work for the school system for a price of $930. This amount has not, as of yet, been collected.

g. The city's golf course made a first payment of $25,000 on the bond issued in (c). Of this balance, $5,000 covered current interest charges with the remainder applied to the principal.

h. By the end of the year, the print shop consumed $2,600 of supplies.

i. The club house for the golf course was completed and the contractor paid $477,000.

j. Depreciation on the printing equipment was calculated as $4,700.

k. The appropriate portion of the money collected from the toll roads was conveyed to the state government.

29. The city of Merlot operated a central garage to provide repairs and maintenance for all city-owned vehicles. The Central Garage Fund was established by a contribution of $200,000 from the General Fund on July 1, 1996, at which time the building was acquired. The after-closing trial balance at June 30, 1998, was as follows:

	Debit	Credit
Cash.	$150,000	
Due from General Fund	20,000	
Inventory of materials and supplies	80,000	
Land	60,000	
Building	200,000	
Accumulated depreciation—Building		$ 10,000
Machinery and equipment	56,000	
Accumulated depreciation—Machinery and equipment		12,000
Vouchers payable.		38,000
Contribution from General Fund		200,000
Retained earnings		306,000
Totals	$566,000	$566,000

The following information applies to the fiscal year ended June 30, 1999:

a. Materials and supplies were purchased on account for $74,000.

b. The inventory of materials and supplies at June 30, 1999, was $58,000, based on the physical count taken.

c. Salaries and wages paid to employees totaled $230,000.

d. An invoice from the city's water and electrical utility totaling $30,000 was paid.

e. Depreciation for the period was computed as follows: building—$5,000 and machinery and equipment—$8,000.

f. Billings to other departments for services rendered to them were as follows:

General Fund	$262,000
Water and Sewer Fund	84,000
Special Revenue Fund	32,000

g. Unpaid interfund receivable balances at June 30, 1999, were as follows:

General Fund	$ 6,000
Special Revenue Fund.	16,000

h. Vouchers payable at June 30, 1999, were $14,000.

Required:

a. For the period July 1, 1998, through June 30, 1999, prepare journal entries to record all of the transactions in the Central Garage Fund accounts.

b. Prepare closing entries for the Central Garage Fund at June 30, 1999.

(AICPA adapted)

30. The following transactions were incurred by the city of Metropolis. Prepare all appropriate journal entries for the following fund categories:

Enterprise Funds
Internal Service Funds
Pension Trust Funds
Nonexpendable Trust Funds
Agency Funds

a. A transfer of $360,000 was made from the city's General Fund to finance a data processing center being established to provide services for all government operations.

b. A gift of $88,000 in cash was received by the city from a local school teacher with the provision that all earnings be used to provide scholarships for local students.

c. The municipal airport reported revenues of $460,000 ($320,000 from assessments made to the airline companies and $140,000 from rental charges). Only $97,000 of the rents have been collected. The airport has also incurred the following expenses:

Salaries	$160,000
Depreciation	80,000
Advertising	9,000
Maintenance	79,000

Although the advertising has already appeared in the newspaper, the cost has not yet been paid.

d. A contract was signed to acquire a $154,000 building for the data processing center. This facility is presently under construction.

e. The city collected $160,000 in general sales taxes. Of this amount, 20 percent will eventually be transferred to the state.

f. The building was completed for the data processing center and payment was made.

g. The municipal airport signed an $800,000 note payable and immediately used these funds to acquire a new hangar.

h. The appropriate amount of sales taxes collected in (e) was conveyed to the state.

i. Cash of $27,000 was transferred from the city's General Fund to the Pension Trust Fund representing the government's current year contribution.

j. The data processing center did the following work; as of yet, no amounts have been collected:

General Fund	$4,000
Special Revenue Fund	900
Municipal Airport	1,400

k. The municipal airport paid the first $8,000 interest installment on the note signed in (g).

l. Income of $12,000 was received on the gift donated in (b). This money was transferred to an Expendable Trust Fund to be used in the stipulated manner.

m. Retired city employees were paid benefits of $44,000 in cash.

31. An examination of the accounts of the city of Delmas, as of June 30, 1998, revealed the following:

a. On December 31, 1997, the city paid $315,000 out of General Fund revenues to acquire a central garage to service its vehicles, with $167,500 of this amount being paid for a building with an estimated life of 25 years, $44,500 for land, and $103,000 for machinery with an estimated life of 15 years. An additional $12,200 cash contribution was received by the garage from the General Fund to finance daily operations.

b. The garage maintained no formal accounting records, but a review of deposit slips and canceled checks for the period revealed the following:

Collections for services to city departments financed from the General Fund	$30,000
Office salaries paid	6,000
Utilities	700
Mechanics' wages	11,000
Materials and supplies	9,000

c. At June 30, 1998, the garage also had uncollected billings of $2,000, accounts payable for materials and supplies of $500, and an inventory of materials and supplies of $1,500.

d. On June 30, 1998, the city issued $200,000 in special assessment bonds at par to finance a street improvement project estimated to cost $225,000. The project was to be paid by a $15,000 contribution from the city and a $210,000 levy against property owners (payable in five equal annual installments beginning on October 1,

1998). The levy was made on June 30. A $215,000 contract was signed on July 2, 1998, but work has not yet begun. The city has agreed to guarantee payment on the bonds in case any forfeitures occur.

e. On July 1, 1996, the city issued $400,000 in 30-year, 6 percent general obligation term bonds at par to finance the construction of a public health center. Construction was completed and the contractors were fully paid a total of $397,500 on May 9, 1998.

f. For the health center bonds, the city set aside General Fund revenues of $20,000 on each October 1 to cover future interest and principal payments.

Required:

The preceding information was recorded only in the General Fund. Prepare the formal entries as of June 30, 1998, to adjust all funds other than the General Fund.

(AICPA adapted)

32. Gotham City was incorporated on July 1, 1998. The following transactions occurred during its first fiscal year, July 1, 1998, to June 30, 1999:

a. The city council adopted a budget for general operations during the fiscal year ending June 30, 1999. Revenues were estimated at $900,000. Legal authorizations for expenditures were $724,000 along with transfers out of $170,000.

b. Property taxes were levied in the amount of $790,000; 2 percent of this amount was estimated to be uncollectible. These taxes were considered available as of the date of levy to finance current expenditures.

c. During the year, a resident of the city donated marketable securities valued at $50,000 to the city. The terms of the trust agreement stipulated that the principal amount be kept intact; use of revenue generated by the securities was restricted to financing college scholarships for needy students. Dividends earned and received on these marketable securities amounted to $5,500 through June 30, 1999. This money was transferred to an Expendable Trust Fund for expenditure in the following period.

d. A General Fund transfer of $5,000 was made to establish an Internal Service Fund to provide for a permanent supply of materials and other items to be used by other funds.

e. The city decided to install lighting on several local streets. A special assessment project was authorized with a budgeted cost of $175,000. Budgetary entries were not formally recorded. A bond was issued for $175,000, with the city guaranteeing payment. The lights were installed. Residents were then assessed $165,000, with the remainder to come from the General Fund. No payments have yet been received.

f. During the year, the Internal Service Fund purchased supplies at various times at a total cost of $4,900.

g. Cash collections recorded by the General Fund during the year were as follows:

    Property taxes $779,000
    Licenses and permits   33,000

h. The city council decided to build a municipal swimming pool at an estimated cost of $500,000. Bonds bearing an annual interest rate of 8 percent were issued for financing purposes. On June 30, 1999, a contract was signed for this project but no expenditures have been made.

i. Revenues of $66,000 were earned by a local parking garage used by the citizens of Gotham City. Maintenance expenses were $12,000 and depreciation, $53,000.

j. A fire truck was purchased for $85,000, and the voucher approved and paid by the General Fund. This expenditure was previously encumbered for $82,700.

Required:

Prepare journal entries to properly record each of the previous transactions in the appropriate fund(s) or group of accounts of Gotham City for the fiscal year ended June 30, 1999.

33. The following information relates to Dane City during its fiscal year ended December 31, 1998:

■ On October 31, 1998, to finance the construction of a city hall annex, Dane issued 8 percent 10-year general obligation bonds at their face value of $600,000. Construction expenditures during the period equaled $364,000.

■ Dane reported $109,000 from hotel room taxes, restricted for tourist promotion, in a Special Revenue Fund. The fund paid $81,000 for general promotions and $22,000 for a motor vehicle.

■ 1998 General Fund revenues of $104,500 were transferred to a Debt Service Fund and used to repay $100,000 of 9 percent 15-year term bonds and to pay $4,500 of interest. The bonds were used to acquire a citizens' center.

■ At December 31, 1998, as a consequence of past services, city firefighters had accumulated entitlements to compensated absences valued at $86,000. General Fund resources available at December 31, 1998, are expected to be used to settle $17,000 of this amount, and $69,000 is expected to be paid out of future General Fund resources.

■ At December 31, 1998, Dane was responsible for $83,000 of outstanding General Fund encumbrances, including the $8,000 for supplies indicated below.

■ Dane uses the purchases method to account for supplies. The following information relates to supplies:

Inventory—1/1/98	$39,000
12/31/98	42,000
Encumbrances outstanding—	
1/1/98	8,000
12/31/98	8,000
Purchase orders during 1998	190,000
Amounts credited to vouchers payable during 1998	181,000

Required

For the following items, determine the amounts based solely on the information provided:

a. What is the amount of 1998 General Fund operating transfers out?

b. How much should be reported as 1998 General Fund liabilities from entitlements for compensated absences?

c. What is the 1998 reserved amount of the General Fund balance?

d. What is the 1998 Capital Projects Fund balance?

e. What is the 1998 fund balance on the Special Revenue Fund for tourist promotion?

f. What is the amount of 1998 Debt Service Fund expenditures?

g. What amount should be included in the general fixed assets account group for the cost of assets acquired in 1998?

h. What amount stemming from 1998 transactions and events decreased the liabilities reported in the general long-term debt account group?

i. Using the purchases method, what is the amount of 1998 supplies expenditures?

j. What was the total amount of 1998 supplies encumbrances?

(AICPA adapted)

Accounting for Government-Owned Colleges and Universities

QUESTIONS TO CONSIDER

- Why does a public college or university utilize fund accounting and what fund types are employed by these not-for-profit organizations?

- Why do the expenditures recorded in a college or university's Restricted Current Funds equal the total amount of revenues recognized in that same fund?

- Why do the 1992 financial statements for Southern Methodist University indicate depreciation expense of nearly $9 million, while the statements for the University of Virginia for the same year state that "consistent with current generally accepted accounting principles for public colleges and universities, depreciation on plant assets is not recorded"?

- What hierarchy has been developed of the authoritative pronouncements produced to guide the financial reporting of for-profit businesses and not-for-profit organizations?

I n its 1995 financial statements, the University of Washington reported holding investments in its endowment valued at more than $294 million. For the year ended June 30, 1996, Auburn University disclosed that $78 million of its revenues came from tuition and fees, while $189 million resulted from government grants and contracts. Statements for Clemson University indicated that $266 million had been expended during that year on instruction, $8 million on capital additions, and $9 million on debt service. Figures reported by Utah State University showed revenues of $262 million of which, $116 million was restricted.

Students, parents, alumni, donors, and any other interested parties can discover a wealth of information in the financial statements of a college or university. Although these organizations are not-for-profit by nature, they differ considerably from the state and local governments discussed in Chapter 17. Such schools do not have the ability to tax their citizens to gain financial support. Rather, they must compete for students and other types of funding. Therefore, although some similarities do exist, accounting appropriate for a public college or university varies significantly from that of a state or local government. Although these educational institutions employ fund accounting, they have developed a distinctly different approach to the gathering and reporting of financial information.

ACCOUNTING FOR COLLEGES AND UNIVERSITIES

Among the more significant activities of state governments is the operation of public colleges and universities. For example, expenditures for Wisconsin's university system exceeded $2 billion for the year ended June 30, 1996. While the University of Wisconsin system is included in the state government's Annual Report, each institution in the system prepares its own financial reports. Thousands of public colleges and universities are in operation throughout the United States. These range from the gigantic state universities with tens of thousands of students to small colleges serving only a few hundred.

Based on their ownership and organizational purpose, and regardless of size, colleges and universities fall into these three categories:

1. *Public colleges and universities.* Governments own or control public organizations. Like other governmental organizations, they follow GASB reporting standards, using fund basis accounting. Public colleges and universities range in size from major state universities, such as the Ohio State University or the University of Texas, to community colleges or government-owned vocational schools.

2. *Private, not-for-profit colleges and universities.* Neither investors nor governments own private, not-for-profit organizations. The operations of private colleges and universities may be very similar to public colleges and universities. Nevertheless, the financial reporting for not-for-profit entities follows *FASB Statements 116 and 117*; thus, they do not present financial information on a fund basis. Private colleges and universities include Harvard University, the University of Miami, the University of Notre Dame, and Southern Methodist University.

3. *Proprietary schools.* Investors or educators own proprietary schools; they are in business to provide training and education with the purpose of making a profit. These institutions frequently provide training in technical or vocational areas such as electronics, cosmetology, secretarial services, and bartending. Like other business enterprises, the financial reporting for these entities follows FASB statements other than those statements relating exclusively to not-for-profits.

Identifying the types of educational organizations is very important because the various types use different accounting standards. Proprietary schools that follow normal business accounting and reporting standards are not described in detail in this text. Private, not-for-profit colleges and universities follow the same accounting and reporting standards as charities, churches, and foundations. These standards are described in the next chapter.

The term *public* indicates that colleges and universities are owned or controlled by governments. Public colleges and universities utilize a *modified total financial resources measurement focus* and the accrual basis of accounting. Unlike governments using a modified accrual basis, public colleges and universities recognize revenue when it is earned rather than available for spending. Unlike private not-for-profits that recognize expenses such as depreciation, public colleges and universities recognize *expenditures*. As a result, the accounting and reporting standards of public colleges and universities are unlike any other organizations and are the topic of this chapter.[1]

At present, generally accepted accounting principles for these educational institutions are best described in two sources:

- *Audits of Colleges and Universities*, the AICPA's industry audit guide.
- *College and University Business Administration (CUBA)*, a guidebook produced by the National Association of College and University Business Officers (sometimes referred to as the *Manual*).

---

[1]Because local school districts (elementary, middle, and high school systems) have the ability to levy taxes to support their operations, they are considered to be governments and follow accounting standards described in the preceding two chapters for governmental entities.

These two sources are not radically different. As the AICPA's audit guide admits, "much of the material in this guide is presented as it appears in the Manual."[2]

As is discussed subsequently, in recent years the GASB has become actively involved in setting accounting standards for colleges and universities. Some impact on the financial reporting process already has been seen that will almost certainly expand in the coming years. Certain procedures might eventually become standardized while others are eliminated as inappropriate. The flexibility that has been a characteristic of college and university accounting will probably be narrowed as the GASB issues additional pronouncements.

Despite the limited quantity of authoritative literature created to date, a number of standard (and unique) procedures have evolved over the years in connection with public college and university accounting. The present reporting process resembles that utilized by state and local governments in two important aspects: first, determination of the school's profitability is not an accounting emphasis. Educational institutions are primarily involved with furnishing services rather than with generating income. The most visible goals of a college or university are to provide an education for enrolled students while also encouraging scholarly research. Neither of these goals can be measured accurately in pure profits. Thus, as in governmental accounting, income determination does not serve as a basic financial reporting objective.

Second, fund accounting is utilized by public colleges and universities. Like a city or county, the operation of a college or university necessarily encompasses a broad range of dissimilar activities. Library operations, research grants, cafeterias, athletic teams, bookstores, computer centers, and the like, all fall under the financial control of most colleges and universities. The number as well as the diversity of these functions mandate some degree of separation within the accounting process. Hence, once again, the use of fund accounting becomes appropriate.

> Service, rather than profits, is the objective of an educational institution; thus, the primary obligation of accounting and reporting is one of accounting for resources received and used rather than for determination of net income. . . . In order to account properly for a diversity of resources and their use, there has developed, over a period of years, the principles and practices of "fund accounting."[3]

Fund accounting is considered especially important to colleges and universities because of the significant amount of restricted donations that are received. To ensure that each gift is expended as stipulated, individual funds are established and monitored. If a donation, for example, is made to finance the study of Shakespeare, the school must take the necessary precautions to ensure that the money is used as specified. Fund accounting is one aspect of that control structure. As stated in a note to the financial statements of the University of Maryland, "in order to ensure observance of limitations and restrictions placed on the use of resources available to the College Park campus, the accounts are maintained in accordance with the principles of fund accounting."

Fund Accounting for Public Colleges and Universities

Understanding the accounting procedures utilized by government-owned colleges and universities requires a familiarity with the various fund categories. Six fund groups exist within the accounting records of most colleges and universities:

Current Funds	Annuity and Life Income Funds
Loan Funds	Plant Funds
Endowment and Similar Funds	Agency Funds

---

[2]AICPA, *Audits of Colleges and Universities* (New York: AICPA, 1992), par. 1.02.

[3]AICPA, *Audits of Colleges and Universities* (New York: AICPA, 1994), par. 2.01.

As in governmental accounting, several of these fund headings are further divided into subgroups to enable schools to account for specific activities or monetary amounts. The Current Funds category, for example, is actually comprised of two distinct fund types: Unrestricted Current Funds and Restricted Current Funds. To provide a basis for the subsequent discussion of college and university accounting, a brief synopsis of each individual fund type follows:

1. *Current Funds*
    a. *Unrestricted Current Funds.* Unrestricted Current Funds account for all currently expendable resources to be used in accomplishing the primary objectives of the institution, such as education and research. Because of the general operating nature of this category, a majority of the financial transactions of any college or university is normally recorded in the Unrestricted Current Funds. Clemson University, as an example, reported unrestricted revenues and other additions of $278 million for the year ending June 30, 1995, along with expenditures and other deductions of nearly $271 million. These figures represented 72 percent of the university's total revenues and additions and 78 percent of all expenditures and deductions.

        Revenues to be recognized in the Unrestricted Current Funds include general student tuition and fees, unrestricted grants and gifts, and amounts generated by a school's auxiliary operations such as the cafeteria and bookstore. Likewise, expenditures cover a broad spectrum of payments made in connection with ongoing activities including professors' salaries, student services, general maintenance, library acquisitions, and other similar costs. For Clemson University, the largest revenue was state appropriations of $131 million and the largest expenditure was $80 million for instruction.

    b. *Restricted Current Funds.* Restricted Current Funds are utilized by colleges and universities to account for resources to be spent for current operating purposes. *However, as the title implies, external restrictions have been placed on the ultimate usage of the money.* Such stipulations are common in connection with gifts as well as with many government grants. A donation made to a university under the provision that the money must be used to buy library books would be accounted for within restricted current funds.

        As an example, for the fiscal year ending June 30, 1995, the University of Washington reported revenues of approximately $181 million within restricted current funds. According to the university's financial statements, this balance was generated from six primary sources:

        Tuition and fees.
        Government grants and contracts.
        Private grants and contracts.
        Sales and services of educational departments.
        Endowment income.
        Realized gains and losses on investments.

        The eventual use of this entire $181 million in revenues was designated by outside parties for specified operating purposes. In 1995, the largest portion ($73 million) went to fund instruction with another $41 million for research. To ensure the appropriate handling of these gifts and grants, the assets were recorded separately within the Restricted Current Funds.

2. *Loan Funds.* Loan Funds account for loans made by the institution. Such money is granted primarily to students to assist them in financing their educations although loans to the school's faculty and staff are also possible. This category maintains a record of the monetary resources available as well as the outstanding loan balances currently owed to the university. Utah State University's balance sheet, for example, showed the following assets as of June 30, 1996:

Cash	$ 16,712
Temporary investment—at cost	655,837
Notes receivable—student loans	9,985,626

3. *Endowment and Similar Funds.* This third general category is extremely important because endowment gifts are significant to the financing of most schools. A number of universities, including the University of Texas, have managed to accumulate endowments of more than $1 billion. To ensure adequate safeguards, these monies are separated and accounted for within several individual classifications:

   a. *Endowment Funds.* College and university Endowment Funds parallel the Nonexpendable Trust Funds found in state and local governments. More specifically, Endowment Funds account for gifts or grants awarded to a school with the stipulation that the principal must be kept intact. Future earnings derived from the gift may be expended, usually for a purpose specified by the original donor. These assets are considered to be permanently restricted because the principal can never be expended.

   b. *Term Endowment Funds.* This classification is identical to Endowment Funds except that the principal also may be spent after an established time or following the occurrence of a specific event. Consequently, these assets are referred to as temporarily restricted.

   c. *Quasi-Endowment Funds.* Historically, one of the more unusual aspects of college and university accounting has been the use of Quasi-Endowment Funds. This category records unrestricted monetary balances voluntarily set aside by the school rather than being applied to current operations. In other types of not-for-profit accounting, the use of Endowment (or Nonexpendable Trust) Funds is normally restricted to amounts given with donor-restrictions. However, colleges and universities can reclassify money into Endowment Funds based solely on the decision of the governing board. Auburn University, for example, reported on June 30, 1996, a total endowment of $79 million with $65 million of this amount being labeled as Quasi-Endowment Funds. Although maintained in the Endowment Funds, those $65 million in assets have no external restriction.

   The use of Quasi-Endowment Funds has been questioned at times because transfers between Unrestricted Current Funds and Quasi-Endowment Funds are discretionary. Therefore, a college or university has the ability to alter the reported size of its Unrestricted Current Funds by moving money into or out of these Quasi-Endowment Funds.[4]

   However, the possible impact of this practice has been limited in recent years. The AICPA audit guide mandates (in paragraph 2.08) that "a clear distinction between the balances of funds which are externally restricted and those which are internally designated within each fund

---

[4]For example, see Kavasseri V. Ramanathan and William L. Weis, "How to Succeed in Nonbusiness without Really Trying: A University Case Study," *Journal of Accountancy*, October 1980.

group should be maintained in the accounts and disclosed in the financial reports." Typically, this is disclosed in the fund balance section of the balance sheet. Thus, readers can distinguish restricted from unrestricted amounts.

4. *Annuity and Life Income Funds*

    a. *Annuity Funds.* "The annuity funds group consists of funds acquired by an institution subject to agreements whereby assets are made available to the institution on the condition that the institution bind itself to pay stipulated amounts periodically to designated individuals. Payments of such amounts terminate at a time specified in the agreements."[5] Obviously, such arrangements are designed to allow a donor (or the donor's family or friends) to continue receiving specified cash inflows for a time from property or other assets that have been legally conveyed to a college or university. Giving to a school is encouraged in this manner because an individual can make a donation without jeopardizing future income levels.

    b. *Life Income Funds.* Similar in nature to Annuity Funds, the major difference is that all income earned on the principal of a gift is distributed to the designated individual(s) rather than just a set amount. Once again, a time limitation is normally imposed on the payments; oftentimes they must continue until the death of the recipient.

5. *Plant Funds*

    a. *Unexpended Plant Funds.* As the title implies, this fund accounts for a school's monetary balances that have been designated for the future acquisition of physical properties such as a library addition or a science laboratory. For example, the 1995 financial statements for the University of Washington disclosed that $70 million was spent during the period for property acquisition, construction, and renovation using the resources held in that school's Unexpended Plant Funds. The monetary amounts maintained in this fund may be derived from numerous sources including gifts, the income earned on earlier donations, or discretionary transfers made from the university's Unrestricted Current Funds.

    b. *Funds for Renewals and Replacements.* A fund that accounts for all money eventually used to update or replace assets presently in service. As an alternative, these assets may be maintained in the Unexpended Plant Funds.

    c. *Funds for Retirement of Indebtedness.* In a manner similar to that of a government's Debt Service Fund, this category records "funds set aside for debt service charges and for the retirement of indebtedness on institutional properties."[6] The June 30, 1995, report of the University of Washington indicated $13 million had been expended on principal and $17 million on interest on the University's outstanding long-term debt.

    d. *Investment in Plant.* This final Plant Fund subgroup reports the cost of all long-lived assets owned by the college or university. In addition, any debts incurred in connection with the procurement of these properties are accounted for here. The University of Washington, as an example, reported more than $1.7 billion in land, buildings, and equipment and an additional $113 million in library books within its Investment in Plant Fund as of June 30, 1995. This fund also reported approximately $280

---

[5]AICPA, *Audits*, par. 10.01.

[6]Ibid., par. 9.01.

million in notes and bonds payable relating to the acquisition of these properties.

6. *Agency Funds.* As in governmental accounting, the Agency Funds category maintains a record of all monies held by a school as a fiduciary for other parties. Often, for example, a college or university serves as a financial caretaker for various student organizations. Auburn University held more than $500,000 in student deposits on June 30, 1996. Although such monetary balances are frequently accounted for within a separate Agency Fund, an alternative is simply to report them as liabilities in the Unrestricted Current Funds.

Application of Accrual Accounting

Several aspects of the reporting process utilized by colleges and universities resemble that of state and local governments. For example, numerous funds are set up (each with its own Fund Balance account) to record the various resources and expenditures. However, significant accounting differences do exist. Probably the most important variation is that these educational institutions employ accrual accounting rather than modified accrual accounting. "Revenues should be reported when earned and expenditures when materials or services are received. Expenses incurred at the balance sheet date should be accrued and expenses applicable to future periods should be deferred."[7]

Depreciation Expense

Traditionally, colleges and universities have been permitted but not required to report depreciation expense. Not surprisingly, because of the impact on current balances (and the work necessary to compute amounts), few public institutions chose to include annual depreciation figures. Instead, as in state and local government accounting, the cost of long-lived assets was recognized immediately (usually in the Unexpended Plant Funds) as an expenditure. The properties themselves were then listed in the school's Investment in Plant Fund in much the same fashion as a government records its long-lived assets in a General Fixed Assets Account Group.

In discussing depreciation, the argument was frequently made that profitability is not a goal of these organizations so that the calculation and recording of this expense is inappropriate. College officials usually have contended that the recording of expenditures is applicable for a governmental organization. Furthermore, new acquisitions are commonly financed by fund-raising projects (rather than from operations) so that ensuring the availability of adequate resources through the recognition of depreciation is not considered necessary.

However, in August 1987, the FASB issued *Statement No. 93*, "Recognition of Depreciation by Not-for-Profit Organizations." This pronouncement required the recognition of depreciation by all not-for-profit organizations (other than state and local governments). The rule pertained to both purchased assets and properties acquired by donation and was aimed at colleges and universities as well as religious institutions and other not-for-profit organizations. The FASB justified this action by stating in paragraph 20:

> Using up assets acquired involves a cost to the organization because the economic benefits (or service potential) used up are no longer available to the organization. That is as true for assets acquired without cost as it is for assets acquired at a cost.

---

[7]Ibid., par. 2.09.

At that time, several types of not-for-profit organizations (governmental colleges and universities, public benefit corporations and authorities, public employee retirement systems, governmental utilities, and governmental hospitals and other health care providers) had been directed to follow the pronouncements of the GASB. However, if the accounting treatment of a transaction or event was not explicitly specified by a GASB pronouncement, applicable FASB pronouncements had to be utilized. Thus, the GASB found itself in the position of having to respond to each statement of the FASB unless it wanted the provisions to apply automatically to this list of governmental not-for-profit organizations.

Consequently, in January of 1988, the GASB countered with a pronouncement of its own, *Statement 8*, "Applicability of FASB Statement No. 93, *Recognition of Depreciation by Not-for-Profit Organizations*, to Certain State and Local Governmental Entities." This standard exempted public colleges and universities (as well as other governmental not-for-profit institutions) from the necessity of recording depreciation. According to paragraph 4,

> Some governmental entities that engage in activities similar to private, not-for-profit organizations covered by *FASB Statement 93* follow governmental fund accounting and reporting principles. Those governmental entities follow GASB standards for depreciation and are therefore not affected by *FASB Statement 93*.

Suddenly, colleges and universities found themselves being guided by two different bodies. Public schools, such as the Ohio State University and the University of Texas, were to follow GASB so that the recording of depreciation was voluntary. In contrast, private institutions such as Harvard and Duke came under the auspices of the FASB and had to report depreciation expense. A power struggle quickly resulted with colleges and universities caught in the middle. "I see the two groups as somewhat entrenched in their positions," said Carl Hanes, the vice president for administration at the State University of New York at Stonybrook. "I see it as a real mess. We have two credible, professional organizations with different voices, and the imposition of their views on the different types of institutions could generate financial information that's not comparable."[8]

College and university officials reacted with dismay at the dual set of rules that had been established. Debates arose as to whether depreciation was truly applicable to these types of not-for-profit organizations. Many school administrators (but certainly not all) seemed to prefer the traditional view that the cost of generating depreciation data would outweigh any possible benefits.

> "Depreciating the university's 160 buildings and equipment worth over $1 billion could cost us up to $200,000 for new computer software to do the figuring each year," estimates William J. Hogan, comptroller of the University of Chicago, a private institution. "It really isn't worth it."[9]

versus

> Depreciation accounting not only ought to be adopted, but it should be adopted in the operating statement and funded by mandatory transfer to the plant funds. Only in this way will financial statements show the true impact and cost of depreciation, providing users of such statements with more accurate information.[10]

---

[8]John B. Thomas, "Higher Education Is the Victim in FASB-GASB Dispute," *Business Officer*, January 1988, p. 20.

[9]Lee Berton, "Several Private Colleges May Ignore New Accounting Rule on Depreciation," *The Wall Street Journal*, February 4, 1988.

[10]Phillip Jones, Sr.; Clarence Jung, Jr.; and Herbert Peterson, "Why Not Depreciate and Why Not in Operations?" *Business Officer*, April 1989, p. 33.

Just before *Statement No. 93* was scheduled to take effect, the FASB postponed the effective date to allow time for a compromise to be developed. No one appeared to want the establishment of two sets of rules. The Financial Accounting Foundation (FAF), which oversees and funds both the FASB and the GASB, stepped in to help mediate a solution to the territorial argument. Numerous compromises were proposed. On October 30, 1989, the FAF voted to give the FASB jurisdiction over both public and private not-for-profit organizations. Thus, only one set of accounting standards would apply to such entities.

However, that ruling did not stop the controversy. Ten different government groups immediately threatened to stop supporting the GASB unless all public entities (such as state universities) remained under its jurisdiction.[11] Faced with a problem having no end in sight, the FAF reversed itself and gave the GASB authority over governmental not-for-profit organizations. Thus, the FASB now requires the reporting of depreciation expense by private colleges and universities (and other private not-for-profit organizations) whereas public schools (and other public not-for-profit organizations) follow the GASB and show depreciation on a voluntary basis. For this reason, the University of Richmond (a private school) reported depreciation expense of approximately $6 million in its 1992 financial statements while Virginia Commonwealth University (a public school just five miles away) indicated that "no provision for depreciation is made."

With the return of standard setting jurisdiction over public colleges and universities to the GASB, the Board acted to return public college and university reporting to the standards in effect before the depreciation controversy. In October, 1991, the GASB issued *Statement No. 15*, "Governmental College and University Accounting and Financial Reporting Models." The statement permits the use of the standards described in the AIPCA's industry audit guide, *Audits of Colleges and Universities* (as amended by AICPA *Statement of Position 74-8*) or the use of governmental accounting practices described in the previous two chapters. Most four-year public institutions use the AICPA model while many community colleges use the governmental model.[12] The AIPCA model is illustrated in the appendix to this chapter and is the *traditional* college and university reporting model.

The GAAP Hierarchy

At some point, the relationship between governmental not-for-profit organizations and FASB pronouncements almost had to be redefined. The GASB could not stop its ongoing work every time a FASB statement was issued to evaluate whether the new standard should be voided for governmental not-for-profit organizations. Apparently, an adequate resolution has been crafted by the AICPA Auditing Standards Board in its *Statement on Auditing Standards 69*, "The Meaning of 'Presents Fairly in Conformity with Generally Accepted Accounting Principles' in the Independent Auditor's Report" issued in 1991. This standard creates a hierarchy for determining whether an accounting treatment should be judged as being in compliance with generally accepted accounting principles (GAAP). For both nongovernmental entities as well as state and local governments, accounting pronouncements and other potential guidelines are grouped into five layers. The higher levels are more authoritative than the lower levels.

The GAAP hierarchy created by *SAS 69* is presented in Exhibit 18–1. For state and local governments, GASB statements and interpretations are placed at the highest level. This same ranking is appropriate for AICPA and FASB pronouncements *but*

---

[11]See, for more information, "The Great GASB," *Forbes*, December 11, 1989, p. 60.

[12]John H. Engstrom and Leon E. Hay, *Essentials of Accounting for Governmental and Not-for-Profit Organizations*, 4th ed. (Burr Ridge, IL: Richard D. Irwin, 1996), p. 286.

Exhibit 18–1
GAAP Hierarchy Summary

Nongovernmental Entities	State and Local Governments
Established Accounting Principles	
FASB Statements and Interpretations, APB Opinions, and AICPA Accounting Research Bulletins	GASB Statements and Interpretations, plus AICPA and FASB pronouncements if made applicable to state and local governments by a GASB Statement or Interpretation
FASB Technical Bulletins, AICPA Industry Audit and Accounting Guides, and AICPA Statements of Position	GASB Technical Bulletins, and the following pronouncements if specifically made applicable to state and local governments by the AICPA: AICPA Industry Audit and Accounting Guides and AICPA Statements of Position
Consensus positions of the FASB Emerging Issues Task Force and AICPA Practice Bulletins	Consensus positions of the GASB Emerging Issues Task Force† and AICPA Practice Bulletins if specifically made applicable to state and local governments by the AICPA
AICPA accounting interpretations, "Qs and As" published by the FASB staff, as well as industry practices widely recognized and prevalent	"Qs and As" published by the GASB staff, as well as industry practices widely recognized and prevalent
Other Accounting Literature*	
Other accounting literature, including FASB Concepts Statements; APB Statements; AICPA Issues Papers; International Accounting Standards Committee Statements; GASB Statements, Interpretations, and Technical Bulletins; pronouncements of other professional associations or regulatory agencies; AICPA *Technical Practice Aids*; and accounting textbooks, handbooks, and articles	Other accounting literature, including GASB Concepts Statements; pronouncements in the first four categories of the hierarchy for nongovernmental entities when not specifically made applicable to state and local governments; APB Statements; FASB Concepts Statements; AICPA Issues Papers; International Accounting Standards Committee Statements; pronouncements of other professional associations or regulatory agencies; AICPA *Technical Practice Aids*; and accounting textbooks, handbooks, and articles

†As of the date of this Statement, the GASB had not organized such a group.

*In the absence of established accounting principles, the auditor may consider other accounting literature, depending on its relevance in the circumstances.

only if they are made applicable to state and local governments by a GASB Statement or Interpretation. Thus, even though a GASB statement may not provide specific guidance in a particular area of financial reporting, FASB statements no longer become automatically appropriate for governmental not-for-profit organizations. Instead, the GASB can study and evaluate each new pronouncement and act if it believes that the guidelines should be followed.

The uncertainty regarding appropriate standards involves more than just colleges and universities. Enterprise funds operated by governments follow accrual accounting that was established historically by the FASB and its predecessors. To further clarify which standards are appropriate, the GASB issued *Statement No. 20*, "Accounting and Financial Reporting for Proprietary Funds and Other Governmental Entities that Use Proprietary Fund Accounting." The standard requires enterprise funds to follow all GASB standards and any FASB standards issued before November 1989, provided the FASB standard does not conflict with a GASB standard. In addition, the entity can either follow all FASB standards issued subsequent to November 1989 that do not conflict with GASB standards or not follow all such standards.

The remainder of this chapter describes the accounting and reporting practices of public (governmental) colleges and universities. The financial reporting practices of private colleges and universities are described in the next chapter.

Traditional Financial Statements for Public Colleges and Universities

Historically, most colleges and universities have produced financial statements in conformity with examples found in *Statement of Position 74-8*, "Financial Accounting and Reporting by Colleges and Universities," issued on August 31, 1974, by the Accounting Standards Division of the AICPA. That pronouncement indicated that three basic financial statements are normally prepared by colleges and universities (often referred to as the AICPA college guide model):[13]

- A statement of changes in fund balances.
- A statement of current funds revenues, expenditures, and other changes.
- A balance sheet.

Each of these statements is presented in a columnar format to provide financial information about the various fund types. Financial statements produced for Utah State University using this format are included in the appendix to this chapter.

Statement of Changes in Fund Balances   In broad categories, the first statement reports:

- Revenues and other fund balance additions.
- Expenditures and other deductions.
- Interfund transfers.

As can be seen in the appendix to this chapter, this information is included for each of the various fund types. Readers learn the underlying cause of all changes occurring during the year in the Fund Balance account for Unrestricted Current Funds, Restricted Current Funds, Loan Funds, and so forth. As an example, this statement reports that Utah State University recognized $157 million in unrestricted revenues in its Unrestricted Current Funds during the year ended June 30, 1996, whereas $124 million was expended for education and general purposes in this same period. These total figures are explained in more detail in the next financial statement.

Statement of Current Funds Revenues, Expenditures, and Other Changes   The second statement provides information for just the two current funds. Since these fund types record all of the ongoing activities of a college or university, this statement presents more detailed information about the operating transactions of the fiscal period. The revenue totals for both the Unrestricted Current Funds and the Restricted Current Funds are broken down to disclose specific figures for sources such as student tuition and fees, federal grants, endowment income, sales made by auxiliary operations, and so on.

Expenditures made from these two funds then are identified individually including amounts paid for instructional costs, research, public service, academic support, and student services. Explanatory figures also indicate any transfers made to or from other funds as well as any other changes in the fund balances.

---

[13]A second model (known as the governmental model because it was established by the *National Council of Governmental Accounting Statement 1*) is available but it is much less frequently encountered.

DISCUSSION QUESTION

Are Two Sets of GAAP Really Needed for Colleges and Universities?

A public college or university normally does not report depreciation on its buildings and equipment. A private college or university must calculate depreciation on each of these long-lived assets and recognize that figure in its financial statements.

A public college or university reports a balance sheet and a statement of changes in fund balance for each of its fund types. A statement of revenues, expenditures, and other changes is produced for the Unrestricted Current Funds and the Restricted Current Funds. A private college or university should report a statement of financial position, a statement of activities, and a statement of cash flows. These statements are designed to reflect the school as a whole rather than focusing on any of the individual fund types.

Many readers of college and university financial statements make comparisons between the data presented by various institutions. The use of this information is especially important to potential donors attempting to evaluate each school's effectiveness and efficiency in utilizing the funding that it receives. Are these readers well served by the division that appears to be growing between the financial reporting that is appropriate for public colleges and universities and that utilized by private colleges and universities?

Balance Sheet   The final financial statement prepared by a college or university indicates assets, liabilities, and the final fund balance for each of the separate fund categories (or major fund subgroups). As presented in the appendix to this chapter, the columnar presentation that conveys data about all of the funds resembles the state and local government accounting format. Although total figures for the educational institution as a whole are not required on either the balance sheet or the statement of changes in fund balances, most schools do provide them.

ACCOUNTING FOR CURRENT FUNDS

Because most college and university financial transactions are recorded within the Current Funds, the primary emphasis in the remainder of this chapter is on analyzing the accounting and reporting of the Unrestricted Current Funds and the Restricted Current Funds. At times, these funds interface with every other fund category through transfers and other interactions. Thus, the following coverage must necessarily involve some introduction to virtually all fund classifications. To assist in explaining applicable accounting procedures in more depth, several additional transactions relating primarily to the noncurrent funds are included at the end of the chapter.

Unrestricted Current Funds

As mentioned previously, the transactions recorded within the Unrestricted Current Funds cover the entire range of ongoing university activities: instruction, research, student services, administration, and the like. Since the accrual basis is in use, timely recognition of all transactions is essential.

Tuition and Fees   Students may be surprised that few state universities charged tuition until the 1970s. At first the amounts were small but tuition increases persisted as the cost of an education at a four-year public university rose 235 percent between 1980 and 1995.[14] Presently, tuition revenues represent a significant source of operating funds for most state universities. Student tuition and fees of $5 million, for

---

[14]Gene Jaffe, "Georgia's Scholarships Are Open to Everyone and that's a Problem," *The Wall Street Journal*, June 2, 1997, p. A1.

example, are entered into the financial records as follows. This entry assumes that 5 percent of this balance will prove to be uncollectible.

Unrestricted Current Funds

Accounts Receivable	5,000,000	
Expenditures—Bad Debts	250,000	
Revenues—Student Tuition and Fees		5,000,000
Allowance for Doubtful Accounts		250,000

    To record billings for tuition and fees with 5 percent
    estimated as being uncollectible.

Just as in governmental accounting, expenditures are recorded by colleges and universities. However, the preceding recognition of bad debts indicates that the Expenditure classification is used here for more than just the recording of financial resource outflows. This redefinition of expenditures is necessary because governmental colleges and universities recognize revenues under the accrual basis as they are earned. The difference between the amount earned and the amounts collected are termed *expenditures* even though they don't result in a cash outflow or a liability being incurred.

A variation of the previous entry may be necessary for summer school tuition and fees. The fiscal year for many colleges and universities ends each June 30, a date that may fall during the middle of a summer school session. Revenues generated by any courses that operate in both fiscal periods are to be recognized *in the year in which most of the instruction occurs*. For example, a course that begins on June 20 but does not end until August 1 should have all of its revenues recorded in the year beginning July 1. Consequently, a deferred revenue account must be recorded in the first period and then reclassified as revenue in the second.

Contributions   Other revenues recognized within the Unrestricted Current Funds include gifts, endowment income, and government appropriations. In each case, *inclusion in this category is only appropriate if expenditure of the money has not been restricted by the donor*. To illustrate the mechanics of the recording process, assume that an individual gives $250,000 in cash to a local university. Of this amount, $50,000 is completely unrestricted but another $120,000 is earmarked for a specific research project. The remaining $80,000 must be used for renovation of present physical facilities. Because the donation is designated for such diverse activities, several separate fund subgroups are involved:

Unrestricted Current Funds

Cash	50,000	
Revenues—Contribution		50,000

    To record unrestricted portion of gift from private donor.

Restricted Current Funds

Cash	120,000	
Fund Balance—Temporarily Restricted for Research		
Project		120,000

    Gift received to finance specified research project.

Funds for Renewals and Replacements

Cash	80,000	
Fund Balance—Temporarily Restricted for Facilities		
Renovation		80,000

    Gift to be used for renovation of physical facilities.

The recording here of an increase in the Fund Balance account for the Restricted Current Funds and the Funds for Renewal and Replacements may seem perplexing since the specific source of the change is not noted. However, within the financial statements, a college or university must disclose the identity of the increases and decreases that occur in its net assets. Therefore, for reporting purposes, the $120,000 and $80,000 asset inflows are identified as contributions. Traditionally, in the internal recording of a school's noncurrent funds, net asset inflows and outflows have been made directly to the Fund Balance account as shown here. Subsidiary ledgers usually are maintained to record the actual nature of each change.

These three entries demonstrate one of the primary objectives of fund accounting for colleges and universities: to monitor the institution's stewardship and ultimate employment of resources restricted for diverse activities. Educational institutions can receive enormous amounts of money with numerous stipulations attached. The accounting system must be able to ensure that all such funding is expended for the appropriate purposes. Although the foregoing donation was received as a single amount, the balances have been segregated within the financial records to ensure proper utilization.

Donated Assets Other than Cash   One of the major reporting problems of all not-for-profit organizations is the handling of donated assets other than cash. The AICPA audit guide states (in paragraph 2.11):

> Gifts, bequests, grants, and other receipts restricted as to use by outside grantors or agencies are recorded as additions directly in the fund group appropriate to the restricted nature of the receipt. Unrestricted gifts, bequests, and grants are recorded as unrestricted current funds revenues.

To illustrate, assume that a donor gives the following to a college or university:

Item	Use	Fair Market Value
Note receivable	Unrestricted	$ 21,000
Investments	Income to be used for student scholarships	40,000
Building (near campus)	Administrative offices	150,000

Following the guidelines of the AICPA audit guide, the following journal entries would have been recorded by this college or university. Receipt of the note is recorded immediately as revenue since its use is unrestricted. Because of the external restrictions included, donation of both the investments and the building increase fund balance accounts (the Investment in Plant account is used for the building rather than a fund balance since no monetary resources are maintained in that fund).

Unrestricted Current Funds

Note Receivable	21,000	
Revenues—Contribution		21,000

To record unrestricted gift of note.

Endowment Funds

Investments	40,000	
Fund Balance—Permanently Restricted for Student Scholarships...............................		40,000

To record investments given to university with stipulation that subsequent income is to be used for student scholarships.

Investment in Plant

Building..	150,000	
Investment in Plant		150,000

To record gift of building that will be used by the school for administrative offices.

Pledges   Before leaving the reporting procedures that are applied to donations, one additional accounting consideration should be mentioned. Often, a college or university receives a definite pledge of support prior to the actual conveyance of any money or other assets. Fund-raising campaigns seeking hundreds of millions of dollars are now relatively common. Most large gifts begin with a pledge followed by periodic payments made over a specified number of years. The AICPA's audit guide states that such pledges should either be disclosed in the financial statement footnotes or actually recognized as an asset.

> Pledges of gifts, including uncollected subscriptions, subscription notes, and estate notes, should be disclosed in the notes unless they are reported in the financial statements. . . . If the pledges are reported in the financial statements, they should be accounted for at their estimated net realizable value in the same manner as gifts received (except as to asset classification, for which pledges would be reported as a receivable), and credited to unrestricted revenues, deferred income, current restricted funds, plant funds, etc., as appropriate.[15]

The financial statements of the Ohio State University indicate one approach to the reporting of pledges. This university discloses the amount of outstanding pledges in a note to its statements: "The University does not report pledges in the financial statements until the gifts are received. The University's gift records indicate that approximately $138,058,000 in pledges are outstanding at June 30, 1990. Since those pledges are often payable either at the discretion of the donors or through their estates, neither the realizable value nor the period of collection can be estimated."

Unfortunately, in accounting for pledges, many schools apparently have chosen to ignore the need for either recording or disclosure:

> In reporting on a review of financial statements of colleges and universities, the author of the report made this striking statement: "Hundreds of colleges found violating accounting rules in finance reports." Leading to this statement was a finding that "415 of 598 responding institutions did not record or disclose donors' pledges, either on their balance sheets or in notes to their financial statements."[16]

The FASB has created guidelines for the recognition of pledges by private not-for-profits. However, no authoritative guidelines exist for public colleges and universities; therefore, practices vary across institutions.

Accounting for Expenditures   The Unrestricted Current Funds also must record the great variety of operating expenditures incurred by any college or university. Faculty salaries, research support, student service costs, and operations of the physical plant are just a few examples of the necessary costs that fall under this heading. Although numerous entries would be made each day in connection with operating expenditures, the following single example demonstrates the impact of these recordings. This entry assumes that all but $85,000 of the current year expenditures have been paid.

Unrestricted Current Funds

Expenditures—Instruction	1,900,000	
Expenditures—Research	325,000	
Expenditures—Student Services	61,000	
Expenditures—Operation and Maintenance of Plant	56,000	
Cash		2,257,000
Accrued Liabilities		85,000
To record current operating expenditures. Payment is made for all but $85,000.		

One further cost incurred by most colleges and universities is the loss of revenue stemming from scholarship grants and other tuition reductions. For example, Auburn

---

[15]AICPA, *Audits*, par. 2.12–2.13.

[16]Arthur R. Kagle and William P. Dukes, "Financial Reporting for Pledges at Educational Institutions," *The CPA Journal*, January 1988, p. 40. The article being discussed within this quotation is by Robert L. Jacobson, "Hundreds of Colleges Found Violating Accounting Rules in Finance Reports," *The Chronicle of Higher Education* 32, no. 6 (April 9, 1986).

University reported tuition waivers totaled $6 million during fiscal year 1996. Often schools decrease or eliminate their fees entirely based on a student's financial needs, academic excellence, or athletic abilities. In addition, faculty and staff members (as well as their families) may be granted similar reductions because of past service to the institution. To provide a measure of the financial impact of such reductions, "tuition and fees should be recorded as revenue even though there is no intention of collection from the student. The amounts of such remissions or waivers should be recorded as expenditures and classified as Scholarships and Fellowships or as staff benefits associated with the appropriate expenditure functional category to which the personnel relate."[17]

Assume, as an illustration, that the normal tuition to be charged a group of students by a college is $1,900,000. However, this amount is reduced during the year by $300,000 because academic scholarships have been granted to several of these individuals. An additional $200,000 will not be assessed because the students have relatives who are faculty or staff members employed by the school. Thus, only $1,400,000 of the tuition is actually subject to collection; that information is recorded through the following journal entry. *By recording both the revenue in total along with separate expenditures for the reductions, the school is better able to mirror the events that have occurred as well as the impact of the various reductions.*

Unrestricted Current Funds

Accounts Receivable	1,400,000	
Expenditures—Student Aid	300,000	
Expenditures—Staff Benefits	200,000	
Revenues—Student Tuition and Fees		1,900,000

To accrue revenues along with reductions for students receiving financial aid and tuition remissions.

The National Association for College and University Business Officers (NACUBO) has recently issued an advisory report about scholarship allowances (tuition discounts) that requires them to be shown as a deduction from tuition revenues rather than as an expense. This report provides industry guidance for private institutions, but may be applicable to public institutions if proposed changes in public college and university reporting requirements are adopted. Like many areas of governmental accounting, accounting for scholarships is in a state of change.

Auxiliary Enterprises   A final group of ongoing activities reported within the Unrestricted Current Funds are the auxiliary enterprises operated by a school: food services, athletic programs, bookstores, and the like. Auxiliary enterprises are essentially self-supporting business entities and activities that provide goods and services to students, faculty, staff, and visitors. Clemson University, for example, reported that $55 million of the revenues reported in 1996 by the Unrestricted Current Funds were generated by such auxiliary endeavors. Auxiliary enterprise expenditures at this school for the same period totaled only $51 million (including $4 million in transfers for debt service).

Although detailed subsidiary ledgers are necessary to monitor the many specific transactional activities, general journal entries record the total revenues and expenditures of these enterprises. Thus, entries such as the following would be prepared periodically by a college or university:

Unrestricted Current Funds

Cash	2,860,000	
Revenues—Auxiliary Enterprises Control		2,860,000

Revenues generated during the period by the various auxiliary operations of the school.

---

[17]AICPA, *Audits*, Appendix A, pp. 53–54.

```
Expenditures—Auxiliary Enterprises Control . . . . . . . . . . . . .   2,018,000
    Cash . . . . . . . . . . . . . . . . . . . . . . . . . . . . . . . . . . . . . . . .                2,018,000
    Payments made in connection with operating expenditures of
    auxiliary activities.
```

Interfund Transfers   Revenues and expenditures do not provide the only means by which the net assets of the Unrestricted Current Funds can be affected. As in governments, transfers to and from other fund categories are commonly encountered in colleges and universities. Such interfund transactions may be discretionary in nature, made voluntarily to reflect the allocation of unrestricted financial resources. In 1996, for example, Auburn University decided to transfer approximately $12 million from Unrestricted Current Funds to Unexpended Plant Funds for future acquisitions and construction.

In many instances, transfers are contractually mandated. A bond indenture might, as an example, require that specific cash amounts be physically set aside each year to ensure eventual payment. For this reason, Auburn University also made more than $13 million in mandatory transfers into its Fund for Retirement of Indebtedness during 1996. As shown in the chapter appendix, all such interfund transfers are reported in the statement of changes in fund balances after the revenues and expenditures.

To illustrate, assume that a college is required by a bond contract to transfer $50,000 in cash each year to its Fund for Retirement of Indebtedness. In addition, the school's board of trustees votes to set aside $80,000 in unrestricted cash to finance student loans and an additional $150,000 for future building construction. The board also decides to transfer $90,000 to a Quasi-Endowment Fund with subsequent earnings to supplement faculty salaries. These four interfund transfers appear in the following Unrestricted Current Funds entry. In each case, a corresponding entry is made in the fund receiving the money (Fund for Retirement of Indebtedness, Loan Fund, etc.) increasing the specific Fund Balance account.

This journal entry draws a clear distinction between mandatory and discretionary (or nonmandatory) transfers. For disclosure purposes, this same identification is made within the published financial statements.

Unrestricted Current Funds

```
Mandatory Transfer for Bond Principal and
    Interest Repayment . . . . . . . . . . . . . . . . . . . . . . . . . . . . .   50,000
Discretionary Transfer for Student Loans . . . . . . . . . . . . . . .   80,000
Discretionary Transfer for Future Building Construction . . . . . .  150,000
Discretionary Transfer to Quasi-Endowment Fund
    for Faculty Salaries . . . . . . . . . . . . . . . . . . . . . . . . . . . . .   90,000
    Cash . . . . . . . . . . . . . . . . . . . . . . . . . . . . . . . . . . . . . . . .             370,000
    To record mandatory and discretionary transfers made by
    college's board of trustees.
```

Restricted Current Funds

Like the Unrestricted Current Funds, the Restricted Current Funds category of a college or university operates on an accrual basis. Therefore, a natural presumption would be that these two current fund subgroups utilize the same accounting principles. One significant difference, however, does exist. All financial resources of the Restricted Current Funds are provided by outside parties who have stipulated the operational usage to be made of the gift or grant. If the school does not follow these provisions, the money may have to be returned. *Hence, these restricted funds are considered to be earned only at the time that the specified expenditure is made.*

For this reason, the actual spending of the money (rather than the original receipt) secures the contribution. Thus, donations, grants, and any other similar inflows that are restricted for current operating purposes initially are recorded as increases in the Fund Balance account of the Restricted Current Funds and not as revenues. Subsequently, when the expenditure is eventually made to achieve the stated goal, the revenue is recognized by means of a reclassification entry. The earnings process is said to be completed by spending the money for the appropriate purpose.

To demonstrate the recording process that provides such precise equilibrium, assume that $120,000 in cash is donated to a university with the provision that this money must be spent to acquire new library books. Several weeks after receiving the gift, the first $50,000 is used for this specified purpose. The journal entries necessary to record these transactions would be as follows. The revenue is recognized at the point of appropriate expenditure.

Restricted Current Funds
Initial Entry

Cash	120,000	
Fund Balance—Temporarily Restricted for Acquisition of Library Books		120,000

Gift received by school to be used in purchasing library books.

Subsequent Entries

Expenditures—Libraries	50,000	
Cash		50,000

Library books acquired with money received as a restricted gift.

Fund Balance—Temporarily Restricted for Acquisition of Library Books	50,000	
Revenues—Gifts and Private Grants		50,000

To recognize as revenue money received and appropriately expended for library books.

Accounting for Noncurrent Funds

A detailed discussion of all possible transactions that could occur within the noncurrent fund categories and subgroups of a college or university would require several chapters. However, an overview of common transactions can be used to provide coverage of the basic reporting techniques incorporated by this type of public organization. Hence, descriptions of three transactional situations frequently encountered by educational institutions, with the journal entries that would result, follow:

1. A university receives a cash grant of $100,000 from an individual donor to finance student loans. Of this amount, $80,000 is immediately distributed to students who have temporary financial needs while the remainder is invested in stocks and bonds. The school estimates that 2 percent of the loan balances will eventually prove to be uncollectible. By year's end, cash of $75,000 is received with $1,000 of the remaining receivables being formally written off as bad accounts. During the period, $3,000 in interest is earned on the investments.

   The appropriate entries to record this series of events are as follows. As indicated previously, subsidiary ledger entries would be necessary to monitor the individual changes in the Fund Balance account.

Loan Funds

Cash	100,000	
Fund Balance—Permanently Restricted for Student Loans		100,000

Private grant received.

Notes Receivable—Students	80,000	
Investments	20,000	
Cash		100,000

Loans and investments made.

Fund Balance—Permanently Restricted for Student		
Loans	1,600	
Allowance for Uncollectible Loans		1,600
Bad accounts are estimated (2%).		
Cash	75,000	
Allowance for Uncollectible Loans	1,000	
Notes Receivable—Students		76,000
Loans are collected with $1,000 written off as uncollectible.		
Cash	3,000	
Fund Balance—Permanently Restricted for Student		
Loans		3,000
Earnings received on investments.		

2. A cash contribution of $400,000 is made to a university with the provision that all income derived from this money be distributed as supplements to faculty salaries. This gift is immediately invested, and $50,000 in income is earned during the year. Because expenditure of this money has been restricted, the income is transferred to the Restricted Current Funds and subsequently paid to the appropriate faculty members. For these transactions, the following journal entries are appropriate:

Endowment Funds

Cash	400,000	
Fund Balance—Permanently Restricted		400,000
Donation received; income to be used for faculty salaries.		
Investments	400,000	
Cash		400,000
Investments are acquired.		

Restricted Current Funds

Cash	50,000	
Fund Balance—Temporarily Restricted for Faculty		
Salaries................................		50,000
Endowment income received.		
Expenditures—Instruction	50,000	
Cash		50,000
Expenditures made to faculty members as stipulated.		
Fund Balance—Temporarily Restricted for Faculty		
Salaries...................................	50,000	
Revenues—Endowment Income		50,000
Revenue recognized at time of appropriate expenditure.		

3. Cash of $100,000 that had been previously transferred from a college's Unrestricted Current Funds to its Unexpended Plant Funds is spent for new science laboratory equipment. At the same time, the school pays $60,000 held in its Funds for Retirement of Indebtedness to extinguish a bond payable. While the laboratory equipment was purchased with funds that were not subject to external restriction, the debt was retired with money that had been specifically designated by a donor for that purpose.

    As mentioned previously, the Investment in Plant account shown in the final entry is the equivalent of an account group. The reported figure represents the fixed assets of the school in excess of the related liabilities. Thus, both the acquisition of land, buildings, and equipment and the payment of long-term debt relating to such acquisitions increase this balance.

Unexpended Plant Funds

Fund Balance—Unrestricted	100,000	
Cash		100,000
Payment made to purchase lab equipment.		

Investment in Plant

Equipment	100,000	
Investment in Plant		100,000
To record acquired lab equipment.		

Funds for Retirement of Indebtedness

Fund Balance—Temporarily Restricted	60,000	
Cash		60,000
Payment made to retire debt.		

Investment in Plant

Bonds Payable	60,000	
Investment in Plant		60,000
To record retirement of debt.		

PROPOSALS FOR CHANGES IN PUBLIC COLLEGE AND UNIVERSITY FINANCIAL REPORTS

In April 1997 the GASB issued the Exposure Draft, "Basic Financial Statements—and Management's Discussion and Analysis—for Public Colleges and Universities." If adopted by the Board, the proposed statement would be effective for fiscal years ending in 2001. The exposure draft calls for a dual perspective display of the financial position and results of operations for government owned colleges and universities as well as a management discussion and analysis. The proposal has much in common with the proposed governmental model changes discussed in the previous chapter. Like the proposed governmental model, governments would provide financial statements from both *fund* and *entitywide* perspectives.

Changes in the Fund Perspective Financial Statements

The proposal does not change the focus of accounting for fund perspective statements. Therefore, relatively minor changes in the journal entries would be necessary to record the activities of the funds.[18] Most of the changes at the fund perspective level involve presentation of information in the fund perspective financial statements. These changes include:

1. Plant fund subgroups (unexpended, renewals and replacement, retirement of indebtedness, and investments in plant) would be combined into a single fund group.
2. The two existing operating statements (statement of current funds revenue, expenditures, and other changes and the statement of changes in fund balances would be combined into a single comprehensive statement of revenues, expenditures, and other changes in fund balance for all fund groups.
3. Fund balances would be segregated into three components: restricted, unrestricted, and invested in capital assets net of related debt.

---

[18]One minor exception is that contributions to permanent endowments would be shown as "other support" rather than revenue and presented below the line "excess of revenues over expenditures," similar to transfers.

Entitywide Perspective Financial Statements

Like the proposed entitywide statements for state and local governments, the purpose of the college or university entitywide financial statements is to provide a comprehensive view of the institution's operations. The entitywide perspective financial statements include a statement of net assets and a statement of changes in net assets. Unlike the proposed entitywide statements for state and local governments, colleges and universities also would present a statement of cash flows.

The accrual basis of accounting would be used to measure changes in economic resources and obligations in the entity perspective statements. Similar to private colleges and universities, the proposed statement would require public institutions to include depreciation as a charge to operations each period. Presently it is very difficult to determine: (1) the cost of services provided, or (2) whether a public college or university is raising sufficient revenue to pay these costs. The entitywide perspective statements are intended to address these two issues. In addition, the entitywide perspective statements should prove more comparable to the statements prepared by private colleges and universities that also use the accrual basis and economic resources focus of accounting.

SUMMARY

1. The three types of colleges and universities differ in ownership interest and organizational purpose. Public institutions are owned or controlled by governmental entities and follow GASB reporting standards. Private not-for-profit institutions follow FASB statements including FASB statements 116 and 117 for not-for-profit organizations. *FASB Statement Nos. 116* and *117* are described in the following chapter. Proprietary schools are in business to provide a return to the investors or owners; therefore, they measure net income using standard business accounting and reporting.

2. Fund accounting is appropriate for colleges and universities because of their diverse activities and the many restricted gifts they receive. Funds are grouped into six general classifications: Current Funds, Loan Funds, Endowment and Similar Funds, Annuity and Life Income Funds, Plant Funds, and Agency Funds. Subgroups exist for many of these fund types.

3. The Current Funds category of a public college or university is divided into Unrestricted and Restricted Current Funds. Unrestricted Current Funds account for presently expendable resources used in accomplishing the primary operating objectives of the school. A majority of the institution's transactions are normally reported within this fund including recognition of tuition, unrestricted grants, cafeteria services, maintenance expense, and faculty salaries. Transfers, which are common in college and university accounting, are classified as either mandatory or discretionary to reveal the underlying nature of the transaction.

4. One unique aspect of the accounting process for colleges and universities is the method by which tuition reductions are reported. Financial aid and scholarships frequently decrease the amount to be collected from students. Schools report the tuition at the gross figure charged to reflect the amount earned. Any corresponding reduction is then recorded as an expenditure. Maintaining separate balances presents a better view of the financial events that have occurred.

5. The Restricted Current Funds account for operating resources that have been designated by the donor or grantor for a specified purpose. Only the restricted nature of these assets separates this category from the Unrestricted Current Funds. Because the monetary resource is ultimately earned by making the stipulated expenditure, the gift or grant is initially recorded as an increase in the Fund Balance account. When an appropriate expenditure is subsequently made, an equal dollar amount is reclassified from the Temporarily Restricted Fund Balance into a Revenue account. Thus, for Restricted Current Funds, revenues always equal expenditures.

6. The remainder of the funds utilized by a college or university are designated to maintain a record of assets being held for specific, nonoperational purposes. Loan Funds, for example, report the financial assistance provided to students. Unexpended Plant Funds monitor the monetary balances held by the school for future acquisitions of physical properties. The Investment in Plant Fund maintains a record of all long-lived assets as well as liabilities incurred in acquiring these properties.

7. Three financial statements have traditionally been produced by a college or university. Each of these is segmented to provide information about each fund type. A statement of changes in fund balances is presented for each fund category and major fund subgroup. Using broad categories, this statement reports revenues and other fund additions, expenditures and other deductions, and transfers. A statement of current fund revenues, expenditures, and other changes then follows to reflect current operations in much more specific detail. Finally, a balance sheet is prepared that includes information describing the financial position of each fund category.

8. Historically, the recording of depreciation expense has been allowed but not required of colleges and universities. However, in 1987, the FASB's *Statement 93* mandated the reporting of depreciation by private not-for-profit organizations. Shortly thereafter, the GASB exempted public institutions from this requirement. Since that time, a hierarchy of generally accepted accounting principles has been created to provide guidance for the production of financial statements. Based on this hierarchy, FASB statements only apply to governmental not-for-profit organizations if accepted by the GASB. Consequently, private colleges and universities must report depreciation whereas public schools are not required to do so.

9. Contributions are recorded as increases in a fund balance account if restricted and as revenue if not. Most colleges and universities do not report pledges although they are allowed to do so.

COMPREHENSIVE ILLUSTRATION

Problem

(*Estimated Time: 25 to 30 Minutes*) State College incurs the following financial transactions during the current fiscal period. Prepare all journal entries including an indication of the fund category or subgroup in which the recording should be made.

1. Students were charged $1 million in tuition for the academic year but the college anticipated receiving only $890,000 of this amount. Uncollectible balances were expected to equal 5 percent of the total (or $50,000). In addition, fees of $60,000 related to faculty members and their families. Because of school policy, these individuals were not actually assessed tuition charges.

2. A gift of $900,000 was conveyed to the school by a private donor. Of this total, $100,000 was restricted for replacement of classroom facilities. The remaining $800,000 was split evenly between a Life Income Fund and an Endowment Fund. Earnings from the Life Income Fund will be paid to the donor's sister until her death with the money then to be used by the school for athletics. All income generated by the Endowment Fund was restricted to the acquisition of equipment for the college's engineering department.

3. Loans of $100,000 were awarded by the school's Loan Funds. When making these payments, the school estimated that 8 percent would eventually prove to be uncollectible.

4. A government grant of $200,000 for biological research was received by the college. The school immediately distributed $160,000 to qualifying projects.

5. Faculty salaries of $400,000 were paid from Unrestricted Current Funds. Additionally, a transfer of $300,000 was made into Unexpended Plant Funds. Another $600,000 of unrestricted funds was set aside with the subsequent income to be used for scientific research. These transfers reflected decisions made by the college's board of trustees.

6. Income of $50,000 was generated by the Life Income Fund created in (2) with the money being immediately distributed to the appropriate recipient.

7. The school paid $1.5 million for a new wing for its art school building. This money had been set aside several years earlier from unrestricted funds.

Solution

1. ### Unrestricted Current Funds

Accounts Receivable	940,000	
Expenditures—Staff Benefits	60,000	
Expenditures—Bad Debts	50,000	
Revenues—Student Tuition and Fees		1,000,000
Allowance for Uncollectible Accounts		50,000

To recognize current revenues, remissions, and estimated bad accounts.

2. ### Funds for Renewals and Replacements

Cash	100,000	
Fund Balance—Temporarily Restricted for Replacement of Classroom Facilities		100,000

To record restricted gift made to college.

Life Income Funds

Cash	400,000	
Fund Balance—Temporarily Restricted		400,000

To record gift made to college with income being paid to the donor's sister until death.

Endowment Funds

Cash	400,000	
Fund Balance—Permanently Restricted		400,000

To record endowment gift—income to be used to buy equipment for engineering department.

3. ### Loan Funds

Notes Receivable—Students	100,000	
Fund Balance—Permanently Restricted for Student Loans . . .	8,000	
Cash		100,000
Allowance for Uncollectible Accounts		8,000

To record granting of student loans and estimation of bad accounts.

4. ### Restricted Current Funds

Cash	200,000	
Fund Balance—Temporarily Restricted for Research . . .		200,000

Government grant received—must be used for biological research.

Expenditures—Research	160,000	
Cash		160,000

Partial distribution is made of government grant.

Fund Balance—Temporarily Restricted for Research	160,000	
Revenues—Government Grants		160,000

To recognize revenue in connection with appropriate expenditure of government biological research grant.

5. ### Unrestricted Current Funds

Expenditures—Instruction	400,000	
Discretionary Transfer to Quasi-Endowment Fund for Scientific Research	600,000	
Discretionary Transfer to Unexpended Plant Funds	300,000	
Cash		1,300,000

To record faculty salaries and transfers made of unrestricted cash balances.

Quasi-Endowment Funds

Cash	600,000	
Fund Balance—Unrestricted		600,000

To record receipt of funds set aside for scientific research by board of trustees.

Unexpended Plant Funds

| Cash .... | 300,000 | |
| Fund Balance—Unrestricted .... | | 300,000 |

To record receipt of funds transferred from Unrestricted Current Funds by board of trustees.

6.   **Life Income Funds**

| Cash .... | 50,000 | |
| Due to Stated Recipient .... | | 50,000 |

To recognize income generated from investments held in Life Income Funds.

| Due to Stated Recipient .... | 50,000 | |
| Cash .... | | 50,000 |

To distribute entire income of Life Income Funds to recipient as specified by donor.

7.   **Unexpended Plant Funds**

| Fund Balance—Unrestricted .... | 1,500,000 | |
| Cash .... | | 1,500,000 |

To pay for newly constructed addition to art school.

Investment in Plant

| Buildings .... | 1,500,000 | |
| Investment in Plant............................. | | 1,500,000 |

To record cost of art school addition.

APPENDIX

Financial Statements for a University

Following are the financial statements for Utah State University for June 30, 1996, and the year then ended. These statements have been produced using the AICPA college guide model. The notes to these financial statements have not been included.

Exhibit 18–2

UTAH STATE UNIVERSITY
Statement of Current Funds Revenues, Expenditures, and Other Changes
For the Year Ended June 30, 1996

	1996			1995
	Unrestricted	**Restricted**	**Total**	**1995**
Revenues				
Educational and general				
Tuition and fees	$37,714,255	$ 5,219,234	$ 42,933,489	$ 40,072,009
Federal appropriations		3,788,315	3,788,315	5,399,153
State appropriations	72,734,900	23,663,820	96,398,720	91,412,215
Federal grants and contracts	10,014,896	56,377,761	66,392,657	69,407,747
State grants and contracts	220,273	8,050,883	8,271,156	6,908,194
Local grants and contracts	443,343	794,266	1,237,609	1,242,344
Private gifts, grants, and contracts	1,665,162	11,390,056	13,055,218	10,638,994
Endowment income	89,069	964,190	1,053,259	1,130,709
Investment earnings	1,103,592		1,103,592	673,130
Interest on loan and leases receivable	17,248		17,248	
Sales and services of educational departments	3,119,074	1,251,929	4,371,003	4,537,771
Conferences and institutes (noncredit)		3,202,184	3,202,184	2,998,321
Service departments	3,048,421		3,048,421	2,525,432
Other	1,274,368	1,208,259	2,482,627	1,836,174
Total educational and general revenues	131,444,601	115,910,897	247,355,498	238,782,193
Auxiliary enterprises	24,283,272		24,283,272	23,558,145
Total current revenues	155,727,873	115,910,897	271,638,770	262,340,338
Expenditures and mandatory transfers				
Educational and general				
Instruction	53,998,838	16,495,697	70,494,535	67,701,691
Research	4,718,371	60,769,887	65,488,258	65,861,068
Public service	2,166,363	20,103,582	22,269,945	21,924,890
Academic support	17,670,366	1,833,672	19,504,038	18,313,947
Student services	5,312,774	1,593,316	6,906,090	7,284,717
Institutional support	18,902,110	1,953,795	20,855,905	17,675,513
Operation and maintenance of plant	14,693,308	206,697	14,900,005	13,596,826
Scholarships and fellowships	6,194,789	12,660,889	18,855,678	17,622,603
Service departments	935,870	11,839	947,709	1,484,738
Mandatory transfers	509,248		509,248	450,000
Total educational and general expenditures and mandatory transfers	125,102,037	115,629,374	240,731,411	231,915,993
Auxiliary enterprises				
Expenditures	24,162,103	281,523	24,443,626	23,420,734
Mandatory transfers	2,002,484		2,002,484	1,811,131
Total auxiliary enterprises	26,164,587	281,523	26,446,110	25,231,865
Total expenditures and mandatory transfers	151,266,624	115,910,897	267,177,521	257,147,858
Other transfers and additions/(deductions)				
Excess of restricted receipts over transfers to revenues		2,373,748	2,373,748	3,247,852
Net change in liability for compensated absences	(363,330)	(159,035)	(522,365)	(762,954)
Net change in liability for early retirement	362,739	(100,534)	262,205	215,304
Refunded to grantors		(2,219)	(2,219)	(69,236)
Other additions/(deductions)—net	1,403,981	(22,130)	1,381,851	19,125
Nonmandatory transfers—net	(3,967,787)	(574,450)	(4,542,237)	(4,351,534)
Total other transfers and additions/(deductions)	(2,564,397)	1,515,380	(1,049,017)	(1,701,443)
Net increase/(decrease) in fund balances	$ 1,896,852	$ 1,515,380	$ 3,412,232	$ 3,491,037

Exhibit 18-3

UTAH STATE UNIVERSITY
Statement of Changes in Fund Balances
For the Year Ended June 30, 1996

	Current Funds		Loan Funds	Endowment and Similar Funds
	Unrestricted	Restricted		
Revenues and other additions				
Educational and general	$130,234,692			
Auxiliary enterprises	24,283,272			
Tuition and fees		$ 4,962,516		
Federal appropriations		3,758,815	$ 212,123	
State appropriations		23,767,601	70,710	
Federal grants and contracts		66,654,278		
State grants and contracts		8,950,684		
Local grants and contracts		894,542		
Private gifts, grants, and contracts		12,284,128		$ 2,308,584
Land grant revenues				
Interest on loans receivable	17,248		235,500	
Building fees				
Retirement of bonded debt				
Retirement of contractual debt (includes $241,215 current fund expenditures)				
Expended for capital assets (includes $13,242,718 current fund expenditures)				
Endowment income	89,069	839,173	3,110	
Investment earnings	1,103,592	1,470,611	41,601	1,132,451
Bond proceeds				
Insurance recovery				
Sales and services of educational departments		1,708,978		
Conferences and institutes (noncredit)		3,261,918		
Decrease in liability for early retirement	362,739			
Other	1,549,194	1,046,664	15,496	38,428
Total revenues and other additions	157,639,806	129,599,908	578,540	3,479,463
Expenditures and other deductions				
Educational and general	124,592,351	115,629,374		
Auxiliary enterprises	24,162,541	281,523		
Refunded to grantors		2,219		
Indirect costs recovered		10,782,562		
Administrative fees		532,701		
Retirement of bonded debt				
Retirement of contractual debt				
Increase in bonded debt				
Increase in contractual debt				
Interest expense				
Loan cancellations			121,383	
Uncollectible loans assigned to federal government			13,241	
Expended for plant facilities (including $1,216,013 not capitalized) . . .				
Disposal of assets				
Increase in liability for compensated absences	363,330	159,035		
Increase in liability for early retirement		100,534		
Other	145,213	22,130	14,695	55,802
Total expenditures and other deductions	149,263,435	127,510,078	149,319	55,802
Transfers among funds—additions/(deductions)				
Mandatory transfers—net	(2,511,732)			
Nonmandatory transfers—net	(3,967,787)	(574,450)	(76,932)	1,855,736
Total transfers among funds	(6,479,519)	(574,450)	(76,932)	1,855,736
Net increase/(decrease)	1,896,852	1,515,380	352,289	5,279,397
Fund balances at beginning of year as previously reported	12,557,649	14,566,517	10,304,890	27,506,142
Restatement for change in Space Dynamics Laboratory consolidation . . .	5,107,699	(5,107,699)		
Fund balances at beginning of year as restated	17,665,348	9,458,818	10,304,890	27,506,142
Fund balances at end of year	$ 19,562,200	$ 10,974,198	$10,657,179	$32,785,539

| | Plant Funds | | |
Unexpended	Repairs and Replacements	Retirement of Indebtedness	Investment in Plant
$ 350			
1,945,998			
54,920			
240,649			$ 2,761,572
63,713			
1,436,027			
3,886,657			4,230,000
			834,980
			31,904,866
11,207			
774,914	$ 28,183	$ 54,165	
		2,714,528	
222,254			
27,179			
8,663,868	28,183	2,768,693	39,731,418
		4,230,000	
		593,765	
			6,601,185
			81,882
3,783		2,216,011	
19,878,161			
			6,721,945
		35,370	
19,881,944	0	7,075,146	13,405,012
1,253,297		1,258,435	
113,215	(31,020)	2,681,238	
1,366,512	(31,020)	3,939,673	0
(9,851,564)	(2,837)	(366,780)	26,326,406
15,770,982	507,444	3,029,947	332,372,354
15,770,982	507,444	3,029,947	332,372,354
$ 5,919,418	$504,607	$2,663,167	$358,698,760

UTAH STATE UNIVERSITY
Balance Sheet
June 30, 1996

	Current Funds		
	Unrestricted Current Funds	**Restricted Current Funds**	**Total Current Funds**
Assets			
Cash	$ 219,916	$ 15,976	$ 235,892
Equity in Cash Management Investment Pool	33,131,062	10,141,948	43,273,010
Investments	1,481,293	278,892	1,760,185
Deposits with trustees			
Cash on deposit with state agencies		29,848	29,848
Accounts, credits, notes, and interest receivable (net of allowances:			
1996—$289,496	2,599,607	14,554,394	17,154,001
Inventories	3,366,629	37,420	3,404,049
Prepaid expenses, deposits, and other assets	284,109	51,055	335,164
Due from other funds—net			
Deferred compensation assets in 457 plans			
Investment in plant			
Total assets	$41,082,616	$25,109,533	$66,192,149
Liabilities and fund balances			
Liabilities			
Accounts payable and accrued expenses	$11,492,131	$ 7,940,965	$19,433,096
Liabilities for compensated absences and early retirement	6,356,433	3,344,150	9,700,583
Deferred revenues, deposits, and other liabilities	3,652,641	2,850,220	6,502,861
Funds held for others			
Due to other funds—net	19,211		19,211
Bonds, notes, and contracts payable			
Total liabilities	21,520,416	14,135,335	35,655,751
Fund balances	19,562,200	10,974,198	30,536,398
Total liabilities and fund balances	$41,082,616	$25,109,533	$66,192,149
Fund balances consist of:			
Unfunded compensated absences and early retirement benefits	($ 6,356,433)	($ 3,344,150)	($ 9,700,583)
U.S. Government grants refundable			
Endowments			
Quasi-endowments—restricted			
Quasi-endowments—unrestricted			
Externally restricted		14,318,348	14,318,348
Internally committed	25,918,633		25,918,633
Net investment in plant			
Total fund balances	$19,562,200	$10,974,198	$30,536,398

	Other Funds			Total All Funds	
Loan Funds	Endowment and Similar Funds	Plant Funds	Agency Funds	1996	1995
$ 16,712	$ (5,455)		$ 134,884	$ 382,033	$ 435,758
655,837	13,404,043	$ 5,267,278	217,674	62,817,842	53,596,618
	17,286,554			19,046,739	18,689,893
	1,574,195	8,676,637		10,250,832	7,898,648
		3,343,622		3,373,470	13,400,142
9,985,626	192,834		22,078	27,354,539	29,070,803
				3,404,049	3,303,844
		710,504		1,045,668	801,325
	333,367			333,367	267,133
			10,734,947	10,734,947	8,850,384
		391,229,157		391,229,157	363,284,665
$10,658,175	$32,785,538	$409,227,198	$11,109,583	$529,972,643	$499,599,213
$ 996		$ 2,109,811	$ 67,588	$ 21,611,491	$ 21,882,088
				9,700,583	9,440,423
		108,872	10,869,331	17,481,064	15,804,546
			172,664	172,664	220,922
		314,156		333,367	267,133
		38,908,407		38,908,407	35,368,176
996	$ 0	41,441,246	11,109,583	88,207,576	82,983,288
10,657,179	32,785,538	367,785,952		441,765,067	416,615,925
$10,658,175	$32,785,538	$409,227,198	$11,109,583	$529,972,643	$499,599,213
				$ (9,700,583)	$ (9,440,423)
$ 8,886,164				8,886,164	8,646,110
	$17,839,843			17,839,843	15,282,445
	14,715,076			14,715,076	11,987,267
	230,619			230,619	236,430
1,771,015		$ 8,231,308		24,320,671	37,728,661
		855,884		26,774,517	19,803,081
		358,698,760		358,698,760	332,372,354
$10,657,179	$32,785,538	$367,785,952	$ 0	$441,765,067	$416,615,925

QUESTIONS

1. Why have colleges and universities traditionally exhibited a significant degree of flexibility in their financial reporting practices?

2. From what sources are the generally accepted accounting principles of colleges and universities derived?

3. In what ways does the reporting process for a public college or university resemble that of a state or local governmental unit?

4. What six general fund groups can be encountered in a public college or university?

5. What transactions or events are normally accounted for within the Unrestricted Current Funds? Within the Restricted Current Funds?

6. What are the various types of Endowment and Similar Funds utilized within college and university accounting?

7. Describe the individual Plant Funds in a college or university's accounting records.

8. Which funds or subgroups of a college or university most resemble the General Fixed Assets Account Group and General Long-Term Debt Account group of a state or local government?

9. How are revenues and expenditures recorded by the various funds in a college or university?

10. What is the GAAP hierarchy? Where was it developed? How has it affected colleges and universities in selecting appropriate accounting principles?

11. A college not only awards a number of scholarship grants but also reduces tuition for the children of its employees. How are these transactions reflected within the school's financial records?

12. When are revenues recognized in the Restricted Current Funds?

13. A gift of $1 million is given to a university with the stipulation that it be used to build a new dormitory. The money is ultimately spent for that purpose. How are these events recorded by the school?

LIBRARY ASSIGNMENTS

1. Read the following articles and any other published information discussing the recording of depreciation expense by colleges and universities:

   "Accounting-Standards Boards' Rift Irks Many Colleges, May Hurt Private Ones," *The Wall Street Journal*, August 31, 1987.
   "The Impact of SFAS 93 on Colleges and Universities," *The CPA Journal*, July 1991.
   "High Dudgeon in the Ivory Tower," *Forbes*, April 4, 1988.
   "Depreciation for Colleges and Universities: Is It Useful Information?" *Government Accountants Journal*, Winter 1987–1988.
   "How College and University Business Officers View Depreciation," *Government Accountants Journal*, Spring 1988.

   Write a short report recommending whether depreciation should be reported by a college or university and give the justification for this opinion.

2. Write to the vice president of financial affairs at one or more colleges and universities and request a copy of the most recent financial statements. Using these statements, answer the following questions:
   - How large is the school's endowment?
   - Is the school a public or private institution?
   - What was the largest source of revenues in the Unrestricted Current Funds?
   - What was the largest source of revenues in the Restricted Current Funds?
   - What was the largest expenditure in the Unrestricted Current Funds?
   - What was the largest expenditure in the Restricted Current Funds?
   - What was the cost of the school's land, buildings, and equipment?
   - Does the school record depreciation expense?
   - Does the school record its pledges? Is the amount of pledges currently outstanding disclosed?

■ Were any interfund transfers made during the period? If so, were they mandatory or discretionary?

PROBLEMS

1. Which of the following should be used in accounting for public colleges and universities?
   a. Fund accounting and accrual accounting.
   b. Fund accounting but not accrual accounting.
   c. Accrual accounting but not fund accounting.
   d. Neither accrual accounting nor fund accounting.
   (AICPA adapted)

2. A large cash gift was made to State University with the following specific instructions: the income earned on this money was to be used to buy library books for five years. Thereafter, all of the principal can be spent to improve facilities in the dining hall. Within which of the school's fund types is this money initially recorded?
   a. Nonexpendable Trust Funds.
   b. Life Income Funds.
   c. Annuity Funds.
   d. Term Endowment Funds.

3. Money is given to a public college or university with the stipulation that it be used solely for the acquisition of new equipment for the physics laboratory. Within which fund is this money recorded?
   a. Capital Projects Funds.
   b. Investment in Plant Fund.
   c. Unexpended Plant Funds.
   d. Endowment Funds.

4. The current funds group of a public university includes which of the following subgroups?

	Term Endowment Funds	Life Income Funds
a.	No	No
b.	No	Yes
c.	Yes	Yes
d.	Yes	No

   (AICPA adapted)

5. Why are Quasi-Endowment Funds somewhat unique to college and university accounting?
   a. Money held within the school's endowment is classified according to the source of the gift.
   b. Internally restricted amounts are classified separately from unrestricted funds.
   c. Assets other than cash are held within the school's endowment.
   d. Several types of gifts are merged together to form a single endowment fund.

6. Which of the following fund types is most similar?
   a. General Fund of a state or local government and the Unrestricted Current Funds of a college or university.
   b. Capital Projects Funds of a state or local government and the Endowment Funds of a college or university.
   c. Debt Service Funds of a state or local government and the Loan Funds of a college or university.
   d. Nonexpendable Trust Funds of a state or local government and the Restricted Current Funds of a college or university.

7. Which of the following fund types is most similar?
   a. Capital Projects Funds of a state or local government and the Investment in Plant of a college or university.

b. Special Revenue Funds of a state or local government and the Restricted Current Funds of a college or university.

c. Enterprise Funds of a state or local government and the Quasi-Endowment Funds of a college or university.

d. Internal Service Funds of a state or local government and the Unrestricted Current Funds of a college or university.

8. Apteck University computes normal tuition charges of $480,000. However, of this amount, $140,000 is to be covered by scholarships. How does the school report this information?

a. As revenues of $340,000.

b. As revenues of $480,000 less an allowance balance of $140,000.

c. As revenues of $340,000 and expenditures of $140,000.

d. As revenues of $480,000 and expenditures of $140,000.

9. The following information was available from Forest College's accounting records for its current funds for the year ended March 31, 1998 (it is a public school):

Restricted gifts received
    Expended $100,000
    Not expended   300,000
Unrestricted gifts received
    Expended   600,000
    Not expended   75,000

What amount should be included in current funds revenues (restricted and unrestricted) for the year ended March 31, 1998?

a. $600,000.

b. $700,000.

c. $775,000.

d. $1,000,000.

(AICPA adapted)

10. For 1998, Hawkeye University charges its students $1.7 million, covering tuition and fees for educational and general purposes. However, only $1.5 million was expected to be realized because scholarships totaling $150,000 were granted to these students, and tuition remissions of $50,000 were allowed to faculty members' children attending the school. What amount should be included in the Unrestricted Current Funds as revenues from student tuition and fees?

a. $1,500,000.

b. $1,550,000.

c. $1,650,000.

d. $1,700,000.

(AICPA adapted)

11. An endowment gift was donated to a public college with the stipulation that the subsequent income was to be spent on medical research. During 1998, endowment revenue was $60,000 but only $47,000 was spent for the research. Which of the following is correct?

a. Revenues of $47,000 are reported in Restricted Current Funds.

b. Expenditures of $47,000 are reported in the Endowment Funds.

c. Revenues of $60,000 are reported in Restricted Current Funds.

d. Revenues of $47,000 are reported in the Endowment Funds.

12. A $100,000 cash gift was made to a public university at the beginning of 1997. The money was to be spent to enhance the salaries of valued professors who write textbooks. During 1997, $42,000 of the money was spent for this purpose. What reporting is made at the end of the year in the Restricted Current Funds?

a. Fund Balance—0; Revenues—$100,000; Expenditures—$42,000

b. Fund Balance—$58,000; Revenues—$42,000; Expenditures—$42,000

c. Fund Balance—$100,000; Revenues—$58,000; Expenditures—0

d. Fund Balance—$58,000; Revenues—$100,000; Expenditures—$42,000

13. In college and university accounting, where are the operations of auxiliary activities (such as the campus bookstore) normally reported?

  a. Restricted Current Funds.
  b. Endowment Funds.
  c. Quasi-Endowment Funds.
  d. Unrestricted Current Funds.

14. A public college holds money in its Unexpended Plant Fund to be used to buy new laboratory equipment. During 1998, a total of $650,000 was spent in this way. What internal recording is made of this $650,000?

   a. A $650,000 reduction is recorded to the Fund Balance of the Unexpended Plant Fund, and Equipment of $650,000 is recorded in the Investment in Plant.
   b. Equipment of $650,000 is recorded in the Unexpended Plant Fund.
   c. An Expenditure of $650,000 is recorded in the Unexpended Plant Fund, and Equipment of $650,000 is recorded in the Unrestricted Current Funds.
   d. A Discretionary Transfer of $650,000 is recorded in the Unexpended Plant Fund, and both an Expenditure and Equipment of $650,000 are reported in the Investment in Plant.

15. The following receipts were among those recorded by Allied College (a public school) during 1998:

Unrestricted gifts	$500,000
Restricted current funds (expended for current operating purposes)	200,000
Restricted current funds (not yet expended)	100,000

   The total amount that should be included in current funds revenues is
   a. $800,000.
   b. $700,000.
   c. $600,000.
   d. $500,000.

   (AICPA adapted)

16. For the spring semester of 1998, Manning University assessed its students a total of $4.4 million, covering tuition and fees for educational and general purposes. However, scholarships of $600,000 were granted to selected students. Tuition reductions of $100,000 were also allowed to faculty members' children attending the school. An additional $75,000 in bad debt expenses are expected.

   How much should Manning recognize as current funds revenues from student tuition and fees?

   What journal entry should be recorded at the time the assessment is made?

   Assume that some of the classes are in summer school and start in one fiscal year and end in the next. How is the revenue to be recognized?

17. A state university transferred cash of $100,000 from unrestricted funds to be held as eventual financing for the construction of a dormitory. A bond of $830,000 was issued at face value. A contract was signed for $908,000. The dorm was built with the final cost being $898,000. That amount was paid.

   Prepare all necessary journal entries for these transactions. Identify the fund type for each entry.

18. An outside donor gave cash of $140,000 to a public university to study frogs. The first $97,000 was spent in that manner. Make the proper journal entries. Identify the fund type for each entry.

19. The following assets were being held in various funds by State Tech at July 1, 1998:

Funds to be used for acquisition of additional properties for university purposes	$1,450,000
Funds set aside for debt service charges and for retirement of indebtedness on university properties	2,657,000

   In what funds will these two amounts be maintained? Assume that $500,000 was expended from the first fund to buy new equipment for the science laboratories. Assume that $700,000 was expended from the second fund to pay off a bond payable ($650,000) and interest ($50,000). What journal entries are required?

20. The following transactions were incurred by Garrison Tech, a public university in the southeastern section of the United States. Prepare all necessary journal entries. Include the fund types in which each entry would be recorded. Amounts are not to be presented.

- Students were assessed tuition charges for the current year. A percentage of this amount was expected to be uncollectible. Another portion was to be covered by academic scholarships.
- A cash gift was awarded to the school with the stipulation that all future income generated from this money should be used to finance genetic research.
- A pledge was received from a donor who specified that the amount would be paid in two years for use in that period.
- A patron of the school donated a collection of paintings by Gris to be added to the permanent collection of the art museum on campus.
- A cash transfer was made from unrestricted funds to finance student loans. Another amount of unrestricted cash was set aside by school officials. This money will be invested with future income to be used for library acquisitions.
- Student loans were awarded for the current year. A portion of this money will never be collected.
- Income was generated from the preceding gift that was restricted for genetic research. This money has not yet been expended.
- A portion of the income just earned was appropriately expended for genetic research.
- An addition was built to the school of business. Money previously set aside by school officials was used to pay a portion of the costs of the construction. A long-term liability was signed to cover the remainder.

21. During the year ended June 30, 1998, Central State College began to conduct a cancer research project financed by a $10 million donation from an alumnus. This entire amount was pledged by the donor on August 1, 1997. The first payment of $3 million was made at that time. The remaining money was given exactly one year later. The gift was restricted to the financing of this particular research project. Central State spent $2 million per year on this project for five consecutive years beginning with the year ended June 30, 1998. Central State follows a policy of recording all pledges.

    How much revenue should Central State report in 1998 and in what fund should it be recognized?

    What journal entry was recorded when the pledge was received?

    What entries are required for the first year's expenditures?

22. The following series of issues concern the accounting procedures utilized by colleges and universities. Prepare answers to each question.
    a. A cash donation is made to a university with the stipulation that the money must be used for biology research. Discuss the accounting procedures necessitated by this gift.
    b. One of the subgroups found within the Plant Funds of a college accounting system is the Investment in Plant. What is the purpose of this subgroup?
    c. The recording of depreciation expense by colleges and universities has become the subject of controversy. What are the positions and what are the justifications for each?
    d. The current funds category of a university has two subgroups. Identify these subgroups and explain their differences.
    e. How are student scholarships recorded in college and university accounting?
    f. Debt Service Funds and Capital Projects Funds are found in the accounting for state and local government units. Which fund types found in college accounting parallel these two funds?
    g. For colleges and universities, what is the significance of the GAAP hierarchy that has been created?
    h. The governing body of a college transfers previously unrestricted money into the Loan Funds. How is this transfer recorded?
    i. What is a Quasi-Endowment Fund? What makes the use of this fund somewhat controversial from an accounting perspective?
    j. What method of recording should be used for pledges of money received by a college or university?
    k. What accounting should be made of contributions made to the permanent collection of a not-for-profit organization?

23. The following series of transactions is for Orlando University. For each, prepare all needed journal entries including an identification of the fund types.
    a. An unrestricted cash donation of $44,000 was given to the school by a former student.

    b. A cash gift of $78,000 was presented to the school with the specification that the money be used to study political processes in Bosnia.

    c. An investment portfolio valued at $50,000 was given to the school with the stipulation that all income generated from these assets must be used to research computer applications in education.

    d. A cash gift of $231,000 was conveyed to the school with the stipulation that the money eventually be used to help pay for the construction of a new chemistry building.

    e. The money from (*a*) was used to pay faculty salaries.

    f. The money from (*b*) was used for the specified purpose.

    g. Cash dividends of $7,000 are received from the investments in (*c*). This money will be spent for the intended purpose but not until next year.

    h. The chemistry building mentioned in (*d*) was built at a cost of $1,950,000. The $231,000 was used as a first payment and a note was signed for the remaining $1,719,000.

24. Jurgeson State College incurred the following transactions during its 1998 fiscal year. Prepare all necessary journal entries indicating the fund category or fund subgroup within which the entry is recorded.

- An Annuity Fund reported income of $30,000. By the provisions of the original gift, 80 percent of all income goes to the donor's mother with the remainder to be used by the college for a cancer research project. Both amounts were appropriately expended during the current year.

- The college borrowed $900,000 during the year to begin construction of a new gymnasium. The building is completed before the end of the year and the $900,000, plus a previously received gift of $340,0000, were used to pay for the construction. The first $25,000 installment on the loan was paid; this amount included $11,000 in interest expense.

- A government grant of $70,000 (received during the previous year to investigate health disorders) was spent for that purpose.

- The college's athletic teams reported a $200,000 loss for the year based on revenues of $1,400,000 and expenditures of $1,600,000.

- Student tuition of $600,000 was assessed. Of this total, 4 percent was assumed to be uncollectible and an additional 10 percent was covered by financial aid scholarships.

- The college's board of trustees transferred $100,000 at the beginning of the year to a Quasi-Endowment Fund. All future income derived from this principal was to be used for law student scholarships. Earnings of $8,000 were reported during the current year and granted to two students.

- Depreciation of $620,000 was recorded on the long-lived assets being reported in the Investment in Plant Fund.

- Student loans of $90,000 were made with the anticipation that only 92 percent would actually be repaid. Interest of $3,000 accrued on these loans during the current year.

25. The following journal entries have been taken from the financial records of the University of Jonesville. In each case, the fund category or fund subgroup in which each entry has been recorded is identified. For each transaction, indicate the correcting entry or entries that should be prepared by the university. If no correction is needed, indicate this fact.

a.
Endowment Fund

Cash	13,000	
Revenues Control.		13,000
Expenditures Control.	13,000	
Cash		13,000

To record revenue earned on endowment gift and subsequent expenditure as per original specifications attached to gift.

b.
Unrestricted Current Funds

Expenditures—Student Loans.	50,000	
Cash		50,000

Money transferred to loan fund to finance future student loans.

Loan Funds

Cash	50,000	
Revenues—Transfer from Unrestricted Funds		50,000

Money transferred by administration to finance student loans.

c.   **Unrestricted Current Funds**

Depreciation Expense	73,000	
Accumulated Depreciation		73,000

Depreciation of university property recorded for the current year.

d.   **Restricted Current Funds**

Cash	100,000	
Revenues—Government Grant		100,000
Expenditures—Research Project	33,000	
Cash		33,000

To record grant made by federal government to finance a project to study molecular structures as well as the initial expenditures made to start this project.

e.   **Unexpended Plant Funds**

Cash	125,000	
Revenues—Philanthropic Gift		125,000

To record gift made to university with the stipulation that the money be used in construction of a new library.

f.   **Unrestricted Current Funds**

Pledges Receivable	50,000	
Deferred Revenues		50,000

Pledge made by university supporter for an unrestricted cash gift to be made in five years.

g.   **Unexpended Plant Funds**

Building	600,000	
Cash		200,000
Bonds Payable		400,000

To record construction of new dormitory—part of cost paid through an earlier gift with the rest covered by the issuance of long-term bonds payable.

h.   **Unrestricted Current Funds**

Accounts Receivable	480,000	
Revenues—Student Tuition and Fees		480,000

To record billings for current tuition—5 percent of above total is considered uncollectible while an additional $60,000 has not been recorded because that amount relates to student scholarships.

26. The following transactions were incurred by the University of South Central. For each, prepare all needed journal entries including an identification of the fund types.
  a. Students were charged $378,000 for tuition. Of this amount, $22,000 is anticipated as being uncollectible.
  b. A cash gift of $85,000 was made to the school with the stipulation that this money be used to finance fine arts performances at the school.
  c. The university paid its faculty $54,000 in cash for normal salaries.
  d. A building was acquired for $800,000. Of the total, previously designated funds of $300,000 were used with the remainder covered by the signing of a note payable.
  e. From the receivables in (*a*), $210,000 in cash was collected. An additional $43,000 was covered by scholarships.
  f. A discretionary transfer of $40,000 was made from unrestricted funds into a quasi-endowment fund.
  g. Of the $85,000 received in (*b*), 40 percent was spent for the intended purpose.
  h. A loan of $110,000 was made to students.

27. Following is the current funds balance sheet of Burnsville University (a public school) as of June 30, 1998, the end of the school's fiscal year.

BURNSVILLE UNIVERSITY
Current Funds Balance Sheet
June 30, 1998

Assets

Current funds:
  Unrestricted:
    Cash $210,000
    Accounts receivable—student tuition and fees, less
      allowance for doubtful accounts of $9,000 341,000
    State appropriations receivable 75,000 $626,000
  Restricted:
    Cash 7,000
    Investments 60,000   67,000
Total current funds................................. $693,000

Liabilities and Fund Balances

Current funds:
  Unrestricted:
    Accounts payable .... $ 45,000
    Deferred revenues............................ 66,000
    Fund balances 515,000 $626,000
  Restricted:
    Fund balances 67,000
Total current funds................................. $693,000

The following transactions occurred during the fiscal year ended June 30, 1998:

- On July 7, 1997, a gift of $100,000 in cash was received from an alumnus with the request that one-half be used for the purchase of books for the university library with the remainder used for the establishment of a scholarship fund. The alumnus further specified that the income generated by the scholarship fund be awarded annually to a qualified disadvantaged student. On July 20, 1997, the board of trustees resolved that the funds of the newly established scholarship fund be invested in high-grade bonds. On July 21, 1997, these bonds were purchased.
- Revenue from student tuition and fees applicable to the year ended June 30, 1998, amounted to $1,900,000. Of this amount, $66,000 had been collected in the prior year and $1,686,000 was received during the current year ended June 30, 1998. In addition, by June 30, 1998, the university had received cash of $158,000 representing fees for the session beginning in September 1998.
- During the year ended June 30, 1998, the university collected $349,000 of the outstanding accounts receivable at the beginning of the year. The balance was deemed to be uncollectible and was written off against the allowance account. At June 30, 1998, the allowance account was increased by $3,000.
- Interest charges of $6,000 were earned and collected during the year on late student fee payments.
- During the year, the state appropriation was received. An additional unrestricted appropriation of $50,000 was made by the state but had not been paid to the university as of June 30, 1998.
- An unrestricted gift of $25,000 cash was received from alumni of the university.
- During the year, investments of $21,000 were sold for $26,000. Dividend and interest income amounting to $1,900 was also received.
- Unrestricted operating expenses of $1,777,000 were accrued during the period. At June 30, 1998, $59,000 of these expenses remained unpaid.
- Restricted current funds of $13,000 were spent for authorized purposes during the year.
- The accounts payable at June 30, 1997, were paid during July 1997.
- During the current year, $7,000 interest was earned and received on the bonds purchased in accordance with the board of trustees resolution, as discussed above.

Required

    a. Prepare journal entries to record these transactions for the year ended June 30, 1998. Label each entry to indicate which funds would be involved.

    b. Prepare a statement of changes in fund balances for the year ended June 30, 1998, for the Unrestricted Current Funds and the Restricted Current Funds.

(AICPA adapted)

28. Following are descriptions of balances found in the various accounts of the University of Northwest Wichita as of December 31, 1997:

Inflow of Net Assets

Revenue generated by bookstore	$ 85,000
Gifts received from graduates designated to buy a new dormitory	100,000
Note is signed to buy new dormitory	300,000
Research grants made to fund cancer research	120,000
Income earned on an endowment where money must be spent on researching fog	30,000
Charges for tuition (does not include reductions of $50,000 because of scholarships and $10,000 because of class cancellations)	545,000

Outflow of Net Assets

Spent for new dormitory	400,000
Spent for faculty salaries	300,000
Spent for research on fog (money was earned in endowment)	30,000
Loaned to students	65,000
Spent for cancer research	75,000

Other

Money restricted by board of trustees for future studies of endangered animals	100,000

Answer each of the following questions:

    a. What is the total revenue recorded in the Unrestricted Current Funds and what are the components?

    b. What is the total revenue recorded in the Restricted Current Funds and what are the components?

    c. Identify the journal entry or entries recorded in the Investment in Plant fund.

    d. How is the money recorded that is being set aside to study endangered animals?

    e. What is the total Expenditures balance to be shown in the Unrestricted Current Funds?

    f. Identify the journal entry or entries recorded when the gift is received for the new dormitory.

29. Record each of the following transactions as if it were incurred by a state or local government. Then, record each transaction as if it were incurred by a college or university. In each case, indicate the fund or fund type in which the entry would be being recorded. Optional entries should be made.

    a. A budget was passed for normal operating activities. Income was anticipated as $760,000 with approved spending amounting to $740,000.

    b. A contract was signed with a construction company for a new building at a cost of $8 million.

    c. Bonds were sold for $8 million (face value) to finance construction of the new building.

    d. The new building was completed and payment of $8 million immediately made.

    e. Cash of $1 million was transferred from unrestricted funds to be set aside to pay off the bonds sold in (*b*).

    f. The $1 million was paid to retire this portion of the bonds before maturity.

    g. Annual assessments were sent out; they are to be collected with the money to be used in this period. The receivables are for $800,000 and the cash collected will be unrestricted. Only 94 percent of the assessment will actually be collected.

    h. Cash of $70,000 was received as a gift which must be spent for a designated operating purpose.

    i. Of the cash in (*h*), $40,000 was spent for the specified purpose.

    j. Investments of $300,000 were received as a gift. Future income that is received from this donation will be used for a stipulated operating purpose.

C H A P T E R

19

Accounting and Reporting for Private Not-for-Profit Organizations

QUESTIONS TO CONSIDER

- Individuals, foundations, and businesses contribute large amounts of resources to not-for-profit organizations. What financial information do contributors want regarding the not-for-profit organization?

- How can a contributor to a charity determine the utilization being made of the resources contributed?

- How should a not-for-profit organization recognize pledges of support?

- Should a not-for-profit record donations of services?

- What is the accounting treatment of charity allowances, bad debts, and contractual adjustments for hospitals and other health care providers?

The Governmental Accounting Standards Board was established in 1984 to set accounting standards for state and local governments as well as organizations owned by state and local governments, such as state universities. In contrast, the Financial Accounting Standards Board (FASB) has authority for establishing accounting standards for business organizations and *private not-for-profit* organizations. The term *private* indicates that the organization is not owned by a government, while the term *not-for-profit* indicates the absence of a profit objective. Private not-for-profits include churches, charities, voluntary health and welfare organizations, many hospitals, and private colleges and universities.

Until recently, even though the FASB had standard-setting authority, the accounting standards for private not-for-profits were established by industry audit guides issued by the American Institute of Certified Public Accountants (AICPA). The accounting standards established by these industry audit guides differed among the various types of not-for-profits. In 1993 the FASB standardized the reporting of private not-for-profit organizations with the issuance of two standards: *FASB Statement No. 116*, "Accounting for Contributions Received and Contributions Made," established guidelines for determining when not-for-profit organizations should recognize contributions and for the reporting of contributions in the financial statements. *FASB Statement No. 117*, "Financial Statements of Not-for-Profit Organizations," established the required financial statements and financial statement format for private not-for-profit organizations.[1]

---

[1]In 1996 the AICPA issued a new audit and accounting guide, *Not-for-Profit Organizations*, to provide guidelines for preparing and auditing financial statements prepared under the FASB standards. The industry guide replaces previous guides (*Colleges and Universities, Voluntary Health and Welfare Organizations*, and *Certain Nonprofit Organizations*) and provides additional guidance and examples for determining how to apply *FASB Statements 116* and *117*.

As a result of these two standards, the financial statements of private colleges and universities are very similar to those of voluntary health and welfare organizations, civic organizations, labor unions, and political parties. However, because government-owned colleges and universities continue to follow accounting standards established by the GASB, the financial statements of public universities differ greatly from those of private universities.

FINANCIAL REPORTING

Many private not-for-profit organizations operate throughout the world. The purpose of each is to achieve one or more stated objectives such as the cure of a particular disease or the cleanup of the environment. Many individuals (especially current and potential contributors) are interested in how the organization spends the money it receives. They want to know:

- Which of these organizations should receive money and how much?
- Is contributing to a particular charity a wise allocation of resources?
- Will donated funds be used effectively by an organization to accomplish its specified purpose or will the money be wasted?

Such questions are faced by every not-for-profit relying on voluntary contributions from the general public, (i.e., *public support*). Future gifts and grants are based, at least in part, on the organization's ability to convince donors that resources are being used wisely to accomplish stated goals. The financial statements are vital to this objective since they report the resources generated and the spending decisions that have been made.

Several basic ideas form the framework for the FASB's standards for not-for-profit organizations. These include:

1. The financial statements should focus on the entity as a whole.
2. Requirements for not-for-profit organizations should be similar to business entities unless there are critical differences in the information needs of financial statement users.

The first idea is important because the organization's financial statements should not be centered around the funds that many not-for-profit organizations use for internal record-keeping. The second idea is important because not-for-profits should use many of the same accrual basis techniques used by business entities for recording and reporting most transactions. Consequently, existing FASB standards for capital leases, pensions, contingent liabilities, and many other issues do not have to be rewritten for not-for-profit organizations.

Although not-for-profit organizations have much in common with business entities, such as accrual based measurement of assets and liabilities, the FASB identified three critical differences between not-for-profit organizations and commercial entities. First, the contributions not-for-profit organizations receive create transactions that have no counterparts in commercial accounting. Second, contributions often have donor-imposed restrictions. And third, no single indicator can describe performance as effectively as net income does for commercial entities, thus other indicators are necessary. These differences suggest the need for a different basic set of financial statements for not-for-profit organizations.

FASB Statement 117, "Financial Statements of Not-for-Profit Organizations," requires three financial statements:

1. The *statement of financial position* reports the assets, liabilities, and net assets of private not-for-profits. The final category, net assets, is used in place of owners' equity or fund balance. Net assets are allocated to unrestricted, temporarily restricted, and permanently restricted as shown in the appendix to this chapter (see Exhibit 19–5).

2. The *statement of activities and changes in net assets* reports revenues, expenses, gains, and losses for the period. Revenues and expenses are determined using the accrual basis of accounting, including depreciation of fixed assets. The statement presents the *change in net assets* for the period and reconciles to net assets appearing on the statement of financial position as shown in the appendix (see Exhibit 19–6).

3. The *statement of cash flows* uses the standard FASB classifications of cash flows from operations, investing activities, and financing activities. Cash flows from operating activities may be prepared on the direct or indirect basis as shown in the appendix (see Exhibit 19–7).

In addition to these statements, voluntary health and welfare organizations are required to prepare a *Statement of Functional Expense* (see Exhibit 19–3). Voluntary health and welfare organizations are entities which promote humanitarian activities, such as public health clinics, homeless shelters, the American Diabetes Association, and Save the Children Federation. These organizations typically receive some revenues from their activities, but rely on support from United Way allocations, government grants, gifts from individuals and foundations, and similar sources to support their activities. The statement of functional expense provides a detailed schedule of expenses by function (such as various programs and administrative activities) and by object (salaries, supplies, depreciation, etc.).

Statement of Financial Position

Exhibit 19–1 presents the statement of financial position for Save the Children Federation, Inc. The asset and liability sections resemble those of business enterprises with assets organized according to liquidity and current liabilities presented before long-term liabilities. Unlike business enterprises, individuals and organizations provide resources to not-for-profit organizations without the expectation of earning a return on their investment. As a result, the concept of owners' equity does not apply to not-for-profit organizations. In the place of paid-in-capital and retained earnings, the final section of the statement presents net assets, the excess of assets over liabilities.

Net assets are presented in three categories: unrestricted, temporarily restricted, and permanently restricted. Restrictions must be imposed by donors from outside the organization before an asset is classified as restricted. Board designated or internally restricted assets are classified as unrestricted for financial statement purposes. Save the Children chooses to display board-designated assets and investments in land, buildings, and equipment as separate categories of unrestricted net assets.

Temporarily restricted assets are restricted for a particular use or for use in a future time period. For example, a private college might receive a grant for drug research. The amounts received from the grant are temporarily restricted for a particular use. Alternatively, the college might receive a grant supporting education programs over the next three years. The amounts received or promised for future periods also are restricted temporarily. The key with temporarily restricted assets is that the resources are expected to be released from restriction on performance of some act or the passage of time.

In contrast, permanently restricted assets are expected to remain restricted for as long as the organization exists. The most common form of permanently restricted assets are endowments in which the principal must remain intact. Additionally, land

Exhibit 19–1

SAVE THE CHILDREN FEDERATION, INCORPORATED
Balance Sheet
(Statement of Financial Position)
September 30, 1996
(In thousands)

Assets
Cash and cash equivalents	$ 6,654
Grants and contracts receivable	2,992
Investments	18,323
Prepaid expenses and other assets	1,345
Contributions receivable	3,049
Assets of pooled income fund	768
Loan program fund assets held in trust for others	1,993
Land, buildings, and equipment, net	7,375
Assets held in trust by others	506
Total assets	$43,005

Liabilities and Net Assets
Liabilities:
Accounts payable and accrued liabilities	9,960
Deferred amounts received under grants and contracts	3,847
Deferred revenue of pooled income fund	462
Severance benefits for foreign national employees	2,392
Long-term debt	2,662
Loan program funds due communities	1,993
Postretirement benefits other than pensions	2,477
Total liabilities	23,793

Net assets:
Unrestricted:
Undesignated	2,633
Board designated	3,804
Investment in land, buildings, and equipment, net	7,375
Total unrestricted net assets	13,812
Temporarily restricted	3,044
Permanently restricted	2,356
Total net assets	19,212
Total liabilities and net assets	$43,005

or works of art are classified as permanently restricted if they are donated with stipulations that they be used for a specified purpose and not sold.

Statement of Activities and Changes in Net Assets

Exhibit 19–2 presents the statement of activities for Save the Children Federation. Note the use of separate columns for the three categories of net assets: unrestricted, temporarily restricted, and permanently restricted. The bottom line agrees with the net asset balances presented on the statement of financial position. *Change in net assets*, the excess of revenue over expenses, is used in place of net income on the statement of cash flows (not presented) in the reconciliation of change in net assets to cash flows from operations.

Measured on the accrual basis, revenues and expenses follow the same standards applicable to business enterprises. The unique feature of not-for-profit organizations is that they receive significant resources through contributions. *FASB Statement No. 116*, "Accounting for Contributions Received and Contributions Made," requires not-for-profit organizations to recognize contributions as revenue in the period the contribution is made. Save the Children reports contributions of $13.370 million for the year ended September 30, 1996. Unconditional promises to give (including

Exhibit 19-2

SAVE THE CHILDREN FEDERATION, INCORPORATED
Statement of Activities
Year Ended September 30, 1996
(In thousands)

	Unrestricted	Temporarily Restricted	Permanently Restricted	Total
Operating revenue:				
Sponsorships	$ —	$ 23,575	—	$ 23,575
Contributions	8,210	5,160	—	13,370
Grants and contracts	67,471	—	—	67,471
Agricultural commodities and ocean freight	7,030	—	—	7,030
Bequests	509	257	—	766
Investment income and net gains	1,487	130	—	1,617
Craft shop and catalog	913	—	—	913
Fee for service contracts	1,687	—	—	1,687
Other	870	—	—	870
Total operating revenue	88,177	29,122	—	117,299
Net assets released from restrictions	30,059	(30,059)	—	—
Total operating revenue and net assets released	118,236	(937)	—	117,299
Operating expenses:				
Program services:				
Agriculture and resource management	6,382	—	—	6,382
Education	22,690	—	—	22,690
Primary health	12,407	—	—	12,407
Economic opportunity	5,027	—	—	5,027
Emergency, refugee, and civil society	47,832	—	—	47,832
Total program services	94,338	—	—	94,338
Supporting services:				
Management and general	7,293	—	—	7,293
Fund-raising	13,782	—	—	13,782
Total supporting services	21,075	—	—	21,075
Total operating expenses	115,413	—	—	115,413
Excess (deficiency) of operating revenue and net assets released over expenses	2,823	(937)	—	1,886
Nonoperating revenue:				
Contributions and change in value of split interest agreements	—	175	477	652
Total nonoperating revenue	—	175	477	652
Change in net assets. before cumulative effect of change in accounting principle	2,823	(762)	477	2,538
Cumulative effect of change in accounting principle	(2,355)	—	—	(2,355)
Total change in net assets	468	(762)	477	183
Net assets at beginning of year, as restated	13,344	3,806	1,879	19.029
Net assets at end of year	$ 13,812	$ 3,044	$2,356	$ 19,212

pledges) are recognized as both a receivable and revenue in the period promised. Save the Children's statement of financial position (Exhibit 19-1) reflects Contributions Receivable of $3.049 million.

Expenses are reported only in the unrestricted column of Exhibit 19-2. Frequently, some of the expenses relate to activities funded through restricted contributions or grants. In such cases, the expense is still reflected as a change in unrestricted net assets. To the extent the expenses meet donor restrictions, net assets are released from temporary restriction. This reclassification is reflected in the statement of activities, in the section following operating revenues, and is shown as a reduction in

Exhibit 19–3

SAVE THE CHILDREN FEDERATION, INCORPORATED
Statement of Functional Expenses
Year ended September 30, 1996
(In thousands)

	Program Services		
	Agriculture and Resource Management	Education	Primary Health
Salaries	$1,849	$ 5,071	$ 3,466
Employee fringe benefits	482	1,323	904
Payroll taxes	136	374	256
Total salaries and related expenses	2,467	6,768	4,626
Agricultural commodities and ocean freight	—	—	—
Inland transportation of commodities	—	—	—
Grants to other agencies	201	1,558	816
Professional fees and contract services	266	731	500
Supplies, material, and equipment	1,398	3,833	2,620
Other project costs	791	6,343	1,482
Telecommunications	133	366	250
Postage and shipping	87	239	164
Advertising	5	13	9
Printing	50	138	94
Occupancy	301	827	565
Travel	598	1,639	1,121
Interest	—	—	—
Miscellaneous	13	36	24
Total expenses before depreciation	6,310	22,491	12,271
Depreciation of buildings and equipment	72	199	136
Total expenses	$6,382	22,690	12,407

restricted net assets and an increase in unrestricted. For the year ended September 30, 1996, Save the Children reclassified $30.059 million of temporarily restricted net assets to unrestricted because either the organization had performed the activities designated by the donors or the donor-imposed time restrictions had passed.

Contributors are major users of the financial statements of not-for-profit organizations. The primary concern of contributors is determining the extent to which the not-for-profit is using the resources provided to fulfill the organizational mission. Expenses are presented in two broad categories, *program services* and *supporting services*. Program services are activities relating to the social services, research, or other objectives of the organization. Within this category, organizations may report several programs or only one. Save the Children reports five program categories. Supporting services consist of administrative costs and fund-raising. These activities generally are regarded as not directly related to one of the organization's stated missions. Frequently analysts use the ratio of program service expenses to total expenses to rank not-for-profits.[2] The Better Business Bureau suggests that ratio values of less than 60 percent are not desirable. Save the Children Federation reports a ratio of 82 percent ($94.338 million/$115.413 million) for the year ended September 30, 1996.

FASB *Statement 124*, "Accounting for Certain Investments Held by Not-for-profit Organizations" requires that investments in equity securities with readily determin-

---

[2]Ellen Stark, "The Top U.S. Charities," *Money*, December 1994, pp. 156–70.

| Program Services | | | Supporting Services | | | |
Economic Opportunity	Emergency, Refugee and Civil Society	Total Program Services	Management and General	Fund-Raising	Total Supporting Services	Total Expenses
$1,426	$ 5,958	$17,770	$2,985	$ 3,239	$ 6,224	$ 23,994
372	1,554	4,635	456	455	911	5,546
105	440	1,311	240	301	541	1,852
1,903	7,952	23,716	3,681	3,995	7,676	31,392
—	7,030	7,030	—	—	—	7,030
—	2,362	2,362	—	—	—	2,362
260	18,514	21,349	21	5	26	21,375
205	859	2,561	1,740	1,577	3.317	5,878
1,078	4,504	13,433	265	734	999	14,432
610	2,548	11,774	—	—	—	11,774
103	430	1,282	84	339	423	1,705
67	281	838	52	879	931	1,769
3	15	45	19	3,990	4,009	4,054
39	163	484	69	1,312	1,381	1,865
232	971	2,896	221	221	442	3,338
461	1,927	5,746	305	409	714	6,460
—	—	—	262	—	262	262
10	42	125	376	241	617	742
4,971	47,598	93,641	7,095	13,702	20,797	114,438
56	234	697	198	80	278	975
5,027	47,832	94,338	7,293	13,782	21,075	115,413

able market values and all debt investments be reported at fair market value. The resulting unrealized gains and losses are reported in the statement of activities. Gains and losses on investments, along with dividend and interest income, are reported as increases or decreases in unrestricted net assets, unless the income is explicitly restricted by the donor or by a law that extends a donor's restrictions to them. Save-the-Children reports *investment income and net gains* of $1,617,000 for the year ended September 30, 1996. Of this amount, $130,000 is temporarily restricted and the remainder is unrestricted.

Statement of Functional Expense

Exhibit 19–3 presents the statement of functional expense for Save the Children Federation. Because contributors are concerned with how their gifts are used, this statement provides a detailed analysis of expenses by both function and object. The columns represent functions and include five programs as well as the supporting services of management and fund-raising. These are the same programs reported on the statement of activities, and column totals agree with operating expenses reported on the statement of activities. The rows list expenses according to their nature; for example, salaries, supplies, travel, and depreciation.

Allocations of joint costs between functions is permitted, although the practice is sometimes controversial, particularly when fund-raising costs are allocated to program services.[3] From an accounting perspective, the rationale for allocating joint costs is easy to understand. If both a program service and supporting service are being carried out by a single cost, it should be divided between them in some manner. Unfortunately, a few charities use allocations for the purpose of reducing the fund-raising cost amount. Some charities report an additional program service with a title such as professional or public education. Direct mail and other solicitation costs are charged partially to program services and justified on the basis that educational materials were included with the request for funds. By allocating part of the costs of solicitation to educational services, the charity is able to report a smaller amount as the cost of its fund-raising activities.

ACCOUNTING FOR CONTRIBUTIONS

Contributions are a major source of support for many not-for-profits. *FASB Statement 116* defines contributions as unconditional transfers of cash or other resources to an entity in a voluntary nonreciprocal transaction. According to *Statement 116*, contributions are recognized as revenue in the period received at their fair market value. Conditional promises to give are not recognized as revenue until the conditions are met. Conditions, however, are different from restrictions. Conditional promises require some future action on the part of the not-for-profit organization before the asset will be transferred and are not recognized as revenue until the condition is met. Restricted contributions specify how the contributions are expected to be used and are recognized as permanently or temporarily restricted revenue when the promise is received.

Cash is not the only type of support received by not-for-profits. Many organizations receive donations of materials intended either to be used by the charity itself (such as vehicles, office furniture, and computers) or distributed to needy groups or individuals (food, clothing, and toys). For organizations such as the Salvation Army and Goodwill Industries, these donations provide a central resource essential to the charity's ongoing operations.

Because donated supplies and other materials provide support for the organization, these contributions should be reported. The 1996 accounting and audit guide, *Not-for-Profit Organizations*, requires contributions of goods to be recorded as support unless they cannot be used or sold by the organization. Although a value is sometimes apparent (for example, if a new vehicle is given), donations such as used clothing, furniture, and toys can be difficult to assess. In such cases, the guide allows the use of estimates and averages, provided they reasonably approximate the results of detailed measurements.

Assume, as an illustration, that a local voluntary health and welfare organization begins a drive to gather furniture and clothing for needy families living in the area. The following items are received:

Bed	$200 fair market value
Tables and chairs	130 fair market value
New clothing	500 fair market value
Used clothing	75 estimated resale value
Total	$905

In addition, one merchant donates a new desk (with an established sales price of $400) for use in the organization's office. Assume that the furniture and clothing are distributed to needy individuals as soon as they are received. The following journal entries would be recorded by the not-for-profit organization:

---

[3]Rhonda L. Rundle, "A Crackdown on 'Charity' Sweepstakes," *The Wall Street Journal*, March 6, 1989, p. B1.

Inventory of Donated Materials   905
     Unrestricted Support—Contributions   905
    Gifts made to organization to be distributed to needy individuals.

Community Service Expenses—Assistance to Needy   905
     Inventory of Donated Materials   905
    Distribution of furniture and clothing to needy individuals.

Furniture—Office   400
     Unrestricted Support—Contributions   400
    Organization received donated office furniture; the asset will be
    depreciated over estimated useful life.

Donations of Works of Art and Historical Treasures

In 1990, the FASB issued an exposure draft that would have required all contributions, including art works and museum pieces, to be recorded as assets with a corresponding increase in revenues. Perhaps no accounting proposal ever put forth created such adverse public reaction. The FASB was deluged with more than 1,000 letters, virtually all of them in opposition. The argument against recognizing *additions to collections* is that the contribution does not provide the same kinds of benefits as contributions of cash or investments. Items held for research or public exhibit create little or no direct increase in cash flows. Thus, they are not assets in the traditional sense. Opponents of the exposure draft argued that recognizing donations as revenues would mislead potential donors who were evaluating the operating results of the organization.

The opposition apparently influenced the Board, because *Statement No. 116* exempted gifts of art works, historical treasures, and similar assets. Recognition of these contributions is not required if (1) they are added to a collection for public exhibition, education, or research; (2) they are protected and preserved; and (3) they are ever sold, any receipts will be used to acquire other collection items.

Unconditional Promises to Give

Statement 116 requires recognizing pledges and other unconditional promises to give as receivables in the period pledged. The 1996 accounting and auditing guide, *Not-for-Profit Organizations*, provides guidance for distinguishing between unconditional promises to give and *intentions* to give. In particular, pledge statements that allow donors to change their minds are intentions to give and not recorded until they become unconditional or the contribution is received.

Because contribution revenue is recognized at fair-market value, the estimated uncollectible portion of pledged amounts should be deducted from contribution revenue and an allowance account established to present the receivable at expected *net realizable value*. Additionally, promises that are not expected to be collected within a year are discounted to present value using an appropriate interest rate, such as the organization's incremental borrowing rate or rate of return on its investment portfolio.[4]

Contributed Services

Donated services are an especially significant means of support for many not-for-profits. The number of volunteers working in some organizations can reach into the thousands. Charities rely heavily on these individuals to fill administrative positions as well as to service fund-raising and program activities.

Contributed services are recognized as revenue if the service (1) creates or enhances a nonfinancial asset, or (2) requires a specialized skill possessed by the

---

[4]AICPA audit and accounting guide, *Not-for-Profit Organizations*, 1994.

contributor and would have had to be purchased if not donated. Examples of the first type include donated labor by carpenters, electricians, and masons. The fair value of the services received would be recognized as an increase in both fixed assets and revenue. Examples of the second type include contributed legal or accounting services and would be recognized as both an expense and revenue when contributed. Contributed services (such as volunteer servers at a soup kitchen) that fail to meet these criteria are not recognized as revenue. This is not because the services have no value, but because of the difficulty in measuring their fair value.

Assume that a certified public accountant donated accounting services that would have cost a local charity $2,000 if not donated. Further, assume that a carpenter donated materials ($4,000) and labor ($3,500) to construct an addition to the charity's facilities. The following journal entries would be recorded by the not-for-profit organization:

General and Administrative Expenses—Accounting Services	2,000	
Unrestricted Support—Contributed Services		2,000
Contribution of professional services.		

Buildings and Improvements	7,500	
Unrestricted Support—Contributed Services		3,500
Unrestricted Support—Contributed Materials		4,000
Contribution of professional services and materials.		

Exchange Transactions

Exchange transactions are *reciprocal* transfers where both parties give and receive something of value. All or a portion of membership dues are frequently reciprocal transfers; the member typically receives benefits in the form of newsletters, journals, and use of organization facilities and services. Because these transactions do not meet the definition of a contribution, they follow normal accrual basis accounting and are recognized as revenue when earned. In contrast to contributions, reciprocal transfers received in advance are recorded as unearned revenue, a liability, rather than as revenue.[5] For example, assume a not-for-profit association received $5,000 in dues for the next fiscal year and that membership dues are deemed to be a reciprocal transaction because members receive a journal and other organization publications. The journal entry to record the receipt would be as follows:

Cash	5,000	
Unearned Revenue—Membership Dues		5,000
Collection of dues for the next fiscal year.		

In the next year, the following journal entry would be made:

Unearned Revenue—Membership Dues	5,000	
Revenue—Membership Dues		5,000
Recognition of dues earned in the current period, but collected in the previous year.		

TYPICAL JOURNAL ENTRIES

The following transactions demonstrate some typical journal entries for a private not-for-profit. Since *FASB Statement 117* does not require using a fund basis, it is not necessary to record transactions in separate funds. However, many not-for-profits choose to use a fund format for internal management purposes and frequently design

---

[5]Guidance for determining how much of a member's dues are contributions is provided in the AICPA accounting and audit guide, *Not-for-Profit Organizations*. For example, membership dues have characteristics of an exchange transaction if nonmembers can obtain similar benefits for a fee.

their general ledger using separate funds. *FASB Statement 117* permits reporting by funds as supplemental information, provided all interfund transactions are eliminated.[6]

Assume Shenandoah Seminary, a private college, began the year 1998 with unrestricted net assets of $1,250,000 and a permanent endowment of $700,000. During 1998 the seminary received the following contributions from alumni and friends:

Unrestricted pledges due within 12 months	$130,000
Cash contributions to the endowment	50,000

The seminary estimated that it will collect 85 percent of the unrestricted pledges and made the following entry:

1. Cash	50,000	
Pledges Receivable	130,000	
Allowance for Uncollectible Pledges		19,500
Unrestricted Support—Contributions		110,500
Restricted Support—Contributions		50,000
To record contributions received.		

Before the end of the fiscal period, the seminary collected $100,000 of the amount pledged and $5,000 of the pledges were written off, as reflected in this journal entry:

2. Cash	100,000	
Allowance for Uncollectible Pledges	5,000	
Pledges Receivable		105,000
To record pledges collected and written off.		

In addition, the seminary collected tuition of $500,000 and an additional $20,000 restricted by an outside donor to be used to support a series of lectures by visiting scholars. The seminary would make the following journal entry:

3. Cash	520,000	
Tuition Revenue		500,000
Restricted Support—Contributions		20,000
To record tuition and restricted contributions.		

The seminary incurred liabilities of $640,000 ($575,000 for operating expenses and $65,000 for equipment). Of this, $625,000 was paid before year-end. The seminary would make the following journal entries:

4. Instruction Expenses	250,000	
Student Services Expenses	120,000	
Scholarships	15,000	
Maintenance Expense	75,000	
Administrative Expenses	115,000	
Accounts Payable		575,000
To record expenses for the year.		

5. Equipment	65,000	
Accounts Payable		65,000
To record purchases of equipment.		

6. Accounts Payable	625,000	
Cash		625,000
To record partial payment of outstanding accounts payable.		

---

[6]The American Accounting Association's 1996 Annual Report presented the association's financial position and results of operations using *FASB Statement 117*. In a supporting schedule, however, the association elected to report balances and activity for four fund categories.

Depreciation on buildings and equipment amounted to $135,000 for the year, as shown in the following journal entry:

7. Depreciation Expense—Instruction	80,000		
Depreciation Expense—Student Services	20,000		
Depreciation Expense—Adminstration	35,000		
Accumulated Depreciation, Buildings, and Equipment		135,000	
To record depreciation on fixed assets.			

Closing Entry

The year-end closing entry must reflect the changes in net assets within the three categories of net assets. In preparing the closing entry, not-for-profits consider any temporarily restricted resources that may have been released from restriction through performance of some activity or the passage of time. Assume that the instructional expenses include $15,500 of expenses relating to the series of lectures by visiting scholars. The following table summarizes changes in unrestricted, temporarily restricted, and permanently restricted net assets for the year:

Calculation of Change in Net Assets

Journal Entry	Unrestricted Net Assets	Temporarily Restricted Net Assets	Permanently Restricted Net Assets
1	$ 110,500		$50,000
3	500,000	$ 20,000	
4	(575,000)		
7	(135,000)		
Net assets released from restriction	15,500	(15,500)	
Increase (decrease) in net assets	$ (84,000)	$ 4,500	$50,000

Because all expenses are reflected as a decrease in unrestricted net assets, the $15,500 decrease in temporarily restricted net assets is added to unrestricted net assets. Journal entries 2, 5, and 6 are not reflected in the preceding table because they did not change the seminary's net assets. As a result of the transactions summarized in the preceding table, the seminary would record this closing entry:

Unrestricted Support—Contributions	110,500	
Restricted Support—Contributions	70,000	
Tuition Revenue	500,000	
Unrestricted Net Assets	84,000	
Temporarily Restricted Net Assets		4,500
Permanently Restricted Net Assets		50,000
Instruction Expenses		330,000
Student Services Expenses		140,000
Scholarships		15,000
Maintenance Expense		75,000
Administrative Expenses		150,000
To close revenues, support, and expenses to appropriate net asset accounts.		

The financial statements and journal entries in the preceding sections describe features common to the various types of private not-for-profit organizations. The following section describes the financial reporting features unique to health care organizations.

ACCOUNTING FOR HEALTH CARE ORGANIZATIONS

From a quantitative perspective, the providers of health care services are quite prevalent throughout the United States with many thousands of institutions in operation; virtually every city and town has hospitals, nursing homes, and medical clinics. The large number of enterprises is not surprising; health care expenditures now make up more than 12 percent of the gross national product in this country.[7]

One major factor influencing the financial reporting of health care organizations is the presence of third-party payors such as insurance companies, Medicare, Medicaid, and Blue Cross/Blue Shield. These organizations, rather than the individual patient, pay all or some of the cost of medical services received. For example, third-party payors may be responsible for more than 90 percent of the fees from hospital care. Because of the significant monetary amounts involved, third-party payors are constantly seeking reliable financial data, especially concerning the costs of patient care. Auditors also are concerned because third-party payors retroactively adjust payment rates as allowable costs are determined. Frequently the final settlements are determined after year-end.

Financial Reporting by Health Care Organizations

Because of the unique nature of the health care industry, specialized reporting standards have been developed. In 1996 the AICPA issued two audit and accounting guides in response to *FASB Statement Nos. 116* and *117*. *Not-for-Profit Organizations* provides guidance for the audits and financial reporting of not-for-profit entities except for not-for-profit providers of health care services. The AICPA audit and accounting guide, *Health Care Organizations*, provides guidance for hospitals, HMOs, nursing homes, laboratories, and group or individual medical practices. Not limited to not-for-profit organizations, this guide provides accounting standards for these three classes of health care providers:

1. *Investor-owned health care enterprises.* Owned by investors or medical practitioners, these businesses provide goods or services to make a profit. Like other business enterprises, the financial reporting for these entities follows FASB statements other than those statements relating exclusively to not-for-profits.

2. *Not-for-profit organizations.* Not owned by investors or by governments these organizations receive some contributions, but for the most part they are self-sustaining from the fees charged for goods and services. Like other not-for-profit entities, their financial reporting follows *FASB Statements 116* and *117* for not-for-profits and other applicable FASB statements.

3. *Governmental health care organizations.* These organizations are either controlled by governments or meet the definition of a governmental entity. Like other governmental organizations, they follow GASB reporting standards. Because these entities are typically treated as enterprise funds, they use accrual basis measurement and reporting. Unlike government-owned colleges and universities, the financial reports of government-owned health care organizations are similar to those of private not-for-profits.

Identifying the type of health care organization is necessary because various types use different accounting standards. For example, *FASB Statement 95* and *GASB Statement 9* establish standards for the statement of cash flows. Hospitals operated by state or local governments would prepare cash flow statements with the four category format of *GASB Statement 9*. Meanwhile, private not-for-profit hospitals and for-profit hospitals would prepare cash flow statements with the three category format of *FASB Statement 95*.

Despite the differences in the ownership and purpose of various types of health care organizations, all three types use accrual accounting in recording both revenues

---

[7]Leon E. Hay and John Engstrom, *Essentials of Accounting for Governmental and Not-for-Profit Organizations,* 4th ed. (Burr Ridge, IL: Richard D. Irwin, 1996), p. 246.

and expenses. In addition, they calculate and recognize depreciation expense each year for all buildings, equipment, and other long-lived assets (other than land). Because of these procedures, the reporting process used by health care organizations resembles that of commercial enterprises.

The most apparent difference between the three types of organizations is in the equity section of the statement of financial position. The equities of investor-owned health care enterprises include common stock and retained earnings. The difference between total assets and total liabilities of private not-for-profit enterprises is reflected in unrestricted, temporarily restricted, and permanently restricted net assets. The equity section of government-owned health care organizations includes unrestricted and restricted fund balances.

Regardless of the type of health care organization, the 1996 AICPA audit and accounting guide requires these four basic financial statements:[8]

- Balance sheet.
- Statement of operations.
- Statement of changes in equity (or net assets/fund balance).
- Statement of cash flows.

The Statement of operations for private not-for-profit organizations follows *FASB Statement 117* requirements for reporting changes in unrestricted net assets. Changes in temporarily restricted and permanently restricted net assets are included on the statement of changes in net assets. A statement of operations and a statement of changes in net assets are illustrated in Exhibit 19–4.

Generally the accounting for not-for-profit health care organizations resembles that of charities and other private not-for-profit organizations. However, health care organizations have particular requirements for the display of items within the statement of operations. Many of these requirements resulting from the unique nature of health care organizations are described in the following sections.

Accounting for Patient Service Revenues

The largest source of revenues normally comes from patient services. These include fees for surgery, nursing services, medicine, laboratory work, X rays, blood, housing, food, and so forth.

Patient (or Resident) Service Revenues and Reductions   For a variety of reasons, health care entities (especially hospitals) often receive less than the total payment normally charged for patient services. Bad debts as well as other fee reductions can be significant. One survey indicated that the median in the state of Virginia is the collection of only 68 percent of hospital charges because of bad debts, charity care, and discounts.[9] *However, to provide complete financial data about the operations of the organization, revenues are still recorded at standard rates if the intention of full collection is present.*

Assume, for example, that patient charges for the current month at a local hospital total $750,000. Of this amount, $170,000 is due from patients with the remaining $580,000 billed to third-party payors: Medicare, Medicaid, Blue Cross/Blue Shield, and various insurance companies. Regardless of expected receipts, the hospital should record revenues through the following journal entry:

Accounts Receivable—Third-Party Payors	580,000	
Accounts Receivable—Patients	170,000	
Patient Service Revenues		750,000
To accrue patient charges for current month.		

---

[8]AICPA audit and accounting guide, *Health Care Organizations*, 1996, paragraph 1.05.

[9]Beverly Orndorff. "Report Shows Case Mix Affects Hospital Costs," *Richmond Times-Dispatch*, October 20, 1990, p. C1.

Exhibit 19–4

MEMORIAL HOSPITAL: A NOT-FOR-PROFIT HOSPITAL
Statement of Operations
Year Ended December 31, 1997
(in thousands)

Unrestricted revenues, gains, and other support:	
Net patient service revenue	$76,100
Cafeteria, gift shop revenue	12,000
Unrestricted investment income	5,000
Net assets released from restrictions used for medical research	300
Total revenues, gains, and other support	93,400
Expenses:	
Salaries and benefits	52,000
Medical supplies and medicines	15,000
Depreciation and amortization	7,000
Interest	2,000
Provision for bad debts	9,000
Other	4,000
Total expenses	89,000
Excess of revenues, gains, and other support over expenses	4,400
Change in net unrealized gains and losses on other than trading securities	(500)
Increase in unrestricted net assets	$ 3,900

Statement of Changes in Net Assets
Year Ended December 31, 1997
(in thousands)

Unrestricted net assets:	
Excess of revenues over expenses	$ 4,400
Net unrealized losses on investments, other than trading securities	(500)
Increase in unrestricted net assets	3,900
Temporarily restricted net assets:	
Contributions for medical research	500
Net assets released from restrictions	(300)
Increase (decrease) in temporarily restricted net assets	200
Permanently restricted net assets:	
Contributions for endowment funds	150
Net realized and unrealized gains on investments	20
Increase in permanently restricted net assets	170
Increase in net assets	4,270
Net assets—beginning of year	22,000
Net assets—end of year	$26,270

The entire $750,000 is initially reported as patient service revenue by this hospital although complete collection is doubtful. This approach is considered the best method of allowing the hospital to monitor activities during the period.

To continue with this illustration. assume that $20,000 of patient receivables are estimated to be uncollectible. Furthermore, not-for-profit hospitals and other similar entities often make no serious attempt to collect amounts owed by indigent patients. In many cases, these facilities were originally created to serve the poor. Assume, therefore, that $18,000 of the accounts receivable will never be collected because several patients earn incomes at or below the poverty level. Thus, to mirror these anticipated revenue reductions, the hospital records two additional entries. Of the S170,000 due from patients, collection of $38,000 is not expected.

As shown here, the handling of the two reductions is not the same. The bad debts create an expense but the revenue and receivable for the charity care are removed entirely. The AICPA audit and accounting guide holds that no reporting should be made if the entity has no intention of making the collection.

Bad Debt Expense	20,000	
Allowance for Uncollectible and Reduced Accounts		20,000

To record estimation of receivables that will prove to be uncollectible.

Patient Service Revenues	18,000	
Accounts Receivable—Third-Party Payors		18,000

To remove accounts that will not be collected because patients' earned income is at the poverty level.

Contractural Agreements with Third-Party Payors The adjustments just recorded reflect amounts that will not be collected from patients. An additional reduction is usually encountered but only in connection with receivables due from third-party payors. Organizations such as Medicare and Blue Cross/Blue Shield often establish contractual arrangements with health care providers stipulating that set rates are to be paid for specific services. The entity agrees, in effect, to accept *as payment in full* an amount computed by the third-party payor as reasonable (based frequently on the average cost within the locality for the service rendered). Thus, although a patient is charged $3,000, for example. the health care entity might collect only $2,700 (or some other total) from a third-party payor if the lower figure is determined to be an appropriate cost. The remaining $300 must be written off by the hospital and is commonly referred to as a *contractual adjustment*.

Some third-party payors have switched in recent years to an alternative method of determining the amount to be paid: prospective payment plans. Under this system, reimbursement is not based on the cost of the health services being provided but on the diagnosis of the patient's illness or injury. Thus, if a patient has a broken leg, as an example, the hospital would be entitled to a set reimbursement regardless of the actual expense incurred.

Such plans were developed in an attempt to encourage a reduction in medical costs since no additional charge is collected if a patient remains in a hospital longer than necessary. "Intent on controlling rampant increases in Medicare spending, [the federal government] implemented a prospective payment system (PPS) in 1983. Under this plan hospitals are paid a predetermined amount per case. Since that time, more and more third-party payors have followed suit, limiting in advance what they'll pay for healthcare services."[10]

In many cases, the health care entity is not certain of the amount to be collected under these reimbursement plans. The AICPA audit and accounting guide (paragraph 1.11) requires that this amount be estimated and any reductions recognized in the same period as the patient service revenue. "Consequently, a reasonable estimate of the amount receivable from or payable to these payors should be made in the same period that the related services are rendered."

In the example just presented, the hospital probably does not anticipate collecting the entire $580,000 billed to third-party payors. Assume, for illustration purposes, that this hospital projects only $520,000 of the $580,000 charge will actually be received. To establish a proper value for the hospital's revenues, another $60,000 adjustment must be recorded.

Contractual Adjustments	60,000	
Allowance for Uncollectible and Reduced Accounts		60.000

To recognize estimated reduction in patient billings because of contractual arrangements made with third-party payors.

---

[10]Richard G. Kleiner, Martha Garner, and Robin G. Colbert, "A Preview of the New Healthcare Audit Guide." *Journal of Accountancy*, September 1989, p. 33.

To determine the exact amount to be paid (especially under cost-reimbursement plans), the health care entity's costs are usually subject to audit by the third-party payors. Although payment is normally made currently, adjustments may be made later based on this examination. Thus, a facility might receive additional payments at a later date or be required to make reimbursements based on subsequent cost calculations made by the third-party payor. In 1990, St. Mary's Hospital of Richmond explained this arrangement through the following financial statement footnote (number 8):

> The Hospital participates in the Medicare and Medicaid Programs. . . . Payment rates for inpatient services provided to program beneficiaries are governed by the applicable regulations and implementation provisions thereunder, based generally on prospectively determined rates using clinical, diagnostic and other factors. However, services such as skilled nursing and certain outpatient services and capital costs are subject to cost-based reimbursement principles, subject to certain limitations. . . . *Programs utilizing cost based reimbursement principles are subject to review and final determination by appropriate program representatives.* (emphasis added)

Thus, some amounts to be collected are based on cost figures developed by the hospital and subject to audit by the payor at a later time. Consequently, current payments may either be increased or decreased in a subsequent year. Under that circumstance, a question must be addressed: should any differences that arise between the expected collection and the final total be carried back to the period of accrual to correct the originally recorded contractual adjustment? If the hospital in the previous example recognizes a $60,000 contractual adjustment because it expects to collect $520,000, what accounting is made if the correct amount is ultimately determined to be only $509,000?

As no error has occurred in an accounting sense, GAAP is followed; any change needed to alter the initial estimation is recorded in the subsequent year. A prior period adjustment would not be considered appropriate.

> Although final settlements are not made until a subsequent period, they are usually subject to reasonable estimations and are reported in the financial statements in the period in which services are rendered. Differences between original estimates reported in the financial statements and subsequent revisions, final settlements, are included in the statement of operations in the period in which the revisions are made.[11]

Assume that in the previous illustration $520,000 is collected as anticipated. However, in the subsequent year, an audit of the hospital's costs by a third-party payor indicates that only $509,000 was appropriate. Thus, an $11,000 reimbursement from the hospital would now be required. Although this change relates to the first time period, no retroactive restatement is permitted.

Initial Period

Cash	520,000	
Allowance for Uncollectible and Reduced Accounts	60,000	
Accounts Receivable—Third-Party Payor		580,000

To record collection from third party based on initial analysis of costs.

Subsequent Period

Allowance for Uncollectible and Reduced Accounts (or Contractual Adjustments)......................................	11,000	
Cash		11,000

To record reimbursement paid to third-party payor based on audit indicating that costs were too high.

---

[11]AICPA Audits, par. 5.07.

Reductions—Financial Statement Presentation   The AICPA audit and accounting guide requires that bad debts be shown as expenses rather than as reductions to patient service revenues. Furthermore, charity care deductions are not recorded at all if the health care entity has no intention of collecting, Finally, contractual adjustments reduce patient service revenues but are not shown explicitly on the financial statements. Rather, patient service revenues are shown as a net figure after removing all such reductions. Since the entity has little chance of collecting the entire balance, reporting total revenues could mislead readers. "Increasing amounts of hospital revenue no longer bear any relationship to established charges. Consequently, gross patient service revenue (that is, the hospitals' charges) has come to have little meaning for financial statement users."[12] Thus, if an organization charges $10 million but anticipates contractual adjustments of $3 million, the statement of revenues and expenses would report net patient service revenues of $7 million.

Accounting for Other Revenues and Contribution

As previously noted, patient service revenues is just one of the revenue categories utilized by a health care entity. The proceeds from gift shops, cafeterias, educational programs, snack bars, newsstands, and parking lots, are all recorded under this heading. Also included in other revenues would be the fair market value of any donated medicines, linen, office supplies, or other materials if used in the major and central activities of the hospital.

To illustrate the accounting for such contributions, assume that a gift of medicine (with a value of $10,000) is made to a nursing home by an outside party. The first of the following journal entries records the receipt of this donation while the second presents the eventual usage of this asset.

Initial Entry

Drugs and Medicine	10,000	
Other Revenues—Donations		10,000
To record gift of medicines.		

Subsequent Entry

Supplies and Other Expenses	10,000	
Drugs and Medicines		10,000
To record use of medicines that had been donated to the nursing home.		

Additional sources of other revenues are the designated grants and gifts often received by hospitals and other health care entities. The accounting for these contributions follows *FASB Statement 116*, "Accounting for Contributions Received and Contributions Made." It requires contributions to be recognized at their fair market value when the contribution is made.

Donated Services   Health care entities have traditionally reported the value of services voluntarily provided as nonoperating gains. However, because guidelines in this area were vague, accounting procedures have tended to vary among organizations. A consistent method of reporting is an important issue because the volume of such contributions can be quite significant. In one study, approximately 90 percent of the not-for-profit hospitals surveyed indicated the utilization of contributed services. Of this group, 88 percent estimated that *more than 10,000 hours of such services were received each year.*[13]

---

[12]"Preview," p. 41.

[13]Jane B. Adams, Ronald J. Bossio, and Paul Rohan, *Accounting for Contributed Services: Survey of Preparers and Users of Financial Statements of Not-for-Profit Organizations* (New York: FASB, 1989), pp. 7–8.

As discussed earlier in the chapter, the FASB now requires the recognition of contributions by *private* not-for-profit organizations. The FASB has stated that donated services should be recognized if the services received either create or enhance nonfinancial assets or require specialized skills, are provided by individuals possessing those skills, and would need to be purchased if not provided by donation.[14]

Accounting for Pledges

As with a college or university, a health care entity frequently receives a verbal commitment or pledge of a gift or grant from a donor prior to the physical transfer of assets. *FASB Statement No. 116* requires that a receivable be immediately recorded if the promise is an unconditional promise to give. Because of the inherent uncertainty involved in collecting such receivables, an adequate provision for doubtful accounts also must be established. If the pledge is to be collected during a future period, the amount should be recorded at a discounted present value. In recording a pledge where the eventual use of the money is specified by the donor, the receivable should be presented with an increase to the temporarily or permanently restricted net asset category.

Donor Restrictions

Historically, both government-owned and private not-for-profit health care organizations used fund accounting. *FASB Statement 117* does not preclude organizations from using funds for internal purposes and many private not-for-profits continue to use funds for management and control purposes. However, for purposes of external reporting, each of the internal funds must be categorized as unrestricted net assets, temporarily restricted net assets, or permanently restricted net assets. As discussed earlier in the chapter, restricted net assets must have donor imposed restrictions. Temporarily restricted net assets are released from restriction either by the passage of time or by actions taken by the organization, such as use of the funds for the purpose intended. Permanently restricted net assets (such as endowments) are not released from restriction as long as the not-for-profit controls the asset.

In contrast, government-owned organizations continue to use fund accounting for both internal and external reporting purposes. The funds used by health care organizations fall into two categories: general funds and donor-restricted funds. Donor-restricted funds maintain a record of resources given by outside parties for a stipulated purpose.

Unlike governmental and public university accounting, government-owned health care organizations record all unrestricted transactions in their general funds. This includes the issuance and payment of long-term liabilities, purchases of land, buildings and equipment, and depreciation on fixed assets. The general funds of government-owned health care organizations resemble the enterprise funds of state and local governments.

Donor-restricted funds of government-owned health care organizations include:

Specific Purpose Funds   Specific purpose funds account for any donation or grant made to a government-owned health care entity for a stipulated operating purpose, such as financing a research project.

Plant Replacement and Expansion Funds   Plant replacement and expansion funds record any monetary resource given to a government-owned health care entity with

---

[14]*FASB Statement of Financial Accounting Standards No. 116*, "Accounting for Contributions Received and Contributions Made," par. 9.

DISCUSSION QUESTION

Is This Really an Asset?

Mercy Hospital is located near Springfield, Missouri. The hospital was created over 70 years ago by a religious organization to meet the needs of area residents who could not otherwise afford adequate health care. Although the hospital is open to the public in general, its primary mission has always been to provide medical services for the poor.

On December 23, 1997, a gentleman told the hospital's chief administrative officer the following story: "My mother has been in your hospital since October 30. The doctors have just told me that she will soon be well and can go home. I cannot tell you how relieved I am. The doctors, the nurses, and your entire staff have been just wonderful; my mother could not have gotten better care. She owes her life to your hospital.

"I am from Idaho. Now that my mother is on the road to recovery, I must return immediately to my business. I am in the process of attempting to sell an enormous tract of land in Idaho. When this acreage is sold, I will receive $15 million in cash. Because of the services that Mercy Hospital has provided for my mother, I want to make a donation of $5 million of this money." The gentlemen proceeded to write this promise on a piece of stationery that he dated and signed.

Obviously, all of the hospital's officials were overwhelmed by the gentleman's generosity. This $5 million gift was 50 times larger than the biggest gift ever received. However, the controller was a bit concerned about preparing the financial statements for 1997. "I have a lot of problems with recording this type of donation as an asset. At present, we are having serious cash flow problems; but if we show $5 million in this manner, our normal donors are going to think we have become rich and don't need their support."

What problems are involved in accounting for the $5 million pledge and how should the amount be reported by Mercy Hospital?

the provision that the asset must be spent on land, buildings, equipment, or retirement of capital debt.

Endowment Funds   Endowment funds record assets donated with the stipulation that only subsequently earned income may be spent.

SUMMARY

1. *FASB Statement No. 117* establishes reporting requirements for private not-for-profit organizations. The intent is to provide financial statement users, including contributors, an overall view of the organization's financial position and results of operations.

2. The required financial statements for not-for-profit organizations include: statement of financial position, statement of cash flows, and statement of activity and changes in net assets. Voluntary health and welfare organizations also are required to issue statements of functional expense.

3. The statements must distinguish between assets, liabilities, revenues, and expenses that are permanently restricted, temporarily restricted, and unrestricted. Such restrictions are donor-imposed. Temporarily restricted assets are expected to be released from restriction due to the passage of time or the performance of some act by the not-for-profit. Permanently restricted net assets are expected to be restricted for as long as the organization exists.

4. Expenses should be reported by their functional classification such as major classes of program services and supporting services. Program services are goods or services provided to beneficiaries or customers that fulfill the purpose or mission of the organization. Supporting services are general administration, fund-raising, and membership development.

5. *FASB Statement 116* establishes accounting and reporting requirements for contributions. Contributions are unconditional transfers of cash or other resources to an entity in a voluntary nonreciprocal transaction.

6. Contributions received by not-for-profit organizations, including unconditional written or oral promises to give, are recognized as revenues or support in the period received at their fair-market value. Contributions made to not-for-profit organizations (generally by for-profit organizations) including unconditional promises to give, are recognized as expenses in the period made at their fair market value.

7. Not-for-profit organizations must distinguish between contributions that are permanently restricted, temporarily restricted, and unrestricted. Such restrictions are donor-imposed.

8. Contributed services are recognized as revenues or support if they either create or enhance nonfinancial assets or require a specialized skill (e.g., accountant, architect, nurse) and would have to be purchased if not provided by donation.

9. Health care organizations fall into three types: First, investor-owned health care enterprises that follow FASB accounting and reporting standards other than those standards relating exclusively to not-for-profits. Second, private, not-for-profit health care organizations that follow *FASB Statements 116* and *117* for not-for-profits and other applicable FASB statements. Third, governmental health care organizations that follow GASB reporting standards.

10. The required financial statements for health care organizations include the statement of financial position, statement of cash flows, and statement of operations, and statement of changes in equity, net assets, or fund balance. The form of the last statement depends on the type of health care organization.

11. Health care organizations frequently receive less than the full amount of patient charges. Contractual adjustments with third-party payors are shown as a deduction from revenue in reporting *net patient service revenue*. Bad debts are estimated and reported as an expense. Charity care charges are not recorded as revenue.

COMPREHENSIVE ILLUSTRATION

Problem

(Estimated time: 30 to 45 minutes) Augusta Regional Hospital is a private not-for-profit hospital offering medical care to a variety of patients, including some with no ability to pay for the services received. In addition, the hospital sponsors a consortium on childhood diseases with the financial support of a private foundation. The hospital maintains an endowment, the principal of which must be maintained, but the earnings are available to provide charity care. During 1998, the hospital has the following financial transactions:

1. The hospital rendered $900,000 in services to patients, of which $700,000 is charged to third-party payors. The administration estimates that only $750,000 will be collected. Of the $150,000 difference, $85,000 is estimated contractual allowances with insurance and Medicare providers, $20,000 is charity care, and $45,000, estimated bad debts.

2. Payment of $105,000 is received from 1997 charges made to third-party payors. Originally, these groups had been billed $127,000, but subsequent audits indicated that the lower amount constituted reasonable costs for the services. The hospital originally estimated in 1997 that collection would be $107,000.

3. A local business donated linens with a fair value $3,000.

4. Cafeteria sales to nonpatients and gift shop receipts totaled $76,000.

5. The hospital incurred expenses of $12,000 in connection with the childhood disease consortium. Funding for this consortium had been received in 1997.

6. The hospital received unrestricted, unconditional pledges of $12,500. The administration expects only 80 percent of these to be collected. In addition, securities with a market value of $8,000 were received and designated for the endowment.

7. A computer consultant donated his services to upgrade several of the hospital's computer systems. The value of these services was $3,000 and would have been acquired if not donated.

8. The hospital incurred the following liabilities:
   $102,000 for purchase of supplies
   $699,000 for salaries
   $50,000 for purchase of equipment

9. End of year adjustment included supplies expense of $99,000 and depreciation expense of $72,000.

Required

a. Prepare the journal entries for these transactions.
b. Prepare a schedule showing the change in unrestricted, temporarily restricted, and permanently restricted net assets.
c. Prepare the closing entry.

Solution

1.	Accounts Receivable—Patients	200,000	
	Accounts Receivable—Third-Party Payors	700,000	
	Patient Service Revenues		900,000
	To accrue billings for the current period.		
	Contractual Adjustments	85,000	
	Allowance for Contractual Adjustment		85,000
	To recognize estimated amounts not expected to be collected from third-party payors.		
	Patient Service Revenue	20,000	
	Accounts Receivable—Patients		20,000
	To remove amount for charity care where no intention exists to collect.		
	Bad Debt Expense	45,000	
	Allowance for Uncollectible Accounts		45,000
	To recognize estimated amounts not expected to be collected from patients.		
2.	Cash	105,000	
	Allowance for Contractual Adjustment	22,000	
	Accounts Receivable—Third-Party Payors		127,000
	To record collection of prior year receivables after reduction for contractual adjustments.		
3.	Inventory of Supplies	3,000	
	Other Revenues—Unrestricted Contributions		3,000
	To recognize fair value of donated items.		
4.	Cash	76,000	
	Other Revenues—Cafeteria and Shops		76,000
	To record cafeteria and shops revenue.		
5.	Consortium Expenses	12,000	
	Cash		12,000
	To record expenses in connection with the childhood disease consortium.		
6.	Pledges Receivable	12,500	
	Investments	8,000	
	Allowance for Uncollectible Pledges		2,500
	Other Revenues—Unrestricted Contributions		10,000
	Other Revenues—Restricted Contributions		8,000
	To record pledges and investments received at estimated fair value.		
7.	Expenses for Profession Services	3,000	
	Other Revenues—Unrestricted Contributions		3,000
	To record donated services.		

8. Supplies Inventory 102,000
   Equipment 50,000
       Accounts Payable 152,000
   To record goods received.

   Salaries Expense 699,000
       Accrued Salaries Payable 699,000
   To record salaries payable.

9. Supplies Expense 99,000
       Supplies Inventory 99,000
   To record supplies expense for the period.

   Depreciation Expense 72,000
       Accumulated Depreciation........................ 72,000
   To record depreciation expense for the period.

Calculation of Change in Net Assets

Journal Entry	Unrestricted Net Assets	Temporarily Restricted Net Assets	Permanently Restricted Net Assets
1	$ 900,000		
	(85,000)		
	(20,000)		
	(45,000)		
3	3,000		
4	76,000		
5	(12,000)		
6	10,000		$8,000
7	(3,000)		
	3,000		
8	(699,000)		
9	(99,000)		
	(72,000)		
Net assets released from restriction – childhood disease consortium	12,000	$(12,000)	
Increase (decrease) in net assets	$ (31,000)	$(12,000)	$8,000

Closing entry

Patient Service Revenues................................	880,000	
Other Revenues—Unrestricted Contributions	3,000	
Other Revenues—Cafeteria and Shops	76,000	
Other Revenues—Unrestricted Contributions	10,000	
Other Revenues—Restricted Contributions	8,000	
Other Revenues—Unrestricted Contributions	3,000	
Unrestricted Net Assets	*31,000*	
Temporarily Restricted Net Assets	*12,000*	
Permanently Restricted Net Assets.......................		*8,000*
Contractual Adjustments...............................		85,000
Bad Debt Expense		45,000
Consortium Expenses		12,000
Expenses for Profession Services......................		3,000
Salaries Expense		699,000
Supplies Expense		99,000
Depreciation Expense.................................		72,000

APPENDIX

Financial Statements for Private Not-for-Profit Colleges or Universities

Following are examples of the financial statements for private colleges and universities (and other private not-for-profit organizations) required by the FASB in its *Statement No. 117*, "Financial Statements of Not-for-Profit Organizations." The notes to these financial statements have not been included.

The FASB offered several formats for the statement of activities but only one has been included here. In addition, both the direct method and the indirect method were demonstrated for the statement of cash flows. The direct method is shown in Exhibit 19–7.

Exhibit 19–5

PRIVATE NOT-FOR-PROFIT COLLEGE OR UNIVERSITY
Statement of Financial Position
June 30, 1999 and 1998
(in thousands)

	1999	1998
Assets:		
Cash and cash equivalents	$ 75	$ 460
Accounts and interest receivable	2,130	1,670
Inventories and prepaid expenses	610	1,000
Contributions receivable	3,025	2,700
Short-term investments	1,400	1,000
Assets restricted to investment in land, buildings, and equipment	5,210	4,560
Land, buildings, and equipment	61,700	63,590
Long-term investments	218,070	203,500
Total assets	$292,220	$278,480
Liabilities and net assets:		
Accounts payable	$ 2,570	$ 1,050
Refundable advance	—	650
Grants payable	875	1,300
Notes payable	—	1,140
Annuity obligations	1,685	1,700
Long-term debt	5,500	6,500
Total liabilities	10,630	12,340
Net assets:		
Unrestricted	115,228	103,670
Temporarily restricted	24,342	25,470
Permanently restricted	142,020	137,000
Total net assets	281,590	266,140
Total liabilities and net assets	$292,220	$278,480

Exhibit 19–6

		PRIVATE NOT-FOR-PROFIT COLLEGE OR UNIVERSITY		
		Statement of Activities and Changes in Net Assets		
		Year Ended June 30, 1999		
		(in thousands)		

	Unrestricted	Temporarily Restricted	Permanently Restricted	Total
Revenues, gains, and other support:				
Contributions	$ 8,640	$ 8,110	$ 280	$ 17,030
Tuition and fees	5,400	—	—	5,400
Investment income on long-term investments	5,600	2,580	120	8,300
Other investment income	850	—	—	850
Net unrealized and realized gains on long-term investments	8,228	2,952	14,620	25,800
Other	150	—	—	150
	28,868	13,642	15,020	57,530
Net assets released from restrictions	14,740	(14,740)	—	—
Total revenues, gains, and other support	43,608	(1,098)	15,020	57,530
Expenses and losses:				
Program services:				
Instruction	13,100	—	—	13,000
Research	8,540	—	—	8,540
Public service	5,760	—	—	5,760
Management and general	2,420	—	—	2,420
Fund raising	2,150	—	—	2,150
Total expenses	31,970	—	—	31,970
Fire loss	80	—	—	80
Actuarial loss on annuity obligations	—	30	—	30
Total expenses and losses	32,050	30	—	32,080
Change in net assets:				
Before changes related to collection items not capitalized	11,558	(1,128)	15,020	25,450
Paintings purchased for art collection but not capitalized	—	—	(10,000)	(10,000)
Change in net assets	11,558	(1,128)	5,020	15,450
Net assets at beginning of year	103,670	25,470	137,000	266,140
Net assets at end of year	$115,228	$24,342	$142,020	$281,590

Exhibit 19-7

PRIVATE NOT-FOR-PROFIT COLLEGES AND UNIVERSITIES
Statement of Cash Flows
Year Ended June 30, 1999
(in thousands)

Cash flows from operating activities:	
Cash received from tuition	$ 5,220
Cash received from contributors	8,030
Cash collected on contributions receivable	2,615
Interest and dividends received	8,570
Miscellaneous receipts	150
Interest paid	(382)
Cash paid to employees and suppliers	(23,808)
Grants paid	(425)
Net cash used by operating activities	(30)
Cash flows from investing activities:	
Insurance proceeds from fire loss on building	250
Purchase of equipment	(1,500)
Proceeds from sale of investments	86,100
Purchase of paintings	(10,000)
Purchase of investments	(74,900)
Net cash used by investing activities	(50)
Cash flows from financing activities:	
Proceeds from contributions restricted for:	
Investment in endowment	200
Investment in term endowment	70
Investment in plant	1,210
Investment subject to annuity agreements	200
	1,680
Other financing activities:	
Interest and dividends restricted for reinvestment	300
Payments of annuity obligations	(145)
Payments on notes payable	(1,140)
Payments on long-term debt	(1,000)
	(1,985)
Net cash used by financing activities	(305)
Net decrease in cash and cash equivalents	(385)
Cash and cash equivalents at beginning of year	460
Cash and cash equivalents at end of year	$ 75
Reconciliation of change in net assets to net cash used by operating activities:	
Change in net assets	$ 15,450
Adjustments to reconcile change in net assets to net cash used by operating activities:	
Depreciation	3,200
Fire loss	80
Actuarial loss on annuity obligations	30
Increase in accounts and interest receivable	(460)
Decrease in inventories and prepaid expenses	390
Increase in contributions receivable	(325)
Increase in accounts payable	1,520
Decrease in refundable advance	(650)
Decrease in grants payable	(425)
Contributions restricted for long-term investment	(2,740)
Interest and dividends restricted for long-term investment	(300)
Unrealized gains on investments	(14,300)
Realized gain on sale of investments	(1,500)
Net cash used by operating activities	$ (30)

QUESTIONS

1. What organization is responsible for issuing reporting standards for private not-for-profit colleges and universities?

2. What organization is responsible for issuing reporting standards for public colleges and universities?

3. What information do financial statement users want to know about a not-for-profit organization?

4. What are the required financial statements for private not-for-profit colleges and universities? What are the required financial statements for public colleges and universities?

5. What are temporarily restricted assets?

6. What are permanently restricted assets?

7. What are the two general types of expenses reported by not-for-profit organizations?

8. What ratio is frequently used to assess not-for-profit organizations?

9. Why is a statement of functional expense prepared for a voluntary health and welfare organization?

10. When are donated services recorded by a not-for-profit organization?

11. What is the current controversy surrounding the allocation of joint costs between program service expenses and supporting service expenses?

12. Why is depreciation recorded by a not-for-profit organization?

13. How should the estimated uncollectible portion of pledges be recorded by a not-for-profit organization?

14. What is the difference between an unconditional promise to give and an intention to give?

15. When should membership dues be considered revenue rather than contributions?

16. What accounts are used to close the revenues, support, and expenses of a not-for-profit organization?

17. What is a third-party payor, and how does the presence of third-party payors affect the financial accounting of a health care organization?

18. What are the three types of health care organizations and what accounting and reporting standards should each follow?

19. What are three types of revenue reported by health care organizations? Give examples of each.

20. What is a contractual adjustment? How is a contractual adjustment accounted for by a health care organization? How should a contractual adjustment related to a prior year be recorded?

21. How are charity care reductions accounted for?

LIBRARY ASSIGNMENTS

1. Locate an annual report for a voluntary health and welfare organization. If one cannot be found in the school library, obtain a copy by calling the local office of an organization such as the American Lung Association, American Cancer Society, or National Multiple Sclerosis Society.

   Using the annual report obtained, answer the following questions about the voluntary health and welfare organization:

   How many different program services are being offered?

   What percentage of total expenses went to supporting services?

   Did the organization have a program service entitled public or professional education?

   Do the notes to the financial statements indicate that any contributed services are recognized within the financial statements?

   What dollar amount was spent on fund-raising?

   How much public support was received and how much revenue was earned?

What is the largest expense category?

What amount of depreciation was recognized for the period?

2. Read the following concerning the allocation of joint costs by not-for-profit organizations:

"Organized Charities Pass Off Mailing Costs as 'Public Education'," *The Wall Street Journal*, October 29, 1990, p. Al.

"Reasonable Joint Cost Allocations in Nonprofits," *Journal of Accountancy*, November 1992.

AICPA, *Statement of Position 87-2*, "Accounting for Joint Costs of Information Materials and Activities of Not-for-Profit Organizations that Include a Fund-Raising Appeal," paragraphs 14-22.

Write a short report indicating whether the costs of direct solicitations made by voluntary health and welfare organizations that also contain informational material should be allocated between program service expenses and supporting service expenses. If allocation is considered appropriate, indicate how that allocation should be made.

3. Read the following discussing the accounting for private not-for-profit colleges and universities:

"Several Private Colleges May Ignore New Accounting Rule on Depreciation," *The Wall Street Journal*, February 4, 1987.

"Why Colleges Cost Too Much," *Time*, March 17, 1997.

PROBLEMS

1. A hospital has the following account balances:

Revenue from newsstand	$ 50,000
Amounts charged to patients	800,000
Interest income	30,000
Salary expense—nurses	100,000
Bad debts	10,000
Undesignated gifts	80,000
Contractual adjustments	110,000

What is the hospital's net patient service revenue?
a. $880,000.
b. $800,000.
c. $690,000.
d. $680,000.

2. A large not-for-profit organization's statement of activities should report the net change for net assets that are

	Unrestricted	Permanently Restricted
a.	Yes	Yes
b.	Yes	No
c.	No	No
d.	No	Yes

(AICPA adapted)

3. Which of the following normally should be considered ongoing or central transactions for a not-for-profit hospital?
I. Room and board fees from patients
II. Recovery room fees
  a. Neither I nor II.
  b. Both I and II.
  c. II only.
  d. I only.

(AICPA adapted)

4. *FASB Statement No. 117,* "Financial Statements of Not-for-Profit Organizations," focuses on
   a. Basic information for the organization as a whole.
   b. Standardization of funds nomenclature.
   c. Inherent differences of not-for-profit organizations that impact reporting presentations.
   d. Distinctions between current fund and noncurrent fund presentations.

   (AICPA adapted)

5. On December 30, 1997, Leigh Museum, a not-for-profit organization, received a $7,000,000 donation of Day Co. shares with donor stipulated requirements as follows:
   - Shares valued at $5,000,000 are to be sold with the proceeds used to erect a public viewing building.
   - Shares valued at $2,000,000 are to be retained with the dividends used to support current operations.

   As a consequence of the receipt of the Day shares, how much should Leigh report as temporarily restricted net assets on its 1997 statement of financial position?
   a. $0
   b. $2,000,000
   c. $5,000,000
   d. $7,000,000

   (AICPA adapted)

6. The Jones family lost its home in a fire. On December 25, 1998, a philanthropist sent money to the Amer Benevolent Society, a not-for-profit organization, to purchase furniture for the Jones family. During January 1999, Amer purchased this furniture for the Jones family. How should Amer report the receipt of the money in its 1998 financial statements?
   a. As an unrestricted contribution.
   b. As a temporarily restricted contribution.
   c. As a permanently restricted contribution.
   d. As a liability.

   (AICPA adapted)

7. Pel Museum is a not-for-profit organization. If Pel received a contribution of historical artifacts, it need not recognize the contribution if the artifacts are to be sold and the proceeds used to
   a. Support general museum activities.
   b. Acquire other items for collections.
   c. Repair existing collections.
   d. Purchase buildings to house collections.

   (AICPA adapted)

8. In April 1998, Delta Hospital purchased medicines from Field Pharmaceutical Co. at a cost of $5,000. However, Field notified Delta that the invoice was being canceled and that the medicines were being donated to Delta. Delta should record this donation of medicines as
   a. A memorandum entry only.
   b. A $5,000 credit to nonoperating expenses.
   c. A $5,000 credit to operating expenses.
   d. Other operating revenue of $5,000.

   (AICPA adapted)

9. A private college receives a cash gift of $300,000 that must be used to assist in building a new dormitory in several years. How is this amount recorded?
   a. Under governmental college accounting practices, it would be recorded as revenue in the Unrestricted Current Funds but the FASB has required it be shown as an increase in temporarily restricted net assets.
   b. Under governmental college accounting practices, it would be recorded as an increase in the fund balance of Unexpended Plant Funds but the FASB has required it be shown as restricted support increasing the temporarily restricted net assets.

   c. Under governmental college accounting practices, it would be recorded as a deferred revenue in the Restricted Current Funds but the FASB has required that it be recognized immediately as a revenue increasing the temporarily restricted net assets.

   d. Under governmental college accounting practices, it would be recorded as an increase in the Investment in Plant of the school but the FASB has required that it be recognized as an increase in permanently restricted net assets.

10. In the accounting for health care providers, what are third-party payors?

   a. Doctors who reduce fees for indigent patients.

   b. Charities who supply medicines to hospitals and other health care providers.

   c. Friends and relatives who pay the medical costs of a patient.

   d. Insurance companies and other groups who pay a significant portion of the medical fees in the United States.

11. Inazu Hospital's accounting records disclosed the following information:

Cost of property and equipment net of accumulated depreciation $19,000,000
Board designated funds 6,000,000

What amount should be included as part of the Unrestricted Net Assets?

   a. $25 million.

   b. $19 million.

   c. $6 million.

   d. $0.

(AICPA adapted)

12. Mercy for America, a not-for-profit health care facility located in Durham, North Carolina, charged a patient $8,600 for services. This amount was actually billed to a third-party payor. The third-party payor submitted a check for $7,900 with a note stating that "the reasonable amount is paid in full." Which of the following statements is true?

   a. The patient was responsible for paying the remaining $700.

   b. The health care facility will rebill the third-party payor for the remaining $700.

   c. The health care facility recorded the $700 as a contractual adjustment that will not be collected.

   d. The $700 was retained by the third-party payor and will be conveyed to the health care facility at the start of the next fiscal period.

13. What is a contractual adjustment?

   a. An increase in a patient's charges caused by revisions in the billing process utilized by a health care entity.

   b. A year-end journal entry to recognize all of a health care entity's remaining receivables.

   c. A reduction in patient service revenues caused by agreements with third-party payors that allows them to pay a health care entity based on their determination of reasonable costs.

   d. The results of a cost allocation system that allows a health care entity to determine a patient's cost by department.

14. A not-for-profit hospital provides its patients with services that would normally be charged at $1 million. However, a $200,000 reduction is estimated because of contractual adjustments. Another $100,000 reduction is expected because of bad debts. Finally. $400,000 will not be collected because the amounts are deemed to be charity care. Which of the following is correct?

   a. Patient service revenues = $1 million; net patient service revenues = $300,000.

   b. Patient service revenues = $1 million; net patient service revenues = $400,000.

   c. Patient service revenues = $600,000; net patient service revenues = $300,000.

   d. Patient service revenues = $600,000, net patient service revenues = $400,000.

15. A local citizen gives a not-for-profit hospital a donation that is restricted for research activities. The money should be recorded in:

   a. Unrestricted Net Assets.

   b. Temporarily Restricted Net Assets.

   c. Permanently Restricted Net Assets.

   d. Deferred Revenue.

16. Late in 1998, a not-for-profit nursing home accepts a $75,000 cash gift with the stipulation that this money must be expended for operating supplies. The money is spent for that purpose but not until the early part of 1999. In which year should the entity recognize this contribution as support?

    a. The donation would not be recorded as revenue of any kind, but an increase in fund balance.

    b. 1998.

    c. 1999.

    d. May be recognized in either 1998 or 1999.

17. Theresa Johnson does voluntary work for a local hospital as a community service. She replaces without charge an administrator who would have otherwise been paid $31,000. Which of the following statements is true?

    a. A nonoperating gain of $31,000 should be recognized.

    b. Public support of $31,000 should be recognized.

    c. An expense reduction of $31,000 should be recognized.

    d. No entry should be made.

18. In 1998, Wells Hospital received an unrestricted bequest of common stock with a fair market value of $50,000. The testator had paid $20,000 for the stock in 1991. Wells should record the bequest as a:

    a. Nonoperating gain of $50,000.

    b. Nonoperating gain of $30,000.

    c. Nonoperating gain of $20,000.

    d. A memorandum entry only.

(AICPA adapted)

19. An organization of high school seniors performs services for the patients at a nearby nursing home. These students volunteer to perform services that the nursing home would not otherwise provide, such as wheeling patients in the park and reading to them. The nursing home has no employer-employee relationship with these volunteers, who donated more than 5,000 hours of service to the nursing home in 1998. At the minimum wage rate, these services would amount to $21,320, while the actual market value of these services is estimated to be $27,400. In the nursing home's 1998 statement of revenues and expenses, what amount should be reported as nonoperating gain?

    a. $27,400.

    b. $21,320.

    c. $6,080.

    d. $0.

(AICPA adapted)

20. A voluntary health and welfare organization receives a gift of new furniture having a fair market value of $2,100. The group gives the furniture to needy families following a flood. How should the receipt and distribution of this donation be recorded by the organization?

    a. No entry should be made.

    b. Public support of $2,100 should be recorded along with community assistance of $2,100.

    c. Recognize revenue of $2,100.

    d. Recognize revenue of $2,100 and community expenditures of $2,100.

21. George H. Ruth takes a leave of absence from his job to work full-time for a voluntary health and welfare organization for six months. Ruth fills the position of finance director, a position that normally pays $38,000 per year. Ruth accepts no remuneration for his work. How should these donated services be recorded?

    a. As public support of $19,000 and an expense of $19,000.

    b. As public support of $19,000.

    c. As an expense of $19,000.

    d. No entry should be recorded.

22. A voluntary health and welfare organization produces a statement of functional expenses. What is the purpose of this statement?

    a. Separates current unrestricted and current restricted funds.

    b. Separates program service expenses from supporting service expenses.

    c. Separates cash expenses from noncash expenses.

    d. Separates fixed expenses from variable expenses.

23. A voluntary health and welfare organization has the following expenditures:

Research to cure disease	$60,000
Fund-raising costs	70,000
Work to help disabled	40,000
Administrative salaries	90,000

How should these be reported by the organization?
a. Program service expenses of $100,000 and supporting service expenses of $160,000.
b. Program service expenses of $160,000 and supporting service expenses of $100,000.
c. Program service expenses of $170,000 and supporting service expenses of $90,000.
d. Program service expenses of $190,000 and supporting service expenses of $70,000.

24. Why do voluntary health and welfare organizations record and recognize depreciation of fixed assets?
a. Fixed assets are more likely to be material in amount in a voluntary health and welfare organization than in other types of not-for-profit organizations.
b. Voluntary health and welfare organizations purchase their fixed assets, and therefore have a historical cost basis from which to determine amounts to be depreciated.
c. A fixed asset used by a voluntary health and welfare organization has alternative uses in private industry, and this opportunity cost should be reflected in the organization's financial statements.
d. Contributors look for the most efficient use of funds, and since depreciation represents a cost of employing fixed assets, a voluntary health and welfare organization should reflect this expense as a cost of providing services.

(AICPA adapted)

25. A voluntary health and welfare organization receives $32,000 in cash from solicitations made in the local community. The organization receives an additional $1,500 from members in payment of annual dues. How should this money be recorded?
a. Revenues of $33,500.
b. Public support of $33,500.
c. Public support of $32,000 and a $1,500 increase in the fund balance.
d. Public support of $32,000 and revenue of $1,500.

26. During the year ended December 31, 1998, the Anderson Hospital (operated by a not-for-profit organization) received and incurred the following:

Fair market value of donated medicines	$ 54,000
Fair market value of donated services (replaced salaried workers)	38,000
Fair market value of additional donated services (did not replace salaried workers)	11,000
Interest income on board-designated funds	23,000
Regular charges to patients	176,000
Charity care	210,000
Bad debts	66,000

How should this hospital report these various items?

27. The following questions concern the appropriate accounting for a not-for-profit health care entity. Write complete answers for each question.
a. What is a third-party payor and how have third-party payors affected the development of accounting principles for health care entities?
b. What is a contractual adjustment and how is this figure recorded in accounting for a health care entity?
c. What are the three types of revenues and gains recognized by a health care entity? Give examples of each.
d. What are board-designated funds and where are these amounts reported?
e. How are donated materials and services accounted for by a not-for-profit health care entity?

28. For each of the following items recorded by a not-for-profit hospital or other health care provider, indicate the specific classification to be used for reporting purposes (unrestricted revenues, temporarily restricted revenues, or permanently restricted revenues):
■ Donated materials.
■ Cafeteria revenues.

- Revenues earned on board-designated funds.
- Charges for educational classes.
- Charges for X rays.
- Unrestricted gifts.
- Grant received from state for research costs that have been incurred.
- Donated nursing services.

29. Under Lennon Hospital's rate structure, the hospital earned patient service revenue of $9 million for the year ended December 31, 1998. However, Lennon did not expect to collect this amount because $1.4 million was deemed to be charity care and contractual adjustments were estimated to be $800,000.

    During 1998, Lennon purchased bandages and other supplies from Harrison Medical Supply Company at a cost of $4,000. Harrison notified Lennon that the supplies were being donated to the hospital.

    At the end of 1998, Lennon had board-designated assets consisting of cash of $60,000 and investments of $800,000.

    How much should Lennon record as patient service revenue and how much as net patient service revenue? How should Lennon record the donation of the bandages? How are the board-designated assets shown on the balance sheet?

30. The Wilson Center is a voluntary health and welfare organization. During 1998, unrestricted pledges of $600,000 were received by the center, 60 percent of which were payable in 1998, with the remainder payable in 1999 (for use in 1999). Officials estimate that 15 percent of these pledges will be uncollectible.

    How much should the Wilson Center report as revenue for 1998?

    In addition, a local social worker, earning $9 per hour working for the state government, contributed 600 hours of time to the Wilson Center at no charge. Except for these donated services, an additional staff person would have been hired by the organization.

    How should the Wilson Center record the contributed service?

31. Cura Foundation, a voluntary health and welfare organization supported by contributions from the general public, included the following costs in its statement of functional expenses for the year ended December 31, 1998:

Fund-raising	$500,000
Administrative (including $70,000 for data processing)	300,000
Research	100,000

    What should Cura report as program service expenses? What should be reported as supporting service expenses?

    (AICPA adapted)

32. A local not-for-profit health care entity incurred the following transactions during 1998. Record each of these transactions in appropriate journal entry form. Prepare a schedule calculating the change in unrestricted, permanently restricted, and temporarily restricted net assets.

    a. The governing board of the organization announced that $160,000 in previously unrestricted cash will be used in the future for the acquisition of equipment. The funds are invested until the purchase eventually occurs.

    b. A donation of $80,000 was made to the entity with the stipulation that all income derived from this money be used to supplement nursing salaries.

    c. The health care entity expended $25,000 for medicines. The money was received the previous year as a restricted gift for this purpose.

    d. The organization charged its patients $600,000. Of this amount, 80 percent is expected to be covered by third-party payors.

    e. The health care entity collected $78,000 from third-party payors who were billed during the preceding year for $84,000. Administrative officials had only anticipated collecting $75,000 of this amount.

    f. Interest income of $15,000 was received on the investments acquired by the board in the first transaction.

    g. The health care entity estimated that $20,000 of current accounts receivable from patients will not be collected and amounts owed by third-party payors will be reduced by $30,000 because of contractual adjustments.

h. The medicines acquired in (*c*) were consumed.

i. The investments acquired in (*a*) were sold for $172,000. All restricted cash and $25,000 that had been previously given to the organization (with the stipulation that the money be used to acquire plant assets) are spent for new equipment.

j. This health care entity receives pledges for $126,000 in unrestricted donations. Ten percent of the pledges are paid immediately with the remainder to be received and used in future years. Officials estimate that $9,000 of this money will never be collected.

33. Prepare the following journal entries for Ames Hospital, a not-for-profit hospital:

a. Patients were charged $300,000 for work done. Of this amount, $50,000 was actually charged to the patients although hospital officials anticipate that $12,000 will be bad accounts. The remaining $250,000 was billed to insurance companies and other third-party payors. Officials believe that these companies will only pay $220,000 after determining reasonable costs for the procedures performed.

b. Insurance companies and other third-party payors paid $187,000 to cover 80 percent of the charges in (*a*). The remaining invoices are under investigation.

c. An unrestricted pledge for $40,000 was received from a wealthy individual but the money cannot be spent for several years.

d. Interest income of $1,000 was received.

e. The administration decided to set aside $100,000. Investments were acquired for that amount with this money to be held to cover part of the cost of building a new wing to the hospital.

f. A local volunteer contributes services to the hospital to replace a retired worker. The value of these services is $9,000.

34. The following questions concern the accounting principles and procedures applicable to a voluntary health and welfare organization. Write out answers to each of these questions.

a. What is the difference in revenue and public support?

b. What is the significance of the statement of functional expenses?

c. What accounting process is used in connection with donated materials?

d. What is the difference in the two types of restricted net asset found in the financial records of a voluntary health and welfare organization?

e. Under what conditions should donated services be recorded?

f. What controversy has arisen as to the handling of costs associated with direct mail and other solicitations for money that also contain educational materials?

35. The following four transactions or events are independent.

■ Unrestricted cash of $25,000 was disbursed for the purchase of new equipment.

■ An unrestricted cash gift of $100,000 was received from a donor.

■ Investments in stocks with a book value of $50,000 were sold by an endowment fund for $55,000. No restrictions exist on this gain.

■ Bonds payable with a face value of $1 million were sold at par. The proceeds had to be used solely for the construction of a new building. The structure was eventually completed at a cost of $1 million and payment is made with the funds generated by the bond issuance.

Required

a. Prepare journal entries for the previous four transactions (including the fund in which each entry is being made) for a state or local government.

36. The following adjusted trial balances are for the Community Association for Handicapped Children, a voluntary health and welfare organization, at June 30, 1997. For internal purposes the association maintains its books on a fund basis.

Required

a. Prepare a statement of activity and changes in net assets for the year ended June 30, 1997.

b. Prepare a balance sheet as of June 30, 1997.

(AICPA adapted)

COMMUNITY ASSOCIATION FOR HANDICAPPED CHILDREN
Adjusted Current Funds Trial Balances
June 30, 1997

	Unrestricted		Restricted	
	Dr.	Cr.	Dr.	Cr.
Cash............................	$ 40,000		$ 9,000	
Bequest receivable..................			5,000	
Contributions receivable.............	12,000			
Accrued interest receivable...........	1,000			
Investments (at cost, which approximate market value)	100,000			
Accounts payable and accrued expense ...		$ 50,000		$ 1,000
Deferred revenue..................		2,000		
Allowances for uncollectible pledges.....		3,000		
Fund balances, July 1, 1996:				
Temporarily restricted.............		12,000		
Unrestricted...................		26,000		
Permanently restricted				3,000
Transfers of endowment fund income		20,000		
Contributions		300,000		15,000
Membership dues		25,000		
Program service fees		30,000		
Investment income.................		10,000		
Deaf children's program.............	120,000			
Blind children's program	150,000			
Management and general services	45,000		4,000	
Fund-raising services	8,000		1,000	
Provision for uncollectible pledges	2,000			
	$478,000	$478,000	$19,000	$19,000

37. Children's Agency, a voluntary health and welfare organization, began operations on July 1, 1997. It conducts two programs: a medical services program and a community information services program. This charity had the following transactions during the year ended June 30, 1998:

a. Received the following contributions:

Unrestricted pledges	$800,000
Restricted cash	95,000
Building fund pledges	50,000
Endowment fund cash	1,000

b. Collected the following pledges:

Unrestricted	450,000
Building fund	20,000

c. Received the following unrestricted cash revenues:

From theater party (net of direct costs)	12,000
Bequests..	10,000
Membership dues	8,000
Interest and dividends	5,000

d. Program expenses incurred (vouchers created for these amounts):

Medical services	60,000
Community information services...............................	15,000

e. Service expenses incurred (vouchers created for these amounts):

General administration	150,000
Fund raising	200,000

f. Fixed assets purchased with unrestricted cash..................... 18,000

g. Depreciation of all buildings and equipment in the Land, Buildings, and Equipment Fund was allocated as follows:

Medical services program	4,000
Community information services program	3,000
General administration	6,000
Fund raising	2,000

h. Paid vouchers payable 330,000

Required

- Prepare journal entries for these transactions.
- Calculate the balances in
    - Unrestricted Net Assets.
    - Temporarily Restricted Net Assets.
    - Permanently Restricted Net Assets.

38. This problem uses the same facts as Chapter 18, problem 23:
    Assume that Orlando University is a private not-for-profit university; prepare a schedule showing the change in: (1) unrestricted net assets, (2) temporarily restricted net assets, and (3) permanently restricted net assets.

39. This problem uses the same facts as Chapter 18, problem 24:
    Assume that Jurgeson College is a private not-for-profit university; prepare a schedule showing the change in: (1) unrestricted net assets, (2) temporarily restricted net assets, and (3) permanently restricted net assets.

CHAPTER

20

Accounting for
Estates and Trusts

QUESTIONS TO CONSIDER

- If a person dies without having written a valid will, how are the estate's assets managed and distributed?

- If the assets held by an estate are insufficient to satisfy all claims against the estate as well as all bequests made by the decedent, what distributions are made?

- How can an individual or a couple limit the federal estate taxes that must be paid so that the amount of assets being conveyed to beneficiaries is maximized?

- In accounting for an estate or trust, why is the distinction between principal and income often considered to be especially significant?

- What are the most common types of trust funds? What is each type of trust designed to accomplish?

ndividuals labor throughout their lives in part to accumulate property that eventually can be conveyed for the benefit of spouses, children, relatives, friends, charities, and the like. After amassing such funds, human nature usually seeks to achieve two goals:

- To minimize the amount of these assets that must be surrendered to the government.

- To ensure that the ultimate disposition of all property is consistent with the person's own wishes.

Therefore, accountants (as well as attorneys and financial planners) often assist individuals who are developing estate plans or creating trust funds. At a later date, the accountant may serve in the actual administration of the estate or trust. In either estate or trust planning, the person's intentions must be spelled out in clear detail so that no misunderstanding can ever arise. All available techniques also should be considered to limit the impact of taxes. To carry out all of these varied responsibilities properly, a knowledge of the legal and reporting aspects of estates and trusts is of paramount importance.

Although many of the complex legal rules and regulations in these areas are beyond the scope of an accounting textbook, an overview of both estates and trusts can serve as an introduction to the issues frequently encountered by members of the accounting profession.

ACCOUNTING FOR AN ESTATE

While none of us want to contemplate our death, or that of our spouse, we all need an estate plan. If you need motivation to reach this decision, remember that every dollar you keep from the folks in Washington goes to someone you like a heck of a lot better—such as your kids, your younger sister, or your alma mater.[1]

[1]Ellen P. Gunn, "How to Leave the Tax Man Nothing," *Fortune*, March 18, 1996, p. 94.

The term *estate* simply refers to the property owned by an individual. However, in this chapter, an estate is more specifically defined as a separate legal entity holding title to the assets of a deceased person. *Thus, estate accounting refers to the recording and reporting of financial events from the time of a person's death until the ultimate distribution of all property.* To ensure that this disposition is as intended and to avoid disputes, each individual should prepare a will, "a legal declaration of a person's wishes as to the disposition of his or her property after death."[2] If an individual dies *testate* (having written a valid will), this document serves as the blueprint for settling the estate and disbursing all remaining assets.

Whenever a person dies *intestate* (without a legal will), state inheritance laws must be followed. Although these legal rules vary from state to state, they are normally designed to correspond with the most common patterns of distribution. When inheritance laws rather than a will are applicable, real property is conveyed based on the *laws of descent* whereas personal property transfers are made according to the *laws of distribution.*

Laws governing wills and estates are established by each individual state and are known as *probate laws.* A *Uniform Probate Code* has been developed by the National Conference of Commissioners on Uniform State Laws in hopes of creating consistent treatment in this area. To date, approximately half of the states have officially adopted the Uniform Probate Code. In many of the other states, the rules and regulations applied are somewhat similar to the Uniform Probate Code. In practice, though, an accountant should become familiar with the specific laws of the state having jurisdiction over an estate.

Administration of the Estate

Regardless of the locale, probate laws generally are designed to achieve three goals:

1. Gather and preserve all of the decedent's property.
2. Carry out an orderly and fair settlement of all debts.
3. Discover the decedent's intent for the remaining property held at death and then follow those wishes.

This process usually begins with the filing of a will with the probate court or an indication that no will has been discovered. If a will is presented, the probate court must rule on the document's validity. A will must meet specific legal requirements to be accepted. For example, would the following signed and dated statement constitute a valid will?

> "I want my children to have my money."

Since the writer is dead, the intention of this statement cannot be verified. Was this an idle wish made without thought or did the decedent truly intend this one sentence to constitute a will conveying all money to these specified individuals upon death? Did the decedent mean for all noncash assets to be liquidated with the proceeds being split among the children? Or, did the writer strictly mean that just the cash on hand at the time of death should be transferred to these individuals? Obviously, in some cases, the validity (and the intention) of a will are not easily proven.

If deemed to be both authentic and valid, the will is admitted to probate and the decedent's specific intentions will be carried to conclusion. Whether a will is present or not, an estate administrator must be chosen to serve in a stewardship capacity. All property of the decedent must be located, debts paid, and distributions appropriately

[2]Stuart Berg Flexner, Editor-in-Chief, *The Random House Dictionary of the English Language,* 2nd ed. (New York: Random House, 1987), p. 2175.

conveyed. This individual serves in a fiduciary position and is responsible for (1) satisfying all applicable laws and (2) making certain that the decedent's wishes are achieved (if known and if possible).

If a specific person is named in the will to hold this position, the individual is referred to as the *executor of the estate*. If the will does not designate an executor or if the named person is unwilling to serve in this capacity (or if the decedent dies without a will), the courts must select a personal representative. A court-appointed individual is known legally as the *administrator of the estate*. An executor/administrator is not forced to serve in this role for free; that person is legally entitled to reasonable compensation for all services rendered.[3]

The executor is normally responsible for fulfilling several tasks:

- Taking possession of all the decedent's assets and completing an inventory of this property.
- Discovering all of the claims against the decedent and settling these obligations.
- Filing estate income tax returns, federal estate tax returns, and state inheritance or estate tax returns.
- Distributing property according to the provisions of the will, or according to state laws if a valid will is not available.
- Making a full accounting to the probate court to demonstrate that the executor has properly fulfilled the fiduciary responsibility.

Property Included in the Estate

The basis for all estate accounting is the property held by the decedent at death. These assets are used to settle claims and pay taxes. Any property that remains is distributed according to the decedent's will (or applicable state laws). For reporting purposes, all items are shown at fair market value; the historical cost originally paid by the deceased individual is no longer relevant. Fair market value is especially important since the sale of some or all properties may be required to obtain enough cash to satisfy claims against the estate. If valuation problems arise, hiring an appraiser might become necessary.

Normally, an estate includes assets such as

- Cash.
- Investments in stocks and bonds.
- Interest accrued to the date of death.
- Dividends declared prior to death.
- Investments in businesses.
- Unpaid wages.
- Accrued rents and royalties.
- Valuables such as paintings and jewelry.

At the time of death, certain assets are legally owned by the decedent. The executor is merely trying to locate and value each item belonging to the estate as of that date.

Some states specify that real property such as land and buildings (and possibly certain types of personal property) are conveyed directly to the beneficiary at the time of death. Therefore, in these states, these assets are not included in the inventory of estate property that is developed by the executor for probate purposes. However,

---

[3]To avoid having to use convoluted terminology, the term *executor* is generally used throughout this textbook to indicate both executors and administrators.

in the filing of estate and inheritance tax returns, such items must still be listed because a legal transfer has occurred.

Discovery of Claims against the Decedent

An adequate opportunity should be given to the decedent's creditors to allow them to file claims against the estate. Usually, the printing of a public notice in an appropriate newspaper is required one time per week for three weeks. In many states, all claims have to be presented within four months of the first of these notices. The validity of these claims must be verified by the executor and placed in order of priority. If insufficient funds are available, this ordering becomes quite important in establishing which parties receive payment. Consequently, claims in category 4 of the following list have the greatest chance of going unpaid.

Order of Priority

1. Expenses of administering the estate. Without this preferential treatment, the appointment of an acceptable executor and the hiring of lawyers, accountants, and/or appraisers could become a difficult task in estates with limited funds.
2. Funeral expenses and the medical expenses of any last illness.
3. Debts and taxes given preference under federal and state laws.
4. All other claims.

To ensure that some amount of protection is available for a surviving spouse and/ or the decedent's minor and dependent children, relatively small allowances are conveyed to these parties prior to the payment of claims. The Uniform Probate Code specifies that a $5,000 homestead allowance is provided to a surviving spouse and/or minor and dependent children. Thus, even an estate heavily in debt would still furnish some financial relief for the members of the decedent's immediate family. In addition, a family allowance of $500 per month (up to a total of $6,000) is recommended for these same individuals during the period of estate administration.

These family members also are entitled to exempt property such as automobiles, furniture, and jewelry having a value not to exceed $3,500 in total. *All other property is included in the estate to pay claims and be distributed as per the decedent's will or state inheritance laws.* Consequently, in most states, a surviving spouse along with minor and dependent children are entitled to receive the following from an estate, regardless of the claims made against the assets:

Homestead allowance	$5,000
Family allowance	6,000 (if the estate administration lasts a full year)
Exempt property	3,500 (fair market value)

Estate Distributions

If a will has been located and probated, property remaining after all claims are settled is conveyed according to that document's specifications.[4] A gift of real property such as land or a building is referred to as a *devise* whereas a gift of personal property such as stocks or furniture is a *legacy* or a *bequest*. A devise is frequently specific: "I leave three acres of land in Henrico County to my son," or "I leave the apartment building on Monument Avenue to my niece." Unless the estate is unable to pay all claims, a devise is simply conveyed to the intended party. However, if claims cannot

---

[4]Property legally held in joint tenancy with one or more individuals will pass to the surviving joint tenants at death and not be subject to the provisions of a will or intestate distribution.

be otherwise satisfied, the executor may be forced to sell the property despite the will's intention.

In contrast, a legacy may take one of several forms. The identification of the type of legacy becomes especially important if the estate has insufficient resources to meet the specifications of the will.

A *specific legacy* is a gift of personal property that is directly identified. "I leave my collection of pocket watches to my son" is an example of a specific legacy because the property is named.

A *demonstrative legacy* is a cash gift made from a particular source. The statement "I leave $10,000 from my savings account in the First National Bank to my sister" is a demonstrative legacy because the source is identified. If the savings account does not hold $10,000 at the time of death, the beneficiary will receive the amount available. In addition, the decedent may specify alternative sources if sufficient funds are not available. Ultimately, any shortfall usually is considered a general legacy.

A *general legacy* is a cash gift with the source being undesignated. "I leave $8,000 in cash to my nephew" is a gift viewed as a general legacy.

A *residual legacy* is a gift of any remaining estate property. Thus, assets left after all claims, taxes, and other distributions are conveyed according to the residual provisions of the will. ("The balance of my estate is to be divided evenly between my two brothers.")

An obvious problem arises if an estate does not have enough funds to satisfy all of the legacies specified in the will. The necessary reduction of the various gifts is referred to as the *process of abatement*. For illustration purposes, assume that a will lists the following provisions:

I leave 1,000 shares of AT&T to my brother. (a specific legacy)
I leave my savings account of $20,000 to my sister. (a demonstrative legacy)
I leave $40,000 cash to my son. (a general legacy)
I leave all remaining property to my daughter. (a residual legacy)

Example One   *Assume that the estate holds the shares of AT&T stock, the $20,000 savings account, and $46,000 in other cash.* The first three parties (the brother, sister, and son) get the assets stated in the will, while the residual legacy (to the daughter) would be the $6,000 cash balance left after the $40,000 general legacy is paid.

Example Two   *Assume that the estate holds the shares of AT&T stock, the savings account, but only $35,000 in other cash.* The first two individuals (the brother and sister) get the specified assets but the son can claim only the remaining $35,000 cash rather than the promised $40,000. Based on the process of abatement, the daughter receives nothing; no amount is left after the other legacies have been distributed.

Example Three   *Assume that the estate holds the shares of AT&T stock but the savings account has a balance of only $12,000 rather than the promised $20,000. Other cash held by the estate totals $51,000.* The stock is distributed to the brother, but the sister gets just the $12,000 cash in the savings account. In most cases, the courts would hold that the remaining $8,000 is a general legacy. Consequently, the sister gets the additional $8,000 in this manner and the son receives the specified $40,000. The daughter is then left with only $3,000 in cash that remains.

Example Four   *Assume that the shares of AT&T stock were sold by the decedent before death and that the savings account holds $22,000. Other cash amounts to $30,000.* The brother receives nothing from the estate since the specific legacy did not exist at death.[5] The sister collects the promised $20,000 from the savings account with the remaining $2,000 being added to the general legacy. Therefore, the son receives a total of $32,000 from the two cash sources. Since the general legacy was not fulfilled, no remainder exists as a residual legacy; thus, the daughter collects nothing from the estate.

Insufficient Funds   The debts and expenses of the administration are paid first in settling an estate. If the estate has insufficient available resources to satisfy these claims, the process of abatement is again utilized. Each of the following categories is exhausted completely to pay all debts and expenses before money is taken from the next:

Residual legacies.

General legacies.

Demonstrative legacies.

Specific legacies and devises.

Estate and Inheritance Taxes

Taxes incurred after death can be quite costly. For example, Helen Walton received $5.1 billion in stock at the death of her husband Sam Walton (founder of Wal-Mart Stores). At this value, these shares could eventually cost her heirs as much as *$2.8 billion* in taxes at her death: $2.2 billion to the United States government and $640 million to the state of Arkansas.[6]

Federal estate tax rates are as high as 55 percent with an additional 5 percent surcharge on extremely large estates (from $10 million to approximately $21 million).[7] States can also impose a separate inheritance or estate tax (commonly known as a "death tax").[8] The federal government allows a limited credit for such taxes assessed by the state. The effect of this credit is to reduce the federal estate tax by exactly the amount paid to the state so that the estate is not double-taxed. However, the amount of this credit (commonly referred to as the pickup or sponge tax) that can be taken is limited. As an illustration, the allowable credit is $99,600 on an estate with a value for federal tax purposes of $2 million. Any amount charged by a state above this ceiling may reduce the size of the estate but is not a direct credit against the federal estate tax.

Many states simply assess death taxes at the pickup tax rate so that the state can share in the distribution without penalizing the estate. Historically, though, a number of states have charged death taxes in excess of the pickup rate. Recently, the trend has been to reduce such taxes. Because many elderly citizens have moved from states having an excess assessment, reducing the death tax rate to the pickup rate is viewed as a way of actually increasing state revenues.

Federal Estate Taxes   The federal estate tax is an excise tax assessed on the right to convey property. The computation begins by determining the fair market value of

---

[5]The legal term *ademption* refers to a situation where a specific bequest or devise fails because the property is not available for distribution. As a different possibility, a bequest or devise is said to lapse if the beneficiary cannot be located or dies before the decedent. This property then becomes part of the residuary estate.

[6]Warren Midgett, "Mrs. Walton's Options," *Forbes,* October 19, 1992, pp. 22–23.

[7]The 5 percent surcharge eliminates the effect of graduated tax rates so that all estates of $21,040,000 or more are taxed at a flat 55 percent.

[8]Coverage of the many and varied state inheritance and estate tax laws is beyond the scope of this textbook. An overview is provided by "How to Minimize State Death Tax Liabilities," by Paul J. Lochray in the July 1990 issue of the *Journal of Financial Planning,* pp. 120–23.

all property held at death. Therefore, even if real property is transferred immediately to the beneficiary and is not subject to probate, the value must still be included for federal estate tax purposes.[9] In establishing fair market value, the executor may choose an alternative valuation date if that decision will reduce estate taxes. This date is six months after death (or the date of disposition for any property disposed of within six months after death). Thus, the federal estate tax process starts by determining all asset values at death or this alternative date. However, a piecemeal valuation cannot be made; one of these two must be used for all properties.

The gross estate figure is then reduced by several items to arrive at the taxable value of the estate:

■ Funeral expenses.
■ Estate administration expenses.
■ Liabilities.
■ Casualties and thefts during the administration of estate.
■ Charitable bequests.
■ Marital deduction for property conveyed to spouse.

The remaining figure is taxed at graduated rates that, as indicated before, rise to a maximum of 55 percent. Individuals then are allowed to deduct a unified transfer credit of $192,800. *The credit was set at this figure so that (based on current tax rates) estates of $600,000 and less may avoid any taxation.*[10] For example, if an estate tax of $210,000 is computed, the required payment is only $17,200 after deducting the $192,800 credit. Also, as mentioned earlier, state inheritance or estate taxes serve as another credit (to the upper limitation allowed) in arriving at the final amount to be paid to the federal government.

The impact of the unified transfer credit may be reduced, though, if the decedent made any taxable gifts while alive. Although annual gifts not in excess of $10,000 per person may be made tax free (the amount is $20,000 per year if conveyed by a married couple), gifts above this level are taxed by the federal government in the same manner as an estate tax since they are both transfers to beneficiaries. To avoid or reduce this gift tax, the donor is allowed to apply the unified transfer credit. *However, any portion of this credit used to shelter gifts from taxation reduces the $192,800 credit available to the estate after death.*

Federal Estate Taxes—Example One   The determination of the taxable estate is obviously an important step in determining estate taxes. Assume for illustration purposes that a person dies holding assets valued at $3 million. Assume further that no taxable gifts were made during the individual's lifetime. Total debts of $400,000 were owed at death. Funeral expenses had a cost of $20,000, and estate administration expenses amounted to $10,000. In this person's will, $300,000 has been left to charitable organizations, with the remaining $2,270,000 (after debts and expenses) given to the surviving spouse.[11] Under this set of circumstances, no taxable estate exists:

---

[9]Life insurance policies with named beneficiaries also are included in the value of the estate as long as the decedent had the right to change the beneficiary.

[10]The Taxpayer Relief Act of 1997 began a gradual increase in the amount of estate assets that can be excluded from taxation. The $600,000 figure rises to $625,000 in 1998 and goes up over the subsequent years to $1 million in the year 2006. As a more immediate benefit, estates that include family-owned businesses can escape tax on $1.3 million of assets as of 1998.

[11]Although not applicable in this case, surviving spouses do have the right in many states to denounce the provisions of a will and take an established percentage (normally 1/3) of the decedent's estate. Such laws protect surviving spouses from being disinherited.

Gross estate (fair market value)		$ 3,000,000
Funeral expenses	$ 20,000	
Administration expenses	10,000	
Debts	400,000	
Charity bequests	300,000	
Marital deduction	2,270,000	(3,000,000)
Taxable estate		—0—
Estate tax		—0—

Federal Estate Taxes—Example Two   For estate planning purposes, having a taxable estate of exactly $600,000 is often considered wise since that amount can be conveyed tax free. In the preceding example, if the couple has already identified the recipient of the estate at the eventual death of the second spouse (their children, for example), a conveyance at the time of the first death may be advantageous. The second estate will then be $600,000 smaller for subsequent taxation purpose. Frequently, a trust fund is established for this purpose as a means of protecting the money and ensuring its proper distribution.

To illustrate, assume that the previous will is identical except that only $1,670,000 is conveyed to the surviving spouse with $600,000 being placed in a trust for the couple's children (a nondeductible amount for estate tax purposes). The estate tax return must now be adjusted to appear as follows:

Gross estate		$ 3,000,000
Funeral expenses	$ 20,000	
Administration expenses	10,000	
Debts	400,000	
Charity bequests	300,000	
Marital deduction	1,670,000	(2,400,000)
Taxable estate (conveyed to trust)		$ 600,000
Estate tax on $600,000 value		$ 192,800
Unified transfer credit		(192,800)
Taxes to be paid		—0—

Once again, no taxes are paid by the estate, but only $1,670,000 is added to the surviving spouse's taxable estate rather than $2,270,000. Thus, an eventual decrease in the couple's *total* estate taxes of $192,800 has been established.

However, for couples, this strategy may not work unless the title to their assets is properly designated. This illustrates a situation where the success of estate planning can hinge on a proper understanding of how the laws function.

> The trick is to divide the first $1.2 million of your assets between you so that you and your spouse have separate estates that can each receive the tax credit. The standard individual credit is $192,800, essentially the tax that would be due on an estate of $600,000. If everything is jointly owned, you'd get that deduction only once because the tax man considers jointly held assets to constitute a single estate that isn't taxed until the second death.[12]

Legally, if a couple holds property as joint tenants or tenants by the entirety, the property passes automatically to the survivor at the death of the other party. Thus, if all property were held in one of these ways, the decedent would have no estate and would not be able to get the benefit of the $600,000 tax-free amount. However, if property is held by the couple as tenants in common, the portion owned by the decedent is included in that person's estate and up to $600,000 can be conveyed tax free.

Other Approaches to Reducing Estate Taxes   Until recently, one technique used by families with large fortunes to reduce estate taxes was the transfer of assets to

---

[12]Gunn, "Leave the Tax Man Nothing," p. 94.

grandchildren or even great-grandchildren. In this manner, the number of separate conveyances (each of which would be subject to taxation at a top rate of 55 percent) from parent to child to grandchild was reduced. However, the government effectively eliminated the appeal of this option by establishing a generation-skipping transfer tax. This flat-rate tax of 55 percent is assessed on any transfers after a $1 million exemption by gift, bequest, or trust distribution to individuals who are two or more generations younger than the donors or decedents.

However, estate taxes may still be reduced by making tax-free gifts prior to death. As just stated, gifts of $10,000 (or $20,000 for a married couple) can be made to an unlimited number of individuals each year without incurring any tax. The size of the donor's taxable estate is gradually reduced over time. "If properly planned, shifting assets can accomplish your objectives and ensure that the rewards of a lifetime of work pass to your heirs and not to the IRS."[13] "You can also give away your money in $10,000 chunks as run-of-the-mill gifts, of course. Tidy sums on their own, they soon add up to small fortunes for your beneficiaries."[14]

A more complicated method of reducing estate taxes is the creation of a family limited partnership. In such cases, parents form a partnership for a legitimate business purpose. The parents are the general partners and retain control during their lives. However, each year a limited partnership interest is conveyed to each child (or other beneficiary). At the time of this gift, the interest is limited and not general; therefore, the value is discounted rather dramatically when computing the amount of required gift taxes. Thus, an interest in property is being conveyed but taxes are computed at a value that can be less than 60 percent of fair market value.[15]

State Inheritance Taxes State inheritance taxes are assessed on the right to receive property with the levy and all other regulations varying, as discussed earlier, based on state laws. However, the actual impact on the individual beneficiaries is determined by the specifications of the will. Many wills dictate that all inheritance tax payments are to be made out of any residual amounts held by the estate. Consequently, any individuals receiving residual legacies are forced to bear the entire burden of this tax.

If the will makes no provisions for state inheritance taxes (or if the decedent dies intestate), the amounts conveyed to each party must be reduced proportionately based on the fair market value received. Thus, the recipient of land valued at $200,000 would have to contribute twice the inheritance tax of a beneficiary collecting cash of $100,000. Decreasing a cash legacy to cover the cost of inheritance taxes creates little problem for the executor. However, a direct reduction of an estate asset such as land, buildings, or corporate stocks might be virtually impossible. Normally, the beneficiary in such cases is required to pay enough cash to satisfy the applicable inheritance tax. Often, life insurance policies are established in the estate planning process to provide cash for such payments.

Estate Income Taxes Although all estates require time to be settled, the period can become quite lengthy if complex matters arise. From the date of death until ultimate resolution, the estate is viewed legally as a taxable entity and must file and pay income taxes to the federal government if gross income is $600 or more. The return is due by the 15th day of the fourth month following the close of the estate's taxable year. The calendar year may be adopted for this purpose or any other fiscal year may be chosen as the taxable year.

[13]*Strategies for Individual Planning 1990–1991* (New York: KPMG Peat Marwick, 1990), p. 64.

[14]Gunn, "Leave the Tax Man Nothing," p. 95.

[15]For a more complete description of family limited partnerships, see "Family Planning, the Smart Tax Move," by Suzanne Barlyn in *Fortune*, March 18, 1996, pp. 96–97.

Applicable income tax rules are generally the same as those utilized by individual taxpayers. Therefore, dividend, rental, interest, and other income earned by the estate in the period following death are taxable to the estate unless of a type that is specifically nontaxable (such as municipal bond interest).

A personal exemption of $600 is provided as a decrease to the taxable balance. In addition, a reduction is allowed for (1) any taxable income donated to charity as well as (2) any taxable income for the year distributed to a beneficiary. In 1996, federal tax rates were 15 percent on the first $1,600 of taxable income per year with various rates levied on any excess income earned up to $7,900. At a taxable income level more than $7,900, a 39.6 percent rate is incurred.

As an illustration, assume that an estate earns net rental income during the current year of $30,000 and dividend income of $8,000. The dividend income is distributed immediately to a beneficiary, while $6,000 of the rental income is given to charity. Estate income taxes for the year would be computed as follows:

Rental income	$30,000
Dividend income	8,000
Total revenue	$38,000
Personal exemption	(600)
Gift to charity	(6,000)
Distributed to beneficiary	(8,000)
Taxable income	$23,400
Income tax:	
15% of first $1,600	$ 240
28% on next $2,200 ($3,800–$1,600)	616
31% on next $2,000 ($5,800–$3,800)	620
36% on next $2,100 ($7,900–$5,800)	756
39.6% on remaining $15,500 ($23,400–$7,900)	6,138
Income tax payable	$ 8,370[16]

The Distinction between Income and Principal

In many estates, the executor is faced with the problem of differentiating between income and principal transactions. For example, a will might state "all income earned on my estate for five years after death is to go to my sister, with the estate then being conveyed to my children." The recipient of the income is known as an *income beneficiary* whereas the party that ultimately receives the principal (also known as the *corpus*) is called a *remainderman*. As the fiduciary for the estate, the executor must ensure that all parties are treated fairly. Thus, if amounts are distributed incorrectly, the executor can be held legally liable by the court.

The definitional difference between principal and income appears to pose little problem. The estate principal encompasses all assets of the decedent at death; income is the earnings on these assets after death. However, many transactions are not easily categorized as either principal or income. As examples,

■ Are funeral expenses charged to principal or income?

■ Is the executor's fee charged to principal or income?

■ Are dividends that are declared before death but received after death viewed as principal or income?

---

[16]As fiduciary entities, estates and trusts are taxed at the same income tax rates. Note that their top rate of 39.6 percent becomes applicable at a taxable income level of $7,900. In comparison, a married couple filing a joint income tax return in 1996 did not hit this top rate until taxable income was $263,750. Historically, fiduciary entities have had lower income tax rates so that taxpayers would move income-producing property into trusts to lower the taxes to be paid. As can be seen, Congress has changed the rate schedules so that it is now advantageous to keep income-producing property out of trusts.

- If stocks are sold for a gain, is this gain viewed as income or an increase in principal?
- Are repairs to rental property considered a reduction of principal or of income?

Clearly, the distinction between principal and interest is not always obvious. For this reason, in writing a will, an individual may choose to spell out the procedure by which principal and income are to be calculated. If defined in this manner, the executor merely has to follow these instructions.

However, in many cases, no guidance is provided by the decedent as to the method by which transactions are to be classified. State laws must then be applied by the executor to determine these two figures. The *Revised Uniform Principal and Income Act* has been adopted as a standard by many states for this purpose. However, some states have created their own distinct laws while still others have adopted modified versions of the *Revised Uniform Principal and Income Act.* Generally accepted accounting principles are not applicable; the distinction between principal and income is defined solely by the decedent's intentions or by state laws.

Although differences exist because of unique state laws or the provisions of a will, the following transactions are normally viewed as adjustments (either increases or decreases) to the *principal of the estate:*

- Life insurance proceeds if the estate is named as the beneficiary.
- Dividends declared prior to death and any other income earned prior to death.
- Liquidating dividends even if declared after death.
- Debts incurred prior to death.
- Gains and losses on the sale of corporate securities or rental property.
- Major repairs (improvements) to rental property.
- Investment commissions and other costs.
- Funeral expenses.
- Homestead and family allowances.

The *income of the estate* includes all revenues and expenses recognized after the date of death. Within this calculation, the following items are included as reductions to income:

- Recurring taxes such as property taxes.
- Ordinary repair expenses.
- Water and other utility expenses.
- Insurance expenses.
- Other ordinary expenses necessary for the management and preservation of the estate.

Several costs such as the executor's fee, court costs, and attorney's and accountant's charges must be apportioned between principal and interest in some fair manner.

Recording the Transactions of an Estate

The accounting process used by the executor of an estate is quite unique. *Since this individual has been given responsibility by the probate court over the assets of the estate, the accounting system is designed to demonstrate the proper distribution of these properties.* Thus, several features of estate accounting should be noted:

- All estate assets are recorded at fair market value to indicate the amount of the executor's accountability. Any assets that are subsequently discovered are disclosed separately so that these adjustments to the original estate value can be noted when reporting to the probate court. The ultimate disposition of all properties must then be recorded to provide evidence that the fiduciary responsibility has been fulfilled.

■ Debts, taxes, or other obligations are only recorded at the date of payment. In effect, the system is designed to monitor the disposition of assets. Thus, claims are relevant to the accounting process only at the time that the assets are disbursed. Likewise, distributions of legacies are not entered into the records until actually conveyed. As mentioned earlier, devises of real property are often transferred at death so that no accounting is necessary.

■ Because of the importance in many estates of separately identifying income and principal transactions, the accounting system must always note whether income or principal is being affected. Quite frequently, two cash balances are maintained to assist in this process.

To illustrate, assume that James T. Wilson dies on April 1, 1998. The following valid will has been discovered:

I name Bob King as executor of my estate.

I leave my house, furnishings, and artwork to my aunt, Ann Wilson.

I leave my investments in stocks to my uncle, Jack E. Wilson.

I leave my automobile and personal effects to my grandmother, Nancy Wilson.

I leave $38,000 in cash to my brother, Brian Wilson.

I leave any income earned on my estate to my niece, Karen Wilson.

All remaining property is to be placed in trust for my children.

The executor will have to (1) make a search to discover all estate assets and (2) allow an adequate opportunity for every possible claim to be filed. The assets should be recorded immediately at fair market value along with the creation of an Estate Principal account. This total represents the amount of assets for which the executor is accountable. The following journal entry establishes the values for the assets owned by James T. Wilson at his death that have been found to date:

Cash—Principal	11,000	
Interest Receivable on Bonds	3,000	
Dividends Receivable on Stocks	4,000	
Life Insurance—Payable to Estate	40,000	
Residence	90,000	
Household Furnishings and Art Work	24,000	
Automobile	4,000	
Personal Effects	2,000	
Investment in Bonds	240,000	
Investment in Stocks	50,000	
Estate Principal		468,000

Following is a list of subsequent transactions incurred by this estate along with each appropriate journal entry. Since estate income is to be conveyed to one party but the remaining principal is to be placed in trust, careful distinction between these two elements is necessary.

Transaction 1   Funeral expenses of $4,000 are paid by the executor.

Funeral and Administrative Expenses	4,000	
Cash—Principal		4,000

Transaction 2   The life insurance policy payable to the estate (shown in the initial entry) is collected.

Cash—Principal	40,000	
Life insurance—Payable to Estate		40,000

Transaction 3   The title to four acres of land is discovered in a safe deposit box. This asset was not included in the original inventory of estate property. An appraiser sets the value of the land at $22,000.

Land	22,000	
Assets Subsequently Discovered		22,000

Transaction 4   The executor receives claims totaling $24,000 for debts incurred by the decedent prior to death. This figure includes medical expenses covering the decedent's last illness ($11,000), property taxes ($4,000), utilities ($1,000), personal income taxes ($5,000), and other miscellaneous expenses ($3,000). The executor pays all of these claims.

Debts of the Decedent	24,000	
Cash—Principal		24,000

Transaction 5   Interest of $8,000 is collected on the bonds held by the estate. Of this amount, $3,000 was earned prior to the decedent's death and was included as a receivable in the initial recording of the estate assets.

Cash—Principal	3,000	
Cash—Income	5,000	
Interest Receivable on Bonds		3,000
Estate Income		5,000

Transaction 6   Dividends of $6,000 are collected from the stocks held by the estate. Of this amount, $4,000 was declared prior to the decedent's death and was included as a receivable in the initial recording of the estate assets.

Cash—Principal	4,000	
Cash—Income	2,000	
Dividends Receivable on Stocks		4,000
Estate Income		2,000

Transaction 7   The executor now has a problem. The Cash—Principal balance is currently $30,000:

Beginning balance	$11,000
Funeral expenses	(4,000)
Life insurance	40,000
Payment of debts	(24,000)
Interest income	3,000
Dividends	4,000
Current balance	$30,000

However, the decedent's brother has been bequeathed $38,000 in cash. This general legacy cannot be fulfilled without the sale of some property. Most of the assets have been promised as specific legacies and cannot, therefore, be used to satisfy a general legacy. Two assets, though, are residual: the investment in bonds and the land that was discovered. The executor must sell enough of these properties to generate the remaining funding needed for the $38,000 conveyance. In this illustration, assume that the executor chooses to dispose of the land and negotiates a price of $24,000. Because a principal asset is being sold, the extra $2,000 received above the recorded value is considered an adjustment to principal rather than an increase in income.

Cash—Principal	24,000	
Land		22,000
Gain on Realization		2,000

Robert Sweingart died during December 1994 at the age of 96. Sweingart had outlived many of his relatives including the person named in his will as executor of his estate. Thus, the decedent's nephew Timothy J. Lee was selected by the probate court as administrator. Lee promptly began his duties including the reading of the will and the taking of an inventory of Sweingart's properties. Although the will had been written in 1959, Lee could see that most of the provisions would be easy to follow. Sweingart had made a number of specific and demonstrative legacies that could simply be conveyed to the beneficiaries. Also included in the will was a $20,000 general legacy to a local church with a residual legacy to a well-known charity. Unfortunately, after all other legacies were distributed, the estate would only have about $14,000 cash.

One item in the will concerned the administrator. Sweingart had made the following specific legacy: "I leave my collection of my grandfather's letters which are priceless to me to my cousin, William." Lee discovered the letters in a wall safe in Sweingart's home. About 40 letters existed, all in excellent condition. They were written by Sweingart's grandfather during the Civil War and described in vivid detail the Second Battle of Bull Run and the Battle of Gettysburg. Unfortunately, Lee could find no trace of a cousin named William. He apparently had died or vanished during the period since the will was written.

Lee took the letters to two different antique dealers. One stated: "A museum that maintains a Civil War collection would love to have these. They do a wonderful job of explaining history. But a museum would not pay for them. They have no real value since many letters written during this period still exist. I would recommend donating them to a museum."

The second dealer took a different position: "I think if you can find individuals who specialize in collecting Civil War memorabilia they might be willing to pay a handsome price especially if these letters help to fill out their collections. A lot of people in this country are fascinated by the Civil War. The number seems to grow each day. The letters are in great condition. It would take some investigation on your part but they could be worth a small fortune."

Lee now has to prepare an inventory of his uncle's property for probate purposes. How should these letters be reported? What should Lee do next with the letters?

Transaction 8   Fees of $1,000 charged for administering the affairs of the estate are paid. Of this amount, $200 is considered to be applicable to estate income.

Funeral and Administrative Expenses	800	
Expenses—Income	200	
Cash—Principal		800
Cash—Income		200

Transaction 9   On October 13, 1998, the house, furnishings, and artwork are given to the decedent's aunt (Ann), the stocks are transferred to the uncle (Jack), and the grandmother (Nancy) receives the decedent's automobile and personal effects.

Legacy—Ann Wilson (residence, furnishings, and artwork)	114,000	
Legacy—Jack E. Wilson (stocks)	50,000	
Legacy—Nancy Wilson (automobile and personal effects)	6,000	
Residence		90,000
Household Furnishings and Artwork		24,000
Investment in Stocks		50,000
Automobile		4,000
Personal Effects		2,000

Charge and Discharge Statement

As necessary, the executor files periodic reports with the probate court to disclose the progress being made in settling the estate. This report is referred to as a *charge and discharge statement*. If income and principal must be accounted for separately, the statement is prepared in two parts. For both principal and income, the statement should indicate:

Exhibit 20–1
Executor's Charge and
Discharge Statement

ESTATE OF JAMES T. WILSON
Charge and Discharge Statement
April 1, 1998–October 13, 1998
Bob King, Executor
As to Principal

I charge myself with:

Assets per original inventory			$468,000
Assets subsequently discovered: land (Trans. 3)			22,000
Gain on sale of land (Trans. 7)			2,000
Total charges			$492,000

I credit myself with:

Debts of decedent (Trans. 4):			
Medical expenses	$ 11,000		
Property taxes	4,000		
Utilities	1,000		
Personal income taxes	5,000		
Others	3,000	$ 24,000	
Funeral and administrative expenses (Trans. 1 and 8)		4,800	
Legacies distributed (Trans. 9):			
Ann Wilson (house, furnishings, and artwork) . . .	114,000		
Jack E. Wilson (stocks)	50,000		
Nancy Wilson (automobile and personal effects) . .	6,000	170,000	
Total credits			198,800
Estate principal			$293,200

Estate principal:

Cash			$ 53,200
Investment in bonds			240,000
Estate principal			$293,200

As to Income

I charge myself with:

Interest income (Trans. 5)			$ 5,000
Dividend income (Trans. 6)			2,000
Total charges			7,000

I credit myself with:

Administrative expenses charged to income (Trans. 8)			200
Balance as to income			$ 6,800

Balance as to income:

Cash			$ 6,800

1. The assets under the control of the executor.
2. Disbursements made to date.
3. Any property still remaining.

Thus, Exhibit 20–1 can be produced by the executor of James T. Wilson's estate immediately after Transaction 9. (Transaction numbers are included in parenthesis for clarification purposes.)

At this point in the illustration, only three transactions remain: distribution to the decedent's brother of the $38,000 cash, conveyance to the niece of the $6,800 cash generated as income since death, and establishment of the trust fund with the remaining principal. The trust fund will receive the $240,000 in bonds and the $15,200 in cash that is left in principal ($53,200 total less $38,000 paid to the brother).

Legacy—Brian Wilson	38,000	
Cash—Principal		38,000
Distribution to Income Beneficiary—Karen Wilson	6,800	
Cash—Income		6,800
Principal Assets Transferred to Trustee	255,200	
Cash—Principal		15,200
Investment in Bonds		240,000

A final charge and discharge statement would then be prepared by the executor followed by closing entries to signal the conclusion of the estate as a reporting entity.

ACCOUNTING FOR A TRUST

A trust is created by the conveyance of assets to a fiduciary (or trustee) who manages the assets and ultimately disposes of them to one or more beneficiaries. The trustee may be an individual or an organization such as a bank. Over the years, trust funds have become quite popular in this country for a number of reasons. Often they are established to reduce the size of a person's estate and, thus, the amount of estate taxes that must eventually be paid. As one financial advisor has stated: "Who needs to establish a trust? You do, and so does your spouse. There may be several good reasons, but start with this: if you don't set up trusts, your heirs may pay hundreds of thousands of dollars in unnecessary estate taxes."[17]

Estate taxes are not the only reason for establishing a trust. People form trust funds as a means of protecting assets and ensuring that eventual use of these assets is as intended. Trusts can also result from the provisions of a will, specified by the decedent as a means of guiding the distribution of estate property. In legal terms, an *inter vivos trust* is one started by a living individual, whereas a *testamentary trust* is created by a will.

Frequently, the *trustor* (the person who funds the trust) will believe that a chosen trustee is simply better suited to manage complicated investments than is the beneficiary. A young child, for example, would not be capable of directing the use of a large sum of money. The trustor may have the same opinion of an individual who possesses little business expertise. Likewise, the creation of a trust for the benefit of a person with a mental or severe physical handicap might be considered a wise decision.

During recent years, one specific type of trust fund, a revocable living trust, has become especially popular as well as controversial. The trustor usually manages the fund and receives most, if not all, of the income until death. After that time, future income and possibly principal payments are made to one or more previously named beneficiaries. Because the trust is revocable, the trustor can change these beneficiaries or other terms of the fund at any time.

> You want to leave knowing your loved ones have the best financial breaks possible. That's why the idea of a revocable living trust may sound so promising. During your lifetime, you turn over all assets to a trust. But you act as your own trustee, so you determine how the assets will be managed and distributed. Then, happy in the knowledge that you can change the trust at any time, you have the joy of knowing you're setting up a financial plan for your life and after death.[18]

Revocable living trusts offer several advantages that appeal to certain individuals. First, this type trust avoids the delay and expense of probate. At the death of the trustor, the trust continues with future payments being made as defined in the trust agreement. In some states, this advantage can be quite important, but in others the cost of establishing the trust may be more expensive than the potential probate costs.

Second, conveyance of assets through a trust can be made without publicity whereas a will is a public document. Thus, anyone who values privacy may want to consider the revocable living trust. The entertainer Bing Crosby, for example, set up such a trust so that no outsider would know how his estate was distributed.[19]

----

[17]Jeff Burger, "Which Trust Is Best for Your Family?" *Medical Economics,* August 1, 1988, p. 141.

[18]Estelle Jackson, "Living Trust May Sound Promising," *Richmond Times-Dispatch,* October 13, 1991, p. C1.

[19]Ibid., p. C5.

Although the number of other types of trust funds is quite large, several of the more common include:

- *Credit Shelter Trust* (also known as a Bypass Trust or Family Trust). A credit shelter trust is designed for couples. Each spouse agrees to transfer at death an amount of up to $600,000 to a trust fund for the benefit of the other. Thus, the income generated by these funds goes to the surviving spouse, but at the time of this individual's subsequent death, the principal is conveyed to a different beneficiary. As discussed in the previous section, this arrangement can be used to reduce the estate of the surviving spouse and, therefore, the amount of estate taxes paid by the couple.

- *Qualified Terminable Interest Property Trust* (known as a QTIP Trust). A QTIP trust is frequently created to serve as a credit shelter trust. Property is conveyed to the trust with the income, and possibly a portion of the principal, being paid to the surviving spouse (or other beneficiary). At a specified time, the remainder is conveyed to a designated party. Such trusts are popular because the spouse is provided with a steady income, but the principal can be guarded by the trustee and then conveyed at a later date to the individual's children or other designated parties.

- *Charitable Remainder Trust.* All income is paid to one or more beneficiaries identified by the trustor. After a period of time (or at the death of the beneficiaries), the principal is given to a stated charity. Thus, the trustor is guaranteeing a steady income to the intended parties while still making a gift to a charitable organization. These trusts are especially popular if a taxpayer holds property that has appreciated greatly (such as real estate or stocks) that is to be liquidated. By conveying it to the trust prior to liquidation, the sale is viewed as that of the charity and is, hence, nontaxable. Thus, tax on the gain is avoided and significantly more money remains available to generate future income for the beneficiaries (possibly the original donor). "This trust lets you leave assets to your favored charity, get a tax break, but retain income for life."[20]

- *Charitable Lead Trust.* This trust is the reverse of a charitable remainder trust. Income from the trust fund goes to benefit a charity for a specified time with the remaining principal then being given to a different beneficiary. For example, a charity might receive the income from trust assets until the donor's children reach their 21st birthdays. "Jacqueline Kennedy Onassis used this technique and ended up sheltering roughly 90 percent of the trust assets from estate taxes. Setup and operating costs, however, preclude the use of this type of trust unless the assets involved are substantial. As such this is a vehicle for the very wealthy, allowing them to keep an asset in the family but greatly reducing the cost of passing it on."[21]

- *Grantor Retained Annuity Trusts* (known as GRATs). The trustor maintains the right to collect fixed payments from the trust fund with the principal being given to a beneficiary after a stated time or at the death of the trustor. For example, the trustor might retain the right to receive an amount equal to 7 percent of the initial investment annually with any remaining balance of the trust fund to go to his or her children at death.

- *Minor's Section 2503(c) Trust.* Established for a minor, this trust fund usually is designed to receive a tax-free gift of up to $10,000 each year ($20,000 if

---

[20]Lynn Asinof, "Estate-Planning Techniques for the Rich," *The Wall Street Journal,* January 11, 1995, p. C1.

[21]Ibid., p. C15.

the transfer is made by a couple). Over a period of time, especially if enough beneficiaries are available, a significant amount of assets can be removed from a person's estate. In this particular trust, though, principal and income must be conveyed to the minor prior to the 21st birthday.

■ *Spendthrift Trust.* A trust that is established so that the beneficiary cannot transfer or assign any unreceived payments. Such trusts are usually established in hopes of preventing the beneficiary from squandering the assets being held by the fund.

■ *Irrevocable Life Insurance Trust.* Money is contributed to the trust to buy life insurance on the donor. If a couple is creating the trust, usually the life insurance policy is designed so that proceeds are paid only after the second spouse dies. The proceeds are not part of the estate and the beneficiary can use the cash to pay estate and inheritance taxes.

■ *Qualified Personal Resident Trust (QPRT).* The donor's home is given to the trust but the donor retains the right to live in the house for a period of time rent free. This removes what is often an individual's most valuable asset from the estate.

The term of the trust can be as short or as long as desired. The longer the term the lower the value of the gift. If the grantor dies before the term of the trust expires, however, the property will revert back to the estate of the deceased and be subject to estate taxes at its current value. Therefore, a term should be picked that the grantor believes he or she will outlive for the benefits of the QPRT to be effective.[22]

As can be seen from these examples, many trust funds generate income for one or more beneficiaries (known as *life tenants* if the income is to be conveyed until the person dies). At death or at the end of a specified period, the remaining principal is transferred to a different beneficiary (a *remainderman*). Therefore, as with estates, differentiating between principal and income is ultimately important in accounting for trust funds. This distinction is especially significant because trusts frequently exist for decades and can control and generate enormous amounts of assets.

The reporting function is also important because of the legal responsibilities of the trustee. This fiduciary is charged with carrying out the wise use of all funds and may be sued by the beneficiaries if actions are considered to be unnecessarily risky or in contradiction to the terms of the trust arrangement. To avoid potential legal problems, the trustee is normally called on to exercise reasonable and prudent care in managing the assets of the fund.

Record-Keeping for a Trust Fund

Trust accounting is quite similar to the procedures that were demonstrated previously for an estate. However, because of the many different trusts that can be created as well as the extended time period that might be involved, the accounting process may become more complex than for an estate. As an example, an apartment house or a significant portion of a business could be placed in a trust for 20 years or longer. Thus, the possible range of transactions to be recorded becomes quite broad. In such cases, the fiduciary might choose to establish two separate sets of accounts: one for principal and one for income. As an alternative, a single set of records could be utilized with the individual accounts identified as to income or principal.

In the same manner as an estate, the trust agreement should specify the distinction between transactions to be recorded as income and those to be recorded as principal.

---

[22]Michael Mingione, "Trust Your House," *The CPA Journal,* September 1996, p. 40.

If the agreement is silent or if a transaction is incurred that is not covered by the agreement, state laws are applicable. Generally accepted accounting principles usually are not considered appropriate. For example, the cash method rather than accrual accounting is utilized by trusts in recording most transactions. Although a definitive set of rules is not possible, the following list indicates the typical division of principal and income transactions.

Adjustments to the Trust's Principal:

Investing costs and commissions.
Income taxes on gains added to the principal.
Costs of preparing property for rent or sale.
Extraordinary repairs (improvements).

Adjustments to the Trust's Income:

Rent expense.
Lease cancellation fees.
Interest expense.
Insurance expense.
Income taxes on trust income.
Property taxes.

Trustee fees and the cost of periodic reporting must be allocated evenly between trust income and principal.

Accounting for the Activities of a Trust

For an inter vivos trust, reporting on an annual basis (or perhaps more frequently) is made to all of the income and principal beneficiaries. However, testamentary trusts come under the jurisdiction of the courts so that additional reporting becomes necessary. Normally, a statement resembling the charge and discharge statement of an estate is adequate for these purposes. Two accounts, Trust Principal and Trust Income, are established to monitor changes that occur. For a testamentary trust, the opening principal balance is the fair market value used by the executor for estate tax purposes.

To illustrate, assume that the following events occur in connection with the creation of a charitable remainder trust. In the will of Samuel Statler, a trust is created with the income earned each year to go to his niece for 10 years with the principal then being conveyed to a local university.

1. Cash of $80,000 and stocks (that originally cost $39,000 but are now worth $47,000) are transferred from the estate to the First National Bank of Michigan because this organization has agreed to serve as trustee for these funds.
2. Cash of $76,000 is invested by the trustee in bonds paying 11 percent annual cash interest.
3. Dividends of $6,000 are collected on the stocks, and interest of $7,000 is received on the bonds. No receivables had been included in the estate for these amounts.
4. At the end of the year, an additional $3,000 in interest is due on the bonds.
5. As trustee, the bank charges $2,000 for services rendered for the year.
6. The niece is paid the appropriate amount of money from the trust fund.

As the trustee, the bank should record these transactions as follows:

1. Cash—Principal 80,000
   Investment in Stocks 47,000
      Trust Principal   127,000
      To record trust assets at the fair market value figure used for
      estate tax purposes.

2. Investment in Bonds 76,000
      Cash—Principal   76,000
      To record acquisition of bonds using cash in trust fund.

3. Cash—Income 13,000
      Trust—Income   13,000
      To record dividends and interest collected.

4. No entry is recorded. These earnings cannot be paid to the income beneficiary until collected so that accrual provides no benefit. Therefore, a cash system rather than accrual accounting is used by the trustee.

5. Expenses—Income 1,000
   Expenses—Principal 1,000
      Cash—Income   1,000
      Cash—Principal   1,000
      To allocate the trustee's fees evenly between principal and
      income.

6. Equity in Income: Beneficiary 12,000
      Cash—Income   12,000
      To record yearly payment made to income beneficiary.
      Amount is computed as the dividends and interest of $13,000
      less expenses of $1,000.

SUMMARY

1. An estate is the legal entity that holds title to a decedent's property until a final settlement and distribution can be made. State laws, known as probate laws, govern this process. These laws become particularly significant if the decedent died intestate (without a will).

2. An executor to oversee the estate should be named in the decedent's will. If not, the probate court selects an administrator. The executor takes possession of all properties, settles valid claims, files tax returns, pays taxes due, and distributes any remaining assets according to the provisions of the decedent's will or state inheritance laws. The executor must issue a public notice so that all creditors have adequate opportunity to file a claim against the estate. Prior to paying these claims, a homestead allowance and a family allowance are provided to the members of the decedent's immediate family. Claims are then ranked in order of priority to indicate the payment schedule if existing funds prove to be insufficient. For example, administrative expenses and funeral expenses are at the top of this priority listing.

3. Devises are gifts of real property; legacies (or bequests) are gifts of personal property. Legacies can be classified legally as specific, demonstrative, general, or residual depending on the type of property and the identity of the source. If insufficient funds are available to fulfill all legacies, the process of abatement is applied to determine the loss allocations. After residual legacies are reduced to zero, general legacies are decreased if necessary. Demonstrative legacies are reduced next followed by specific legacies.

4. Federal estate taxes are assessed on the value of estate property. Reductions in the total value of an estate are allowed for funeral and administrative expenses as well as for liabilities, charitable gifts, and all property conveyed to a spouse. In addition, a unified transfer credit is available so that estates worth less than $600,000 are not taxed. A

portion (or all) of the decedent's unified transfer credit could have been used prior to death to reduce or avoid the payment of taxes on gifts of more than $10,000 per person per year (or $20,000 per couple). Federal estate taxes are reduced by amounts paid, within defined limits, to the states for inheritance or estate taxes.

5. In both estates and trusts, the distinction between income and principal is frequently an important issue. Income may be assigned to one party with the principal eventually going to a different beneficiary. Such arrangements are especially common in trust funds such as charitable remainder trusts. The decedent (for an estate) or the trustor (for a trust) should have identified the method of classification to be used for complicated transactions. If no guidance is provided, state laws become applicable. For example, major repairs and investment costs usually are considered reductions in principal, whereas expenses such as property taxes and ordinary repairs are charged to income. The bookkeeping procedures for estates and trusts are designed to separate and then reflect the transactions affecting principal and income.

6. To provide evidence of the fiduciary's proper handling of an estate or trust, a charge and discharge statement is produced. This statement reports the assets over which the individual has been given responsibility. The statement also indicates all disbursements of assets as well as the property remaining at the current time. Separate reports are prepared for income and principal.

COMPREHENSIVE ILLUSTRATION

Problem   *(Estimated Time: 30 to 40 minutes)*

Part A

The will of James Daily contains the following provisions:

I leave my house, my personal effects, and my investments in corporate stocks to my wife, Nora.
I leave the balance in my savings account up to a total of $26,000 to my son, George.
I leave $6,000 in cash to my niece, Susan.
I direct that all remaining assets, including my rental properties, be placed in trust. The income from this trust will go to my wife. At her death, the principal of this trust fund will be conveyed to the First United Church of Burlington, Alabama.

The executor of this estate has now paid all claims and the following properties remain (fair market value is indicated)

House and personal effects	$320,000
Savings account	23,000
Cash	9,000
Investment in bonds	35,000

All rental property as well as corporate stocks were sold by Daily prior to his death.

Required

a. Identify the following:
- Trustor.
- Life tenant.
- Remainderman.
- General legacy.
- Demonstrative legacy.

b. Answer the following questions:
- Is this trust an inter vivos trust or a testamentary trust?
- What specific type of trust has been created?
- To whom will the properties be distributed?

Part B

The will of Susan York contains the following provisions:

I leave my house and personal effects to James J. York.
I leave $9,000 in cash to M. J. York.
I leave all my investments to Bishop University.
Any income earned on my investments prior to distribution I leave to the Freedom Church of Lubbock, Texas.
I leave the remainder of my estate to Cindy Ruark.

The executor, Brendan Jaminson, takes an inventory and discovers the following assets. An appraisal is made of every item to determine its fair market value at the time of York's death.

Cash	$ 46,000
House and personal effects	310,000
Investments:	
Stocks	21,000
Bonds	44,000
Land (rental property)	65,000
Collection of antiques	19,000
Dividends receivable	1,000
Interest receivable	2,000
Rent receivable	4,000
Total	$512,000

The following valid claims are made against the estate and paid by the executor:

Funeral expenses	$17,000
Executor charges	9,000
Medical expenses	11,000
Debts	5,000

The following cash collections are received by the estate:

Dividends	$ 2,000
Interest	3,000
Rent	7,000
Sold antique collection	21,000

Prior to June 25, 1998, the current date, the executor made complete distributions to both James J. York and M. J. York.

Required

Prepare a charge and discharge statement for this estate. The date of death was January 23, 1998.

Solution

Part A

a.

- James Daily established the trust fund and would, therefore, be legally referred to as the trustor.
- James Daily's wife, Nora, will receive the benefits of the trust fund until her death. She is a life tenant.
- The First United Church of Burlington, Alabama, has been designated to receive the principal of the trust fund after the death of Nora Daily. Thus, the church is termed the remainderman of the fund.
- Since the $6,000 gift to Daily's niece Susan does not come from a designated source, it is known as a general legacy.
- The cash gift to Daily's son is to be taken from a savings account. A conveyance that is to be derived from a specified source is known as a demonstrative legacy.

b.

- This trust fund is a testamentary trust because it was created by the provisions of the decedent's will.
- This trust is an example of a charitable remainder trust. For a stated time, the earnings generated by the trust are to be conveyed to an income beneficiary. After

that date (the death of Nora Daily, in this case), the principal is transferred to a charitable organization.

■ The following distributions should be made by the executor of this estate:

House and personal effects are given to Nora Daily. Since investments in corporate stocks are no longer held by the estate, this portion of the will cannot be fulfilled.

The $23,000 cash found in the savings account is conveyed to George Daily. Although a maximum of $26,000 was promised, the account is not large enough to reach the upper limit specified by the will. However, because the provisions as written have been fulfilled, the remaining $3,000 is not a general legacy.

Cash of $6,000 is given to Daily's niece.

The remaining property (the investment in bonds and the $3,000 cash) is placed in the trust.

Part B

ESTATE OF SUSAN YORK
Charge and Discharge Statement
January 23, 1998–June 25, 1998
Brendan Jaminson, Executor

As to Principal

I charge myself with:

Assets per original inventory...................			$512,000
Gain on sale of antiques.......................			2,000
Total charges			$514,000

I credit myself with:

Debts of decedent:			
Medical expenses	$ 11,000		
Other debts	5,000	$ 16,000	
Funeral and administrative expenses ($17,000 + $9,000)		26,000	
Legacies distributed:			
James J. York (house and personal effects)	$310,000		
M. J. York (cash)	9,000	319,000	
Total credits			$361,000
Estate principal			$153,000

Estate principal:

Cash (see below)	$ 23,000
Investments:	
Stocks.....................................	21,000
Bonds.....................................	44,000
Land.......................................	65,000
Estate principal	$153,000

Cash balance:

Beginning balance	$ 46,000
Sale of antique collection	21,000
Collection of receivables (dividends $1,000, interest $2,000, and rent $4,000)	7,000
Payment of debts and expenses (funeral expenses $17,000, executor charges $9,000, medical expenses $11,000, and debts $5,000)	(42,000)
Legacy distribution (M. J. York)	(9,000)
Cash balance...........................	$ 23,000

As to Income

I charge myself with:

Dividend income ($2,000 collection less $1,000 receivable at death)	$ 1,000
Interest income ($3,000 less $2,000)	1,000
Rent income ($7,000 less $4,000)	3,000
Balance as to income...................	$ 5,000

Balance as to income:

Cash......................................	$ 5,000

QUESTIONS

1. What is the meaning of the terms *testate* and *intestate*?
2. If a person dies without having written a will, how is the distribution of property regulated?
3. What are probate laws? What are their objectives?
4. What responsibilities are given to the executor of an estate?
5. At what value are the assets within an estate reported?
6. How are the claims against an estate discovered by an executor?
7. What claims against an estate have priority?
8. What are homestead and family allowances?
9. What is the difference between a devise and a legacy?
10. Describe and give examples of the four types of legacies.
11. What is the purpose of the process of abatement? How is this process utilized by the executor of an estate?
12. How is the federal estate tax computed?
13. What is the unified transfer credit and how is this credit applied?
14. What is a taxable gift?
15. For couples, why is the establishment of a $600,000 trust fund considered a good estate planning technique?
16. What deductions are allowed in computing estate income taxes?
17. In accounting for an estate or trust, how is the distinction between principal and income determined?
18. What transactions are normally viewed as changes in the principal of an estate? What transactions are normally viewed as changes in the income of an estate?
19. What is the alternative date for valuing the assets of an estate? When should this alternative date be used?
20. In the initial accounting for an estate, why does the executor only record the assets?
21. What is the purpose of the charge and discharge statement that is issued by the executor of an estate?
22. What is a trust fund? Why have trust funds become especially popular in recent years?
23. What is an inter vivos trust? What is a testamentary trust?
24. What are QTIP trusts, GRATs, and charitable remainder trusts?
25. Why is the distinction between principal and income so important in accounting for most trusts?

LIBRARY ASSIGNMENT

Read the following and any other published materials on estate planning:

"Advantages of Planned Giving," *The CPA Journal,* September 1992.

"Special Needs Trusts: Financial and Estate Planning for the Disabled," *Journal of Accountancy,* July 1991.

"Charitable Remainder and Wealth Replacement Trusts: Too Good to Be True?" *Journal of Accountancy* (Personal Financial Planning Section), April 1992.

"A Primer on Trusts," *Journal of Accountancy,* May 1993.

"Get Your Estate in Shape," *Money,* May 1997.

"Charitable Remainder Trusts," *The CPA Journal,* September 1996.

"Estate-Planning Techniques for the Rich," *The Wall Street Journal,* January 11, 1995.

"How to Leave the Tax Man Nothing," *Fortune,* March 18, 1996.

"Who Will Inherit Your Wealth?" *Fortune,* December 16, 1994.

"Caveat Testator," *Forbes,* June 16, 1997.

"Revocable Trusts: Appealing, But Beware," *Journal of Accountancy,* October 1991.

Write a report describing the various techniques used in estate planning to both reduce estate taxes and ensure that a decedent's assets are utilized as intended.

PROBLEMS

1. Which of the following is not a true statement?
   a. *Testate* refers to a person having a valid will.
   b. Personal property is conveyed by the laws of descent if an individual dies without a valid will.
   c. *Intestate* refers to a person having no valid will.
   d. A specific legacy is a gift of personal property that is specifically identified.

2. Why might real estate be omitted from an inventory of estate property?
   a. Real estate is subject to a separate inheritance tax.
   b. State laws prohibit real property from being conveyed by an estate.
   c. State laws require a separate listing of all real estate.
   d. In some states, real estate is considered to be conveyed directly to a beneficiary at the time of death.

3. What is the purpose of the laws of distribution?
   a. They guide the distribution of personal property when an individual dies without a will.
   b. They are used to verify the legality of a will, especially an oral will.
   c. They guide the distribution of real property when an individual dies without a will.
   d. They outline the functions of the executor of an estate.

4. A bond was owned by a deceased individual. Which of the following amounts is included in the estate principal?
   a. All interest collected prior to distributing the bonds to a beneficiary is considered part of the estate principal.
   b. Only the first cash payment after death is included in the estate principal.
   c. Interest that was not collected prior to death is excluded from the estate principal.
   d. Interest earned prior to death is considered part of the estate principal even if received after death.

5. Which of the following is not a goal of probate laws?
   a. To gather and preserve all of the decedent's property.
   b. To ensure that each individual produces a valid will.
   c. To discover the decedent's intent for property held at death and then to follow those wishes.
   d. To carry out an orderly and fair settlement of all debts and distribution of property.

6. How are claims against a decedent's estate discovered by an executor?
   a. Public notice must be printed in an appropriate newspaper to alert all possible claimants.
   b. The executor waits for nine months until all possible bills have been received.
   c. All companies that the decedent did business with are contacted directly by the executor.
   d. Claims to be paid by the estate are limited to all of the bills received, but not paid, prior to the date of death.

7. Why are claims against an estate put into an order of priority?
   a. To help the executor determine the due date for each claim.
   b. To determine which claims are to be paid if funds are insufficient to pay all claims.
   c. To assist in determining which specific assets are to be used to satisfy these claims.
   d. To list the claims in order of age so that the oldest can be paid first.

8. Which of the following claims against an estate does not have priority?
   a. Funeral expenses, since the amounts incurred are usually at the discretion of family members.
   b. Medical expenses associated with the decedent's last illness.
   c. The costs of administering the estate.
   d. Unpaid rent on the decedent's home if not paid for the three months immediately prior to death.

9. How does a devise differ from a legacy?
   a. A devise is a gift of money and a legacy is a nonmonetary gift.
   b. A devise is a gift to an individual and a legacy is a gift to a charity or other organization.
   c. A devise is a gift of real property and a legacy is a gift of personal property.
   d. A devise is a gift made prior to death and a legacy is a gift made at death.

10. What is the homestead allowance?
   a. A reduction of $20,000 that is made in estate assets prior to computing the amount of federal estate taxes.
   b. The amount of property conveyed in a will to a surviving spouse.
   c. An allotment of $5,000 cash made from an estate to a surviving spouse and/or minor and dependent children before any claims are paid.
   d. A decrease made in the value of property on which state inheritance taxes are assessed. The reduction is equal to the value of property conveyed to a surviving spouse.

11. Which of the following is a specific legacy?
   a. The gift of all remaining estate property to a charity.
   b. The gift of $44,000 cash from a specified source.
   c. The gift of $44,000 cash.
   d. The gift of 1,000 shares of stock in IBM.

12. A will has the following statement: "I leave $20,000 cash from my savings account in the Central Fidelity Bank to my sister, Angela." This gift is an example of:
   a. A residual legacy.
   b. A general legacy.
   c. A demonstrative legacy.
   d. A specific legacy.

13. What is the objective of the process of abatement?
   a. To give legal structure to the reductions that must be made if an estate has insufficient assets to satisfy all legacies.
   b. To ensure that all property distributions take place in a timely manner.
   c. To provide adequate compensation for the estate executor and any appraisers or other experts that must be hired.
   d. To ensure that all legacies are distributed to the appropriate party as specified by the decedent's will or state laws.

14. For estate tax purposes, what date is used for valuation purposes?
   a. Property is always valued at the date of death.
   b. Property is always valued at the date of distribution.
   c. Property is valued at the date of death unless the alternative date is selected which is the date of distribution or six months after death whichever comes first.
   d. Property is valued at the date of death although a reduction is allowed if the value declines within one year of death.

15. Which of the following statements is true concerning the unified transfer credit?
   a. It is reduced by any charity bequests made by the decedent during the three years just prior to death.
   b. It only applies to decedents who produced valid wills.
   c. It is reduced by nontaxed gifts to individuals made during the decedent's lifetime if over $10,000 per person per year.
   d. It enables estates valued at $900,000 or less to avoid federal estate taxes.

16. In computing federal estate taxes, deductions from the value of the estate are allowed for all of the following except
   a. Charitable bequests.
   b. Losses on the disposal of investments.
   c. Funeral expenses.
   d. Debts of the decedent.

17. The estate of John Lexington has a taxable value of $550,000. The estate of Dorothye Alexander has a taxable value of $650,000. The estate of Scotty Fitzgerald has a taxable value of $750,000. None of these individuals made any taxable gifts during their lifetimes. Which of the following statements is true?

    a. Only Fitzgerald's estate will have to pay federal estate taxes.

    b. All three of the estates will have to pay federal estate taxes.

    c. None of these estates is large enough to necessitate the payment of estate taxes.

    d. Only the estates of Alexander and Fitzgerald are large enough to necessitate the payment of estate taxes.

18. Sally Anne Williams dies on January 1, 1998. All of her property is conveyed to several relatives on April 1, 1998. For federal estate tax purposes, the executor chooses the alternative valuation date. On what date is the value of the property determined?

    a. January 1, 1998.

    b. April 1, 1998.

    c. July 1, 1998.

    d. December 31, 1998.

19. M. Wilson Waltman dies on January 1, 1998. All of his property is conveyed to beneficiaries on October 1, 1998. For federal estate tax purposes, the executor chooses the alternative valuation date. On what date is the value of the property determined?

    a. January 1, 1998.

    b. July 1, 1998.

    c. October 1, 1998.

    d. December 31, 1998.

20. Which of the following is true concerning gift taxes?

    a. A couple may make gifts of $25,000 each year to a person without having to pay a gift tax.

    b. A gift tax can be avoided by applying the unified transfer credit but this use reduces the amount of the credit that can be applied by the donor's estate after death.

    c. Gift tax computations and estate tax computations are unrelated.

    d. Gift taxes can be avoided by making all gifts to blood relatives.

21. A couple has written a will that leaves part of their money to a trust fund. The income from this trust will benefit the surviving spouse until death with the principal then going to their children. Why was the trust fund created?

    a. To reduce the estate of the surviving spouse and, thus, decrease the total amount of estate taxes to be paid by the couple.

    b. To make certain that the surviving spouse is protected from lawsuits filed by the children of the couple.

    c. To give the surviving spouse discretion over the ultimate use of these funds.

    d. Trust funds generate more income than other investments so that the earning potential of the money is maximized.

22. The executor of an estate is filing an income tax return for the current period. Revenues of $12,000 have been earned. Which of the following is not a deduction allowed in computing taxable income?

    a. Income distributed to a beneficiary.

    b. Funeral expenses.

    c. A personal exemption.

    d. Charitable donations.

23. What is a remainderman?

    a. A beneficiary that receives the principal left in an estate or trust after a specified time.

    b. The beneficiary of the decedent's life insurance policy.

    c. An executor or administrator after an estate has been completely settled.

    d. If a legacy is given to a group of people, the remainderman is the last of the individuals to die.

24. In an estate, which of the following is charged to income rather than to principal?

    a. Funeral expenses.

    b. Investment costs.

    c. Property taxes.

    d. Losses on the sale of investments.

25. In recording the transactions of an estate, when are liabilities recorded?

    a. When incurred.

    b. At the date of death.

    c. When the executor takes responsibility for the estate.

    d. When paid.

26. What is the difference between an inter vivos trust and a testamentary trust?
    a. A testamentary trust conveys money to a charity, while an inter vivos trust conveys money to individuals.
    b. A testamentary trust is created by a will, while an inter vivos trust is created by a living individual.
    c. A testamentary trust conveys income to one party and the principal to another, while an inter vivos trust conveys all monies to the same party.
    d. A testamentary trust ceases after a specified period of time, while an inter vivos trust is assumed to be permanent.

27. Which of the following is a charitable lead trust?
    a. The income of the trust fund goes to an individual until death with the principal then being conveyed to a charitable organization.
    b. Charitable gifts are placed into the trust until a certain dollar amount is achieved that is then transferred to a specified charitable organization.
    c. The income of a trust fund goes to a charitable organization for a specified time with the principal then being conveyed to a different beneficiary.
    d. A charity conveys money to a trust that generates income for use by the charity in its various projects.

28. The estate of Nancy Hanks reports the following information:

Value of estate assets	$1,400,000
Conveyed to spouse	700,000
Conveyed to children	100,000
Conveyed to charities	420,000
Funeral expenses	50,000
Administrative expenses	20,000
Debts	110,000

    What is the taxable estate value?
    a. $70,000.
    b. $100,000.
    c. $180,000.
    d. $420,000.

29. An estate has the following income:

Rental income	$5,000
Interest income	3,000
Dividend income	1,000

    The interest income was immediately conveyed to the appropriate beneficiary. The dividends were given to charity as per the decedent's will. What is the taxable income of the estate?
    a. $4,400.
    b. $5,000.
    c. $8,000.
    d. $8,400.

30. Define each of the following terms:
    ■ Will.
    ■ Estate.
    ■ Intestate.
    ■ Probate laws.
    ■ Trust.
    ■ Inter vivos trust.
    ■ Charitable remainder trust.
    ■ Remainderman.
    ■ Unified transfer credit.
    ■ Executor.
    ■ Homestead allowance.

31. Answer each of the following questions:
    ■ What are the objectives of probate laws?
    ■ What tasks are performed by the executor of an estate?

- What assets are normally included as estate properties?
- What claims have priority to the distributions made by an estate?

32. The will of Victor Laslo has the following stipulations:

    Antique collection goes to Ilsa Lunn.
    All money in the First Savings Bank goes to Richard Blaine.
    Cash of $9,000 goes to Nelson Tucker.
    All remaining assets are put into a trust fund with the income going to Lucy Van Jones. At her death, the principal is to be conveyed to Howard Amadeus.

    Identify the following:
    a. Remainderman.
    b. Trustor.
    c. Demonstrative legacy.
    d. General legacy.
    e. Specific legacy.
    f. Life tenant.

33. The will of Carson M. Newman has the following provisions:
    "I leave the cash balance deposited in the First National Bank (up to a total of $50,000) to Jack Abrams. I leave $18,000 cash to Suzanne Benton. I leave 1,000 shares of Coca-Cola Company stock to Cindy Cheng. I leave my house to Dennis Davis. I leave all of my other assets and properties to Wilbur N. Ed."
    a. Assume that the estate has the following assets: $41,000 cash in the First National Bank, $16,000 cash in the New Hampshire Savings and Loan, 800 shares of Coca-Cola stock, 1,100 shares of Xerox stock, a house, and other property valued at $13,000. What distributions will be made from this estate?
    b. Assume that the estate has the following assets: $55,000 cash in the First National Bank, $6,000 cash in the New Hampshire Savings and Loan, 1,200 shares of Coca-Cola stock, 600 shares of Xerox stock, and other property valued at $22,000. What distributions will be made from this estate?

34. The estate of Jeb Stewart reports the following information:

Value of estate assets	$2,300,000
Conveyed to spouse	1,000,000
Conveyed to children	230,000
Conveyed to trust fund for benefit of spouse	500,000
Conveyed to charities	260,000
Funeral expenses	23,000
Administrative expense	41,000
Debts	246,000

    What is the taxable estate value?

35. An estate has the following assets (all figures approximate market value):

Investments in stocks and bonds	$900,000
House	260,000
Cash	70,000
Investment land	60,000
Automobiles (three)	51,000
Other assets	100,000

    The house, cash, and other assets are left to the decedent's spouse. The investment land is contributed to a charitable organization. The automobiles are to be given to the decedent's brother. The investments in stocks and bonds are to be put into a trust fund. The income generated by this trust will go to the decedent's spouse annually until all of the couple's children have reached the age of 25. At that time, the trust will be divided evenly among the children.

    The following amounts are paid prior to distribution and settlement of the estate: funeral expenses of $20,000 and estate administration expenses of $10,000.
    a. What is the value to be reported as the taxable estate for federal estate tax purposes?
    b. How does the Unified Transfer Credit affect the computation of federal estate taxes? How is this credit used in computing gift taxes during the decedent's lifetime?

36. During the current year, an estate generates income of $20,000:

Rental income $9,000
Interest income 6,000
Dividend income 5,000

The interest income is conveyed immediately to the beneficiary stated in the decedent's will. Dividends of $1,200 are given to the decedent's church.

What amount of federal income tax must be paid by this estate?

37. The executor of the estate of Wilbur Stone has listed the following properties (at fair market value):

Cash................................ $300,000
Life insurance receivable 200,000
Investments in stocks and bonds 100,000
Rental property 90,000
Personal property....................... 130,000

The following transactions occur in the months following the decedent's death:

- Claims of $80,000 are made against the estate for various debts incurred before the decedent's death.
- Interest of $12,000 is received from bonds held by the estate. Of this amount, $5,000 had been earned prior to death.
- Ordinary repairs costing $6,000 are made to the rental property.
- All debts ($80,000) are paid.
- Stocks recorded in the estate at $16,000 are sold for $19,000 cash.
- Rental income of $14,000 is collected. Of this amount, $2,000 had been earned prior to the decedent's death.
- Cash of $6,000 is distributed to Jim Arness, an income beneficiary.
- The proceeds from the life insurance policy are collected with the money being immediately distributed to Amanda Blake as specified in the decedent's will.
- Funeral expenses of $10,000 are paid.

Required

a. Prepare journal entries to record each of the preceding transactions.
b. Prepare in proper form a charge and discharge statement.

38. The executor of the estate of James Cooper has recorded the following information:

Assets discovered at death (at fair market value):
Cash $600,000
Life insurance receivable 200,000
Investments:
    Walt Disney Company 11,000
    Polaroid Corporation........................ 27,000
    Ford Motor Company 34,000
    Compaq Computer Corporation 32,000
Rental property 300,000

Cash outflows:
Funeral expenses .... $ 21,000
Executor fees 12,000
Ordinary repairs of rental property 2,000
Debts 81,000
Distribution of income to income beneficiary 4,000
Distribution to charitable remainder trust 300,000

Cash inflows:
Sale of Polaroid stock .... $ 30,000
Rental income ($4,000 earned prior to death) 11,000
Dividend income ($2,000 declared prior to death) 12,000
Life insurance proceeds 200,000

Debts of $17,000 still remain to be paid. The shares of Compaq have been conveyed to the appropriate beneficiary.

Required

Prepare a charge and discharge statement for this estate.

39. The will of Jane T. Simmons has the following provisions:
    - $150,000 in cash goes to Thomas Thorne.
    - All shares of Coca-Cola go to Cindy Phillips.
    - Residence goes to Kevin Simmons.
    - All other estate assets are to be liquidated with the resulting cash going to the First Church of Freedom, Missouri.

    Prepare journal entries for the following transactions:

    a. The executor of this estate has discovered the following assets (at fair market value):

Cash	$ 80,000
Interest receivable	6,000
Life insurance policy	300,000
Residence	200,000
Shares of Coca-Cola Company	50,000
Shares of Polaroid Corporation	110,000
Shares of James River	140,000

    b. Interest of $7,000 is collected.
    c. Funeral expenses of $20,000 are paid.
    d. Debts of $40,000 are discovered.
    e. An additional savings account of $12,000 is located by the executor.
    f. Title to the residence is conveyed to Kevin Simmons.
    g. Life insurance policy is collected.
    h. Additional debts of $60,000 are discovered. Debts totaling $100,000 are paid.
    i. Cash of $150,000 is conveyed to appropriate beneficiary.
    j. The shares of Polaroid are sold for $112,000.
    k. Administrative expenses of $10,000 are paid.

40. After the death of Lawrence Pope, his will was read. It contained the following provisions:
    - $110,000 in cash goes to decedent's brother, Ned Pope.
    - Residence and other personal property go to his sister, Sue Pope.
    - Proceeds from the sale of Ford stock go to uncle, Harwood Pope.
    - $300,000 goes into a charitable remainder trust.
    - All other estate assets are to be liquidated with the cash going to Victoria Jones.

    The following transactions subsequently occur:

    a. The executor of this estate discovers the following assets (at fair market value):

Cash	$ 19,000
Certificates of deposit	90,000
Dividend receivable	3,000
Life insurance policy	450,000
Residence and personal effects	470,000
Shares of Ford Motor Company	72,000
Shares of Xerox Corporation	97,000

    b. Life insurance policy is collected.
    c. Dividends of $4,000 are collected.
    d. Debts of $71,000 are discovered.
    e. Title to the residence is conveyed to Sue Pope along with the decedent's personal effects.
    f. Title to land valued at $15,000 is discovered by the executor.
    g. Additional debts of $37,000 are discovered. All of the debts, totaling $108,000, are paid.
    h. Funeral expenses of $31,000 are paid.
    i. Cash of $110,000 is conveyed to Ned Pope.
    j. The shares of Ford are sold for $81,000.
    k. Administrative expenses of $16,000 are paid.
    l. The appropriate payment is made to Harwood Pope.

Required

    a. Prepare journal entries for the preceding transactions.

    b. Prepare a charge and discharge statement.

41. James Albemarle creates a trust fund at the beginning of 1998. The income from this fund will go to his son, Edward. When Edward reaches the age of 25, the principal of the fund will be conveyed to United Charities of Cleveland.

    Prepare all necessary journal entries for the trust to record the following transactions:

    a. Cash of $300,000, stocks worth $200,000, and rental property valued at $150,000 are transferred by James Albemarle to the trustee of this fund.

    b. Cash of $260,000 is immediately invested in bonds issued by the U.S. government. Commissions of $3,000 are paid on this transaction.

    c. Permanent repairs of $7,000 are incurred so that the property can be rented. Payment is made immediately.

    d. Dividends of $4,000 are received. Of this amount, $1,000 had been declared prior to the creation of the trust fund.

    e. Insurance expense of $2,000 is paid on the rental property.

    f. Rental income of $8,000 is received.

    g. The trustee collects $4,000 from the fund for services rendered.

    h. Cash of $5,000 is conveyed to Edward Albemarle.

42. An inter vivos trust fund is created by Henry O'Donnell. O'Donnell owns a large department store in Higgins, Utah. Adjacent to the store, he also owns a tract of land used as an extra parking lot when the store is having a sale or during the Christmas season. O'Donnell expects the land to appreciate in value and eventually be sold for an office complex or additional stores.

    O'Donnell places this land into a charitable lead trust which will hold the land for 10 years until O'Donnell's son is 21. At that time, title will be transferred to the son. The store will pay rent to use the land during the interim. The income generated each year from this usage will be given to a local church. The land is currently valued at $320,000.

    During the first year of this arrangement, the trustee records the following cash transactions:

Cash inflows:	
Rental income	$60,000
Cash outflows:	
Insurance	$ 4,000
Property taxes	6,000
Paving (considered an extraordinary repair)	4,000
Maintenance	8,000
Distribution to income beneficiary	30,000

Prepare all journal entries for this trust fund including the entry to create the trust.

Financial Reporting and the Securities and Exchange Commission

21

QUESTIONS TO CONSIDER

- How does the U.S. government ensure that adequate reliable information is available to encourage investors to buy and sell securities so that sufficient capital can be raised by businesses for financing purposes?

- What companies are subject to the rules and regulations of the Securities and Exchange Commission?

- How does the SEC influence the development of accounting principles in the United States?

- What is the purpose of the registration statements filed with the SEC? What various periodic filings must also be made?

- What steps usually occur in the registration process?

- Which types of securities are exempt from registration with the SEC?

The Securities and Exchange Commission was born on June 6, 1934—a time of despair in the markets. Americans were still suffering from the 1929 market crash after a roaring 1920s when they bought about $50 billion in new securities—half of which turned out to be worthless. Their confidence also was eroded by the 1932 indictment (later acquittal) of Samuel Insull for alleged wrongs in the collapse of his utility "empire," and by the 1933–34 Senate hearings on improper market activity.[1]

The financing of the American industrial complex is very much dependent on raising vast amounts of monetary capital. During every business day in the United States, billions of dollars of stocks, bonds, and other securities are sold to thousands of individuals, corporations, trust funds, pension plans, mutual funds, and other institutions. Such investors cannot be expected to venture their money without forethought. They have to be able to assess the risks involved: the possibility of either a profit or loss being returned to them as well as the expected amount.

Consequently, disclosure of sufficient, accurate information is absolutely necessary to stimulate the inflow of large quantities of capital. Enough data must be available to encourage investors to consider buying and selling securities in hopes of generating profits. *Without adequate information on which to base these decisions, investing becomes no more than gambling.*

THE WORK OF THE SECURITIES AND EXCHANGE COMMISSION

In the United States, the responsibility for ensuring that complete and reliable information is available to investors lies with the Securities and Exchange Commission (SEC), an independent agency of the federal government created by the Securities

---

[1]"D-Day for the Securities Industry, 1934," *The Wall Street Journal*, May 9, 1989, p. B1.

Exchange Act of 1934. Although the SEC's authority applies mainly to publicly held companies, the commission's guidelines and requirements surely have been a major influence in the United States on the development of all generally accepted accounting principles.

> The SEC is an independent, nonpartisan, quasijudicial regulatory agency with responsibility for administering the federal securities laws. The purpose of these laws is to protect investors in securities markets that operate fairly and to ensure that investors have access to disclosure of all material information concerning publicly traded securities. The Commission also regulates firms engaged in the purchase or sale of securities, people who provide investment advice, and investment companies.[2]

The SEC is headed by five commissioners appointed by the president of the United States (with the consent of the Senate) to serve five-year staggered terms. To ensure the bipartisan nature of this group, no more than three of these individuals can belong to the same political party. The chairman is from the same political party as the president. The commissioners provide leadership for an agency that has grown over the years into a large organization with more than 3,000 employees and composed of more than a dozen divisions and major offices including the following:

- The *Division of Corporation Finance* has responsibility for ensuring that disclosure requirements are met by publicly held companies. This division reviews registration statements as well as tender offers and proxy solicitations.

- The *Division of Market Regulation* oversees the securities markets in this country and is responsible for registering and regulating brokerage firms.

- The *Division of Enforcement* helps to ensure compliance with federal securities laws. This division investigates possible violations of securities laws and recommends appropriate remedies.

- The *Division of Investment Management* works to ensure compliance with regulations concerning the registration, responsibility, and practices of investment companies and investment advisors.

- The *Office of Compliance Inspections and Examinations* determines whether brokers, dealers, and investment companies and advisors are in compliance with federal securities laws.

- The *Office of the Chief Accountant* is responsible for all accounting and auditing matters that arise in connection with the securities laws.

The SEC's budget for 1996 was nearly $350 million. A breakdown of this appropriation gives some indication of the work of the organization:

Major Programs—Percentage of Overall Budget

Prevention and suppression of fraud	30 percent
Investment management regulation	22 percent
Full disclosure	19 percent
Supervision and regulation of securities markets	13 percent
Program direction	10 percent
Legal and economic services	6 percent

This chapter provides an overview of the workings of the Securities and Exchange Commission along with the agency's relationship to the accounting profession. Unfortunately, a complete examination of the organization is beyond the scope of this textbook. Therefore, only a portion of the SEC's functions are discussed here. This

---

[2]"The U.S. Securities and Exchange Commission," SEC Web Site, May 1997. Available from http://www.sec.gov; INTERNET.

coverage provides an introduction to the role the agency currently plays in the world of American business.

Purpose of the Federal Securities Laws

Before examining the SEC and its various functions in more detail, a historical perspective should be established. The development of laws regulating companies involved in interstate commerce were discussed as early as 1885. In fact, the Industrial Commission created by Congress suggested in 1902 that all publicly held companies should be required to disclose material information including annual financial reports. However, only the crisis following the stock market crash of 1929 and the subsequently discovered fraud prompted Congress to act in hopes of reestablishing the trust and stability needed for capital markets.

> The securities market activities of the 1920s are legend. While trading and investment were brisk, the underlying strength of the market was eroding as a result of certain common practices. The first was price manipulation. It was not uncommon for brokers or dealers to indulge in "wash sales" or "matched orders," in which successive buy and sell orders created a false impression of activity and forced prices up. This maneuver allowed those involved to reap huge profits before the price fell back to its true market level.[3]

Eventually, Congress enacted two primary pieces of securities legislation:

- The Securities Act of 1933 regulates the initial offering of securities by a company or underwriter.
- The Securities Exchange Act of 1934 regulates the subsequent trading of securities through brokers and exchanges.

These laws put an end to the legality of many abuses that previously had been common practices such as the manipulation of stock market prices and the misuse of corporate information by officials and directors (often referred to as *inside parties*[4]) for their own personal gain. Just as important, these two legislative actions were designed to help rebuild public confidence in the capital market system. Because of the large losses suffered during the market crash and subsequent depression, many investors had begun to avoid buying stocks and bonds. This reduction in the pool of available capital dramatically compounded the economic problems of the day.

The creation of federal securities laws did not end with the 1933 Act and the 1934 Act. During the decades since the first commissioners were appointed, the SEC has administered rules and regulations created by a number of different congressional actions. Despite the passage of subsequent legislation, the major objectives of this organization have remained relatively constant. Over the years, the SEC has attempted to achieve several interconnected goals that include:

- Ensuring that full and fair information is disclosed to all investors before the securities of a company are allowed to be bought and sold.
- Prohibiting the dissemination of materially misstated information.
- Preventing the misuse of information especially by inside parties.
- Regulating the operation of securities markets such as the New York Stock Exchange and American Stock Exchange.

---

[3]K. Fred Skousen, *An Introduction to the SEC* (Cincinnati: South-Western Publishing, 1991), p. 4.

[4]Inside parties usually are identified as the officers of a company as well as its directors and any owners of more than 10 percent of any class of equity security. An individual's level of ownership is measured by a person's own holdings of equity securities as well as ownership by a spouse, minor children, relatives living in the same house as the person in question, and a trust in which the person is the beneficiary.

As judged by the dollar amounts exchanged each day in the trading of securities, the capital market system in the United States is flourishing. At least part of the responsibility for this success lies with the SEC and the agency's ability to attain the preceding goals. Today, most investors apparently believe in the overall integrity of the market system as well as the sufficiency and fair presentation of the data that they receive. Even the insider trading indictments during recent years and the stock market plunges of 1987 and 1989 have not appeared to shake investor faith appreciably. Thus, any introduction to the SEC must examine the methods used to maintain public confidence as it regulates the honest distribution of both financial and nonfinancial information.

Full and Fair Disclosure

Probably no responsibility of the SEC is more vital than the task of ensuring that sufficient, reliable information is disclosed by a company before its stocks, bonds, or other securities can be publicly traded. Unless specifically exempted, all publicly held companies (frequently referred to as *registrants*) must file detailed reports with the SEC periodically. These filings are required and regulated by the Securities and Exchange Commission as a result of a number of laws passed by Congress over the years:

1. Securities Act of 1933: Requires the registration of new securities offered for public sale so that potential investors can have adequate information. The act is also intended to prevent deceit and misrepresentation in connection with the sale of securities.[5]

2. Securities Exchange Act of 1934: Requires continuous reporting by publicly owned companies and registration of securities, security exchanges, and certain brokers and dealers. This act prohibits fraudulent and unfair behavior such as sales practice abuses and insider trading.

3. Public Utility Holding Company Act of 1935: Requires registration of interstate holding companies of public utilities covered by this law. This act was passed because of abuses in the 1920s where huge, complex utility empires were created to minimize the need for equity financing.

4. Trust Indenture Act of 1939: Requires registration of trust indenture documents and supporting data in connection with the public sale of bonds, debentures, notes, and other debt securities.

5. Investment Company Act of 1940: Requires registration of investment companies that engage in investing and trading in securities.

6. Investment Advisers Act of 1940 and Securities Investor Protection Act of 1970: Requires registration of investment advisers. Also requires them to follow certain standards created to protect investors.

7. Foreign Corrupt Practices Act of 1977: Affects registration only indirectly through amendment to the Securities Exchange Act of 1934. This act requires the maintenance of accounting records and adequate internal accounting controls.

8. Insider Trading Sanctions Act of 1984 and Insider Trading and Securities Fraud Enforcement Act of 1988: Also affects registration only indirectly. Increases the penalties against persons who profit from illegal use of inside information and who are associated with market manipulation and securities fraud.

---

[5]Interestingly, one of the provisions originally suggested for this act would have created a federal corps of auditors. The defeat of this proposal (after some debate) has allowed for the rise of the independent auditing profession as it is currently structured in the United States. For more information, see "The SEC and the Profession, 1934–1984: The Realities of Self-Regulation," by Mark Moran and Gary John Previts, *Journal of Accountancy*, July 1984.

Because of these laws, approximately 12,000 companies are subject to federal securities regulation. Although these companies make up only about one-third of 1 percent of the corporations in this country, the overall size of this group is staggering. In 1995, security registrations totaled $824 billion. Initial public offerings totaled $82 billion and foreign companies registered $41 billion in securities. The SEC staff reviewed 1,150 initial offering statements, and more than 1,000 registration statements. Nearly 3,000 annual reports received either a full review by staff accountants or a financial statement review.

SEC Requirements   As is obvious from the previous list of laws, the filing requirements administered by the SEC are extensive. Thus, accountants who specialize in working with the federal securities laws must develop a broad knowledge of a great many reporting rules and regulations. The SEC specifies most of these disclosure requirements in two basic documents, *Regulation S–K* and *Regulation S–X*, which are supplemented by periodic releases and staff bulletins.

Regulation S–K establishes requirements for all nonfinancial information contained in filings with the SEC. A description of the registrant's business as well as its securities are just two items covered by these regulations. A partial list of other nonfinancial data to be disclosed includes specified data about the company's directors and management, a discussion and analysis by the management of the current financial condition and the results of operations, and descriptions of both legal proceedings and the company's properties.

Regulation S–X prescribes the form and content of the financial statements (as well as the accompanying notes and related schedules) included in the various reports filed with the SEC. Thus, before being accepted, all financial information must meet a number of clearly specified requirements.

The SEC's Impact on Financial Reporting to Stockholders   The SEC's disclosure and accounting requirements are not limited to the filings made directly with that body. *Rule 14c–3* of the 1934 Act states that the annual reports of publicly held companies furnished to stockholders in connection with the company's yearly meeting should include financial statements that have been audited. This information (referred to as *proxy information* because it accompanies the management's request to cast votes for the stockholders at the annual meeting) must present balance sheets as of the end of the two most recent fiscal years along with income statements and cash flow statements for the three most recent years. *Rule 14c–3* also states that additional information, as specified in *Regulation S–K*, should be included in this annual report.

In recent years, the SEC has moved toward an *integrated disclosure system*. Under this approach, much of the same reported information that is required by the SEC must also go to the shareholders. Thus, the reporting process is simplified because only a single set of information must be generated in most cases. The integrated disclosure system is also intended as a way of improving the quality of the disclosures received directly by the shareholders.

Information required in proxy statements includes the following:

1. Five-year summary of operations including sales, total assets, income from continuing operations, and cash dividends per share.
2. Description of the business activities including principal products and sources and availability of raw materials.
3. Three-year summary of industry segments, export sales, and foreign and domestic operations.
4. Listing of company directors and executive officers.
5. Market price of the company's common stock for each quarterly period within the two most recent fiscal years.

6. Any restrictions on the company's ability to continue paying dividends.
7. Management's discussion and analysis of financial condition, changes in financial condition, and results of operations. Discussion should include liquidity, trends and significant events, causes of material changes in the financial statements, and the impact on the company of inflation.

In addition, the SEC has required certain disclosures in proxy statements describing the services provided by the registrant's independent external auditor. This information is intended as a means of helping to ensure that true independence is not endangered. Such disclosure must include:

1. All nonaudit services provided by the independent auditing firm.
2. A statement as to whether the board of directors (or its audit committee) approved all nonaudit services after considering the possibility that such services might impair the external auditor's independence.
3. The percentage of nonaudit fees to the total annual audit fee. This disclosure helps indicate the importance of the audit work to the firm versus the reward from any other services provided to the registrant.
4. Individual nonaudit fees that are larger than 3 percent of the annual audit fee.

The SEC's Authority over Generally Accepted Accounting Principles

Since financial reporting standards can be changed merely by amending *Regulation S–X*, the SEC holds the ultimate legal authority for establishing accounting principles for most publicly held companies in this country. In the past, the SEC has usually restricted the application of this power to disclosure issues while looking to the private sector (with the SEC's oversight) to formulate accounting principles. For this reason, the Financial Accounting Standards Board rather than the SEC is generally viewed today as the main standards-setting body for financial accounting in the United States. "Under federal law, the SEC has the mandate to determine accounting principles for publicly traded companies. But it has generally ceded that authority to private-sector accounting bodies such as the Financial Accounting Standards Board."[6]

However, the Securities and Exchange Commission does retain the ability to exercise its power with regard to the continuing evolution of accounting principles. The chief accountant of the SEC is responsible for providing the commissioners and the commission staff with advice on all current accounting and auditing matters and also helps to draft rules for the form and content of financial statement disclosure and other reporting requirements. "Perhaps the most powerful accounting position in the United States is that of Chief Accountant of the SEC."[7] The work of the chief accountant can lead to amendments being passed by the SEC as needed to alter various aspects of *Regulation S–X*.

Financial Reporting Releases (FRR) are issued currently by the SEC as needed to supplement *Regulation S–X* and *Regulation S–K*. They explain desired changes in the reporting requirements. By the end of 1996, 46 FRRs had been issued.[8] In addition,

---

[6]Kevin G. Salwen and Robin Goldwyn Blumenthal, "Tackling Accounting, SEC Pushes Changes with Broad Impact," *The Wall Street Journal*, September 27, 1990, p. Al.

[7]Skousen, *An Introduction to the SEC*, p. 16.

[8]From 1937 until 1982, more than 300 *Accounting Series Releases* (ASRs) were issued by the SEC to (1) amend *Regulation S–X*, (2) express interpretations regarding specific accounting and auditing issues, and (3) report disciplinary actions against public accountants. The ASRs that dealt with financial reporting matters of continuing interest were codified by the SEC in 1982 and issued as *Financial Reporting Release No. 1*.

the staff of the SEC publishes a series of *Staff Accounting Bulletins* (SAB) as a means of informing the financial community of its views on current matters relating to accounting and disclosure practices.[9] For example, *SAB 97* was released in 1996 to address two business combination accounting issues where official guidance did not appear to be present. First, this SAB established specific rules when two companies merged just prior to offering the stock of the combined companies to the public. In such cases, it was held that historical cost of both companies could only be retained if the 12 requirements of a pooling of interests had been met. Second, *SAB 97* specified that in a purchase combination the shareholder group receiving the largest ownership interest is to be viewed as the acquirer even though less than 50 percent of the ownership may have been acquired. However, a different acquirer could be identified if there was objective and verifiable evidence available.

Additional Disclosure Requirements   Historically, the SEC has tended to restrict use of its authority to the gray areas of accounting where official guidance is not available. New reporting problems arise each year while many other accounting issues, even after years of discussion, have never been completely addressed by any authoritative body. In such cases, the commission may require the disclosure of additional data if current rules are viewed as insufficient.

> It was in the 1970s that the SEC seemed to single out disclosure as the area in which it would take the standard-setting lead, leaving measurement issues to the FASB. This was when the SEC was expanding the coverage of Management's Discussion & Analysis (MD&A), an extensive narrative disclosure that is required to be appended to the financial statements.[10]

For example, in the early part of 1997, while the FASB worked on a project concerning the accounting for derivatives, the SEC approved rules so that more information would be available immediately. Footnote disclosure had to include more information about accounting policies in use. In addition, information was required about the risk of loss from market rate or price changes inherent in derivatives and other financial instruments. By means of these disclosures, the SEC enabled investors to have data about the potential consequences of the company's financial position.

Moratorium on Specific Accounting Practices   The commission also can exert its power by declaring a moratorium on the use of specified accounting practices. When authoritative guidance is not present, the SEC can simply prohibit a particular method from being applied. As an example, in the 1980s, companies were utilizing a variety of procedures to account for computer software costs because no official pronouncement had yet been issued. Hence, the SEC

> imposed a moratorium that will prohibit companies that plan to go public from capitalizing the internal costs of developing computer software for sale or lease or marketed to customers in other ways. . . . The decision doesn't prevent companies currently capitalizing internal software expenses from continuing, but the companies must disclose the effect of not expensing such costs as incurred. The moratorium continues until the Financial Accounting Standards Board issues a standard on the issue.[11]

When the FASB eventually arrived at a resolution of this question by issuing *Statement 86*, "Accounting for the Costs of Computer Software to Be Sold, Leased, or Otherwise Marketed," the SEC dropped the moratorium. Hence, the FASB was

---

[9]The SEC also releases *Accounting and Auditing Enforcement Releases (AAER)* when SEC enforcement activities are involved.

[10]Stephen A. Zeff, "A Perspective on the U.S. Public/Private-Sector Approach to the Regulation of Financial Reporting," *Accounting Horizons*, March 1995, pp. 58–59.

[11]"SEC Imposes 'Software Costs' Moratorium," *Journal of Accountancy*, September 1983, p. 3.

allowed to set the accounting rule, but the SEC ensured appropriate reporting until that time.

Challenging Individual Statements   As described above, officially requiring additional disclosure and prohibiting the application of certain accounting practices are two methods used by the SEC to control the financial reporting process. Forcing a specific registrant to change its filed statements is another, less formal approach that can create the same effect. For example:

> Advanced Micro Devices, Inc., agreed to settle an investigation by the Securities and Exchange Commission of the semiconductor company's public disclosures. The SEC found AMD "made inaccurate and misleading statements" concerning development of its 486 microprocessor. In 1992 and 1993, AMD "led the public to believe that it was independently designing the microcode for its 486 microprocessor without access" to the code of its rival chipmaker, Intel Corp., the SEC said, "when, in fact, AMD had provided its engineers . . . with Intel's copyrighted 386 microcode to accelerate the company's development efforts." Without admitting or denying the commission's findings, AMD, based in Sunnyvale, California, consented to an order barring it from committing future violations of SEC rules. No fines were imposed.[12]

Following the action taken by the SEC, any company involved in a similar event would certainly be well advised to provide the suggested disclosure.

Overruling the FASB   The SEC's actions are not necessarily limited, however, to the gray areas of accounting. Although the commission has allowed the FASB (and previous authoritative groups) to establish accounting principles, the SEC retains the authority to override or negate any pronouncements produced in the private sector. This power was dramatically demonstrated in 1977 when the FASB issued *SFAS 19* "Financial Accounting and Reporting by Oil and Gas Producing Companies." After an extended debate over the merits of alternative methods, this statement was issued requiring oil and gas producing companies to apply the successful-efforts method when accounting for unsuccessful exploration and drilling costs.

In response, the SEC almost immediately invoked a moratorium on the use of this practice until an alternative approach could be evaluated. Thus, companies filing with the SEC were not allowed to follow the method established by the FASB (after years of formal study and deliberation). Although the commission's reaction toward the accounting profession was a unique instance, the handling of this one issue clearly demonstrates the veto power that the SEC maintains over the work of the FASB.[13]

Filings with the SEC

Because of legal regulations, registrants may be required to make a number of different filings with the SEC. The SEC actually receives approximately 700,000 filings per year.[14] However, for the overview being presented here, the reporting process is divided into two broad categories:

- Registration statements.
- Periodic filings.

---

[12]"SEC Inquiry on Disclosure to Public Is Being Settled," *The Wall Street Journal*, October 1, 1996, p. B4.

[13]For a detailed account of the activities surrounding the SEC's rejection of *SFAS 19*, see "The SEC Decision Not to Support SFAS 19: A Case Study of the Effect of Lobbying on Standard Setting," by Donald Gorton in *Accounting Horizons*, March 1991.

[14]Sandra Block, "SEC Gets Closer to Electronic Filing," *The Wall Street Journal*, August 30, 1991, p. C1.

Registration statements ensure the disclosure of sufficient, relevant financial data before a security can be *initially offered* to the public by either a company or its underwriters. The dissemination of such information is mandated by the Securities Act of 1933. Registration is necessary except in certain situations described at a later point in this chapter. The SEC charges a registration fee that was decreased in 1996 to an amount equal to 1/33rd of 1 percent of the value of the securities offered. In 1995, the SEC collected $559 million in fees, an amount that was nearly twice its cost of operations. Thus, in 1996, Congress made known its intent that the SEC collect only enough fees to cover the government's cost. At that time, a nine-year program was begun to reduce certain fees and remove others to eliminate the surplus generated by the SEC.

After initial registration, periodic filings with the SEC are required of registrants by a number of federal laws, the most important of which is the Securities Exchange Act of 1934. This legislation has resulted in the *continual reporting of specified data* by all companies that have securities publicly traded on either a national securities exchange or an over-the-counter market.[15]

For registration statements as well as periodic filings, the SEC has established forms that provide the format and content to be followed in providing required information. "These forms contain no blanks to be filled in as do tax forms. Instead, they are narrative in character, giving general instructions about the items of information to be furnished. Detailed information must be assembled by the companies using the form designed for the type of security being offered as well as the type of company making the offer."[16]

Registration Statements   As indicated, a registration statement must be filed with and made effective by the Securities and Exchange Commission before a company can offer a security publicly. A security is broadly identified to include items such as a note, stock, treasury stock, bond, debenture, investment contract, evidence of indebtedness, or transferable share.

The SEC's role is not to evaluate the quality of the investment. Rather, the SEC seeks to ensure that the content and disclosure of the filing complies with all applicable regulations. The responsibility for the information always rests with corporate officials. The SEC is charged with ensuring full and fair disclosure of relevant financial information. The registrant has the responsibility to provide such data, and the decision to invest must remain with the public.

A number of different forms are available for this purpose, depending on the specific circumstances. Some of the most commonly encountered registration statement forms are:

- **S–1**   Used when no other form is prescribed. Usually used by new registrants or by companies that have been filing reports with the SEC for less than 36 months.
- **S–2**   Used by companies that have filed with the SEC for 36 months or longer but are not large enough to file a Form S–3.
- **S–3**   Used by companies that are large in size and already have a significant following in the stock market (at least $75 million of its voting stock is held by nonaffiliates). Disclosure is reduced for these organizations because the public is assumed to already have access to a considerable amount of information.

---

[15]A company that has securities traded on an over-the-counter market does not have to file under the 1934 act unless it has at least $10 million in assets and 500 shareholders.

[16]Skousen, *An Introduction to the SEC*, p. 47.

- ■ S–4   Used for securities issued in connection with business combination transactions.
- ■ SB–1   Used by small business issuers to register up to $10 million of securities but only if the company has not registered more than $10 million of securities offerings during the previous 12 months. A small business issuer has annual revenues of less than $25 million and less than $25 million of voting securities held by nonaffiliates.
- ■ SB–2   Used by small business issuers to register securities to be sold for cash.

The use of Form S–2 and especially Form S–3 offers a distinct advantage to established companies that are issuing securities. Rather than duplicate voluminous information already disclosed in other filings with the SEC—frequently the annual report to shareholders—the registrant can simply indicate the location of the data in these other documents, a process referred to as *incorporation by reference*.

Registration Procedures   The actual registration process is comprised of a series of events leading up to the permission to "go effective" by the SEC. Since the registrant is seeking to obtain significant financial resources through the issuance of new securities in public markets, each of these procedures is of vital importance.

After selecting the appropriate form, information is accumulated by the company according to the requirements of *Regulation S–K* and *Regulation S–X*. If problems or questions are anticipated, a prefiling conference with the SEC staff may be requested by the company to seek guidance prior to beginning the registration. For example, if uncertainty exists concerning the handling or disclosure of an unusual transaction, a prefiling conference can save all parties considerable time and effort.

> The Commission has a long-established policy of holding its staff available for conferences with prospective registrants or their representatives in advance of filing a registration statement. These conferences may be held for the purpose of discussing generally the problems confronting a registrant in effecting registration or to resolve specific problems of an unusual nature which are sometimes presented by involved or complicated financial transactions.[17]

When received by the SEC, the registration statement is reviewed by the Division of Corporation Finance.[18] An analyst makes a determination as to whether all nonfinancial information complies with the SEC's disclosure requirements in *Regulation S–K*. At the same time, an accountant verifies that the financial statement data included in the filing meet the standards of *Regulation S–X* and have been prepared according to generally accepted accounting principles. *Since a formal audit is not conducted by the SEC, the report of the company's independent CPA is essential to this particular evaluation.* In addition, an SEC lawyer also reviews the registration statement to verify the legal aspects of the document.

The Division of Corporation Finance almost invariably requests clarifications, changes, or additional information, especially for those filings involving an initial registration. A *letter of comments* (also known as a *deficiency letter*) is issued to the company to communicate these findings. In most cases, the registrant attempts to provide the necessary data or changes to expedite the process. However, in contro-

---

[17]Michael A. Walker and Daniel Schechtman, *SEC Compliance*, vol. 3 (New York: Warren Gorham Lamont, 1997), par. 30,641.

[18]All registration statements filed by issuers offering securities to the public for the first time are carefully reviewed. Subsequent registration statements and periodic filings are only reviewed on a selective basis. Because of the enormous increase in filings over the past decade, concern has been raised as to whether the SEC continues to have adequate staffing capabilities to review a sufficient number of these filings. See, for example, "Busy SEC Must Let Many Cases, Filings Go Uninvestigated," by Bruce Ingersoll in the December 16, 1985, issue of *The Wall Street Journal*, p. A1.

versial areas, the issuer may begin discussions directly with the SEC staff in hopes of resolving the problem without making the requested adjustments or disclosure or, at least, with limited inconvenience.

When the Division of Corporate Finance is eventually satisfied that all SEC regulations have been fulfilled, the registration statement is made effective and the securities can be sold. *Effectiveness does not, however, indicate an endorsement of the securities by the SEC.* With most offerings, the stock is actually sold by the company to one or more underwriters (stock brokerage firms) that market the shares to their clients to earn commissions.

For convenience and to save time and money, large companies are allowed to use a process known as *shelf registration*. They file once with the SEC and are then allowed to offer those securities at any time over the subsequent two years without having to go back to the SEC. In a similar manner, in recent years the SEC has considered moving more toward a system of registering companies rather than registering individual transactions to ease the burden of extensive reporting requirements. A company could possibly register on a periodic basis to cover all issuances during a set time.

The registration statement is physically composed of two parts. Part I, referred to as a *prospectus*, contains extensive information that include:

1. Financial statements for the issuing company audited by an independent CPA along with appropriate supplementary data.
2. An explanation of the intended use of the proceeds to be generated by the sale of the new securities.
3. A description of the risks associated with the securities.
4. A description of the business and the properties owned by the company.

The registrant must furnish every potential buyer of the securities with a copy of this prospectus, thus ensuring the adequate availability of information for their investment analysis.

One interesting movement in recent years has been the proposal that portions of each prospectus be written in "plain English" to promote the investor's ability to understand the information. In the early part of 1997, the SEC proposed that the cover page of the prospectus as well as the summary and risk factors sections be written using six principles of clear writing: active voice, short sentences, everyday language, tabular presentation of complex material, no legal jargon, and no multiple negatives. For example,

> *Before Plain English:* "The proxies solicited hereby for the Heartland Meeting may be revoked, subject to the procedures described herein, at any time up to and including the date of the Heartland Meeting."

> *In Plain English:* "You may revoke your proxy at any time up to and including the day of the meeting by following the directions on page 18."[19]

Part II of the registration statement is primarily for the informational needs of the SEC staff. Additional data are disclosed about the company and the securities being issued such as marketing arrangements, expenses of issuance, sales to special parties, and the like. The registrant is not required to provide this information to prospective buyers, although the entire registration statement is available to the public through the SEC.

Securities Exempt from Registration   According to the 1933 Act, not all securities issued by companies and their underwriters require registration. For example, securi-

---

[19]"SEC Proposes Mandating Plain English," *Journal of Accountancy*, April 1997, p. 10.

ties sold strictly to the residents of the state in which the issuing company is chartered and principally doing business are exempted. However, these offerings are still regulated by the securities laws of the individual states (commonly known as *blue sky laws*) which vary significantly across the country.[20]

Other exempt offerings include but are not limited to the following:

■ Securities issued by governments, banks, and savings and loan associations.

■ Securities issued that are restricted to a company's own existing shareholders where no commission is paid to solicit the exchange.

■ Securities issued by nonprofit organizations such as religious, educational, or charitable groups.

■ Small offerings of no more than $5 million. In most cases, though, a Regulation A offering circular must still be filed with the SEC and given to prospective buyers. However, much less information is required of a company in an offering circular than in a registration statement.

■ Offerings of no more than $1 million made to any number of investors within a 12-month period. No specific disclosure of information is required. General solicitations are allowed. The issuer must give notice of the offering to the SEC within 15 days of the first sale.

■ Offerings of no more than $5 million made to 35 or fewer purchasers in a 12-month period. No general solicitation is allowed for securities issued in this manner. Accredited investors (such as banks, insurance companies, and individuals with net worth of more than $1 million) are not included in the restriction on the number of buyers. Unaccredited investors must still be furnished with audited financial statements and other specified information. Parties making purchases have to hold the securities for at least two years or the filing exemption is lost.

■ The private placement of securities to no more than 35 sophisticated investors (having knowledge and experience in financial matters) who already have sufficient information available to them about the issuing company. Again, the number of accredited investors is unlimited and general solicitation is not permitted. These private placement rules have become quite important in recent years. Private placements in the United States rose from $16 billion in 1980 to more than $200 billion in 1996. The SEC estimated that private placements in 1989 represented 35 percent of all corporate financings.

Periodic Filings with the SEC   Once a company has issued securities that are publicly traded on a securities exchange or an over-the-counter market, information must be continually filed with the SEC so that adequate disclosure is available. As with registration statements, several different forms are utilized for this purpose. However, for most companies with actively traded securities, three of these are common: Form 10–K (an annual report), Form 10–Q (a quarterly report), and Form 8–K (disclosure of significant events). Smaller businesses use Form 10–KSB for annual reports and Form 10–QSB for quarterly reports.

In addition, as mentioned previously, proxy statements must be filed with the SEC. These statements are issued to a company's owners by the management or other interested party in hopes of securing voting rights to be used at stockholders' meetings.

Form 10–K   A 10–K form is an annual report filed with the SEC within 90 days of the end of a registrant's fiscal year to provide information and disclosures required by

---

[20]"These early laws became known as 'blue sky' laws after a judicial decision characterized some transactions as 'speculative schemes which have no more basis than so many feet of "blue sky".'" (Skousen, *An Introduction to the SEC*, p. 3.)

Regulation S–K and *Regulation S–X*. Fortunately, because of the integrated disclosure system, the annual report that is distributed by companies to their stockholders includes most of the basic financial disclosures required by the SEC in Form 10–K. Thus, many companies simply attach the stockholders' annual report to the Form 10–K each year and use the incorporation by reference procedure to meet most of the SEC's filing requirements. This process is sometimes known as a *wrap around* filing.

Form 10–K, as with the various other SEC filings, is constantly undergoing assessment to determine if investor needs are being met. Thus, the SEC's reporting requirements are evolutionary and change over time.

> The Securities and Exchange Commission issued guidelines aimed at making public companies provide a more detailed look at the trends and business changes that management expects in the future. . . . In the main part of yesterday's interpretation, the commissioners said that in the 10–K reports, companies must discuss "trends, demands, commitments or events" that it knows are "reasonably likely" to occur and have a material effect on financial condition or results.[21]

As indicated by this quote, the SEC has become especially interested during recent years in the quality of the information provided by the Management's Discussion and Analysis (MD&A) section of a registrant's filings. Basically, the management should describe verbally the company's past, present, and future. This information can give a nonquantified feel for the prospects of the company; it is a candid narrative to provide statement readers with a sense of management's priorities, accomplishments, and concerns. The MD&A is a feature carefully reviewed by the SEC staff.[22] "If the management of a company knows something that could have a material impact on earnings in the future, officials have an obligation to share that information with shareholders."[23]

Form 10–Q A 10–Q form contains condensed interim financial statements for the registrant and must be filed with the SEC within 45 days of the end of each quarter. However, no Form 10–Q is required following the fourth quarter of the year since a Form 10–K is forthcoming shortly thereafter. A Form 10–Q does not have to be audited by an independent CPA.

Information to be contained in each Form 10–Q includes the following:

- Income statements must be included for the most recent quarter and for the year to date as well as for the comparative periods in the previous year.
- A statement of cash flows is also necessary, but only for the year to date as well as for the corresponding period in the preceding year.
- Two balance sheets are reported: one as of the end of the most recent quarter with the second showing the company's financial position at the end of the previous fiscal year.
- Each Form 10–Q should also include any needed disclosures pertaining to the current period including the management's discussion and analysis of the financial condition of the company and results of operations.

Form 8–K An 8–K form is used to disclose a unique or significant happening. Consequently, the 8–K is not filed at regular time intervals but rather within 15

---

[21]Paul Duke, Jr., "SEC Issues Guidelines for 10–K Filings Seeking More Details on Trends, Changes," *The Wall Street Journal*, May 19, 1989, p. A2.

[22]See, for example, "Annual Reports: The SEC Cracks the Whip," by Tim Smart in *Business Week*, April 10, 1989.

[23]Kevin G. Salwen, "SEC Charges Caterpillar Failed to Warn Holders of Earnings Risk Posed by Unit," *The Wall Street Journal*, April 2, 1992, p. A3.

calendar days of the event (or within 5 business days in certain specified instances). During 1996, the SEC received more than 20,000 8–K reports. According to the SEC's guidelines, Form 8–K may be filed to report any action that company officials believe is of importance to security holders. However, several events are designated for required disclosure in this manner; this list includes the following:

- Resignation of a director.
- Changes in control of the registrant.
- Acquisitions or dispositions of assets.
- Changes in the registrant's certified accountants.
- Bankruptcy or receivership.

Proxy Statements   As was mentioned in a previous section, most of the significant actions undertaken by a company first must be approved at stockholders' meetings. For example, the members of the board of directors are elected in this manner to oversee the operations of the company. Although such votes are essential to the operations of a business, few (if any) major companies could possibly assemble enough shareholders at any one time and place for a voting quorum. The geographic distances are simply too great. Hence, before each of the periodic meetings, the management (or any other interested party) usually requests signed proxies from shareholders granting the legal authority to cast votes for the owners in connection with the various actions to be taken.[24]

Because of the power conveyed by a proxy, any such solicitation sent to shareholders (by any party) must include specific information as required by the SEC in its *Regulation 14A*. This proxy statement has to be filed with the SEC at least 10 days before being distributed. A number of the disclosed items were described previously. Other data that must be reported to the owners include:

- The proxy statement needs to indicate on whose behalf the solicitation is being made.
- The proxy statement must disclose fully all matters that are to be voted on at the meeting.
- In most cases, the proxy statement has to be accompanied (or preceded) by an annual report to the shareholders.

As with all areas of disclosure, the SEC's regulation of proxy statements has greatly enhanced the information available to investors. Historically, shareholders have not always been able to get adequate information.

> Thus was the president of one company able to respond cavalierly to a shareholder's request for information, "I can assure you that the company is in a good financial position. I trust that you will sign and mail your proxy at an early date." Quaint. But that was nothing. One unlisted company printed its proxy on the back of the dividend check—so when you endorsed the check you voted for management.[25]

> From a 1902 annual report to shareholders: "The settled plan has been to withhold all information from stockholders and others that is not called for by the stockholders in a body. So far no request for information has been made in the manner prescribed by the directors."[26]

---

[24]Any person who owns at least 5 percent of the company's stock or has been an owner for six months or longer has the right to look at a list of shareholders to make a proxy solicitation.

[25]Laura Jereski, "You've Come a Long Way, Shareholder," *Forbes*, July 13, 1987, p. 282.

[26]Skousen, *An Introduction to the SEC*, p. 75.

DISCUSSION QUESTION:

Is the Disclosure Worth the Cost?

Filing with the SEC requires a very significant amount of time and effort on the part of the registrant. Companies frequently resist every attempt by the commission to increase the levels of disclosure. Usually, the argument is made that additional information will not necessarily be useful to a great majority of investors. Regardless of the issue, the cost of the extra data is said to far outweigh any benefits that might be derived from this disclosure.

Such contentions are not necessarily made just to avoid disclosing information. One survey estimated the cost of SEC disclosures to be more than $400 million in 1975 alone. "The table reports an estimated $213,500,000 for the fully variable costs of 10–K, 10–Q and 8–K disclosures in 1975. To this should be added the separate estimate (not shown) of $191,900,000 for disclosure related to new issues in 1975, for a total estimate of about $400,000,000 for SEC disclosure costs in 1975. These estimates are biased downward because they do not include various fixed costs."[27] Such costs are either passed along to the consumer in the form of higher prices or serve to retard the growth of the reporting company.

The author of one survey (that has been widely discussed and debated over the years) held that federal securities laws are not actually helpful to investors.

I found that there was little evidence of fraud related to financial statements in the period prior to the enactment of the Securities Acts. Nor was there a widespread lack of disclosure. . . . Hence, I conclude that there was little justification for the accounting disclosure required by the Acts. . . . These findings indicate that the data required by the SEC do not seem to be useful to investors.[28]

The SEC was created, in part, to ensure that the public has fair and full disclosure about companies that have their securities publicly traded. However, the commission must be mindful of the cost of such disclosures. How can the SEC determine whether the cost of a proposed disclosure is more or less than the benefits that will be derived by the public?

Electronic Data Gathering, Analysis, and Retrieval System (Edgar)

During recent years, the SEC has become almost overwhelmed by the sheer mountain of documents that it receives, reviews, and makes available to the public. Filings with the SEC are estimated to contain 5 million pieces of paper each year.

In 1984, the SEC began to develop an electronic data gathering, analysis, and retrieval system nicknamed Edgar. As originally envisioned, all filings would arrive at the SEC on disks or through some other electronic transmission. Each filing could be reviewed, analyzed, and stored by SEC personnel on a computer so they would no longer constantly have to shift through stacks of paper. Perhaps more importantly, investors would have the ability to access this data through the Internet. Thus, investors throughout the world could have information available for their decisions literally minutes after the documents are made effective by the SEC.

Because of the ambitious nature of the Edgar project, approximately a decade was required to get the system effectively operational. For years, Edgar was the object of much scorn; "one member of the House Energy and Commerce Committee suggested renaming the project Mr. Ed, 'since the SEC has a much better chance of finding a talking horse than it does of achieving an efficient computer filing sys-

---

[27]J. Richard Zecher, "An Economic Perspective of SEC Corporate Disclosure," *The SEC and Accounting: The First 50 Years*, ed. Robert H. Mundheim and Noyes E. Leech (Amsterdam: North-Holland, 1985), pp. 75–76.

[28]George J. Benston, "The Value of the SEC's Accounting Disclosure Requirements," *The Accounting Review*, July 1969, p. 351.

tem' ".[29] However, the beginning of the explosive use of the Internet in the mid-1990s corresponded with the widescale availability of information on Edgar. Not surprisingly, Edgar's popularity grew rapidly.

> If you're suspicious about a certain stock, then go to www.sec.gov/cgi-bin/srch-edgar.[30] That's the Securities & Exchange Commission's Edgar database—chockablock with annual reports, prospectuses and all the other paperwork demanded of public companies.[31]

> For a thorough financial history of a company or mutual fund, or to view a prospectus, there's no more complete source than EDGAR, a Web site established by the SEC. Quarterly 10–Q and annual 10–K financial reports and other mandatory filings from public companies are posted on EDGAR within 24 hours after they are submitted to the SEC, as are prospectuses issued by public companies and mutual funds.[32]

This system is designed to benefit the registrant as well as the investor. The SEC hopes to make the entire filing system simpler for all parties.

> General Motors Acceptance Corporation, which has been filing on the Edgar pilot program for several years, reports that Edgar has substantially reduced the amount of time it takes to get SEC approval for GMAC deals. . . . Mr. Folbigg, of GMAC, agrees that small companies should be able to convert from paper to electronic filing without much trouble. "The key to the Edgar system is a good secretary who can follow instructions," he says. GMAC does its filings via a personal computer.[33]

SUMMARY

1. In the United States, the Securities and Exchange Commission (SEC) has been entrusted with the responsibility for ensuring that complete and reliable information is available to investors who buy and sell securities in public capital markets. Since being created in 1934, this agency has administered numerous reporting rules and regulations created by congressional actions starting with the Securities Act of 1933 and the Securities Exchange Act of 1934.

2. Before a company's securities (such as either equity or debt) can be publicly traded, appropriate filings must be made with the SEC to ensure that sufficient data are made available to potential investors. Disclosure requirements for this process are outlined in two documents: *Regulation S–K* (for nonfinancial information) and *Regulation S–X* (describing the form and content of all included financial statements).

3. The ability to require the reporting of specified information gives the SEC enormous legal power over the accounting profession in the United States. Traditionally, this authority has been wielded only to increase disclosure requirements and to provide guidance where none was otherwise available. However, in a significant demonstration of its authority, the SEC overruled the FASB's decision in 1977 as to the appropriate method to account for unsuccessful exploration and drilling costs incurred by oil and gas producing companies.

4. Filings with the SEC are divided generally into two broad categories: registration statements and periodic filings. Registration statements are designed to provide information about a company prior to its issuance of a security to the public. Depending on the circumstances, several different registration forms are available for this purpose. After the statement is produced by the registrant and initially reviewed by the SEC, a letter of comments is furnished describing desired explanations or changes. These concerns must be resolved before the security can be sold.

5. Not all securities issued in the United States require registration with the SEC. As an example, formal registration is not necessary for securities sold by either government

---

[29]Block, "SEC Gets Closer to Electronic Filing," p. C1.

[30]Another address for Edgar is www.sec.gov/edgarhp.htm

[31]Joseph R. Garber, "Click Before you Leap," *Forbes*, February 24, 1997, p. 162.

[32]Randy Myers, "The Wired World of Investment Information," *Nation's Business*, March 1997, pp. 58–59.

[33]Block, "SEC Gets Closer to Electronic Filing," pp. C1 and C5.

units or banks. Certain issues for relatively small amounts are also exempt although some amount of disclosure is normally required. Securities sold solely within the state in which the business operates are not subject to federal securities laws but must comply with state laws frequently referred to as *blue sky laws.*

6. Companies that have their stocks or bonds publicly traded on a securities exchange must also submit periodic filings to the SEC to ensure that adequate disclosure is constantly maintained. Among the most common of these filings are Form 10–K (an annual report) and Form 10–Q (condensed interim financial information). Form 8–K also is required to report any significant events that occur. In addition, proxy statements (documents that are used to solicit votes at stockholders' meetings) also come under the filing requirements monitored by the SEC.

Because no computations were presented in this chapter, a Comprehensive Illustration is not included.

QUESTIONS

1. Why were federal securities laws originally passed by Congress?
2. What is covered by *Regulation S–K*?
3. What is covered by *Regulation S–X*?
4. What are some of the major divisions within the SEC?
5. What is covered by the Securities Act of 1933?
6. What is covered by the Securities Exchange Act of 1934?
7. What are the goals of the SEC?
8. What information is required in a proxy statement?
9. Why is the content of a proxy statement considered to be so important?
10. How does the SEC affect the development of generally accepted accounting principles in the United States?
11. What is the purpose of Financial Reporting Releases and Staff Accounting Bulletins?
12. What was the SEC's response to the FASB's handling of accounting for oil and gas producing companies, and why was this action considered so significant?
13. What is the purpose of a registration statement? Under what law is a registration statement filed?
14. What are the two parts of a registration statement? What is contained in each part?
15. How does the SEC generate revenues?
16. Three forms commonly used in the registration process are Form S–1, Form S–3, and Form SB–2. Which registrants should use each of these forms?
17. What is incorporation by reference?
18. What is a prefiling conference, and why might it be helpful to a registrant?
19. What is a letter of comments? By what other name is a letter of comments often referred?
20. What is a prospectus? What is contained in a prospectus?
21. What is a shelf registration?
22. Under what circumstances is a company exempt from filing a registration statement with the SEC prior to the issuance of securities?
23. What is a private placement of securities?
24. What are blue sky laws?
25. What is a wrap around filing?
26. When is a Form 8–K issued by a company? What specific information does a Form 8–K convey?
27. What is the purpose of the Management's Discussion and Analysis?
28. What is the difference in a Form 10–K and a Form 10–Q?
29. What is the purpose of creating the Edgar system?

LIBRARY ASSIGNMENTS

1. Locate a recent annual report of a publicly traded company such as Ford Motor Company or IBM. Read the Management's Discussion and Analysis for the most recent years. Write a report to answer the following questions:
   - What information is provided in the MD&A that is not found in the financial statements?
   - What were the most important pieces of information in the MD&A?
   - Was anything included in the MD&A that was purely speculation on the part of the management?
   - Was anything omitted from the MD&A that would have been helpful information?

2. Read the following as well as any other published information on the work of the SEC:

   "Tackling Accounting, SEC Pushes Changes with Broad Impact," *The Wall Street Journal*, September 27, 1990, p. A1.

   "Annual Reports: The SEC Cracks the Whip," *Business Week*, April 10, 1989.

   "A Perspective on the U.S. Public/Private-Sector Approach to the Regulation of Financial Reporting," *Accounting Horizons*, March 1995.

   "The SEC and the Profession, 1934–84: The Realities of Self-Regulation," *Journal of Accountancy*, July 1984.

   "Arthur Young Professors' Roundtable: The SEC—Past, Present, Future," *Journal of Accountancy* (News Feature Section), March 1985.

   Write a report discussing the work of the SEC. Give a historical perspective as well as information on its current activities.

PROBLEMS

1. Which of the following statements is true?
   a. The Securities Exchange Act of 1934 regulates intrastate stock offerings made by a company.
   b. The Securities Act of 1933 regulates the subsequent public trading of securities through brokers and markets.
   c. The Securities Exchange Act of 1934 is commonly referred to as blue sky legislation.
   d. The Securities Act of 1933 regulates the initial offering of securities by a company.

2. What is the purpose of *Regulation S–K*?
   a. Defines generally accepted accounting principles in the United States.
   b. Establishes required disclosure of nonfinancial information with the SEC.
   c. Outlines enforcement procedures carried out by the SEC.
   d. Indicates which companies must file with the SEC on an annual basis.

3. What is the difference between *Regulation S–K* and *Regulation S–X*?
   a. *Regulation S–K* establishes reporting requirements for companies in their initial issuance of securities whereas *Regulation S–X* is directed toward the subsequent issuance of securities.
   b. *Regulation S–K* establishes reporting requirements for companies smaller than a certain size whereas *Regulation S–X* is directed toward companies larger than that size.
   c. *Regulation S–K* establishes regulations for nonfinancial information filed with the SEC whereas *Regulation S–X* prescribes the form and content of financial statements included in SEC filings.
   d. *Regulation S–K* establishes reporting requirements for publicly held companies whereas *Regulation S–X* is directed toward private companies.

4. The Securities Exchange Act of 1934:
   a. Regulates the public trading of previously issued securities through brokers and exchanges.
   b. Prohibits blue sky laws.
   c. Regulates the initial offering of securities by a company.
   d. Requires the registration of investment advisors.

5. What is a registration statement?
   a. A statement that must be filed with the SEC before a company can begin an initial offering of securities to the public.
   b. A required filing with the SEC before a large quantity of stock can be obtained by an inside party.
   c. An annual filing made with the New York Stock Exchange.
   d. A filing made by a company with the SEC to indicate that a significant change has occurred.

6. Which of the following is a registration statement used by large companies that already have a significant following in the stock market?
   a. Form 8–K.
   b. Form 10–K.
   c. Form S–1.
   d. Form S–3.

7. What was the significance of the controversy in 1977 over the appropriate accounting principles to be used by oil and gas producing companies?
   a. Several major lawsuits resulted.
   b. Companies refused to follow the dictates of the SEC.
   c. Partners of a major accounting firm were indicted on criminal charges.
   d. The SEC overruled the FASB on the handling of this matter.

8. Which of the following must be provided to every potential buyer of a new security?
   a. A letter of comments.
   b. A deficiency letter.
   c. A prospectus.
   d. Form S–16.

9. What is meant by the term *incorporation by reference*?
   a. The legal incorporation of a company in more than one state.
   b. Filing information with the SEC by indicating that the information is already available in another document.
   c. A reference guide indicating informational requirements specified in *Regulation S–X*.
   d. Incorporating a company in a state outside of its base of operations.

10. What is a letter of comments?
    a. A letter sent to a company by the SEC indicating needed changes or clarifications in a registration statement.
    b. A questionnaire supplied to the SEC by a company suggesting changes in *Regulation S–X*.
    c. A letter included in a Form 10–K to indicate the management's assessment of the company's financial position.
    d. A letter composed by a company asking for information or clarification prior to the filing of a registration statement.

11. What is a prospectus?
    a. A document attached to a Form 8–K.
    b. A potential stockholder as defined by *Regulation S–K*.
    c. A document filed with the SEC prior to the filing of a registration statement.
    d. The first part of a registration statement that must be furnished by a company to all potential buyers of a new security.

12. Which of the following is not exempt from registration with the SEC under the Securities Act of 1933?
    a. Securities issued by a nonprofit religious organization.
    b. Securities issued by a government unit.
    c. A public offering of no more than $5.9 million.
    d. An offering made to only 26 sophisticated investors.

13. Which of the following is usually not filed with the SEC on a regular periodic basis?
    a. Form 10–Q.
    b. A prospectus.
    c. A proxy statement.
    d. Form 10–K.

14. What is a shelf registration?
    a. A registration statement that is formally rejected by the SEC.
    b. A registration statement that is rejected by the SEC due to the lapse of a specified period of time.
    c. A registration process for large companies that allows them to offer securities over a period of time without seeking additional approval by the SEC.
    d. A registration form that is withdrawn by the registrant without any action having been taken.

15. What is Edgar?
    a. A system used by the SEC to reject registration statements that do not contain adequate information.
    b. The enforcement arm of the SEC.
    c. A system being designed for the SEC to allow electronic filings.
    d. A branch of the government that oversees the work of the SEC.

16. Identify each of the following as they pertain to the SEC:
    - Blue sky laws.
    - S–1 Statement.
    - Letter of deficiencies.
    - Prospectus.

17. Discuss the objectives of the Securities Act of 1933 and the Securities Exchange Act of 1934. How are these objectives accomplished?

18. What are the steps involved in filing a registration statement with the SEC?

19. Discuss the methods by which the SEC can influence the development of generally accepted accounting principles in the United States.

20. Which forms do most companies file with the SEC on a periodic basis? Explain the purpose of each form and its primary contents.

21. Which forms do most companies file with the SEC in connection with the offering of securities to the public?

22. What is the importance of a Form 8-K? What is the importance of a proxy statement?

23. Discuss each of the following terms:
    - Financial reporting releases.
    - Wrap around incorporation.
    - Incorporation by reference.
    - Division of corporation finance.
    - Integrated disclosure system.
    - Management's discussion and analysis.
    - Chief accountant of the SEC.

24. Which organizations are normally exempted from the registration requirements imposed by the SEC?